The Encyclopedia of Public Choice

Volume I

The Editors

CHARLES K. ROWLEY, Duncan Black Professor of Economics, George Mason University and General Director, The Locke Institute; and Dr. Dr. h.c.mult. **FRIEDRICH SCHNEIDER**, Department of Economics, The University of Linz

Advisory Board

JAMES M. BUCHANAN, *Buchanan House, George Mason University*

BERNARD GROFMAN, *Department of Political Science, University of California, Irvine*

ARYE L. HILLMAN, *Department of Economics, Bar-Ilan University*

MARTIN PALDAM, *Department of Economics, Aarhus University*

WILLIAM F. SHUGHART II, *Department of Economics, University of Mississippi*

ROBERT D. TOLLISON, *Department of Economics, Clemson University*

DENNIS C. MUELLER, *Department of Economics, University of Vienna*

MICHAEL C. MUNGER, *Department of Political Science, Duke University*

PETER C. ORDESHOOK, *Humanities and Social Sciences, Cal Tech*

GORDON TULLOCK, *School of Law, George Mason University*

HANNELORE WECK-HANNEMANN, *Institut Fur Finanzwissenschaft, Universitat Innsbruck*

The Encyclopedia of Public Choice

Editors

CHARLES K. ROWLEY
*The Locke Institute, and
George Mason University*

and

FRIEDRICH SCHNEIDER
*Johannes Kepler University of Linz,
Institute of Economic Policy*

Kluwer Academic Publishers

DORDRECHT / BOSTON / LONDON

Distributors for North, Central and South America:
Kluwer Academic Publishers
101 Philip Drive
Assinippi Park
Norwell, Massachusetts 02061 USA
Telephone (781) 871-6600
Fax (781) 871-6528
E-Mail <kluwer@wkap.com>

Distributors for all other countries:
Kluwer Academic Publishers Group
Post Office Box 322
3300 AH Dordrecht, THE NETHERLANDS
Telephone 31 78 6576 000
Fax 31 78 6576 474
E-Mail <orderdept@wkap.nl>

    Electronic Services <http://www.wkap.nl>

Library of Congress Cataloging-in-Publication

The encyclopedia of public choice / editors, Charles Rowley and Friedrich Schneider.
    p. cm.
   Includes bibliographical references and index.
   ISBN 0-7923-8607-8 (alk. paper)
   ISBN 0-306-47828-5 (electronic)
   ISBN 0-306-47830-7 (electronic plus print)
    1. Policy sciences–Encyclopedias. 2. Economic policy–Encyclopedias.
3. Social policy–Encyclopedias. I. Rowley, Charles Kershaw. II. Schneider, Friedrich.

H41.E57 2004
320'.6'03–dc21
                                                              2003046109

Copyright © 2004 by Kluwer Academic Publishers. Second Printing 2004.

All rights reserved. No part of this publication may be reproduced, stored in a retrieval system or transmitted in any form or by any means, electronic, mechanical, photo-copying, microfilming, recording, or otherwise, without the prior written permission of the publisher, with the exception of any material supplied specifically for the purpose of being entered and executed on a computer system, for exclusive use by the purchaser of the work.
Permissions for books published in the USA: permissions@wkap.com
Permissions for books published in Europe: permissions@wkap.nl
Printed on acid-free paper.

*We dedicate 'The Encyclopedia of Public Choice'
to the memory of*

Duncan Black
23 May 1908 to 14 January 1991

The Founding Father of Public Choice

TABLE OF CONTENTS

Preface xiii

Acknowledgments xvii

ESSAYS

Public Choice and Constitutional Political Economy
Charles K. Rowley 3

Public Choice: An Introduction
Dennis C. Mueller 32

Are Vote and Popularity Functions Economically Correct?
Martin Paldam 49

Constitutional Political Economy
James M. Buchanan 60

Corruption
Susan Rose-Ackerman 67

Dictatorship
Ronald Wintrobe 77

Environmental Politics
Hannelore Weck-Hannemann 91

Experimental Public Choice
Arthur J.H.C. Schram 96

Gordon Tullock at Four Score Years: An Evaluation
Charles K. Rowley 105

Interest Group Behavior and Influence
Frans van Winden 118

International Trade Policy: Departure from Free Trade
Arye L. Hillman 129

James M. Buchanan
Robert D. Tollison 139

**Milton Friedman, 1912: Harbinger of the
Public Choice Revolution**
Charles K. Rowley and Anne Rathbone 146

Monetary Policy and Central Bank Behavior
Manfred Gärtner 159

**The Political Economy of Taxation: Positive and
Normative Analysis when Collective Choice Matters**
Stanley L. Winer and Walter Hettich 173

Public Choice from the Perspective of Economics
Robert D. Tollison 191

Public Choice from the Perspective of the History of Thought
Charles K. Rowley 201

Public Choice Theory from the Perspective of Law
Francesco Parisi 214

Public Choice from the Perspective of Philosophy
Hartmut Kliemt 235

Public Choice from the Perspective of Sociology
Viktor J. Vanberg 244

Public Finance
Harvey S. Rosen 252

Regulation and Antitrust
William F. Shughart II 263

Scholarly Legacy of Mancur Olson
Melvin J. Hinich and Michael C. Munger 284

Shadow Economy
Friedrich Schneider 286

Social Choice, Contracts and Logrolling
Peter Bernholz 296

Spatial Theory
Melvin J. Hinich and Michael C. Munger 305

Trade Liberalization and Globalization
Arye L. Hillman 312

William H. Riker
John Aldrich 321

BIOGRAPHIES

ALDRICH, John Herbert **327**

ANDERSON, Lisa Reneé **328**

BAUMOL, William J. **328**

BAVETTA, Sebastiano **329**

BENNETT, James Thomas **330**

BENSON, Bruce Lowell **330**

BERNHOLZ, Peter **332**

BESLEY, Timothy John **334**

BESOCKE, Portia DiGiovanni **335**

BOETTKE, Peter J. **335**

BORCHERDING, Thomas Earl **336**

BRADBURY, John Charles **337**

BRAMS, Steven J. **338**

BUCHANAN, James McGill **339**

CAIN, Michael J.G. **340**

CAPLAN, Bryan Douglas **341**

CONGLETON, Roger Douglas **341**

COUGHLIN, Peter Joseph **343**

COWEN, Tyler **344**

CRAIN, William Mark **344**

CREW, Michael Anthony **346**

DA EMPOLI, Domenico	347
DAVIS, Otto Anderson	348
EKELUND, Robert Burton Jr.	349
FISCHEL, William A.	351
FROHLICH, Norman	352
GARRETT, Thomas A.	353
GOFF, Brian L.	354
GROFMAN, Bernard N.	355
HANSON, Robin Dale	357
HETTICH, Walter	357
HINICH, Melvin J.	358
HOLCOMBE, Randall Gregory	359
HOLLER, Manfred Joseph	361
HOLT, Charles A.	362
KAEMPFER, William Hutchison	363
KEIL, Manfred Werner	364
KENNY, Lawrence Wagner	365
KLEINDORFER, Paul Robert	366
KURRILD-KLITGAARD, Peter	367
LABAND, David Neil	368
LANGBEIN, Laura	369
LEE, Dong Won	370
LEE, Dwight R.	370
LOHMANN, Susanne	372

LÓPEZ, Edward John 373

MATSUSAKA, John G. 374

McCHESNEY, Fred Sanderson 375

MUDAMBI, Ram 375

MUNGER, Michael Curtis 376

NAVARRA, Pietro 377

OPPENHEIMER, Joe 378

PADOVANO, Fabio 379

PALDA, Filip 381

PARISI, Francesco 382

PEACOCK, Alan Turner 383

PECORINO, Paul 384

RATHBONE, Anne Elissa 385

REKSULAK, Michael 385

ROMER, Thomas 386

ROWLEY, Charles Kershaw 387

RUBIN, Paul Harold 388

SASS, Tim Roger 390

SCHMID-LUEBBERT, Stefanie 391

SCHNEIDER, Friedrich Georg 391

SCHOFIELD, Norman James 392

SCULLY, Gerald William 393

SENED, Itai 394

SHUGHART, William Franklin II 395

SMITH, Vernon L. 396

SOBBRIO, Giuseppe 398

SOBEL, Russell Steven 399

STEPYKINA, Ekaterina 400

STRATMANN, Thomas 400

THOMPSON, Earl 401

THORNTON, Mark 401

TIDEMAN, Thorwald Nicolaus 402

TOLLISON, Robert Dewitt 403

TOWER, Edward 405

TULLOCK, Gordon 406

TWIGHT, Charlotte Augusta Lewis 407

URKEN, Arnold Bernard 408

VACHRIS, Michelle Albert 409

VANBERG, Viktor J. 410

VAUBEL, Roland 412

WAGNER, Richard E. 413

WECK-HANNEMANN, Hannelore 414

WILLETT, Thomas Dunaway 415

WILLIAMS, Walter E. 417

WINER, Stanley Lewis 418

WITTMAN, Donald Alan 419

WU, Wenbo 420

Index 421

PREFACE

The Encyclopedia provides a detailed and comprehensive account of the subject known as *public choice*. However, the title would not convey sufficiently the breadth of the Encyclopedia's contents which can be summarized better as the fruitful interchange of economics, political science and moral philosophy on the basis of an image of man as a purposive and responsible actor who pursues his own objectives as efficiently as possible.

This fruitful interchange between the fields outlined above existed during the late eighteenth century during the brief period of the Scottish Enlightenment when such great scholars as David Hume, Adam Ferguson and Adam Smith contributed to all these fields, and more. However, as intellectual specialization gradually replaced broad-based scholarship from the mid-nineteenth century onwards, it became increasingly rare to find a scholar making major contributions to more than one.

Once Alfred Marshall defined economics in neoclassical terms, as a narrow positive discipline, the link between economics, political science and moral philosophy was all but severed and economists redefined their role into that of 'the humble dentist' providing technical economic information as inputs to improve the performance of impartial, benevolent and omniscient governments in their attempts to promote the public interest. This indeed was the dominant view within an economics profession that had become besotted by the economics of John Maynard Keynes and Paul Samuelson immediately following the end of the Second World War.

Even during this 'dark age' for political economy, however, a little known Scot named Duncan Black was sowing the seeds for a *renaissance* that would once again provide for a reunion between economics and political science. Black launched the public choice research program in 1948 with a seminal paper on the rationale of group decision-making and in so doing earned later fame as the founding father of public choice.

Black's seminal contribution was extended in 1951 by Kenneth Arrow in his famous 1951 monograph entitled *Social Choice and Individual Values*. A further major extension occurred in 1957, when Anthony Downs published his seminal book entitled *An Economic Theory of Democracy*.

In 1962, James Buchanan and Gordon Tullock, in their famous book *The Calculus of Consent*, extended the perspective of public choice by shifting attention away from direct elections and parliamentary democracy, to outline a rational choice approach to the logical foundations of a constitutional republic. In 1965, Mancur Olson opened up the discussion of interest group behavior to rational choice analysis in his famous book entitled *The Logic of Collective Action*. In 1971 William A. Niskanen opened up the discussion of bureaucratic behavior to rational choice analysis in his book entitled *Bureaucracy and Representative Government*.

These six contributions constitute the foundations of the public choice research program. Two other books also contributed to the early public choice tradition, namely the 1951 monograph by Black and Newing entitled *Committee Decisions with Complementary Valuation* and the 1962 masterpiece by William Riker entitled *The Theory of Political Coalitions*. All these works are as relevant to scholars of public choice now as they were several decades ago when they were written.

Since public choice first emerged during the years of reconstruction from the devastation of the Second World War, the world's political environment has evolved and changed dramatically. The Marshall Plan enabled Western Europe to eliminate its dictatorships and to establish and/or to reinforce democracy. The European colonial powers eased themselves out of their imperial roles, releasing their former colonies into independence, albeit in many cases an independence that rapidly deteriorated into the one party state, outright dictatorship or even kleptocracy. Even Latin-America slowly has eased itself into democracy, albeit in many cases of a fragile and unstable nature.

The United States utilized its economic strength and its political resilience to confront and to contain the USSR throughout the Cold War and eventually to defeat it, thus opening up Eastern Europe and even Russia itself to varying forms of democratic or semi-democratic government. The remaining communist dictatorships, notably The People's Republic of China, Cuba and North Korea, clearly are endangered species, unlikely to survive the first decade of the new century. The last bastions of non-communist, non-sub-Saharan African dictatorship, mostly located in the Middle East, are finding it increasingly costly and difficult to fend off the democratic desires of their down-trodden and mostly impoverished subjects. For the first time in the history of the world, a majority of individuals now live under conditions of democracy, a state that public choice is uniquely qualified to analyze.

Given the enormity of the political changes outlined above, it is very reassuring to discover, not least through the contributions to this Encyclopedia, that public choice has retained its ability to explain and to predict the behavior of all actors in political markets — even the behavior of al-Qaeda terrorists — within the framework of the rational choice approach.

The Encyclopedia of Public Choice is a monumental offering. It consists of 306 entries each assigned to one of three headings, namely essays, concepts and biographies. The Encyclopedia is an entirely new work, all its contributions being newly commissioned. Drafts of the entries were received from the authors over the period October 2001 through September 2002, most of them arriving during the six months March 2002 through August 2002.

The essays are designed to be far-ranging discussions of central issues in the public choice literature, and evaluations of the lives and works of some of the founding fathers, each written by authors who have worked extensively in those fields. The authors were asked to avoid writing surveys, but rather to present their own views on the topic under review.

The concepts are designed to be more narrowly-focused contributions, offering up-to-date introductions and first-rate bibliographies. Once again, the authors were expected to explicate their own views and not to attempt to write a comprehensive survey. In several cases, where the issue was deemed to be sufficiently controversial, authors with differing viewpoints provide competing interpretations.

Every contributor to the essay and/or the concepts sections of the Encyclopedia was invited to contribute his or her own biography. The large majority complied. These are short outlines modeled on Mark Blaug's *Who's Who in Economics*. They provide interested readers with a short biography, a limited list of publications and a brief statement of the scholar's self-perceived career contribution to public choice.

The allocation of entries across these three categories is as follows: 28 essays, including two introductions, one by Charles K. Rowley and one by Dennis C. Mueller; 186 concepts; and 92 biographies. The Encyclopedia itself consists of well in excess of one million words. The contributors, and the editors, have taken care to make the language of the Encyclopedia as non-technical and comprehensible as possible. For this reason, the Encyclopedia should be accessible to all scholars, all graduate and undergraduate students of economics, political science, and public choice as well as to most scholars and students of such closely related disciplines as law, philosophy, sociology and psychology. The Encyclopedia should be an indispensable companion to all practitioners of public policy.

The editors have made every effort to present a well-balanced and comprehensive body of public choice scholarship from the early beginnings of the discipline to its current flourishing state. By and large, we believe that we have achieved this goal. However, as always, the proof of the pudding is in the eating. We trust that you will enjoy the rich banquet that is set before you.

CHARLES K. ROWLEY
Duncan Black Professor of Economics
George Mason University and
General Director
The Locke Institute

and

PROFESSOR DR. DR. h.c.mult. FRIEDRICH SCHNEIDER
Department of Economics
University of Linz

REFERENCES

Arrow, K.F. (1950). "A difficulty in the concept of social welfare." *Journal of Political Economy*, 58: 328–346.

Arrow, K.J. *Social Choice and Individual Values*. New York: Wiley.

Black, D. (1948). "On the rationale of group decision-making." *Journal of Political Economy*, 56: 23–34.

Black, D. and Newing, R.A. (1951). *Committee Decisions with Complementary Valuation*. London: W. Hodge.

Blaug, M. (2000). *Who's Who in Economics*. Cheltenham, UK and Northampton, USA: Edward Elgar Publishing.

Buchanan, J.M. and Tullock, G. (1962). *The Calculus of Consent*. Ann Arbor: University of Michigan Press.

Downs, A. (1957). *An Economic Theory of Democracy*. New York: Harper & Row.

Niskanen, W.A. (1971). *Bureaucracy and Representative Government*. New York: Aldine-Atherton.

Olson, M. *The Logic of Collective Action*. Cambridge: Harvard University Press.

Riker, W. (1962). *The Theory of Political Coalitions*. New Haven: Yale University Press.

ACKNOWLEDGMENTS

Our acknowledgments are due first to each scholar who has contributed to this Encyclopedia, and most especially to those who have made multiple contributions. Their enthusiasm and commitment to the project made our editorial task much easier than it would otherwise have been. We are especially indebted to the members of the distinguished Advisory Board (listed separately at the beginning of this volume) whose responses to our request for advice and help were always friendly and helpful. In particular we are indebted to William F. Shughart II and Robert D. Tollison whose help and intellectual support went far beyond anything that we could possibly expect.

We are also indebted to Marilea Polk Fried and Marian Scott at Kluwer Academic Publishers, both for their editorial help, and for their persistence in making sure that we adhered to deadlines.

The project was organized through the auspices of The Locke Institute in Fairfax, Virginia. The Locke Institute acknowledges with deep gratitude the financial support of the following individuals and foundations, without whose generosity, we could not successfully have completed this project: James T. Bennett; Robert S. Elgin; Daniel Oliver; Gordon Tullock; The Chase Foundation of Virginia and the Sunmark Foundation.

Charles Rowley is grateful to the James M. Buchanan Center for Political Economy for Summer research support, and to Anne Rathbone for project support.

Essays

PUBLIC CHOICE AND CONSTITUTIONAL POLITICAL ECONOMY

1. Introduction

Public choice – or the economics of politics – is a relatively new science located at the interface between economics and politics (Rowley 1993, Mueller 1997, and Shughart and Razzolini 2001). It was founded in 1948 by Duncan Black, who died in 1991 without ever achieving full recognition as the Founding Father of the discipline (Tullock 1991). Its practitioners seek to understand and to predict the behavior of political markets by utilizing the analytical techniques of economics, most notably the rational choice postulate, in the modeling of non-market decision-making behavior.

Public choice – thus defined, is a positive science concerned with what is or what conditionally might be. Its dedicated journal is *Public Choice*, introduced by Gordon Tullock in 1966 and now ranked among the thirty most important journals in social science worldwide. Its intellectual home is The Center for Study of Public Choice, now located in The James M. Buchanan Center for Political Economy at George Mason University in the Commonwealth of Virginia.

The public choice research program was launched in 1948 by Duncan Black's paper on the rationale of group decision-making. This paper demonstrated that, under certain conditions, at most one motion is capable of securing a simple majority over every other motion. Specifically, if voter preferences are single-peaked over a single-dimensional issue space, a unique equilibrium exists in the motion most preferred by the median voter. For Black (1948), this result was the political science counterpart of competitive market equilibrium in his own discipline of economics.

In 1950, Arrow seized upon this insight to demonstrate that when Black's condition of single-peaked preferences does not hold the unique vote equilibrium will not hold and voting cycles may prevail. Arrow incorporated this insight into his famous, 1951 book, *Social Choice and Individual Values* outlining a difficulty in social welfare. These papers fundamentally challenged Black's theoretical notion of political stability and offered an alternative theoretical viewpoint that political markets are inherently unstable. These alternative viewpoints would be subjected to extensive empirical evaluation throughout the first half century of the public choice research program.

In 1957, Anthony Downs moved public choice from its early beginnings in analyzing committee decisions and direct elections in an environment essentially devoid of institutions to its subsequent preoccupation with the institutions of democracy and representative government. In a far-reaching contribution, he laid the foundations for an ambitious research program that would apply rational choice theory to every aspect of the political market place. Without apparently having read Black's (1948) contribution, and having no clear concept of the importance of the median (Rowley 2003), Downs utilized the spatial economic theory of Harold Hotelling (1929) to emphasize the predictable dominance of the middle voter in two party democracies, thus offering a falsifiable theory of democracy that would attract a large volume of high quality empirical research.

However, even while re-establishing the notion that political markets, under favorable circumstances, may reflect the preferences of the middle voter, even while forcing the rational choice analysis of economists down the throats of political scientists, Downs sowed seeds of doubt that subsequently generated fruitful public choice research. He noted that, in an environment where information is complex, costly to acquire, and offering little economic return to those who acquire it, members of the electorate may economize in its acquisition, relying on ideology as represented by political party brand images to direct their voting decisions. He also noted that members of the electorate might rationally abstain from voting in situations where they could not distinguish between the policy positions of rival candidates or political parties.

Such doubts, notwithstanding, Downs (1957) essentially replicated the work of Black (1948) in rejecting the sophistry of Arrow (1950, 1951) and in reinforcing the notion that political markets inherently are stable and reflect the preferences of the middle voter. His original contribution consists of extending the 1948 insight of Black to the real world institutions of politics.

The classics of public choice reviewed so far focused attention exclusively on voting in unconstrained democratic environments. As such they were only of limited significance for a constitutional republic such as the United States of America, a republic that deliberately was not designed to be a democracy as usually defined. In 1962, Buchanan and Tullock ingeniously shifted the public choice perspective well away from the environment of parliamentary democracy as envisaged by Downs (1957) to reflect the institutions of constitutional republicanism envisaged by the authors of *The Federalist* almost two centuries earlier.

The Calculus of Consent (Buchanan and Tullock 1962) differed sharply from earlier contributions in the emphasis provided by Buchanan and Tullock on methodological individualism and universal consent. More important for public choice and constitutional political economy, however, was the insight provided by Buchanan and Tullock's constitutional economic theory. The authors were able to demonstrate that at the constitutional stage, an individual rationally would choose to abide by a vote ratio that minimized the sum of his expected external costs and his expected decision-making costs from collective action. Whether this vote ratio would be some minority vote, a simple majority or some supra-majority vote would depend on the slopes of the two aggregated functions. This result was a direct challenge to the political scientists who almost universally at that time endorsed the normative advantages of majority rule.

The Calculus of Consent also challenged the new welfare economics of Samuelson and Arrow that systematically paved the way for government intervention in free markets on the grounds of widespread market failure. Buchanan and Tullock noted that all categories of market failure – monopoly power, public goods, externalities, limited and asymmetric information and moral hazard – were evident much more in political than in ordinary markets, not least because of the ubiquity of indivisibilities in political markets.

By this insight, Buchanan and Tullock leveled the playing field in the debate over the respective merits of political and economic markets (Goetz 1991). By directing attention to the difference between choices over rules and choices subject to rules, the book also provided the logical foundations for the constitutional political economy research program.

Although both Downs and Buchanan and Tullock discussed the role for interest groups in political markets, neither of them analyzed interest group behavior from the perspective of rational choice theory. This *lacuna* was filled by the fifth and final founding father of public choice, Mancur Olson, whose book *The Logic of Collective Action* (1965) fundamentally challenged the conventional political science view of interest group behavior.

Whereas political science viewed interest groups as reflective of underlying voter preferences and as suppliers of relevant information to political markets, Olson offered a radically different interpretation. Because the objectives pursued by interest groups have profound publicness characteristics, rational choice predicts that their efforts typically will be eroded by free-rider problems, so that groups will be difficult to form and to motivate.

However, such difficulties are not uniform across groups. Existing groups have decisive advantages over potential groups in the competition for political favors; groups offering concentrated benefits are more effective than groups offering dispersed benefits; small groups are more effective than large groups; groups that can coerce supply (e.g. professional associations and trade unions) are more effective than those that cannot; and that successful large groups must rely on providing selective (private) benefits to members in order to attract support for policies with public good/bad characteristics (for a critique of this view see Stigler 1974).

Thus the logic of collective action suggests that competition among interest groups does not simply reinforce the underlying voter-directed political equilibrium. Rather, it predictably distorts the underlying political equilibrium in favor of policies favored by the more effective interest groups, policies typically that provide concentrated benefits for the few financed by dispersed taxes on the many.

2. Alternative Perspectives in Public Choice

Like all successful intellectual innovations, public choice has given birth to a new generation of scholars, journals and research institutions, offering a diversity of approaches and methods, not all of which correspond to those adopted by the 'founding fathers' (Mitchell 1988, 1989, 2001). Three schools currently dominate the public choice landscape, each worthy of a brief discussion, namely Rochester, Chicago and Virginia.

Rochester

The intellectual entrepreneur of the Rochester school of positive political theory was William Riker, who began to consider the applicability of the rational choice approach and game theory in political science during the late 1950's (Riker 1962). In 1964, he strengthened this presence by transforming his introductory text on American government into the first rational choice book aimed at undergraduate majors in political science (Riker 1964).

By rejecting the then fashionable behavioral school in favor of rational choice theory, Riker indicated that he was stepping outside conventional political science in order to embrace the challenge from economics on its own terms. By employing game theory, Riker indicated that conflict and conflict resolution was an integral part of public choice, a view that was not universally shared by the leading Virginian scholars at that time (Buchanan and Tullock 1962).

By 1973, Riker and Ordeshook felt able to define politics as 'the mystery of how social science evolves out of individual preferences' (Riker and Ordeshook 1973, p. 6). Their book demonstrated that the mystery would be resolved by mathematical political science buttressed by the use of rigorous statistical method. Once again, Buchanan and Tullock, the joint leaders of the Virginia School were uncomfortable with this choice of scientific method.

The Rochester School encompasses such well-known scholars as Riker, Aranson and Banks (all now deceased), Ordeshook, Brams, Enelow, Hinich, Munger, Aldrich, Schofield, McKelvey, Fiorina, Ferejohn, Shepsle, Weingast, Romer and Austin-Smith. It consistently applies positive political science to the study of elections, party strategies, voting agenda manipulation, interest groups, coalition formation, legislative behavior and bureaucratic behavior. The rational choice approach is deployed unremittingly in this research program.

Until the early 1980's, with the notable exceptions of Riker and Aranson, the Rochester School focused primarily on abstract theoretical analysis largely ignoring institutional details. In part, this reflected a reaction against the institutionalism of conventional political science. In part, it reflected the preoccupation of Rochester scholars with spatial voting models (Enelow and Hinich 1984). As public choice analysis gradually eroded confidence in the vote motive as a primary determinant of political market behavior, and as Virginia School interest-group theories began to play an ever more important role, the research program of the Rochester School appeared to be in significant decline.

The program was rescued during the early 1980's by such scholars as Kenneth Shepsle and Barry Weingast who shifted direction and initiated influential research into the institutions of the US legislature and the federal bureaucracy. Drawing heavily on recent research findings in the new institutional economics, these scholars have blended political science with economics to the extent that it is now extremely difficult to unravel the primary focus. Initially, this Rochester program was chauvinistic, directed almost exclusively at US institutions and surprisingly narrow, ignoring the complex interactions between the separate branches of a compound republic. More recently, it has extended its focus to the international arena and has begun to model the interactive behavior of the separate branches of the US government.

The Rochester program, for the most part, eschews normative discussion. Its practitioners, whatever their personal philosophies, report neutrally on such matters as cyclical majorities, log-rolling, interest-group politics, legislative stability, bureaucratic discretion and the like. Some, like Shepsle (1982) are skeptical about constitutional reforms. Others like Fiorina (1983) are hostile to studies that find fault with the federal bureaucracy. Riker and Aranson were notable exceptions to this apolitical neutrality. However, they are no longer with us.

Chicago

The Chicago political economy research program (CPE) was a relatively late starter, launched by George Stigler's 1971 article on economic regulation. Like so much of Chicago scholarship, this program largely ignored preceding non-Chicago work in the field and still fails to cite such work in its own publications. In rebuilding the wheel, however, it made distinctive contributions to the literature.

Although Stigler retained the mantle of leadership until his death in 1991, leading Chicago economists such as Gary Becker, Sam Peltzman and William Landes and leading legal scholars such as Richard Posner quickly joined the program. Although the Chicago School itself has a lengthy pedigree in normative as well as in positive analysis – Frank Knight, Jacob Viner, Henry Simons and Milton Friedman – CPE under the deconstructive influence of Stigler was overtly positive, asserting for the most part that 'what is is technically efficient'. Although economists could observe, explain and predict, attempts to change the course of history by and large were deemed to be futile, wasteful uses of scarce resources (Rowley 1992, 38–41).

CPE is a body of literature that analyses government from the perspective of rational choice theory and neoclassical price theory (Mitchell 1989, Tollison 1989). It views government primarily as a mechanism utilized by rational, self-seeking individuals to redistribute wealth within society. Homo economicus is modeled almost exclusively as an expected wealth-maximizing agent (Reder 1982). From this perspective, 'fresh-water economics' mocks the 'salt-water economics' of the east coast academies for their adherence to the public interest theory of government: 'Get your heads out of the sand you hay-bags!'

Ironically, however, CPE ends up with a view of the political process that is not far distant from that of the public interest school. Specifically, political markets are viewed as technically efficient mechanisms for satisfying the preferences for redistribution of individual citizens working through efficient pressure groups. This interpretation of the political process emanates from a fundamentally flawed application of Chicago microeconomics to the political marketplace.

CPE draws on the tight prior equilibrium methodology applied by Chicago economists in their analysis of private markets (Reder 1982) in its study of transfer politics. The thrust of this methodology is toward instantaneous and durable equilibria, with political markets always clearing. In equilibrium no individual can raise his expected utility (wealth) without reducing the expected utility (wealth) of at least one other individual. Political agents (brokers) clear political markets without invading them as principals. They are driven by constraints, not by preferences. There is no role for ideology in the CPE research program.

The auxiliary hypotheses of the CPE program ensure that political market equilibria are tight and instantaneous. It is assumed that all political actors are price-takers; that there is no discretionary power in political markets; that the prices at which individuals agree to contract are market-clearing prices consistent with optimizing behavior; that such prices reflect all economically relevant information; that individuals engage in optimal search; that all constraints on political market behavior are efficient, reflecting expected utility maximizing behavior on the part of those who create or modify them.

The auxiliary conditions imposed by CPE do not produce political market equilibria based on perfect foresight. Random disturbances cannot be accommodated. Nor will political actors utilize uneconomic information. The system responds with stochastic analogs of determinist general equilibrium. A particular feature of CPE, as of the Chicago School more generally, is the presumption that only propositions derived from tight prior equilibrium theory are valid. In a sense, CPE demands that the findings of empirical research must be consistent with the implications of standard price theory (Reder 1982). This is a dangerous perversion of the methodology of positive economics advanced in 1953 by Milton Friedman.

Ultimately, the Chicago presumption must give way if confronted with relentlessly adverse evidence. But this can take a very long time, given the malleability of statistical techniques and of political-economic data. When Gary Becker (1976) remains willing to defend in-kind transfers as carrying lower excess burdens than lump sum transfers of income, when George Stigler (1992) argues that all long-lived trade protection tariffs are efficient, while William Landes and Richard Posner (1987) defend U.S. tort law as being economically efficient, and while the *Journal of Political Economy* publishes papers that defend the U.S. federal farm program as an efficient mechanism for transferring income to poor farmers, there is justifiable cause to worry whether CPE scholars and their journal editors ever look out from their ivory towers and survey the real world.

Virginia

The Virginia School, with its early roots in the economics of Frank Knight and Henry Simons at the University of Chicago (Mitchell 1988, 2001) is the most far-reaching program in public choice, provocative because many of its practitioners do not hesitate to step across the divide separating science from moral philosophy. Under the early intellectual leadership of James M. Buchanan and Gordon Tullock, the Virginia School established itself in the teeth of active opposition both from orthodox neoclassical economics and from conventional political science. It has challenged successfully, *inter alia*, Keynesian macroeconomics, Pigovian welfare economics, conventional public finance and the veneration of simple-majority democracies.

From the outset, the Virginia School differentiated its research program from the early public choice contributions of Duncan Black (1948) and Anthony Downs (1957) through its focus on the logical foundations of a constitutional democracy. In 1962, Buchanan and Tullock published *The Calculus of Consent*, arguably the single most important text ever written in public choice and constitutional political economy.

This book demonstrates that individuals are capable of long-run expected utility maximization when establishing the rules of the game, even though they will resort to short-run expected utility maximization when playing under rules. Because constitutional rules are designed to be durable, individuals confront generalized uncertainty with respect to the impact of such rules on their individual lives. This generalized uncertainty makes possible near-universal consent regarding rules even among a heterogeneous electorate without reliance on the artificial assumptions later used by John Rawls in his famous book, *A Theory of Justice* (1971).

The Virginia tradition commenced in earnest in 1957, with the founding by James Buchanan and Warren Nutter of *The Thomas Jefferson Center for Studies in Political Economy* at the University of Virginia. For a decade, Buchanan, Tullock, and Ronald Coase pioneered a research program that would fundamentally change the playing field of political economy throughout the Western World by providing an effective scientific counter-balance to the early postwar onslaught by neoclassical economists targeted against the capitalist system.

Throughout the period 1945 – 1957, Keynesian macroeconomists, Pigovian welfare economists, Arrovian social choice theorists and Musgravian public finance scholars had waged an unrelenting war against free markets, alleging near-universal market failure and exploring the appropriate public sector responses by benevolent and impartial democratic governments. Even such an old-style free market economist as Milton Friedman (1963) was forced onto the defensive, devising ever more exotic methods of government intervention designed to minimize the discretionary power of government while recognizing that private markets were widely beset by such problems as monopoly, externalities, public goods and bounded rationality. Even Harold Demsetz, whose writing always stressed the importance of a comparative institutions approach to policy formation, had no theory of government from which to launch a scientific counter-attack.

In a *tour de force*, Buchanan and Tullock (1962) provided the missing theory of government and placed the advocates of market failure on the defensive (Goetz 1991). If problems of monopoly, externalities, public goods and bounded rationality afflicted private markets, they simply ravaged political markets that confronted individuals with massive indivisibilities and severely limited exit options. The scene was set for a program of scientific endeavor that would expose government failures and for a program of moral philosophy that would support constitutional reforms designed to restrict the scope and size of government.

The Virginia School does not focus primarily on the vote motive as the fulcrum of political markets, in part because of the paradox of voting implicit in rational ignorance and rational abstentions in large numbers elections (Rowley 1984), in part because of the lengthy period between elections (Mitchell 1988) and in part because of agenda control problems (Romer and Rosenthal 1978). Instead, a great deal of analysis is focused on the behavior of interest groups, the legislature, the executive, the judiciary and the bureaucracy. The results of such scientific inquiry rarely show the political market in a favorable light. Only through constitutional interventions do Virginians see much prospect of utility-enhancing institutional reforms (Buchanan, Rowley and Tollison 1987).

The Virginia research program analyses government, from the perspective of neoclassical price theory, as a vehicle used by rational self-seeking individuals to redistribute wealth (Rowley 1992). In this respect, the protected core of the research program closely resembles that of Chicago. Yet, its central hypotheses – suggestive of widespread government failure – could not be more different.

Important differences in the auxiliary statements of the two programs explain this divergence. Virginia, unlike Chicago, does not assume that individuals are always price takers in political markets; significant discretionary power is recognized. Virginia does not assume as generally as Chicago that political markets clear instantaneously and completely. Virginia does not assume that decision-makers in political markets are always fully informed about the present or that they are capable of forming rational expectations over the future. Virginia does not excise human error from its theory of political market behavior, and does not ignore institutions in favor of black-box theory (Rowley 1997, Rowley and Vachris 1994).

That its central hypotheses differ so sharply from those of a school that applies unmodified private market theory to political market analysis is only to be expected.

3. The Vote Motive

The early contributions to public choice (Black 1948, Downs 1957) viewed the vote motive as a key determinant of political market equilibrium. Black (1948) deduced the median voter theorem whereby competing political candidates would be driven by vote considerations to converge in policy space to a unique and stable equilibrium that reflected the policy preferences of the median voter.

Downs (1957) reinvented Black's wheel albeit without reference to the median voter. He focused on systems of two party representative governments and demonstrated that vote maximizing politicians would formulate policies to win elections rather than seek political victory in order to implement preferred policies. He also noted the tendency for such political competition to converge to the center of the voter distribution, albeit without distinguishing between the mode, the median and the mean since he deployed normal distributions throughout his analyses.

This equilibrium offered little discretion to political parties unless they had no serious aspiration to govern. As such, it should have been attractive to those wedded to majoritarian political outcomes. In reality, it was anathema to conventional political scientists because of its strict adherence to the rational choice approach.

In the event, the median voter theorem, while still attracting attention among public choice scholars promised more than it could deliver. It rests on a stringent set of assumptions that coincide only rarely in political markets (Rowley 1984):

1. Two political parties must contest the election;
2. The policies at issue must collapse into one dimension of left-right space;
3. Voter preferences must be single-peaked over policy space;
4. Political parties must be able and willing to move across policy space;
5. Political parties must be well informed regarding the preferred policies of the voters;
6. Voters must be well informed regarding the policy positions of the competing parties;
7. Voters must not abstain in significant numbers from voting in elections;
8. Voters must punish governments that deviate from their electoral manifesto.

Once these assumptions are relaxed, individually or severally, to take account of the realities of political markets, the median solution is much less dominant, especially where the distribution of voter preferences is skewed or multi-modal (Rowley 1984). In some circumstances, the mean dominates the median (Romer and Rosenthal 1979). In others, the political equilibrium cycles in single or in multi-dimensional policy space (Black 1948, Arrow 1951). In yet other circumstances, there is no equilibrium as the political parties become immobilized at separate positions in policy space (Rowley 1984). In consequence the grip of voter majorities over the election manifestos must be viewed as much looser than either Black or Downs was willing to acknowledge.

Enelow and Hinich (1984) challenged the assumption, central both to Black and to Downs, that competing political parties (or presidential candidates) are mobile over policy space. Their counter-hypothesis is that political parties are immobilized in the short run by the recent history of their political behavior. In such circumstances, political parties (candidates) must advertise to consolidate the voter preference distribution around their respective positions in policy space. Rationally ignorant voters are vulnerable to such persuasive advertising. To the extent that they are correct, and elections are determined by campaign expenditures, the concept of revealed voter preferences is rendered suspect and, with it, the underlying connection between political equilibrium and majoritarian politics.

The probability that an individual vote will prove to be decisive in a major election is minute (less than one in a million in U.S. presidential elections (Stigler 1971). This implies that the differential expected benefit to any voter from voting decisively in an election is also trivial, far less than the cost of voting. Only some notion of civil duty or some major miscalculation of probabilities will drive the rational voter to the polls. Only an active consumption interest will motivate the rational individual to become informed about the political market. Otherwise, he will remain rationally ignorant, whether or not he casts his vote, and will rely on opaque ideology indicators to determine his electoral strategy (Downs 1957). Alternatively, knowing that his vote is indecisive, he will vote expressively, following his heart rather than his interest. This serious consequence of the indivisibility of the vote mechanism opens up tempting avenues for interest groups to invade the political process (for a counter view see Peltzman 1984).

Elections are discrete events in a continuous political process. The vote motive, at its best, is only as influential as elections are in controlling the post-election behavior of incumbents (Tullock 1976). Such control is limited by the high rate of voter memory decay that protects deviant governments from adverse electoral consequences. It is further weakened by the ability of political parties to full-line policy bundles intermingling popular with less popular policy proposals in the electoral process.

Once again, these weaknesses open up opportunities for effective interest groups to divert the supply of policies well away from the preferences of the median voter (for a useful survey of spatial models see Ordeshook 1997).

4. The Special Interests

A special interest issue is one that generates substantial personal benefits for a small number of constituents while imposing a small individual cost on a large number of other potential voters (Gwartney and Wagner 1988). As James Madison recognized in *The Federalist* (Number 51, 1787), a majority-based system of representative government is biased toward the adoption of special interest (or faction-based) policies, even when such policies are generally harmful to society. The Founding Fathers wrote the separation of powers and the bicameral legislature into the United States Constitution to curtail this perceived political bias. The 'Bill of Rights' (the first ten amendments to the Constitution) were clearly designed to protect individuals from the excesses of federal and state governments.

Arguably, these constitutional constraints have failed to hold firm against special interest pressures. Facilitated by a weak Supreme Court, that became increasingly deferential toward the legislative branch of government after 1936, parchment has ceded victory to the guns of the special interests and has allowed factions to roam freely across constitutional constraints (Wagner 1987).

Special interests emerge to take advantage of rational ignorance within the legislature, through the mechanism of persuasive campaign contributions, to obtain advantages for their members more than commensurate with their relative voting strength. Their success depends on their relative abilities to offer political gains, in the forms of votes and money, to politicians who broker policies beneficial to concentrated interests and detrimental to diffused interests (Ekelund and Tollison 2001). Legislatures infested with such parasites typically manifest weak party allegiance and relatively high incumbent electoral success rates.

The logic of collective action (Olson 1965) demonstrates that interest groups are far from easy to organize. Because many of the benefits to be derived from effective interest group lobbying have public good or public bad characteristics, free riding by members of the group is rational. Such free riding diminishes the pressure that can be exerted on the legislature. The free riding problem is not dispersed equally, however, across potential interest groups. Some groups, notably in the United States, trade unions and professional groups, are able to coerce supply. Other groups, notably producer groups, successfully engage in collective action, in the absence of coercion, because they are small and homogeneous. These groups predictably will be differentially successful in the political process.

Large, diffuse groups confront the free riding problem in its most devastating form. In many instances, for example consumers and taxpayers, they simply cannot form an effective coalition. If such interest groups are to be politically effective, they must organize themselves primarily to provide private (or selective) benefits to the membership, bundling their public objectives into the subscription fee as a by-product of their activities. The by-product solution, coupled with the tax privileged status of most such groups, explains the existence and relative success of organizations active on behalf of the elderly, of abortion rights, of the environment etc., each of which is plagued by public good or public bad characteristics.

To the extent that Olson's (1965) theory is correct, and there is a great deal of accumulated evidence in its favor, the implications for the political process are serious. Interest group pressures will divert the political equilibrium away from the median voter even under circumstances outlined by Duncan Black (1948). Moreover, because such diversions are most effectively achieved through redistributions that are opaque and not transparent, interest group politics will impose high excess burdens on society, as regulations and complex in-kind subsidies are favored over lump sum transfers (Olson 1982).

The logic of collective action constitutes a core element of Virginia Political Economy. It has been challenged, inevitably, by the Chicago School, notably in the scholarship of Gary Becker (1983, 1985) and more recently of Donald Wittman (1989, 1995). Gary Becker modeled interest groups within a general equilibrium framework, on the assumption that they can be formed and reorganized at a minimal cost, that their policy benefits, for the most part, are private and not public in nature, and that free riding can be limited by low cost monitoring. It is not surprising that these assumptions result in a much more benign view of such organizations.

Specifically, Becker suggests that interest groups redistribute wealth efficiently, minimizing the deadweight costs to society. Groups that impose high deadweight excess burdens, in this view, are replaced by more efficient alternatives. This *Panglossian* view has its advocates, mostly from the University of Chicago. The public choice evidence almost universally refutes the predictions of the model (Ekelund and Tollison 2001). There are, for example, virtually no instances of lump sum redistribution in any democracy. Sadly, the post-Friedman Chicago is less interested in positive methodology (Friedman 1953, Lakatos 1978) and more interested in the elegance of theory, in this sense following the standard bias of modern neoclassical economics.

5. Rent Seeking and Rent Extraction

Rents are here defined as returns in excess of opportunity cost engineered in a market economy by the regulatory intervention of government (Tollison, 1982, 1997, Rowley, Tollison and Tullock, 1988). The availability of such rents gives rise to rent seeking on the part of interest groups, whose members rationally expend resources in a competition to secure the present value of the rents that are potentially available. Whether rent seeking outlays constitute welfare neutral transfers or whether they constitute welfare-reducing wastes of resources depends on the institutional structure, although the general presumption is that some waste occurs even within a well-designed political system. The extent of rent seeking outlays in response to any given aggregate of available rents depends on attitudes towards risk, the nature of returns to scale in rent seeking and the nature of the rent seeking game (Tullock 1980).

As with so many important contributions to public choice, the original insight came from Gordon Tullock, this time in his seminal 1967 paper in *The Western Economic Journal* challenging the then conventional wisdom that the only loss of welfare from monopoly was the deadweight loss characterized as the *Harberger Triangle* (Harberger 1954). Tullock focused attention on the *Tullock Rectangle* of producer's surplus created as a consequence of monopoly and posed the simply but crucially important question: would not producers when competing for that monopoly rationally expend aggregate resources, in the limit, equal to the present value of that rent? His positive reaction to that question shook the throne of the new welfare economics, and ultimately destroyed the latter's widely endorsed presumption against free markets.

In 1971, Tullock returned to the theme of his 1967 paper, which as yet had made little headway in mainstream economics, shifting attention to the cost of transfers. Drawing from his experience in China, where beggars mutilated themselves as a means of making themselves pitiful to potential donors, Tullock argued that many would be recipients of government transfers in the Western democracies engaged in similar forms of activity. Rejecting the notion that all political redistribution of wealth is voluntary, Tullock focused attention on the resource cost of competitive lobbying of politicians and bureaucrats both by those who sought transfers and by those who sought to prevent them. He noted that the resources invested in such activities were socially wasteful, irrespective as to whether the transfers were made or not.

By recognizing that government regulatory activities are endogenous, the self-seeking response to resource outlays by influential pressure groups, Tullock explicitly challenged the public interest theory of government. In 1974, Anne Krueger coined the term rent seeking to characterize these activities, a term that would take a central place in the public choice litany.

The rent seeking insight plays a central role in Virginia Political Economy, suggesting as it does that that there are significant welfare costs to government activity. By the same coin, the concept presents a fundamental challenge to Chicago School notions that democracies are efficient and that the cost of redistribution does not exceed the normal cost of government.

Indeed, in recognizing that successful rent seeking results in a transitional gains trap that obstructs efficient economic reforms (Tullock 1975), the research program explains why clearly inefficient regulations remain on the statute books and offers a clear warning to those who are rationally well-informed to work hard to obstruct the passing of new regulations, however attractive the latter may appear to be.

A recent empirical study by Laband and McClintock (2001) suggests that, for the United States, supposedly a relatively efficient constitutional republic, the annual cost of rent seeking and rent protection amounts at least to $400 billion. Evidently, this is not the normal cost of government, even if rent seeking continues to be downplayed or ignored entirely by Chicago economists. (See also Laband and Sophocleus 1988).

The rent seeking literature assumes that politicians are passive brokers of policies that create rents, responding to rent-seeking bids essentially as auctioneers bent on maximizing the size of their brokerage fees. A recent literature (McChesney 1987, 1997, 2001), however, presents a yet more dismal picture, by recognizing that politicians may abandon their brokerage roles in order to obtain yet more lucrative returns by threatening adverse legislation unless they are paid off in terms of protection moneys. Rent extraction, as this Mafia-like protection racket is labeled, is highly costly in terms of resource mis-allocation. Yet, like 'the dog that did not bark' it does not manifest itself at all in the public accounting system. Even should it be revealed, the politicians who benefit from it, unlike members of *La Cosa Nostra*, are immune from legal penalties.

6. The Legislature

Under conditions of democracy, elected politicians serve for specified or flexible terms in legislatures as representatives of the electorate. Legislatures typically are either unicameral or bicameral in nature. They may or they may not be constrained by written or by conventional constitutional rules.

Organized on the basis of political parties, or coalitions of parties, or committees and sub-committees, politicians essentially are political brokers, pairing demanders and suppliers of legislation, i.e., those willing to pay most for a particular law or transfer with those who are willing to pay the least to prevent such a law of transfer. Typically, such politician-brokers concentrate on legal arrangements that benefit well-organized and concentrated groups at the expense of diffuse interests, each of which latter is taxed a little to fund the transfer or legislation (Tollison 1988).

Although politicians have ideologies of their own, competition among them, together with the contestability of their positions, constrains their ability to pursue such ideologies unless they conform to those of the constituents who secured their election. Of course, that does not imply that some politicians will not risk an election loss by pursuing a goal to which they are especially attracted. Nor does it imply that politicians will misjudge the will of the electorate on ideologically charged issues. Fundamentally, however, politicians are brokers and not purveyors of policy (Rowley 1992).

Politicians expend resources in specific wealth transfer markets in return for brokerage fees that typically take the form of some mixture of campaign contributions, post-political career remuneration and promised votes. The size and continuity of such brokerage fees depend significantly upon the perceived durability of the wealth transfers. Durability, in a political system characterized by cycles, depends upon institutional constraints designed to protect the status quo. Such constraints vary significantly across the world's democratic legislatures. However, both politicians and interest groups share a common interest in promoting institutional arrangements that enhance the durability of laws (Tollison 1988).

In Westminster models of parliamentary democracy, where parliament is supreme and there is no effective separation of powers, durability of laws in a polity characterized by cycles is not easy to achieve. In such systems, the executive branch of government, the prime minister and the cabinet, are drawn from the elected legislature and are dependent for their continuation in office on the majority support of the legislature. The cabinet possesses agenda power in preparing legislation, but this is modified by the ongoing threat that alienated members of the majority party may withdraw parliamentary support and force the government to resign. Coalition governments, typical in many democracies in Continental Europe, are yet more vulnerable to cycles. Predictably, campaign contributions will be relatively low and interest group activity relatively less forceful, *ceteris paribus,* under all such systems of government than under more severely constrained models.

The United States legislature is just such a constrained model, both by constitutional design and by evolved institutional structure. Its bicameral format increases the difficulty both of passing and of repealing laws. The separation of powers allows for bills passed by both chambers to be vetoed by the President, forcing it back onto two-third supra-majority votes to override the veto. The independent federal judiciary patrols the borders of its legislation, in principle, at least to ensure that the Constitution has not been infringed. These constitutional constraints arguably enhance the durability of its determinations (Landes and Posner 1975, Anderson, Shughart and Tollison 1988, Tollison 1988, Mueller 1996).

In an alternative and important explanation of the stability and durability of legislative equilibrium, Shepsle (1978) and others have focused attention on the role of committees and the nature of committee assignments in both chambers of the United States Congress, but more especially in the House, as coalition-builders. In this analysis, committees substitute for more vulnerable logrolling (Tullock 1959) in overcoming the high transaction costs of contracting in political markets. They do so by providing a division of labor within the legislature, in which representatives specialize in the political issues relevant to their own districts.

The committee structure of Congress is grounded in 'property rights' granted to each committee of jurisdiction, allowing it almost exclusive rights in 'gate keeping' (i.e., in deciding whether or not to allow potential bills onto the floor of the chamber). It is also grounded in the 'deference' accorded to each committee by non-committee members, grounded both in reciprocity, in threat, and in the power of 'ex post settling up' accorded to committees with jurisdiction by the convention that conference committees between the two chambers are manned primarily by members of those original committees (Shepsle and Weingast 1981). In such circumstances, committees can protect the status quo, or their own bills from non-empty win-sets (Black and Newing 1951) thereby providing protection against cycling in an environment of instability.

Despite the growing literature based on the new institutional economics that focuses attention on the gains-from-trade aspect of 'politics-as-it-is', there is another, darker side of the legislative process that must not be ignored. Politics is not primarily concerned with gains-from-trade, but with obtaining power over the public authority (Moe 1987, 1990). When two poor voters and one rich voter comprise the electorate, the rich voter is in trouble. He is not in trouble because of political cycles and the instability of the political process. He is in trouble because the poor majority may decide to steal his wealth, using the political; process as a less costly mechanism than theft. To the extent, that the legislative process is concerned more with redistribution than with wealth creation, so the fear of the rich voter must be increased.

Because there are no long-term property rights in the public authority, the governing political party must exercise caution when legislating its institutions. Political opponents, should they access the power of those institutions, may deploy that power to reward their own constituents. For this reason, the agencies of government are often tightly constrained by legislation, or even are designed to fail in their express purposes (Moe 1990).

7. The Presidency

In countries exemplified by the United States, where the separation of powers is enshrined in the Constitution, the President is elected by an independent vote and holds his position for a fixed term quite independently from the wishes of the majority of the legislature. The United States Constitution arms the president with a veto power over bills emanating from the legislature. To override the presidential veto each chamber of the Congress must re-pass the affected bill with at least a two-third supra-majority vote. The veto threat effectively allows the President to serve as a third chamber of the legislature, logrolling with the other chambers in the shaping of legislation (Carter and Schap 1987). The President also enjoys significant regulatory powers delegated to him by Congress. These powers can be utilized to reward or to punish legislators who choose to pursue goals contrary to the preferences of his key constituents in the Electoral College (Moe 1987).

Potential differences in the interest group constituencies of the Congress and the president emanate in part from their different bases of representation. Special interests are much more effective when targeting their rent seeking on the specialized districts of the House than they are state-wide in the Senate. They are least effective in targeting the nation-wide constituency of the president. The special interests are most effective when working in opaque environments (Crew and Rowley 1988). Presidential politics are much more transparent than congressional politics.

One view that has some currency in the public choice literature (see Crain and Tollison 1979) is that the President and Congress override the separation of powers and the intent of the Founding Fathers and impose a collusion of powers designed to enhance the durability of legislation and thus to raise the brokerage fees provided by the special interests. While this perspective has some credibility when the presidency and the Congress are both controlled by a single political party, it is difficult to justify when the party of the president does not control the Congress.

When the Congress and the President are at odds with each other, it is by no means clear which branch will dominate. Madison (*The Federalist*, No. 53) envisaged the legislature as the dominant branch and worried about the power that this would accord to factions. Powerful presidents, (most notably Ronald Reagan) however, have influenced policy even when their parties have been in a legislative minority. Certainly, presidents are able to destabilize political equilibrium when the policies at issue are high priority and transparent.

8. The Judiciary

The United States federal judiciary was established by the Founding Fathers as a co-equal independent branch of government designed to function as an effective counter-weight to the legislative and the executive branches. To limits its powers, the federal judiciary is dependent on the President and the Congress for its appointments, dependent on the executive branch for enforcing its judgments, and on the Congress for appropriating its budget. Within these constraints, however, the judiciary patrols the behavior of the executive and the legislative branches to ensure that the Constitution is not violated.

To secure independence, federal judges are granted lifetime tenure, albeit subject to the sanction of impeachment. Their salaries cannot be reduced in nominal terms during their tenure. Their judgments, especially those of the Supreme Court, are accorded enormous respect even when they run counter to majority popular opinion. Even so, the federal judiciary has not escaped public choice scrutiny.

Because judges and justices are appointed through a political process, it is extremely unlikely that the 'best and the brightest' will be successful. Typically, they will have made contributions too controversial for the tender souls of the politicians. Potential appointees are scrutinized closely in terms of ideological bias and past political service.

Where the President's party controls the Senate, and thus the Judiciary Committee, candidates of the alternative political persuasion will not be nominated. Only stealth candidates who provide a false image of their views (notably in recent years Justice Souter) will wriggle through the selection process. Where the party of the president does not control the Senate, serious candidates will have to display mediocre intellects and enhanced deference to the legislature (in recent years Justice Kennedy is a good example) or to be willing to play the color card (Justice Thomas).

The interest-group theory of politics (McCormick and Tollison 1981) models legislatures as firms supplying wealth transfers to competing interest groups by means of contracts termed 'laws'. In one interpretation (Anderson 2001), the judiciary confirms such contracts by adjudicating in favor of the short-term interests of pressure groups who successfully bid for political influence. As the balance of pressure groups changes so the courts will shift their judgments, irrespective of the original intent of the legislation.

An alternative interpretation (Landes and Posner 1975), focuses on the long-run effects of judicial independence, arguing indeed that such independence may be an integral component of the interest-group theory of government. They argue that the function of judges is to provide stability to the bargains agreed between the legislature and organized pressure groups, thus increasing the value of the rents that are dispersed. Precisely because the judiciary is independent from the current legislature, the judiciary is able to resolve disputes concerning the interpretation or constitutionality of a law by reference to the intentions of the originally enacting legislative body. Landes and Posner (1975) provide weak empirical support for this proposition. The proposition remains suspect, however, because such long-run stabilization of contracts inevitably reduces the prospects for the forging of new contracts (Benson 2001). Legislators who control the budget appropriations to the judiciary are unlikely to allow strong judicial independence where it threatens their current brokerage fees in the rent-seeking market.

9. Bureaucracy

The bureaucracy of government, responsible for the implementation of policies that are legislated and signed into law, is located in the executive branch of government. However, bureaus are dependent on the legislature for budget appropriations, are subject to its oversight authority, and are vulnerable to new legislation where their activities place them at odds with the current legislative majority.

The traditional political science perspective envisaged senior bureaucrats as being impartial, and public-spirited in the sense of pursuing either the original intent of the legislation that created their bureaus or the current wishes of their legislative overseers. This perspective has been closely scrutinized by public choice scholars who have focused on the rational choice approach in which senior bureaucrats are viewed as maximizing their personal utilities subject to relevant institutional constraints.

Within the public choice perspective, the senior bureaucrats who exercise authority over the budget are viewed as self-seeking maximizers of utility that is defined as some balance between expected wealth, ideology, patronage, discretionary power and ease of management (Tullock 1965, Downs 1967, Niskanen 1971). Budget maximization (Niskanen 1971) or discretionary budget maximization (Niskanen 1975, 2001) is deployed as a plausible proxy for these various objectives. Senior bureaucrats commit a total output in return for a total budget appropriation. They seek the maximum budget compatible with satisfying this output commitment.

In negotiating such budgets with the legislature, senior bureaucrats are viewed as possessing information advantages because of the monopoly nature of their provisions. Their legislative overseers have little access to independent information regarding the bureau's production function. Because of the indivisible nature of the budgetary negotiations, the senior bureaucrats are able to operate as discriminating monopolists, extracting the total surplus from the legislature (Niskanen 1971).

The nature of the budgetary outcome under these bargaining conditions depends on two factors. First is the nature of the budgetary environment, specifically whether the bureau is demand-constrained or budget constrained (Niskanen 1971). In circumstances of relaxed oversight, or demand constraint, the budget-maximizing bureau simply maximizes the sixe of its bureau unconstrained by output constraints. In circumstances of tightened oversight, or budget constraint, the bureau maximizes the size of its budget at a lower level than would be possible under conditions of demand constraint.

In both circumstances, the output of the bureau is significantly higher than the median voter would prescribe. In the former case, the bureau is additionally technically inefficient, supplying its output at costs significantly higher than those minimally available to it. In the latter case, the bureau is technically efficient according to this model (Niskanen 1971).

Once discretionary budget maximization replaces budget maximization, the outcome of budget negotiations changes. Senior bureaucrats no longer negotiate deals that extend output beyond that optimally demanded by the legislature. Instead they focus their attention on maximizing the budget surplus that can be deployed in pursuit of other goals (Niskanen 1975). A key implication of this outcome is that bureaus are always technically inefficient, securing budgets significantly in excess of the minimal cost of providing output even if the level of their output is not in excess of the optimal requirements of the oversight committee.

Members of the bureaucracy predictably enter the political market place on the demand as well as on the supply side as special interests that are unconstrained by free-rider considerations (Rowley, Shughart and Tollison 1987). They tend to be differentially well-informed concerning the predictable response of legislators to specific initiatives. They are rationally well informed concerning the policies that their bureaus will administer. Predictably, senior bureaucrats favor non-transparent policy initiatives, not only to conceal special interest allocations from electoral scrutiny, but also to maximize their own discretionary power in the provision of commodities subject to their control (Crew and Rowley 1988).

Following Niskanen's seminal work, the public choice analysis of bureaus has reverted somewhat from his 1971 theory of bureau dominance to the view that oversight committees exercise significant control and that bureaus respond to a significant degree to the dictates of their political masters (Weingast and Moran 1983). The congressional dominance theory assumes that congressmen on the relevant committees possess sufficient incentives and sufficient sanctions to establish effective governance over the agencies that they monitor.

The federal bureaus and agencies established by statute usually, though not universally, are subject to oversight both by the Congress and by the President. Their budgets are appropriated by both chambers of the Congress but are subject to review and potential veto by the President. In such circumstances, it is relevant to analyze bureaucratic behavior from the perspective of a multiple principal-agent relationship (Rowley and Vachris 1993).

The congressional dominance theory (Weingast and Moran 1983) assumes that congressmen on the relevant oversight and appropriations committees possess sufficient incentives and sufficient sanctions to establish governance over the agencies that they monitor. Although the committees are not endowed with sufficient resources to engage in continuous monitoring, special interests keep them well informed about agency performance. By choking of appropriations to recalcitrant agents, by harassing them through the oversight process, and by threatening interventionist legislation, congressional committees are viewed as influential monitors. The threat of *ex post* sanctions and the promise of *ex post* settling up create ex ante incentives for agents to reflect the preferences of the majority vote on the relevant congressional committees.

The hub of the efficient governance hypothesis is the assumption that congressional committees exercise a near monopoly jurisdiction over their respective agents, thus benefiting from clearly defined property rights that encourage circumspect monitoring. To the extent that congressmen self-select the committees on which they serve, the near monopoly power that they access provides leverage over precisely those issues relevant to their individual political support and, hence, to their expectations of re-election.

If this hypothesis is correct, there are two testable predictions that should survive empirical testing, namely (1) that specific oversight/appropriations committees should exercise more influence than Congress as a whole over the behavior of particular agents and (2) that if the political complexion of a particular committee should shift, then so should the political relevant behavior of the associated agent. Early tests have not refuted either of these hypotheses (Weingast and Moran 1983, Weingast 1984, Grier 1991).

Nevertheless, because of the competition among multiple principals for agency control, agents will not be efficiently monitored. Considerable agency discretion will survive (Rowley and Vachris 1993). The multiplicity of principals arises from at least four sources, namely (1) jurisdictional overlaps among oversight committees in each chamber of the Congress, (2) duality of oversight responsibilities in a bicameral legislature, (3) jurisdictional conflicts between oversight and appropriations committees composed of different members and (4) the competing jurisdictions of the Congress and the President, especially when the Congress and the presidency are controlled by different political parties (Rowley and Vachris 1993).

10. Constitutional Political Economy

According to Buchanan (1990) there is a 'categorical distinction' to be made between constitutional economics and ordinary economics, a distinction in the ultimate behavioral object of analytical attention (*ibid.*, 2). In ordinary economics, analysis is concentrated on choices made *within* constraints that are imposed exogenously to the person or persons making that choice. Constitutional economics, in contrast, directs analytical attention to the choice *among* constraints, choices that are made *ex ante* by individuals in seeking to restrict their own and others' subsequent choice sets in the ordinary political sphere.

The seminal contribution to constitutional political economy is *The Calculus of Consent*, co-authored in 1962 by Buchanan and Tullock. This book outlined for the first time an individualistic theory of the constitution, assigning a central role to a single decision-making rules – that of general consensus or unanimity.

By focusing attention on the nature of expected external costs and expected decision-making costs under decision-rules short of unanimity, and by recognizing that constitutional rules are derived under conditions of generalized uncertainty, Buchanan and Tullock explained why rules of less than unanimity (not necessarily a simple majority rule) would be chosen unanimously by rational individuals at the constitutional stage: 'At best, majority rule should be viewed as one among many practical expedients made necessary by the costs of securing widespread agreement on political issues when individual and group interests diverge' (Buchanan and Tullock 1962).

The Calculus of Consent effectively leveled a playing field in political economy that had tilted dangerously against free markets during the late 1940's and 1950's. Advocates of the new welfare economics, led by Paul

Samuelson and Kenneth Arrow, had developed a sophisticated attack on free markets, claiming that they were plagued by problems of monopoly, externalities, public goods, and information deficiencies. By so doing, they had placed even Milton Friedman, the most formidable defender of the capitalist system, on the defensive (Friedman 1962).

Buchanan and Tullock (1962) redressed this imbalance by demonstrating that political markets were riddled by these exact same weaknesses, but much more generally because of the indivisibility of collective decision-making. Recognition of this reality by individuals deliberating under conditions of uncertainty in constitutional decision-making was precisely why they designed constitutions that would limit the range and extent of government and thus rein in the potential abuse of individual rights. In this sense, constitutional political economy explains why public choices are constrained by the unanimous consent of rational and free individuals.

The hard core of the constitutional political economy research program combines the assumptions of rational choice, methodological individualism and *homo oeconomicus* in a manner that distinguishes it sharply from all mainstream economic research programs designed to evaluate the nature and the role of the state (Brennan and Hamlin 2001). Over the following forty years, the auxiliary assumptions of the model have adjusted to reflect changing circumstances. Those working within the field, however, have not found it necessary to adjust the hard-core assumptions.

As the political environment in the United States deteriorated from the rosy scenario of the second Eisenhower administration through the civil rights crisis, and the Vietnam fiasco of the Kennedy and Johnson administrations, culminating in the Watergate crisis of the Nixon administration, Buchanan in particular became less enamored of the positive gains-from-trade approach of *The Calculus of Consent*. In *The Limits of Liberty* (1975), he effectively deployed the philosophy of Thomas Hobbes – the threat of beckoning anarchy – to protect the hard core of his research program in a much less favorable external environment. From this insight came some of the best scholarship of the program, most notably in 1977 *Democracy in Deficit* by Buchanan and Wagner.

There then occurred through the decade of the 1980's a shift of direction from science to moral philosophy as Brennan and Buchanan (1980, 1985) injected propositions from John Rawls (1971) into the protective belt of their theory. With the breakdown of the Soviet Empire in the early 1990's, scholars recognized that Rawls's 'veil of ignorance' played no role in the process of constitution making that followed in the wasteland left behind by socialism. In 1990, Buchanan returned to science in an important paper introducing his new journal, *Constitutional Political Economy*. Since then the constitutional political economy research program has proceeded successfully along the rational choice lines from whence it originated (Mueller 1996, Brennan and Hamlin 2001).

11. Bioeconomics of Non-Human Societies

Innovative public choice scholarship is extending the frontiers of the discipline well beyond the domain of rational economic man to encompass the behavior of other species, notably bees and fishes. Janet Landa, a law-and-economics scholar and a prominent bioeconomist, has written two important papers dealing with these species.

Her 1986 paper on the political economy of swarming in honeybees offers a fascinating study of collective action in biological systems. Landa explains the organization of bee swarming as a means whereby honeybees economize on information and decision-making costs when establishing a new nest site. She uses the Buchanan and Tullock (1962) theory choice of Pareto-optimal voting rules to explain why scout bees use the unanimity rule when deciding where to establish a new nest.

On the one hand, the external costs of using the 'any bee' rule would be very high for the whole bee swarm should the one bee find an unsuitable home. On the other hand, the decision-making costs of using the unanimity rule are low both because scout bees constitute only about 5 per cent of the whole swarm and because they are a homogeneous group, being experienced former foragers. Because of the high external costs relative to decision-making costs, the use of the rule of unanimity by scout bees is efficient.

Just as honeybees 'vote with their wings' (Landa 1986), when swarming out of their nest in search of a new home, so many species of fish 'vote with their fins' (Landa 1998), when forming schools in order to migrate to spawn, to search for new foraging areas, to hunt for prey and to organize for defense. In her 1998 paper, Landa applies public choice analysis to the biological literature on schooling fish, using a selfish fish, club-theoretic paradigm.

On this basis she hypothesizes that a selfish fish (a) joins the fish school because it derives hydrodynamic benefits (a club good), (b) has no incentive to completely free-ride because it will be left behind by the school if it attempts so to do, (c) has no incentive to shirk a leadership role because of role reversibility between leaders and followers, (d) derives defense benefits against predators from its membership of the school, and (e) has no incentive to discriminate against odd-looking outsiders since odd-looking fish in a school are attacked more frequently by predators than are look-alikes. On the other hand, outsiders display xenophobia towards insiders because outsiders do not wish to become prime targets for predators. As a consequence, fish schools tend to be homogeneous.

Finally, Landa applies the Buchanan and Tullock (1962) theory of choice of optimal voting rules to explain why the 'any leader' rule for making the collective choice to escape, the main anti-predator defense strategy, is optimal for members of a fish school. In so doing, Landa explains the leaderless, completely decentralized form of organization of fish schools, in contrast to bee swarms. Evidently, the reach of *The Calculus of Consent* extends well beyond *Homo Sapiens* into the bioeconomics (consilience of economics with biology) of non-human societies.

Charles K. Rowley
Duncan Black Professor of Economics
James M. Buchanan Center for Political Economy
George Mason University

and

General Director
The Locke Institute
Fairfax, Virginia

REFERENCES

Aldrich, J.H. (1997). 'When is it rational to vote?' in D.C. Mueller (ed.) *Perspectives on Public Choice*. Cambridge: Cambridge University Press.

Anderson, G. (2001). 'The judiciary'. In W.F. Shughart and L. Razzolini (eds.) *The Elgar Companion to Public Choice*. Cheltenham, UK and Northampton, USA: Edward Elgar Publishing, 293–309.

Anderson, G.A., Shughart, W.F. and Tollison, R.D. (1988). 'On the Incentive of Judges to enforce Legislative Wealth Transfers'. *Journal of Law and Economics*, 31, 215–228.

Arrow, K.J. (1950). 'A Difficulty in the Concept of Social Welfare', *Journal of Political Economy* 58, 328–46.

Arrow, K.J. (1951). *Social Choice and Individual Values*. New York: John Wiley.

Becker, G.S. (1976). 'Comment on Peltzman' *Journal of Law and Economics* XIX (2), 245–248.

Becker, G.S. (1983). 'A theory of competition among pressure groups for political influence'. *Quarterly Journal of Economics*, 63, 371–400.

Benson, B. (2001). 'Law and economics' In W.F. Shughart and L. Razzolini (eds.) *The Elgar Companion to Public Choice*, Cheltenham, UK and Northampton, USA: Edward Elgar Publishing, 547–589.

Black, D. (1948). 'On the rationale of group decision-making'. *Journal of Political Economy*, 56, 23–34.

Brennan, H.G. and Buchanan, J.M. (1980). *The Power to Tax*. Cambridge: Cambridge University Press.

Brennan, H.G. and Buchanan, J.M. (1985). *The Reason of Rules*. Cambridge: Cambridge University Press.

Brennan, H.G. and Hamlin, A. (2001). 'Constitutional choice' In W.F. Shughart and L. Razzolini (eds.) *The Elgar Companion to Public Choice*. Cheltenham, UK and Northampton, USA: Edward Elgar Publishing, 117–139.

Buchanan, J.M. (1975). *The Limits of Liberty: Between Anarchy and Leviathan*. Chicago: Chicago University Press.

Buchanan, J.M. (1987). 'The constitution of economic policy'. *American Economic Review*, 77 (3), 243–250.

Buchanan, J.M. (1990). 'The domain of constitutional economics'. *Constitutional Political Economy*, 1 (1), 1–18.

Buchanan, J.M., Rowley, C.K. and Tollison, R.D. (1987). *Deficits*. Oxford: Basil Blackwell.

Buchanan, J.M. and Tullock, G. (1962). *The Calculus of Consent*. Ann Arbor: University of Michigan Press.

Buchanan, J.M. and Wagner, R.E. (1977). *Democracy in Deficit: The Political Legacy of Lord Keynes*. New York: Academic Press.

Carter, J.R. and Schap, D. (1987). 'Executive veto, legislative override and structure-induced equilibrium'. *Public Choice*, 52, 227–44.

Coase, R.H. (1960). 'The Problem of Social Cost'. *Journal of Law and Economics*, 3, 1–44.

Crain, W.M. (2001). 'Institutions, durability, and the value of political transactions'. In W.F. Shughart and L. Razzolini (eds.) *The Elgar Companion to Public Choice*. Cheltenham, UK and Northampton, USA: Edward Elgar Publishing, 183–196.

Crain, W.M. and Tollison, R.D. (1979a). 'Constitutional Change in an Interest Group Perspective'. *Journal of Legal Studies*, 8, 156–175.

Crain, W.M. and Tollison, R.D. (1979b). 'The Executive Branch in the Interest-Group Theory of Government'. *Journal of Legal Studies*, 8, 555–567.

Crew, M.A. and Rowley, C.K. (1988). 'Toward a Public Choice Theory of Regulation'. *Public Choice*, 57, 49–67.

Downs, A. (1957). *An Economic Theory of Democracy*. New York: Harper & Row.

Downs, A. (1967). *Inside Bureaucracy*. Boston: Little Brown.

Ekelund, R.B. and Tollison, R.D. (2001). In W.F. Shughart and L. Razzolini (eds.) *The Elgar Companion to Public Choice*. Cheltenham, UK and Northampton, USA: Edward Elgar Publishing, 357–378.

Enelow, J.M. and Hinich, M.J. (1984). *The Spatial Theory of Voting*. Cambridge: Cambridge University Press.

Fiorina, M. (1983). 'Flagellating the Federal Bureaucracy'. *Society*, 66–73.

Friedman, M. (1953). 'The Methodology of Positive Economics' In M. Friedman, *Essays in Positive Economics*. Chicago: University of Chicago Press, 3–43.

Friedman, M. (1962). *Capitalism and Freedom*. Chicago: University of Chicago Press.

Goetz, C.J. (1991). *Uncommon Common-Sense vs. Conventional wisdom: The Virginia School of Economics*. Fairfax: Center for Study of Public Choice.

Grier, K. (1991). 'Congressional Influence on US Monetary Policy: An Empirical Test'. *Journal of Monetary Economics*, 28, 202–220.

Gwartney, J. and Wagner, R.E. (1988). *Public Choice and Constitutional Economics*. Greenwich: JAI Press.

Harberger, A.C. (1954). 'Monopoly and Resource Allocation', *American Economic Review* 44, 77–87.

Hotelling, H. (1929). 'Stability in Competition', *American Economic Review* 39, 41–57.

Lakatos, I. (1978). *The Methodology of Scientific Research Programs*. Cambridge: Cambridge University Press.

Laband, D.N. and McClintock, G.C. (2001). *The Transfer Society*. Washington, DC: The Cato Institute.

Laband, D.N. and Sophocleus, J.P. (1988). 'The social cost of rent seeking: first estimates'. *Public Choice*, 58, 269–276.

Landa, J. (1986). 'The political economy of swarming in honeybees: voting-with-wings, decision-making costs, and the unanimity rule'. *Public Choice*, 51, 25–38.

Landa, J. (1998). 'Bioeconomics of schooling fishes: selfish fish, quasi-free riders, and other fishy tales'. *Environmental Biology of Fishes*, 53, 353–364.

Landes, W.E. and Posner, R.A. (1975). 'The Independent Judiciary in an Interest Group Perspective'. *Journal of Law and Economics*, 18, 875–902.

Landes, W.E. and Posner, R.A. (1987). *The Economic Structure of Tort Law*. Cambridge: Cambridge University Press.

Madison, J. (1788). *The Federalist* 51, Publius, February 6.

Madison, J. (1788). *The Federalist* 53, Publius, February 9.

McChesney, F.S. (1987). 'Rent extraction and rent creation in the economic theory of regulation'. *Journal of Legal Studies*, 16, 101–118.

McChesney, F.S. (1997). *Money for Nothing: Politicians, Rent Extraction, and Political Extortion*. Cambridge, MA: Harvard University Press.

McChesney, F.S. (2001). 'Rent seeking and rent extraction' In W.F. Shughart and L. Razzolini (eds.) *The Elgar Companion to Public Choice*. Cheltenham, UK and Northampton, USA: Edward Elgar Publishing, 379–395.

McCormick, R.E. and Tollison, R.D. (1981). *Politicians, Legislation and the Economy: An Inquiry into the Interest-Group Theory of Government*. Boston: Martinus Nijhoff.

Mitchell, W.C. (1988). 'Virginia, Rochester and Bloomington: Twenty-five Years of Public Choice and Political Science'. *Public Choice*, 56, 101–120.

Mitchell, W.C. (1989). 'Chicago Political Economy: A Public Choice Perspective'. *Public Choice*, 63, 282–292.

Mitchell, W.C. (2001). 'The old and the new public choice: Chicago versus Virginia' In W.F. Shughart and L. Rozzalini (eds.) *The Elgar Companion to Public Choice*. Cheltenham, UK and Northampton, USA: Edward Elgar Publishing, 3–30.

Moe, T.N. (1987). 'An Assessment of the Positive Theory of Congressional Dominance' *Legislative Studies Quarterly*, 12, 475–520.

Moe, T.N. (1990). 'Political Institutions: The Neglected Side of the Story'. *Journal of Law, Economics and Organization*, 6, 213–253.

Moe, T.N. (1997). 'The positive theory of public bureaucracy' In D.C. Mueller (ed.) *Perspectives on Public Choice*. Cambridge: Cambridge University Press, 455–480.

Mueller, D.C. (1989). *Public Choice II*. Cambridge: Cambridge University Press.

Mueller, D.C. (1996). *Constitutional Democracy*. Oxford: Oxford University Press.

Mueller, D.C. (ed.) (1997). *Perspectives on Public Choice*. Cambridge: Cambridge University Press.

Niskanen, W.A. (1971). *Bureaucracy and Representative Government*. New York: Aldine-Atherton.

Niskanen, W.A. (1975). 'Bureaucrats and Politicians'. *Journal of Law and Economics*, 18, 617–643.

Niskanen, W.A. (2001). 'Bureaucracy', in W.F. Shughart and L. Razzolini (eds.) *The Elgar Companion to Public Choice*. Cheltenham, UK and Northampton, USA: Edward Elgar Publishing, 258–270.

Olson, M. (1965). *The Logic of Collective Action: Public Goods and the Theory of Groups*. Cambridge, MA: Harvard University Press.

Olson, M. (1982). *The Rise and Decline of Nations: Economic Growth, Stagflation and Social Rigidities*. New Haven: Yale University Press.

Ordeshook, P.C. (1997). 'The spatial analysis of elections and committees: Four decades of research' in D.C. Mueller (ed.) *Perspectives on Public Choice*. Cambridge: Cambridge University Press, 247–270.

Peltzman, S. (1976). 'Toward a More General Theory of Regulation'. *Journal of Law and Economics*, 19 (2), 211–240.

Peltzman, S. (1984). 'Constituent Interest and Congressional Voting'. *Journal of Law and Economics*, 27, 181–210.

Peltzman, S. (1990). 'How Efficient is the Voting Market?'. *Journal of Law and Economics*, 33, 27–64.

Rawls, J. (1971). *A Theory of Justice*. Cambridge: Belknap Press.

Reder, M.W. (1982). 'Chicago Economics: Permanence and Change'. *Journal of Economic Literature*, 20, 1–38.

Riker, M.W. (1962). *The Theory of Political Coalitions*. New Haven: Yale University Press.

Riker M.W. (1964). *Federalism: Origins, Operation Significance*. Boston: Little, Brown and Co.

Riker, W.H. and Ordeshook, P.C. (1973). *An Introduction to Positive Political Theory*. Englewood Cliffs: Prentice Hall.

Romer, T. and Rosenthal, H. (1978). 'Political Resource Allocation: Controlled Agendas and the Status Quo', *Public Choice*, 33, 27–43.

Romer, T. and Rosenthal, H. (1979). 'The Elusive Median Voter', *Journal of Public Economics*, 12, 143–170.

Rowley, C.K. (1984). 'The relevance of the median voter theorem', *Journal of Institutional and Theoretical Economics*, 140, 104–135

Rowley, C.K. (1991). 'The Reason of Rules: Constitutional Contract versus Political Market Conflict', *Annual Review of Conflict Knowledge and Conflict Resolution*, 2, 195–228.

Rowley, C.K. (1992). *The Right to Justice*. Aldershot UK and Brookfield, USA: Edward Elgar Publishing.

Rowley, C.K. (1993). 'Introduction' In C.K. Rowley (ed.) *Public Choice Theory*, Volume 1, Aldershot, UK and Brookfield, USA: Edward Elgar Publishing, ix–xxix.

Rowley, C.K. (1997). 'Donald Wittman's *The Myth of Democratic Failure*', *Public Choice*, 92, 15–26.

Rowley, C.K. (2001). 'The international economy in public choice perspective' In W.F. Shughart and L. Razzolini (eds.) *The Elgar Companion to Public Choice*. Cheltenham UK and Northampton, USA: Edward Elgar Publishing, 645–672.

Rowley, C.K. (2003). 'Public Choice from the Perspective of the History of Thought', in this volume, 199–211.

Rowley, C.K., Shughart, W.F. and Tollison, R.D. (1987). 'Interest Groups and Deficits' In J.M. Buchanan, C.K. Rowley and R.D. Tollison (eds.) *Deficits*. Oxford: Basil Blackwell, 263–280.

Rowley, C.K., Tollison, R.D. and Tullock, G. (eds.) (1988). *The Political Economy of Rent Seeking*. Boston and Dordrecht: Kluwer Academic Publishers.

Rowley, C.K. and Vachris, M.A. (1993). 'Snake Oil Economics versus Public Choice' in C.K. Rowley (ed.) *Public Choice Theory*, Volume III, Aldershot, U.K. and Brookfield, USA: Edward Elgar Publishing, 573–84.

Rowley, C.K. and Vachris, M.A. (1994). 'Why democracy does not necessarily produce efficient results', *Journal of Public Finance and Public Choice*, 12, 95–111.

Shepsle, K.A. (1978). *The Giant Jigsaw Puzzle*. Chicago: Chicago University Press.

Shepsle, K.A. and Weingast, B.R. (1981). 'Structure-Induced Equilibrium and Legislative Choice'. *Public Choice*, 37, 503–520.

Shepsle, K.A. (1982). 'The Budget: Will a Constitutional Amendment Help?' *Challenge*, 53–56.

Shughart, W.F. and Razzolini, L. (eds.) (2001). *The Elgar Companion to Public Choice*, Cheltenham, U.K. and Northampton, USA: Edward Elgar.

Stigler, G.J. (1971). 'The Theory of Economic Regulation'. *Bell Journal of Economics and Management Science*, 2, 137–146.

Stigler, G.J. (1974). 'Free riders and collective action: an appendix to theories of regulation'. *Bell Journal of Economics and Management Science*, 5, 3–21.

Stigler, G.J. (1988). *Chicago Studies in Political Economy*. Chicago: Chicago University Press.

Stigler, G.J. (1992). 'Law or economics', *Journal of Law and Economics*, 35, 455–468.

Tollison, R.D. (1982). 'Rent seeking: A survey'. *Kyklos*, 35, 575–602.

Tollison, R.D. (1988). 'Public Choice and Legislation'. *Virginia Law Review*, 74, 339–371.

Tollison, R.D. (1989). 'Chicago Political Economy'. *Public Choice*, 63 (3), 293–298.

Tollison, R.D. (1997). 'Rent seeking' In D.C. Mueller (ed.) *Perspectives on Public Choice*. Cambridge: Cambridge University Press, 506–525.

Tullock, G. (1959). 'Problems in majority Voting'. *Journal of Political Economy*, 67, 571–579.

Tullock, G. (1965). *The Politics of Bureaucracy*. Washington, DC: Public Affairs Press.

Tullock, G. (1967). 'The Welfare Costs of Tariffs, Monopolies and Theft'. *Western Economic Journal*, 5, 224–232.

Tullock, G. (1971). 'The cost of transfers'. *Kyklos*, 4, 629–643.

Tullock, G. (1975). 'The Transitional Gains Trap'. *The Bell Journal of Economics and Management Science*, 6, 671–678.

Tullock, G. (1976). *The Vote Motive*, London: Institute of Economic Affairs.

Tullock, G. (1980). 'Efficient Rent-Seeking' In J.M. Buchanan, R.D. Tollison and G. Tullock (eds.) *Toward the Theory of the Rent-Seeking Society*. College Station: Texas A & M University Press, 97–112.

Tullock, G. (1981). 'Why So Much Stability?'. *Public Choice*, 37, 189–202.

Tullock, G. (1989). *The Economics of Special Privilege and Rent-Seeking*. Boston: Kluwer Academic Publishers.

Tullock, G. (1991). 'Duncan Black: The Founding Father', *Public Choice* 71, 125–128.

Weingast, B.R. (1981). 'Republican Reregulation and Deregulation: The Political Foundations of Agency-Clientele Relationships'. *Journal of Law and Contemporary Problems*, 44, 147–173.

Weingast, B.R. (1984). 'The Congressional Bureaucratic System: A Principal-Agent Perspective'. *Public Choice*, 44, 147–191.

Weingast, B.R. and Marshall, W.J. (1988). 'The Industrial Organization of Congress'. *Journal of Political Economy*, 96, 132–163.

Weingast, B.R. and Moran, N.J. (1983). 'Bureaucratic Discretion or Congressional Control?'. *Journal of Political Economy*, 91, 765–800.

Wicksell, K. (1896). *Finanztheoretische Untersuchungen*. Jena: Gustav Fisher.

Wittman, D. (1989). 'Why Democracies Produce Efficient Results'. *Journal of Political Economy*, 97, 1395–1424.

Wittman, D. (1995). *The Myth of Democratic Failure: Why Political Institutions are Efficient*. Chicago: University of Chicago Press.

PUBLIC CHOICE: AN INTRODUCTION

1. Origins

Public Choice has been defined as the application of the methodology of economics to the study of politics. This definition suggests that public choice is an inherently interdisciplinary field, and so it is. Depending upon which person one selects as making *the* pioneering contribution to public choice, it came into existence either in the late 18th century as an offshoot of mathematics, or in the late 1940s as an offshoot of economics. The case for the earlier date rests on the existence of publications by two French mathematicians, Jean-Charles de Borda (1781) and the Marquis de Condorcet (1785). Condorcet was the first person, as far as we know, to discover the problem of *cycling*, the possibility when using the simple majority rule that an alternative x can lose to y in a vote between the two, y can lose to another alternative z, but z will also lose to x. The existence of such a possibility obviously raises the issue of how a community can decide among these three alternatives, when a cycle exists, and what the normative justification for any choice made will be. No cycle exists, of course, if some alternative, say y, can defeat both x and z. The literature has commemorated Condorcet's contribution by naming such an issue like y a *Condorcet winner*. A vast number of papers and books have analyzed both the normative and positive implications of the existence of cycles.

Condorcet gave his name to one other important part of the public choice literature, when he proved what he called a theorem about juries, and what we now call the *Condorcet jury theorem*. This remarkable theorem provides both a justification for making collective decisions with the simple majority rule, and for the institution of democracy itself. It rests on three assumptions: (1) The community faces a binary choice between x and y, with only one of the two choices being the "right" choice for the community. (2) Everyone in the community wants to make the right choice. (3) The probability p that a citizen votes for the right choice is greater than 0.5. The theorem states that the probability that the community makes the right choice when it uses the simple majority rule increases as the number of voters increases approaching one in the limit.

That the theorem provides a normative case for the simple majority rule is obvious, if one accepts its premises. Condorcet described the collective decision as one regarding the determination of whether a person had committed a particular crime or not — hence the theorem's name. For this type of collective decision the definition of "the right decision" is fairly controversial — the person is declared innocent only if she is in fact innocent. The assumption that everyone wants to make the right choice in this situation also seems uncontroversial.

The argument that the theorem also provides a justification for democracy is more subtle, and under it the assumptions underpinning the theorem become more controversial. Imagine, however, that everyone in the community agrees that they would like a "good government" that would be honest and provide goods and services and levy taxes so as to maximize the welfare of the community. Two parties compete for the honor of becoming the government, and each citizen votes for the party that he believes will form the best government. If each citizen has a greater than 0.5 probability of picking the party that will form the best government (two-party) democracy chooses the best government in a large electorate with near certainty.

The second and third assumptions take on extreme importance, when the theorem is used as a defense of democracy. Citizens share a common goal — good government. Each citizen has a greater than 0.5 probability of picking the party that will provide the best government. Citizens do not merely flip coins to decide how to vote, they study the parties and make an *informed* choice.

The assumption that everyone agrees on what good government is, becomes more controversial when we are thinking of the whole panoply of things governments do. If citizens disagree about what government should do, there will be no "right choice" for all citizens. This being the case, parties will compete not only on the basis of how good they will be at advancing the community's welfare, but how that welfare should be defined. Finally, when one is thinking of a large electorate, even the assumption that voters are well-informed becomes controversial.

Many studies in public choice employ some of the assumptions needed to apply the Condorcet jury theorem to the study of politics, many others do not. All of the work on party competition that uses "spatial modeling" assumes, for example, that voters are well-informed, that they know the positions of the parties in the issue space. At the same time, however, this literature does not assume that voters agree on where the parties should be located in the issue space. Conflicts of interest or preferences are assumed, and thus voters do not agree on which party is best even when they are certain about what the parties will do in office — assuming that is that the parties will do different things. There is another branch of the public choice literature, however, that *does* assume common interests among citizens, and thus does accord with the second assumption underlying the jury theorem. This work often focuses on decisions made at the constitutional stage of the political process and today often goes by the name of constitutional political economy.

Thus, directly or indirectly Condorcet's pioneering work raised many of the questions with which the modern public choice literature has been concerned. Do individuals share common interests? Is democracy stable or not (produce cycles)? Are voters sufficiently well-informed that one gains information by aggregating their preferences? What voting rule should be used to aggregate these preferences?[1]

Borda was critical of the use of the simple majority rule to aggregate preferences, and proposed instead a rule which today carries his name. If there are n possible outcomes to a collective decision, each voter assigns a one to his most preferred choice, a two to his second most preferred choice, and so on. The scores awarded are then added across all voters, and the Borda-count rule selects as the winner the alternative receiving the lowest score. With only two alternatives from which to choose, the Borda-count is equivalent to the simple majority rule. When $n > 2$, it avoids cycling and has additional desirable properties that make it attractive.[2]

Three more names deserve brief mention before we end this discussion of the forerunners to public choice. Another mathematician, the Reverend Charles L. Dodgson, better known today as Lewis Carroll, wrote a series of pamphlets analyzing the properties of voting procedures roughly a century after the work of Borda and Condorcet.[3] John Stuart Mill's *Considerations on Representative Government* (1861) must also be mentioned, since he was one of the great economists of the 19th century, although the work is arguably an early contribution to political science rather than to public choice, since it makes no noticeable use of economic reasoning. Nevertheless, the great thinker's logical mind is quite evident, and it is one of the few works in political science from the 19th century that still warrants reading by students of public choice.

The same can be said of Knut Wicksell's (1896) classic essay on *Just Taxation* written as the 19th century came to a close. As the title suggests, it is as much or more a contribution to public finance than to the study of politics, but it contains an early normative economic justification for the state, and a spirited defense of the unanimity rule for aggregating individual preferences.

2. Early Classics

The modern literature on public choice came into being with the publication of articles by Duncan Black (1948a,b), James Buchanan (1949) and Kenneth Arrow (1950) in the late 1940s and 1950. Retrospectively, one can identify three important contributions between Wicksell and Black, namely Hotelling (1929), Schumpeter (1942) and Bowen (1943), but it was Black, Buchanan and Arrow who got the public choice ball rolling.

Duncan Black's two articles, first published in 1948 and then republished with extensions and an interesting account of the history of ideas lying behind his work, take up the problem of cycling under the simple majority rule and provide a proof of the famous median voter theorem. This theorem has been frequently invoked to describe equilibria in theoretical studies and has been the analytical foundation for much of the empirical work in public choice.

Arrow proved that no procedure for aggregating individual preferences could be guaranteed to produce a complete social ordering over all possible choices and at the same time satisfy five, seemingly reasonable, axioms. Indirectly Arrow's theorem invoked the problem of cycling again, since one of his axioms was intended to ensure that cycling did not occur. Arrow's 1950 article and 1951 book spawned much controversy and a huge literature.

Although Buchanan published several important articles prior to 1962, it was the book *The Calculus of Consent*, published in that year and coauthored with Gordon Tullock that established Buchanan and Tullock as leading scholars in the field. Although the book contains many interesting discussions of the properties of the simple majority rule, logrolling and the like, its most lasting contribution to the literature has been to introduce the distinction between the constitutional stage of collective decision making in which the voting rules and other institutions of democracy are selected, and the applications of these rules to the actual work of making collective choices.

In *Capitalism, Socialism and Democracy*, Schumpeter put forward "another theory of democracy" in which the social function of democracy is fulfilled incidentally by the competitive struggle for power between parties, just as the social function of markets is fulfilled incidentally by the competitive struggle for profits among firms (Schumpeter, 1950, Ch. 22). Anthony Downs did not cite this argument of Schumpeter directly, but he did state that "Schumpeter's profound analysis of democracy forms the inspiration and foundation for our whole thesis" (1957, p. 27, n. 11). Downs was a student of Kenneth Arrow, and it appeared that with his dissertation he wished to develop Schumpeter's insight and demonstrate how political competition between parties could produce a welfare maximum and thus avoid the dire implications of Arrow's impossibility theorem. Downs ultimately failed in this endeavor, but succeeded in introducing a mode of analysis of competition using spatial modeling that was to have a profound impact on the development of the field, particularly among practitioners trained in political science. Building again on insights from Schumpeter (1950, pp. 256–64), Downs also developed a model of the rational voter who, among other things, rationally chooses to remain ignorant of most of the issues in an election (Chs. 11–14).

Another doctoral dissertation that was to have a profound impact on both the public choice field and political science in general was that of Mancur Olson published in book form in 1965.[4] Just as Downs had shown that the logic of rational decision making led individuals to invest little time in collecting information to help them decide how to vote, "the logic of collective action" would prevent individuals from voluntarily devoting time and money to the provision of public goods. Mancur Olson did not invent the "free-rider problem," but no one has put it to better use than he did in this and his subsequent contributions to the literature.

All of the "early classics" discussed so far were written by economists. One contribution by a political scientist that certainly falls into this category is William Riker's *The Theory of Political Coalitions* (1962). In this book Riker developed the logic of coalition formation into a theory that could explain among other things why "grand coalitions" were short lived. Riker's book foreshadowed a large literature that would apply game theoretic tools to political analysis.

Deciding when the early classics end and the "late" ones begin is a somewhat subjective judgment. Perhaps from the vantage point of 2002, however, the definition of early can be extended up through the early 1970s to include three more sets of works. First, of these in chronological order would be an article published by Gordon Tullock in 1967. This article might be dubbed a "hidden classic," since its seminal nature did not become apparent to the profession at large until its main idea was rediscovered and developed by Anne Krueger (1974) and Richard Posner (1975) sometime later. It was Krueger who gave the idea the name of rent seeking. Up until Tullock's 1967 article appeared, standard discussions of "the social costs of monopoly" measured these costs solely in terms of the "deadweight triangle" of lost consumers' surplus resulting from the monopolist's restriction of output. The rectangle of monopoly rents was treated as a pure transfer from consumers to the monopolist and as such devoid of any welfare significance. Tullock pointed out, however, that the right to supply the monopolized product or service was a valuable right, and that individuals could be expected to invest time and money to obtain or retain this right. These investments constitute a pure social waste as they only serve to determine the identity of the monopoly rent recipient. They have no positive impact on the allocation of resources.

The social costs of rent seeking are potentially very large. Numerous articles have appeared since the pioneering contributions of Tullock and Krueger. One branch has analyzed theoretically the conditions under which the total resources invested in rent seeking fall short of, equal, or exceed the size of the rents pursued. A second branch has sought answers to the same questions empirically.[5] One of the curiosities of this literature has been that it has by and large analyzed rent seeking as if it were exclusively a problem of the public sector, even though the logic of rent seeking applies with equal validity to the private sector.[6]

While Tullock's rent-seeking article has proved to be a hidden classic, Sen's (1970) article about the Paretian liberal might be dubbed an "unassuming classic." Sen put forward another sort of paradox, in the spirit of the Arrow paradox, but neither the author nor any of the readers of this six page note is likely to have appreciated at the time it appeared the impact it was to have on the literature.[7] Where Arrow proved that it was impossible *not to have a dictator* and satisfy four other axioms, Sen proved that it was impossible *to allow someone to be a dictator* over even one simply choice — as for example whether he sleeps on his back or his stomach — and satisfy three other axioms.

The last early contribution that qualifies as a classic is William Niskanen's (1971) book on bureaucracy. Niskanen posited that bureaucrats seek to maximize the size of their budgets and then proceeded to derive the implications of this assumption. A by now huge literature has been built on the analytical foundation that he laid.[8]

3. The Second Generation

3.1. More Impossibilities

During the 1970s several papers appeared, which extended the dire implications of Arrow's impossibility theorem and the literature it spawned. Satterthwaite (1975) and Gibbard (1977) demonstrated the incompatibility of having a preference aggregation procedure that was both nondictatorial and *strategyproof*, where by strategyproof was meant that everyone's best strategy was to faithfully reveal their true preferences. These theorems illustrated the close relationship between Arrow's independence-of-irrelevant-alternatives axiom and the goal of having a preference aggregation procedure in which individuals did not have an incentive to behave strategically.

McKelvey (1976) and Schofield (1978) drew out a further implication of a procedure's failure to satisfy the transitivity axiom. When a procedure leads to voting cycles it is possible to move anywhere in the issue space. An agenda setter can take advantage of this feature of cycling to lead a committee to the agenda setter's most preferred outcome.

3.2. The Veil of Tears Rises

The theorems of McKelvey and Schofield might be regarded as the capstones — or should we say tombstones — for the literature initiated by Arrow. It paints a very negative picture of the capacity for democratic procedures to aggregate information on voter preferences in a normatively appealing matter. Collective decisions were likely to be arbitrary or dictatorial. Free riding and the strategic concealment of individual preferences undermined democracy's legitimacy. Rent seekers and bureaucrats contributed to the "waste of democracy." William Riker's (1982) attack against "populist democracy" — the idea that democratic procedures could aggregate individual preferences reasonably — accurately conveys the flavor of this literature. Even before Riker's book appeared, however, several developments in the public choice literature were taking place that painted a far more cheery picture of democracy's potential. The first of these concerned the potential for direct revelation of preferences.

3.2.1. Voting Rules
In his classic article deriving the conditions for the Pareto optimal allocation of private and public goods, Paul Samuelson (1954) matter-of-factly proclaimed that it would be impossible to get people to honestly reveal their

preferences, because no person could be excluded from consuming a pure public good. So things stood for nearly 20 years, when Clarke (1971) and Groves (1973) showed that individuals could be induced to reveal their preferences for public goods honestly by charging them a special "incentive tax" equal to the costs that their participation in the collective choice process imposed on the other voters. This class of procedures was first discovered in another context by William Vickrey (1961), and has come to be known in the public choice literature as "demand revelation" processes.

Mueller (1978, 1984) showed that the preference revelation problem could be solved using a three-step procedure in which each individual first makes a proposal — say a quantity of public good and a tax formula to pay for it; and then following a random determination of an order of veto voting removes (vetoes) one element from the set of all proposals.

Hylland and Zeckhauser (1970) added to the list of preference-revelation procedures by showing that individuals will allocate a stock of "vote points" across a set of issues to reveal the intensities of their preferences on these issues, if the quantities of public goods provided are determined by adding the square roots of the points each individual assigns to an issue. During the decade of the 1970s, one new method appeared after another to solve the heretofore seemingly insoluble problem of inducing people to reveal their preferences for public goods honestly.

3.2.2. Two-party Competition

During the decade of the 1980s, several papers appeared that suggested that two-party representative governments were far better at aggregating individual preferences than had previously been demonstrated. One set of these articles simply replaced the assumption of the Downsian voter model, that each individual votes with probability one for the candidate promising her a higher utility, with the assumption that the probability of an individual's voting for a candidate increases when the candidate promises her a higher utility. Substituting this "probabilistic voting" assumption for the standard Downsian deterministic voting assumption allowed Coughlin and Nitzan (1981a,b) and Ledyard (1984) to prove that the competition for votes between two candidates led them to select an equilibrium pair of platforms that maximized some form of social welfare function. Schumpeter's assertion that the competition for votes between parties resulted in a form of "invisible hand theorem" for the public domain was, after forty years, finally proved.

In a multidimensional issue space, every platform choice by one party can be defeated by an appropriate choice of platform by the other, and the two candidates might cycle endlessly, under the Downsian assumption of deterministic voting. Such cycling could in theory take the candidates far away from the set of most preferred points of the electorate. A platform x, lying far from the set of most preferred points of the electorate would, however, be dominated by some other point y, lying between x and the set of most preferred points of the electorate, in the sense that y could defeat every platform that x could defeat, and y could also defeat x. By restricting one's attention to points in the issue space that are not dominated in this way, the set of attractive platforms for the two candidates shrinks considerably. The cycling problem does not disappear entirely, but it is reduced to a small area near the center of the set of most-preferred points for the population.[9]

These results clearly sound a more optimistic note about the potential for preference aggregation than many of the early classics and the works discussed in section A. The reader can see how dramatic the difference in perspectives is by comparing the books by Wittman (1995) and Breton (1996) to that of Riker (1982).

3.3. Political Business Cycles

Almost all Nobel prizes in economics have been awarded for contributions to economic theory. All of the early classics in public choice have been theoretical contributions, as have the subsequent contributions reviewed so far.[10] As the public choice field has matured, however, an increasing number of studies has appeared testing every and all of its theoretical propositions. Space precludes a full review of the many empirical contributions to the field that have been made. We have therefore selected only three areas, where a lot of empirical work has been done, beginning with the area of "political business cycles."

One of the most frequently quoted propositions of Anthony Downs (1957, p. 28) is that "parties formulate policies in order to win elections, rather than win elections in order to formulate policies." Among the policies of great concern to voters few stand higher than the state of the economy. If the quoted proposition of Downs is correct, then parties should compete for votes on the basis of their promised macroeconomic policies, and both parties in a two-party system should offer the same set of policies. Kramer (1971) was the first to test for a relationship between the state of the economy and votes for members of the House and the President. Nordhaus (1975) and MacRae (1977) were among the first to develop a Downsian model of the political business cycle in which both parties are predicted to follow the same strategy of reducing unemployment going into an election to induce short-sighted voters to vote for the incumbent party/candidates.

Numerous observers of politics in both the United States and the United Kingdom have questioned the prediction of the one-dimensional Downsian model that both parties adopt identical positions at the most-preferred outcome for the median voter. This prediction appears to be blatantly at odds with the evidence concerning macroeconomic policies, where right-of-center parties clearly seem to be more concerned about inflation, while left-of-center parties are more concerned about unemployment. Early contributions by Hibbs (1977, 1987) and Frey and Schneider (1978a,b) incorporated these "partisan effects" into a political model of macroeconomic policy and provided empirical support for them.

In some areas of public choice, data for testing a particular proposition are difficult to obtain and empirical work is accordingly sparse. Such is not the case with respect to hypotheses linking policy choices to macroeconomic outcomes. Data on variables like unemployment and inflation rates are readily available for every developed country, as are data on electoral outcomes. Each passing year produces more observations for retesting and refining previously proposed hypotheses. The empirical literature on political business cycles is by now vast. The main findings grossly condensed are that partisan differences across parties are significant and persistent, but that both parties of the left and parties of the right do tend to become more "Downsian" as an election approaches and adapt their policies to sway the uncommitted, middle-of-the-road voters.[11]

3.4. Public Choice Goes Multinational

All of the early classics discussed in section II were written by either American or British authors. It is thus not surprising that the literature on representative government, as for example in the political business cycle area, has almost always assumed the existence of a two-party system — even when testing the model using data from countries with multiparty systems. In the last couple of decades, however, considerably more attention has been devoted to analyzing properties peculiar to multiparty systems. This literature has been heavily populated by persons trained in public choice, and is one in which the lines between political science and public choice are particularly blurred.

A salient feature of multiparty systems is that no single party typically wins a majority of seats in the parliament, and thus no single party is able to *form the government*. Consequently, a coalition of parties must come together if the cabinet is to reflect the wishes of a majority of the parliament, or a minority government forms. Two important questions arise: (1) which parties will build the coalition that forms the government, and (2) how long will it last?

Game theory provides the ideal analytical tool for answering the first question, and it has been used to make a variety of predictions of the coalition that will form after an election. Riker's (1962) prediction, that a *minimum winning coalition* forms, receives as much support as any theory, although it accounts for less than half of the governments formed in European countries since World War II.[12] In particular, it fails to predict that many minority governments have existed.

A theory that can account for the existence of minority governments has been put forward by van Roozendaal (1990, 1992, 1993). His theory emphasizes the pivotal position of a party that includes the median member of the parliament (a *central party*), under the assumption that the parties can be arrayed along a single, ideological dimension. Under the assumption that each party favors proposals coming close to their position along the ideological dimension over proposals lying far away, a central party will be a member of every coalition that forms. A large central party is likely to be able to successfully lead a minority government by relying on votes from the left to pass some legislation and votes from the right for other legislation.

When the issue space cannot reasonably be assumed to be one-dimensional, cycling is likely to arise, which in the context of cabinet formation implies unstable party coalitions. Here game theoretic concepts like the covered set and the heart have proven useful for identifying the likely members of the coalitions that eventually form.[13]

A long literature beginning with Taylor and Herman (1971) has measured the length of a government's life and related this length to various characteristics of the government. One of the regularities observed is that minority governments tend to be relatively short lived, governments formed by a single, majority party long lived.[14] One of the likely future growth areas in public choice is likely to be research on multiparty systems.

3.5. Experimental Economics

Experimental economics can be rightfully thought of as a separate field of economics and not just a "topic" in public choice. Two of its pioneering scholars — Vernon Smith and Charles Plott — have also been major contributors to the public choice field, however, and an important stream of the experimental literature has dealt with public choice issues. It thus constitutes an important body of empirical evidence corroborating, or in some cases undermining, certain hypotheses in public choice.

The first experimental study of the new voting mechanisms described in section A was by Vernon Smith (1979). He ran experiments on the Groves and Ledyard (1977) iterative version of the demand revelation process, and a somewhat simpler auction mechanism that Smith had developed. In most experiments the subject chose a public good quantity and set of contributions that was Pareto optimal. The experiments also served to demonstrate the feasibility of using the unanimity rule, as the participants had to vote unanimously for the final set of contributions and public good quantity for it to be implemented.

Hoffman and Spitzer (1982) devised an experiment with an externality to test the Coase theorem and found that in virtually every run of the experiment the subjects were able to reach a bargain that was Pareto optimal.

A third set of experiments that might in some way be thought of as rejecting a prediction of an important theory, but it rejects the theory in favor of alternatives that support the behavioral premises underlying the public choice methodology. Frohlich et al. (1987) presented students with four possible redistribution rules — Rawls's (1971) rule of maximizing the floor, maximizing the average, maximizing the average subject to a floor constraint, and maximizing the average subject to a range constraint. The students were made familiar with the distributional impacts of the four rules and were given time to discuss the merits and demerits of each rule. In 44 experiments in which students were uncertain of their future positions in the income distribution, the five students in each experiment reached unanimous agreement on which redistributive rule to use to determine their final incomes in every case. Not once did they choose Rawls's rule of maximizing the floor. The most popular rule, chosen 35 out of 44 times, was to maximize the average subject to a floor constraint. Similar experiments conducted in Canada, Poland and the United States all found (1) that individuals can unanimously agree on a redistributive rule, and (2) that this rule is almost never Rawls's maximin rule, but rather some more utilitarian rule like maximizing the mean subject to a floor (Frohlich and Oppenheimer, 1992). While these results may constitute bad news for Rawlsians, they lend support to the assumptions that underlie economic and public choice modeling. They suggest further that individuals are not concerned merely with their own welfare, but are also motivated by considerations of fairness and justice, although apparently not in the extreme form posited by Rawls.

The last set of experiments are less comforting for students of public choice. At least since the publication of Mancur Olson's *Logic of Collective Action* in 1965, a basic tenet in the public choice literature is that individuals will *free ride* in situations where contributions to the provision of a public good are voluntarily. Countless experiments have demonstrated that they do free ride, but to a far smaller degree than one might have expected. If 100 is the contribution to the public good that produces the optimum quantity of the good for the collective, and 1 is the contribution that is individually optimal, then the typical finding in an experiment testing for free rider behavior is that the *mean* contribution of the participants is around 50. Some people do free ride, but many make contributions that are far larger than is individually optimal. In aggregate the total contributions fall far short of what would be optimal for the group, but far above what pure free riding behavior would produce.[15]

Many additional types of experiments have been run that have important implications for both public choice and other branches of economics, and many more will be run in the future. Experimental economics seems destined to remain an important source of empirical evidence for testing various theories and propositions from the field.[16]

4. The Next Generation

At the start of the new millennium the public choice field is some fifty years old and befitting its age has begun to resemble other mature fields in economics. Important theoretical breakthroughs are fewer and farther between than during the field's first 25 years. Much current research consists of extending existing theories in different directions, and of filling in the remaining empty interstices in the body of theory. Much current research also consists of empirically testing the many theoretical propositions and claims that have been made up until now. The future development of the field will most certainly parallel that of other mature fields in economics — continually increasing use of sophisticated mathematics in theoretical modeling, continual use of more and more sophisticated econometrics applied to larger and larger data sets when estimating these models.

Two other trends that are apparent at the start of the new millennium are worth commenting upon. Although public choice is destined to remain just one of many fields in economics, it is possible — I would dare to say likely — that it eventually takes over the entire discipline of political science, takes over in the sense that all political scientists will eventually employ rational actor models when analyzing various questions in political science and all will test their hypotheses using the same sorts of statistical procedures that economists employ. Political institutions are sufficiently different from market institutions to require important modifications in the assumptions one makes about the objectives of rational actors in politics and about the constraints under which they pursue these objectives. Nevertheless, the assumption that individuals rationally pursue specific objectives has proven to be so powerful when developing testable hypotheses about their behavior, that this methodology — the methodology of public choice — must eventually triumph in some form throughout the political science field.

With the exception of Duncan Black all of the major contributors to the early public choice literature came from North America, and this continent can be said to be the "home" of public choice for much of its early life. The Public Choice Society was founded there and has grown to a point where its annual meetings attract over 300 participants from around the world. There now is also a Japanese Public Choice Society and an European Public Choice Society, however, with the annual meeting of the latter often attracting well over 200 participants. Thus, the second discernable trend as the third millennium begins is the full internationalization of the discipline. Scholars can be found applying the public choice methodology to the questions pertinent to their country on every continent of the globe, and an increasing fraction of the important contributions to this literature can be expected to come from outside the North American continent.

DENNIS C. MUELLER

NOTES

1. For additional discussion of Condorcet and the jury theorem, see Young (1997).
2. See in particular, Saari (1994).
3. See discussion in Black (1958, Ch. 20).

4. Alt (1999) describes the impact of Olson's work on the political science literature.
5. For recent surveys of this literature, see Magee (1997), Tollison (1997) and Mueller (forthcoming, Ch. 15).
6. The same might be said of the implications of Arrow's impossibility theorem. The theorem establishes that no method for aggregating preferences is consistent with the five "Arrow axioms." The theorem thus casts a shadow over both market and non-market methods for aggregating individual preferences, and yet most discussions of the theorem's import focus only on democratic procedures.
7. See, for example, Sen (1996).
8. For recent surveys of this literature, see Moe (1997), Wintrobe (1997) and Mueller (forthcoming, Chs. 16 and 17).
9. Gordon Tullock's (1967) claim that this was the case was rigorously Miller (1980, 1983) and McKelvey (1986) among others.
10. Riker (1962) demonstrated the explanatory power of his theory of coalitions with historical examples, but the main contribution of the book was to propose a theory.
11. For recent surveys of this literature, see Paldam (1997), Drazen (2000) and Mueller (2003, Ch. 19).
12. See Laver and Schofield (1990). A minimum winning coalition is one which constitutes a majority of the seats in the parliament, but falls to a minority coalition through the defection of any member party.
13. For discussions of these concepts and surveys of this literature, see Laver and Schofield (1990), Schofield (1997), and Mueller (forthcoming, Ch. 13).
14. For a recent survey of this literature see Müller and Strøm (2000).
15. The pioneering contributions to this strand of the literature were by Marwell and Ames (1979, 1980).
16. For recent surveys of this literature, see Ledyard (1995) and Hoffman (1997). Ostrom and Walker (1997) also survey large parts of the literature.

REFERENCES

Alt, James E. (1999). "Obituary: thoughts on Mancur Olson's contribution to political science." *Public Choice*, 98: 1–4.

Arrow, Kenneth J. (1950). "A difficulty in the concept of social welfare." *Journal of Political Economy*, 58: 328–346.

Arrow, Kenneth J. (1951). *Social Choice and Individual Values*. New York: John Wiley and Sons.

Black, Duncan (1948a). "On the rationale of group decision making." *Journal of Political Economy*, 56: 23–34; reprinted in K.J. Arrow and T. Scitovsky (eds.) (1969) 133–146.

Black, Duncan (1948b). "The decisions of a committee using a special majority." *Econometrica*, 16: 245–261.

Black, Duncan (1958). *The Theory of Committees and Elections*. Cambridge: Cambridge University Press.

Borda, Jean-Charles de (1781). *Memoire sur les Elections au Scrutin*. Paris: Histoire de l'Academie Royale des Sciences.

Bowen, Howard R. (1943). "The interpretation of voting in the allocation of economic resources." *Quarterly Journal of Economics*, 58: 27–48.

Breton, Albert. (1996). *Competitive Governments*. Cambridge: Cambridge University Press.

Buchanan, James M. (1949). "The pure theory of government finance: a suggested approach." *Journal of Political Economy*, 57: 496–506.

Buchanan, James M. and Gordon Tullock (1962). *The Calculus of Consent. Logical Foundations of Constitutional Democracy*. Ann Arbor: University of Michigan Press.

Clarke, Edward H. (1971). "Multipart pricing of public goods." *Public Choice*, 11: 17–33.

Condorcet, Marquis de (1785). *Essai sur l'Application de L'Analyse à la Probabilité des Décisions Rendues à la Pluraliste des Voix*. Paris.

Coughlin, Peter and Shmuel Nitzan (1981a). "Electoral outcomes with probabilistic voting and nash social welfare maxima." *Journal of Public Economics*, 15: 113–122.

Coughlin, Peter and Shmuel Nitzan (1981b). "Directional and local electoral equilibria with probabilistic voting." *Journal of Economic Theory*, 24: 226–239.

Dodgson, Charles L. (1876). *A Method of Taking Votes on More than Two Issues*; reprinted in Black (ed.) (1958) 224–234.

Downs, Anthony (1957). *An Economic Theory of Democracy*. New York: Harper and Row.

Drazen, Allan (2000). *Political Economy in Macroeconomics*. Princeton: Princeton University Press.

Frey, Bruno S. and Friedrich Schneider (1978a). "An empirical study of politico-economic interaction in the U.S.." *Review of Economics and Statistics*, 60: 174–183.

Frey, Bruno S. and Friedrich Schneider (1978b). "A politico-economic model of the United Kingdom." *Economic Journal*, 88: 243–253.

Frohlich, Norman and Joe A. Oppenheimer (1992). *Choosing Justice: An Experimental Approach to Ethical Theory*. Berkeley: University of California Press.

Frohlich, Norman, Joe A. Oppenheimer, and Cheryl L. Eavey (1987). "Laboratory results on Rawls's distributive justice." *British Journal of Political Science*, 17: 1–21.

Gibbard, Allan (1977). "Manipulation of schemes that combine voting with chance." *Econometrica*, 45: 665–668.

Groves, Theodore (1973). "Incentives in teams." *Econometrica*, 41: 617–631.

Groves, Theodore and John J. Ledyard (1977). "Optimal allocation of public goods: a solution to the 'free rider' problem." *Econometrica*, 45: 783–809.

Hibbs, Douglas A. Jr. (1977). "Political parties and macroeconomic policy." *American Political Science Review*, 71: 1467–1487.

Hibbs, Douglas A. Jr. (1987). *The Political Economy of Industrial Democracies*. Cambridge: Harvard University Press.

Hoffman, Elizabeth (1997). "Public choice experiments," in D.C. Mueller (ed.) *Perspectives on Public Choice*. Cambridge: Cambridge University Press, pp. 415–426.

Hoffman, Elizabeth and Matthew L. Spitzer (1982). "The coase theorem: some experimental tests." *Journal of Law and Economics*, 25: 73–98.

Hotelling, Harold (1929). "Stability in competition." *Economic Journal*, 39: 41–57.

Hylland, Aanund and Richard Zeckhauser (1970). "A mechanism for selecting public goods when preferences must be elicited." KSG Discussion Paper 70D, Harvard University.

Kramer, Gerald H. (1971). "Short run fluctuations in U.S. voting behavior, 1896–1964." *American Political Science Review*, 65: 131–143.

Krueger, Anne O. (1974). "The political economy of the rent-seeking society." *American Economic Review*, 64(3): 291–303; reprinted in J.M. Buchanan, R.D. Tollison, and G. Tullock (eds.) (1980) 51–70.

Laver, Michael and Norman Schofield (1990). *Multiparty Government*. Oxford: Oxford University Press.

Ledyard, John O. (1984). "The pure theory of large two-candidate elections." *Public Choice*, 44(1): 7–41.

Ledyard, John O. (1995). "Public goods: a survey of experimental research," in J.H. Kagel and A.E. Roth (eds.) *The Handbook of Experimental Economics*. Princeton: Princeton University Press, pp. 111–251.

MacRae, C. Duncan (1977). "A political model of the business cycle." *Journal of Political Economy*, 85: 239–263.

Magee, Stephen P. (1997). "Endogenous protection: the empirical evidence," in D.C. Mueller (ed.) *Perspectives on Public Choice*. Cambridge: Cambridge University Press, pp. 526–561.

Marwell, G. and Ames, R.E. (1979). "Experiments on the provision of public goods I: resources, interest, group size, and the free rider problem." *American Journal of Sociology*, 84: 1335–1360.

Marwell, G. and Ames, R.E. (1980). "Experiments on the provision of public goods II: provision points, stakes, experience and the free rider problem." *American Journal of Sociology*, 85: 926–937.

McKelvey, Richard D. (1976). "Intransitivities in multidimensional voting models and some implications for agenda control." *Journal of Economic Theory*, 12: 472–482.

McKelvey, Richard D. (1986). "Covering, dominance, and institution-free properties of social choice." *American Journal of Political Science*, 30: 283–314.

Mill, John Stuart. (1861). *Considerations on Representative Government*. New York: Bobbs-Merrill, 1958.

Miller, Nicholas R. (1980). "A new solution set for tournaments and majority voting: further graph-theoretical approaches to the theory of voting." *American Journal of Political Science*, 24: 68–96.

Miller, Nicholas R. (1983). "The covering relation in tournaments: two corrections." *American Journal of Political Science*, 27: 382–385.

Moe, Terry M. (1997). "The positive theory of public bureaucracy," in D.C. Mueller (ed.) *Perspectives on Public Choice*. Cambridge: Cambridge University Press, pp. 455–480.

Mueller, Dennis C. (1978). "Voting by veto." *Journal of Public Economics*, 10: 57–75.

Mueller, Dennis C. (1984). "Voting by veto and majority rule." in Horst Hanusch (ed.) *Public Finance and the Quest for Efficiency*. Detroit: Wayne State University Press, pp. 69–85.

Mueller, Dennis C. (2003). *Public Choice III*. Cambridge: Cambridge University Press.

Müller, Wolfgang C. and Kaare Strøm (2000). "Coalition governance in Western Europe," in W.C. Müller and K. Strøm (eds.) *Coalition Governments in Western Europe*. Oxford: Oxford University Press, pp. 559–592.

Niskanen, William A. Jr. (1971). *Bureaucracy and Representative Government*. Chicago: Aldine-Atherton.

Nordhaus, William D. (1975). "The political business cycle." *Review of Economic Studies*, 42: 169–190.

Olson, Mancur, Jr. (1965). *The Logic of Collective Action*. Cambridge: Harvard University Press.

Ostrom, Elinor and James Walker (1997). "Neither markets nor states: linking transformation processes in collective action areas," in D.C. Mueller (ed.) *Perspectives on Public Choice*. Cambridge: Cambridge University Press, pp. 35–72.

Paldam, Martin (1997). "Political business cycles," in D.C. Mueller (ed.) *Perspectives on Public Choice*. Cambridge: Cambridge University Press, pp. 342–370.

Posner, Richard A. (1975). "The social costs of monopoly and regulation." *Journal of Political Economy*. 83: 807–827; reprinted in J.M. Buchanan, R.D. Tollison, and G. Tullock (eds.) (1980) 71–94.

Rawls, John A. (1971). *A Theory of Justice*. Cambridge, MA: Belknap Press.

Riker, William H. (1962). *The Theory of Political Coalitions*. New Haven and London: Yale University Press.

Riker, William H. (1982). *Liberalism Against Populism*. San Francisco: W.H. Freeman.

Samuelson, Paul A. (1954). "The pure theory of public expenditure." *Review of Economics and Statistics*, 36: 386–389.

Saari, Donald G. (1994). *Geometry of Voting*. Berlin: Springer.

Satterthwaite, M.A. (1975). "Strategy-proofness and arrow's conditions: existence and correspondence theorems for voting procedures and social welfare functions." *Journal of Economic Theory*, 10: 187–217.

Schofield, Norman (1978). "Instability of simple dynamic games." *Review of Economic Studies*, 45: 575–594.

Schofield, Norman (1997). "Multiparty electoral politics," in D.C. Mueller (ed.) *Perspectives on Public Choice*. Cambridge: Cambridge University Press, pp. 271–295.

Schumpeter, Joseph A. (1942). *Capitalism, Socialism and Democracy*, 3rd edn, 1950. New York: Harper and Row.

Sen, Amartya (1970). "The impossibility of a paretian liberal." *Journal of Political Economy*, 78: 152–157.

Sen, Amartya (1996). "Rights: formulation and consequences." *Analyse & Kritik*, 18: 153–170.

Smith, Vernon L. (1979). "An experimental comparison of three public good decision mechanisms." *Scandinavian Journal of Economics*, 81(2): 198–215.

Taylor, Michael J. and Herman, V.M. (1971). "Party systems and government stability." *American Political Science Review*, 65: 28–37.

Tollison, Robert D. (1997). "Rent seeking," in D.C. Mueller (ed.) *Perspectives on Public Choice*. Cambridge: Cambridge University Press, pp. 506–525.

Tullock, Gordon. (1967). "The welfare costs of tariffs, monopolies and theft." *Western Economic Journal*, 5: 224–232; reprinted in Buchanan, Tollison and Tullock (eds.) (1980) 39–50.

van Roozendaal, Peter (1990). "Centre parties and coalition formations: a game theoretic approach." *European Journal of Political Research*, 18: 325–348.

van Roozendaal, Peter (1992). "The effect of dominant and central parties on cabinet composition and durability." *Legal Studies Quarterly*, 17: 5–36.

van Roozendaal, Peter (1993). "Cabinets in the Netherlands (1918–1990): the importance of 'dominant' and 'central' parties." *European Journal of Political Research*, 23: 35–54.

Vickrey, William (1961). "Counterspeculation, auctions, and competitive sealed tenders." *Journal of Finance*, 16: 8–37.

Young, H. Peyton (1997). "Group choice and individual judgements," in D.C. Mueller (ed.) *Perspectives on Public Choice*. Cambridge: Cambridge University Press, pp. 201–225.

Wicksell, Knut (1896). "Ein neues Prinzip der gerechten Besteuerung." *Finanztheoretische Untersuchungen*, Jena; translated as "A New Principle of Just Taxation," 1958; reprinted in (1967) Richard A. Musgrave, and Alan T. Peacock (eds.) *Classics in the Theory of Public Finance*. London: Macmillan, pp. 72–118.

Wintrobe, Ronald (1997). "Modern bureaucratic theory," in D.C. Mueller (ed.) *Perspectives on Public Choice*. Cambridge: Cambridge University Press, pp. 429–454.

Wittman, Donald (1995). *The Myth of Democratic Failure: Why Political Institutions are Efficient*. Chicago: University of Chicago Press.

A

ARE VOTE AND POPULARITY FUNCTIONS ECONOMICALLY CORRECT?

1. Introduction

During the last 30 years about 300 papers on Vote and Popularity functions (defined in Table 1) have been written.[1] Most of the research is empirical. The purpose of this article is to survey this literature and discuss how the empirical results fit into economic theory.

It is my experience that when academic economists are confronted with the results of the VP-research they frown, as they go against "our" main beliefs. Voters do not behave like *economic man* of standard theory. In other words, the results are not "economically correct" — as defined in Table 2. Political scientists have other problems depending on their school, so this essay is written to the typical mainstream economist (as the author).

From bedrock theory follows a remarkable amount of nice, sound theory, and everything can be generalized into the general equilibrium, growing along a steady state path maximizing consumption. Politics convert the demand for public good into the optimal production of such goods and minimizing economic fluctuations. The past is relevant only as it allows the agents to predict the future, markets are efficient etc. This nice theory is well-known, and it is a wonderful frame of reference. Especially in the 1980s a strong movement in economics argued that the world was really much closer to the bedrock than hitherto believed. If the noise terms are carefully formulated, the world is log-linear and everybody maximizes from now to infinity.

Bedrock theory suffers from two related problems. The first is that it is a bit dull. So many models are "set into motion" by some (small) deviation from perfection — for example an observation that seems to contradict the theory.[2] It is almost like a good old crime story. A criminal is needed for the story to be interesting. However, in the end the criminal is caught and all is well once again.

The second problem is *the theodicy problem of economics*.[3] With such rational agents we expect that economic outcomes are rational too. How come we see so many crazy outcomes when we look at the world? Average GDP differs between countries by 100 times. Some countries have pursued policies that have reduced their wealth by a 2–3% per year for several decades (think of Zambia). All countries have irrational institutions such as rent control and (at least some) trade regulation. Discrimination based upon ethnic differences is common etc. Debt crises have frequently occurred. The reader will probably agree that nobody can be closer to *economic man* then the bankers of the island of Manhattan: How come that even they managed to lend so much to Bolivia that at one point in time the debt burden reached 145% of GDP? We will return to the theodicy problem of economics at the end, but let us return to the subject matter.

Economic data tend to be much better — and easily accessible — than political data, so most of the literature on VP-functions concentrates on the economic part of the function. The present essay follows this tradition and uses the setup listed in Table 3.

Many experiments have been made with the lag structure, plenty of economic variables have been tried, and

Table 1: Defining the VP-function

Vote function: $V_t = F_t^e + F_t^p$	Explaining the vote for the government, at the election in time t, by economic, F_t^e, and political variables, F_t^p
Popularity function:	Is a formally similar function explaining the polled popularity of the government
VP-function:	Vote and Popularity functions are formally alike and closely related

Table 2: Characterizing the economically correct model

Bedrock theory: Models are built symmetrically around a *central case* where *rational* agents maximize their utility from now to infinity, given perfect foresight. The key agent is termed *economic man*.

Table 3: The basic quarterly macro VP-function

1. $VP_t = F_t^e + F_t^p$	Model from Table 1
2. $F_t^p = \alpha_g + \gamma t_g + e_{2t}$	Political model (formal)
3. $F_t^e = \beta_1 u_{t-\text{lag}} + \beta_2 p_{t-\text{lag}} + \cdots + e_{1t}$	Economic model (measured variable)
4. $VP_t \approx -0.6 u_{t-(1/4)} - 0.6 p_{t-(1/4)}$ $+ \cdots + \alpha_g - 0.15 t_g + e_t$	Typical coefficients estimated

Greek letters are coefficients to be estimated. e's are residuals
$u_t, p_t, \ldots,$ are economic variables as unemployment (u), inflation (p), etc
α_g and t_g, the political part is reduced to a government specific constant and trend

sometimes more genuine political variables have been included,[4] nonlinear functional forms have been used, etc, but we shall mainly discuss the simple linear expressions (3) and (4) from Table 3.

2. Main Results in the Literature

The literature on VP-functions is large, but most of the findings can be concentrated as in Table 4. The starting point is a simple hypothesis.

The responsibility hypothesis: Voters hold the government responsible for the economy. From this hypothesis follows the reward/punishment-mechanism: Voters punish the government in votes and polls if the economy goes badly, and they reward it if the economy goes well.

The hypothesis is not without problems: Governments may not have a majority, or external shocks may occur, which no sane person can ascribe to the government. A variable giving the *clarity of responsibility* may consequently enter the function. This is referred to as "content" in Table 4 — a subject that will not be discussed at present.

The literature was started by Kramer (1971) writing about vote functions (in the US),[5] while Mueller (1970) and Goodhart and Bhansali (1970) presented the first popularity function — for the US and UK — almost simultaneously.

The most important contributions since then are much more difficult to point out, but the following may be mentioned: Frey and Schneider (1978a,b) and Hibbs (1982) generated a wave of papers, both due to their lively fight and to new developments: Frey and Schneider integrated the VP-function into a set of policy reaction functions, while Hibbs mainly developed the modeling techniques.

The micro-based literature was started by Kinder and Kiewiet (1979). It was further pushed by Lewis-Beck (1988), while the cross-country discussion was started by Paldam (1991). A good sample of papers giving the present stage of the arts can be found in two recent volumes (both results from conferences trying to collect the main researchers in the field): Lewis-Beck and Paldam (2000) and Dorussen and Taylor (2002). This effort has generated the results listed in Table 4.

Each of the items of the table except the last will be discussed in a short section. We will argue that most are contrary to economic correctness, but that they are all possible to rationalize. However, they are at the *opposite extreme* of the *rationality spectrum* from the one normally considered by economists, see Figure 1 at the end: On one side is *economic man* and on the other the actual voter. This essay is written to say that this other side of the spectrum is getting far too little attention in standard theory.

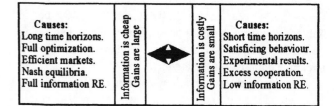

Figure 1: The two ends of the rationality spectrum.

Table 4: Main results in the literature

Section	Finding	Empirical status
3.	*The big two:* Voters react to mainly unemployment and inflation	Uncontroversial
4.	*Myopia:* The time horizon of voters is short — events more than 1 year from an election have small effects only	Uncontroversial
5.	*Retrospective:* Voters react to past events more than to expected future ones, but the difference is small as expectations are stationary	Controversial
6.	*Sociotropic:* In most countries voters are both sociotropic and egotropic[a]	Controversial
7.	*Low knowledge:* Voters know little about the (macro) economy	Uncontroversial
9.	*Grievance asymmetry:* Voters punish the government more for a bad economic situation than they reward it for a similarly sized good one	Controversial
10.	*Cost of ruling:* The average government ruling a normal 4-year period loses $2\frac{1}{2}$% of the votes. This result is independent of party system, voting law, country size, etc	Uncontroversial
Not covered	*Context:* The VP-function only generalizes if set in the same context. In particular, the responsibility pattern generalizes if the government is *clearly* visible to the voter	Only explored in a dozen papers

Note: The status line indicates if the result is *controversial*, i.e., if a minority of the researchers in the field disagrees. The article only considers the responsibility pattern and thus assumes a simple setting where both the government and the opposition are well defined. Complex, changing coalitions and minority governments are not discussed.

[a] Sociotropic: voters care about the national economy. Egotropic: voters care about their own economy.

In Table 3 the models are written as simple relations between levels, assuming all variables to be stationary. The present will largely disregard the substantial problems of estimation. That is, (i) should the model be formulated in levels or in first differences? (ii) should it contain an error correction term? And (iii) should series be pre-whitened? Popularity series are known to have complex and shifting structures in the residuals when modeled. So there are plenty of estimation problems. Many of the papers are from before the cointegration revolution, but new papers keep coming up using state of the arts techniques, though they rarely find new results.

Politologists have found that only 20% of the voters in the typical election are *swing voters*, and the net swing is considerably smaller, see Section 10. It means that 80% vote as they always do. The permanent part of voting is termed the *party identification, Id*. It is not 100% constant, and it needs an explanation, but it should be differently explained from the swing vote. The VP-function concentrates on the swing voters, but it may be formulated with terms handling the more permanent part of the vote as well.

In the more simple formulations one may work with *level estimates* where the committed voters enter into the constants, and with the *first difference estimates* where the committed voters are "differenced out". The choice between the two formulations is then a question of estimation efficiency to be determined by the structure of cointegration between the series, and the (resulting) structure of the error terms.

3. The Big Two: Unemployment (Income) and Inflation

The two variables which are found in most VP-functions are the rates of unemployment and inflation, u_t and p_t. Both normally get negative coefficients, often about -0.6 as listed in model (4) of Table 3. Unemployment is sometimes replaced with income thus confirming Okun's law. The Phillips curve is sufficiently weak so that unemployment and inflation have little colinearity in these functions.

The data for the rate of unemployment and the vote share for the government have roughly the same statistical structure so that it is possible that they can be connected as per the linear version of model (1). Data for the rate of inflation are upward skew. That is, inflation can explode and go as high as the capacity of the printing press allows. Also, people pay little interest to low inflation rates, but once it reaches a certain limit it becomes the key economic problem.[6] Hence, inflation cannot enter linearly in model (1), except of course, if we consider a narrow interval for inflation rates. Fortunately, inflation is often within a narrow interval in Western countries.

An interesting controversy deals with the role of unemployment. It was started by Stigler (1973) commenting on Kramer (1971). Stigler remarked that a change of unemployment of 1 percentage point affected 1% of the workers only — that is $\frac{1}{2}$% of the population. App 80% of those vote for the Left anyhow. The potential for affected swing voters is thus only 0.1% of the voters. How can this influence the vote by 0.6%? Note that Stiegler automatically assumes that voting is egotropic and retrospective. You change the vote if you — yourself — are affected by the said variable.[7] This point deals with the micro/macro experiences and the observability of the variables. It has often reappeared in the literature. Table 5 shows some of the key points.

The table lists the important variables and some other variables that have often been tried, but with little success. Unemployment and income affect individuals differently and are observable both at the micro and the macro level. Inflation is more difficult to observe for the individual at the macro level. We see prices go up, but the individual cannot observe if they rise by 2 or 3%. However, this is covered by the media.

The other variables listed — the balance of payments and the budget deficit — are much discussed in the media and are important in political debates. They are important *predictors for policy changes*, and indicators of *government competence*. However, they have no micro observability. It is interesting that they are rarely found to work in VP-functions.

Table 5: The character of the variables entering in the VP functions

	Micro-experience	Observability	Significant
Unemployment	Very different for individuals	Personal and media	Mostly[a]
Income	Different for individuals	Personal and media	
Inflation	Similar for individuals	Mostly media	Mostly
Balance of payment	None	Only media	Rarely
Budget deficit	None	Only media	Never

[a] The two variables have strong colinearity in VP-functions.

Refined models with competency signaling and full information rational expectations, where voters react to predicted effects of, e.g., budget deficits, are contrary to the findings in the VP-function literature. In fact, when we look at what people know about the economy — see Section 7 — it is no wonder that they do not react to changes in the balance of payments and the budget.

Under the responsibility hypothesis model (1) is an estimate of the *social welfare function*. It comes out remarkably simple. Basically, it is linear, and looks like Model (4) in Table 3. The main problem with such estimates is that they are unstable. Many highly significant functions looking like (4) have been estimated, but they frequently "break down" and significance evaporates.

If (4) is stable, it appears inconceivable that it cannot be exploited politically. And, in fact a whole literature on political business cycles has been written — since Nordhaus (1975) exploring the possibility for creating *election cycles* in the economy. However, most studies have shown that such cycles do not exist in practice. What may exist is rather the reverse, governments may steer the economy as per their ideology and create *partisan cycles*.[8]

4. Voters are Myopic

The voter's myopia result deals with the duration of the effect of a sudden economic change. Imagine a short and sharp economic crisis — like a drop in real GDP lasting one year — how long will this influence the popularity of the government?

One of the most consistently found results in the VP-function literature is the voter's myopia result. Only the events of the past year seem to count. A few researchers (notably Hibbs, 1982) have found that as much as $\frac{1}{3}$ of the effect remained after 1 year, but most researchers have been unable to find any effect after one year. The myopia result has been found even for political crises, which are often sharply defined in time. Consequently, the model looks as follows:

$$VP_t = \int_{-\infty}^{t} f(u_t, p_t) e^{rt} dt \approx \int_{t-1}^{t} f(u_t, p_t) e^{rt} dt \quad \text{(eq (4) in Table 3)} \quad (5)$$

The subscript $(t-1)$ represents a lag of one quarter (or perhaps one year) as before. The welfare maximization of the variable u (say unemployment) leading to the vote is made from $t-1$ to t, where the time unit "1" is a year, and the "discounting" expression e^{rt} has a high discount rate so that everything before $t-1$ is irrelevant.

Formula (5) is surely not how such expressions look in economic textbooks. A key part of economic correctness is that *economic man has a long time horizon and looks forward*. The common formulation of the closest corresponding models is:

$$W_t = \int_{t}^{\infty} f(u_t, p_t) e^{-rt} dt \quad (6)$$

The welfare to be maximized is a function of the relevant economic variable from now to infinity, with a small discount rate, r, perhaps even as small as the long run real rate of interest or the real growth rate. It gradually reduces the weight of future values, but events 20 years into the future count significantly.

Expressions (5) and (6) are hard to reconcile. First, the maximization is *retrospective* in (5) and *prospective* in (6), as will be discussed in Section 5. Second, the time horizons are dramatically different. None of the 300 studies have ever found evidence suggesting that events as far back as 2 years earlier have a measurable impact on the popularity of the government!

Many descriptions have been made of the political decision process by participants in the process and by the keen students of current affairs found among historians, political scientists and journalists. A common finding is that the decision process tends to have a short time horizon. The political life of a decision maker is uncertain and pressures are high. How decisions are made has little in common with the description of "benevolent dictators maximizing social welfare" still found in economic textbooks and many theoretical models.

The outcomes of "benevolent dictator calculations" have some value as a comparative "benchmark", and as ideal recipes for economic policy making.[9] However, some theorists present such exercises as realistic descriptions of policy making, deceiving young economists into believing that this is the way political decisions are made.

5. Voters are Retrospective/Expectations are Static

One of the key facts about economic theory is that it is largely theory driven. One of the main areas over the last 4 decades has been the area of expectation formation. It has been subjected to a huge theoretical research effort. Less interest has been given to research in the actual formation of inflationary expectations where real people are actually polled, as the results have typically been embarrassing. I think that we all know in our heart of hearts that real people cannot live up to our beautiful theories about *economic man*.

In the field of VP-functions about 50 papers have looked at the existing data and found that in many countries RP-pairs — defined in Table 6 — have been collected for such series as unemployment, inflation and real income. The papers have then tried to determine which of the two

Table 6: A polled RP-pair

Economics	Politology	Question in poll
Past experience	Retrospective	How has X developed during the last Z-period?
Expectations	Prospective	How do you expect X will develop during the next Z-period?

Note: X is an economic variable and Z is a time period like a quarter, a year or a couple of years.

variables in the pair are the most powerful one for predicting the vote/popularity of the governments.

Most of the analysis is done on micro-data of individual respondents, so many thousands of observations have been used to determine this controversy. The many papers do not fully agree, so the results of the efforts have to be summarized as follows:

RP1: The two series in the RP pair normally give almost the same results.

RP2: Most results show that the retrospective series are marginally more powerful.[10]

I think that virtually all economists will agree that the correct result in the RP-controversy is that the prospective twin should beat the retrospective one by a long margin. But by a rough count the retrospective twin wins in 2 of 3 cases in the studies made.

Some of the main discussants in this research are Helmut Norpoth for the majority retrospective view and Robert S. Erikson for the minority prospective view. They are working with the same data for the USA. Erikson terms the controversy *bankers or peasants*. Bankers work professionally with the economy and have prospective expectations. Peasants are interested in matters of farming mainly, and hence are retrospective, when it comes to the economy. The question thus is, if the average voter behaves mostly as a banker or as a peasant.[11] Once the question is asked, it appears that the obvious answer must be that the average person is a peasant. However, Erikson finds that voters behave as bankers.[12]

When the results of Erikson and Norpoth are compared, the difference is small. The most disgraceful result actually is (RP1) that the two series in the existing RP-pairs are as similar as identical twins. The only conclusion one can draw is that people form largely static expectations.

The author's own poll of 4788 Danes asking about the RP-pair for inflation found a net difference in the answers of 34 cases, i.e., 0.7% of the respondents (see Nannestad and Paldam, 2000).[13] With such a tiny difference it is no wonder that we were unable to find any difference in the fit of the VP function if we used the prospective or retrospective series. This is typical also for the British and the German results.

This brings us back to the large gap separating formulas (5) and (6). It does solve the apparent contradiction between the direction of the maximization if voters have static expectations. But then surely it is much easier to use the past as in (5). When we look at the vast literature building highly refined theory of inflationary expectations and analyzing the dynamic consequences of the different assumptions it is hard to reconcile with the findings of the VP-literature. Here is surely a field where facts are much duller than fiction.

6. Voters are Mainly Sociotropic — Or Perhaps Not

Once the analysis of VP-functions moved into micro research, data increased dramatically to allow much stronger tests, but new interesting problems came up. The most intriguing was probably the sociotropic/egotropic controversy, where the two terms are defined in Table 7.[14]

Like the RP-pairs also ES-pairs exist in various data sets: The egotropic question is "how has your own economic situation developed in the last Z-period?" The corresponding sociotropic question is: "How has the economic situation of your country developed in the last Z-period?" The "economic situation" is sometimes replaced with "unemployment", and once more Z is typically either a quarter or a year.

The economically correct answer is surely that *economic man* is egotropic. Therefore, it was shocking when Kinder and Kiewiet (1979) demonstrated that the US voter was sociotropic. Several other studies — notably Lewis-Beck (1988) — have confirmed the result also for other countries, even after considerable refinement of the questions. So, for more than a decade there was no doubt that the main result in the literature was that voters are sociotropic, contrary to economic correctness.

Kinder and Kiewiet's model was remarkably simple:

$$VP_i = \gamma_0 + \alpha E_i + \beta S_i + \lambda Id_i + u_i \qquad (7a)$$

Table 7: Defining egotropic and sociotropic

The economic factor in the VP-function is:	
Egotropic	what matters is the personal economy
Sociotropic	what matters is the national economy

Here i is an index for the individual, E_i is the egotropic variable, S_i is the sociotropic variable and Id_i is a party identification variable.

The model of Kinder and Kiewiet was estimated on a cross-section. In an unusually aggressive article Kramer (1983) pointed out that this was not the right approach for the problem. In a cross-section the true sociotropic variable is constant, and hence unable to explain anything. What is estimated as sociotropic can only be different perceptions, ϕ_i, of the same objective variable, Y:

$$VP_i = \gamma_0 + \alpha E_i + \beta \phi_i(Y) + \lambda Id_i + u_i \tag{7b}$$

Kramer did not see that the reformulation makes the economic correctness problem larger, not smaller! Surely, the rational voter perceives Y unbiased — that is, the perception error is white noise — and hence the coefficient β to $\phi_i(Y)$ should be zero. Kinder and Kiewiet's finding that the sociotropic term, β, dominates the egotropic term, α, becomes even more mysterious. The most reasonable interpretation of the finding is thus that the different perceptions estimated must be due to different personal experiences, and hence that what is estimated as a sociotropic effect is really egotropic.

The next generation of models trying to come to grips with the egotropic/sociotropic distinction was introduced by Markus (1988). He reformulated (7b) into a mixed cross-section time series model, which includes a time index, t:

$$VP_{i,t} = \gamma_0 + \gamma E_{i,t} + \beta Y_t + \lambda Id_{i,t} + u_{i,t} \tag{8a}$$

$$VP_{i,t} = \gamma_0 + \gamma E_{i,t} + \beta \phi_{i,t}(Y_t) + \lambda Id_{i,t} + u_{i,t} \tag{8b}$$

In Model (8a) the polled sociotropic variable is replaced with the "objective" one from the national statistical office. It can be compared with (8b) that should be almost the same as (7).

Model (8a) gives rather different results than (7). Now α and β become approximately the same on US data. Several studies have now estimated the various models for more countries. UK is covered by Price and Sanders (1994),[15] Denmark by Nannestad and Paldam (1997a) and Sweden by Jordahl (2001). It appears that both α and β become significant, though not in a predictable mixture.

Thus the old agreement that voting is *only* sociotropic has given way to a more unclear picture, where voting is a *mixture* of egotropic and sociotropic factors. This is less economically incorrect than the old view, but a sizable sociotropic factor still appears in voting in most countries.

7. Voters are Uninformed about the Economy

Many polls have asked people about their knowledge of the economy. It appears that nobody has collected such polls systematically, and few studies have therefore been made comparing results.[16] However, the results show rather decisively that voters know little about the economy.

In our Danish polls (see Nannestad and Paldam, 2000) most voters knew the number of unemployed within a few percentage points. They tended to know that the country had a balance of payments deficit and a budget deficit, *both* when the country had such deficits, and when it did not. When the two balances had the reverse sign, many mixed them up. Virtually nobody knew the sizes of the balances. Also, about $\frac{2}{3}$ of the voters could not give an assessment of the inflation rate within 2 percentage points (that is, if inflation was 3% they were either outside the range of 1–5% or answered "don't know").

However, there was one time during the four years covered, where knowledge increased substantially. This was around a general election. All of a sudden people knew that the balance of payments had changed from red to black figures.

The same type of result has been found about the EU: In European countries with no referenda institution, people know little about the European Union, but in countries with frequent referenda people know a lot more (see Paldam, 2001).

So, either people do seek information in connection with elections or they learn from watching the big show of an election/referendum campaign in TV. The fact that the information level goes up is worth to note as it explains why vote functions have a lower fit than popularity functions. It also explains why party popularities are normally much more volatile around elections than else.

Economic theory predicts that voters know what they need to know. The marginal benefits of information should be equal to the marginal costs:

$$MB(I) = MC(I) \quad \text{(the condition for rationality of information)} \tag{9}$$

One way to *define rational expectations* is to demand that (9) is fulfilled.[17] This is the definition used in the present paper.

The big problem surrounding (9) is what the benefits MB(I) are. Is it possible to argue convincingly that MB(I) is significantly larger than zero?

It is sometimes argued that people do need information on the macro level when they buy and sell shares and bonds (i.e., in connection with financing a house or a business) and when they buy and sell foreign exchange in connection with journeys abroad. But the theory of *market efficiency* — where many professional dealers are present — does effectively cut the link to information here. A (small) dealer in these markets can find no better information than the price.

The one occasion where people need information about the macro economy is when they vote at national elections and at their union, etc. Hence, we write:

$MB(I) = \partial B(V)/\partial I$ (marginal benefit of economic information should be equal to the marginal improvement in the benefits derived from voting better) (10)

This brings us to the problems surrounding MB(V), the marginal benefit of voting. It is the problem known in the paradox of voting, where almost the same equation as (10) can be written:

$MB(V) = MC(V)$ (the condition for rationality of voting) (11)

Much has been written about (11), but nobody has been able to argue convincingly that MB(V) differs significantly from zero. That makes all terms in (10) and (11) zero! However, we know that people do vote even if they do not know much about the economy. Surely, our friend *economic man* is in trouble. He should know nothing about the economy, and never vote. In short, the average voter behaves differently from *economic man*.

8. Two Ways to Rescue *Economic Man*

Two lines of arguments are often used to rationalize this apparent mess described in the last section. One is to argue that the cost of information, C(I), is small too. The second is to show that the cost of voting in an election, C(V), is large, and belongs to the class of social capital observations. Unfortunately, the two attempts are rather in the opposite direction.

C(I) is small too. This argument has been used by researchers such as Wittman (1995), Erikson et al. (2000) and Sanders (2000).[18] They argue the voters know what they need to know, and that this is not much. What they need is to "grasp" what is going on, i.e., to have some *feel* for the way the economy is going. This *feel* is acquired from the media without really trying. If most experts look gloomy, then things are going badly, and if they look relaxed then things are going well. If a feel is enough then it is possible to argue that C(I) is almost zero as well. There is something in this argument, and Sanders does show that soft "feel" questions about the economy can be scaled to track the actual economy reasonably well.

If everything goes on at the extreme low-cost end of the scale, so that $MB(I) = MC(I) = MC(V) = MB(V) \approx 0$ which is almost zero, then things become a bit wooly. Also, it is well-known that people are unable to make utility assessments involving small numbers.

The other approach is to start from *the large size of C(V)*. People do spend a lot of time looking at election campaigns in TV. Many go to some meetings, pay membership fees to political parties. Nearly everybody spends an hour driving to the election location, waiting in line and voting. In short, they have considerable costs *participating in the national democratic process*. Also, we know that parties find it worthwhile to spend millions on their campaigns. The total costs in time and money of a national election are likely to be something like 1% of GDP in the typical democracy.[19] So we have to explain why so much is spent by the individual and the political system.

Voting is a social capital phenomenon It is a well-known observation that people in experiments play the cooperative solution much more than they should if they solve the game as good little *economic men*. The excess frequency with which the cooperative solution is played is a measure of the *social capital* or the *mutual trust* of the players. The key point to note is that trust does not need to be specific. It can be general. Many attempts have been made measuring general trust, and we know that it is much higher in some — generally more successful societies — than in others.[20]

In infinitely repeated games it is possible to uphold cooperative solutions, and it is arguable that society is a large number of games played with many players in different combinations over and over, seemingly without end. We do not bother solving all games in which we participate — and some of the everyday games are too complex to solve. So we develop rules of thumb standards, which can be termed trust. If a country succeeds in reaching a high level of trust then it is an advantage to everyone, as the cooperative solution becomes the one automatically reached in many situations.

The attempts to integrate these observations in standard theory are still going on. It seems likely that they may succeed, and then the paradox of voting may be solved at long last.

Given that this solution works, then we know that people do undertake considerable cost to follow the political scene and participate in the process. Given that these costs are so high, why not imagine that people also try to follow the economy? The fact that they are not so knowledgeable may simply be that it is difficult, as all those of us who teach the subject know.

It is interesting that the two attempts to save *economic man* are so different. In my judgement the second approach is the most promising, but it is not yet integrated into standard theory. However, both approaches agree that *economic man* is the wrong model for the job at hand.

9. Voters have a Grievance Asymmetry

Already the first popularity function study (Mueller, 1970) — discovered that voters react more to a negative economic event than to a corresponding positive one.

It was also found by Bloom and Price (1975) commenting on Kramer (1971). Then, for some time nobody looked for a grievance asymmetry, and the effect was forgotten.

Once the analysis of micro data became organized, it became possible to look for more effects. And, in the 1990s several studies looked carefully and found a rather strong asymmetry. See, e.g., Price and Sanders (1994) and Nannestad and Paldam (1997b). It appears that if e.g., unemployment increases by 1% (point), it has *twice* as large a negative effect as the positive effect of a fall in unemployment of 1% (point). The effect is thus large, and it is highly significant.

This has the consequence that if the economy moves from A to B in a straight line then the voter is more content than if it moves in a more roundabout way. In short, the variation around the growth path causes the government popularity to fall. Consider the average (Avr) and variance (Var) of a positive variable, i.e., a variable where $\partial VP/\partial X > 0$:

$$\partial VP/\partial Avr(X) > 0 \quad \text{and} \quad \partial VP/\partial Var(X) < 0 \quad (12)$$

This is the standard formulation of *risk aversion*, so this is well integrated into economics, as long as it is prospective.

If the variables are retrospective, it is different. Relation (12) now changes from risk aversion to *loss aversion*. This is, in principle, an important change entering into one of the *economic-man*-problems discussed by Kahneman (1994) and other critiques of standard theory. The problematic aspect is that utility becomes path dependent. Costs are not sunk at all.

However, if expectations are stationary then it becomes unclear if we are dealing with risk aversion — which is perfectly nice theory — or loss aversion — which is a bad anomaly!

10. It Costs Governments Votes to Rule

The average government in a mature western democracy loses $2\tfrac{1}{2}$% of the vote just by ruling (see Paldam, 1991; and Nannestad and Paldam, 2002). There is no difference between the average outcome and its standard deviation in such countries as the Netherlands, Sweden, Italy and Japan so it is a surprising fact. Also, it is heavily underresearched.[21]

Per definition the average government rules exactly as the rational voter should expect. So the economically correct prediction must surely be that the voter votes as before. It is hence a strange result that the average government loses a highly significant fraction of the votes. Three theories try to provide an explanation:

The oldest (from Mueller, 1970) is the *coalition of minorities theory*. It essentially says that the governments are formed when parties before elections manage to put together inconsistent coalitions. However, when they rule, the inconsistencies are reviled. So essentially the theory is that you can get away with unrealistic promises when in opposition. In average $2\tfrac{1}{2}$% of the voters form unrealistic expectations at every election. This is a small irrationality, but it is a long-run fault, so it is not a "nice" theory, and it appears that no other evidence exists for the theory.

The second theory is the *median gap model*. It starts from a slightly amended version of the median voter theory. The pure form of the model suffers from the well-known problem that if both parties accept the policy of the median voter, they become perfectly alike and there is no reason to vote. To be distinguishable there has to be a gap around the median position between the voters. If there is a gap of size (some of the voters will get as close as they can come to their ideal policy if the government changes at every election. This has all been worked out as a perfectly respectable model, and it is even possible to calibrate the model with reasonably looking parameters so as to explain the observed fact. Unfortunately, little corroborating evidence exists for the theory.

Finally, the third theory builds upon the *grievance asymmetry* just discussed. Imagine that the outcome is symmetrically distributed around the expected outcome. So, some variables improve and some deteriorate, but the gains and losses are equally large. If the reaction is asymmetric then there must be a loss of popularity in average. It is easy to show that the model produces the typical cost of ruling for reasonably sized VP-functions with the typical grievance asymmetry and realistically noisy economic outcomes.

Let us for a moment assume that the last theory is true. The average government loses votes because it rules and this causes governments to change. This destroys the evidence for the median voter theorem. In a two-party (two-block) system both parties (blocks) converge to 50% of the votes just because they rule when they are larger than 50%. The simplest explanation of the cost of ruling thus undercuts one of the key theorems of political economy.

11. Conclusion: Look at the Other End of the RE-Spectrum

Throughout the above survey it has appeared that the findings in the large VP-literature contradict the notions that the average voter behaves as does *economic man* of standard theory. That is, the symmetric, forward-looking agent, who takes *everything relevant* into consideration for his decisions. This is the fellow we constantly meet in the theoretical literature. However, the voters we meet "out there in the real world" do not optimize forward, but backward, and they have a short time horizon. Also, they have a strong grievance asymmetry, so that it cost votes to rule.

Section 7 argued that it would be irrational if the voter behaved as *economic man*! Voting is a decision where ignorance is rational, even if it is accepted that a "feel" for the economy is enough, we are still faced with complex and unsolved questions.

However, once you start from the notion that politics is a field with much uncertainty, and hence a short time horizon, things start to fall into some order. Under the circumstances it would be inconsistent, if the voters had long memories. This means the election cycles are out of the question, but it is consistent with the notion of partisan cycles. The shorter the time horizon the better does the past predict the future. Surely, within a few quarters nothing is likely to change very much.

The sizeable fraction of sociotropic voting — it is probably 25–50% — also makes a lot of sense when you ask what elections are all about. It does deal with the whole economy, not with the economy of Mrs Voter herself! So perhaps it is not so surprising that people give some consideration to the way they feel the government handles the economy when they vote.

Also, we do have a lot of results showing that the average citizen in all countries has considerable risk aversion (or, for that matter, loss aversion). The whole of the financial sector makes a perfectly good living out of turning risk pooling into a negative sum game for everybody else. So it is natural to expect a clear grievance asymmetry.

Once that is accepted, the cost of ruling follows. It is an important finding as it causes parties to change in power, and governments coalitions to converge to 50% of the vote. This happens irrespective of the median voter theorem and the minimum winning coalition theorem. Or rather it produces exactly the same observable facts in a much simpler way.

In short, it is worthwhile to take the findings in the VP-function literature seriously and use these findings for the development of a more realistic theory. Such a theory will also make it easier to explain the many suboptimal — or even crazy — outcomes we observe.

MARTIN PALDAM

NOTES

1. The author has contributed about 20 of these papers including a couple of surveys, see Paldam (1981), Nannestad and Paldam (1994) and the introduction to Lewis-Beck and Paldam (2000). The text has benefitted from discussions with Peter Nannestad.
2. Also, a lot of papers in economics seem to be theory driven in the sense that change old models using unfashionable assumptions into new models using more appropriate assumptions.
3. The reader probably knows the theologists have struggled with their theodicy problem for the last 2000 years: If God is good and omnipotent, how come we see so much random and human cruelty in the world? Theologists most of the time manage to convince themselves that it is bad theology even to recognize that there is a problem, but then they may encounter a child suffering from terminal cancer.
4. Dummies for special events are common, but some quantitative variables have been tried too. The most famous is the *rally-around-the-flag* variable for foreign policy crisis constructed from political almanacs, where the size of the spikes are assessed by media volume and the speed of the decay after the event is estimated.
5. It appears that Kramer's paper was around as a working paper longer than the other two, even when it was published a year later.
6. This tallies nicely with the findings in the literature dealing with effects of inflation. High inflation is harmful, but whether inflation is 2 or 5% seems to have no effects on the real economy.
7. It is easy to reach a much higher number than did Stiegler. (1) Imagine that the average household has three voters, who have an income loss if one member becomes unemployed. (2) An increase of 1% in the rate of unemployment means that 3 people suffer a spell of unemployment. Hence, 9 people experience a loss when unemployment rises by 1%. The 0.1% in the text now is 0.9% and that is larger than the 0.6% that has to be explained. Also, maybe your welfare is affected by the way your friends fare.
8. The main articles in the field are reprinted and surveyed in Frey (1996). See Gärtner (1994) and Paldam (1997) for recent surveys.
9. The reader should consult Tinbergen (1956) and Johansen (1978, 1979) to find the classical version of how benevolent dictators maximize social welfare, just in case one such ruler ever happened. When reading such descriptions it is sad to contemplate that we are dealing with some of the most brilliant minds in our profession.
10. Recent research from Portugal has found a PR-set which differs considerably, and here the retrospective series works significantly better, see Veiga and Veiga (2002).
11. Compare Nickelsburg and Norpoth (2000) and Erikson et al. (2000) — using almost the same data. It is probably unfair to single out two of the authors from their coauthors, but they are the ones I have heard defending their views most eloquently.
12. Even the farsightedness of bankers can be doubted as mentioned in the introduction.
13. The polls were done quarterly for the years 1990–93, where inflation had a clear downward trend. Nevertheless, only 0.7% of the respondents (net) predicted a fall.
14. Both words are created for the purpose and not in most dictionaries: Sometimes the term egotropic is replaced by more loaded terms as "egocentric" or "egoistic."
15. The studies of the UK are rather numerous as a search in a good library database under the names Harold Clarke, Davis Sanders and Paul Whitley will show.
16. Aidt (2000) is an attempt to find and summarize such polls.

17. Two other definitions are: (1) Data contains no exploitable regularity. (2) Expectations are model consistent.
18. All of the above are politologists, of which Donald Wittman is known as the one, who is making the rational expectations revolution in Political Science.
19. Assume that people use in average 15 hours on the election, and that only half of this is leisure, this is $\frac{1}{2}$% of the normal working year to start with. Then it is normal to declare a school holiday, and the advertisement budget and the opportunity costs of the media coverage, etc. If one also adds the cost of bad government for about half a year before the election and a bit after, then surely 1% of GDP is a low estimate of the costs of a national election.
20. In ongoing work I have measured how much larger social capital is in Denmark than in Russia by a whole battery of questions using the same questionnaire. It is between 2.5 and 4 (times) by *all* measures. The literature on social capital has recently been surveyed by several authors, see e.g., Paldam (2000).
21. The research on the cost of ruling is surveyed and discussed in Nannestad and Paldam (2002), so I am brief at present. The second and third theory are from Paldam and Skott (1995) and Nannestad and Paldam (1997b).

REFERENCES

Aidt, T. (2000). "Economic voting and information." *Electoral Studies*, 19: 349–362.

Bloom, H.S. and Price, H.D. (1975). "The effects of aggregate economic variables on congressional elections." *American Political Science Review*, 69: 1232–1269.

Dorussen, H. and Taylor, M. (eds.) (2002). *Economic Voting*. London and New York: Routledge.

Erikson, R.S., MacKuen, M.B., and Stimson, J.A. (2000). "Bankers or peasants revisited: economic expectations and presidential approval." *Electoral Studies*, 19: 295–312.

Frey, B.S. and Schneider, F. (1978a). "An empirical study of politico-economic interaction in the US." *Review of Economics and Statistics*, 60: 174–183.

Frey, B.S. and Schneider, F. (1978b). "A politico-economic model of the United Kingdom." *Economic Journal*, 88: 243–253.

Frey, B. (1996). *Political Business Cycles*. Aldershot: Edward Elgar.

Gärtner, M. (1994). "Democracy, elections, and macroeconomic policy: two decades of progress." *European Journal of Political Economy*, 10: 85–110.

Goodhart, C.A.E. and Bhansali, R.J. (1970). "Political economy." *Political Studies*, 18: 43–106.

Hibbs, D.A. Jr. (1982). "On the demand for economic outcomes: macroeconomic outcomes and mass political support in the United States, Great Britain, and Germany." *Journal of Politics*, 44: 426–462.

Johansen, L. (1978, 1979). *Lectures on Macroeconomic Planning*, 2 vols. Amsterdam: North-Holland.

Johrdahl, H. (2001). An economic analysis of voting in Sweden. Paper for the EPCS, Econ Department, Uppasala University, Paris.

Kahneman, D. (1994). "New challenges to the rationality assumptions." *Journal of Institutional and Theoretical Economics (JITE)*, 150: 18–36.

Kinder, D.R. and Kiewiet, D.R. (1979). "Economic discontent and political behavior: the role of personal grievances and collective economic judgement in congressional voting." *American Journal of Political Science*, 23: 495–527.

Kramer, G.H. (1971). "Short-term fluctuations in U.S. voting behavior, 1896–1964." *American Political Science Review*, 65: 131–143.

Kramer, G.H. (1983). "The ecological fallacy revisited: aggregate versus individual-level findings on economics and elections and sociotropic voting." *American Political Science Review*, 77: 92–111.

Lewis-Beck, M.S. (1988). *Economics and Elections: The Major Western Democracies*. Ann Arbor: Michigan University Press.

Lewis-Beck, M.S. and Paldam, M. (eds.) (2000). "Economic voting: an introduction." *Electoral Studies (special issue Economics and Elections)*, 19: 113–121.

Markus, G.B. (1988). "The impact of personal and national economic conditions on presidential voting: A pooled cross-section analysis." *American Journal of Political Science*, 32: 137–154.

Markus, G.B. (1988). "The impact of personal and national economic conditions on the presidential vote: a pooled cross-sectional analysis." *American Political Science Review*, 36: 829–834.

Mueller, J.E. (1970). "Presidential popularity from Truman to Johnson." *American Political Science Review*, 64: 18–34.

Nannestad, P. and Paldam, M. (1994). "The VP-function: a survey of the literature on vote and popularity functions after 25 years." *Public Choice*, 79: 213–245.

Nannestad, P. and Paldam, M. (1997a). "From the pocketbook of the welfare man: a pooled cross-section study of economic voting in Denmark, 1986–92." *British Journal of Political Science*, 27: 119–136.

Nannestad, P. and Paldam, M. (1997b). "The grievance asymmetry revisited: a micro study of economic voting in Denmark, 1986–92." *European Journal of Political Economy*, 13: 81–99.

Nannestad, P. and Paldam, M. (2000). "What do voters know about the economy? A study of Danish data, 1990–1993." *Electoral Studies*, 19: 363–392.

Nannestad, P. and Paldam, M. (2002). "The cost of ruling. A foundation stone for two theories," in Dorussen and Taylor (eds.)

Nickelsburg, M. and Norpoth, H. (2000). "Commander-in-chief or chief economist? The president in the eye of the public." *Electoral Studies*, 19: 313–332.

Nordhaus, W.D. (1975). "The political business cycle." *Review of Economic Studies*, 42: 169–190.

Paldam, M. (1981). "A preliminary survey of the theories and findings on vote and popularity functions." *European Journal of Political Research*, 9: 181–199.

Paldam, M. (1991). "How robust is the vote function?" in H. Norpoth, M.S. Lewis-Beck, and J.-D. Lafay (eds.) *Economics and Politics: The Calculus of Support*. Ann Arbor: University of Michigan Press.

Paldam, M. (1997). "Political business cycles," in D.C. Mueller (ed.) *Perspectives on Public Choice. A Handbook*. Cambridge, UK: Cambridge University Press, ch. 16.

Paldam, M. (2000). "Social capital: one or many? Definition and measurement." *Journal of Economic Surveys*, 14: 629–653.

Paldam, M. (2001). "A small country in Europe's integration. Generalizing the political economy of the Danish case." *Public Choice* (forthcoming, maybe in 2003).

Paldam, M. and Skott, P. (1995). "A rational-voter explanation of the cost of ruling." *Public Choice*, 83: 159–172.

Price, S. and Sanders, D. (1994). "Party support and economic perceptions in the UK: a two-level approach," in D. Brouhton et al. (eds.) *British Elections and Parties Yearbook 1994*. London: Frank Cass, pp. 46–72.

Sanders, D. (2000). "The real economy and the perceived economy in popularity functions: how much do the voters need to know? A study of British data, 1974–97." *Electoral Studies*, 19: 275–294.

Stigler, G.J. (1973). "General economic conditions and national elections." *American Economic Review, Papers and Proceedings*, 63: 160–180. Special panel on Kramer (1971).

Tinbergen, J. (1956, 1964). *Economic Policy: Principles and Design*. Amsterdam: North-Holland.

Veiga, F.J. and Veiga, L.G. (2002). "The determinants of vote intentions in Portugal." *Public Choice* (forthcoming maybe in 2003).

Wittman, D. (1995). *The Myth of Democratic Failure. Why Political Institutions are Efficient*. Chicago: Chicago University Press.

C

CONSTITUTIONAL POLITICAL ECONOMY*

1. Constitutional and Nonconstitutional Economics

There is a categorical distinction to be made between constitutional economics and nonconstitutional, or ordinary, economics — a distinction in the ultimate behavioral object of analytical attention. In one sense, all of economics is about choice, and about the varying and complex institutional arrangements within which individuals make choices among alternatives. In ordinary or orthodox economics, no matter how simple or how complex, analysis is concentrated on choices made *within* constraints that are, themselves, imposed exogenously to the person or persons charged with making the choice. The constraints that restrict the set of feasible choice options may be imposed by nature, by history, by a sequence of past choices, by other persons, by laws and institutional arrangements, or even by custom and convention. In the elementary textbook formulation of demand theory, for example, the individual consumer-purchaser confronts a range of goods available at a set of prices, but is restricted by the size of the budget. This budget is not within the choice set of the consumer-purchaser during the period of choice under scrutiny. Indeed it would seem unnatural or bizarre, within the mind-set fostered by ordinary economics, to consider or limit the set of available choice options. Within this mind-set, the utility of the chooser is always maximized by allowing for choices over the whole range allowed by the exogenously determined constraints.

It is precisely at this critical point that constitutional economics, in its most inclusive definition, departs from the conventional framework of analysis. Constitutional economics directs analytical attention to the *choice among constraints*. Once stated in this fashion, economists will recognize that there is relatively little in their established canon that will assist in analyzing choices of this sort. To orthodox economists, only the elementary reality of scarcity makes choice necessary; without scarcity there would be no need to choose. And it would appear to be both methodologically and descriptively absurd to introduce the artificial creation of scarcity as an object for behavioral analysis. Such bedrock conservatism presumably explains much of ordinary economists' inattention and disinterest in constitutional questions, at all levels.

If we move beyond the models of orthodox economics, however, even while remaining at the level of individual behavior, we observe that individuals do, in fact, choose their own constraints, at least to a degree and within some limits. Within recent decades, a few innovative thinkers from economics and other social sciences have commenced to study the choice processes that are involved here (Elster, 1979; Schelling, 1978; Thaler and Shefrin, 1981). The *economics of self-control* has reached the status of a respectable, if minor, research program, which may be destined to become more important in this era of emphasis on diet, exercise, health, and the environment. We must surely be sufficiently catholic to allow analysis in this *individual constitutional economics* to qualify for inclusion in the domain.

As they carry on within their own guaranteed private spaces, however, individuals would presumably subject themselves to a relatively small set of prior constraints. Individuals basically *trust themselves* to choose rationally when confronted with the externally imposed constraints that are dictated in their historically emergent conditions. If the choice among constraints, in all its complexity, is limited to the economics of self-control, or stated conversely, to the economics of temptation, there might be little to be gained in delineating a constitutional economics enterprise.

It is essential to acknowledge, near the outset of discussion, that individuals choose to impose constraints or limits on their own behavior primarily, even if not exclusively, as a part of an *exchange* in which the restrictions on their own actions are sacrificed in return for the benefits that are anticipated from the reciprocally extended restrictions on the actions of others with whom they interact along the boundaries of private spaces and within the confines of acknowledged public spaces. That is to say, a domain of constitutional economics would exist even if individuals, in their private spaces, chose never to impose constraints on their own behavior. Note that by interpreting the individual's choice of a generalized constraint that restricts the actions both of others and himself as a part of a reciprocal exchange, we have moved toward the familiar domain of orthodox economics. So interpreted, the individual who joins in a collective decision to impose a generally applied constitutional rule is not, at base, acting differently from observed behavior in a setting that involves giving up one desired good, apples, for another desired good, oranges.

---

* An extended and somewhat modified version of this essay was published under the title 'The Domain of Constitutional Economics,' in *Constitutional Political Economy* 1 (1, 1990): 1–18.

In the latter example, we can, without violating the meaning of words, say that the individual chooses to constrain or to limit, the potential consumption of apples in exchange for the expanded opportunity to consume oranges. Expressed in this way, all that is required is that we classify the restrictions on others' actions as *goods* in the individual's preference function along with the more natural classification or restrictions on his own actions as *bads*.

In this simplistic and individualistic perspective, the choice of a reciprocally binding constraint by individuals who are related one to another in an anticipated set of interactions becomes fully analogous to trade in ordinary goods and services, and, so treated, becomes quite different from the choice of a self-imposed constraint in the much more difficult economics of self-control, briefly discussed above. Note, in particular, however, that the analysis of individual choice behavior is necessarily shifted from the subject realm of the private to the public or political. The analysis becomes *political economy* almost by definition. *Constitutional economics* morphs into *constitutional political economy*.

Why have the practitioners of orthodox economics seemed so reluctant to extend analysis to include the reciprocal exchange of liberties that are central to the domain of constitutional political economy? In part such reluctance stems from the artificial splitting between the academic disciplines of economics and political science late in the nineteenth century. Economists have been content to confine their attention to market relationships. I can advance several other and related reasons. Economists, along with their peers in the other social sciences as well as other academic disciplines have had no difficulty, through the ages, in implicitly classifying restrictions on some of the activities of some persons in the body politic to be *good*. But the classification procedure has been quite different from the subjective evaluations presumed to be embodied in individuals' preference functions. The nonconstrained voluntary behavior is not classified to be *bad* because an individual simply disprefers such behavior in the ordinary way. Some such behavior is deeded to be bad, and hence its rectification to be good, on the basis of an externally derived criterion of *goodness* or *truth*. The attributes or qualities of goodness and/or badness applied to actions of persons are treated as if they are intrinsically public, in the Samuelsonian taxonomic sense. An action cannot, properly, be adjudged to be good by one person without an implied generalization of such judgment to other persons. In this conceptualization, persons must, ideally, be brought into agreement on some ultimate classification of actions through a process that resembles scientific discourse. Agreement does not emerge from a trading process where different interests are essentially compromised, with each party reckoning to enjoy some benefits while suffering some sacrifice of preferred position.

In some respects, it is surprising that economists have 'jumped out' of their own analytical framework so readily when they consider the possible imposition of generalized constraints on behavior. They have expressed little curiosity in deriving justification for such constraints from a calculus of individual interests. Economists have, instead, been willing intellectual captives of idealistic political philosophers, and they have readily embraced variants of the Platonic and Helenian mind-sets. Amartya Sen's (1970) usage of the term *meddlesome preferences*, by sharp contrast with such terms as *merit goods* and *merit wants*, tends to focus analysis back toward a straightforward calculus of interest and away from nonindividualistic attributes of either goods or actions.

A second, and related, reason for economists' general failure to use the exchange setting when they consider the possible imposition of generalized constraints on individual behavior lies in the methodological dominance of the maximization paradigm. In the latter, *the economic problem* is defined as one of allocating scarce means (resources) among alternative ends. Choice is made necessary by the scarcity of means, and that which is desired (utility) is maximized when like units of resources yield equivalent returns in all uses to which they are put. In this elementary formulation, emphasis is almost exclusively placed on the choices that are made within the scarcity constraints that are, themselves, presumed to be beyond the scope for chooser selection. There is little or no attention paid to the identification of the choosing unit in this abstracted definition, and this feature allows for a relatively unnoticed transference of analysis from individual choice to *social*, *political*, or *collective* choice on the basis of some implicit presumption that collectivities choose analogously to individuals.

This shift from individual to supraindividual choice was supported, and indirectly justified, by the emergence of macroaggregation and macroeconomic theory and policy during the early decades of the post-Robbins half century. Target levels of macroaggregates (national product, rate of growth, levels of employment) were established to be objectively *good* and to serve as guideposts for choices to be made by collective entities (governments) subject only to the constraints imposed by natural scarcities and technological limits. By some implicit extension of the model for individual choice behavior, constrained only by external forces, governments came to be viewed romantically and were deemed capable of achieving the *good*, as defined for them by the economists and other social philosophers. Microeconomists had long been ready at hand to proffer policy advice to governments concerning ways and means to promote greater overall economy efficiency.

A third reason for economists' general failure to extend their analytical apparatus to the derivation of institutional constitutional structure is to be found in their presumption that structural constraints are not, themselves, subject to deliberative choice, and, hence, to change. Economists have not neglected to recognize the relevance of institutional rules in affecting patterns of human behavior. Property rights economics, in particular Alchian (1977), has opened up a research program that concentrates attention directly on the effects of alternative structures. For the most part, however, the emphasis here is on existing arrangements rather than on the comparative analysis involved in extension to structures that might be designed and implemented.

Constitutional political economy differs from nonconstitutional or orthodox economics along each of the dimensions that may be inferred from the reasons for neglect detailed above. Analysis is consistently individualistic, in the several senses that are relevant. The derivation of institutional constraints is based on a calculus of individual interests, which, in turn, requires the introduction and use of an exchange paradigm as opposed to the idealists' search for the unique *good*. Furthermore, there is no extension of the choice calculus from the individual to collectivities, as such. Collective *choice* is factored down into the participatory behavior of individual members. Finally, emphasis is centered directly on the selection of rules, or institutions, that will, in turn, limit the behavior of the persons who operate within them. Institutions, defined broadly, are variables subject to deliberative evaluation and to explicit choice (Buchanan and Tullock, 1962).

As noted, at one extreme constitutional analysis may be applied to the individual in total isolation, who may act solely in private space. At the other extreme, constitutional analysis is applied to the whole set of persons who make up the membership of the polity. This subcategory of research emphasis is the most familiar, since the very word *constitutional* tends to convey political connotations. The derivation of constraints on government does, indeed, occupy much of our attention. But the inclusive domain of constitutional economics also includes the derivation, analysis of, and justificatory argument for rules that constrain both individual and collective behavior in a wide array of membership groupings, larger than the one-unit limit but smaller than the all-inclusive limit of the whole polity. Clubs, trade unions, corporations, parties, universities, associations — these, and many more, exist and operate under constitutions that are amenable to scientific inquiry.

2. Constitutional *Economics* and Constitutional *Politics*

In section 1, I have attempted to distinguish between *constitutional* and *nonconstitutional* economics or political economy. I propose, in this section, to distinguish between constitutional *economics* and constitutional *politics*, as the latter term may be generally and widely interpreted. As I have noted, most constitutional inquiry and analysis is concentrated at the level of the politically organized collectivity and is, in this sense, political. The distinction to be emphasized, however, is one of perspective rather than one that relates directly to either form of organization or to the type of activity. If an exchange rather than a maximizing paradigm is taken to be descriptive of the inclusive research program for the discipline, then *economics* involves inquiry into *cooperative* arrangements for human interaction, extending from the simplest of two-person, two-good trading processes through the most complex quasi-constitutional arrangements for multinational organizations. As noted in the first section, orthodox economics has rarely been extended to noncommercial or political activity, as such, but the exchange perspective readily allows this step to be taken.

The cooperative perspective, however, must be categorically distinguished from the contrasting *conflictual* perspective, which has been applied, almost automatically, to all political interactions, whether or not these are classified as constitutional. It will be useful here to examine the differences between the cooperative and the conflictual perspectives more carefully. The very term *politics* tends to conjure up a mental image of potential conflict among those persons who are members of the politically organized community. This conflict may be interpreted to be analogous to scientific disputes, in which separate participants or groups seek to convince one another of the *truth* of their advanced propositions. The age-old tradition of idealism in political philosophy conceives of all of politics in this light and, as noted earlier, the dominance of this model of politics has tended to discourage economists from political extensions of the exchange or cooperative paradigm. But, even if the teleological interpretation is rejected, politics may seem, by its very nature, to involve conflict between and among individuals and groups within a polity.

From the institutionally determined characteristics of collective decisions, the characteristics that dictate mutual exclusivity among the alternatives for selection (only one candidate can be electorally chosen) imply some ultimate division of the membership into two subsets, *winners* and *losers*. This perspective almost directly suggests that politics is primarily if not exclusively a distributional game or enterprise — a process that involves transfers of value (utility) among and between separately identified coalitions of persons.

Note that the predominance of the distributional elements in the conflictual model of politics need not imply that the game be zero sum, although this limiting case may be useful for some analytical purposes. Conflictual politics may be positive, zero, or negative sum, as gains and losses are somehow aggregated over all participants (members). And this seems to be the natural model for analyzing politics so long as rules for reaching collective decisions require less than full agreement. If a majority, whether simple or qualified, is allowed to be decisive and impose its will on a majority, then the observed opposition of the minority to the alternative preferred by the majority can be taken to indicate that members of the minority expect to suffer utility losses, at least in a lost opportunity sense. In this model of conflictual politics, which appears to be descriptive of ordinary political activity, there seems to be no direct way of introducing a cooperative interpretation. A necessary condition for cooperation in social interaction is the prospect for positive expected gains by all parties, or, in the gainer-loser terminology, the prospect that there be no net losers. At a first descriptive cut, this condition seems to be foreign to the whole political enterprise.

It is precisely at this point, however, that constitutional politics, or politics at the constitutional level of choices among alternative sets of basic rules or constraints, rescues the cooperative model, at least in some potential explanatory and normative sense. As it operates and as we observe it to operate, ordinary politics may remain conflictual, in the manner noted above, while participation in the inclusive political game that defines the rules for ordinary politics may embody positively valued prospects for all members of the polity. In other words, constitutional politics does lend itself to examination in a cooperative analytical framework, while ordinary politics continues to lend itself to analysis that employs conflict models of interaction.

Generalized agreement on constitutional rules that allow for the reaching of ordinary collective decisions by means that do not require general agreement is surely possible, as is empirically demonstrated in the context of almost all organizations. The analytical-scientific inquiry that involves comparisons of the working properties of alternative sets of rules along with the examination of processes through which agreement on rules may be attained defines the domain of primary concern. The usage of the terminology *constitutional political economy* rather than the somewhat more accurate *constitutional politics* is prompted by the linkage in scientific heritage between *economics* and *cooperation*, by the inference of the appropriateness of the exchange as opposed to the conflict paradigm.

3. The Intellectual Traditions of Constitutional Political Economy

In sections 1 and 2, I have attempted to set the research program in constitutional political economy apart from ongoing programs within the interrelated and more inclusive disciplines of economics and political science. It would be totally misleading, however, to infer from my discussion that this research program has emerged full blown, as if divorced from any traditions of intellectual inquiry. As I have noted, constitutional political economy did indeed blossom only in the second half of the century. But the program was not based either on a new scientific discovery, at least as usually defined, or on a new set of analytical tools. Constitutional political economy is best interpreted as a reemphasis, a revival, a rediscovery of basic elements of earlier intellectual traditions that have been put aside, neglected, and sometimes forgotten in the social sciences and social philosophy. These traditions are those of classical political economy and contractarian political philosophy.

Classical political economy, represented especially in the works of Adam Smith (1776), was directed toward offering an explanation and understanding of how an economy (set of markets) would work without detailed political interventions and control. Smith's aim was to demonstrate that the *wealth* of the nation would be larger under a regime of minimal politicization than under the alternative closely controlled mercantilist regime. And the whole thrust of the argument was to the effect that all groups in the economy and especially the laboring classes, could be expected to share in the benefits promised upon the shift in regimes. The emphasis was on the generalization of expected gains over all persons and classes. The suggested change in the structure, or basic rules, that depoliticization involves was, therefore, within the feasible limits of potential agreement by all parties. The normative focus, again especially in Adam Smith, was not explicitly distributional. Only with Marxian extensions of Ricardo's abstract analysis did interclass conflict enter into classical attention.

It is also important to recognize that the Smithean emphasis was not allocational in the modern economists' meaning of this term. The analysis was not designed to show that economic resources would be more effectively allocated to higher valued uses under a market than under a politicized regime, as measured by some external and objective standard of value. The aim was, instead, to show that the market order would allocate resources such that the evaluations (preferences) of individuals would be more fully satisfied, *regardless of what these evaluations might be*. In terms of his familiar example of the butcher, Smith's lesson was to show that self-interest in the marketplace works to supply meat for supper, provided that meat is what consumers want. There is no implication here that self-interest in the marketplace works to supply meat because meat is valuable in some nutritional sense as defined by experts.

So interpreted, therefore, Adam Smith's enterprise falls squarely within the domain of constitutional political economy. In a strictly positive sense, his analysis described both how the existing regime worked and how an alternative regime might work. And, since the alternative seemed to generate more wealth to all parties, as measured by their own standards, the normative extension of the positive analysis was quite straightforward. In this extension, the object upon which collective attention must be placed is the set of rules or constraints within which persons behave in their capacities as consumers-buyers and producers-sellers. The laws and institutions that define the economic-political order become the variables subject to possible adjustment and reform.

I have selected elements from the tradition of classical political economy that seem to provide precursory foundations for the modern research program in constitutional political economy. My treatment would surely be accused of bias, however, if I failed to indicate the presence of considerable ambiguity and confusion in the philosophical underpinnings of the classical economics enterprise. An interpretation of that enterprise in terms of classical utilitarianism would be quite different from my own; this alternative interpretation would stress quite separate elements of the tradition. The interpersonal comparability and aggregate measurability of utility were not explicitly rejected by the classical economists and, in a selected reading, these may be attributed, as presumptions, to their analyses. In this case, the whole enterprise becomes precursory to the maximizing rather than to the exchange paradigm in economics, with both allocational and distributional implications, and with a wholly different avenue for moving from the individual to the collective levels of choice. The categorical distinction between choices among rules and choices within rules all but disappears in the utilitarian configuration.

The elements of Adam Smith's intellectual enterprise become directly precursory to the research program in constitutional economics only when these elements are imbedded within the tradition of contractarian political philosophy, the tradition that was developed prior to but became competitive with and quite different from classical utilitarianism. From the seventeenth century, from the works of Althusius, Hobbes, Spinoza, and Locke in particular, attempts were made to ground justificatory argument for state coercion on agreement by those individuals who are subject to coercion. This intellectual tradition invented the autonomous individual by shucking off the communitarian cocoon. The assignment to the individual of a capacity for rational independent choice, as such, allowed a *science* of economics and politics to emerge — a *science* that embodied a legitimatizing explanation for the emergence of and existence of the state. In agreeing to be governed, explicitly or implicitly, the individual exchanges his own liberty with others who similarly give up liberties in exchange for the benefits offered by a regime characterized by behavioral limits.

The contractarian logic leaves open any specification of the range and scope for consent-based coercive authority. The early contractarians, and notably Hobbes, had no understanding of the efficacy of market order as it might function under the umbrella of the protective or minimal state. This understanding was provided only in the eighteenth century and was fully articulated only in the great work of Adam Smith. Classical political economy, as appended to the contractarian intellectual foundations, allowed the development of a scientifically based analysis aimed at comparing alternative structures of political-legal order — analysis that could introduce and use principles of rational choice behavior of individuals and without resort to supraindividualistic norms. Utilitarianism also rejected all supraindividual norms, as such, and grounded all norms in a calculus of pleasure and pain. Nonetheless, this Benthamite intrusion created ambiguity in the efforts to add up utilities over persons. In this way, the contractarian justification derived from conceptual agreement was obscured, and the way was opened for a nontranscendental utilitarian supercession of individualistic norms. The contractarian philosophical basis upon which classical political economy should have been exclusively developed was, at least partially, undermined and neglected for almost two centuries, only to be rediscovered in the research program of constitutional economics.

4. The Hard Core and its Critics

Throughout this article I have referred to constitutional political economy as a *research program*, thereby deliberately using the Lakatosian classification. In this scheme, there exist elements in the hard core of the program that are rarely, if ever, challenged by those scholars who work inside the intellectual tradition defined by the program. These central elements are taken as presuppositions, as relatively absolute absolutes, and, as such, they become, themselves, the constraints (the constitution) within which the scientific discourse is conducted. External intellectual challenges to the whole enterprise tend to be directed at these elements in the core of the program. The ongoing research within the constraints can, of course, proceed without concern for these external criticisms, but practitioners need to be aware of the core-imposed limits on the persuasive potential of the internalized analytical exercise.

For constitutional political economy, the foundational position is summarized in *methodological individualism*. Unless those who would be participants in the scientific dialogue are willing to locate the exercise in the choice calculus of individuals, *qua* individuals, there can be no departure from the starting gate. The autonomous individual is a *sine qua non* for any initiation of serious inquiry in the research program. Individual autonomy, as a defining quality, does not, however, imply that the individual chooses and acts as if he or she exists in isolation from and apart from the community or communities of other persons with whom he or she may be variously associated. Any form of community or association of individuals may reflect some sharing of values, and, further, any individual's formation of values may be influenced by the values of those with whom he or she is variously associated in communities. The communitarian challenge to methodological individualism must go beyond the claim that individuals influence one another reciprocally through presence in communities. The challenge must make the stronger claim that individuation, the separation of the individual from community, is not conceptually possible, that it becomes meaningless to think of potential divergence between and among individual interests in a community. Stated in this way, it is evident that methodological individualism, as a presupposition of inquiry, characterizes almost all research programs in economics and political science; constitutional economics does not depart from its more inclusive disciplinary bases in this respect.

The communitarian critique does not often appear in such blatant guise. For constitutional political economy, in particular, the critique apparently leaves the individualistic postulates unchallenged, while either implicitly or explicitly asserting the existence of some supraindividualistic source of evaluation. Individual evaluations are superseded by those emergent from God, natural law, right reason, or the state. This more subtle stance rejects methodological individualism, not on the claim that individuation is impossible, or that individual evaluations may not differ within a community, but rather on the claim that it is normatively improper to derive collective action from individual evaluations. To the communitarian who posits the existence of some supraindividualistic value scale, the whole analysis that builds on a base of an individualistic calculus can only be useful as an input in schemes of control and manipulation designed to align individualized preferences with those orderings dictated by the overarching norms for the community.

Concomitant with methodological individualism as a component of the hard core is the postulate of rational choice — a postulate that is shared over all research programs in economics. The autonomous individual is also presumed to be capable of choosing among alternatives in a sufficiently orderly manner as to allow a quality of rationality to be attributed to observed behavior. For constitutional economics, the capacity for rational choice is extended to include a capacity to choose among constraints, both individually and collectively applied, within which subsequent choices may be made.

Rationality implies that choices may be analyzed as if an ordering of alternatives exists, arrayed in accordance with some scalar of *preferredness*. We may, but need not, use the term utility to designate that which the individual calls upon to make up the ordinal ranking. At the analytical level, there is no need that the ranking correspond with any array of the choice alternatives that may be objectively measurable by some outside observer. The test for individual rationality in choice does require, however, the minimal step of classifying alternatives into *goods* and *bads*. The central rationality precept states only that the individual choose more rather than less of goods, and less rather than more of bads. There is no requirement that rationality dictates choice in accordance with the individual's economic interest, as this might be measured by some outside observer of behavior.

The individualistic postulate allows the interests or preferences of individuals to differ, one from another. And the rationality postulate does not restrict these interests beyond the classificatory step noted. *Homo economicus*, the individual who populates the models of empirical economics, may, but need not, describe the individual whose choice calculus is analyzed in constitutional political economy. When selecting among alternative constitutional constraints, however, the individual is required to make some predictions about the behavior of others than himself. And, in such a setting, there is a powerful argument that suggests the appropriateness of something akin to the *Homo economicus* postulate for behavior (Brennan and Buchanan, 1985).

I have briefly discussed the individualistic and the rationality presuppositions for the research program. These elements are not controversial, and they would be listed as components of the hard core both by practitioners and critics of constitutional economics. A less obvious element that is, however, equally fundamental involves the generalization of the individualistic and the rationality postulates to *all* persons in the political community. All individuals must be presumed capable to make rational choices among alternatives in accordance with individually autonomous value scales. And this generalization does not allow derivation of collective action, whether or not directed toward choices among constraints, from individual evaluations on anything other than an *equal weighting*. To introduce a weighting scheme through which the evaluation of some persons in the community are deemed more important than other persons would require resort to some supraindividualistic source, which is, of course, ruled out by adherence to the individualistic postulate. In this sense the whole of the constitutional economics research program rests squarely on a *democratic* foundation.

5. Perception, Vision, and Faith

Nietzsche used the metaphor of viewing the world of reality through differing windows (Kaufman, 1950: 61), and Ortega y Gasset went so far as to define ultimate reality itself as a perspective (Ortega y Gasset, 1961: 45). In a sense, any research program involves a way of looking at, and thereby imposing an order on, that which is perceived. This characterization applies particularly to any program in social science, where the ultimate object of inquiry is behavior in a social interaction process. I have on several occasions referred to the *constitutional perspective*, which I have acknowledged to be different from other perspectives that might be used in examining and evaluating the interaction of individuals in social and/or political settings. This elementary fact that perspectives differ, or may differ, raises difficult issues in epistemology that cannot be ignored.

Consider, first, perception at its simplest level. Presumably, individuals are sufficiently alike, one to another, biologically that we see, hear, taste, smell, and feel physical phenomena similarly if not identically. We all see a wall as a barrier to movement, and no one of us makes an attempt to walk through walls. Someone who failed to perceive a wall as the others of us would be classified to be abnormal in at least one of the basic perceptual senses. As phenomena come to be increasingly complex, however, individuals may come to differ in their perceptions, despite the fact that, biologically, they continue to possess the same perceptual apparatus. Elementary sense perception must be accompanied by imaginative constructions that require some mental processing before a basis for evaluation, and ultimately for action, can be established.

As phenomena increase in complexity, the imaginative elements in perception increase relative to those that emerge directly from the senses. In this progression from the simple to the complex, the similarity in perceptions among persons must decrease. What may be called the *natural* way of observing phenomena fades away at some point along the spectrum. Individuals may then be brought into agreement on that which they observe only by entry into some sort of association of shared values or norms, which members, either explicitly or implicitly, choose. This statement may seem contradictory when first made; it may seem to state that persons choose how they see reality. But the statement becomes less challenging to ordinary notions when we replace *see* with *think about*.

I have been accused of committing the naturalistic fallacy, in some of my own works, of failing to respect properly *the fact — value, positive — normative* distinction, and, hence, of deriving the *ought* from the *is*, at least implicitly. I submit, however, that my critics mount such charges only because of their own confusion about the nature of perception of complex phenomena. If there exists no *natural* way of observing reality, some evaluation and choosing process is a necessary complement to the imaginative step that allows apparent chaos to be converted into order. We select the *is* that defines the hard core of our research program, and this holds true whether or not we are professional scientists. Within this *is*, we can adhere strictly to the precepts laid down for positive analysis. But the normative implications that may be drawn are, indeed, derivative from the chosen perceptive framework, and could not, or would not, be otherwise available.

Constitutional political economy is a domain of inquiry and discourse among scientists who choose to perceive social interaction as a set of complex relationships, both actual and potential, among autonomous persons, each of whom is capable of making rational choices. The domain, as such, cannot be extended to include inquiry by those who choose to perceive social interaction differently. There is simply no common basis for scientific argument, and ultimately agreement, with those who choose to perceive social interaction either in purely conflictual or purely idealistic visions. These visions are, indeed, alternative 'windows' on the world, and the process through which individuals choose among such windows remains mysterious. How can empirical evidence be made convincing when such evidence must, itself, be perceived from only one vantage point at a time? The naivete of modern empirical economists in this respect verges on absurdity.

When all is said and done, *constitutional political economy* must be acknowledged to rest upon a precommitment to, or a faith in, man's cooperative potential. Persons are neither bees in hives, carnivorous beasts in a jungle, nor angels in God's heaven. They are independent units of consciousness, capable of assigning values to alternatives, and capable of choosing and acting in accordance with these values. It is both physically necessary and beneficial that they live together, in many and varying associations and communities. But to do so, they must live by rules that they can also choose.

JAMES M. BUCHANAN

REFERENCES

Alchian, A. (1977). *Economic Forces at Work*. Indianapolis: Liberty Fund.

Althusius, J. (1932). In C.J. Friedrich (ed.) *Politica Methodica Digesta*. Cambridge: Harvard University Press.

Brennan, G. and Buchanan, J.M. (1985). *The Reason of Rules: Constitutional Political Economy*. Cambridge: Cambridge University Press.

Buchanan, J.M. (1987). "Constitutional economics." *The New Palgrave*. London: Macmillan.

Buchanan, J.M. and Tullock, G. (1962). *The Calculus of Consent: Logical Foundations of Constitutional Democracy*. Ann Arbor: University of Michigan Press.

Elster, J. (1979). *Ulysses and the Sirens*. Cambridge: Cambridge University Press.

Hobbes, T. (1943). *Leviathan*. London: Everymans Library.

Kaufman, W. (1950). *Nietzsche*. Princeton: Princeton University Press.

Locke, J. (1955). *Second Treatise of Civil Government*. Chicago: Gateway.

McKenzie, R. (ed.) (1984). *Constitutional Economics*. Lexington, MA: Lexington Books.

Ortega y Gasset, J. (1961). *Meditations on Quixote*. New York: Norton.

Schelling, T. (1978). "Egonomics, or the art of self management." *American Economic Review*, 68: 290–294.

Sen, A.K. (1970). "The impossibility of a paretian liberal." *Journal of Political Economy*, 78: 152–157.

Smith, A. (1979). *The Wealth of Nations*. Oxford: Clarendon Press.

Spinoza, B. (1854). *A Treatise in Politics*. London: Holyoake. (Trans. William McCall.)

Thaler, R. and Shefrin, H.M. (1981). "An economic theory of self-control." *Journal of Political Economy*, 89: 392–406.

CORRUPTION

Corruption is an archetypal topic for students of Public Choice. It brings together the private search for economic gain with the government's efforts to supply public goods, correct market failures, and aid the needy. Public Choice's insistence on viewing politicians and government bureaucrats as motivated by the same economic interests as private individuals and firms provides a background for understanding why corruption occurs and why it is difficult to combat.

Corruption in my formulation is the *misuse* of public office for private gain. This definition leaves open the issue of just what constitutes misuse, but it recognizes that sometimes public office can legitimately provide private benefits to politicians and bureaucrats. Thus, targeted "pork barrel" projects and special interest legislation are not corrupt. They result from the day-to-day operation of a representative political system. If a legislator works to pass a statute that is favored by his or her legal campaign donors, this is not corrupt even if it violates democratic ideals. Those who seek to discredit government across the board often put the "corruption" label on all kinds of government actions. Although many of these phenomena are indeed proper subjects of study and the loci of reform efforts, it will not help the analysis of democracy to put them all into the corruption pot.

There are several reasons for maintaining a distinction between bribery, fraud, and self-dealing, on the one hand, and quid pro quo politics, on the other. First, a political system that encourages legislators to "bring home the bacon" for their constituents may also be one that encourages voters to monitor their representatives to be sure they are not benefiting personally from their position. Voting systems that limit constituency-based politics may encourage corruption (Kunicova and Rose-Ackerman, 2002). Second, strict rules on legal campaign donations may simply drive contributions underground into a corrupt netherworld. Thus, it is valuable to maintain a distinction between legal donations from wealthy interests and illegal, secret gifts. Third, some reform proposals designed to deal with bureaucratic corruption involve the use of legal incentive payments. Mixing financial incentives with the provision of public services is not invariably corrupt. Often it is an efficient method of service delivery.

This entry concentrates on corruption that involves a public official, either a politician or a bureaucrat. However, corrupt incentives can also arise in purely private interactions. Corruption is, in essence, an agency/principal problem. An agent violates the trust of his or her principal through self-enrichment or through illegally enriching a political party. A public official may take a bribe in return for a favorable decision or may simply steal from the state's coffers. Clearly, corporate managers can face similar incentives, and with the growing privatization of former state enterprises, the locus of some forms of corruption will shift into the private sector. Private-to-private corruption has been little studied but ought to be the object of future work (for one example see Andvig, 1995).

I proceed as follows. Section 1 outlines the underlying causes of corruption and its consequences from a political-economic point of view. Section 2 discusses reform options in the light of the discussion in section 1 and the broader literature behind the summary presented here. This note provides only a brief overview of both topics. Readers who want to pursue these issues further should consult my two books — Rose-Ackerman (1978, 1999), a review article by Pranab Bardhan (1997), the framework presented in Shleifer and Vishny (1993), Robert Klitgaard illustrative case studies (1988), and della Porta and Vannucci's reflections on the Italian case (1999). Most of these references also include extensive references to the literature. To access current work, the World Bank Institute maintains a website [http://www.worldbank.org/wbi/governance] as does Transparency International (TI) an international non-governmental organization committed to fighting international bribery [http://www.transparency.org].

1. The Incentives and Consequences of Bribery

I focus on bribery. Ordinary fraud is relatively uninteresting as an analytic matter, and few would argue that stealing from the state is to be encouraged. However, with bribery the story is different. Some economists observe money changing hands and assume that something efficient must be occurring. Some Public Choice scholars who favor a minimal state and who view most state actions as illegitimate exercises of power interpret bribes as a desirable way to avoid the exercise of government power. I want to argue that both of these tolerant views are, as a general matter, mistaken, but to do so requires one to understand the incentives for paying and accepting bribes. My basic message is that even if an individual bribe seems to further efficiency or get around an irrational rule, the systemic effects of widespread tolerance are invariably harmful both for the efficient operation of the economy and for the legitimacy of the state.

The government allocates scarce benefits and imposes costs. Individuals and firms may be willing to pay government agents to gain the former and to avoid the latter. Opportunities for corruption arise whenever the officials' actions involve the exercise of discretion and are impossible to monitor perfectly (Klitgaard, 1988). The level of benefits under official control can vary from the allocation of a driver's license to the award of a major public works contract. The costs avoided can be a traffic ticket, a multimillion dollar tax bill, or a prison sentence. Bribes can also improve quality, notably by speeding up service delivery or jumping someone ahead in a queue.

The potential bribe revenues available to any individual politician or bureaucrat depend upon his or her monopoly power. If potential bribe payers have non-corrupt alternatives, bribes, if they are paid at all, will be low. If the chance of being caught and punished is high, corruption may be deterred. Thus, one can think of corruption in cost\benefit terms where payoffs will be deterred if at least one side of the potential deal faces costs that exceed the benefits. If expected penalties increase more than in proportion to the size of the bribe, only small bribes may be paid and accepted. Conversely, if penalties do not rise in proportion to benefits, small bribes are deterred, and large bribes are unaffected (Rose-Ackerman, 1978).

The mere existence of corrupt opportunities, however, says nothing about their welfare implications. In discussing this issue, it is important to recognize that the level of bribe payments is likely to be a poor measure of their social cost. Sometimes very small bribes have large consequences. Bribe may be low, not because the value of the quid pro quo is low, but because the bribe payer has bargaining power relative to the official. For example, if a majority-rule legislature with weak parties is bribed to approve a law favored by a particular firm, no individual politician has much bargaining power; he or she can easily be replaced by another person formerly outside the corrupt coalition. Thus, my focus is not on situations where bribes are high but on those cases where the social costs are severe.

One might suppose that if a government has scarce benefits to distribute, say a number of restaurant licences, then corruption will distribute them to those with the highest willingness-to-pay, and the winners will be the most efficient restaurateurs. There are several responses to this claim. First, corrupt markets are inefficient compared with the aboveboard sale of licences. Bribe-prices are secret, and entry may be blocked. Thus, the government should simply legally sell the scarce rights if its goal is to allocate the service to those who value it the most in dollar terms. Second, the basic purposes of some public programs would be violated by sales to the highest bidders. For example, selling places in public universities and in subsidized housing would undermine the basic goals of those programs. Third, toleration of corruption gives officials an incentive to engage in the creation of more scarce benefits in order to create more corrupt opportunities. For example, corrupt contracting officials have an incentive to support wasteful public projects designed to make payoffs easy to hide.

Similar points can be made about bribes paid to avoid the imposition of costs. Clearly, if a regulation is onerous and inefficient, then paying for an exemption seems efficient. However, permitting such individualized law compliance can be very harmful. First, profit-maximizing firms and individuals will not distinguish between socially efficient and socially inefficient rules. They will want to be exempted from all of them. The rules will only be enforced against those with a low willingness to pay. This includes not just those for whom the rule is not costly but also poor households and marginal businesses. In the case of tax collection, those exempted from taxes generate higher bills or lower services for others. Selective exemption on the basis of willingness to pay is inefficient and unfair. Second, officials will seek to create even more restrictive rules so that they can be paid to decline to enforce them. Empirical work suggests that in countries where corruption is high, red tape is high, and managers spend considerable time dealing with public officials (Kaufmann, 1997). Thus, even if each individual corrupt decision is rational for the bribing firm, the overall costs of doing business in society are high. Investment and entrepreneurship are discouraged.

The costs of corruption are not limited to its impact on the efficacy of public programs taken one by one. In addition, endemic corruption has implications for the legitimacy of the state in the eyes of its citizens. In highly corrupt states, where both day-to-day interactions with officials and high-level deals are riddled with payoffs, people often express great cynicism about political life. This can lead to vicious spirals. The theoretical work on corruption has produced a number of multiple-equilibria models where both high corruption and low corruption solutions exist (Bardhan, 1997; Rose-Ackerman, 1999: 107–108, 124–125). Some countries, particularly a number of the former socialist countries, illustrate these pathologies. To give a flavor of these models consider two variants. First, suppose that there is a fixed supply of law enforcement personnel. If very few transactions are corrupt, the enforcers can catch most of the illegal deals, thus encouraging more people to be honest in the next round and so forth. If most are corrupt, the law enforcement authorities are spread very thin and only catch a few wrongdoers. This encourages more to enter the corrupt arena next period and so on in a vicious spiral. Similar results occur if we assume that the moral stigma of corruption is a function of the number of others who engage in it. If most are corrupt, the stigma is low, and next period more shift to the corrupt side, and so forth. Second, another kind of spiral can affect the character of those who become politicians or bureaucrats. If most officials are corrupt, this will discourage honest people from working for the government and encourage the dishonest to apply, making the government even more corrupt. If government work makes one rich, those who want to get wealthy choose the public sector and do not become entrepreneurs. Their corruption creates a costly environment for business that further discourages private business activities. This self-selection mechanism can produce an equilibrium in which the dishonest and the greedy have disproportionately chosen public sector employment.

Empirical work has begun to shed light on some of the costs of corruption outlined above. Research on corruption is difficult because the perpetrators seek to keep their transactions secret. Nevertheless, scholars have begun to analyze and measure the impact of corruption on economic and political phenomena and to explain how political and economic conditions contribute to corruption. This work, based on cross-country data, is quite consistent in finding that corruption is harmful to growth and development and that corruption is the result of weak economic and political institutions.

The cross-country research uses data that measure perceptions of corruption, such as the composite Transparency International index, developed by Johann Graf Lambsdorff, or the World Bank Institute's recalculation using similar data. The perceptions are mostly those of international business people and country experts. Studies using these data have found that high levels of corruption are associated with lower levels of investment and growth, and that foreign direct investment is discouraged (e.g., Mauro, 1995; Wei, 2000). Highly corrupt countries tend to under-invest in human capital by spending less on education and to over-invest in public infrastructure relative to private investment (Mauro, 1997; Tanzi and Davoodi, 1997). Corrupt governments lack political legitimacy and hence tend to be smaller than more honest governments, everything else equal (Johnson et al., 2000). Corruption reduces the effectiveness of industrial policies and encourages business to operate in the unofficial sector in violation of tax and regulatory laws (Ades and Di Telia, 1997; Kaufmann, 1997). Turning the causal story around, recent research suggests that autocracies tend to be more corrupt than democracies, but that democracy is not a simple cure. Within the universe of democracies, corruption is facilitated by features of government structure such as presidentialism, closed-list proportional representation, and federalism (Kunicova, 2001; Kunicova and Rose-Ackerman, 2002; Treisman, 2000).

These are important findings, but they are limited by the aggregated nature of the data. Each country is treated as a single data point that is more or less "corrupt." This work shows that corruption is harmful but says little about the precise mechanisms. To counter this weakness, two new types of research are underway: detailed questionnaires that target households, businesses, and public officials; and what might be called "econometric case studies." The questionnaires permit researchers to explore people's actual experiences. The case studies help one understand how corrupt sectors operate and how malfeasance might be controlled.

Here are some examples of the research I have in mind. Several studies questioned small- and medium-sized businesses about the costs of corruption and red tape. Other researchers have used questionnaires and focus groups to examine household attitudes and behavior. Researchers have studied countries as diverse as those in sub-Saharan Africa and in Central and Eastern Europe. Some of the most comprehensive are a study of four countries in

Central and Eastern Europe by William Miller et al. (2001, forthcoming) and work that focuses on the business environment in the same region by Simon Johnson et al. (2000). This research complements the World Bank Institute's work on "state capture" and administrative corruption in post-socialist countries (Hellman et al., 2000).

Sectoral studies are represented by work on how corruption limits the performance of the judiciary in Latin America (e.g., Buscaglia and Dakolias, 1996). Other examples are Wei Li's (forthcoming) estimates of the waste and corruption generated when China had a two-price policy for basic raw materials, and research by Rafael di Tella and Ernesto Schagrodsky (forthcoming) on the benchmarking of product prices in the hospital sector in Argentina that shows how monitoring and civil service pay reform can go hand in hand. As an example of research that can make a difference, consider Ritva Reinikka and Jakob Svensson's (forthcoming) documentation of the severe leakage of federal funds meant for local schools in Uganda. Their study led to a simple, information-based reform that had positive results.

These contributions are very diverse in topic and methodology, but they all share an interest in using detailed data to understand both how corrupt systems operate and which policies have promise. Only if one looks at the fine structure of political and economic systems, can one go beyond a showing that corruption is harmful to an understanding of the way it operates in different contexts. Given that knowledge, reform programs can attack corruption where it has the worst effects.

2. Reform

Reform strategies attack the problem of corruption from several directions: program redesign, law enforcement, improved government performance and accountability. Before presenting this mixture of reform options, however, I begin with a solution that is favored by some Public Choice scholars. Many Public Choice analysts accept the claim that corruption is harmful. However, they argue that the solution should be, not the reform of public programs, but a reduction in the size of government. They argue that the best way to avoid corruption is to shrink government and rely on the market. Of course, this will sometimes be true, but it is not a general solution and would be risky if employed across the board. The most obvious problem with this argument is that it misses the benefits of some, even poorly operating, public programs. Programs to limit external costs, correct for information failures, produce public goods, or aid the needy have no effective private market counterparts. Free rider problems plague efforts at private provision. Furthermore, if a program is reduced in size but not eliminated, corruption may increase instead of decrease. To see this, consider a program to provide public housing to the needy. A cut in the program by half creates scarcity and hence the competition for places. Bribes may increase.

Another form of government "load shedding" has similar difficulties. Privatization is justified as a way of introducing market discipline into the operation of formerly state-owned firms. Competitive pressures and the need to raise capital in the private market will squeeze out waste and encourage a focus on consumer satisfaction. Unfortunately, privatization does not always imply the creation of competitive markets. Sometimes the process of turning over assets has itself been corrupted by collusion between powerful private and public interests. This sometimes implies that public firms are sold too cheaply to insiders and that the terms of the deal give the new owners access to monopoly rents. Corruption in the privatization process in some countries is analogous to corruption in large scale public procurements — powerful politicians and business interests gain at the cost of ordinary citizens. Citizens lose both because the benefits to the state coffers are lower than they should be and because the benefits of expanding the role of competitive markets are lost. Thus, over-enthusiastic efforts to limit the role of government should be avoided, and the cutbacks that are carried out should be carefully designed to avoid the problems outlined here.

If a country faces a vicious spiral of corruption, such as I outlined above, this would seem the best case for the "load shedding" solution. The government is in a dysfunctional low-level trap where piecemeal reform will be ineffective. The state needs a major overhaul in law enforcement and in the recruitment of personnel. However, a simple attempt to shrink the state is unlikely to be effective because it can create a chaotic situation in which a lawless free-for-all replaces the corruption that went before. A new kind of corruption and self-dealing may arise that is based on the attempt to establish some kind of certainty in a situation of fluidity and chaos.

If corruption cannot be countered by single-minded efforts to limit the size of government, then one must also consider ways to reform government from within and to limit the willingness of citizens and firms to pay bribes. Any actual program needs to be adapted to the conditions in a particular country, but the broad outlines can be identified. Anticorruption policies can increase the benefits of being honest, increase the probability of detection and the level of punishment, reduce the corrupt opportunities under the control of public officials, and increase the accountability of government to its citizens. The incentives for corruption are influenced by:

- the level of benefits and costs under the discretionary control of officials,
- the formal laws designed to combat defining corruption, bribery, and conflicts of interest, and to regulate finance spending,
- the credibility of law enforcement against both, those who pay and those who accept bribes,
- the conditions of civil service employment, and the performance incentives officials face,
- the extent of auditing and monitoring within government,
- the ability of citizens to learn about government activities, file complaints, and obtain redress, and
- the level of press freedom and the freedom of individuals to form nongovernmental organizations.

I focus on four broad categories: reductions in the discretion and monopoly power of government officials, enforcement of anticorruption laws, civil service reform, and increased accountability to citizens.

2.1. Reducing the Incentives for Payoffs

The most basic reforms are those that reduce the level of benefits under the control of public officials. As I noted above, the most obvious option is simply to eliminate laws and programs that are permeated with corruption. If the state has no authority to restrict exports or license businesses, no one will pay bribes in those areas. If a subsidy program is eliminated, the bribes that accompanied it will disappear as well. If price controls are lifted, market prices will express scarcity values, not bribes.

In general, any reform that increases the competitiveness of the economy will help reduce corrupt incentives. Thus policies that lower the controls on foreign trade, remove entry barriers for private industry, and privatize state firms in a way that assures competition will all contribute to the fight against corruption.

But any move toward deregulation and privatization must be carried out with care. Deregulating in one area may increase corruption elsewhere. Furthermore, many regulatory and spending programs have strong justifications and ought to be reformed, not eliminated. Corruption in the collection of taxes obviously cannot be solved by failing to collect revenue. One solution is to clarify and streamline the necessary laws in ways that reduce official discretion. Rules could be made more transparent with publicly provided justifications. Governments might favor simple nondiscretionary tax, spending, and regulatory laws as a way of limiting corrupt opportunities. Clear rules of proper behavior could be established so violations can be noticed even if the bribery itself is not. Where possible, procurement decisions could favor standard off-the-shelf items to provide a benchmark and to lower the cost of submitting a bid. Obviously, the value of such reforms depends upon the costs of limiting the flexibility of public officials (Anechiarico and Jacobs, 1996). Sometimes a certain risk of corruption will need to be tolerated because of the benefits of a case-by-case approach to program administration. Transparency and publicity can help overcome corrupt incentives even in such cases, but only if the systems of accountability discussed below exist. If they do not, simple clear rules can simply permit a top ruler more effectively to extract payoffs. This is just one example of the importance of viewing reform in the context of the entire political-economic environment.

Economists have long recommended reforming regulatory laws in such areas as environmental protection by introducing market-based schemes that limit the discretion of regulators. Analysts also recommend user fees for scarce government services. These reforms have the additional advantage of removing corrupt incentives by replacing bribes with legal payments. The sale of water and grazing rights, traceable pollution rights, and the sale of import and export licenses can improve the efficiency of government operations while limiting corruption.

Finally, administrative reforms may lower corrupt incentives. Corruption is often embedded in the hierarchical structure of the bureaucracy. Low level officials collect bribes and pass a share on to higher level officials perhaps in the form of an up-front payment for the job itself. Conversely, higher ups may organize and rationalize the corrupt system to avoid wasteful competition between low-level officials. The top officials may then share the gains of their organizational ability with subordinates, perhaps using them to run errands, transfer funds, and do other risky jobs that expose them to arrest. To break such patterns may require a fundamental reorganization effort.

One possibility is the introduction of competitive pressures within government to lower the bargaining power of individual officials. If bribes are paid for such benefits as licenses and permits, which are not constrained by budgetary limits, overlapping, competitive bureaucratic jurisdictions can reduce corruption. Because clients can apply to any one of a number of officials and can go to a second one if the first turns him down, no one official has much monopoly power. Thus no one can extract a very large payoff. For qualified clients, bribes will be no larger than the cost of reapplication. Unqualified clients will still pay bribes, but even they will not pay much so long as they too can try another official (Rose-Ackerman, 1978). If all officials are corrupt, the outcome is stable. However, if some establish an honest reputation, applicants will prefer those officials, thus reducing the gains to the corrupt. This reduction in benefits may induce some marginal officials to shift to being honest, further reducing the benefits to the remaining corrupt officials and so on. A small number of honest officials can overturn a corrupt system if congestion is not a serious problem. Honesty may drive out dishonesty even if only a few officials are honest on principle (Rose-Ackerman, 1978). If, instead, those who pay bribes are unqualified, the honesty of some officials increases the gains to those who are corrupt, inducing more to become corrupt.

When officials, such as police officers, can impose costs, another type of overlapping jurisdiction model should be considered. Police officers seeking to control illegal businesses can be given overlapping enforcement areas. That way gamblers and drug dealers will not pay much to an individual policeman since a second one may come along later and also demand a payoff. The first one is simply unable to supply protection. Bribes may fall so low that it is not worthwhile for police officers to risk taking them. This system may work better if the law enforcement officers belong to different police forces — state or federal, for example. Then collusion between officers to defeat the system will be less likely (Rose-Ackerman, 1978).

Alternatively, consider the losers in corrupt transactions. The state could introduce ways for the potential losers to appeal unsatisfactory decisions. Sometimes bribe payers view themselves as losers who would be better off in an honest world. They feels themselves to be the victims of extortion. Such bribe payers are potential allies in an anti-corruption effort who will cooperate in efforts to eliminate payoffs. Conversely, in other cases bribery makes both payer and receiver better off with respect to a no-bribery world. Thus control incentives must rest with outsiders not in on the corrupt deal (e.g., disappointed bidders, taxpayers, consumers). The existence of losers, such as disappointed bidders, with a large stake in the outcome can facilitate efforts to limit corruption.

2.2. Anticorruption Laws and Credible Law Enforcement

A basic condition for corruption control is a viable legal framework that enforces the law without political favoritism or arbitrariness. The goal is both to deter those tempted to engage in corrupt acts and to educate the public to resist criminal conduct by officials. Tough laws are not sufficient. Many highly corrupt countries have exemplary formal statutes that have no real meaning because they are seldom enforced. A country serious about reform must have effective investigation and prosecution bodies and a well-functioning judicial system that is not itself corrupt. Because corruption is a two-sided offense, the law must specify the status of both those who make payments and those who receive them. If just one of the parties can be deterred, that is sufficient to prevent the deal from going through.

Designing an optimal deterrence strategy raises a seeming paradox. The more severe the penalties for corruption faced by officials, the lower the incidence of corruption, but the higher the bribes. If the risk of detection is high, officials must receive a high return in order to be willing to engage in bribery. One way around such a result is an expected penalty function that is an increasing function of the size of the bribe (Rose-Ackerman, 1978: 109–135). Conversely, if penalties on bribe payers have deterrent effects, this will lower the demand for corrupt services and the level of bribes at the same time.

An independent judiciary or some other kind of independent tribunal is a necessary condition for the use of law enforcement to check official malfeasance. This is a serious problem in many countries where the judicial system is backlogged and some judges are corrupt. Prosecutors, whether they are formally in the executive branch, as in the United States, or part of the judiciary, as in Italy, must be able to have the independence to pursue corruption allegations and need to be able to reward those who report on corrupt deals with lowered charges and penalties. Some countries have had success with independent anticorruption commissions or inspector generals reporting only to the chief executive or the parliament. These can be useful responses, but a single-minded focus on law enforcement is unlikely to be sufficient if the incentives for corruption are deeply imbedded in the structure of public programs and if law enforcement efforts can be diverted to harass political opponents.

2.3. The Civil Service

Many developing countries have very poorly paid civil servants. Although at independence most former colonies inherited civil service pay scales that exceeded private sector wages, this advantage has eroded over time. Wages relative to private sector wages have fallen in countries in transition in Eastern Europe and the former Soviet Union. The pattern varies across countries and over time. In some parts of the developing world public sector pay is so low that officials must supplement their pay with second jobs or payoffs. Some work suggests that there is a negative correlation between civil service wages (relative to private sector wages) and the level of corruption (Van Rijckeghem and Weder, 2001).

If officials are paid much less than people with similar training elsewhere in the economy, only those willing to accept bribes will be attracted to the public sector. Civil service pay should be set at least equal to equivalent positions in the private sector in order to make it possible to recruit based on merit and to permit those selected to serve without resorting to corruption. If the benefits under the control of officials are very valuable, however, parity may not be sufficient. Instead, civil service wages may need to be set above the going private sector wage with generous benefits, such as pensions, that will be received only if the worker retires in good order. This strategy, however, must be combined with an effective monitoring system. There must be a transparent, merit-based system of selecting civil servants or else people will pay the powerful to be allotted desirable government jobs.

Pay reform is necessary, but not sufficient. Penalties must be tied to the marginal benefits of accepting payoffs. In cases where corruption's only efficiency cost stems from its illegality, the payments should be legalized. In the design of such systems, however, it is important to avoid giving monopoly power to bureaucrats that they can use to extract increased levels of rents.

2.4. Public Accountability

Corruption can be checked by structures that create independent sources of power and information inside and outside the government. Although not sufficiently taken by themselves, these options complement other reform strategies by reducing corrupt opportunities and increasing the risks of paying and accepting payoffs. There are several linked aspects in a system of public accountability over and above the checks provided by periodic democratic elections.

- Outsiders, such as ordinary citizens or the media, can obtain *information* about how the government is operating and have a way of expressing their displeasure about general policies. Nongovernmental organizations can organize easily and face few legal hurdles. They may even be subsidized.
- The structure of government includes *guarantees that protect the individual against the state*. Government actions may be checked by a specific Bill of Rights that limits state power, and individuals can appeal attempts to extort bribes. The legal system provides protection and perhaps rewards to individuals who come forward to "blow the whistle", on corrupt practices, but the state is also constrained by legal rules that protect the accused.
- *Higher level governments and international organizations* can use what leverage they have to constrain the behavior of individual governments.
- The threat of *exit* can be a powerful constraint on governments, reducing corrupt opportunities and limiting the scope for waste.

First, the private sector, particularly an independent media, can be an important check on the arbitrary exercise of power by government, but only if the government provides information, if the press is not controlled, and if people can organize into associations. Accountability to the public requires both that individuals can find out what the state is doing and that they can use this information to hold public actors accountable. Governments must publish budgets, revenue collections, statutes and rules, and the proceedings of legislative bodies. Financial data should be independently audited. Secret funds available to chief executives and top ministers are an invitation to corruption. Procurement regulations must keep the process open and fair. Scandals frequently occur because top officials overrule tender boards or because lower level officials operate without formal controls on their purchasing decisions.

Freedom of information acts in the United States and in a number of European countries are an important precondition for effective public oversight. These laws permit citizens to request information as members of the public without showing that their own personal situation will be affected.

Finding out what is happening is of little value however, unless people can use their knowledge to influence government. Individuals face a familiar free rider problem in seeking to control political and bureaucratic processes and to limit malfeasance. Information may be, in principle, available, but no one may have an incentive to look at it. Laws that make it easy to establish associations and nonprofits will help. For example, Transparency International has local chapters that carry out a range of activities including participation in Integrity Workshops, sometimes organized with the help of aid agencies. These workshops bring together concerned people from both the public and the private sectors to discuss the problem of corruption. Nonprofit organizations can carry out and publish public opinion surveys that reveal public attitudes toward government services. An alternative to NGO surveys of service users is the creation of "hot lines" so that citizens can complain directly to the government. The information from such complaint mechanisms will be less systematic than a survey and may well be self-serving, but hotlines provide a means of making a complaint without the necessity of establishing an organization. This method will only be successful, however, if those who complain can either do so anonymously or are not fearful of reprisals. Furthermore, if the complaints concern individuals, they must have a credible way of defending themselves against false accusations.

The second aspect of accountability is the way the government structure protects individuals against the state. The forms of administrative law and the protection they provide to individuals are of critical importance. If an official tries to extort a bribe from individuals or firms, do they have any recourse? Obviously, if the bribe is to be paid to permit illegal activities or to soften a legal regulation or tax assessment, the answer is no. Corruption of this type is unlikely to be revealed by the parties to the deal unless they have been arrested and are seeking to mitigate their punishment. However, those who face bribe demands as a condition for obtaining a legal benefit may not go along with the demand if they can appeal to an honest forum, such as an appeals board within the agency or the courts. In order to make appeals worthwhile, however, the processes must not only be honest, but also speedy and efficient.

The Ombudsman represents one route for citizen complaints. Many countries have established Ombudsmen to hear complaints of all kinds, not just those related to malfeasance. These offices can help increase the accountability of government agencies to ordinary citizens, but they are seldom a way to uncover large scale systemic corruption and most have no authority to initiate lawsuits.

Ombudsmen and other complaint mechanisms are insufficient if people are unwilling to complain. Reporting the peculations of others can be dangerous. Thus, governments should consider promulgating whistleblower statutes that protect and reward those in the public and the private sector who report malfeasance. However, whistleblower protection is obviously pointless unless the prosecutorial system follows up, the courts are incorruptible and relatively efficiently run, and the penalties are severe enough to deter potential offenders.

The third check on corruption can arise from intergovernmental relations. In a federal system, the national government can constrain the states, and the states, the localities. Similarly, institutions operating internationally may provide a check on national governments. This kind of leverage has problematic aspects since those who exercise it can make no straightforward claim to represent the interests of the affected citizens. There are two cases, however, in which such actions may be justified. First, corruption and waste frequently have cross-border consequences. Corrupt politicians or those engaged in legal joint ventures with private firms may try to use their political power to restrict commerce across state borders. Internationally, officials working in collaboration with corrupt business firms harm the prospects of honest businesses. Second, state and local governments may be under the control of narrow elites that use the apparatus of government for personal gain. Although both oversight from above and competition between jurisdictions for investment resources limit corrupt possibilities at the local level, they do not eliminate them. In fact, cross-country empirical work suggests that federal states are, on balance, more corrupt than unitary states suggesting that the negative effects outweigh the positive (Treisman, 2000).

Exit, the final constraint on corruption, has the advantage of not requiring a concerted organizational effort. In a world with many coequal governments, the corruption and ineffectiveness of government officials is limited by the ability of constituents and business firms to go elsewhere. Multinational firms trying to decide where to locate a manufacturing plant can limit bribe demands by locating several feasible sites. Residents of a village whose officials extract large payoffs for routine services can move elsewhere. The mobility of people and businesses clearly limits the ability of officials to extract payoffs for services to which one is entitled.

Mobility, however, is not always helpful. It will make it more difficult for an individual jurisdiction to control undesirable behavior. Suppose, e.g., that a city government has installed an honest police force that cracks down on illegal gambling. The gamblers may simply move to a friendly suburb that they can control and establish their business there. Several examples of this phenomena exist in United States urban areas. The ease with which funds can cross national borders, coming to rest in various "financial paradises" is another example of how multiple, competing jurisdictions can make control of corruption, fraud, and tax evasion more, not less, difficult. Thus interjurisdictional competition should be encouraged when it reduces the economic rents available for corrupt distribution and helps control waste but should be limited when it facilitates the illegal behavior that corruption often makes possible or requires.

A system of public accountability implies that once a law or regulation is put in place, individuals and groups both inside and outside government have the ability to find out how it is being administered, to complain, and to set in motion a legal or political enforcement process. To be a meaningful anticorruption check, however, knowledge must be combined with the existence of institutions that can take effective action both to promulgate new laws and to enforce existing ones.

3. Conclusions

Corruption has a moral dimension, but it can be understood and combated through the application of political-economic principles. A first step in the understanding of corruption is the documentation of the incentives for private gain built into political and bureaucratic processes. Next is an evaluation of the social costs when officials and private citizens succumb to these incentives. Part of the reform agenda involves explaining the social harm of corruption and trying to change a culture of tolerance both within government and in the citizenry and the business community (Rose-Ackerman, 2002). Moral suasion may work if backed up by concrete arguments for why corruption is harmful to society. Reformers do not simply point to corruption and appeal for people to change their behavior; rather they demonstrate that reducing corruption provides real gains, not just symbolic victories. The key point is to encourage people to look beyond the net gains from any particular corrupt deal to see how tolerance of corruption has negative systemic effects.

However, as Public Choice theory teaches, most people will not behave well simply because they are told that such actions are in the public interest. A change in behavior needs to be in their interest as well. A political-economic approach can go beyond documenting the costs of corruption to suggest ways to lower its incidence and impact. Although reforms in law enforcement and in internal monitoring are part of the story, the most important lessons of a political-economic approach are its recommendations to turn attention to the redesign of individual public programs, on the one hand, and to ways to increase government transparency and accountability on the other. That strategy both reduces the corrupt incentives facing bribe payers and recipients and facilities effective public oversight by the population.

SUSAN ROSE-ACKERMAN

REFERENCES

Ades, Alberto and Rafael Di Tella (1997). "National champions and corruption: some unpleasant interventionist arithmetic." *The Economic Journal*, 107: 1023–1042.

Andvig, Jens Christian (1995). "Corruption in the North Sea oil industry: issues and assessments." *Crime, Law, and Social Change*, 28: 289–313.

Anechiarico, Frank and James B. Jacobs (1996). *The Pursuit of Absolute Integrity: How Corruption Control Makes Government Ineffective*. Chicago: University of Chicago Press.

Bardhan, Pranab (1997). "Corruption and development: a review of issues." *Journal of Economic Literature*, 35: 1320–1346.

Buscaglia, Jr., Edgardo and Maria Dakolias (1996). *Judicial Reform in Latin American Courts: The Experience in Argentina and Ecuador*. World Bank Technical Paper No. 350, Washington DC: World Bank.

della Porta, Donatella and Alberto Vannucci (1999). *Corrupt Exchange*. New York: Aldine.

Di Tella, Rafael and Ernesto Schargrodsky (forthcoming). "The role of wages and auditing during a crackdown on corruption in the city of Buenos Aires," in Donatella della Porta and Susan Rose-Ackerman (eds.) *Corrupt Exchanges: Empirical Themes in the Politics and Political Economy of Corruption*. Frankfurt: Nomos Verlag.

Hellman, Joel S., Gereint Jones, and Daniel Kaufmann (2000). "Seize the stat, seize the day:" state capture, corruption, and influence in transition. Policy Research Working Paper 2444, Washington DC: World Bank.

Johnson, Simon, Daniel Kaufmann, John McMillan, and Christopher Woodruff (2000). "Why do firms hide? bribes and unofficial activity after communism." *Journal of Public Economics*, 76: 495–520.

Kaufmann, Daniel (1997). "The missing pillar of growth strategy for Ukraine: institutional and policy reforms for private sector development," in Peter K. Cornelius and Patrick Lenain (eds.) *Ukraine: Accelerating the Transition to Market*. Washington: IMF, pp. 234–275.

Klitgaard, Robert (1988). *Controlling Corruption*. Berkeley, CA: University of California Press.

Kuniocova, Jana (2001). "Are presidential systems more susceptible to political corruption?" draft, New Haven: Department of Political Science, Yale University.

Kunicova, Jana and Susan Rose-Ackerman (2002). "Electoral rules as constraints on corruption," draft, New Haven, CT: Department of Political Science, Yale University.

Li, Wei (forthcoming). "Corruption and resource allocation: evidence from China," in Donatella della Porta and Susan Rose-Ackerman (eds.) *Corrupt Exchanges: Empirical Themes in the Politics and Political Economy of Corruption*. Frankfurt: Nomos Verlag.

Mauro, Paolo (1995). "Corruption and growth." *Quarterly Journal of Economics*, 110: 681–712.

Mauro, Paolo (1997). "The effects of corruption on growth, investment, and government expenditure: a cross-country analysis," in Kimberly Ann Elliott (ed.) *Corruption and the Global Economy*. Washington DC: Institute for International Economics, pp. 83–108.

Miller, William L., Åse Grødeland, and Tatyana Y. Koshechkina (2001). *A Culture of Corruption: Coping with Government in Post-Communist Europe*. Budapest: Central European University Press.

Miller, William L., Åse Grødeland, and Tatyana Y. Koshechkina (2003). "Values and norms *versus* extortion and temptation," in Donatella della Porta and Susan Rose-Ackerman (eds.) *Corrupt Exchanges: Empirical Themes in the Politics and Political Economy Corruption*. Frankfurt: Nomos Verlag.

Reinikka, Ritva, and Jakob Svensson (2003). "Measuring and understanding corruption at the micro level," in Donatella della Porta and Susan Rose-Ackerman (eds.) *Corrupt Exchanges: Empirical Themes in the Politics and Political Economy of Corruption*. Frankfurt: Nomos Verlag.

Rose-Ackerman, Susan (1978). *Corruption: A Study in Political Economy*. New York: Academic Press.

Rose-Ackerman, Susan (1999). *Corruption and Government: Causes, Consequences and Reform*. Cambridge, England: Cambridge University Press.

Rose-Ackerman, Susan (2002). " 'Grand' corruption and the ethics of global business." *Journal of Banking and Finance*, 26.

Shleifer, A. and Vishny, R. (1993). "Corruption." *Quarterly Journal of Economics*, 108: 599–617.

Tanzi, Vito and Hamid Davoodi (1997). "Corruption, public investment and growth." IMF Working Paper WP/97/139, Washington DC: International Monetary Fund.

Treisman, D. (2000). "The causes of corruption: a cross-national study." *Journal of Public Economics*, 76: 399–457.

Van Rijckeghem, Caroline and Beatrice Weder (2001). "Bureaucratic corruption and the rate of temptation: do wages in the civil service affect corruption, and by how much?" *Journal of Development Economics*, 65: 307–331.

Wei, Shang-jin (2000). "How taxing is corruption on international investors?" *Review of Economics and Statistics*, 82: 1–11.

D

DICTATORSHIP

The literature which takes a public choice approach to dictatorship, largely barren before 1990 except for Tullock's *Autocracy* (1987), is now growing and may be entering a period of prosperity. This survey focuses on the most recent literature, and on three questions in particular: (1) The behavior of dictators, including the the strategies dictators use to stay in power; (2) The relative efficiency of dictatorship: Which is better, dictatorship or democracy, in promoting economic growth and efficiency?; and (3) What policies should the democracies adopt to deal with dictatorships if they are interested in promoting freedom?

1. The Behavior of Dictators

1.1. The Dictator's Dilemma

The standard view of the difference between democracy and dictatorship in political science (e.g., Friedrich and Brzezinski, 1965) is that dictators can use the tool of repression to stay in power. Thus dictators typically impose restrictions on the rights of citizens to criticize the government, restrictions on the freedom of the press, restrictions on the rights of opposition parties to campaign against the government, or, as is common under totalitarian dictatorship, simply prohibit groups, associations, or political parties opposed to the government. To be effective, these restrictions must be accompanied by monitoring of the population, and by sanctions for disobedience. The existence of a political police force and of extremely severe sanctions for expressing and especially for organizing opposition to the government such as imprisonment, internment in mental hospitals, torture and execution are the hallmark of dictatorships of all stripes.

However, the use of repression creates a problem for the autocrat. This is the Dictator's Dilemma (Wintrobe, 1990, 1998) — the problem facing any ruler of knowing how much support he has among the general population, as well as among smaller groups with the power to depose him. The use of repression of course breeds fear on the part of a dictator's subjects, and this fear breeds a reluctance on the part of the citizenry to signal displeasure with the dictator's policies. This fear on their part in turn breeds fear *on the part of the dictator*, since, not knowing what the population thinks of his policies, he has no way of knowing what they are thinking and planning, and of course he suspects that what they are thinking and planning is his assassination. The problem is magnified the more the dictator rules by repression, i.e., through fear. The more his repressive apparatus stifles dissent and criticism, the less he knows how much support he really has among the population.

From a theoretical point of view, the Dictator's Dilemma originates from the lack of an enforcement mechanism in politics. It is advantageous for the dictator to "buy off" some of his constituents, especially those who may be too powerful to repress, and those whose demands are easily satisfied. So a simple trade of rents or policies for support would solve the dictator's dilemma, and also allow his subjects to rest easily. But there is no mechanism analogous to legal contractual enforcement which would enforce this trade. Another way to put it is that the dictator and his subjects have a mutual *signaling* problem. In general, the easiest way to overcome the problem of obtaining support is to "overpay" supporters, i.e., to pay them more than they are worth by distributing rents to them. The support of workers can be obtained through paying them excessive wages, of capitalists by giving them monopoly privileges, of particular regions by locating manufacturing facilities in places where they don't really belong but where they are politically valuable, of ethnic groups by giving them special privileges and so on. Of course, similar practices are widespread in democracy where they are known as "pork barrel politics". They are often described as a failure of democracy. But if democracy may be likened to a pork barrel, the typical dictatorship is a temple of pork! That is, these practices appear to be much more widespread under dictatorship than under democracy.

In sum, while there is always a class of people who are repressed under a dictatorship, there is also, in any successful dictatorship, another class — the overpaid. As far as the people in the middle are concerned, the sad thing is that they can side with either group. The general population may be repressed in that their civil liberties may be taken away, but other aspects of the regime may compensate for this as far as they are concerned.

However, *the use of repression doesn't mean that dictators aren't popular*. Indeed, it sometimes appears from the historical record that the more repressive they were, the more popular they became! All the evidence indicates that Hitler was very popular. Communism was *popular* at one time; when it became unpopular, the regimes fell. Reports in the newspapers suggest that Castro and Saddam Hussein were often popular with their peoples.[1]

That dictatorships use two instruments — repression and loyalty or popularity — to stay in power suggests a useful classification of regimes. Four types can be distinguished: tinpots (low repression and loyalty), tyrants (high repression, low loyalty), totalitarians (high levels of both), and timocrats (low repression, high loyalty). Thus, totalitarian regimes combine high repression with a capacity to generate loyalty. Under tyranny, the regime stays in power through high repression alone and loyalty is low. A tinpot regime is low on both counts. And timocracy implies that loyalty is high even at low levels of repression. These four types or *images* have tended to recur over and over in the literature on dictatorship.[2]

This classification may be thought of in three ways. On one level, the regimes simply represent different combinations of the variables loyalty and repression. However, the classification also illuminates behaviour, because *the regimes differ in their response to economic change.* Suppose, e.g., that there is an increase in economic growth which raises the dictator's popularity. Tinpots and timocrats both respond to an increase in popularity by lowering the level of repression; tyrants and totalitarians, by raising it.

A third way to think about the regimes is that they simply represent different solutions (levels of repression and loyal support) to the same general model. Thus, assume that all dictators have the same utility function, where the arguments are consumption (C) and power (π).

$$U = U(\pi, C) \tag{1}$$

Power may be desired either for its own sake, or because dictators wish to impose their ideas of the common good on society.[3] The tinpot ruler represents the special or "corner" solution where the sole aim is to maximize consumption. On the other hand, the leaders of tyrannies and totalitarian regimes represent the opposite extreme of dictators who maximize power. Finally, timocracy[4] represents the case of benevolent dictatorship, where the dictator's objective is the welfare of its people. While many if not all dictators profess this objective, it is hard to think of an instance where it explains much about their behavior.[5]

Combining this utility function with a constraint which shows how money can be converted into power and power into money provides an illuminating explanation of the limits to a dictator's power. Totalitarian dictators in particular appeared to maximize the control of the state over the individual. For example in Nazi Germany, one official suggested that "the only time an individual has a private life is when he is asleep." What limits a dictator's pursuit of power? It would be arbitrary to specify that the dictator's power is limited by a revenue-maximizing tax. For, so long as the dictator has sufficient power, he can raise more funds by imposing new tax bases and by finding other ways to raise money. In short, if there is no limit to his power, there is no limit to his resources either. And *vice versa*. In the end, the constraint on his behavior does not arise from an artificially fixed budget, nor from arbitrary limits to his power, but from the ultimately diminishing possibilities of transforming money into power and *vice versa*. So the limits to budgetary resources and to power must be simultaneously determined.

More precisely, the dictator is constrained in two ways. The first constraint — the costs of accumulating power — is governed by the political institutions of the regime, and the second — the capacity to use his power to increase revenue — by the dictator's economy. These constraints are combined in equation

$$B(\pi) = P_\pi \pi (B - C) + C \tag{2}$$

The left-hand side of the constraint (2) shows the dictator's budget B as a function of power (π), i.e., it shows how the dictator's power may be used (through taxation, regulation or the provision of public goods) to obtain budgetary resources. The right-hand side shows how the funds are "spent": either on consumption, C, or accumulating power π via the money-to-power relation $\pi(B-C)$, with each unit of π multiplied by P_π — the "price" of power in terms of money.

The solution (first-order conditions) may be obtained by choosing π and C to maximize (1) subject to the constraint (2). Rearranging terms, it is expressed simply as

$$\frac{U_c}{U_\pi} = \frac{1}{P_\pi(1 - \frac{1}{\varepsilon^\pi}) - B_\pi} \tag{3}$$

Equation (3) displays in a particularly transparent way the elements that enter into the dictator's calculus — the marginal costs of accumulating power $p_\pi[1-(1/\varepsilon^\pi)]$, where $\varepsilon^\pi \equiv (\partial \pi / \partial P_\pi)(P_\pi/\pi) > 0$, is the elasticity of π with respect to its price; the marginal effect of power on the dictator's budget (B_π), and U_C/U_π — the dictator's preferences for power vs. consumption.

The first term (P_π) is governed by the dictator's political apparatus for building loyalty and for repression and the productivity of these instruments in producing power. The second (B_π) shows what the exercise of power does to the dictator's budget via its effects on the economy, e.g., its effects on economic growth, economic efficiency, and the capacity to implement taxes. Sometimes (e.g., if power is used to provide a public input, or to raise or implement taxes) the exercise of state power will raise revenue, i.e., $B_\pi > 0$. Sometimes (i.e., if power is used to impose inefficient regulation on industry) power will lower state revenue

($B_\pi < 0$). The third factor (U_C/U_π) simply represents the dictator's preferences between consumption and power. Sometimes one can see some of the factors at work molding these preferences — e.g., how Party organization or the nature of the dictator's support can drive him in the direction of maximizing power. But, perhaps more than any other political or economic agent, political dictators have some freedom to put their stamp on society.

This equilibrium provides the limit to power. At the equilibrium, the dictator cannot obtain more power (its marginal cost in money is larger than the extra power required to support this budget) and cannot obtain more revenue (the power required to do so is larger than the revenue necessary to support this level of power). Note the simultaneous equilibrium of money and power.

In turn the model also simultaneously determines the dictator's consumption, equilibrium level of repression and loyal support. So this model of a utility maximizing dictator can be put together with various types of economic system (communist, apartheid, capitalist-authoritarian, etc. each of which contain values of B_π, ε_π and P_π) to derive implications about the behaviour of different regimes — comparative static changes in Π and B, as well as in levels of repression, loyalty, etc. Put differently, the three elements in equation (3), determine the nature of the dictatorship — whether the regime resembles more closely that of a tinpot, totalitarian, tyrant, or timocrat.

As far as the economy is concerned, what turns out to be crucial is not whether the dictator's intervention helps or hurts the economy on the whole, but the effects of *marginal* (further) interventions on economic growth, efficiency, or the dictator's budget. If this marginal effect (B_π) is positive, whether the total effect is positive or negative within a considerable range, the dictator will tend to be oriented more towards power rather than consumption. On the other hand, if the use of power tends to retard growth and other dimensions of economic efficiency rather than favoring it, the dictator tends to be a tinpot. So the marginal economic effects of the dictator's power helps to determine whether the dictator is tinpot, totalitarian or tyrant.

Winer and Islam (2001) test Wintrobe's theory of non-democratic regimes using a large sample of both non-democratic and democratic countries. Some additional hypotheses about the differences between democratic and non-democratic countries suggested but not explicitly considered by Wintrobe are also considered. The results indicate clearly that the relationship between an index of civil and political freedoms and economic growth varies substantially across all regime types. Other aspects of the theory are partially confirmed. In particular, positive growth leads to a reduction in the degree of freedom in totalitarian regimes (that attempt to maximize power), and negative growth (falling levels of per capita real income) appears to reduce freedom in tinpot regimes (that just attempt to maintain power), as predicted by the Wintrobe theory. On the other hand, positive growth in tinpots and negative growth in totalitarians also reduces freedom, contrary to the theory, although in the case of tinpots, the absolute value of the effect on the index of freedom appears to be bigger for negative than for positive growth, as predicted by Wintrobe's model. Some results concerning differences across regimes in the effect of schooling on freedom are also provided.

1.2. New Work on Repression: Dynamics, Ideology and Genocide

The theory of repression has been extended by Philip Verwimp (2001), who attempts to understand the behavior of the Habyarimana regime in Rwanda, and in particular to explain the origins of the tragic genocide that took place there. The paper applies Wintrobe's model in a new way (by using the price of coffee as an index of the capacity of a dictatorial regime to generate loyalty) and it extends the model to explain genocide. Verwimp suggests that the Habyarimana regime, frustrated by its loss of power, attempted to split the population along ethnic lines and set one group against the other, culminating in rewarding Hutus for the extermination of Tutsis. Thus the genocide is interpreted as the attempt by the regime to remain in power by accentuating the ethnic split the population into two groups, ultimately singling out one for extermination by the other.

Spagat (2001) studies the optimal strategy for a dictator hanging onto power by choosing how much repression to apply in every period. State variables are the amount of "hate" and "fear" in society which are both increasing in the amount of repression from the previous period. Hate, fear and a random shock determine the quantity of repression required for the dictator to survive. They show that in every period there are only two possible optimal choices: the minimal repression necessary to retain power ("no demonstration") or the maximum possible repression ("demonstration"). The state space can be divided into two regions separated by an increasing function such that "no demonstration" is optimal in one and "demonstration" in the other. Under some conditions the opportunity for international borrowing makes demonstration optimal when it would not have been without this option.

Bernholz (2001) develops a model of the evolution of totalitarian regimes. In the model there are "believers" who are convinced that others have to be converted to the supreme values of their ideology for their well-being and, possibly, enemies of their creed whose presence is obnoxious to them. Believers spend resources on winning new converts and to win the secular power of the state. Whether they succeed in this endeavour depends on the costs of converting new believers and on the amount of resources they are prepared to spend for this purpose, given their incomes and their propensity to consume. Their chances of success are greater if a crisis occurs, an event which is usually outside of their control. Once secular power has been secured, the resources of the state can be used to win more converts, to drive into exile or to kill inconvertibles and to try to reach the imperialistic aims implied by the ideology. If the latter is not the case, the regime may turn into a mature "ideocracy" after having reached its domestic aims. This would for instance be the case, if all inconvertibles had been removed and all the other population been converted. In this case no further terror and (or) repressions characteristic of totalitarian regimes are required. If the ideology implies ambitious imperialistic aims, for instance the conversion of all people on earth (except for inconvertibles) or the domination of the whole globe by the believers, it is highly probable that these aims cannot be reached. As a consequence either a war is lost and this leads to the removal of the totalitarian regime, or the ends have to be adapted to maintain the credibility of the ideology. But then the totalitarian state may again turn into a mature ideocracy, if the ideology has been reinterpreted to remove its unrealistic imperialistic aims. Or the change of the ideology weakens the regime in a way that it loses its proselytizing character altogether, and turns into an ordinary autocratic regime.

1.3. The Irony of Absolutist Monarchy

Another important analysis of the limits on the power of dictatorship is provided by the "irony of absolutism." The problem is described in a series of works by North, Weingast, Root and others (e.g., North, 1981; North and Weingast, 1989; Root, 1994). In North's (1981) model of the monarchy, the King maximizes revenue, and the central problem is that the structure of property rights which is appropriate for this purpose is not usually that which is efficient from the economic point of view. More subtly, there is a tradeoff between power and revenue. As Root describes the "Irony of Absolutism", absolute power gave the King the capacity to repudiate debts, but

> Creditors took into account the king's reputation for repudiating debts and therefore demanded higher interest rates than would otherwise have been needed to elicit loans. Actually, *because he was above the law, the king had to pay more for loanable funds than did his wealthy subjects*. In short, the Crown had a problem asserting its credit because it had a history of reneging on commitments. [Italics added.][6]

North and Weingast suggest that this problem gave rise to the Glorious Revolution in England, in which power over the Treasury was devolved on Parliament. In this way the King could credibly commit to repay. No such devolution of power occurred in France. The result was that the English King solved the problem of how to raise funds and could finance his army and other expenditures while the French King did not, leading to the chronic shortage of revenue that was one of the factors leading to the French revolution.[7]

Congelton (2002) extends this analysis by pointing out that all kings share power. He suggests a generalized template, "King and Council" for looking at these issues. In practice one rarely observes pure forms of dictatorship that lack a council, or pure forms of parliament that lack an executive. Generally government policies emerge from organizations that combine an executive branch of government, "the king," with a cabinet or parliamentary branch, "the council." Congleton provides an explanation for this regularity: The bipolar "king and council" constitutional template has a number of properties which give it great practical efficiency as a method of information processing and collective choice. First, a council generally has a wider array of direct experience and/or knowledge than the king does, and therefore is in position to be a better estimator of "policy consequences" than the king alone tends to be. Second, a bipolar design can reduce losses from conflict in cases where significant power centers other than the king exist. Third, a king and council template which provides agenda control to the king, tends to reduce the extent to which majoritarian cycles may arise in the council. Fourth, the king and council templates allow gradual evolutionary shifts of power between the executive and parliament as circumstances change without the necessity of violent conflict. Insofar as a form of majority rule is used by the council and is stable, the recommendations of council tend to be both robust as estimators and moderate in their policy recommendations.

2. Growth and Economic Efficiency Under Dictatorship

There has been a lot of research asking the question, which is better for the economy, democracy or dictatorship? The answer is complex, mainly because the economic systems under autocracies vary so much. Those who believe there is some simple formula for distinguishing the economy of dictatorship from that of democracy should compare, for example, the economies of Nazi Germany, Apartheid South Africa, Papa Doc's Haiti, Pinochet's Chile and the Former Soviet Union.

2.1. Democratic Inaction

One general proposition which is true of all these systems is that dictators have a greater capacity for *action*, good or bad. If a dictator wishes to raise taxes, declare war, or take tough measures vs. crime, he may have to deal with some opposition to these policies among his advisers, but by and large, he can do so. Democracies, on the other hand are often mired in *inaction*.[8] The basic reason is that democratic leaders can only act when they can build support for their policies and there may be no consensus as to what to do. Even on problems where there is agreement that something should be done, there may be no agreement on *what* should be done. In extreme cases, the political system of a democratic country may become paralyzed by conflicts or opposing viewpoints.[9] In these circumstances, politicians often prefer to do nothing, to shroud their positions in ambiguity, or to pretend to be on all sides of an issue. The result is that the population can become cynical, and lose trust in the promises of any politician. This can set in motion a downward spiral, since the more this happens and trust is lost, the harder it becomes for politicians to do something by forging a compromise. This is more likely to happen when the pressures for political action on an issue are particularly conflicting, when positions are far apart, when issues are particularly divisive, when the population is divided along racial or ethnic lines, and when there is relatively little trust in politicians by the citizens.

2.2. Economic Growth and Efficiency

2.2.1. Introduction
Some new theorizing and empirical work compares the economic performance of democracies and dictatorships directly. A convenient place to start is Barro's empirical work (1996a,b). Barro stresses the advantages of dictatorship, which are that it controls rent seeking and other redistributory pressures, i.e., the autocrat, unlike the democratic politician, is capable of shutting down or simply ignoring the redistributory demands of interest groups characteristic of democracy (Barro, 1996b, p. 2). His empirical work suggests that more democracy raises growth at low levels of political freedom but depresses growth when a moderate amount of freedom has already been attained. However, the effect of an increase in political freedom on economic growth is not very large and the overall effect "not statistically different from zero" (Barro, 1996b, p. 6). Barro's results are only obtained once certain variables are held constant, including free markets, the rule of law, and small government consumption. So, really, again, only certain *kinds* of dictatorship are being discussed. The paper also, finds, perhaps surprisingly, that democracy does not necessarily promote the rule of law.

Przeworski et al. (2000) find that basically there is no difference between the rates of growth in dictatorships vs democracies in their comprehensive examination of the performance of these two kinds of regimes in 141 countries over the 40 years or so after the second world war. But the same study confirms the importance of politics on economic growth. They show that changes in office (political instability) and other forms of unrest such as strikes, demonstrations and riots reduce economic growth substantially under dictatorship, whereas while these are more frequent under democracy they do not cause a reduction in the rate of growth there (Przeworski et al. (2000) pp. 192–193).

Sen (1993) calls the general idea that dictatorship is better suited to economic development than democracy the Lee thesis, after Lee Kwan Yew, the autocratic but economic efficiency-minded ruler of Singapore for many years. Sen raises many questions about Lee's ideas and suggests instead that democracy is intrinsically important to the process of development. In particular, Sen's observation that famines only seem to occur under dictatorship is provocative. However, no general theoretical model is presented that compares democracy with dictatorship.

2.2.2. The Predatory State
The most prominent theoretical idea in this literature is undoubtedly Olson's concept of an autocrat as a "stationary bandit" — at one point he refers to it as "the other invisible hand" — that guides rulers to use their power to at least some extent in the public interest. In his (2000) book, this concept is approached through a criminal metaphor. Each theft reduces the wealth of society and therefore the amount available for the thief to steal. Does this lead the thief to curtail his activity, in order to preserve the wealth of his prey? For the typical criminal, the answer is "no" because his interest is too narrow. The wealth of the society on which he preys is like a public good to the typical small scale criminal, his effort to preserve it would have only a minuscule effect, and so he is better off free riding rather than attempting to conserve it. On the other hand, the Mafia and other criminal organizations which have a monopoly on crime in their area, do have a sufficiently *encompassing* interest to take the effects of their thefts on

the wealth of society as a whole. Thus, Olson asserts, they typically do not steal at all but engage in protection instead, charging the citizens a fee to ensure the safety of their victims both from others and from the protectors themselves.

This criminal metaphor then becomes the foundation for the origins of government. The logic is the same as that just outlined with respect to government by a "roving" vs. that by a "stationary" bandit: the stationary bandit, unlike the roving one, has an encompassing interest in preserving the wealth of the society from which he steals, and therefore limits his "theft" (taxes) and even provides public goods — both to the point where the marginal benefit to him is sufficient to account for his costs in terms of foregone income. The history of the forms of government is then simple to derive: autocracy (the stationary bandit) arises out of anarchy as the bandit(s) with the greatest capacity for violence take over the area and substitutes an encompassing for a narrow interest; democracy arises out of dictatorship when autocracy is overthrown and none of the individuals or leaders involved in the coup has sufficient power to make themselves autocrats.

In the end, just two variables are necessary to compare and analyze governments:

(i) how encompassing (breadth of self interest) is the interest of the ruler,
(ii) how long (time horizon) is his interest.

Thus, in the same way that dictatorship is superior to anarchy because the dictator has an encompassing interest in the society he rules, so democracy is superior to dictatorship because democratic majorities are more encompassing than the interest of the dictator. Secondly, dictators or democracies with long time horizons have more of an interest in preserving or enhancing the wealth of the society they rule than those who rule only for the short term.

Some evidence is presented in Keefer et al. (1996), who argue that any incentive an autocrat has to respect property rights comes from his interest in future tax collections and national income and increases with his planning horizon. They find an empirical relationship between property and contract rights and an autocrat's time in power.

So, comparing dictatorships, the basic implication is, the more encompassing, the better. Political scientists indeed have a classification that appears to match this: between "mobilizational" regimes which encourage political participation among the ruled and regimes which simply try to stamp out opposition. The problem with Olson's analysis is that, comparing dictatorships, the worst regimes in human history appear to be precisely those such as Nazi Germany, Soviet Russia, or Cambodia which appear to have been the most encompassing. The reason is simple: it was those regimes that wanted to remold the citizens and the societies under their rule and therefore intervened most dramatically and thoroughly into the lives of their citizens. Whether it is their brutal treatment of minorities or their record on the environment, it is an understatement to suggest that the historical record of these regimes offers little that is to be admired. So the theory appears to be capable, not just of misleading with respect to the understanding of autocratic regimes, but of "getting it wrong" in a spectacular fashion.

The same problem appears with respect to the second variable, the time horizon of the dictator. In Olson's model, the longer the time horizon, the better, i.e., the more the dictator tends to rule in the social interest. But regimes with a long time horizon have been precisely those in which the leaders had a tighter grip on power, and hence were more capable of molding the society and the individuals within it, i.e., the mobilizational regimes just discussed. Those where the regime is just interested in looting the society typically have a shorter time horizon.

In short, from the point of view of citizens of these regimes, or more specifically from that of the peasants under Stalin, the Jews under Hitler, the blacks in South Africa, and so on, it would no doubt have been better if their bandits had been less stationary!

The alleged superiority of dictatorship over anarchy is also challenged in a major article by Moselle and Polak (2001). In their model, the existence of a state can result in lower levels of both output and welfare than would occur under anarchy. This occurs if the state is "predatory" in the sense that the rulers extract taxes from the population for their own ends. In this framework, even a weak state can be bad for output and welfare and that a "corrupt" state that makes side deals with bandits can be especially bad.

Perhaps the most basic problem with Olson's framework is, I suspect, the lack of emphasis on competition. Once the struggle for power is assumed away, many of the most interesting aspects of the behaviour of dictators become idiosyncratic features of their preferences, and hence largely unpredictable, instead of being derived from the principle of competition. Thus the wars among the monarchies, etc are all aspects of "princely consumption". And how would the model explain Stalin's war against the peasantry, Hitler's treatment of the Jews, and the persecution of minorities in other dictatorships? On the bandit model, the only way to understand these forms of behaviour is that dictators have some monopoly power, and that they use this power to implement their preferences which happen to be weird preferences. The reason for this is that the model does not deal with the competitive struggle to acquire and maintain dictatorial powers. So the behavior of the dictator cannot be understood as motivated by competition or survival in office but simply as consumption.

Two other contributions address the problem of why some dictatorships, most notably regimes in East Asia and Chile, appear to be pro-growth while in others the autocrat is "predatory" and simply plunders the economy. Robinson (1997) argues that the likelihood of predatory behaviour may be positively related to the extent to which a regime is encompassing and values the future. He develops a model in which whether or not a state is predatory hinges on the relationship between development and the distribution of political power. Development is typically inconsistent with the preservation of the political status quo and this gives those in power an incentive to oppose it. Predatory behaviour is also more likely the lower the level of income and the more unequal the society. To put it bluntly, from the dictator's point of view, ruining the economy can sometimes be a good thing! And the regimes of Mobutu and Papa Doc, who both did this, were extremely long lived. A democratic politician cannot hope to profit in the same way.

Michael Spagat's (2001) paper addresses this problem by suggesting that there is a "bifurcation point" or level of capital below which it does not pay the dictator to try and develop the economy, and above which the dictator pursues rapid growth in order to maximize his personal consumption over time. He develops this idea in a simple formal model. A particularly novel feature of it is that there is an endogenous probability of a political catastrophe which removes the dictator from power, and this in turn depends on the dictator's capacity to satisfy certain groups which depends on the level of the capital stock. Hence a dictator's economy sometimes grows faster than a social planner's might, as capital accumulation wards off the possibility of catastrophe. The authors use simulation analysis to show the existence of bifurcation and to show how it depends on various parameters, and they provide some empirical evidence using Gastil data of the existence of bifurcation, and of their basic prediction that the variance of growth rates in dictatorship is higher than that under democratic regimes.

2.2.3. The Contest for Power

In contrast to economic models which stress the incentives of a ruler, *once he is in office*, Wintrobe (2002) focuses on the conditions under which the ruler obtains power, and how he can be deprived of it. All political systems contain a mechanism which determines the allocation of political power, and if and how it is reallocated when a transfer would improve the functioning of the system. Among the most obvious and commonly considered types of political system — democracy, dictatorship, anarchy, and hereditary monarchy — *only* democracy appears to possess a relatively low-cost procedure or mechanism which makes it possible to transfer political power on a regular and systematic basis, where the transfer is accepted by those who lose power as well as those who gain it, and which offers some possibility that these reallocations will tend to shift power into the hands that can use it most effectively.

Thus there is a strict analogy between democracy, based on human rights, and capitalism, based on property rights: democracy makes power transferable just as capitalism makes the ownership of capital assets transferable. This gives democracy an enormous advantage over these other political systems.

To elaborate, the main economic advantage of the election mechanism would seem to be that it allows for the transfer of power at relatively low cost. It solves the *contest for power* problem. If there are no elections, the only ways to transfer power are by such means as revolutions, insurrections, coups and wars. Compared to these, democratic elections on the basis of inalienable human rights would seem to be, in a word, cheap. Thus the economic attractiveness of the election mechanism is simple: it provides a formal and agreed-upon procedure to decide on the allocation of political power, and one that is explicitly accepted by or consented to in advance by the parties who lose the contest. Among the most commonly discussed systems of government — anarchy, hereditary monarchy, dictatorship and democracy — only democracy possesses this advantage.

Granted that democracies can transfer power at relatively low cost, does power typically transfer from lower to higher valued uses? Do democracies allocate power properly? In the models of Stigler (1971); Peltzman (1976); Olson (1982), democracy is inefficient because it is dominated by interest groups and the policies pursued by interest groups are inefficient and wasteful. In the rent-seeking framework, it is the contest itself which is inefficient and wasteful. These theories are the foundations of Barro's (1996) empirical work. However, Becker (1983) showed that under democracy the losses from inefficient policies enter into the workings of the political system and affect its allocation of power. The reason is that the larger the deadweight losses from a policy, the more opposition there will be to it from the groups which bear these losses. Alternatively the more inefficient a subsidy, the less the group which gains from the subsidy will exert pressure to obtain it. Consequently, even in a model such as Becker's, which focuses solely on interest group competition, the contest is not wasteful, and it tends to select efficient over inefficient policies. To put it simply, if power ends up in the "wrong" hands the democratic political process takes account of this and tends to set it right.[10]

What about dictatorship? The basic difference between dictatorship and democracy is that dictators have the capacity to repress opposition to their policies (as outlined above). They can silence demonstrations, censor the media, ban opposition parties, put leaders of troublesome groups in jail, and, not uncommonly, torture or execute them. As a consequence, the repressed are, in effect, not allowed to spend resources to exert political pressure: instead they are silenced by the government. It follows that if the costs of public policies can be made to fall on those who are repressed, these costs do not enter into the competition among interest groups.[11]

Assume for a moment that this is the case, i.e., all of the costs of inefficient policies fall on those whose political demands are effectively repressed by the regime. Since the losses make the repressed worse off, this weakens the capacity of those who are opposed to the regime to resist it.[12] This is the strategy of "immiserization" practised most notably, perhaps, by Papa Doc of Haiti.[13] Another nice illustration of this is the effect of sanctions against Saddam Hussein, discussed by Kaempfer et al. (2001). The sanctions generate rents, and these are appropriated by those who are close to Saddam. The losses from the sanctions are borne by those who are opposed to the regime, and this in turn weakens their capacity to oppose it, leading to his further entrenchment in power. To put it simply, the sanctions against Saddam Hussein don't necessarily weaken his hold on power at all.

On the other hand, to the extent that the repressed cannot be made to bear all of the costs of the public sector, some of these costs will fall on other groups — actual supporters, potential supporters and largely passive acceptors of the regime. To the extent that the costs of public expenditures and regulations fall on these groups, they would indeed enter into the competition among groups for subsidies and other rents from the regime under dictatorship, just as they do under democracy. However, even in this case, the mechanism does not work as well as under democracy. The reasons are: (1) The information problem deriving from the Dictator's Dilemma: In a democracy the different groups competing for redistributory policies or public goods are free to openly debate and criticize existing policies and to expose flaws in each others' proposals. Under dictatorship, any form of attack on policies which have been or might be favored by the regime can be interpreted as a sign of disloyalty,[14] and for this reason people may not be eager to report problems to the autocrat. (2) What incentive is there for the dictator to correct bad policies? After all, among the fruits of dictatorship is "the quiet life" — freedom from competitive pressures so long as he is safely in office. (3) Finally, once decisions are made there may be no mechanism by which to correct them except by the overthrow of the dictator. Since there is no peaceful and regularized way to replace an autocrat, he may tend to oppose any attempt to change the policies, since any change may be threatening to his survival in office.

To sum up, the economic losses from inefficiency may or may not enter into the dictator's political budget equation, depending on who experiences them. Let us take the two cases in turn: (1) Suppose the losses are experienced by actual or potential supporters. The lack of political competition under dictatorship still implies that the economy may be allowed to deteriorate more (compared to a democracy) before some attempt is made to change the policies or replace the dictator; (2) On the other hand, suppose the economic losses are experienced primarily or wholly by those who are opposed to and repressed by the system. In this case the losses typically weaken rather than strengthen the capacity of those who are opposed to the regime to actually topple it, and this raises the attractiveness of inefficient policies from the point of view of the dictator.

A final issue is the relative influence of producer vs consumer groups under dictatorship vs democracy. Ever since the work of Downs, it has been a standard proposition in the economics of politics that democracy favors producer groups over consumer groups (Downs, 1957; Stigler, 1971; Peltzman, 1976; Olson, 1982; Becker, 1983). The main reasons advanced are that since these groups are small, it is relatively easy for them to overcome the free rider problem, and since their *per capita* benefits would be large from any subsidy, they have a substantial interest in applying pressure to obtain it. On the other hand, consumer groups are large, and the *per capita* benefit from any subsidy would be small.

I pointed out above that dictators cannot survive in office on the basis of repression alone but need support as well. Which groups can be expected to support dictators? Consumer groups, environmental groups and other groups with a large number of potential supporters, each of which has a small stake in issues like the prices of goods or the state of the environment have difficulty surviving or forming under autocracy. There are typically no laws protecting human rights under dictatorship. Without such laws, it is difficult for large groups — such as consumers — to organize. There is no free press to call attention to pricing or environmental or labour abuses and to aid in the formation of a mass membership and there are no independent courts in which to sue violators. And it is difficult for supporters of human rights, who have been crucial in generating the "rights revolution" (Epp, 1998; Ignatieff, 2000) to mobilize support. In brief, the common weapons of mass organizations — publicity and the courts — are more easily countered by a dictator than a democratic politician.

On the other hand, the weapons of small producer groups such as cash donations actually thrive in the closed environment and tame courts of a dictatorship. In exchange, dictators obviously have much to offer producers for their support including tariffs, subsidies and other rents, fewer problems from labor unions, and the removal of unfavorable regulations. So the possibilities of a trade of rents for support between the dictator and the small, concentrated interest group is actually *enhanced* under dictatorship, just as trades with representatives of broader public opinion are diminished. This implies that *producers typically have more power under dictatorship than democracy*.

This analysis also provides an alternative explanation for Barro's evidence cited above: that the rate of growth is slightly higher under dictatorship than democracy at low levels of dictatorship and lower at high levels of repression. Since producers especially benefit from economic growth, their greater political weight under dictatorship implies that dictators would emphasize this policy. Note, however, that this growth comes as the result of the greater influence of producer groups and is not necessarily a Pareto improvement. Thus the growth could arise to the detriment of the environment, the consumer, etc. Moreover, at high levels of repression, this positive effect on growth is increasingly overwhelmed by the information problems generated by the Dictator's Dilemma, which increasingly hamper growth and ultimately strangle it.

Finally it is worth pointing out that an extension of the theory of property rights used in this analysis provides a simple economic justification of human rights. Economic efficiency justifies the ownership of private property on the ground that property should be allocated to the party who is most highly motivated to maximize its value. Who is it that can be counted to manage or take care a piece of property best? The owner. Human rights give this privilege of "ownership" of the individual (if you like, of his human capital) to that individual himself or herself. Under dictatorship, it resides with the sovereign. But the dictator, as Sen (1993) suggested, tends to regard the people under his rule as "stock" and cannot be expected to care for their lives the way they would themselves. Perhaps this explains Przeworski et al.'s striking result that the average life span is systematically lower under dictatorship (see Przeworski et al., 2000, chapter 5).

3. Policy towards Dictatorship

3.1. Aid: A Single Standard

What policies should be followed towards dictatorship by democratic regimes interested in promoting freedom? Suppose, idealistically, that the only goal of Western policy is to reduce repression. The "weapons" in our arsenal are sanctions, trade agreements, imposing human rights constraints, and aid packages. Take a classic example of a tinpot dictator like Ferdinand Marcos. Should we have given aid to his regime? Suppose Marcos' only goal was to consume as much as possible — in his case, this meant buying shoes for his wife Imelda. What limited his consumption? Why didn't he spend all of the GNP of the Philippines on shoes for her? The constraint is that he had to stay in office, so he could not allow his power to fall so low that he was in danger of being deposed. As a tinpot, the levels of both repression and loyalty under his regime were just high enough to stay in office.

Suppose first that the tinpot is safely in office, which, at one point, according to accounts of the regime, Marcos felt he was. Then there is no point in giving him aid, because all he will do with the money is to buy more shoes. A trade agreement would have the same effect. On the other hand, suppose he is in danger of being deposed. Then the aid simply props up the regime. So, *in neither case does the aid reduce repression*. An alternative policy would be to insist on human rights observances as a condition of receiving aid. But if the levels of repression and loyalty were previously just sufficient to stay in office, Marcos will simply be deposed if he lowers repression. So he would have refused this offer, and the policy is ineffectual.

On the other hand, suppose the aid is tied to human rights observances in a particular way. In order to keep receiving the aid, repression must be steadily relaxed over time. Then the dictator has an incentive to use the aid to improve the welfare of his people. The reason is that if their welfare improves, and he can claim credit for this, loyalty or support for him will tend to increase. As a result, he can afford to relax repression, and still buy the same number of shoes for Imelda as before.

Now look at totalitarian regimes or tyrannies, defined as regimes whose rulers are uninterested in consumption, but in power. Should we aid them? Again, suppose that, as the result of either policy, economic growth improves. This gives the rulers an opportunity to accumulate more power, and since power is the only thing they care about, they take this opportunity, in the same way that a businessman who is already rich will grab an opportunity to make more money. So, for these regimes, aid which is untied to human rights observances is not merely wasted, but counterproductive — repression *increases* when the economy improves. This is what happened under Hitler and Stalin: the more popular they were, the more they took these opportunities to put the screws to all those elements of the population whose absolute loyalty was uncertain. In the same way, the enormous economic growth in China has resulted in not the slightest degree of relaxation in the level of repression there.

It might seem obvious that we would not aid these regimes, since the aid money would be spent on accumulating more power over the population, including repressing them. But, again, if the aid is tied to a human rights constraint, which becomes progressively more stringent over time, the policy will work in the right direction. If the economy improves as a result, support increases, and the rulers can afford to relax repression and still have the same level of power as before. The human rights observances constraint is absolutely necessary if this is to lead to a fall in repression and not an increase.

So we have a very simple guide — a *single standard* — to the policies which should be pursued by foreign governments interested in reducing repression. This is to make human rights observance the cornerstone of Western policy. Aid to any type of regime can be expected to produce beneficial effects provided it is accompanied by a long term human rights constraint, one which becomes progressively more stringent over time. Without the human rights standard, the effects of aid will be ineffectual or perverse.

3.2. Trade

Another policy dilemma is whether to trade with dictatorships. Trade policy is a bit more complicated than aid. We can distinguish the following effects:

1. Trade may be expected to increase national income of the target regime, as productivity there will rise due to the availability of imported inputs at a lower price, and the demand for the target's exports increase. To the extent that the regime can successfully claim the credit for this improvement in welfare, loyalty to the regime may be expected to increase.

2. The rise in income will also increase tax revenues, giving the dictator more resources at his disposal. These may be used either for his own consumption, or to further his hold on power through increased expenditures on either repression or loyalty.

3. Since the richer people are, the more they tend to demand liberty, the increase in income tends to reduce loyalty to the dictatorship as people increasingly demand their rights (Bilson, 1982; Londregan and Poole, 1996). However, note that the estimated size of this effect is very small. Thus, as Londregan and Poole conclude their analysis of this effect in non-European countries, "Those expecting income growth to promote the development of democratic institutions must be very patient indeed" (pp. 22–23).

4. The increase in trade creates further links to foreign businesses and among domestic producers, possibly resulting in the development of independent power bases within the target regime. This is particularly likely when the trade is not organized through the central government (as it is in Cuba, for example). Thus, in China, regional governments in particular have built up substantial connections with outsiders and with the private sector, and are much more independent of the central government for revenue than they were before Deng launched his "social market" revolution. To the extent that this happens, loyalty to the regime may fall. On the other hand, it has been argued that trade between different types of civilizations actually increases mistrust, as the increased intensity of contacts simply breeds hostility. For example, World War I occurred at precisely the last peak of the "openness" of the international system. In that case, while there may be a short-run fall in loyalty due to the initial increase in contacts, in the longer run, further contacts simply breed nationalism and possibly *increased* support for the dictatorship in the target regime.

To disentangle the implications for policy, suppose first that the net effect of these changes, is, as seems likely, that support for the regime increases as the result of the trade agreement. Suppose also that the ruler is a tinpot. Then it can be argued that, with increased support, the tinpot will be himself motivated to relax repression (so that he can buy more shoes for his wife), and there is no need for a human rights constraint. But note that, even in this case, the human rights constraint does no harm; it simply asks the dictator to do what he would do in any case, and therefore it should be acceptable to him. On the other hand, if, on balance, loyalty to the regime were to decrease, the tinpot would want to raise repression in order to stay in office, and the human rights constraint is absolutely necessary for the trade agreement to lower, not raise, repression.

Suppose now that we are dealing with a totalitarian dictator. Again, if loyalty were to increase, on balance, as the result of the trade agreement, the dictator would tend to raise repression, and the binding human rights constraint is necessary to prevent a loss of freedom. The only case for a trade agreement with a totalitarian regime is where the opposite happens, and loyalty to the regime decreases from the trade agreement. In that case, repression falls as well. *This is the only case where trade with a totalitarian regime makes sense.* But note that, the totalitarian leader, in pursuing this trade agreement, cannot fail to be aware of the likely consequences of the trade agreement for his hold on power; namely, that his capacity for repression, the loyalty to him of the citizenry, and his power are all going to diminish as a result of his signing up. So, if this analysis were correct, it requires us to believe that the totalitarian is either unaware of, or deliberately acting contrary to, his own long run interest.[15] It is noteworthy also that all the totalitarian regimes which have collapsed historically did so as the result of falling, not rising real income, and that the increase in income in China has resulted in not the slightest relaxation of repression there after almost two decades of reform and spectacular economic growth. The case for trade with totalitarian regimes, therefore is particularly weak.[16]

Finally, suppose that the human rights constraint cannot be implemented, either because the target regime is too powerful, or because no agreement can be reached among the countries involved in implementing the policy. Or alternatively suppose the dictator promises to abide by the human rights constraint and then reneges. Then there is a difficult choice between a policy of sanctions, on the one hand, and trade agreements with no effective human rights constraint, on the other. Of course, the actual choices are never this stark, and the actual policies followed will be a mixture of trade and sanctions, but the basic principle involved in the choice remains one of engagement or isolation. In that case, the analysis here implies that the least harm is likely to come from a trade agreement with a tinpot regime, the most harm from trade with a totalitarian, with tyranny an intermediate case.

3.3. Sanctions

Historically, the most important alternative to a policy of aid to motivate dictatorships to behave is to use sanctions to punish those that do not. However, it is vital to realize that sanctions are not just the reverse of aid, and that policies like those pursued by the United States and the United Nations vis-à-vis regimes like Castro's Cuba, Saddam Hussein's Iraq or Milosevic's Serbia may superficially resemble those described here, but in fact they work very differently. In all these cases, the U.S. or the UN imposed sanctions, and offered to lift them as a reward for better behavior. Such policies are not necessarily wrongheaded, but they do not work in the manner of those advocated here. The reason is that the sequence is reversed: the regime has to liberalize *first*, i.e., before the sanctions are lifted, trade allowed to resume and aid to flow. This means that the regime has no chance to use the benefit of aid or trade to build loyalty prior to liberalization, as with the policies advocated here. So the dictator who agrees to liberalize puts himself in immediate danger of being deposed, and it is no surprise that dictators like Castro, Hussein and Milosevic were all reluctant to do so.

Kaempfer et al. (2001) extend Wintrobe's 1998 model of dictatorship and combine it with the public choice analysis of sanctions. They note that 85% of the time that sanctions are imposed they are imposed on a non-democratic regime. They point out that damaging economic sanctions can be counterproductive, undermining the political influence of the opposition. In the public choice approach, sanctions work through their impact on the relative power of interest groups in the target country. An important implication of this approach is that sanctions only work if there is a relatively well organized interest group whose political effectiveness can be enhanced as a consequence of the sanctions. For example, as the authors note, sanctions vs Iraq have had a devastating on the country but have been ineffective in destabilizing the Hussein regime. The reason, they argue is the fragmentation of the Iraqi opposition. At the other extreme, sanctions against South Africa were highly effective, because, in that case, there was a well organized opposition. The authors suggest that the effectiveness of the opposition is key to the effectiveness of sanctions and they try to show why this is true and to derive implications of this insight.

They also extend the model by adding two exogenous variables to it, s the impact of sanctions on the terms of trade; and q, the level of opposition; moreover q depends on s, $q_s > 0$, and by making the price of repression P_R (constant in Wintrobe's model) a variable which depends on q and s (in addition to their other effects on the model) as well as on the country's economic performance.

In their model sanctions have two main and opposing effects on the dictator's budget: (1) the budget of the dictator rises through the appropriation of sanctions rents; (2) the budget falls due to the increase in opposition. There are two cases. In the first case, the opposition is significant enough that $q_s > 0$. If, in addition, the second effect is large enough, the budget falls. If in addition, loyalty to the dictator falls due to the sanctions then sanctions are effective.

In the second case, there is no significant opposition. Then the net effect on the dictator's budget of sanctions is that it *rises* due to the appropriation of sanctions rents. If in addition loyalty *rises* because those close to the dictator are happy about their increased capacity to appropriate these rents, then the sanctions are entirely counterproductive, and the budget of the regime, its power, and the level of repression all increase.

4. Conclusion

In recent years a small but now growing literature has looked at dictatorship from the point of view of public choice. While there is no consensus in the literature and it would be too soon to look for one, a number of ideas are attracting interest. The literature looks at (1) the objectives of dictators; (2) the constraints on their behavior; (3) their strategies for staying in office; (4) their incentives to provide public goods compared to that under democracy; (4) the economic efficiency of dictatorship compared to democracy; and (5) policy towards dictatorships. On the *objectives* of dictators, some models simply assume that dictators maximize lifetime consumption, as in standard economic models. However although this is certainly true of small scale dictators, it hardly fits many of the most important dictatorships like those of Hitler or Stalin and other models explicitly posit a taste for power or, in common with many models of democracy, ideological objectives. Since dictators are by definition monopolistic, the case for including such other objectives is particularly strong. Wintrobe looks at the *strategies* used by dictators to stay in office and emphasizes the Dictator's Dilemma — the tradeoff between using repression and building support, noting that only the latter provides a firm foundation for autocratic rule. Recent contributions extend this framework to consider dynamic models of repression, the issue of genocide and the efficacy of sanctions against dictatorships.

The *constraint* on autocratic maximization is sometimes specified as the maximum revenue available. Other models specify the so-called "irony of absolutism" as the chief limit to a dictator's power. Wintrobe reasons that as long as more power is available there are ways to extract more revenue from the private sector. Similarly, as long as more revenue is available, it is possible to accumulate more power: For these reasons in his model the equilibrium power and budget of the dictator are determined simultaneously.

The model of the dictator as "stationary bandit" originated by Mancur Olson shows that even a dictator has an *incentive to provide public goods* in order to raise revenue though arguing that this incentive is less under dictatorship than under democracy.

There is, as always, disagreement about the *economic efficiency* of dictatorship vs democracy but the disagreement appears to be narrowing. On both theoretical and empirical grounds there appears to be a consensus that high levels of repression are inimical to economic efficiency. Empirical work by Barro and others provides some (very slim, as acknowledged) evidence that growth rates are higher under dictatorship at low levels of repression though even this is challenged in a major empirical study by Przeworski and others. Theoretically, such a result can be explained by a reduction of rent seeking or redistributory pressures, as Barro does, or by the greater influence of producer groups under dictatorship, in which case the growth might come about at the expense of consumers or workers and need not signal greater efficiency. The "contest for power" framework, on the other hand, emphasizes that only democracy provides a mechanism for getting incompetent or corrupt rulers out and suggests that democracy might be more economically efficient than dictatorship when this factor is taken into account.

On policy the Wintrobe model provides a simple guide to the policies that should be pursued by foreign governments interested in reducing repression. This is to implent human rights observances, which become more stringent over time, as a condition for receiving aid or trade. One problem with this is that the dictator may promise to abide by human rights and then renege. The literature continues the standard skepticism of economists on the effectiveness of economic sanctions as a tool for getting dictators to lower repression.

RONALD WINTROBE

NOTES

1. See for example, John Deutsch, Options: Good and Bad Ways To Get Rid of Saddam, *Hte New York Herald Tribune*, February 24, 1999, p. 8 on Saddam Hussein's popularity.
2. For details, see Wintrobe (1998), chapter 1.
3. The model does not distinguish between the desire for power for its own sake (as an end in itself) and the desire for power as a means to implement some other objective, e.g., in order to implement some personal or party preference as government policy. Bernholz (2001, discussed further below) stresses that dictators pursue power in order to implement a vision of society, e.g., Nazism with respect to racial objectives or communism with respect to equality. Wittman emphasized the same point with respect to politicians in a democracy: that they are interested in ideological objectives as well as being elected (Wittman, 1983). In my book I did not rule out other objectives for dictators besides power and consumption, but I tried to see how far one could go with this simple and basic public choice perspective. Of course, sometimes an ideology interferes with the pursuit of power; this could be incorporated into the model in the same way as consumption benefits already are. However, ideology is in part a tool (often incorporated in propaganda) to accumulate power, so the pursuit of power and that of an ideological objective are often difficult to distinguish in practise.
4. The Greek root of timocracy is *Thymos* — *to* love. The term is borrowed from Plato's *Republic*.
5. In my book I suggest the example of the Age of the Antonines, following Gibbon's description of this time as "the happiest the world has ever known", in his *Decline and Fall of the Roman Empire* (1981).
6. Root (1994), p. 177.
7. Note that the irony of absolutism is already incorporated into equation (3) above: it means that $B_\pi < 0$, i.e., that an increase in the autocrat's power π reduces budgetary revenue B. Presumably this would be true at high levels of π.
8. Some formal conditions for the existence of equilibrium inaction, as well as the circumstances under which this is

inefficient, are discussed in Howitt and Wintrobe (1995) and in Wintrobe (1998), chapter 11.
9. There is a large literature in political science which associates the historical breakdown of democracy in various countries with precisely these variables: inaction, lack of credibility, and their mutually reinforcing effects (for details and references see Wintrobe, 1998, chapter 13).
10. Newer, dynamic models of democratic decision-making cast doubts on the efficiency of democracy in a dynamic context. The basic problem discussed there (e.g., in Besley and Coate, 1998) is the inability of a representative democracy to commit to future policy outcomes. The question from the point of view of this survey is of course, whether a dictatorship could be expected to do better in this respect. To my knowledge nothing has been written on this issue but it is worth noting the evidence in Przeworski et al. that the average life of a dictatorship is less than democracy.
11. Thus in Becker's model, equation (13) would not hold for a repressed group since the group cannot spend resources to pressure the government; neither would equation (14), in which each person maximizes his income from producing pressure.
12. Contrast this proposition with Becker's point that under democracy larger deadweight losses increase pressure from the group experiencing them to lobby against the policies.
13. For more details, see Wintrobe (1998).
14. As an illustration, Mao Tse Tung's personal physician, Li Zhisui, appeared to be afraid to criticize Mao even on the smallest matters. See Zhisui (1994). Other illustrations of this point for various regimes can be found in Wintrobe (1998).
15. Note that the situation is very different for a tinpot, for whom the relaxation of repression following a trade agreement serves his interest, rather than acting contrary to it, as is the case for a totalitarian.
16. The analysis of the effects of trade on tyranny is identical to that for totalitarian regimes; the only difference is that the magnitude of the change in the supply of loyalty is smaller.

REFERENCES

Barro, Robert (1996a). "Democracy and growth." *Journal of Economic Growth*, 1.

Barro, Robert (1996b). *Getting It Right*. Boston: MIT Press.

Becker, Gary (1983). "Theory of competition among interest groups for political influence." *Quarterly Journal of Economics*, 98: 371–400.

Besley, Timothy and Stephen Coate (1998). "Sources of inefficiency in a representative democracy: a dynamic analysis." *American Economic Review*, 88: 139–156.

Bernholz, Peter (2001). "Ideocracy and totalitarianism: a formal analysis incorporating ideology." *Public Choice*, 108(1–2): 33–75.

Bilson, John (1982). "Civil liberties — an econometric investigation." *Kyklos*, 35: 94–114.

Coase, Ronald (1960). "The problem of social cost." *Journal of Law and Economics*, 1–44.

Congleton, Roger (2002). "From dictatorship to democracy without revolution," paper delivered at the American Economic Association meetings, Atlanta.

Downs, Anthony (1957). *An Economic Theory of Democracy*.

Epp, Charles (1998). *The Rights Revolution*. Chicago, IL: University of Chicago Press.

Freedom House (1978–2001). "Freedom in the world: the annual survey of political rights and civil liberties." *Freedom Review*. New York: Freedom House.

Friedrich, Karl and Zbigniew Brzezinski (1965). *Totalitarian Dictatorship and Autocracy*. Cambridge, MA: Harvard University Press.

Howitt, Peter and Ronald Wintrobe (1995). "The political economy of inaction." *Journal of Public Economics*, 56: 329–353.

Ignatieff, Michael (2000). *The Rights Revolution*. Toronto: Anansi Press for the CBC.

Islam, Muhammed and Stanley L. Winer (2001). "Tinpots, totalitarians (and democrats): an empirical investigation of the effects of economic growth on civil liberties and political rights," ms., Carleton University, Ottawa, Canada.

Kaempfer, W., Anton Lowenberg, and William Mertens (2001). "International economic sanctions against a dictator," paper delivered at the Public Choice Society Meetings, San Antonio, Texas.

Keefer, Philip, Christopher Clague, Stephen Knack, and Mancur Olson (1996). "Property and contract rights under democracy and dictatorship." *The Journal of Economic Growth*, 1(2): 243–276.

Londregan, John and Keith T. Poole (1996). "Does high income produce democracy"? *World Politics*, 49: 1–30.

McFaul, Michael (1995). "State power, institutional change, and the politics of privatization in Russia." *World Politics*, 47: 210–243.

Moselle, Boaz and Benjamin Polak (2001). "A model of a predatory state." *Journal of Law, Economics and Organization*, 17: 1–33.

North, Douglas (1981). *Structure and Change in Economic History*. New York: W.W. Norton.

North, Douglas and Barry Weingast (1989). "Constitutions and commitment: the evolution of institutions governing public choice in seventeenth century England." *Journal of Economic History*, XLIX: 808–832.

Olson, Mancur (1982). *The Rise and Decline of Nations*. New Haven and London: Yale University Press.

Olson, Mancur (1993). "Democracy and development." *American Political Science Review*, 87: 567–575.

Olson, Mancur (2000). *Power and Prosperity: Outgrowing Communist and Capitalist Dictators*. New York: Basic Books.

Peltzman, Samuel (1976). "Towards a more general theory of regulation." *Journal of Law and Economics*, 19: 211–240.

Posner, R.A. (1975). "The social costs of monopoly and regulation." *Journal of Political Economy*, 83: 807–827.

Przeworski, Adam, Michael E. Alvarez, Jose Antonio Cheibub, and Fernando Limongi (2000). *Democracy and Development: Political Institutions and Well-Being in the World 1950–1990*. New York: Cambridge University Press.

Robinson, James (1997). "When is a state predatory," ms., USC.

Root, Hilton (1994). *The Foundation of Privilege: Political Foundations of Markets in Old Regime France and England*. Berkeley: University of California Press.

Schumpeter, Joseph (1943, 1976). *Capitalism, Socialism and Democracy*. London: George Allen and Unwin.

Sen, Amartya (1993). "Political Rights and Economic Needs," The John M. Olin Lecture in Law and Economics at the University of Toronto Law School, October 1.

Spagat, Michael (2001). "Political instability and growth in dictatorships," ms., Royal Holloway College, England.

Stigler, G. J. (1971). "The Theory of Economic Regulation" *Bell Journal of Economics and Management Science* 2, 137–146.

Tullock, Gordon (1987). *Autocracy*. Dordrecht: Martinus Nijihoff.

Verwimp, Philip (2001). "The political economy of coffee and dictatorship in Rwanda," ms., Department of Economics, Leuven, Belgium.

Wintrobe, Ronald (1990). "The tinpot and the totalitarian: an economic theory of dictatorship." *American Political Science Review*, 84: 849–872.

Wintrobe, Ronald (1998). *The Political Economy of Dictatorship*. New York: Cambridge University Press.

Wintrobe, Ronald (1998b). "Some lessons on the efficiency of democracy from a study of dictatorship," in S. Borner and M. Paldam (eds.) *The Political Dimension of Economic Growth*. McMillan: International Economic Association.

Wintrobe, Ronald (2002). "The contest for power: property rights, human rights, and economic efficiency," paper presented at the American Economic Association meetings, Atlanta.

Wittman, Donald (1983). "Parties as utility maximizers." *American Political Science Review*, 77, 142–157.

Wittman, Donald (1995). *The Myth of Democratic Failure*. Chicago: University of Chicago Press.

Zhisui, Li (1994). *The Private Life of Chairman Mao*. New York: Random House.

E

ENVIRONMENTAL POLITICS

Building on the seminal contributions by Pigou (1920), Coase (1960) and Baumol and Oates (1971), economists have extensively explored the role that economic incentives might play in bringing a more efficient allocation of natural resources. The theory of environmental economics suggests that pricing instruments are an adequate means to internalize external costs. More specifically, there is widespread agreement within the scientific community that from a theoretical point of view pricing instruments are preferable to alternative measures due to their efficiency advantages (Frey et al., 1985). However, though economists see pricing instruments as an attractive policy tool, most attempts to introduce economic incentives in environmental policy have failed and the acceptance of these mechanisms in the political debate is still rather limited (Hahn, 1989; Frey and Schneider, 1997).

There are many possible reasons why incentive instruments as a means to internalize external costs have been rarely applied in the past. It certainly would be too simple just to refer to imperfect information on the part of decision-makers about the advantages of incentive-based instruments. On the contrary, there seem to be good reasons why politicians, voters, bureaucrats and/or representatives of interest groups are rather reluctant to favor price instruments on a large scale in environmental politics.

It is the purpose of the political economy of environmental policy to point out these reasons by concentrating on the process of political decision-making and the incentives of the political agents to implement alternative environmental instruments. Public choice methodology can be used to explain the discrepancy between economic theory and political reality also in environmental politics. Though public choice theory has been applied extensively in politico-economic modeling of popularity and voting functions, in analyzing political business cycles, in explaining rent-seeking behavior and the persistence of protectionism, for example, it is relatively less developed in environmental economics. Originated by the seminal study of Buchanan and Tullock (1975), the literature on the political economy of environmental policy has mainly focused on the comparative analysis of alternative policy measures and their chances for implementation, respectively (see, e.g., Frey, 1972; Dewees, 1983; Hahn, 1990; Downing, 1991; Horbach, 1992; Weck-Hannemann, 1994; Pearson, 1995; Congleton, 1996; Frey and Schneider, 1997; Dijkstra, 1999; Kirchgässner and Schneider, 2003). Besides, the public choice approach has been applied to analyze international environmental problems (for a survey see, e.g., Schulze and Ursprung, 2001; Bommer, 1998; Kirchgässner, 1999).

In their initial study, Buchanan and Tullock (1975) argue that direct control measures have better chances to be favoured and implemented in the political process than incentive based instruments like taxes on pollution. More generally, it is argued in the public choice literature on environmental politics that incentive oriented instruments are neither in the interest of the decision-makers on the supply side nor they are favored by the most influential groups of voters on the demand side in the political market. It is hypothesized that if any instrument of environmental policy is used at all, the main actors of environmental policy have a strong interest to apply command and control measures instead of incentive based instruments.

More recently, however, ecological taxes as well as tradable permits became more popular and voluntary agreements have been implemented. According to the Kyoto protocol, market based instruments are intended to play a more prominent role also in international environmental policy. Kirchgässner and Schneider (2003), therefore, conclude that "while we are still far away from general acceptance and widespread application of market based environmental instruments, the situation has changed at least somewhat". Consequently, it has to be asked whether the old diagnosis by Robert Hahn (1989) and the papers in the public choice tradition still holds, i.e., that the patients don't follow the doctor's orders in that environmental policy is dominated by command and control measures and, if applied at all, market based instruments deviate from the therapy economists typically prescribe.

Generally, public choice theory not only intends to analyze how the agents in the political sector (i.e., in particular, politicians and public bureaucrats) influence the state of the economy but also how the state of the economy in turn influences voters' preferences and thereby the evaluation of policies and parties. The level and structure of public interventions are determined endogenously in the political market for state interventions. In order to analyze the process of environmental policy it is important to identify the various actors involved and their interests and impact in the political decision-making process, respectively. The usual way is to single out four groups of actors which are examined in more detail, i.e., voters, politicians, public bureaucrats and interest groups representing the private sector.

Political economists view the policy measures that governments and parliaments adopt as outcomes of an exchange process. Elected officials supply the policies that voters and interest groups demand. In exchange for regulation, politicians receive votes, money and information. From a political economy perspective, it is useful to think about the negative externalities of private production and consumption as transfers to specific groups which are allowed to make use of resources without bearing the full opportunity costs. The introduction of alternative environmental policies then increases transfers to some groups and decreases the transfers to others. Whether or not it is possible to devise a pricing scheme that will find political acceptance not only depends on the changes in welfare brought about by pricing but also on the relative influence of groups in the political game.

In highly stylized models of political competition with two parties and a single policy dimension, the preferences of the median voter determine policy (Downs, 1957). In practice, however, elected officials are not this tightly bound to citizen preferences for a number of reasons: First, voters are rationally ignorant in the sense that they acquire political information up to the point where the marginal cost of acquiring additional knowledge equals marginal benefits. These benefits are low because an individual has only a miniscule impact on policy-making. If voters are unaware of what elected officials do, the latter can deviate from citizen preferences. Second, in representative democracies, voters simultaneously decide a large number of issues when electing their representatives. In contrast to unemployment or general tax policy, environmental issues are not particularly salient during general election campaigns. As a consequence, the influence of voter preferences on policy-making is weaker in the area of environmental policy. Third, the lack of political information on the part of voters allows interest groups to influence policy-making. Even in a competitive political environment, elected officials are willing to distort policies in favor of organized interests because the campaign contributions from these interests allow candidates to increase their popularity with voters. And finally, as voters have little political information, it is often simplest for them to evaluate the relative performance of their elected officials. The resulting 'yardstick competition' implies that there is little pressure on politicians to implement effective environmental instruments as long as other jurisdictions do not have successful programs of their own.

Once rational ignorance and the influence of groups are taken into account, the set of environmental policy instruments that is employed in political equilibrium can deviate significantly from the instruments citizens as voters (or, all the more, a social planner) would use. Nevertheless, there is little doubt that voter preferences constitute a significant constraint on political decision-making and public opinion is influential in setting policy. There is evidence that the sensitivity of voters to environmental issues has increased over the last decades resulting in environmental issues being considered as fairly important by many voters. On the other hand, there is also ample evidence that voters are less than enthusiastic about bearing high costs for better environmental quality. Faced with the trade-off between higher real individual income and the production of better environmental quality that largely is a public good, it is reasonable that in many cases voters care more about their economic short-term well being than the prospective environmental situation.

Voters also seem to prefer a policy of direct regulations and command and control measures to price incentives. There is evidence that pricing is not considered to be a fair allocation mechanism either as a mechanism to eliminate excess demand (Kahneman et al., 1986) nor in public good contexts. As regards the latter, Frey and Oberholzer-Gee (1996) document that willingness-to-pay is seen as the least fair of seven allocation mechanisms using a locally unwanted, but socially beneficial facility as their example. Moreover, there is considerable evidence that the introduction of economic incentives in one area can have negative consequences in others (Lepper and Greene, 1978; Frey, 1997). Such negative spillovers exist if pricing crowds out intrinsic motivation. This does not imply that price incentives fail to work but they become less effective, and there may be negative spillovers to other areas where no incentives for environmental protection exist. Altogether, these arguments contribute to explain why voters may be reluctant to accept effective environmental policies in general terms, and market based instruments particularly.

According to the public choice approach, alternative policy measures are supplied by politicians in the political market pursuing their own goals subject to various constraints. Politicians are hypothesized to have a self-interest in implementing specific instruments being either in line with their ideology or increasing their discretionary power or their personal income. In order to be re-elected they have to take into account voters' interests. The more binding the re-election constraint is, the less discretionary power the politicians have at their disposal in order to pursue their self-interest and the more they are linked to the demand side of the political process.

Given competition among alternative political parties and the re-election constraint being restrictive, politicians have to trade off benefits and costs (in terms of gains and losses in votes) when evaluating alternative policy measures. In political equilibrium, policies match the preferences of well-organized interests better than the preferences of more dispersed groups. In general, smaller groups are easier to organize than larger groups, and associations that find it less difficult to produce a mix of private and public goods ('selective incentives') are more likely to overcome the free-rider problem associated with interest group activities (Olson, 1965). If groups are not already organized it is unlikely that they will exercise decisive influence in any policy debate, whereas existing organizations can be counted on to exert considerable influence. In particular, producer interests (i.e., employers and employees) are better organized than consumers, and industry and business associations are more important players in the political game compared to environmental interest groups. By making campaign contributions and information available to politicians using them in order to attract additional voters, special interest groups can afford to be successful although their preferred policies are not in line with the preferences of the majority of voters.

The ability of groups to overcome free-rider problems is one of the determinants of the level of transfers to different groups. Another is the cost of transfers. The Chicago school of political economy emphasizes that political competition will ensure that the most efficient method of redistribution is chosen (Becker, 1983). If ecological taxes or tradable permits are in fact the most efficient means to allocate environmental resources, the Chicago school suggests that interest groups will prefer this form of transfers to other forms. Thus, given the will to reduce negative external effects with environmental policy, pricing schemes should be a politically attractive policy instrument.

However, the Chicago view of political economy, which emphasizes that lawmakers and interest groups seek efficient ways to make transfers, stands in stark contrast to the Virginia school, which emphasizes that politicians will use inefficient means of transfer if this allows them to hide the cost of redistribution. Tullock (1983), and Coate and Morris (1995) show that inefficient transfers will occur if voters have ex-post difficulty distinguishing efficient from inefficient policies and if they are uncertain if the elected officials work in their best interest. In many political situations, these assumptions appear to be fairly realistic. Thus, politicians favor policies whose costs are difficult to see. Benefits, on the other hand, should be highly visible. Consequently, it can be stated that environmental policies are less promising than alternative policy issues (as, e.g., employment policies), and regulation policies are more attractive than pricing instruments. Charging drivers, for example, the prices for road usage directly keeps the costs of using roads highly visible, reminding voters of the policy every time they stop at toll booths or look at their electronically generated charges. While the costs remain highly visible, the benefits of the policy — reduced road congestion and better environmental quality — are much less salient (Oberholzer-Gee and Weck-Hannemann, 2002).

Public choice theory applied to environmental politics generally suggests that direct control measures have better chances to be realized than incentive based instruments though the latter are more efficient. Both, a policy of command and control and incentive based instruments involve costs for reducing the emissions. In the case of taxes or tradable permits, however, the polluters have to pay for remaining emissions which under a policy of command and control is avoidable resulting in an additional rent (Buchanan and Tullock, 1975). Moreover, polluting industries may consider that with direct control measures there is some leeway for negotiations with the environmental protection agency. Polluting industries can make use of their informational advantage in arguing for less strict regulations and exceptions from the rule. Thus, taken together, there seem to be good reasons why regulated industries prefer command and control measures to pricing instruments provided that they are not successful to avoid any environmental regulation at all.

Besides politicians, officials in the public bureaucracy have a considerable influence in the political market by preparing and formulating alternative policy proposals. They also have to implement and to examine the policy measures adopted. According to public choice theory, public bureaucrats aim to increase their discretionary power and to weaken the budget constraint. In contrast to politicians, they are not faced with a re-election constraint. Their discretionary power arises out of the specific principal-agent relationship between the representatives in the political sector and public bureaucracy. They are expected to favor policy measures which have to be administered explicitly (providing them with discretionary power vis-à-vis government and the private sector) and as a result, they generally prefer direct control instruments and oppose the application of market based instruments in environmental policy.

Nevertheless, environmental taxes and tradable permits might be attractive means to seek for individual rents on the part of the relevant actors in the political debate. Generally, policy-makers favor instruments that weaken the government's budget constraint. In this respect, environmental taxes recommend themselves because they generate additional funding. Thus, besides regulatory measures also pricing instruments may well serve the self-interest of policy-makers provided that the additional resources are at the disposal of policy-makers themselves.

In recent years, economists and lawmakers have considered the option of linking the phasing in of environmental taxes to reductions in taxes on labor, a reform project that is often referred to as an ecological tax reform. If the revenues from environmental taxes were used to lower other taxes, it is theoretically possible to reduce the overall cost of transfers in an economy, thereby making such a pricing scheme politically more attractive. While there is little disagreement about the existence of a 'green' dividend — ecological taxes are generally expected to increase environmental quality — it is less clear if a 'blue' dividend exists, where 'blue' refers to a reduction in the overall distortions in the tax system and a subsequent increase in employment (for a survey of the double dividend debate see, e.g., Goulder, 1995).

Bovenberg and DeMooij (1994) show that environmental taxation can in fact reduce employment and economic welfare. Their argument, based on optimal taxation theory, is that "taxing a broad base will lead to less distortions than taxing a narrow base. If the environmental tax is ultimately borne by labor, taxing the narrow bases energy or CO_2 will lead to larger distortions than taxing the larger base labor." (Kirchgässner, 1998: 44).

Altogether, theoretical and empirical work does not support the idea that an ecological tax reform will bring about notable efficiency gains that help establish environmental taxes. Keeping in mind a political economy perspective, however, an ecological tax reform may still bring about additional benefits for two reasons. First, by definition, a narrower tax base allows citizens to more easily substitute away from the taxed activities, making tax increases less attractive from the perspective of a revenue-maximizing politician and keeping the size of government more limited (Brennan and Buchanan, 1980). Secondly, unlike taxes on labor, proportional (indirect) taxes have the advantage of not automatically increasing with labor productivity (Kirchgässner, 1998).

While these arguments may be appealing for voters, politicians are not attracted by ecological taxes for these reasons. Their concern is neither to tame *Leviathan* nor primarily to improve the natural environment. Rather, they may be concerned about the situation on the labor market and the reduction of the unemployment rate in order to weaken their re-election constraint or they are interested in taxes creating additional revenue at their discretionary disposal. Thus, in contrast to the previously dominant view in public choice theory, governments may argue in favor of environmental taxes and by this way aim at improving the environment but "for the wrong reasons" (Kirchgässner and Schneider, 2003).

In addition, if pricing revenues are returned to citizens, politicians can try to channel these funds toward their own constituencies. Pricing revenues could also be used to compensate those who lose when economic incentives are introduced. Well-organized groups can be expected to support pricing measures provided that the revenues are used to finance infrastructure and services being in their own interest. On the other hand, they are assumed to be less in favor of pricing measures given that the purpose is explicitly and exclusively to internalize external costs combined with lump sum transfers or a reduction of other taxes. In effect, this is an argument to target revenues from environmental taxes to projects that benefit polluters. There is some empirical evidence that taxes can be introduced if they are channeled back to those opposing the price measure. Kimenyi et al. (1990), for example, show for the US in general that, in comparison to general fund financing, earmarking leads to increased tax revenues. Hence, given the re-election constraint to be decisive, pricing instruments may even so have a chance if they are introduced in such a way that well-organized groups are benefited most and the costs are spread to less influential and latent interest groups. Earmarking of revenues in this case may be an essential feature to achieve the respective aim on the part of politicians and most powerful interest groups.

Beyond that, the opposition to environmental taxes by main polluters may be mitigated by accepting exceptions and tax allowances (Hahn, 1989). If emission taxes are fixed at a relatively low rate and thus avoidance costs in the case of emission standards exceed the tax burden, this solution is in effect favorable for polluters. If likewise exemptions are made for the most polluting sectors, e.g., the energy intensive producing industries in the case of CO_2 taxes (see, e.g., Ekins and Speck, 1999), this implies that the resistance of those producers who produce most emissions can be weakened. However, this also reduces the environmental impact of such a policy significantly.

Likewise, tradable permits may be implemented in such a way that those groups mostly affected get an additional rent (Hahn, 1989; Kirchgässner and Schneider, 2003). If the permits are auctioned, there is an additional revenue for the government which can be used either in their own interest or to the benefit of taxpayers or to the advantage of effectively lobbying interest groups. If, on the other hand, grand-fathering is used the existing firms get the pollution rights for free and are put in a position to sell them. Moreover, grand-fathering creates a barrier to entry against new firms because these have to pay for all the permits they need or the permit market may be so much restricted that no significant trade occurs and newcomers are kept away by this way. It follows that existing firms may well favor the grand-fathering of tradable permits. And indeed, according to Svendsen (1999), the position of private business interest groups seems to have changed in the United States from less advocating a command and control policy in favor of a grandfathered permit market.

Thus, all in all, the dominant interest groups are expected to orient their lobbying activities towards preventing any effective policy measures. As far as alternative environmental instruments are concerned they most likely accept direct control measures but, nevertheless, incentive based instruments may also have a chance to be implemented if the following conditions hold: the less pronounced the incentive effect of the pricing measures turns out (i.e., moderate changes in prices with only a limited incentive effect); the more likely it is for special interest groups to realize exceptions from the rule (e.g., when those groups particularly affected by these measures are exempted or at least admitted a reduced rate or a transitional arrangement); the more likely it is to shift the burden on to latent interest groups or groups without voting rights (as, e.g., foreigners); and if earmarking of the revenues ensures that there are not only costs but also benefits (e.g., when revenues from pricing instruments are earmarked to the use of maintaining and improving the infrastructure of services which benefits the producers, operators and users of the corresponding services).

Recently, another instrument that is also often labelled as a market-based instrument is increasingly used. Yet, voluntary agreements are in no way such an instrument but instead the main purpose of their support is to prevent the use of effective instruments of environmental policy. As Kirchgässner and Schneider (2003) emphasize, the only possibility to make voluntary agreements effective is to combine them from the beginning with the threat that the government will intervene if the negotiated results will not be reached. But, in this case the voluntary agreement is actually superfluous and just a kind of symbolic policy.

Also, in international environmental policy, the willingness to introduce market based instruments, such as internationally tradeable permits or 'joint implementation' or 'clean development mechanism' projects, might be of a more symbolic nature: in demanding to introduce such instruments of which it is obvious that the distributional problems bring about that their implementation has no real political chance may be an effective way to prevent the implementation of more effective and enforceable policy measures (Kirchgässner and Schneider, 2003).

Altogether, considering these new developments, the moderate increase in the use of economic instruments of environmental policy does not invalidate the arguments put forward by the public choice approach. There is still only limited support of the use of incentive based instruments, and their application in many respects deviates from the ideal therapy. The synopsis given by Kirchgässner and Schneider (2003) seems to be well targeted when they state that economic instruments, at best, "will be introduced for other (non-environmental) reasons and/or in a way which is not very helpful for the environment. But, on the other hand, it is a step in this direction and one might hope that over time citizens become more familiar with such instruments and their advantages which might — in the long run — increase their acceptance in the electorate."

One might also think about adequate institutional conditions contributing to improve the chance that incentive based instruments as the most efficient means in environmental policy have a better chance to be implemented in the political decision-making process. Referring to a process-oriented approach, it can be argued that the political process itself has to ensure that all relevant arguments have an equal chance to enter into the discussion resulting in efficiency to be reached endogenously, i.e., via the process and not via the evaluation of alternative outcomes. All the pros and cons have to enter in the political process without distortion. This is best guaranteed if voters have a direct say in political matters and can act as agenda setters as well as if the principle of fiscal equivalence and institutional congruence is realized. With the institutions of direct democracy and the right of initiative and institutional congruence it can be expected that politicians are forced to be more responsive to voters' interests than in a system of representative democracy with spillovers of external effects.

At the constitutional level the decision-makers do not know their specific individual position but the social consequences of alternative policy programs. This 'veil of uncertainty' enables that fair and efficient rules are adopted. However, in order to elicit such fair and efficient rules, the 'veil of uncertainty' has to be sufficiently strong. This might be approximated in the following ways (Kirchgässner, 1994): if rules are discussed with respect to uncertain future events, if individuals decide for their descendants, and if the time span is long enough between the decision about the rules and the coming into force of these rules. Consequently, the acceptance and implementation of pricing instruments in environmental policy might be furthered by assigning them as long-term general measures instead of discussing the issue in a predominantly short-term and concrete context.

HANNELORE WECK-HANNEMANN

REFERENCES

Baumol W.J. and Oates, W.E. (1971). "The use of standards and prices for the protection of the environment." *Swedish Journal of Economics*, 73: 42–54.

Becker, G.S. (1983). "A theory of competition among pressure groups for political influence." *The Quarterly Journal of Economics*, 98(3): 371–400.

Bommer, R. (1998). *Economic Integration and the Environment. A Political-Economic Perspective.* Cheltenham: Edward Elgar.

Bovenberg, A.L. and DeMooij, R.A. (1994). "Environmental levies and distortionary taxation." *American Economic Review*, 84: 1085–1089.

Brennan, G. and Buchanan, J.M. (1980). *The Power to Tax. Analytical Foundations of a Fiscal Constitution.* Cambridge, MA: Cambridge University Press.

Buchanan, J.M. and Tullock, G. (1975). "Polluters' profits and political response: direct controls versus taxes." *American Economic Review*, 65: 139–147.

Coase, R.H. (1960). "The problem of social cost." *Journal of Law and Economics*, 3: 1–44.

Coate, S. and Morris, S. (1995). "On the form of transfers in special interests." *Journal of Political Economy*, 103(6): 1210–1235.

Congleton, R.D. (ed.) (1996). *The Political Economy of Environmental Protection: Analysis and Evidence.* Ann Arbor: University of Michigan Press.

Dewees, D.N. (1983). "Instrument choice in environmental policy." *Economic Inquiry*, 21: 53–71.

Dijkstra, B.R. (1999). *The Political Economy of Environmental Policy.* Cheltenham: Edward Elgar.

Downing, P.B. (1991). "A political economy model of implementing pollution laws." *Journal of Environmental Economics and Management*, 8: 255–271.

Downs, A. (1957). *An Economic Theory of Democracy.* New York: Harper & Row.

Ekins, P. and Speck, S. (1999). "Competitiveness and exemptions from environmental taxes in Europe." *Environmental and Resource Economics*, 13: 369–396.

Frey, B.S. (1972). *Umweltökonomie*, 3rd edn. Göttingen: Vandenhoeck.

Frey, B.S. (1997). *Not Just for the Money. An Economic Theory of Personal Motivation.* Cheltenham/Brookfield: Edward Elgar.

Frey, B.S. and Oberholzer-Gee, F. (1996). "Fair siting procedures: an empirical analysis of their importance and characteristics." *Journal of Policy Analysis and Management*, 15: 353–376.

Frey, B.S. and Schneider, F. (1997). "Warum wird die Umweltökonomie kaum angewendet"? *Zeitschrift für Umweltpolitik*, 2: 153–170.

Frey, B.S. Schneider, F., and Pommerehne, W.W. (1985). "Economists' opinions on environmental policy instruments: analysis of a survey." *Journal of Environmental Economics and Management*, 12(1): 62–71.

Goulder, L.H. (1995). "Environmental taxation and the double dividend — a reader's guide." *International Tax and Public Finance*, 2: 157–183.

Hahn, R.W. (1989). "Economic prescriptions for environmental problems: how the patient followed the doctor's orders." *Journal of Economic Perspectives*, 3(2): 95–114.

Hahn, R.W. (1990). "The political economy of environmental regulation: towards a unifying framework." *Public Choice*, 65: 21–47.

Horbach, J. (1992). *Neue Politische Ökonomie und Umweltpolitik.* Frankfurt/Main: Fischer.

Kahneman, D., Knetsch, J., and Thaler, R. (1986). "Fairness as a constraint on profit seeking: entitlements in the market." *American Economic Review*, 76: 728–741.

Kimenyi, M.S., Lee, D.R., and Tollison, R.D. (1990). "Efficient lobbying and earmarked taxes." *Public Finance Quarterly*, 18(1): 104–113.

Kirchgässner, G. (1994). "Constitutional economics and its relevance for the evolution of rules." *Kyklos*, 47(3): 321–339.

Kirchgässner, G. (1998). "The double dividend debate: some comments from a politico-economic perspective." *Empirica*, 25(1): 37–49.

Kirchgässner, G. (1999). "International environmental policy: problems and possible solutions." *Aussenwirtschaft*, 54(2): 269–290.

Kirchgässner, G. and Schneider, F. (2003). "On the political economy of environmental policy." *Public Choice* (forthcoming).

Lepper, M. and Greene, D. (eds.) (1978). *The Hidden Costs of Reward: New Perspectives on the Psychology of Human Motivation.* New York: Erlbaum.

Oberholzer-Gee, F. and Weck-Hannemann, H. (2002). "Pricing road use: politico-economic and fairness considerations." *Transportation Research Part D* (forthcoming).

Olson, M. (1965). *The Logic of Collective Action.* Cambridge MA: Harvard University Press.

Pearson, M. (1995). "The political economy of implementing environmental taxes," in L. Bovenberg and S. Cnossen (eds.) *Public Economics and the Environment in an Imperfect World.* Boston; Kluwer, pp. 37–57.

Pigou, A.C. (1920). *The Economics of Welfare.* London: MacMillan.

Schulze, G.G. and Ursprung, H.W. (eds.) (2001). *International Environmental Economics — A Survey of the Issues.* Oxford: Oxford University Press.

Svendsen, G.T. (1999). "U.S. interest groups prefer emission trading: a new perspective." *Public Choice*, 101: 109–128.

Tullock, G. (1983). *Economics of Income Redistribution.* Boston: Kluwer.

Weck-Hannemann, H. (1994). "Politische ökonomie der umweltpolitik," in R. Bartel. and F. Hackl. (eds.) *Einführung in die Umweltökonomie.* München: Vahlen, pp. 101–117.

EXPERIMENTAL PUBLIC CHOICE

1. Introduction

A few decades ago, most economists believed that their discipline was non-experimental. Economic phenomena should be studied theoretically or empirically. The ideal paper was one where rigorous theory was tested using advanced econometric methods. The fact that the empirics were usually based on (often incomplete) field data only remotely related to the problem at hand was no problem: this is why we had econometrics.

Over the past decades, Economics has rapidly become an experimental science, however. It has become obvious to many that laboratory experiments provide the means to control conditions in a way that allows for a systematic test of economic theories. Contrary to econometric testing, laboratory testing allows one to systematically test essential elements of a theory. In addition, experiments can be used to explore potential paths of new research, in situations where no theory exists or where existing theory is shown to be inadequate. Finally, experiments have the advantage that they can be replicated, allowing for a systematic analysis of the robustness of the findings.

The use of laboratory experiments in public choice research has also increased rapidly in the last thirty years or so. At meetings of the various public choice societies, it has become very common to encounter experimental papers. This is no coincidence but has been actively solicited by the societies themselves. For example, it is a well-established tradition that the North American Public Choice Society organizes its yearly spring conference together with the Economic Science Association (the international society of experimental economists). The bylaws of the European Public Choice Society even explicitly state that *"The Society's interest is in theoretical rigor, empirical and experimental testing, and real world applications."*

The increased use of experiments in public choice is definitely an enrichment to this literature. Much of the literature on non-market decision-making is based on theoretical assumptions about individual behavior (see Schram, 2000) or on field data from elections or surveys that are not particularly tailored to answer the questions raised by the theory. In both cases, experiments provide a method that is complementary to the existing methods. Together with theory and empirics based on field data, experiments allow us to understand public choice phenomena in more depth.

Two types of experimental studies can be important for public choice. One group is concerned with individual behavior and motivations. Its conclusions with respect to individuals' motivations and preferences (Schram, 2000), or the role of emotions and bounded rationality (Bosman, 2001; Bosman and van Winden, 2001), for example, can have important consequences for the assumptions made in many public choice theories. This type of studies is not discussed in detail in this essay, however. A brief evaluation of their importance is given in the concluding section. A detailed discussion of their relevance to public choice can be found in Schram, 2000. Instead, this essay focuses on a second group of studies: those where experiments are used to analyze a number of traditional public choice topics.[1]

This essay is organized as follows. The next section briefly describes the experimental methodology. This is followed by four sections on experiments in public choice: public goods (section 3), voter turnout and participation games (section 4), rent seeking and lobbying (section 5), and spatial voting (section 6). A concluding discussion is presented in section 7.

2. Experimental Economics

In a laboratory experiment, behavior is studied in a controlled environment. Participants (in most cases university students) are invited to a computer laboratory, where they are asked to make decisions in a framework designed by the experimenter. Decisions are 'real,' e.g., in the sense that they have monetary consequences for the subjects. At the end of the experiment, they are paid in cash an amount that depends on their own decisions and (in many cases) on the decisions of other participants. An excellent description of what an experiment in economics entails and how one can set up an experiment is provided in Davis and Holt (1993).

Traditionally (e.g., Smith, 1994), one distinguishes the environment, institutions and behavior in an experiment. The environment refers to the structural characteristics of an economic problem, such as the number of agents, the information structure, preferences, endowments, cost structure, etc. According to Davis and Holt (1993), economists traditionally viewed economic problems almost exclusively in terms of these characteristics. Institutions refer to the rules governing the interaction of economic agents, such as the market or auction rules, or the government decision-making procedures. For a long time, it was argued that it is possible to control the environment and institutions in an experiment and to study behavior. By varying institutions, for example, one could investigate how they affect behavior.

Two *caveats* can be made with respect to this traditional distinction, however. First of all, one can argue that many non-experimental economists have considered the importance of institutions as well. The boom in institutional economics and game theory has highlighted the important effects they may have on behavior. Second, it is not obvious that one can control the environment completely. Especially preferences might be difficult to control in a laboratory. Though one tries to induce preferences by offering a payoff scheme, one cannot control individual preferences for other things than the own private earnings. Nevertheless, it is obvious that the laboratory allows for a much higher level of control than was possible before.

Experimental results can therefore carry much weight. The control in a laboratory allows one to address very specific research questions. For example, if we are interested in studying committee voting on two proposals under two different voting rules (see section 6), there is no better setting to study this than in an experiment where the only treatment variable is the voting rule. Keeping all other aspects of the problem constant (e.g., number of members, payoff to each member if either proposal is accepted, etc.) the environment is stripped of all the confounding elements we typically observe in the outside world. What remains is exactly what we want to study: the effect of the voting rule. If we combine an analysis along these lines with a theoretical analysis and an empirical analysis using field data, this will likely lead to a much more complete understanding of the problem at hand than we would be able to achieve without the laboratory data.

Of course there are also disadvantages related to using the experimental method. Many of theses are discussed in the standard texts in this field (Davis and Holt, 1993 or Kagel and Roth, 1995). Plott (1982) systematically discusses questions raised by economists about the validity of laboratory experiments. Here, we briefly discuss the issue of external validity, i.e., is the evidence obtained in a laboratory relevant for the 'outside world?'

Naturally, the external validity of an experiment depends on the experimental design. There is no reason why the external validity of all laboratory experiments *per se* should be doubted, however. Subjects participating in an experiment are real people. They are facing real monetary incentives that (in a carefully designed experiment) are salient. Hence, if we observe certain behavior in an experiment it is economic behavior.[2] Nevertheless, every experimental design should be critically assessed with respect to the structure and its relationship with the problem being studied. In general, a thorough theoretical analysis of the problem at hand is useful in this assessment.

3. Public Goods Experiments

Public goods experiments usually study voluntary, individual, contributions to a public good. Given the role that government plays in providing public goods and the possibility that government provision crowds out individual contributions, this is of obvious importance in public choice. It is therefore no surprise that one of the first major papers on this topic was published in the journal Public Choice (Isaac et al., 1984). Since then, studies on voluntary contributions to public goods have been a major part of the experimental literature.

The typical setup of a public goods experiment is as follows. Subjects are allocated into groups of size N (typically, N = 4 or 5). Each is given an endowment of 'tokens.' These must each be invested in either a 'private account' or a 'public account.' Each token in the private account gives a payoff A to the subject alone. Each token in the public account gives a payoff B to every participant in the group. Hence, an investment in the public account is a voluntary contribution to a pure public good. The interesting cases are where $B < A < NB$, because this implies that contributing nothing to the public good is a dominant strategy, whereas contributing all tokens is efficient. The relative payoff to the two accounts, A/B, gives the marginal rate of substitution (hereafter, mrs) between private and public account.[3]

Ledyard (1995) presents a first extensive survey of experiments of this type. Some important regularities listed in his survey are:

i) contributions to the public good start at a relatively high level (typically 40–60% of the endowments);

ii) with repetition, these contributions decrease to 0–30%; very often they do not decrease to zero, however (Isaac et al., 1994);

iii) the contribution levels are a decreasing function of the mrs.

To these regularities, one can add:

iv) contributions increase with group size (Isaac et al., 1994);

v) many subjects split their tokens across the two accounts, i.e., they don't contribute everything to one of the two accounts (Palfrey and Prisbrey, 1997; Brandts and Schram, 2001);

vi) there is considerable subject heterogeneity: systematic differences across subjects exist; some consistently contribute, some never do; others switch from contributing to not contributing (Palfrey and Prisbrey, 1997; Brandts and Schram, 2001);

vii) if group composition is held constant across periods, contributions get more concentrated in groups as the experiment moves on (Brandts and Schram, 2001).

The type of public goods experiments described is by far the type most often studied. The linear production function for public goods is easy for subjects to understand and provides an interesting tradeoff between private earnings and group welfare.[4] Over the last few years many extensions to the setup have been studied, often in an attempt to study other regarding preferences or reciprocity (see Schram, 2000, or Fehr and Gächter, 2000a, for an overview). These extensions include the study of situations where there is no efficiency gain to be made from cooperation (Palfrey and Prisbrey, 1997; Brandts and Schram, 2001); cross-cultural comparisons (Cason et al., 2002; Brandts et al., 2002); framing (Andreoni, 1995a; Sonnemans et al., 1998); and the effect of allowing costly punishment of free riders (Fehr and Gächter, 2000b).

The bottom line in this whole body of literature is that subjects in public goods experiments contribute voluntarily to the public goods, to a much larger extent than the selfish individually rational prediction of free riding would have them do. In addition, contributions cannot simply be attributed to erratic behavior of the subjects (Andreoni, 1995b; Brandts et al., 2002). On the other hand, contributions tend to be lower than the efficient level, many subjects do free ride and contributions decrease with repetition. There is an ongoing discussion about what motivates subjects to behave in this way.

From a public choice point of view, the relationship between group size and free riding is of interest. Mancur Olsen's idea that free riding will increase with group size is not supported by the experimental data. On the contrary, contributions increase with group size (see regularity iv, above).[5] Isaac et al. (1994) show that it is not group size *per se* that matters, but the interaction between group size and mrs. Keeping the mrs constant, the 'pure' group size effect is positive (if the mrs is large enough). At this stage, it is difficult to understand this apparent anomaly. One possibility is that it is related to the gains from cooperation (Brandts and Schram, 2001). For any given mrs, a specific number k of contributors is needed to make them better off (as a subgroup) than if none of them would contribute. The larger the group, the more likely it is that there will be k contributors. From an individual's point of view, in a large group it is less likely that he will be a 'sucker', for whom the cooperative gain is smaller than the individual contribution to the public good.

4. Voter Turnout as a Participation Game

The paradox of voter turnout has been the subject of academic debate for decades (for an early survey, see Schram, 1991). The debate probably started with Downs' (1957) formulation of the problem. He notes that, due to the low probability of being decisive, the expected benefits from voting in a large-scale election are generally outweighed by the cost of the act. Nevertheless a very large number of voters actually turns out to vote in general elections. Many theoretical and empirical papers have been published trying to explain the paradox, but only few rational choice models have been developed that show that turning out to vote might sometimes be rational in an instrumental sense (see Ledyard, 1984, or Schram, 1991, and the references given there).

Palfrey and Rosenthal (1983) model the turnout problem as a participation game and study it game-theoretically. In this game, there are two or more teams. Everyone has to make a private decision that is beneficial to every member in one's own team and harmful to members of other teams. The decision is whether or not to 'participate' in an action, where participation is costly. Palfrey and Rosenthal show that in many cases, Nash-equilibria with positive levels of participation exist. Note that there are two types of conflicts in a participation game. Within the group, there is an incentive to free-ride on the costly participation of other group members. Between groups, there is an incentive to compete and out-vote the other group. Note the difference with the incentives in the public goods games of the previous section, were only the free-riding incentive exists.

It is difficult to study voter turnout using field data.[6] Participation games provide a structure to study this decision experimentally, however. This was first done by Bornstein (1992) and Schram and Sonnemans (1996a,b). Here, we shall describe the experiment used in the latter two papers. In the experiments, subjects are split in two groups of 6 individuals. Each subject had to decide whether or not to buy a token at a given price. The number of tokens bought in each group determines the payoffs. There were two payoff schedules, representing a winner-takes-all election (*WIN*) and proportional representation (*PR*). In *WIN*, each member of the group that bought the most tokens (won the elections) received a fixed sum and the payoff for the other group was zero (with ties broken randomly). In *PR* the payoff to any group-member was proportional to the relative turnout of the groups. In addition to these experiments, two *WIN* sessions were run with groups of 14 subjects and two where one group consisted of 8 and the other of 6 participants. The results obtained show:

i) Nash equilibrium is a poor predictor of turnout;
ii) participation is higher in winner-takes-all than in proportional representation; this is in line with the comparative statics of the pure strategy equilibria;
iii) participation is higher with repetition in fixed groups;
iv) participation increases substantially after five minutes of free communication;
v) there is no significant effect of group size on relative turnout;
vi) when groups size is unequal, relative turnout is higher in the smaller group.

To date, there have not been many other published experimental studies on participation games. A number of recent working papers are dedicated to these games, however. These include Cason and Mui (2001) on the role of participation costs and uncertainty with respect to the benefits of voting. They find that increasing costs cause decreasing participation rates. Uncertainty has mixed effects, depending on which subjects are facing it.

With different co-authors, Großer studies three extensions to the participation games: (1) the introduction of group size uncertainty (Großer and Kugler, 2002); (2) the endogenization of policy (and group) formation (Großer et al., 2002); and (3) the introduction of information about the turnout decision of some other voter (Großer and Schram, 2002). The results in these papers include:

vii) uncertainty about group size decreases turnout;
viii) a mix of allied and floating voters in a group yields higher turnout rates than a situation without allied voters;
ix) endogenous political ties between voters and candidates are observed, i.e., over a series of elections, candidates design policies for specific groups of voters who reward them with their votes;
x) higher turnout rates are observed when subjects are informed about the decision of other participants.

The bottom line in the research on participation games is that (as in elections) traditional theory is a bad predictor of turnout. Participants often do react to a change of incentives (e.g., an increase in the costs of voting) in a predictable way, however. Moreover, the results of the recent experiments on group size uncertainty and information about other voters show how experimentation might be useful in a further analysis of the turnout paradox. Another interesting development is that some of the results observed in participation games can be explained in a quantal response framework McKelvey and Palfrey (1995). Goeree and Holt (2000) show that the results reported in Schram and Sonnemans (1996a,b) are consistent with a quantal response equilibrium.

5. Rent-seeking and Lobbying

van Winden (1999, 2002) provides detailed surveys of the experimental literature on lobbying. He distinguishes three types of studies that are relevant in this respect: experiments on common agency problems, signaling models and rent seeking. We will briefly discuss the first two categories (see van Winden's surveys for more details) and elaborate a bit on the rent seeking experiments.

Common agency experiments (see Kirchsteiger and Prat, 2000) study the effect of campaign contributions in exchange for favorable policies. Lobbyists compete in offering a politician a 'contribution schedule' which depicts the (possible) campaign contribution as a function of potential policies. The politician chooses a policy and collects the contribution. One interesting experimental result is that lobbyists tend to focus on the most preferred result and do not offer significant contributions for less preferred alternatives.

In signaling games, the focus is on the strategic transmission of (relevant) information from a lobbyist to a politician. This (credibly) assumes that the lobbyist may have information that is relevant to the politician, when making his decision. Of course, there may be an incentive for the lobbyist to transmit untruthful information. The experiments of Potters and van Winden (1992) study this environment. Though their results cast doubt on the predictive power of the theoretical literature in this field, they do find that mutual beneficial (costly) transmission of information takes place from the lobbyist to the politician.

In the experimental rent seeking literature the role of the policy maker is replaced by some commonly known mechanism. The focus is on the competition between lobbyists. They typically compete for a 'prize' (rent) by placing bids. The mechanisms used are typically that the highest bid wins the prize or that the probability of winning the prize is proportional to the (relative) bid. An important characteristic of this setup is that all bids are irreversible (like in an all-pay auction). This yields possible inefficiencies (overdissipation) in the lobbying process, because the sum of the bids may be higher than the value of the prize.

The main experimental studies on rent-seeking are Millner and Pratt (1989), Davis and Reilly (1998), Potters et al. (1998), and Weimann et al. (2000). Here, we will describe the experiments in Potters et al. The mechanism used in this study to determine a winner is part of the experimental design, which distinguishes perfectly and imperfectly discriminating contests. This distinction allows the authors to compare a situation where the equilibrium strategies yield positive probabilities of overdissipation (i.e., inefficiency), with one where the probability of overdissipation is zero. In other words, the equilibrium in one experimental treatment attributes a positive probability to the event that the sum of the bids is higher than the prize, whereas another attributes zero probability to this event. The main results are:

i) the (Nash) equilibrium predictions are not supported;
ii) overdissipation is more likely when theory predicts that it will be. In other words, the point predictions derived from game theory are rejected but the predicted comparative statics are supported;
iii) subjects 'learn' to play more according to theory as they gain more experience through repetition over rounds.

The bottom line in this line of research is that only limited support for the theoretical literature on lobbying is found. This may be due to the fact that some subjects do play in line with theory, whereas others do not (Potters et al., 1998), yielding an aggregate outcome that does not provide support.

6. Spatial Voting Experiments

Two types of voting experiments can be observed in the literature, both starting in the late seventies and early eighties at the California Institute of Technology. Both are basically experiments on spatial voting models, one focussing on committee voting, and the other on the median voter model.[7] An early survey of these experiments is presented in McKelvey en Ordeshook (1990). Because many of these studies were undertaken more than a decade ago, this survey still covers many of the important experiments in this field. A more recent survey is included in van Winden and Bosman (1996).

In the committee voting experiments, the typical setup is one, where a committee of n members has to choose a point (x,y) on some two dimensional issue space. Each committee member is assigned a personal ideal point in this space and the individual payoffs are a (declining) function of the distance between this ideal point and the point chosen by the committee. A commonly known decision-making institution determines how a committee decision is determined. These institutions describe, e.g., the agenda setting, the communication and the majority rule used. Examples of this type of experiment include Berl et al. (1976), Fiorina and Plott (1978), Hoffman and Plott (1983), and Eavey and Miller (1984), who argue that this model can be considered to be a test of the Niskanen (1971) model of bureaucracy. The conclusions include:

i) if decisions are made by simple majority rule and a Condorcet winner exists, the committee decision is close to that outcome;

ii) if decisions are made by simple majority rule and no Condorcet winner exists, stable outcomes are often observed, though as yet no theoretical predictions for these outcomes are known;

iii) communication does not have a large effect on the outcome;

iv) the Niskanen model does not find support, in the sense that an agenda setter (bureaucrat) does not manage to make his ideal point the committee decision.

The median voter experiments study the interaction between political candidates and voters. The latter are given an ideal point in a one- or two dimensional policy space. Once again, their payoffs are a declining function of the distance between the chosen point and the ideal point. Candidates choose a position in the policy space, hoping to attract voters. If elected, their position is chosen and determines the voters' payoffs. Candidates' payoffs are positively related to the number of votes they receive (e.g., the winner receives a fixed amount and the loser receives nothing). Examples of this type of experiments include Collier et al. (1987), Williams (1991), McKelvey en Ordeshook (1993), and Olson and Morton (1994). The conclusions include:

i) with complete information on ideal points and payoffs, the median voter model finds support;

ii) even with incomplete information, there is convergence to the median, when it exists;

iii) costly information on candidates' positions does not affect the rate of convergence to the median.

The bottom line of both types of voting experiments is that quite some support for theoretical predictions (Condorcet winner, median voter) is observed. Moreover, stable outcomes when no Condorcet winner exists and convergence to the median voter even in case of incomplete information indicate that the voting mechanism can lead to even more robust results than predicted by theory.

7. Concluding Discussion

As mentioned in the introduction, there is a large body of experimental literature that is not directly related to public choice topics, but still very relevant for the analysis of these topics. This is the literature on individual motivations and (bounded) rationality. Most of public choice theory is based on the *homo economicus*, who pursues his selfish preferences in a perfectly rational way.

Both of these elements have been questioned, based on experimental results (see Schram, 2000, for an overview). Many authors argue that preferences are only selfish in certain circumstances. Instead, it is argued that other regarding preferences such as altruism or fairness can be widely observed for many subjects. This observation has led to theoretical models incorporating these preferences (e.g., Fehr and Schmidt, 1999; Bolton and Ockenfels, 2000). By now, there is enough material to try to incorporate other regarding preferences in some of the traditional public choice theory.

The assumption of perfect rationality also needs to be adjusted. It is becoming increasingly clear that emotions (Bosman, 2001) and limits to rationality (Camerer, 1998) can have major impacts on behavior. In this case it is less clear how existing models could be adapted to accommodate these results, however. As yet, there is no model of bounded rationality that seems to be applicable. On the other hand, these results do create space for theories based on 'reasonable' behavioral assumptions other than perfect rationality.

The examples given in this essay show that a variety of typical public choice topics has been studied in a laboratory environment. In some cases, this has given support to existing theories and ideas (e.g., the median voter model). In others (e.g., rents seeking), it raises doubts about the validity of the theory in its present form. In yet other cases (e.g., the turnout paradox), the experimental results can give hints as to ways to develop the theory further. In this way, experimental studies have proven to be a welcome addition to the public choice literature.

ARTHUR J.H.C. SCHRAM

NOTES

1. A third group of studies observed is that of 'political engineering:' experiments are used to help design political systems. See Riedl and van Winden (2001) for an example.
2. It is, of course, possible that the behavior observed is specific to the particular kind of subject in the experiment (usually students). This is a problem related to common experimental procedures as opposed to the experimental method as such, however.
3. It is also quite common to refer to B/A (i.e., 1/mrs) as the marginal per capita return (mpcr); see Isaac et al., 1984.
4. Another widely studied case is where the production technology uses a threshold: a minimum amount of contributions needs to be collected for the public good to be produced. These 'step-level public goods' are extensively studied in Offerman et al. (1996). A meta-analysis is given by Croson and Marks (2000).
5. On the other hand, Offerman et al. (1996) show that voluntary contributions decrease with group size in a step-level public goods game.
6. Güth and Weck-Hanneman (1997) and Blais and Young (1999) use field experiments to study the paradox of voter turnout. In both cases, the turnout decision of a group of students in a real election is monitored. Güth and Weck-Hannemann study the value of a vote by offering a payment in return for abstention. Blais and Young study the effect of being exposed to a presentation about the turnout paradox.
7. A limited number of other topics related to voting have been studied experimentally. These include vote trading (McKelvey and Ordeshook, 1980), voting on jury decisions (McKelvey and Palfrey, 1998), voting to prevent public bads (Sutter, 1999), and the aggregation of information through elections (Wit, 1997).

REFERENCES

Andreoni, J. (1995a). "Warm-glow versus cold-prickle: the effects of positive and negative framing on cooperation in experiments." *Quarterly Journal of Economics*, 110: 1–22.

Andreoni, J. (1995b). "Cooperation in public-goods experiments: kindness or confusion"? *American Economic Review*, 892: 891–904.

Berl, J., McKelvey, R., Ordeshook, P., and Winer, M. (1976). "An experimental test of the core in a simple n-person cooperative non-side payment game." *Journal of Conflict Resolution*, 20: 453–479.

Blais, A. and Young, R. (1999). "Why do people vote? An experiment in rationality." *Public Choice*, 99: 39–55.

Bolton, G. and Ockenfels, A. (2000). "ERC: a theory of equity, reciprocity and competition." *American Economic Review*, 90: 166–193.

Bosman, R. (2001). Emotions and economic behavior. PhD-thesis, University of Amsterdam.

Bosman, R. and van Winden, F. (2001). "Emotional hazard in a power-to-take experiment." *Economic Journal*, 112: 147–169.

Bornstein, G. (1992). "The free-rider problem in intergroup conflicts over step-level and continuous public goods." *Journal of Personality and Social Psychology*, 62: 597–606.

Brandts, J. and Schram, A. (2001). "Cooperation and noise in public goods experiments: applying the contribution function approach." *Journal of Public Economics*, 79: 399–427.

Brandts, J., Saijo, T., and Schram, A.J.H.C. (2002). "A four country comparison of spite and cooperation in public goods games," mimeo, University of Amsterdam.

Camerer, C. (1998). "Bounded rationality in individual decision making." *Experimental Economics*, 1: 163–183.

Cason, T., Saijo, T., and Yamato, T. (2002). "Voluntary participation and spite in public good provision experiments: an international comparison." *Experimental Economics* (forthcoming).

Cason, T., and Mui, V. (2001). "Uncertainty and resistance to reform in laboratory participation games," mimeo, Purdue University.

Collier, K., McKelvey, R., Ordeshook, P., and Williams, K. (1987). "Retrospective voting: an experimental study." *Public Choice*, 53: 101–130.

Croson, R.T.A. and Marks, M.B. (2000). "Step returns in threshold public goods: a meta- and experimental analysis." *Experimental Economics*, 1: 239–259.

Davis, D.D. en Holt, C.A. (1993). *Experimental Economics*. Princeton: Princeton University Press.

Davis, D.D. and Reilly, R.J. (1998). "Do too many cooks always spoil the stew? An experimental analysis of rent-seeking and the role of a strategic buyer." *Public Choice*, 95: 89–115.

Downs, A. (1957). *An Economic Theory of Democracy*. New York: Harper and Row.

Eavey, C. and Miller, G. (1984). "Fairness in majority rule games with a core." *American Journal of Political Science*, 28(3): 570–586.

Fehr, E. and Gächter, S. (2000a). "Fairness and retaliation." *Journal of Economic Perspectives*, 14: 159–181.

Fehr, E. and Gächter, S. (2000b). "Cooperation and punishment in public goods experiments." *American Economic Review*, 90: 980–994.

Fehr, E. and Schmidt, K.M. (1999). "A theory of fairness, competition and cooperation." *Quarterly Journal of Economics*, 114: 817–868.

Fiorina, M. and Plott, Ch. (1978). "Committee decisions under majority rule: an experimental study." *American Political Science Review*, 72: 575–598.

Goeree, J. and Holt, Ch. (2000). "An explanation of anomalous behavior in binary-choice games: entry, voting, public goods, and the volunteers' dilemma," mimeo, University of Virginia.

Großer, J. and Kugler, T. (2002). "The impact of group size uncertainty on voter turnout—an experiment on a 'standard' and 'modified' participation game," mimeo, University of Amsterdam.

Großer, J., Elberfeld, W., and Giertz, T. (2002). "An experimental study of the polity game," mimeo, University of Amsterdam.

Großer, J. and Schram, A. (2002). "The influence of neighborhood information exchange on voter turnout — an experimental study of a modified participation game," mimeo, University of Amsterdam.

Güth, W. and Weck-Hannemann, H. (1997). "Do people care about democracy? An experiment exploring the value of voting rights." *Public Choice*, 91: 27–47.

Hoffman, E. and Plott, Ch. (1983). "Pre-meeting discussions and the possibility of coalition-breaking procedures in majority rule committees." *Public Choice*, 40: 421–439.

Isaac, R.M., Walker, J., and Thomas, S. (1984). "Divergent evidence on free riding: an experimental examination of possible explanations." *Public Choice*, 43(1): 113–149.

Isaac, R.M., Walker, J., and Williams, A. (1994). "Group size and the voluntary provision of public goods: experimental evidence utilizing large groups." *Journal of Public Economics*, 54: 1–36.

Kirchsteiger, G. and Prat, A. (2001). "Inefficient equilibria in lobbying." *Journal of Public Economics*, 82(3): 349–375.

Ledyard, J. (1984). "The pure theory of large two-candidate elections." *Public Choice*, 44: 7–41.

Ledyard, J. (1995). "Public goods: a survey of experimental research," in J. Kagel and A. Roth (eds.), *The Handbook of Experimental Economics*. Princeton University Press, pp. 111–194.

Kagel, J.H. and Roth, A.E. (eds.) (1995). "*The Handbook of Experimental Economics*." Princeton: Princeton University Press.

McKelvey R. en Ordeshook, P. (1980). "Vote trading: an experimental study." *Public Choice*, 35(2): 151–184.

McKelvey R. en Ordeshook, P. (1990). "A decade of experimental research on spatial models of elections and committees," in J.M. Enlow and M.J. Hinich (eds.) *Readings in the Spatial Theory of Voting*. Cambridge, England: Cambridge University Press, pp. 99–144.

McKelvey en Ordeshook (1993). "Information and elections: retrospective voting and rational expectations," in D. Kinder and T. Palfrey (eds.) *Experimental Foundations of Political Science*. The University of Michigan Press, pp. 333–362.

McKelvey, R. en Palfrey, T. (1998). "An experimental study of jury decisions," Discussion Paper, California Institute of Technology.

McKelvey, R. and Palfrey, T. (1995). "Quantal response equilibria in normal form games." *Games and Economics Behavior*, 7: 6–38.

Millner, E.L. and Pratt, M.D. (1989). "An experimental investigation of efficient rent-seeking." *Public Choice*, 62: 139–151.

Niskanen, W. (1971). *Bureaucracy and Representative Government*. Aldine-Atherton.

Offerman, T., Sonnemans, J., and Schram, A. (1996). "Value orientations, expectations, and voluntary contributions in public goods." *Economic Journal*, 106: 817–845.

Olson, M. (1965). *The Logic of Collective Action*. Cambridge: Harvard University Press.

Olson, M. and Morton, R. (1994). "Entry in spatial competition and strategic uncertainty," Discussion Paper, Tinbergen Institute, (TI 94-123), University of Amsterdam.

Palfrey, T.R. and Prisbrey, J.E. (1997). "Anomalous behavior in linear public goods experiments: how much and why?" *American Economic Review*, 87: 829–846.

Palfrey, T.R. and Rosenthal, H. (1983). "A strategic calculus of voting." *Public Choice*, 41: 7–53.

Plott, C.R. (1982). "Industrial organization theory and experimental economics." *Journal of Economic Literature*, 20: 1485–1587.

Potters, J., de Vries, C.G., and van Winden, F. (1998). "An experimental examination of rational rent-seeking." *European Journal of Political Economy*, 14: 783–800.

Potters, J., and van Winden, F. (1992). "Lobbying and asymmetric information." *Public Choice*, 74: 269–292.

Riedl, Arno and van Winden, Frans A.A.M. (2001). "Does the wage tax system cause budget deficits?" *Public Choice*, 109: 371–394.

Schram, A.J.H.C. (1991). *Voter Behavior in Economic Perspective*. Heidelberg: Springer Verlag.

Schram, A. (2000). "Sorting out the seeking: rents and individual motivation." *Public Choice*, 103: 231–258.

Schram, A. and Sonnemans, J. (1996a). "Voter turnout as a participation game: an experimental investigation." *International Journal of Game Theory*, 25: 385–406.

Schram, A. and Sonnemans, J. (1996b). "Why people vote: experimental evidence." *Journal of Economic Psychology*, 17: 417–442.

Smith, V.L. (1994). "Economics in the laboratory." *Journal of Economic Perspectives*, 8: 113–131.

Sonnemans, J., Schram, A., and Offerman, T. (1998). "Public good provision and public bad prevention: the effect of framing." *Journal of Economic Behavior and Organization*, 34: 143–161.

Sutter, M. (1999). "Public bad prevention by majority voting on redistribution — experimental evidence," mimeo, University of Innsbruck.

Weimann, J., Yang, C-L., and Vogt, C. (2000). "An experiment on sequential rent-seeking." *Journal of Economic Behavior and Organization*, 41: 405–426.

Williams, K. (1991). "Candidate convergence and information costs in spatial elections: an experimental analysis," in T. Palfrey (ed.) *Laboratory Research in Political Economy*. The University of Michigan Press, pp. 113–135.

van Winden, F. (1999). "On the economic theory of interest groups: towards a group frame of reference in political economics." *Public Choice*, 100: 1–29.

van Winden, F. (2003). "Experimental investigation of collective action." in S. Winer and H. Shibate (eds.) *Political Economy and Public Finance: The Role of Political Economy in the Theory and Practice of Public Economics*. Edward Elgar.

van Winden, F. and Bosman, R. (1996). "Experimental research in public economics," in *Experiments in Economics — Experimente in der Ökonomie*. Ökonomie und Gesellschaft, Jahrbuch 13, Campus Verlag, Frankfurt.

Wit, J. (1997). Dynamics and information aggregation in elections and markets. PhD-thesis, University of Amsterdam.

G

GORDON TULLOCK AT FOUR SCORE YEARS: AN EVALUATION

1. Biographical Details

Gordon Tullock was born in Rockford, Illinois on February 16, 1922, four score years ago. His father, George was a hardy Midwesterner of Scottish ancestry, his mother, Helen, was of equally hardy Pennsylvania Dutch stock. He obtained his basic education in the public schools of that city, displaying from early childhood a superior intellectual ability that clearly distinguished him from his peers. In 1940, Tullock left for the School of Law at the University of Chicago to combine a two-year program of undergraduate courses with a four-year formal law program. In fact, he completed the initial two-year program in a single year.

His law school program was interrupted by his being drafted into military service as an infantry rifleman in 1943, but not before he had all but completed a one semester course in economics taught by Henry Simons. This course was to be Tullock's only formal exposure to economics, a fact that no doubt enhanced rather than hindered his future success in contributing highly original ideas in that discipline.

Tullock served in the US military until shortly after the end of hostilities, returning to civilian life in December 1945. He took part in the Normandy landings on D-Day + 7 as a member of the Ninth Infantry. His life almost certainly was spared by the good fortune of his being left behind at division headquarters to defend three anti-tank guns. The original members of the Ninth Infantry were decimated on their hard-fought route across France and into Germany.

Following behind, Tullock eventually would cross the Rhine, he claims, while still asleep. Ultimately, he would end up in the Russian sector. Although Tullock modestly dismisses his wartime service as uneventful, this can only be with the advantage of hindsight. Participation in a major land war as part of 'the poor bloody infantry' is never without the gravest of risks.

Following this three-year wartime interruption, Tullock returned to Chicago and obtained a *Juris Doctor* degree from the Chicago Law School in 1947. He failed to remit the $5 payment required by the University and thus never received a baccalaureate degree.

His initial career, as an attorney with a small but prestigious downtown Chicago law firm, was controversial and, perhaps, mercifully brief. During his five-month tenure, Tullock handled two cases. The first case he won when he was expected to lose, and only after one of the partners in his firm had advised his client not to pursue the matter. The second case he lost when he should have won and he was admonished by the court for his poor performance (Brady and Tollison, 1991, 1994, 2). Fortunately for the world of ideas, these events persuaded him to seek out an alternative career.

Prior to graduation, Tullock had passed the Foreign Service Examination. He joined the Foreign Service in Fall 1947 and received an assignment as vice consul in Tientsin, China. This two-year assignment included the Communist takeover in 1948. Following Tullock's return to the United States, the Department of State dispatched him to Yale University (1949–1951) and then to Cornell University (1951–1952) for advanced study of the Chinese language.

In late 1952, he joined the 'Mainland China' section of the Consulate General in Hong Kong. Some nine months later he was reassigned to the political section of the U.S. Embassy in Korea. Tullock returned to the United States in January 1955, where he was assigned to the State Department's Office of Intelligence and Research in Washington. He resigned from the Foreign Service in Fall 1956.

Over the next two years, Tullock held several positions, including most notably that of research director of the Princeton Panel, a small subsidiary of the Gallup organization in Princeton. Essentially, he was in transition, marking time until he was ready to make a bid for entry into academia.

Unusually, Tullock had already published in leading economics journals articles on hyperinflation and monetary cycles in China and on the Korean monetary and fiscal system even during his diplomatic service, thus whetting his own appetite for an academic career and signaling an unusual facility for observing his environment as the basis for creative thinking. Furthermore, he had read and had been intellectually excited by the writings of such scholars as Joseph Schumpeter (1942), Duncan Black (1948) and Anthony Downs (1957), scholarship that provided the basis for reintegrating economics with political science within a strictly rational choice framework. In short, Tullock was ready to play a significant role in extending the empire of economics into the territory of contiguous disciplines.

In Fall 1958, at age 36, he accepted a one-year postdoctoral fellowship at the Thomas Jefferson Center for Political Economy at the University of Virginia. Still a relatively unknown quantity at that time, Tullock nevertheless brought with him to the Center two indispensable assets, namely a brilliant and inquiring, if still-unfocused, intellect and an unbounded enthusiasm for his adopted discipline of political economy. Quickly he forged a bond with the Director of the Center, James M. Buchanan, a bond that would result in some of the most original and important political-economic scholarship of the mid-twentieth century.

His fellowship year at the Center was productive, resulting in an important publication on the problem of majority voting (Tullock, 1959). In Fall 1959, Tullock was appointed as Assistant Professor in the Department of International Studies at the University of South Carolina. Publications continued to flow (Tullock, 1961a,b) while Tullock crafted a seminal draft paper entitled 'An Economic Theory of Constitutions' (Tullock, 1959) that would become the fulcrum for *The Calculus of Consent* (Buchanan and Tullock, 1962).

On this basis, Tullock quickly advanced to the rank of Associate Professor before returning to the University of Virginia, and renewing his relationship with James Buchanan, in February 1962, just as the University of Michigan Press was publishing their seminal book, *The Calculus of Consent*. In 1966, Tullock edited and published the first issue of *Papers on Non-Market Decision Making*, the precursor to *Public Choice*. Between 1962 and 1967, Tullock published innovative books on bureaucracy (Tullock, 1965), on method (Tullock, 1966) and on public choice (Tullock, 1967a) as well as a rising volume of scholarly papers that earned him international recognition as a major scholar.

Despite this distinguished resume, Tullock would be denied promotion to Full Professor of Economics on three consecutive occasions by a politically hostile and fundamentally unscholarly University administration. In Fall 1967, Buchanan protested these negative decisions by resigning to take up a position at the University of California at Los Angeles. Tullock also resigned to become Professor of Economics and Political Science at Rice University. With Ronald Coase having resigned for similar reasons in 1964 to take up a position at the University of Chicago, it appeared that the nascent Virginia School of Political Economy might have been deliberately nipped in the bud by the left-leaning administration of the University of Virginia.

As a result of a successful initiative by Charles J. Goetz, the University of Virginia plot failed. Goetz succeeded in attracting Tullock to Virginia Polytechnic Institute and State University in Blacksburg as Professor of Economics and Public Choice in Fall 1968. Goetz and Tullock immediately established the *Center for Studies in Public Choice* in 1968, as the basis for promoting scholarship in the field and as a means of attracting James Buchanan to join them at VPI. This initiative bore fruit in 1969, when James Buchanan joined the VPI faculty and assumed the General Directorship of the Center, which was immediately renamed as the *Center for Study of Public Choice*. Simultaneously, Tullock renamed his journal *Public Choice* and the new sub-discipline set down fruitful roots in the foothills of the Appalachian Mountains.

Henceforth, Tullock would never again look back. Over the next one-third of a century he forged for himself a reputation as a brilliant entrepreneurial scholar and a formidable debater. To this day he refuses to rest on well-earned laurels as a Founding Father of three sub-disciplines of economics, namely public choice, law and economics and bio-economics.

Universities have recognized his contributions by appointing him to a sequence of Distinguished Chairs (VPI & SU 1972–1983, George Mason University 1983–1987 and 1999–, and the University of Arizona 1987–1999). Professional associations have honored him by electing him to their presidencies (Public Choice, the Southern Economic Association, the Western Economic Association, the International Bio-Economics Society, the Atlantic Economic Society and the Association for Free Enterprise Education). In 1992, an Honorary Doctorate of Laws was conferred on him by the University of Chicago, in 1996 he was elected to the American Political Science Review Hall of Fame and in 1998 he was recognized as a Distinguished Fellow of the American Economic Association. These awards and honors reflect powerful entrepreneurial contributions across three major scholarly disciplines.

2. A Natural Economist?

James Buchanan has described Gordon Tullock as a *natural economist*, where natural is defined as having "intrinsic talents that emerge independently of professional training, education, and experience" (Buchanan, 1987, 9). A natural economist, therefore, "is someone who more or less consciously thinks like an economist" (*ibid.*, 9). In Buchanan's judgment, there are very few such natural economists and most of those who claim competence in economics as a discipline are not themselves natural. Buchanan identifies Gary Becker and Armen Alchian along with Gordon Tullock as prominent members of the rare natural economist species.

Buchanan recognizes that all economists of repute rely upon the rational choice model as the basis for analyzing the market interactions of human beings. Human beings are depicted as self-interested, utility maximizing agents for whom social interchange is initiated and exists simply as a preferred alternative to isolated action. Even though the large majority of economists do not fully endorse this model as an accurate depiction of individuals in society, they utilize it in market analysis on an 'as-if' basis.

Yet many of them waver or object when confronted with extending the rational choice model to the analysis of non-market behavior especially, one might conjecture, prior to Tullock's successful contributions in the 1960s. The behavior of such agents as politicians, voters, bureaucrats, judges, preachers, research scholars, family members, criminals, revolutionaries, terrorists and media anchors, they argue, cannot be effectively captured in terms of the rational self-interest model. The natural economist has no such inhibitions.

In this perspective of Tullock's work, individuals exist as isolated islands in an ocean of exchange, solipsist in vision and poised irreversibly on the edge of the jungle (Rowley, 1987a, 20). Because the natural economist is imbued comprehensively with a Hobbesian vision of the world, he cannot comprehend the contractarian promise expounded by Hume, Locke and the young John Stuart Mill. He cannot model man as rising above his narrow self-seeking instincts.

George Stigler once suggested that a major difference between his own scholarship and that of Milton Friedman was that whereas Friedman sought to change the world he (Stigler) sought merely to understand it. This distinction holds with equal force with respect to the scholarship of Buchanan and Tullock. Precisely because Tullock seeks to understand — even when what he learns is unappetizing — he adopts no subterfuge in his analytical approach.

If consent exists, Tullock notes and explores its rationale. If conflict is manifest, Tullock investigates the social dilemma to the extent possible with the tools of neoclassical economics. No judgment is passed; no policy recommendations are advanced. Tullock chronicles observed events as part of the pattern of a diverse universe that he is ever eager to explore. In this sense, Buchanan's insight, as I shall demonstrate, is accurate with respect to much of Tullock's scholarship, but inaccurate in important respects.

I should close this section by noting, however, that a natural economist need not manifest extreme solipsism in his own behavior. There is no reason why those who utilize self-seeking assumptions in scientific analysis should be seduced by the assumptions that they deploy into adopting an entirely solipsist mode of personal behavior.

Certainly, Tullock does not live the life of *homo oeconomicus*, as the many faculty visitors and graduate students who have diverted him from his writings to share his intellectual curiosity, his ideas and his wit will readily testify. If Tullock is generous with respect to his time, he is equally generous with respect to his modest wealth, as those who have dined — and dined well — at his table and those who he has supported financially in times of need will also testify. He may well raise *homo oeconomicus* as his indomitable standard on the field of intellectual battle. This standard is by no means the appropriate measure for evaluating his life (Rowley, 1987a, 22).

3. The Calculus of Consent

The two most widely cited of Gordon Tullock's many contributions are *The Calculus of Consent* (co-authored with James Buchanan) published in 1962, and "The Welfare Costs of Tariffs, Monopolies and Theft" published in 1967. Let us focus briefly on Tullock's contributions to *The Calculus* as a means both of assessing his insights and of teasing out the limits of the natural economist hypothesis.

The Calculus is a momentous work of scholarship, the first major foray by Buchanan and Tullock into the terrain of political science and the cornerstone of the Virginia political economy program. The principal objective of the book was to rationalize the Madisonian enterprise in strictly economic terms and to provide a logical rational choice foundation for constitutional democracy.

Fundamentally, the book was an exercise in team production, yet with each author bringing distinctive qualities to the enterprise (Rowley, 1987b, 45). Buchanan brought to the task an emphasis on modeling politics-as-consentaneous-exchange under the influence of Knut Wicksell. Tullock focused on modeling all agents in the constitutional endeavor in strict self-interest terms. By resolving this tension the co-authors wrote a masterpiece. In Tullock's contributions on logrolling and its implications for the simple majority voting rule (Chapter 10), and in his contributions on the bicameral legislature and the separation of powers (Chapter 16), we see the natural economist in his most unrelenting guise.

However, Tullock's central contribution to *The Calculus* was the economic theory of constitutions (Chapter 6) written at the University of South Carolina in 1959. This economic theory provides the logical foundation for constitutional democracy and indeed it is the anvil on which *The Calculus of Consent* was forged. Ironically, it is a chapter in which Tullock suppresses the self-interest axiom in its most myopic form as a means of identifying the unanimity principle as a rational individual decision-making rule for effecting constitutional choices.

In Chapter 6, Tullock assumes that the domain of collective action has already been determined and that the specific institutions through which collective action occurs are already in place. On this basis, he analyzes the choice of optimal rules by any random individual in society as a function of minimizing expected costs. Tullock distinguishes between two categories of expected cost, namely the expected external costs imposed on them by collective action and the expected costs of making decisions through collective action.

By recognizing that individuals fear the imposition of external costs upon them by government, Tullock challenged head-on the Platonic model of beneficent government that then dominated the political science literature. Only a rule of unanimity can protect any random individual from the imposition of such costs. By recognizing that expected decision-making costs are a monotonically increasing function of the number of individuals who must agree in order to effect collective action, Tullock was able to check the unanimity instincts of James Buchanan and to demonstrate that only voting rules short of unanimity are capable of minimizing the combined expected external and decision-making costs of collective action.

The rational individual, at the stage of constitutional choice, thus confronts a calculus not unlike that which he must face in making everyday economic choices. By agreeing to more inclusive rules, he accepts the additional burdens of decision-making in exchange for additional protection against adverse outcomes and *vice versa* (Buchanan and Tullock, 1962, 72). Tullock recognizes that differences in the burden of these costs with respect to specific constitutional choices will result in the selection by rational individuals of more or less inclusive rules. This insight explains the choice of supra-majority rules for collective actions involving such fundamental collective choices as life, liberty and property in combination with the choice of significantly less inclusive rules for collective choices involving lower perceived external costs.

At this point, however, Tullock retreats from the concept of *homo oeconomicus* in its narrow myopic form in order to focus on the mechanism through which random individuals who have selected optimal constitutional rules for themselves translate these choices into universally endorsed constitutional rules for society. This is a significant issue. Individuals differ in many ways and, at any specific time, such differences will obstruct the achievement of universal consent.

Agreement, according to Tullock, is more likely regarding general rules for collective choice than for later choices to be made within the confines of certain agreed-on rules, because in the former case individuals are separated from their particular interests by a veil of uncertainty. Because general rules are expected to govern choices over lengthy time periods, individuals cannot predict with any degree of certainty whether they are likely to be in winning or losing coalitions on any specific issue. Their own self-interest in such circumstances will lead them to choose rules that maximize the expected utility of a randomly selected individual.

Consent will not occur without discussion. This is not the hypothetical world depicted by John Rawls in *A Theory of Justice* (1971). The discussion envisaged in *The Calculus of Consent* can be likened to that among players determining the rules of a card game before the cards are dealt. It is in the self-interest of each player at this stage to devise a set of rules that will constitute the most interesting game for the representative player. Once the cards are dealt, of course, no such agreement is likely as *homo oeconomicus* re-emerges to follow his self-serving instincts.

For universal consent over rules to be feasible, Tullock recognizes that participants must approach the constitutional convention as equals in the sense that differences are accepted without rancor and that there is no discernible dominant group that holds political power. For such a group would not rationally divest itself of its authority. Therefore, *The Calculus of Consent* has little relevance for a society characterized by sharp distinctions between social classes, religious or ethnic groupings where one such grouping has a clearly advantageous position at the constitutional stage.

In 1787, this may not have appeared to be a problem for the United States because the limited suffrage went largely unchallenged. By 1860, it clearly was sufficiently important to destroy the Union. It is very surprising that Tullock completely failed to anticipate that this problem would re-emerge in the United States during the mid 1960s as long-term minorities began seriously to question the rules that had subjugated them to the whims of a dominant majority. The collapse of the US Constitution in 1860, and its near collapse between 1968 and 1974, in any event strongly conform to the predictions of the economic model.

Like all original insights, Buchanan and Tullock presented *The Calculus of Consent* to its intellectual audience in an embryonic form. Some forty years after its birth, significant and unresolved problems remain as is inevitable for any theory that purports to rationalize universal consent for less than unanimous decision-making rules in the real world.

Foremost among these problems is the silence of *The Calculus* with respect to the characteristics of the state of nature in the pre-constitutional environment. Written as the book was in the late 1950s it is reasonable to infer that the authors envisaged a Lockeian state of nature governed by natural law that allowed individuals to protect inalienable rights to life and liberty and imprescriptible rights to private property.

In such an environment, individuals predictably will consent only to a set of rules that will require government to protect their natural rights (i.e., that limit the domain of collective action to government as a minimal state). Because government will be so constrained, individuals anticipate that decision rules will be fully enforced by government as a referee and that collective action within those rules will not be reneged upon in the post-constitutional environment.

Once collective action bursts out of this restricted domain, as occurred in the United States in 1937 in the Supreme Court judgment of *West Coast v. Parrish* that destroyed forever the primacy of liberty to contract, considerations of conflict rapidly overwhelm those of consent, and constitutional rules are reformulated in a much less promising, more Hobbesian environment. This environmental shift was recognized simultaneously in 1974 at the peak of the Watergate crisis, by both co-authors of *The Calculus of Consent*.

Tullock's response was to write *The Social Dilemma* (1974) and to focus forever after on positive public choice in a Hobbesian environment. Under pressure, Tullock's natural economist instincts have resurfaced with a vengeance as his intellectual focus has switched from the potential for gains-from-trade to the reality of generalized prisoners' dilemmas and intractable hold-out situations.

Buchanan's response, in contrast, was to write *The Limits of Liberty* (1975) striving to rationalize the survival of consentaneous decision-making in a Hobbesian world. Thereafter, Buchanan has focused almost exclusively on constitutional political economy, frequently changing tack to protect limited government from the adverse consequences of the predatory state (Brennan and Buchanan, 1980, 1985; Buchanan, 1990; Buchanan and Congleton, 1998). Under pressure, Buchanan has reached beyond *homo oeconomicus* in his attempt to provide an intellectual platform through which concerned private citizens might forestall the re-emergence of *Leviathan* in the United States.

4. The Political Economy of Rent Seeking

If Tullock dips his standard in *The Calculus of Consent*, he resurrects it with a vengeance in his seminal contributions to the rent seeking literature. Here we see the natural economist in his favorite role as he analyzes narrow self-seeking by individuals in the unrelenting Hobbesian environment of the redistributive state.

Economic rent is a familiar concept to economists. It is simply defined as any return to a resource owner in excess of the owner's opportunity cost. Economic analysis identifies various categories of such returns — monopoly rents, quasi-rents, infra-marginal rents — that arise in market economies as a consequence of the less than perfect supply elasticity of factor inputs. Within a competitive market, the search for rents is nothing more than the normal profit seeking incentive that shifts resources to their most highly valued uses and creates new products and values (Tollison, 1987, 144). Positive temporary rents induce new entry and negative temporary rents compel exit in both cases impacting beneficially on economic output.

Tullock's rent seeking insight focuses attention on a malignant rather than a benign phenomenon. The notion that individuals and groups dissipate wealth by utilizing scarce resources to seek rents created for them by government is a classic insight by Gordon Tullock (Tullock, 1967b). The insight is of pivotal importance for Virginia political economy. Arguably, it is the single most important contribution to the public choice research program and it remains, some thirty-five years after its inception, a major engine motivating public choice scholarship.

Tullock's insight was first presented in 1967 in an article published by *The Western Economic Journal* following its rejection by the well known editors of three leading economics journals. The term 'rent seeking' was associated with Tullock's insight some seven years later by Anne Krueger (1974) in a paper that failed to reference Tullock's several prior contributions to the literature.

Tullock's attention was energized by a growing tendency for 1960s' economists to dismiss the welfare costs of monopolies and tariffs as unimportant in view of the minute values associated with Marshallian deadweight loss triangles of consumers' surplus imposed by such instruments (one tenth of one-percent of US gross domestic product according to one measure devised by Arnold Harberger (1954, 1959). Instinctively, Tullock sensed that such complacency was ill founded, and noted that "the classical economists were not concerning themselves with trifles when they organized against tariffs, and the Department of Justice is not dealing with a miniscule problem in its attacks on monopoly" (Tullock, 1967b).

Tullock identified the Harberger fallacy by introducing a shift of emphasis based on a classic public choice insight. Generally, governments do not impose tariffs and do not create monopolies in a political market vacuum. They must be lobbied or pressured into so doing by the expenditure of resources in political activity by those who stand to benefit from such market protections. According to Tullock, rational producers would invest resources in lobbying, say for a tariff, until the expected marginal return on the last dollar so spent was equal to its expected marginal cost. Those who opposed the transfer would expend resources similarly in the opposite direction. All such outlays dissipate the rents expected by those who lobby. In certain adverse circumstances, such dissipation constitutes a complete waste of society's resources.

Tullock went on to demonstrate that rent seeking is not limited to the lobbying of government by private interests. In his 1975 article on 'Competing for Aid,' (Tullock, 1975b) he demonstrated how rent seeking for fiscal aid from the federal or state governments occurred among lower levels of government. This insight came from Tullock's experience in China where he observed how individuals deliberately mutilated themselves to make themselves attractive as recipients of charity. Similarly the City of Blacksburg deliberately under-maintained its own roads in order to become eligible for road-fund support from the Commonwealth of Virginia.

One of the major activities of modern government is the granting of special privileges to various politically influential organizations. Tullock observed that with notable exceptions, the profit record of such groups does not differ systematically from that of unprotected sections of the economy. In part, this may be because the rents either have been dissipated up front or eroded by new entrants. In part, however, the phenomenon is due to the capitalization of monopoly rents so that only the original beneficiaries of the privilege make abnormal gains. Market capitalization gives rise to a transitional gains trap where the revoking of a government privilege imposes capital losses on second generation rent recipients (Tullock, 1975a). It would seem, as David Friedman has put it, that "the government cannot even give anything away." It is also evident that rational individuals will lobby virulently to avoid the imposition of capital losses, making it extremely difficult for politicians to support the abolition of special privileges once they have been bestowed.

As with *The Calculus of Consent* so it is the case with rent seeking, that Tullock's original insight was presented to public choice in embryonic form. Many of the gaps have now been closed (see Tullock, 1993). Two significant problems yet remain unresolved.

The first is the ad hoc nature of rent seeking theory that constrains the generality of its predictive power and that allows critics such as Stiglitz (1991) to contend that "while these theories share with stock market analysts the ability to provide ready interpretations of whatever occurs, their success in predicting these political forces is much more limited". This is a fair criticism. Following the collapse of the Soviet Empire in 1989 and the collapse of Enron in 2001, rent seeking rationalizations abound. However, no public choice scholar predicted either of these collapses in advance.

The second is the marked disparity between the magnitude of rents created by the US federal government and the relatively small level of observed rent seeking outlays. Even if the efficient rent-seeking model (Tullock, 1980a) is adjusted to take account of risk aversion and increasing returns in rent seeking, this gap by no means is reconcilable. In his 1989 book on *The Economics of Special Privilege and Rent Seeking* Tullock ingeniously rescues the rational choice model by suggesting that rent seekers succeed in opaque rather than transparent markets and thus are forced to utilize inefficient techniques in rent seeking in order to escape voter scrutiny. Such inefficient techniques are very costly and reduce the returns to rent seeking. Ironically, the very inefficiency of their methods reduces the total of rent seeking in society and ultimately mitigates the loss of wealth to society.

In this context, consider two types of worlds. In one, Tullock waste is exact and complete. Here the incentive to create monopoly is low because there are no excess returns from so doing. However, the social cost per instance of realized monopoly is high. In the other world, politicians succeed in converting rent-seeking costs into transfers. There are significant excess returns to monopoly creation. Hence there will be many more realized monopolies and many more Marshallian triangles of deadweight loss imposed on society. It is not clear a priori which type of world is preferable from the viewpoint of wealth maximization.

Let me conclude this discussion with an accolade to Gordon Tullock from one of his former colleagues, Robert Tollison, much of whose career has been expended on researching the rent-seeking research program initiated by Tullock:

> The theory of rent-seeking is here to stay. As I have observed in another context the most interesting thing about Tullock's ingenious insight is how simply he put it. Like Coase, he communicated his vision in terms that every lay economist could follow. This is a criterion by which greatness in science is measured. In economics, the Tullocks of our profession are more indispensable than ever. To wit, the scarcest thing in any science is a good idea, clearly communicated. (Tollison, 1987, 156)

5. The Vote Motive

The truly original insights into the vote motive must be ascribed to Duncan Black, whose writings during the late 1940s on the median vote theorem and the problem of vote cycles make him the undisputed Founding Father of public choice, and to Anthony Downs, whose 1957 book introduced rational choice analysis to the study of democracy and representative government and defined the paradox of voting implicit in the rational abstention of voters when confronted with large-scale elections. Tullock, nevertheless, leaves firm footprints on the sand with respect to this area of public choice scholarship.

First, Tullock has focused attention on the relevance of logrolling and vote trading for majority voting in representative assemblies. In 1959, his paper on 'Problems of Majority Voting' demonstrated that majority voting mechanisms in the absence of logrolling and vote trading deny voters the opportunity to seek gains from trade available to them where varying minorities care more passionately than varying majorities over specific programs in the policy bundles potentially available through the political process.

However, utility-maximizing logrollers, in the absence of binding contracts among each other, typically induce excessive public provisions (in terms of median preferences) under majority rule. Only by requiring supra-majorities can this weakness be avoided. This insight, provides powerful support for a constitutional requirement that legislatures should always operate under supra-majority vote-rule constraints.

In 1981, Tullock returned to his earlier work on logrolling to address a perceived paradox in legislative behavior, namely the perceived stability of policy outcomes in a spatial environment seemingly conducive to endless cycling. His innovative paper entitled 'Why so much stability?' initiated a major research program on the topic now referred to as 'structure-induced-equilibrium.' Although Tullock's contribution is generally referred to as logrolling, in truth it falls directly within the structure-induced paradigm.

Tullock's contribution is based on the recognition that most government actions have the characteristic of providing a relatively intense benefit to a small group at a small cost to each member of a large group. Such bills are passed by several small groups getting together to logroll across their separately preferred programs. In line with his work in *The Calculus of Consent* (1962), Tullock distinguishes between two forms that logrolling can take, namely individual bargains and formal coalitions.

Individual bargains predictably involve everyone since anyone excluded can offer lower prices for his vote in order to get back in. Tullock claims that a stable equilibrium is likely in such circumstances, though it will not be a Pareto optimum. In this judgment he is incorrect. As Bernholz (1974) established, if there is a cycle in the voting, there is also a logrolling cycle, unless individuals somehow can commit themselves to a specific bargain.

Tullock recognizes the instability of formal coalitions, given that those excluded from the majority coalition can destabilize it through counter-offers, since there will be over-investment in projects favored by members of the coalition and under-investment in projects favored by the minority. Moreover, there is little evidence either of formal coalitions in legislative bodies, or of any systematic exploitation of specific minorities. Rather, as Tullock observes, the committee structure of Congress creates stability to protect itself from the chaos of endless cycles:

> One simple procedure is to have the relevant committee which will, of course, contain representatives from both parties, canvass the House and decide which particular rivers and harbors bills would, in fact, pass if implicit logrolling were used on votes on each individual bill. This collection of specific projects can then be put together in one very large bill and presented to Congress as a unit. (Tullock, 1981, 199–200)

This was the first attempt to explain the observed stability of political equilibrium under conditions conducive to cycling within the framework of a strictly rational choice model.

Second, (in 1967a) Tullock re-focused the rational voter abstention model of Downs (1957) in order to take account of the phenomenon of rational voter ignorance. If information is costly and if voters rationally economize in obtaining it, then the original equation of Downs, where the expected payoff to the individual from voting in an election is:

$R = BP - C + D$

changes to:

$R = BPA - C_v - C_i + D$

where B refers to the net personal benefit expected from the victory of the voter's preferred party or candidate, P refers to the probability that the voter's vote is decisive, A refers to the voter's subjective estimate of the accuracy of his judgment, C_v refers to the cost of voting, C_i refers to the cost of obtaining additional information and D refers to the consumption benefit received from voting.

Suppose, in such latter circumstances, argues Tullock, that C_v is negative as a consequence of social pressures, in which case voting is always rational. The cost of becoming adequately informed is much more expensive. In such circumstances, it would rarely be rational for the individual voter to cast a well-informed vote. In essence, most voters will be rationally ignorant (Tullock, 1967a, 114).

The fact that the average voter is rationally ignorant opens up incentives for highly motivated members of the mass media to attempt to influence others in their voting behavior. Tullock also addresses this issue (Tullock, 1967a). The expected payoff associated with such behavior is:

$R = BP_p - C_i - C_p$

where P_p is the probability that persuasion is decisive and C_p is the cost of persuasion. For individuals working in the mass media, P_p is much larger than P and C_p is likely to be zero. Advocacy therefore is a highly predictable activity in political markets. Advocacy will be directed most heavily at rationally ignorant swing voters whose behavior typically determines the outcome of political elections.

So far Tullock discusses the provision and consumption of political information without specific reference to the important issue whether or not such information is deliberately deceptive, although he recognizes that there is a fine distinction between persuasion and lies. In a further essay, on the economics of lying, Tullock (1967a) Tullock focuses on the incentives for politicians to lie to rationally ignorant voters in the course of election campaigns.

The expected benefit associated with a political lie comes from its success in securing votes. This is the product of the probability that the lie will be believed and the probability that it will persuade individuals to switch their votes in favor of the liar. The expected cost of a political lie is the sum of any cost to conscience and the product of the probability that the lie will be detected and the loss of votes associated with such detection. According to Tullock (1967a), the rational vote-seeking politician will lie to the point where the marginal expected benefits are equated with the marginal expected cost. Predictably, politicians will lie more extensively to the rationally ignorant than to the well-informed voters.

Because competing politicians have clear incentives to expose each others' lies, explicit lies are less likely than lies by inference. Politicians are well versed in such nuances of expression. Negative campaigning, where the respective campaign staffs of competing politicians, rather than the candidates themselves, lie about each other's candidate and accuse each other of lying is an excellent example of such nuanced vote-seeking behavior.

Tullock's natural economist instincts dominate in his approach to the vote motive. The current faddish popularity of theories of expressive voting, for example, wherein rational voters are assumed to vote their conscience rather than their interest, leaves Tullock unmoved and unconvinced. If individuals go to the polls, they vote their interest, as best such interest is perceived to be through the fog of rational ignorance, persuasion and lies.

One senses (and shares) Tullock's skepticism concerning public choice scholars who relinquish the rational choice model in this field in favor of sociological explanations of human action. If Tullock's understanding of the vote motive speaks little for the net benefits of democracy, this does not concern him, nor should it concern us. Tullock views the world as it is and not as it ideally might be. From this perspective, democracy is a very weak reed on which to rest the well-being of a nation, save when the domain of collective action is strictly and effectively curtailed by constitutional rules (Tullock, 1998, 2000).

6. Bureaucracy

Tullock's 1965 book, *The Politics of Bureaucracy*, is the first application of the positive rational choice approach to a field that until then was dominated by 'a normative mishmash of Max Weber's sociology and Woodrow Wilson's vision of public administration' (Niskanen, 1987, 135). In this tradition, senior bureaucrats were viewed for the most part as impartial and well-informed servants of the prevailing public good as determined by each ruling government. The one prior book on bureaucracy by an economist (Ludwig von Mises, 1944) was essentially devoid of analytic content. Tullock's (1965) contribution, therefore, inevitably was a voyage of discovery that opened up a fertile field for future research by challenging the fundamental premise that dominated the political science literature. Tullock is clearly influenced by Machiavelli's *The Prince* and by *Parkinson's Law* in modeling the behavior of senior bureaucrats and their subordinates.

Tullock models bureaucracy as a hierarchical system in which individuals advance by merit, as determined by senior bureaucrats. Ambitious self-interest motivates the behavior of all bureaucrats. The organizational system selects against moral rectitude. A man with no morals has a marked advantage over a more moral colleague who is willing to sacrifice career opportunities, at the margin, in pursuit of moral goals.

The moral quality of senior bureaucrats, therefore, with rare exceptions, is extremely low, not least because they must respond to the amoral behavior of ambitious underlings who seek to usurp their positions. There is no market check on the harmful organizational consequences of such unbridled personal ambition. It is also pointless to train bureaucrats in ethics, since self-interest dominates moral rectitude in this perverse non-market environment.

Because bureaus are hierarchical systems in which top-down decision-making is the norm, Tullock identifies two major problems that lead to organizational inefficiency. First, instructions are unlikely to pass down the hierarchy without distortion even in the absence of malevolent design. Tullock refers to this as the problem of *whispering down the lane*. Second, senior bureaucrats cannot access fully the information available at lower levels of the hierarchy. If they delegate they lose control. If they fail to delegate, their decisions will be ill-informed. Thus, Tullock shreds the central postulates of the political science research program and sets the scene for the economic analysis of bureaucracy.

Tullock (1965) focuses entirely on the internal organization of a bureau. Later work by Niskanen (1971) and by Weingast and Moran (1983) tightened the economic analysis and identified the link between bureaus and their sponsor organizations. This shift of emphasis opened up the path to important empirical analysis that strongly supports the rational choice approach. Tullock's insights, culled from his personal experience in the Department of State, were indispensable to establishing this research program.

7. The Law

Tullock, the natural economist, rarely strays from positive rational choice analysis to engage in normative discussion. His first book on the law, *The Logic of Law* (1971a), however, is an exception to this rule. Here Tullock adopts utilitarian philosophy as first outlined by Jeremy Bentham, but as modified by Lionel Robbins (1938), by Nicholas Kaldor (1939) and by Hicks (1939).

Bentham's brand of utilitarianism comprises a combination of three conditions (Sen, 1987, 39), namely:

1. *Welfarism*, which requires that the goodness of a state of affairs should be a function only of utility information regarding that state of affairs;
2. *Sum-ranking*, which requires that utility information regarding any state of affairs should be assessed in terms of the sum of all individuals' utilities concerning that state of affairs; and
3. *Consequentialism*, which requires that every choice in society should be determined by the goodness of the consequent state of affairs.

Tullock's only formal training in economics was the course provided in the Chicago Law School by Henry Simons, who is best known for *A Positive Program for Laissez Faire* (1934), a propagandist tract, more an essay in utilitarian political philosophy than in economics (Coase, 1993, 240). It is not surprising, therefore, that Tullock followed in his master's footsteps, albeit modifying the utilitarian ethic to suppress the sum-ranking condition in favor of the Pareto principle.

In *The Logic of the Law*, the first book ever published in law-and-economics, Tullock explicitly refers to Bentham's failed reforms of the English legal system, and claims that: '[s]ince we now have a vast collection of tools that were unavailable to Bentham, it is possible for us to improve on his work' and '[h]opefully this discussion, together with empirical research, will lead to significant reforms' (Tullock, 1971a, xiv). On this basis, Tullock launches a critical review of substantive law and legal procedure within the United States as they existed in the late 1960s.

Tullock recognizes the limitations posed by the ordinal nature of utility and the inability to make interpersonal comparisons of utility. To overcome these restrictions, he falls back on the approach first developed in *The Calculus of Consent* (1962), in which individuals are viewed as focusing on potential reforms from a long-term *ex ante* perspective behind a veil of uncertainty. In such circumstances, legal reforms that myopic individuals who suffer a short-term loss of utility might be expected to veto, nevertheless satisfy the unanimity requirement of the modified Pareto principle.

Tullock's critical eye takes in most areas of substantive law in the United States — contract, tort, theft, robbery, tax, and family — but focuses most savagely on legal procedures within the Anglo-Saxon legal system, a focus that he has sharpened even more with the passage of time as he has become yet more enamored with Napoleon (the civil code) and yet more skeptical of Wellington (the adversarial procedures of the common law).

The Logic of the Law (1971a), *Trials on Trial* (1980) and *The Case Against the Common Law* (1997) all utilize a writing style more appropriate for policy-makers than for lawyers, rejecting the minutiae of legal footnotes for the straight-forward prose and anecdotal evidence for which Tullock is renowned. Not surprisingly, Tullock has failed to achieve the same level of influence over the legal profession as he has, with respect to public choice, over economists and political scientists.

Most lawyers are rent-seekers rather than scholars, slaves to the complex details of the law that provide them with their remuneration and profoundly mistrustful of ideas that appear to threaten their monopoly rents. It should come as no surprise that lawyers and legal scholars have responded much more favorably to the sophistry of Richard Posner a fellow lawyer who advises them that their pursuit of private wealth through lucrative adversarial litigation indubitably contributes to the wealth of society (Posner, 1973).

Undeterred by this apparent failure to influence the American legal profession, Tullock continues to launch successive assaults upon Anglo-Saxon legal procedure. In so doing, he identifies the weak link of Chicago law-and-economics. For, if litigation leads to incorrect legal outcomes and legal errors are not automatically corrected by future litigation, the assertion that the common law is efficient is extremely difficult to sustain.

In his most recent, and arguably his best book on this subject, *The Case Against the Common Law* (1997) Tullock deploys the rational choice approach to powerful effect, demonstrating that a socialistic court system, with salaried bureaucrats (judges) and below average intelligence jurors responding to the competing arguments of self-seeking lawyers, buttressed by the paid lies of their respective expert witnesses, within a system that is designed to restrict relevant evidence, is extremely unlikely to contribute positively to the efficiency of the law and to the aggregate wealth of society.

The fact that legal scholars of all brands, from Yale and Harvard to Chicago, choose to remain silent concerning the issues that Tullock raises, rather than to attempt to refute them, is suggestive that they know just how potentially devastating is his logic of the law for the continuation of the high incomes that they earn. Lawyers and legal scholars are sufficiently well-trained in the Socratic technique to recognize the importance of voiding it when confronted with such a formidable debater, so better armed than they are in the logic of the law (Goetz, 1987; Rose-Ackerman, 1987; Schwartz, 1987).

8. Bio-economics

In 1957, shortly after leaving the Department of State and while working in Princeton, Gordon Tullock became interested in social insects and in other aspects of biology. He prepared a manuscript that would be published in a much revised form only one third of a century later, dealing with issues of coordination without command in the organization of insect societies. In this early draft, he deployed economic tools to analyze the internal structure of ants, termites and a few other insect species. Tullock's monograph was well in advance of the pioneering work of Edward O. Wilson who is formally and correctly credited with founding the field of sociobiology.

Tullock's full bibliography contains a surprising number of publications in journals of biological science as well as a number of more popular publications in this field. One of these, his 1971b paper that applied economic principles to explain the behavior of the coal tit as a careful shopper, inspired a doctoral dissertation that provided a supportive empirical test of the avian feeding habits of the coal tit (Goetz, 1998, 629).

Together with Janet Landa, Michael Ghiselin and Jack Hirshleifer, Gordon Tullock ranks as one of the founding fathers of bio-economics. Most of his contributions were collected into his 1994 research monograph entitled: *The Economics of Non-Human Societies*. In this monograph, Tullock analyses the extraordinary feats of cooperation and adaptation to changes in their environments accomplished by ants, termites, bees, mole rats, sponges and (his favorite) slime molds, species that have literally microscopic or non-existent brains.

Tullock assumes that animals, plants, ameboid single-cells of sponges and the individual cells of slime molds all possess the functional equivalent of the preference function of human beings. This preference function is extremely primitive and is not necessarily mediated by way of a nervous system. A process of Darwinian selection and inheritance determines the success of such species in social coordination. He details the behavior patterns of such primitive species in terms of this rational choice model. It must be said that anyone who is prepared to argue the applicability of the rational choice model to the behavior of slime molds is indeed a natural economist!

9. The Editorial Initiative

Tullock's career as journal editor began inconspicuously in 1966 when he edited the first issue of *Papers in Non-Market Decision Making*, the precursor to the journal *Public Choice* that would become the spear-head of the public choice revolution and arguably one of the most influential policy-oriented journals of the last third of the twentieth century. From the outset, Tullock displayed enormous entrepreneurial talent in launching and directing this editorial initiative (Rowley, 1991).

Historians of scientific revolution (Kuhn, 1970) observe that textbooks and scholarly journals serve for the most part to consolidate rather than to initiate new research programs. The scholarly journals, in particular, tend to be conduits facilitating the preoccupation with 'puzzle-solving' that normal science epitomizes. In this sense, journals are vehicles of normal science constrained by the vision of the past and, at most, are reluctant agents in the process of scientific revolution.

Tullock was well aware from the outset of the preoccupations of journal editorship, indeed he had investigated the nature of the problem in his 1966 book entitled *The Organization of Inquiry* completed prior to embarking on his own editorial career (Rowley, 1991). In that book, Tullock placed *homo oeconomicus* center stage in the non-market decision making environment of the typical scholarly journal and deduced on this basis an economic explanation of conventional editorial predilections for normal puzzle-solving science.

To understand the behavior of journal editors, Tullock argues, it is necessary to take account of the non-market environment of the academy, the institution central to the scholarly journal's success or failure. Universities, with few exceptions, are either publicly-owned socialist institutions or are non-profit organizations in each case offering bureaucratic services in exchange for block appropriations and grants supplemented by fee income.

The senior bureaucrats responsible for their operations have few incentives to become acquainted with the details of their institutions' outputs, particularly with respect to the nature and quality of advanced research and scholarship. Yet, they have strong incentives to utilize low cost filters for evaluating scholarly output as a basis for appointing, tenuring, promoting and remunerating their academic work-force. As a consequence, "[t]he whole responsibility for evaluating research, in essence, is left to the editors of the learned journals" (Tullock, 1966, 37).

Unfortunately, most editors exercise only a subordinate role in the evaluation of scholarship, essentially providing a brokerage function between scholars on the supply and the demand side of the market for ideas. As Tullock observes: "the job of journal editor, although respectable, is not of sufficient attraction to get the very best personnel" (Tullock, 1966, 141). In the typical case, where the editor is a respected but not a leading scholar in his discipline, truly important and innovative pieces of scholarship often will lie beyond his evaluation capacity.

In such circumstances, the use of anonymous readers becomes a lifeline for the intellectually overwhelmed editor. Recourse to this lifeline predictably will fail to protect the path-breaking contribution. Leading scholars often either refuse to referee papers or provide only cursory evaluations. Hard-pressed editors thus submit manuscripts "to relatively junior scientists since such men are rather flattered at the honor and are unlikely to delay and delay" (Tullock, 1966, 143). Under the shield of anonymity, the referee "is also not under any great pressure to reach the correct decision" (Tullock, 1966, 143).

In such circumstances, Tullock argues, editors tend to discriminate against ground-breaking articles because of risk-aversion in the face of augmented uncertainty:

> The probability of error on the part of the original investigator is greater, the possibility of error by the editor in misjudging the article is also great, and it is certain that the article, if published, will be very carefully examined by a large number of specialists. Under the circumstances, the possibility that the editor's own reputation will suffer from publication of such articles is a real one. It is not surprising, therefore, that these articles are sometimes hard to place. The problem is compounded by the fact that the prestige of a journal is affected by those it accepts; it is not affected by those it turns down. This probably leads the editors to some degree, at any rate, to play safe." (Tullock, 1966, 147)

Yet, in his own lengthy editorial career (1966–1990), Tullock did not reflect his own logic, did not play safe, did not hide behind the anonymity of referees, did not slip from the cutting edge of public choice and did not step down from the editorship of *Public Choice* even as his reputation became assured as one of the two leading scholars in the discipline. Instead, he deployed his journal as an active agent, seeking out contributions in areas where he detected important research deficiencies — vote models, logrolling, rent-seeking, the stability of political equilibrium, demand-revealing bureaucracy and autocracy are noticeable examples.

He placed the journal firmly behind empirical research, recognizing the problem of obtaining good data, and allowing authors scope to experiment with respect both to the use of proxy variables and to method (Tullock, 1991). Variable though the quality of published papers undoubtedly was, scholars of public choice were attracted like magnets to each issue of the journal for the gems that they might find — and might find only in *Public Choice* — because its editor was a genius and because rival editors both in economics and in political science, quite simply, were not. Once again, Tullock's behavior diverged from that of the natural economist in its public-spirited, self-effacing, contribution to the development of an important discipline.

10. Tullock's World View

In many respects, Tullock does manifest the characteristics outlined by Buchanan (1987) as defining the natural economist. However, as this essay demonstrates, Tullock is much more than this. He is a warm-hearted and deeply-concerned person with a powerful vision of the good society and a willingness to explore the reforms necessary to move mankind onto a better path.

In this regard, Tullock's philosophy is utilitarian in the modified sense of the Pareto principle, further adjusted to allow for individual decision-making behind a veil of uncertainty. This philosophy, first spelled out in *The Calculus of Consent*, has been applied systematically by Tullock ever since wherever he has engaged in public policy discussion. Tullock is not an anarchist. He believes that there is a positive role for the state. No doubt that role extends in his mind beyond that of the minimal or 'night-watchman' state.

However, any such extension, is extremely limited. Unlike many professed classical liberals, Tullock has not allowed himself to be diverted onto a normative Hobbesian path by the events of September 11, 2001. Rather he has maintained a principled Lockeian position that a free society should never over-react to perceived violence and that basic constitutional rights should not be trampled on. He is a true friend of liberty, always watchful and vigilant in its defense. His good sense and common decency is much needed and highly valued in this increasingly troubled world.

CHARLES K. ROWLEY

REFERENCES

Bernholz, P. (1974). "Logrolling, arrow-paradox and decision rules: a generalization." *Kyklos*, 27: 49–72.

Black, D. (1948). "On the rationale of group decision-making." *Journal of Political Economy*, LVI: 23–34.

Brady, G.L. and Tollison, R.D. (1991). "Gordon Tullock: creative maverick of public choice." *Public Choice*, 71(3): 141–148.

Brady, G.L. and Tollison, R.D. (1994). "Gordon Tullock: creative maverick of public choice." in G.L. Brady and R.D. Tollison (eds.) *On the Trail of Homo Economicus*. Fairfax: George Mason University Press, pp. 1–6.

Brennan, H.G. and Buchanan, J.M. (1980). *The Power to Tax*. Cambridge: Cambridge University Press.

Brennan, H.G. and Buchanan, J.M. (1985). *The Reason of Rules*. Cambridge: Cambridge University Press.

Buchanan, J.M. (1975). *The Limits of Liberty: Between Anarchy and Leviathan*. Chicago: University of Chicago Press.

Buchanan, J.M. (1987). "The qualities of a natural economist." in C.K. Rowley (ed.) *Democracy and Public Choice: Essays in Honor of Gordon Tullock*. Oxford: Basil Blackwell.

Buchanan, J.M. (1990). "The domain of constitutional economics." *Constitutional Political Economy*, 1(1): 1–18.

Buchanan, J.M. and Tullock, G. (1962). *The Calculus of Consent*. Ann Arbor: University of Michigan Press.

Buchanan, J.M. and Congleton, R.D. (1998). *Politics by Principle, Not by Interest*. Cambridge: University of Cambridge Press.

Coase, R.H. (1993). "Law and economics at Chicago." *Journal of Law and Economics*, 36: 239–254.

Downs, A. (1957). *An Economic Theory of Democracy*. New York: Harper and Row.

Goetz, C.J. (1987). "Public choice and the law: the paradox of Tullock." in C.K. Rowley (ed.) *Democracy and Public Choice: Essays in Honor of Gordon Tullock*. Oxford: Basil Blackwell.

Goetz, C.J. (1998). "Tullock, Gordon (1922-)," in P. Newman (ed.) *The New Palgrave Dictionary of Economics and the Law*, Vol. 3. London: Macmillan, pp. 628–629.

Harberger, A.C. (1954). "Monopoly and resource allocation." *American Economic Review*, 44: 77–87.

Harberger, A.C. (1959). "Using the resources at hand more effectively." *American Economic Review*, 49: 134–146.

Hicks, J. (1939). *Value and Capital*. Oxford: Clarendon Press.

Kaldor, N. (1939). "Welfare propositions of economics and interpersonal comparisons of utility." *Economic Journal*, 49: 549–552.

Krueger, A. (1974). "The political economy of the rent-seeking society." *American Economic Review*, 64: 291–303.

Kuhn, T. (1970). *The Structure of Scientific Revolutions*, 2nd ed. Chicago: University of Chicago Press.

Mises, L. von. (1944). *Bureaucracy*. New Haven: Yale University Press.

Niskanen, W.A. (1971). *Bureaucracy and Representative Government*. Chicago: Aldine Press.

Niskanen, W.A. (1974). "Bureaucracy," in C.K. Rowley (ed.) *Democracy and Public Choice: Essays in Honor of Gordon Tullock*. Oxford: Basil Blackwell.

Niskanen, W.A. (1987). "Bureaucracy," in C.K. Rowley (ed.) *Democracy and Public Choice*. Oxford: Basil Blackwell, 130–140.

Posner, R.A. (1973). *Economic Analysis of Law*. Boston: Little Brown and Company.

Rawls, J. (1971). *A Theory of Justice*. Cambridge: Belknap Press.

Robbins, L. (1938). "Interpersonal comparisons of utility: a comment." *Economic Journal*, 48: 635–641.

Rose-Ackerman, S. (1987). "Tullock and the inefficiency of the common law," in C.K. Rowley (ed.) *Democracy and Public Choice: Essays in Honor of Gordon Tullock*. Oxford: Basil Blackwell, pp. 181–185.

Rowley, C.K. (1987a). "Natural economist or popperian logician"? in C.K. Rowley (ed.) *Democracy and Public Choice: Essays in Honor of Gordon Tullock*. Oxford: Basil Blackwell, pp. 20–26.

Rowley, C.K. (1987b). "The calculus of consent." in C.K. Rowley (ed.) *Democracy and Public Choice: Essays in Honor of Gordon Tullock*. Oxford: Basil Blackwell.

Rowley, C.K. (1991). "Gordon Tullock: entrepreneur of public choice." *Public Choice*, 71(3): 149–170.

Schwartz, W.F. (1987). "The logic of the law revisited," in C.K. Rowley (ed.) *Democracy and Public Choice: Essays in Honor of Gordon Tullock*. Oxford: Basil Blackwell, pp. 186–190.

Schumpeter, J.A. (1942). *Capitalism and Democracy*. New York: Harper and Row.

Sen, A. (1987). "Rational behavior," in J. Eatwell, M. Milgate, and P. Newman (eds.) *The New Palgrave: A Dictionary of Economics*, Vol. 4. London: Macmillan, pp. 68–76.

Simons, H. (1934). In H.D. Gideonse (ed.) *A Positive Program for Laisser-Faire: Some Proposals for Liberal Economic Policy*. Chicago: Chicago University Press.

Stiglitz, J.E. (1991). "Another century of economic science." *Economic Journal*, 101: 134–141.

Tollison, R.D. (1987). "Is the theory of rent-seeking here to stay"? in C.K. Rowley (ed.) *Democracy and Public Choice: Essays in Honor of Gordon Tullock*. Oxford: Basil Blackwell, pp. 143–157.

Tullock, G. (1959). "Problems of majority voting." *Journal of Political Economy*, 67: 571–579.

Tullock, G. (1961a). "An economic analysis of political choice." *Il Politico*, 16: 234–240.

Tullock, G. (1961b). "Utility, strategy and social decision rules: comment." *Quarterly Journal of Economics*, 75: 493–497.

Tullock, G. (1965). *The Politics of Bureaucracy*. Washington DC: Public Affairs Press.

Tullock, G. (1966). *The Organization of Inquiry*. Durham: Duke University Press.

Tullock, G. (1967a). *Toward a Mathematics of Politics*. Ann Arbor: University of Michigan Press.

Tullock, G. (1967b). "The welfare costs of tariffs, monopolies and theft." *Western Economic Journal*, 5: 224–232.

Tullock, G. (1971a). *The Logic of the Law*. New York: Basic Books.

Tullock, G. (1971b). "The coal tit as a careful shopper." *The American Naturalist*, 105: 77–80.

Tullock, G. (1971c). "The cost of transfers." *Kyklos*, 24: 629–643.

Tullock, G. (1974). *The Social Dilemma: The Economics of War and Revolution*. Blacksburg, VA: Center for Study of Public Choice.

Tullock, G. (1975a). "The transitional gains trap." *The Bell Journal of Economics and Management Science*, 6: 671–678.

Tullock, G. (1975b). "Competing for aid." *Public Choice*, 21: 41–52.

Tullock, G. (1980a). "Efficient rent-seeking," in J.M. Buchanan, R.D. Tollison, and G. Tullock (eds.) *Towards a Theory of the Rent-Seeking Society*. College Station: Texas A & M. University Press.

Tullock, G. (1980b). *Trials on Trial: The Pure Theory of Legal Procedure*. New York: Columbia University Press.

Tullock, G. (1981). "Why so much stability"? *Public Choice*, 37(2): 189–202.

Tullock, G. (1989). *The Economics of Special Privilege and Rent-Seeking*. Boston: Kluwer Academic Publishers.

Tullock, G. (1991). "Casual Recollections of an Editor". *Public Choice*, 71(3): 129–140.

Tullock, G. (1993). "*Rent seeking*," Shaftesbury Paper No. 3. Aldershot: Edward Elgar Publishing.

Tullock, G. (1994). *The Economics of Non-Human Societies*. Tucson: Pallas Press.

Tullock, G. (1997). *The Case Against the Common Law*. The Blackstone Commentaries, No 1, Fairfax, Virgina: The Locke Institute

Tullock, G. (2000). *Exchanges and Contracts*. The Blackstone Commentaries, No. 3. Fairfax, Virginia: The Locke Institute.

Weingast, B.R. and Moran, M.J. (1983). "Bureaucratic discretion or congressional control: regulatory policy making by the federal trade commission." *Journal of Political Economy*, 91: 765–800.

I

INTEREST GROUP BEHAVIOR AND INFLUENCE

1. Introduction

During the last two decades economics has witnessed a remarkable upsurge in theoretical as well as empirical studies of the behavior and political influence of interest groups. Recent books by Sloof (1998), Drazen (2000), Persson and Tabellini (2000), and Grossman and Helpman (2001) refer to a wealth of evidence of the significance of organized interests in the political arena, besides presenting surveys of theoretical studies. Political economics definitively seems to move away from the common assumption of atomistic demand in 'political markets' (the median voter model) towards a more realistic framework. In a sense it is picking up and deepening some older strands of literature inspired by classical writers on political economy (like Marx and Pareto), the so-called pluralists in political science (like Bentley and Truman), and others, who were concerned with the political impact of particular social groups under the label of 'factions', 'classes', or 'elites' (see e.g., Bottomore, 1970; Moe 1980). The modern political economic literature to be surveyed in this paper, however, is characterized by much greater rigor, through the use mathematical modeling, and keener attention for individual incentives. Strict adherence to methodological individualism would require the modeling of the following chain of events regarding the interaction between policymakers and interest groups: group formation/adjustment → group decision making → group activity → political decision making → government policies (plus other relevant events) → group formation/adjustment. Due to the complexity involved, group formation and adjustment (influenced by policy outcomes) are typically neglected by taking the existence of interest groups as given, thereby sidestepping the thorny issue of the individual incentives for participation in collective action (Olson, 1965). In addition, interest groups are commonly assumed to act as single (unitary) actors. Nevertheless, our conclusion will be that there has been substantial theoretical progress, opening up many promising paths for important and exciting research.

In this paper we will focus on formal theoretical models of interest group behavior and influence, with emphasis on the positive aspects.[1] Early modeling of interest groups, during the 1970s and the beginning of the 1980s, had difficulty in dealing simultaneously with the behavior of interest groups and policymakers. In response short cuts were taken in the form of higher levels of abstraction or by focusing on one side of the interaction between the agents. The former short cut is used in the cooperative game and compromise function models described in section 2, the latter by the so-called influence and vote function models discussed in section 3. In the wake of the rise of non-cooperative game theory in the 1980s the modeling of interest group behavior became much more general and sophisticated. Two strands of literature will be highlighted. Section 4 discusses common agency models of contributions offered to policymakers in exchange for policies or to help finance electoral campaigns, while section 5 deals with models of strategic information transmission. Section 6 is concerned with extended models investigating the multiple means and channels of influence that are in general available to groups. Section 7 concludes.

2. Cooperative Games and Compromise Functions

Characteristic of cooperative game models is the focus on coalitions rather than individual agents, and outcomes (reasonable compromises) rather than strategic moves. Although less explicit, it avoids problems of arbitrariness in the specification of moves. By requiring collective rationality, policy outcomes of these models are (constrained) efficient, that is, they are in accordance with the maximization of a weighted representation of the utilities of the players involved. More formally, suppose that n interest groups can be meaningfully distinguished for the policy x, and that $v^i(x)$ represents the related net benefits or utility of group i ($i = 1,\ldots,n$). Let μ^i denote the 'political influence weight' of the group. Then, the behavioral assumptions underlying the models imply that x follows from the maximization of the function $P(x) = \Sigma_i \mu^i v^i(x)$. Although this function looks like a social welfare function, it should not be labelled such because the influence weights are based on a positive instead of normative (ethical) analysis. We will therefore call it a *political welfare function*. Two types of models will be discussed: the *power to tax* model (Aumann and Kurz, 1977) and the *interest function approach* (van Winden, 1983). These models differ in the assumptions underlying the function $P(x)$ and the nature of the influence weights.

The *power to tax* model concerns a redistribution game where the so-called Harsanyi-Shapley-Nash value is used as solution concept. The income distribution is determined by majority voting. Players in the game are all n individuals in society (making up the set N), who are endowed with a pre-tax income y^i. Redistribution is constrained by the requirement that total after-tax income ($\Sigma_i x^i$) equals total pre-tax income ($\Sigma_i y^i$). Groups enter the picture because a majority coalition is required for redistribution. Any majority coalition, C, can redistribute all income from those outside the coalition, $N\backslash C$, to itself. The crucial point is that the outside coalition $N\backslash C$ can threaten to destroy its own pre-tax income, leaving nothing to be redistributed to C. The outcome of this game is determined by using the Nash Bargaining Solution (which assumes that players can make binding agreements, committing themselves to carry out threats if no agreement is reached). Proceeding in this way for all possible coalitions, an individual's 'power' (Shapley value) can be derived from the individual's (expected) contribution to all possible coalitions. They show that this power over the *resulting* income distribution ($x = x^1, \ldots, x^n$) corresponds with $\mu^i = 1/v_x^i$, that is, an individual's influence weight equals the reciprocal of her or his *ex post* marginal utility v_x^i. Since commitments are possible threats are never carried out, because they are anticipated by the players, preventing inefficient outcomes. Furthermore, no coalitions (interest groups) actually form. Thus, one could say that x results from the anticipation of pressure activities that could but do not actually occur. The model has been extended in several directions. For example, Aumann et al. (1983) apply a similar analysis to public goods, Gardner (1981) introduces a government as player, Osborne (1984) studies the differential taxation of goods that can (like labor-time via strikes) or cannot (like land) be 'destroyed', while Peck (1986) takes incentive effects of taxation into account.[2]

The *interest function approach* takes a less abstract perspective on policymaking. It is argued that in capitalist economies, analytically, four basic social groups can be distinguished, based on their position with respect to production in the economy: capitalists, private sector workers, public sector workers (politicians and bureaucrats), and dependants (unemployed, disabled, retired). The political interests of a group are represented by an 'interest function' $v^i(x, y)$. The value of x is determined by the public sector workers, while $y = (y^1, y^2)$ stands for the actions taken by the capitalists and private sector workers, respectively. The latter two groups play a non-cooperative game, where each group takes the actions of the government and the other group as given. This determines their actions as a function of x: $y = (y^1, y^2) = y(x)$. The crucial assumption is that public sector workers, when deciding on x, will to some extent take account of the interests of the other groups. The extent to which they will do so is related to the potential influence of 'ideology' (including altruism), multiple positions (simultaneous membership of different groups), mobility (probability of becoming a member of a different group), and pressure (influence attempts by private sector groups).[3] The resulting policy x is assumed to have the character of a compromise (a generalized Nash Bargaining Solution), equivalent to the maximization of the 'complex interest function' $P(x)$ above, where the influence weights are determined by the aforementioned factors. No explicit behavioral model is provided, though, for the relationship between these weights and the proposed determinants of pressure (threat potential, group cohesion, and an information factor). Later models, discussed below, do provide such a microfoundation.[4] The approach has been theoretically as well as empirically applied in several ways. For example, dynamic models including elections — showing politically induced economic cycles of various lengths — are analyzed by van Winden (1983) and van Winden et al. (1987). Borooah and van der Ploeg (1983) and van Velthoven (1989) study macroeconomic models with endogenous government behavior (see also Przeworski and Wallerstein, 1988). van Velthoven and van Winden (1985) and Verbon (1989) focus on social security. Renaud (1989) presents (empirical) analyses of fiscal federalism and public sector growth. Mazza and van Winden (1996) study the impact of labor migration, and Drissen (1999) analyzes a computable general equilibrium model with redistribution and public production. Also, with some empirical support (Renaud and van Winden, 1988; van Velthoven, 1989) the relative numerical strengths of these groups have been used to study with a theoretical model the dynamics of endogenous influence weights (van Velthoven and van Winden, 1985).

Another strand of literature, with roots in Stigler's (1971) theory of regulation and its formalization by Pelzman (1976), simply postulates a compromise function to endogenize policy, using as arguments typically the weighted surpluses of consumers and producers. Maximization by the policymaker is usually (implicitly) justified by the presumed goal of maximal electoral support. However, as noted by Hirshleifer (1976), policymakers (regulators) themselves constitute an interest group with an interest in wealth, implying that political support can only be an instrumental and partial aim.

3. Influence and Vote Functions

Policies can be affected by interest groups in two ways: directly, by influencing the behavior of policymakers, and indirectly, by influencing the behavior of voters. The influence function and vote function models discussed next are concerned with these two channels of influence. Characteristic is the focus on interest group behavior, whereas the impact on policymaking or voting behavior is simply assumed. Furthermore, while the precise nature of the activity is often left obscure in the first type of models, campaign contributions are focused on in the latter.

3.1. Influence Functions

Political decision making is often modeled as a kind of all-pay-auction. Policymakers offer certain policies (public goods, transfers, regulation), while demand comes from interest groups. The 'price' the latter have to pay is determined by the resources spent on the acquisition of the goods. Let x represent the policies, y^i the resources spent by interest group i, and $v^i(x, y^i)$ its net benefits. Many studies assume a fixed positive relationship between policies and resources spent, an *influence function*: $x = I(y, z)$, where both y and z are vectors and z represents exogenous variables (like group sizes). Examples are Findlay and Wellisz (1983), Cairns (1989), and Coggins et al. (1991). In one part of the literature, based on the pressure model of Becker (1983), x represents the amount of a transfer or public good. In the rent seeking literature, originating with Tullock (1967, 1980), x usually denotes the probability that a particular good (a monopoly license, for instance) is obtained. The equilibrium level of the resources spent by the groups are determined under the assumption of non-cooperative (Cournot-Nash) behavior. In both literatures the resources spent by the interest groups typically entail a pure social cost, that is, their activity has no productive aspect. Competition has a better side in Becker's model, where efficiency costs of the policies (transfers) as such are taken into account. Under some reasonable assumptions, an increase in the efficiency cost of taxes (subsidies) induces an increase (decrease) in the resources spent by the taxed (subsidized) group, leading to a fall in the tax and subsidy level. Another interesting result follows if an increase in group size induces free riding. If the negative free riding effect is sufficiently strong, this will lead to fewer resources being spent. The implication is that "groups can more readily obtain subsidies when they are small relative to the number of taxpayers" (Becker, 1983, p. 395).[5] This second result qualifies the importance of sheer numbers in politics. However, this result only bites if influence via elections (votes) is dominated by interest group pressure.[6] If not, larger groups can be expected to focus relatively more on pressuring politicians interested in votes than bureaucrats. Also, larger groups will be relatively more inclined to produce pressure in the pursuit of group-specific public goods (like a trade tariff), because of the fewer spoils to the individual member in case of private goods (like transfers).[7]

An important issue that rent-seeking models are concerned with is the extent to which the benefits of the rent (x) are dissipated in the competition among groups to obtain the rent. Other issues explored are the effects of: risk attitude, nature of the rent (private or public good), groups versus individuals as players, intergroup mobility, multiple rents (prizes), endogeneity of the order of moves, asymmetry of information (e.g., regarding valuation or capabilities), budget constraints, and sharing rules (for surveys, see Nitzan, 1994; Tollison, 1997).[8]

Although competition among interest groups may be less detrimental to efficiency than the rent seeking literature suggests, in the Becker model "all groups could be made better off by reduced expenditures" (Becker, 1983, p. 387), because of the assumed wasteful character of these expenditures. This brings us to an important limitation of influence function models. Since the influence of expenditures (pressure) is assumed but not explained, it is not clear why policymakers would behave this way. The government is a 'black box', and there is no benchmark showing the consequences of having no interest group activity. It is also not clear on what kind of activities resources are spent by the (exogenously given) interest groups.

3.2. Vote Functions

More specific regarding interest group activity are models focusing on campaign contributions. Although the importance of this type of activity is not undisputed, for the US at least, a relative abundance of data makes this focus attractive.[9] Two types of models can be distinguished. In *exchange models* contributions to a candidate are assumed to elicit a preferred policy response (e.g., Welch, 1980).[10] Because of the simply assumed positive relationship between contributions and policies (platforms) these models are similar to the models just discussed. One interesting outcome is that groups will generally split contributions between candidates, while contributions will rise with the probability of electoral success (assumed to be given).

In contrast, *support models* of campaign contributions assume that interest groups take policies as given but try to increase the number of votes for the favored candidate (e.g., Brock and Magee, 1980; Hillman and Ursprung, 1988; Pedersen, 1995; Persson and Tabellini, 2000). In this case, the probability of electoral success is assumed to be positively related to contributions. Under some plausible additional assumptions the following results are obtained (see Potters and van Winden, 1996): (a) groups will only contribute to the favored candidate, (b) the more preferred the policy of the favored candidate the higher the contribution, (c) no contributions are made if platforms are identical, and (d) contributions are higher the 'closer' the election. Regarding the optimal behavior of the candidates it is typically assumed that (informed) voters will punish candidates for adjusting policies in the direction favored by the campaign donors. Consequently, candidates may on balance (at some point) start to lose votes when (further) catering to interest groups to raise campaign contributions (Denzau and Munger, 1986).[11]

Compared to influence function models, a strong point of these models is not only their explicitness regarding interest group activity but also that they open up the 'black box' of policymaking by introducing candidates. The assumption of a vote function introduces another 'black box,' however, concerning the nature of the mechanism through which money buys votes.[12]

4. Common Agency Models of Contributions

One approach actually explaining why influence occurs is the common agency or menu auction model of Bernheim and Whinston (1986), which got widely applied through the influential work of Grossman and Helpman (1994, 2001). To illustrate, suppose that part of the electorate is organized in n interest groups or lobbies. Let the joint welfare of the members of interest group i be denoted by $v^i(x)$, and that of the unorganized by $v^u(x)$, where x represents government policy. Before the policy is determined, the lobbies offer contributions to the policymaker contingent on the value of x, denoted by the contribution schedules $c^i(x)$. The net welfare of group i equals $w^i(x) = v^i(x) - c^i(x)$. The policymaker is assumed to care about total contributions $c(x) = \Sigma_i c^i(x)$ (for campaign spending or other reasons) and aggregate welfare $v(x) = \Sigma_i v^i(x) + v^u(x)$ (due to re-election concerns, for instance; see below). More specifically, it is assumed that the policymaker's objective is to maximize $c(x) + \gamma v(x)$, with $\gamma \geq 0$.[13] The game between the lobbies and the policymaker consists of two stages: first, the interest groups simultaneously commit to a contribution schedule, followed by the policymaker committing to a policy. In equilibrium, contribution schedules $\{c^i(x)\}$ are such that each lobby maximizes the net joint welfare of its members, given the schedules of the other groups and the anticipated policy response of the policymaker, while the policy x is such that it maximizes the policymaker's objective, taking the contribution schedules as given. Focusing on 'truthful Nash equilibria',[14] this model has the interesting property that the policymaker sets policy x in accordance with the maximization of $(1 + \gamma)\Sigma_i v^i(x) + \gamma v^u(x)$, which is clearly a function of the form $P(x)$ above. Thus, it provides a microfoundation for such a political welfare function and an explicit behavioral model for the link between influence weights and pressure in the interest function approach. Note that the welfare of individuals represented by the lobbies has a larger weight, and that the numerical strength of social groups plays a role (since v^i and v^u denote joint welfare). Not surprisingly, competition by other groups can dramatically affect the benefits from lobbying. Only a single (monopolistic) lobby can capture all the surplus from lobbying — by just compensating the policymaker for selecting a different policy — because it leaves no alternative for the policymaker.

Applications of the model concern international trade policies (Grossman and Helpman, 1994, 1995), electoral competition (Grossman and Helpman, 1996; Prat, 2000), public goods (Besley and Coate, 2001), redistribution (Dixit et al., 1997; Grossman and Helpman, 1998), local public goods and fiscal federalism (Mazza and van Winden, 2002a; Persson, 1998; Persson and Tabellini, 1994), capital taxation (Marceau and Smart, 2002), environmental policies (Aidt, 1998), labor market policies (Rama and Tabellini, 1998), and legislative bargaining (Persson, 1998; Dharmapala, 1999a).

Extensions are presented by Dixit et al. (1997) who allow for preferences that are not quasi-linear,[15] Bergemann and Välimäki (1998) who extend the model to a multi-period game, and Prat and Rustichini (1999) who consider a multi-agent setting. Variants of the model include sequential lobbying (Prat and Rustichini, 1998), and so-called 'natural equilibria' where principals offer contributions for at most one instead of all possible policy alternatives (Kirchsteiger and Prat, 2001).

Interestingly, Grossman and Helpman (1996) demonstrate that the function maximized by the policymaker can be endogenously obtained in an electoral competition model where parties maximize their seat shares in a legislature and where contributions can influence platforms as well as voting behavior (through campaign expenditures).[16] Dixit et al. (1997), furthermore, show that more efficient policy instruments will be used in equilibrium when they are available, which supports the argument of Becker (1983). However, in contrast with Becker's 'black box' model, interest groups may prefer the government to be institutionally restricted to inefficient redistributive policies, because distortions (accompanied by welfare losses) make it more difficult to exploit them.

Although providing an explicit behavioral model of interest group influence, which is a major achievement, existing common agency models rely on some strong assumptions. For example, interest groups are exogenously given, of fixed size, and assumed to behave as unitary actors. Also, players are supposed to stick to their choices, which may be due to reputation concerns in a repeated game (Harrington, 1993), but is simply assumed here. Moreover, essentially complete information is assumed, a major restriction which is relaxed in the models discussed next.

5. Information Transmission Models

An important kind of interest group activity neglected in the models discussed so far is the transmission of information. Think of the endorsement of electoral candidates or the information conveyed to candidates regarding issues that are important to electoral groups. Not restricted to elections, moreover, is the essential role they play in informing policymakers of the likely consequences of policies. Interest groups are often better informed about issues that are relevant to them. Due to conflicts of interests, strategic behavior (dissembling) by interest groups may be expected, however, which makes the study of this topic not at all trivial. To illustrate, I will discuss the basic signaling model of lobbying of Potters and van Winden (1992). Suppose that a policymaker has to choose between two policies, x_1 and x_2. The payoffs of these policies to the policymaker and an interest group are determined by the 'state of the world', which is either t_1 or t_2, in the following way:

	t_1	t_2
x_1	$a_1, 0$	$0, 0$
x_2	$0, b_1$	a_2, b_2

with a_i (b_i), denoting the normalized payoff to the policymaker (interest group), assumed to be positive ($a_i, b_i > 0$, $i = 1, 2$).[17] Thus, the policymaker prefers x_i if the state is t_i, while the interest group always prefers x_2: there is a partial conflict of interest.[18] Which state prevails is assumed to be private information to the group; that is, the group knows its 'type,' which is either 't_1' or 't_2.' The policymaker only knows the probability, p ($1-p$), that the group is of type t_2 (t_1). Assuming that $p < a \equiv a_1/(a_1 + a_2)$ the policymaker will pick x_1 on the basis of her prior belief p. However, before the policymaker decides, the group can either send a message (m) against a fixed cost ($c > 0$), or no message (n), which is costless. Let s_i denote the probability that type t_i sends a message (m), and $r(s)$ the probability that the policymaker responds with x_2 after signal $s = m, n$. Then, the following (sequential) equilibrium of this signaling or sender-receiver game is obtained: (1) if $b_1 < c < b_2$: $s_1 = 0$, $s_2 = 1$, $r(n) = 0$ and $r(m) = 1$; (2) if $c < b_1 < b_2$: $s_1 = p(1-a)/(1-p)a$, $s_2 = 1$, $r(n) = 0$ and $r(m) = c/b_1$.[19] In regime (1) lobbying costs are prohibitive for the 'bad' type t_1 (who wants to dissemble), but not for the 'good' type t_2 (who wants to convey the truth). Consequently, only the latter sends a message, enabling the policymaker to make fully informed decisions. If lobbying costs are not prohibitive, regime (2), the good type (with the larger stake) again always lobbies, whereas the bad type does so only from time to time. Fully mimicking the good type would induce the policymaker to stick to x_1, because she would not be able to distinguish between the types. By sometimes responding to a message with this policy, however, the policymaker discourages the bad type from doing so. Since a message may come from both types, lobbying is clearly less informative in this regime. Note that lobbying increases with p (reflecting the inclination of the policymaker to choose x_2), with lower costs, and higher stakes (via a switch from regime (1) to (2)). The influence of lobbying, $r(m)$, increases with higher costs, and lower stakes (b_1). In this equilibrium (with $p < a$) lobbying can never be detrimental to the policymaker or the interest group (*ex ante*, that is). In case that $p > a$ an equilibrium exists, however, where the group, irrespective of its type, always lobbies, although the response of the policymaker (x_2) remains the same as with no lobbying. This shows that lobbying may be a pure social waste.

The model illustrates that lobbies should somehow be able to distinguish themselves in order to influence policies through information transfer. Fixed lobbying costs provides one such opportunity. The model can be extended in several directions, generally increasing the scope for information transfer (for surveys, see Austen-Smith, 1997; Sloof, 1998; Grossman and Helpman, 2001). Consider, for instance, endogenous lobbying costs. If the interest group can determine the cost, a full revelation equilibrium can always be obtained by having the good type profitably outspend the bad type (in the example, by choosing c at least equal to b_1; Potters and van Winden, 1992). However, also the policymaker can make lobbying costly, by demanding a fee or contributions for access (Austen-Smith, 1995; Lohmann, 1995). The reason may be a time constraint, the intrinsic valuation of contributions, or to screen the lobbies. Also in this way the scope for information transfer increases, by forcing lobbies to reveal their preferences. Other extensions, with a similar outcome, include multiple senders (Potters, 1992; Austen-Smith and Wright, 1992), multiple receivers (Ainsworth and Sened, 1993), multidimensional policies (Battaglini, 2002), receiver uncertainty about whether the sender is informed (Austen-Smith, 1994), auditing and verification by the policymaker or an intermediary agent (Potters and van Winden, 1992; Austen-Smith and Wright, 1992; Rasmusen, 1993), and persuasion games (Lagerlöf, 1997; Bennedsen and Feldman, 2000). In a persuasion game the sender can transmit or withhold evidence, but cannot 'lie.' This assumption is sometimes justified by referring to reputational concerns in a repeated game.[20] In the above example, the interest group would only be able to reveal its type (t_i) or to abstain from lobbying. This obviously increases the scope for information transfer. Actually, a persuasion game can be seen as one extreme of a more general static model with exogenous cost of lying (which are infinite, then), and the basic signaling game (where lying is costless) as the other extreme. These costs can be endogenized in a repeated signaling game model, where an interest group may want to report truthfully to build up or maintain its reputation. Moreover, apart from costly messages ('words'), sanctions through the enforcement of threats ('deeds') become available then as a means of influence. See the integrated model of Sloof and van Winden (2000).

Applications concern: fiscal policies and regulation (Potters and van Winden, 1992; Lohmann, 1998; Esteban and Ray, 2000), legislative voting and its institutional features (Austen-Smith and Wright, 1992; Ainsworth, 1993; Austen-Smith, 1993; Bennedsen and Feldman, 2000, 2002), international trade negotiations (Milner and Rosendorff, 1985), the emergence of lobbyists (Ainsworth and Sened 1993), legislative control of bureaucracy (Epstein and O'Halloran, 1995; Sloof, 2000), and issues related to political campaigning, like contributions and endorsements (Cameron and Jung, 1992; Austen-Smith, 1995; Lohmann, 1995; Potters et al., 1997; Grossman and Helpman, 1999; Sloof, 1999; Prat 2000a,b).

Models of information transmission also typically assume that interest groups are of fixed size and behave like a unitary actor.[21] Their comparative strength relates to the fact that they deal with a crucial problem in actual politics, the lack of information. Furthermore, often no (exogenous) commitment assumption is relied on. However, this is bought with simplicity in terms of issues and institutions investigated, which restricts their usefulness. Another worrisome feature concerns the strong rationality assumptions (see Sadiraj et al., 2001, 2002). Nevertheless, as a benchmark these models serve a useful purpose. For one thing, due to the relationship between lobby expenditures and influence — qualified by the incentives of interest groups — an informational microfoundation is provided for the use and possibly the specification of an influence function (Lohmann, 1995) as well as a political welfare function (Potters and van Winden, 1990).

6. Multiple Means and Channels

So far attention has been focused on one means of influence (contributions or information transmission) and one channel of influence (mostly the nexus with politicians). In practice, however, interest groups can use multiple means and multiple channels. Drawing conclusions from studies focusing on just one means or channel can be treacherous, because the use and impact of these different instruments is not likely to be independent. For instance, common agency models predict that contributions buy policies. However, if contributions simultaneously transmit information on the lobby's type or only serve to gain access, signaling models suggest that this relationship is much more subtle and may even be absent. We now turn to the relatively few models dealing with this multiplicity.

6.1. Multiple Means

The following means of influence can be distinguished:[22] (1) lobbying, (2) pressure, (3) structural coercion, and (4) representation. Models of lobbying — the use of 'words' — typically involve costly messages in the transmission of information. However, if preferences are sufficiently aligned cheap talk messages may also be informative and influential. Austen-Smith and Banks (2002) focus on the consequences of adding the option for a sender to inflict self-imposed utility losses and demonstrate that the scope for information transfer and influence increases. In case of pressure — the use of 'deeds' — (opportunity) costs are inflicted on the policymaker. Contributions in common agency models are one example, where in general contributions may stand for anything that is valued by the policymaker and costly to the interest group (campaign contributions, bribes, ghost writing, etc.). Another example is punishment (instead of reward) through the enforcement of a threat, like a labor or investment strike or a terrorist act. Bennedsen and Feldmann (2001) combine a common agency model with a persuasion game to allow an interest group the choice between lobbying and pressure via contributions. According to their analysis contributions are a more effective means of influence, which may crowd out the search for and transmission of information. Sloof and van Winden (2000) investigate the choice between lobbying and pressure via the enforcement of threats in a repeated signaling game. It turns out that pressure — in contrast to lobbying — only occurs when the interest group's reputation is 'low' (think of a new group). Moreover, (repeated) lobbying cannot completely substitute for pressure, but may be necessary to maintain a reputation. It is concluded that pressure is typically exerted to build up a reputation while lobbying is used to maintain a reputation.

Structural coercion refers to constraints on the behavior of a policymaker which are not related to influence attempts. The behavior of voters (with negligible individual influence) forms a constraint of this type. Through the use of endorsements, or campaign contributions after policies have been determined, interest groups may affect voting and thereby influence the political process. Potters et al.

(1997) investigate an interest group's choice between endorsement and contributions, using a signaling game, and show that the group may prefer contributions (indirect endorsements) when the preferences of the group and the voter are not sufficiently aligned. This model also provides a microfoundation for the impact of campaign expenditures on voting.

In case of 'representation', finally, interest groups try to get their interests directly represented among the policymakers.[23] This may be achieved in different ways: through 'multiple positions' (a form of penetration where, for example, via an election a position of policymaker is obtained), 'revolving doors' (offering future career opportunities), and the development of 'social ties' (affective bonds; see Harsanyi, 1962). To our knowledge, there are no models yet incorporating this means of influence. Extension of the so-called citizen-candidate model of representative democracy (Osborne and Slivinski, 1996; Besley and Coate, 1997) may be helpful, though, to deal with penetration, while the model of van Dijk and van Winden (1997) may be useful for social ties.

6.2. Multiple Channels

In practice, interest groups have many different channels of influence available. For example, they can choose between different legislators, bureaucrats,[24] or political candidates (at home, but also abroad).[25] They may also approach several of them to expand supportive coalitions. Moreover, policymakers may be targeted at different tiers within a single governmental body (e.g., the legislative and the bureaucratic tier) as well as at different governmental levels (like the municipal, state, or national level). In addition, an interest group can go for it alone, hire professionals, form an alliance with others, or support an intermediary organization.

Austen-Smith (1993) studies the lobbying of legislators at the agenda setting stage (committee) and the voting stage (House). His signaling model predicts that only agenda stage lobbying is generically influential. Dharmapala (1999a,b) demonstrates with a common agency model the impact of legislative committee structure on policy outcomes when interest groups can offer contributions to different legislators. Prat (2001) provides a microfoundation for split contributions to candidates (cf. section 3), using a common agency model. Models concerning the efforts of interest groups to expand supportive coalitions are lacking (cf. Hojnacki and Kimball, 1998).

Several studies investigate the choice between legislators and bureaucrats. Moore and Suranovic (1992) look at the case where import-competing industries can pursue import relief via administered protection or via lobbying politicians directly (assuming exogenous probabilities of success). Their analysis suggests that reform restricting one of these options may cause welfare losses through substitution effects. Mazza and van Winden (2000, 2002a), using a common agency model, look at various issues related to the interaction between a legislator (deciding on a budget) and a bureaucrat (deciding on the allocation of the budget) when both can be offered contributions by interest groups. Their results show that competition between interest groups may function as a substitute for legislative control, while the budget may be used as a second-best instrument of control (a smaller government being the legislative response to bureaucratic capture). Sloof (2000) studies a politician's decision whether or not to delegate policy authority to a bureaucrat when both can be lobbied. His signaling game analysis shows that politicians may prefer a biased bureaucracy and an interest group with a large stake, because the informational gains may outweigh the distributional losses. Moreover, interest groups would typically lobby politicians to further delegation.

Hoyt and Toma (1989), using an influence function model, consider the choice between state and local governmental levels as targets for interest groups, when states mandate expenditure and revenues of local governments. Their analysis suggests that payoffs from influence at the state level generally will exceed that at the local level.

Interest groups may also delegate the influencing of decision making at another level to a policymaker. Mazza and van Winden (2002b) investigate this issue with a common agency model where a local policymaker may transfer part of the contributions received to a higher level policymaker. In fact, using policymakers as an intermediary also occurs when campaign contributions are offered to candidates to affect voting behavior. The choice between working alone and hiring a lobbyist is modeled by Johnson (1996), while van Winden (1983) addresses the budget allocation decision regarding the alternative of joining an alliance (like a trade organization); both authors use influence functions. These choices clearly relate to the internal organization of an interest group, a neglected topic in the literature (see, e.g., Moe, 1980, Rothenberg, 1988).

7. Concluding Remarks

An important achievement of the literature surveyed in this paper is the successful incorporation of interest group behavior and influence in the formal positive analysis of political decision making. It has helped to redress the imbalance in Public Choice created by a disproportional attention for the electoral nexus between policymakers and voters. Interest groups impact government policies also outside elections by employing resources that are valuable in both contexts (particularly, money and information). Gradually, a more rigorous and also more positive view of the functioning of interest groups has been established.

Notwithstanding the progress made, there are still many blind spots in our understanding of the political economic role played by interest groups. Firstly, notwithstanding the huge number of empirical studies there are relatively few 'stylized facts,' basically showing that contributions and lobbying, the size of organized membership, and an interest group's stake are positive determinants of influence, whereas the presence of an oppositional force in the political arena, electoral pressures, and the presence of a well-informed electorate are negative determinants (Potters and Sloof, 1996). The main problems are a serious lack of data and a shortage of hypotheses derived from theoretical models that provide structure and a base for embedding. Laboratory experimentation forms an important complementary research method, because of the opportunity it offers to study behavior under controlled conditions and to check the robustness of findings through replication. However, until now only few experiments have been carried out, with mixed success for the models (see van Winden, 2002). Also, to compensate for the extreme simplicity of many formal models, which may lead to a distorted view of the multi-faceted interaction between interest groups and policymakers (cf. Saint-Paul, 2000), computer experiments (simulations) allowing for greater complexity and dynamics should receive more attention (examples are Fafchamps et al., 1999; Sadiraj et al., 2001, 2002).

Secondly, existing models typically assume a level of rationality which seems unrealistic, though useful as a benchmark. There is mounting evidence that people are quite myopic, use rather simple adaptive rules of decision making, and concentrate on issues at hand (e.g., Ortoni et al., 1988; Kagel and Roth, 1995). A related issue concerns the impact of emotions and feelings. Although investigated in a few studies of political behavior,[26] the subject has been neglected in the literature on interest groups. Interestingly, allowing for affective social ties in the interaction between a policymaker and an interest group would not only imply that the former may be willing to benefit the latter without compensation, but also that the interest group may care about the interests of the policymaker.[27]

Thirdly, research needs to go beyond the common assumption of exogenously given groups that are of fixed size and behave as unitary actors. The formation, dynamics, and internal politics of interest groups are badly neglected topics.[28] Why do only some interests get organized, or are induced to do so by policymakers? Why, for instance, are the retired in the US well organized in the intergenerational 'redistribution game' while there is no comparable organization for the younger people (Lohmann, 1998)? Furthermore, what is the nature, cause, and impact of the decision-making procedures maintained by organized interests? And how do government policies feed back into the development of groups?

The considerable theoretical progress made in recent years will serve as a fresh source for the derivation and testing of competing hypotheses and for structuring the search for new data. In addition, it has helped developing a framework for the interpretation, coordination, and planning of future research. Notwithstanding the substantial progress, much remains to be done.

FRANS VAN WINDEN

NOTES

1. The (field) empirical literature is surveyed in Potters and Sloof (1996). van Winden (2002) discusses the relatively small number of experimental studies. In this paper we draw on Potters and van Winden (1996) and van Winden (1999). For an earlier survey of models, see Mitchell and Munger (1991). Hillman (1989), Morton and Cameron (1992), Nitzan (1994), and Austen-Smith (1997) provide more specific reviews.
2. Dougan and Snyder (1996) present another cooperative game model of income redistribution. Zusman (1976) deals with consumer and producer groups in a regulated market.
3. Mobility can be an important reason why the interests of dependants are taken into account (see Renaud and van Winden, 1988). Another reason why social groups may count is 'structural coercion', that is, the systematic reactions by private sector agents to government policies when these are taken as given. In that case policymakers may be induced to sort these agents into groups (which need not be organized). In this way interest groups play a role in *probabilistic voting models*, for example (see Coughlin et al., 1990; Coughlin, 1992; Hettich and Winer, 1999). To illustrate, suppose an incumbent party has to choose its platform x in a forthcoming election. The electorate comprises N groups, where each member of a group (say, group i, with n_i members) derives the same utility $v_i(x)$ from the party's policy. In addition, member j has a personal utility 'bias' b_{ij} in favor of (>0) or against (<0) this party, where b_{ij} is uniformly distributed over the interval (l_i, r_i). Let utility from the challenging party be zero, then voter ij votes for the incumbent if $v_i(x) + b_{ij} > 0$. Interestingly, maximization of expected plurality (assuming $l_i < v_i(x) < r_i$) implies that $P(x)$ above is maximized, with $\mu_i = n_i/(r_i - l_i)$. Thus, numerical strength and group homogeneity determine the influence weights.
4. See the common agency model in section 4. Further support is provided by the (pressure) model of strategic information transmission of Potters and van Winden (1990). See also the probabilistic voting model discussed in the previous note.
5. This result also follows if the efficiency cost to taxpayers decreases when the tax per individual falls due to an increase

in the number of taxpayers. The opposition by taxpayers to subsidies decreases in that case.
6. According to Becker this happens via the persuasion of 'rationally ignorant' voters.
7. The last two results concerning group size are demonstrated in Potters and van Winden (1996).
8. Neary (1997) compares rent seeking models with economic models of conflict. For a recent rent seeking model incorporating a constitutional stage, see Sutter (2002).
9. According to Wright (1990) the ratio of campaign contributions to lobbying expenditure is about 1 to 10.
10. In some models contributions are exchanged for services which are assumed to be independent from policies (e.g., Baron, 1989). Apart from the fact that it is difficult to visualize such services (cf. Morton and Cameron, 1992), these models are of little help in analyzing the influence of interest groups on policies (for more discussion, see Austen-Smith, 1997).
11. Usually, candidates are assumed to play Nash amongst each other and to act as Stackelberg leaders with respect to the interest group(s). Edelman (1992) reverses the latter assumption.
12. Austen-Smith (1987) assumes that campaign expenditures enable a candidate to clarify her or his policy position, which is appreciated by risk-averse voters because it reduces the variance of the perceived policy. This reduction is exogenously given, though, and only bites out of equilibrium. See also Coate (2001).
13. A similar function holds if the policymaker cares about net (of contributions) welfare, given that contributions are higher valued than the same amount in the public's purse.
14. Bernheim and Whinston (1986) show that the set of best responses to any strategies played by opponents includes a strategy that is 'truthful', which means that it reflects the true preferences of the interest group; moreover, such equilibria are 'coalition proof', in the sense that players cannot improve their lot through costless pre-play communication which carries no commitment.
15. Quasi-linear preferences imply constant marginal utility of income which frustrates a concern for redistribution (via money transfers).
16. Note that this microfoundation of a political welfare function hinges on the sorting of individuals into organized interest groups, and not on the grouping of individual voters by policymakers because of their shared characteristics (as in probabilistic voting models).
17. In terms of payoff functions $v^i(x)$, with the policymaker (interest group) denoted by $i = 1$ (2), it is assumed that: $v^1(x_1;t_1) - v^1(x_2;t_1) > 0$, $v^1(x_2;t_2) - v^1(x_1;t_2) > 0$ and $v^2(x_2;.) - v^2(x_1;.) > 0$.
18. If $b_1 < 0 < b_2$, there is no conflict of interests and no problem for information transmission, since the group has no incentive to dissemble. Even costless messages can be effective, then. If $b_2 < 0 < b_1$, there is a full conflict of interests with no scope for information transfer, because the group always wants to dissemble which is anticipated by the policymaker. The fact that 'cheap talk' (costless messages) can be informative if the sender's preferences regarding the receiver's actions are dependent on the former's private information is shown more generally in the seminal paper by Crawford and Sobel (1982).
19. Note the condition that $b_2 > b_1$. If the reverse of this 'sorting condition' would hold, the 'bad' type t_1 has a larger stake in persuading the policymaker. Since the latter will then be inclined to interpret a message as coming from t_1 rather than t_2, no messages will be sent in that case.
20. This may also jusitify the (exogenous) cost of lying in the model of Austen-Smith and Wright (1992). In this model (two) interest groups have to pay a cost to get informed (observed by the policymaker) but can subsequently send a costless message (which would be uninfluential 'cheap talk' were it not for the anticipated cost of lying).
21. An exception is Sadiraj et al. (2002). In this dynamic 'bounded rationality' model the participation of voters in interest groups is endogenous. The fees paid by those who join are (conditionally) supplied to political candidates to finance polling (for learning the preferences of voters).
22. See van Winden (1983, in particular pp. 16 and 94). Pressure is here distinguished from lobbying.
23. Interestingly, the empirically often observed lobbying of friendly legislators instead of opponents may be related to a bias in representation, since committees tend to share the same biases as the interest groups surrounding them (Kollman, 1997).
24. Relatively few studies focus on the influence of interest groups on the bureaucracy; see e.g., Spiller (1990), Laffont and Tirole (1991), and Banks and Weingast (1992).
25. See Hillman and Ursprung (1988), Hillman (1989).
26. A theoretical example is the 'minimax regret strategy' (Ferejohn and Fiorina, 1974) to explain voting in large-scale elections. For empirical studies, see Abelson et al. (1982), Marcus and Mackuen (1993), and Bosman and van Winden (2002).
27. See van Dijk and van Winden (1997) for a theoretical model and van Dijk et al. (2002) for experimental support.
28. Some recent attempts to endogenize group formation include Dougan and Snyder (1996) and Mitra (1999).

REFERENCES

Abelson, R.P., Kinder, D.R., Peters, M.D., and Fiske, S.T. (1982). "Affective and semantic components in political person perception." *Journal of Personality and Social Psychology*, 42: 619–630.

Aidt, T. (1998). "Political internalization of economic externalities and environmental policy." *Journal of Public Economics*, 69: 1–16.

Ainsworth, S. (1993). "Regulating lobbyists and interest group influence." *The Journal of Politics*, 55: 41–56.

Ainsworth, S. and Sened, I. (1993). "The role of lobbyists: entrepreneurs with two audiences." *American Journal of Political Science*, 37: 834–866.

Aumann, R. and Kurz, M. (1977). "Power and taxes." *Econometrica*, 45: 1137–1161.

Aumann, R. and Kurz, M., and Neyman, A. (1983). "Voting for public goods." *Review of Economic Studies*, 50: 677–693.

Austen-Smith, D. (1987). "Interest groups, campaign contributions, and probabilistic voting." *Public Choice*, 54: 123–139.

Austen-Smith, D. (1993). "Information and influence: lobbying for agendas and votes." *American Journal of Political Science*, 37: 799–833.

Austen-Smith, D. (1994). "Strategic transmission of costly information." *Econometrica*, 62: 955–963.

Austen-Smith, D. (1995). "Campaign contributions and access." *American Political Science Review*, 89: 566–581.

Austen-Smith, D. (1997). "Interest groups: money, information and influence," in D.C. Mueller (ed.) *Perspectives on Public Choice*. Cambridge: Cambridge University Press.

Austen-Smith, D. and Banks, J.S. (2002). "Costly signaling and cheap talk in models of political influence." *European Journal of Political Economy*, 18: 263–280.

Austen-Smith, D. and Wright, J.R. (1992). "Competitive lobbying for a legislator's vote." *Social Choice and Welfare*, 9: 229–257.

Banks, J.S. and Weingast, B.R. (1992). "The political control of bureaucracies under asymmetric information." *American Journal of Political Science*, 36: 509–524.

Baron, D. (1989). "Service-induced campaign contributions and the electoral equilibrium." *Quarterly Journal of Economics*, 104: 45–72.

Battaglini, M. (2002). "Multiple referrals and multidimensional cheap talk." *Econometrica*, 70: 1379–1401.

Becker, G. (1983). "A theory of competition among pressure groups for political influence." *Quarterly Journal of Economics*, 98: 371–400.

Bennedsen, M. and Feldmann, S.E. (2000). "Lobbying legislatures," mimeo.

Bennedsen, M. and Feldmann, S.E. (2001). "Informational lobbying and political contributions," mimeo.

Bennedsen, M. and Feldmann, S.E. (2002). "Lobbying and legislative organization, the effect of the vote of confidence procedure," mimeo.

Bergemann, D. and Välimäki, J. (1998). "Dynamic common agency." Cowles Foundation Working Paper, Yale University.

Bernheim, B.D. and Whinston, M.D. (1986). "Menu auctions, resource allocation, and economic influence." *Quarterly Journal of Economics*, 101: 1–31.

Besley, T. and Coate, S. (1997). "An economic model of representative democracy." *Quarterly Journal of Economics*, 112: 85–114.

Besley, T. and Coate, S. (2001). "Lobbying and welfare in a representative democracy." *Review of Economic Studies*, 68: 67–82.

Borooah, V. and van der Ploeg, F. (1983). *Political Aspects of the Economy*. Cambridge: Cambridge University Press.

Bosman, R. and van Winden, F. (2002). "Emotional hazard in a power-to-take experiment." *The Economic Journal*, 112: 147–169.

Bottomore, T.B. (1970). *Elites and Society*. Harmondsworth: Penguin Books.

Brock, W. and Magee, S. (1980). "Tariff formation in a democracy." in J. Black and B. Hindley (eds.) *Current Issues in Commercial Policy and Diplomacy*. London: MacMillan.

Cairns, R. (1989). "Dynamic rent-seeking." *Journal of Public Economics*, 39: 315–334.

Cameron, C.M. and Jung, J.P. (1992). "Strategic endorsements," mimeo, New York: Columbia University.

Coate, S. (2001). "Political competition with campaign contributions and informative advertising." Working Paper 8693, NBER, Cambridge.

Coggins, J., Graham-Tomasi, T., and Roe, T. (1991). "Existence of equilibrium in a lobbying economy." *International Economic Review*, 32: 533–550.

Coughlin, P. (1992). *Probabilistic Voting Theory*. Cambridge: Cambridge University Press.

Coughlin, P., and Mueller, D., and Murrell, P. (1990). "Electoral politics, interest groups, and the size of government." *Economic Inquiry*, 29: 682–705.

Crawford, V. and Sobel, J. (1982). "Strategic information transmission." *Econometrica*, 50: 1431–1451.

Denzau, A. and Munger, M. (1986). "Legislators and interest groups: how unorganized interests get represented." *American Political Science Review*, 80: 89–106.

Dharmapala, D. (1999a). "Comparing tax expenditures and direct subsidies: the role of legislative committee structure." *Journal of Public Economics*, 72: 421–454.

Dharmapala, D. (1999b). Legislative bargaining and vote buying under the influence of lobbying, mimeo, Cambridge: Harvard University.

van Dijk, F. and van Winden, F. (1997). "Dynamics of social ties and public good provision." *Journal of Public Economics*, 323–341.

van Dijk, F., and Sonnemans, J., and van Winden, F. (2002). "Social ties in a public good experiment." *Journal of Public Economics*, 85: 275–299.

Dixit, A., Grossman, G.M., and Helpman, E. (1997). "Common agency and coordination: General theory and application to government policy making." *Journal of Political Economy*, 105: 752–769.

Dougan, W.R. and Snyder, J.M. Jr. (1996). "Interest-group politics under majority rule." *Journal of Public Economics*, 61: 49–71.

Drazen, A. (2000). *Political Economy in Macroeconomics*. Princeton: Princeton University Press.

Drissen, E. (1999). *Government Decisions on Income Redistribution and Public Production*. Amsterdam: Thela Thesis.

Edelman, S. (1992). "Two politicians, a PAC, and how they interact: two extensive form games." *Economics and Politics*, 4: 289–305.

Epstein, D. and O'Halloran, S. (1995). "A theory of strategic oversight: congress, lobbyists, and the bureaucracy." *Journal of Law, Economics, and Organization*, 11: 227–255.

Esteban, J. and Ray, D. (2000). "Wealth constraints, lobbying and the efficiency of public allocation." *European Economic Review*. 44: 694–705.

Fafchamps, M., De Janvry, A., and Sadoulet, E. (1999). "Social heterogeneity and wasteful lobbying." *Public Choice*, 98: 5–27.

Ferejohn, J.A. and Fiorina, M.P. (1974). "The paradox of not voting: a decision theoretic analysis." *American Political Science Review*, 68: 525–536.

Findlay, R. and Wellisz, S. (1983). "Some aspects of the political economy of trade restrictions." *Kyklos*. 36: 469–481.

Gardner, R. (1981). "Wealth and power in a collegial polity." *Journal of Economic Theory*, 25: 353–366.

Grossman, G.M. and Helpman, E. (1994). "Protection for sale." *American Economic Review*, 84: 833–850.

Grossman, G.M. and Helpman, E. (1995). "Trade wars and trade talks." *Journal of Political Economy*, 103: 675–708.

Grossman, G.M. and Helpman, E. (1996). "Electoral competition and special interest politics." *Review of Economic Studies*, 63: 265–286.

Grossman, G.M. and Helpman, E. (1998). "Intergenerational redistribution with short-lived governments." *The Economic Journal*, 108: 1299–1329.

Grossman, G.M. and Helpman, E. (1999). "Competing for endorsements." *American Economic Review*, 89: 501–524.

Grossman, G.M. and Helpman, E. (2001). *Special Interest Politics*. Cambridge: MIT Press.

Harrington, J.E. (1993). "The impact of reelection pressures on the fulfilment of campaign promises." *Games and Economic Behavior*, 5: 71–97.

Harsanyi, J. (1962). "Measurement of social power, opportunity costs, and the theory of two-person bargaining games." *Behavioral Science*, 7: 67–80.

Hettich, W. and Winer, S.L. (1999). *Democratic Choice and Taxation*. Cambridge: Cambridge University Press.

Hillman, A. (1989). *The Political Economy of Protection*. Chur: Harwood.

Hillman, A. and Ursprung, H. (1988). "Domestic politics, foreign interests, and international trade policy." *American Economic Review*, 78: 729–745.

Hirshleifer, J. (1976). "Comment (on: Peltzman 1976)." *Journal of Law and Economics*, 19: 240–244.

Hojnacki, M. and Kimball, D.C. (1998). "Organized interests and the decision of whom to lobby in Congress." *American Political Science Review*, 92: 775–790.

Hoyt, W.H. and Toma, E.F. (1989). "State mandates and interest group lobbying." *Journal of Public Economics*, 38: 199–213.

Johnson, P.E. (1996). "Corporate political offices in a rent-seeking society." *Public Choice*, 88: 309–331.

Kagel, J.H. and Roth, A.E. (eds.) (1995). *The Handbook of Experimental Economics*. Princeton: Princeton University Press.

Kirchsteiger, G. and Prat, A. (2001). "Inefficient equilibria in lobbying." *Journal of Public Economics*, 82: 349–375.

Kollman, K. (1997). "Inviting friends to lobby: interest groups, ideological bias, and congressional committees." *American Journal of Political Science*, 41: 519–544.

Laffont, J. and Tirole, J. (1991). "The politics of government decisionmaking: a theory of regulatory capture." *Quarterly Journal of Economics*, 106: 1089–1127.

Lagerlöf, J. (1997). "Lobbying, information, and private and social welfare." *European Journal of Political Economy*, 13: 615–637.

Lohmann, S. (1995). "Information, access, and contributions: a signaling model of lobbying." *Public Choice*, 85: 267–284.

Lohmann, S. (1998). "An informational rationale for the power of special interests." *American Political Science Review*, 92: 809–827.

Marceau, N. and Smart, M. (2002). "Corporate lobbying and commitment failure in capital taxation." CESifo Working Paper No. 676.

Marcus, G.E. and Mackuen, M.B. (1993). "Anxiety, enthusiasm, and the vote: the emotional underpinnings of learning and involvement during presidential campaigns." *American Political Science Review*, 87: 672–685.

Mazza, I. and van Winden, F. (1996). "A political economic analysis of labor migration and income redistribution." *Public Choice*, 88: 333–363.

Mazza, I. and van Winden, F. (2000). "An endogenous policy model of hierarchical government." CREED Working Paper, University of Amsterdam.

Mazza, I. and van Winden, F. (2002a). "Does centralization increase the size of government? The effects of separation of powers and lobbying." *International Tax and Public Finance*, 9: 379–389.

Mazza, I. and van Winden, F. (2002b). "Delegation of lobbying to a policymaker." CREED Working Paper (in preparation), University of Amsterdam.

Milner, H.V. and Rosendorff, B.P. (1996). "Trade negotiations, information, and domestic politics: the role of domestic groups." *Economics and Politics*, 8: 145–189.

Mitchell, W.C. and Munger, M.C. (1991). "Economic models of interest groups: an introductory survey." *American Journal of Political Science*, 35: 512–546.

Moe, T.M. (1980). *The Organization of Interests*. Chicago: University of Chicago Press.

Moore, M.O. and Suranovic, S.M. (1992). "Lobbying vs. administered protection." *Journal of International Economics*, 32: 289–303.

Morton, R. and Cameron, C. (1992). "Elections and the theory of campaign contributions: a survey and critical analysis." *Economics and Politics*, 4: 79–108.

Neary, H.M. (1997). "A comparison of rent-seeking models and economic models of conflict." *Public Choice*, 93: 373–388.

Nitzan, S. (1994). "Modelling rent-seeking contests." *European Journal of Political Economy*, 10: 41–60.

Olson, M. (1965). *The Logic of Collective Action*. Cambridge: Harvard University Press.

Ortoni, A., Clore, G.L., and Collins, A. (1988). *The Cognitive Structure of Emotions*. Cambridge: Cambridge University Press.

Osborne, M.J. (1984). "Why do some goods bear higher taxes than others?" *Journal of Economic Theory*, 32: 111–127.

Osborne, M.J. and Slivinski, A. (1996). "A model of political competition with citizen candidates." *Quarterly Journal of Economics*, 111: 65–96.

Peck, R. (1986). "Power and linear income taxes: an example." *Econometrica*, 54: 87–94.

Pedersen, K.R. (1995). "Rent-seeking, political influence and inequality: a simple analytical example." *Public Choice*, 82: 281–305.

Pelzman, S. (1976). "Toward a more general theory of regulation." *Journal of Law and Economics*, 19: 211–240.

Persson, T. (1998). "Economic policy and special interest policy." *The Economic Journal*, 108: 310–327.

Persson, T. and Tabellini, G. (1994). "Does centralization increase the size of government?" *European Economic Review*, 38: 765–773.

Persson, T. and Tabellini, G. (2000). *Political Economics*. Cambridge: MIT Press.

Potters, J. (1992). "Lobbying and pressure." Tinbergen Institute Research Series No. 36, Amsterdam.

Potters, J. and Sloof, R. (1996). "Interest groups. A survey of empirical models that try to assess their influence." *European Journal of Political Economy*, 12: 403–442.

Potters, J., and Sloof, R., and van Winden, F. (1997). "Campaign expenditures, contributions and direct endorsements: the strategic use of information and money to influence voter behavior." *European Journal of Political Economy*, 13: 1–31.

Potters, J., and van Winden, F. (1990). "Modelling political pressure as transmission of information." *European Journal of Political Economy*, 6: 61–88.

Potters, J. and van Winden, F. (1992). "Lobbying and asymmetric information." *Public Choice*, 74: 269–292.

Potters, J. and van Winden, F. (1996). "Models of interest groups: four different approaches," in N. Schofield (ed.) *Collective Decision-Making, Social Choice and Political Economy*. Boston: Kluwer, pp. 337–362.

Prat, A. (2000a). "Campaign spending with office-seeking politicians, rational voters, and multiple lobbies." *Journal of Economic Theory*.

Prat, A. (2000b). "An economic analysis of campaign finance." *World Economics*, 1: 13–28.

Prat, A. (2001). "Campaign advertising and voter welfare." *Review of Economic Studies*.

Prat, A., and Rustichini, A. (1998). "Sequential common agency." Discussion Paper No. (9895). CentER, Tilburg University.

Prat, A. and Rustichini, A. (1999). "Games played through agents." Discussion Paper No. (9968). CentER, Tilburg University.

Przeworski, A. and Wallerstein, M. (1988). "Structural dependence of the state on capital." *American Political Science Review*, 82: 1–29.

Rama, M. and Tabellini, G. (1998). "Lobbying by capital and labor over trade and labor market policies." *European Economic Review*, 42: 1295–1316.

Rasmusen, E. (1993). "Lobbying when the decisionmaker can acquire independent information." *Public Choice*, 77: 899–913.

Renaud, P.S.A. (1989). *Applied Political Economic Modelling*. Heidelberg: Springer Verlag.

Renaud, P. and van Winden, F. (1988). "Fiscal behaviour and the growth of government in the Netherlands," in J. Lybeck and M. Henrekson (eds.) *Explaining the Growth of Government*. Amsterdam: North Holland, pp. 133–156.

Rothenberg, L.S. (1988). "Organizational maintenance and the retention decision in groups." *American Political Science Review*, 82: 1129–1152.

Sadiraj, V., Tuinstra, J., and van Winden, F. (2001). "A dynamic model of endogenous interest group sizes and policymaking." CREED/CENDEF Working Paper, University of Amsterdam.

Sadiraj, V., Tuinstra, J., and van Winden, F. (2002). "Interest groups and social dynamics in a model of spatial competition." CREED/CENDEF Working Paper, University of Amsterdam.

Saint-Paul, G. (2000). "The new political economy: recent books by Allan Drazen and Torsten Persson and Guido Tabellini." *Journal of Economic Literature*, 38: 915–925.

Sloof, R. (1998). *Game-Theoretic Models of the Political Influence of Interest Groups*. Boston: Kluwer.

Sloof, R. (1999). "Campaign contributions and the desirability of full disclosure laws." *Economics and Politics*, 11: 83–107.

Sloof, R. (2000). "Interest group lobbying and the delegation of policy authority." *Economics and Politics*, 12: 247–274.

Sloof, R., and van Winden, F. (2000). "Show them your teeth first!" *Public Choice*, 104: 81–120.

Spiller, P.T. (1990). "Politicians, interest groups, and regulators: a multi-principals agency theory of regulation, or 'let them be bribed'." *Journal of Law and Economics*, 33: 65–101.

Stigler, G. (1971). "The theory of economic regulation." *Bell Journal of Economics and Management*, 2: 3–21.

Sutter, D. (2002). "Constitutional prohibitions in a rent seeking model." *Public Choice*, 111: 105–125.

Tollison, R.D. (1997). "Rent seeking," in D.C. Mueller (ed.) *Perspectives on Public Choice*. Cambridge: Cambridge University Press, pp. 506–525.

Tullock, G. (1967). "The welfare costs of tariffs, monopolies, and theft." *Western Economic Journal*, 5: 224–232.

Tullock, G. (1980). "Efficient rent-seeking," in J.M. Buchanan, R.D. Tollison, and G. Tullock (eds.) *Toward a Theory of the Rent-Seeking Society*. College Station: Texas A&M University Press, pp. 97–112.

van Velthoven, B. (1989). *The Endogenization of Government Behaviour in Macroeconomic Models*. Berlin: Springer Verlag.

van Velthoven, B. and van Winden, F. (1985). "Towards a politico-economic theory of social security." *European Economic Review*, 27: 263–289.

Verbon, H. (1989). *The Evolution of Public Pension Schemes*. Berlin: Springer Verlag.

Welch, W. (1980). "The allocation of political monies: economic interest groups." *Public Choice*, 35: 97–120.

van Winden, F. (1983). *On the Interaction between State and Private Sector*. Amsterdam: North Holland.

van Winden, F. (1999). "On the economic theory of interest groups: towards a group frame of reference." *Public Choice*, 100: 1–29.

van Winden, F. (2002). "Experimental investigation of collective action," in S.L. Winer and H. Shibata (eds.) *Political Economy and Public Finance*. Cheltenham: Edward Elgar.

van Winden, F., Schram, A., and Groot, F. (1987). "The interaction between economics and politics: modelling cycles." *European Journal of Political Research*, 15: 185–202.

Wright, J.R. (1990). "Contributions, lobbying, and committee voting in the U.S. House of Representatives." *American Political Science Review*, 84: 417–438.

Zusman, P. (1976). "The incorporation and measurement of social power in economic models." *International Economic Review*, 17: 447–462.

INTERNATIONAL TRADE POLICY: DEPARTURE FROM FREE TRADE

In a world with no international boundaries and no sovereign governments, all trade would be domestic and there could be no international trade policy. Governments and national sovereignty introduce *international* trade, but the gains from free trade (Kemp, 1962; Samuelson, 1962) remain unaffected. Yet nonetheless governments have often chosen to depart from free trade. Economic research has taken two approaches to the departures from free trade. A conventional view in the international economics literature has been normative in developing a research agenda that shows how departure from free trade can enhance efficiency and maximize social welfare. A political-economy view synonymous with public (or rational) choice has approached departure from free trade from a positive perspective (explaining and predicting rather than recommending), and has shown why trade policy might *compromise* the efficiency of free trade for political and income-distribution reasons. The conventional normative views have origins in classical 19th century justifications put forward as exceptions to the case for the efficiency of free trade.

1. The Terms of Trade

A classical 19th century argument recognized that departure from free trade may increase the welfare of a population by improving the terms of trade. Gain through the terms of trade requires a population collectively to have monopsony power in the world market for imported goods. The usual outcome of a tariff (income effects can result in unusual outcomes) is an increased domestic (relative) price of imports and reduced domestic demand, and the terms of trade improve if the reduced domestic demand decreases world demand so that the relative price of imported goods falls in world markets. The cheaper imports are the source of social benefit. There are accompanying losses because of declines in the amount of trade and domestic inefficiency because of the tariff. An *optimum tariff* balances these losses against the gains from improvement in the terms of trade.

Since the gain to a population through an optimum tariff is at expense of people in other countries whose terms of trade have deteriorated, the optimum tariff is known as a beggar-thy-neighbor policy. World efficiency is also compromised for the benefit of a local population. Populations in countries that do not seek gain at the expense of others will not wish to have their governments impose optimum tariffs. There may in any event be no prospect of gain through an optimum tariff, since there may be no goods for which a country's population has a sufficiently large share of world consumption for collective monopsony power to be present. Whenever populations face given market-determined world prices, there is no collective monopsony power and the optimum tariff is zero.

There are problems other than willingness to take advantage and feasibility in seeking gain through optimum tariffs. Where feasible, optimum tariffs may result in foreign retaliatory tariffs that reverse beneficial terms of trade changes while further reducing the volume of trade (although terms of trade gains from an optimum tariff may be sustainable despite retaliation, Johnson, 1953–54). Benefits to a population also require that revenue from the tariff be used to finance increased public spending or to reduce other taxes. For example, a government of a country whose population has collective monopsony power might decide to use a tariff on coffee to reduce the world price of coffee and so improve the country's terms of trade as an importer of coffee. Domestic consumers of coffee lose when the domestic price of coffee increases. The offsetting gain to consumers is through the tariff revenue that the government has collected. There is however considerable evidence of wasteful government spending (Tanzi and Schuknecht, 2000). A government that does not spend the revenue in a socially beneficial way, or does not reduce other taxes, fails to deliver the offsetting gain. The legacy of the tariff for domestic consumers is the higher domestic price of coffee. The country's tariff will have provided benefits to coffee consumers in other countries through the reduced world price of coffee.

Market power in world markets has generally been exercised through monopoly (e.g., the OPEC oil cartel) rather than through monopsony. Documented cases of optimum tariffs improving the terms of trade are uncommon in the empirical literature. Also uncommon is documentation of governments declaring that the purpose of a tariff is to mobilize monopsony power of the domestic population to improve the terms of trade.

2. Infant Industries

The optimum tariff is one of two classical cases for departure from free trade. The second classical argument justified temporary protection to allow a new or infant domestic industry to establish itself (Kemp, 1960). The theme of the infant industry argument has also reappeared in a literature that rediscovered learning externalities to explain why diminishing returns do not constrain growth. More direct domestic policies can correct for the market imperfections that underlie the infant-industry argument (Baldwin, 1969). The infant industry argument is therefore a *second-best* case for public policy when first-best corrective policies are unavailable. Uncompensated private learning externalities, which are often proposed as underlying a case for infant industry protection, call for compensating subsidies as a first-best response. Unless the infant industry is a monopoly, protection does not compensate a domestic producer for beneficial externalities provided to other domestic competitors. There are, in addition, moral hazard problems associated with protection of infant industries. Since the reward for doing well is the end of protection, it may be preferable for a producer with infant status never to perform too well, and so to remain a protected infant. Since there are many potential infant industries, a government also has to decide which industry to protect, and has to avoid political favors.

3. Distortions or the Theory of the Second Best

In second-best situations there are uncorrectable domestic market inefficiencies (or "distortions"). The unresolved domestic inefficiencies can be due to externalities as in the case of the infant industry, or can be due to domestic monopoly, public goods, or restrictions on prices in markets such as minimum wages. The theory of the second best proposes that, if *all* domestic market imperfections cannot be corrected, departures from free trade may be efficient and increase social welfare. Minimum wages provide one example. In the minimum-wage case, a country's international comparative advantage is in labor-intensive production. The direction of international trade has however been distorted by the minimum wage, which has artificially increased the domestic cost of labor. The first-best policy is to eliminate the minimum wage. With the minimum wage, however, present, the realized direction of international trade may be contrary to true comparative advantage, since domestic labor looks scarce or expensive because of the minimum wage but is actually relatively abundant and cheap. Second-best theory in that case proposes elimination of the "incorrect" international trade.

Another example of a second-best case for departure from free trade is based on the presence of environmental externalities. Computation of the true cost of production of a good when environmental costs are included can switch a country's comparative advantage. The first-best response is to correct the environmental externality domestically at its source. If however correction of the externality cannot take place at the domestic source, the "second-best" trade policy may no longer be free trade. The efficient second-best policy depends on whether the domestic industry that is the source of environmental damage is an exporter or confronts import competition. If the industry exports its output, an export tax decreases domestic production and thereby reduces domestic environmental damage. If a polluting industry confronts import competition, a government subsidy to imports is the appropriate second-best policy, since, by making competing imports cheaper, the government reduces domestic output of the local industry. There is a compendium of cases where the theory of the second best shows how efficiency gains can be achieved through departures from free trade (Bhagwati, 1971).

4. Strategic Trade Policy

Strategic trade policy is a second-best proposal for government intervention where the second-best enters because of imperfect competition in international markets. When international markets are not competitive, rents (or excess profits) may be present. Strategic trade policy devises means of capturing the rents for a country's own nationals rather than leaving the rents with foreigners. Strategic trade policy arose as an adjunct to a body of literature that called itself the "new" international trade theory. The new theory differed from the old in recognizing that international markets might not be competitive and in emphasizing the potential importance of economies of scale. Many variants of strategic trade policy have been proposed (Brander, 1995). In the basic Cournot duopoly model, for example, a domestic firm was described as confronting a foreign firm in a third market. A subsidy by the government to its domestic firm allowed the firm to credibly expand output beyond the Cournot equilibrium output, and profits or rents of the domestic firm then increased at the expense of the foreign firm. The same type of rent transfer to a domestic firm could take place through an import duty if a foreign firm were selling in the home market.

Proposals for strategic trade policy proposal are related to the two classical cases for departure from free trade. Like the optimum tariff, strategic trade policy is based on gains in non-competitive markets at the expense of foreigners, while, in third markets, problems of retaliation arise, since a foreign government can neutralize gains from strategic trade policy by subsidizing its own national firm. Since resources and personnel attracted to an industry favored by strategic trade policy are unavailable for other industries, policies that favor one domestic firm or industry are at the expense of other domestic firms or industries (Dixit and Grossman, 1986). As with the infant-industry case, a belief in the effectiveness of strategic trade policy requires an accompanying belief that political decision makers can maximize social welfare by knowing "how to pick winners and losers" from among the domestic firms that are eligible under the theory for government assistance. All domestic firms facing foreign competition in imperfect markets are in principle eligible for assistance through strategic trade policy.

Strategic trade policy envisages policies as chosen to maximize social welfare (defined as profits of the domestic firm plus welfare of domestic consumers when intervention is in domestic and not in third markets). Nonetheless strategic trade policy benefits the firms whose profits increase (unless all profit increases can be discriminately taxed). Given the broad scope of eligibility, beneficiaries of strategic trade policy can be selected to reward political support such as provided by campaign contributions, which is a different problem from government having inadequate information to pick winners and losers.

Global capital markets allow individual shareholders to diversify risk by owning stock in both "domestic" and "foreign" firms. A diversified shareholder has no need for strategic trade policy. Indeed, calls for strategic trade policy introduce extraneous uncertainty into asset diversification decisions, since, in deciding on an asset portfolio, investors need to guess whether a government will heed a proposal of intervention on behalf of a firm (Feeney and Hillman, 2001).

Characteristics of strategic trade policy appear present in government policies toward agriculture (Bagwell and Staiger, 2001). Studies have also pointed to the world duopoly of aircraft frames and have considered possibilities in semi-conductors and automobiles. With the exception perhaps of agricultural subsidies, cases of policy makers following recommendations of strategic trade policy are uncommon.

5. Revenue Motives

Government revenue can be a motive for taxes on international trade. Taxation of internationally traded goods has the administrative advantage of goods passing through a limited number of geographic locations where revenue can be collected. Because of ease of collection, taxes on international trade (or taxes for right of passage) were often the first taxes historically levied. Taxes on international trade have remained significant government revenue sources where domestic taxes cannot be levied because of ineffective tax administration. Where possible, domestic taxes however provide broader tax bases than taxes on international trade. A domestic sales tax has in particular a broader base for taxation than an import tariff, which only taxes imported goods.

Taxes on imports have often too high to maximize revenue: with sufficiently high import duties, there is of course no tax revenue at all, since there are no imports. If a country's population has the collective monopsony power necessary for an optimum tariff, the revenue-maximizing tariff exceeds the optimum tariff. By maximizing revenue from the tariff, a government would be shifting real income abroad.

More significantly, a revenue motive is at odds with restrictions on international trade through import quotas that are freely assigned to private importers. Governments seeking revenue would auction the quotas, but auctions have been rare. In another type of import quota known as a voluntary export restraint, governments have forgone revenue by assigning rights to sell in domestic markets to foreign firms. Historical cases and contemporary instances where poorer countries lack effective tax administrations aside, revenue needs do not explain departure from free trade.

6. Protection and Political Economy

The normative descriptions of beneficial consequences of departure from free trade have in common the point of departure that markets have failed to provide efficient outcomes. Second-best policies specify uncorrectable market inefficiencies. Strategic trade policy is based on rents in inefficient non-competitive markets. In the classical precursors, the optimum tariff argument required non-competitive markets that allowed realization of monopsony power; and the infant-industry argument was based on markets that were inefficient because of non-internalized beneficial externalities. A political economy or public choice view in contrast accepts that markets and therefore free trade policies are proximately efficient, and looks for political incentives for policy makers to choose departures from free trade. Economic theory shows how some groups benefit from the inefficiency of a departure from free trade. Protectionist policies can benefit broad factor classes. More particularly, beneficiaries tend to be identified with incomes from non-diversified industry-specific sources (Jones, 1971). Rather than second-best *corrections* for inefficiency, the public choice or political economy view has approached departure from free trade as *creating* inefficiency, for political gain related to incomes in import-competing industries.

Feasible policies depend on (that is, are endogenous to) institutions and laws. Policy outcomes also depend on abilities of interest groups to organize and mobilize resources for collective political action (Olson, 1965). Organized interests groups are generally better able to influence policy decisions than the broad population. The per capita stakes of special interests are also higher: special interests are seeking to increase their incomes, while the losses of consumers from protection of any one industry are small, because spending on the products of the industry in general comprises only a small part of an individual's or household's total spending. A public choice view predicts that, under these conditions, political-economy considerations can result in socially undesirable protectionist policies. Incumbent governments or politicians may seek maximal political support by trading off the political benefits from providing increased income to organized industry interests against the political cost of dissatisfaction of disorganized voters with departures from free trade (Hillman, 1982). The incumbent policy maker may confront many organized interest groups and may be able to design a combination of policies to maximize the payments received from selling protection to the different organized interests (Grossman and Helpman, 1994). Rather than decided by incumbents, policies may be determined through proposals made by candidates competing for political office (Hillman and Ursprung, 1988; Magee et al., 1989). Political-support considerations have also been linked to the sudden collapse of domestic industries that have lost comparative advantage (Cassing and Hillman, 1986), and to the choice of the means of protection (Cassing and Hillman, 1985; Hillman and Ursprung, 1988). Empirical studies have confirmed that departures from free trade are in general not the consequence of second-best intent to improve efficiency or maximize social welfare, but reflect protection related to political support and domestic income distribution (Baldwin, 1984; Hillman, 1989, chapter 11; Rodrik, 1995).

7. Contingent Protection

Contingent protection differs from protection in place. A level of protection defines protection in place. Contingent protection is defined through legal rules that specify conditions under which protection can be provided. Anti-dumping duties are a form of contingent protection. Producers can successfully undertake legal proceedings to request anti-dumping duties, if foreign firms can be shown to be causing injury through unfair competitive practices. Evidence of unfair practices (or unfair trade) may be domestic sales by foreign producers at less than cost, or sales in the domestic market at prices less than in the foreign producers' home markets. A claim of dumping is similar to a claim of predatory pricing (where firms are claimed to be selling at below cost with the intent of eliminating rivals from a market). Anti-dumping and predatory-pricing laws are complex, and are open to ambiguities in interpretation, since costs may be difficult to define and competitors reduce prices in the normal course of competition. While proven cases of predatory pricing are uncommon, claims of injury through the trade-related counterpart of dumping tend to be more often accepted by courts.

A second form of contingent protection consists of import duties that neutralize (or countervail) subsidies that foreign producers are shown to be receiving from their governments. Or the subsidies may be implicit within ownership of foreign competitors by foreign governments.

Contingent protection can also be provided without the requirement of demonstrating unfair foreign competition through escape clause or safeguard provisions. The escape is from prior trade liberalization commitments, to safeguard an industry that is being injured by import competition. The relief from import competition is intended to be temporary (as in the infant industry case), to give a domestic industry time to adjust to competition from imports.

Contingent protection is encoded in the rules of the World Trade Organization (WTO) and the pre-1995 predecessor General Agreement on Tariffs and Trade (GATT) (Jackson, 1997). Trade liberalization agreements are negotiated under conditions of uncertainty about future comparative advantage. Contingent protection facilitates ex-ante trade liberalization agreements under conditions of uncertainty, since governments know that liberalization can be reversed in cases where ex-post contingencies call for protection (Ethier, 2002).

The legalistic language of contingent protection differs from concepts of economic theory. The unfair competition and injury defined in laws on contingent protection contradict the perspective of economic theory that competition is socially beneficial. The harm or injury defined in contingent-protection laws is incurred by producers, who benefit from less competition rather than more. The benefit from competition in economic theory is to consumers or society at large. Contingent-protection laws therefore reflect political sensitivity to producer interests and unemployment in import-competing industries.

It is irrational for foreign producers to pay anti-dumping duties if the duties can be avoided by charging higher prices. The initiation (or threat thereof) of anti-dumping procedures is therefore often sufficient to lead foreign producers to increase prices (Prusa, 1992; Schuknecht, 1992). Anti-dumping laws can thereby sustain non-competitive pricing in domestic markets by disciplining foreign producers to cooperate in accepting the price leadership role of domestic producers in domestic markets (Hillman, 1990).

Escape clause or safeguard provisions introduce moral hazard into incentives of producers to claim injury. There can be asymmetric information: producers may know, but the government and the courts may not know, whether producer injury is due to imports, or is due to reasons such as a decline in domestic demand or inept management of domestic firms. The asymmetric information allows spurious claims of injury to be made in order to obtain the benefits of protection (Leidy and Hoekman, 1991).

A mechanism of contingent protection that is not part of formal national trade law or GATT/WTO procedures takes the form of voluntary restraints on exports negotiated between governments of importing and exporting countries. The restraints set limits on total allowable foreign sales in the domestic market. To ensure adherence to the limit on imports, foreign exporters are assigned domestic market quotas. As with anti-dumping duties, pre-conditions are established for non-competitive practices. Domestic producers can set domestic prices or quantities to be sold with foreknowledge of supply by the foreign cartel that has been created by the inter-governmental agreement (Hillman, 1990). The price to domestic consumers increases, and domestic and foreign producers earn higher profits in the domestic market. The higher profits of domestic firms reflect the successful protectionist objective. The higher profits of foreign firms are compensation for the protection that has been provided to domestic producers (Hillman and Ursprung, 1988; Hillman, 1990; Ethier, 1991, 2002). There are similarities and also links (Rosendorff, 1996; Ethier, 2002) between voluntary export restraints and anti-dumping duties. In both cases, trade policies allow non-competitive behavior that increases domestic and foreign producer profits.

8. Protectionism as Insurance

Contingent protection suggests insurance. Through the rules of contingent protection, import-competing producers are provided with insurance against cheaper imports. Since contingent protection is usually discriminatory, it also provides insurance to third-countries whose exports are not constrained (Ethier, 1991, 2002). Protectionism has been interpreted as insurance against trade-related income losses provided by government maximizing social welfare (Eaton and Grossman, 1985). Protectionism as social insurance (insurance provided by government) is another normative second-best case for departure from free trade. Social insurance is a second-best policy, because private insurance markets do not provide the income protection that people in seek. Protection as social insurance has also been proposed as a positive theory to explain observed conservative income-maintaining policies in industries confronting import competition (Corden, 1974).

There is a problem with a second-best normative interpretation of protection as social insurance. Asymmetric information that prevents private insurance markets from efficiently providing insurance also prevents government from replicating missing insurance markets (Dixit, 1992).

A public choice perspective also notes that political motives for providing protection can look like replication of missing or incomplete insurance markets. In an expanding industry there are ambiguities in distinguishing politically provided benefits from incomes earned through personal merit and effort. The same ambiguities about sources of benefit are not present when protection increases incomes in an industry in decline because of lost comparative advantage. It is therefore politically advantageous to assist declining industries, because the benefits from political favors are clear to the beneficiaries (Hillman, 1982). Characteristics of insurance are present when protection provides benefits to industries in decline. If protection is insurance, the insurance coverage is however selective and incomplete. Only import-competing industries are eligible, and import-competing industries do not benefit equally from the insurance provided by government. Industry collapse can take place in the face of cheaper imports (Cassing and Hillman, 1986). The selective insurance reflects different political benefits from ex-post protection. In cases in particular of contingent protection where an insurance motive is explicitly indicated, ambiguities about the existence and source of injury have allowed decisions about whether to provide protection to become politicized (Finger et al., 1982; Schuknecht, 1992).

9. Domestic Political Objectives and the Terms of Trade

Domestic political objectives have been linked to effects through the terms of trade (Bagwell and Staiger, 1999). The domestic efficiency costs of protectionist policies are reduced or are not incurred at all, if the efficiency costs can be shifted to people abroad through improvements in the terms of the trade. In contrast to the optimum tariff argument, the objective of government in this scenario is not necessarily gain to society through improved terms of trade, but to provide protection. Whether governments can provide politically motivated protection while felicitously increasing social welfare is an empirical question. Feasibility depends on terms of trade gains to offset domestic efficiency losses.

Whether efficiency costs of protection can be moved to foreigners at all is also an empirical question. The answer depends on the ability to influence the terms on the trade, and, if the terms of trade can be influenced, on the absence of retaliation and the realization of social benefits through government revenue. If social welfare increases because of terms of trade changes even though there is a political interest in providing protection, there is a normative case for departure from free trade. In this case, pursuing a political objective of protection can be socially beneficial.

10. Rent Seeking

A rent is income that can be increased or taken away without changing behavior. Rents are therefore earned by industry-specific factors of production that have no substitution possibilities in production, and the activity of seeking policies that increase incomes or prevent income declines in import-competing industries is therefore a form of rent seeking (Tullock, 1967). Protectionist policies also provide rents for importers who obtain quota rights (Krueger, 1974). Anti-dumping laws and voluntary export restraints negotiated between governments provide rents for both domestic producers and for foreign sellers. Rents and rent seeking are therefore parts of a political-economy view of international trade policy. The social losses due to trade-related rent seeking depend on how resources used in rent seeking influence political decisions, and on whether the rents that are sought are income transfers from others through protection or are in place through import (or export) quotas (Hillman and Riley, 1989). The efficiency losses from willingness to depart from free trade consist of the resources attracted to rent seeking, and are an addition to the losses from protection due to substitution effects in production and consumption. Although not incorporated in the conventional normative analyses, incentives for rent seeking are also part of strategic trade policy. A government considering following the recommendations of strategic trade policy would face rent-seeking activity from the diverse potential beneficiaries of government assistance.

11. Voting

When trade policy is decided by majority voting as an election issue, there is no assurance that free trade will be chosen. A self-interested median voter will want free trade only if his or her personal assets and income sources correspond to the average asset composition and income sources for the economy at large (Mayer, 1984). Trade policy can be the dominant issue in an election (Irwin, 1994). In general, however, unless voters happen to live in Switzerland (Weck-Hannemann, 1990), voters do not have opportunities to vote on trade policy directly. Political representatives are then in a position to decide on trade policy.

12. Why is Trade Policy Used to Redistribute Income?

There remains the question why political decision makers should wish to use protectionist trade policy to redistribute income. A country whose population has collective monopsony power in world markets has reason to use a tariff to achieve a domestic income distribution objective because of the benefits from terms of trade improvements *that offset, in whole or in part,* the domestic inefficiencies of tariffs. Part of the cost of protection can thereby be transferred to foreigners. Yet, if there are gains from an optimum tariff and a government has no qualms about imposing costs on foreigners for the benefit of the local population, we might expect the government to seek to impose the optimum tariff in any event without regard for the domestic income distribution objective. Also, optimum tariffs do not seem all that relevant for many goods and many governments.

If world prices are more or less independent of domestic demand, protectionist policies create domestic inefficiencies without offsetting terms of trade changes. The domestic inefficiencies could be avoided if non-distorting lump-sum taxes and subsidies were available to redistribute income. Since non-distorting means of redistributing income are in practice not feasible, policy makers have no choice but to use some form of inefficiency-creating mechanism to redistribute income. Still, this does not answer the question why trade policy should be used to redistribute income, since there are in general income transfer mechanisms that incur smaller efficiency losses (Mayer and Riezman, 1990). Governments should be expected to use these more efficient means of income transfer, since, by consensus, everybody in the population would wish the inefficiency associated with redistribution to be minimized.

The consensus in favor of efficiency has been the basis for a prediction that political redistribution *is in practice always undertaken* in the most efficient way (Wittman, 1995). If that were so, departures from free trade should be observed as a means of income distribution only when more efficient means of redistribution are unavailable. All observed trade restrictions could then be interpreted ex-post as having been the most efficient ex-ante means of achieving policy makers' income redistribution objectives.

Choice of the efficient means of income redistribution is however compromised by political benefits from information asymmetries. Information about government policy has political consequences. Political decision makers gain by not publicizing to voters at large policies that benefit special interests. Surreptitious or hidden income transfers are politically more advantageous. Departures from free trade are obtuse means of transferring income. Voters may not be aware that a tariff that taxes foreign goods is at the same time a subsidy to domestic import-competing producers. The rhetoric of unfair foreign competition or protecting domestic jobs against foreign competition may be used. Voluntary export restraints are a particularly obtuse means of income redistribution through trade restrictions. The government sets limits on permissible quantities of imports and directs foreign exporters to set market shares. Foreign exporters thereby establish a cartel for supply to the domestic market. The restricted domestic supply increases the domestic price, which provides the protectionist income transfer to import-competing domestic producers. The benefits to domestic producers from protection have been achieved through voluntary compliance with foreign competitors

If the information is not personally useful, voters have reason to be "rationally ignorant" of trade policy issues. Voters are however not equally ignorant of all income transfer mechanisms. A direct income transfer that is "hidden" in a line item of a government's budget can be found if someone is looking. The transfer of income via a tariff from consumers to protected producers is indirect and less obvious. Tariffs have the politically expedient characteristic that domestic buyers directly make income transfers to domestic producers through the increased domestic price facilitated by the tariff. The income transfer using through protectionism does not require intermediation of government through taxation and budgetary allocations. The indirect nature of redistribution by trade policy therefore explains why international trade restrictions are used as means of income redistribution when more efficient but more obvious means of income transfer are available (Stephen Magee et al., 1989). Protection then makes clear to the beneficiaries that the government has provided them with benefits, when voters at large have reason to be "rationally ignorant" of trade policy issues.

13. Agriculture

Agriculture has been a special case for government intervention. Rarely have governments left agriculture to the intervention-free determination of markets (Anderson and Josling, 1993). Agriculture is often taxed in poorer countries, where agriculture is a large part of national income and agricultural goods are exported. An export tax is sometimes directly levied or government enforces a position for itself as monopsonistic domestic buyer and pays farmers a low price and sells in the world market at a higher price. To obtain revenue from an export tax or domestic monopsony, the government needs to be effective in preventing smuggling, which creates a need for resources for policing of borders. The benefits from goods escaping export tax or the monopsony price and reaching the market outside the country introduce gains from corruption through the participation of border officials in smuggling activities. If the corruption reaches into the government, smuggling can be extensive and little official government revenue may be provided.

The taxes on agriculture in poorer countries reflect the search for extensive and available tax bases, and also, since agricultural sectors are large in poorer countries, the taxes on agriculture also reflect the principle that larger groups face higher costs of collective action. Since many of these countries are dictatorships or quasi-dictatorships, the taxes also reflect the fact that those with power exploit the powerless.

The principle of organizational advantage applied to the effectiveness of organization of small groups underlies government assistance to agriculture in richer countries, where agriculture has been extensively subsidized or protected. The policies that support agriculture in richer countries are also sometimes explained as justified by an objective of sustaining traditional rural life and avoiding depopulation of the countryside. The beneficiaries of agricultural subsidies are however often large firms rather than smaller family farms.

Trade conflicts involving agriculture have often been framed in terms of motives other than protection. For example, European restrictions on imports of U.S. beef have been framed in terms of the purported health hazard from hormones given to U.S. cattle. Protectionism has reflected former colonial ties in discrimination by the European Union in favor of imports of bananas from former European colonies, to the disadvantage of bananas grown (often on U.S.-owned plantations) in Central America.

14. National Security

Protection of agriculture is often justified on grounds of national security. Consequences of vulnerability to foreign suppliers were demonstrated when the international oil cartel OPEC imposed export embargos. There have also been cases where countries under threat from foreign aggressors found that defense equipment, which had been ordered and paid for, was withheld by foreign suppliers. In other cases, when foreign-purchased defense equipment has been required for self-defense, foreign governments have withheld spare parts. Trade embargos provide a normative case for self-reliance because of national security concerns (Mayer, 1977; Arad and Hillman, 1979). Countries also impose restrictions on exports because of national security concerns.

15. Views of Government

With national security and some other limited cases as exceptions (for example, trade in heroin), there is a compelling case for free trade independent of international boundaries. Departures from free trade have however often taken place. The political economy premises of the public choice approach point to political motives and income distribution as underlying the departures from free trade and to inefficiencies incurred, including through rent seeking. Theories set out in the conventional normative view have, in contrast, described how governments can act in the public interest by correcting inefficiencies when departing from free trade.

Since the political economy premises of public choice offer positive conclusions and the conventional theories offer normative recommendations, the two approaches have been complementary. Open lines of communication between the approaches require however a maintained clear distinction become normative and positive analysis. The distinction is lost and lines of communication are not present when a normative belief that government *should* act in the public interest becomes a prediction that government *will* always act in the public interest, because government *should* be benevolent. The censorship that is then implicitly imposed limits politically correct economic analysis to normative theory where government can do no wrong (Hillman, 1998). Since non-virtuous government is by hypothesis excluded from economic analysis, the consequent theories *can only* be normative. Addressing *why* governments have chosen to depart from free trade may require introducing non-virtuous government into economic analysis. A public choice perspective would advise caution in pursuing a research agenda that provides a repertoire of normative arguments consistent with departure from free trade by virtuous government. When policy makers are politically motivated, the normative proposals can be misused to justify politically expedient policy decisions.

In the mid-1990s, the political economy premises of public choice began to be widely adopted in descriptions of departure from free trade (e.g., Grossman and Helpman, 2002). With the exception of agriculture and national security, and limited incidents of contingent protection, governments were at the same time, after extensive liberalization, no longer significantly departing from free trade (*see trade liberalization and globalization*).

ARYE L. HILLMAN

REFERENCES

Anderson, K. and Josling, T. (1993). "The challenge to economists of multilateral trade negotiations on agricultural protection." *Food Research Institute Studies*, 24: 275–304; reprinted (1995) in G.H. Peters (ed.) *Agricultural Economics. International Library of Critical Writings in Economics*, ch. 21. Cheltenham, U.K: Edward Elgar.

Arad, R.W. and Hillman, A.L. (1979). "Embargo threat, learning and departure from comparative advantage." *Journal of International Economics*, 9: 265–275.

Bagwell, K. and Staiger, R.W. (1999). "An economic theory of GATT." *American Economic Review*, 89: 215–248.

Bagwell, K. and Staiger, R.W. (2001). "Strategic trade, competitive industries, and agricultural trade disputes." *Economics and Politics*, 13: 113–128.

Baldwin, R.E. (1969). "The case against infant-industry protection." *Journal of Political Economy*, 77: 295–305.

Baldwin, R.E. (1984). "Trade policies in developed countries," in R. Jones and P. Kenen (eds.) *Handbook of International Economics*. Amsterdam: North-Holland, pp. 571–619.

Bhagwati, J.N. (1971). "The generalized theory of distortions and welfare," in J.N. Bhagwati, R.W. Jones, R.A. Mundell, and J. Vanek (eds.) *Trade, Balance of Payments, and Growth: Essays in Honor of Charles P. Kindleberger*. Amsterdam: North-Holland, pp. 69–90.

Brander, J.A. (1995). "Strategic trade policy," in G.M. Grossman and K. Rogoff (eds.) *Handbook of International Economics*. Amsterdam: North-Holland, pp. 1395–1455.

Cassing, J.H. and Hillman, A.L. (1985). "Political influence motives and the choice between tariffs and quotas." *Journal of International Economics*, 19: 279–290.

Cassing, J.H. and Hillman, A.L. (1986). "Shifting comparative advantage and senescent industry collapse." *American Economic Review*, 76: 516–523; reprinted (2004) in J.N. Bhagwati and B.P. Rosendorff (eds.) *Readings in the Political Economy of Trade Policy*. Cambridge, MA: MIT Press.

Corden, W.C. (1974). *Trade Policy and Economic Welfare*, 2nd edn, 1997. Oxford: Oxford University Press.

Dixit, A. and Grossman, G.M. (1986). "Targeted export promotion with several oligopolistic industries." *Journal of International Economics*, 21: 233–249.

Dixit, A. (1992). "Trade policy with imperfect information, in R.W. Jones and A.O. Krueger (eds.) *The Political Economy of International Trade: Essays in Honor of Robert E. Baldwin*. Oxford: Blackwell, pp. 9–24.

Eaton J. and Grossman, G.M. (1985). "Optimal commercial policy when markets are incomplete." *Canadian Journal of Economics*, 18: 258–272.

Ethier, W.J. (1991). "The economics and political economy of managed trade," in A.L. Hillman (ed.) *Markets and Politicians*: Boston: Kluwer Academic Publishers, pp. 283–306.

Ethier, W.J. (2002). "Unilateralism in a multilateral world." *Economic Journal*, 112: 266–292.

Feeney, J. and Hillman, A.L. (2001). "Privatization and the political economy of strategic trade policy." *International Economic Review*, 42: 535–556.

Finger, J.M., Hall, H.K., and Nelson, D.R. (1982). "The political economy of administered protection." *American Economic Review*, 72: 452–466.

Grossman, G.M. and Helpman, E. (1994). "Protection for sale." *American Economic Review*, 84: 833–850; reprinted (2004) in J.N. Bhagwati and B.P. Rosendorff (eds.) *Readings in the Political Economy of Trade Policy*. Cambridge, MA: MIT Press.

Grossman, G.M. and Helpman, E. (2002). *Interest Groups and Trade Policy*. Princeton, NJ: Princeton University Press.

Hillman, A.L. (1982). "Declining industries and political-support protectionist motives." *American Economic Review*, 72: 1180–1187; reprinted (2004) in J.N. Bhagwati and

B.P. Rosendorff (eds.) *Readings in the Political Economy of Trade Policy*. Cambridge, MA: MIT Press.

Hillman, A.L. (1989). *The Political Economy of Protection*. Chur: Harwood Academic Publishers.

Hillman, A.L. (1990). "Protectionist policies as the regulation of international industry." *Public Choice*, 67: 101–110.

Hillman, A.L. (1992). "International trade policy: benevolent dictators and optimizing politicians." *Public Choice*, 74: 1–15.

Hillman, A.L. (1998). "Political economy and political correctness." *Public Choice*, 96: 219–239 (Presidential Address, European Public Choice Society, Prague, April 1997).

Hillman, A.L. and Ursprung, H.W. (1988). "Domestic politics, foreign interests and international trade policy." *American Economic Review*, 78: 729–745; reprinted (2004) in J.N. Bhagwati and B.P. Rosendorff (eds.) *Readings in the Political Economy of Trade Policy*. Cambridge MA: MIT Press.

Hillman, A.L. and Riley, J. (1989). "Politically contestable rents and transfers." *Economics and Politics*, 1: 17–39; reprinted (2004) in J.N. Bhagwati and B.P. Rosendorff (eds.) *Readings in the Political Economy of Trade Policy*. Cambridge MA: MIT Press.

Irwin, D. (1994). "The political economy of free trade: voting in the British general election of 1906." *Journal of Law and Economics*, 37: 75–108.

Jackson, J.H. (1997). *The World Trading System: Law and Policy of International Relations*, 2nd edn. Cambridge, MA: MIT Press.

Johnson, H.G. (1953–54). "Optimum tariffs and retaliation." *Review of Economic Studies*, 21: 142–153.

Jones, R.W. (1971). "A three-factor model in theory, trade, and history," in J.N. Bhagwati, R.W. Jones, R.A. Mundell, and J. Vanek (eds.) *Trade, the Balance of Payments, and Growth: Essays in Honor of Charles B. Kindleberger*. Amsterdam: North-Holland, pp. 3–21.

Kemp, M.C. (1960). "The mill-bastable infant-industry dogma." *Journal of Political Economy*, 68: 65–67.

Kemp, M.C. (1962). "The gains from international trade." *Economic Journal*, 72: 803–819.

Krueger, A.O. (1974). "The political economy of the rent seeking society." *American Economic Review*, 64: 291–303; reprinted (1980) in J.M. Buchanan, R.D. Tollison, and G. Tullock (eds.) *Toward a Theory of the Rent-Seeking Society*. Texas A&M Press, pp. 51–70.

Leidy, M.P. and Hoekman, B.M. (1991). "Spurious injury as indirect rent seeking: free trade under the prospect of protection." *Economics and Politics*, 3: 111–137.

Magee, S., Brock, W.A., and Young, L. (1989). *Black Hole Tariffs and Endogenous Policy Theory*. Cambridge, MA: Cambridge University Press.

Mayer, W. (1977). "The national defense tariff argument reconsidered." *Journal of International Economics*, 7: 363–377.

Mayer, W. (1984). "Endogenous tariff formation." *American Economic Review*, 74: 970–985; reprinted (2004) in J.N. Bhagwati and B.P. Rosendorff (eds.) *Readings in the Political Economy of Trade Policy*. Cambridge MA: MIT Press.

Mayer, W. and Riezman, R. (1990). "Voter preferences for trade policy instruments." *Economics and Politics*, 2: 259–273.

Olson, M. (1965). *The Logic of Collective Action: Public Goods and the Theory of Groups*. Cambridge, MA: Harvard University Press.

Prusa, T.J. (1992). "Why are so many anti-dumping petitions withdrawn?" *Journal of International Economics*, 33: 1–20.

Rodrik, D. (1995). "Political economy of trade policy," in G.M. Grossman and K. Rogoff (eds.) *Handbook of International Economics*. Amsterdam: North-Holland, pp. 1457–1495.

Rosendorff, B.P. (1996). "Voluntary export restraints, antidumping procedure, and domestic politics." *American Economic Review*, 86: 544–561; reprinted (2004) in J.N. Bhagwati and B.P. Rosendorff (eds.) *Readings in the Political Economy of Trade Policy*. Cambridge MA: MIT Press.

Samuelson, P.A. (1962). "The gains from trade once again." *Economic Journal*, 72: 820–829.

Schuknecht, L. (1992). *Trade Protection in the European Community*. Chur: Harwood Academic Publishers.

Tanzi, V. and Schuknecht, L. (2000). *Public Spending in the 20th Century*. New York: Cambridge University Press.

Tullock, G. (1967). "The welfare costs of tariffs, monopoly, and theft." *Western Economic Journal*, 5, 224–232; reprinted (1980) in J.M. Buchanan, R.D. Tollison, and G. Tullock (eds.) *Toward a Theory of the Rent-Seeking Society*. Texas A&M Press, pp. 39–50.

Weck-Hannemann, H. (1990). "Protection under direct democracy." *Journal of Theoretical and Institutional Economics*, 146: 389–418.

Wittman, D. (1995). *The Myth of Democratic Failure: Why Democratic Institutions are Efficient*. Chicago: The University of Chicago Press.

J

JAMES M. BUCHANAN

1. Introduction

James M. Buchanan was born on October 3, 1919, in Murfeesboro, Tennessee. He grew up on a farm in this area of the United States. His post-secondary school education consists of a B.A. degree from Middle Tennessee State University (1940), an M.A. degree in economics from the University of Tennessee (1941), and a Ph.D. degree in economics from the University of Chicago (1948). He served in the U.S. Navy in the Pacific during World War II, where he received a Bronze Star. He has taught at the following universities: Tennessee, Florida State, Virginia, University of California, Los Angeles, Virginia Polytechnic Institute, and George Mason University where he still works today. He also maintains an office at Virginia Polytechnic Institute. He has held endowed chairs in economics at Virginia, Virginia Polytechnic Institute, and George Mason University. He was Department Chair at Florida State. He was Department Chair and Director and cofounder of the Thomas Jefferson Center for Political Economy at Virginia. He was General Director of the Center for Study of Public Choice at both Virginia Polytechnic Institute and George Mason. He has also served as a visiting professor at the University of Miami, Brigham Young University, the London School of Economics, and Cambridge University. He spent a year in Italy as a Fulbright Research Scholar. He is a former President of the Mont Pelerin Society, the Western Economic Association, and the Southern Economic Association. He has been awarded many honorary doctorates, including ones from University of Catania and the New University of Lisbon. He is a Distinguished Fellow of the American Economic Association. He received the Alfred Nobel Memorial Prize in Economics in 1986, the last year the award was tax-free.

2. My Plan

My approach to a Buchanan biography will be linear in nature. Basically, I will follow him in a straight line, where divisions of time are marked by his university affiliations. In this way I can review his work and perhaps say a few words about his contemporaneous colleagues and doctoral students. My focus, however, will be on his intellectual work at each school, beginning with graduate school at the University of Chicago and proceeding to his present residence at George Mason University. So rather than discussing Buchanan's ideas by category, I am going to trace their evolution over time at different work stations.

I am only going to hit the high points of Buchanan's contributions in these various locales. That he is a prolific scholar is well known. The interested reader may refer to the 20 volumes of his collected works published by Liberty Fund.[1]

3. Graduate School

I am fortunate in the respect that Buchanan has written an autobiographical memoir (Buchanan, 1992), that provides invaluable guidance to his view of the various stages of his career. I begin with his graduate student years at the University of Chicago.

Two features of his graduate student experience stand out. One was his introduction to Frank Knight, and the other was his discovery of the work of Knut Wicksell. From what I can gather, his attraction to Knight was based on Knight's personality and his general approach to intellectual affairs and not especially on Knight's economics. Basically, he was impressed by Knight as a person. Knight came from a rural background outside the establishment. Buchanan had similar roots. To Buchanan, Knight was a truth-seeker (but there were no truths to be sought), who cared not one whit for anything else. This was what Buchanan wanted to be; this is what he took from Knight; Knight is his role model.

Buchanan (1992) also credits Knight with his conversion from socialism by teaching him how markets work. The conversion apparently came about six weeks into a price theory course taught by Knight. I am not so sure about this recounting, mostly because it is hard to conceive of Buchanan as a budding socialist. In any event Buchanan was not much of a socialist, if at all, although residues remain, such as his antipathy towards inherited wealth.

Buchanan's second formative experience at Chicago was his happenstance discovery of Wicksell's dissertation (Wicksell, 1896). This is the famous work (part of which was later translated and published by Buchanan) that emphasized the use of more qualified (stricter) voting rules in defining the efficiency of public spending proposals. Wicksell's ideas were to play a significant role in shaping Buchanan's approach to political economy as it evolved over the upcoming years. Not only had Buchanan found a calling at Chicago (economics and scholarship), but he had found some useful guides about how and where to go in Knight and Wicksell.

4. Early Academics and Italy

Buchanan began his academic career at the University of Tennessee in 1948. He moved to Florida State University in 1951, where he was a Full Professor and Department Head from 1954 to1956. He spent an eventful year in Italy as a Fulbright Research Scholar, after which he moved to the University of Virginia in 1956.

Over this period he wrote and published two pieces in the *Journal of Political Economy* which presaged his later work in public choice (Buchanan, 1954a,b). Both papers were written in response to Arrow's famous work on social welfare (Arrow, 1951). One paper (1954b) is the original and classic statement of the differences in terms of individual choice behavior between voting and the market. Voting, for example, is a more "bundled" choice than market choices. The second paper (1954a) is a fundamental critique of Arrow's analysis. Buchanan makes a variety of points here, with perhaps the most important being that there is nothing special about majority rule as opposed to a unanimity rule, where the latter will yield consistent collective choices analogous to the way that markets work. Basically, he argued that outcomes and rules were related and that Arrow ignored this linkage in his analysis.

I do not have the time and space to review these papers in detail. The point is that they clearly were important early precursors of public choice analysis. Buchanan, in this early period, was already thinking deeply about voting processes and the implications of voting processes for economic well being. These papers were the seed corn of the public choice revolution, and clearly contained echoes of Wicksell.

The year that Buchanan spent in Italy was intellectually fruitful. He was introduced to the Italian tradition in public finance, in which an individual choice perspective was employed and spending and taxes were linked and not treated separately. This methodological insight was later to fuel many of Buchanan's contributions to the theory of public finance.

He also had an epiphany about public debt theory which led to his major work in this area (Buchanan, 1958). The latter involved the individual choice approach to fiscal analysis, in which Buchanan clearly exposited how the burden of the debt was shifted to future taxpayers. We clearly did not simplistically owe the debt to ourselves. Though the Keynesians howled in protest, time has been kind to Buchanan's analysis, as it now seems to have strong currency among present day analysts and observers of public debt policy. Paying down the debt so as not to leave a burden on our children has virtually become a political mantra in some quarters.

5. Charlottesville

It is hard to call one period of Buchanan's academic life more productive than another, but the amount and quality of the work he did at the University of Virginia is simply amazing. Most of this work is so well known that I need only mention it in passing.[2]

It was over this period that Buchanan met Gordon Tullock, and Tullock joined the Economics Department in Charlottesville.[3] An intellectual association was thus formed that would produce seminal work and carry forward for many years into the future. The seminal work was, of course, *The Calculus of Consent*, published in 1962. This is one of three or four major works in early public choice that are rightly considered classics. The book was a *tour de force*, covering methodological issues, constitutional economics, analyses of voting rules, and still other topics that continue to occupy public choice scholars today.

What is so amazing about this period of Buchanan's life is that he also made lasting and fundamental contributions to public expenditure theory and to the theory of taxation. He wrote his famous papers on externalities (Buchanan and Stubblebine, 1962a), tax earmarking (Buchanan, 1963), and clubs (Buchanan, 1965), each of which heavily influenced the subsequent literature of public economics. Indeed, the clubs paper by itself has created an industry of further applications to such topics as alliances and fiscal federalism.

He wrote and published a major treatise on public finance (Buchanan, 1967), in which he introduced an individual choice approach to public finance theory, as well as rehabilitating and extending such concepts as fiscal illusion. This is my favorite work by Buchanan, and it still merits rereading today. As Buchanan shows time and again in this work, understanding the efficiency of taxation and spending programs requires analyzing both sides of the fiscal account at the same time.

He wrote and published a major book on public goods theory (Buchanan, 1968). This book is deceptively technical, and is still the most creative work on public goods theory in the literature. It also treats the "supply" as well as the "demand" for public goods, an aspect of analysis which makes this book unique in the area of public goods theory.

Buchanan published his little book on subjective cost (Buchanan, 1969) during this time. Here, we have a prime example of Buchanan's dalliance with Austrian ideas, a link that he personally cares about but which really is not all that important in the general context of his work. Buchanan cannot be claimed by the Austrians; his work is much bigger than their narrow methodological hiding place. And while costs may be subjective, this has not stopped Buchanan from forging ahead as a creative economic theorist.

Finally, he made major contributions to the discussion of methodology in the 1960s. For some of this work, see Buchanan (1962b) and Buchanan (1964).

On top of all this, there were numerous other papers, lectures, and academic duties. The Public Choice Society was cofounded by Buchanan in 1963, and as noted earlier, he served as President of the Southern Economic Association in 1963. This was at a time when being President of the Southern actually meant something.

Moreover, many of Buchanan's best doctoral students studied and wrote their dissertations under his direction at Virginia. These include (in no special order): Matt Lindsay, Dick Wagner, Charlie Goetz, Charlie Plott, Mark Pauly, Toby Davis, and Craig Stubblebine, to mention a few.[4]

This is a good place to discuss Buchanan as a teacher. In the classroom he was at his remarkable best. He was a hard teacher, who set a good example for his students. His method was to assign short papers, due every two weeks, about whatever he was working on at the time. These papers and his classes made the students feel as if they were working on the frontiers of economics and participating in an exciting discussion of ideas. Grades were based on one's originality in approaching a topic, not on technique or the derivation of results. Creativity was the key to a good grade in Mr. Buchanan's class.

Oftentimes, these class papers led to later publications by students, which, of course, helped them immensely in their careers. The best example of this is Mark Pauly's paper on moral hazard (Pauly, 1968). This was a very important contribution to economic theory, and it was written and published while Pauly was a graduate student at Virginia.

Buchanan's class was transforming for students. Typically, one entered the program at Virginia (as I did) to obtain a doctorate and return to a small liberal arts college to teach. The idea of being a research economist had never really occurred to many of these students.

Yet under the tuteledge and encouragement of Buchanan, they got their degrees at Virginia and headed off to Harvard, Northwestern, Cornell, Iowa State, Purdue, Illinois, UCLA, Carnegie-Mellon, and other major universities to publish or perish. And almost to a person, these young economists have emerged in their own right as important scholars.

One significant aspect of these students is that they are all different, working in different areas and approaches to economics, some of which bear little resemblance to Buchanan's work. Buchanan did not produce homogeneous graduate students, who all worked in his tradition. He produced a colorful array of creative people who found their own way in the world. They were able to do this because Buchanan did not beat them down as students, and make them feel as if there was nothing they could do. He rather gave them encouragement and inspiration, showing them that they too could participate at a high level in the economics profession. This is the mark of a gifted teacher. Like a Zen Master, Buchanan gave visions and aspirations to his students that he did not possess himself.

In 1969, Buchanan left Virginia to take a position at the University of California, Los Angeles. After an uneventful intellectual year there, he joined Gordon Tullock and Charlie Goetz at Virginia Polytechnic Institute, where they had taken up residence previously. Tullock had left the University of Virginia earlier and gone to Rice University, but was lured to Blacksburg by Goetz, where, with Goetz, he helped to entice Buchanan back to the Commonwealth of Virginia. The story of why Buchanan and Tullock left Virginia revolved around that university's failure to promote Tullock to full professor. Virginia's loss was clearly Virginia Polytechnic Institute's gain.

6. Blacksburg

Buchanan's return to Blacksburg was a happy one. There, he joined Tullock and Goetz to form the Center for Study of Public Choice, where he was to work productively for the next 14 years. He was also joined in Blacksburg by Mrs. Betty Tillman, who had been his Executive Assistant at Virginia and whose role in the public choice movement would grow tremendously in Blacksburg and later in Fairfax. The Center was housed in Blacksburg in the old president's house, a large mansion atop a hill overlooking the Duck Pond. Center offices were palatial by normal academic standards.

This idyllic setting attracted an array of talented scholars to the Center, both as permanent faculty and as visitors, and to my mind this period represents the high water mark of the Center in terms of the level of work and quality of faculty there. Over this period, the faculty included people such as (in no special order): Dick Wagner, Tom Borcherding, Charlie Goetz, Winston Bush, Geoff Brennan, Mel Hinich, Bob Mackay, Art Denzau, Mark Crain, Roger Faith, Dwight Lee, and Nic Tideman, and, of course, Buchanan and Tullock.[5] Visitors to the Center were commonplace, and such notable scholars as Dennis Mueller, Charles Rowley, Fritz Schneider, Peter Bernholz, Dick McKenzie, Eddie West, and many others spent time in Blacksburg over this period. Numerous doctoral students completed their degrees at the Center at this time, and went on to careers as well known scholars. These include (in no particular order): Randy Holcombe, Carolyn Weaver, Henry Butler, Dick McKenzie, Genia Toma, Mark Toma, David Laband, Roger Congleton, and Janet Landa. Laband, Congleton, and Landa wrote under Buchanan.

Buchanan was literally in charge. He generally opened the door in the morning, and closed it at night, putting in 10 to 12 hours a day in between, Saturdays and Sundays being only partial exceptions (6 hours). I would say also that most of the external financial support that came to the Center in Blacksburg (and later in Fairfax) was due to Buchanan and his presence in these locales. That Buchanan was unfailingly generous in supporting others' research efforts ought to be noted.

Buchanan's work over this period continued his earlier emphasis on issues of constitutional economics and public finance from a public choice perspective. In addition, there were side excursions to topics in which he was interested. Let me explain.

One of his major works over this period was *The Limits of Liberty* (Buchanan, 1975a). The book is dedicated to Winston Bush, a colleague in Blacksburg, who died tragically in a local car accident. Bush had attracted Buchanan's interest to the issue of analyzing how individuals act in a setting of anarchy (no government) and in how individuals make the leap to civil society with rules and laws. This, of course, is precisely the constitutional paradigm that Buchanan already knew so well, but Bush's approach opened up new vistas. In *Limits*, Buchanan offers the best statement of his intellectual position. The step to civil society contains risks (Leviathan), and it should not be approached without careful thought about how to do it. In particular, Buchanan stresses the criterion of agreement on rules as being the acid test of validation for the formation of governmental institutions. Hence, Buchanan emerges in this book not only as a major voice in constitutional economics, but in contractarian philosophy as well. Space does not permit me to do justice to this work; suffice it to say that it has had a major impact in both philosophy and economics.

On the public finance side of the street, Buchanan began a collaboration with Geoffrey Brennan in Blacksburg that proved to be fruitful and important. Indeed, Brennan would become Buchanan's most prolific collaborator, and a genuine colleague and friend in all ways. Building upon the foundation laid in *Limits*, these authors pioneered a new approach to public finance based on the idea that government could be expected to act like a Leviathan and to seek to maximize whatever advantage it was given when civil society emerged from anarchy. That is, the state would be a tax-revenue maximizer, a regulatory rent maximizer, and so on. Buchanan and Brennan (1980) traced out the novel implications of this approach for taxation, spending, and the size of government, and also explored how certain rules could be designed to constrain the tendencies of the Leviathan state. This work literally flipped the existing theory of public finance on its head. Instead of using economic analysis to show government how to collect taxes more efficiently, Buchanan and Brennan used it to show how to guard against the potential for a bloated, tyrannical public sector.

Buchanan's other book over this period was written with Dick Wagner, and it represents what I have called an excursion into an interesting side issue (Buchanan and Wagner, 1977). They use basic public choice analysis to explain why Keynesian economic principles are abused by self-interested politicians to run perennial budget deficits. This is not a technical book, but it is a very persuasive application of basic public choice theory. Buchanan's support for a balanced budget amendment to the U.S. Constitution grew out of this earlier critique of Keynesian economics.

I have, of course, only mentioned books so far. In addition, there are numerous major journal articles. This was the time period in which Tullock's earlier work on rent seeking (Tullock, 1967) was consolidated and extended (Buchanan et al., 1980). Buchanan played a major role in this effort. His paper (Buchanan, 1980) on "Rent Seeking and Profit Seeking" remains the clearest statement in the literature of the rent seeking idea. Other major papers over this period include Buchanan and Tullock (1975) on regulation, Buchanan (1975b) on the Samaritan's Dilemma, and Buchanan and Brennan (1977) on tax limits, to name only three.

Buchanan also became very interested in the work of John Rawls during the Blacksburg era, and he wrote several papers (see, for example, Buchanan, 1972), in which he drew parallels between the Rawlsian approach to deriving a social contract (minimax) and his own approach to constitutional choice (expected utility maximization under uncertainty about future position). In my view, the interest of Buchanan in Rawls was another excursion into a side issue, where Buchanan was looking for individuals who shared his general interest in the problems of constitutional choice at least in a broad sense. Today, I would say that Buchanan's position on constitutional economics is purely Buchanan's, and bears little or no resemblance to that of Rawls. Indeed, I see virtually no imprint of the Rawlsian interlude in Buchanan's work.

Alas, paradise was lost. An academic civil war erupted in Blacksburg, quite unexpectedly, and after all was said and done, Buchanan actually won the war. But fearing that too much capital had been burned up in the process, Buchanan and his Center colleagues accepted an offer to move *en masse* (at given pay and rank) to George Mason University in Fairfax, Virginia. George Mason's gain was VPI's loss.

Buchanan, however, only moved his professional address to Fairfax. In Blacksburg, he had returned to a rural lifestyle with relish, and escounced himself deep in the Appalachian Mountains, where he grew his own vegetables and chopped his own wood. This is still his main residence, as he commutes back and forth to Fairfax, and he shares this dominion with his wife, Ann, and a host of cats and dogs.

A final note about Blacksburg is that it was a very social place. People worked hard, but they played hard too. Jim and Ann Buchanan were at the center of this society. To be asked over to dinner by Jim meant that there was good eating and good conversation in your future. In addition, there were poker games to be played, blackberries to be picked, Super Bowls to be watched, and foozball games after work. Needless to say, Buchanan did not play foozball, but otherwise he was the center of a unique and lively little universe. Before the war, Blacksburg was fun.

6. Fairfax

Buchanan did not move to Fairfax because he wanted to advise government. He moved there because he found the academic environment there congenial. Moreover, this time, George Mason's gain really was VPI's loss. Barely over two years in residence at Mason, Buchanan was awarded the Nobel Prize in Economics (1986). The Prize changes most people, but I do not think that Buchanan changed very much at all after 1986. He still worked long hours, he was still interested primarily in ideas, he remained (s) productive, and he continued to stay on course. I mostly remember the incredible surge of pride that swept through the Center and through the hundreds of friends and colleagues of Buchanan and the Center on the day of the Nobel announcement. A ragtag band of public choicers basked in reflected sunlight.

As I said, the Mason environment was congenial. Mason is a former community college in a suburban setting. The Center was given facilities in an old Methodist church in a copse of woods on the edge of campus. I forget who occupied the preacher's old office.

There has been a great deal of turnover of Center faculty at Mason, but over the last 19 years, the faculty has included (in no special order): Dick Wagner, Charles Rowley, Gordon Tullock, Roger Congleton, Mark Crain, Tyler Cowen, David Levy, Ron Heiner, Geoff Brennan, Dwight Lee, Bill Shughart, Victor Vanberg, and, of course, Buchanan.[6] The Center also has educated a slew of doctoral students over this era, far more than at any other locale. Among these students are (in no special order): Gary Anderson, Pam Brown, Brian Goff, Don Leavens, Joe McGarrity, and many, many others. Buchanan directed only two doctoral dissertations at George Mason (Frank Forman and Nimai Mehta).

After Buchanan's Nobel the university allowed the Center to rehabilitate (at its own expense) an old house across the street from the main Center building. This is now the Buchanan House, which houses Buchanan, Mrs. Tillman, and Mrs. Jo Ann Burgess, the Librarian of the Buchanan House. Many Buchanan artifacts are displayed in the Buchanan House, including a replica of his Nobel medal.

Buchanan's work over the Fairfax period has continued unabated. In 1983, he and Brennan published a follow-on study to *The Power to Tax*, ingeniously called *The Reason of Rules* (Buchanan and Brennan, 1985). This work is a treatise on constitutional economics that seeks to make the case for an "economics of rules" as opposed to an "economics of politics." The book stepped out of the normal box in which economics operates, and asked the question, how should we go about selecting the rules of play in the box? This is, of course, the life-long question that has held Buchanan's interest.

Buchanan published one other book over this period, a work with Roger Congleton on *Politics by Principle, not Interest* (Buchanan and Congleton, 1998). This book expresses in modern analytical terms many of the ideas that Buchanan was writing about earlier. In particular, Buchanan and Congleton show how general rules of taxation, for example, increase the efficiency and productivity of government. Simply put, flat taxes may be better than progressive taxes because they reduce rent seeking and tax evasion in a post-constitutional society. This work has received several nice reviews.

Buchanan's other intellectual work at Mason has been extensive. He has issued several important collections of his papers (for example, see Buchanan, 1991). He has consolidated and extended his intellectual position (for example, see Buchanan, 1990). He has explored new areas of economic theory (for example, see Buchanan, 1994). Moreover, he is still hard at work, pushing well beyond the 20 volumes of his *Collected Works*.

Mason was not as social as VPI had been. The urban setting raised the costs of socializing. Everyone seemed to go their own way. Buchanan instituted and funded a Virginia Political Economy Lecture Series, which served as a social occasion each March. Speakers have included many of the people mentioned in this paper.

This pretty much exhausts the Buchanan time line. We are up to date. Buchanan is still in residence at George Mason, but he also keeps an office at VPI. They have also named a Center in his honor at George Mason, called the James M. Buchanan Center for Political Economy.

7. Essences

The science of essences concerns those things which define the elements of what makes something smell or taste so good. What is the essence, then, of Buchanan? I will list these by way of closing this account of his life to date. My methodology is that of the pointillists (Georges Seurat), hoping to achieve a general impression from a series of interconnected dabs of paint.

- Buchanan changed the subject matter of modern economics by stressing agreement on the rules of the game as a separate and important inquiry in its own right.
- Buchanan exposed the vacuous nature of modern welfare economics by stressing agreement and not an arbitrary social welfare function as the key to the validity of institutional choices.
- Buchanan led the way in showing scholars how to analyze political processes using the methodology of economics.
- Buchanan pioneered in bringing individual choice analysis back into public finance theory.
- Buchanan refocused economics in methodological terms on those areas (individual choice behavior) where it has the greatest value.
- Buchanan has made many contributions to positive economic analysis.
- Buchanan is primarily a normative theorist.
- Buchanan is a great teacher, who trained many good students.
- Buchanan is a good colleague, reading and commenting on thousands of papers by colleagues.
- Buchanan created and largely financed an intellectual network at three universities in Virginia.
- Buchanan's contractarianism has had a major impact on philosophy.
- Buchanan is one of the most cited scholars of his generation.
- Buchanan does not suffer fools gladly.
- Buchanan is honest, and does not hesitate to state his mind, sometimes hotly.
- Buchanan has a loyal network of friends and colleagues in this country and abroad.
- Buchanan is a prolific lecturer, having given thousands of invited lectures, seminars, and talks, in a variety of venues, from Rotary Clubs to the great universities of the world (as well as the not so great).
- Buchanan is an incessant traveler, especially to Europe.
- Buchanan is an avid reader of both fiction and non-fiction.
- Buchanan grows his own food and chops his own wood.
- Buchanan is an active correspondent, having produced thousands of pages of accumulated correspondence.
- Buchanan does not like to talk on the telephone.
- Buchanan types his own work from handwritten notes, either on an old typewriter or, more recently, on a computer.
- Buchanan's memos are on yellow onionskin paper.
- Buchanan is a regular attendee and participant in professional meetings and conferences (especially Liberty Fund conferences).
- Buchanan is one of the best writers in the economics profession.
- Buchanan is virtually a whole university by himself as well as an effective academic infighter.
- Buchanan is a hard coauthor to keep up with; he has a paper drafted and back to you before you have time to take a deep breath.
- Buchanan is a good friend to animals, especially dogs and cats.
- Buchanan is an armchair theorist with an aversion to econometrics.
- Buchanan is a social man, who loves a good joke and a good conversation.

If this reminds you of Buchanan just a little bit, my methodology has worked, and I can draw this essay to a close. They say that only poets and singers achieve immortality. But surely the work of great economists lasts long enough and reverberates across time in such a way that they are practically immortal. Anyway, what is the difference between a half-life of 250 years and immortality? Buchanan has reached this level. And it is a good guess that his ideas will grow in importance over time as young scholars reshape modern social science along the lines that he has laid out.

ROBERT D. TOLLISON

NOTES

1. See Brennan et al. (1999–present). Note that these volumes do not include work that Buchanan has produced since 1999, work which continues unto this day.
2. Note also that the previously discussed book on the public debt was published in 1958 while Buchanan was at Virginia.
3. Other members of Virginia's Economics Department at this time were Warren Nutter, Leland Yeager, and Ronald Coase.
4. I also wrote under Buchanan at Virginia, finishing in 1969.
5. I was Professor of Economics and Executive Director of the Center from 1976–1981 in Blacksburg.
6. I was Director of the Center at George Mason from 1984–1998; I also held the Duncan Black Chair in Economics over most of that period.

REFERENCES

Arrow, K.J. (1951). *Social Choice and Individual Values*. New York: Wiley.

Brennan, G., Kliemt, H., and Tollison, R. (eds.) (1999–present). *The Collected Works of James M. Buchanan*. Indianapolis: Liberty Fund.

Buchanan, James M. (1954a). "Social choice, democracy, and free markets." *Journal of Political Economy*, 62: 114–123.

Buchanan, James M. (1954b). "Individual choice in voting and the market." *Journal of Political Economy*, 62: 334–363.

Buchanan, James M. (1958). *Public Principle of Public Debt*. Homewood: Irwin.

Buchanan, James M. and Stubblebine, C. (1962a). "Externality." *Economica*, 29: 371–384.

Buchanan, James M. (1962b). "The relevance of Pareto optimality." *Journal of Conflict Resolution*, 6: 341–354.

Buchanan, James M. (1963). "Earmarking versus general-fund financing." *Journal of Political Economy*, 71: 457–469.

Buchanan, James M. (1964). "What should economists do?" *Southern Economic Journal*, 30: 213–222.

Buchanan, James M. (1965). "An economic theory of clubs." *Economica*, 32: 1–14.

Buchanan, James M. (1967). *Public Finance in Democratic Process*. Chapel Hill: North Carolina Press.

Buchanan, James M. (1968). *The Demand and Supply of Public Goods*. Chicago: Rand McNally.

Buchanan, James M. (1969). *Cost and Choice*. Chicago: Markham.

Buchanan, James M. (1972). "Rawls on justice as fairness." *Public Choice*, 13(Fall): 123–128.

Buchanan, James M. (1975a). *The Limits of Liberty*. Chicago: Chicago Press.

Buchanan, James M. (1975b). "The samaritan's dilemma," in E.S. Phelps (ed.) *Altruism, Morality, and Economic Theory*. New York: Russell Sage, pp. 71–85.

Buchanan, James M. (1980). "Rent seeking and profit seeking," in J.M. Buchanan, R.D. Tollison, and G. Tullock (eds.) *Toward a Theory of the Rent-Seeking Society* College Station: Texas A&M Press, pp. 3–15.

Buchanan, James M. (1990). "The domain of constitutional economics." *Constitutional Political Economy*, 1: 1–18.

Buchanan, James M. (1991). *The Economic and Ethics of Constitutional Order*. Ann Arbor: Michigan Press.

Buchanan, James M. (1992). *Better than Plowing*. Chicago: University of Chicago Press.

Buchanan, James M. (1994). "The economic, and the ethics of idleness." *In Ethics and Economic Progress*. Norman: Oklahoma Press, pp. 112–128.

Buchanan, James M. and Brennan, H.G. (1977). "The logic of tax limits: alternative constitutional constraints on the power to tax." *National Tax Journal*, 32: 11–22.

Buchanan, James M. and Brennan, H.G. (1980). *The Power to Tax*. Cambridge: Cambridge Press.

Buchanan, James M. and Brennan, H.G. (1985). *The Reason of Rules*. Cambridge: Cambridge Press.

Buchanan, James M. and Congleton, R.C. (1998). *Politics by Principle, Not Interest*. Cambridge: Cambridge Press.

Buchanan, James M., Tollison, R.D., and Tullock, G. (eds.) (1980). *Toward a Theory of the Rent-Seeking Society*. College Station: Texas A&M Press.

Buchanan, James M. and Tullock G. (1962). *The Calculus of Consent*. Ann Arbor: Michigan Press.

Buchanan, James M. and Tullock, G. (1975). "Polluters' profits and political response: direct controls versus taxes." *American Economic Review*, 65: 139–147.

Buchanan, James M. and Wagner, R.E. (1977). *Democracy in Deficit*. New York: Academic Press.

Pauly, Mark (1968). "The economics of moral hazard." *American Economic Review*, 58: 531–537.

Tullock, G. (1967). "The welfare costs of tariffs, monopolies, and theft." *Western Economic Journal*, 5: 224–232.

Wicksell, Knut (1896). *Finanztheoretische Untersuchurgen*. Jena: Gustav Fischer.

M

MILTON FRIEDMAN, 1912: HARBINGER OF THE PUBLIC CHOICE REVOLUTION

1. Introduction

Throughout the first fifteen years following the end of World War II the economics profession throughout the Western World was characterized by a touching belief in the omniscience and impartiality of government as the servant of the public good and by a cynical belief in the endemic failure of free markets to maximize social welfare as defined by the Pareto Principle supplemented by the Kaldor-Hicks-Scitovsky potential compensation test. It was also characterized by the hegemony of Keynesian economics with its support for large and fiscally interventionist governments and its contempt for monetary instruments of macro-economic intervention.

The behemoths who bestrode the economics profession throughout that period were Paul Samuelson, Kenneth Arrow, John Kenneth Galbraith, James Tobin, Robert Solow and Joan Robinson. Classical political economy was dead, buried by the Great Depression and by the writings of John Maynard Keynes (1936). Free market economics was on the ropes, with few advocates and even those forced into perpetual defense in an environment in which public choice analysis played no role. The future for economic liberty and capitalism was bleak indeed.

In a world in which free markets were systematically derided, there would be no effective role for the emergence of public choice to analyse political market failure and to even the playing field between the competing advocates of government and of free markets. First, it would be necessary for some brave soul to step forward and to clear the brush from the forest by re-formulating the case both for capitalism and for monetary policy as the fundamental basis for individual freedom. Then and only then would it be possible for the public choice revolution to begin. Such a soul was Milton Friedman, arguably the most influential economist of the twentieth century, one of that century's greatest economic advocates of liberty, and certainly a necessary pre-condition for and harbinger of the public choice revolution.

2. The Early Years

Milton Friedman was born on July 31, 1912 in Brooklyn, New York City, the only son and the youngest of four children. His father, Jeno Saul Friedman (1878) and his mother, Sarah Ethel Landau (1881) were both born in the small, mostly Jewish town of Beregszasz in Carpetho-Ruthenia. Carpetho-Ruthenia was then in the Hungarian part of Austro-Hungary. After World War I, it became part of Czechoslovakia; after World War II, it became part of the USSR; after the demise of the USSR it became part of Ukraine. The town is now called Berehovo.

At the age of sixteen (1894) Friedman's father migrated to the United States and settled in Brooklyn. His mother migrated to the United States when she was fourteen (1895). Shortly after her arrival, Friedman's mother went to work as a seamstress in a sweatshop, a welcome opportunity for her to earn a living while she learned English and adjusted to the new country. Shortly after his arrival, Friedman's father went into business on his own, first as a sweatshop owner, later as the owner of a retail dry goods store and an ice-cream parlor. He remained self-employed for the remainder of his life (Friedman and Friedman 1998, 20).

In these respects, both of Friedman's parents benefited from late nineteenth century capitalism as it was practiced in the United States. Their family income was always small and uncertain and they sometimes resorted to post-dated checks. For the most part, however, the family struggled to balance its budget while investing to the best of its ability in the education of its young (Friedman and Friedman, 1998, 21).

In 1913, little more than a year after Milton Friedman's birth, the Friedman family moved from Brooklyn to Rahway, a small town in New Jersey that served mostly as a bedroom city for commuters to New York and Newark. For most of Friedman's youth, his mother ran the store while his father commuted to New York where he worked as a jobber or petty trader. The common language within the household was English, since this was deemed to be essential for the family to function economically in the New World. Milton Friedman never became proficient in Hungarian, but he picked up enough Yiddish to understand the conversation of adults (Friedman and Friedman, 1988, 21).

Until shortly before his bar mitzvah at the age of thirteen, Milton Friedman was fanatically religious, attending Hebrew School at the local synagogue and conforming in every detail to the complex dietary and other requirements of Orthodox Judaism. By the age of twelve, however, he decided that there was no valid basis for his religious beliefs and he shifted to complete agnosticism, becoming fanatically anti-religious, although he did go through the bar mitzvah ceremony for the sake of his parents.

Friedman's father suffered for many years from angina and died from a heart attack at the age of forty-nine when his son was only fifteen years of age and was preparing to enter his senior year in high school. Milton Friedman inherited this genetic defect and would have died himself in his sixties had he not benefited from the perfection of by-pass surgery techniques. Friedman's mother and sisters worked to support the family while Milton, as the male sibling, was encouraged to complete his education.

From 1924 to 1928, Friedman attended Rahway High School, graduating with a good grounding in languages, mathematics and history. He ascribes his enduring love of mathematics to a civics teacher who put the classic proof of the Pythagorean theorem on the blackboard while quoting from the poet Keats' *Ode on a Grecian Urn*: "Beauty is truth, truth beauty — that is all ye know on earth, and all ye need to know" (Friedman and Friedman, 1998, 24). Although the Friedman household could afford few books, the young Friedman became a voracious reader, almost exhausting the contents of the small local public library.

Encouraged by two of his high school teachers who were recent graduates of Rutgers University and by his success in competing for a partial scholarship at this then small New Brunswick college, Friedman entered Rutgers University in 1928 as a residential scholar. He worked his way through college as a part-time clerk in the men's department of a local department store, and he earned his lunch by waiting tables at a restaurant across the street from his dormitory (no doubt this embedded in the young Friedman, through an experience that was not available to his more pampered peers, an understanding that there is indeed no such thing as a free lunch).

Together with a fellow Jewish student, Friedman also engaged in a profitable entrepreneurial venture, buying and selling second-hand undergraduate books within the campus community, in so doing, bringing upon himself the wrath of the university bookstore, whose margins he undercut. During the summer vacations, Friedman covered his living expenses by selling fireworks for the Fourth of July Celebration, and by setting up a summer school for failing high school students, teaching classes in a number of subjects at fifty cents per hour. From an early age, Friedman showed an interest in buying and selling for profit and a predilection for entrepreneurial activity, having learned from his parents to embrace the capitalist market economy.

Friedman's original intention when entering Rutgers University was to major in mathematics with the objective of becoming an actuary. Although his actuarial results were extraordinarily good for an undergraduate, Friedman soon discovered that actuarial work was not the only paying occupation that used mathematics. Fortunately, he discovered economics and ended his degree program with the equivalent of a double major in economics and mathematics.

This decision changed his life, primarily because of his exposure to two remarkable men, Arthur F. Burns, who later would become Chairman of the Federal Reserve System and Homer Jones who later would become Vice-President of Research at the St. Louis Federal Reserve Bank. Burns inspired in Friedman a passion for scientific integrity, for scrupulous accuracy in the checking of sources and for openness to criticism. Jones provided Friedman with a sound grounding in insurance and statistics, while first introducing him to the Chicago School's pre-occupation with individual freedom.

In 1932, at the age of nineteen, Friedman graduated from Rutgers University with a degree in mathematics and economics. With the United States in the depths of economic depression and job opportunities very few, he applied for scholarships to a number of universities and received two offers of tuition scholarships, one from Brown University in applied mathematics and the other from the University of Chicago in economics. Had Homer Jones not taught at Rutgers University thus exposing Friedman to the excitement of Chicago economics, Friedman would never have applied to Chicago, or even if he had applied there he would not have received the scholarship that made it possible for him to attend. As it was, he left Rahway for Chicago in the fall of 1932, journeying west of the Delaware River for the very first time.

Studying economics at the University of Chicago was an eye-opening experience for the young Friedman. In 1932, as for the rest of the twentieth century, the Economics Department had the deserved reputation of being one of the best in the United States. Jacob Viner and Frank Knight were the acknowledged stars of the faculty. Henry Schultz, Paul Douglas, Henry Simons (who would move to the law school in 1939), Lloyd Mints, Harry A. Millis and John Nef constituted a talented supporting cast. Debate over economic issues was fierce, the intellectual atmosphere was open and the search for truth dominated scholarly discourse. Friedman was exposed for the first time in his life to a brilliant group of graduate students drawn to this vibrant intellectual atmosphere from all over the world (Friedman and Friedman, 1998, 35).

In his first quarter at Chicago, Friedman took the course on price and distribution theory taught that year by Jacob Viner. This course revealed to Friedman the logical and coherent nature of economic theory as a set of tools to be judged primarily by its usefulness in understanding and interpreting important economic events. Because the students in that class were seated alphabetically, Friedman was also introduced to Rose Director, his future wife and future co-author of two important books on classical liberalism.

During his year at Chicago, Friedman also took Frank Knight's class on the history of economic thought. He was greatly impressed by Knight's unrelenting commitment to the pursuit of truth and by his unfailing suspicion of government intervention, attributes that he himself would unfailingly observe in his own career. He was also exposed to Chicago monetary theory in courses taught by Lloyd Mints that focused on the fundamentals and not on the institutional arrangements. He strengthened his technical expertise with courses drawn from the department of mathematics and with a course in econometrics taught by Henry Schultz. Friedman became acquainted during his years at Chicago with fellow graduate students George J. Stigler and Allen Wallis both of whom would later make important contributions to economics. He received his master's degree at Chicago in 1933.

At the urging of Henry Schultz, Friedman moved to Columbia University for the second year of his graduate work so that he could study with Harold Hotelling. Hotelling would provide him with the same kind of feeling for mathematical statistics that Viner had imbued in him for economic theory. Wesley C. Mitchell introduced him to the empirical analysis of business cycles and John Maurice Clark introduced him to institutional economics. Fritz Machlup, a fellow student, introduced him to Austrian economics.

If Chicago had provided Friedman with the powerful tools of neoclassical price theory, and a favorable regard for free market capitalism, Columbia gave him the institutional framework and the facts relevant for testing those tools (Breit and Ransom, 1998, 227). Having satisfied the course requirements for a Ph.D., Friedman returned to Chicago for the academic year 1934–35 as research assistant to Henry Schultz working with him on his pathbreaking *magnum opus* on demand analysis. By the year's end, Friedman had also satisfied the course requirements for a Ph.D. at Chicago.

There were few academic jobs available in the United States at this stage of the Great Depression and Friedman's prospects were further lowered by the existence of anti-Semitism within the U.S. academy. Therefore, Friedman left Chicago in the fall of 1935 to take up a well-paid New Deal position in Washington with the National Resources Committee, where he spent two years designing and working on an extensive empirical study of consumer budgets. The experience that he acquired there working with practical statistics would prove to be invaluable throughout his scientific career. The final report on the results of this study was published in two volumes in 1938 and 1939.

Drawing from his work at the Committee, Friedman published an article on a new statistical technique — the use of ranks to avoid the assumption of normality implicit in the analysis of variance — in the December 1937 issue of the *Journal of the American Statistical Association*. The work he performed at the Committee also formed the basis of a book published in 1957 as *The Theory of the Consumption Function*. Friedman claims that this is his most important scientific work (Friedman and Friedman, 1998, 66).

In the fall of 1937, Friedman moved to New York to begin what would prove to be a long association with the National Bureau of Economic Research and with his former mentor at Rutgers University, Arthur Burns. Friedman worked at the NBER under the supervision of Simon Kuznets to fill in a major *lacuna* on data on income and wealth, namely the distribution of income and wealth by size. He edited the first three conference volumes on *Studies in Income and Wealth* for the NBER.

He also revised and completed a preliminary manuscript that Kuznets had drafted on the incomes of professional practitioners. The final product was a book, *Incomes from Independent Practice* completed in 1940 but published only in 1945 because of a hostile reception to the authors' conclusions by the then-powerful American Medical Association (Friedman and Friedman, 1998, 74–76). Friedman and Kuznets determined that approximately one half of the observed excess earnings of physicians over dentists was explained by the success of the American Medical Association in limiting entry into medicine.

In addition to working at the NBER from 1937 to 1940, Friedman was able to secure a part-time teaching appointment at Columbia Extension. This was Friedman's first experience of formal teaching. In 1938, Friedman married Rose Director, six years after first meeting her in Chicago. They would have a daughter, Janet, born in 1943 and now an attorney, and a son, David, born in 1945 and now a well-known professor of law and economics. Rose would be an active partner in her husband's professional life, co-authoring with him two extremely influential books on political economy.

Harold Groves, who had become acquainted with Friedman at the Income Conference offered Friedman a visiting professorship at the University of Wisconsin for the year 1940–41. Despite efforts by Groves to make this position permanent, and despite an excellent teaching performance in statistics and economics, Friedman would be denied such a position in part at least because of overt anti-Semitism within the Department of Economics (Breit and Ransom, 1998, 227; Friedman and Friedman, 1998, 91–104).

From 1941 to 1943, Friedman joined Carl Shoup at the U.S. Treasury as a Principal Economist in the Tax Research Division. During this period, Friedman according to his wife, Rose, made the worst intellectual mistake of his career (Friedman and Friedman, 1998, 123). In order to raise taxes for the war effort, he helped to devise a scheme for withholding income tax at the source of the income. This innovation (for which Friedman was not solely responsible) arguably is the most important single cause of the growth of government in the United States during the second half of the twentieth century.

Tax withholding tends to obscure the full burden of federal and state tax liabilities on individual taxpayers and thus provides an illusionary reduction in the cost of government. By developing the idea and advocating its implementation as a policy tool, Friedman showed no instinct for the likely public choice implications and no concern for the adverse impact of such a policy for individual liberty (Rowley, 1999, 416).

Friedman soon tired of his work on tax reform and moved to New York in 1943 to join a close friend, Allen Wallis as Associate Director of the Statistical Research Group at Columbia University. There he joined a group of distinguished statisticians, including Abraham Wald, Jacob Wolfowitz and Harold Hotelling in work directly relevant to the war effort. Together with Wallis and Wald, he would develop a method of sequential sampling designed to help the U.S. Navy in its sampling inspection of wartime production of munitions. Sequential analysis became the standard method of quality control inspection.

At the same time, Friedman at last turned to his doctoral dissertation drawing upon his NBER study. He completed the dissertation in 1945 and received his doctorate from Columbia University in 1946, more than ten years after completing his course-work for the degree. Of course, the war was a special circumstance. However, it would now be virtually impossible for an American student to drag out his degree program over such a lengthy period and still be allowed to graduate. It is fortunate for economics that Columbia University was flexible. Without a doctorate, Friedman would have found it all but impossible to enter the postwar American academy.

Although Friedman's early career appears to have been a patchwork of short-term appointments, it formed the basis for all of his subsequent work. Well-versed in mathematics and statistics, formidably well-trained in economic theory and well-experienced in economic policy-making, he would be uniquely equipped to confront a postwar economics profession obsessed with Keynesian macroeconomics, seduced by socialist dogma and aggressively hostile to classical liberal political economy.

The Allied victory over Japan in August 1945 coincided with the end of the 'Wilderness Years' for Milton Friedman, years that had been immensely enjoyable and productive despite the absence of any permanent academic position. With the help of George Stigler, Friedman secured a one-year appointment for the academic year 1945–46 at the University of Minnesota, where he taught courses in statistics and economics. Long before the academic year was over, he would accept a tenured position at Minnesota with the rank of associate professor.

During his year at Minnesota, Friedman co-authored with George Stigler a pamphlet attacking rent control, with the catchy title of *Roofs or Ceilings*. The National Association of Real Estate Boards circulated 500,000 copies of this pamphlet as part of its campaign against rent controls. Friedman's first foray into classical liberalism marked him as a rising star among the small group of classical liberal scholars in the United States. It also marked the early signs of a willingness to stand firmly against mainstream economic thinking when such thinking could be shown to run counter to sound economic theory (Friedman and Friedman, 1998, 150).

In the spring of 1946, Stigler received an offer from the Department of Economics at the University of Chicago, contingent upon approval by the central administration after a personal interview. President Ernest Colwell vetoed the appointment on the grounds that his work was excessively empirical. Ironically, Friedman was offered the position initially offered to Stigler and the New Chicago School was born with an unrelenting emphasis on empirical analysis that has continued throughout the remainder of the twentieth century.

Friedman returned to the University of Chicago in the fall of 1946 as associate professor of economics, succeeding his mentor Jacob Viner in the teaching of microeconomic theory. In 1948, he was promoted to full professor. In 1951, he became the third recipient of the prestigious John Bates Clark medal. In 1963, he was appointed Paul Snowden Russell Distinguished Service Professor. In 1967, he was elected president of the American Economic Association. In 1976, he was awarded the Nobel Prize in Economic Science. Friedman retired from the University of Chicago in 1977, moving to the Hoover Institution at Stanford University as a senior research fellow.

3. The Path to Scientific Recognition

Unlike several of his classical liberal contemporaries — James M. Buchanan, Ronald H. Coase and Gordon Tullock — Milton Friedman forged his scientific reputation not by traveling less well-trodden paths but by a sequence of brilliant challenges to mainstream economics. The Royal Swedish Academy of Science, in awarding him the Nobel Prize in Economic Science in 1976, cited Friedman "for his achievements in the fields of consumption analysis, monetary history and theory and for his demonstration of the complexity of stabilization policy." This section focuses on these contributions and assesses their implications for classical liberal political economy and for the public choice revolution:

3.1. The Methodology of Positive Economics

During his graduate years at Chicago, Friedman had been taught by Frank Knight who evidenced extreme skepticism towards empirical economic analysis. None of the leading scholars at Chicago during the 1930s showed any real interest in numbers. Quite possibly, Friedman would have embraced that skepticism, had he been able to move directly into an academic position in 1935. Experience at the NRC and the NBER during his Wilderness Years, however, taught him to respect empirical analysis and led him to think deeply about the methodology of positive economics. When he returned to Chicago in 1946, he determined to make sense of the kind of work that he had undertaken with Kuznets and Burns. In so doing, he would make an important contribution to methodology that would be the defining characteristic of the new Chicago School of Economics.

During the 1930s the economics profession had become enamored of a view advanced by Lionel Robbins that the veracity of an economic model should be tested primarily by the correspondence between its assumptions and the facts (Walters, 1987, 423). Specifically Robbins explained: "But the final test of the validity of any such definition is not its apparent harmony with certain usages of every day speech, but its capacity to describe exactly the ultimate subject matter of the main generalizations of science" (Robbins, 1932, 4–5). Thus Robbin's view was that the assumptions of good science must directly reflect empirical reality.

This view encouraged significant challenges to the model of perfect competition from critics such as Joan Robinson and Edward Chamberlin who claimed that the assumptions of the perfectly competitive model failed to conform to the reality of twentieth-century markets. It also stimulated attacks on all theories that incorporated the assumption that firms maximize profits. More fundamentally, the Robbins test was being widely deployed to attack the laissez-faire model of economics (Samuelson, 1963, 213).

As early as 1947, Friedman was able to circulate in draft form a radically different view of the proper methodology for positive economics than that espoused by Robbins. Six years later, in 1953, Friedman's article on the methodology of positive economics would make a controversial but long-lasting entry into the litany of economics.

In preparing his essay, Friedman benefited slightly both from a brief conversation with Karl Popper (whose great book *Logik der Forschung* was not yet available in the English language) and from his collaboration with James Savage whose book *The Foundations of Statistics* would shortly revolutionize the philosophical foundations of statistics (Friedman and Friedman, 1998, 215). Ultimately, however, the methodology outlined in Friedman's 1953 essay is uniquely his own.

At the outset of his Essay Friedman states that: "The ultimate goal of a positive science is the development of a 'theory' or 'hypothesis' that yields valid and meaningful (i.e., not truistic) predictions about phenomena not yet observed." (Friedman, 1953, 7). He reinforces this view in the following terms: "Viewed as a body of substantive hypotheses, theory is to be viewed by its predictive power for the class of phenomena which it is intended to 'explain'" (Friedman, 1953, 8). In this respect, a hypothesis can be falsified but never verified:

> The hypothesis is rejected if its predictions are contradicted ("frequently" or more often than predictions from an alternative hypothesis); it is accepted if its predictions are not contradicted; great confidence is attached to it if it has survived many opportunities for contradiction. Factual evidence can never "prove" a hypothesis; it can only fail to disprove it, which is what we generally mean when we say somewhat inexactly, that the hypothesis has been "confirmed" by experience. (Friedman, 1953, 8–9)

This emphasis on prediction leads Friedman to reverse the epistemic order presumed in orthodox methodology (Hirsch and Marchi, 1990, 76). Instead of reasoning from true causes to implications, Friedman reasons from observed implications to possible premises. In this view, the premises of a successful theory are accepted to the extent to which they yield a set of predictions that has not been falsified by the available evidence. The simpler and the more fruitful the premises involved, the more acceptable they are, given the accuracy of the predictions that they generate.

From this perspective, Friedman launched a controversial and in retrospect almost certainly an exaggerated attack on the ruling convention that a theory should be tested by the realism of its assumptions.

> Truly important and significant hypotheses will be found to have "assumptions" that are wildly inaccurate descriptive representations of reality, and, in general, the more significant the theory, the more unrealistic

the assumption......A hypothesis is important if it "explains" much by little, that is if it abstracts the common and crucial elements from the mass of complex and detailed circumstances surrounding the phenomena to be explained and permits valid predictions on the basis of them alone. (Friedman, 1953, 14)

Friedman immediately modified this startling and memorable assertion with a more cautious explanation:

The relevant question to ask about the "assumptions" of a theory is not whether they are descriptively "realistic", for they never are, but whether they are sufficiently good approximations for the purpose in hand. And this question can be answered only by seeing whether the theory works, which means whether it yields sufficiently accurate predictions. (Friedman, 1953, 15)

Friedman's statement of methodology did not meet with widespread early acceptance within an economics profession yet unacquainted with the writings of Karl Popper. Most of the early critiques were ad hoc in nature, more designed to buttress the ongoing attack on neoclassical theory than to provide profound insights. In 1963, however, Paul Samuelson entered the debate with a more formal attempted rebuttal of the Friedman's methodology (Samuelson, 1963).

Samuelson focused attention on Friedman's assertions (1) that a theory is vindicated if some of its consequences are empirically valid to a useful degree of approximation (2) that the empirical unrealism of the theory itself, or of its assumptions, is quite irrelevant to its validity and worth and (3) that it is a positive merit of a theory that some of its content and assumptions are unrealistic.

According to Samuelson (1963), this methodology is incorrect as a matter of logic. Define a theory (call it B) as a set of axioms, postulates or hypotheses that stipulate something about observable reality. Fundamentally, this theory contains everything — assumptions as well as consequences — and is refuted or not as a whole by reference to how well it conforms to the relevant evidence. Friedman denies this and argues instead that B has consequences (call them C) that somehow come after it and assumptions (call them A) that somehow are antecedent to it. What are the implications of this separation?

According to Samuelson $A = B = C$. If C is the complete set of consequences of B, it is identical with B. B implies itself and all the things that itself implies. Thus, if C is empirically valid, then so is B. Consider, however, a proper subset of C (call it $C-$) that contains some but not all the implications of B and consider a widened set of assumptions that includes A as a proper subset (call it $A+$). Now suppose that C has complete empirical validity. Then so has B and so has A. However, the same cannot be said for $A+$. Similarly, the empirical validity of $C-$ does not of itself impart validity to A or to B.

If Samuelson is correct, Friedman's methodology is scientifically flawed. For example, it may well be the case that certain characteristics of the model of perfect competition conform to reality ($C-$ as Friedman would argue). However, other parts do not (A as Friedman would acknowledge). In such circumstances, the model (B in Samuelson's broader sense) has not been validated and economists should proceed with extreme care in making use of it even if the evidence strongly and consistently conforms to $C-$.

Samuelson's deconstruction is valid, however, only for a methodology that views theory as moving from cause to effect, the very methodology that Friedman rejected in his 1953 essay. The real question for Friedman is to gauge the extent to which the assumptions of a theory are adequate for the job in hand, which is to generate predictions that conform with the available evidence. He rejects on methodological grounds the notion advanced by Samuelson (1963) that a theory must be realistic in all its aspects.

To put Friedman's central thesis in a nutshell it is that 'the ultimate test of the validity of a theory is not conformity to the canons of formal logic, but the ability to deduce facts that have not yet been observed, that are capable of being contradicted by observation, and that subsequent observation does not contradict' (Friedman, 1953, 300). In this respect, Friedman's 1953 views on methodology, though contentious at the time, proved to be consistent with those of Karl Popper and provided the intellectual foundations first for the new Chicago School of Economics and subsequently for a significant section of the economics profession.

This shift of methodology proved to be very important for Friedman's subsequent empirical re-evaluation of Keynesian economics and for his empirical work on the role of money in the macro-economy. By persuading many economists that economic science could be advanced by exposing the predictions of very simple models to the evidence, Friedman would be able to demonstrate, for example, that the quantity equation was a better predictor of economic behavior than the Keynesian income–expenditure equation. This result would have enormous implications for reining in fiscal interventions that threatened individual liberties.

3.2. Fiscal Policy is Overrated

In evaluating the evolution of a scholar's career, it is important not to do so from the end-point of that career from the perspective of hindsight. This is particularly so when evaluating Friedman's critique of Keynesian economics. Ultimately, the success of this critique would constitute his most important contribution to classical liberal political economy and a significant assist to the public choice revolution. However, Friedman's critique of Keynesian economics was piecemeal in nature, and certainly did not start out as a grand design.

Friedman was always more impressed with the scholarship of Maynard Keynes than with that of the Keynesians. Indeed, Friedman viewed Keynes, like himself, as a purveyor of the economics of Alfred Marshall (Hirsch and Marchi, 1990, 187). Keynes's *General Theory* (1936) made an indelible impression on economic thinking during the immediate postwar years, and the young Friedman was sufficiently impressed by it to allow the Keynesian model to dictate much of his research agenda during the 1940s and 1950s.

Friedman's early preoccupation with the Keynesian model was motivated not by ideological concerns but rather by empirical puzzles surrounding a relationship at the core of the Keynesian system, namely the consumption function. According to the Keynesians, current consumption expenditure was a stable function of current income. A fundamental psychological rule of any modern community dictated that the marginal propensity to consume was less than one and that the average propensity to consume declined with income.

These two conjectures became matters of policy importance. Governments seized on the first as a scientific justification for deficit spending during periods of recession. Economists seized on the latter to consolidate the secular stagnation thesis and to suggest that advanced economies would be condemned to stagnation in the absence of deficit financing. In both instances, the fallacy of a free lunch enticed the unwary into embracing the palliative of government growth given that government apparently could exploit the consumption function, increasing household incomes by increasing government expenditures, in order to achieve a leveraged impact on the macro economy through the multiplier mechanism.

In his book, *A Theory of the Consumption Function* (Friedman, 1957), Friedman addressed a number of empirical puzzles surrounding this theory. Early work using US data for the interwar period had seemed to support the theory (Friedman, 1957, 3). However, postwar studies were more problematic. Estimates of saving in the United States made by Kuznets for the period since 1899 revealed no increase in the percentage of income saved during the past half century despite a substantial rise in real income (Kuznets, 1952, 507–526). The ratio of consumption expenditure to income was decidedly higher than had been computed from the earlier studies.

Examination of budget studies for earlier periods strengthened the appearance of conflict. The average propensity to consume was roughly the same for widely separated dates despite substantial differences in average real income. Yet each budget study separately yielded a marginal propensity decidedly lower than the average propensity. Finally, the savings ratio in the period after World War II was sharply lower than that predicted by the relationships estimated for the interwar period. According to Friedman's methodology something was seriously amiss. The Keynesian consumption function had failed a basic empirical test (Friedman, 1957, 4).

In his book, *A Theory of the Consumption Function* (Friedman, 1957), Friedman adapted a dynamic theory of Irving Fisher (1930) to explain some of the empirical anomalies that had arisen in attempts to test the static Keynesian model against time series and cross-section data on consumption and income (Sargent, 1987). This book is Friedman's best purely scientific contribution and the work that best reflects his methodology of positive economics (Walters, 1987).

Irving Fisher (1930) had posited that consumption should be a function of the present value of income, not of its current value. Friedman accepted the dynamic implications of this theory, but replaced Fisher's concept with the concept of *permanent income*. He posited that consumers separated their current income into two parts, namely a permanent part equivalent to the income from a bond and a transitory part equivalent to a non-recurring windfall. In testing the theory of the consumption function against cross-section data, econometricians must resolve a signal extraction problem in order to estimate the permanent component of income from observations on the sum of the permanent and the transitory components of income.

To model the time series data, Friedman introduced the concept of *adaptive expectations* to create a statistical representation of permanent income. Agents were assumed to form expectations about the future path of income as a geometric distributed lag of past values. The decay parameter in the distributed lag ought to equal the factor by which the consumer discounted future utility. Friedman estimated his model on time series data using the method of maximum likelihood.

On this basis Friedman (1957) demonstrated that there exists a ratio between permanent consumption and permanent income that is stable across all levels of permanent income, but that depends also on other variables, most notably the interest rate and the ratio of wealth to income. The transitory components of income have no effect on consumption except as they are translated into permanent income.

From the perspective of the 1950s, Friedman's analysis had very important consequences for macroeconomic policy. First, it suggested that the immediate fiscal policy multiplier was markedly lower than that posited by the Keynesians. Second, it indicated that the dynamic responses of income to fiscal policy shocks were much more complicated than those indicated by textbook IS-LM curves. Both results suggested caution in the use of fiscal policy as a stabilization device.

Although the Keynesians argued that fiscal policy should be used even-handedly across the business cycle, countering recessions with budget deficits and booms with budget surpluses, the political system confounded such naïve expectations (Buchanan and Wagner, 1977). The political incentives to maintain budget deficits during booms as well as slumps simply overwhelmed economic logic. Therefore, to the extent that Friedman's theory dampened economists' enthusiasm for an active fiscal policy, it thus helped to dampen the rate of growth of government. Friedman's book, although devoid of any notions of public choice, nevertheless provided an invaluable foundation for the later work in 1977 by Buchanan and Wagner on the political economy of deficit-finance.

It is important to note that Friedman has never argued that fiscal policy is completely impotent. His own theory of adaptive expectations indeed supposes that individual responses to fiscal policy occur with lags, allowing fiscal policy to exert an influence on the macro-economy during the period of adjustment. Friedman's crucial insight is that monetary policy typically is more effective than fiscal policy as an instrument of macro-economic policy.

It is also important to note, that New Keynesian views are now very much the mainstream in macro-economics, albeit operating within a rational expectations framework that offers only limited scope for fiscal intervention and a much greater role for monetary policy than was envisaged by the original followers of Keynes.

3.3. Money Matters

Friedman's interest in the role of money in the macro-economy was first sparked in 1948 when Arthur Burns at the NBER asked him to research the role of money in the business cycle. Thus began a thirty-year program of research with Anna Schwartz that would demonstrate that money matters — indeed that it matters a great deal — and that would further erode the perceived empirical importance of the Keynesian model.

By 1948, Keynesian economic theory ruled triumphant throughout the academies of the Western World. The classical quantity theory for the most part had been eliminated from textbook economics; and where it was mentioned it was treated as a *curiosum*. The conventional view throughout the economics profession was that money did not matter much, if at all. What really mattered was autonomous spending, notably in the form of private investment and government outlays. Fiscal policy was crucial; monetary policy was all but irrelevant in the sense that 'you cannot push on a string.'

Only the University of Chicago, through the teachings of Henry Simons, Lloyd Mints, Frank Knight and Jacob Viner, had stood at all resolutely against this pervasive doctrine during the late 1930s and 1940s as Keynesian doctrine swept through the academy. Friedman was well-versed in the subtle version of the quantity theory expounded at Chicago, a version in which the quantity theory was connected and integrated with general price theory and became 'a flexible and sensitive tool for interpreting movements in aggregate economic activity and for developing relevant policy prescriptions' (Friedman, 1956, 3).

Systematically, over the period 1950–80, Friedman and his research associates would challenge the empirical relevance of the Keynesian model by demonstrating the empirical superiority of the quantity theory as expounded at Chicago. By the time that his research program was complete, and prior to the rational expectations revolution, almost all economists would recognize that money did matter, that what happened to the quantity of money had important effects on economic activity in the short run and on the price level in the long run (Friedman and Friedman, 1998, 228).

Before Keynes, the quantity theory of money had played an important role in classical economics. Using the behavioral equation $MV = PY$, classical theorists had argued that the income velocity of circulation of money, V, was a constant; that real income, Y, was unaffected by changes in the quantity of money (the so-called classical dichotomy); and therefore that changes in the supply of money, M, directly affected the price level, P. Keynes (1936) derided this naïve textbook version of the quantity theory, arguing instead that V was not a constant but was highly variable and that it served as a cushion to prevent any change in the supply of money from exerting an impact on either real income or the level of prices.

In conjunction with his work at the NBER, Friedman established a Workshop in Money and Banking at the University of Chicago. The first product of this Workshop was a book: *Studies in the Quantity Theory of Money* (1956) which Friedman edited. In retrospect, this publication was the first major step in a counter-revolution that succeeded in restoring the quantity theory to academic respectability. There is no evidence that Friedman was aware at that time of the dimensions of the impending battle. His express intent in writing the introductory essay was simply to "set down a particular 'model' of a quantity theory in an attempt to convey the flavor of the (Chicago) oral tradition" (Friedman, 1956, 4). Of course, the impact of his essay would be much more dramatic than he and his colleagues at that time could possibly foresee.

Friedman's introductory essay provided a subtle and sophisticated restatement of the quantity theory of money as a stable money-demand function (Breit and Ransom, 1998, 228). Unlike the classical economists, Friedman rejected the notion that V, the income velocity of circulation of money, was a constant. Instead, he modeled V as a stable function of several variables, since money was an asset, one way of holding wealth. Within this framework, he posited that V would respond to nominal monetary expansion in the short run by accentuating rather than by cushioning the impact of such expansion on nominal income. This restatement became recognized as the theoretical position of the Chicago School on monetary economics.

The four empirical studies in the book — dealing with inflationary and hyperinflationary experiences in Europe and the United States — provided support for the quantity theory in its restated form by demonstrating a striking regularity in economic responses to monetary changes. The most significant finding was that velocity was a stable function of permanent income. Since money is a luxury good, the demand for which rises as income increases, velocity would tend to decline over time as income rose. The monetary authority therefore must increase the stock of money to offset this decline in velocity, if it wished to maintain price stability (Breit and Ransom, 1998, 230).

These results met with skepticism from Keynesian economists who counter-claimed that the supply of money merely accommodated demand and did not impact independently on the macro-economy. It would take Friedman and his colleagues the better part of a decade of high-quality theoretical and empirical analysis to mount a persuasive case for the quantity theory.

One important component of this research program was the comparative test (Friedman and Meiselman, 1963) in which a simple version of the income–expenditure theory, $C = a + kA$ was compared with a simple version of the quantity theory, $C = b + vM$. For the period 1897 to 1958, using annual data, and for a shorter period using quarterly data, the quantity theory performed better than the income–expenditure theory, implying that v was more stable than k, except for the period of the Great Depression.

More influential, ultimately, was the monumental book co-authored with Anna Schwartz, *A Monetary History of the United States, 1867–1960* (Friedman and Schwartz, 1963). This monumental piece of empirical research offered substantial support for the restated quantity theory and sent shock waves through the economics profession by explaining the Great Depression in terms of the failure of the federal reserve to deploy effective open-market operations that would have prevented the banking crisis that brought about a significant decline in the supply of money (Breit and Ransom, 1998, 239).

Subsequent research by Friedman determined (1) that the impact of a fiscal deficit on nominal income was short lived whereas, after a lag, an increased rate of growth of the nominal money supply permanently augmented the rate of price inflation; (2) that the adjustment of nominal income to an increased rate of monetary growth occurred with a long and variable lag; (3) that in the long run additional monetary growth affected only the rate of inflation and exerted virtually no effect on the level or rate of growth of real output (Walters, 1987, 425).

So successful was Friedman's empirical work in supporting the quantity theory that economists began to clamor for an explicit theory of the role of money in income determination, a theory capable of generating the propositions supported by the empirical investigations. In response Friedman published two strictly theoretical articles (Friedman, 1970, 1971) that sparked critical reviews from leading Keynesian scholars. The debate between the Keynesians and the quantity theorists would continue for another decade before the worldwide stagflation of the 1970s brought a close to decisive victory for Friedman's position (Gorden 1978).

The restoration of the quantity theory undoubtedly weakened the reliance by governments on fiscal policy as a means of countering the business cycle. This alone was a major contribution to classical liberalism, weakening as it did the justification for government macro-economic intervention through fiscal policy. However, Friedman would fail to persuade the economics profession and the wider public that monetary policy also should be eschewed in favor of a non-discretionary rate of increase in the nominal money supply at the underlying rate of growth of productivity. This was unfortunate because governments that wished to use the inflation tax to evade the real debt implications of deficit-financing, now knew just how to go about their business. Although Friedman was very slow to recognize it, failure in this regard reflected more the pressures of public choice than any weakness in Friedman's research on the long and variable lags in the relationship between changes in the nominal supply of money and changes in the behavior of nominal income (Rowley, 1999, 419). The Federal Reserve Board and its influential staff in the United States and central bank systems elsewhere would not easily be dislodged from playing an active role in monetary policy.

Failure was also, in part, the consequence of Friedman's success in promoting free markets. Deregulation of the banking system made it difficult from the early 1980s onwards to determine just which M should be subjected to the non-discretionary rule. Perhaps most important, however, was Friedman's neglect (typical of the Chicago School) of any detailed institutional analysis of the banking sector. In the absence of such an analytical framework, the call for non-discretionary policy too easily could be categorized as dogma rather than as science.

Fundamentally, of course, the case in favor of the non-discretionary rule collapsed during the 1980s once it became apparent that the demand for money was unstable in the wake of banking deregulations.

3.4. The Fallacy of the Phillips Curve

An important component of the Keynesian orthodoxy during the 1960s was the notion that there existed a stable negative relationship between the level of unemployment and the rate of price inflation. This relationship was characterized as the *Phillips curve* in recognition of the celebrated 1958 paper by A.W. Phillips that plotted unemployment rates against the rates of change of money wages and found a significant statistical relationship between the two variables.

Keynesian economists had focused on this apparent relationship to persuade government that there existed a permanent trade-off between price inflation and unemployment, allowing choices to be made between alternative rates of unemployment and alternative rates of price inflation. By accepting a modest increase in prices and wages, politicians, if they so wished, could lower the rate of unemployment in an economy.

Friedman had questioned the validity of the Phillips curve in the early 1960s, but without any significant intellectual impact. In his Presidential Address to the American Economic Association in December 1967 (Friedman, 1968), Friedman was able to raise the tone of this questioning, arguing convincingly that the concept of the stable Phillips curve was an illusion and that any trade-off that existed between the rate of inflation and the rate of unemployment was strictly temporary in nature. Once again, Friedman placed himself directly against the thrust of Keynesian doctrine deconstructing it from the perspective of Marshallian economics (De Vroey, 2001).

Keynes had rendered money non-neutral and had made fiscal policy potent in its effects on output by withdrawing one equation (the labor supply schedule) and one variable (money wages) from the classical model (Sargent, 1987, 6). The Keynesian model was thus short one equation and one variable by comparison with the classical model. To close that gap, the Keynesians had incorporated the Phillips curve as a structural relationship. In so doing, they mis-interpreted the true nature of labor market equilibrium.

Friedman in his 1967 Address re-asserted the classical assumption that markets clear and that agents' decision rules are homogeneous of degree zero in prices. When agents confront inter-temporal choice problems, the relevant price vector includes not only current prices but also expectations about future prices. This the proponents of the stable Phillips curve had failed to recognize.

The trade-off between inflation and unemployment captured in the Phillips curve regression equations represented the outcomes of experiments that had induced forecast errors in private agents' views about prices. If the experiment under review was a sustained and fully anticipated inflation, Friedman asserted, then there would exist no trade-off between inflation and unemployment. The Phillips curve would be vertical and the classical dichotomy would hold.

Friedman in his 1967 paper utilized a version of adaptive expectations to demonstrate that any trade-off between inflation and unemployment would be strictly temporary and would result solely from unanticipated changes in the inflation rate. The natural rate of unemployment, defined essentially in terms of the 'normal equilibrium' of Marshall rather than in the Walrasian terms of the subsequent rational expectations school (De Vroey, 2001, 130), was a function of real forces. If monetary expansion fools the workers temporarily so that they do not recognize that their real wage has been lowered, it might stimulate a temporary reduction in the level of unemployment below the 'normal equilibrium (or natural rate). As soon as the money illusion dissipates, unemployment will drift back to the natural rate. To keep unemployment below the natural rate requires an ever-accelerating rate of inflation.

On the basis of this logic, Friedman predicted that the apparent Phillips curve trade-off evident in the data from the 1950s and 1960s would disappear once governments systematically attempted to exploit it. In the 1970s, the Phillips curve trade-off vanished from the data. Indeed, estimated Phillips curves became positive as rising rates of inflation began to coincide with rising rates of unemployment.

Once again Friedman's positive economic analysis paved the way for a reduction in the extent of government economic intervention now through monetary policy. Economic events would ultimately invalidate the Phillips curve hypothesis. However, by directing the attention of economists to model mis-specification, Friedman hastened the process, further weakening the economic case for government intervention in the macro-economy.

3.5. The Reason of Rules

Friedman's views on monetary policy were greatly influenced by Henry Simons' teachings on the superiority of rules over discretionary policy (Breit and Ransom, 1998, 241). From the outset of his career, but with increased vigor following his empirical work on the quantity theory of money, not least his analysis of the Great Contraction (Friedman and Schwartz, 1963), Friedman argued in favor of committing macro-economic policy to a series of monetary and fiscal rules designed to reduce the degree of discretionary power available to government agents. It should be noted, however, that this argument was not based on any knowledge of public chocie. Rather, Friedman was concerned that central banks typically failed to predict the pattern of the business cycle and the distributed lags of monetary intervention, thus destabilizing the macro-economy.

Friedman's advocacy of rules stemmed from recognition that monetary policy could not peg interest rates, could not generate full employment and could not stabilize cyclical fluctuations in income (Butler, 1985, 177). Yet, monetary policy had a considerable power for mischief, since it affected every part of the economy. Therefore, it deserved great respect. In particular, because changes in the supply of money exerted an impact on the macro-economy only with long and variable lags, the potential for destabilizing policy intervention was high even at the hands of a benevolent government.

At different times, Friedman advocated two comprehensive and simple plans for coordinating monetary and fiscal policies. In 1948, he advocated an automatic adjustment mechanism that would overcome the problem of the lag and that would be more likely to move the economy in the right direction than would discretionary monetary policy.

Friedman advocated (1) the imposition of 100 percent reserve requirements on the banks, making the supply of money equal to the monetary base and (2) a prohibition on government placing interest-bearing debt with the public. The Federal Reserve would be required to monetize all interest-bearing government debt, so government deficits would lead to increases in the monetary base, and government surpluses would lead to reductions in that base. Such a mechanism would act as an automatic stabilizer and would also assign a clear responsibility for growth in the money supply (and in inflation) to its primary determinant, the federal deficit (Sargent, 1987, 9).

If implemented, Friedman's proposed rule would have eliminated much of the discretionary power that enabled governments to implement Keynesian macroeconomic policy. For that reason alone, it was doomed during the era of Keynesian hegemony. In addition, it implied the abolition of the central banking institutions that determine the course of monetary policy. Such powerful pillars of the economic establishment would not easily surrender their power and wealth by stepping down in favor of an automatic rules-based system.

By 1960, Friedman pragmatically recognized that central banks, open market operations and fractional reserve banking were here to stay, at least for the foreseeable future. In such circumstances, he advanced an alternative rules-based mechanism that was in some respects quite contradictory to his earlier, preferred ideal. Its essential element would be a legislated monetary rule designed to ensure the smooth and regular expansion of the quantity of money.

According to this mechanism, the Federal Reserve would be required by statute to follow a rule of increasing high-powered money by a constant k-percent per annum, where k was a small number designed to accommodate productivity growth in the economy. This rule would permanently limit the fiscal authorities' access to the printing press to the stipulated k-percent increase and would force them to finance current deficits only by credibly promising future surpluses (Sargent, 1987, 9).

Cyclical movements in real income would not be avoided by this non-discretionary mechanism. However, the non-discretionary nature of the rule would prevent some of the wilder swings induced by inept and ill-timed monetary measures (Butler, 1985, 185).

So far, this advocacy has failed, not least because of public choice pressures combined with some skepticism as to the importance of high-powered money as the key monetary variable. Nevertheless, Friedman's advocacy has not been in vain. Monetary authorities in the United States and elsewhere are now aware of the relationship between the quantity of money and the price level. Throughout the world, there is far more reliance on monetary restraint as the basis for price stability than was the case during the Keynesian era. Such monetary restraint has increased the political costs of fiscal expansion. Once again, a largely positive program of economic analysis has served well the cause of liberty.

4. On Liberty

Individuals are born with free wills, and, if they so choose, they are able to forge judgments that are conditioned neither by their particular circumstances nor by the environment in which they find themselves. Nevertheless, particular circumstances and environments influence judgments even though, ultimately, they do not shape them. Milton Friedman's views on the nature and importance of liberty surely were influenced by his particular circumstances and environment.

Friedman is a second-generation central European immigrant and a Jew, characteristics that were not viewed favorably in the United States during the first half of the twentieth century; characteristics, indeed, that attracted hostile discrimination from public bodies and their agents, themselves protected from the discipline of the competitive market-place. Growing up in such circumstances demonstrated to Friedman in a very personal way the powerful and even-handed protection against prejudice provided by the capitalist system.

Much of Friedman's scholarly career has been played out against the international backcloth of unequivocal political evil, in the form of totalitarian fascist nightmares epitomized by Adolf Hitler's Third Reich and in the form of totalitarian socialist nightmares, epitomized by Josef Stalin's USSR. The 'days of the devils' (Johnson, 1983) may now be largely over. However, their evil mark is printed indelibly on everything that Friedman writes and says and does.

Domestically in the United States, Friedman's career has played out against a background of monotonic growth in the size of government and in the reach of its interventionist tentacles. Not for him has there been the privilege of nineteenth century British classical liberals who lived out their lives in environments that largely matched their philosophical beliefs. Circumstances and environments combine, in Friedman's case, to demand an aggressive classical liberalism, designed to roll back tyranny as well as to preserve and to protect established liberties. That demand has called forth an unwavering supply.

Friedman outlines his special brand of classical liberalism very clearly in the introductory paragraphs of *Capitalism and Freedom*:

> The free man will ask neither what his country can do for him nor what he can do for his country. He will ask rather "What can I and my compatriots do through government" to help us discharge our individual responsibilities, to achieve our several goals and purposes, and above all, to protect our freedom? And he will accompany this question with another: How can we keep the government we create from becoming a Frankenstein that will destroy the very freedom we establish it to protect? Freedom is a rare and delicate plant. Our minds tell us, and history confirms, that the great threat to freedom is the concentration of power. Government is necessary to preserve our freedom, it is an instrument through which we can exercise our freedom; yet by concentrating power in political hands, it is also a threat to freedom. (Friedman, 1962, 2)

In three important books — *Capitalism and Freedom* (Friedman, 1962), *Free to Choose* (Friedman and Friedman, 1979) and *Tyranny of the Status Quo* (Friedman and Friedman, 1983) — as well as in many other essays (see Leube, 1987 for a representative selection) and in numerous *Newsweek* columns — Friedman outlined a view of classical liberalism closely related to the philosophy of the young John Stuart Mill.

Friedman's philosophy, like that of Mill, is one in which freedom is viewed as indivisible, with economic freedoms equally as important as political freedoms. Like Mill, Friedman also holds that government should be as decentralized as possible in order to allow alienated citizens to vote with their feet. Like Mill Friedman also holds that "the only purpose for which power can be rightfully exercised over any member of a civilized community against his will, is to prevent harm to others" (Mill, 1865, 6). It is a philosophy like that of Mill in which "[O]ver himself, over his own body and mind, the individual is sovereign" (Mill, 1865, 6).

This said, Friedman does not believe that most debates over economic policy are debates over value judgments (Friedman, 1967). Disagreements exist, for the most part because economists accept differing tentative hypotheses about the relationship between economic phenomena. Friedman maintains an optimistic perspective that most of these disagreements will disappear over time as competing hypotheses are subjected to empirical testing. He has qualified this optimism, however, with the passage of time recognizing, in the wake of the public choice revolution, that economists and policy-makers are not always driven by considerations of high moral purpose (Friedman, 1986).

In Friedman's normative ideal, government should be strong and yet severely constrained. The major function of government is to protect the freedom of the people from outside and from inside intervention (i.e., to protect negative freedom in the sense most clearly defined by Isaiah Berlin, 1969). To achieve this objective, government must be empowered to provide an effective system of defense and to provide internally for the protection of property rights, the enforcement of private contracts and the maintenance of competitive markets. These powers, however, should not be unlimited. Government itself should remain strictly subject to the rule of law.

Unlike modern anarcho-capitalists, Friedman does not believe that private forces are capable of effectively providing these indispensable prerequisites of the free society. Nor is he comfortable with restricting government to the functions of the minimal (or night-watchman) state. Although he expresses a strong preference in favor of voluntary co-operation and private enterprise, he also recognizes that government upon occasion may enable individuals to accomplish jointly arrangements that would be more difficult or more expensive for them to accomplish severally (Friedman, 1962, 2). In particular, Friedman is sensitive to the problem of poverty and argues in *Capitalism and Freedom* (1962) in favor of a negative income tax to set a limit below which no family income could fall.

In contemplating such arrangements, however, Friedman unequivocally focuses on the harmful consequences of institutional arrangements that shield individuals from taking personal responsibility for their own decisions or that reflect paternalistic value judgments imposed by philosopher-kings on their fellow citizens. He is driven in this presumption by a recognition that the great advances in civilization have never come from centralized government, that centralized government can never duplicate the variety and diversity of individual action and that centralized government always substitutes uniform mediocrity for the variety that is essential for successful entrepreneurial innovation (Friedman, 1962, 4).

A basic human value that underpins Friedman's philosophy is tolerance based on humility (Friedman, 1991). An individual has no right to coerce someone else, not only because of fundamental principles of classical liberalism, but also because no individual can be sure that he is right and the other person wrong. In this respect, Friedman sets himself aside from Utopian classical liberals such as Ludwig von Mises (Mises, 1963) who protect their arguments from empirical criticism on *a priori* grounds. Friedman rejects *praxeology* of the kind advanced by Mises on the ground that it converts a body of substantive conclusions into a religion.

Friedman argues that democracy is the appropriate form of government to foster political freedom. However, the prerequisite to democracy is a capitalist economy that separates economic from political power, allowing the one to offset the other (Breit and Ransom, 1998, 257). In this regard, Friedman fails to take full account of public choice arguments that there is a predictable tension between democracy and free markets in the absence of self-enforcing constitutional constraints on government authority (Rowley, 1999).

Much of Friedman's normative message is now commonplace in the debate over public policy. For example, several experimentations in the use of school vouchers are currently under way in the United States and many more are under consideration. The 1960's Great Society programs that attempted to provide a welfare state from cradle to the grave are systematically, if slowly, being dismantled in favor of market-based alternatives. Affirmative-action policies that rely on bureaucratic controls rather than on competitive capitalism are increasingly the subject of criticism, even among those for whom those policies were ostensibly designed. Conscription in the military has given way to the market-based volunteer force. Fixed exchange rate regimes systematically have given way to flexible exchange rate regimes throughout the large majority of the Free World. In all these areas, Friedman's once controversial ideas have begun to overwhelm the forces of mercantilism, mirroring the success of Adam Smith two centuries earlier.

It should not be forgotten, however, that Friedman's success was bitterly fought and courageously achieved against powerful forces in a western world then dedicated to the elimination of individual freedom in favor of democratic socialism. Ranged against Friedman in this regard were eminent members of the economics profession (including Paul Samuelson, Kenneth Arrow, John Kenneth Galbraith, James Tobin, Robert Solow and Joan Robinson) who consistently demonstrated anti-free market prejudices combined with a high regard for big government and an easy willingness to sacrifice economic freedoms on the altar of Keynesian macroeconomic policies.

When intellectual battles are won and lost, the victor rarely receives his justly earned accolades. Those whose arguments have failed, and who seek continued academic respect, shift their positions and rely on myopia to protect them from the consequences of their earlier mistakes.

Rest assured, however, that those leopards who argued so confidently in the middle years of the twentieth century for the institutional arrangements of democratic socialism would not have changed their spots to the extent that they have in the absence of Friedman's firm and convincing voice in defense of economic freedom, a voice that penetrated the citadels of coercion in the West as well as in the East, a voice that gave hope for a freer and more prosperous future during a dangerous half century for those who cherish freedom. Without that clear and convincing voice in favor of capitalism it is doubtful whether the public choice revolution would have made the inroads that it has into the widely held postwar mis-conception that government is the omniscient and impartial servant of the public good.

CHARLES K. ROWLEY
ANNE RATHBONE

Acknowledgments

We wish to thank Amanda J. Owens for invaluable collaboration in preparing biographical materials. We are extremely grateful to Milton Friedman for ensuring that the essay is factually correct. We wish to thank also William Breit, James M. Buchanan, Tyler Cowen, David Fand, J. Daniel Hammond, Robert Higgs, Henry G. Manne, Fred McChesney and Andrew Sellgren for helpful suggestions. The Locke Institute is indebted to the Earhart Foundation for financial support.

SELECTED WORKS

(1945). *Income from Independent Professional Practice.* (With Simon Kuznets). New York: National Bureau of Economic Research.

(1946). *Roofs or Ceilings? The Current Housing Problem*. (With George J. Stigler). Irvington-on-the-Hudson, New York: Foundation for Economic Education.

(1953). *Essays in Positive Economics*. Chicago: University of Chicago Press.

(1956). *Studies in the Quantity Theory of Money* (ed.). Chicago: University of Chicago Press.

(1957). *A Theory of the Consumption Function*. Princeton: Princeton University Press.

(1962). *Capitalism and Freedom*. Chicago: University of Chicago Press.

Friedman, M. and Meiselman, D. (1963). "The Relative Stability of Monetary Velocity and the Investment Multiplier in the United States, 1897–1958," in *Stabilization Policies*. Prentice Hall, pp. 165–268.

(1963). *A Monetary History of the United States, 1867–1960*. (With Anna J. Schwartz). Princeton: Princeton University Press.

(1966). *Price Theory: A Provisional Text*. (With David I. Fand and Warren J. Gustus). Chicago: Aldine Press.

(1967). "Value judgments in economics," in Sidney Hook (ed.) *Human Values and Economic Policy*. New York: New York University Press, pp. 4–8.

(1978). *Milton Friedman's Monetary Framework: A Debate with His Critics*. (Edited by Robert J. Gordon). Chicago: University of Chicago Press.

(1980). *Free to Choose*. (With Rose D. Friedman). New York: Harcourt Brace Jovanovich.

(1984). *Tyranny of the Status Quo*. (With Rose D. Friedman). San Diego, New York and London: Harcourt Brace Jovanovich.

(1986). "Economists and economic policy." *Economic Inquiry*, XXIV: 1–10.

(1987). *The Essence of Friedman*. (Edited by Kurt R. Leub, with a Foreword by W. Glenn Campbell and an Introduction by Anna J. Schwartz). Stanford: Hoover Institution Press.

(1991). "Say 'no' to intolerance." *Liberty*, 4(6): 17–20.

(1998). *Two Lucky People*. (With Rose D. Friedman). Chicago: University of Chicago Press.

BIBLIOGRAPHY

Blaug, M. (1985). *Great Economists Since Keynes*. Totowa, New Jersey: Barnes and Noble Books.

Breit, W. and Spencer, R.W. (1995). *Lives of the Laureates: Thirteen Nobel Economists*, 3rd edn. Cambridge, MA: MIT Press.

Breit, W. and Ransom R.L. (1998). *The Academic Scribblers*. Princeton: Princeton University Press.

Buchanan, J.M. and Wagner, R.E. (1977). *Democracy in Deficit: The Political Legacy of Lord Keynes*. New York: Academic Press.

Butler, E. (1985). *Milton Friedman: A Guide to His Economic Thought*. New York: Universe Books.

De Vroey, M. (2001). "Friedman and Lucas on the Phillips curve: from a disequilibrium to an equilibrium approach". *Eastern Economic Journal*, 27(2): 127–148.

Dohert, B. (1995). "Best of both worlds." *Reason*, June, 32–38.

Fisher, I. (1930). *The Theory of Interest*. London and New York: Macmillan.

Frazer, W. (1988). *Power and Ideas: Milton Friedman and the Big U-Turn*, vols I and II. Gainsville, Florida: Gulf/Atlantic Publishing Company.

Friedman, M. and Meiselman, D. (1963). "The Relative Stability of Monetary Velocity and the Investment Multiplier in the United States, 1897–1958", in *Stabilization Policies*. Prentice Hall, 165–268.

Hirsch, A. and de Marchi, N. (1990). *Milton Friedman: Economics in Theory and Practice*. Ann Arbor: University of Michigan Press.

Johnson, P. (1983). *Modern Times: The World from the Twenties to the Eighties*. New York: Harper and Row.

Keynes, J.M. (1936). "The General Theory of Employment, Interest and Money". New York and London: Harcourt, Brace and Co.

Kuznets, S. (1952). "Proportion of Capital Formation to National Product". *American Economic Review*, 42: 507–526.

Mill, J.S. (1865). *On Liberty*. London: Longman, Green & Co.

Mises, Ludwig von (1963). *Human Action*. New Haven: Yale University Press.

Robbins, L.C. (1932). *An Essay on the Nature and Significance of Economic Science*. London: Macmillan.

Rowley, C.K. (1999). "Five market friendly nobelists." *The Independent Review*, III(3): 413–431.

Rowley, C.K. (1999). "Review of 'Milton and Rose Friedman, Two Lucky People." *Public Choice*, 99(3–4): 474–480.

Samuelson, P.A. (1963). "Comment on Ernest Nagel's 'assumptions in economic theory.'" *American Economic Review*, May, 211–219.

Sargent, T.J. (1987). *Some of Milton Friedman's Scientific Contributions to Macroeconomics*. Stanford: Hoover Institution.

Walters, A. (1987). "Milton Friedman: born 1912," in John Eatwell, Murray Milgate, and Peter Newman (eds.) *The New Palgrave: A Dictionary of Economics*, volume 2. London and New York: Macmillan, pp. 422–427.

MONETARY POLICY AND CENTRAL BANK BEHAVIOR

1. Introduction

There are few areas in which public choice has had as much success in making inroads into mainstream economics and, in particular, in influencing real-life developments as in the design of monetary institutions and the day-to-day conduct of monetary policy. This survey tracks these developments, from the humble beginnings in the 1970s related to Nordhaus' (1975) account of the opportunistic political business cycle to the widespread academic and political discussion on monetary policy rules and targets of today.[1] Section 2 contains a compact review of the two classical ideas in political macroeconomics, the political business cycle and the inflation bias. Section 3 moves on to more modern, stochastic models, in which the desire for undistorted stabilization of supply shocks calls for refined remedies to the time-inconsistency problem, such as performance contracts and inflation targets for central banks.

Section 4 moves on to a discussion of current developments which focus on instrument and targeting rules for monetary policy. Finally, section 5 briefly assesses these developments.

2. How it Started: Political Business Cycles and all that

Today's academic discussion and recent developments in monetary policy and institutions rest on three main pillars: The traditional theory of economic policy in the spirit of Theil (1961) and Tinbergen (1952); the endogenisation of economic policy, the groundwork for which was laid in many classical writings in public choice, although the main influence stems from the compact and compelling formalizations by Nordhaus (1975) and MacRae (1977); and, the rules-versus-discretion debate that came in the wake of the rational expectations revolution, with implications for endogenous policy making that were initially formalized by Kydland and Prescott (1977) but worked out and popularized by Barro and Gordon (1983). We will focus here on the public-choice-related roots of modern monetary policy conduct and design.

The birth of New Political Macroeconomics, as it would be called decades later, and, hence, also of positive analyses of monetary policy, was Nordhaus' concise formal demonstration of what opportunistic governments might do to an economy. In strong contrast to Theil–Tinbergen-type benevolent policymakers, opportunism takes the form of vote maximization at periodically held elections. Voters derive instantaneous or period utility from the state of the economy, as represented by inflation π and the logarithm of income y (or, alternatively, unemployment):

$$u = -0.5\pi^2 + \xi y \qquad (1)$$

Votes cast on election day then reflect total utility and, hence, the course of the economy during the incumbent governments recent term in office, with more distant periods receiving less weight due to voter forgetfulness.

Operating within a natural-rate aggregate-supply framework in which income (or, again, unemployment) depend on inflation surprises,[2]

$$y = \pi - E_{-1}\pi \qquad (2)$$

and inflation expectations are adaptive, governments maximize reelection prospects by resorting to expansionary policies, fiscal or monetary, in the run-up to an election, while deliberately driving the economy into a recession once the election is over, thus creating election-related swings in economic activity known as the *political business cycle*.

From the perspective of mainstream macroeconomics, the Nordhaus model (and its cousin, the partisan theory proposed by Hibbs (1977), which suggested that election-related swings were due to ideologically motivated differences between the preferences of party constituencies) was almost dead on arrival. Despite the extraordinary interest it drew from public choice scholars, its key building blocks were at that time being discarded by macroeconomists: a non-vertical long-run Phillips curve (which was not essential to the political business cycle, however), adaptive inflation expectations, and backward-looking voters. A number of authors[3] quickly pointed out that little in terms of added rationality in inflation expectations formation was required in order to eliminate the political business cycle.

While efforts by Alesina (1987), Persson and Tabellini (1990) and others gave the study of election-related macroeconomic cycles a vigorous second life under the labels of *Rational partisan theory* and *Rational political business cycles*, political business cycles do not feature prominently on today's research agenda any longer.[4]

Instead, research interest has shifted towards the rational-expectations equilibrium implications of endogenous policy making, with a particular emphasis on monetary policy. The starting point for this work, overlooked by most early critics, is the insight that while rational inflation expectations do indeed eliminate the political business cycle, they do leave the economy and policy trapped in a suboptimal, inefficient equilibrium. If monetary policy is driven by preferences such as (1), either because it caters to the electorate, or because this describes the government's or the central bank's very own preferences, the model's discretionary rational-expectations solution in the context of a one-shot game between the government and the economy is

$$\pi = \xi \qquad (3)$$

Thus, despite the desire for full price stability inherent in (1), discretionary monetary policy cannot deliver.[5] The reason is the time-inconsistency of price stability. Once it is achieved with income being at its potential level, the central bank can always raise its own utility, or public support, by generating some inflation and a lot of income gains. While this mechanism and insight had already been described by Kydland and Prescott (1977), it attracted little attention until it was restated and popularized by Barro and Gordon (1983). The latter work triggered a still ongoing discussion of what institutional arrangements would lead to the best macroeconomic outcomes, in particular, a reduction of the inflation bias. Initially, Barro and Gordon (1983) had suggested that reputational forces may take care of the inflation bias. However because such forces are strongly weakened when the government's horizon does not extend to infinity, Rogoff's (1985) suggestion to put monetary policy into the hands of a conservative central bank, characterized by total oblevity towards income developments, received the most attention. In the above context, an arch conservative monetary policy guided by preferences $\hat{\xi} = 0$ delivers full price stability without any detrimental effects on income. To achieve such policy, the governing body of the central bank must have preferences $\hat{\xi} = 0$, and the central bank needs to be made completely independent of the government (which political competition forces to attend to the preferences of voters represented by ξ).[6] Condoned by the apparent empirical support for this proposition in the form of significant negative correlations between long-run inflation and measures of central bank independence,[7] the long ruling orthodoxy was that central banks must be completely independent and as conservative (meaning inflation averse) as possible.[8]

3. Enter the Stabilization Bias

Two innovations rekindled interest in the basic Nordhaus scenario and kept the discussion alive and vigorous up to the present.

The first was a modification of the utility function that gave inflation and income *symmetric* treatment. Nordhaus (1975), Kydland and Prescott (1977), Barro and Gordon (1983), and virtually hundreds of papers since, had employed an asymmetric functional form, assuming that utility depended nonlinearly on inflation, but linearly on income (or unemployment). This did help simplify the math, yet still sufficed to derive the political business cycle under adaptive inflation expectations and the inflation bias when expectations were rational.

The second innovation was to conduct the analysis in a more realistic stochastic context in which the economy was subject to supply shocks, and the potential need for stabilization entered the picture.

3.1. The Trade between Price Stability and Shock Stabilization

In order to demonstrate the implications of these two innovations, let us proceed from a hybrid utility function that comprises both the original asymmetric treatment (for $\alpha = 0$) and the later symmetric treatment (for $\alpha = 1$):

$$u = -0.5\pi^2 - \alpha\xi(y-k)^2 + (1-\alpha)\xi y \qquad (3)$$

$k > 0$ is society's income target which is assumed to exceed potential income (which has been normalized to zero) because the latter is inefficiently low (also carrying involuntary unemployment) due to distortive taxes, monopolistic trade unions, legal constraints, and other imperfections in goods and labour markets.

Aggregate supply is subject to surprise inflation plus supply shocks ε that are white noise with zero mean and variance σ_ε^2:

$$y = \pi - E_{-1}\pi + \varepsilon \qquad (4)$$

Maximizing equation (3) subject to (4) yields the following rational-expectations solutions for inflation and income:

$$\pi = (1-\alpha)\xi + \alpha\xi k - \frac{\alpha\xi}{1+\alpha\xi}\varepsilon\alpha \qquad (5)$$

$$y = \frac{1}{1+\alpha\xi}\varepsilon \qquad (6)$$

Equations (5) and (6) convey three important insights:

1. The first two terms on the right-hand side of (5) constitute the inflation bias that monetary policy cannot get rid of, even in the absence of shocks. If utility is linear in y ($\alpha = 0$) this bias equals ξ. If utility is nonlinear in y, with decreasing marginal utility ($\alpha = 1$), this bias amounts to ξk. It is positive if k exceeds potential income. Then the marginal utility of income is positive at the no-surprise equilibrium level, and inflation must be positive in order to generate a marginal disutility of inflation large enough to counterbalance the net temptation to raise income. At full price this does not apply because the marginal disutility of inflation is zero.

2. The coefficients in the stochastic terms of both (5) and (6) indicate how supply shocks are split into inflation and income responses. Note that the absolute values of the two coefficients sum up to one.[9] So only $1/(1+\alpha\xi)$ percent of any given adverse supply shock are actually permitted to drive income down, while the remaining $\alpha\xi/(1+\alpha\xi)$ percent materialize in increased inflation.

3. When utility is linear in y ($\alpha = 0$) the solutions simplify to $\pi = \xi$ and $y = \varepsilon$. Inflation is always constant at a level reflecting the conservativeness of monetary policy. Supply shock are never permitted to affect inflation, independently of the conservativeness of monetary policy.

The third insight states the specific conditions under which the famous monetary-policy conservativeness result holds: In order to achieve second-best outcomes, that is, full price stability and the exact extent of shock stabilization society requests, monetary policy needs to be as conservative as possible in the sense that it should only look at the goal of price stability while ignoring movements of income altogether.[10]

If, however, more realistically, the utility function is symmetric ($\alpha = 1$), a dilemma pops up. To see this, note that the solutions for inflation and income now become

$$\pi = \xi k - \frac{\xi}{1+\xi}\varepsilon \qquad (7)$$

$$y = \frac{1}{1+\xi}\varepsilon \qquad (8)$$

The key insight here is that in a stochastic context with decreasing marginal utility from income gains, delegating monetary discretion to an arch conservative central bank (characterized by $\hat{\xi} = 0$) constitutes a fourth-best solution only. All it ensures is that we achieve price stability. The price to be paid are distorted responses to supply shocks. The variance of inflation is minimized at var $(\pi) = 0 \cdot \sigma_\varepsilon^2 = 0$, but this goes at the cost of maximum variance of income at var $(y) = \sigma_\varepsilon^2$. Society would prefer an intermediate solution, namely var $(\pi) = [\xi/(1+\xi)]^2\sigma_\varepsilon^2$ and var $(y) = [1/(1+\xi)]^2\sigma_\varepsilon^2$. In the face of this trade-off between inflation bias and stabilization bias, a superior outcome, a third-best result, is achieved if society picks a more moderately conservative central bank, one that is more conservative than society, but not arch conservative ($\xi > \hat{\xi} > 0$) [Rogoff (1985)].

Figure 1 may help clarify the trade-offs involved and serve as a background for issues addressed later on. The convex line constitutes the trade-off between income variability and inflation variability implied by the model. Society's preferences, represented by concave indifference curves, determine the desired split between income and inflation variability. We can move down along this line from the point on the ordinate (which obtains for $\hat{\xi} = 0$) towards the point on the abscissa (which obtains for $\hat{\xi} \to \infty$). The dilemma is that in order to remove the inflation bias we need $\hat{\xi} = 0$. This would put us into point A on the variance trade-off line with the variance of income being at a maximum at σ_ε^2 and the variance of inflation being at a minimum at zero. Society would prefer B. As we move from A towards B by raising $\hat{\xi}$, we reduce the stabilization bias, but pay by increasing the inflation bias. All we can achieve is a third-best optimum in a point such as C, where society's net marginal benefit from increasing $\hat{\xi}$ is zero.

The 1990s brought an avalanche of research on how to move beyond the third-best outcome generated by a moderately conservative central bank. This quest for second-best outcomes in a stochastic macroeconomic framework focussed on two main suggestions: To equip central bank chiefs with a *performance contract*, or to commit them to an *inflation target*.[11]

3.2. Performance Contracts

Equipped with a linear performance contract of the form $s = -\lambda \pi$, where s is a variable component of the central bank's governing body's salary that depends on inflation, the central bank's derived utility function changes into

$$u = -0.5\pi^2 - 0.5\hat{\xi}(y-k)^2 - \lambda\pi \qquad (9)$$

Now optimal policy under discretion leads to the following behaviour of inflation and income:

$$\pi = \hat{\xi}k - \lambda - \frac{\hat{\xi}}{1+\hat{\xi}}\varepsilon \qquad (10)$$

$$y = \frac{1}{1+\hat{\xi}}\varepsilon \qquad (11)$$

These results show that a properly designed linear performance contract can indeed lead to second best results. The inflation bias, comprising the first two terms on the right-hand side of (10), is removed if $\lambda = \hat{\xi}\pi$. And shock stabilization is prevented when the central bank's preferences are representative of society's ($\hat{\xi} = \xi$). This actually is ensured best if the central bank is not independent of the government. Whatever tendencies towards a higher inflation bias this may carry can easily be taken care of by setting the punishment coefficient in the performance contract appropriately.[12]

3.3. Inflation Targets

Inflation targets have been very popular in academic research as a probably more realistic and viable alternative to performance contracts. Inflation targets also do provide a natural link from the literature discussed here to the

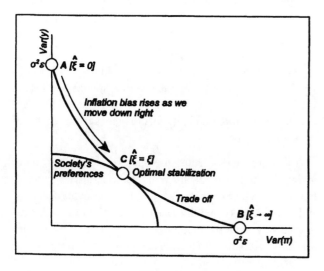

Figure 1:

recent intensive discussion of general monetary policy rules and targets at which we will look below. The general idea is that society (via the government) can communicate an inflation target π^T to the central bank. The questions to be answered are, what this target should be, how target misses are to be punished, and what preferences the central bank should have.

After adding the inflation-target term to the central bank's utility function, the derived utility function reads

$$u = -0.5\pi^2 - 0.5\hat{\xi}(y-k)^2 - 0.5\lambda(\pi - \pi^T)^2 \qquad (12)$$

Under discretion, the inflation rate follows

$$\pi = \frac{1}{1+\lambda}\hat{\xi}k - \frac{\lambda}{1+\lambda}\pi^T - \frac{\hat{\xi}}{1+\lambda+\hat{\xi}}\varepsilon \qquad (13)$$

while income is determined by

$$\frac{1+\lambda}{1+\lambda+\hat{\xi}}\varepsilon \qquad (14)$$

Again, a second-best optimum can be achieved. The condition for the inflation bias to disappear is $\pi^T = -\hat{\xi}k/\lambda$. This is an awkward result, however. No only because the central bank must be told to deflate, but even more so because the central bank systematically misses the assigned target. In the aspired zero-inflation equilibrium, the deviation from the inflation target must be large enough to offset any temptation to inflate that results from the central bank's own preferences.[13]

The condition for avoiding a stabilization bias is that the shock's coefficient in, say, (14), which describes the central bank's response, must be the same as the shock's coefficient in (8), which states society's desired response. This is accomplished if $\hat{\xi} = (1+\lambda)\xi$, meaning that now the government must pick a central banker who is *less conservative*, less inflation-averse than society.

Table 1 summarizes the consolidated knowledge about central bank independence and conservativeness in this section's macroeconomic environment. The important point it does highlight is that little scientific support remains for the quest for the most independent, most conservative central bank that did and still does seem to shape the design and development of institutions in many of the world's countries and regions.[14]

3.4. A Macroeconomic Framework with Income Persistence

The above findings do not change dramatically if, more in line with our empirical knowledge about the time series properties of income and other macroeconomic variables, we let shocks have lasting effects on income due to some degree of persistence, as in equation (15).

$$y = \beta y_{-1} + \pi - E_{-1}\pi + \varepsilon \qquad (15)$$

Because inflation surprises and shocks now affect all future incomes, policy choices are being made so as to maximize the expected present value $E_{t-1} U_t$ of current and future period utilities:

$$E_{t-1} U_t = \sum_{i=0}^{\infty} \delta^i E_{t-1} u_{t+i} \qquad (16)$$

Under discretion, there is still an inflation bias, which now takes the form

$$\pi = \frac{\xi k}{1-(\alpha+b)\delta} - cy_{-1} - d\varepsilon \qquad (17)$$

b, c and d are coefficients composed of the structural equations parameters that we do not need to spell out here.[15] This bias features a constant part which is similar to the bias in the natural rate framework discussed above. In addition to the familiar dependence on preferences ξ this bias also depends on the degree of persistence β. The straightforward explanation is that the more persistent income is, the longer income gains generated by current inflation surprises last. But then the temptation to inflate is larger, and because this is anticipated by the labour market, we end up with a higher inflation bias.

Table 1: How conservative should the central bank be?

Macroeconomic and monetary policy framework	Optimal degree of central bank conservatism
• Deterministic macroeconomic framework	
— Baseline model (perfect discretion)	— arch conservative ($\hat{\xi}=0$)
• Stochastic macroeconomic framework	
— Baseline model (perfect discretion), 3rd best	— moderately conservative ($\xi > \hat{\xi} > 0$)
— Added performance contract; 2nd best	— as conservative as society ($\hat{\xi} = \xi$)
— Added inflation target; 2nd best	— less conservative than society ($\hat{\xi} > \xi$)

The second term defining the inflation bias is endogenous, time-dependent. It states that this inflation bias is the higher, the lower income was last period. The mechanism at play here is that the marginal utility of income is higher when an adverse supply shock hit income last period and persistence will thus tend to keep income below potential income this period also. The central bank will thus be prepared to inject a larger inflation hike into the economy in the hope of income gains. But since again the labour market anticipates this, these income gains do not really accrue, and all we are left with is an inflation bias above average.

3.4.1. State-dependent Performance Contracts
While the math to demonstrate this is labourious, it is intuitively clear that a linear inflation performance contract cannot do a way with this type of *variable* inflation bias. The required extension of the optimal contract is straightforward, though. Since the inflation bias is variable, dependent on last period's income, the performance contract must also be state-dependent of the form

$$s_t = -(\lambda_1 - \lambda_2 y_{t-1})\pi_t \tag{18}$$

This contract may specify λ_1 so as to eliminate the constant inflation bias, as in the natural-rate framework discussed above. And it may specify λ_2 such as to counterbalance the added incentive to inflate after income fell, thus removing the state-dependent inflation bias. Once the performance contract is designed optimally, central bank preferences should be identical to society's in order not to bias stabilization. This mimics the result obtained in the natural-rate context.

3.4.2. State-dependent Inflation Target
In the presence of income persistence inflation targets must be path dependent, comprising a constant term to take care of the fixed inflation bias and a term that follows lagged income to take care of the variable inflation bias: $\pi_t^T = \beta_0 + \beta_1 y_{t-1}$. As Svensson (1997a) shows, however, even a state-dependent inflation target cannot get rid of both types of inflation bias, and keep stabilization undistorted. It must be combined with the appropriate central bank preferences that compensate for the stabilization bias introduced by the inflation target.

4. Current Developments

Current research on monetary policy and central banks is looking for answers to three important questions:

1. How can the stabilization options be improved? Rather than discussing how different targets within a given family can be optimized so as to achieve second-best solution within a given trade-off, researchers turn to completely different target variables and how they may affect the trade-off options. We will exemplify this by comparing inflation targets as discussed above to price level targets.

2. Is the consolidated knowledge as surveyed in section 3 reasonably robust to changes in the macroeconomic environment within which monetary policy operates? A key role in this discussion is being played by the so-called New Keynesian aggregate supply curve which, in line with recent methodological changes in macroeconomics, is being derived from solid microfoundations and features forward-looking inflation expectations.

3. How can some of the more abstract theoretical insights of political macroeconomics be brought to bear on the actual conduct of monetary policy. This question is being discussed in a separate strand of research focussing on policy rules, which has close ties to the topics discussed so far.

4.1. The Choice of Targets and their Effects on Trade-offs

The question which macroeconomic variable monetary policy should target is not a trivial one. To demonstrate how that choice of target variables affects the variability of macroeconomic variables, as well as the implied trade offs between these variabilities, let us compare inflation targets with price level targets. In order to focus on the issue at hand, assume, as much of the literature does, that society can assign a target to the central bank in the strict sense that the target *overrides* any pertinent preferences the central bank itself may have (rather than *adding* it to the central bank's preferences, as assumed previously). Equipped with such an assigned inflation target, the central bank utility function reads

$$u = -0.5(\pi - \pi^T)^2 - 0.5\hat{\xi}(y - k)^2 \tag{19}$$

The discretionary optima for inflation and income that follow are

$$\pi = \hat{\xi}k - \pi^T - \frac{\hat{\xi}}{1+\hat{\xi}}\varepsilon \tag{20}$$

and

$$y = \frac{1}{1+\hat{\xi}}\varepsilon \tag{21}$$

The volatility trade-off from which society may choose by selecting $\hat{\xi}$ is characterized by $\text{var}(\pi) = [\hat{\xi}/(1+\hat{\xi})]^2 \sigma_\varepsilon^2$ and $\text{var}(y) = [1/(1+\hat{\xi})]^2 \sigma_\varepsilon^2$, and depicted as the lower

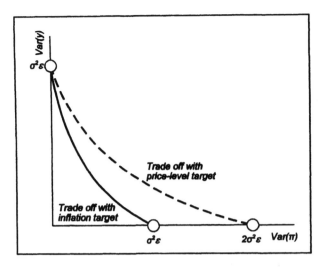

Figure 2:

convex line in Figure 2. The specific target value π^T neither affects the trade-off, nor where we end up on it. Actually, the depicted curve is an efficiency frontier. As long as monetary policy is governed by preferences coming from this very family of utility functions, comprising inflation and income as arguments that enter in quadratic form, we end up somewhere on this line. All society can do is move up or down this curve into its preferred point by picking $\hat{\xi}$.

Now other families of utility functions exist, comprising different variables or functional forms. An argument that is often advanced against in inflation targets for monetary policy is that it makes the variance of the price level go towards infinity as we increase the time horizon, making it difficult for individuals and firms to form expectations. In an attempt to remedy this, the government may assign a price level target to the central bank instead, even though society's preferences are still as given in equation (3) with $\alpha = 0$. The central bank's utility function then reads

$$u = -0.5(p - p^T)^2 - 0.5\hat{\xi}(y - k)^2 \qquad (22)$$

where p is the logarithm of the price level. Note that the aggregate-supply function (4) may be rewritten as

$$y = p - E_{-1}p + \varepsilon \qquad (23)$$

since inflation is the first difference in the log of the price level. Maximizing (22) subject to (23) mimics the maximization of (19) subject to (4), except that the price level p has taken the place of inflation π. Hence the solution for the price level is equal to the solution we previously derived for inflation,

$$p = \hat{\xi}k - p^T - \frac{\hat{\xi}}{1 + \hat{\xi}}\varepsilon \qquad (24)$$

whether we assign an inflation target or a price level target has no effect on income which again follows

$$y = \frac{1}{1 + \hat{\xi}}\varepsilon \qquad (25)$$

Since $\pi \equiv p - p_{-1}$, the behaviour of inflation is directly derived from (24):

$$\pi = -\frac{\hat{\xi}}{1 + \hat{\xi}}(\varepsilon - \varepsilon_{-1}) \qquad (26)$$

This implies an inflation variance of var $(\pi) = 2[\hat{\xi}/(1 + \hat{\xi})]^2\sigma_\varepsilon^2$, which is twice as large as when the central bank pursued an inflation target. As Figure 2 illustrates, this dramatically worsens the options for stabilization policy and is likely to affect society's pick of central bank conservativeness. In fact, a second-best optimum cannot even be achieved because $[\xi/(1 + \xi)]^2 = 2[\hat{\xi}/(1 + \hat{\xi})]^2$ — which would provide the right inflation variability — and $1/(1 + \xi) = [1/(1 + \hat{\xi})]$ — which would provide the desired variability of income — cannot be met at the same time. Independently of society's preferences, which we may not know, we can state that assigning a price-level target is inefficient. Switching to an inflation target permits lowering the variance of inflation (income) without raising the variance of income (inflation).[16]

The example used here goes to show that the choice of a target variable, or variables, is a delicate one with obvious welfare implications. The inefficiency of price level targeting relative to inflation targeting is not robust, however, to changes in the macroeconomic framework. This is not really surprising, since the trade off is generated by the complete model, comprising both the macroeconomic structure and the incentives governing monetary policy. Svensson (1999b) demonstrates that, when faced with an economy with a sufficient degree of income persistence, society may be well advised to assign price-level targeting even though it possesses preferences cast in terms of an optimal inflation rate, because it results in lower inflation variability. Dittmer and Gavin (2000) show that in a model with a New Keynesian Phillips curve, as discussed in the following section, price-level targeting always generates a more favourable trade off between income and inflation variability, even if income is not persistent.

4.2. The New Keynesian Aggregate-supply or Phillips Curve

Roberts (1995) uses the Calvo (1983) model (in which prices are sticky because during any given period a firm has a fixed probability, strictly smaller than 1, that it may adjust prices) to show that a loglinear approximation about the steady state of the aggregated pricing decisions of individual firms reads

$$y = \beta y_{-1} + \pi - E\pi_{+1} + \varepsilon \qquad (27)$$

While this aggregate supply curve looks very similar to the neoclassical supply curve with persistence that we used above, the inclusion of tomorrow's expected rate of inflation rather than today's has important implications.[17] One is that any movement in inflation, and particularly when it is rationally anticipated, affects income.[18] Clarida et al. (1999) look at how this bears on the issues discussed in the preceding sections of this paper. Major findings are:

1. There is an inflation bias if the central bank has an income target that exceeds potential income. This is most easily rationalized if we think of monetary policy as a series of one-shot games in which policymakers take next period's expected inflation as given. It also holds in a more general setting, however, when the central bank has a longer horizon.

2. The inflation bias is negatively correlated with central bank conservativeness, that is, with the weight that the income target has in its utility function. An inflation nutter ($\hat{\xi} = 0$), as an arch conservative central bank is sometimes referred to, would entirely eliminate the inflation bias.

3. As a final analogue to results obtained within the Neoclassical framework, only a moderately conservative central bank would strike the right balance between the desires to reduce the inflation bias and to keep shock stabilization as undistorted as possible.

The framework used by Clarida et al. (1999), being somewhat richer than the one reported here, with shocks on the supply side and on the demand side, permits a host of other insights not directly comparable to the consolidated knowledge acquired within the neoclassical framework. A key issue that has been raised within this context, however, is whether preferences do indeed feature an income target which exceeds potential income, thus generating a problem of time inconsistency. This is an important question, because if there was no inflation bias, or if it had different causes than presumed since spelled out by Kydland and Prescott (1977) and Barro and Gordon (1983), there might not exist the dilemma of choosing between inflation-bias reduction and less distortion of stabilization policy, making things much simpler for monetary policy.

As Cukierman (2002) has demonstrated, though, an income target exceeding normal or potential income is not necessary for an inflation bias to occur. All that is needed is an asymmetry in the central bank's utility function. Suppose preferences are such that the central bank wants income to rise, but only until it reaches potential income. It does not want to push it beyond that level, but, if it exceeds potential income due to a favourable supply shock, it refrains from trying to drive it down. As a consequence, whenever a positive shock hits and income is above potential income, inflation remains at zero. Whenever a negative shock drives income below normal levels, monetary policy cushions that fall by creating inflation. As a result, average and expected inflation are strictly greater than zero. We have an inflation bias in equilibrium. In this context, much of the same remedies and policy recommendations would apply, with the math being a bit more cumbersome due to the employed piecewise utility functions.

4.3. The Quest for Monetary Policy Rules

This is probably the most active topic on today's research agenda on monetary policy. The field is still in a flux, and there are several perspectives from which to look at it. In order to understand the current discussion, we need to introduce some definitions.[19]

From a simplifying perspective there are two kinds of monetary policy rules. The first category comprises *instrument rules*. These specify how some instrument of monetary policy, typically an interest rate or monetary aggregate, responds to a set of macroeconomic variables. If these variables are predetermined at the time the instrument is being set, we speak of an *explicit instrument rule*. An *implicit instrument rule* specifies the instrument as a function of forward-looking variables that are not predetermined, of course. Due to this simultaneity between instrument and determining variables, this must be considered an *equilibrium condition* rather than a rule.

The second group of monetary policy rules comprises *targeting rules*. Characteristic for a targeting rule is the "assignment" of a loss function to the central bank. If this loss function features only one target variable, say inflation, we have a *strict* targeting rule. If additional variables are included, say income, we speak of a *flexible* targeting rule. To the extent that the right or best target variables are difficult to control or to observe, the use of loss functions with *intermediate targets* is sometimes proposed. These targets should be highly correlated with the true goal, but easier to control and to observe.

Current research on monetary policy rules is related to the work reported in section 3. But it also differs in a few major aspects.

1. There is a deliberate shift from a predominantly analytical towards a sophisticated yet practical monetary

policy analysis, with strong doses of pragmatism and a quest for quantitative results. As consequence research interests of academics and central banks have begun to meet in this area.[20]

2. Employed models have been stripped of time inconsistency. So there is no more inflation bias and no more potential for conflict between price stability and stabilization policy. Stabilizing inflation and income around their desired values remains the only challenge. The discarding of the inflation bias appears to come as a response to criticism by a group of central bank notables and academics that the underlying story [Barro and Gordon (1983)] was unconvincing and empirically inaccurate. As a result, models are being employed in which a loss function or rule is imposed on the central bank that features an income target coinciding with potential income.[21]

3. While the New Classical or Lucas aggregate supply curve, more recently with added persistence, had completely dominated the literature discussed in section 3, there is no such consensus in the rules discussion. By contrast, this discussion accepts that no consensus regarding the right model of the macroeconomy has emerged yet, and emphasizes that this calls for thorough checks as to whether any derived rules are robust in the sense that they still function reasonably well within alternative macroeconomic models. These models cover a wide range of possibilities. Some reduce to a single equation. Some comprise up to a hundred equations. Some are derived from intertemporal optimizing behaviour of representative agents. Some are made up of equations purported to mimic the dynamic relationships we see in empirical VARs.

4. A final innovation characteristic of the rules discussion is the use of analytical and empirical methods that have become standard in real business cycle and dynamic general equilibrium analyses. This includes the calibration of models, stochastic simulations, and judgement of the empirical validity by means of comparing distributions of and correlations between simulated time series to those encountered in reality.

4.3.1. The Taylor Rule and Other Instrument Rules
Instrument rules for monetary and fiscal policy have a long tradition in economics. In the past, the most famous such rule was the Friedman rule, proposing that the money supply should grow at a fairly constant rate equal to the trend growth rate of income. Such a rule is an explicit, if not an exogenous rule, since it hardly allows for any feedback from current economic variables into monetary policy, certainly not in the short run.[22]

Among the recent crop of more sophisticated monetary policy rules, which includes McCallum's (1988) rule for the monetary base, the Henderson and McKibbin (1993) rule for the federal funds rate, and dozens of other rules, the rule that has swept the field is the one proposed by Taylor (1993). The Taylor rule states that the central bank has a real interest rate target, from which it deviates if inflation and/or income are off target. Solving this for the nominal interest rate yields

$$i = r^T + \pi + 0.5(\pi - \pi^T) + 0.5(y - y^*) \qquad (28)$$

When following the Taylor rule the central bank sets its instrument, the federal funds rate, at r^T when inflation and income are at their optimal levels. An increase in inflation makes the central bank raise the nominal interest rate by a factor of 1.5. This raises the real interest rate, dampening effect aggregate demand. While it does not include any forward-looking variables, the Taylor rule can nevertheless call for preemptive strikes against future inflation. This is the case if rising income, which also drives up the real interest rate, drives up inflation with a lag.

Initially proposed as a descriptive and expository devise that can be used to account for the general flavour of monetary policy in the US and explain the Fed's policy shift during the Volcker era, the Taylor rule has become much more. And the meanwhile quite voluminous amount of empirical research suggests that Taylor's rule is indeed a quite reasonable description of policy behaviour of many central banks, including the Bundesbank, which is usually considered the most extreme, inflation nutter in recent history.[23] The rule also has come to fame in financial circles, where it is now a common tool for forecasting changes in the interest rate.

4.3.2. Inflation Targeting and Other Targeting Rules
As mentioned, a targeting rule is characterized by the assignment of a loss or utility function to the central bank, In section 3 we showed this in a parsimonious framework for inflation and income. Many possible targets are being discussed in the literature, such as the price-level, inflation, nominal GDP or nominal GDP growth, with inflation targeting drawing the most academic interest and being the most successful among central banks.[24] The term inflation targeting is a misnomer, however, because only *strict* inflation targeting refers to a utility function of the form $u = -0.5(\pi - \pi^T)^2$. If additional target variables enter the utility function, this is being referred to as *flexible* inflation targeting. An example is the familiar utility function

$$u = -0.5(\pi - \pi^T)^2 - 0.5\xi(y - y^*)^2 \qquad (29)$$

which, for obvious reasons, might just as well be referred to as flexible *income targeting.*

In an effort to facilitate practical implementation or monitoring, a target rule is often expressed as a set of equations the target variables must fulfill. In the case of equation (29), if there is perfect control over the target variables and there is no trade-off, we obtain these equations from the first-order conditions for the unrestricted maximum of the utility function as $\pi = \pi^T$ and $y = y^*$. If control is imperfect, the expected values must equal the targets. Things do become much more complicated, however, when, as is always the case, we have trade-offs between macroeconomic variables, be it within periods or intertemporarily. While first-order conditions usually still exist, they may be too complicated for practical purposes. It may then be advisable to switch to intermediate target variables which, ideally, should be "highly correlated with the goal, easier to control than the goal, easier to observe than the goal, and transparent" [Svensson (1999a), p. 619]. In terms of how to pursue the target, Svensson (1999a) further reports that the target variable included in the loss function is usually not the best indicator for the instrument to respond to.

4.3.3. Comparing Instrument and Targeting Rules

From a purely technical viewpoint, instrument and targeting rules are simply two sides of the same coin. Maximization of any utility function or target subject to a macroeconomic model leads to an optimal instrument rule. For example, maximization of (29) with respect to the instrument π, subject to (4), gives the instrument rule $\pi = \pi^T - \varepsilon\xi/(1 + \xi)$. This may be rewritten. After solving (4) for ε and substituting the result, we obtain

$$\pi = \pi^T - \xi(E_{-1}\pi - \pi^T) - \xi(y - y^*) \qquad (30)$$

The result is a Taylor-like instrument rule in which the instrument π depends on the income gap and on the expected deviation of inflation from the inflation target. We may note here that (28) is not an explicit instrument rule. The endogeneity of income on the right-hand side makes this rule implicit, an equilibrium condition.[25]

Just as the optimization of a given utility or loss function generates an explicit or implicit instrument rule, any given instrument rule can be traced back to a utility function that is being optimized. This mapping from preferences to instrument rule or back does, of course, crucially depend on the macroeconomic model to which it is attached, and it may not be unique.

The competition between instrument and target rules thus boils down to the question of which one is more practical. A starting point for this discussion must be that realistic models of the macroeconomy are much more complex than the models we looked at. While this need not affect the utility function to be assigned to the central bank, it leads to immensely complicated optimal instrument rules, which will also be very difficult to monitor. On the other hand, it will also bear heavily on how a central bank pursues its assigned targets. It is flexible in doing so, however, and free to incorporate any progress the science of economics may make. As our view of how the economy functions change, the target(s) need not be adjusted. An instrument rule, by contrast, would have to be adjusted continuously, which may lead into credibility problems. But this is where the conceded uncertainty about the proper macroeconomic model comes into play. Robustness studies of instrument rules produced two interesting results.[26]

First, complex, optimal instrument rules derived from one specific model perform poorly when plugged into a different model. So using such a rule would be very risky if we have serious doubts about the true nature of macroeconomic transmission channels and interaction.

Second, simple instrument rules, taken from the same family as the Taylor rule, do not perform much worse than the complex optimal rule.

Third, and this is actually implied in the second result, the near-optimal performance of simple rules is rather robust across a wide spectrum of models.

Ball (1999) addresses the issue of preference uncertainty, referring to ξ, the relative weight of income stabilization in society's utility function. In terms of Figure 2 he proceeds from the assumption that we do not know society's indifference curves. Then the best we can do is focus on efficiency and identify those rules or targeting variables that generate lower trade-off lines, so that society can be made better off, now matter what the weight parameter is in its utility function. Employing a calibrated version of the macroeconomic model shown in note 25, Ball compared inflation targeting, nominal GDP growth targeting, and the Taylor rule. In this framework inflation targeting is efficient and nominal GDP growth targeting is inefficient. The verdict for the Taylor rule is mixed. In its original form reported as equation (28), i.e., endowed with the coefficients of 0.5 advocated by Taylor, the rule is inefficient. In order to make a rule with the same structure as the Taylor rule efficient, the interest rate response to output gaps would have to be about twice as high. This rule can be derived from the efficient inflation target.

5. Assessment

Monetary policy is an exciting field to work in these days, both for its intellectual and methodological challenges and for its close interaction with policy makers and institutions. From a public choice perspective, nevertheless, and despite the enormous progress that is being achieved, recent developments may cause mixed feelings. In a way one may

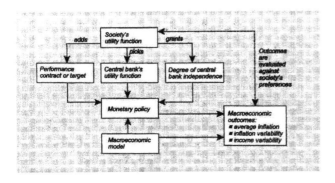

Figure 3:

wonder whether, on an undisputedly higher level of theoretical and methodological sophistication, we are not coming back full circle to fostering and refining the seemingly extinct art of optimal economic policy making as envisaged by Tinbergen and Theil. The resurgence of a more technocratic approach becomes obvious when we interpret recent developments against the political macroeconomics approach that was dominating the discussion until a few years ago and that we traced in the first half of this survey. Its main structure is sketched in Figure 3.

The political-macroeconomics approach has three building blocks: the preferences of society (or voters), the preferences of the policymaker (here the central bank), and a macroeconomic model (usually degenerated into an aggregate supply equation). Monetary policy conducted within the stochastic macroeconomic model generates economic outcomes which are then evaluated by society on the basis of its preferences. The key result is that monetary policy governed by society's preferences produces an inefficient outcome featuring an undesired, high level of price instability. Society can improve on this suboptimal outcome in a number of ways. One way to achieve price stability without distorting the stabilization of shocks is to set new incentives for the central bank by picking a progressive central bank which cares a lot about income, making it independent of the government, and adding an inflation target to its environment.

The current applied discussion of rules and targets questions all three building blocks that characterize the public choice approach:

1. Society has no more desire for income to exceed potential income. So preferences are compatible with what can be achieved in the long run, both regarding price stability and the level of income. This eliminates the inflation bias, and, hence, the dilemma of a potential trade-off between an inflation and a stabilization bias. In fact, monetary policy governed by society's preferences generates an optimal long-run equilibrium and stabilization as desired.

2. The central bank has no preferences of its own. It can "either be assigned" a loss function (as for instance in the inflation targeting approach), or a reaction function.

3. Finally, and this is one of the strong points, current research about rules and targets accepts as a fact that economists do not agree on a correct macroeconomic model.

On the issue of whether there is a basis for time inconsistency and excessive inflation, it is hard to see why society should settle for potential income as its optimal choice. If potential income is indeed the result of a series of distortions, as is argued for most industrial countries, and comes along with such burdens as involuntary unemployment, shouldn't we want higher income. Do Europeans really not want their 10 percent a-priori risk of being unemployed to fall? This is, in effect what we are claiming when we argue that the desire for income not to exceed potential income is in our *preferences*. It is something entirely different if we decide that we do not want to draw one monetary policy to raise income. This would be the result of a cost-benefit calculation on the basis of the macroeconomic options, from which we *might* conclude that a short-lived income hike was not worth the price of a lasting increase in inflation. Our preferences are an element in this calculation, but must not be confused with the calculation itself.[27]

Discarding the central bank's generic preferences and assuming it can simply be assigned any utility function or instrument rule is similarly worrisome. This might be a plausible approximation when fines for deviations from the assigned instrument or targeting rules are so large that personal preferences are dwarfed. But this does not really seem to and cannot really be the idea in a world of change in which rules are at best a frame of reference for policy decisions. None of these rules tells us how to adjust target levels in an evolving macroeconomic environment, how to implement a rule or switch from one to another, how to respond to financial bubbles or other phenomena outside our standard models.

So, measured against what political macroeconomics achieved and contributed to monetary policy making and designed, current developments may be seen as a setback. Devising optimal rules and targets is certainly useful, but so are plans of how to eat right. The problem is that even its proponents see and sell monetary policy rules as a general framework with plenty of discretion. But then, what are optimality and robustness studies that are based on the strict application of a particular rule worth, if we do not know under what circumstances, how often, and in what direction central banks will deviate from or even change the rule? Such questions obviously cannot be addressed without returning the preferences of society and the central bank back into the equation and, hence, reactivating the public-choice element in monetary policy research.

MANFRED GÄRTNER

NOTES

1. This survey puts particular emphasis on recent, policy-related developments. Older developments are selectively discussed in order to bring out the public-choice roots of many current developments and provide a theoretical background for current discussions. For more detail on these earlier developments, readers may consult two previous surveys of mine which focus on political business cycles and the first-generation discussion of time-inconsistency (Gärtner, 1994) and the second-generation discussion of tune-inconsistency including a refined macroeconomic framework with persistence and the interaction with fiscal policy (Gärtner, 2000).
2. We do not make a distinction between a Phillips curve and an aggregate supply curve. So simplify notation, we usually normalize the log of potential income, y^*, to zero and give the aggregate supply curve unity slope.
3. See, for example, Frey and Ramser (1976) and McCallum (1977).
4. This, by any means, should not be read to mean that political business cycles are dead. See, for example, the contribution by Drazen (2000b).
5. The inferiority of this result obtained under discretion is usually demonstrated by comparing it with the optimal inflation rate $\pi = 0$ that obtains when the central bank has to *commit* to an inflation rate *before* expectations are being formed.
6. See Eijffinger and Hoeberichts (1998).
7. See Alesina and Summers (1993).
8. See, however, Forder's (1998a,b) illuminating and sobering account of the validity of empirical evidence on central bank independence and inflation.
9. This is because the aggregate supply curve has been given a slope of one. In the general case, the slope coefficient would also feature in the stabilization terms.
10. For a result to be classified as first best, income also would have to be as required. Since this is considered to be beyond the reach of monetary policy, optimal monetary policy is only judged by whether it achieves second-best results.
11. The discussion on performance contracts was initiated by Persson and Tabellini (1993), Waller (1995) and Walsh (1995). Major contributors to the early academic discussion of inflation targets in the current context were Herrendorf and Lockwood (1997), Muscatelli (1995) and Svensson (1997a). See also Bernanke and Mishkin (1997), and Walsh (1998), chapter 8.
12. A linear contract focussing on the performance of aggregate income could be tailored to achieve the same second-best result, of course. The literature emphasizes inflation performance contracts, however.
13. Svensson (1997) proposes that the central bank can simply be assigned a utility function which completely overrides any generic preferences which the central bank actually has. This formally solves the problem of a negative inflation target which is never met, but is arbitrary and unconvincing, not only from a public choice perspective.
14. The most prominent example is probably the European Central Bank, the blueprint for which does not seem to take account of the trade-offs and refined results emerging in a stochastic macroeconomic context.
15. For details, see Sevensson (1997).
16. Note that a price-level target here is only inefficient from the partial perspective of shock stabilization. Things are more complex when we bring the inflation bias into the picture, because, as we move down from the no-bias point on the ordinate, the bias increases as we move along the inflation-target trade-off, but not as we move along the price-level-target trade-off.
17. For a detailed discussion of this and related New Keynesian aggregate supply curves and their implications for monetary policy see Clarida et al. (1999).
18. Incidentally, a vote-maximizing government facing a backward-looking electorate and a New Keynesian aggregate supply curve with $\beta = 0$ would create a political business cycle with some of the same features as the Nordhaus cycle. In fact, in a two period setting it would be the very same cycle that a government creates when aggregate supply is neoclassical and inflation expectations are of the simplest adaptive mould ($E_{-1}\pi = \pi_{-1}$).
19. We follow Svensson (1999), who is one of the most active contributors to this discussion.
20. There has been a host of conferences with "monetary policy rules" in the title, sponsored or hosted by central banks. A first example is the conference jointly sponsored by the Sveriges Riksbank and the Institute for International Economic Studies at Stockholm University, held June 12–13, 1998, in Stockholm.
21. Among those who have criticized the premise of central banks pursuing income targets which exceed potential income from the background of their hands-on experience with monetary policy making is Blinder (1995). Academic criticism of this idea has come, among others, from McCallum (1997) and Taylor (1983).
22. For an account of how the Friedman rule fared in practice, see Hafer and Wheelock (2001).
23. See, for example, Clarida et al. (1998), who estimate policy reaction functions for the G3 (Germany, Japan, and the US) and the E3 (UK, France, and Italy) countries, and Peersman and Smets (1998), who explore the Taylor rule as a benchmark for analysing monetary policy in the euro area.
24. It is generally believed that quite a number of central banks, including those of Australia, Canada, New Zealand, Sweden and the U.K. have adopted some form of inflation targeting during the last ten to fifteen years.
25. The Taylor rule maximizes a utility function such as (29) only then as a strict instrument rule, if sufficient lags make inflation and income predetermined when the interest rate is being set. A pragmatic macroeconomic structure, purported to parsimoniously represent results from typical VARs that interest rates affect income after one year and inflation after two years, that serves this purpose comprises a dynamic *IS* curve,

$$y = -\beta r_{-1} + \gamma y_{-1} + \varepsilon$$

and an accelerationist aggregate supply curve (without expectations),

$$\pi = \pi_{-1} + \delta y_{-1} + \eta$$

where all variables are measured as deviations from their targets. Minimization of the loss function $\text{var}(\pi) + \xi \text{var}(y)$, which directly relates to (29), yields an explicit interest rate rule:

$$r = \hat{\alpha}\pi + \hat{\beta}y$$

where the coefficients depend on the model's structural coefficients. See Ball (1999).

26. See the conference volume edited by Taylor (1999), which focusses on the issue of how robust various policy rules perform in a variety of different macroeconomic frameworks.
27. For further arguments on the pros and cons of an income target in excess of potential income, see Walsh (1998), p. 370f.

REFERENCES

Alesina, A. (1987). "Macroeconomic policy in a two-party system as a repeated game." *Quarterly Journal of Economics*, 102: 651–678.

Alesina, A. and Summers, L. (1993). "Central bank independence and macroeconomic performance." *Journal of Money, Credit, and Banking*, 25: 157–162.

Ball, L. (1999). "Efficient rules for monetary policy." *International Finance*, 2: 63–83.

Barro, R. and Gordon, D. (1983). "Rules, discretion, and reputation in a model of monetary policy." *Journal of Monetary Economics*, 12: 101–121.

Bernanke, B.S. and Mishkin, F.S. (1997). "Inflation targeting: a new framework for monetary policy." *Journal of Economic Perspectives*, 11: 97–116.

Blinder, A. (1995). "Central banking in theory and practice: lecture II: credibility, discretion, and independence." *Marshall Lecture*, University of Cambridge, May.

Calvo, G. (1983). "Staggered prices in a utility maximizing framework." *Journal of Monetary Economics*, 383–398.

Clarida, R., Gali, J., and Gertler, M. (1998). "Monetary policy rules in practice: some international evidence." *European Economic Review*, 42: 1033–1067.

Clarida, R., Gali, J., and Gertler, M. (1999). "The science of monetary policy: a new Keynesian perspective." *Journal of Economic Literature*, 37: 1661–1707.

Dittmer, R. and Gavin, W.T. (2000). "What do New-Keynesian Phillips curves imply for price-level targeting?" *Federal Reserve Bank of St. Louis Review*, March/April, 21–27.

Drazen, A. (2000a). *Political Economy in Macroeconomics*. Princeton: Princeton University Press.

Drazen, A. (2000b) "The political business cycle after 25 years." *NBER Macroeconomics Annual*, May.

Eijffinger, S. and Hoeberichts, M. (1998). "The trade off between central bank independence and conservativeness." *Oxford Economic Papers*, 50: 397–411.

Forder, J. (1998a). "The case for an independent European central bank: a reassessment of evidence and sources." *European Journal of Political Economy*, 14: 53–71.

Forder, J. (1998b). "Central bank independence — conceptual clarifications and interim assessment." *Oxford Economic Papers*, 50: 307–334.

Frey, B.S. and Ramser, H.-J. (1976). "The political business cycle: a comment." *Review of Economic Studies*, 43: 553–555.

Gärtner, M. (1994). "Democracy, elections and macroeconomic policy: two decades of progress." *European Journal of Political Economy*, 10: 85–109.

Gärtner, M. (2000). "Political macroeconomics: a survey of recent developments." *Journal of Economic Surveys*, 14: 527–561.

Hafer, R.W. and Wheelock, D.C. (2001). "The rise and fall of a policy rule: monetarism at the St. Louis Fed, 1968–1986." *Federal Reserve Bank of St. Louis Review*, January/February, 1–24.

Henderson, D.W. and Mc Kibbin, W.J. (1993). "An assessment of some basic monetary policy regimes pairs: analytical and simulation results from simple multi-region macreocnomic models," in R.C. Bryant, P. Hooper, and C.L. Mann (eds.) *Evaluating Policy Regimes: New Research in Empirical Macroeconomics*. Washington DC, The Brookings Institution, pp. 45–218.

Herrendorf, B. and Lockwood, B. (1997). "Rogoff's conservative central banker restored." *Journal of Money, Credit and Banking*, 29: 476–495.

Hibbs, D.A. (1977). "Political parties and macroeconomic policy." *American Political Science Review*, 71: 1467–1487.

Kydland, F.E. and Prescott, E.J. (1977). "Rules rather than discretion: the inconsistency of optimal plans." *Journal of Political Economy*, 85: 473–491.

MacRae, D.C. (1977). "A political model of the business cycle." *Journal of Political Economy*, 85: 239–263.

McCallum, B.T. (1977). "The political business cycle: an empirical test." *Southern Economic Journal*, 43: 504–515.

McCallum, B.T. (1988). "Robustness properties of a rule for monetary policy." *Carnegie-Rochester Conference Series on Public Policy*, 29: 173–204.

McCallum, B.T. (1997). "Critical issues concerning central bank independence." *Journal of Monetary Economics*, 39: 99–112.

Muscatelli, A. (1995). "Delegation versus optimal inflation contracts: do we really need conservative central bankers?" Discussion Paper No. 9511, University of Glasgow.

Nordhaus, W.D. (1975). "The political business cycle." *Review of Economic Studies*, 42: 169–190.

Peersman, G. and Smets, F. (1998). "Uncertainty and the Taylor rule in a simple model of the euro-area economy," mimeo.

Persson, T. and Tabellini, G. (1990). *Macroeconomic Policy, Credibility and Politics*. Chur: Harwood Academic Publishers.

Roberts, J.M. (1995). "New Keynesian economics and the Phillips curve." *Journal of Money, Credit, and Banking*, 27: 974–984.

Rogoff, K. (1985). "The optimal degree of commitment to an intermediate monetary target." *Quarterly Journal of Economics*, November, 1169–1189.

Svensson, L.E.O. (1997). "Optimal inflation targets, 'conservative' central banks, and linear inflation contracts." *American Economic Review*, 87: 98–114.

Svensson, L.E.O. (1999a). "Inflation targeting as a monetary policy rule." *Journal of Monetary Economics*, 43: 607–654.

Svensson, L.E.O. (1999b). "Price-level targeting versus inflation targeting: a free lunch?" *Journal of Money, Credit, and Banking*, 31: 276–295.

Taylor, J.B. (1983). "Comments on, rules, discretion and reputation in a model of monetary policy by R.J. Barro and D.B. Gordon." *Journal of Monetary Economics*, 12: 123–125.

Taylor, J.B. (1993). "Discretion versus policy rules in practice." *Carnegie-Rochester Conference Series on Public Policy*, 39: 195–214.

Taylor, J.B. (ed.) (1999). "Monetary policy rules." A National Bureau of Economic Research Conference Report. Chicago: University of Chicago Press.

Theil, H. (1961). *Economic Forecasts and Policy*, 2nd edn. Volume XV of Contributions to Economic Analysis. Amsterdam: North-Holland.

Tinbergen, J. (1952). *On the Theory of Economic Policy*, 2nd edn. Volume I of Contributions to Economic Analysis. Amsterdam: North-Holland.

Wagner, H. (1999). "Inflation targeting versus monetary targeting." *Kredit und Kapital*, 610–632.

Waller, Ch. J. (1995). "Performance contracts for central bankers." *Federal Reserve Bank of St. Louis Review*, September/October, 3–14.

Walsh, C.E. (1995). "Optimal contracts for central bankers." *American Economic Review*, 85: 150–167.

Walsh, C.E. (1998). *Monetary Theory and Policy*. Cambridge, MA: MIT Press.

P

THE POLITICAL ECONOMY OF TAXATION: POSITIVE AND NORMATIVE ANALYSIS WHEN COLLECTIVE CHOICE MATTERS

1. Introduction

There are many reasons for studying taxation. As the ancient Roman writer Cicero pointed out so succinctly, when he called it the sinews of the state, taxation is central to the existence and functioning of a nation, as well as to the functioning of its lower levels of government. Taxing citizens is a vital method of financing the most essential public sector activities, such as the courts, the legal system, national defense and police protection. In addition, it provides the means for producing social programs, such as public health services, education and welfare. Finally, taxation is one of the most important ways in which a community's distributional goals may be attained.

The study of collective choice is an essential part of any comprehensive analysis of taxation. The activities of communities differ in nature from activities carried out by the private sector. Provision of most publicly provided goods or services cannot be accomplished and organized through markets. Instead, collective choice procedures are needed to allocate required resources and to decide the level and extent of public provision. In democratic countries, governmental expenditures, and the ways of raising the necessary revenues, are usually determined by some type of majority rule, although such rule may be limited or attenuated by constitutional provisions and constrained by the operation of a competitive system of political parties. Taxation thus represents an essential tool for decision makers who want to command scarce resources for use in the public sector as part of the democratic process.

In this paper we review both positive and normative aspects of taxation. We examine how to study why taxes and revenue structures have taken their present form and why they are used in a particular way as part of the democratic process. In addition, we also consider the classic normative questions, namely what makes a good tax system and how to assess the efficiency of taxation. In dealing with both aspects of the tax literature, we attempt to set out a plan for a more complete and comprehensive analysis of taxation in the face of collective choice than is attempted in most of the available literature on fiscal issues.

Since our emphasis is on the positive and normative study of tax structure and tax systems, we pay only limited attention to the political economy of redistribution. Some branches of the fiscal literature make the link between progressive taxation and redistribution their main focus, while trying to analyze how income tax rates are determined as part of the political struggle over a society's income shares. While we shall consider studies of this nature, we conceive fiscal analysis as an enterprise of broader scope than is implied by the approach adopted in this work. In our view, questions of efficiency as well as of redistribution are involved in studying political equilibria, and fiscal policy encompasses the use of many different kinds of taxation as well as of other policy instruments such as regulation that affect the drawing of resources into the public sector.

Although most dictatorial regimes also make use of taxation, we deal primarily with fiscal choices in democratic states in this essay. The reader with a special interest in the analysis of authoritarian regimes may want to consult the recent work by Wintrobe (1996), where a theory of such states is developed. Comparative international analysis relevant to this topic can be found in Musgrave (1969) and Kenny and Winer (2001), where tax systems in a large sample of countries are examined in an econometric framework.

In view of space constraints, references to the literature will be illustrative rather than exhaustive. The essay emphasizes theoretical ideas and empirical issues relevant to the study of tax systems and tax structure. Further bibliographic material can be found in Hettich and Winer (1999); in Boadway and Keen (2000) concerning the political economy of redistribution; in Gould and Baker (2002) and Kirchgaessner (2002) with respect to taxation and political institutions; and in Webber and Wildavsky (1986) concerning fiscal history.[1]

2. Basic Issues

2.1. Two Major Approaches

There are two broad approaches to the study of taxation, both with an extensive and well-developed literature. The first one is associated with the work of Wicksell (1896) and Lindahl (1919), two of its most important early proponents, as well as with work of Buchanan (e.g., 1968, 1976). Here, taxation is seen as part of an exchange — albeit an imperfect one — between citizens and their government. Tax payments are made to obtain public goods and services, and to some extent, to participate in collectively determined redistribution. The emphasis is on taxation as a price for public output consumed by voters, and on institutions or methods designed to link the fiscal and the expenditure sides of the budget.

A second approach sees taxation as a set of policies that are linked only indirectly to the expenditure side via the government budget restraint. Taxation is analyzed as the coercive taking of resources to finance largely unspecified government activities. The emphasis is on ways to minimize the efficiency costs of taxation through the policy choices of a social planner. Such a planner may also take account of distributional aims in achieving his or her objectives, by including distributional weights in the design of fiscal policy. Such weights will be derived from an exogenously given welfare function, rather than being the outcome of a political process. The second approach has its origins in the work of Edgeworth (1925), Ramsay (1927), and Pigou (1952) and has been developed with great analytical sophistication by Mirrlees (1971) and others in the recent literature on optimal taxation.[2]

Although the two approaches to taxation are quite distinct in emphasis and in the results that they reach, both must contend with the same central problem, namely the separation of taxing and spending. Governments provide goods and services that are different in nature from those provided through private markets. So-called public goods, such as defense, are consumed equally by all members of the collectivity, and it is not possible to ration such goods according to price, as is done in markets for private goods. The same is true for goods that are mixed in nature, having both public and private characteristics. The difficulty of excluding those who do not pay voluntarily from enjoying the benefits of public output gives rise to the problems of preference revelation and free-riding. In response, most collectivities use coercive taxation to finance public output, creating tax systems where there is only a diffuse and distant link between additional consumption of publicly provided goods and increases in tax liability.

The separation of taxing and spending gives rise to welfare losses over and above the losses due to the tax payment itself, a primary focus of the tax literature.[3] Individual taxpayers will respond to tax rates by adjusting their activities so as to reduce their tax liability, with such adjustments being quite unrelated to the consumption of publicly provided goods. If an income tax is levied, for example, taxpayers may reduce work effort and consume more leisure, in order to maximize utility in the face of such taxation. This results in a reduction of economic welfare in comparison to a situation where payment for the same public output elicits no such trade-off or evasive adjustment. The size of this loss — the excess burden or deadweight cost of taxation — is used in the literature as a measure of the inefficiency created by a particular tax. The same type of analysis can also be used to compare the efficiency (or inefficiency) of different available tax instruments.

Separation of taxing and spending also has implications for redistribution. Since markets cannot be used to allocate public goods and their costs among users, and to determine what level of such goods should be produced, other mechanisms must be employed to reach such decisions.[4] All available collective decision processes create their own incentives for redistribution between those in the majority and those in the minority with regard to a particular fiscal issue. In addition, the separation of the two sides of the budget makes it more difficult to understand the distributional implications of various ways of providing and financing of public programs. This opaqueness may be exploited by those who are in a position to use public resources for their own purposes.[5]

Although both basic approaches to taxation must confront the separation of taxing and spending, they deal with its implications in quite different ways. The first approach focuses on collective decision processes and fiscal structures designed to create a closer link between taxing and spending, or on institutional and fiscal constraints that would have the effect of limiting coercion. Wicksell was the first to suggest ways to reduce coercion, and thus separation, by proposing unanimity, or qualified unanimity, as a budgetary decision criterion. Increases in budgets, as well as the ways of financing them, could only be adopted if they passed according to this criterion. Lindahl further formalized the analysis by providing a theoretical process where tax shares and the output of public goods were jointly decided in bargaining among the affected decision makers.[6]

The second basic approach adopts a rather different perspective. Decision processes are taken as exogenous, and their effects are not examined as part of the analysis. This is exemplified by the assumption of a social planner who makes decisions on behalf of the collectivity according to an exogenously given welfare function. In this literature, the emphasis is shifted to the identification and measurement of welfare losses, and to the design of tax systems that maximize social welfare, given the assumed analytical framework.

2.2. A Comprehensive Approach with Collective Choice

In describing the two approaches, we have emphasized what may be called normative questions. Tax analysis has an additional dimension, however. Although it is interesting to ask how efficiency in taxation should be defined, and how it can be measured, it is of equal importance to examine the nature of existing fiscal systems. In this context, we ask why tax systems have the characteristics that we observe and what may explain the variations in revenue systems among different jurisdictions. This type of examination is usually called positive analysis.

The study of actual revenue systems reveals that there is a similar underlying structure despite of the many variations that are observed (Hettich and Winer, 1999). Taxes are imposed on several major bases, such as personal income, corporate profits or property. Each tax has a rate structure, which may be simple or more complex. In addition, there are special provisions that affect the definition of the base and that may specify separate rates for particular components of the base, such as capital gains. In practice, tax policy is a manipulation of some aspect, or a combination of characteristics, of this *tax skeleton*. If we follow the methodological approach that underlies all economic theory, we can interpret observed tax systems as equilibrium outcomes of economic and political processes and forces.

A comprehensive or complete approach to taxation will include both positive and normative analysis. It will allow us to analyze observed tax systems, as well as guide us in asking questions about possible improvements in the many existing features of such systems. To achieve this, we need models that encompass theoretical analysis of both positive and normative questions and that allow statistical testing of hypotheses derived from them (Hettich and Winer, 2002).

If we briefly return to consider the two approaches to taxation reviewed earlier, we see that only the first one provides a suitable starting point for the development of a comprehensive analysis. Observed tax systems arise from decisions made through collective choice processes. To explain them, we must start by modeling such processes and by linking actual revenue systems to the predictions of our models. The assumption of a social planner does not provide a starting point for meaningful theoretical or empirical research of this nature. Although we can derive a sophisticated normative analysis with the planner framework, we cannot fully link it to the results of positive analysis as required by a comprehensive approach.[7]

Creation of an inclusive fiscal policy analysis is not an easy task. Although the literature contains many of the necessary elements, they have not been assembled as yet into a fully integrated theoretical system. Figure 1 gives a schematic presentation of the different elements in a complete analysis and shows their interrelation. As in traditional microeconomics, we start with the behavioral assumptions of essential decision makers. In democratic countries, decision makers include voters, who have additional roles as taxpayers and consumers of public goods, and who also participate in the private economy. In most models, they are assumed to maximize their utility. We also have politicians who propose policies or platforms and whose goal is to be elected. The interactions of voters and politicians takes place in a given constitutional framework (written or unwritten), a postulate that parallels the assumption of a set of existing property rights in the study of private markets.

To be useful, any proposed model must yield stable equilibria and must be accompanied by proofs of their existence. Otherwise, it is not possible to carry out comparative static analysis of the kind common in economics. The model should yield predictions or hypotheses useful for positive analysis, whether based on partial equilibrium analysis or on a more general framework, so that they can be tested with accepted statistical techniques. A comprehensive approach can also be used for computational general equilibrium analysis that includes an explicit voting mechanism in the modeling of the public sector. This will allow investigation of how exogenous shocks or changes in policy affect the economic welfare of different voting groups, and how these changes in welfare feed back to determine the choice of tax and other policy instruments via the collective choice mechanism represented in the model.

It is desirable that the same framework can also be used for normative analysis. This requires that, under specified conditions, political equilibria satisfy certain characteristics, such as Pareto Optimality. If this demonstration can be accomplished, the framework can also be used for work described in the boxes on the right-hand side in Figure 1. One should note the similarity between the proposed scheme and the approach common in economics applied to the private sector, where positive and normative analysis are both based on the same model of competitive markets, where the First Theorem of Welfare Economics (the "invisible hand" theorem) links positive and normative analysis, and where the study of market failure is used as an aid to restore the operation of decentralized market forces. However, any examination of optimality must now refer to *political* markets, not to their private counterpart. The same is true when we turn to the study of deviations from optimality. We now deal with political market failure, rather than with the malfunction of private markets.

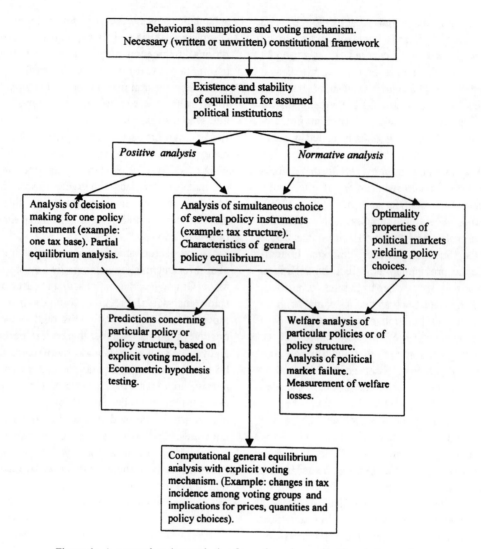

Figure 1: A comprehensive analysis of taxation when collective choice matters.

3. Political Equilibria and the Partial and General Equilibrium Study of Tax Systems

A comprehensive approach to the political economy of taxation begins with positive theory, represented schematically by the left side of Figure 1. In proceeding down the left side of the figure, we confine the discussion by and large to two frameworks that have been most widely used for positive theoretical and empirical work. These are the median voter and probabilistic voting models. Subsequently, we will turn to the use of these models in normative theorizing. While it will become apparent that neither of them is entirely satisfactory from the perspective presented here, there is much that has been learned about the political economy of taxation from exploration of these approaches.

We begin the discussion of each model with a brief description of its constitutional structure and key behavioral assumptions, and then turn to the question of the existence of equilibrium. We shall see that the manner in which this question is dealt with has a determining influence on the development of the theory.

3.1. The Median Voter Model and its Extensions

One of the first models of the public sector to explicitly incorporate a collective choice mechanism was based on the median voter theorem of Duncan Black (1958). This is a model of direct democracy where alternatives to the status quo may be proposed without cost, and in which the institutions of representative democracy do not play an explicit role. Behavioural assumptions for individuals are straightforward: citizens vote sincerely for the policy platform that maximizes their welfare, given the structure of the private economy, and there is no uncertainty about how any voter will behave at the polls.

The model focuses on the problem of coercion made possible by the use of majority rule and aggravated by the separation of spending and taxing.[8] It is successful in explaining coercive redistribution, despite the tendency for redistributive voting games to lack equilibria (see McKelvey, 1976; Schofield, 1978), because the analysis is carried out in a carefully limited framework. With some exceptions, mentioned below, application of the median voter theorem to describe a political equilibrium requires that the fiscal system be reducible to one independent parameter over which (indirect) preferences are single-peaked. Even if preferences are well-behaved in more than one dimension, endless cycling over alternative proposals rather than an equilibrium tends to occur, and the model is then of little help in understanding observed tax policy, which exhibits considerable stability over time and place.

A standard model involves a single rate of tax (usually in a linear progressive system) that is chosen by majority rule, and a uniform subsidy or one pure public good on which all revenue is expended. Voting over the average tax rate, or equivalently over the size of the subsidy provided, continues until one rate emerges — the Condorcet winner — that cannot be defeated by any other proposal in a pair-wise majority vote. This tax rate and the implied subsidy level maximize the welfare of the median voter — the voter whose preferred tax rate is at the median of those most desired by each voter (see, for example, Romer, 1975; Meltzer and Richard, 1981). If the median voter's income is below the average, the median voter demands and receives a positive tax rate and corresponding subsidy.

The extent of redistribution toward the median voter and the corresponding size of government are limited by behavioral responses to taxation. In the linear income tax case, the equilibrium tax rate, and thus the degree of average tax progressivity, depends on the elasticity of labour supply. As this elasticity increases, more substitution from work to leisure occurs at any rate of tax. This in turn causes a reduction in the aggregate size of the tax base and in the fiscal surplus (the difference between benefits received and the full cost including excess burden of the taxes paid) that can be enjoyed by the median voter. In equilibrium, the tax rate demanded by the decisive voter therefore declines.[9]

Extension of the median voter model to a non-linear income tax system is possible, such as when a second parameter that controls the degree of marginal rate progressivity is added to the average rate of tax. In this case, establishing existence of an equilibrium requires either that further restrictions be placed on the nature of voter preferences (see, Roberts, 1977; Meltzer and Richard, 1981; Gans and Smart, 1996), or it must be assumed that each fiscal parameter is decided by majority rule in a separate "committee" of a legislature or in a separate election in which the median voter is decisive (as in Meltzer and Richard, 1985).[10,11] Then, in addition to the skewness of income as indicated by mean relative to median income, the variance of income also affects the equilibrium size of government. With a higher variance, incomes at the high end of the income scale are even bigger, and this can lead to even more redistribution being demanded by the median voter whose income is below the average (Cukierman and Meltzer, 1991).

A further application of the median voter model allows for private supplementation of publicly provided private goods, such as with healthcare (Gouvia, 1997; Epple and Romano, 1996a,b). When equilibria in the model extended in this way can be established — a difficult issue in this more complex policy setting — an intriguing "ends against the middle" result can be established. It may be that middle income earners who favor a large public sector are opposed by the poor who want lower taxes because they do not value the publicly supplied good highly relative to private consumption, and by the rich who want lower taxes so they can finance even higher levels of the publically supplied private good than will ever be forthcoming from the public sector. In the equilibrium, the middle income group may win out at the expense of both the poor and the rich.[12]

Before turning to the probabilistic voting framework, one may note that the splitting of dimensions that has sometimes been used to justify extension of the median voter model to multi-dimensional fiscal systems is an alternative way of establishing a political equilibrium (Shepsle, 1979; Shepsle and Weingast, 1981). Those who adopt this approach relate particular legislative rules and procedures, or norms of behaviour, (called the "structure") to the nature and stability of policy outcomes in institutional settings where a vote cycle would otherwise occur.

The approach usually takes one beyond the median voter framework, where a single decisive voter gets what he or she wants. A norm of behavior among politicians on a specific committee of a legislature, for example, may survive because members receive a return to co-operating, inducing them not to vote according to their narrow self-interest. They will do this because they recognize that voting according to broader criteria will eliminate the uncertainty that would result from cycling over alternatives.

A major challenge in using the structure-induced framework lies in identifying the specific institutional arrangements that result in a particular feature of the observed tax skeleton. This difficulty limits the application of the approach to taxation, including applications to non-linear tax systems. An exception is the work of Inman and Fitts (1990), who use the approach to focus on universalism and reciprocity ("you scratch my back and I will scratch yours") as a norm of behavior that emerges to overcome political instability in legislatures, with each legislator agreeing to support the allocations most preferred by every other member. As long as the benefits of public spending are concentrated within particular electoral constituencies, while the costs are spread by the tax system over the country as a whole, the norm leads legislators to agree to larger budgets and greater use of special tax provisions than would occur if benefits and costs were matched more closely within each district.[13]

3.2. Probabilistic Voting

The application of the median voter model points to the role of the skewness of income in determining the extent of coercive redistribution through the fiscal system, as well as to behavioral responses to taxation and the resulting welfare losses as factors limiting the overall size of government. Because of the manner in which equilibrium is established, the model has little to say about the tax skeleton or tax structure as a whole.

The probabilistic voting model provides a basis for analyzing the tax skeleton as a whole, and it does so by using an approach to the problem of establishing equilibrium that does not require the number of tax instruments to be severely restricted. This is a model of representative democracy in which political parties are forced to compete for votes in order to win the struggle for power. Just as in the median voter framework, the specific institutions that maintain and shape electoral competition are not formally represented in the model.

In addition to differences in constitutional setting, the probabilistic voting model also adopts an alternative approach to political behavior. While economic behavior and the structure of private markets are essentially the same in both frameworks, individual voting, while still sincere, is no longer deterministic, a fact suggested by the model's name. In a probabilistic setting, political parties do not know with certainty how any voter will behave at the polls. This is the key assumption allowing for the possibility that an equilibrium may exist, even if the tax system is multidimensional (Hinich, 1977; Coughlin and Nitzan, 1981; McKelvey and Patty, 2001).

When voting is strictly deterministic, as in the median voter model, each voter will abruptly switch support from the incumbent to the opposition (or vice versa) if promised a sufficiently favorable policy outcome. The points at which voters switch their support from one party to another become the objects of a bidding war between the parties, leading almost inevitably to vote-cycling over alternative platforms. However, if voting behavior is probabilistic, a small change in a policy platform directed at any voter will lead at most to a small change in the probability of support from that voter, not to a total loss of his or her support. If, in addition to the probabilistic nature of voting, the objective functions of the parties — total expected votes or expected plurality — are also concave in policy choices for each platform of the opposition, a Nash equilibrium in the electoral game may exist despite the complexity of the fiscal system being decided upon.[14] In this setting, each party is forced by competition to maximise its total expected vote defined across all citizens, and the equilibrium in the model represents a balancing of the heterogeneous and conflicting economic interests of all citizens. Here every voter, and not just the median voter, has some direct political influence on the equilibrium fiscal system.

It should be noted that if the policies of opposing parties become very polarized, the probability that some radical voters will support the party at the other end of the spectrum may fall to zero. If this happens, the expected vote functions of both parties may not be sufficiently concave over the entire policy space, and a vote-cycle may reemerge (Usher, 1994). Thus the instability of majority rule continues to cast a shadow, even in this framework. For this reason, use of the probabilistic voting model implies the important assumption that issues that would lead to extreme polarization of the electorate are kept out of the political arena, thereby limiting the domain over which policy instruments can be defined.

Since it is reasonable to assume that expected support for any party will rise with an increase in expected welfare for any voter, every party has an incentive to adjust the tax mix so as to make the aggregate excess burden of taxation as small as possible, although increases in the welfare cost of taxation will be tolerated if this allows for greater satisfaction of particular, politically sensitive or influential groups. For this reason, the probabilistic voting model is well suited to the study of how the full costs of taxation, including excess burden, are taken into account in determining the nature of the tax skeleton.

Each tax instrument, such as a particular tax base or special provision, will have a different loss of expected votes or political cost associated with it, reflecting factors such as the costs of organizing political opposition and the welfare losses resulting from the economic adjustments to the use of the instrument. Governments that are forced by competition to maximize expected support will thus aim for a tax skeleton that equalizes the marginal political costs of raising another dollar of revenues across tax sources. This logic will be familiar to those who adopt the optimal tax approach to fiscal design, although such logic must be substantially adapted in the present context. First we must allow for the difference between social welfare and expected political support, and second, we must acknowledge that the task is to characterize a political equilibrium that may or may not be efficient. (We consider the efficiency of political equilibria in the models we are discussing in section 6 below.)

In the probabilistic voting framework it is possible to understand how tax policy instruments may arise endogenously, if we acknowledge that systems which are costly to administer reduce the level of services and subsidies and hence the level of political support that can be obtained with a given total revenue (Hettich and Winer, 1988, 1999; Warskett et al., 1998). Tax bases, rate structures and special provisions can be explained in this manner. To economize on the administrative costs of actually operating a tax system, governments must group related activities into composite tax bases to lower transaction costs for themselves — the costs of becoming informed about taxpayers, of designing tax structures, and of enforcing tax laws. In a similar manner, they combine taxpayers into rate bands, rather than taxing each individual at a unique rate. However, such grouping creates a loss in expected support, since differentiated treatment of heterogeneous taxpayers would maximize expected political support in a frictionless world. Governments must balance this loss against the gain in support from spending fewer resources for administrative activities and more resources for the provision of public goods.

By extension, similar arguments can also be used to explain the existence of special provisions. If there is a group which offers effective opposition to the inclusion of a specific economic activity in a particular base, it may be cheaper to placate it with a special provision, rather than with the creation of a separate base for the disputed item. Thus, capital gains may become part of a fairly broadly defined income tax, while being taxed at a rate that differs from the rate applied to other types of income. It should be noted that in this framework, special provisions are a rational response by governments who expect to compete with opposition parties in future elections. They cannot be interpreted as deviations from some ideal tax base designed to satisfy particular normative criteria, which in actuality may have limited support among voters. Nor are they introduced primarily as a hidden substitute for direct subsidies, as is so often argued in the tax expenditure literature.[15] Special tax provisions would exist even in a world where no attempt is made to give direct subsidies to encourage particular activities.

Moreover, since revenue structures are equilibrium outcomes, they should be expected to adjust whenever a significant exogenous shock occurs, such as when some exogenous factor alters the size of a potential tax base and thus changes the economic and political consequences of relying on that tax source.[16] We should therefore expect tax systems to change frequently, although this will not be a sign of political instability or of "tax reform."

The focus on the equilibrium mix of policies also has other important implications for positive tax analysis. For example, it casts doubt on the separate treatment of particular sources of revenue, such as tariffs, debt or seignorage, which have often been studied without reference to the rest of the fiscal system. Tariffs are an instrument of protection, but they were also a major source of revenue of the advanced democracies in the 19th century and are still important revenue producers in many less developed countries today. In the probabilistic voting framework, the setting of tariffs will involve tradeoffs between protection and revenue, as well as tradeoffs between tariffs and other sources of revenue (Winer and Hettich, 1991). Similar arguments will also apply to the study of debt or to seignorage, or for that matter, to the study of other single revenue sources.

At a more abstract level, the issue raised here concerns the difference between partial and general equilibrium analysis of tax instruments, a distinction made on the left side of Figure 1. Analysis of a part of the whole tax system is often a productive way to proceed, just as limiting the analysis to one private market allows for greater focus and detail. But at the same time, such an analysis must be carried out while remaining cognizant of the broader equilibrium setting.

A further illustration of general equilibrium analysis applied to the tax skeleton that is made possible by probabilistic voting concerns the so-called "flat" tax, which we will interpret for argument's sake as a uniform proportional tax on a single base with only limited exemptions. If special provisions are indeed a means of making the fiscal system politically more efficient, helping to adapt taxation to the characteristics of voters in an administratively effective manner, as was suggested above, it will be unlikely that a policy can succeed that removes this type of policy instrument completely. We may therefore expect democratic tax systems to be complex. While "reforms" can occur that simplify tax laws to some extent, if this becomes a politically popular aim, the result will probably be a fiscal system that retains considerable complexity.

Finally, one should note the implications of taxation for the use of other policy instruments. Any constraint on the use of a particular fiscal instrument, such as imposition of a "flat" tax on income, may lead to the introduction of more special provisions in other tax bases, or to the increased use of policy instruments such as regulation, which can have similar economic effects on voters. Forced simplicity in taxation may thus lead to additional, and perhaps more obscured, complexity in other places.

In summary, the probabilistic framework predicts stable equilibrium outcomes for choices in multiple dimensions. It emphasizes the incentives that governments have to deal with the full costs of taxation, while taking the relative political influence of various groups of taxpayers into account and making it possible to show how the tax skeleton arises endogenously. On the other hand, the model has not been used extensively to study coercive redistribution, and it lacks specific institutional features and detailed references to actual governing arrangements, a limitation that also affects the median voter model.

4. Statistical Research

A complete program of work on the political economy of taxation will include statistical modeling and testing of hypotheses in addition to theoretical work. It may also involve the construction and use of computable general equilibrium models. In this and the next section, we complete the coverage of the elements of a comprehensive approach depicted on the left side of Figure 1 by considering how the two approaches have been used to inform empirical research.

Statistical analysis using the median voter and probabilistic voting models can be compared by imposing restrictions on the following system of semi-reduced form equations:

$$s_k = s_k(s_1, s_2, \ldots, s_{k-1}, \ldots, s_{k+1}, \ldots, s_K, G, x);$$
$$s_k \geq 0; \quad k = 1, 2, \ldots, K. \tag{1a}$$

$$G = G(s_1, s_2, \ldots, s_K, x); \quad G > 0. \tag{1b}$$

Here time subscripts and error terms are omitted, revenue structure $s = \{s_1, s_2, \ldots, s_K\}$ includes all tax bases, rate structures and special provisions that define the tax skeleton, G equals the level of public expenditure, and x is a vector of conditioning variables including, in principle, all exogenous or predetermined factors relevant to decisions by economic and political agents.

These equations are consistent with a wide variety of models of political equilibrium. They acknowledge that in an equilibrium, the use of any policy instrument depends in general on the setting of all other instruments. For example, tax structure depends on how much revenue in total is to be raised, and the reliance on any particular type of tax depends on how much revenue is raised in other ways.

While the equations are quite general, they still omit many aspects of fiscal structure. In particular, the formation of the tax instruments themselves is suppressed as is the structure of public expenditures. Relationships between fiscal instruments and other policies such as regulations and laws are ignored. Moreover, fiscal institutions are not explicitly represented, although their effects will be embedded in the coefficients of the estimating equations and might be included to some extent in the vector of exogenous factors.

To our knowledge, no one has yet estimated such a system to explain a complete tax structure consisting of bases, rates and special provisions. The problems of doing empirical research with such general systems resemble the difficulties associated with empirical work in any general equilibrium context. In fact, the problems are more acute here than is the case in the study of the private economy since the equilibrium framework must take account of the interaction between the private economy and the political system. In such a setting, it is often useful to proceed by simplifying further, while justifying why some particular part of the larger fiscal system is deserving of special attention.

Researchers who base their work on the median voter model have focused on the implications of coercive redistribution for the overall level of taxation. In this case, the number of fiscal instruments is usually reduced to two (i.e., usually $K = 1$), such as a single proportional tax rate in addition to the overall level of public expenditure. Specific estimating equations are derived by maximization of the median voter's utility subject to the relevant constraints. The vector x of exogenous variables reflects the median voter's characteristics, such as his or her income, and the factors that determine behavioral responses to taxation.

When K is equal to one, the government budget restraint will determine one of the two policy variables, and estimation of only one equation has to be carried out (see, for example, Meltzer and Richard, 1983). It should be noted that modeling the average tax rate on a particular base, such as income, rather than modeling an overall average rate, is not a proper empirical application of the median voter model. This must be so unless one believes that coercive redistribution is only exercised via income taxation.

Implementation of the estimating equation requires that the researcher first figure out who the median voter is, and this usually involves additional assumptions so that the median voter can be identified as the person with median income. The ratio of mean to median income is a critical explanatory variable resulting from application of the model, with skewed distributions hypothesized to lead to larger public sectors, and with more elastic behavioral responses expected to offset this tendency.

Another approach to applying the median voter model starts with an assumption that a complex tax structure is fixed independently of public spending. The median voter model is then solved for the level of public expenditure most desired by the median voter as a function of exogenously given tax shares and other factors (Borcherding and Deacon 1972; Bergstrom and Goodman, 1973).

There is an extensive body of empirical work, which we cannot review here, in which the median voter model is used to explain the overall size of government for different political jurisdictions. It is fair to say that over the last three decades, this approach has dominated empirical public choice.

More recently, the probabilistic voting model has been applied to model tax systems where K in (1a) and (1b) is equal to two or more. In these applications, the instrument set s is usually interpreted as the shares of total revenue coming from several sources such as profits, personal income, consumption, trade, property, seignorage and public debt. Instead of including characteristics of the median voter, the vector x now consists of exogenous factors that determine the marginal political costs associated with relying on each revenue source. These include the factors determining the full economic costs of each tax source, such as the size of potential tax bases, and the factors determining how the full costs of raising revenue in each way are translated into political opposition.[17]

Empirical work of this nature has been conducted by Pommerehne and Schneider (1983) who model the revenue structure of Australian national governments, by Winer and Hettich (1991) for the government of Canada in the 19th century and by Kenny and Winer (2001) for a sample of 100 countries. Some research in this vein considers just one or two parts of the larger equilibrium system. Moomau and Morton (1992), for example, limit themselves to the property tax, Winer and Hettich (2002) look at the relationship between state income taxation and special provisions for the property tax, while Kenny and Toma (1997) examine the choice between income taxation and the inflation tax in the U.S. Chernick and Reschovsky (1996) use a partial approach to study determinants of tax progressivity among U.S. states.

4.1. Some Evidence Concerning the Role of Institutions

The role of political institutions is only implicit in the empirical work described above, as it is in the theoretical models that underlie these applications. By estimating reduced form equations across electoral systems, or by doing analogous case studies, interesting stylized facts about the role of institutions can be generated.

There is a growing body of work of this kind, much of it dealing with the consequences of alternative electoral systems for the overall level and composition of spending (see, Kirchgaessner, 2002 and Gould and Baker, 2002 for reviews; Persson and Tabellini, 2001 and Milesi-Ferretti et al., 2002 for recent contributions). As yet, few studies relate electoral systems or other aspects of governance to specific features of the tax system except at an aggregate level. However, existing research points to future directions for work applied more directly to taxation.

Of particular interest is a branch of the literature that investigates the relationship between electoral systems or structural characteristics of government and overall fiscal discipline. Persson and Tabellini (2001), for example, find that aggregate spending and deficit financing is less responsive to the economic shocks in presidential regimes and under majoritarian elections (where a first-past-the-post rule is coupled with single member constituencies) than in parliamentary regimes using proportional representation.

Using data on OECD countries, Ashworth and Heyndels (2002) investigate how volatility in tax systems is affected by the degree to which government is fragmented, while Volkerink and de Haan (2000) ask similar questions with regard to reliance on deficit financing. Fragmentation is measured by the number of decision makers involved in fiscal decisions or by the number of parties in a governing coalition. Their studies show that fragmented governments tend to have tax systems that exhibit more persistence in the face of exogenous shocks, and larger deficits.

The effects of legislative rules and laws for insuring that at an aggregate level at least, spending is kept in line with revenues have also been investigated. Many of these studies, reviewed in Kirchgaessner (2002) and Poterba (1997), use data from U.S. states. It appears that balanced-budget rules and other types of limitations have to some extent been successful in linking spending to available revenues and in inducing somewhat more rapid fiscal adjustments.

There is also some statistical evidence concerning the role of specific policy processes in linking spending and taxing. In an analysis of European Union countries, von Hagen (1992) finds that overall fiscal discipline is stronger where there is a top-down budgetary process run by a strong Prime Minister, and where parliament has limited powers of amendment.[18]

Finally, there is some exploratory work on institutions that bears on the nature of the tax skeleton. Hettich and Winer (1999, chapter 11) use descriptive statistics to show that the Canadian tax system is less complicated and involves more frequent major reforms than that of the U.S., a result they explain with the greater transactions costs facing politicians in the congressional system, characterized by checks and balances, than in the Canadian parliamentary setting. And Steinmo (1993) uses the case study method in an interesting attempt to relate stylized differences in tax structures among Sweden, the U.K. and the U.S. to differences in their political systems.

This is a rapidly evolving literature. It would be of much interest if research of this nature could be grounded in the application of formal structural models in which the tax skeleton is represented. To accomplish this is particularly difficult for electoral systems based on proportional representation because of the well recognized problem of modeling the post-election bargaining among prospective coalition members that affects final equilibrium policy outcomes.[19]

5. Computable Equilibrium Modeling and the Representation Theorem

Another way to further our understanding of taxation is by constructing an applied or computable equilibrium model that can be used for simulation. Rather than being estimated econometrically, these models are calibrated either to synthetic or real data sets for specific jurisdictions at a point in time.

In applying the median voter framework, one must specify how the private economy depends on the tax instrument or size of government that is determined in political equilibrium. (The structure must be such as to insure that voters' preferences are single peaked over the relevant policy instrument.) Public policy is chosen so that, given the relationship between the median voter's well-being and the private economy, the median voter's welfare is maximized. When a computable model of a federal system is constructed and the median voter model is applied at each level, it is necessary to assume that voters make their decisions about whom to support in each election without considering the consequences for policy at other levels of government.

Nechyba (1997, 1999) explores various issues, including the setting of property tax rates and the effects of school vouchers, in a large scale median voter model of the relationship between state and local governments. The model allows for tax competition between cities and inter-jurisdictional migration and is calibrated to data for New Jersey. Voting decisions at each level of government are assumed to be independent in the minds of the voters, and at each level the median voter is decisive. Holtz-Eakin (1992) has constructed a synthetic political economy in order to compare the results of various experiments based on the median voter theorem to results when a probabilistic voting approach is used with the same data.

In a computable version of a probabilistic voting model, what is optimized by the choice of (several) policy instruments is a political support function defined across all voters, rather than the median voter's utility. This technique is illustrated at some length below. Work of this sort includes Rutherford and Winer (1999, 2002) and Hotte and Winer (2001), who use the model to work out the effective political influence that must be imputed to each of several groups of voters so that the model replicates a benchmark fiscal system (the U.S. rate of tax on labor, capital and the size of government in 1973 and 1983). These weights are then used to construct counterfactuals that allow changes in the benchmark system over time to be decomposed into a part due to changing economic structure and a part due to changes in relative political influence. Since it will be useful in the next section where normative issues are considered, we illustrate the derivation of the optimization problem referred to above that can be used to compute an equilibrium in a probabilistic model. This derivation is based on the work of Coughlin and Nitzan (1981).

To simplify, we limit the discussion to a situation with two political parties, two tax bases, two tax rates and one public good. To acknowledge tax administration and information costs implicitly, we assume that the number of tax rates is less than the number of voters and that taxation is proportional rather than lump sum. Indirect utility for voter h is $v_h(t_1,t_2,G)$ and, after substitution of the general equilibrium structure of the private economy, the government budget restraint can be written as $G = R_1(t_1,t_2,G) + R_2(t_1,t_2,G)$.

Each party chooses tax rates and the size of public expenditure to maximize its total expected vote. The probability that voter h supports the incumbent as perceived by the party, f_{hi}, depends on the difference in the voter's evaluation of his or her welfare under the incumbent's policies (i) and those of the opposition (o): $f_{hi} = f_h(v_{hi} - v_{ho})$. The expected vote for the incumbent government then is $EV_i = \Sigma_h f_h(v_{hi} - v_{ho})$, and the vote for the opposition is defined analogously. In addition, we assume that knowledge of the probability density functions describing voting behavior and of the structure of the private economy is common to the competing parties.

Given the platform of the opposition, first order conditions for the choice of tax rates that maximize EV_i subject to the budget restraint are of the form

$$\frac{\sum \partial f_h/\partial v_h \cdot \partial v_h/\partial t_1}{\partial(R_1+R_2)/\partial t_1} = \frac{\sum \partial f_h/\partial v_h \cdot \partial v_h/\partial t_2}{\partial(R_1+R_2)/\partial t_2}. \quad (2)$$

From (2) it can be seen that the platform chosen by the incumbent equalizes the marginal effect of tax policies on expected votes per dollar of revenue across tax sources. The condition illustrates the equalization of "marginal political costs" across tax instruments referred to earlier. A Nash equilibrium, if it exists, is a simultaneous solution to such first order conditions for both incumbent and opposition parties.[20]

After substitution of equilibrium values of the partial derivatives in (1), the resulting condition can also be used to characterize the tax system that emerges in a Nash equilibrium. Let $\theta_h = \partial f_h/\partial v_h$ be the particular values at a Nash equilibrium of the sensitivities of voting to a change in welfare, and let the other partial derivatives also be evaluated at the equilibrium. Then the first order conditions characterizing optimal equilibrium strategies take the form:

$$\frac{\sum \theta_h \cdot \partial v_h/\partial t_1}{\partial(R_1+R_2)/\partial t_1} = \frac{\sum \theta_h \cdot \partial v_h/\partial t_2}{\partial(R_1+R_2)/\partial t_2}. \quad (3)$$

Now it can be seen that this equilibrium condition may be replicated by solving a particular optimization problem. It is straightforward to show that maximization of the following "political support function" (S) by choice of the same policy instruments, subject to the same government budget constraint, leads to the identical condition:[21]

$$S = \Sigma_h \theta_h v_h. \quad (4)$$

The use of this optimization problem to compute a political equilibrium constitutes what we shall call the Representation Theorem.[22] Note that since S is maximized in a political equilibrium, it makes sense to think of the weights θ_h in the support function as measures of the effective influence exerted by different voters on equilibrium policy outcomes.

As well as permitting the probabilistic voting model to be operationalized, the Representation Theorem has important implications for the normative evaluation of tax systems.

6. Normative Analysis

In our initial discussion of the elements depicted in Figure 1, we pointed out that a fully general approach would have a normative as well as a positive dimension. Although there is an extensive literature using collective choice models as a basis for positive theoretical and empirical research, there is only a limited body of work on how to explicitly link them to normative questions. Filling in the boxes on the right side of Figure 1 remains a challenging task. In this section we consider some of the issues involved in using the median voter and probabilistic voting models to do so. We also briefly consider some other contributions to the normative literature in the light of the comprehensive approach to political economy.

In normative analysis, we evaluate imperfect situations by comparing them to a state that has defined optimal properties. Three steps are needed in this kind of work. To start with, one must define a counterfactual or standard of reference representing an optimal allocation of resources. The underlying theoretical analysis must prove that this allocation exists and that it is a stable equilibrium outcome of a relevant or acceptable collective choice process. (It should be recalled that public goods and the corresponding taxes cannot be allocated or distributed without recourse to a collective choice process.)

Once this has been accomplished, a second step becomes possible. Imperfect situations can be contrasted with the socially optimal, democratically arrived at allocation. Finally, the loss in welfare resulting from the imperfect operation of the decision process is measured in monetary terms.

The three steps are well-known from neoclassical welfare economics relating to competitive markets, where the First Theorem serves to define the ideal counterfactual or standard of reference, and where the second step is represented by the analysis of market failure. In a final step, the implications of imperfect markets are then measured by quantifying the resulting welfare losses.

Although the same sequence of steps must be followed in a normative analysis of taxation that includes collective choice as a significant component, there are important differences of interpretation. Since the relevant equilibria must now refer to a political process, the counterfactual, as well as the analysis of imperfections, must refer to the working of political mechanisms rather than to the operation of private markets. Thus, we are interested in the identification and measurement of the consequences of *political* market failure. This involves identifying the sources of such failures, and then relating such failures to specific identifiable parts of tax structure that are undesirable as a result. Such a political market failure analysis of tax policy remains to be accomplished.[23]

The importance of establishing a normative analysis that includes collective choice in such a systematic manner can be better understood if we use it to evaluate a well-known result derived from the social planner model where politics play no role. The latter approach has been widely used to argue for tax policies that minimize excess burdens measured in relation to lump sum taxation. To achieve such minimization, it is necessary to adjust the tax system so as to equalize the marginal excess burden created by raising an additional dollar of revenue across all different tax sources.

The limitations of this sort of policy recommendation can be seen clearly if we ask the same questions in a framework based on a collective choice model such as probabilistic voting. In a probabilistic voting model, political competition tends to force parties to adopt Pareto efficient policies. Otherwise the possibility remains that the opposition can propose a Pareto improving policy platform and thereby increase its expected electoral support. This tendency is readily apparent from the Representation Theorem stated in the previous section, which shows that under certain conditions, the equilibrium can be replicated by maximizing a particular weighted sum of utilities subject to the general equilibrium structure of the economy.[24]

This does not imply, however, that marginal excess burdens per dollar, or marginal efficiency costs, will be equalized across tax sources, thereby minimizing total excess burden. The reason is that voters differ in their effective political influence even when the franchise is universal. Hence in directing resources towards voters who the governing party thinks are especially influential, the incumbent party will accept an increase in the marginal efficiency cost of a particular tax source above that of other taxes if it thinks this will improve the chances for reelection. We can clarify this point by continuing with the development of the model introduced in section 5. Using condition (3) in the special case where the equilibrium political influence weights (the θ_h's) for all voters are equal, we can substitute the change in aggregate welfare defined by $W_k = \Sigma_h \partial v_h / \partial t_k$ into (3), subtract 1 from each side, and simplify to get

$$\frac{W_1 - \partial(R_1 + R_2)/\partial t_1}{\partial(R_1 + R_2)/\partial t_1} = \frac{W_2 - \partial(R_1 + R_2)/\partial t_2}{\partial(R_1 + R_2)/\partial t_2}. \quad (5)$$

Here the numerator on each side of the equation is the marginal excess burden of the corresponding tax change — the change in welfare over and above the change in revenue — while the quotient on each side of (5) represents the marginal efficiency cost of each tax source.

Thus if the θ's are all equal, the tax system equalizes the marginal costs per dollar across tax sources and hence minimizes the total excess burden of taxation. On the other hand, if political influence is distributed unequally as in (3) and (4), unweighted marginal welfare losses for different tax sources may vary significantly as parties trade off the welfare of and support from different voters, even though Pareto efficiency is being achieved.

In other words, by weighting welfare changes for different people equally, traditional normative analysis imputes all observed inequality of marginal efficiency costs to the inefficiency of tax policy. This is an extreme view, given the existence of vigorous political competition for the support of rational economic agents.[25] Even if we allow for the existence of political market failures, which we have not done here, at least some part of the inequality of marginal efficiency costs in equilibrium will still be due to the pursuit of support from voters who differ in their effective political influence. (What part of the inequality is actually due to political market failure is unknown, and little studied.) Moreover, proceeding as if the marginal efficiency costs should be equalized when political influence actually differs across groups of voters may lead to reforms that only serve to move society along or possibly even inside of the Pareto efficiency frontier.[26]

Cost-benefit analysts have long recognized the problem of determining the proper direction of reform when the weights attached to various groups of people are not equal.[27] They have tried to infer such distributional weights (as they are called in this literature) from existing data and to use them in aggregating losses and gains for different groups.[28] Whether weights derived from existing political equilibria, which may be imperfect, are appropriate for normative analysis is unclear.

There is as yet no consensus on what institutional characteristics of the voting process would be required to yield an ideal outcome, or on what weights would be embedded in the equilibria arising in such a system. As a result, definition of a counterfactual ideal and measurement of losses as a consequence of political market imperfections remain unsolved analytical problems in the approach based on probabilistic voting, and in related or similar approaches.

What is the nature of normative analysis in work based on the median voter framework? While the probabilistic voting model emphasizes the problems of reconciling conflicting and heterogeneous interests, the median voter model draws our attention primarily to the consequences of coercion under majority rule.

There is an analogue to the role of the Representation Theorem in normative work based on the median voter model. It involves the demonstration that total revenue, or the aggregate tax rate, are efficient in equilibrium under certain special circumstances. The question of what the required conditions are has been extensively explored, with rather discouraging results. Efficiency of the public sector in this world will only occur in the special and rather unlikely case where preferences are symmetrically distributed around those of the median voter, so that the consequences of coercion for the welfare of voters on either side of the median just balance out.

Individual preferences are usually taken as given and inviolable. So it would be understandable if a policy analyst in search of efficiency, who based his analysis on the median voter model, were led to propose changes in the basic voting rule, rather than in particular policies, as a way of improving the allocation of resources.

6.1. Limiting Majority Rule

Proposals for reform of the basic voting rule have a long history in the literature on taxation. There have also been several proposals to constrain the use of policy instruments as a way of indirectly limiting the exercise of coercion. Such proposals are not usually associated with either of the two formal models we have been analyzing. Nonetheless, to complete the discussion of normative tax analysis, it is of interest to briefly consider some of this work. The discussion will also point to the difficulties of normative theorizing without the use of a comprehensive framework.

As we noted earlier, Wicksell (1896) advocated the adoption of a qualified or approximate unanimity rule to limit coercive redistribution through the public sector. Of course he did not use the median voter model as a basis for his proposal. But he clearly understood the essential link between collective choice and the allocation of resources, and realized the dangers that are inherent in majority rule. He proposed an institutional solution in his perceptive analysis of what would be required to generate a more efficient political equilibrium in a democratic society.

Wicksell's analysis is an example of a "process-oriented" approach to reform. His analysis does not include a blueprint for tax structure, and is confined to reform of the policy process. A concern with the coercive power of government also lies behind more recent process-oriented proposals. These involve detailed tax blueprints, the purpose of which is to make it difficult for democratic governments to engage in coercive actions while still permitting them to finance needed public services.

Simons (1938) was a successful advocate of an process-oriented approach to restricting the power of government to coerce private citizens. He was not primarily concerned with coercive redistribution between rich and poor, and was content to leave the determination of vertical equity to the political process. He argued instead for a tax levied on comprehensively defined income as a way of limiting the ability of governments to interfere in private markets (or, as he put it, to "dip deeply into great incomes with a sieve"). Buchanan and Congleton (1998) have recently proposed a flat tax without exemptions, based on concerns similar to those expressed by Wicksell and Simons.

Normative tax theory after 1945 was dominated by discussion of the comprehensive income tax system advocated by Simons, until Optimal Taxation replaced his approach in the early 1970s. Simons' work also stimulated several important tax commissions during the period. This occurred even though the political foundations of Simons' argument for the comprehensive income tax were not generally appreciated.[29]

While not clearly connected to a formal model of political equilibrium, the arguments of Simons and Buchanan and Congleton carry with them a statement of what the ideal tax system should look like. As a result, they allow identification of the parts of existing tax systems that are undesirable, and measurement of departures from the ideal then becomes possible. These are key steps in a comprehensive normative analysis of taxation.

However, there is a serious flaw in the design of the tax blueprints advocated by those concerned with the coercive power of government. These proposals are at odds with the understanding of political equilibrium developed using the probabilistic voting approach. In this framework, political competition creates pressures for any government to implement a tax system that is, to some extent, adapted to deal with excess burdens. As we have already seen, competition in such a political system pushes the government to implement a complicated tax skeleton which is unlikely to resemble the fiscal structures advocated by Simons or by Buchanan and Congleton.

7. Conclusion

There has been much work in the past two decades that approaches public sector problems from a political economy perspective. This is true for issues relating to taxation as well as for topics touching on other aspects of the public economy. Most of this research has not been part of a broad, comprehensive framework of the sort outlined in Figure 1 however. Authors have mostly focused on one specific aspect or problem, and have used a particular collective choice model to deal with a question or topic of limited scope.

We show in this chapter that public sector analysis can be carried out as part of a comprehensive theoretical framework. Although the discussion is concerned primarily with taxation, it has implications for all research on the public economy that acknowledges the necessity for collective choice. A truly general framework will allow for analysis of positive as well as of normative questions and will link the two areas of inquiry in a meaningful fashion. While most individual studies will continue to focus on some particular aspect of the government sector, their implications for related questions can be better understood when they are evaluated against the background of an inclusive approach.

Taxation is a crucial topic in public finance. It touches directly on the need for a collective choice mechanism, and it involves analysis of coercive redistribution arising from the use of majority rule. In addition, it requires an understanding of how tax systems are structured to deal with the welfare losses stemming from the separation of spending and taxing, a separation that arises from the very nature of public goods.

When using collective choice models to examine these issues, we must confront the theoretical problems related to existence and stability of equilibrium. Otherwise, predicted policy outcomes may be only transitory phenomena, unsuitable for comparative static analysis, the method of research that has provided the logical underpinning of most work in economics. Moreover, equilibrium must now include political as well as economic forces.

In this chapter, we focus on the two main collective choice models that have been used to examine taxation, namely the median voter model and probabilistic voting. In each case, we examine the nature of equilibrium analysis, along with the contributions of the model to the understanding of major fiscal issues. Although both approaches have given rise to extensive literatures from which many useful insights can be derived, our review shows that probabilistic voting is able to encompass a wider range of questions. In particular, this model allows for the examination of both positive and normative questions, while the median voter model has little to say on the efficiency of taxation. Regarding theoretical and empirical research, median voter analysis has provided a strong focus for the examination of coercive redistribution, but it has not proved suitable for the study of tax structure and tax design due to its limited success in dealing with multi-dimensional issues. Probabilistic voting provides an appropriate basis for studying the nature of observed tax systems, and it can, at least in principle, also be used to shed light on coercive redistribution.

Both models still fall short of integrating into the analysis the wealth of existing fiscal institutions within which the exchange between citizens and governments occurs. While there is work on fiscal institutions, it is largely limited to linking them to the aggregate level of spending or to attempts to control budget deficits. Research in this area only rarely deals with specific features of observed tax systems or fiscal structure. A framework that encompasses taxation as an instrument of coercive redistribution, that can explain the tax skeleton and its relationship to excess burden, that accounts for the role of administration costs, and that assigns an explicit role to fiscal institutions remains to be constructed.

Whatever approach is chosen in future work, the nature of equilibrium remains crucial. If it is ignored, analytical results may be doomed to irrelevance or disregard in the political arena, a fate that has befallen a large number of proposals for a comprehensive income or consumption tax or a generalized flat tax. Advocates of such taxes have never demonstrated that they represent equilibrium outcomes of an acceptable and democratic collective choice process. Research based on probabilistic voting strongly suggests that democratic regimes will inevitably create complex tax systems with multiple bases, varied rate structures and a myriad of special provisions.

Although a comprehensive approach remains to be fully developed, consideration of existing work against the background of a generalized framework helps in seeing the strengths and weaknesses of available models and is useful in guiding the researcher in future work. It also makes clear that much has already been accomplished, and that the collective choice literature devoted to taxation is a rich and valuable source of analytical and policy-relevant insights.

STANLEY L. WINER
WALTER HETTICH

NOTES

1. There are also several excellent studies of the political and economic aspects of specific taxes or episodes in tax history of particular countries. This literature notably includes Witte (1985) on the income tax system of the United States and Gillespie (1991) on the tax structure of Canada.
2. For a review of Optimal Taxation, see, for example, Stiglitz (1987).
3. See Creedy (1998) for extended discussion of the meaning and measurement of excess burden.
4. This problem has given rise to several normative approaches to the distribution of the tax burden as alternatives to taxation according to benefits received, including most notably the principle of taxation according to ability to pay. See, for example, Musgrave (1959, chapter 5).
5. Wagner (1976), Buchanan and Wagner (1977), West and Winer (1980) and others have considered the role of fiscal illusion in the political manipulation of taxation and public debt.
6. On the concept of a Lindahl equilibrium, see also, Foley (1977), Johansen (1965) and Head (1974).

7. In addition to bypassing the essential role of collective choice, a social planning approach imputes motives to public decision makers that differ from those of their self-interested private counterparts included in the same framework. Brennan and Buchanan (1980), Kau and Rubin (1981), Levi (1988), Wilson (1989), Edwards and Keen (1996) and others have drawn attention to the importance of motivation by public officials in the analysis of taxation.

8. Even if there are no public goods, the use of majority rule allows coercion to exist. Separation of spending and taxing, which is necessarily present when public goods are provided, opens up additional routes by which coercion may be exercised.

9. One longstanding and as yet unanswered question that may be raised at this point is why the extension of the franchise in the 19th century to those with lower incomes did not lead to the expropriation of capital through the fiscal system. A possible answer provided by the median voter, as well as by the alternative framework considered later, lies in the negative implications for wealth and income of high taxes on the rich, although this remains a conjecture. On this point, see for example Winer and Rutherford (1992), who explore the argument in a computable equilibrium model calibrated to the U.K. economy in the 19th century.

   Roemer (2001) constructs an interesting model where equilibrium is established because of the need by every political party to construct a coalition of members with various interests, all of whom prefer its policies to that of the opposition. The difficulty of maintaining this coalition severely constrains the ability of political entrepreneurs to engineer a winning coalition, regardless of what the opposition proposes. This may be considered as an alternative general way of modeling political equilibrium. In such a framework, redistribution can be limited by a party's need to appeal to particular groups of voters — such as the poor and also religious voters, some of whom may be rich.

10. The restriction on preferences is related to the Mirrlees-Spence single crossing property, so that incomes and abilities of all voters are monotonically related. The application of this kind of restriction to allow another dimension of policy in the median voter model are reviewed in Boadway and Keen (2000). It appears that such restrictions cannot be used to allow a median or decisive voter model to extend to the analysis of the tax skeleton as a whole.

11. It should be noted that when we assume that decisions on different tax parameters are made sequentially in different election or committees, each policy parameter must have an independent relationship to welfare in the minds of those involved. Such a procedure requires indirect preferences to be Euclidean (represented by concentric circles), so that an optimal choice for any voter in a given dimension is independent of the choice of policies in other dimensions (Ordeshook, 1992, 283–285).

12. The triumph of the middle class in such a context is often referred to as Director's Law (Stigler, 1970).

13. There are also a few explorations of U.S. tax reform in the structure-induced equilibrium tradition, including Stewart (1991) and McCubbins (1991), who concentrate on the implications of a divided Congress for the politically feasible set of tax proposals.

14. See Enelow and Hinich (1989) for a discussion of the conditions underlying the concavity of expected vote functions.

15. The tax-expenditure literature is derived from the work of Henry Simons (1938) who argued for a tax on comprehensively defined income as the mainstay of the tax system. A tax-expenditure is a deviation of actual tax payments from tax liabilities that would apply if taxation was levied on this ideal base. We consider Simons' approach to taxation further in section 6.

16. If the size of a potential tax base expands, we may expect the marginal excess burden of relying more heavily on that source to fall relative to the excess burden from using other bases. Opposition to increasing reliance on the growing base may also decline because the fixed costs of organizing opposition are spread across more taxpayers.

17. See Hettich and Winer (1999, chapter 8) and Kenny and Winer (2001) for further details.

18. But see also Bohn and Inman (1996). Breton (1996) models the power of a Prime Minister in a parliamentary system to control spending and compares this power to that of the President in a U.S. congressional system of checks and balances. He suggests that a strong Prime Minister backing a strong Minister of Finance coupled with traditions of budgetary secrecy and cabinet solidarity combine to offer distinct advantages for maintaining the overall balance of spending and taxing.

19. Austen-Smith (2000) builds on the median voter model, and on models of agenda control by Romer and Rosenthal (1978) to formally compare the average rate of tax in an electoral system with a FPTP to one in a three-party system with PR. Austen-Smith's study is motivated by the desire to model the observation that average income tax rates appear to be higher and post tax distributions of income flatter in countries with proportional representation, than in countries with a first-past-the-post electoral system. The key to his explanation appears to lie in differences between electoral systems regarding the pivotal or decisive voter and the incentives created for taxpayers to choose among available occupations.

20. Neither the existence of an equilibrium (nor the convergence of platforms that occurs in this version of the model) is guaranteed under all conditions.

21. Second order conditions sufficient to insure the existence of a constrained maximum must also be satisfied. For further details see Coughlin (1992) and Hettich and Winer (1999).

22. Note also that the support function S is not a social welfare function. The weights in S are determined *within* the model by voting behavior, and different types of behavior will give rise to different support functions (see Coughlin, 1992).

23. Political failures may occur as a result of lobbying and the use of advertising to sway voters, or in a dynamic context where the problem is to insure the consistency of policies over time. Contributions on the first aspect of political economy are reviewed in Grossman and Helpman (2001) and on the second in Drazen (2000, chapters 4–6). The link to specific features of tax systems in this literature remains to be more fully developed. In this regard, see also footnote 25 below. Political market failure may also result from unregulated tax competition between jurisdictions: the relevant literature is reviewed by Wilson (1999).

24. We have implicitly assumed that political competition is perfect, in the sense that parties must continually maximize expected votes, and that no one can systematically influence voters with advertising misrepresenting how policies will affect individual welfare. If these conditions are not met, the equilibrium will not be efficient, and the optimization problem that is used to replicate the equilibrium will be different from what has been stated above. See Hettich and Winer (1999, chapter 6). Other situations may also lead to political market failure.
25. An important general lesson here is that normative analysis that is not informed by a model of political equilibrium is likely to be misleading. Another interesting example of this is provided by the literature on the time-consistency of public policy. A policy is not time consistent if it requires a course of action today (about today and tomorrow) that will subsequently become undesirable. It is often argued that the inability of governments to commit to consistent policy over time will result in a loss of social welfare compared to a situation where governments are prevented from adopting discretionary policies based on period by period political optimization (see, for example, Fischer, 1980). The problem with this and similar arguments is that it does not allow for the constraints on misuses of discretionary power that exist in a democracy (Hettich and Winer, 1985; Marceau and Smart, 2002). People in democratic societies are not powerless in opposing unwanted government actions using normal political channels. Moreover, we may also find the legal system being altered to make it difficult for governments to unilaterally expropriate private property. As a result, it is not obvious that further restrictions on the ability of governments to respond to changing events, which must have social costs as well as benefits, are warranted to counteract possible time inconsistency.
26. For related but different arguments concerning the problems of doing welfare analysis without taking political equilibrium into account, see Coate (2000) and Besley and Coate (2002).
27. See, for example, the text by Boardman et al. (1996, chapter 2).
28. Rutherford and Winer approached this issue by calibrating the weights so that maximization of the support function replicated the benchmark equilibrium.
29. See Hettich and Winer (1985, 1999) for review of the relevant literature on this point. It is of interest to note that measurement of deviations from the broadly based personal income tax, following Surrey (1973) and others, is the basis of tax-expenditure budgets, which have even been enshrined into law in some countries.

REFERENCES

Ashworth, John and Bruno Heyndels (2002). "Political fragmentation an the evolution of national tax structures in the OECD." *International Tax and Public Finance*, 8(3): 377–393.

Austen-Smith, David (2000). "Redistributing income under proportional representation." *Journal of Political Economy*, 108(6): 1235–1269.

Bergstrom, Theodore C. and Robert P. Goodman (1973). "Private demands for public goods." *American Economic Review*, 63(3): 280–296.

Besley, Timothy and Stephen Coate (2003). "On the public choice critique of welfare economics." *Public Choice* 114: 253–273.

Black, Duncan (1958). *The Theory of Committees and Elections*. Cambridge, UK: Cambridge University Press.

Boadway, Robin and Michael Keen (2000). "Redistribution," in A.B. Atkinson and F. Bourguignon (eds.) *Handbook of Income Distribution*, Volume 1. North-Holland: Elsevier, pp. 677–790.

Boardman, Anthony E., Aidan Vining, and David Weimer (1996). *Cost Benefit Analysis: Concepts and Practice*. Prentice-Hall.

Bohn, H. and Robert P. Inman (1996). "Balanced-budget rules and public deficits: evidence from the U.S. States." *Carnegie-Rochester Conference Series on Public Policy*, 45: 13–76.

Borcherding, Thomas F. and Robert T. Deacon (1972). "The demand for the services of non-federal governments." *American Economic Review*, 62: 891–901.

Brennan, Geoffrey and Buchanan, James (1980). *The Power to Tax: Analytical Foundations of a Fiscal Constitution*. New York: Cambridge University Press.

Breton, Albert (1996). *Competitive Governments: An Economic Theory of Politics and Public Finance*. New York: Cambridge University Press

Buchanan, James M. (1968). *The Demand and Supply of Public Goods*. New York: Rand McNally.

Buchanan, James M. (1976). "Taxation in fiscal exchange." *Journal of Public Economics*, 6: 17–29.

Buchanan, James M. and Wagner, Richard E. (1977). *Democracy in Deficit: The Political Legacy of Lord Keynes*. New York: Academic Press.

Buchanan, James M. and Roger D. Congleton (1998). *Politics by Principle, Not Interest: Towards a Nondiscriminatory Democracy*. New York: Cambridge University Press.

Chernick, Howard and Andrew Reschovsky (1996). "The political economy of state and local tax structure," in G. Pola, G. France, and G. Levaggi (eds.) *Developments in Local Government Finance*. Cheltenham, UK: Edward Elgar, pp. 253–272.

Coate, Stephen (2000). "An efficiency approach to the evaluation of policy changes." *Economic Journal*, 110(463): 437–455

Coughlin, Peter (1992). *Probabilistic Voting Theory*. New York: Cambridge University Press.

Coughlin, Peter and Shmuel Nitzan (1981). "Electoral outcomes with probabilistic voting and Nash social welfare maxima." *Journal of Public Economics*, 15: 113–121.

Creedy, John (1998). *Measuring Welfare Changes and Tax Burdens*. Cheltenham, UK: Edward Elgar.

Cukierman, Alex and Meltzer, Allan H. (1989). "A political theory of government debt and deficits in a neo-ricardian framework." *American Economic Review*, 79(4): 713–732.

Cukierman, Alex and Allan H. Meltzer (1991). "A political theory of progressive income taxation," in A. Meltzer, A. Cukierman and S. Richard (eds.) *Political Economy*. Oxford: Oxford University Press, pp. 76–108.

Drazen, Allan (2000). *Political Economy in Macroeconomics*. Princeton, NJ: Princeton University Press.

Edgeworth, F.Y. (1925). *Papers Relating to Political Economy*. London: Macmillan.

Edwards, J. and M. Keen (1996). "Tax competition and leviathan." *European Economic Review*, 40: 113–134.

Enelow, James and Melvin Hinich (1989). "A general probabilistic spatial theory of elections." *Public Choice*, 61(2): 101–113.

Epple, Dennis and Richard E. Romano (1996a). "Ends against the middle: determining public service provision when there are private alternatives." *Journal of Public Economics*, 62: 297–325.

Epple, Dennis and Richard E. Romano (1996b). "Public provision of private goods." *Journal of Political Economy*, 104(1): 57–84.

Fischer, Stanley (1980). "Dynamic inconsistency, cooperation and the benevolent dissembling government." *Journal of Economic Dynamics and Control*, 2: 93–107.

Fitts, Michael and Inman, Robert P. (1992). "Controlling congress: presidential influence in domestic fiscal policy." *Georgetown Law Journal*, 80(5): 1737–1785.

Foley, Duncan (1977). "Resource allocation and the public sector." *Yale Economic Essays*, 7(1): 45–98.

Gans, J.S. and Michael Smart (1996). "Majority voting with single-crossing preferences." *Journal of Public Economics*, 59: 219–237.

Gillespie, W. Irwin (1991). *Tax, Borrow and Spend: Financing Federal Spending in Canada, 1867–1990*. Ottawa: Carleton University Press.

Gould, Andrew C. and Peter J. Baker (2002). "Democracy and taxation." *Annual Review of Political Science*, 5: 87–110.

Gouvia, Miguel (1997). "Majority rule and public provision of a private good." *Public Choice*, 93: 221–224.

Grossman, Gene M. and Elhanan Helpman (2001). *Special Interest Politics*. Cambridge, MA: MIT Press.

Head, John (1974). *Public Goods and Public Welfare*. Durham, Duke University Press.

Hettich, Walter (2002). "Better than what? Policy analysis, collective choice and the standard of reference," in S. Winer and H. Shibata (eds.) *Political Economy and Public Finance: The Role of Political Economy in the Theory and Practice of Public Economics*. Cheltenham, UK: Edward Elgar.

Hettich, Walter and Stanley L. Winer (2002). "Rules, politics and the normative analysis of taxation," in R. Wagner and J. Backhaus (eds). *Handbook of Public Finance*. Kluwer Academic Publishers.

Hettich, Walter and Stanley L. Winer (1999). *Democratic Choice and Taxation: A Theoretical and Empirical Analysis*. New York: Cambridge University Press.

Hettich, Walter and Stanley L. Winer (1988). "Economic and political foundations of tax structure." *American Economic Review*, 78: 701–713.

Hettich, Walter and Stanley L. Winer (1985). "Blueprints and pathways: the shifting foundations of tax reform." *National Tax Journal*, 38(4): 423–445.

Hinich, Melvin (1977). "Equilibrium in spatial voting: the median voter result is an artifact." *Journal of Economic Theory*, 16: 208–219.

Holtz-Eakin, Douglas (1992). "Elections and aggregation: interpreting econometric analyses of local governments." *Public Choice*, 74(1): 17–42.

Hotte, Louis and Stanley L. Winer (2001). "Political influence, economic interests and endogenous tax structure in a computable equilibrium framework: with application to the United States, 1973 and 1983." *Public Choice*, 109(1): 66–99.

Inman, Robert P. and Michael A. Fitts (1990). "Political institutions and fiscal policy: evidence from the U.S. historical record." *Journal of Law, Economics and Organization*, 6(Special Issue): 79–132.

Johansen, Leif (1965). *Public Economics*. Amsterdam: North Holland Press.

Kau, James B. and Paul H. Rubin (1981). "The size of government." *Public Choice*, 37(2): 261–274.

Kenny, Lawrence W. and Stanley L. Winer (2001). "Tax systems in the world: an empirical investigation into the importance of tax bases, collection costs, and political regime." Carleton Economic Papers. Available at www.ssrn.com.

Kenny, Lawrence W. and Mark Toma (1997). "The role of tax bases and collection costs in the determination of income tax rates, seignorage and inflation." *Public Choice*, 92(1): 75–90.

Kirchgaessner, Gebhard (2002). "The effects of fiscal institutions on public finance: a survey of the empirical evidence," in S. Winer and H. Shibata (eds.) *Political Economy and Public Finance: The Role of Political Economy in the Theory and Practice of Public Economics*. Cheltenham, UK: Edward Elgar.

Levi, Margaret (1988). *Of Rule and Revenue*. Los Angeles: University of California Press.

Lindahl, Eric (1919). "Just taxation: a positive solution" (translation by Elizabeth Henderson), in R.A. Musgrave and A.T. Peacock (eds.) *Classics in the Theory of Public Finance*. London: Macmillan (1958), pp. 168–176.

Marceau, Nicolas and Michael Smart (2002). "Corporate lobbying and commitment failure in capital taxation." CESifo Working Paper 676, February.

McCubbins, Mathew D. (1991). "Party politics, divided government, and budget deficits," in S. Kernell (ed.) *Parallel Politics: Economic Policy Making in the United States and Japan*. Washington DC: The Brookings Institution, pp. 83–118.

McKelvey, Richard D. (1976). "Intransitivities in multidimensional voting models and some implications for agenda control." *Journal of Economic Theory*, 12(3): 472–482.

McKelvey, Richard D. and John W. Patty (2001). "A theory of voting in large elections." Working Paper, California Institute of Technology, December.

Milesi-Ferretti, Gian Maria, Roberto Perotti with Massimo Rostagno (2002). "Electoral systems and public spending." *Quarterly Journal of Economics*, 117(2): 609–657.

Meltzer, Allan H. and Scott F. Richard (1981). "A rational theory of the size of government." *Journal of Political Economy*, 89: 914–927.

Meltzer, Allan H. and Scott F. Richard (1983). "Tests of a rational theory of the size of government." *Public Choice*, 41(3): 403–418.

Meltzer, Allan H. and Scott F. Richard (1985). "A positive theory of in-kind transfers and the negative income tax." *Public Choice*, 47: 231–265.

Mirrlees, James A. (1971). "An exploration in the theory of optimum income taxation." *Review of Economic Studies*, 38: 175–208.

Moomau, Pamela H. and Morton, Rebecca B. (1992). "Revealed preferences for property taxes: an empirical study of perceived tax incidence." *Review of Economics and Statistics*, 74(1): 176–179.

Mueller, Dennis (1990). "Public choice and the consumption tax," in M. Rose (ed.) *Heidelberg Conference on Taxing Consumption*. Springer-Verlag, pp. 227–246.

Mueller, Dennis (1989). *Public Choice II*. Cambridge: Cambridge University Press.

Musgrave, Richard (1969). *Fiscal Systems*. New Haven: Yale University Press.

Musgrave, Richard (1959). *The Theory of Public Finance*. McGraw-Hill.

Nechyba, Thomas J. (1997). "Local property and state income taxes: the role of interjurisdictional competition and collusion." *Journal of Political Economy*, 105(2): 351–384.

Nechyba, Thomas J. (1999). "School finance induced migration and stratification patterns: the impact of private school vouchers." *Journal of Public Economic Theory*, 1(1): 5–50.

Ordeshook, Peter (1992). *A Political Theory Primer*. New York: Routledge.

Persson, Torsten and Guido Tabellini (2001). "Political institutions and policy outcomes: what are the stylized facts?" Center for Economic Studies and IFO Institute for Economic Research, Munich Germany, Working Paper 459, April.

Peters, Guy B. (1991). *The Politics of Taxation: A Comparative Perspective*. Cambridge, MA: Blackwell.

Pigou, A.C. (1951). *A Study in Public Finance*, Third Edition. London: Macmillan.

Pommerehne, Werner W. and Schneider, Friedrich (1983). Does government in a representative democracy follow a majority of voters' preferences? — an empirical examination," in Horst Hanusch (ed.) *Anatomy of Government Deficiencies*. Springer, pp. 61–84.

Poterba, J.M. (1997). "Do budget rules work?," in A. Auerbach (ed.) *Fiscal Policy: Lessons From Economic Research*. Cambridge, MA: MIT Press, pp. 329–336.

Ramsey, F.P. (1927). "A contribution to the theory of taxation." *Economic Journal*, 37: 47–61.

Roberts, K.W.S. (1977). "Voting over income tax schedules." *Journal of Public Economics*, 8: 329–340.

Roemer, John (2001). *Political Competition: Theory and Applications*. Cambridge, MA: Harvard University Press.

Romer, Thomas (1975). "Individual welfare, majority voting and the properties of a linear income tax." *Journal of Public Economics*, 4: 163–168.

Romer, Thomas and Howard Rosenthal (1978). "Political resource allocation, controlled agendas and the status quo." *Public Choice*, 33: 27–43.

Rutherford, Thomas and Stanley L. Winer (1999). "Endogenous policy in a computational general equilibrium framework, with application to the United States 1973 and 1983," in W. Hettich and S. Winer (eds.) *Democratic Choice and Taxation*, Chapter 7. Cambridge: Cambridge University Press.

Rutherford, Thomas and Stanley L. Winer (2002). "Endogenous policy in a computational general equilibrium framework." Research Report 9007, University of Western Ontario, June 1990, in S. Winer (ed.) *Political Economy in Federal States: Selected Essays of Stanley L. Winer*, Chapter 12. Cheltenham UK: Edward Elgar.

Schofield, Norman (1978). "Instability of simple dynamic games." *Review of Economic Studies*, 45: 575–594.

Schumpeter, Joseph A. (1981). "The crisis of the tax state," Translated (1954) in A. Peacock et. al. (eds.) *International Economic Papers* 4. London: MacMillan & Co., pp. 29–68.

Shepsle, Kenneth A. (1979). "Institutional arrangements and equilibrium in multi-dimensional voting models." *American Journal of Political Science*, 23: 27–59.

Shepsle, K.A. and Weingast, B.R. (1981). "Structure-induced equilibrium and legislative choice." *Public Choice*, 37: 503–519.

Simons, Henry (1938). *Personal Income Taxation: The Definition of Income as a Problem of Fiscal Policy*. Chicago: University of Chicago Press.

Steinmo, Sven (1993). *Taxation and Democracy: Swedish, British and American Approaches to Financing the Modern State*. New Haven: Yale University Press.

Stewart, Charles H. Jr. (1991). "The politics of tax reform in the 1980s," in A. Alesina and G. Carliner (eds.) *Politics and Economics in the Eighties*. University of Chicago Press.

Stigler, George J. (1970). "Director's law of public income redistribution." *Journal of Law and Economics*, 13: 1–10.

Stiglitz, Joseph E. (1987). "Pareto efficient and optimal taxation and the new new welfare economics," in Auerbach and M. Feldstein (eds.) *Handbook of Public Economics*, Volume II, North-Holland: Elsevier, pp. 992–1042.

Surrey, Stanley S. (1973). *Pathways to Tax Reform: The Concept of Tax Expenditures*. Cambridge, MA: Harvard University Press.

Usher, Dan (1994). "The significance of the probabilistic voting theorem." *Canadian Journal of Economics*, 27(2): 433–445.

van Winden, Frans A.A.M. (1983). *On the Interaction Between State and Private Sector*. Amsterdam: North-Holland.

von Hagen, J. (1992). "Budgetary procedures and fiscal performance in the European communities." Commission of the European Communities, Economic Papers No. 96, October.

Volkerink, Bjorn and Jacob de Haan (2000). "Fragmented government effects on fiscal policy: new evidence." Unpublished Paper, University of Groningen, May.

Wagner, Richard E. (1976). "Revenue structure, fiscal illusion, and budgetary choice." *Public Choice*, 25: 45–61.

Warskett, George, Stanley L. Winer, and Walter Hettich (1998). "The complexity of tax structure in competitive political systems." *International Tax and Public Finance*, 5: 127–155.

Webber, Carolyn and Wildavsky, Aaron B. (1986). *A History of Taxation and Expenditure in the Western World*. New York: Simon and Schuster.

Weingast, B.R. (1979). "A rational choice perspective on congressional norms." *American Journal of Political Science*, 23: 245–262.

West, Edwin G. and Stanley L. Winer (1980). "Optimal fiscal illusion and the size of government." *Public Choice*, 35(5): 607–622.

Wicksell, Knut (1896). "A new principle of just taxation," in Richard Musgrave and Alan Peacock (eds.) *Classics in the Theory of Public Finance*. New York: Macmillan (1958), pp. 72–118.

Wilson, John D. (1999). "Theories of tax competition." *National Tax Journal*, 52(2): 269–304.

Wilson, John D. (1989). "An optimal tax treatment of leviathan." *Economics and Politics*, 1(2): 97–118.

Winer, Stanley L. and Walter Hettich (2002). "Explaining the use of related instruments," in S. Winer (ed.) *Political Economy in Federal States: Selected Essays of Stanley L. Winer*, Chapter 3. Cheltenham, UK: Edward Elgar.

Winer, Stanley L. and Walter Hettich (1998). "What is missed if we leave out collective choice in the analysis of taxation." *National Tax Journal*, 51(2): 373–389.

Winer, Stanley L. and Hettich, Walter (1991). "Debt and tariffs, an empirical investigation of the evolution of revenue systems." *Journal of Public Economics*, 45: 215–242.

Winer, Stanley L. and Rutherford, Thomas (1992). "Coercive redistribution and the franchise: a preliminary investigation using computable general equilibrium modeling," in A. Breton et al. (eds.) *Preferences and the Demand for Public Goods*. Dordrecht: Kluwer Academic, pp. 351–375.

Wintrobe, Ronald (1996). *The Political Economy of Dictatorship*. New York: Cambridge University Press.

Witte, John F. (1985). *The Politics and Development of the Federal Income Tax*. University of Wisconsin Press.

PUBLIC CHOICE FROM THE PERSPECTIVE OF ECONOMICS

1. Introduction

I address public choice from the perspective of economics in this essay. The "perspective of economics" is taken to mean the application of the principles of maximizing behavior and demand and supply to institutions and behavior in the political world. I begin with a discussion of this familiar methodology, and then proceed to illustrate how the principles of maximizing behavior and demand and supply can be applied to the various component parts of a representative democracy, including the legislative, executive, and judicial branches, as well as interest groups, bureaucracy, and voters. This will be in no sense a review of the literature. The point is to illustrate how economic principles can be applied to political behavior in each of the above contexts. In each case a single and simple illustration will be given. In such a way the reader can decide whether the economic perspective really adds anything to the understanding of political behavior over and above alternative analyses. For example, do we learn more about a legislator's behavior with an assumption that he acts in his self-interest or in the "public interest"? Finally, although many of the illustrations are related to U.S. political processes, I endeavor in each case to generalize the discussion to an international setting.

2. The Perspective of Economics

In the movie, *A Few Good Men*, a Marine officer, who is testifying at a court martial, is asked if a soldier was in danger from his colleagues. He does not answer the question, so the interrogator repeats the question, adding, "in mortal danger?" The officer responds, "Is there any other kind?" This response represents my basic approach to the topic of this essay. When given the assignment to discuss the contributions of economics to public choice, my instinct was to echo the answer of the Marine officer, "Is there any other kind?"[1]

Public choice emerged from the maximizing paradigm of modern microeconomics, and it remains to this day within that approach. This tried and tested model colonized the traditional intellectual territory of political science. Even the key political scientists who participated in the public choice revolution, such as Riker (1962), assumed that politicians and their coalitions were maximizing some objective subject to constraints (for example, the pro rata gains to the minimum winning coalition). The simple transfer of the economist's model of individual self-interest to the subject matter of political science was the seed corn of the public choice revolution.

In this essay I discuss the transfer of economic methodology to the theory of public choice, and attempt to assess whether the application of the economist's model of human behavior has been more or less successful. First, I briefly stretch the economist's model, and then I describe what it means to argue that its application to politics has been "successful."

Any conventional textbook on microeconomics lays out the economist's model of individual behavior.[2] Individuals are assumed to have transitive and stable preferences, which they pursue by making trade-offs among desired goods as a function of their relative costliness. The law of demand, for example, is an empirical proposition about such behavior. In effect, the economic model predicts that individuals will seek to minimize the effect of constraints, such as income and prices, on their behavior. If "price" rises, they economize on the use of the more costly "good"; if "price" falls, they expand their usage of the less expensive "good." The quotation marks around "price" and "good" are there to indicate that the economic model is general. The model applies to any context which includes "prices" and "goods," ranging from obvious cases like the price of chocolate to other cases, such as a market for legislation, in which "prices" and "goods" may not be so obvious. Any subject is fair game for the application of the economic model, including the world of politics. The only thing that limits the expansion of the economic approach to other areas is the creativity of the analyst. Economics, of course, may not explain or predict behavior very well in these applications, but there is no subject matter to which economic reasoning cannot be deployed. Arguably, there is nothing in the world that is "non-economic."[3]

The economic model is a simple model of behavior, but not a simplistic model. Preferences, as noted, are assumed to be given and stable. This places preferences outside the purview of economists. People want what they want; economists cannot say why people like chocolate. Taking preferences as given, the maximizing model is quite general. Sometimes individuals will maximize utility, and sometimes they will maximize wealth (a special case). Individuals are "selfish" only to the extent that they pursue their goals purposively. The goals can be anything the individual chooses, be it piggish wealth accumulation or some notion of a higher life including service to others. The economic model says to the analyst, give me the constraints or "prices" and I will give you predictions about how individuals will respond. All behavior is economic; if the "price" of altruism falls, individuals will be more altruistic. Even the altruist will seek to help others in the most effective manner, given the "price" of altruism.

The stability of preferences is an empirical issue. Typically, economic analysis proceeds on the basis that individuals reach "equilibrium" states of behavior. That is, a constraint or price changes, individuals rearrange their behavior so as to minimize the effect of the change on their lives, and then settle down into a new equilibrium mode of behavior. Obviously, unstable preferences would undermine the explanatory value of the economic model, which is based on tracing out the effects of constraint changes in the face of given preferences. This does not mean that preferences never change or evolve, only that they are stable enough for the economic approach to make reliable predictions. In both markets and politics equilibrium behavior seems pervasive. Consumption decisions are repetitive; political transactions are durable and last for a long time (for example, the Interstate Commerce Commission or Social Security).

How does one evaluate the "success" of the economic model in analyzing politics? The primary criterion is how well the economic model explains or predicts political behavior relative to competing models, say in the sense of a statistical test or an R^2. This criterion cannot always be applied because it is not feasible to test all theories empirically. In some cases we have to use our judgement about what is going on or about what actually "explains" events. Is the pattern of predictions consistent with economizing behavior or with some other model in the absence of a defining empirical test? In the discussion of the success of economic models in this paper, however, I will primarily adhere to the testability criterion for success; that is, how well have these models fared in empirical tests?[4]

The key point, then, to keep in mind as I proceed is that the economic content of public choice is taken to mean that political actors, like private actors, pursue their ends effectively, but the constraints they face in the process are different. Hence, political actors (bureaucrats) will behave differently than private actors (corporate executives) for this reason, and not because they are different types of people. My effort in this regard will be to cover selected areas of public choice analysis in order to assess how well the economist's model has performed in explaining political behavior and institutions. I will not try to be copious in the sense of a literature review; I will rather try to be concise in offering an example of how to apply the economic model to selected areas of public choice analysis, beginning with the legislature.

One final proviso is in order. There is no doubt that the economic approach has come under heavy assault in recent times (Thaler, 1992; Green and Shapiro, 1996). For the most part, in my view, economic methodology has withstood these attacks. For every anomaly, there is a rational choice explanation. Nonetheless, this debate will continue in the literature, but in the meantime, this essay will offer an unashamedly thick rationality approach to the subject matter of public choice.[5]

3. The Legislature

The legislature is the most analyzed institution of representative democracies in modern public choice analysis. From the perspective of economics are the principles of demand and supply relevant to the legislature? To explore this question the labor market for legislator services is analyzed. Specifically, I address the problem of how legislators are paid, using U.S. state legislators as the example to be analyzed. My explanation of legislative pay will seem familiar to economists. Nonetheless, it will contrast markedly with the explanations and approaches to the same problem offered by other observers of such matters. For example, "Most states fail to pay their lawmakers anything approximating a living wage" (Staayer, 1973: 93).

In effect, I view legislators as participants in a labor market, and I try to explain differences in the legal (above board) pay of legislators by factors that affect the supply of and demand for their services. The supply of legislative services is analogous to the supply of any service where labor is extensively used in (roughly) fixed proportions to other inputs. The quantity-supplied of legislative services (which I will measure in man-years per year) is therefore determined by the relative wage, the price of inputs other than labor, and technology. Each state has a separate supply function, but I do not expect the conditions of supply to vary greatly across states. Potential legislators are never a finite fraction of the available labor in a state, and the occupational composition of legislatures is similar across states. These positions are held primarily by members of professions that can capitalize (through extra-legal pay) readily on certain aspects of being a legislator. Lawyers often continue to draw a wage from their law firms while serving. Farmers can be legislators where sessions are held between growing seasons. The reasons that banking, insurance, and real estate people gravitate to these offices are not hard to discern.

In each state there is some demand for legislative influence. The demand for legislative influence implies a derived demand for legislators. The technical relationship between influence and legislators is not one of proportionality because an excessive number of legislators would dilute the influence of each and might not be able to pass any laws. I further expect that, given the lack of low-cost substitutes for legislative action within a state, the elasticity of the demand for representation with respect to the legislative wage rate must be close to zero over the relevant range. Across states, in contrast to the relative invariability of supply in this market, I expect that the demand for representation will shift as a function of state income, population, budget size, and so forth.

With this background in mind, note that wage determination takes essentially two forms across states. In some states legislative pay is set in the constitution and is difficult to change. A new wage would require the passage of a constitutional proposal. Such proposals typically emanate from the legislature under relatively strict voting and quorum rules and must be signed by the governor and passed in a statewide referendum. In other states pay is set by a statute passed by both houses of the legislature and signed by the governor. These pay bills are subject to legislative consideration under normal voting and quorum rules and do not require a statewide referendum.

I contend that legislative determination of pay by statute amounts to a strong form of union power. Unions typically achieve higher relative wages by restricting entry. In this case entry is somewhat more loosely controlled through constitutional limitations on the size of the legislature and on the procedures for gaining a seat, and legislators are given a direct hand in wage determination. I would expect to observe the impact of this monopoly power in higher relative wages for legislators in these states.

The conditions in the legislative labor market for a single state are depicted in Figure 1. Each legislature is

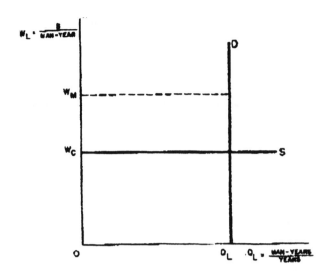

Figure 1: Determination of legislative pay.

treated as a separate labor market. A measure of legislative output (Q_L) in terms of man-years per year is on the horizontal axis, and annual legal pay (W_L) measured as dollars per man-year is on the vertical axis. The competitive supply curve for successful applicants for these seats is given by S. This relationship represents the wage that must be forthcoming for a given level of output to persuade prospective legislators to run for and to accept office. Following the previous argument, I draw a completely inelastic demand curve over the relevant range for the services of legislators. In the absence of any contrary evidence I assume that existing wages clear the market for the given constraint on legislative size in both union and nonunion states. That is, there is no excess supply.

In states where the legislative wage is constitutionally determined, some given wage, W_C, will prevail. Candidates will adjust to the given wage, and supply or marginal opportunity costs will shift accordingly as more- or less-qualified individuals seek election, so that the market clears. In states that allow legislative control over pay, the wage is adjusted by legislators to maximize the present value of a seat. This wage is, for the moment, arbitrarily drawn in Figure 1 at W_M.

The main issue confronting this theory concerns the forces which constrain legislators from setting an infinite wage in Figure 1. Since I argue that the demand for legislator time is completely inelastic over the relevant range, this pay problem reduces to a question of what limits the wage-setting ability of the legislature under these conditions.

Basically, the present value of a seat will be inversely related to the wage rate after some point, because higher wages will attract new entrants and alienate voters, both of which dampen reelection prospects and offset the effect of increasing the wage on the present value of seats. Incumbents must thus trade off union wage gains and other benefits from being in office against the extra costs associated with increased competition to retain seats. There is thus a determinate upper bound on the monopoly wage in the problem.

As a result of monopoly power in this labor market, then, wages in states where legislators can set their own wage will be higher on average (W_M) relative to states where the wage is set in the constitution (W_C). The legislative union predictably will have a substantial impact on relative wages because the demand for legislator services will be quite inelastic, as suggested earlier. This condition follows from the rules of derived demand in two related senses. First, there is only one legislature per state, so there is not a nonunion sector from which to buy output. Second, there are in general poor substitutes for the services of legislators (for example, legal versus private cartels).

This model of legislator pay offers a robust explanation of state legislator pay in the U.S. In fact, the amount of relative wage-setting power ceded to the set-your-own-pay legislatures is higher than for any known labor union (300 to 400 percent).[6] It should thus be clear that the principles of supply and demand can be readily adapted to the public choice context of the legislature. At the core of the legislative process are markets and allocation mechanisms familiar to modern economics and a great distance removed from the view that legislators are undercompensated.[7]

Moreover, this lesson applies with appropriate modifications to the legislatures of other countries. Stigler (1976), for example, discusses the determinants of legislative size across countries, and finds that such factors as population provide a common explanation for legislative size in different national legislatures. And the work of Marvel (1977) on the British Factory Acts clearly puts the British Parliament into an interest-group context as early as the 1830s. So too does Weck-Hanneman's (1990) work on direct democracy in Switzerland suggest that using the voters as the legislature is no insurance against protectionist outcomes. Public choice analysis of the legislature and related institutions is not confined to the U.S.

4. The Judiciary

No other institution of democratic government is more insulated from the political process than the judiciary. In the American political system constitutional rules provide the courts with a high degree of independence from the other branches of government. At the federal level, for example, judges are granted life tenure; their nominal salaries cannot be reduced; and they can be removed only by means of impeachment for high crimes and misdemeanors. While most state judges typically serve more limited terms, their offices are generally much more secure than those of their counterparts in the legislative and executive branches. Judicial independence limits the ability of these other branches of government to sway courts' decisions, and because judges face heavy sanctions in cases of detected corruption, they are arguably unlikely to be influenced by the economic interests of the parties before them. In short, the standard view is that the judiciary is — and, indeed, should be — above the fray of interest-group politics.

Given their effective independence from ordinary political pressures, what motivates judges to behave in any particular way? There are three major hypotheses regarding the nature and consequences of judicial independence. First, one view holds that an independent judiciary operates as a necessary counterweight to the legislative and executive branches. The judiciary acts to protect society from unconstitutional encroachments by the other government branches, and judges are therefore motivated by their concern for the public's interest. A second view regards the independent judiciary as an agent not of the general public's interest, but of the interests of groups that otherwise are unrepresented (or under-represented in other political forums). Whereas the legislature faithfully responds to the wishes of the majority, judges interpose their wills to protect the interests of politically vulnerable minorities. Finally, the independent judiciary may actually be something of a loose cannon. Posner (1986), for example, argues that because judges are insulated from interest-group politics and receive no monetary payoffs from deciding a case in a particular manner, the economic self-interest of judges cannot explain judicial decisionmaking. He suggests instead that judges seek to maximize their own utility by imposing their personal preferences and values on society.

In an important contribution to public choice theory, Landes and Posner (1975) contend that these popular models of the functioning of the independent judiciary are ad hoc and unconvincing. They propose an alternative economic theory in which the courts increase the durability of wealth transfers purchased from the legislature by interest groups. By reason of its effective independence from the sitting legislature and practice of interpreting laws on the basis of original legislative intent, the judiciary confers to legislation something of the character of a binding long-term contract. By construing statutes in this manner, the judiciary increases the durability of legislative contracts and, hence, raises the price interest groups are willing to pay for wealth transfers in their own favor.

In the interest-group theory of government legislatures are modeled as firms that supply wealth transfers in the form of special-interest legislation. Legislatures assign property rights in wealth transfers to the highest bidder by means of legislative contracts, i.e., statutes. Domestic producers purchase tariff and non-tariff barriers to protect them from import competition, farmers purchase production-restricting marketing orders and price subsidies to increase their incomes at consumers' expense, and so on.

But while there are many similarities between legislative markets and ordinary markets in this regard, the two differ in at least one important respect: the mechanisms available for enforcing contracts once they have been negotiated. There are basically two contract-enforcing mechanisms in private markets. One is enforcement by a third party. In this case the contracting parties agree to rely on an independent arbitrator or the courts to resolve disputes and sanction noncompliance. Alternatively, when explicit agreements are absent or incomplete by reason of being costly to negotiate, self-enforcing mechanisms help maintain a contractual relationship. Each party relies upon the threat of withdrawal of future business to provide assurance that implicit agreements will be honored (Klein and Leffler, 1981). In political markets, however, the legislature can, in principle, break its legislative contracts at any time, and leave any "injured" party with no immediate avenue of redress. An interest group cannot bring suit against the legislature for modifying or repealing an existing legislative contract simply because of shifts in the political winds. Landes and Posner (1975: 879) provide an example in which the dairy industry buys a tax on the sale of margarine in one session of Congress, but the margarine producers buy the removal of the tax in the next session.

This example illustrates the dynamic insight that contract negotiations between legislatures and interest groups will be thwarted if political fortunes are easily reversed. Uncertainty with respect to the length of time over which an interest group can expect to collect the benefits it has purchased will tend to lower the present value of the transfer, and therefore reduce the price it is willing to pay. Given that individual legislators face a limited time horizon due to frequent electoral challenges, resulting in unpredictable shifts in the composition of the legislature, markets for legislative wealth transfers would not function very efficiently in the absence of institutional constraints capable of mitigating this source of contractual instability.[8] Interest groups are not likely to expend time and treasure to secure the passage of legislation if, once enacted, it tends to be easily amended or repealed. It should therefore not be surprising that wealth-maximizing legislatures have adopted various measures designed to enhance the stability of legislative contracts and thereby increase the demand prices for legislative output.

Landes and Posner divide these institutional arrangements into two categories. The first is composed of the constitutive rules of the legislature itself. Procedural norms on such matters as bill introductions, committee hearings, floor action, and filibusters serve to increase the continuity, regularity, and stability of the legislature's operations. By making it more difficult to enact legislation in the first place, such measures also make it more difficult to amend or repeal existing laws.

The existence of an independent judiciary also enhances the durability of legislative contracts. Legislation is not self-enforcing; recourse to the courts is necessary to give effect to often vague or ambiguous statutory language. If judges act at the behest of the sitting legislature in interpreting previously enacted legislation, decide cases with an eye toward protecting otherwise under-represented groups, or simply indulge their own personal preferences, they might refuse to enforce the bargained-for statute. Such behavior would render earlier contracts null and void.

In contrast, if independence means that judges can be relied upon to interpret and enforce legislation in accord with the original legislative intent, judges will tend to protect the integrity of the legislature's contracts with interest groups. By providing such durability, the courts enhance the value of present and future redistributive legislation and facilitate the operation of the market for wealth transfers. On the other hand, if the legislative marketplace more closely resembles a Hobbesian jungle, such legislative contracts will be worth little, and governmental wealth transfer activity will greatly diminish.

In the Landes-Posner model, the judiciary is part of the institutional structure that induces equilibrium in the market for wealth transfers. By virtue of its independence and by interpreting legislation on the basis of original intent (i.e., a reversion point), the judiciary functions to limit cycling in majority rule decisions. This judicial function tends to increase the present value of legislative wealth transfers to special interest groups. As Landes and Posner explain, however, the value of the courts to the legislature in this regard and, not coincidentally, the ability of the judiciary to maintain its independence, depend on how well the courts play their assigned role.

What motivates judges to behave in the ways predicted by the Landes-Posner model? Landes and Posner provide a theoretical reason why legislatures might benefit from the existence of an independent judiciary, but not why judges themselves would benefit from enforcing legislative contracts with interest groups in the face of political pressure. Legislative procedural rules may make it costly for margarine producers to buy the repeal of a tax enacted at the dairy industry's behest, but what prevents the courts from declaring the tax unconstitutional? Subsequent empirical tests of the Landes-Posner model have furnished two possible answers to these questions. One is that judges are rewarded for behaving independently. The other is that alternative contract-enforcement mechanisms exist which tend to be relied on more heavily in jurisdictions where the judiciary is less independent. An independent judiciary is only one of several institutions of democratic government that play complementary roles in promoting the durability of legislative wealth transfers.

First, in a direct test of the Landes-Posner model Anderson et al. (1989) examined the relationship between the annual salaries of judges serving on state courts of last resort, measures of their opportunity costs for serving on the court, prospective workloads, measures of judicial independence, and the courts' propensities to overturn legislation on due process grounds. The goal was to determine whether judges are in fact rewarded by legislatures (in the form of higher pay or budgets) for behaving independently in the Landes-Posner sense. In sum, the evidence from due process challenges to legislative acts suggests that "self-interested judges can be shown to behave in manner consistent with the functioning of efficient markets for coercive wealth transfers for the same reasons that other participants in those markets participate — wealth maximization (Anderson et al., 1989: 3).

Second, in any principal-agent relationship the optimal amount of judicial discretion depends on the configuration of the costs and benefits of delegating decision-making authority to that branch. Some judicial independence is beneficial to the sitting legislature (i.e., judges enforcing contracts with respect to their original meanings), but too much independence (judges indulging their own personal preferences) may inhibit the well-ordered functioning of the market for wealth transfers. These observations suggest the existence of an optimal amount of judicial independence and, hence, an optimal mix of institutional constraints for promoting the durability of contracts with interest groups in particular circumstances.

Constitutional provisions, or what Landes and Posner term "legislation of a higher order," represent an alternative institution in the interplay between the legislative and judicial branches. Such provisions are worth more than ordinary legislation to interest groups because they are more durable. They are also more costly to obtain in the first place. Whereas the enactment of ordinary laws typically fall under the normal majority voting rules of the legislature, constitutional amendments are subject to stricter procedures, typically requiring approval by legislative super-majorities and subsequent ratification by popular vote.

Whether or not an interest group will pursue the more costly route of constitutional amendment to secure a wealth transfer in it own favor consequently depends on the expected durability of wealth transfers secured through the normal legislative processes. Crain and Tollison (1979) used data from U.S. states to test the Landes-Posner model in this context. The model assumed that because interest groups could depend on the courts to enforce legislative contracts in jurisdictions where judicial independence is high in the Landes-Posner sense, they would rationally tend to rely more on normal legislative processes in those jurisdictions. On the other hand, constitutional amendment would be worth more to interest groups in states with less independent judges. At the margin interest groups will demand ordinary legislation or extraordinary constitutional change to the degree of a state's particular judicial independence. The results of this empirical model supported the predicted tradeoff of the Landes-Posner theory. The frequency of constitutional amendment tended to be higher in states with lower judicial independence, other things being equal.

Other institutions of democratic government also appear to substitute for judicial independence in ways predicted by Landes and Posner. For example, as legislator tenure and the size of the voting bloc controlled by the legislature's majority party increase, the value of an independent judiciary declines because legislators will be less likely to renege on the bargains they strike with interest groups. Reputations for honoring commitments are as valuable to politicians and political parties as they are to suppliers of more ordinary goods and services. Evidence from the states adduced by Crain et al. (1988) suggests that the sizes of legislative majorities trade off with measures of judicial independence in ways consistent with functioning of a well-ordered market for wealth transfers.

Two final points about the public choice analysis of the judiciary should be noted. The empirical evidence supporting the Landes and Posner theory is scanty at best, especially the evidence presented by the authors themselves. Other work, as cited above, has proven more supportive, but, still, the empirical evidence is weak. Moreover, when one moves to the international arena, it is clear that the separation of powers is important. Rowley (2000), for example, details differences between the U.S. and England in which this point is highlighted with respect to budgetary process. It is also apparent that the type of legal system (civil versus common law) plays an important role in economic growth and development, with common law being the growth-friendly legal system (Wessel, 2001). For international comparisons, these important points must be kept in mind.

5. The Executive

Previous work on the U.S. presidency has examined the president's formal and informal powers. Neustadt (1960) focused on the president's informal power and his ability to persuade or bargain with Congress in an institutional setting which places the two branches in conflict. The formal powers of the president (vetoes and appointments) have been examined using the structurally-induced-equilibrium (SIE) models introduced by Shepsle and Weingast (1981).

Although economists and political scientists have derived equilibrium results from the bargaining game and SIE models by including a presidential preference set, the content of this preference set has remained a black box. Since these models do not specify the policies preferred by the president, few predictions can be made about the bills the president will veto, the budget he will propose, the people he will appoint, or the regulations he will promulgate and enforce.

The few works that have advanced positive theories of presidential behavior make the essential point that the U.S. president is not a popular vote maximizer but an electoral vote maximizer. Wright (1974), in an important early paper, showed that New Deal spending in the 1930s could be explained as a function of a measure of electoral votes across states. Anderson and Tollison (1991) found this same result while controlling for measures of congressional influence. Grier et al. (1995) argued that winner-take-all voting in states and the unequal distribution of electoral votes across states in presidential elections makes incumbent presidents rationally place more weight on the preferences of voters in closely contested, larger states when making policy decisions. They tested this hypothesis by examining whether presidential veto decisions are influenced by the floor votes of senators from these electorally crucial states. In a pooled sample of 325 individual bills from 1970 through 1988, they found significant evidence of this behavior by incumbent presidents. That is, the more senators from electorally important states oppose a bill, the more likely the president is to veto it, even when controlling for a wide variety of conditioning variables, including the overall vote on the bill.

Several basic points should be kept in mind here. First, the behavior of the executive branch of government is among the least studied parts of modern public choice analysis. This literature is in its infancy. Second, more so than other areas, this literature is tied exclusively to U.S. political institutions, namely, the Electoral College system of electing presidents. Third, the literature is rife with measurement issues. Some authors use electoral votes per capita, some use raw electoral votes (a proxy for population), and some use closeness weighted electoral votes (either per capita or raw).

Nonetheless, in keeping with the central point of this essay, presidential behavior in this approach is modeled as maximizing electoral votes subject to constraints. Essentially, the president is analyzed as a careful shopper for electoral votes in his effort to be elected or reelected. States in which the incumbent president or candidate expects to win or lose by a wide margin can safely be ignored in this process. States that are predicted to be close will be the recipients of presidential largesse and visits. The constraints on this activity include time, campaign resources, congressional influences over federal pork, and so on.[9] Such a model has thus far provided a strong predictive theory of presidential behavior in a variety of areas. It also represents a core example of how simple economic theory can add to our understanding of political behavior.

The basic operation of the theory is simple. In the U.S. presidents are not elected by the popular vote but by an Electoral College. Each state has a number of electoral votes equal to its number of representatives and senators (2). A simple majority of the popular vote in a state suffices to win all its electoral votes. The winner of the majority of electoral votes (270) is elected president, a fact which raises the odd but thankfully rare prospect that a candidate could lose the overall popular vote and still be elected president (Gore v. Bush 2000).

An economic model of presidential and presidential candidate behavior maps into this situation easily. When faced with a choice among states with respect, for example, to new funding initiatives, the president will estimate the possibility that he will win the state times the number of electoral votes. States with higher expected values will receive the funding, following an equi — marginal rule of funding allocation. States that are not expected to be close (win or lose) or small states are left out in the cold in this calculation.[10] Obviously, all forms of presidential behavior and not simply funding can be analyzed with this model. The relevant constraints on the president are the obvious ones — time and money.

This approach has been successfully employed, as noted above, to explain the allocation of New Deal spending across states, presidential vetoes, campaign stops by presidential candidates (Brams and Davis, 1974; Colatoni et al., 1975), and still other aspects of presidential decision making (Anderson and Tollison, 1991). Though still in its infancy, this approach, at least for the U.S., has the potential to fill in the black box of presidential preferences and to offer a positive economic explanation of presidential behavior. It also clearly finds its roots in the basic economic methodology of maximizing expected value subject to constraints.

The chief executive outside of the U.S. setting, especially in parliamentary democracies, is coincidential with the leader of his party in the legislature. In this context parties represent coalitions of interests that are not necessarily driven by the same type of geographic imperatives as in the U.S. There is also the problem of forming coalitions in the parliament in order to fashion a governing majority. Rowley (2000) provides a clear discussion, for example, of how the office of prime minister functions in England. Again, however, these chief executives are vote-maximizers, only in a more complex and less geographically-oriented system than the U.S. And, generally, Moe and Caldwell (1994) outline the relevant public choice consequences of presidential and parliamentary systems.

6. Interest Groups

The economic analysis of an interest-group economy is relatively straightforward, and can be stated more or less in conventional demand and supply terms (McCormick and Tollison, 1981). The demand for transfers is based upon the organizational costs facing potential interest groups. Net demanders of transfers will be those groups that can organize for collective action in a cost-effective fashion. In other words, net demanders will be those groups that can organize to lobby for $1 for less than $1. Net "suppliers" are simply the inverse of the demand function for transfers, namely, those for whom it would cost more than $1 to organize to resist losing $1 in the political process. "Suppliers" is in quotation marks because individuals clearly would not engage in such a "transaction" voluntarily without being coerced by the state.

The equilibrium amount of transfers is determined by the intersection of the demand and "supply" curves, and this equilibrium is facilitated by the actions of the agents of the political process, such as elected officials. The incentives of these agents are to seek out "efficient" transfers by targeting "suppliers", who will generally be unorganized with low per-capita losses from transfers and regulation (why spend $1 to save $0.10?), and by targeting demanders who will be well organized and active in the political process. If political agents miscalculate and transfer too much or too little wealth, the political process will discipline them, for example, through elections.

There are various testable implications of this framework, which boil down to predictions about the costs and benefits of lobbying. When the benefits of lobbying are higher and the costs lower, there will be more transfers and more lobbying (and lobbyists). Cross-sectional empirical research on the American states (McCormick and Tollison, 1981; Shughart and Tollison, 1985; Crain and Tollison, 1991) and on the OECD countries (Mueller and Murrell, 1986) have illustrated many such results. For example, larger legislatures have been shown to be more costly environments in which to lobby, as well as bicameral legislatures with more disparate house and senate sizes (McCormick and Tollison, 1981).

7. Bureaucracy

Bureaucracy, in a sense, constitutes a fourth branch of government. The public choice approach to bureaucratic behavior has evolved over time, dating from Niskanen's (1971) seminal work on the subject. In *Bureaucracy and Representative Government*, Niskanen argued that because of its superior information, a bureau had greater bargaining power with regard to its budget than did the bureau's oversight committee. Thus, the economic content in this approach is that the bureau maximizes its budget subject to all-or-none demand curve for its output, and this budget tends to be about twice as large as it "ought" to be (under the assumption of linearity). Much of the subsequent work on the economic theory of bureaucracy has been in this tradition. Wintrobe (1997) offers a masterful summary of these developments.[11]

It is worth noting, however, that different bureaus may reflect differing circumstances. For example, Niskanen wrote based on his experience in the U.S. Department of Defense. He also later moved away from the budget maximizing model and allowed the possibility that bureaus may pursue the maximization of the discretionary budget, in which case excessive bureau outputs disappear (Niskanen, 1975). Nonetheless, Weingast and Moran (1985) offered an alternative to Niskaven's theory, which predicts that the oversight committee (the principal) has most of the relevant bargaining power, including the ability to remove or to hamper the career of the bureau head (the agent). They tested this theory with data concerning the Federal Trade Commission (FTC).

The issue raised in this debate is an important one. Are government bureaus out of control and bloated in size or are they merely docile agents following the commands of voters as expressed through their elected representatives on the relevant committees? The Weingast approach suggests that political incentives should be compatible as between the legislature and the bureaucrat. The legislator observes a particular political trade-off in the election. Imposing that trade-off on his bureaucratic agent is in the legislator's self-interest. That is, the bureaucrat's role is to transfer wealth or to implement legislation and policy in the direction of the legislator's preferred trade-off. In this approach bureaucracy is not out of control but is closely monitored and controlled by Congress. Bureaucrats who cannot be made to behave in accordance with the legislature's wishes are moved out of power.

The agent-principal problem is an economic problem. The principal is a residual claimant who holds an "ownership" right in the activities that his agent performs. The problem of the principal is to devise contractual and monitoring arrangements so that his interest is reflected in the labors of the agent. This stylized economic setting has stimulated a great deal of economic research and interest among economists because it obviously applies to many activities in an economy, such as the corporation, the labor union, the not-for-profit firm, and so on.

The agency problem has also had an impact on the economic theory of regulation and legislation. The issue can be put as follows. A bureau head, say a regulatory bureau head, is the agent. Members of Congress serving on an oversight committee are the principals. The members of Congress evaluate and set political trade-offs by reading their election returns. The issue is how effective are the politicians in seeing to it that the bureaus under their jurisdiction make the appropriate political trade-offs and transfers?

As suggested above, the answer, in an emerging literature pioneered by Weingast (Weingast and Moran, 1983), appears to be that bureaus are quite attuned to the preferences of their overseers. Weingast has studied the FTC and the SEC, and in both cases he found strong support for such an hypothesis. Contrary to the common impression, then, government agencies do not appear to have a lot of discretion or to be out of the control of the voters through their elected representatives. They appear to heed the electoral trade-offs perceived by their political overseers when it comes to supplying wealth transfers and public policies.

These same principles of bureaucratic behavior also apply across countries in an international context. Wintrobe (1997) makes this clear in his survey article. Nonetheless, "international organizations" *per se* may represent a particularly nettlesome case of agencies "out of control" (Frey and Gygi, 1990). The moral of such analyses is simply that the relevant controls on the behavior of international bureaucrats are much laxer than those on their domestic counterparts. Hence, their carpets are thicker, and their lunches are longer.

What is at stake here for students of regulation and government is to pierce the black box of bureaucracy and to understand its inner workings better. How does one explain the process of economic regulation and, more generally, bureaucratic performance? The agent-principal framework offers a sensible route by which to develop a better understanding of such issues. Moreover, the agent-principal framework represents modern economic theory at work in public choice analysis. Subject to the costs of monitoring bureaucratic behavior, legislators are able to influence the goals and purposes of public policies in directions that maximize their reelection prospects.

8. Voters

So far, it is clear that the major components of democratic government can be fruitfully approached using economic methods. It is tempting to stop here and rest my case. However, voters represent a basic unit of public choice analysis because voters are the ones who convey the property rights to the rational agents in the foregoing analysis that empower these actors to run the government. Unfortunately, the behavior of voters in public choice analysis has been characterized as being only loosely related to the operation of thick rationality. Fortunately, there is a fairly easy resolution of this problem.

Public choice analysts customarily discuss voting behavior in terms of the paradox of voting. That is, on straight economic grounds (a comparison of the personal costs and benefits of voting) voting is not worthwhile yet turnouts in most elections are nontrivial. Hence, voting behavior is rationalized as consumption-type rather than investment-type behavior. People vote, for example, to express their patriotic duty rather than to express their self-interest in legislation. In contrast with other parts of public choice theory in which behavior is modeled with maximizing, self-interested agents at the helm, the economic role of voters is comparatively unarticulated in the conventional version of public choice theory. In the standard approach voters maximize utility rather than narrow economic self-interest, so that their behavior in the ballot box is less predictable. Needless to say, this is a weakness of public choice theory wherein rational economic agents are assumed to gain their property rights to run the government from unpredictable voters. There are two basic routes out of this problem.

First, Stigler (1972), in particular, has questioned the consumption approach to understanding voter behavior. He argued that in politics a little more or a little less plurality matters. In this world votes will matter to politicians and parties at the margin, and they will invest rationally in a supply of votes in order to have an impact on political and legislative outcomes. In such an instance the paradox of voting is a moot issue. Interest groups will invest in a supply of votes for politicians in exchange for a higher probability of seeing a favorite bill passed. Such investments will be made on cost-benefit grounds — e.g., if it takes 1 percent more plurality to ensure the power to put a bill through, the interest group will compare the costs of turning out voters in this amount with the benefits of the legislation. In such a way voting behavior can be incorporated into the economic theory of government. In other words, the management of votes supplied by interest groups provides an alternative way to view the voting process, a way that is consistent with the general drift of the economic theory of legislation.

Second, the Stigler approach has not had much impact on the literature. Rather, an alternative argument is made. Although the investment motive is weak, this does not challenge the rational choice model. Voters are rationally ignorant after all, which opens up opportunities for interest groups. In other words, the standard concentrated benefits/diffused costs model of interest-group legislation rests on the rational ignorance and abstention of voters. Otherwise, such legislation would not be possible. In this more plausible approach to voting behavior, the rational choice model is seen to be consistent with and strongly complementary to the interest-group theory of government. Moreover, this latter theory of voter behavior applies across countries, so that there is no difficulty in generalizing this aspect of public choice analysis to an international context.

9. Conclusion

It is thus fairly easy to see how economic methodology permeates the modern theory of public choice. In each case examined above, the use of economic methods leads to a general result; that is, it leads to an organizing principle that offers an explanation for the behavior of a particular set of governmental actors. Moreover, in each case there is empirical support for the economic approach as outlined.

Obviously, I have only touched upon modern public choice analysis lightly. My examples are meant to be explanatory and illustrative and not at all comprehensive in covering modern public choice analysis. Needless to say, other scholars work in other public choice traditions, and the purpose here is not to slight these traditions. Modern public choice analysis has a unified methodology regardless of whether the analyst adheres to an interest-group approach to explaining government (as I do) or to some other approach. This methodology finds its origin and home in the maximizing paradigm of modern economics. Public choice analysis descended from economic analysis, so that when asked about the influence of economics on public choice, I find it reasonable to answer, is there any other kind?

ROBERT D. TOLLISON

NOTES

1. The reader may want to contrast this approach to that given in Cohn (1999), in which political science, specifically Riker's Rochester School of Political Science, is given the credit for the invention of public choice. While I do not quarrel that Riker and his students have been important figures in modern public choice theory, they are most surely not the only ones when one considers such names as Downs, Buchanan, Tullock, Stigler, Niskanen, and others too numerous to mention, all of whom wrote as economists.
2. See Silberberg (1995) for an excellent discussion.
3. Politics is not the only area of study that has been colonized by the economic approach. Other areas include the family, crime, religion, and law.
4. It should not go unnoted, however, that the public choice paradigm has had great acceptance in the larger sense of being a useful way to think about politics and political institutions. Political actors are generally seen today as self-interested and not disinterested agents; government is no longer treated as an exogenous, unexamined institution in economic and political models ($\bar{G}$); and public choice analyses permeate the work of modern economics and political science. Public choice is no longer an interloper; it is a paradigm.
5. Thick nationality is a term used by Green and Shapiro (1996), which means rationality in the sense of wealth maximization rather than the more general case of utility maximization.
6. See McCormick and Tollison (1978, 1981) for empirical results.
7. There are related issues here concerning the potential for extra-legal (below board) compensation to legislators, which are linked to the legislator's occupation. Lawyers, for example, are more effective at combining legislative service with making money on the side, so that there will predictably be more lawyers in low legal pay legislatures. Again, see McCormick and Tollison (1981).
8. In the limit such wealth transfers would tend toward zero.
9. Even if the candidate is a lame duck and cannot run for reelection, the party has strong incentives to control shirking so that the lame duck behaves as if he were actually running for reelection.
10. Note that closeness is more than just a previous victory margin in a state. Volatility of the vote also matters. A state with a previous victory margin of seven points and a standard deviation of 2 percent is safer that a state with a previous victory margin of 12 points and a standard deviation of 5 percent.
11. Niskanen's heavy use of conventional price theory in presenting his theory of bureaucracy should be noted here.

REFERENCES

Anderson, G.M., Shughart, W.F., and Tollison, R.D. (1989). "On the incentives of judges to enforce legislative wealth transfers." *Journal of Law and Economics*, 32: 215–228.

Anderson, G.M. and Tollison, R.D. (1991). "Congressional influence and new deal spending, 1933–1939." *Journal of Law and Economics*, 34: 161–175.

Anderson, G.M. and Tollison, R.D. (1991). "Political influence on civil war mortality rates: the Electoral College as a battlefield." *Defence Economics*, 2: 219–234.

Brams, S.J. and Davis, M.D. (1974). "The 3/2's rule in presidential campaigning." *American Political Science Review*, March, 113–134.

Cohn, J. (1999). "Irrational exhuberance." *The New Republic*, October 25, 25–31.

Colatoni, C.S., Levesque, T.J., and Ordeshook, P.C. (1975). "Campaign resource allocation under the electoral college." *American Political Science Review*, March, 141–160.

Crain, W.M., Shughart, W.F., and Tollison, R.D. (1988). "Legislative majorities as nonsalvageable assets." *Southern Economic Journal*, 55: 303–314.

Crain, W.M. and Tollison, R.D. (1979). "Constitutional change in a interest-group perspective." *Journal of Legal Studies*, 8: 165–175.

Crain, W.M. and Tollison, R.D. (1991). "The price of influence in an interest-group economy." *Rationality and Society*, 15: 437–449.

Frey, B.S. and Gygi, B. (1990). "The political economy of international organizations." *Aubenwintschaft*, 45: 371–394.

Green, D.P. and Shapiro, I. (1996). *Pathologies of Rational Choice Theory: A Critique of Applications in Political Science*. New Haven: Yale Press.

Grier, K.B., McDonald, M., and Tollison, R.D. (1995). "Electoral politics and the executive veto." *Economic Inquiry*, 33: 427–440.

Klein, B. and Leffler, K.B. (1981). "The role of market forces in assuring contractual performance." *Journal of Political Economy*, 89: 615–641.

Landes, W. and Posner, R. (1975). "The independent judiciary in an interest-group perspective." *Journal of Law and Economics*, 18: 875–901.

Marvel, H.P. (1977). "Factory regulation: a reinterpretation of early English experience." *Journal of Law and Economics*, 20: 379–402.

McCormick, R.E. and Tollison, R.D. (1978). "Legislatures as unions." *Journal of Political Economy*, 86: 63–78.

McCormick, R.F. and Tollison, R.D. (1981). *Politicians, legislation, and the economy*. Boston: Kluwer.

Moe, T.M. and Caldwell, M. (1994). "The institutional foundations of democratic government: a comparison of presidential and parliamentary systems." *Journal of Institutional and Theoretical Economics*, 150: 171–195.

Mueller, D.C. and Murrell, P. (1986). "Interest groups and the size of government." *Public Choice*, 48: 125–145.

Neustadt, R.E. (1960). *Presidential Power*. New York: Wiley.

Niskanen, W.A. (1971). *Bureaucracy and Representative Government*. Chicago: Aldine Atherton.

Niskanen, W.A. (1975). "Bureaucrats and politicians." *Journal of Law and Economics*, 18: 617–644.

Posner, R.A. (1986). *Economic Analysis of the Law*. Boston: Little, Brown.

Riker, W.H. (1962). *The Theory of Political Coalitions*. New Haven: Yale Press.

Rowley, C.K. (2000). "Budget deficits and the size of government in the U.K. and the U.S.: a public choice perspective on the Thatcher and Reagan years," in K.C. Chrystal and R. Pennant-Rea (eds.) *Public Choice Analysis of Economic Policy*. London: St. Martin.

Shepsle, K.A. and Weingast, B.R. (1981). "Structure-induced equilibrium and legislative choice." *Public Choice*, 37(3): 503–519.

Shughart, W.F. and Tollison, R.D. (1985). "Corporate chartering: an exploration in the economics of legal charge." *Economic Inquiry*, 23: 585–599.

Silberberg, E. (1975). *Principles of Microeconomics*. Englewood Cliffs: Prentice Hall.

Stigler, G.J. (1972). "Economic competition and political competition." *Public Choice*, 13(Fall): 91–106.

Stigler, G.J. (1976). "The sizes of legislatures." *Journal of Legal Studies*, V: 1–16.

Straayer, J.A. (1973). *American State and Local Government*. Columbus, OH: Merrill.

Thaler, R.H. (1992). *The Winners Curse: Paradoxes and Anolomies of Economic Life*. New York: Macmillan.

Weck-Hanneman, H. (1990). "Protectionism in direct democracy." *Journal of Institutional and Theoretical Economics*, 146: 389–418.

Weingast, B.R. and Moran, M.J. (1983). "Bureaucratic discretion or congressional control?" *Journal of Political Economy*, 91: 765–800.

Wessel, D. (2001). "The legal dna of good economies." *Wall Street Journal*, September 6, 1.

Wintrobe, R. (1997). "Modern bureaucratic theory," in D.C. Mueller (ed.) *Perspectives on Public Choice: A Handbook*. Cambridge: Cambridge Press, pp. 429–454.

Wright, G. (1974). "The political economy of new deal spending: an econometric analysis." *Review of Economics and Statistics*, 56: 30–38.

PUBLIC CHOICE FROM THE PERSPECTIVE OF THE HISTORY OF THOUGHT

1. Introduction

Public choice is a relatively new discipline located at the interface between economics and political science. Its modern founding was the achievement of Duncan Black whose 1948 (a–c) articles are widely viewed as the seminal contributions that launched scholarship in the application of economic analysis into the traditional domain of political science. Yet its true founding goes back almost two centuries in time, to the late eighteenth century contributions of two French *Encyclopedistes*, the Compte de Borda and the Marquis de Condorcet. The two French noblemen shared a conviction that social sciences were amenable to mathematical rigor, and made significant contributions to the theory of voting. These contributions form the foundations on which much of modern public choice has been crafted.

In his pioneering work on elections, Condorcet (1785) sought to 'inquire by mere reasoning, what degree of confidence the judgement of assemblies deserves' (1785, iv). In modern jargon he posed what is now known as the jury problem or the vote problem. The starting point, well-known to the *Encyclopedistes*, is that majority voting is unambiguously the best voting rule when only two candidates are on stage. How might this rule be extended to three or more candidates? The naive but widely held answer is plurality voting, where each voter casts a vote for one candidate and the candidate with most votes is elected.

Condorcet raised doubts as to the general acceptability of the plurality vote rule. Suppose that 60 voters have opinions about three candidates A, B and C as shown in Table 1.

In the illustration, candidate A wins by plurality. Yet, if A is opposed only by B he loses (25 to 35) and if A is opposed only by C he loses again (23 to 37). Thus the plurality rule does not convey accurately the opinion of the majority.

Using identical premises, in 1781 Borda had initiated the discussion of voting rules by questioning the effectiveness of the simple majority vote rule and by proposing the method of marks as a more appropriate rule. In this method, each candidate receives 2 points from a voter who places him first, 1 point from a voter who places him second and 0 points from a voter who places him third. Hence, C is elected with a score of 78 points. Condorcet, however, in following up on the insight of Borda, sought a different solution.

Condorcet posited a simple binomial model of voter error. In every binary comparison, each voter has a probability $1/2 < p < 1$ of ordering the candidates correctly. Thus the relevant data is contained in the 'majority tournament'

that results from taking all pairwise votes: B beats A 35 to 25; C beats A 37 to 23; C beats B 41 to 19. Condorcet proposed that candidates should be ranked according to 'the most probable combination of opinions' (1785, 125). In modern terminology, this is a maximum likelihood criterion.

In the above example, the most probable combination is given by the ranking CBA, since this agrees with the greatest total number of votes. Condorcet's ranking criterion implies that an alternative that obtains a majority over every other alternative must be ranked first. Such an alternative, if one exists, is now known as a 'Condorcet winner'. However, as Condorcet established, some configurations of opinions may not possess such a winner because the majority tournament contains a cycle. Such an occurrence is now known as Condorcet's paradox and is illustrated in Table 2.

In this illustration, A beats B, 33 to 27; B beats C, 42 to 18; C beats A, 35 to 25. In such circumstances, pairwise voting results in intransitivity. According to Condorcet's maximum likelihood criterion, the cycle should be broken at its weakest point, namely A over B, which yields the ranking of B over C over A. Therefore, in this case, B would be declared the winner.

Condorcet's *Essai* contains other useful, insights that now play an important role in public choice. Perhaps the most important is the issue of strategic manipulation, which is hinted at in several places, although it is never systematically explored (Moulin and Young, 1987). For example, on page clxxix of the *Discours Preliminaire*, Condorcet criticizes Borda's method of marks as being vulnerable to a *cabale*. When confronted with this criticism, Borda was merely moved to comment: 'My scheme is only intended for honorable men' (Rowley, 1987). It has since been established by modern game theory that any configuration of individual opinions that guarantees the existence of a Condorcet winner also defines a strategy proof voting rule. This remains an important argument in favor of Condorcet consistent rules designed to elect the Condorcet winner whenever it exists (Moulin, 1983).

Because the publications by Condorcet and Borda were not widely circulated in the late eighteenth century, because they were somewhat densely written and because they were written in French, their ideas disappeared for some 150 years

Table 1

	23	19	16	2
Top	A	B	C	C
	C	C	B	A
Bottom	B	A	A	B

Table 2

23	17	2	10	8
A	B	B	C	C
B	C	A	A	B
C	A	C	B	A

until they were rediscovered and proselytized by Duncan Black in 1958. Since then, the ideas have strongly influenced public choice theorists and have played a central role in many of the discipline's recent developments.

2. The Insights of Duncan Black

Ideas that are lost do not constitute any part of the litany of science. Duncan Black essentially rediscovered ideas that had been advanced earlier by the two 18th century French noblemen only to be lost, then to be rediscovered late in the nineteenth century (1884) by Charles Dodgson (Lewis Carroll), then to be lost again. Since Black's discovery has not been lost, he must be viewed as the true founder of public choice (Rowley, 1991). The work of Borda, Condorcet, and Dodgson is known today only because Black researched their writings and made them available to his own generation of scholars (Grofman, 1987).

Duncan Black's vision as a young economist was that of developing a pure science of politics that would place political science on the same kind of theoretical footing as economics. All of his work was underpinned by the deceptively simple insight of modeling political phenomena 'in terms of the preferences of a given set of individuals in relation to a given set of motions, the same motions appearing on the preference schedule of each individual' (Black, 1972, 3).

In this search, Black rediscovered Condorcet's paradox of cyclical majorities (Black, 1948a, 32–33) and thereby opened up an extremely fruitful avenue of public choice research. It is important to acknowledge Black's achievement because recognition for the rediscovery of the Condorcet paradox is frequently and incorrectly given to Kenneth Arrow. Black (1948a,b,c) raised a number of important questions and offered some preliminary answers related to this paradox (Grofman, 1981). A first question asks whether the paradox is inevitable; a second asks how frequently the paradox can be expected to occur; a third asks how easy it is to detect a paradox from the available evidence on majority rule outcomes; and a fourth asks how large will a cycle be.

Black's answer to the first question was that the paradox is not inevitable. Embedded in this answer is the famous median voter theorem that will be outlined and evaluated later in this section. In answering the second question, Black focused attention on the special case of three voters and three alternatives for what is now known as the 'impartial culture' i.e., a committee in which all strong preference orderings are equally likely.

Black recognized the wider significance of this question. He suggested that the likelihood of the paradox of cyclical majorities occurring would increase rapidly as the number of motions under consideration and the number of committee members increased (Black, 1958, 51). In this judgment he has been proved correct by subsequent analysis (Grofman, 1981, 15).

In answering the third question, how easy is it to detect a paradox, Black provided two useful results. The first result is that under standard amendment procedures, given sincere voting, a voting paradox will always be revealed if there are as many rounds of voting as there are alternatives less one. The second result is the theorem that the voting paradox is always revealed if data is available on all paired comparisons. This is a powerful result since Black also shows that if a majority winner exists no voter has an incentive to vote insincerely in such a complete balloting.

The fourth question, querying how many alternatives are likely to be located in a *top cycle*, was not directly addressed by Black. However, he did provide a number of insights on interrelationships between cycles. For example, he noted that if two intersecting cycles have one motion in common, it must be possible to form a cycle that includes all the motions of both cycles (Black, 1958, 48). He also examined the case of three nonintersecting cycles (where every motion in the first defeats every motion in the second, and where every motion in the second defeats every motion in the third). He demonstrated, in such circumstances, that every motion in the third may still defeat every motion in the first (Black, 1958, 50). As subsequent analysis has confirmed, winning cycles are likely to include all alternatives (McKelvey, 1976).

Black's answer to the first question, concerning the inevitability of the paradox of the voting cycle, has been left to the end because it is his most important legacy to public choice. His insight came in February 1942, while 'fire-watching' in case of air raids, late at night in the magnificent green drawing room of Warwick Castle (Black, 1972, 4). While playing with diagrams that represented motions as points on a line and with preferences represented as single-peaked utility functions, Black saw 'in a shock of recognition' (*ibid.*) the property of the median optimum, or what we now refer to as the median voter theorem.

The idea of single-peakedness can be defined in a number of different ways. Black provided a graphical interpretation that is illustrated in Figure 1. A set of preference schedules is said to be single-peaked if there occurs an ordering of the alternative motions such that the preference schedules of all committee members can be graphed as single-peaked curves (i.e., as curves that change direction at most once, up or down).

Where this condition holds, Black established that a unique alternative exists capable of attracting a simple

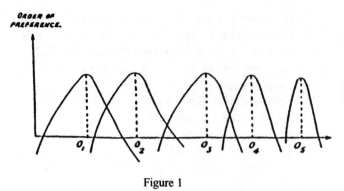

Figure 1

majority in pairwise competition against all other alternatives. This majority winner is the most preferred alternative of the median voter. Hence, for single-peaked preferences, Black established that there is a stable majority choice at the median of the voter distribution. Furthermore, under this condition, majority rule gives rise to a transitive ordering of alternatives.

In Figure 1, the median outcome is at point O_3 in policy issue space. It is important to note that Black's theorem is restricted to the case (illustrated in Figure 1) where policy issue space is defined in terms of a single dimension. As we now know (Black, 1958), where the median voter theorem holds, majority rule always selects a Condorcet winner.

3. The Insight of Kenneth J. Arrow

Although Duncan Black's 1948 article is best known for its derivation of the median voter theorem, Black was clearly aware of the potential for cycling, should the condition of single-peaked preferences fail to hold. In 1949, Black and Newing attempted to define the necessary conditions for the existence of a stable voting equilibrium in multidimensional space, focusing on the three-person case. In this contribution they clearly anticipated the contributions of Kenneth Arrow. Their paper was submitted to *Econometrica* in November 1949. The referee, Kenneth Arrow, reported favorably on the paper.

In a stroke of misfortune, *Econometrica* delayed by some 18 months in reaching a decision on the paper. When it did so, the Managing Editor, Ragnar Frisch, informed the authors that he would recommend the article for publication 'if the interrelationships with Arrow's recent monograph could be brought out clearly throughout the paper' (Coase, 1981). Arrow's 1950 article and his 1951 monograph apparently had pre-empted the Black and Newing article as a consequence of inexcusable editorial delay. Black and Newing withdrew the article from *Econometrica* and published it in 1951 in a little read booklet. By such chance events are Nobel Prizes sometimes won and lost (Rowley, 1991).

In any event, Arrow's 1951 book has exerted a significant impact on the evolution of public choice, even though its primary concern was normative rather than positive in nature, focusing as it did on the desirable characteristics of alternative mechanisms of social choice. This impact stems from Arrow's rediscovery of Condorcet's paradox of cyclical fluctuations.

Arrow (1950, 1951) responded to the apparent collapse during the 1930s of Benthamite utilitarianism as economists systematically retreated from the notion that utility is measurable on a cardinal scale and comparable across individuals. If the weak Pareto principle is all that remains of the once mighty utilitarian doctrine, what are the normative implications for the available mechanisms of effecting social choices? In his famous impossibility theorem, Arrow proved that any social welfare function involving at least three individuals choosing over at least three alternatives must violate at least one of six reasonable axioms of social choice, namely rationality, unbounded domain, the Pareto principle, non-dictatorship, non-imposition and independence of irrelevant alternatives.

Most important, from the perspective of public choice, was Arrow's proof that a social welfare function based on majority rule has the unsatisfactory property of being intransitive when at least three individuals vote over at least three alternatives, even when the preferences of each person are strictly transitive. Arrow did not infer that majority rule would always produce cycles in such circumstances. Given an unbounded domain, it sufficed for him to demonstrate that certain configurations of individual preferences would result in the Condorcet paradox.

Although this insight is not original to Arrow, nevertheless, it is he who has gained recognition for it. Undoubtedly, Arrow's emphasis on the instability of majority rule contrasts sharply with Black's emphasis on the stability of the median voter outcome. Since these two impulses still course strongly through much of public choice analyses of the vote motive, it is convenient, if not strictly accurate, to distinguish them by reference to the two scholars.

4. The Insight of Anthony Downs

Both Black and Arrow analyzed the majority vote mechanism in abstract terms, deliberately seeking generality at the cost of sacrificing institutional detail. Although their contributions, especially those of Arrow, sparked an almost obsessive interest among students of social choice, perhaps because of their abstractness, they failed to make much initial inroad into political economy and political science.

In 1957, Anthony Downs filled this institutional vacuum with a book entitled *An Economic Theory of Democracy* that would become a fulcrum for public choice analysis. Downs was a student of Kenneth Arrow whose work on social choice theory clearly motivated his contribution. Surprisingly, Downs displayed no knowledge of Black's contributions despite Arrow's evident acquaintance with them. Ironically, despite the fact that most public choice scholars identify Downs with the median voter theorem, the theorem is referred to nowhere in the book.

Rather Downs adapted the spatial economic model of Harold Hotelling (1929) to demonstrate that competition between two political parties under conditions of parliamentary democracy often results in both parties converging in policy issue space to adopt identical platforms that reflect the preferences of a majority of the electorate. Since Downs depicted normally distributed voter preference distributions, there is no means in his analysis of distinguishing between the mean, the median and the mode as the relevant point of party convergence.

The real contribution of Downs was not the median voter theorem (unequivocally the insight of Black) but rather the introduction of the rational choice approach to the study of political science. Pitting himself against the well-entrenched tradition of behavioral analysis among political scientists, Downs laid the foundations for a major research program that would apply rational choice theory to every aspect of the political market place.

By rational action, Downs meant action that is efficiently designed to achieve the consciously selected political and/or economic ends of every actor in the political market place. From this perspective he developed an economic theory of democracy designed to understand and to predict political behavior within an environment of two-party representative democracy.

From the self-interest axiom sprang Down's view of what motivates the political actions of party members. They act 'solely in order to attain the income, prestige, and power which comes from being in office' (Downs, 1957, 28). Politicians, in this model, never seek office as a means of promoting particular policies. Their only goal is to reap the rewards of holding office. The fundamental hypothesis of Down's model is that 'parties formulate policies in order to win elections, rather than win elections to formulate policies' (Downs, 1957, 28). Thus, the application of the self-interest axiom leads Downs to the hypothesis of vote-maximizing government.

Downs also applied the self-interest axiom to voter behavior, hypothesizing that each citizen casts his vote for the party that he expects to provide him with the most benefits. As Downs recognized, the concept of rational voting is deceptively complex, ambiguous and, hence, deserving of close scrutiny. The benefits that voters consider in making their decisions are streams of utility (referred to as utility income) derived from government activity.

Not all utility income is relevant to the vote decision, since utility income includes benefits that the recipient does not realize that he will receive and also benefits that he is aware of without knowing their exact source. However, only benefits of which rational voters are conscious at the time of the election can influence their voting decisions.

The unit of time over which voters evaluate utility income flows is the election period, defined as the time elapsing between elections. At least two such election periods enter into the calculus of the rational voter, namely, the period ending at the time of the election and the period following that election. Both periods are relevant to his determination of the expected party differential in utility income, the measure that will determine which party will secure his vote.

In placing his vote, the voter is helping to select the government that will govern him during the coming election period. His rational decision must reflect the expected future performances of the competing parties. Yet, he knows that political parties are neither obligated to honor nor always capable of carrying out their platform commitments.

In such circumstances, the most recent election period experience of the party in power is the best possible guide to its future behavior, assuming that its policies have some continuity. This performance must be weighed against the performance the opposition would have produced had it been in power. Downs asserted that it is rational for the voter to ground his voting decision primarily on current events, while applying two future-orienting modifiers to his current party differential.

The first modifier is the trend factor, an adjustment made by each citizen to his current party differential to account for relevant trends in the behavior of the government during the current election period. The second modifier is the tie breaker adjustment utilized only when the voter cannot distinguish between the parties. In such circumstances, voters cast their votes by comparing the performance of the incumbent government with that of its immediate predecessor. Voters who still cannot distinguish between the competing parties rationally abstain from voting.

Because Downs was not aware of the median voter theorem, his discussion of the basic logic of government decision-making was less precise than it might have been.

In general, he suggested that vote-maximizing incumbents will follow the majority principle, subjecting each decision to a hypothetical poll and always choosing the alternative that the majority of voters prefer. He recognized that such a strategy would not guarantee victory in every election.

The opposition party might defeat a majority-pleasing government by adopting one of three possible strategies. The first such strategy is adoption of a program identical in every detail with that of the incumbent. Such a strategy forces the electorate to decide their vote by comparing the performance of the incumbent with those of previous governments. Only rarely would such a strategy be effective.

The second such strategy is that of opposing the incumbent by supporting minority positions on carefully selected issues, building a coalition of minorities into a majority vote for the next election. Such a strategy can succeed only where the preferences of those in the minority are more intensely held than the preferences of those in the majority, i.e., where consensus is weak. In the case of passionate majorities, a sufficiently large coalition of minorities will not emerge.

The third such strategy is available to an opposition once again only when there is a lack of consensus in the electorate. In this case, the lack of consensus takes the form of the Condorcet paradox of cyclical majorities. In such circumstances, any alternative that the government chooses can be defeated in a paired election by some other alternative. As long as the government must choose first, and must remain committed to this choice, a prescient opposition can always defeat it.

Downs correctly recognized that his model appears to disintegrate at this point because of the false assumption of certainty. In reality, political parties do not fully know what voters prefer and voters do not fully know the consequences of government acts. If uncertainty is introduced into the model, the incumbents are saved from almost inevitable defeat at each succeeding election, but appear also to be freed from the grip of the majority principle. Therefore, Downs devoted a major part of his book to the effects of uncertainty on the behavior of political markets.

According to Downs, uncertainty divides voters into groups endowed with varying degrees of confidence in their voting decisions. Those who feel least well-informed are vulnerable to persuasion by voters who are well-informed and who provide correct but biased information favorable to their own causes. Interest groups that want government to adopt policies favorable to their causes pose as representatives of the popular will, simultaneously creating public opinion supportive of their views and convincing government that such public opinion exists. Political parties, once they have formed their policies, endeavor to extend electoral support for those policies.

Uncertainty thus forces rational governments to regard some voters as more important than others. By so doing, it modifies the equality of influence that universal suffrage was designed to ensure.

Uncertainty limits the ability of the voter to relate every act of the government to his own view of good policy. The rational voter in such circumstances may lower his information costs by identifying party ideologies as a substitute for detailed policy platforms. Each political party in turn will develop an ideology consistent with its policy actions as a short cut to gaining votes. According to Downs, all parties are forced by competition to be relatively honest and responsible in regard both to policies and ideologies.

From this economic perspective, Downs utilized the theory of spatial competition invented by Harold Hotelling (1929), as refined by Arthur Smithies (1941), to elaborate a theory of political party competition under conditions of representative democracy. His version of Hotelling's spatial market consisted of a linear scale running from zero to 100 in the usual left-right fashion. He assumed that all voters would agree on the ordering of both parties across this single dimensional left-right space, essentially by reference to the projected ideologies of the parties.

Downs further assumed that every voter's preferences are single-peaked over this left-right issue space implying that each voter always prefers a position closer to his ideal point over one that is further away and that he always votes for the political party that is closer to his ideal point. If these conditions hold, and if all voters always vote, the two parties will converge to the center of the voter preference distribution in order to maximize their respective votes. Figure 2 illustrates this outcome with both parties converging at point 50 in left-right space.

However, if voters located at the two extremes of left-right space become alienated as the political parties move towards the center their threats to abstain may halt this process of convergence well short of the center of the distribution. In such circumstances the ideologies of the two parties may differ sharply and political consensus may

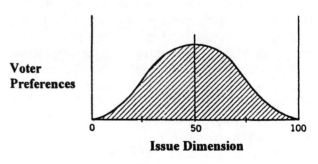

Figure 2

not emerge. Figure 3 illustrates this outcome with the two parties ending up located respectively at points 25 and 75 in issue dimension space.

If the condition of single-peaked preferences does not hold, and the distribution of voters across left-right issue space is bimodal, with modes located near each extreme, parties will locate themselves in proximity with their respective modes. The victorious party will implement policies radically opposed by the opposition. In such circumstances, Downs predicted that government policy will be unstable and that democracy may induce chaos, leading perhaps to its replacement by some form of autocracy. Figure 4 illustrates such an outcome with the two parties located respectively at points A and B across left-right space.

In the view of Downs, multi-party systems are likely to occur whenever the distribution of voters over issue space is multi-peaked or polymodal. In such circumstances, the Hotelling model (1929) is likely to hold with political parties maneuvering in left-right space until the distance between each party and its immediately adjacent neighbors is the same for all parties. Figure 5 illustrates this outcome with the four competing parties located respectively at points A, B, C and D in issue space.

Downs focused particular attention on the causes and effects of rational voter abstention, recognizing that many citizens who are eligible to vote in democratic elections fail

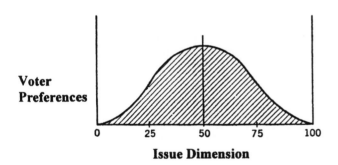

Figure 3

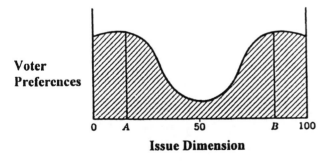

Figure 4

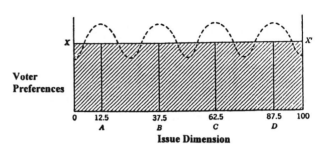

Figure 5

to do so. Downs assumed that a citizen's reward for voting is the value of his vote, i.e., his party differential discounted to allow for the influence of other voters upon the election's outcome. On this basis, he demonstrated that when voting is without cost every citizen who prefers one party over the other votes and every citizen who is indifferent between the parties abstains.

In reality, voting is always costly, because every act takes time. The cost of voting may outweigh the returns, even for citizens who prefer one party to the other. Indeed, because the expected return to voting is often miniscule, even low voting costs may result in rational abstentions for citizens who view voting in elections solely from an instrumental perspective.

The importance of rational abstentions depends on its impact on political power. This impact in turn stems from two potential biases. The first potential impact arises from the distribution of the ability to bear the costs of voting. If the cost of voting consists primarily of poll taxes, loss of earnings and transportation costs, upper income citizens obtain a political advantage since the ability to bear such costs typically varies inversely with income. If the cost of voting primarily is the loss of leisure, no income-correlated disparity exists.

The second potential impact arises from biases in the distribution of high returns. The total return each citizen receives from voting depends on (1) the benefits he obtains from democracy, (2) how much he wants a particular party to win, (3) how close he thinks the election will be and (4) how many other citizens he thinks will vote. Since the expected return predictably is higher for the high-income than for the low-income citizen, the former has a greater incentive to become politically informed. He also has a greater incentive to vote on the basis of expected benefits.

5. The Insight of James M. Buchanan and Gordon Tullock

After a gap of five years, there followed the most far-reaching and the only philosophical founding contribution, namely *The Calculus of Consent* by James M. Buchanan and Gordon Tullock (1962). Neither author was trained formally in philosophy or in political science. Yet, this book explicitly moved the analysis to the interface between economics, philosophy and political science, applying the tools of economics and economic philosophy to a detailed and far-ranging evaluation of political institutions in an attempt to delineate the logical foundations of constitutional democracy.

Buchanan and Tullock rejected the emphasis placed by Downs on the group behavior of political parties in favor of a model of collective decision-making that is more closely analogous to the theory of private choice. Collective action is viewed as the action of individuals when they choose to accomplish goals collectively rather than individually. Government is viewed as a set of processes that allows collective action to take place. From this perspective of methodological individualism, the rule of unanimity is advanced as a weak ethical criterion for the 'good' in evaluating both new constitutions and initiatives for constitutional change.

Buchanan and Tullock embedded their analysis firmly within the framework of rational choice, acknowledging albeit that *homo economicus* may not always be as narrowly self-seeking as neoclassical economics frequently assumes. They further acknowledged that in the effecting of collective choices, the individual has no way of knowing the final outcome at the time that he makes his own contribution. For this reason, individuals lose that full sense of personal responsibility inherent in the making of private choices.

The rational self-seeking individual will contemplate collective action only when such action increases his expected utility. In an environment devoid of any kind of Pareto-relevant externality, the state would have no utilitarian support. Buchanan and Tullock therefore rationalized the existence of collective action as a means for individuals to combine in order to reduce the burden of external costs imposed upon them by purely private or voluntary actions. In contemplating such collective action, the rational individual is concerned to minimize his relevant expected costs, defined as the sum of his expected residual external costs and of his expected costs of decision-making within a collective framework.

In deciding whether any particular activity belongs within the realm of collective rather than private choice, the rational individual must take account of the expected cost of voluntary cooperative arrangements. If such costs are zero, all Pareto-relevant externalities would be eliminated by voluntary private behavior (here we note an early application of the 1960 Coase theorem).

If the environment is one of positive transaction costs, however, the choice between non-cooperative private behavior, cooperative private behavior and collective political action must rest on the relative expected costs of these alternatives. The existence of Pareto-relevant external effects of private behavior is neither a necessary nor a sufficient condition for an individual to entrust that activity to the realm of collective choice. In this regard, Buchanan and Tullock, *for the first time in formal economic analysis*, called specific attention to the fact that the collective organization of activities must also impose expected external costs upon the individual unless the collectivity itself is constrained to make decisions through a rule of unanimity.

Thus, the expected costs that collective choices impose on the individual depend on decision-making rules that govern such choices. In such circumstances, the individual will compare the expected costs of private choice with the expected costs of the most efficient form of collective action when making his decision whether or not to submit to collective action.

Buchanan and Tullock designed a generalized economic theory of constitutions specifically to analyze the problem of individual choice among alternative collective decision-making rules. This economic theory, now widely recognized as the most important and enduring insight of *The Calculus of Consent*, is outlined in Figures 6–9.

Figure 6 outlines the nature of the relationship between the present value of an individual's expected external costs and the number of individuals required to take collection action. Buchanan and Tullock suggested that the curve **CN** will slope downwards throughout its range, reaching zero

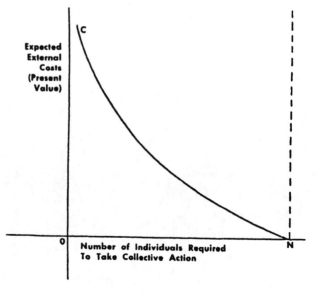

Figure 6

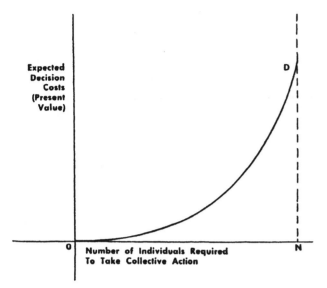

Figure 7

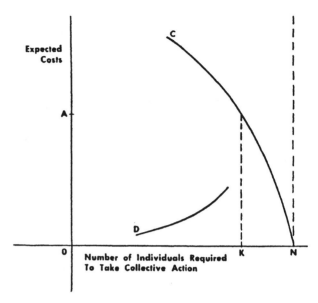

Figure 9

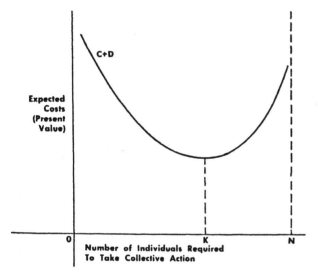

Figure 8

only where the rule of unanimity is in place. The point **C** on this curve represents the (high) external costs that the individual expects will be imposed on him if *any* single individual in the group is authorized to undertake action for the collectivity. Note that **C** represents a randomly selected and not a uniquely designated individual, since the latter situation would be one of dictatorship.

As the decision rule becomes more and more inclusive, the individual's expected external costs of collective action decline, since there will be fewer decisions that the individual expects to run counter to his own desires. Only with the rule of unanimity will such costs be zero. For reasons outlined in Figure 7, the rational individual will rarely choose unanimity as his most preferred rule when collective action is chosen over both private action and voluntary cooperation.

Figure 7 outlines the relationship between the present value of an individual's expected decision-making costs and the number of individuals required to take collective action. Buchanan and Tullock suggested that the curve **OD** will slope upwards throughout its range, reaching its highest point at **D** when the rule of unanimity is in place. At this point, the costs of strategic bargaining are so high as to render any form of agreement almost impossible.

Figure 8 sums the expected external costs and the expected decision-making costs functions vertically to create a curve that relates expected costs to the number of individuals required to take collective action. The rational individual will seek to minimize the expected costs of collective action by choosing the rule that requires **K/N** of the group to agree in order to act collectively. If the expected cost of private action or of voluntary cooperation is less than **OB** in Figure 8 the rational individual will not endorse collective action.

As Buchanan and Tullock emphasized, the calculus of individual consent does not require that all potential collective action should be organized through the operation of the same decision-making rule. In their view, two categories of potential collective action can be separated even at this conceptual stage. In the first category are located those potential collective actions that are characteristically undertaken by government. Figure 8 effectively depicts the calculus of individual consent for this category.

In the second category are located those potential collective actions that modify the structure of established individual rights and property rights. The rational individual will foresee that collective action in this area potentially may inflict him with very severe costs. Figure 9 illustrates that the rational individual at best will require a much more inclusive rule as the basis for consenting to this category of collective actions. In the limit, the calculus of individual consent will break down entirely, and the individual will decline to enter into political society but will choose instead to protect this category of rights by private actions and/or by voluntary cooperation.

In Figure 9, the expected external costs curve remains relatively high throughout the range of collective action rules short of unanimity. In such circumstances, the expected decision-making costs curve scarcely becomes a factor. In Figure 9, for example, where the expected costs of private organization are depicted as **OA**, the expected external costs of collective action exceed the expected costs of private organization for all rules less inclusive than that shown by **K/N**. Given that expected decision-making costs rise exponentially in this latter range, the prospects for an individual agreeing to collective action under any rule short of unanimity are small.

Throughout this analysis, Buchanan and Tullock centered attention on the calculus of a single individual as he confronts the constitutional choice concerning rules of decision-making. What we should now perceive as a weakness in their book is the limited attention that Buchanan and Tullock devoted to dealing with the way in which individuals reach agreement concerning the rules that must govern various forms of collective action. Since individuals are aware of their own relative positions in society, at the moment of constitutional choice, they are also aware that decision-making rules short of unanimity may impose different expected external costs upon them.

For the most part, Buchanan and Tullock evaded this issue, commenting that '[W]e prefer to put this issue aside and to assume, without elaboration, that at this ultimate stage, which we shall call the constitutional, the rule of unanimity holds' (Buchanan and Tullock, 1962, 77). In fact, they did not completely put the issue aside. They relied upon the extended time horizon of the individual in making his constitutional choices to explain his greater willingness to consent to rules that potentially are harmful to his shorter-term interests.

Constitutional rules, by their nature, are expected to be long-lived, since constitutional change is usually subject to highly inclusive rules of decision-making. The rational individual, confronted with constitutional choice, is inevitably uncertain of his particular interest at some unspecified future time. In such circumstances, he will selfishly tend to choose rules of collective decision-making that maximize the utility of some random individual. Such far-sightedness in constitutional decision-making differs sharply from the more myopic, sectional-based approach of the individual in the ordinary business of politics.

Buchanan and Tullock recognized that uncertainty alone would not necessarily guarantee unanimity in the prior judgment of individuals as to the rules of collective decision-making that would minimize costs. Nevertheless, they argued that any initial conflicts of opinion over rules should be amenable to reasoned compromise.

Buchanan and Tullock likened the resolution of such conflicts to the discussion that might take place between potential participants as to the appropriate rules under which a game shall be played. Since no player can anticipate which specific rules might benefit him during a particular play of the game, he will not find it difficult to concur with others in devising a set of rules that will constitute the most interesting game for the average or representative player.

Buchanan and Tullock recognized that the process of constitutional decision-making set out in their book has little relevance for any society that is deeply divided by reference to social class, race, religion, or ethnicity. Unanimity over a collective decision-making rule is especially unlikely when one of these coalitions is perceived to hold an especially advantageous position. Needless to say, this implies that *The Calculus of Consent* could not have been written in its existing form with relevance for the United States, the constitutional democracy explicitly central to their analysis, had the co-authors joined forces in the late 1960s rather than in the late 1950s.

In any event, the analysis of Buchanan and Tullock provided a number of important insights into constitutional political economy. First, it is rational to have a constitution, in the sense that there is more than one rule for collective decision-making. Second, there is no necessary justification for majority rule as the basis for collective decision-making. At best, majority rule should be viewed as one among many practical expedients made necessary by the costs of securing widespread agreement on political issues when individual interests diverge.

Third, it is rational to have a constitution that requires a more inclusive rule of collective decision-making with respect to incursion on individual rights and property rights than with respect to less fundamental issues. Fourth, the more inclusive the decision-making rule, the more willing will individuals be to the entrustment of decision-making to collective choice. The range of collective decision-making, thus, is not independent of the rules that govern such activities in societies that respect the primacy of individual choice.

Finally, the analysis of Buchanan and Tullock suggests that the over-all costs of collective decision-making are lower, with respect to any constitutional rule, in communities characterized by a more than by a less homogeneous population. From this perspective alone, a more homogeneous community would adopt a more inclusive rule for collective choice. However, the homogeneity characteristic affects expected external costs as well as expected decision-making costs. On balance, Buchanan and Tullock, predict that the more homogeneous the community, the less inclusive will be the rules of collective choice and the more extensive will be the range of actions encompassed within the collective sphere.

Buchanan and Tullock deployed the rational choice model to offer a number of important insights into the logic of constitutional design. A comprehensive review of these applications is beyond the scope of this essay. However, their evaluation of the rule of simple majority voting is illustrative of the general approach.

Buchanan and Tullock grounded their discussion of the simply majority vote rule on the generalized assumption that individuals vary in the intensity of their preferences for or against specific collective actions. In such circumstances, the rule of simple majority, applied to a single issue of collective choice, may provide minor gains in utility for a majority at the cost of imposing major losses in utility upon a minority (abstracting from the issue of the problem of measuring utility across individuals). Rational individuals will recognize this danger when engaging in constitutional decision-making and will protect themselves from its most serious consequences by providing institutional opportunities for logrolling (or the trading of votes).

An institutional environment in which logrolling cannot occur is the standard referendum on a single issue determined by a simple majority vote conducted by secret ballot. The rational individual, concerned about the potential tyranny of the majority, will therefore be extremely wary about endorsing decision-making by referenda as the basis for determining collective choices.

Buchanan and Tullock noted that logrolling opportunities are prevalent in many of the political institutions of the Western democracies. Explicit logrolling is a common feature of all representative assemblies where exchanges of votes are easy to arrange and to observe. Such exchanges of votes significantly affect the political process. Implicit logrolling dominates the electoral process since the leaders of the political parties formulate complex mixtures of policies into electoral platforms designed to attract voters support by appealing to intensely held preferences.

Buchanan and Tullock suggested that both explicit and implicit logrolling tend to improve the efficiency of the political process, even though these practices are widely criticized on ethical grounds. They demonstrated, however, that even when logrolling is possible, simple majority rule is likely to produce undesirable collective decisions, for example by over-investing in the public sector. Indeed, they further demonstrated that a system in which the open buying and selling of political votes is encouraged tends to improve the efficiency of simple majority rule as evaluated in terms of the Pareto criterion.

Recognition of the fact that preference intensities over policy alternatives differ among the electorate may encourage the rational individual to favor the bicameral over the unicameral legislature as a basis for constitutional design. A properly designed bicameral legislature, offering different bases of representation, will discriminate automatically between legislation potentially affecting intense minorities and legislation on which the intensity of desires is more or less equal. This will significantly improve the efficiency of the political process.

A further improvement in political market efficiency occurs when the constitution provides a president with veto power, effectively establishing a third house of the legislature. This third house represents the entire body of voters in one grand constituency, raising the minimum size of the logrolling coalitions and further protecting the individual voter from the excesses of rule of simple majority voting.

In this manner, Buchanan and Tullock outlined the sort of calculus that the individual must undergo when he considers the question: can the pursuit of individual self-interest be turned to good account in politics as well as in economics? They were able to show that, even under the behavioral assumption of extreme self-interest, something akin to the constitutional democracy conceived of by the American Founding Fathers would tend to emerge from the rational individual calculus. They concluded their epic on an extremely optimistic note, a note perhaps that some forty years on they would no longer feel able to hold:

> With the philosophers of the Enlightenment we share the faith that man can rationally organize his own society, that existing organization can always be perfected, and that nothing in the social order should remain exempt from rational, critical, and intelligent discussion. Man's reason is the slave to his passions and recognizing this about himself, man can organize his own association with his fellows in such a manner that the mutual benefits from social interdependence can be effectively maximized. (Buchanan and Tullock, 1962, 306)

6. The Insight of Mancur Olson

Prior to 1965, public choice had been developed with a primary emphasis on the vote motive. It is true that Downs (1957) and Buchanan and Tullock (1962) both acknowledged the relevance of pressure group activities in the political process. Neither of them accorded to interest groups the central role that they evidently play in the determination of political outcomes in the Western democracies. In his important 1965 book, *The Logic of Collective Action*, Mancur Olson filled this *lacuna* in the public choice literature with his rigorous application of the rational choice approach to the analysis of interest groups.

Prior to Olson's book, economists, sociologists and political scientists had taken for granted the notion that groups of individuals with common interests usually attempted, often successfully, to further those interests by the application of political pressure. This notion played a central conceptual role in early American theories of labor unions, in the 'group theory' of the pluralists in political science, in John Kenneth Galbraith's concept of 'countervailing power' and in the Marxian theory of class conflict. This theory of interest group behavior essentially transferred the logic of the rational choice theory of individual behavior to that of groups.

In *The Logic of Collective Action*, Olson provided a dramatically different view of collective action. If individuals in some group share a common interest, furtherance of that common interest automatically benefits each individual in that group whether or not he bears any of the costs of collective action to further that interest. Thus the existence of a common interest need not provide any incentive for individual action in the common interest, especially when any one member's efforts are highly unlikely to make the difference between group success and group failure.

From an analytical viewpoint, Olson demonstrated that the benefits of collective action take the form of public goods in the sense that individual members of the group cannot easily be excluded from any benefits that accrue. Economists recognized that voluntary and spontaneous market mechanisms either do not arise or seriously underprovide public goods, as a consequence of the free-rider problem. This under-provision of markets is paralleled exactly by the under-provision of pressure in the case of large groups attempting to pursue a common interest.

Since many groups with common interests do not have the power to tax their memberships, Olson's theory predicts that many groups that would benefit from collective action will fail to organize effectively in pursuit of their common interests. This prediction is supported by evidence. There is no major country in which organizations of consumers effectively support consumer interests. There is no major country in which groups of unemployed workers are effectively organized for collective action. Neither are taxpayers nor are most of the poor typically organized to act in their respective common interests.

Although the logic of collective action indicates that some groups can never act collectively, Olson suggested that other groups, with the assistance of ingenious leadership, may be able to overcome the difficulties of collective action. He posited three conditions, any of which is ultimately sufficient to make collective action possible, namely (1) that the relevant group is small in size, (2) that the group has access to selective incentives or (3) that the group can coerce the supply of pressure.

Suppose that a group is composed of a small number of members each with identical preferences in favor of some common interest. An example of such a group would be an industry made up of two large firms that would gain equally from the provision of a government subsidy or a tax loophole. Since the lobbying activity of each firm, if successful, will exert a significant impact on profits, strategic bargaining between them predictably will result in a group optimal outcome. As the number of firms in the industry increases, however, the incentive to act collectively erodes.

Even in an industry composed of many firms effective lobbying may occur where one firm has a differentially high absolute demand for collective action. In such circumstances, such a firm may engage in collective action, notwithstanding the inability of other firms to provide pressure of their own. This leads to the paradoxical exploitation of the great by the small. Olson illustrated the existence of this phenomenon in a variety of military alliances, in international organizations and in metropolitan areas in which collective goods are provided across an entire metropolis by independent municipalities of greatly different size.

If large groups are to organize themselves effectively to supply pressure, Olson argued that they must engage in the provision of selective incentives to their members. These selective incentives are functionally equivalent to the taxes that enable governments to supply public goods, except that interest group members, unlike taxpayers, cannot be coerced into accepting selective benefits.

Selective benefits either punish or reward individuals depending on whether or not they have borne a share of the costs of collective action. One example of this device is the provision of life insurance and medical policies to paid-up members of the American Association of Retired Persons at rates that would not be available to individual consumers. Another example is the mechanism whereby farm associations in the United States obtain most of their membership by deducting the dues owed by farm organizations from the patronage dividends or rebates of farm cooperatives and insurance companies associated with those organizations.

Large groups that fail to provide selective benefits may nevertheless overcome the free-rider problem associated with collective action where they are able to devise mechanisms for coercing the supply of pressure. An obvious device of this kind is the combination of the closed shop and the picket line utilized by some trade unions to make union membership a condition of employment and to control the supply of union labor during strikes. Another conspicuous example is the statutory requirement extracted by state bar associations in the United States that only paid-up members of the bar are allowed to engage in the practice of law.

Olson's application of the rational choice approach to the analysis of collective action offered disturbing insights into the political process. Since access to collective action is uneven, the application of pressure by groups in pursuit of common membership goals will be uneven across society. Legislatures that respond systematically to such uneven pressures (by taking advantage of rational ignorance among the electorate or by utilizing the campaign contributions to manipulate voters' preferences) may be able systematically to evade the centripetal pressures of two-party spatial politics while effectively providing tenure to incumbent representatives.

7. Conclusions

The five contributions evaluated in this essay together comprise the founding content of the public choice research program. By rejecting both the philosopher-king approach of economic science and the behavioral approach of political science, in favor of the rational choice approach, the Founding Fathers revolutionized our understanding of the political process.

One important consequence of these contributions has been a dampening of the enthusiasm with which social scientists proffer policy advice to governments. A second important consequence has been the dampening of enthusiasm for active government even among scholars who still nurse strong suspicions concerning the behavior of private markets.

The Founding Fathers of public choice, in some cases by design and in other cases by accident, effectively leveled the playing field in the debate over the relative merits of governments and private markets. This playing field, by the mid-1950s, had become undeniably prejudiced in favor of an allegedly omniscient and impartial government.

In balancing this playing field, the Founding Fathers of public choice played an indispensable role in stimulating the Western democracies to abandon their mid-twentieth century flirtation with socialism, thereby paving the way for a resurgence of market processes. The insights provided by the public choice research program rank among the most important of all advances in economic science during the second half of the twentieth century, when measured in terms of their contribution to the wealth of nations and to the expansion of individual liberty.

CHARLES K. ROWLEY

REFERENCES

Arrow, K.J. (1950). "A difficulty in the concept of social welfare." *Journal of Political Economy*, 58: 328–346.

Arrow, K.J. (1951). *Social Choice and Individual Values*. New York: Wiley.

Black, D. (1948a). "On the rationale of group decision making." *Journal of Political Economy*, 56(1): 23–34.

Black, D. (1948b). "The decisions of a committee using a special majority." *Econometrica*, 16(3): 245–261.

Black, D. (1948c). "The elasticity of committee decision with an altering size of majority." *Econometrica*, 16: 261–272.

Black, D. (with R.A. Newing) (1951). *Committee Decisions with Complementary Valuation*. Glasgow: William Hodge.

Black, D. (1958). *The Theory of Committees and Elections*. Cambridge: Cambridge University Press.

Black, D. (1972). "Arrow's work and the normative theory of committees." (unpublished manuscript).

Borda, J-P de (1781). Memoire sur les Elections au Scrutin. *Histoire de l'Academie Royale des Sciences*. Paris.

Buchanan, J.M. and Tullock, G. (1962). *The Calculus of Consent*. Ann Arbor: University of Michigan Press.

Coase, R.H. (1981). "Duncan Black: a biographical sketch," in Gordon Tullock (ed.) *Toward a Science of Politics*. Blacksburg: Center for Study of Public Choice.

Condorcet, M. (1785). *Essai sur l'application de l'analyse a la probabilite des decisions rendues a la pluralite des voix*. Paris.

Downs, A. (1957). *An Economic Theory of Democracy*. New York: Harper & Row.

Grofman, B. (1981). "The theory of committees and elections: the legacy of Duncan Black," in Gordon Tullock (ed.) *Toward a Science of Politics*. Blacksburg: Center for Study of Public Choice.

Grofman, B. (1987). "Black, Duncan," in J. Eatwell, M. Milgate, and P. Newman (eds.) *The New Palgrave: A Dictionary of Economics*. London: Macmillan, pp. 250–251.

Hotelling, H. (1929). "Stability in Competition," *Economic Journal*, 39, 41–57.

McKelvey, R.D. (1976). "Intransitivities in multidimensional voting models and some implications for agenda control." *Journal of Economic Theory*, 18(1): 1–22.

Moulin, H. (1983). *The Strategy of Social Choice*. Amsterdam: North Holland.

Moulin, H and Young, H.P. (1987). "Condorcet, M," in J. Eatwell, M. Milgate, and P. Newman (eds.) *The New Palgrave: A Dictionary of Economics*. London: Macmillan, pp. 566–567.

Olson, M. (1965) *The Logic of Collective Action*. Cambridge, MA: Harvard University Press.

Rowley. C.K. (1987). "Borda, Jean-Charles de (1733–1799)," in J. Eatwell, M. Milgate, and P. Newman (eds.) *The New Palgrave: A Dictionary of Economics*. London: Macmillan, pp. 262–263.

Rowley, C.K. (1991). "Duncan Black: pioneer and discoverer of public choice." *Journal of Public Finance and Public Choice*, 2: 83–87.

PUBLIC CHOICE THEORY FROM THE PERSPECTIVE OF LAW

The enlightened conception of separation of powers holds that law should be made by the legislature, interpreted by the judiciary, and enforced by the executive branch of government. Public choice theory provides a solid foundation for the appraisal of this traditional formula. The findings of public choice theory, while supporting much of the traditional wisdom, pose several challenges to the theoretical foundations of these constitutional principles. In the following pages I shall revisit these important question considering the issue of institutional design through the lenses of public choice theory.

1. Sources of Law and the Institutional Design of Law-Making

According to a fundamental principle of constitutional design, powers should be allocated to the branch and level of government or society that can best exercise them. This principle can be applied to the question of law-making in order to select sources of law that will exploit the comparative advantage of different legal and social institutions in the production of legal rules.

I consider three main criteria for evaluating the relative advantages of alternative sources of law, focusing on the political economy of production of ordinary (i.e., non-Constitutional in nature) law.

1.1. Minimization of Agency Problems

First, the mechanisms for law creation should be able to reflect the underlying preferences of the individuals subject to the law.

For the case of political processes of law formation, this requires the choice of collective decision making procedures that will promote the alignment of the incentives of political representatives and the incentives of the represented citizens. In the presence of perfect incentive alignment, agency problems in political representation will disappear.

Likewise, in an ideal world judge-made law should approximate the rules that private parties would have chosen if engaging in an *ex ante* choice of applicable law. This claim, known as the efficiency of the common law hypothesis, constitutes an important premise of the law and economics movement. According to this hypothesis, the common law (i.e., judge-made law) is the result of an effort — conscious or not — to induce efficient outcomes. The same proponents of this hypothesis suggests that common law rules enjoy a comparative advantage over legislation in the creation of efficient legal rules because of the evolutionary selection of common law rules induced by adversarial adjudication.

The case of customary law is quite different from those of the other sources of law. Customary law avoids the interface of third party decision makers (such as legislators and judges) and is directly derived from the observation of the behavioral choices of individuals in society. In a customary law setting the group of lawmakers coincides with the subjects of the law and agency problems are generally absent from such process of law formation. In the following discussion, we will consider the different group of problems that however affect the process of customary law formation.

In all the above cases, the institutional design of lawmaking should induce incentive alignment in order to minimize the extent of agency problems, with a minimization of rent seeking and a resulting optimal supply of public goods.

1.2. Minimization of Rulemaking Costs

The second criterion for evaluating alternative sources of law is that of cost minimization of collective decision-making. According to this criterion, the mechanisms for law creation should be chosen in order to minimize the transaction costs of collective decision making and political bargaining.

This cost minimization problem involves the evaluation of two different costs:

(a) direct costs of decision making, such as the costs of reaching a majoritarian consensus in a political context, or the cost of litigation or adjudication in a judicial context;

(b) indirect or external costs, such as the cost imposed on a minority group by the rules chosen by a majority coalition.

Different levels of transaction costs of types (a) and (b) are inherent in the different processes of law formation.

1.2.1. Direct Costs of Lawmaking

In a legislative process, individual preferences are captured by the collective decision making process through the imperfect interface of political representation. Bargaining among political representatives is costly, due to the strategic behavior of large number bargaining (i.e., free riding, hold ups, and other collective action problems) and the absence of legal enforcement mechanisms for political bargains. In this dimension, lawmaking through politics is likely to impose the highest level of transaction costs among the alternative sources of law that we consider.

Transaction and information costs are also present in the case of judge made law. The process of judicial creation of legal rules faces the obvious constraint given by the costly access to information regarding alternative legal rules. If we analogize the law-making process to a production process in the marketplace, the common law may indeed appear as a quite inefficient production process. The common law process, when shifting some of the law making functions to the judiciary, entrusts courts with the task of conceiving and refining legal rules while adjudicating specific cases.

From a production point of view, such process foregoes the economies of scale and scope that might be exploited by a specialized legislative process. On the other hand, the common law process, by relying on the adversarial efforts of the parties, utilizes information available to the parties. Parties have direct information on the costs and benefits of alternative rules and courts may be regarded as having an informational advantage over central legislative bodies, given the opportunity of judges to infer the litigants' preferences from the choices they make during the case.

Courts have a further informational advantage in observing the revealed preference of the parties with respect to applicable law. Modern legal systems generally provide a set of default rules that apply if the parties fail to choose alternative provisions to govern their relationship. When parties opt out of the default rules (through ex ante choice of differing provisions or ex ante choice of law), they reveal their preferences over alternative legal rules. If courts observe a large number of parties routinely opting out of the default rules, it becomes evident that such rules have failed their cost-minimization task under the circumstances and do not approximate the will of the majority of the contracting parties. In these cases, courts would have a comparative informational advantage over legislators in designing and revising default legal rules.

For the case of customary law, we should distinguish two distinct costs: (a) the cost of decentralized creation of a customary legal rule; and (b) the cost of judicial finding of an existing rule of customary law.

The costs of creation are relatively minimal. Most rules of customary law are derived from the observation of widespread practice followed by individuals in society. In this context, customary rules are a costless byproduct of the economic and social interactions of individuals in society. Such practices are not being carried out with the objective of giving birth to binding rules of customary law and the legal recognition of such practices as binding customs adds no cost to the activities involved.

The costs for courts to identify a rule of customary law may, however, be considerable. Customs are intangible sources of law and their content does not enjoy any objective articulation in written law. The identification of custom thus requires knowledge of past practice and investigation of the beliefs shared by those who engaged in the practice: a process that can be costly and difficult to carry out.

A point of advantage of customary sources of law is related to the fact that custom is formed through the independent action of individuals in society, without the need for their express agreement to the emerging rule. Since most rules of custom require a very high level of participation without yet necessitating a unanimous consensus, hold up problems and other transaction-associated costs are generally avoided in the formation of customary legal rules. No single individual in society can prevent the emergence and recognition of a general custom.

1.2.2. External Costs of Lawmaking

The various sources of law also have different levels of external costs. As public choice theory has shown, in the case of political decision making direct costs and external costs of lawmaking are negatively correlated (Buchanan and Tullock, 1962). The tradeoff between direct and external costs is easily illustrated by the consideration of the two limit cases of unanimity and dictatorship in a voting context. If deliberations require a unanimity vote, the risk of external costs disappears, since unanimity gives every voter a veto power against undesired proposals. Transaction costs are instead very high under a unanimity rule. In the opposite case of dictatorship, the risk of external costs is much higher, since a dictator can single-handedly impose costs on all other individuals. Conversely, the direct costs of lawmaking are lowest under dictatorship, given that no consensus and political bargaining is necessary under a dictatorial decision rule.

Analogous tradeoffs between direct and external costs exist for the other sources of law, but the content and interpretation of such costs differ substantially in each case.

Thus, for example, rules of customary law require a very high level of participation and consensus. This reduces the risk of external costs imposed on unwilling minorities, but, as a result of such high threshold of required participation, customary laws are relatively slow in their emergence and evolution.

In evaluating the various sources of law, it will be necessary to give careful consideration to the different performance of alternative lawmaking processes from the vantage point of this criterion of cost minimization.

1.3. Stability and Transitivity of Collective Outcomes

The third problem of institutional design is to minimize the cost of instability and ensure rational and transitive collective choices. As it has been observed in the literature (e.g., Cooter, 2000; Stearns, 1994; Parisi, 1997), when political cooperation fails and the lawmaking mechanisms do not generate Condorcet winners, several legal institutions and doctrines come to the rescue to minimize instability and select among cyclical alternatives. In particular, Cooter (2000) explains how democratic constitutions pursue these goals of stability by separating powers among the branches of government, by guaranteeing individual rights, and creating a framework of competition for political office. Parisi (1998) considers the role of logrolling as an instrument of stability in a legislative setting. With reference to judge made law, Stearns (1994) considers the role of standing doctrines and stare decisis as evolved institutions aimed at reducing instability in the absence of a Condorcet majority consensus. In the different setting of customary law, Parisi (1997) discusses the process of formation and evolution of customary law, unveiling the ability of customary law to generate stable rules in different game-theoretic situations.

2. Law through Politics: The Political Economy of Legislation

Comparative differences in legal systems often reflect different ideologies and conceptions of political economy of lawmaking. In recent years, all countries of the modern world have been giving written statutes increasingly greater importance among the sources of law. The supremacy of written law over other sources of legal order is not, however, a universal characteristic of all modern legal systems.

Comparative legal scholars usually distinguish between civil law and common law systems. The distinction is based on a dichotomous conception of legal traditions. Systems of the civil law tradition give greater weight to written and statutory sources of law. Generally speaking, these systems are historically derived from a legal tradition that recognized the authority of a comprehensive body of written law (e.g., the Roman Corpus Juris) and were not relying on the casuistic evolution of case-by-case decision making in the absence of a coherent skeleton of codified law. This dichotomous distinction, while useful as a preliminary classificatory tool, should not be overestimated.

During the last several decades, legal systems of the world have converged toward a middle ground. In the civil law tradition, the dogmas of supremacy of legislation over case-law have gradually given way to a more balanced conception of sources of law, where statutes and case-law more or less happily coexist with one another. Likewise, in the common law tradition, the proliferation of legislative intervention has gradually corroded the traditional dominance of judge-made sources.

2.1. Lawmaking and Political Representation

During the nineteenth century, the enlightened conception of democratic governance and the renewed trust in political decision-making fostered an increased importance of statutory law. Ideals of democratic legislation gradually replaced the historic conception of statutory law as a written articulation of laws of a higher and older origin. Laws were not the mere expression of preexisting natural or fundamental rights, but rather they were the primary source, if not the sole origin, of individual rights. Rights were derived from laws, rather than laws being derived for the protection of individual rights. Legislative bodies were making (i.e., creating) law as opposed to finding (i.e., recognizing) preexisting legal norms. With the exception of some minimal Constitutional constraints on law making, national Parliaments and Congresses acted as sovereign lawmakers. Such unbounded legislative powers were justified by the alleged function of legislative organs as faithful agents and political representatives of the people.

The unfolding of history has, however, revealed the true face of democratic decision making and the limits of mechanisms of political representation in lawmaking.

There are two theoretically distinct problems that affect the mechanisms of political representation. These problems have become the respective focus of several important contributions in the public choice and social choice literature.

Within the public choice tradition, we learn that political representatives are agents of the individuals they represent. Such political representation is often affected by pervasive agency problems. The correction of these problems requires the choice of collective decision making procedures that promotes the alignment of the incentives of political representatives with the incentives of the represented citizens, or else an effective monitoring and accountability of political agents. If incentives are effectively aligned, agency problems of this type do not affect political representation. Much of the public choice and the constitutional design literature addresses these fundamental problems.

The second problem emerges even in the absence of agency problems in representation. This problem is one of selection of appropriate criteria for aggregating individual preferences. If the interests of politicians align with the interests of the people whom they represent, politics can be viewed as a framework for bargaining among political agents of the various factions in society. The question is whether political bargaining can successfully yield a consensus among the various political factions, such that political outcomes can be legitimately and unambiguously identified with the "will of the people".

As the social choice literature has often pointed out, even if we contemplate a world of perfect incentive alignment between political representatives and the represented citizens (i.e., even if we assume away agency problems in political representation), there is no assurance that the mechanisms of law creation are responsive to the underlying preferences of individuals in society.

2.2. Political Decision Making and the Market for Votes

One of the main insights from social choice theory is that the correlation between preference and choice is weaker for groups than for individuals (Shubik, 1982: 124). According to Arrow's (1951) possibility theorem, it may indeed be too much to expect methods of collective decision making to be at the same time rational and egalitarian. Arrow's theorem shows that any social decision that is adopted must violate at least one of six self-evident axioms of normative political theory, commonly described by the following terms: range, universal domain, unanimity, nondictatorship, independence of irrelevant alternatives, and rationality. Arrow's negative conclusion and its various corollaries pose a dramatic threat to the legitimacy of political decisions. The observation that the likelihood of cycling majorities decreases in situations where the number of decision-makers is much greater than the number of choices does not affect the practical relevance of Arrow's analysis applied to the political process, where the large number of decision-makers is actually concentrated into a restricted number of interest groups with "group" votes.

The heart of Arrow's theorem states that there are no non-dictatorial rules or procedures for collective decision-making that reflect the combined preferences of voters to a consistent collective outcome (Arrow, 1951). The implications of Arrow's theorem concern the existence of cyclical majorities which are capable of repealing any resolution that has been adopted previously. Parisi (1998) suggests that, if all voters are allowed to enter into binding agreements over the policy outcome to be adopted by the majority coalition, collective preferences in a multi-dimensional policy space will be transitive as long as individual preferences are single-peaked.

This intuition runs contrary to the common thought in public and social choice theory (see, e.g., Bernholz, 1973; N.R. Miller, 1977; and Th. Schwartz, 1977). Most of the literature on the stability implications of log-rolling considers log-rolling in the context of bargaining for the formation of coalitions where side-payments are only instruments for entering the majority coalition, and no side-payments are made by those who are not part of the majority.

The political reality is often different from that contemplated by these scholars. Bargaining is certainly permitted even between minority and majority voters, with exchanges taking place among all coalitions.

As shown by Parisi (1998), if we allow for a broader role for bargaining and side-payments and contemplate binding and enforceable political bargains across different coalitions, the results would be quite different.

2.3. One Man One Vote, and the Market for Votes

In situations in which no strong political consensus is reached on a given issue, intransitivity may result. Intransitivity implies that a different order in the decision making process may affect the outcome and that any winning coalition may be undermined by the reintroduction of an alternative it previously defeated. The structure of the voting process does not allow the cycle to be broken by looking at the intensity of voters preferences. The outcome is arbitrarily determined by the order of motions, with no guarantee that the ultimate result will yield a higher level of social welfare than that potentially afforded by any other defeated policy alternative. The inability of the democratic process to capture the intensity of the voters' preferences is a by-product of the generally espoused principle that every individual is entitled to one — and only one — vote. The "one man, one vote" rule is further explained by the fact that individual voters do not face the opportunity cost of casting their vote. Whether their preference is strong or weak, voters will cast their vote in favor of their favored option. Even if specifically designed to allow voters to indicate the intensity of voters' preferences, the voting ballot could not possibly capture such intensity. Absent a mechanism to extract the true intensity of their preferences, individual voters would tend to overstate their preference in order to maximize the impact of their votes.

Democracy gives equal weight to all votes when they are counted, regardless of how strongly the voters feel about the issue. In this way, numerically equal groups have equal political say in the process. However, if the distribution of sentiments on an issue is not symmetrical, and the minority holds strong preferences, the outcome would be inefficient. By introducing the possibility of bargaining and vote-trading in the process, the intensity of preferences will be reflected in the decision-making process. With bargaining and side-payments, the "one man, one vote" rule would provide the initial entitlement for each voter-trader. The exchange mechanism would then reveal the relative strength of individual preferences.[1]

Political bargaining may provide a solution to the intensity problem, and at the same time correct for the cyclicality problem. Politicians know well that under certain conditions the outcome may depend on the sequence of decisions and therefore on agenda-setting. For example, in a situation with intransitive preferences, the agenda-setter may influence the process in favor of his preferred policy by determining the sequence of decisions and introducing his preferred policy in the last motion. This point is well known among public choice theorists and legal practitioners. Judge Easterbrook (1983) has noted that "someone with control of the agenda can manipulate the choice so that the legislature adopts proposals that only a minority support." (See also Levine and Plott, 1977; Long and Rose-Ackerman, 1982.)

Agenda-setting increases the internal predictability of the outcome for those who are involved in the process and have full information about it. Legislators sharing similar information on their respective prospects will have an opportunity to bargain under conditions of symmetric information, trading votes for issues on which they hold weak preferences in exchange for votes on issues which have more value for them. Economic theory teaches us that bargaining between politicians will continue until the marginal utility of gaining one vote on a certain issue equals the marginal cost of giving up one vote for another issue. We should further consider whether the outcome selected by majorities in a such an environment of costless and enforceable political bargaining maximizes the combined welfare of the platforms. Parisi (1998) suggests that both stability and efficiency will be obtained through bargaining, as long as the exchanges are enforceable and relatively costless to carry out. The implications are very far-reaching and can be articulated in the following two propositions:

(a) If the conditions for the Coase theorem are present for all voters (i.e., if political agents can enter into coalition contracts with other agents and such contracts are enforceable as stipulated, unless mutually dissolved by all parties), the composition of the initial majority coalition is irrelevant for the policy outcome.

(b) If the Coase theorem holds, voters' preferences are strictly concave, and vote-exchange agreements are enforceable, cycling in a multi-dimensional policy space is excluded.

Thus, if political bargains are possible at no cost and political agreements are enforceable, the resulting political equilibrium will be unique and will occur at a point of social maximum. Any point other than the global maximum will be unstable, since there will always be enough surplus to allow for side payments to voters in exchange for policy concessions. Once the socially optimal point is reached, there will be no opportunity to destabilize the policy arrangement.

2.4. Enforcing Political Bargains

The above conclusions rest on a quite formidable assumption. Political agreements are assumed to be enforceable, just like ordinary contracts in a private law setting. This implies that any attempt to modify the bargained for policy choice would have to be accepted by all parties — contracts can be resolved only with the consent of the contracting parties.

More generally, the Coasian bargaining assumption implies that all political promises are enforceable In this setting, minority voters can join the coalition and have a marginal effect on the policy outcome by out-bidding or "bribing" all members of the pre-existing majority. With enforceable contracts members of a majority coalition cannot cheat on each other. Collectively, they will entertain offers made by minority voters who will influence the status quo with their side payments, but they will not be able to break away from an existing coalition, since such coalition agreements can be modified only with the consent of all parties. Finally, as well-known in the collective action literature groups with lower collective action costs can be more effective in gathering the most effective bribe, as public choice theory has extensively shown in the various rent-seeking contexts (Olson, 1965; Kahn, 1990).

As pointed out by Cooter (2000), in real politics bargaining is afflicted by a special problem that is usually absent in private contracts. Political agents are limited in the extent to which they can enter into enforceable political bargains. For example, coalitions agreements are only good until a new coalition is formed. Likewise, there is no way to bind future voting decisions in a logrolling context, or to constrain the choices of future office-holders.

In a traditional contract setting, a contractual agreement can be undone only with the consent of all original contracting parties. Conversely, in informal political agreements, any political agent can betray the original agreement and destabilize the original coalition. There are no direct legal remedies to render such agreements enforceable.

In general, no agreement between current members of Congress regarding future voting is enforceable under the law. For example, majority deliberations cannot be perpetuated prohibiting future amendments or requiring that such amendments be carried out with a super-majority vote.

Legislators sometimes have to be creative to make contracts enforceable in the real-world market for votes. In several occasions political actors attempt to signal the enforceability of their bargains (and ensure its influence against the status quo) in a future vote by publicly stating that they would not "go back and undo the things that they pledged that they would do." In other situations, the repeat interaction among politicians may induce the fulfillment of some political bargains, thus facilitating political cooperation.

However, the general non enforceability of political bargains limits the deals that can be struck among political representatives and among branches of government.

2.5. Limits of the Politics-Like-Markets Analogues

In real politics, legislative and political bodies seldom work like markets. Cooter (2000) points out three main challenges to the politics-like-market analogy. The first reason why political markets do not work like ordinary markets is that the value of a legislator's vote often depends upon how the other legislators' vote. There are pervasive externalities and resulting free riding incentives in political action. The second reason is that real life politics has too many political actors for each one to bargain with everyone else. Unlike the atomistic marketplace of traditional economics, bilateral negotiations would be prohibitively expensive in real life politics. Third, Cooter points out the diffuse hostility to a rationalization of politics as a market for consensus. Ordinary citizens with little information about legislative bargains and would resist any institutionalization of political bargaining, objecting to their representatives participating in open logrolling.

Indeed, a full analysis of the politics-like-market analogy cannot be accomplished in a vacuum, but rather must be exposed to the reality of democratic politics. The following corrollaries are discussed by Parisi (1998) and are illustrative in this regard: (1) on issue bundling; (2) on free riding and bargaining failures; and (3) on agency problems and the political dilemma.

2.5.1. Issue Bundling

In the real world of politics, transaction costs are present. As a way to minimize the effect of transaction costs, policy "packages" are traded and voted upon in the usual course of dealing. Political deals are indeed characterized by a bundling of different issues. Congressional voting normally requires a binomial vote on legislation supplying a bundle of bargained-for provisions. And House and Senate rules do not prevent amendments that are unrelated to the subject matter of the bill at issue (Dixon, 1985; Riggs, 1973). For example, when Congress sent President Clinton the 1997 appropriations bill that funds White House operations, it included legislative riders ranging from the repeal of a law allowing states to share in federal price discounts from the pharmaceutical industry, to a provision to clarify that imports manufactured by indentured child labor are prohibited (Rogers, 1997). Although the item veto enabled President Clinton to remove particular items from such bundles, he has thus far utilized that power narrowly and selectively (Penny, 1997).

From an efficiency perspective, bundling — just like tying in a commodity market — may generate suboptimal outcomes. In order for a vote exchange process to work at its best, all dimensions of the policy space should be the potential object of bargaining and trade. Bundling reduces the dimensions of the bargaining space. At the limit, all policy dimensions may collapse down to a two-dimensional policy space, limiting the domain of the optimization process.

In an ideal world with no transaction costs, no bundling should exist, in order to maximize the beneficial functioning of the political market. In a real world with positive transaction costs, a positive amount of bundling is to be expected and is part of the global optimization process. Elhauge (1991: 31) has noted that where there is issue bundling, "diffuse interests can be systematically underrepresented even if voters face no collective action problem." But the market will adjust to reach the optimal tradeoffs between the savings on transaction costs and the inefficiencies of tying.

2.5.2. Free Riding and Bargaining Failures

An important assumption of the Coase theorem is the absence of transaction costs. A costless transaction requires the absence of strategic behavior in the bargaining process. This condition is highly problematic in the context of multi-party voting. The opportunity for individual strategic behavior is elevated where two polar groups seek compromise. In the real-world market for votes, the term "triangulation" has been to describe the result of efforts to legislate in the middle ground between ideological extremes, where vote-trading transaction costs are high (Broader (1997), attributing the "triangulation" concept to former Clinton-advisor Dick Morris).

All cyclicality problems require the presence of at least three voters. Bargaining among three voters in a two dimensional space is highly sensitive to free riding and other forms of strategic preference revelation.

If we think of this triangular situation in a spatial voting setting, we can realize that any movement in the policy space will generate benefits or losses for at least two parties. In the great majority of cases, all three parties will be affected by a potential policy change. Under such conditions, any bargaining carried out by one voter has the potential of creating side benefits for another voter. Any policy change "purchased" by one voter is potentially a free good (or a free bad) for another voter. In a three-party bargaining, voters are thus faced with a collective action problem. The problem is exacerbated by an increase in the number of voters. In a multi-voter setting, strategic behavior may indeed plague the bargaining process.

The collective action problem described above is not different from any other free riding problem in a Coasian setting. Olson (1997) has discussed the collective action problem in the context of a Coasian bargaining, questioning the practical validity of the Coasian proposition in a multi-party context. If the object of one individual's bargaining generates a benefit to other individuals who are not involved in the bargain, what is obtained through the bargaining of one individual creates a positive externality to other individuals. Thus the incentives to undertake the bargaining may be seriously undermined. Every individual wishes to be the free rider, having somebody else pay the price of the common good. Thus, similar to any public good situation, there will be a sub-optimal level of bargaining for the common interest.

2.5.3. Agency Problems and the Political Dilemma

The analysis of the hypothetical market for votes considered in this article takes the will of the voters as a given. Further analysis should consider the effect of agency problems in the bargaining mechanism. In the real world of politics, most collective decisions are carried out by political representatives, who undertake collective decisions as agents of the represented individuals. Political representation is often undermined by serious agency problems. Public choice theory provides ample analysis of the factors of such incentive misalignment, including (a) rational abstention; (b) rational ignorance; and (c) regulatory capture and resulting special interest legislation. Such discrepancies are most visible when an agency problem in political representation occurs at the margin of a crucial vote.

If bargaining is carried out in the absence of agency problems, the bargaining result maximizes the voters' utility, as illustrated above. But where the bargaining is carried out by interested representatives, the opportunity is present for departures from the optimality outcome described above.

In general terms, if market mechanisms are allowed to operate in political contexts, the collective decision-making mechanism is lubricated. In the absence of representation failures, the collective outcome will approximate the allocative outcome of a competitive market. If bargaining is carried out by agents whose underlying incentives differ from those of their principals, the market mechanism may generate greater discrepancies between the ideal and the real political outcomes, including the fact that agents may be induced to abandon their principals' core values.

2.6. The Cost of Legislation

The absence of legal enforcement mechanisms in political contracts increases transaction costs and often represents an unsurmountable obstacle to political cooperation. According to Cooter (2000), the institutional design of lawmaking should promote institutional arrangements that minimize the transaction costs of political bargaining.

With respect to legislation as a source of law, the previous sections have shown that the politics-like-markets analogues risk overlooking the difficulties of correcting political failures through political bargaining. The existence of effective exchange mechanisms within politics accentuates the features of the underlying political system. In a world of good politics, it allows for better outcomes. In a world of political failures, it may exacerbate the existing problems.

In a world where political bargaining exists, however, the existence of enforcement mechanisms within politics will promote stability and reduce costly intransitivity of collective outcomes.

As discussed above, stability cannot be used as a proxy for efficiency. It is indeed well-known in the social and public choice literature that a "Condorcet winner" can at times be inefficient, but at least it can always be trusted to satisfy the preferences of the majority of voting individuals. Absent mechanisms to induce voters to reveal the true intensity of their preferences, democratic legislative systems cannot improve on Condorcet winners and should maintain rules that allow such alternatives to prevail when they exist.

If Condorcet winners do not exist, the method and sequence of voting (i.e., agenda setting, etc.) determines the political outcome. In these cases, as Cooter (2000) aptly puts it "democratic politics becomes a contest, not to satisfy the preferences of a unique majority, but to determine which majority's preferences will be satisfied". In these situations, institutions should be designed in order to minimize the welfare costs of voting intransitivity and instability. The existence of enforceable contractual mechanisms for political exchange may be a valuable instrument of stability.

These results confirm Buchanan and Tullock's (1962: 153) important observation that "with all side payments prohibited, there is no assurance that collective action will be taken in the most productive way." Likewise, they provide a conjectural solution to Tullock's (1981) puzzle as to why there is so much stability in the political process.

3. Common Law and the Economics of Judicial Lawmaking

Judge made law and doctrines of stare decisis have varying degrees of importance in the various legal system of the world. As well known, there is a substantial historical difference between the role played by precedents in the common law and civil law traditions. In early legal systems, written legislation was utilized with great parsimony and great weight was given to customary sources of law. Occasionally, sources of customary law were unable to provide solutions to emerging legal issues and to satisfy the changing needs of society. In these cases, precedents were recognized and followed as a matter of outright necessity.

With the gradual expansion of statutory law, the recognition of precedents as sources of law was no longer a practical necessity. In these setting, contemporary legal systems have developed a variety of doctrines to determine the effective role of judicial decisions in the presence of legislation and to guarantee an effective separation between these two branches of government. Principles of separation of powers provide the Constitutional foundations for balancing the institutional roles played by courts and legislators.

3.1. Separation of Powers and the Independent Judiciary

One key feature of most Constitutional systems of the Western legal tradition is the principle of separation of powers, with particular importance placed on an independent judiciary to ensure the fair adjudication of law. The principle of separation of powers implies that, unlike the legislative and executive branches, most judges are (or should be) systematically shielded from political or economic influence.

As a matter of institutional design, the independence of judges can be achieved by either turning the judiciary into a bureaucracy-type institution, where judges are selected and promoted according to pre-established standards of performance on the bench, or through political appointment with life-tenure, with the consequent elimination of any ties with the appointing political body (Cooter, 2000). The first approach is generally followed by most Civil law jurisdictions, while the second approach finds its typical incarnation in the Federal judiciary of the United States.

Landes and Posner (1975) examine the effect of the independent judiciary on lobbying, the de jure system of interest group purchase of legislative policy. Economic analysis of the role of the courts shows how an independent judiciary can make viable a governmental process that emphasizes interest group participation in policy formation. By enforcing laws validly passed, even in a previous legislative session, the judiciary ensures integrity in the Constitutional process by imposing prohibitive costs on public interest purchase of judicial decisions.

Landes and Posner work from the perspective of interest group analysis, pointing out that interest groups will not purchase policy programs if they cannot assume that desired policy will last. In the absence of an enforceable contract, some other power must provide that guarantee. In the first instance, the high transaction costs associated with cumbersome process of enacting legislation supply stability. Accordingly, if courts, which must enforce legislation, were agents of the Congress in session, the legislature could cheaply arrange a de facto repeal by asking its courts to rewrite legislation by taking advantage of interpretive leeway. If, on the other hand, the judiciary is independent and interprets legislation in accordance with the enacting Congress' intent, it then supports, rather than interferes with, purchase of legislation by interest groups. However, the independent judiciary may also impose costs by declaring the law unconstitutional or interpreting it in a way that reduces gains to the group that paid for the law.

Some questions have been raised in the literature regarding the actual level of independence of the judiciary. After all, in the U.S. legal system Congress does have powers, such as appropriations of funds, creation of new judgeships, and rewriting jurisdiction by which they might compel judicial acquiescence. However, self-interested judges can increase their independence by rendering predictable decisions in accord with the original meaning of the statute. According to Landes and Posner (1975) this increases the value of the judiciary to the current legislature because its members know that the courts will enforce the contracts they make. According to the authors, the structure of the judiciary — life tenure, rules against ex parte contact, and impeachment for accepting bribes — also prevents interest groups from influencing judges directly.

Landes and Posner (1975) further explore the positive implications of the economic theory of the judiciary. First, they consider the case of 'dependent' judiciaries, such as those established in specialized agencies, making a consistent finding that such entities are established when the chance of judicial nullification of political and legislative bargains is high. Mild judicial review allows the agencies to keep the terms of a particular legislative deal, but since that review is not wholly effective, administrative adjudication becomes far less consistent over time, as would be expected from a dependent judiciary that is not protected from shifts political emphasis. The authors further consider the effect the economic system of legislation coupled with an independent judiciary has on the form of interest group legislation. Building upon public choice models of rent-seeking, the authors suggest that interest groups purchase legislation that does not require substantial annual appropriations. Legislative rents that require yearly Congressional funding are quickly dissipated as it would be necessary to lobby each new Congress to support the program, the costs of which eat into the net present value of the legislation for its intended beneficiaries. Since the judiciary cannot help to enforce new annual appropriations, interest groups tend not to purchase such legislation.

The law and economics literature also considers the role of the independent judiciary in enforcing the Constitution. According to Landes and Posner (1975) judicial independence has two purposes in this context. First, it establishes ground rules for a system of interest group politics enforced by the independent judiciary. Second, the Constitution confers specific protective legislation on powerful interests groups willing to purchase such a provision in their favor. For example, broad interpretation of the First Amendment is a form of protective legislation purchased by publishers as an interest group. The Constitution's purpose, supported by the independent judiciary, is to protect groups powerful enough to obtain a constitutional provision or a special interest legislation in their favor.

The conclusions reached by this literature stress that the independent judiciary is an essential element in the observed struggle among interest groups, which is a major component of political practice. Although the judiciary is a critical player in this process, it itself is not 'political,' but rather is above politics because it fulfills its role by enforcing the legislative deals of earlier legislatures, not because it has special wisdom, integrity, morality, or commitment to principle.

3.2. The Hypothesis that the Common Law is Efficient

To the extent to which judicial bodies are independent from political forces and shielded from interest group pressure, the process of judicial lawmaking can be considered immune from the collective decision making failures considered in the previous section.

In this setting, law and economics scholars formulated a conjecture, known as the efficiency of the common law hypothesis — according to which the common law (i.e., judge-made law) is the result of an effort — conscious or not — to induce efficient outcomes. This hypothesis was first intimated by Coase (1960) and was later systematized and greatly extended by Posner in numerous books and articles: common law rules attempt to allocate resources in either a Pareto or Kaldor-Hicks efficient manner. Further, common law rules are said to enjoy a comparative advantage over legislation in fulfilling this task because of the evolutionary selection of common law rules through adjudication. Several important contributions provide the foundations for this claim; the scholars who have advanced theories in support of the hypothesis are, however, often in disagreement as to its conceptual basis.

Rubin (1977) provides an important contribution to the emerging efficiency of the common law hypothesis. He maintains that the efficiency of the common law is best explained by an evolutionary model in which parties will more likely litigate inefficient rules than efficient ones. The pressure for the common law to evolve to efficiency, he argues, rests on the desire of parties to create precedent because they have an interest in future similar cases. Rubin thus considers three basic situations: where both parties are interested in creating precedent, where only one party is interested in creating precedent, and where neither party has such an interest.

Where both parties have an interest in future similar cases, and the current legal rule is inefficient, the party held liable will have an incentive to force litigation. Parties will continue to use the courts until the rule is changed. If the current rule is efficient, however, there is no incentive to change it, so it will remain in force. Where only one party has an interest in future similar cases, the incentive to litigate will depend on the allocation of liability. If liability falls on a repeat player, litigation will likely occur, whereas the other party would have no incentive to litigate. As a result, precedents will evolve in the interested party's favor, whether or not the rule is efficient. In the event that neither party is interested in precedents, the legal rule — whether efficient or not — will remain in force, and parties will settle out of court because they lack the incentive to change the current rule. Rubin thus concludes that the common law becomes efficient through an evolutionary process based on the utility maximizing decisions of litigants, rather than on judges' desires to maximize efficiency.

Rubin's analysis was extended by Priest (1977), who articulated the idea that the common law tends to develop efficient rules independently of judicial bias in decision-making. Indeed, he asserts, efficient rules will develop even despite judicial hostility toward efficient outcomes. Priest parts with Rubin, however, on the source of the tendency toward efficiency, rejecting Rubin's conclusion that this tendency occurs only where both parties to a dispute have an interest in future similar cases and therefore have an incentive to litigate. Instead, he asserts that litigation is driven by the costs of inefficient rules, rather than the desire for precedent.

According to Priest's analysis, inefficient rules impose greater costs on the parties subject to them than do efficient rules, thereby making the stakes in a dispute greater. Where the stakes are greater, litigation is more likely than settlement. Consequently, out of the complete set of legal rules, disputes arising under inefficient rules will tend to be litigated and relitigated more often than disputes arising under efficient rules. This means that the rules not contested will tend to be efficient ones. Because they are less likely to be reviewed, including by judges hostile to efficient outcomes, these rules tend to remain in force. Further, as inefficient rules are reviewed, the process of review provides the chance that they will be discarded in favor of efficient rules which, in turn, are less likely to be reviewed. Thus, the selection of efficient legal rules will continue through the adjudication process.

3.3. Litigation as a Rule Selection Mechanism

An important component of the theories advanced by Rubin (1977) and Priest (1977) is the criteria for the selection of disputes for litigation. In fact, only a small fraction of disputes go to trial, and even fewer are appealed. Priest and Klein (1984) develop a model of the litigation process that explores the relationship between the set of disputes litigated and the set of disputes settled. According to their one-period model of dispute resolution, the proportion of plaintiff victories in any set of cases will be influenced by the shape of the distribution of disputes, the absolute magnitude of the judgment, litigation and settlement costs, and the relative stakes of the parties. Priest and Klein show that the set of disputes selected for litigation, rather than settlement, will therefore constitute neither a random nor a representative sample of the set of all disputes. They then derive a selection hypothesis: where both parties have equal stakes in the litigation, the individual maximizing decisions of the parties will create a strong bias toward a success rate for plaintiffs at trial (or appellants on appeal) of 50 percent, regardless of the substantive standard of law.

When the assumption that both parties have equal stakes in the dispute is relaxed (e.g., where one of the parties is a repeat player and has a stake in future similar cases), the rate of success in litigation begins to deviate from the hypothesized baseline, and the model predicts that the repeat player will prevail more frequently. Priest and Klein present a great deal of data, both derived from their own empirical investigations and from the major empirical studies of the legal system since the 1930s. While they caution, because of measurement problems, against the conclusion that these data confirm the selection hypothesis, the data are nonetheless encouraging.

Legal disputes are resolved at various stages of a sequential decision-making process in which parties have limited information and act in their own self-interest. An efficient resolution occurs when legal entitlements are assigned to the parties who value them the most, legal liabilities are allocated to the parties who can bear them at the lowest cost, and transaction costs are minimized. Following these premises, Cooter and Rubinfeld (1989) review economic models of legal dispute resolution, attempting to synthesize a model that provides a point of reference necessary to both an understanding of the courts, and deliberation over proposed changes in legal rules. In the first stage of a legal dispute, the underlying event, efficiency requires balancing the cost of harm against the cost of harm avoidance. Because Coasian bargaining is typically not possible, the social costs of harm are externalized. Therefore, an initial allocation of entitlements is essential to creating incentives for efficient levels of activity and precaution. During the second stage, the harmed party decides whether or not to assert a legal claim. This requires the balancing of immediate costs, such as hiring an attorney, and the expected benefits from asserting a claim. In the third stage, after a legal claim is asserted, but before trial, courts encourage parties to bargain together to reach a settlement. If the parties cannot privately settle their dispute, the court performs this function in the final stage, trial. Using their hybrid economic model of suit, settlement, and trial, Cooter and Rubinfeld come to examine the incentives parties face as they proceed through the litigation process, and make predictions based on the decisions available to the parties, with a discussion of some of the concerns that arise from the pursuit of efficiency which pervades normative economic analysis.

3.4. Judicial Incentives and the Common Law

To understand judicial behavior, the first step is to analyze the incentives faced by judges in their judicial role. In the federal system, law and economics has had difficulty explaining judicial behavior in economic terms, in part because the federal judiciary is structured so as to shield judges from direct political or economic constraints. Posner (1994) articulates a positive economic theory of the behavior of federal appellate judges, using a model in which judicial utility is primarily a function of income, leisure, and judicial voting. He argues that appellate judges are ordinary, rational people whose behavior is somewhat analogous to that of managers of nonprofit enterprises, voters, and theatrical spectators.

In Posner's view appellate judges are like nonprofit managers in that it is difficult to determine the quality or value of the desired output (neutral "justice") from the full range of their services (rulemaking, private dispute resolution, and interposition between the government and its citizens). A rational public is reluctant to buy such services from a profit-making enterprise because a competitive market is not feasible, and they are reluctant to delegate such services to elected officials whose use of political criteria would not be easily monitored. The judiciary is called on to apply neutral justice with much discretionary power but without monetary or political compensation incentives.

The judiciary's nonprofit structure enables competent people to be attracted to judging at lower wages by not forcing judges to work as hard as comparable lawyers might in private practice. However, because most judges continue their judicial activity beyond the usual retirement age of their private sector counterparts, Posner postulates that judges must derive utility in judging beyond just money and leisure. Posner believes that an appellate judge's utility function additionally contains preferences for a good reputation, popularity, prestige, and avoiding reversal. He explicitly excludes from the judicial utility function a desire to promote the public interest because he says such preference cannot be assumed across the board for all individuals. While it might explain the decisions of a few judges, it is not a good standard overall.

Posner analogizes judicial decision making to political voting. There is pure utility in voting, as evidenced by participation in popular elections in which individuals incur a net cost in order to participate in the political process. This analogy suggests that voting on cases is one of the most important sources of judicial utility due to the deference judges' opinions receive by lawyers and the public. Judges further derive a consumption value in deciding for whom or what to vote. Judges balance this consumption against the opportunity cost of decision-making. Leisure-seeking by judges with weak preferences may result in "going along" voting: insistence that a particular decision is coerced by the law, joining opinions containing much dictum with which they disagree, or using procedural rules to avoid difficult or politically sensitive issues. Posner further suggests that this leisure-seeking explains why judges adhere to *stare decisis*, but not rigidly, given the partially offsetting utility of discretionary power.

Posner's approach supports the theory that the conditions of judicial employment enable and induce judges to vote their values (among which Posner believes efficiency to be particularly influential), and his hypothesis generates a number of testable economic predictions about judicial behavior which have engaged an entire generation of legal and economic scholars.

3.5. Rules, Standards and the Economics of Legal Rulemaking

Often a judge must choose between a rule that is precise and one that provides better results in most cases but has higher adjudication costs. Posner's foundational work on the economics of legal rulemaking is often associated with the general theory of adjudication advanced in Ehrlich and Posner (1974). The choice of the degree of precision in the formulation of legal commands is largely based on the desire to minimize social costs. Specific legal rules and general legal standards lie at opposite ends of the precision spectrum. Ehrlich and Posner articulate the criteria for determining the optimal degree of specificity, given cost minimization as a dominant consideration. The authors begin with a static cost-benefit analysis of the optimum level of detail in legal rules.

Ehrlich and Posner (1974) discuss the benefits that precision brings to the legal system, including increased predictability and the consequential reduction in litigation expenditures, increased speed of dispute resolution, and reduced information costs associated with adjudication. The authors suggest that greater precision benefits the legal system. Such benefit results from increasing the marginal productivity of prosecuting the guilty relative to the innocent and reducing the marginal productivity of a guilty defendant's litigation expenditures relative to the innocent. Greater precision allocates scarce judicial resources more efficiently. It makes outcomes more predictable and thus encourages settlement. It decreases the number of legal issues and thus makes dispute resolution more speedy. It reduces information costs in dispute resolution by summarizing what has been learned in prior adjudications, and it facilitates monitoring of judicial agency costs by making incompetent or corrupt outcomes more detectable.

With these benefits, precision also brings costs: the costs of rule formulation (often substantial, given the high transaction costs of statutory decisions) and allocative inefficiency arising from both the over-inclusive and under-inclusive effects of rules. Greater specificity generates inefficiencies from imperfect fits between the coverage of a rule and the conduct it seeks to regulate. Greater precision imposes costs in obtaining and evaluating information and formulating rules (which increases with the number of decision-makers involved). Greater specificity increases the information barriers for laymen, who are more likely to understand general standards than specific rules which employ technical language. Additionally, it increases expenditures on legal counsel because most rules are not nearly as intuitive as standards. Lastly, specificity increases the rate of obsolescence of the rules under changing economic and social conditions.

4. Customary Law and the Economics of Decentralized Lawmaking

The hypothesis that legal rules evolve toward efficiency by a process similar to natural selection was originally formulated with reference to judge-made common law rules. While wealth-maximizing hypotheses of the common law have served as a baseline for the analysis of other sources of law, different theoretical frameworks are used to explain the economic structure of non-judge-made rules.

As part of this undertaking, law and economics scholars have examined whether and how far the theory that law is an instrument for maximizing social wealth or efficiency can be extended to other decentralized processes of law formation, such as customary law and social norms.

4.1. Adjudicating Social Norms

According to the theory of spontaneous law, customary law has a comparative advantage over other institutional sources. The intellectual basis of this claim is related to the proposition that any social arrangement that is voluntarily entered upon by rationally self-interested parties is beneficial to society as a whole.

The inductive process which underlies spontaneous law builds upon the role of individuals giving direct effect to their revealed preferences, without the interface of third-party decision-makers. To the extent that social practices have emerged under competitive conditions (i.e., so long as there is an implicit cost for indulging in inefficient equilibria) without Pareto relevant externalities, we may be able to draw plausible conclusions regarding the desirability of emerging customs. It is in this latter sense that custom may reclaim full dignity as a source of law. The evolutionary and game-theoretic appraisals of the lawmaking process have indeed shed new light on the normative foundations of spontaneous law, but they require an appropriate analysis of the incentive structure in the originating social environment (Cooter, 1992).

Evolutionary theories of cooperation have indeed explained the ability of rationally self-interested individuals to cooperate for the sake of mutual gain. Evolutionarily stable cooperative strategies serve efficiency goals and may emerge as social norms recognized by the community to be obligatory. Once emerged, customary rules generate the expectations of the other members of society and those expectations in turn demand judicial enforcement. In some instances, peer pressure and spontaneous processes of norm internalization will support their enforcement.

The legal system may further this process by recognizing and enforcing welfare-maximizing social norms. In this regard, Cooter (1994) argues that legal recognition and enforcement should consequently be denied in the case of non-cooperative practices, under a test that amounts to a structural analysis of the social incentives that generated the norm. He further argues that in the process of common law adjudication, a distinction must necessarily be made between cooperative norms and non-cooperative practices. Courts are not specialized in the adjudication of most norms. They must therefore resort to a structural approach, first inquiring into the incentives underlying the social structure that generated the norms, rather than attempting to weigh their costs and benefits directly.

4.2. The Process of Customary Law Formation

A fundamental insight of the economic analysis of law is the notion that legal sanctions are "prices" set for given categories of legally relevant behaviour. This idea develops around the positive conception of law as a command backed by an enforceable sanction. Law and economics uses the well-developed tools of price theory to predict the effect of changes in sanctions on individual behaviour. One essential question, however, remains unanswered: How can the legal system set efficient prices if there is no market process that generates them? In other words, how can legal rules reflect the level of social undesirability of the conduct being sanctioned?

Although the legal system sometimes borrows a price from the actual market (e.g., when the sanction is linked to the compensatory function of the rule of law), there is a wide range of situations in which legislative and judicial bodies set prices in the absence of a proper market mechanism. In a law and economics perspective, customary law can be viewed as a process for generating legal rules that is analogous to a price mechanism in a partial equilibrium framework.

Both the emergence of custom from repeated contractual practice and the role of custom as a non-contractual solution to game inefficiencies have been the object of study in both the economic and philosophical literature. Law and economics has revisited this familiar theme, considering the spontaneous emergence of customary law, and, more recently, emphasizing the issue of legal and institutional change in an evolutionary setting (see, e.g., Cooter, 1994; Parisi, 1995 and 1998; E. Posner, 1996; Bernstein, 1996). Further, Parisi (2000) has considered the public choice dimension of the process of customary law formation, considering the potential for norm manipulation and the desirability of an increased recognition and incorporation of customary norms by the legal system.

4.3. Customary Law in the Age of Legislation

In the "social contract" framework, customary rules can be regarded as an implied and often non-verbalized exercise of direct legislation by the members of society. Those legal systems that grant direct legal force to customary rules regard custom as a primary, although not exclusive, source of law. In such legal traditions, courts enforce customary rules as if they had been enacted by the proper legislative authority. Custom thus amounts to a spontaneous norm which is recognized by the legal system and granted enforcement as a proper legal rule.

Modern legal systems generally recognize customary rules that have emerged either within the confines of positive legislation (*consuetudo secundum legem*) or in areas that are not disciplined by positive law (*consuetudo praeter legem*). Where custom is in direct conflict with legislation (i.e., *custom contra legem*) the latter normally prevails. In some instances, however, a custom supersedes prior legislation (i.e., *abrogative custom*), and some arguments have been made in support of emerging practices that conflict with obsolete provisions of public international law (*desuetudo*, or abrogative practice) (Kontou, 1994).

Judicial recognition of customary practice amounts to a declaratory (rather than constitutive) function that treats custom as a legal fact. The legal system "finds" the law by recognizing such practices, but does not "create" the law. The most notable illustration is the system of international law, where, absent a central legislative authority, custom stands next to treaties as a primary source of law. (See, e.g., Article 38(1) of the *Statute of the International Court of Justice*; and Restatement 102 of the *Foreign Relations Law of the United States*.)

Whenever they are granted legitimate status in a legal system, customary rules are usually given the same effect as other primary sources of law. Although often subordinated to formal legislation, customary rules derive their force from the concurrence of a uniform practice and a subjective belief that adherence to them is obligatory (*opinio iuris*), without necessarily being formally incorporated into any written body of law. For this reason, they are usually classified as "immaterial" sources of law (H.L.A. Hart, 1961: 246–247; Brownlie, 1990). This notion implies that the custom remains the actual source of law even after its judicial recognition. In this setting, the judicial decisions that recognize a custom offer only persuasive evidence of its existence and do not themselves become sources of law. In turn, this prevents the principle of *stare decisis* from crystallizing customary law.

4.4. The Anatomy of Customary Law

The theory of customary law defines custom as a practice that emerges outside of legal constraints, and which individuals and organizations spontaneously follow in the course of their interactions out of a sense of legal obligation. Gradually, individual actors embrace norms that they view as requisite to their collective well-being. An enforceable custom emerges from two formative elements: (a) a quantitative element consisting of a general or emerging practice; and (b) a qualitative element reflected in the belief that the norm generates a desired social outcome.

4.4.1. The Quantitative Element
The quantitative requirements for the formation of customary law concern both the length of time and the universality of the emerging practice. Regarding the time element, there is generally no universally established minimum duration for the emergence of customary rules. Customary rules have evolved from both immemorial practice and a single act. Still, French jurisprudence has traditionally required the passage of forty years for the emergence of an international custom, while German doctrine generally requires thirty years. (See Tunkin, 1961; Mateesco, 1947.) Naturally, the longer the time required to form a valid practice, the less likely it is for custom to effectively anticipate the intervention of formal legislation, and to adapt to changing circumstances overtime.

Regarding the condition of universality, international legal theory is ambivalent. Charney (1986) suggests that the system of international relations is analogous to a world of individuals in the state of nature, dismissing the idea that unanimous consent by all participants is required before binding customary law is formed. Rather than universality, recent restatements of international law refer to "consistency" and "generality." (See D'Amato, 1971.) Where it is impossible to identify a general practice because of fluctuations in behavior, the consistency requirement is not met. (See *Asylum case* (1950), at 276–277; and *Wimbledon case* (1923), Ser. A, no. 1.) Similarly, more recent cases in international law restate the universality requirement in terms of "increasing and widespread acceptance." (See, e.g., *Fisheries Jurisdiction case* (1974), at 23–26; *North Sea Continental Shelf cases* (1969), at 42), allowing special consideration for emerging general norms (or local clusters of spontaneous default rules) that are expected to become evolutionarily stable over time.

With regard to rules at the national or local level, the varying pace with which social norms are transformed suggests that no general time or consistency requirement can be established as an across-the-board condition for the validity of a custom. Some variance in individual observation of the practice should be expected because of the stochastic origin of social norms. A flexible time requirement is particularly necessary in situations of rapid flux, where exogenous changes are likely to affect the incentive structure of the underlying relationship.

4.4.2. The Qualitative Element

The second formative element of a customary rule is generally identified by the phrase *opinio iuris ac necessitatis*, which describes a widespread belief in the desirability of the norm and the general conviction that the practice represents an essential norm of social conduct. This element is often defined in terms of necessary and obligatory convention. (Kelsen, 1939, D'Amato, 1971; Walden, 1977). The traditional formulation of *opinio iuris* is problematic because of its circularity. It is quite difficult to conceptualize that law can be born from a practice which is already believed to be required by law.

The practical significance of this requirement is that it narrows the range of enforceable customs: only those practices recognized as socially desirable or necessary will eventually ripen into enforceable customary law. Once there is a general consensus that members of a group ought to conform to a given rule of conduct, a legal custom can be said to have emerged when some level of spontaneous compliance with the rule is obtained. As a result, observable equilibria that are regarded by society as either undesirable (e.g., a prisoner's dilemma uncooperative outcome) or unnecessary (e.g., a common practice of greeting neighbours cordially) will lack the subjective and qualitative element of legal obligation and, therefore, will not generate enforceable legal rules.

The concept of *opinio iuris* introduces a distinction between mere behavioural regularities and internalized obligations. This distinction may be related to the parties' awareness of the expected aggregate payoffs from the game, a distinction that is crucially important in the normative setting. Two categories of social rules are generally distinguished: (a) those that reflect mere behavioural patterns that are not essential to the legal order; and (b) those that reflect an internalized belief that the practice is necessary or socially desirable. A mere behavioural regularity, lacking the qualitative element of *opinio iuris*, does not generate a customary rule. In legal jargon, such behaviour is a mere usage; in economic terms it simply represents an equilibrium convention. On the other hand, norms considered necessary for social well-being are treated as proper legal customs and can enter the legal system as primary sources of law.

4.5. The Domain of Customary Law

The literature on social norms proceeds by considering the appropriate domain of customary law and studying the situations that are more easily governed by spontaneous law.

The earliest economic models of spontaneous norm formation consider the role of morality and internalized obligations as a means for inducing cooperation in conflict games (see, e.g., Gauthier, 1986; Ullmann-Margalit, 1977). Internalization of the norm is a source of spontaneous compliance. For example, individuals internalize obligations when they disapprove and sanction other individuals' deviations from the rule, or when they directly lose utility when the norm is violated. In this setting, Cooter (1994) suggests that a legal custom will successfully evolve when the *ex ante* individual incentives are aligned with the collective public interest. Cooter (1994: 224) calls this proposition the "alignment theorem."

The perfect alignment of individual interests rarely occurs in real life situations, however, so proxies for structural harmony (such as role reversibility and reciprocity) have been considered by the more recent literature.

4.5.1. Reciprocity and Incentive Alignment

Individuals choose among alternative rules of behaviour by employing the same optimization logic they use for all economic choices. True preferences are unlikely to be revealed when individual interests are not aligned. Traditionally, strategic preference revelation is viewed as a hindrance to the spontaneous emergence of cooperation. Such a problem is likely to be minimized in situations of role reversibility or stochastic symmetry (Parisi, 1995). Role reversibility and stochastic symmetry induce each member to agree to a set of rules that benefits the entire group, thus maximizing her expected share of the wealth.

These conditions in fact occurred during the formative period of the medieval law merchant (*lex mercatoria*), when traveling merchants acted in the dual capacity of buyer and seller. If they articulated a rule of law which was favourable to them as sellers, it could have the opposite effect when they acted as buyers, and vice-versa. This role reversibility changed an otherwise conflicting set of incentives (buyer versus seller) into one that converged toward symmetrical and mutually desirable rules.

The law merchant therefore illustrates a successful system of spontaneous and decentralized law (see Benson, 1989, 1990; Greif, 1989). Fuller (1969: 24) observes that frequent role changes foster the emergence of mutually recognized and accepted duties "in a society of economic traders. By definition the members of such a society enter direct and voluntary relationships of exchange.... Finally, economic traders frequently exchange roles, now selling, now buying. The duties that arise out of their exchanges are therefore reversible, not only in theory but in practice."

Certainly, the emergence of consensus for a given rule does not exclude the possibility of subsequent opportunistic deviation by some individuals when roles are later reversed. This is a typical enforcement problem, however, and the possibility of strategic defection does not undermine the rule's qualitative features. The general acceptance of (or acquiescence to) a custom depends primarily on its anticipated effect on the group. Those strategies that maximize the expected payoff for each participant if reciprocally undertaken evolve into norms. This conception of spontaneous law is examined by Stearns (1994: 1243–1244), who observes that if the participants were unable to devise rules governing future interactions, and unforeseen circumstances placed them in a forced market relationship requiring post-contractual negotiations, courts and legislatures might have a comparative advantage over the participants in devising market facilitating rules. Unlike market participants, courts and legislatures choose from among alternative solutions as if the underlying events had not yet occurred, without attempting to maximize strategically the advantage caused by unforeseen circumstances (see also Shubik, 1987).

Where rules are breached following role reversal, norms play a collateral yet crucial role in sanctioning case-by-case opportunism. A merchant who invokes a particular rule when buying yet refuses to abide by the same rule when selling would be regarded as violating a basic norm of business conduct, and would suffer reputational costs within the business community. Conditions of role reversibility, coupled with norms that generate disincentives to adopt opportunistic double standards, are therefore likely to generate optimal rules via spontaneous processes. The group's ability to impose a sanction obviously depends on an individual's accountability for his past behaviour. Benson (1992: 5–7) explores the role of reputation in situations of repeated market interaction, observing that reputation serves as a source of collective knowledge regarding past actions.

4.5.2. Reciprocity Rules in Customary Legal Systems
When unilateral defection promises higher payoffs and there is no contract enforcement mechanism, players are tempted to depart from optimal strategies, often generating outcomes that are Pareto inferior for all (e.g., the well-known prisoner's dilemma game). Prisoner's dilemma-type games are plagued by the dominance of opportunistic behaviour because of the potential accessibility of off-diagonal, non-cooperative outcomes. Schotter (1981), Lewis (1969) and Leibenstein (1982) analyze the role of conventions in correcting prisoner's dilemma situations.

Among the devices capable of correcting prisoner's dilemma-type games, the players can bind their strategic choices to those of their opponents, drastically changing the equilibrium of the game. Ensuring automatic reciprocity by binding a player's strategy to that of his opponent eliminates access to off-diagonal outcomes and renders the reward for unilateral defection unobtainable. Just as no rational player will employ defection strategies in the hope of obtaining higher payoffs from unilateral cheating, neither will a rational player be induced to select defection strategies as a merely defensive tactic. Automatic reciprocity mechanisms thus guarantee the destabilization of mutual defection strategies and the shift toward optimizing cooperation. (For a similar argument relying on tit-for-tat strategies, see, generally, Axelrod, 1981.)

Interestingly, where custom is recognized as a primary source of law, mechanisms of automatic reciprocity are generally regarded as meta-rules of the system. One may consider the following two illustrations, drawn respectively from ancient law and modern international law, which reveal substantial structural similarities.

Lawless environments are characterized by structural reciprocity. In such environments, rules of reciprocity emerge as fundamental customary norms. In the absence of an established legal system or commonly recognized rule of law, reciprocity implies that parties can do unto others what has been done to them, subject to the limits of their reciprocal strengths. Ancient customs of retaliation, based on conceptions of symmetry and punitive balance, provide an intriguing illustration of the principle of reciprocity at work. (See, e.g., Exodus 21:23; and Code of Hammurabi Paragraphs 108 and 127.)

Similarly, in the so-called law of nations (the system that governs the relationships between states), the voluntary recognition of rules by sovereign states implies that absent a commonly accepted standard of conduct, lawless freedom applies. Positions that are unilaterally taken by one state generate a standard which may be used against the articulating state in future occasions.

Thus, in both ancient law and modern international law, the principle of reciprocity serves as a crucial pillar for the process of law formation. Often, situations of post-contractual behaviour capable of modifying states' obligations arise in the law and practice of international relations. The international law formation process provides states with numerous occasions for opportunistic behaviour, including hold-out strategies and free riding. Left unconstrained, states' unilateral defection strategies would dominate in equilibrium. To cope with this reality, basic norms of reciprocity are generally recognized as rules of the game.

As a further illustration, one can consider Art. 21(1)b of the 1969 Vienna Convention, which articulates an established custom of reciprocity, creating a mirror-image mechanism in the case of unilateral reservations: "A reservation established with regard to another party ... modifies those provisions to the same extent for that other party in its relations with the reserving state." The effects of this automatic reciprocity mechanism are similar to a tit-for-tat strategy without the need for active retaliation by states: whenever a treaty is modified unilaterally in favour of one state, the result will be as if all the other states had introduced an identical reservation against the reserving state. As shown by Parisi (1995), by imposing a symmetry constraint on the parties' choices, this rule offers a possible solution to prisoner's dilemma problems.

It should be noted that, while the principle of reciprocity solves conflict situations characterized by a prisoner's dilemma structure (in both symmetric and asymmetric cases), alone it is incapable of correcting other strategic problems. For example, when a conflict occurs along the diagonal possibilities of the game (such that the obtainable equilibria are already characterized by symmetric strategies), a reciprocity constraint will not eliminate the divergence of interests between the players and will not affect the results of the game (e.g., in a "Battle of the Sexes" game, reciprocity is ineffective). The same holds for pure conflict (i.e, zero-sum) situations.

4.5.3. Other Environmental Conditions that Foster Efficient Customs

Evolutionary models further examine the role of long-term relationships in the equilibrium of the game. In long-term human interactions, reciprocity and close-knittedness provide individuals with incentives to choose globally optimizing strategies. Introducing interdependent utility functions into the model, the horizons of individual maximization are extended to include payoffs from future interactions with a direct computation of the well-being of close members within the group. Such a theoretical framework obviously allows for a far more optimistic prediction of spontaneous order. This insight is consistent with the predictions of evolutionary models of social interaction, where low discount rates for future payoffs and the close-knittedness of the group are found to be positively correlated with the emergence of optimal social norms. Models based on interdependent utility and close-knittedness generate results that are qualitatively similar to those discussed for the case of role reversibility.

If the models are further modified to allow the intensity of sentiments of social approbation or disapprobation to vary with the relative frequencies of the two strategies in the population, the degree of spontaneous norm enforcement is likely to increase with a decrease in the proportion of defectors in society. Likewise, norms that are followed by a large majority of the population are more likely to be internalized by marginal individuals in the absence of coercion. Generally, if the measure of spontaneous enforcement and internalization of the norm depends on the proportion of the population that complies with the norm's precepts, the dynamic adjustment will become even more conspicuous. Along with the adjustments taking place in the initial time period, an additional "internalization effect" will occasion a dynamic adjustment of the equilibrium. An initial change in the players' level of norm internalization reproduces the conditions of instability occasioned by the initial emergence of the norm. In this setting, norms become self-reinforcing in that they are likely to occasion an increase in both spontaneous compliance and expected payoffs to the norm-abiding players, with a threshold level of compliance marking the "tilt point" for the survival of the norm.

The various models formulated in the literature suggest that iterated interactions with role reversibility, reciprocity constraints, and structural integration facilitate the emergence and recognition of customary law. The dynamic of the norm formation may unveil the existence of a "tilt point" beyond which emerging beliefs become stable and self-sustaining. In light of reciprocal constraints undertaken by other members of the community, individuals who frequently exchange roles in their social interactions have incentives to constrain their behaviour to conform to socially optimal norms of conduct. Buchanan (1975) insightfully anticipated this result, suggesting that even stronger logic explains the emergence of cooperation in situations of induced reciprocity. In both cases, the non-idealistic and self-interested behaviour of human actors will generate optimal norms.

4.6. Articulation Theories of Customary Law

Notable scholars have considered the conditions under which principles of justice can emerge spontaneously through the voluntary interaction and exchange of individual members of a group. As in a contractarian setting, the reality of customary law formation relies on a voluntary process through which members of a community develop rules that govern their social interaction by voluntarily adhering to emerging behavioural standards. In this setting, Harsanyi (1955) suggests that optimal social norms are those that would emerge through the interaction of individual actors in a social setting with impersonal preferences. The impersonality requirement for individual preferences is satisfied if the decision makers have an equal chance of finding themselves in any one of the initial social positions and they rationally choose a set of rules to maximize their expected welfare. Rawls (1971) employs Harsanyi's model of stochastic ignorance in his theory of justice. However, the Rawlsian "veil of ignorance" introduces an element of risk aversion in the choice between alternative states of the world, thus altering the outcome achievable under Harsanyi's original model, with a bias toward equal distribution (i.e., with results that approximate the Nash criterion of social welfare). Further analysis of the spontaneous formation of norms and principles of morality can be found in Sen (1979), Ullmann-Margalit (1977), and Gauthier (1986).

Legal theorists and practitioners have addressed a similar issue when considering the requirements of *opinio iuris*. In attempting to solve one of the problems associated with the notion of *opinio iuris*, namely the troublesome problem of circularity, legal scholars (notably, D'Amato, 1971) have considered the crucial issue of timing of belief and action in the formation of customary rules. The traditional approach emphasizes the awkward notion that individuals must believe that a practice is already law before it can become law. This approach basically requires the existence of a mistake for the emergence of a custom: the belief that an undertaken practice was required by law, when instead, it was not. Obviously, this approach has its flaws. Placing such reliance on systematic mistakes, the theory fails to explain how customary rules can emerge and evolve overtime in cases where individuals have full knowledge of the state of the law.

In this context, legal theorists have proposed to look past the notions of *opinio iuris* and usage concentrating on the qualitative element of "articulation." Articulation theories capture two important features of customary law: (a) customary law is voluntary in nature; and (b) customary law is dynamic. According to these theories, in the process of ascertaining the qualitative element of *opinio iuris*, relevance must be given to the statements and expressions of belief (i.e., articulations) of the various players. Individuals and states articulate desirable norms as a way to signal that they intend to follow and be bound by such rules. In this way, articulation theories remove the guessing process from the identification of *opinio iuris*.

Consistent with the predicament of the economic models, articulation theories suggest that greater weight should be given to beliefs that have been expressed prior to the emergence of a conflict. Here, it is interesting to point out a strong similarity between the legal and the economic models. Articulations that are made prior to the unveiling of conflicting contingencies can be analogized to rules chosen under a Harsanyian veil of uncertainty.

States and individuals will have an incentive to articulate and endorse norms that maximize their expected welfare. Given some degree of uncertainty as to the future course of events, the emerging rules will be such as to maximize the expected welfare of the community at large. Conversely, rules that are articulated after an outburst of conflict may be strategically biased. Once the future is disclosed to them, parties will tend to articulate rules that maximize their actual welfare, rather than the expected welfare to be derived from an uncertain future. Thus, ex ante norms should be given greater weight in the adjudication process.

This predicament seems to be contradicted, however, by the empirical and anecdotal evidence on commercial customary law. Bernstein (1996) examines customary rules that have developed in various modern commercial trades. Her findings seem to indicate that in the adjudication of business disputes, commercial tribunals tend to enforce customary rules that are quite different from the business norms spontaneously followed by the parties in the course of their relationship. Rather, customary rules develop around practices developed during the conflictual phase of a relationship. In this setting, Bernstein distinguishes between relationship norms and end-of-the-game norms. When adjudicating a case, courts are faced with parties who have reached the end point in their relationship. The end-of-the-game norms of the conflictual phase thus tend to be enforced, while the cooperative norms developed in the course of their relationship remain outside the domain of adjudication.

4.7. The Limits of Customary Law

Customary rules are generally accepted by the community, with a larger share of rules followed spontaneously by the community and a consequent reduction in law enforcement costs. In the decentralized dynamic of spontaneous law, individual decision-makers directly perceive the costs and benefits of alternative rules, and reveal their preferences by supporting or opposing their formation. The formative process of customary law proceeds through a purely inductive accounting of subjective preferences. Through his own action, each individual contributes to the creation of law. The emerging rule thus embodies the aggregate effects of independent choices by various individuals that participate in its formation. This inductive process allows individuals to reveal their preferences through their own action, without the interface of third-party decision-makers.

The analogy between customary rules and spontaneous market equilibria, however, calls for an assessment of the potential insufficiencies of the spontaneous processes of law formation. The literature in this area is relatively thin and much work still needs to be done to develop a coherent understanding of the limits of spontaneous sources of law.

4.7.1. Path Dependence and the Idiosyncracies of Customary Law

Norms and conventions, vary from place to place. Any theory about the efficiency of spontaneous law should explain the diversity of norms and conventions across time and space. In my view, there are two primary ways to provide such an explanation.

The first is to look for idiosyncratic environmental or institutional factors which might attribute to the diversity of observed rules. If the underlying social, economic, or historical realities are found to be different from one another, different norms or conventions should be expected. Rules, norms and conventions develop in response to exogenous shocks through a natural process of selection and evolution. This "survival of the fittest" explanation would suggest that whatever exists in equilibrium is efficient, given the current state of affairs. This belief, borrowed from Darwinian evolutionism, is pervasive in the law and economics literature, and, when applied to spontaneous law, risks becoming a tautological profession of faith. Ironically, we should note that the originators of such a claim, socio-biologists, have now widely refuted its validity.

The second way to reconcile the efficiency claim to the observed diversity of spontaneous rules is to consider the role of path dependence in the evolution of norms and conventions. Evolution toward efficiency takes place with some random component. Random historical and natural events (the random element of chaos theory) determine the choice of the initial path. This may be the case particularly where initial choices are made under imperfect information. Evolution then continues toward efficiency along different paths, with results that are influenced and constrained by the initial random conditions.

If we agree that path dependence has something to do with the emergence and evolution of customary law, we should follow this logic to its conclusion, revisiting the very foundations of the efficiency claim. The main question is whether path dependence could ever lead to inefficient results. According to current research (Roe, 1996), path dependence may lead to inefficient equilibria. Once a community has developed its norms and conventions, the costs of changing them may outweight the benefits. Less efficient rules may persist if the transition to more efficient alternatives is costly. Thus, if one allows for some randomness and path dependence, norms and conventions, although driven by an evolution-toward-efficiency dynamic, may stabilize around points of local, rather than global, maximization. Our history, in this sense, constrains our present choices. We may wish we had developed more efficient customs and institutions, but it would be foolish now to attempt to change them. The claim of efficiency of spontaneous law thus becomes a relative one vis-à-vis the other sources of law. The point then becomes that of weighing the relative advantages of spontaneous law-making against the attributes of engineered legislation, taking full account of the pervasive public choice and information problems underlying such alternatives.

4.7.2. Rational Abstention and Norm Manipulation

A public choice analysis of customary law should further consider the vulnerability of norms and customs to the pressure of special interest groups. This line of analysis — relatively undeveloped in the current literature — should search for parallels between the legislative process and the dynamic of norm formation. In that setting, the opportunity for collective beliefs and customs to be manipulated by special interest groups should be analyzed. Any claim that customary sources are superior to proper legislation will have to rest on a solid understanding of the relative sensitivity of each source to possible political failures.

The application of a well known theorem of public choice to the study of customary law generates very interesting results. Unlike legislation in a representative democracy, customary law rests on the widespread consensus of all individuals affected by the rule. If principal-agent problems are likely to arise in a political world characterized by rational ignorance and rational abstention of voters, no such problems appear to affect customary sources. Individuals are bound by a customary rule only to the extent that they concurred — actively or through voluntary acquiescence — in the formation of the emerging practice.

Imperfect information, however, may induce voluntary acquiescence — or even active concurrence — to an undesirable practice. Economic models of cascade or bandwagon behaviour have shown how inferior paths can be followed by individuals who rely on previous choices undertaken by other subjects, and value such observed choices as signals of revealed preference. Economic models have shown that, when information is incomplete, excessive weight can be attached to the signal generated by others. Others' choices may be followed even when the agent's own perception conflicts with the content of the observed signal. In this way, a biased or mistaken first-mover can generate a cascade of wrong decisions by all his followers, with a result that may prove relatively persistent under a wide array of conditions.

Cascade arguments may also unveil the relative fragility of spontaneous sources of law in light of the possible manipulation of collective beliefs through biased leadership. If information is imperfect, the input of politically biased first-movers may generate undesirable norms. These norms may persist because of the weight attached to the choices of our predecessors. Thus, once generated, wrong beliefs may become stable and widespread in any community of imperfect decision makers.

4.7.3. Collective Action Problems in Customary Legal Regimes

Another potential weakness of customary law is revealed by the application of a collective action framework to the study of the formation and enforcement of customary rules. We can start the analysis by observing that legal rules and law enforcement are public goods. In the case of customary rules, collective action problems may thus arise at two distinct stages: first, in the formative process of customary rules; and second, in the enforcement of the emerged customs.

The process of a custom formation relies on the spontaneous and widespread acceptance of a given rule by the members of a group. Individuals often face a private cost when complying with the precepts of the rule, and they generally derive a benefit because of the compliance of others with existing rules. Thus, the formation of customary law can be affected by a public good problem. When discussing the conditions under which customary rules can effectively develop, I illustrated the analysis with a game-theoretic framework. The public good problem considered here is in many respects similar to the strategic tension that we have examined in the context of customary law formation. If individuals face a private cost and generate a public benefit through norm creation, there will be a suboptimal amount of norms created through spontaneous processes. Any individual would like others to observe a higher level of norm compliance than he or she observed. The resulting level of norm compliance would thus be suboptimal. Collective action problems in the formation of customary rules have traditionally been corrected by norms which sanctioned opportunistic double standards, and by metarules imposing reciprocity constraints on the parties.

More serious collective action problems emerge in the enforcement of spontaneous norms. If the enforcement of norms is left to the private initiative of individual members of the group, a large number of cases will be characterized by a suboptimal level of enforcement. Punishing violators of a norm creates a public good because of the special and general deterrent effect of the penalty. Yet imposition of the penalty is left to private initiative, punishers would be willing to enforce norms only to the point which the private marginal cost of enforcement equals its private marginal benefit. This equilibrium obviously diverges from the social optimum, where enforcement would be carried out until the marginal cost equals the social, rather than private, marginal benefit.

This consideration explains why the customs of ancient societies recognized and sanctioned only a limited category of wrongs. Generally speaking, only those wrongs that had a well-identified victim were likely to be addressed through a system of private law enforcement. For the system of private law enforcement to function properly, it was necessary for the victim or his clan to have a strong interest in carrying out the punishment. This also explains why other categories of wrong with a broader class of victims tend to emerge during more advanced stages of legal development, when law enforcement is delegated to a central authority.

In sum, collective action problems may be pervasive in the enforcement of customary rules, with a consequential risk that enforcement will be suboptimal. This conclusion suggests that the decentralized process of law formation may be successfully coupled with a centralized mechanism of law enforcement. In this way, the advantages that customary sources have in gathering diffuse information will be available, free from the collective action problems that typically affect decentralized processes of law enforcement.

5. Conclusion: Public Choice and Functional Law and Economics

Law and economics scholarship has traditionally been labeled as normative or positive. In both such versions, law and economics focuses on the role of law as an instrument of behavioral control, and treats the political process and institutions as exogenous.

A new generation of literature — developed at the interface of law, economics and public choice theory — pushes the boundaries of economic analysis of law, studying the origins and formative mechanisms of legal rules. The resulting approach, which can be labeled "functional" approach (Posner and Parisi, 1998) is quite skeptical of both the normative and the positive alternatives.

The functional approach is weary of the generalized efficiency hypotheses espoused by the positive school. In this respect, the functionalists are aligned with the normative school. Nothing supports a generalized trust in the efficiency of the law in all areas of the law. Even more vocally, the functional school of law and economics is skeptical of a general efficiency hypothesis when applied to sources of the law other than common law.

The functional approach is also critical of the normative extensions and ad hoc corrective policies, which are often advocated by the normative schools. Economic models are a simplified depiction of reality and, according to the functionalists, it is often dangerous to utilize such tools to design corrective or interventionist policies on the basis of such imperfect assumptions. In this respect, the functionalists are aligned with the positive school in their criticism of the normative approach. According to both the positivists and the functionalists, normative economic analysis often risks overlooking the many unintended consequences of legal intervention.

Public choice theory provides strong methodological foundations for the functional school of law and economics. Public choice theory provides indeed the tools for the appraisal of the traditional assumptions of law and economics. The findings of public choice theory, while supporting much of the traditional wisdom, pose several challenges to the theoretical foundations of the neoclassical law and economics approach.

In the above pages we have revisited the important questions concerning the institutional design of lawmaking through the lenses of public choice theory. Alternative sources of law are evaluated considering their respective advantages in the production of legal rules. The functionalist approach to legal analysis sheds new light on the process of law formation suggesting that the comparative evaluation of alternative sources of law requires an appropriate analysis of the incentive structure in the originating environment.

In spite of the sophisticated mathematical techniques of economic analysis, scholars, judges and policymakers in many situations still lack the expertise and methods for evaluating the efficiency of alternative legal rules. Courts and policymakers can thus resort to a functional approach, first inquiring into the incentives underlying the legal or social structure that generated the legal rule, rather than attempting to weigh the costs and benefits of individual rules directly. In this way, the functionalist approach to law and economics, building upon the solid grounds of public choice theory can extend the domain of traditional law and economics inquiry to include both the study of the influence of market and non-market institutions (other than politics) on legal regimes, and the study of the comparative advantages of alternative sources of centralized or decentralized lawmaking in supplying efficient rules.

Undoubtedly, the field is still far from a point of maturity. The relationship between competing sources of social and legal order remains for the great part still to be evaluated in light of the important criteria that should govern the institutional design of lawmaking.

FRANCESCO PARISI

NOTE

1. From an efficiency perspective, in fact, weight should be given to intensive preferences.

BIBLIOGRAPHY

Arrow, Kenneth J. (1951). *Social Choice and Individual Values*. New Haven: Yale University Press.

Axelrod, R.M. (1981). "The emergence of cooperation among egoists." *American Political Science Review*, 75: 306–318.

Benson, B.L. (1989). "The spontaneous evolution of commercial law." *Southern Economic Journal*, 55: 644–661.

Benson, B.L. (1990). *The Enterprise of Law: Justice Without the State*. San Francisco: Pacific Research Institute.

Benson, B.L. (1992). "Customary law as a social contract: International Commercial Law." *Constitutional Political Economy*, 3: 1.

Bernholz, Peter (1973). "Logrolling, arrow-paradox and cyclical majorities." *Public Choice*, 15: 87–95.

Bernstein, L. (1996). "Merchant law in a merchant court: rethinking the code's search for immanent business norms." *University of Pennsylvania Law Review*, 144: 1765.

Broder, David S. (1997). "Catatonic Politics." *Washington Post*, November 11, A19.

Brownlie, I. (1990). *Principles of Public International Law*. Oxford: Clarendon Press.

Buchanan, J.M. (1975). *The Limits of Liberty: Between Anarchy and Leviathan*. Chicago: University of Chicago Press.

Buchanan, J.M. and Tullock, G. (1962). *The Calculus of Consent. Logical Foundations of Constitutional Democracy*. Ann Arbor, MI: University of Michigan Press.

Charney, J.I. (1986). "The persistent objector rule and the development of customary international law." *British Yearbook of International Law*, 56: 1.

Coase, Ronald H. (1960). "The problem of social cost." *Journal of Law and Economics*, 3: 1–44.

Cooter, R.D. (1992). "Against legal centrism." *California Law Review*, 81: 425.

Cooter, R.D. (1994). "Structural adjudication and the new law merchant: a model of decentralized law." *International Review of Law and Economics*, 14: 215–231.

Cooter, R.D. (2000). *The Strategic Constitution*. Princeton, NJ: Princeton University Press.

Cooter, R.D. and Rubinfeld, D.L. (1989). "Economic Analysis of Legal Disputes and their Resolution", *Journal of Economic Literature*, 27, 1067–97.

D'Amato, A. (1971). *The Concept of Custom in International Law*. Ithaca, NY: Cornell University Press.

Dixit, Avinash and Olson, and Mancur Jr. (1997). "Does voluntary participation undermine the coase theorem"? Aug. 6, 1997 (unpublished manuscript on file with the *George Mason Law Review*).

Dixon, Alan J. (1985). "Line-item veto controversy." *Congressional Digest*, 64: 259, 282.

Easterbrook, Frank H. (1983). "Statutes' Domains." *University of Chicago Law Review*, 50: 533.

Ehrlich, Isaac and Posner, Richard A. (1974). "An economic analysis of legal rulemaking." *Journal of Legal Studies*, 3: 257–286.

Elhauge, Einer R. (1991). "Does interest group theory justify more intrusive judicial review?" *Law Journal*, 101: 31.

Fuller, L.L. (1969). *The Morality of Law*, Revised Edition. New Haven, CT: Yale University Press.

Gauthier, D. (1986). *Morals by Agreement*. Oxford: Clarendon Press.

Greif, A. (1989). "Reputation and coalitions in medieval trade: evidence on the maghribi traders." *Journal of Economic History*, 49: 857.

Harsanyi, J.C. (1955). "Cardinal welfare individualistic ethics, and interpersonal comparisons of utility." *Journal of Political Economy*, 63: 315.

Hart, H.L.A. (1961). *The Concept of Law*. Oxford: Clarendon Press.

Hirshleifer, J. (1982). "Evolutionary models in economics and the law: cooperation versus conflict strategies." *Research in Law and Economics*, 4: 1.

Kahn, Peter L. (1990). "The politics of unregulation: public choice and limits on government," *Cornell Law Review*, 75(280, 312): 101.

Kelsen, H. (1939). "Théorie du Droit International Coutumier." *Revue Internationale de la Théorie du Droit*, 1(New Series): 263.

Kontou, N. (1994). *The Termination and Revision of Treaties in the Light of New Customary International Law*. Oxford: Clarendon Press.

Landes, William M. and Posner, Richard A. (1975). "The independent judiciary in an interest-group perspective." *Journal of Law and Economics*, 18: 875–901.

Leibenstein, H. (1982). "The prisoners' dilemma in the invisible hand: an analysis of intrafirm productivity." *American Economic Review Papers and Proceedings*, 72: 92.

Levine and Plott (1977). "Agenda influence and its implications." *Virginia Law Review*, 63: 561.

Lewis, D. (1969). *Convention: A Philosophical Study*. Cambridge, MA: Harvard University Press.

Long and Rose-Ackerman (1982). "Winning the contest by agenda manipulation." *Journal of Policy Analysis and Management*, 2: 123.

Mateesco, N.M. (1947). *La Coutume dans les Cycles Juridiques Internationaux*. Paris.

Miller, N.R. (1977). "Logrolling, vote trading and the paradox of voting: a game theoretical overview." *Public Choice*, 30: 51.

Olson, Mancur (1965). *The Logic of Collective Action*. Cambridge, MA: Harvard University Press.

Olson, Mancur (1997). "*The coase theorem is false?*" Paper presented at the 1997 American Law and Economics Association annual conference held in Toronto, Canada.

Parisi, F. (1995a). "Private property and social costs." *European Journal of Law and Economics*, 2: 149–173.

Parisi, F. (1995b). "Toward a theory of spontaneous law." *Constitutional Political Economy*, 6: 211–231.

Parisi, F. (1997a). "The cost of the game: a topology of social interactions." *European Journal of Law and Economics*.

Parisi, F. (1997b). "The economics of customary law: lessons from evolutionary socio-biology," in B. Bouckaert, and G. De Geest (eds.) *The Production of Law: Essays in Law and Economics*. Antwerpen: Maklu Publisher.

Penny, Timothy J. (1997). "Pork is safe from this president's line-item vetoes." *Wall Street Journal*, November 13: A22.

Posner, Eric (1996a). "Law, economics, and inefficient norms." *University of Pennsylvania Law Review*, 144: 1697.

Posner, Eric (1996b). "Norms, formalities, and the statute of frauds: a comment." *University of Pennsylvania Law Review*, 144: 1971.

Posner, Richard (1994). "What do judges and justices maximize? (the same thing everybody else does)." *Supreme Court Economic Review*, 3: 1.

Posner, Richard and Parisi, Francesco (1998). "Scuole e Tendenze nella Analisi Economica del diritto." *Biblioteca della Liberta*, 147: 3–19.

Priest, George L. and Klein, Benjamin (1984). "The selection of disputes for litigation." *Journal of Legal Studies*, 13: 1–55.

Priest, George (1977). "The common law process and the selection of efficient rules." *Journal of Legal Studies*, 6: 65–82.

Rapoport, A. (1987). "Prisoner's dilemma," in *The New Palgrave: A Dictionary of Economics*. New York: Norton.

Rawls, John (1971). *A Theory of Justice*. Cambridge, MA: Harvard University Press.

Riggs, Richard A. (1973). "Riggs, separation of powers: congressional riders and the veto power." *University of Michigan Journal of Law Reform*, 6: 735, 743–745.

Roe, Mark (1996). "Chaos and evolution in law and economics." *Harvard Law Review*, 109: 641–668.

Rogers, David (1997). "Clinton warns he's prepared to veto spending bills if changes aren't made." *Wall Street Journal*, October 2.

Rubin, Paul H. (1977). "Why is the common law efficient?" *Journal of Legal Studies*, 6: 51–63.

Schotter, A. (1981). *Economic Theory of Social Institutions*. Cambridge, MA: Harvard University Press.

Schwartz, Th. (1977). "Collective choice, separation of issues and vote trading." *American Political Science Review*, 72.

Sen, A.K. (1979). "Rational fools: a critique of the behavioral foundations of economic theory," in F. Hahn, and M. Hollis (eds.) *Philosophy and Economic Theory*. Oxford: Clarendon Press.

Shubik, M. (1987). *Game Theory in the Social Sciences: Concepts and Solutions*, Fourth Edition. Boston: M.I.T. Press.

Stearns, Maxwell L. (1994). "The misguided renaissance of social choice." *Yale Law Journal*, 103: 1219.

Tullock, Gordon (1981). "Why so much stability." *Public Choice*, 37(2): 189–202.

Tunkin, G.I. (1961). "Remarks on the juridical nature of customary norms in international law." *California Law Review*, 49: 419.

Ullmann-Margalit, E. (1977). *The Emergence of Norms*. Oxford: Clarendon Press.

Walden, R.M. (1977). "The subjective element in the formation of customary international law." *Israel Law Review*, 12: 344.

PUBLIC CHOICE FROM THE PERSPECTIVE OF PHILOSOPHY

The ascent of public choice theory[1], including the public choice society and its journal, is clearly one of the great success stories of post-war social and political theory. To look at it from the point of view of philosophy poses nevertheless a task of critical appraisal rather than uncritical applause. Public choice theory as interpreted here essentially forms an economic approach to politics and to public law. Therefore I shall focus on the role of economic's core assumption of opportunistically rational and selfish behavior in public choice. As shown in the first part (1) the views expressed by some classics of philosophy are at root of modern public choice theory. Beyond that some of them should be taken seriously as systematic contributions to present discussions about public choice in general and the role of the basic behavioral assumption of rational economic man in particular. On the basis of the discussion of the first part the second (2) assesses the public choice account of constitutional democracy in terms of individually rational choice. Philosophically promising amendments from the "neo-classical repair shop" that might conceivably solve some of the "paradoxes" of the standard economic approach to constitutional democracy are discussed. The third part (3.) summarizes and concludes what may be seen as a "philosopher cum economist's" view on public choice.

1. From Classics to Moderns

1.1. Knave Proof Institutions

David Hume said that in politics "every man must be supposed a knave" ((Hume, D., 1985), VI, 42). Many modern public choice theorists, in particular James M. Buchanan, endorse the Humean view. Yet, "it appears somewhat strange, that a maxim should be true in *politics* which is false in *fact*." ((Hume, D., 1985), VI, 42–43). The Humean suggestion seems incompatible with the fundamental methodological norm that the facts should be accepted for what they are and be reported truthfully (see (Albert, Hans, 1985)). The criterion for evaluating the quality of an empirical theory is its truth. In empirical science per se no good is to be expected from using models that are known to be false. So, can we defend the advice of counter-factually adopting a point of view according to which everybody is looked at *as if* being a knave?

A typical modern public choice theorist will tend to interpret the term "knave" as "opportunistically rational economic man".[2] Doing so he may want to adapt Dennis Robertson's (see (Robertson, D. H., 1956)) social functional justification of economics in general to public choice theory in particular and suggest that the task of normative public choice theory is to "economize on love". In particular if we engage the task of "mechanism design" (see Myerson, Roger B., 1991) in public choice under the behavioral assumption that all individuals behave like "(rational) knaves" then we should end up with proposals that can work properly without requiring "love" as "input". The mechanisms will work even if all pursue their narrow self-interest in opportunistic ways. They will therefore be "knave proof" in the specific sense of allowing for opportunistically rational behavior throughout and make it "the interest even of bad men, to act for the public good" ((Hume, D., 1985), III, 16).

Contrary to what is often suggested, the assumption of opportunistically rational selfish behavior does not necessarily lead to the worst case scenario in politics. In politics the worst is to be expected from misguided unselfishness (see Arendt, Hannah, 1951). From Hitler to Stalin, to the attack on the world trade center, human unselfishness and sacrifice rather than opportunism and selfishness are at root of all large scale evil.[3] Therefore, if the Humean principle is seen to aim at worst case scenarios, we cannot interpret it as implying opportunistically rational behavior in the sense of the standard model of rational economic man. To put it otherwise, the public choice theorist who is relying on the model of rational economic man in her explanations of public choice processes may be too optimistic. Engaging the task of understanding "politics without romance" (see Buchanan, James M., 1979) by using the model of rational economic man as a universal behavioral assumption may indeed systematically underestimate the evil influence of romanticism based on superstition and enthusiasm (see again Hume, D., 1985, X).

Though the assumption of opportunistically rational selfish behavior may not lead to the worst case scenario in politics, rendering an institution "knave proof" may be the only way to eliminate the incentive of rational but risk averse individuals who are not knaves to behave as if they were. Seen in this light it is not the case that individuals are selfishly seeking their own advantage — for example out of "greed" — it is rather their resentment or fear of being exploited by others that motivates their actions. Hobbes came close to such a view when insisting that the lack of certainty rather than any base motive on the side of actors in a state of nature (not necessarily a stateless situation but one that ensues beyond the limits of norms enforced by selective sanctions) induces them to engage in pre-emptive action against other individuals. As long as individuals are not certain that others will behave well — or that others have at least a selfish motive to behave well — the risk that others might not behave well justifies and induces rational actors to act in ways that they would deem unacceptable otherwise.

For instance, in a collective goods setting individuals might be willing to contribute voluntarily their own due. They would resist the temptation to choose the dominant free-riding strategy if they knew that others would not free-ride. For them what is a prisoner's dilemma game in objective or material payoffs is an assurance game in subjective payoffs. Their most preferred choice is not the unilateral exploitation of the good conduct of others. Yet being afraid that others might choose the strategy that is dominant in objective payoffs, risk averse individuals might rationally choose the free-ride strategy themselves. More specifically, would such individuals know that all others or a "sufficient" number of them had contributed already they would prefer to contribute themselves (see more or less in this vein Jasay, A. de, 1989; Margolis, H., 1982; Taylor, Michael and Hugh Ward, 1982) but they strongly resent the risk of being exploited. In such a world "defection" would not anymore be a dominant alternative and the game theoretic paradigm would not be an n-person prisoner's dilemma but rather an n-person assurance game.[4]

It is a fundamental insight of public choice theory that the mere awareness that there may be knavish behavior together with loss aversion (in the sense of (Kahneman, Daniel and Amos Tversky, 1984)) may induce individuals who are not knaves to behave as if they were. If these individuals believe that too much institutional trust in the good conduct of people may in fact "invite" or induce others to behave badly they may "react" with knavish acts to the anticipated knavish behavior of others (or the mere suspicion thereof). This is a factual behavioral assumption that in turn may justify the use of the counter-factual assumption of opportunistically rational selfish behavior in institutional design. Such design may minimize the risk to trigger knavish behavior in otherwise well-intentioned individuals.

Normative public choice theory at least in the Buchanan and Tullock variant suggests that institutions be chosen as to minimize risks of too much trust. However, insufficient trust may have negative effects too. Behaviorally, treating those who are not knaves as if they were, may crowd out their trustworthiness (see on crowding out Frey, Bruno S., 1997). Treating individuals as if they were knaves may be a major policy mistake in all realms in which behavior is not fully controllable. For instance, honesty in taxpaying may actually decrease if the controls on taxpaying behavior are tightened. In a business firm intrinsically motivated employees who are providing "trust goods" may be driven out if their superiors start to control their behavior too tightly by specific incentives, rewards and punishments. More generally speaking social order could not exist without non-opportunistic behavior and without some amount of trust in individuals' good conduct. If public choice theory suggests a solution of the problem of social order that is in this respect mistaken, it may undermine the foundations of the very order on which public choice practice rests.

1.2. Public Choice Theory and the "Hobbesian Problem of Social Order"

Since Robinson on his island is one of the heroes of modern economic story telling let us look at an "islandic" story about Robinson and Friday which illustrates the "Hobbesian problem of social order" (see Parsons, T. 1968).[5] Robinson and Friday live "before public choice" (see Buchanan, James M., 1972). In that state of nature, Robinson may legitimately take action against Friday (even take Friday's life) to eliminate any uncertainty originating from the mere presence of Friday. If Robinson lets Friday live — as he in fact does in Defoe's original story — he must incur that risk for a reason as, for instance, his hope to gain from the division of labor and exchange.

Once certainty prevails Hobbes expects individuals to behave in ways that are quite the opposite of what we expect from rational opportunists. For instance, imagine that in a bilateral exchange Friday has acted as a first-mover and delivered his goods as agreed in a preceding mutual promise (see Hardin, Russell, 1982). After Friday has acted there is no uncertainty anymore about Friday doing his part. Friday has executed his promise. Therefore — according to Hobbes — Crusoe as a second-mover is under an obligation to reciprocate. According to Hobbes Crusoe must do his due even in the absence of the "shadow of the future" (see Axelrod, Robert, 1984); and more generally on the underlying folk theorem (Fudenberg, Drew and Jean Tirole, 1992). He must perform even without a rational incentive. However, without such an incentive Crusoe's reciprocal act is not opportunistically rational (or not sub-game perfect in the sense of Selten, Reinhard, 1965, 1975). Yet it is, according to Hobbes, what we (legitimately) can expect from a second mover who is *not* uncertain about the first mover's actions.

Hobbes clearly smuggles in norm-oriented behavior here.[6] He not only believes that individuals are sometimes under an obligation not to act opportunistically but also thinks that they will in fact behave non-opportunistically sometimes. The emergence of social order becomes more intelligible by this Hobbesian concession but at the price of rendering a Hobbesian approach to norm compliant behavior less stringent and clearly incompatible with a strict economic and public choice approach.[7]

In a Hobbesian approach some of the sociologists' claims that men would not always act opportunistically are already accepted. To avoid this the hard-nosed economist and public choice theorist should turn to Spinoza rather than to Hobbes. Spinoza endorses an "economic" approach to norm-guided behavior according to which everybody will in each instance of choice act opportunistically rational. Because of their centrality for the relationship between philosophy and public choice Spinoza's views deserve to be cited in some length:[8]

> Now it is a universal law of human nature that no one ever neglects anything which he judges to be good, except with the hope of gaining a greater good, or from the fear of a greater evil; nor does anyone endure an evil except for the sake of avoiding a greater evil, or gaining a greater good. That is, everyone will, of two goods, choose that which he thinks the greatest; and of two evils, that which he thinks the least. I say advisedly that which he thinks the greatest or the least, for it does not necessarily follow that he judges right. This law is so deeply implanted in the human mind that it ought to be counted among the eternal truths and axioms.
>
> As a necessary consequence of the principle just enunciated, no one can honestly forego the right which he has over all things, and in general no one will abide by his promises, unless under the fear of a greater evil, or the hope of a greater good ... Hence though men make promises with all the appearances of good faith, and agree that they will keep to their engagement, no one can absolutely rely on another man's promise unless there is something behind it. Everyone has by nature a right to act deceitfully, and to break his compacts, unless he be restrained by the hope of some greater good, or the fear of some greater evil. (Spinoza, Benedikt de, 1951, 203–204)

This contains in a nutshell an economic theory of norm-guided behavior. In this theory in particular the norms of law are seen exclusively as external constraints to individual action. The opportunistically rational individual will show norm-compliant behavior if and only if in the instance of choice the expected future consequences of norm-compliant behavior are preferred to non-compliant behavior. The "should" attached to norms derives from self-interest and opportunism not from using the norm itself as standard. Norms do not have any motivational force of their own but serve as instruments in predictions of sanctions (positive or negative).

The preceding view is clearly as mistaken as the "over-socialized" model of man according to which people follow internalized norms no matter what. Human beings can and sometimes do make opportunistically rational choices but we must not assume away the human faculty to "internalize" norms.[9] They sometimes follow norms because of an "intrinsic motivation" to do so. They can and do in fact adopt an "internal point of view to norms or rules". They can accept norms or rules as standards and guidance of their behavior rather than treating them merely as external constraints to which they try to adapt in an opportunistically rational fashion.[10]

Standard public choice theory has no room for an internal point of view to norms. However, without an adequate understanding of the faculty to adopt an internal point of view to norms we cannot adequately understand power and authority and thus an essential aspect of all public choice (excellent on this (Barry, Norman, 1981)). The "easiness with which the many are governed by the few; and the implicit submission by which men resign their own sentiments and passions to those of their rulers" (Hume, D., 1985, IV, 32) cannot plausibly be explained without some element of non-opportunistic behavior. Convictions and beliefs are not merely indicating knowledge of what will happen but express "opinions" on what should be chosen to happen.

Since a wider model of human behavior than that of Spinoza or, for that matter, standard public choice theory is needed economists and in particular public choice theorists run into problems. They cannot have it both ways: on the one hand, bash the sociologists for their assumption of non-opportunistic behavior and on the other hand wheel in non-opportunistic behavior whenever that seems convenient.[11] Either we strive to explain each and every single act of norm-compliant behavior in terms of the expected causal consequences, in particular the future rewards and punishments that the single act is expected to bring about, or we have already given up the core assumption of the model of economic man and thus are not any longer pursuing a purely economic approach to politics.

For instance, an economist who "explains" non-subgame perfect (non-opportunistic) behavior of an individual by demonstrating that it is in the self-interest of the actor to be so committed gives the game away. Drawing attention to the fact that it is in the selfish interest of the committed individual to become committed is no explanation at all. Using such an "explanation" in constitutional political economy amounts to the same as to explaining Crusoe's use of a can opener by pointing out that it is in Crusoe's self-interest to have one (see also (Brennan, H. Geoffrey and Hartmut Kliemt, 1990)). But self-interest per se does not explain the existence of the tin opener. Without a can opener being there Crusoe cannot use it — likewise, without commitment power he as a rational economic man cannot commit.

More generally speaking, a rational actor cannot give up her rationality and opportunism merely because this would be in her self-interest. In game theory, which has taken this aspect of rationality most seriously and thereby to its extreme, cases in which rationality and self-interest are in conflict abound. For instance the whole problem of credible threats and promises emerges only because individuals cannot suspend their faculty to act opportunistically at will. Smuggling commitment power in where it is not part of "the rules of the game" amounts to violating the very premise on which the economists' own criticism of other approaches (in particular sociological) to human behavior is based (see on this more extensively, Kliemt, H., 1987); (Kliemt, Hartmut, 1993).[12] Still, if truth rather than coherence or elegance is the aim of theorizing then a modified model of human behavior is needed. It must accommodate behavior that is boundedly rational in the sense of being subject to limits of information processing as well as in the sense of being intrinsically bound by or to norms.

The philosophical classics used "opinion" to accomplish this task. Hobbes, for instance, said: "... the power of the mighty hath no foundation but in the opinion and belief of the people..." (Hobbes, Thomas, 1682/1990, 16). Even more significantly Hume spoke of "opinion of interest" and of "opinion of right" (see Hume, D., 1985, IV, 33) as central determinants of political behavior. Turning to public choice theory's account of the essential institutions of constitutional democracy and in particular of voting it will become obvious that including the role of "opinion" and the related distinction between low and high cost situations leads to a fruitful modification of the basic behavioral model underlying public choice theory (see for early hints (Tullock, G., 1971) and generalizing (Brennan, H. Geoffrey and James M. Buchanan, 1984), originally 1982; Brennan, G. and L. Lomasky, 1983; Brennan, H. Geoffrey and Loren Lomasky, 1984; Brennan, H. Geoffrey and Loren Lomasky, 1985, Brennan, H. Geoffrey and Loren E. Lomasky, 1989).[13]

2. Constitutional Democracy and Public Choice

Constitutional democracy is commonly associated with "voting procedures for selecting rules and rulers" on the one hand and with "rule of law and the protection of individual rights" on the other hand. Both of these central aspects of the political process in a constitutional democracy cannot be understood adequately if we stick to the standard neo-classical model of opportunistically rational and selfish behavior of individuals. Since the likelihood that a single vote will be decisive in a general election is smaller than the probability of being hit by an asteroid on the way to the voting booth, participation can hardly be explained in terms of expected causal effects on the collective outcome (see Tullock, G. 1967; Downs, A., 1957). Though policies impose significant costs on citizens, voters, in view of the low probability to be decisive, decide behind a "veil of insignificance" (Kliemt, Hartmut, 1986). So why do they participate at all?

2.1. From the Old to the New Public Choice Account of Voter Participation

As is well known public choice theorists have tried to argue that people go to the polls because they are extremely risk averse, because they systematically misperceive the probability that their own vote is decisive or because they fear damage for their general reputation if they are recognized as non-voters. Taking these factors into account voter turn out at the polls might be somewhat higher than the mixed equilibrium to be expected otherwise (see on that equilibrium, Palfrey, Thomas R. and Howard Rosenthal, 1984), however the theoretically plausible values are significantly below any level of participation observed in the real world. To explain the low rates of abstention that we as a matter of fact do observe it is necessary to wheel in intrinsic motivation or a kind of preference for voting as formed by internalization of values and norms.[14]

The account of expressive voting behavior that involves merely insignificant costs of alternative voter choices as fully developed in Geoffrey Brennan's and Loren Lomasky's "Democracy and Decision" (see Brennan, H. Geoffrey and Loren E. Lomasky, 1994 and also Brennan, H. Geoffrey and Loren E. Lomasky, 1989) may in the last resort come directly from the shelf of what has been ironically characterized as "the neo-classical repair shop". Nevertheless, if we intend to stick reasonably close to the economic home turf it is a major step towards a more convincing and coherent (modified) neo-classical account of voting. In Brennan's and Lomasky's explanation of voting behavior causal effects of voting on public outcomes or choices are separated from the private consequences for the choosing individual. For instance the private consequence of fulfilling "her duty" towards the poor will emerge with certainty if a rich woman votes for higher tax redistribution favoring the poor. She can "consume" the "warm glow of fulfilling her duty" while her vote itself will be insignificant for whether or not she will indeed have to pay higher taxes. Casting her vote according to the interests of the rich she would forego with certainty the satisfaction derived from acting according to a standard of morals that puts a high self-esteem-premium on unselfish behavior while gaining only a completely insignificant decrease in the likelihood of having to pay higher taxes. So in view of the intrinsic motivation to maintain the self-image as a moral person the rich woman will rationally choose to go to the polls — provided that it is not too inconvenient and that she does not expect her own vote to be decisive with any significant likelihood.

The spatial model of voting according to which individuals vote for those parties that are located closest to their own position on the ideological field will in principle stand after this modification. Distance in the "opinion" space matters. But that it matters is not explained by the expected causal effects of individual voting behavior on the collective outcome. Voting being "expressive" the spatial model must be seen from a completely different angle. Though it is still framed in terms of individually rational choice the utilities and expectations on which the whole argument is based are much closer to traditional philosophical views of government. Elections resemble opinion polls in which individuals express their views of what they deem right or wrong for the collectivity at large rather than strategic situations in which individuals seek to bring about collective results by exerting some strategic influence.

If we look at things with a philosophical eye we may note here more generally that it is perhaps harder to explain how particular interests can in fact be pursued at the polls effectively than to explain how generalized moral aims are pursued through voting. That this difficulty does indeed exist seems to be supported by the observation that practically all particular interests in public presentation camouflage themselves as general ones. One could, of course, argue here that this serves the purpose of increasing information costs for those who might otherwise be stirred up to take action against the pursuit of special interests. However, a much more plausible view might be that individuals at the polls will tend to prefer what they think is "right" for the public at large rather than what is in their direct particular interest. Those who are trying to further particular interests at the polls must be in a position to argue that the public at large should endorse those interests from a moral or impartial point of view. This is necessary not because the public must be deceived but rather to mobilize and coordinate the particular interest to be served (this is also an amendment to another great book of public choice, namely (Olson, M., 1965)). The particular interest must be presented as a legitimate interest to those who have the particular interest but would not pursue it without moral license at the polls.

If responses of "morally motivated" individuals to this "trick" or "re-framing" lead to results that would also be predicted as the outcome of rational strategic choices in the classical model then this — in view of the veil of insignificance and its effects — is an astonishing phenomenon requiring some explanation or other. What is seen as an explanans (an explanation) in public choice theory may become an explanandum (something to be explained) if expressive voting and the like are factored in. For example, if farmers are particularly successful in serving their particular interests then the strength of these interests and the relative ease with which they are organized is perhaps not the explanation of political phenomena but rather the phenomenon to be explained. If voting is low cost and if expressive components will in all likelihood dominate strategic considerations why is it so that groups seem to be able to act strategically as groups at the polls? The vote of the farmer is as insignificant as that of any consumer. So why would farmers (or more generally producers) go to the polls and vote according to their private interests while their customers cannot in the same way co-ordinate?

Of course, information costs do play a role but they cannot explain in full what we observe. More easy access to information on the income than on the spending side may be a factor but there must be some motive to act on information even at low costs. Within the expressive voting framework as laid out here some ideas come forward easily. For instance there is a "natural" claim to legitimacy going along with producers' interests and this must be taken into account in public choice theory. For it is not interest per se that is guiding individuals in their choices as voters but rather their "opinion" that they are expressing "legitimate interests" at the polls.

Now, one might be tempted to say that it is not important whether interests directly and strategically dominate voting behavior or only indirectly through expressing opinion of interest or right as filtered by criteria of legitimacy. But this is quite obviously mistaken if the dimension of influencing voter choice is taken into account. For traditional models have no room for legitimacy concerns as a *factual* determinant of choice. The philosophical or methodological criticism of public choice theory here is not a normative one but rather that the theory leads to inadequate explanations, predictions and also misguided policy recommendations if it comes to influencing "opinion" as expressed in voter choice.

2.2. Is there "Public" Choice at all?

In the proper sense of the term only individuals can choose. Individuals can make their choices "in public" but it is not the "public" that chooses we only describe it — quite misleadingly — as a choosing entity. For instance, imagine again the simplest case of a general majority election selecting one of two candidates who run for office. In such a case we tend to describe our act of voting as "choosing one of the candidates". However, literally speaking no person is performing the act of "choosing the candidate" (as opposed to, say, choosing one's bride). The only act that is performed is that of choosing to vote for or against a certain candidate — or not to vote at all.

Nobody makes public choices: they rather emerge, as Buchanan has always insisted (see Buchanan, James M., 1954). If it comes to overall results of the process there is no difference between market and political choice. The results are emergent rather than chosen. Of course, we can look at the market, too, *as if* it were a choosing entity. We then describe outcomes that emerge on the market as "collective or public choices". We can always describe something as if it were something else.[15] But it seems strange and certainly not fruitful to look at the collective results of market interaction as collective choices. But then it should seem strange as well to describe the outcomes of politics as collectively chosen. At least we use a "systematically misleading expression" (see Ryle, Gilbert, 1931–32) whenever we speak of "public choice".[16] The older term "non-market decision making" may have been more suitable than the term "public choice" in this regard.

To insist that there are only individual and no collective choices as emerging either from market or non-market decision making does not deny that there are other relevant differences. For instance, in voting the collective result is clearly intended. Voters say yes or no with the vision that the collective result is to be brought about while on the market the collective result is typically neither on the agenda nor on individuals' minds. Unless consumers do things like buying "politically correct coffee" they are not intentionally trying to bring about or influence overall market results. Nevertheless the differences in the costs of choice making rather than an alleged difference between collective as opposed to individual choices is essential to "public choice". Cost asymmetries are also essential for deriving a more adequate account of the very existence of the rules that transform individual choices into public outcomes.

2.3. How do Public Choice Rules Emerge and Manage to Exist?

As has been noted before constitutional democracy besides being characterized by voting is also characterized by rule of law and the respect of individual rights. Again the model of opportunistically rational, selfish behavior is in no way sufficient to explain how rules manage to exist or are brought into existence. The Spinozist or standard public choice account cannot conceivably be true in full. As a specific example, think of the behavior of judges. True enough there are aspects of the judges' behavior that can be accounted for in terms of opportunistically rational and selfish behavior. Judges do not like it if higher courts reject or revise their verdicts since this may be detrimental to their career prospects. They economize on their own effort etc. In short, judges like everybody else can and do act opportunistically rationally some of the time. They respond to incentives and external constraints. Yet it is quite strange to assume that they would not often simply try to form their opinion on what the law requires and act upon this. Besides extrinsic motivation by external incentives judges — at least some, some of the time — are intrinsically motivated to find according to the law.

In principal and agent relationships we generally utilize institutionally that individuals can be expected to show genuine norm-following behavior if the costs of doing so are relatively minor. Hume, whose directly related remarks on opinion were already mentioned, uses the instructive example of the emperor of Rome who could treat his subjects like "wild beasts" but had to lead his Praetorian guards "like men" by their "opinion". Since the physical strength of the emperor would in no way suffice to overcome resistance of any greater number of individuals it is surprising initially how easily he can govern his subjects. Yet if we take into account how the division of labor is extended to the enforcement and creation of rules most of the surprise vanishes.

Those who are policing rules like the Praetorian guards should in general bear only minor costs when doing so. At the same time the emperor must try to feed both their "opinion of interest" — namely that on average they will be better off obeying his orders — as well as their "opinion of right" — namely that he legitimately claims obedience.

The Praetorians must be induced to stick to opinions that bring so-called "power conferring rules" into existence. Rules create power if they are accepted as standards and applied by sufficiently many sufficiently influential individuals in a non-opportunistic manner to single out those who are seen as authorized to give orders or to enact rules. The mighty are mighty because sufficiently many sufficiently influential individuals tend to follow their orders in a non-opportunistic manner. At the same time others obey the mighty because they are mighty. The latter obey out of a rational calculus in particular because they are afraid of encountering sanctions imposed voluntarily by those who follow orders to impose the sanctions.

To understand the role of self-interest here it is important to note that a rule can be adopted out of self-interest while the within rule choices are afterwards made by applying the rule as a standard rather than according to a calculation of the consequences of the singular acts. That individuals apply rules in a non-opportunistic manner which goes beyond case by case considerations changes the character of social interaction fundamentally even if the genuine rule following behavior is shown only if the rules are in the interest of those who follow them and opportunity costs of that behavior are relatively low. Constitutions and the individual rights they may confer exist because power conferring rules are followed.[17] Like all collective structures they must be created by individual behavior and must be explained as results of individual choices which cannot be opportunistically rational throughout.

3. Conclusions

In all social contexts the same "entities" (human beings) are acting. Therefore predictions and explanations of human market behavior like buying and selling should be based on the same model as predictions and explanations of human political behavior like voting or rent-seeking. Likewise the so-called within rule choices should be explained according to the same logic as the choices of rules (see Brennan, G. and J.M. Buchanan, 1985). Norm-guided behavior should be explained by the same model as opportunistically rational behavior — the one or the other triggered by different circumstances. If markets can fail as instruments of coordinating individual choices then politics can fail as an instrument of coordination as well.

Human behavior is to a large extent purposeful action under constraints regardless of the institutional settings or natural circumstances imposing the constraints. It is, however, very doubtful whether the standard model of opportunistically rational choice that is egoistically motivated by "objective payoffs" leads to a realistic account of purposeful action under constraints. All people are sometimes opportunistic. Perhaps all are sometimes even behaving like knaves. Still, social interaction would be quite a different ball game if all people were behaving opportunistically all the time. If that were true neither the very existence of a normative or legal order nor such central public choice behavior as voting in a large electorate could be adequately explained. People at least sometimes simply do what they deem right rather than advantageous for themselves. Without taking this into account our view of "public choice" is distorted and the very possibility of "public choice" as a rule-guided enterprise of determining collective outcomes is a riddle.

The modifications of the neo-classical behavioral model suggested in particular by Brennan and Lomasky on the basis of older ideas of Buchanan and Tullock may lead us a long way. But as we know and experimental economics indicates in some high-stake experiments, humans do show non-selfish behavior even in situations of high costs.[18] The assumption of forward-looking rational choice throughout is, however, doubtful in any event. In the end going to the neo-classical repair shop will not rescue public choice theory as a purely economic theory in the traditional sense of a discipline based on rational choice throughout. In public choice it may be even less rewarding than in more traditional branches of economics since from a philosophical methodological point of view it seems even more doubtful that without major revisions of the underlying behavioral model public choice theory can in fact lead to true explanations of public choice.

On the other hand, traditional public choice theory very well serves our philosophical desire for a rational choice account of society. An account of the workings of society in general and of public choice in particular in terms of opportunistically rational choice is the only one that really appeals to our favorite self-image as rational beings.[19] James M. Buchanan's economic philosophy represents this self-image in its most mature "contractarian public choice" variant (see Buchanan, James M., 1999, in particular Buchanan, James M. 1999a,b). But psychology and cognitive science as well as experimental economics (see Kagel, John H. and Alvin E. Roth, 1995), are knocking at the door of public choice and political philosophy (see for an example Frohlich, Norman and Joe A. Oppenheimer, 1992). Once this door opens in full, new insights into public choice and how it might be improved in theory and practice will emerge.

HARTMUT KLIEMT

NOTES

1. In my discussion of the relationships between public choice and philosophy I shall generally use the term "public choice" for "public choice theory" as well as for the thing itself (but often I shall also differentiate explicitly between the two).
2. For Hume's own justification see Hume, D. (1985). *Essays. Moral, Political and Literary*. Indianapolis: Liberty Fund.
3. There have been public choice analyses of the selfish rent-seeking motives of people who profited, for instance, from the persecution of the Jews by the Nazis; yet these arguments, though very useful and illuminating; cannot explain the full scale of engagement for the "good cause". For the rent seeking argument see Anderson, Gary M. and Robert D. Tollison, 1993. "Wealth Maximization in Hell.:" 13. Fairfax, VA: Center for Study of Public Choice.
4. Possibly, of course, an iterated prisoner's dilemma in which the dominance properties of defection are also altered and cooperation according to folk theorem logic may become sequentially rational may be studied; see for a philosophically particularly useful study of this kind Taylor, Michael (1987). *The Possibility of Cooperation*. Cambridge: Cambridge University Press.
5. For an "Icelandic" story on anarchy and law one may turn to Njal's Saga. For an account of law without the state it is interesting to consult Benson, Bruce (1990). *The Enterprise of Law. Justice Without the State*. San Francisco: Pacific Research Institute for Public Policy.
6. That even the folk theorem does so has been convincingly argued as well see, Güth et al., 1991. "On supergames and folk theorems: a conceptual analysis," in R. Selten (ed.) *Game Equilibrium Models. Morals, Methods, and Markets*. Berlin et al.: Springer, pp. 56–70.
7. For a philosophical account of Hobbes that may be particularly interesting for the public choice theorist see Hampton, Jane, 1988. *Hobbes and the Social Contract Tradition*. Cambridge: Cambridge University Press.
8. Buchanan in his appendix to the calculus of consent which is devoted to the topic of "reading political philosophy" also emphasizes the importance of Spinoza, though for a different reason (see appendix to Buchanan, James M. and Gordon Tullock (1962). *The Calculus of Consent*. Ann Arbor: University of Michigan Press).
9. A rich literature on experiments on ultimatum bargaining shows this; see for an overview Roth, Alvin E (1995). "Bargaining Experiments," in John H. Kagel and Alvin E Roth (eds.) *The Handbook of Experimental Economics*. Princeton: Princeton University Press, pp. 253–348. And originally the seminal paper Güth et al. (1982). "An experimental analysis of ultimatum bargaining". *Journal of Economic Behavior and Organization*, 3: 367–388.
10. The leading legal philosopher Herbert Hart developed his basically adequate theory of how a legal order works and can manage to exist in criticism of "economic" or Spinozist accounts. He criticized legal philosophers as John Austin in ways that directly apply as well to many views expressed by public choice theorists; see Hart, Herbert L.A. (1961). *The Concept of Law*. Oxford: Clarendon Press; Austin, John (1954). *The Province of Jurisprudence Determined*. London.
11. See also Güth, Werner and Hartmut Kliemt (1998). "Towards a fully indirect evolutionary approach". *Rationality and Society*, 10(3): 377–399. The paper programmatically indicates how both the shadow of the past and that of the future can be integrated into a single model systematically.
12. Since the utility functions are formally also part of the rules it might be added that using appropriate modifications of the utility function whenever needed is ad hoc in an unacceptable way, too.
13. The distinction between high and low costs has been around in ethical theory, and in common sense ethics, since antiquity. According to this view we may legitimately demand and expect other-regarding or generally norm-oriented behavior if costs are low while high costs of performance form an excuse and a motivationally sufficient reason to violate normative requirements (see Heyd, David (1982). *Supererogation. Its Status in Ethical Theory*. Cambridge et al.: Cambridge University Press; Urmson, J.O. (1958). "Saints and heroes", in I. Melden (ed.) *Essays in Moral Philosophy*. Seattle/London: University of Washington Press, pp. 198 ff.).
14. If people are asked why they go to the polls they say that they feel obliged to act that way.
15. An instructive argument against the philosophical practice of the same kind can be found in Jasay, Anthony de (1996). "Justice as something else". *The Cato Journal*, 16(2): 161–173.
16. It may also be noted in passing that aspects like cycling in voting are game theoretically and strategically interesting with respect to the working properties of systems of rules but not with respect to some concept of a genuinely collective choice of results.
17. Otherwise a variant of the ancient problem "quis custodiet custodes ipsos?" would emerge or "who is going to control the controllers themselves?"
18. For ways of incorporating even this into neo-classical economics see for instance Frank, R. (1987). "If homo economicus could choose his own utility function, would he want one with a conscience?" *The American Economic Review*, 77(4): 593–604.
Frank, R. (1988). *The Passions within Reason: Prisoner's Dilemmas and the Strategic Role of the Emotions*. New York: W.W. Norton.
19. It should be noted that to the first meeting of the small group that formed the nucleus of what later on was to become the public choice society, besides obvious suspects like J.M. Buchanan, J. Coleman, W. Mitchell, M. Olson, V. Ostrom, W. Riker, and G. Tullock, the philosopher J. Rawls was invited and actually participated in the second meeting. Rawls always insisted that for normative political theory we need to know how political institutions in fact work and that therefore philosophy has to come down from the skies. Still, he took the counterfactual economic model as acquired from his reading of the economic literature as factual at least in part and in that sense just switched skies — in Rawls' "A Theory

of Justice" there are many traces of the introductory text by Baumol, William J. (1972). *Economic Theory and Operations Analysis*. London: Prentice Hall International.

REFERENCES

Albert, Hans (1985). *Treatise on Critical Reason*. Princeton: Princeton University Press.

Anderson, Gary M. and Robert, D. Tollison (1993). *Wealth Maximization in Hell*. Volume 13. Fairfax, VA. Center for Study of Public Choice.

Arendt, Hannah (1951). *The Origins of Totalitarianism*. New York: Harcourt.

Austin, John (1954). *The Province of Jurisprudence Determined*. London: Macmillan.

Axelrod, Robert (1984). *The Evolution of Cooperation*. New York: Basic Books.

Barry, Norman (1981). *An Introduction to Modern Political Theory*. London and Basingstoke: Macmillan.

Baumol, William J. (1972). *Economic Theory and Operations Analysis*. London: Prentice Hall International.

Benson, Bruce (1990). *The Enterprise of Law. Justice Without the State*. San Francisco: Pacific Research Institute for Public Policy.

Brennan, G. and Buchanan, J.M. (1985). *The Reason of Rules*. Cambridge: Cambridge University Press.

Brennan, G. and Lomasky, L. (1983). "Institutional aspects of 'merit goods' analysis." *Finanzarchiv, N.F.*, 41(2): 183–206.

Brennan, H. Geoffrey and James M. Buchanan (1984). "Voter choice: evaluating political alternatives." *American Behavioral Scientist*, 28(2): 185–201.

Brennan, H. Geoffrey and Hartmut Kliemt (1990). "Logo logic." *Journal of Constitutional Political Economy*, 1(1): 125–127.

Brennan, H. Geoffrey and Loren Lomasky (1984). "Inefficient unaminity." *Journal of Applied Philosophy*, 1(1): 151–163.

Brennan, H. Geoffrey and Loren Lomasky (1985). "The impartial spectator goes to Washington." *Economics and Philosophy*, 1: 189–211.

Brennan, H. Geoffrey and Loren E. Lomasky (1989). *Large Numbers, Small Costs — Politics and Process — New Essays in Democratic Thought*. Cambridge: Cambridge University Press.

Brennan, H. Geoffrey and Loren E. Lomasky (1994). *Democracy and Decision*. Cambridge: Cambridge University Press.

Buchanan, James M. (1954). "Individual choice in voting and the market." *Journal of Political Economy*, 62: 334–343.

Buchanan, James M. (1972). "Before public Choice," in Gordon Tullock (ed.) *Explorations in the Theory of Anarchy*. Blacksburg, Va.: Center for Study of Public Choice, pp. 27–37.

Buchanan, James M. (1979). "Politics without romance: a sketch of positive public choice theory and its normative implications." *IHS Journal, Zeitschrift des Instituts für Höhere Studien — Wien*, 3: B1–B11.

Buchanan, James M. (1999a). *The Logical Foundations of Constitutional Liberty*. Indianapolis: Liberty Fund.

Buchanan, James M. (1999b). *Moral Science and Moral Order*. Indianapolis: Liberty Fund.

Buchanan, James M. (1999 ff). *The Collected Works of James M. Buchanan*. Indianapolis: Liberty Fund.

Buchanan, James M. and Gordon Tullock (1962). *The Calculus of Consent*. Ann Arbor: University of Michigan Press.

Downs, A. (1957). *An Economic Theory of Democracy*. New York: Harper & Row.

Frank, R. (1987). "If homo economicus could choose his own utility function, would he want one with a conscience?" *The American Economic Review*, 77(4): 593–604.

Frank, R. (1988). *The Passions within Reason: Prisoner's Dilemmas and the Strategic Role of the Emotions*. New York: W.W. Norton.

Frey, Bruno S. (1997). *Not Just For the Money. An Economic Theory of Personal Motivation*. Cheltenham: Edward Elgar.

Frohlich, Norman and Joe, A. Oppenheimer (1992). *Choosing Justice. An Experimantal Approach to Ethical Theory*. Berkeley et al.: University of California Press.

Fudenberg, Drew and Jean Tirole (1992). *Game Theory*. Cambridge, London: The MIT Press (Massachusetts Institute of Technology).

Güth, Werner and Hartmut Kliemt (1998). "Towards a fully indirect evolutionary approach." *Rationality and Society*, 10(3): 377–399.

Güth, Werner, Rolf Schmittberger, and Bernd Schwarze (1982). "An experimental analysis of ultimatum bargaining." *Journal of Economic Behavior and Organization*, 3: 367–388.

Güth, Werner, Wolfgang Leininger, and Günther Stephan (1991). "On supergames and folk theorems: a conceptual analysis," in R. Selten (ed.) *Game Equilibrium Models. Morals, Methods, and Markets*. Berlin et al.: Springer, pp. 56–70.

Hampton, Jane (1988). *Hobbes and the Social Contract Tradition*. Cambridge: Cambridge University Press.

Hardin, Russell (1982). "Exchange theory on strategic basis." *Social Science Information*, 2: 251 ff.

Hart, Herbert L.A. (1961). *The Concept of Law*. Oxford: Clarendon Press.

Heyd, David (1982). *Supererogation. Its Status in Ethical Theory*. Cambridge et al.: Cambridge University Press.

Hobbes, Thomas (1682/1990). *Behemoth or The Long Parliament*. Chicago: Chicago University Press.

Hume, D. (1985). *Essays. Moral, Political and Literary*. Indianapolis: Liberty Fund.

Jasay, A. de (1989). *Social Contract — Free Ride*. Oxford: Oxford University Press.

Jasay, Anthony de (1996). "Justice as something else." *The Cato Journal*, 16(2): 161–173.

Kagel, John H. and Alvin E. Roth (eds.) (1995). *The Handbook of Experimental Economics*. Princeton: Princeton University Press.

Kahneman, Daniel and Amos Tversky (1984). "Choices, values and frames." *American Psychologist*, 39: 341–350.

Kliemt, Hartmut (1986). "The veil of insignificance." *European Journal of Political Economy*, 2(3): 333–344.

Kliemt, H. (1987). "The reason of rules and the rule of reason." *Critica*, XIX: 43–86.

Kliemt, Hartmut (1993). "Constitutional commitments," in Ph. Herder Dorneich (ed.) *Jahrbuch für Neuere Politische Ökonomie*. pp. 145–73.

Margolis, H. (1982). *Selfishness, Altruism, and Rationality. A Theory of Social Choice*. Cambridge: Cambridge University Press.

Myerson, Roger B. (1991). *Game Theory — Analysis of Conflict*. Cambridge, London: Harvard University Press.

Olson, M. (1965). *The Logic of Collective Action*. Cambridge, MA.

Palfrey, Thomas R. and Howard Rosenthal (1984). "Participation and the provision of discrete public goods: a strategic analysis." *Journal of Public Economics*, 24: 171–193.

Parsons, T. (1968). *Utilitarianism. Sociological Thought*. New York and London: Macmillan.

Robertson, D.H. (1956). *Economic Commentaries*. London: Staples Press.

Roth, Alvin E. (1995). "Bargaining experiments," in John H. Kagel and Alvin E Roth (eds.) *The Handbook of Experimental Economics*. Princeton: Princeton University Press, pp. 253–348.

Ryle, Gilbert (1931–32). "Systematically misleading expressions." *Proceedings of the Aristotelian Society*, XXXII: 139–170.

Selten, Reinhard (1965). "Spieltheoretische Behandlung eines Oligopolmodells mit Nachfrageträgheit." *Zeitschrift für die gesamte Staatswissenschaft*, 121: 301–24, 667–689.

Selten, Reinhard (1975). "Reexamination of the perfectness concept for equilibrium in extensive games." *International Journal of Game Theory*, 4: 25–55.

Spinoza, Benedikt de (1951). *A Theologico-Political Treatise. A Political Treatise*. New York: Dover.

Taylor, Michael (1987). *The Possibility of Cooperation*. Cambridge: Cambridge University Press.

Taylor, Michael and Hugh Ward (1982). "Chickens, whales, and lumpy goods: alternative models of public-goods provisions." *Political Studies*, 30: 350–370.

Tullock, G. (1967). *Toward a Mathematics of Politics*. Ann Arbor: University of Michigan Press.

Tullock, G. (1971). "The charity of the uncharitable." *Western Economic Journal*, 9: 379–392.

Urmson, J.O. (1958). "Saints and heroes," in I. Melden (ed.) *Essays in Moral Philosophy*. Seattle/London: University of Washington Press, p. 198 ff.

PUBLIC CHOICE FROM THE PERSPECTIVE OF SOCIOLOGY

One of the most significant developments in modern social science is, without doubt, the expansion of economic analysis beyond the customary boundaries of economics into the domains of other disciplinary fields such as law, history, sociology and political science, a development often referred to as "economic imperialism" (Tullock, 1972; Radnitzky and Bernholz, 1987; Swedberg, 1990: 14; Frey, 1999: viii). *Public Choice* or, as it has also been called, the *New Political Economy* or *Non-Market-Economics* has played a prominent role in this development that has significantly changed the relationship between economics and its scientific neighbors. In contrast to the exclusive focus on the mechanics of market forces and the pronounced tendency towards disciplinary isolation that has characterised neoclassical, mainstream economics, the new political economy has systematically extended the "economic perspective" into areas of inquiry that have traditionally been regarded as the domain of other social sciences.

Public choice theory has had its most visible influence in political science while its impact in sociology has been much weaker. Yet, sociology is at the same time the social science that feels most fundamentally challenged by the new, generalised economics. In sociology, more than in any other social science, "economic imperialism" is perceived as a threat to the field's disciplinary identity. Why this is so can be better understood if one takes a look at the history of the relation between economics and sociology, the two neighbouring social sciences that "have been estranged from each other far too long" (Swedberg, 1990: 3).

1. On the History of the Relation between Economics and Sociology

As has often been noted, public choice theory, in particular in its Virginia tradition (Buchanan, 1986: 10ff.), is not bringing an entirely new perspective to economics. It is in essence a revival and systematic extension of a research program that was very much inherent in the classical beginnings of economics as a scientific enterprise, in particular so in the political economy of Adam Smith (Buchanan ibid.: 10; Buchanan, 1978: 18, 1987a: 585; West, 1990). It is only because this research program had largely been forgotten during the neoclassical period in economics, that the new political economy can be said to be "new." Adam Smith held a chair in "moral philosophy," a field that in modern terminology may be most adequately described as *social science* (Lindenberg, 1986: 21). Smith and others who, in the history of ideas, are commonly referred to as *Scottish Moral Philosophers*, including, in particular, David Hume and Adam Ferguson, developed in the second half of the 18th century a research program that was not at all confined to economic issues in a technical sense but constituted a general paradigm in social theory, integrating economic, legal, political and social analysis (Rowley, 1998: 474ff.; Vanberg, 1975: 5ff.). It is a paradigm based on methodological individualism and centred around the idea that social aggregate phenomena should be explained as the largely unintended outcomes "of individual actions directed toward other people and guided by their expected behavior" (Hayek, 1948: 6).

The advantages of specialisation about which Adam Smith wrote have, of course, shaped the development of academia no less than that of other areas of human activity. Since Smith's time "moral philosophy" has become subdivided in a growing number of specialised social sciences, just as its counterpart, "natural philosophy" has split up into the various specialised natural sciences. Yet, while among the latter the subdivision into specialised fields was largely a matter of a pragmatic division of labour, the situation in the social sciences was different. In particular the separation between sociology and economics turned into a paradigmatic divide, leading to two fundamentally different theoretical traditions.

In the case of sociology the manner in which the French sociologist Emile Durkheim (1855–1917) defined the field was critical in its early emergence as an academic discipline. It is largely due to his influence that sociology came to found its claims for disciplinary identity on the assertion that its own theoretical perspective is categorically different from the individualistic, utilitarian perspective of economics, and that the latter, for inherent reasons, is incapable of accounting for important aspects of social reality, in particular for its normative and institutional dimensions. According to Durkheim, the science of sociology has its origins in 18th century French social philosophy, the polar counterpart to the individualist paradigm of the Scottish Moralists (Vanberg, 1975: 134ff.), and in particular in the social philosophy of Auguste Comte, who was the first to use the term "sociologie" in his *Cours de Philosophie Positive*, published between 1830 and 1842. Though Durkheim rejected Comte's historicist claims, i.e., his concern with laws of history that supposedly govern the development of human society, he fully endorsed Comte's anti-individualist premises and his claim that society must be looked at as a specific kind of reality apart from its individual constituents and governed by its own laws (Durkheim [1900] 1964a, [1915] 1964b).

In his ambition to secure for sociology a distinct place in an academic environment in which disciplines like psychology and economics had already established themselves, Durkheim defined sociology in a twofold manner. On the one hand he defined it in terms of its subject matter, namely "as the science of institutions, of their genesis and of their functioning" (Durkheim [1895] 1938: lvi), while, on the other hand, he defined it in methodological terms, namely as a science that has its own, non-individualist theory. It was his methodological commitment that implied that "sociology cannot be based upon a theory that treats the individual as the *starting point* of analysis" (Giddens, 1971: 211) and that, therefore, it had to be based on fundamentally different theoretical principles than economics. For economists, he censured, "there is nothing real in society but the individual" (Durkheim, 1978: 49). Even worse, their concept of the individual is empirically inadequate, ignoring "all circumstances of time, place, and country in order to conceive of man's abstract type in general" (ibid.), "the sad portrait of an isolated egoist" (ibid.).

Even if later generations of sociologists were not quite as explicit in their programmatic anti-individualism as Durkheim, and even if there were prominent exceptions such as Max Weber, in its mainstream, sociology has been dominated ever since by the silent premise that the "utilitarian tradition" on which economics is based can, for principal reasons, not be an adequate foundation for sociological theory (Camic, 1979). In modern sociology the Durkheim program has most forcefully been restated by Talcott Parsons who proclaimed that "anything like a satisfactory sociological theory could not have been developed at all within the utilitarian framework," and that only "the break with utilitarian premises" allowed for the "emergence of sociological theory" (Parsons, 1968: 234).

While sociology, in the manner described above, committed itself to excluding a priori as sociologically inadequate any explanation of social phenomena that starts from assumptions about individual human behaviour, post-Smithian economics retained the individualist paradigm of its classical origins, yet it increasingly focused its analytical interest on an ever more narrowly defined aspect of social reality, namely the properties of a highly stylised market, described in terms of a highly stylised model of man. Compared to the much broader outlook of Adam Smith's political economy, the writings of David Ricardo marked the beginnings of a shift in emphasis about which Harold Demsetz (1982: 6f.) has said: "Markets became empirically empty conceptualizations of the forums in which exchange costlessly took place. The legal system and the government were relegated to the distant background by the simple device of stating, without clarification, that resources where 'privately owned.'" This shift in the theoretical orientation of economics found its most influential statement in Leon Walras' *Éléments D'Économie Politique Pure* of 1874 which defined the neoclassical research program of modern economics. It was Walras' ambition to develop a "science of pure economics" in the same spirit as "a physico-mathematical science like mechanics or hydrodynamics" (Walras [1874] 1954: 71). His pure economics was to be concerned with "how prices result from a hypothetical régime of absolutely free competition" (ibid.: 256), supposing "that the market is perfectly competitive, just as in pure mechanics we suppose, to start with, that machines are perfectly frictionless" (ibid.: 84). Phenomena which he "classified under the heading of institutions" (ibid.: 63) Walras explicitly excluded from the domain of pure economics, without denying, though, that they can be a proper subject of economics more broadly understood. Even though the study of institutional phenomena fell, in his view, outside of "economics as an exact science" (ibid.: 47), he considered it the appropriate subject of what he called "social economics" (ibid.: 79). However, the part that his "social economics" would have had to play in a more broadly conceived economics was never developed, not by Walras himself nor in what has come to be known as the Walrasian tradition. Neoclassical mainstream economics remained occupied with advancing and formalising in ever more refined ways Walras' program for "a scientific theory of the determination of prices" (ibid.: 40), and left unattended the institutional issues that Walras had assigned to "social economics."

2. Convergences between Economics and Sociology

A sociology that would have concentrated on the study of institutional phenomena, without pre-committing to a non-individualist theoretical perspective, and an economics that would have primarily concerned itself with the study of market processes, without excluding categorically the institutional dimension from its explanatory enterprise, such a sociology and such an economics could have productively co-evolved as two disciplines that, in a pragmatic division of labor, focus on different kinds of issues, but share in the same theoretical foundation and they could have easily supplemented each others explanatory contributions wherever the task at hand required it. Yet, the diverging developments described above created a paradigmatic divide between a non-individualist sociology claiming institutional phenomena as its own domain and an individualist economics studying the mechanics of markets, explicitly disregarding the institutional dimension. As a consequence, these developments left a " 'no-man's land' between economics and sociology" (Swedberg, 1990: 316), namely the systematic study of institutional phenomena and, more generally, non-market phenomena from an individualist perspective. The significance of *Public Choice* and related theoretical approaches that emerged within economics during the second half of the 20th century lies in the very fact that they have embarked on a systematic exploration of this "no-man's land."

James M. Buchanan has explicitly characterised public choice theory as "an attempt to close up the analysis of social interaction systems" (Buchanan, 1972: 11). It is an effort to pursue the development "of an internally consistent social science" (ibid.: 23) by systematically extending the individualist economic approach beyond its traditional domain as "a highly developed theory of market behavior" (ibid.: 11) to the " 'public choices' that define the constraints within which market behavior is allowed to take place" (ibid.) and, more generally, to non-market behavior (ibid.: 23). Along with other approaches to a *new institutional economics*, public choice is about the extension of the "*homo oeconomicus* postulate from market to collective institutional settings" (Buchanan, 1983: 12). It is an effort to analyse institutional and non-market phenomena within the same general paradigm as market phenomena, i.e., "with individual decision-makers as the basic units" (ibid.: 9). Characterising the various related approaches that seek to go beyond the boundaries of traditional mainstream economics, Ronald Coase (1994: 36) notes that "economists are extending the range of their studies to include all of the social sciences." Hans Albert (1979: 8) speaks of these approaches as a revival of the "general sociological research program" that was present at the classical origins of economics, a research program that constitutes a principal alternative to theoretical perspectives prevalent in sociology, and that can well be developed into "a general paradigm for social science" (ibid.: 23). And Bruno S. Frey describes the generalised economic perspective that is "known under such terms as 'Non-Market Economics,' 'New Political Economy,' or 'New Institutionalism' " (Frey, 1999: viii) as "a *new paradigm* for the *social sciences*" (ibid.: vii), as an outlook that "applies the same theoretical approach to many different areas," thus advancing the "unity of the social sciences" (ibid.: 15).

Just as within economics the discontent with the narrow focus of the Walrasian research program led to efforts to revive the general social science perspective of classical political economy, in sociology the discontent with the a priori methodological commitment of the Durkheim program led to attempts to advance an individualist sociological theory, expressly compatible with the behavioural foundations of economics and, in fact, with direct connections to public choice theory (Vanberg, 1983). Even though these approaches have hardly begun to grow out of their somewhat marginal existence within the sociological profession, they deserve attention in the present context. It was the Harvard sociologist George C. Homans who initiated the modern emergence of an individualist sociology with his 1958 article "Social Behavior as Exchange," in which he argued that all human interaction can be looked at as exchange, in much the same way that economists look at market behavior. In his 1964 presidential address to the

American Sociological Association, Homans challenged his colleagues with his plea to "bring man back" into sociology, and to acknowledge the fact that beneath their programmatic anti-individualism sociologists have actually no other operable theory to work with than conjectures about human behavior. Calling for an end to what he chastised as "intellectual hypocrisy," Homans (1964: 818) noted: "It would unite us with the other social sciences, whose actual theories are much like our actual ones, and so strengthen us all." And he invited his fellow sociologists to see as their task to explain how relatively enduring social structures are "created and maintained by the actions of individuals, actions of course taken under the influence and constraint of the actions of other individuals" (Homans, 1975: 64).

The fact that Homans' own work remained very much focused on the analysis of "elementary social behavior" (Homans, 1974) made it easy for mainstream sociologists to discount his challenge as not really demonstrating that social phenomena at the structural and institutional level can be explained satisfactorily on the basis of assumptions about individual human behavior, without recourse to a "genuine sociological theory." A more direct challenge to the traditional doctrine arose in the work of James S. Coleman (1990), who said about himself that he had been converted by Homans' arguments from a "Durkheimian" to an advocate of methodological individualism (Coleman in Swedberg, 1990: 49; Coleman, 1986: 2). Coleman applied the individualist paradigm explicitly to the institutional and organisational level, notably with his theory of corporate action, a theory that seeks to answer, on the basis of assumptions about individual behavior, the question of how men act collectively through corporate units such as households, firms, organisations, political parties, nation-states etc. (Vanberg, 1982: 8ff.). Distancing himself from the standard self-image of his fellow-sociologists he called for a sociological approach that "does not afford itself the luxury of beginning with already formed units of social organisation. Instead, it must begin with persons, and move up from there, or if, in an application, it begins at a level above persons, it must be ultimately analysable into relations among persons" (Coleman, 1975: 85f.).

Coleman has been one of the early members of the Public Choice Society, and he has explicitly argued that sociology can build on the same theoretical foundation as microeconomics, namely the "purposive actor model" (Coleman, 1975: 88). He has added, though, that borrowing their basic behavioural model from economics does not dispense sociologists from their task to build sociological theory (ibid.: 93). In the introduction to a collection of his essays, entitled *Individual Interest and Collective Action* he describes the articles included as "attempts to investigate some of the most important problems of sociology ... beginning with a paradigm of rational action borrowed from economics (and slightly elaborated)" (Coleman, 1986: 10f.).

Coleman's work has become the focal point of an international group of like-minded sociologists that includes, among many others, such scholars as Raymond Boudon in France, Michael Hechter and Douglas D. Heckathorn in the United States, Siegwart Lindenberg and Werner Raub in the Netherlands, Karl-Dieter Opp and Thomas Voss in Germany, or Toshio Yamagishi in Japan. This group of individualist sociologists is often subsumed under the umbrella-name of *rational choice sociology*, even though not all of them are firmly wedded to the rational choice model, and one of their main outlets for their publications is the journal *Rationality and Society* that Coleman founded in 1989. In his "Editorial Introduction" to the journal's inaugural issue Coleman (1989: 6) notes that *Rationality and Society* "explicitly espouses methodological individualism" and that its focus is "on the paradigm of rational action," a paradigm on which he comments: It is a "paradigm in social science that offers the promise of bringing greater theoretical unity among disciplines than has existed until now. ... It is the paradigm on which economic theory rests. It is the basis for the expanding domain of public choice within political science. It is the paradigm of the burgeoning field of law and economics. ... Social exchange theory is one of the manifestations of this paradigm in sociology" (ibid.: 5).

3. Sociology as a "Multi-paradigm Science"

From the perspective of rational choice sociology there is obviously no reason to perceive public choice theory along with the other branches of the new generalised economics as an "imperialistic" threat. Instead, both sides can be seen as perfectly compatible research programs that build on the same theoretical foundations, even if, due to the different substantive interests of their respective home-disciplines, they typically apply their shared basic paradigm to different kinds of explanatory issues. Yet, as noted before, the group of sociologists who explicitly subscribe to methodological individualism represents only a minority fraction within the sociological profession at large. As it has been since its origins as a separate academic discipline, sociology continues to be dominated by a methodological commitment to a non-individualist, anti-utilitarian outlook, in spite of the fact that this commitment, quite apparently, even after more than a century since its inception has not come to fruition in the sense of producing a theoretical paradigm that would unite the field. Instead, as soon as one looks beyond the surface of a generally — explicitly or tacitly — shared anti-individualist outlook, modern sociology presents itself as a theoretically fragmented discipline, lacking even a consensus on what criteria one could possibly employ to judge what may count as a "theory," let alone as a "good theory." In his introduction to a textbook on contemporary sociological theories one author describes the state of the field in these terms: "Beneath the surface of professional association membership are numerous disagreements, tensions, and disputes that threaten to break up even the formal unity of sociologists. ... Such disputes reveal that sociologists are as yet unsure of the foundation of their discipline and to some, the foundations have yet to be laid" (Wells, 1978: 1).

Euphemistically, sociology may be described as a "multi-paradigm science" (Ritzer, 1975), reflecting the variety of distinct theoretical perspectives that one typically finds discussed in surveys on "sociological theory," perspectives such as functionalism, structuralism, conflict theory, critical theory, marxism, symbolic interactionism, ethno-methodology, post-modernism, and others. In a more critical assessment of the current state of sociological theory one might suspect that it's a priori commitment to a non-individualist outlook may have led sociology into a blind alley. As George C. Homans has put it, misled by its self-imposed programmatic restrictions sociology has looked "for its fundamental principles in the wrong places and hence without success" (Homans, 1967: 73).

A brief comment should be added here on Max Weber (1864–1920) who was mentioned earlier as a prominent exception to the dominant programmatic commitment in sociology. Trained as an economist in the tradition of the German Historical School, Weber was sympathetic to the analytical economics of the Austrian tradition, and one of his aims in developing his research program of social economics (*Sozialökonomik*) was to reconcile the conflicting views in the "Methodenstreit" that had erupted with the controversy between Carl Menger and Gustav Schmoller. As a sociologist, Weber clearly considered himself a *methodological individualist*, even if he did not use the term that was not yet common in his time, defining sociology as a science that seeks to explain social and economic phenomena through "understanding" the human actions that, collectively and interactively, bring them about. He once explicitly stated (in a letter, dated March 9, 1920, to his colleague Robert Liefmann) that when he moved from economics into sociology he made it his mission to fight the widespread misuse of collectivist notions and to insist that the individualist approach is the only adequate method in sociology (Vanberg, 1975: 103f.).

Max Weber's theoretical outlook could have well become the focal point of an individualist tradition in sociology, yet this is not what happened. Even though, since decades, he has been and continues to be one of the most often cited "authorities" in matters of sociological theory, it is not his methodological individualism but rather other aspects of his work that gained him popularity, such as his concept of "ideal types" and his emphasis on the method of "Verstehen," or his historical studies on the rise of capitalism and other subjects. In fact, even those sociologists who explicitly regard themselves as working in the Weberian tradition are typically no less convinced than their fellow-sociologists that the individualist-utilitarian approach of economics is entirely inadequate as a foundation of sociological theory. Very few of them are likely to form an alliance with rational choice sociologists.

4. Economic Imperialism?

In light of the history, briefly traced above, of the relation between economics and sociology it is both unfortunate and misleading that the label *economic imperialism* has come to be used to describe the efforts within public choice and related approaches to reconstitute economics as a general *social science*. The use of this label is unfortunate because with "imperialism" one tends to associate the notions of invasion and conquest, notions that make it appear as if what is at stake is a hostile take-over of other social sciences by economics. Such framing of the issue is, for obvious reasons, unlikely to invite an open discourse on the relative merits of alternative theoretical approaches. Instead, it is bound to provoke little more than defensive reactions on part of the prospective victims of economics' expansionist ambitions. The label *economic imperialism* is, however, also misleading, and this in two ways. First, it distracts from the fact that the real issue is not about the relation between different disciplines within the social sciences but about the explanatory potential of alternative theoretical paradigms *for the social science*s. And second, it is misleading because it distracts attention from the fact that the theoretical foundations of "the economic approach" cannot remain unaffected in the process, but that its generalised application makes apparent the need to reform the "economic model of man" in certain ways. Both aspects are briefly discussed below.

The true significance of what is misleadingly labelled as "economic imperialism" lies not in the fact that economics is expanding its domain at the expense of other social sciences, or that economists were about to claim a general competence in the various areas traditionally covered by other disciplines. Economists should be the last to ignore that division of labor is of no lesser importance in academia than in other realms of life. What is at stake is the *theoretical unity of the social sciences*, not the ambition to turn the various social sciences into branches of economics. As was described above, it was the paradigmatic split in the social sciences, in particular between sociology and economics, that made a thoroughgoing methodological individualism the trademark of the "economic approach." But, apart from the fact that economics has been the only social science that has been predominantly and consistently committed to methodological individualism, there is nothing specific "economic" about an individualist approach. Therefore, to show how an individualist methodology can be successfully used to solve explanatory problems traditionally studied by other social sciences is not about exporting a uniquely "economic approach." It means only to show that a theoretical approach that has been used in economics, and largely remained confined to economics, has a much broader explanatory potential than previously recognised. In this sense the reorientation in the social sciences that public choice and related approaches in modern economics have initiated is, in essence, about the consistent application of an individualist methodology throughout the social sciences. It does not put in question that there can be a meaningful division of labour between various specialised disciplines. What it does put in question is the theoretical or paradigmatic divisions that have fragmented the social sciences in the past and that have robbed them from the opportunity to communicate effectively among each other.

As noted, there is a second sense in which the label "economic imperialism" is misleading. It suggests that the need to change and to adapt their theoretical orientation is exclusively on the side of the "invaded" disciplines, while the invading "economic paradigm" remains essentially unaffected in the process. To be sure, that the new generalised economics departs from the neoclassical tradition in that it explicitly seeks to account for institutional aspects is, as has been noted above, well recognised. What is not equally well recognised is the fact that the explanatory potential of neoclassical theory is not only limited by its focus on highly stylised markets, but also by the fact that it employs a highly stylised model of man, of *homo oeconomicus*, the perfectly rational, fully informed maximiser of his own welfare. Reconstituting economics as a general social science does, however, not only require one to rectify the institutional deficiency of the neoclassical tradition, it also requires one to modify its problematic behavioural assumptions. Someone who in his thorough critique of the Walrasian tradition has always emphasised both aspects is Hans Albert. While maintaining that the research program of classical political economy represents a general theoretical approach in social science, he blames the "model-Platonism" of neoclassical economics for its disregard of institutional aspects as well as for its behavioural deficiency, i.e., for the fact that it turned the broadly utilitarian psychology of the classics into a purely formal "*decision logic* or logic of choice" (Albert, 1979: 9), instead of developing it into an empirically contentful theory of human behaviour. And while he acknowledges that the new institutionalism in economics "has undoubtedly rehabilitated one of the important ideas of the economic research program" (ibid.: 20), he leaves no doubt that in his view serious problems remain with the behavioral foundations of the economic approach.

5. The Behavioural Foundations of Economics as a Social Science

One may well agree with Ronald Coase's (1994: 45) supposition that "the success of economists in moving into other social sciences is a sign that they possess certain advantages in handling the problems of those disciplines." The crucial question, however, is which of the specific attributes that may define the economic approach confer to it the advantages that account for its success. There are good reasons to presume that methodological individualism and the general notion of self-interested human behaviour are the crucial contributing factors here, not, however, the particular model of "rational choice" in its standard interpretation. Doubts about the explanatory power of the latter are, in fact, voiced by Coase (ibid.: 43) when he notes: "To say that people maximize utility... leaves us without any insight into why people do what they do." James Coleman who, as noted above, expressly calls for a sociology based on rational choice theory, also voices some caution when he argues: "For the moment, it is the only well developed conception of rational action that we have; and though it may well be replaced when cognitive psychology is more fully developed, there is nothing to replace it now" (Coleman 1975: 81). Such a waiting attitude is not what Dennis C. Mueller (1986) has recommended to his colleagues. In his presidential address to the 1986 Public Choice Society Meeting, he made a case for replacing what he calls the "rational egoism postulate" of economics by a behavioural theory that, while maintaining the assumption of self-interested, payoff-oriented behaviour, puts less emphasis on *rational choice* than on *adaptive learning*. Specifically, Mueller advocates "starting with behaviorist psychology" (ibid.: 15), which, incidentally, is the same choice that George C. Homans' had made for his individualist sociology, noting: "We believe that the propositions of behavioral psychology are the general explanatory propositions of all the social sciences. Accordingly, they are the general propositions of economics" (Homans, 1974: 74). In a similar spirit Mueller notes as an advantage of "starting with behaviorist psychology" that "it allows us to begin with a unified view of human behavior" and that it "is less of a methodological leap for a social scientist who works with rational egoist models than going to some competing sociological-psychological theories" (Mueller, 1986: 15).

Whether a more behaviorist approach, as suggested by Mueller, or a model closer to cognitive psychology, as suspected by Coleman, is a more likely candidate for replacing the traditional rational choice model, remains to be seen. It should be apparent, though, that economists who — be it in public choice or in other branches of the new generalised economics — seek to re-establish, in the spirit of classical political economy, the economic approach as a "general paradigm for social science" (Frey) cannot evade the task of rectifying not only its *institutional* but also its *behavioral* deficiency. In fact, it is more and more recognised that, ultimately, institutional phenomena cannot be consistently explained without substituting the standard rational choice model with a behavioral theory that accounts for the element of *rule-following* in human conduct. The fact that rational choice theory with its focus on the incentive-contingencies of *single choices* tends to emphasise the role of situational calculation in human behavior and to ignore the extent to which such behavior is a matter of habits, routines and rule-guided conduct, has been a principal obstacle in the relation between economics and sociology. Durkheim was surely right when he argued that "mores and the prescriptions of law and morality would be impossible if man were not capable of acquiring habits" (Durkheim, 1978: 51), and he had reason to conclude that an economics that models man as a case-by-case maximiser is unable to systematically explain the role of habits.

While Durkheim erred when he diagnosed that a non-individualist alternative to the approach of economics is needed to account for the role of norms and institutions in social life, his challenge to the economic model of man remains to be answered. Habits, routines and other forms of individual rule-guided behavior are, indeed, the building blocks of what we call institutions (Nelson, 2002: 21ff.), and a model of man on which explanations of institutional phenomena are to be founded must be able to provide a systematic explanation for the obvious rule-following element in human behavior. The reluctance of economists to part with their traditional model of man may be somewhat softened by recent theoretical developments in cognitive psychology and evolutionary theory that converge towards a model of rule-based or program-based behaviour. This model maintains much of what has made rational choice theory so attractive to economists but provides at the same time a systematic bridge between the notion of pay-off governed individual behavior on the one hand and institutional phenomena on the other (Vanberg, 2002).

6. Conclusion

As has been described above, sociology was established as an academic discipline in explicit opposition to the individualist-utilitarian approach of economics, and the conviction that this approach cannot provide an adequate foundation for sociological theory still very much dominates — if only as a tacit premise — the profession. From the viewpoint of the majority of the profession, public choice is, therefore, perceived as "economic imperialism" that threatens the very identity of sociology. The apparent failure of the Durkheim-program to produce a non-individualist, genuine "sociological" theory that would be able, through its explanatory success, to unite the field, has led, however, to the emergence of individualist approaches in sociology, in particular *rational choice sociology*, with close affinities to public choice and other branches of the new generalised economics. Viewed from the perspective of rational choice sociology, public choice is not perceived as an imperialist threat at all but as a promising development towards a theoretically unified social science. Rational choice sociologists would readily agree with James Buchanan's (1987b: 234) diagnosis that public choice and related approaches in modern economics "point toward a fundamental revision of existing orthodoxy, and an emerging consensus on what may be called a general theory of social structures, which will surely include political organization as only one among an array of forms. These developments should help to break down the barriers among the disciplinary specializations in the social sciences, barriers which have been, at best, arbitrarily erected and maintained."

VIKTOR J. VANBERG

REFERENCES

Albert, Hans (1979). "The economic tradition: economics as a research program for theoretical social science," in K. Brunner (ed.) *Economics and Social Institutions*. Boston: Martinus Nijhoff, pp. 1–27.

Buchanan, James M. (1972). "Toward analysis of closed behavioral systems," in J.M. Buchanan and R.D. Tollison (eds.) *Theory of Public Choice — Political Applications of Economics*. Ann Arbor: The University of Michigan Press, pp. 11–23.

Buchanan, James M. (1978). "From private preferences to public philosophy: the development of public choice," in *The Economics of Politics*. London: The Institute of Economic Affairs, pp. 1–20.

Buchanan, James M. (1983). "The public choice perspective." *Economia Delle Scelte Pubbliche* 1: 7–15, reprinted in Buchanan 1986, pp. 19–27.

Buchanan, James M. (1986). *Liberty, Market and State: Political Economy in the 1980s*. New York: New York University Press.

Buchanan, James M. (1987a). "Constitutional economics." *The New Palgrave : A Dictionary of Economics*, Volume 1. London: Macmillan, pp. 585–588.

Buchanan, James M. (1987b). "An individualistic theory of political process," in *Economics: Between Predictive Science and Moral Philosophy*. College Station: Texas A&M University Press, pp. 223–235 (first published in D. Easton, ed., *Varieties of Political Theory*, Englewood Cliffs: Prentice-Hall, 1966).

Camic, Charles (1979). "The utilitarians revisited." *The American Journal of Sociology*, 85: 516–550.

Coase, Ronald H. (1994). "Economics and contiguous disciplines," in R.H. Coase *On Economics and Economists*. Chicago and London: The University of Chicago Press, pp. 34–46.

Coleman, James S. (1975). "Social structure and a theory of action," in P.M. Blau (ed.) *Approaches to the Study of Social Structure*. New York: The Free Press, pp. 76–93.

Coleman, James S. (1986). *Individual Interests and Collective Action: Selected Essays*. Cambridge: Cambridge University Press.

Coleman, James S. (1989). "Editor's introduction: rationality and society." *Rationality and Society*, 1: 5–9.

Coleman, James S. (1990). *Foundations of Social Theory*. Cambridge, MA. and London: The Belknap Press of Harvard University Press.

Demsetz, Harold (1982). *Economic, Legal, and Political Dimensions of Competition*. Amsterdam: North-Holland.

Durkheim, Emile (1938). *The Rules of Sociological Method*. Glencoe, IL: The Free Press (originally published in 1895).

Durkheim, Emile (1964a). "Sociology and its scientific field," in K.H. Wolff (ed.) *Essays on Sociology and Philosophy by Emile Durkheim*. New York: Harper & Row, pp. 354–375 (originally published in 1900).

Durkheim, Emile (1964b). "Sociology," in K.H. Wolff (ed.) *Essays on Sociology and Philosophy by Emile Durkheim*. New York: Harper & Row, pp. 376–385 (originally published in 1915).

Durkheim, Emile (1978). *Emile Durkheim on Institutional Analysis* (edited, translated and with an introduction by Mark Traugott). Chicago and London: University of Chicago Press.

Frey, Bruno S. (1999). *Economics as a Science of Human Behavior: Towards a New Social Science Paradigm*, extended Second Edition. Boston/Dordrecht/London: Kluwer Academic Publishers.

Giddens, Antony (1971). "The 'individual' in the writings of Emile Durkheim." *Archives européennes de sociologie*, 12: 210–228.

Hayek, Friedrich A. (1948). *Individualism and Economic Order*. Chicago: The University of Chicago Press.

Homans, George C. (1958). "Social behavior as exchange." *The American Journal of Sociology*, 62: 597–606.

Homans, George C. (1964). "Bringing men back in." *American Sociological Review*, 29: 809–818.

Homans, George C. (1967). *The Nature of Social Science*. New York: Harcourt, Brace & World.

Homans, George C. (1974). *Social Behavior: Its Elementary Forms*, Revised Edition. New York: Harcourt, Brace & World.

Homans, George C. (1975). "What do we mean by social 'structure'?" in P.M. Blau (ed.) *Approaches to the Study of Social Structure*. New York: The Free Press, pp. 53–65.

Homans, George C. (1982). "The present state of sociological theory." *The Sociological Quarterly*, 23: 285–299.

Lindenberg, Siegwart (1986). "How sociological theory lost its central issue and what can be done about it," in S. Lindenberg, J.S. Coleman, S. Nowak, (eds.) *Approaches to Social Theory*, New York: Russel Sage Foundation, pp. 19–24.

Mueller, Dennis C. (1986). "Rational egoism versus adaptive egoism as fundamental postulate for a descriptive theory of human behavior." *Public Choice*, 51: 3–23.

Nelson, Richard R. (2002). "Bringing institutions into evolutionary growth theory." *Journal of Evolutionary Economics*, 12: 17–28.

Parsons, Talcott (1964). *Essays in Sociological Theory*, Revised Edition. New York: The Free Press.

Parsons, Talcott (1968). "Utilitarianism: sociological thought." *International Encyclopedia of the Social Sciences*, Volume 16. New York: Macmillan & The Free Press, pp. 229–236.

Radnitzky, Gerard and Peter Berholz (eds.) (1987). *Economic Imperialism. The Economic Method Applied Outside the Field of Economics*. New York: Paragon.

Ritzer, George (1975). *Sociology: A Multiple Paradigm Science*. Boston: Allyn and Bacon.

Rowley, Charles K. (1998). "Law-and-economics from the perspective of economics." *The New Palgrave Dictionary of Economics and the Law*. London: Macmillan, pp. 474–486.

Swedberg, Richard (1990). *Economics and Sociology — Redefining their Boundaries: Conversations with Economists and Sociologists*. Princeton, NJ: Princeton University Press.

Tullock, Gordon (1972). "Economic Imperialism," in J.M. Buchanan and R.D. Tollison (eds.) *Theory of Public Choice: Political Applications of Economic*, Ann Arbor: The University of Michigan Press, pp. 317–329.

Vanberg, Viktor (1975). *Die zwei Soziologien: Individualismus und Kollektivismus in der Sozialtheorie*. Tübingen: J.C.B. Mohr (Paul Siebeck).

Vanberg, Viktor (1982). *Markt und Organisation — Individualistische Sozialtheorie und das Problem korporativen Handelns*. Tübingen: J.C.B. Mohr (Paul Siebeck).

Vanberg, Viktor (1983). "The rebirth of utilitarian sociology." *The Social Science Journal*, 20: 71–78.

Vanberg, Viktor (2002). "Rational choice vs. program-based behavior: alternative theoretical paradigms and their relevance for the study of institutions." *Rationality and Society*, 14: 7–53.

Walras Leon (1954). *Elements of Pure Economics or the Theory of Social Wealth* (translated by W. Jaffé). Homewood, IL: Richard D. Irwin (originally published in 1874).

Wells, Alan (ed.) (1978). *Contemporary Sociological Theories*. Santa Monica: Goodyear.

West, Edwin G. (1990). "Adam Smith and public choice," in E.G. West *Adam Smith and Modern Economics: From Market Behaviour to Public Choice*. Aldershot: Edward Elgar, pp. 105–131.

PUBLIC FINANCE

1. Scope of the Field

Public Finance is the branch of economics that studies the taxing and spending activities of government. The term is something of a misnomer, because the fundamental issues are not financial (that is, relating to money). Rather, the key problems relate to the use of real resources. For this reason, some practitioners prefer the label *public sector economics* or simply *public economics*. Public finance encompasses both *positive* and *normative analysis*. Positive analysis deals with issues of cause and effect, for example, "If the government cuts the tax rate on gasoline, what will be the effect on gasoline consumption?" Normative analysis deals with ethical issues, for example, "Is it fairer to tax income or consumption?"

Modern public finance focuses on the microeconomic functions of government, how the government does and should affect the allocation of resources and the distribution of income. For the most part, the macroeconomic functions of government — the use of taxing, spending, and monetary policies to affect the overall level of unemployment and the price level — are covered in other fields.

2. Methodological Basis

Mainstream economic theory provides the framework for public finance. Indeed, it would not be unreasonable to view public finance as just an area of applied microeconomics. As is the case in other fields of economics, the normative framework of public finance is provided by *welfare economics*, the branch of economic theory concerned with the social desirability of alternative economic states.[1] Much of welfare economics focuses on the conditions under which the allocation of resources in an economy is *Pareto-efficient*, defined as an allocation such that the only way to make one person better off is to make another person worse off. Pareto efficiency seems a reasonable normative criterion — if the allocation of resources is not Pareto efficient, it is "wasteful" in the sense that it is possible to make someone better off without hurting anybody else. A stunning result of welfare economics is that if two assumptions are satisfied, then an economy will achieve a Pareto-efficient allocation of resources without any government intervention. The assumptions are: 1) All producers and consumers act as perfect competitors; that is, no one has any market power. 2) A market exists for each and every commodity. In a way, this result formalizes an old insight: When it comes to providing goods and services, free enterprise systems are amazingly productive.

Suppose for the moment that these two assumptions are satisfied. Does the government have any role to play in the economy? Only a very small government that protects property rights and provides law and order would seem appropriate. However, even if an allocation of resources is Pareto-efficient, it may not be socially desirable. A society may be willing to trade some efficiency in return for a fairer distribution of resources among its members (although "fairer" may be hard to define). Hence, even if the economy is Pareto efficient, government intervention may be necessary to achieve a fair distribution of real income.

Furthermore, real world economies may not satisfy the two assumptions required for Pareto efficiency. The first assumption is violated when firms have market power and raise their prices above competitive levels. Monopoly is an extreme example. The issues associated with market power are generally dealt with in the field of Industrial Organization, not Public Finance. The second assumption is violated when markets for certain commodities do not emerge. After all, if a market for a commodity does not exist, then we can hardly expect the market to allocate it efficiently. For example, there is no market for clean air. In effect, individuals can use up clean air (that is, pollute) at a zero price. That particular resource is not used efficiently.

Nonexistence of markets occurs in a variety of situations; each one opens potential opportunities for the government to intervene and improve welfare. In effect, then, the list of market failures provides the public finance agenda.

3. Public Expenditure

The theory of welfare economics focuses our attention on market failure and distributional considerations as reasons for considering governmental intervention. This section illustrates these issues.

3.1. Public Goods

A *public good* has two characteristics. First, once it is provided, the additional cost of another person consuming the good is zero — consumption is *nonrival*. Second, preventing anyone from consuming the good is either very expensive or impossible — consumption is *nonexcludable*. A classic example of a public good is national defense. One person's consumption of the services provided by the army does nothing to diminish another person's consumption of the same services. Further, excluding any particular person from the benefits of national defense is all but impossible. In contrast, a private good (such as food) is both rival and excludable.

To see why the market may not provide public goods in efficient amounts, note that, for a private good, the market in effect forces each person to reveal what his true preferences are. If the value of the commodity to a person is greater than or equal to the market price, he buys it; otherwise not. There is no incentive to hide one's true preferences. In contrast, people have incentives to hide their true preferences for public goods. Each person knows that once national defense is provided, he can enjoy its services, whether he pays for them or not. Therefore, he may claim that defense means nothing to him, hoping that he can get a "free ride" after other people pay for it. Everyone has the same incentive, so that defense may not be funded, even though it is in fact beneficial. In short, the market cannot be relied upon to provide a public good in efficient amounts; some kind of collective decision making process may be better (Samuelson, 1954).

While important, this finding does not provide a firm set of guidelines for deciding when the government rather than the private sector should provide some commodity. The result depends in part on whether the public and private sectors pay different amounts for labor and materials, the extent to which the government can address the diversity of tastes for the commodity among the citizenry, and whether or not government provision will have a more favorable (somehow defined) impact on the distribution of real income. Whether public or private provision is better must be decided on a case by case basis. The fact that this can be difficult is reflected in the ongoing political debates in many countries about the merits or *privatization* — taking services that are supplied by the government and turning them over to the private sector.

3.2. Externalities

When the activity of one entity (a person or firm) directly affects the welfare of another in a way that is outside the market mechanism, that effect is called an externality. The classic example is a polluter, who imposes losses on other individuals by degrading the environment. In general, efficiency requires that individuals pay a price for any commodity that reflects its value in alternative uses. But there is no market for (say) clean air. Individuals treat it as if its price is zero, and hence use it in inefficiently large amounts.

There are a number of ways in which government intervention can potentially enhance efficiency in the presence of an externality. 1) It can levy a tax on the externality producing activity. Basically, the tax makes up for the fact that the price being faced by the polluter is too low. 2) It can create a market for the right to pollute. Recall that the fundamental problem is that there is no market for the resource being polluted. In some cases, the government can create such a market. The government announces it will sell permits to spew a given quantity of some pollutant into the environment. Firms bid for the rights to own these permissions to pollute, and the permissions go to the firms with the highest bids. Again, firms are forced to confront a cost for using up the resource. 3) It can simply order each polluter to reduce pollution by a certain amount. A major problem with such a command-and-control solution is that the reduction in pollution may be greater or less than the efficient amount. That is, the reduction that the government orders may not be the same reduction that would occur if the firm were facing the true price of the resource.

In general, most countries rely on command-and-control mechanisms for dealing with environmental problems. However, in recent years market-oriented approaches have made some inroads. In the United States, for example, there is now an active market in allowances to emit sulfur dioxide into the air. An important area for future research is to see if it is possible to expand the scope of such policies, and to determine whether the efficiency gains that theory predicts actually occur (Stavins, 2002).

3.3. Social Insurance

One way to obtain some protection against the uncertainties of life is to purchase insurance. In private insurance markets, people pay premiums to an insurance company, and receive benefits in the event of certain unlucky occurrences. In addition, a number of government programs also replace income losses that are consequences of events at least partly outside personal control. These programs, collectively referred to as *social insurance*, are among the largest components in the budgets of western governments.

Is there a rationale within conventional welfare economics for such substantial government involvement in insurance markets? There are reasons to believe that private insurance markets will fail to operate efficiently. To see why, note that we can expect an individual who knows he is especially likely to collect benefits to have an especially high demand for insurance, a phenomenon known as *adverse selection*. Due to adverse selection, in order to break even, the insurance company must charge a higher premium for individual coverage than it would if a random group of people were buying insurance. However, these higher premiums exacerbate the adverse selection problem. Only individuals who know they are at great risk will pay the high prices. This, in turn, requires a further increase in premiums, and the pattern continues. The market fails to provide an efficient amount of insurance.[2] In essence, mandatory social insurance solves this problem by forcing everybody into one big group — the country.

Government retirement programs, which, in effect, provide insurance against the possibility that people will outlive the resources they have accumulated for retirement, are particularly important forms of social insurance. Typically, such programs have been funded on a *pay-as-you-go* basis, meaning that the benefits paid to current retirees come from payments made by those who are presently working. The problem is that in most countries, the ratio of retirees to workers will be increasing in coming years. Hence, other things being the same, it will be necessary either to increase the tax rate on current workers or reduce the benefits received by retirees. The best way to cope with this problem is a major academic and political controversy (Feldstein and Liebman, 2001). Considerable attention has been given to privatizing the systems. Under privatization, workers' contributions are earmarked for their own accounts. Workers then invest the funds in various financial assets, and finance their retirements out of the accumulations in the accounts. Major issues in privatization schemes include how to pay benefits to the current generation of retirees, and how to provide a socially acceptable living standard to individuals who are unable to accumulate enough wealth in their accounts during their working lives.

Other forms of social insurance are unemployment insurance and health insurance. Unemployment insurance provides benefits to workers who lose their jobs. The major problem is how to devise systems that provide protection but do not at the same time make unemployment too attractive (Meyer, 1995). One of the main issues in health insurance is the extent to which the government should directly provide insurance as opposed to providing people with incentives to purchase insurance on the private market. Various nations have come up with quite different solutions. In Canada, for example, health care services are produced by the private sector, with the reimbursements negotiated by the government. In the United Kingdom, health services are produced by the public sector through the National Health Service. In the United States, there is publicly provided insurance only for certain groups, basically the elderly (through Medicare) and for the poor (through Medicaid). A particularly contentious and important issue is the effect that the various systems have on people's health status (Fuchs, 1998).

3.4. Income Redistribution

As noted above, even in the absence of market failures, government intervention in the economy may be necessary to achieve a "fair" distribution of real income. A key question in this context is whether the government needs to intervene directly in markets in order to enhance fairness. For example, should it impose ceilings on the prices of commodities consumed by the poor? The answer is no. Roughly speaking, it is a better policy for the government to redistribute income suitably and then let markets work. Put another way, the issues of efficiency and distributional fairness can be separated. If society determines that the current distribution of resources is unfair, it need not interfere with market prices and impair efficiency. Of course, the government needs some way to reallocate resources, and problems arise if the only available mechanisms for doing so (such as taxes) themselves induce inefficiencies. These issues are discussed below.

This whole area is complicated by the fact that there is no consensus on what a fair income distribution looks like. Some believe that the government should engineer complete equality. Others believe that society should move toward equality, but take into account the losses in efficiency that are engendered by taxing high-income people and subsidizing low-income people. Still others believe that attention to the distribution of income at a given point in time is misguided; what matters is whether there is social mobility over time. The idea here is that even if people at the bottom of the income distribution are quite poor, it may not be a major social problem if the identities of these people change over time (Atkinson, 1983).

In many countries, income distribution programs rely primarily on *in-kind transfers* — payments from the government to individuals in the form of commodities or services rather than cash. In-kind transfers include medical care, food, housing, and energy consumption. A natural question is why governments do not simply give the poor cash and let them spend the money as they want? One possibility is that policy makers care about the distribution of certain commodities rather than income *per se*. For example, they may want every family to consume housing of a given quality. In addition, in-kind transfers may help curb welfare fraud. In-kind transfers may discourage ineligible persons from applying because some well-off people may be willing to lie to receive cash, but be less willing to lie to obtain some commodity they do not really want (Nichols and Zeckhauser, 1982). Finally, in-kind transfers are attractive politically because they help not only the beneficiary but also the producers of the favored commodity. Thus, for example, agricultural interests can be expected to support programs for subsidizing food consumption by the poor.

One of the most contentious issues in this area is how income maintenance policies affect the behavior of the poor. Most attention has been focused on work effort — do beneficiaries reduce their work effort and if so, by how much. In the belief that welfare reduces work effort, several countries have introduced work requirements — in order to be eligible for welfare, recipients have to agree to accept work or job-training programs. The efficacy of such programs is not yet well understood. Another open question is whether income maintenance programs lead to the creation of a "welfare culture" — children brought up in households receiving welfare come to view it as a way of life and hence are unlikely to acquire the skills necessary to earn a living. It is indeed the case that a mother's participation in welfare increases the probability that her daughter eventually also ends up on welfare. However, it is not clear whether the exposure to welfare "causes" the daughter to go on welfare, or if other correlated aspects of the family environment are responsible (Blank, 1997).

3.5. A Caveat

We have discussed a number of situations in which the government can improve welfare by enhancing efficiency and fairness. However, the fact that the market-generated allocation of resources is imperfect does not mean the government is necessarily capable of doing better. For example, in certain cases the costs of setting up a government agency to deal with some market failure could be greater than the cost of the market failure itself. Moreover, governments, like people, have only imperfect information, and hence can make mistakes. Finally, it is not clear that government decision-makers will have maximizing social welfare as their goal; we return to this theme at the end of this essay. Hence, it is best to think of welfare economics as helping us identify situations in which government intervention *may* enhance efficiency and fairness; whether it actually will needs to be evaluated on a case by case basis.

4. The Theory of Taxation

Taxes are the most important source of revenue for modern economies. The theory of taxation explores how taxes should be levied to enhance economic efficiency and to promote a "fair" distribution of income. Just as in the case of expenditures discussed in Section 3, welfare economics provides the underlying analytical framework. Various aspects of the theory are discussed in this section.

4.1. Tax Incidence

Policy debates about taxation are usually dominated by the question of whether its burden is distributed fairly. To discuss this normative issue requires some understanding of the positive question of how taxes affect the distribution of income. A simple way to determine how taxes change the income distribution would be to conduct a survey in which each person is asked how many dollars he or she pays to the tax collector each year.

Although such an approach is convenient, it is quite likely to produce misleading answers. To see why, suppose that the government levies a tax of one dollar on the sellers of a certain commodity. Suppose that prior to the tax, the price of the commodity is $20, and that after the tax is levied, the price increases to $21. Clearly, the sellers receive as much per unit sold as they did before. The tax has not made them worse off. Consumers pay the entire tax in the form of higher prices. Suppose that instead, the price increases to $20.25. In this case, sellers are worse off by 75 cents per unit sold; consumers are worse off by 25 cents per unit sold. The burden of the tax is shared between the two groups. Yet another possibility is that after the tax is imposed, the price stays at $20. If so, the consumer is no worse off, while the seller bears the full burden of the tax.

The *statutory incidence* of a tax indicates who is legally responsible for the tax. All three cases above have exactly the same statutory incidence. But the situations differ drastically with respect to who really bears the burden. The *economic incidence* of a tax is the change in the distribution of private real income induced by the tax.

The example above suggests that the economic incidence problem is fundamentally one of determining how taxes change prices. In the conventional supply and demand model of price determination, the economic incidence of a tax depends on how responsive supply and demand are to prices.[3] In general, the more responsive supply is to price relative to demand, the greater the share of the tax that will be shifted to consumers. Intuitively, the more responsive demand is to price, the easier it is for consumers to turn to other products when the price goes up, and therefore more of the tax must be borne by suppliers. Conversely, if consumers purchase the same amount regardless of price, the whole burden can be shifted to them. In cases where the responses of supply and demand to price are well understood, then fairly reliable estimates of the economic incidence of a tax can be obtained. In some areas, the behavioral responses are not well understood, and incidence analysis is on less firm ground. For example, there is still great controversy over the burden of taxes on corporations — to what extent are they borne by owners of capital, and to what extent by laborers? This is an important topic for research.

4.2. Excess Burden

Taxes impose a cost on the taxpayer. It is tempting to view the cost as simply the amount of money that he or she pays to the government. However, this is only part of the story. A tax distorts economic behavior — in general, consumers buy fewer taxed goods and more untaxed goods than otherwise would have been the case. Their decisions are not based entirely on the merits of the commodities themselves. In the same way, business owners make investments based in part on tax considerations, as opposed to economic fundamentals. Because a tax distorts economic activity, it creates a loss in welfare that actually exceed the revenues collected. This is referred to the *excess burden* of the tax.

In general, the more responsive behavior is to the tax, the greater the excess burden, other things being the same. Intuitively, because excess burdens arise because of distortions in behavior, the more that behavior is capable of being distorted, the greater the excess burden. Another important result is that the excess burden of a tax increases with the square of the tax rate — doubling a tax quadruples its excess burden, other things being the same. This means that, in general, it makes sense to spread taxes over as large a group of commodities as possible — a small tax on a number of commodities has a smaller excess burden than a very large tax on one commodity.[4]

This discussion suggests that, just like the incidence problem discussed above, the excess burden of a tax depends on the behavioral response to the tax. Estimating such behavioral responses and computing excess burdens is an important role for public finance economists. Some estimates suggest that the excess burdens for real-world tax systems are quite high. One recent survey suggested that in the United States, the average excess burden per dollar of tax revenue is 18 cents. While any particular figure must be taken with a grain of salt, virtually all estimates suggest that the tax system is highly inefficient in the sense of generating large excess burdens (Jorgenson and Yun, 2001).

The fact that a tax generates an excess burden does not mean that the tax is bad. One hopes, after all, that it will be used to obtain something beneficial for society either in terms of enhanced efficiency or fairness. But to determine whether or not the supposed benefits are large enough to justify the costs, sensible policy requires that excess burden be included in the calculation as a cost to society.

4.3. Optimal Taxation

Public finance economists have devoted a great deal of attention to the problem of the design of optimal taxes. Of course, this is a normative issue, and it cannot be answered without a statement of ethical goals. To begin, suppose that the goal is to raise a given amount of money with the smallest amount of excess burden possible. There are a variety of ways to characterize the result. One of the most elegant is the rule that as long as goods are unrelated in consumption (that is, are neither substitutes nor complements), then the more responsive demand is to price, the lower should be the tax rate on that commodity. The intuition behind this rule is straightforward. Efficient taxes should distort decisions as little as possible. The potential for distortion is greater the more responsive the demand for the commodity is to its price. Therefore, efficient taxation requires that relatively high rates of taxation be levied on goods whose demands are relatively unresponsive to their price.

This result strikes many people as ethically unappealing. For example, the demand for food is relatively unresponsive to changes in its price. Is it really desirable to tax food at relatively high rates? Most people would argue that it is not desirable, because their ethical views indicate that a tax system should have *vertical equity*: It should distribute burdens fairly across people with different abilities to pay. Public finance economists have shown how to modify the efficiency rule to account for the distributional consequences of taxation. Suppose, for example, that the poor spend a greater proportion of their income on commodity X than do the rich, and vice versa for commodity Y. Then even if the demand for X is less responsive to price than the demand for Y, optimal taxation may require a higher rate of tax on Y than X. True, a high tax rate on Y creates a relatively large excess burden, but it also tends to redistribute income toward the poor. As in other areas of public finance, the optimal policy depends on the extent to which society is willing to tradeoff efficiency for fairness (Auerbach and Hines, 2002).

With its focus on efficiency and fairness issues, the theory of optimal taxation falls directly within the framework of conventional welfare economics. There are other criteria for tax design that are not reconciled so easily with welfare economics. The main one is *horizontal equity*, the notion that people in equal positions should pay equal amounts of taxes. One problem with implementing this principle is defining equal positions. The most common criterion is income, but wealth and consumption are also possible. A problem with all three measures, however, is that they are the outcomes of people's decisions. Two individuals may have exactly the same wage rate, but one chooses to work 1000 hours per year while another chooses to work 2000 hours per year. Despite the fact that they have different incomes, in a meaningful sense they are in "equal positions" because their potential to earn income is the same.

Things are complicated further by the fact that adjustments in market prices may render some horizontal inequities more apparent than real. Suppose, for example, that in one type of job a large part of compensation consists of amenities that are not taxable — pleasant offices, access to a swimming pool, and so forth. In another occupation, compensation is exclusively monetary, all of which is subject to income taxation. This would appear to be a violation of horizontal equity, because the person in the job with a lot of amenities has too small a tax burden. But, if both arrangements coexist and individuals are free to chose, then the net after-tax rewards (including amenities) must be the same in both jobs. Otherwise, people would leave the job with the lower net after-tax rewards. In short, the fact that amenities are not taxed is not unfair, because the before- tax monetary compensation falls by just enough to offset this advantage. Put another way, introducing taxation for such amenities would *create* horizontal inequities (Feldstein, 1976).

We conclude that horizontal equity is a rather amorphous concept. Yet it has enormous appeal as a principle of tax design. Notions of fairness among equals, regardless of their vagueness, will continue to play an important role in the development of tax policy.

5. Revenue Raising Instruments

Public finance economists have used the theoretical framework discussed in Section 4 above to analyze the various revenue sources used by modern governments. This section discusses briefly some of the key issues associated with each kind of tax.

5.1. Income Tax

Taxes on income play a major role in the fiscal systems of all western countries. A starting point for the analysis and evaluation of real world income tax systems is a definition of income. Traditionally, public finance economists use the so-called *Haig-Simons* definition: Income is the money value of the net increase in an individual's power to consumer during a period. This is equal to the amount actually during the period plus net additions to wealth. Net additions to wealth — saving — must be included in income because they represent an increase in potential consumption. Importantly, the Haig-Simons criterion requires the inclusion of *all* sources of potential increases in consumption, regardless of whether the actual consumption takes place, and regardless of the form in which the consumption occurs. While not uncontroversial, the Haig-Simons definition provides a useful guide.

The Haig-Simons definition encompasses those items ordinarily thought of an income: wages and salaries, business profits, rents, royalties, dividends, and interest. These forms of income are relatively easy to measure and to tax. However, in other contexts, implementing the Haig-Simons criterion can lead to major problems. [5] Some examples follow:

- Only income net of business expenses increases potential consumption power. But distinguishing between consumption and costs of obtaining income can be difficult. To what extent is a desk bought for an office at home just furniture, and to what extent is it a business expense?
- A capital gain is the increase in the value of an asset — say, a share of stock — during a period of time. From a Haig-Simons point of view, a capital gain is income whether or not the stock is actually sold, because the capital gain represents an increase in potential to consume. However, captial gains and losses may be very difficult o measure, particularly when the assets are not sold. Indeed, in general, no attempts are made to tax capital gains of assets that have not actually been sold.
- In-kind services are not easy to value. One important example is the income produced by people who do housework rather than participate in the market.

Such difficulties in implementing a Haig-Simons concept of income are of great practical significance. To the extent that income that comes in certain forms cannot be taxed, individuals' decisions are biased in the direction of taking their income in those forms. Thus, for example, there is a bias in favor of capital gains (which are taxed only when the asset is sold) as opposed to dividend income (which is taxed as it is earned). Such biases create efficiency losses to the economy. Further, complicated rules are often needed to determine whether a certain type of income falls in a category that is favored by the tax system. Capital gains again provides a good example; it is not always obvious whether the return that an individual receives from a company is a dividend or a capital gain. Such complexity leads to substantial compliance costs.

In additions, several forms of income that would be administratively relatively easy to tax are partially or altogether excluded from the income tax bases of most countries. An important example is the return on saving that is deposited in retirement accounts. Indeed, given the extent to which income that is saved in various forms is excluded from taxation, it is a misnomer to characterize these systems as income taxes. They are more a hybrid between income and consumption taxes.

5.2. Corporation Income Tax

Corporations are independent legal entities and as such are subject to taxes on their incomes. Most public finance economists believe that it makes little sense to levy a special tax on corporations. Only real people can pay a tax; hence, it would make more sense to tax the incomes of corporation *owners* via the personal income tax. Again, this distinction is of more than academic importance. Treating the corporation as a freestanding entity for tax purposes leads to important distortions in economic activity. To see why, note that when a corporation earns income it is taxed once at the corporate level, and then again when it is paid out to shareholders in the form of dividends. In effect, then, corporate income that is paid out in the form of dividends is double taxed. This biases businesses against organizing in corporate form. Moreover, double taxation of corporate income effectively increases the tax rate on the return to corporate investments. This reduces the volume of investment undertaken by corporations, although there is substantial disagreement about the magnitude of this effect.

The incidence of the corporation tax is highly controversial. In one highly influential model due to Harberger (1962), the tax on corporate capital leads to a migration of capital from the corporate sector until after-tax rates of return are equal throughout the economy. In the process, the rate of return to capital in the noncorporate sector is depressed so that ultimately all owners of capital, not just those in the corporate sector, are affected. The reallocation of capital between the two sectors also affects the return to labor. Most public finance economists believe that the burden of the corporation tax is split between labor and capital, although there is significant disagreement about the exact division.

If corporate income was untaxed, individuals could avoid personal income taxes by accumulating income with corporations. Evidently, this would lead to serious equity and efficiency problems. The question is whether there is a way to integrate personal and corporate income taxes into a single system so as to avoid the distortions associated with double taxation. The most radical solution to this problem is called *full integration*. Under this approach, all earnings of the corporation during a given year, whether they are distributed or not, are attributed to stockholders just as if the corporation were a partnership. The corporation tax as a separate entity is eliminated. This approach has not been implemented in any country, in part because of administrative problems. The *dividend relief approach* is less extreme. With it, the corporation can deduct dividends paid to stockholders. Although this approach eliminates the double taxation of dividends, it still maintains the corporation tax as a separate entity. Variants on this approach are used in a number of European nations.

5.3. Consumption Taxes

The base of a consumption tax is the value (or quantity) of commodities sold to a person for *actual* consumption, as opposed to an income tax, whose base is the change in *potential* consumption. Consumption taxes take a variety of forms. A *retail sales tax* is levied on the purchase of a commodity. In the United States, retail sales taxes are not a significant component of revenue at the national level, but they are at the state level. Even there, though, the rates generally do not exceed 7 percent or so.

In Europe, the most important type of consumption tax is a *value-added tax (VAT)*. The *value-added* at each stage of production of a commodity is the difference between the firm's sales and the purchased material inputs used in production. If a firm pays $100 for its material inputs and sells its output for $150, then its value added is $50. A VAT is a percentage tax on value-added at each stage of production. For example, if the VAT rate were 10 percent, then the firm's tax liability would be $5. Note that the total value of a commodity when it is finally sold is equal to the sum of the value-added at each stage of production. Hence, a VAT of 10 percent applied to each stage is equivalent to a 10 percent tax on the final product. In Europe, VAT rates are as high as 25 percent. With rates at such levels, evasion is likely to be a problem for retail sales taxes; VATs are easier to administer, which accounts for their popularity.[6]

A distinguishing feature of both VATs and retail sales taxes is that the tax liability does not depend on the characteristics of the buyer. Whether one is rich or poor, the rate is the same. This prompts concerns over equity, which have been dealt with by applying lower rates to commodities such as food and medicine. But this may not be an effective way to deal with equity concerns. For example, even if it is true that food expenditures on average play an especially important role in the budgets of the poor, there are still many upper-income families whose food consumption is proportionately very high. In recent years, public finance economists have given a great deal of attention to the problem of designing *personal* consumption taxes. Such taxes require individuals to file tax returns and write checks to the government, allowing tax liabilities to depend on personal circumstances.

One example is a *cash-flow* tax. Each household files a return reporting its annual consumption expenditures during the year. Just as under the personal income tax, various exemptions and deductions can be taken to allow for special circumstances, and a progressive marginal rate schedule applied to taxable consumption. From an administrative viewpoint, the major question is how to compute annual consumption. Taxpayers would report their incomes, and then subtract all saving. To keep track of saving, qualified accounts would be established at various financial institutions. Whether a cash-flow tax is administratively feasible is very controversial.[7] Many analysts believe that its record-keeping requirements would make it very difficult or impossible administratively.

5.4. Wealth Taxes

Wealth is the value of the assets an individual has accumulated as of a given time. Wealth taxes do not play a major role in the fiscal systems of any western countries. One justification of taxing wealth is that it is a good measure of an individual's ability to pay taxes. This is a controversial issue. Suppose that a miser has accumulated a huge hoard of gold that yields no income. Should she be taxed on the value of the hoard? Some believe that as long as the miser was subject to the income tax while the hoard was accumulating, it should not be taxed again. Others would argue that the gold *per se* generates satisfaction and power for the individual, and should therefore be subject to tax. Perhaps the major problem with this argument is that many rich people have a substantial component of their wealth in *human* capital — their stock of education, skills, and so on. However, there is no way to value human capital except by reference to the income it yields. This logic points back to income as the appropriate base.

Some nations levy taxes on wealth only when it is transferred at the time of the death of the owner. These are referred to as *estate taxes*. Estate tax proponents argue that it is a valuable tool for creating a more equal distribution of income. Further, many believe that ultimately, all property belongs to society as a whole. During an individual's life, society permits her to dispose of the property she has managed to accumulate as she wishes. But at death, the property reverts to society, which can dispose of it at will. Opponents argue that it is fundamentally wrong to argue that a person holds wealth only at the pleasure of "society," or that "society" ever has any valid claim on personal wealth.[8]

A controversial issue is the incentives created by an estate tax. Suppose that an individual is motivated to work hard during his lifetime to leave a large estate for his children. The presence of an estate tax might discourage his work effort. On the other hand, with an estate tax, a greater amount of wealth has to be accumulated to leave a given after-tax bequest, so the tax might induce the individual to work harder to maintain the net value of his estate. Consequently, the effect of an estate tax on a donor's work effort is logically indeterminate. Similarly, one cannot predict how the tax will affect the amount of saving. There is currently very little in the way of empirical evidence on these incentive issues.

To the extent that an estate tax reduces saving, it may actually *increase* inequality. If there is less saving, then there is less capital investment. With less capital with which to work, the real wages of workers decrease and under certain circumstances, the share of income going to labor falls. To the extent that capital income is more unequally distributed than labor income, the effect is to increase inequality. This scenario is hypothetical. It simply emphasizes a point made above in a variety of different contexts — to understand the impact of a tax, one must take into account how taxpayers respond to it.

5.5. Deficit Finance

In addition to taxation, the government's other major source of revenue is borrowing. The *deficit* during a time period is the excess of spending over revenues. The *national debt* at a given time is the sum of all past budget deficits. That is, the debt is the cumulative excess of past spending over past receipts. Future generations either have to retire the debt or else refinance it. It would appear, then, that future generations must bear the burden of the debt. But the theory of incidence tells us that this line of reasoning is questionable. Merely because the legal burden in on future generations does not mean that they bear a real burden. Just as in the case of tax incidence, the answer depends on economic behavior.

Assume that the government borrows from its own citizens. One view is that such an internal debt creates no burden for the future generation. Members of the future generation simply owe it to each other. There is a transfer of income from those who do not hold bonds to the bondholders, but the generation as a whole is no worse off in the sense that its consumption level is the same as it would have been.

This story ignores the fact that economic decisions can be affected by government debt policy. According to the *neoclassical model of the debt*, when the government borrows, it competes for funds with individuals and firms who want the money for their own investment projects. Hence, debt finance leaves the future generation with a smaller capital stock, other things being the same. Its members therefore are less productive and have smaller real incomes than otherwise would have been the case. Thus, the debt imposes a burden on future generations, through its impact on capital formation. The key assumption in this argument is that public spending crowds out private investment. Whether crowding out actually occurs is a controversial issue; the empirical evidence is mixed (Elmendorf and Mankiw, 1999).

A further complication is introduced when we consider individuals' transfers across generations. Suppose that when the government borrows, people realize that their heirs will be made worse off. Suppose further that people care about the welfare of their descendants and do not want their descendants' consumption levels reduced. What can they do about this? They can save more to increase their bequests by an amount sufficient to pay the extra taxes that will be due in the future. The result is that nothing really changes. Each generation consumes exactly the same amount as before the government borrowed.

The striking conclusion is that private individuals undo the intergenerational effects of government debt policy so that tax and debt finance are essentially equivalent. This view is sometimes referred to as the *Ricardian model* because its antecedents appeared in the work of the 19th century economist David Ricardo. (However, Ricardo was skeptical about the theory that now bears his name.) Some public finance economists have challenged the plausibility of the *Ricardian model*. They believe that information on the implications of current deficits for future tax burdens is not easy to obtain. Another criticism is that people are not as farsighted and not as altruistic as supposed in the model. A number of statistical studies have examined the relationship between budget deficits and private saving. The evidence is rather mixed, and the Ricardian model has both critics and adherents among professional economists.

From time to time, events such as natural disaster and wars lead to temporary increases in federal government expenditures. An old question in public finance is whether such expenditures should be financed with taxes or borrowing.

6. Fiscal Federalism

The analysis so far has assumed that a nation has one government that sets tax and expenditure policies. In contrast, many countries have a federal system, which consists of different levels of government that provide public goods and services and have some scope for making decisions. The subject of *fiscal federalism* concerns the activities of the various levels of government and how they relate to each other. A key question is the optimal allocation of responsibilities among different levels of government. Posed within the framework of welfare economics, the question is whether a centralized or decentralized system is more likely to enhance efficiency and equity (Oates, 1999).

Among the disadvantages of a decentralized system is that individual communities may ignore the externalities they create. Suppose, for example, that some jurisdiction provides excellent public education for its children. If some of the children eventually emigrate to other jurisdictions, the other communities benefit from having a higher quality work force. But in deciding how much education to provide, the jurisdiction only considers its own welfare. Therefore, it may provide an inefficiently low amount of education. More generally, if each community cares only about its own members, then any positive or negative externalities it creates for other communities are overlooked. According to the standard arguments made above, resources are allocated inefficiently.

Another disadvantage of a decentralized system relates to the fact that for certain public services, the cost per person falls as the number of users increases. Suppose that the more people who use a public library, the lower the cost per user. If each community sets up its own library, costs per user are higher than necessary. A central government, on the other hand, could build one library for the region, allowing people to benefit from scale economies. Of course, various activities are subject to different scale economies. The optimal scale for library services might differ from that for fire protection, and both surely differ from the optimal scale for national defense. This observation helps rationalize a system of overlapping jurisdictions — each jurisdiction can handle those services with scale economies that are appropriate for the jurisdiction's size.

Decentralized systems can also lead to inefficiencies with respect to raising revenues. Taxes levied by decentralized communities are unlikely to be efficient from a national standpoint. Instead, communities are likely to select taxes on the basis of whether they can be exported to outsiders. For example, jurisdictions that have a near-monopoly on certain natural resources such as coal may impose large taxes on these commodities, figuring that they will be shifted largely to coal users outside the community.

A major advantage to a decentralized system is that it allows communities to tailor their public services to the tastes of their residents. Tastes for public services, just like the tastes for all other commodities, vary across people. A centralized government tends to provide the same level of public services throughout the country, regardless of the fact that people's tastes differ. It is inefficient to provide individuals with more or less of a public good than they desire if the quantity they receive can be more closely tailored t their preferences. Under a decentralized system, individuals with similar tastes for public goods group together, so communities are more likely to provide the types and quantities of public goods desired by their inhabitants.

Another advantage is that decentralized systems foster intergovernmental competition. If citizens can choose among communities, then substantial government mismanagement may cause citizens to chose to live elsewhere. This threat may create incentives to government managers to produce more efficiently and be more responsive to their residents.

Finally, a decentralized system may enhance experimentation and innovation in locally provided goods and services. For many policy questions, no one is certain what the right answer is, or even whether there is a single solution that is best in all situations. One way to find out is to let each community choose its own way, and then compare the results. For example, some jurisdictions might choose to provide innovative job-training programs for individuals who lose their jobs. If the innovations are successful, other jurisdictions can imitate them. If not, the costs to the country as a whole are small.

This discussion makes it clear that a purely decentralized system cannot be expected to maximize social welfare. Efficiency requires that those services that affect the entire country, such as national defense, be provided at the national level. On the other hand, it seems appropriate for goods that affect only the members of a particular jurisdiction to be provided locally. This leaves us with the in-between case of community activities that create externalities that are not national in scope. While one solution would be to create a single regional government, a larger jurisdiction carries the cost of less responsiveness to local differences in tastes. An alternative method is a system of taxes and subsidies. The central government can subsidize activities that create positive externalities. In some countries, central governments give grants to communities that roughly follow this model.

7. Public Finance and Public Choice

Traditionally, the field of public finance has tended to convey a rather rosy view of government. With a tax here, an expenditure there, the state readily corrects all market imperfections, meanwhile seeing to it that incomes are distributed in an ethically desirable way. The implicit assumption is that the government is a neutral and benign force. In contrast, the field of public choice assumes that individuals view government as a mechanism for maximizing their self interest. Such a viewpoint can lead to rather different conclusions from those of conventional public finance.

A good example is provided by optimal tax theory. Suppose that in a certain society, there are three commodities, X, Y, and leisure. Labor is totally fixed in supply, and therefore, income is fixed. Note that a proportional tax at the same rate on X and Y is equivalent to a tax on income. Now, suppose that currently, this society levies a tax on X, but its constitution forbids taxing Y. Viewing this situation, a student of optimal tax theory might say something like,

"You are running an inefficient tax system. You could eliminate excess burden if you taxed X and Y at equal rates — an income tax. I recommend that you lower the tax on X and impose a tax at the same rate on Y. Set the rates so that the same amount of revenue is collected as before."

Suppose, however, that the citizens suspect that if they allow taxation of Y, their politicians will not lower the tax rate on X. Rather, they will simply take advantage of the opportunity to tax something new to make tax revenues as large as possible. Therefore, by constitutionally precluding the taxation of Y, the citizens may be rationally protecting themselves against an inefficiently large public sector. In other words, if government does not necessarily act in the interest of its citizens, then what looks inefficient from the point of view of optimal tax theory may be efficient in a public choice setting.[9]

In recent years, public choice has had substantial influence on the field of public finance. In both theoretical and empirical work, public finance economists study the incentives facing government decision-makers, and how these incentives affect policy outcomes. In making their own policy recommendations, there is a heightened awareness that a policy that emerges from the legislative process may look quite different from the original proposal, and one should take this into effect in formulating recommendations. In the future, one can expect both Public Finance and Public Choice to continue to enjoy the benefits of intellectual cross-fertilization.

HARVEY S. ROSEN

NOTES

1. Bator (1957) provides a classic exposition of welfare economics.
2. For a more general treatment of this phenomenon, see Akerlof (1970).
3. For a treatment of tax incidence in other models of price determination, see Fullerton and Metcalf (forthcoming).
4. For a proof, see Auerbach and Hines (forthcoming).
5. Bradford (1986) provides a careful discussion of issues relating to the implementation of an income tax.
6. See Cnossen (1998) for a discussion of issues relating to the implementation of VATs.
7. The difficulties and advantages of this system are discussed in Pechman (1980).
8. See Gale and Slemrod (2000) for further details.
9. Holcombe (1998) provides further comparisons between optimal tax theory and a public choice approach.

REFERENCES

Akerlof, George (1970). "The market for lemons: quality uncertainty and the market mechanism." *Quarterly Journal of Economics*, 84: 488–500.

Atkinson, Anthony B. (1983). *The Economics of Inequality*. Oxford: Oxford University Press.

Auerbach, Alan and James R. Hines, Jr., (2002). "Taxation and economic efficiency," in Alan Auerbach and Martin Feldstein (eds.) *Handbook of Public Economics*.

Bator, F.M. (1957). "The simple analytics of welfare maximization." *American Economic Review*, 47: 22–59.

Blank, Rebecca (1997). *It Takes a Nation — A New Agenda for Fighting Poverty*. New York: Russell Sage Foundation.

Bradford, David (1986). *Untangling the Income Tax*. Cambridge, MA: Harvard University Press.

Cnossen, Sijbren (1998). "Global trends and issues in value-added taxation." *International Tax and Public Finance*. 5: 399–428.

Elmendorf, Douglas W. and Gregory Mankiw, N. (1999). "Government debt," in John B. Taylor and Michael Woodford (eds.) *Handbook of Macroeconomics*. Amsterdam: North-Holland.

Feldstein, Martin (1976). "On the theory of tax reform." *Journal of Public Economics*, 6: 77–104.

Feldstein, Martin and Jeffrey B. Liebman (2001). "Social security." Working Paper No. 8541, National Bureau of Economic Research, September.

Fullerton, Don and Gilbert Metcalf. (2002). "Tax incidence," in Alan Auerbach and Martin Feldstein (eds.) *Handbook of Public Economics*.

Fuchs, Victor (1998). "Health, government, and Irving Fisher." Working Paper No. 8490, National Bureau of Economic Research, August.

Gale, Willaim G. and Joel B. Slemrod (2000) "A matter of life and death: reassesing the estate and gift tax." *Tax Notes*, August 14, 927–932.

Hargberber, Arnold C. (1962). "The incidence of the corporation income tax." *Journal of Political Economy*, LXX: 215–240.

Holcombe, Randall (1998). "Tax policy from a public choice perspective." *National Tax Journal*, LI: 359–371.

Jorgenson, Dale W. and Kun_Young Yun (2001). *Investment Volume 3: Lifting the Burden*. Cambridge: The MIT Press.

Meyer, Bruce D. (1995). "Lessons from the US unemployment insurance experiments." *Journal of Economic Literature*, 33: 91–131.

Nichols, Albert L and Richard J. Zeckhauser (1982). "Targeting transfers through restrictions on recipients." *American Economic Review Papers and Proceedings*, 72: 372–377.

Oates, Wallace E. (1999). "An essay on fiscal federalism." *Journal of Economic Literature*, 37: 1120–1149.

Pechman, Joseph A. (ed.) (1980). *What Should Be Taxed: Income or Expenditure?* Washington: The Brookings Institution.

Samuelson, Paul A. (1954). "The pure theory of public expenditure." *Review of Economics and Statistics*, 36: 387–389.

Stavins, Robert N. (2002). "Experience with market-based environmental policy instruments," in Karl-Goran Maler and Jeffrey Vincent (eds.) *The Handbook of Environmental Economics*. Amsterdam: North-Holland/Elsevier Science.

R

REGULATION AND ANTITRUST

> The state — the machinery and power of the state — is a potential resource or threat to every industry in the society. With its power to prohibit or compel, to take or give money, the state can and does selectively help or hurt a vast number of industries. (Stigler, 1971: 3)

In theory, public policies toward business — the regulation of prices and conditions of entry into specific industries, and the enforcement of antitrust laws that circumscribe the conduct of firms more broadly — serve as bulwarks of a freely functioning market economy. Without such public-sector controls, profit-seeking firms, it is commonly thought, inevitably would acquire market power and exploit it by restricting output and raising price, benefiting themselves at consumers' expense. Government agents must therefore vigilantly stand guard, intervening when necessary to limit the potential abuses of monopoly. Such intervention supposedly is guided by the goals of ensuring that prices are kept in line with costs, that scarce productive resources remain fully employed, that technological progress is rapid, and that economic growth is vigorous.

From this point of view, regulation and antitrust are thrust upon unwilling producers in order to channel and redirect their behavior away from privately rational, but socially harmful ends. Business decisions motivated solely by the quest for profit are displaced by those of public policymakers who pursue broader objectives. Assigning greater weight to the interests of society as a whole, the antitrust and regulatory authorities act quickly and appropriately to correct the failures that seem to flourish in unfettered markets, thereby redistributing wealth back to consumers and enhancing economic efficiency.

Public choice theory, by contrast, resists modeling public policymakers as disinterested maximizers of society's welfare (Buchanan and Tullock, 1962). Built on a foundation of methodological individualism, public choice closes the behavioral system by assuming that all human actors, in or out of government, pursue similar objectives (utility maximization) and employ the same rational-choice calculus to select the alternative that yields the greatest personal benefit net of cost (Buchanan, 1972). This assumption of universal self-interest, coupled with the logic of collective action (Olson, 1965), implies that the individuals responsible for formulating and executing public policies toward business will have powerful incentives, not selflessly to promote the public interest, but to enhance their own wellbeing by catering to the demands of politically well-organized special-interest groups.

Applied to public utilities, common carriers and other 'natural monopolies', the economic theory of regulation has revolutionized the study of public policies toward business. As a result of the empirical evidence accumulated over the past quarter century, lending broad support to the theory's implications, few economists now take seriously the naïve view 'that regulation is a device for protecting the public against the adverse effects of monopoly' (Posner, 1971: 22). The public interest 'theory' of regulation (Hotelling, 1938; Joskow and Noll, 1981), which is not in fact a theory in the accepted scientific sense (Posner, 1974; Aranson, 1990), has been displaced by models that bring the tools of microeconomics to bear in analyzing regulation as the product of the supply and demand for wealth transfers. Initially articulated as a theory of regulatory agency 'capture' in which, 'as a rule, regulation is acquired by the industry and operated primarily for its benefit' (Stigler, 1971: 3), the theory has been generalized and extended to allow for more complex patterns of wealth transfers amongst the many and varied groups having stakes in regulatory outcomes (Peltzman, 1976; McCormick and Tollison, 1981; Becker, 1983). The constellation of forces at work has been shown to include the industry's customers (Posner, 1974), subsets of heterogeneous producers (Marvel, 1977; Maloney and McCormick, 1982; Anderson and Tollison, 1984; Anderson et al., 1989), and politicians themselves (Crain and McCormick, 1984; McChesney, 1987, 1991, 1997). While disputes continue about the efficiency of the regulatory process (Becker, 1985; Wittman, 1989, 1995; Lott, 1997; Rowley, 1997) — that is, whether competition in the market for wealth transfers is sufficiently robust so as to minimize regulation's deadweight social costs — the economic theory of regulation, which models regulation exclusively as a mechanism of wealth redistribution, is now the reigning paradigm of regulatory analysis.

Such a revolution has not yet materialized fully in the study of antitrust policy. Despite efforts to bring public choice principles to bear in explaining the origins (Baxter, 1980; DiLorenzo, 1985; Stigler, 1985; Libecap, 1992; Boudreaux et al., 1995; Ekelund et al., 1995; Troesken, 2000) and enforcement of the antitrust laws (Faith et al., 1982; Shughart and Tollison, 1985; Shughart, 1990; McChesney and Shughart, 1995), the conventional wisdom that antitrust serves the interests of that most unorganized of groups — consumers — still holds sway. Even the late George Stigler, who did much to undermine the idea 'that regulation is instituted primarily for the benefit of the public at large' (Stigler, 1971: 3), once called antitrust a 'public interest law in the same sense in which...private property, enforcement of contracts, and suppression of crime are public-interest phenomena' (Hazlett, 1984: 46).

The scholarly disconnect between antitrust and regulation rests partly on a failure to appreciate the regulatory character of many antitrust decrees (Easterbrook, 1984). In addition, while regulatory policies normally are tailored narrowly to apply to specific firms and industries — and the interest groups having stakes in regulatory outcomes can therefore be identified easily — the antitrust laws supply a broad set of proscriptions on firm behavior that apply to the economy generally. Antitrust's wide reach complicates the identification of winners and losers. Because no one group consistently benefits from antitrust enforcement, the special-interest basis of antitrust policy is less apparent than is the case with other forms of regulation. Last, there is widespread resistance to the idea that the law enforcement agencies and judges who interpret and give effect to the vague language of the antitrust statutes are vulnerable to political influence.

As we shall see, however, antitrust *is* regulation and, hence, both can be analyzed with the same set of tools. Despite the tenacity of the public-interest view of competition policy (McCormick, 1984), the economic theory of regulation, embellished by public choice principles, helps to illuminate the causes and consequences of antitrust and to situate it within a general economic model of public policies toward business.

1. Policy Responses to 'Market Failure'

Orthodox welfare economics (Pigou, 1932) justifies government intervention into the private economy on the basis of a perceived failure of market institutions always "to sustain 'desirable' activities or to estop 'undesirable' activities" (Bator, 1958: 351). Such situations arise when the benefits or costs of a decision or choice at the level of the individual diverge from the corresponding benefits or costs at the level of society, that is, when the parties interacting in a market cannot capture the full social benefits — or do not bear the full social costs — of their resource-allocation decisions. Potential gains from trade remain unexploited when private benefits and costs are not equal to social benefits and costs and, in principle, society's welfare can be improved by appropriate policy intervention.

Consider the case of environmental pollution. In the stylized Pigouvian world, manufacturers of goods that generate toxic wastes as byproducts of the production process have little incentive to take account of the costs the pollutants impose on others. The marginal private cost of production, which consists only of the explicit and implicit costs borne by the firm's owners in bringing the product to market, is consequently less than the marginal social cost of production, which includes the additional health care expenses and other costs incurred by third parties exposed to the environmental contaminants. Because private costs are less than social costs, the firm produces a quantity of output that is greater than is optimal from society's point of view. Intervention in the form of an effluent fee equal to the difference between private and social costs is the prescribed policy response. Such a tax forces the firm to "internalize the externality", thereby reducing production to the socially optimal rate and supplying tax revenue that can in principle be used to compensate those who are injured by the residual pollutants.

Private markets may likewise fail to achieve ideal results when the social benefits of an activity exceed its private benefits. In deciding whether to be inoculated against a communicable disease, for instance, rational individuals understandably pay greater attention to the expected reduction in their own risks of infection than to the benefits conferred on others, whose risks are also lowered by virtue of immunity that is more widespread. Because inoculated individuals cannot appropriate personally the positive spillover effects of their choices, a public subsidy for vaccines helps align private benefits with social benefits, inducing more individuals to become inoculated than otherwise and thereby correcting the market's undersupply of immunizations. Market failures are also thought to be common when transaction-relevant information is distributed asymmetrically between buyers and sellers and the better-informed parties can exploit their superior knowledge strategically: purchasers of insurance may misrepresent their own risk characteristics in order to obtain coverage at actuarially favorable rates, for example. Similarly, sellers of 'experience goods' may, because quality claims cannot be verified prior to purchase, misrepresent product attributes in order to increase their profits at buyers' expense (Nelson, 1970). Public intervention to ensure appropriate information provision is routinely called for in such circumstances. In the limit, private markets may fail completely — and production rights must therefore be assigned to the public sector if any output is to be supplied at all — in the case of certain 'public goods' (national defense, for example) whose consumption is nonrivalrous and from whose benefits nonpayers cannot easily be excluded (Samuelson, 1954).

As the foregoing discussion suggests, conventional welfare economics assumes (often implicitly) that while markets are beset with imperfections, the public policy process is not so encumbered. The costs of transacting, including the costs of acquiring, collating and utilizing information about resource values and of contracting for their exchange — costs that may prevent private economic actors from exploiting all available gains from trade — are ignored when corrective government action is prescribed. Social welfare is invariably enhanced when government intervenes because policymakers are presumed to be fully informed about the social costs and social benefits of resource allocation decisions not taken into account by private decision makers and, moreover, unselfishly to select the appropriate policy response.

This line of reasoning commits what Harold Demsetz (1969) calls the 'nirvana fallacy'. Market outcomes are generated in a setting in which information is costly to acquire, the future is uncertain, and choices consequently are 'boundedly rational' (Simon, 1957). Nevertheless, market performance is usually evaluated, not by way of comparison with other, necessarily imperfect alternatives, but rather in light of the outcomes that would materialize in some idealized and unattainable world in which decision makers are fully informed and endowed with perfect foresight.

Modern approaches to the study of the imperfections associated with externalities, asymmetric information and public goods raise doubts about their empirical importance (Demsetz, 1970; Coase, 1974; Cawley and Philipson, 1999). More fundamentally, the Coase Theorem (Coase, 1959, 1960) highlights the incentives of private parties to take account of the external costs and benefits of their resource allocation decisions and to contract their own way around 'market failure'. Consider apple growing and beekeeping (Cheung, 1973). Apple growers benefit from the pollination services of bees and beekeepers benefit from a ready supply of apple blossom nectar. A complex set of bilateral contracts has evolved that compensates each party for their joint contributions to the apple and honey crop. Such contractual solutions to market failures require only that property rights be defined clearly and that transaction costs be less than expected gains. Indeed, the contours of the efficient solution (but not the distribution of income) are invariant to the initial property rights assignments. The Coase Theorem emphasizes that not every potential market failure demands a government response: private parties may fail to reach agreement, not only because the costs of doing so are high, but also because the anticipated benefits are low. The Theorem emphasizes in addition that, even when social welfare potentially can be enhanced by government intervention, the knowledge limitations confronting policymakers and the costs of government intervention must be considered before corrective action is taken.

1.1. The Regulatory Nirvana

Nowhere is the nirvana fallacy committed more regularly than in the analysis of perceived market failures due to monopoly, to which regulatory and antitrust policies have arisen in response. The textbook model of 'perfect competition' remains the standard by which the conduct of flesh-and-blood producers is evaluated by those who formulate and execute public policies toward business. In that model, rivalry between firms, by any commonsensical definition of the concept, is assumed away. Competition is 'perfect' in the model of perfect competition because large numbers of firms offering identical products for sale interact with large numbers of consumers making offers to buy, there are no barriers to the entry of new firms into the market (and no barriers to the exit of old ones), and all transaction-relevant information, including information about the locations of sellers and the prices they charge, the quality attributes of their products, and the requirements and creditworthiness of buyers, is freely available to all.

Under such circumstances, long-run market equilibrium is characterized by *allocative efficiency* and by *productive efficiency*. Since the product offered for sale by any one firm is, by assumption, identical in all respects to the products offered by its 'rivals', no seller can charge a price greater than marginal production cost. Because there is no product differentiation in the model of perfect competition, buyers select among sellers solely on the basis of price; they are otherwise indifferent as to the identity of the firm from which they make their purchases. The demand curve facing an individual seller consequently is perfectly elastic (horizontal) at the market-determined price (which is equal to marginal cost): any firm attempting to raise its price above marginal cost would immediately see its customers switching their purchases to rivals charging lower prices. No firm possesses *market power*, defined as the ability to raise price without losing all of its sales; each is a *price taker*, whose only decision is how much output to produce at the going market price.

When the firm (and the industry) expands output to the point at which price is equal to marginal cost, the value consumers place on the last unit produced (the amount they are willing to pay for it) is just equal to the value (opportunity cost) of the resources consumed in producing that unit. From society's point of view, price equal to marginal cost yields an efficient allocation of the economy's scarce sources in the sense that producers' decisions about how much to produce dovetail with consumers' decisions about how much to buy. Neither too few nor too many resources are devoted to the production of the good in question. As Goldilocks might say, the quantity of resources consumed by the perfectly competitive industry is 'just right'.

In addition, since there are, again by assumption, no barriers to the entry of new firms into the industry, sellers cannot earn positive economic profits in the long run. The rate of return on invested capital in the perfectly competitive industry is driven to normal levels — equal to the rate of return on the next best alternative investment opportunity. With above-normal profits eliminated by new entry (and below-normal profits eliminated by exit), market price (average revenue) is not only equal to marginal cost, it is equal to average cost as well. Given that marginal cost is equal to average cost only at the latter's minimum point, that is in turn the only point consistent with long-run, zero-profit industry equilibrium. What is true for the industry must also be true for every firm in it. Price equal to marginal cost and zero profits implies that the horizontal demand schedule perceived by price-taking firms must be tangent to the minimum points on their respective average cost curves. This is the hallmark of *productive efficiency*. Given existing technologies and resource prices, the perfectly competitive industry produces its product at the lowest possible cost per unit. Things are once again 'just right': the industry consists of the socially optimal number of firms each of which employs its production capacity at the efficient (cost-minimizing) rate.

1.2. The Welfare Costs of Monopoly

The belief that actual markets frequently fail to achieve ideal textbook results supplies the principal justification for antitrust and regulatory intervention into the private economy. But using the model of perfect competition in this way commits the nirvana fallacy. Real producers do not conduct business in a frictionless world of homogeneous products, zero transaction costs and perfect knowledge. Owing to differences in quality, reputation, location, and so on, each seller's product or service has one or more unique attributes that distinguish it in the minds of consumers from the products or services sold by its rivals. The offerings of sellers in most markets are good, but not perfect substitutes for one another and buyers typically have preferences for one particular brand (and are therefore willing to pay more for it). The demand schedule confronting each firm slopes downward under these very common circumstances and because of this, neither allocative nor productive efficiency can possibly be attained.

In the presence of product differentiation (and the downward-sloping demand curves to which it gives rise), the assumptions of the model of perfect competition no longer apply. In order to attract customers away from the sellers of substitutable products and to increase its own sales, each firm must be prepared to engage in the commonplace types of rivalry assumed away for model-building purposes. They advertise and promote their products, engage in research and development, and offer pre- and post-sale services, warranties, convenient locations and hours of operation, to name a few of the many available methods of nonprice competition. In addition, of course, the quantity sold by a firm facing a downward-sloping demand curve can be increased if its product's price is reduced. Downward-sloping demand also implies market power: the firm can raise its price without losing all of its sales.

The firm with market power does not take price as given, but instead searches for the price that maximizes its profits and, as every sophomore knows, that profit maximum occurs at an output rate that is lower (and a price that is consequently higher) than would be chosen by a perfectly competitive industry facing the same demand and cost conditions. In other words, the firm exploits its market power by restricting the number of units offered for sale below the competitive level. This output restriction reduces the welfare of consumers in two ways. First, because price exceeds average cost, at least in the short run (see below), income is redistributed from buyers to the seller in the form of pure economic profit. (This redistribution, by itself, usually is treated as a pure income transfer having no impact on the welfare of society as a whole: the seller's gains exactly offset consumers' losses.) Second, because price also exceeds marginal cost, additional surplus is transferred away from consumers which, not being captured by the seller, imposes a 'deadweight' welfare loss on society (Harberger, 1954). When all units of output are sold at the same price (i.e., the seller does not engage in price discrimination), this deadweight social welfare loss materializes because, by restricting production below the competitive level, the firm fails to supply units of output for which consumers are willing to pay more than it would cost to produce.

Markets populated by firms possessing market power thus fail to achieve desirable results in the sense that fewer units of output are produced (and fewer resources are therefore allocated to production) than is optimal when benchmarked against the textbook model of perfect competition. Price in excess of marginal cost impairs allocative efficiency. Moreover, although productive efficiency is achieved by firms with market power under constant-cost conditions, only by coincidence will such firms produce their outputs at rates corresponding to minimum average cost with more generic U-shaped cost curves.

The polar case of market power is monopoly, defined as a market served by a single firm producing a product having no close substitutes. Whether any firm possessing market power, including a monopolist, is able to earn above-normal profits in the long run depends critically on the conditions of entry facing newcomers to the industry. Consider a market that is perfectly 'contestable', for example. Firms contemplating entry into such a market do not bear any costs not borne by the established firm(s) — and firms exiting the industry can recoup their prior investments net of depreciation. Under these conditions, prices and profits must stay at competitive levels regardless of the number and size distribution of incumbent producers (Baumol et al., 1982).

1.3. Efficiency or Redistribution?

It is not the distribution of income between producers and consumers that is the stated concern of public policies toward business. Profits, after all, play an indispensable role in market economies, helping guide alert entrepreneurs to redirect scarce productive resources from less highly valued to more highly valued uses. Rather, it is the existence of allocative inefficiency ('deadweight' social welfare loss) that supplies a theoretical justification for government intervention into sectors of the economy ostensibly plagued by market power. Although the deadweight losses due to monopoly do not seem to loom large empirically (Harberger, 1954; Posner, 1975) and therefore are offset by even modest efficiency gains (Williamson, 1968a, 1977), the presumption is that appropriate public policies can and will be employed systematically to identify and correct these market failures, thereby restoring competitive results. In principle, the public's interest will be served — society will experience a net gain from such intervention — as long as the cost of implementing pro-competitive public policies is less than the associated improvement in market efficiency.

The proponents of an activist anti-monopoly policy have also pointed to the possibility of 'X-inefficiency' (Leibenstein, 1966, 1978), the idea that the managers of firms insulated from competitive market forces have weak incentives to deploy the resources at their command cost-effectively. Less competition leads to internal waste and therefore less efficiency. While Leibenstein did not identify the sources of such waste precisely (hence the 'X' in 'X-inefficiency'), he argued that such losses would far outweigh any cost savings (i.e., scale economies) otherwise associated with monopoly. Thus, in contrast to Williamson's tradeoff model, it is productive efficiency, not allocative efficiency, that should loom large in justifying public policies toward business. If freedom from competition makes it possible for managers to be 'X-inefficient', then policies aimed at increasing firms' exposure to competitive market forces will produce significant efficiency gains. Subsequent work has indicated, however, that this remains an open question (Stigler, 1976; Jensen and Meckling, 1976; De Alessi, 1983; Bertoletti and Poletti, 1997; Schmidt, 1997; for a general application of these ideas to regulation and antitrust, see Rowley and Peacock, 1975).

On the other hand, the public choice model stresses that issues of income distribution will tend to carry greater weight in the public policy process than concerns of economic efficiency. Groups that stand to gain or lose wealth because of policies targeting perceived sources of market failure will coalesce around the policy process in order to protect their own parochial interests. Politicians and policymakers will respond rationally to and balance these competing demands, and in doing so tend to give preference to those constituencies best able to support them politically in exchange for favorable treatment. The economic theory of regulation (including antitrust regulation) is thus about the political pressures that impinge on the elected officials who enact the legal rules delineating regulation's scope, and on the agencies whose bureaucrats enforce those rules. Depending on the policy process in question, the beneficiaries of regulation may turn out to be almost any well-organized special-interest group. Owing to the fact that 'the public' is numerous, geographically dispersed, and, in general, unorganized politically, its influence on the policy process is necessarily weak. Public regulation of private industry therefore will rarely, if ever, serve the public's interest.

2. Regulation

> The 'protection of the public' theory of regulation must say that the choice of [oil] import quotas is dictated by the concern of the federal government for an adequate supply of petroleum in the event of war — a remark calculated to elicit uproarious laughter at the Petroleum Club. (Stigler, 1971: 4)

The extent of public regulation of industry in the United States — and elsewhere — is both broad and deep. To name just a few, rules — and agencies to enforce them — have been established to require the disclosure of financial information to investors; to license physicians, hospitals, attorneys, accountants, stockbrokers, barbers, electricians, plumbers, morticians, and taxicab operators; to regulate advertising claims; to enforce environmental quality, workplace safety and product safety standards; and to promote equal opportunity in employee hiring and promotion decisions. While all such regulatory regimes are worthy of study from an interest-group perspective (see, e.g., Stigler, 1988), because of its historical significance in justifying regulatory controls on private industry, the case of immediate interest here is that of so-called natural monopoly.

Natural monopoly 'does not refer to the actual number of sellers in a market but to the relationship between demand and the technology of supply' (Posner, 1969b, 1999: 1). In particular, a monopoly is said to be 'natural' if, first, the production of the good or service in question is characterized by robust economies of scale, that is, long-run average costs fall sharply over the relevant range of output rates. Scale economies will loom large if production technologies are subject to increasing returns (proportional increases in input usage produce greater than proportional increases in output), if large capital investments must be made before production begins, but the cost of producing additional units or of serving additional customers is comparatively low from then on, or both. Second, monopoly is natural if, in the presence of significant economies of scale in production, the demand schedule intersects the long-run average cost curve at a point where the latter is still declining.

The existence of scale economies up to the level of market demand is sufficient for establishing natural monopoly when the firm produces a single product. In modern parlance, scale economies are a strong form of 'cost sub-additivity', meaning that there is no feasible way of subdividing the firm's quantity of output, Q, having each subpart produced by separate firms, without incurring higher total costs. In other words, 'the cost of producing the whole is less than the sum of the costs of producing the parts' (Baumol et al., 1982: 17). Strict cost sub-additivity (and, hence, natural monopoly) in the multi-product case requires both economies of scale and economies of joint production, the latter representing situations in which the total cost of producing the individual products by separate firms is greater than the total cost of having all of them produced by the same firm (Tirole, 1988: 19–20; also see Sherman, 1989; Spulber, 1989).

The efficiency results of free and open competition may not be achievable under the conditions defining natural monopoly. Because of the peculiar relationship between demand and cost, one firm can supply the entire market more efficiently than two or more firms, each of which, owing to the strictures of cost sub-additivity, would necessarily incur higher unit costs. Indeed, an alternative definition of natural monopoly is an industry in which one firm is viable (i.e., earns positive economic profits), but two or more firms are not (Tirole, 1988: 20). Two unhappy outcomes are then possible: 'either the firms will quickly shake down to one through mergers or failures, or production will continue to consume more resources than necessary' (Posner, 1969b, 1999: 1). In the former case, left unrestrained, the sole survivor rationally will restrict the number of units it produces below the competitive level and raise its price to the monopoly profit-maximum. In the latter case, capital investments will be wastefully duplicated from society's point of view in the sense that production on a larger scale by a single firm would yield substantial improvements in economic efficiency.

Regulation of natural monopoly is thus justified normatively on the grounds that, while society would benefit from the production efficiencies achieved by having the market served by a single firm, allocative efficiency will be impaired if the monopolist remains free to exercise his market power. Society can in principle have it both ways if government intervenes by, on the one hand, assigning exclusive rights to produce the good or service in question to one firm and, on the other hand, imposing legal controls that require the franchisee to expand production and lower price, thereby approximating competitive market outcomes.

Construed narrowly, the natural monopoly justification for regulation rests on the fulfillment of extreme assumptions and, as such, applies only to a limited set of 'public utilities'. Water and sewer systems, electric power grids and telecommunication networks, long regulated by local, state and national governments in the United States and elsewhere, are prime examples. Even in these textbook cases, however, the theoretical rationale for regulation is weak. Competition for the field can substitute for competition within it (Demsetz, 1968; Williamson, 1976). Additionally, 'access pricing', whereby rival suppliers pay for the right to utilize the large-scale infrastructure necessary to serve public utility customers, avoids duplicative investments in production capacity and promotes efficient utilization of that capacity (Shy, 2001: 8). It also turns out that if an unregulated natural monopolist operates under conditions of contestability, it will charge Ramsey-optimal prices in all markets (i.e., prices that are inversely proportional to the elasticity of demand in each market; see Ramsey, 1927), subject to a minimum profit constraint that ensures viability (Baumol et al., 1977; Baumol et al., 1982; Tirole, 1988: 308–309). Hence, while the particular configurations of cost and demand defining natural monopoly prevent the attainment of first-best outcomes, they may not preclude second-best optima even in the absence of regulation.

In practice, even otherwise staunch supporters of active government involvement in the economy admit that arguments based on 'trumped-up claims of monopoly' (Scherer, 1980: 482) frequently have been appealed to in order to widen regulation's scope far beyond the limited set of industries for which public-sector controls might theoretically be defensible. Indeed, public regulation of industry in the United States began at the federal level in 1887 with passage of the Act to Regulate Commerce, which established the Interstate Commerce Commission (ICC) and delegated to that agency the authority to ensure that railway rates were 'just and reasonable'. The ICC's regulatory powers ultimately were expanded to include control over most surface (and some subsurface) interstate transportation modes, including inland water carriers, trucks, busses, and crude oil pipelines — industries to which the natural monopoly label does not obviously apply.

Public regulation of industry in the United States in fact predates the Act to Regulate Commerce by a decade. In 1877, the US Supreme Court ruled that when private property is 'affected with a public interest', regulation is constitutionally permissible despite the Fourteenth Amendment's guarantee that 'no State shall ... deprive any person of life, liberty, or property without due process of law'. That ruling was handed down in *Munn* v. *Illinois*, 94 U.S. 113, a case challenging a provision of the Constitution of the State of Illinois designating privately owned grain elevators as public warehouses as well as a law passed by the Illinois legislature in 1871 prescribing maximum rates for grain storage. Munn and Scott, two grain elevator operators, had been convicted of charging higher rates than the law allowed; the Supreme Court upheld their conviction. In the following years, the Court construed the 'public interest' standard strictly, approving state regulation of only a select group of industries, including in addition to grain storage, banks, fire insurance companies and insurance agents. Limited as the early extensions of regulation may have been, none of the newly regulated industries plausibly were monopolies, natural or otherwise.

But the Court rejected even the narrow construction of *Munn* in 1934, declaring that 'the phrase "affected with a public interest" can, in the nature of things, mean no more than that an industry, for adequate reason, is subject to control for the public good' and that 'there can be no doubt that on proper occasion and by appropriate measures the state may regulate a business in any of its aspects, including the prices to be charged for its products or the commodities it sells'. In that 1934 case, *Nebbia* v. *New York*, 291 U.S. 502, a case in which the Court upheld the right of New York's Milk Control Board to regulate milk prices in the state, the Court in effect ruled that there is no constitutional distinction between public utilities and other industries. The states were thereafter free to regulate any business operating within their jurisdictions for any reason public officials could rationalize as promoting the public interest, so long as the regulation was 'neither arbitrary nor discriminatory'.

Thus were the regulatory floodgates opened. Any pretense that natural monopoly conditions explained the onset of economic regulation was gone.

With their stronger and more overt socialist heritages, many European governments adopted a different method for dealing with alleged natural monopolies. At least until recently, public ownership rather than regulation of privately owned firms has been the norm there. (Though much rarer, such a policy approach is not unknown in the United States: the electric power industry, e.g., contains a mix of investor-owned, publicly owned and customer-owned companies; virtually all of America's local public transit systems, many of its municipal refuse collection services and, most infamously, its postal delivery service, are also operated as government enterprises.) As with public regulation in the United States, public ownership in Europe expanded far beyond the bounds set by the peculiar configurations of cost and demand defining natural monopoly. In addition to the traditional public utilities, commercial airlines, railroads, banks, television and radio networks, and telephone systems are (or have been) nationalized. So have the manufacturing of steel, automobiles and aircraft, and the extraction and processing of oil, coal and other natural resources. While an analysis of state-owned enterprises is beyond the scope of the present discussion, it suffices to say that, because of weaker incentives for using resources efficiently (Alchian, 1965; De Alessi, 1982, 2001), publicly owned firms are predicted to perform poorly by market standards. That prediction is borne out by an extensive empirical literature (see, e.g., Shughart, 1997: 295–301). Public enterprise even seems to be inferior to (less technically efficient than) regulation (Rowley and Yarrow, 1981).

The American and European paths continue to diverge even now. Beginning with the domestic commercial airlines, a wave of deregulation has been underway in the United States since the late 1970s. The United Kingdom embarked on a program of privatization the following decade, and the number of state-owned enterprises on Europe's endangered species list increased dramatically with the collapse of the Soviet Union. But public ownership of industry in Europe has been replaced, not by a hands-off approach to the private sector, but by a new emphasis on regulation. A comparison of traditional and interest group theories of regulation helps shed light on these developments.

2.1. The Standard Theory

Given that, absent contestable market conditions, an unregulated natural monopolist rationally would restrict output, raise price, and thereby earn above-normal profits, the case for government intervention rests on the theory that an industry-specific regulatory agency can and will impose controls that allow the substantial economies of single-firm production to be achieved, while at the same time forcing prices and profits to competitive levels. But a serious problem arises at the outset: because marginal cost lies below average cost when the latter is falling, mandating a price equal to marginal cost would cause the regulated firm to incur losses and a subsidy would therefore be necessary for it to remain viable in the long run. Market demand would be satisfied and the regulated firm would be constrained to earning a normal profit if it were allowed to charge a price equal to average cost, but that price would necessarily exceed marginal cost. Thus, all orthodox theories of regulation are inevitably concerned with tradeoffs between productive efficiency, allocative efficiency and sustainability.

There is a second, perhaps more serious, problem confronting the regulators. The ostensible goal of regulation is to induce the regulated firm to produce and price 'optimally' (Train, 1991). If that goal is to be achieved, the regulatory agency must be fully informed about the cost and demand conditions facing the firms it is responsible for regulating. It is reasonable to assume, though, that regulated firms will have both more and better information about their own costs and the values their own customers place on the goods or services they produce than will the regulatory agency's staff, no matter how expert they may be. The very real possibility exists that regulated firms will exploit their superior knowledge to persuade regulators to approve rate requests that depart from optimality. Mechanisms must therefore be designed that provide incentives for regulated firms truthfully to reveal the specialized information in their possession. The complexity of the regulatory process is increased — and strategic misrepresentation of relevant information becomes more likely — owing to the fact that considerations of allocative efficiency and sustainability typically force regulatory agencies to contrive a schedule of allowable rates rather than permitting them to deal with the much simpler problem of approving a single price that all customers will pay.

The necessity of creating a schedule of allowable rates arises whenever customers differ in their marginal valuations of the good or service supplied by the regulated firm. Under such quite common circumstances, requiring the regulated firm to charge the same price to all buyers generates allocative inefficiency even if that price is set at the proper break-even level which allows the firm to earn a normal profit. This allocative inefficiency results from the fact that some customers — those who would choose to purchase the good or service if it were priced at marginal cost — will not be willing to buy at the higher average-cost price. In addition, as noted above, because marginal cost lies continuously below average price under natural monopoly conditions, no single market-clearing price equal to marginal cost exists at which the regulated firm can avoid economic losses.

Price discrimination is the standard solution to this problem. Following this approach, customers are segregated into different classes based on their elasticities of demand for the regulated firm's product and a separate rate is set for each class that is inversely proportional to its demand elasticity (Ramsey, 1927). The result of price discrimination is higher rates for those customers having less elastic demands and lower rates for those customers having more elastic demands. It is not unusual, for example, for industrial customers to be required to pay more for electric power than commercial (small business) customers, who are in turn required to pay more than residential customers. Such discriminatory rate structures help achieve regulation's two-fold objective, at least in principle. First, charging different prices to different classes of customers increases the regulated firm's revenues over and above those that would be earned under a single-price policy. Price discrimination thus makes it more likely that the firm will break even. Second, tailoring prices more closely to customers' marginal valuations works to mitigate allocative inefficiency.

Other regulatory pricing schemes for helping resolve the twin problems of efficiency and sustainability include 'peak-load pricing', which involves charging higher prices to all customers when the demand for the regulated firm's good or service rises systematically relative to normal demand. Differentially higher electricity rates during the summer months and differentially higher public transit fares during 'rush-hour' are relevant examples. 'Multi-part pricing', in which customers pay a fixed service connection charge upfront plus a price per unit of service consumed that approximates the marginal cost of supplying them, is another alternative, as is a rate schedule that declines in stepwise fashion as additional 'blocks' of service are consumed.

It should be obvious, however, that, in the presence of imperfect (and perhaps strategically false) information, diversity in customers' demands and differences in the costs of serving them, 'optimal' regulation will be elusive (Coase, 1946). The orthodox case for regulating natural monopoly is undermined further by considering some rational behavioral responses to it. Traditional public utility regulation requires the regulatory agency to establish schedules of allowable rates consistent not only with the goal of improving allocative efficiency, but also with an eye toward preventing the regulated firm's revenues from breeching an overall profit constraint, thereby ensuring that the firm's owners earn only a normal or 'fair' return on their investments. Under such a regulatory regime, the regulatory agency is obligated to pass through to customers the cost of any physical capital it permits the firm to add to its installed 'rate base' (the value of the stock of capital on which the regulated rate of return is computed) plus an allowance for normal profit. Because prices must be increased by more than the cost of additions to the rate base in order to ensure that the regulated firm continues to earn a 'fair' return, the cost of capital is effectively lowered. As a result, the regulated firm has an incentive to invest in more capital than it would in the absence of regulation (Averch and Johnson, 1962; Baumol and Klevorick, 1970). Rate-of-return regulation may therefore compromise the regulated firm's productive efficiency by inducing it to select an input combination that is too capital-intensive compared with the combination that is optimal from society's point of view. Firms subject to rate-of-return regulation also have incentives opportunistically to evade the regulatory profit constraint by diversifying into unregulated lines of business and then adopting internal-to-the-firm transfer pricing policies that reallocate recorded profits away from core activities subject to regulatory control.

So-called price-cap regulation supplies a somewhat different set of incentives (Acton and Vogelsang, 1989; Train, 1991: 317–319). Adopted by the US Federal Communications Commission in mid 1990 for regulating long-distance telephone rates and by regulatory authorities in the United Kingdom for regulating natural gas, electric power and water utilities, the regulated firm is permitted to earn a rate of return that exceeds the ceiling that would otherwise be imposed in exchange for agreeing not to raise its prices by more than allowed under a predetermined formula. That formula is of the form $CPI - X$, where CPI is the annual rate of increase in an index of retail prices and X is some specified percentage less than the measured economy-wide inflation rate. In other words, the public utility or common carrier is authorized to raise its prices only if the rate of inflation is greater than X, and then only to the extent that the CPI exceeds that threshold.

Price-cap regulation has two advantages over traditional rate-of-return regulation. First, because input prices are not distorted and the regulated firm can keep any and all of the profits it earns under the price cap, it will choose efficient methods of production. In addition, the firm has an incentive to implement any cost-reducing innovations in those production methods, again because it can keep all of the realized profits. (It does not have an incentive to pass those cost savings on to consumers in the form of lower prices, however.) Second, regulatory rate hearings are greatly simplified: requests for price increases are approved automatically, subject only to the regulatory agency's determination that the proposed increase satisfies the agreed-to pricing formula.

It is nevertheless true that, as with all other forms of regulation, the information required to implement price caps largely must be obtained from the regulated firm itself. Depending on how methodically regulatory rate hearings are conducted and how aggressively the regulatory agency adjusts price caps over time to take account of changing conditions of cost and demand, the utility may be able to exploit its superior knowledge to benefit its owners and managers at consumers' expense.

In the end, and in spite of a large and elegant scholarly literature prescribing mechanisms for dealing with the complexities of regulation,

> its contribution to social and economic welfare is very possibly negative. The benefits of regulation are dubious, not only because the evils of natural monopoly are exaggerated but also because the effectiveness of regulation in controlling them is highly questionable. (Posner [1969b] 1999: 106)

The conclusion that regulation often fails to achieve its stated goals garnered empirical support in an initial series of studies examining its actual effects. A study of electric utility regulation, for example, found that it had little or no impact on the level of prices or on the rates of return to investments in that industry (Stigler and Friedland, 1962). In another study, investors were found to have obtained few benefits from the regulatory oversight of new stock issues by the US Securities and Exchange Commission (Stigler, 1964). Indeed, a survey of the early empirical literature supporting the 'capture' theory of regulation suggested that, while regulatory intervention was not always as ineffective as Stigler and Friedland had found — as a matter of fact, they were later shown to have been wrong (Peltzman, 1993) — in those industries where regulation did affect prices and profits, the effects were perverse (Jordan, 1972). In particular, when applied to naturally competitive industries, such as air and surface transportation, regulation uniformly was found to have reduced the number of competitors and to have raised prices. On the other hand, when applied to industries more plausibly characterized by natural monopoly conditions, regulation had no effect on prices.

These empirical findings raised two important questions. If consumers' interests are not materially advanced by regulation, why is regulation adopted in the first place? Given the very real costs of regulation — the costs to taxpayers of defraying the expenses of the regulatory agencies and the costs to society in the form of the resources misallocated by poorly crafted regulatory constraints and the resources consumed in attempts to influence the regulatory process — why does regulation persist?

The initial answer to both of these questions was that, despite their well-intentioned purposes, regulatory agencies are vulnerable to 'capture' by the very firms they were created to oversee. Public institutions ostensibly designed to protect consumers from the abuses of monopoly in practice catered chiefly to the interests of producers. This 'capture' theory of regulation has subsequently been formalized and extended into what is currently known as the economic theory of regulation, to which the discussion now turns.

2.2. The Economic Theory of Regulation

Regulation creates rents for the regulated. By virtue of the exclusive franchises they have been granted, the owners of regulated firms are in position to earn profits in excess of normal levels. Regulatory agencies are of course charged with the responsibility of ensuring that public utilities and other natural monopolies do not exercise their market power, imposing controls on price that allow the owners to earn only 'fair' rates of return on their investments. But if the profits of regulated natural monopolies were in fact typically equal to the rate of return available in the next best alternative investment opportunity, there would be no need for rules governing the conditions of entry into the regulated industry. The regulation of entry into a market with natural monopoly characteristics can be justified on the basis of a social-welfare standard only if prices would be too high after entry, not if they would be too low. If prospective entrants anticipate that entry will cause prices to fall below average cost so that all firms, including the incumbent, stand to incur economic losses, *then they will not enter*. Legal barriers to entry, usually imposed in the form of requirements that newcomers to the market obtain a 'certificate of convenience and necessity' from the regulatory agency prior to entering, consequently supply prima facie evidence that the profits of regulated firms are often above normal levels.

Regulated firms may earn supranormal profits in only some of their markets. Regulatory mandates requiring public utilities to serve all of the customers in their territories regardless of cost (so-called 'universal service' requirements) and rules designating shippers as 'common carriers', may force regulated firms to serve markets they would not serve in the absence of regulation. In such cases, and as an alternative to explicit subsidy, the regulatory agency must permit the regulated firm to make up losses in markets where revenues are less than costs by charging higher prices (and earning profits exceeding normal levels) in more remunerative markets. A case can be made for erecting legal barriers to entry into the firm's paying markets on the grounds that, without the supranormal returns obtainable there, owners would not earn a 'fair' return overall.

Regulatory cross-subsidies of these kinds are quite common, so common in fact that Richard Posner (1971) calls such pricing schemes 'taxation by regulation:' some of the excess returns associated with exclusive natural monopoly franchises are taxed away by regulators in the form of requirements to serve customers that would not be served otherwise. The implication is that regulators allow regulated firms to charge some of their customers prices that exceed the costs of serving them so that other customers can be served at prices that are less actual costs. One allocative inefficiency is introduced to sponsor another.

The history of deregulation (about which more later) suggests, however, that prices exceed costs in most, if not all, regulated markets. The rates paid by long-distance telephone customers, for example, supposedly kept high by regulators in order to subsidize local telephone customers, have fallen dramatically since MCI and other competitors began entering the industry in 1982. (Deregulation was initially opposed by the incumbent regulated monopolist AT&T on the basis that, if MCI was allowed to 'skim the cream' from its most profitable market, AT&T's ability to fulfill its universal local telephone service obligations would be severely compromised.) But local telephone rates are also falling as competition emerges in those markets. To be sure, lower local and long-distance telephone rates are explained in part by the rapid pace of technological change in the telecommunications industry since the early 1980s — events which themselves owe much to the competitive market forces unleashed by deregulation. It is nevertheless reasonable to conclude from this and similar experiences in the commercial airline industry, the trucking industry, and the natural gas transmission industry, among others, that prices (and profits) under regulation tend to exceed normal levels.

Whether rents exist in all or only some of a regulated firm's markets, however, their existence begets rent-seeking (Tullock, 1967; Krueger, 1974). Individuals and groups rationally strive to put themselves in position to earn abovenormal returns and, moreover, are willing to invest resources for the purpose of capturing them equal to the expected value of their anticipated gains (Posner, 1975; Tullock, 1980). In the case at hand, rent-seeking materializes in the form of lobbying activities calculated to influence the regulatory process. George Stigler (1971) modeled regulation largely as a struggle between producers and consumers for access to the rents associated with conditions of natural monopoly. Given that the members of the regulated industry normally would be better informed about the regulatory process, have greater financial stakes in regulatory outcomes, and, owing to their smaller numbers and more cohesive objectives, be better organized and, hence, more effective in bringing influence to bear on the regulatory agency, regulators would tend to favor their interests over those of consumers. The essence of the 'capture' theory of regulation is that 'consumers are the least organized and therefore typically the least effective interest group. The long-run consumer interest in particular has no lobby' (Posner [1969b] 1999: 67).

In Stigler's formulation of the problem, producers dominate the regulatory process and no one should therefore be surprised that, from society's perspective, public regulation of industry is ineffective or perverse: 'Consumers never asked for an Interstate Commerce Commission to prevent new truckers from entering the business. Nor had consumers been heard from when the federal government set up milk marketing boards to restrict the supply of milk and drive up the price. The main players were truckers and milk producers, who wanted to limit competition' (Henderson, 1995: 62).

A subsequent formalization of the economic theory of regulation (Peltzman, 1976) supplies a more general framework for thinking about the problem. In that more general theory, the regulators themselves are portrayed as rational, self-interested actors whose objective is to maximize their own political support. Where they hold elective office, 'political support' can be defined in terms of votes, campaign contributions, or both, in which case regulators are assumed to be motivated by the goal of maximizing their probability of reelection. Where they hold appointive office, regulators strive to maximize their probability of reappointment or some other index of job security. An even more universal behavioral assumption is utility (wealth) maximization, a maximand which includes the regulator's salary and perquisites of public office as well as income received from post-government employment, which, because of the specialized knowledge gained in participating in the regulatory process, not infrequently will be a job in the regulated industry itself. In any case, the interest-group theory of regulation rejects the analytical inconsistencies of the 'public-interest' theory, which places regulators outside the model and does not therefore inquire into their motives. Everyone involved in the regulatory process, including the regulators themselves, is thereby brought within the ambit of positive economic analysis.

As in all economic models of human behavior, the regulator's pursuit of self-interest is not unconstrained. In Peltzman's framework, the regulator selects the price the regulated firm is permitted to charge. This price can be set at the competitive level, in which case the regulated firm earns a normal profit and consumers enjoy all of the gains associated with regulation. The price can also be set at the monopoly profit-maximizing level, in which case producers are regulation's sole beneficiaries. In general, however, the politically self-interested regulator must weigh the demands of both groups. While an increase in price (and profit) elicits greater political support from the regulated firm(s), it also invites greater opposition from consumers. Lower prices invoke the opposite reactions. If the political returns to higher profit or lower price are diminishing at the margin, neither group will get all that it wants from regulation: from the regulator's point of view, the optimal price will lie somewhere between the extremes of competition and monopoly. Where the balance is struck in any particular case depends on the configurations of the costs and benefits of bringing political influence to bear on the regulatory process facing the groups having stakes in the outcome.

Like the public-interest theory, the Stigler-Peltzman model predicts that regulation will target natural monopolies and that, to the extent to which losses in political support from the regulated firm are offset by increases in support from consumers, regulators will require the regulated firm to charge a lower price than it would otherwise. But unlike the public-interest theory, the Stigler-Peltzman model helps explain why regulatory controls have in practice been applied to industries that would otherwise be competitive. If regulators can increase their political support by mandating that prices be raised above competitive levels, they will rationally do so up to the point where the additional support provided by producers equates at the margin to the loss in support from consumers.

Although the discussion thus far places the Stigler-Peltzman model of regulation in its original, highly stylized producer-consumer context, the economic theory of regulation is in fact much more general. Because 'the political process automatically admits powerful outsiders to the industry's councils' (Stigler, 1971: 7), regulatory outcomes will assimilate the interests of any individual or group that can bring effective influence to bear on the regulators. For example, 'it is well known that the allocation of television channels among communities does not maximize industry revenue but reflects pressures to serve many smaller communities' (ibid.). The regulatory subsidies granted to rural electric power and telephone customers are further examples of this point. The economic theory of regulation accommodates such diversity. It places regulation in political context and argues that the observed level and pattern of regulatory intervention into the private economy is the logical outcome of a process that tends to favor groups having comparative advantages in exploiting regulatory institutions and processes to their own self-serving ends.

One of the most fruitful applications of the interest-group model recognizes not only that a constellation of interests frequently impinges on the regulatory process, but also that the groups seeking influence are themselves not monolithic. The producers in any industry, for example, differ as to size, cost-efficiency, geographic location, and so on. Heterogeneity on these and other competitive margins gives rise to the possibility that a subset of firms within an industry will be able to utilize regulatory processes to benefit themselves at the expense of their rivals.

To illustrate, consider an industry whose members employ two distinct production technologies. Assume that one technology is relatively labor-intensive and that the other is relatively capital-intensive. The firms using capital-intensive production methods negotiate a contract with labor union representatives that raises wage rates *industry-wide*. All firms face higher costs as a result, but the costs of the labor-intensive firms rise proportionately more than those of the capital-intensive firms. Marginal producers employing labor-intensive production methods are forced to exit the industry, and if the ensuing increase in market price outweighs the increase in costs for the surviving low-cost producers, their inframarginal rents increase. Moreover, these rents are protected by the fact that the now higher industry wage rates erect a barrier to entry by labor-intensive firms (Williamson, 1968b).

Regulatory processes can be exploited to produce similar intra-industry redistributions of wealth. Consider the Factory Acts adopted by the British government during the 1830s. These laws, which limited the hours women and children could legally work, are widely seen as public-spirited measures designed to end the cruel exploitation of vulnerable members of the labor force. Howard Marvel (1977), however, argues that a key impetus for passage of the Factory Acts was that they benefited the owners of steam-powered textile mills at the expense of the owners of water-powered mills. The latter could operate only when water flows were adequate to power the textile machinery; production had to be curtailed during times of drought. By preventing the water-powered mills from working overtime when streams were in spate, the Factory Acts conferred a considerable competitive advantage on the owners of the steam-powered mills who were not constrained by river conditions and could therefore operate on a regular basis year-round. In addition, Anderson and Tollison (1984) suggest that the interests of senior (male) factory operatives also played a role in the adoption of the Factory Acts insofar as the working-hour restrictions limited the extent to which women and children could compete for their jobs.

The heterogeneous firm approach has likewise been shown to be helpful in explaining the adoption of workplace safety rules (Maloney and McCormick, 1982) and environmental quality regulations (Pashigian, 1985; Bartel and Thomas, 1987). Requiring all producers to employ the same technologies for reducing the risk of on-the-job injuries or for controlling the emission of pollutants can benefit some firms at the expense of others. The actual (as opposed to the stated) purposes of regulation are frequently cloaked in high-minded ideals.

2.3. Deregulation

In seeking to explain why a regulatory policy has been adopted, the economic theory of regulation 'tells us to look, as precisely and carefully as we can, at who gains and who loses, and how much...' (Stigler, 1975: 140). In seeking to explain why a regulatory policy persists, especially in the face of evidence that its actual effects are 'unrelated or perversely related' to its announced goals, the interest-group theory tells us that 'the *truly intended effects should be deduced from the actual effects*' (ibid.; emphasis in original). Errors are of course possible, but in the Stigler-Peltzman framework,

> errors are not what men live by or on. If an economic policy has been adopted by many communities, or if it is persistently pursued by a society over a long span of time, it is fruitful to assume that the real effects were known *and desired*. Indeed, an explanation of a policy in terms of error or confusion is no explanation at all — anything and everything is compatible with that 'explanation.' (ibid.; emphasis added)

Hence, if it is found, for example, that the regulatory policies of the US Civil Aeronautics Board placed the interests of the commercial airlines over those of the flying public, or that the regulatory policies of the Interstate Commerce Commission placed the interests of the railroads and motor carriers over those of their customers, then the interest-group theory teaches that it is reasonable to conclude that regulation was intended to have precisely those effects.

But what of deregulation? While it is relatively easy, after the fact, to identify the winners and losers from regulation's adoption, how is it possible to explain policies freeing an industry from regulatory control, thereby presumably confiscating its hard-won rents? One theory appeals to regulation's 'unintended consequences': designed to ensure that regulated firms would earn profits in excess of normal levels, some regulatory regimes were in practice unable to deliver on that promise. Airline rate regulation under the auspices of the US Civil Aeronautics Board, for instance, has been described as 'sporadic, casual, and uninformed' (Wilcox, 1966: 424). The agency's failure in this regard has been attributed to a number of factors, not the least important of which was the problem of determining 'the' cost of a seat on a particular flight, given the industry's complex mix of routes, traffic schedules and capital equipment (Douglas and Miller, 1976). Lacking sufficient flexibility in the fares they were permitted to charge under regulation, the airlines rationally competed for passengers by a variety of nonprice means, including safety records, quality of in-flight meals, comfort of aircraft cabin interiors, and attractiveness of cabin attendants. The scheduling of frequent flights on major routes, offering passengers convenient departure and arrival times, was one of the more important margins of competition. The result was chronic overcapacity: 'for all flights by all major airlines in 1977, the composite load factor stood at only 55.5 percent, which meant that on average each plane was flying a little more than half full' (McGraw, 1984: 261). Thus, despite regulatory rate fixing, which generated markups ranging from 20% to 95% over the fares charged on unregulated intrastate flights of equal distance (Keeler, 1972), the airlines' profits were eroded by the costs of inefficient scheduling and other forms of nonprice competition. Indeed, the airlines hardly ever earned what the CAB considered to be a 'fair' rate of return (Moore, 1986: Douglas and Miller, 1974).

An important barrier to regulatory reform is what Gordon Tullock (1975) calls 'the transitional gains trap': the promise of above-normal returns motivates resource owners to seek regulatory privileges from the state. But these gains are only transitory. First, the present value of the available rents is in some cases dissipated upfront in the form of expenditures incurred in the pursuit of monopoly rights. To the extent that these rent-seeking investments are 'sunk', deregulation will not necessarily increase society's welfare (McCormick et al., 1984; Shughart, 1999). Second, regulatory rent streams may be eroded ex post by nonprice competition among the privileged franchisees. Last, if the monopoly franchise is subsequently sold, the rents will be capitalized in the purchase price of the monopolist's assets. In all of these cases, the rate of return on investments in the regulated industry is driven to normal levels. As a result, there seems to be no politically acceptable way of abolishing a regulatory program that is inefficient both from the standpoint of consumers, who pay artificially high prices, and from the standpoint of producers, who no longer make exceptional profits: 'those persons and groups who have established what they consider to be entitlements in the positive gains that have been artificially created will not agree to change, and those persons and groups who suffer losses will not willingly pay off what they consider to be immoral gainers' (Buchanan, 1980: 365). The controversy over compensation for the 'stranded costs' of regulated electric utilities — investments made under regulation that are not viable in a competitive market environment — is illustrative (McChesney, 1999).

From a theoretical perspective, the uncomfortable fact of the matter is that the grip of the 'dead hand' of monopoly (Buchanan and Tullock, 1968) has been loosened in the airline industry, the trucking industry, and elsewhere. While economists have not yet fully fleshed out a general theory of institutional change, at least some of the episodes in what has thus far been a highly selective deregulation movement seem amenable to explanation by the economic theory of regulation (Keeler, 1984; Peltzman [1989] 1998).

The railroad industry exemplifies a case in which 'support for ... regulation eroded along with the rent' (Peltzman [1989] 1998: 307). Even though federal regulators kept prices artificially high, a secular decline in demand for rail transport and a regulatory rate structure that accommodated the interests of motor carriers, the ICC's other major constituency, ultimately squeezed railroad profit margins. A spate of bankruptcies in the early 1970s produced a situation in which the only viable political options were nationalization or deregulation. The commercial airline industry, where, as we have seen, profits were dissipated over time by nonprice competition between the major carriers and inefficient capacity utilization, is another instance in which the demand for deregulation seems to have originated from the regulated firms themselves. A demand-side theory of deregulation based on the interests of producers, who expected costs to fall faster than prices, is broadly consistent with the Stigler-Peltzman model. Other examples of deregulation (e.g., stock brokerage, bank deposits, oil) also seem to fit that model, while some (e.g., telecommunications, trucking) do not (Peltzman [1989] 1998).

Supply-side forces may also be at work. Politicians serve as brokers of wealth transfers in a public choice interpretation of the economic theory of regulation (McCormick and Tollison, 1981). If wealth transfers, not social welfare, are all the brokers care about — that is, they are 'factionalist reformers' rather than 'utilitarian reformers' (Tollison and Wagner, 1991) — then in the face of changes in underlying economic conditions or coalitional strength (producing corresponding changes in relative political prices), they may take advantage of opportunities to advance their own interests by deregulating selected industries, thereby redistributing wealth to newly important constituencies, even though the costs to society of doing so exceed the benefits.

In any case, privatization and deregulation pose major challenges to models in which the privileged holders of monopoly franchises and the other beneficiaries of regulation seem well positioned to resist reform when it is not in their interest. Analytical responses to these challenges merit high priority on the research agendas of political economists. This is especially so given that, paradoxically, the selective retreat of traditional economic regulation of price and entry has been accompanied by spirited growth of regulation in the areas of social and environmental policy (McGraw, 1984: 304).

3. Antitrust

> There is a specter that haunts our antitrust institutions. Its threat is that, far from serving as the bulwark of competition, these institutions will become the most powerful instrument in the hands of those who wish to subvert it. More than that, it threatens to draw great quantities of resources into the struggle to prevent effective competition, thereby more than offsetting the contributions to economic efficiency promised by antitrust activities. This is a specter that may well dwarf any other concern about the antitrust processes. We ignore it at our peril and would do well to take steps to exorcise it. (Baumol and Ordover, 1985: 247)

The stated goals of antitrust policy are much the same as those of regulatory policy. It too attempts to influence the pricing and output decisions of private business firms. But enforcement of the antitrust laws proceeds by indirect means rather than by way of the hands-on price and entry controls normally associated with public regulation. Stripped to their essentials, the antitrust laws declare private monopolies to be illegal. Law enforcement is then carried out on a number of fronts, including preventing monopolies from being created in the first place through the merger of former competitors or the striking of collusive agreements among them, requiring the dissolution of large firms that have attained monopoly positions in the past, and limiting the use of certain business practices thought to facilitate the acquisition or exercise of market power.

American common law in the late nineteenth century 'still contained provisions that had been struck from the English common law by statutes', including proscriptions on forestalling and engrossing as well as prohibitions on combinations of workers in restraint of trade (Letwin, 1965: 52). US antitrust policy's legislative history dates to state statutes, many of which were enacted in the 1880s (Libecap, 1992; Boudreaux et al., 1995). It began at the federal level with passage of the Sherman Act (1890), section 1 of which states that 'every contract, combination in the form of trust or otherwise, or conspiracy, in restraint of trade or commerce among the several States, is declared to be illegal'. The law's only other substantive section (section 2) declares that 'every person who shall monopolize, or attempt to monopolize, or combine or conspire with any other person or persons, to monopolize any part of the trade or commerce among the several States, or with foreign nations, shall be deemed guilty of a felony'.

Some commentators have argued that the Sherman Act merely codified the common law treatment of restraints of trade (Demsetz, 1992; Kleit, 1993), layering on an apparatus of public enforcement (by the US Department of Justice) and allowing certain mergers to be deemed unlawful, neither of which innovations produced significant changes in American competition policy. It is clear, however, that at least some freely entered into private contracts were newly brought within statutory reach. Before the Sherman Act, price-fixing agreements were not presumptively illegal. Indeed, 'the common law was inclined to uphold contracts in restraint of trade for the same reasons that moved it to sustain any good contract' (Letwin, 1965: 42). As was the case with the futures contracts banned in a Dutch edict of 1610, which proscribed 'windhandel' or trading in shares not currently in the seller's possession, the courts did not impose sanctions on firms for participating in collusive agreements; 'they simply refused legal enforcement of such contracts' (Garber, 2000: 36). In particular, 'the modern common law on combinations in restraint of trade was established by the *Mogul Steamship* case [2 Chitty 407 (1815)], which laid down the principle that although a trade combination might be destroyed by attack from within, it could not be successfully attacked by an outsider' (Letwin, 1965: 49). Thus, 'the Sherman Act went far beyond the common law when it authorized the Attorney General to indict violators of the Act, and gave injured persons the power to sue them' (ibid.: 52).

The Sherman Act was innovative for a second reason. 'Unlike statute law, common law allows people to contract around it' (De Alessi, 2001: 39). In other words, 'all those parties who do not wish to be bound by a particular [common law] rule, ... generally have the opportunity to adopt any other rule that is mutually satisfactory' (De Alessi and Staaf, 1991: 112). This was no longer possible after 1890. Controlled by the statute's language, individuals and firms were no longer free to enter into contracts that would restrain trade, even if such contracts made them jointly better off.

Be that as it may, desultory enforcement of the Sherman Act early on, combined with negative reactions from antitrust's partisans to early interpretations of it, produced a demand for new legislation that would define more sharply the boundaries of US antitrust policy. Supporters of a vigorous antitrust policy were especially critical of the 1911 landmark decision ordering the dissolution of the Standard Oil trust, in which the Court announced a 'rule of reason', declaring its unwillingness to condemn all restraints of trade, but only those determined to be 'unreasonable'. As a compromise between those pressing for a law that would incorporate a list of specific business practices to be declared unlawful (and made criminal offenses) and those pressing for a law that would provide broad, but unspecified enforcement powers, two additional antitrust statutes were enacted in 1914. One of these was the Clayton Act, which identified and declared illegal four specific business practices — price discrimination (section 2), exclusive dealing and tying contracts (section 3), mergers (section 7) and interlocking corporate directorates (section 8) — where their effect 'may be to substantially lessen competition or tend to create a monopoly'. The other was the Federal Trade Commission Act, which created a five-member law enforcement body and delegated to it the responsibility for prosecuting unspecified 'unfair methods of competition' (FTC Act §5).

Subsequent amendments to these two statutes strengthened and broadened the scope of the powers granted to the federal antitrust authorities. The most important of these were the Robinson-Patman Act (1936), which made it more difficult to mount defenses against charges of unlawful price discrimination; the Wheeler-Lea Act (1938), which added the phrase 'unfair or deceptive acts or practices in or affecting commerce' to section 5 of the FTC Act, thereby granting the commission authority to regulate advertising and other business activities, such as product warranties and credit terms, falling under the rubric of 'consumer protection'; the Celler-Kefauver Act (1950), which closed a 'loophole' in section 7 of the Clayton Act allowing mergers consummated through the acquisition of stock to escape condemnation (but see Ekelund et al., 1995); and the Hart-Scott-Rodino Antitrust Improvement Act (1976), which established a formal pre-merger notification and review process.

Statutory antitrust policy is of much more recent vintage in Europe. Six pieces of legislation delineate its contours in the United Kingdom: the Monopolies and Restrictive Trade Practices Act (1948), the Fair Trading Act (1973), the Restrictive Trade Practices Act (1976), the Resale Prices Act (1976), and the Competition Acts of 1980 and 1998. The first of these laws established the Monopolies and Restrictive Practices Commission, a tribunal having the authority to investigate cases referred to it by the Board of Trade (see Rowley, 1966, for an analysis of the repercussions of the law). The second established the Office of Fair Trading, delegating to it responsibility for monitoring competition and granting it authority to refer to a lay body, the Monopolies and Mergers Commission (MMC), the power to investigate suspected 'monopoly situations' (defined as a single firm or group of firms accounting for 25 percent of sales or purchases in the relevant market). Public utilities and 'anti-competitive practices' were added to the MMC's charge by the Competition Act of 1980. The two 1976 statutes deal with price-fixing agreements and with vertical price restraints (e.g., resale price maintenance), respectively (Hay and Morris, 1991: 612–614); the Competition Act of 1998 aligns British law more closely with its European counterpart (Utton, 2000).

Competition policy in the European Union emanates from the Treaty of Rome (1957). The first of the Treaty's two substantive antitrust provisions prohibits agreements and other concerted actions, be they along horizontal or vertical lines or involve price or nonprice terms, which restrict competition within or among the member states. The second provision condemns abuses of dominant market positions, including 'imposing unfair purchasing or selling prices or other unfair trading conditions', 'limiting production, markets or technical development to the prejudice of consumers', 'applying dissimilar conditions to equivalent transactions with other trading parties' and 'making the conclusion of contracts subject to acceptance by the other parties of conditions which... have no connection with the subject of such contracts' (ibid.: 617). Although not based on any clearly articulated theory of anticompetitive behavior, possible 'abuses of dominant market positions' have been the chief concern of the EU's law enforcers in recent years. Reflecting the emerging globalization of antitrust, worries of incipient market dominance have provoked decisive European opposition to a number of high-profile mergers between major US companies to which US authorities had previously granted clearance.

Despite differences in details, the stated purposes of competition policy in the United States and elsewhere in the western industrialized world rest squarely on the market-failure tradition. Antitrust's staunchest advocates see the laws as embodying values consistent with economic efficiency goals, ensuring that markets remain vigorously competitive and that consumers are thereby protected against the abuses of market power: 'a much more widespread pattern of growth by merger, an efflorescence of collusive agreements of all sorts, and the use of various exclusionary and otherwise anticompetitive practices now forbidden would all follow on the abandonment of a pro-competitive public policy' (Kaysen and Turner, 1959: 5). Indeed, at least one respected student of the legislative history of the Sherman Act has argued forcefully that antitrust's origins were explicitly based on a consumer-welfare standard (Bork, 1966, 1978).

The professed efficiency basis of competition policy has not gone unchallenged (Lande, 1982; DiLorenzo and High, 1988). What is more important, faith in the efficacy of the antitrust laws to deliver net social gains ignores the political pressures that impinge on the agencies created to enforce them, pressures marshaled by groups perceiving opportunities to exploit antitrust processes strategically, not to promote competition, but to subvert it (Baumol and Ordover, 1985). A law that declares mergers to be illegal where their effect 'may be to substantially lessen competition or tend to create a monopoly' is also a law that affords the merger partners' rivals the opportunity to block a transaction that promises to create a larger, more efficient competitor. A law that makes it illegal for a firm to charge different prices to different customers not justified by differences in the cost of serving them is also a law that affords rivals the opportunity to seek relief from prices that are 'predatorily' low. The Robinson-Patman Act was in fact drafted and passed in response to the political influence mobilized by independent grocers, druggists and other small retailers, who complained loudly that, under the Clayton Act's original language, the Federal Trade Commission was either unable or unwilling to prevent the emerging national chain stores from using their mass buying power to sell goods to consumers at prices below those charged by the independents (Ross, 1984).

Observers of the antitrust enforcement process have long been critical of individual applications of it (for recent surveys of the case-study literature, see Armentano, 1990; Rubin, 1995). A typical antitrust case study finds that the evidence presented in behalf of the plaintiff was 'weak and at times bordered on fiction' and that 'neither the government nor the Courts seemed able to distinguish between competition and monopolizing' (Peterman, 1975: 143). Even when the law conceivably has struck at acts and practices that resulted in injury to consumers, the effectiveness of the penalties imposed on guilty defendants has been called into question (Elzinga, 1969; Rogowsky, 1986, 1987). Systematic empirical studies of the antitrust case-selection process have produced *no* support for the hypothesis that the process is guided by social-welfare criteria (Long et al., 1973; Asch, 1975; Siegfried, 1975) or that antitrust law enforcement has had measurable pro-competitive effects on the behavior of firms (Stigler, 1966; Asch and Seneca, 1976; Shaw and Simpson, 1986; Sproul, 1993).

Viewed through the lens of public choice, these apparent empirical anomalies are easily explained: social-welfare criteria carry little or no weight in the objective functions of the politicians and policymakers charged with drafting and enforcing the antitrust laws. Writing in 1969, Richard Posner charged that the Federal Trade Commission's stated mission of promoting competitive markets had been significantly impaired by reason of its dependence on Congress, which must approve budget requests and confirm presidential appointments to senior policymaking positions. He emphasized the obvious point that in a geographically based representative democracy, each member of the legislature is obligated to protect and further the provincial interests of those who have elected him to office. More specifically, 'the welfare of his constituents may depend disproportionately on a few key industries. The promotion of the industries becomes one of his most important duties as a representative of the district' (Posner, 1969a: 83). The ability to do so would accrue disproportionately to the members of the committees and subcommittees of Congress vested with oversight responsibilities with respect to antitrust law enforcement generally and the FTC in particular: a legislator holding such a position will have 'a great deal of power to advance the interests of businesses located in his district however unimportant the interests may be from a national standpoint' (ibid.). A subsequent test of this antitrust 'pork barrel' hypothesis found that cases instituted against firms headquartered in the jurisdictions of key committee members were more likely to be dismissed than cases instituted against firms not so represented (Faith et al., 1982).

Merger law enforcement seems to be particularly vulnerable to political influence. Two studies have found that, holding its staff's evaluation of the merits of a proposed merger constant, the commission is more likely to vote to oppose a transaction the more pressure is brought to bear on it in the form of news coverage and summonses to appear before congressional committees (Coate et al., 1990; Coate and McChesney, 1992). Similarly, the only two factors found to increase the probability of a merger challenge by the UK's Monopolies and Mergers Commission were whether the proposed merger would affect the balance of payments adversely and whether the firm targeted for takeover contested the bid (Weir, 1992). The available evidence from capital market event studies suggests that the mergers challenged by the US antitrust authorities tend to be efficiency enhancing on balance, and that the merger partners' rivals therefore appear to be the chief beneficiaries of merger law enforcement (e.g., Eckbo and Wier, 1985). This evidence offers further support for the contention that, because many investigations of alleged violations of the law are initiated 'at the behest of corporations, trade associations, and trade unions whose motivation is at best to shift the costs of private litigation to the taxpayer and at worst to harass competitors', antitrust seldom serves the public's interest (Posner, 1969a: 87).

In sum, the empirical case for characterizing antitrust processes as a mechanism of wealth redistribution is strong. From the perspective of public choice, antitrust is simply another form of regulation, having the same causes and consequences. Although this conclusion has not yet gained wide acceptance, the mounting evidence of the politicization of antitrust law enforcement produced by recent high-profile cases brought against some of the world's most successful business enterprises — cases instigated not in response to complaints by consumers but at the prompting of competitors and other special pleaders — promises eventually to bring antitrust within the ambit of the economic theory of regulation.

4. Summary

The economic theory of regulation generally and antitrust in particular looks behind the stated intentions of the proponents of government intervention into the private economy to uncover hidden agendas of wealth redistribution. The theory's main thrust is that the formulation and enforcement of public policies toward business has, in fact, tended to protect politically powerful constituencies at the sacrifice of competition and economic efficiency. That is, the theory explains many (if not all) policy decisions as rational political responses to the demands of well-organized pressure groups. These demanders of protectionism offer political support (votes, campaign contributions and the like) in return for favored treatment. These favors include the right to charge prices in excess of costs, the erection of barriers to the entry of new rivals, and the proscription of business practices and contractual agreements that would enhance overall economic efficiency, but harm them personally. Importantly, the strategic exploitation of regulation and antitrust by well-organized groups does not represent 'abuse' of the policy process in any meaningful sense. The demand for protectionism — and the political response to it — is simply rational behavior under a particular set of institutional constraints.

Competing with this general public-choice description of the purposes and effects of government policies toward business is the public-interest 'theory', which contends that regulatory and antitrust policies are the product of well-intentioned, but fallible, public servants. Whether justified or not in the economic theories or situational facts they rely on in any particular case, the function of the relevant laws, regulations and enforcement agencies is to serve what are believed to be the best interests of society as a whole. While mistakes are certainly possible, public policies toward business, or so it is thought, are designed and generally work to improve the allocation of scarce productive resources.

Strongly held a priori beliefs in the efficacy of governmental processes are the principal sources of support for the public-interest theory. The empirical evidence is almost universally consistent with the predictions of the interest-group, public-choice theory. As a result, the benefits of regulation are now seen to accrue chiefly, not to the public at large, but to politically well-organized pressure groups. While antitrust policy has only recently been exposed to the analytical power of the public-choice model, the idea that it, uniquely among public policies toward business, is immune to political influence is now in significant retreat.

WILLIAM F. SHUGHART II*

* I benefited from the comments and suggestions of Fred McChesney, Michael Reksulak, Charles Rowley, Russell Sobel, Alexander Tabarrok and Robert Tollison. As is customary, however, I accept full responsibility for any remaining errors.

REFERENCES

Acton, J.P. and Vogelsang, I. (1989). "Price-cap regulation: introduction." *RAND Journal of Economics*, 20: 369–372.

Alchian, A.A. (1965). "Some economics of property rights." *Il Politico*, 30(4): 816–829.

Anderson, G.M., Ekelund, R.B. Jr, and Tollison, R.D. (1989). "Nassau senior as economic consultant: the factory acts reconsidered." *Economica*, 56: 71–92.

Anderson, G.M. and Tollison, R.D. (1984). "A rent-seeking explanation of the British factory acts," in D.C. Collander (ed.) *Neoclassical Political Economy: The Analysis of Rent-Seeking and DUP Activities*. Cambridge, MA: Ballinger, pp. 187–201.

Aranson, P.H. (1990). "Theories of economic regulation: from clarity to confusion." *Journal of Law and Politics*, 6: 247–286.

Armentano, D.T. (1990). *Antitrust and Monopoly: Anatomy of a Policy Failure*, Second Edition. Oakland, CA: Independent Institute.

Asch, P. (1975). "The determinants and effects of antitrust policy." *Journal of Law and Economics*, 18: 575–581.

Asch, P. and Seneca, J.J. (1976). "Is collusion profitable?" *Review of Economics and Statistics*, 58: 1–12.

Averch, H. and Johnson, L.L. (1962). "Behavior of the firm under regulatory constraint." *American Economic Review*, 52: 1052–1069.

Bartel, A.P. and Thomas, L.G. (1987). "Predation through regulation: the wage and profit effects of the occupational safety and health administration and the environmental protection agency." *Journal of Law and Economics*, 20: 239–264.

Bator, F.M. (1958). "The anatomy of market failure." *Quarterly Journal of Economics*, 72: 351–379.

Baumol, W.J., Bailey, E., and Willig, R. (1977). "Weak invisible hand theorems on the sustainability of prices in a multiproduct monopoly." *American Economic Review*, 67: 350–365.

Baumol, W.J. and Klevorick, A.K. (1970). "Input choices and rate-of-return regulation: an overview of the discussion." *Bell Journal of Economics and Management Science*, 1: 162–190.

Baumol, W.J., Panzar, J.C., and Willig, R.D. (1982). *Contestable Markets and the Theory of Industry Structure*. New York: Harcourt Brace Jovanovich.

Baumol, W.J. and Ordover, J.A. (1985). "Use of antitrust to subvert competition." *Journal of Law and Economics*, 28: 247–265.

Baxter, W.F. (1980). "The political economy of antitrust," in R.D. Tollison (ed.) *The Political Economy of Antitrust: Principal Paper by William Baxter*. Lexington, MA: Lexington Books, pp. 3–49.

Becker, G.S. (1983). "A theory of competition among pressure groups for political influence." *Quarterly Journal of Economics*, 98: 371–400.

Becker, G.S. (1985). "Public policies, pressure groups, and dead weight costs." *Journal of Public Economics*, 28: 329–347.

Bertoletti, P. and Poletti, C. (1997). "X-inefficiency, competition and market information." *Journal of Industrial Economics*, 45: 359–375.

Bork, R.H. (1966). "Legislative intent and the policy of the Sherman act." *Journal of Law and Economics*, 9: 7–48.

Bork, R.H. (1978). *The Antitrust Paradox: A Policy at War with Itself*. New York: Basic Books.

Boudreaux, D.J., DiLorenzo, T.J., and Parker, S. (1995). "Antitrust before the Sherman act," in F.S. McChesney and W.F. Shughart II (eds.) *The Causes and Consequences of Antitrust: The Public-Choice Perspective*. Chicago: University of Chicago Press, pp. 255–270.

Buchanan, J.M. (1972). "Toward analysis of closed behavioral systems," in J.M. Buchanan and R.D. Tollison (eds.) *Theory of Public Choice*. Ann Arbor: University of Michigan Press, pp. 11–23.

Buchanan, J.M. (1980). "Reform in the rent-seeking society," in J.M. Buchanan, R.D. Tollison, and G. Tullock (eds.) *Toward a Theory of The Rent-Seeking Society*. College Station: Texas A&M University Press, pp. 359–367.

Buchanan, J.M. and Tullock, G. (1962). *The Calculus of Consent: Logical Foundations of Constitutional Democracy*. Ann Arbor: University of Michigan Press.

Buchanan, J.M. and Tullock, G. (1968). "The 'dead hand' of monopoly." *Antitrust Law and Economic Review*, 1: 85–96.

Cawley, J. and Philipson, T. (1999). "An empirical examination of barriers to trade in insurance." *American Economic Review*, 89: 827–846.

Cheung, S.N.S. (1973). "The fable of the bees: an economic interpretation." *Journal of Law and Economics*, 16: 11–33.

Coase, R.H. (1946). "The marginal cost controversy." *Economica*, 13: 169–182.

Coase, R.H. (1959). "The federal communications commission." *Journal of Law and Economics*, 2: 1–40.

Coase, R.H. (1960). "The problem of social cost." *Journal of Law and Economics*, 3: 1–44.

Coase, R.H. (1974). "The lighthouse in economics." *Journal of Law and Economics*, 17: 357–376.

Coate, M.B., Higgins, R.S., and McChesney, F.S. (1990). "Bureaucracy and politics in FTC merger challenges." *Journal of Law and Economics*, 33: 463–482.

Coate, M.B. and McChesney, F.S. (1992). "Empirical evidence on FTC enforcement of the merger guidelines." *Economic Inquiry*, 30: 277–293.

Crain, W.M. and McCormick, R.E. (1984). "Regulators as an interest group," in J.M. Buchanan and R.D. Tollison (eds.) *The Theory of Public Choice-II*. Ann Arbor: University of Michigan Press, pp. 287–304.

De Alessi, L. (1982). "On the nature and consequences of private and public enterprise." *Minnesota Law Review*, 67: 191–209.

De Alessi, L. (1983). "Property rights, transaction costs, and X-efficiency: an essay in economic theory." *American Economic Review*, 73: 64–81.

De Alessi, L. (2001). "Property rights: private and political institutions," in W.F. Shughart II and L. Razzolini (eds.) *The Elgar Companion to Public Choice*. Cheltenham, UK and Northampton, MA, USA: Edward Elgar, pp. 33–58.

De Alessi, L. and Staaf, R.J. (1991). "The common law process: efficiency or order?" *Constitutional Political Economy*, 2: 107–126.

Demsetz, H. (1968). "Why regulate utilities?" *Journal of Law and Economics*, 11: 55–65.

Demsetz, H. (1969). "Information and efficiency: another viewpoint." *Journal of Law and Economics*, 12: 1–22.

Demsetz, H. (1970). "The private production of public goods." *Journal of Law and Economics*, 13: 293–306.

Demsetz, H. (1992). "How many cheers for antitrust's 100 years?" *Economic Inquiry*, 30: 207–217.

DiLorenzo, T.J. (1985). "The origins of antitrust: an interest-group perspective." *International Review of Law and Economics*, 5: 73–90.

DiLorenzo, T.J. and High, J.C. (1988). "Antitrust and competition, historically considered." *Economic Inquiry*, 26: 423–435.

Douglas, G.W. and Miller, J.C. III (1974). "Quality competition, industry equilibrium, and efficiency in the price-constrained airline market." *American Economic Review*, 64: 657–669.

Douglas, G.W. and Miller, J.C. III (1976). *Economic Regulation of Domestic Air Transport: Theory and Policy*. Washington, DC: Brookings Institution.

Easterbrook, F.H. (1984). "The limits of antitrust." *University of Texas Law Review*, 63: 1–40.

Eckbo, B.E. and Wier, P. (1985). "Antimerger policy under the Hart-Scott-Rodino act: a reexamination of the market-power hypothesis. *Journal of Law and Economics*, 28: 119–149.

Ekelund, R.B. Jr., McDonald, M.J., and Tollison, R.D. (1995). "Business restraints and the Clayton Act of 1914: public- or private-interest legislation?" in F.S. McChesney and W.F. Shughart II (eds.) *The Causes and Consequences of Antitrust: The Public-Choice Perspective*. Chicago: University of Chicago Press, pp. 271–286.

Elzinga, K.G. (1969). "The antimerger law: Pyrrhic victories?" *Journal of Law and Economics*, 12: 43–78.

Faith, R.L., Leavens, D.R. and Tollison, R.D. (1982). "Antitrust pork barrel." *Journal of Law and Economics*, 25: 329–342.

Garber, P.M. (2000). *Famous First Bubbles: The Fundamentals of Early Manias*. Cambridge and London: MIT Press.

Harberger, A.C. (1954). "Monopoly and resource allocation." *American Economic Review Papers and Proceedings*, 44: 77–87.

Hay, D.A. and Morris, D.J. (1991). *Industrial Economics and Organization: Theory and Evidence*, Second Edition. Oxford: Oxford University Press.

Hazlett, T.W. (1984). "Interview with George Stigler." *Reason*, January: 44–48.

Henderson, D.R. (1995). "Antitrust busters." *Reason*, August/September: 62–64.

Hotelling, H. (1938). "The general welfare in relation to problems of taxation and railway and utility rates." *Econometrica*, 6: 242–269.

Jensen, M.C. and Meckling, W.H. (1976). "Theory of the firm: managerial behavior, agency costs and ownership structure." *Journal of Financial Economics*, 3: 305–360.

Jordan, W.A. (1972). "Producer protection, prior market structure and the effects of government regulation." *Journal of Law and Economics*, 15: 151–176.

Joskow, P. and Noll, R. (1981). "Regulation in theory and practice: an overview," in G. Fromm (ed.) *Studies in Public Regulation*. Cambridge: MIT Press, pp. 1–65.

Kaysen, C. and Turner, D.F. (1959). *Antitrust Policy*. Cambridge: Harvard University Press.

Keeler, T.E. (1972). "Airline regulation and market performance." *Bell Journal of Economics and Management Science*, 3: 399–424.

Keeler, T.E. (1984). "Theories of regulation and the deregulation movement." *Public Choice*, 44(1): 103–145.

Kleit, A.N. (1993). "Common law, statute law, and the theory of legislative choice: an inquiry into the goal of the Sherman Act." *Economic Inquiry*, 31: 647–662.

Krueger, A.O. (1974). "The political economy of the rent-seeking society." *American Economic Review*, 64: 291–303.

Lande, R.H. (1982). "Wealth transfers as the original and primary concern of antitrust: the efficiency interpretation challenged." *Hastings Law Journal*, 34: 65–151.

Letwin, W. (1965). *Law and Economic Policy in America: The Evolution of the Sherman Antitrust Act*. Chicago and London: University of Chicago Press.

Libecap, G.D. (1992). "The rise of the Chicago packers and the origins of meat inspection and antitrust." *Economic Inquiry*, 30: 242–262.

Leibenstein, H. (1966). "Allocative efficiency vs. 'x-efficiency'." *American Economic Review*, 56: 392–415.

Leibenstein, H. (1978). "X-inefficiency xists — reply to an xorcist." *American Economic Review*, 68: 203–211.

Long, W.F., Schramm, R., and Tollison, R.D. (1973). "The determinants of antitrust activity." *Journal of Law and Economics*, 16: 351–364.

Lott, J.R. Jr (1997). "Donald Wittman's *The myth of democratic failure*: review article." *Public Choice*, 92: 1–13.

Maloney, M.T. and McCormick, R.E. (1982). "A positive theory of environmental quality regulation." *Journal of Law and Economics*, 25: 99–124.

Marvel, H.P. (1977). "Factory regulation: a reinterpretation of early English experience." *Journal of Law and Economics*, 20: 379–402.

McChesney, F.S. (1987). "Rent extraction and rent creation in the economic theory of regulation." *Journal of Legal Studies*, 16: 101–118.

McChesney, F.S. (1991). "Rent extraction and interest-group organization in a Coasean model of regulation." *Journal of Legal Studies*, 20: 73–90.

McChesney, F.S. (1997). *Money for Nothing: Politicians, Rent Extraction, and Political Extortion*. Cambridge: Harvard University Press.

McChesney, F.S. (1999). "Of stranded costs and stranded hopes: the difficulties of deregulation." *Independent Review*, 3: 485–509.

McChesney, F.S. and Shughart, W.F. II (eds.) (1995). *The Causes and Consequences of Antitrust: The Public-Choice Perspective*. Chicago: University of Chicago Press.

McCormick, R.E. (1984). "The strategic use of regulation: a review of the literature," in R.A. Rogowsky and B. Yandle (eds.) *The Political Economy of Regulation: Private Interests in the Regulatory Process*. Washington, DC: Federal Trade Commission, pp. 13–32.

McCormick, R.E., Shughart, W.F. II, and Tollison, R.D. (1984). "The disinterest in deregulation." *American Economic Review*, 74: 1075–1079.

McCormick, R.E. and Tollison, R.D. (1981). *Politicians, Legislation, and the Economy: An Inquiry into the Interest-Group Theory of Government*. Boston: Martinus Nijhoff.

McGraw, T.K. (1984). *Prophets of regulation: Charles Francis Adams, Louis D. Brandeis, James M. Landis, Alfred E. Kahn*. Cambridge and London: Belknap Press of Harvard University Press.

Moore, T.G. (1986). "U.S. airline deregulation: its effects on passengers, capital, and labor." *Journal of Law and Economics*, 29: 1–28.

Nelson, P. (1970). "Information and consumer behavior." *Journal of Political Economy*, 78: 311–329.

Olson, M. (1965). *The Logic of Collective Action: Public Goods and the Theory of Groups*. Cambridge: Harvard University Press.

Pashigian, B.P. (1985). "Environmental quality regulation: whose self-interests are being protected? *Economic Inquiry*, 23: 551–584.

Peltzman, S. (1976). "Toward a more general theory of regulation." *Journal of Law and Economics*, 19: 211–240.

Peltzman, S. (1993). "George Stigler's contribution to the economic analysis of regulation." *Journal of Political Economy*, 101: 818–832.

Peltzman, S. (1989, 1998). "The economic theory of regulation after a decade of deregulation," in S. Peltzman (eds.) *Political Participation and Government Regulation*. Chicago: University of Chicago Press, pp. 286–323.

Peterman, J.A. (1975). "The Brown Shoe case." *Journal of Law and Economics*, 18: 81–146.

Pigou, A.C. (1932). *The Economics of Welfare*, Fourth Edition. London: Macmillan.

Posner, R.A. (1969a). "The federal trade commission." *University of Chicago Law Review*, 37: 47–89.

Posner, R.A. (1969b, 1999). *Natural Monopoly and its Regulation*. Washington, DC: Cato Institute.

Posner, R.A. (1971). "Taxation by regulation." *Bell Journal of Economics and Management Science*, 2: 22–50.

Posner, R.A. (1974). "Theories of economic regulation." *Bell Journal of Economics and Management Science*, 5: 335–358.

Posner, R.A. (1975). "The social costs of monopoly and regulation." *Journal of Political Economy*, 83: 807–827.

Ramsey, F.P. (1927). "A contribution to the theory of taxation." *Economic Journal*, 37: 47–61.

Rogowsky, R.A. (1986). "The economic effectiveness of section 7 relief." *Antitrust Bulletin*, 31: 187–233.

Rogowsky, R.A. (1987). "The Pyrrhic victories of section 7: a political economy approach," in R.J. Mackay, J.C. Miller III, and B. Yandle (eds.) *Public Choice and Regulation: A View From Inside the Federal Trade Commission*. Stanford, CA: Hoover Institution Press, pp. 220–239.

Ross, T.W. (1984). "Winners and losers under the Robinson-Patman Act." *Journal of Law and Economics*, 27: 243–271.

Rowley, C.K. (1966). *The British Monopolies Commission*. London: George Allen and Unwin.

Rowley, C.K. (1997). "Donald Wittman's *The myth of democratic failure*: review article." *Public Choice*, 92: 15–26.

Rowley, C.K. and Peacock, A.T. (1975). *Welfare Economics: A Liberal Restatement*. Oxford: Martin Robertson.

Rowley, C.K. and Yarrow, G.K. (1981). "Property rights, regulation and public enterprise: the case of the British steel industry 1957–1975." *International Review of Law and Economics*, 1: 63–96.

Rubin, P.H. (1995). "What do economists think about antitrust? A random walk down Pennsylvania avenue," in F.S. McChesney and W.F. Shughart II (eds.) *The Causes and Consequences of Antitrust: The Public-Choice Perspective*. Chicago: University of Chicago Press, pp. 33–61.

Samuelson, P.A. (1954). "The pure theory of public expenditure." *Review of Economics and Statistics*, 36: 387–389.

Scherer, F.M. (1980). *Industrial market structure and economic performance*, Second Edition. Boston: Houghton Mifflin.

Schmidt, K.M. (1997). "Managerial incentives and product market competition." *Review of Economic Studies*, 64: 191–213.

Shaw, R.W. and Simpson, P. (1986). "The persistence of monopoly: an investigation of the effectiveness of the United Kingdom monopolies commission." *Journal of Industrial Economics*, 34: 355–372.

Sherman, R. (1989). *The Regulation of Monopoly*. Cambridge and New York: Cambridge University Press.

Shughart, W.F. II (1990). *Antitrust Policy and Interest-Group Politics*. New York: Quorum Books.

Shughart, W.F. II (1997). *The Organization of Industry*, Second Edition. Houston, TX: Dame Publications.

Shughart, W.F. II (1999). "The reformer's dilemma." *Public Finance Review*, 27: 561–565.

Shughart, W.F. II and Tollison, R.D. (1985). "The positive economics of antitrust policy: a survey article." *International Review of Law and Economics*, 5: 39–57.

Shy, O. (2001). *The Economics of Network Industries*. Cambridge and New York: Cambridge University Press.

Siegfried, J.J. (1975). "The determinants of antitrust activity." *Journal of Law and Economics*, 17: 559–574.

Simon, H.A. (1957). *Models of Man*. New York: Wiley.

Sproul, M.T. (1993). "Antitrust and prices." *Journal of Political Economy*, 101: 741–754.

Spulber, D.F. (1989). *Regulation and Markets*. Cambridge and London: MIT Press.

Stigler, G.J. (1964). "Public regulation of the securities market." *Journal of Business*, 2: 117–142.

Stigler, G.J. (1966). "The economic effects of the antitrust laws." *Journal of Law and Economics*, 9: 225–258.

Stigler, G.J. (1971). "The economic theory of regulation." *Bell Journal of Economics and Management Science*, 2: 3–21.

Stigler, G.J. (1975). "Supplementary note on economic theories of regulation (1975)," in G.J. Stigler (ed.) *The Citizen and The State: Essays on Regulation*. Chicago: University of Chicago Press, pp. 137–141.

Stigler, G.J. (1976). "The xistence of x-efficiency." *American Economic Review*, 86: 213–216.

Stigler, G.J. (1985). "The origin of the Sherman Act." *Journal of Legal Studies*, 14: 1–12.

Stigler, G.J. (ed.) (1988). *Chicago Studies in Political Economy*. Chicago: University of Chicago Press.

Stigler, G.J. and Friedland, C. (1962). "What can regulators regulate? The case of electricity." *Journal of Law and Economics*, 5: 1–16.

Tirole, J. (1988). *The Theory of Industrial Organization*. Cambridge and London: MIT Press.

Tollison, R.D. and Wagner, R.E. (1991). "Romance, realism, and economic reform." *Kyklos*, 44(1): 57–70.

Train, K.E. (1991). *Optimal Regulation: The Economic Theory of Natural Monopoly*. Cambridge: MIT Press.

Troesken, W. (2000). "Did the trusts want a federal antitrust law? An event study of state antitrust enforcement and passage of the Sherman Act," in J.C. Heckelman, J.C. Moorhouse, and R.M. Whaples (eds.) *Public Choice Interpretations of American Economic History*. Boston: Kluwer Academic Publishers, pp. 77–104.

Tullock, G. (1967). "The welfare costs of tariffs, monopolies and theft." *Western Economic Journal*, 5: 224–232.

Tullock, G. (1975). "The transitional gains trap." *Bell Journal of Economics and Management Science*, 6: 671–678.

Tullock, G. (1980). "Efficient rent seeking," in J.M. Buchanan, R.D. Tollison, and G. Tullock (eds.) *Toward a Theory of The Rent-Seeking Society*. College Station: Texas A&M University Press, pp. 97–112.

Utton, M. (2000). "Going European: Britain's new competition law." *Antitrust Bulletin*, 45: 531–551.

Weir, C. (1992). "Monopolies and mergers commission, merger reports and the public interest: a probit analysis." *Applied Economics*, 24: 27–34.

Wilcox, C. (1966). *Public Policies Toward Business*, Third Edition. Homewood, IL: Irwin.

Williamson, O.E. (1968a). "Economies as an antitrust defense: the welfare tradeoffs." *American Economic Review*, 58: 18–36.

Williamson, O.E. (1968b). "Wage rates as a barrier to entry: the Pennington case in perspective." *Quarterly Journal of Economics*, 82: 85–116.

Williamson, O.E. (1976). "Franchise bidding for natural monopolies — in general and with respect to CATV." *Bell Journal of Economics*, 7: 73–104.

Williamson, O.E. (1977). "Economies as an antitrust defense revisited." *University of Pennsylvania Law Review*, 125: 699–736.

Wittman, D. (1989). "Why democracies produce efficient results." *Journal of Political Economy*, 97: 1395–1424.

Wittman, D. (1995). *The Myth of Democratic Failure: Why Political Institutions are Efficient*. Chicago: University of Chicago Press.

S

SCHOLARLY LEGACY OF MANCUR OLSON

Mancur Olson had the rare ability to explain clearly the subtle nature of how groups of human beings organize to educated readers who are not versed in economic theory and its arcane vocabulary. His first book *The Logic of Collective Action: Public Goods and the Theory of Groups*, first published by the Harvard University Press in 1965, presented the fundamental issues of group formation by self-interested individuals in a way that made sense to most readers. He made a serious and successful effort to connect his theory with the scholarly writings on groups by sociologists and other non-economists. This book influenced the thinking of many academics and non-academics.

The technical term for the principal inherent problem of group formation is called the "free rider problem". If all members of the group receive a benefit from the action of the group and are not forced to contribute to the cost of group action, a self-interested group member has no incentive to contribute. As an example of this "problem" consider the case of the classical music station KMFA in Austin, TX. This station plays classical music of all sorts 24 hours a day. The station does not receive any public funds. The existence of this station depends on voluntary contributions from people who value the existence of the station. The number of people in the Austin area who contribute is a fraction of the people who listen to the station. The bi-annual fund raising drives attempt to shame those listeners who do not contribute to pledge monetary support.

There is no hard evidence about how the appeals to the non-contributing listeners work but the station has been able to raise enough funds to flourish. Most standard treatments of the free rider problem in the modern economics literature involve the use of non-cooperative game theory. This literature uses language and formalism that most educated people cannot comprehend unless they have taken a college level course in game theory. A person with a solid education and an ability to understand a logical argument can understand anything Mancur Olson wrote, however, because of the clarity of his thought and expression. Olson did not "solve" the free rider problem. He explained the problem without jargon and then he addressed how various groups attempt to deal with the problem.

He also developed two other important theoretical propositions, the implications of which will be explored for generations. These propositions have to do with (1) the implications of group development for economic performance and political health of a nation, and (2) the implications of the transition from "roving bandits" to "stationary bandits" as a necessary and sufficient condition for the existence of government. As James Buchanan wrote of him, "Mancur Olson was perhaps more influential in political science than any other of his economist peers." Given Buchanan's own enormous influence, this is a telling statement.

1. Life

> (The Stationary Bandit)... is not like the wolf that preys on the elk, but more like the rancher who makes sure that his cattle are protected and given water. The metaphor of predation obscures the great superiority of stationary banditry over anarchy and the advances in civilization that have resulted from it. No metaphor or model of even the autocratic state can, therefore, be correct unless it simultaneously takes account of the stationary bandit's incentive to provide public goods at the same time that he extracts the largest possible net surplus for himself. (Olson, 1993)

Mancur was born on a ranch in North Dakota in 1932, and he had ample opportunity to watch the wolf stalk the elk firsthand. There was a residual Scandinavian cadence, learned from his parents, in his speech throughout his life. His manner was plain and straightforward, and he was artlessly humble in his dealings with people he met. The version of his curriculum vitae he gave out in response to requests led off with his social security number, as if he might have to identify himself.

He graduated from North Dakota Agricultural College in 1954, and then won a spot as a Rhodes Scholar at University College, Oxford. From Oxford he returned to the U.S. and attended graduate school at Harvard. His dissertation became the remarkably influential book The *Logic of Collective Action* (whose title was selected partly on advice from James Buchanan) when it was later published in 1965. Only Anthony Downs' dissertation, *An Economic Theory of Democracy*, even comes close in terms of impact for a first work in the history of public choice.

Olson was hired at the Economics Department at Princeton, and then took the position of Deputy Assistant Secretary of the US Department of Health, Education and Welfare in the Johnson administration. In his two year at HEW, he had ample opportunity to observe the work of government, and the actions of interest groups, that would figure so prominently in his next book. In 1969 he left the government and accepted a job as Professor of Economics in the rather blue collar environs of the College Park campus of the University of Maryland. He was never seriously tempted by offers at more glamorous institutions, and remained at College Park for the rest of his life.

2. Contributions

Olson's major contribution, explaining the logic of collective action, defies easy categorization. It is problem for the Left, because it argues that the key distinction is between consumers and producers, or between producers at different levels of the supply chain, rather than between capitalists and labor. Further, the problem of free-riding is a direct assault on Marx's ideas about the inevitable construction of a workers' paradise where "from each according to his ability, to each according to his need" is the norm.

But it is also a problem for conservatives, because powerful producers will face no countervailing political force from consumers, wage-earners, or less concentrated industries. The fact that many people free-ride may be no more than an extension of the standard Samuelsonian "public goods" problem, but its political implications would seem to require government intervention to ensure compliance with laws, even if all citizens might support the law in principle. Further, since voting is also subject to the free-rider problem, the claim that voters can be relied on to police corruption is rendered suspect, and questions are raised about the campaign finance system.

Olson's second important book, *The Rise and Decline of Nations* (1982), made the seemingly paradoxical claim that long-term political stability hurts economic performance. This would appear to contradict the conventional wisdom that stability and predictable actions by government enhance growth. But Mancur claimed that interest become entrenched in stable democracies, so that the governments suffer from "institutional sclerosis" as lobbyist manage a system of redistribution that distorts incentives and fails to reward initiative.

The apparent policy implication ("need growth? Fight a war!") was not taken very seriously, but Olson was making a very serious point about the dynamics of economic history. The clearest example is the explanation implied for the economic "miracles" of Germany and Japan after WWII. Their success, as Olson saw, had at least as much to do with the fact that all the entrenched interests in government were swept away along with the governments that were replaced after the war ended.

The larger question of why some nations prosper and others fail to grow, and the role of government in fostering growth or blocking it, occupied Olson in the last fifteen years of his life. His views differed substantially from those of both the Chicago and Virginia public choice schools. Virginians tend to believe that all government is evil (with the possible exception of the Pentagon, and that is located in Virginia). Chicago public choice scholars have moved toward a system of theory in which government is efficient, at least in the way that it conducts transfers. Olson argued that government was neither evil nor efficient. His "Maryland school" centered on the idea that government does some things well, if it has the right incentives. And, surprisingly, it has the right incentives more often than one might think, at least in Olson's view.

The key concept was the "stationary bandit," introduced in his celebrated 1993 paper in the *American Political Science Review*. While many in the public choice movement have argued that government is simply a device for extracting benefits from citizens, Olson claimed that even a bandit, once stationary, had strong incentives to ensure at least minimal prosperity for citizens.

But more than this, the autocrat will recognize that problems of legitimate succession will still rob citizens of incentives to invest and build. The only way to ensure a truly long time horizon is to form a democracy. Further, since democracies appear less likely to go to war with one another, this form of government will have important evolutionary advantages if it can once be implemented. So, the original roving bandit who first settles down is the true father of democracy, and he created the democratic system purely out of his own self-interest in stability and prosperity.

This work is quite controversial, since it raises important questions about the nature of transition to democracy. Was Stalin bad, or was he inevitable? Olson tries to take on this question in portions of his last book, *Power and Prosperity*, published posthumously.

Though Olson studied the collective action problem, he spent most of his professional life providing public goods for free. At conferences, in his office, and in discussing ideas he was happiest when he felt like he was learning something. He came from a generation of scholars who crossed a threshold, taking up very modern techniques but keeping a focus on the classical questions of moral philosophy.

MELVIN J. HINICH
MICHAEL C. MUNGER

REFERENCES

Dougherty, Keith (2001). "Fast forward to Mancur: the theory of public goods before Mancur Olson." Presented at the annual meetings of the Public Choice Society, March 2002, San Diego, CA.

Economist, March 7 (1998). "Mancur, scourge of special interests, Died on February 19, aged 66."

McLean, Ian (2000). "The divided legacy of Mancur Olson." *British Journal of Political Science*, 30: 651–668.

Olson, Mancur (1965). *The Logic of Collective Action*. Cambridge, MA: Harvard University Press.

Olson, Mancur (1982). *The Rise and Decline of Nations: Economic Growth, Stagflation, and Social Rigidities*. New Haven: Yale University Press.

Olson, Mancur (1993). "Dictatorship, democracy, and development." *American Political Science Review*, 87(3): 567–576.

Olson, Mancur (2000). *Power and Prosperity: Outgrowing Communist and Capitalist Dictatorships*. New York: Basic Books.

SHADOW ECONOMY

1. Introduction

Crime and shadow economic activities are a fact of life around the world, and almost all societies engage in trying to control these activities through education, punishment, or prosecution. Gathering statistics about who is active in the shadow economy activities, the frequency with which underground activities occur and the magnitude of these activities, is crucial for making effective and efficient decisions regarding allocating resources in this area. Obviously it is difficult to get accurate information about underground or shadow economy activities because individuals engaged in these activities wish to remain unidentified. Hence, estimation of shadow economy activities can be considered as a scientific passion for knowing the unknowable.

These attempts at measurement are obviously problematic,[1] since shadow economy activities are performed in such a way as to avoid any official detection. Moreover, if you ask an academic, a public sector specialist, a policy or economic analyst, or a politician, what is going on in the shadow economy, and even just how big it is, you will get a wide range of answers.[2] In spite of this, there is growing concern over the phenomenon of the shadow economy, and there are several important reasons why politicians and public sector workers should be especially worried about the rise and growth of the shadow economy.

Among the most important of these are:

- If an increase of the shadow economy is caused mainly by a rise in the overall tax and social security burden, this may lead to an erosion of the tax and social security bases and finally to a decrease in tax receipts, and thus to a further increase in the budget deficit or to a further increase of tax rates with the consequence of an additional increase in the shadow economy, and so on. Therefore, a growing shadow economy can be seen as a reaction by individuals who feel overburdened by state activities.

- With a growing shadow economy, (economic) policy is based on erroneous "official" indicators (like unemployment, official labor force, income, consumption), or at least indicators that are inaccurate in magnitude. In such a situation, a prospering shadow economy may cause politicians severe difficulties because it provides unreliable official indicators, and the direction of intended policy measures may therefore be questionable.

- On the one hand, a growing shadow economy may provide strong incentives to attract (domestic and foreign) workers away from the official economy. On the other hand, at least two-thirds of the income earned in the shadow economy is immediately spent in the official economy[3] resulting in a considerable (positive) stimulating effect on the official economy.

2. What is the Shadow Economy?

Studies trying to measure the shadow economy first face the difficulty of defining it. For instance, one commonly used definition is the shadow economy includes all currently economic activities which contribute to the officially calculated (or observed) Gross National Product.[4] However, Smith (1994, p. 18) defines it as "market-based production of goods and services, whether legal or illegal, that escapes detection in the official estimates of GDP." As these definitions leave open a lot of questions, Table 1 may be helpful for developing a better feeling for what could be a reasonable consensus definition of the legal and illegal underground or shadow economy.

From Table 1 it becomes clear that the shadow economy includes unreported income from the production of legal goods and services, either from monetary or barter transactions hence, all economic activities which would generally be taxable were they reported to the tax authorities. In general, a precise definition seems quite difficult, if not impossible, as "the shadow economy develops all the time according to the 'principle of running water': it adjusts to changes in taxes, to sanctions from the tax authorities and to general moral attitudes, etc." (Mogensen et al., 1995, p. 5).[5] Our survey does not focus on tax evasion or tax compliance. It rather serves as a supplement to the recent survey of Andreoni et al. (1998, p. 819), who excluded the shadow economy: "Unfortunately, there are many important issues that we do not have room to discuss, most notably the vast literature on the underground economy which exists in part as a means of evading taxes."[6]

Table 1: A Taxonomy of types of underground economic activities[1]

Type of activity	Monetary transactions	Nonmonetary transactions
ILLEGAL ACTIVITIES	Trade in stolen goods; drug dealing and manufacturing; prostitution; gambling; smuggling, and fraud	Barter: drugs, stolen goods, smuggling etc. Produce or growing drugs for own use. Theft for own use.
	Tax Evasion	Tax avoidance
LEGAL ACTIVITIES	Unreported income from self-employment; Wages, salaries and assets from unreported work related to legal services and goods; Barter of legal services and goods	Employee discounts, fringe benefits; All do-it-yourself work and neighbor help

[1] Structure of the table taken from Lippert and Walker (1997, p. 5), with additional remarks.

3. Empirical Estimates

The following tables serve to indicate approximate magnitudes of the size and development of the underground economy, defined as productive activities, i.e. using the narrow definition. Table 2 prevents a rough comparison of the size of the underground economies relative to GNP for a selection of Western European countries, Japan and the United States for the end 1990s, using the currency demand approach.

The South European countries (Greece, Italy) have an underground economy almost one third as large as the officially measured GNP: followed by Spain, Portugal and Belgium having a shadow economy between 20 and 24 % (of official) GNP. According to these estimates, the Scandinavian countries also have a sizeable unofficial economy (between 18 and 20 % of GNP), which is attributed mainly to the high fiscal burden. The "central" European countries (Ireland, the Netherlands, France, Germany and Great Britain) have a smaller underground economy (between 13 and 16 % of GNP) probably due to a lower fiscal burden and moderate regulatory restrictions. The lower underground economies are estimated to exist in countries with relatively low public sectors (Japan, the United States and Switzerland), and comparatively high tax morale (United States, Switzerland).

Table 3 provides a rough comparison of the size of the underground economy relative to official GNP for a selection of developing and transition economies for the end of the 1990s, using the physical input (electricity) demand approach. Some of these countries (Nigeria, Egypt, Thailand) are estimated to have an underground sector nearly three quarters the size of officially re-corded GNP. In many countries the size is one quarter to one third of GNP. In

Table 2: Size of the underground economy relative to GNP in various European countries, end 1990s. Estimation based on the currency demand approach

Greece	27–30%
Italy	
Spain	
Portugal	20–24%
Belgium	
Sweden	
Norway	18–23%
Denmark	
Ireland	
France	
Netherlands	13–16%
Germany	
Great Britain	
Japan	
United States	8–10%
Austria	
Switzerland	

Source: Compiled from Schneider and Enste (2000).

Asian countries with a comparatively low public sector, high tax morale or high expected punishment (Hong Kong, Singapore) the underground economy is estimated to be similar to that in many "northern" European countries.

Transition economies are estimated to often have substantial unofficial activities, many around one quarter of GNP. An exception is ex-Czechoslovakia where according to these estimates the underground sector is clearly around ten percent of GNP.

Table 3: Size of the underground economy relative to GNP in various developing and transition countries, end of the 1990s. Estimates based on the physical input (electricity) demand approach

Developing countries
Africa
    Nigeria   68–76%
    Egypt
    Tunisia   39–45%
    Morocco
Central and South America
    Guatemala
    Mexico   40–60%
    Peru
    Panama
    Chile
    Costa Rica
    Venezuela   25–35%
    Brazil
    Paraguay
    Columbia
Asia
    Thailand   70%
    Philippines
    Sri Lanka   38–50%
    Malaysia
    South Korea
    Hong Kong   13%
    Singapore

Transition Economies
Central Europe
    Hungary   24–28%
    Bulgaria
    Poland   16–20%
    Rumania
    Slovakia   7–11%
    Czech Republic
Former Soviet Union Countries
    Georgia
    Azerbaijan   28–43%
    Ukraine
    Belarus
    Russia
    Lithunia   20–27%
    Latvia
    Estonia

Source: Compiled from Schneider and Enste (2000).

Table 4 reports estimates of the growth of the underground economy (relative to GNP) for selected Western countries and the United States, using the currency demand approach.

The Scandinavian (Sweden, Norway, Denmark) and the German speaking countries (Germany, Austria) exhibit a sizeable increase of the underground economy within the 35 years (1960–1999) covered. But also the countries with a low share in the beginning (Switzerland, the United States) show a significant increase, for the U.S. the share more than doubled. Sizeable increases have been estimated, with few exceptions, for all types of countries and all kinds of approaches: the increasing importance of the underground relative to the official economy is a robust phenomenon.

Table 4: Growth of the underground economy relative to GNP for selected West European countries and the United States, 1960–1999. Estimates based on the currency demand approach (rounded figures)

	1960 (%)	1999 (%)	Percentage point increase (%)
Sweden	2	18.5	16.5
Denmark	4.5	17.5	13.0
Norway	1.5	18.0	16.5
Germany	2	14.2	11.2
United States	3.5	9.5	6
Austria	0.5	9	6.5
Switzerland	1	6.7	5.7

Source: Compiled from Schneider and Enste (2000).

4. What are the Main Causes of the Increase in the Shadow Economy?

4.1. Increase of the Tax and Social Security Contribution Burdens

In almost all studies,[7] the increase of the tax and social security contribution burdens is one of the main causes for the increase of the shadow economy. Since taxes affect labor-leisure choices and also stimulate labor supply in the shadow economy, or the untaxed sector of the economy, the distortion of this choice is a major concern of economists. The bigger the difference between the total cost of labor in the official economy and the after-tax earnings (from work), the greater is the incentive to avoid this difference and to participate in the shadow economy. Since this difference depends broadly on the social security system and the overall tax burden, they are key features of the existence and the increase of the shadow economy.

But even major tax reforms with major tax rate deductions will not lead to a substantial decrease of the shadow economy. They will only be able to stabilize the size of the shadow economy and avoid a further increase. Social networks and personal relationships, and the high profit from shadow economy activities and associated investments in real and human capital are strong ties which prevent people from working in the shadow economy. For Canada, Spiro (1993) expected similar reactions of people facing an increase in indirect taxes (VAT, GST). After the introduction of the GST in 1991 in the midst of a recession the individuals, suffering economic hardships because of the recession, turned to the shadow economy, leading to a substantial loss in tax revenue. "Unfortunately, once this habit is developed, it is unlikely that it will be abandoned merely because economic growth resumes" (Spiro, 1993, p. 255). They may not return to the formal sector, even in the long run. This fact makes it even more difficult for politicians to carry out major reforms, because they may not gain a lot from them.[8]

The most important factor in neoclassical models is the marginal tax rate. The higher the marginal tax rate, the greater is the substitution effect and the bigger the distortion of the labor-leisure decision. Especially when taking into account that the individual can also receive income in the shadow economy, the substitution effect is definitely larger than the income effect[9] and, hence, the individual works less in the official sector. The overall efficiency of the economy is, therefore (ceteris paribus), lower and the distortion leads to a welfare loss (according to official GDP and taxation.) But the welfare might also be viewed as increasing, if the welfare of those who are working in the shadow economy were taken into account, too.[10]

While there have been many theoretical studies on tax evasion in the last twenty years, empirical studies of tax evasion are hard to come by.[11] Most of them are based on tax compliance experiments and cover only some parts of the shadow economy.[12] Convincing empirical evidence for the theoretical hypothesis why people evade taxes is hard to find and the results are ambiguous (Pommerehne and Weck-Hannemann, 1992). The results are more convincing for the shadow economy: for example, Schneider (1994a,b), Johnson et al. (1998a,b) found strong evidence for the general influence of taxation on the shadow economy.

The strong influence of indirect and direct taxation on the shadow economy will be further demonstrated by showing empirical results in the case of Austria and the Scandinavian countries. In the case of Austria, Schneider (1994b) finds out, that as the driving force for the shadow economy activities, the direct tax burden (including social security payments) has the biggest influence, followed by the intensity of regulation and complexity of the tax system.

A similar result has been achieved by Schneider (1986) for the Scandinavian countries (Denmark, Norway, and Sweden). In all three countries, various tax variables (average direct tax rate, average total tax rate (indirect and direct tax rate and marginal tax rates) have the expected positive sign (on currency demand) and are highly statistically significant. Similar results are reached by Kirchgaessner (1983, 1984) for Germany, and by Klovland (1984) for Norway and Sweden.

Two other recent studies provide strong evidence of the influence of income taxes on the shadow economy: Cebula (1997), using Feige's data for the shadow economy, found evidence of the impact of government income tax rates, IRS audit probabilities, and IRS penalty policies on the relative size of the shadow economy in the United States. Cebula concludes that a restraint of any further increase of the top marginal income tax rate may at least not lead to a further increase of the shadow economy, while increased IRS audits and penalties might reduce the size of the shadow economy. His findings indicate that there is generally a strong influence of state activities on the size of the shadow economy: For example, if the marginal federal personal income tax rate increases by one percentage point, ceteris paribus, the shadow economy rose by 1.4 percentage points.

More detailed information of the labor supply decision in the underground economy is given by Lemieux et al. (1994), using micro data from a survey conducted in Quebec City, Canada. In particular, their study provides some economic insight into the size of the distortion caused by income taxation and the welfare system. The results of this study suggest that hours worked in the shadow economy are quite responsive to changes in the net wage in the regular (official) sector. It also provides some support for the existence of a Laffer curve. The Laffer curve suggests that an increase of the (marginal) tax rate leads to a decrease of tax revenue when the tax rate is too high. Their empirical results attribute this to a (mis-)allocation of work from the official to the informal sector, where it is not taxed. In this case, the substitution between labor market activities in the two sectors is quite high. These empirical findings clearly indicate that "participation rates and hours worked in the underground sector also tend to be inversely related to the number of hours worked in the regular sector" (Lemieux et al., 1994, p. 235). The findings demonstrate a large negative elasticity of hours worked in the shadow economy with respect to the wage rate in the regular sector and also to a high mobility between the sectors.

In another investigation, Hill and Kabir (1996) found empirical evidence that marginal tax rates are more relevant than average tax rates, and that a substitution of direct taxes by indirect taxes seems unlikely to improve tax compliance. More evidence on the effect of taxation on the shadow economy is presented by Johnson et al. (1998b), who come to the conclusion that it is not higher tax rates *per se* that increase the size of the shadow economy but the ineffective and discretionary application of the tax system and the regulations by governments. Their finding that there is a *negative* correlation[13] between the size of the unofficial economy and the *top* (marginal) tax rates might be unexpected. But since other factors like tax deductibility, tax reliefs, tax exemptions, the choice between different tax systems, and various other options for legal tax avoidance, were not taken into account, it is not all that surprising.[14] For example, hardly anybody is paying the top marginal tax rate in Germany, since there are many legal tax loopholes(of course, mostly used by wealthy people.[15]

Johnson et al. (1998b) find a *positive* correlation between the size of the shadow economy and the corporate tax burden. They come to the overall conclusion that there is a large difference between the impact of direct taxes as compared to the corporate tax burden. Institutional aspects, like the efficiency of the administration, the extent of control rights held by politicians and bureaucrats, and the amount of bribery and especially corruption, therefore, play a major role in this "bargaining game" between the government and the taxpayers.

4.2. Intensity of Regulations

The increase of the intensity of regulations (often measured in the numbers of laws and regulations, like licenses requirements) is another important factor, which reduces the freedom (of choice) for individuals engaged in the official economy.[16] One can think of labor market regulations, trade barriers, and labor restrictions for foreigners. Although Johnson et al. (1998b) did not find overall significant empirical evidence of the influence of labor regulations on the shadow economy, the impact is clearly described and theoretically derived in other studies, for example, for Germany (Deregulation Commission 1990/91). Regulations lead to a substantial increase in labor costs in the official economy. But since most of these costs can be shifted on the employees, these costs provide another incentive to work in the shadow economy, where they can be avoided.

Empirical evidence supporting the model of Johnson et al. (1997), which predicts, inter alia that countries with more general regulation of their economies tend to have a higher share of the unofficial economy in total GDP, is found in their empirical analysis. A one point increase of the regulation index (ranging from 1 to 5, with 5 = the most regulation in a country), ceteris paribus, is associated with an 8.1 percentage point increase in the share of the shadow economy, when controlled for GDP per capita (Johnson et al. (1998b), p. 18). They conclude that it is the enforcement of regulation that is the key factor for the burden levied on firms and individuals, and not the overall extent of regulation mostly not enforced that drive firms into the shadow economy. Friedman et al. (1999) reach a similar result. In their study, every available measure of regulation is significantly correlated with the share of the unofficial economy and the sign of the relationship is unambiguous: more regulation is correlated with a larger shadow economy. A one point increase in an index of regulation (ranging from 1 to 5) is associated with a 10 percent increase in the shadow economy for 76 developing, transition, and developed countries.

These findings demonstrate that governments should put more emphasis on improving enforcement of laws and regulations, rather than increasing their number. Some governments, however, prefer this policy option (more regulations and laws), when trying to reduce the shadow economy, mostly because it leads to an increase in power of the bureaucrats and to a higher rate of employment in the public sector.[17]

4.3. Social Transfers

The social welfare system leads to strong negative incentives for beneficiaries to work in the official economy since their marginal tax rate often equals or nearly reaches 100 percent. This can be derived either from the neoclassical leisure-income model or from empirical results.[18]. Such a system provides major disincentives for individuals who are getting welfare payments to even search for work in the official economy, since their overall income is much higher when they are still receiving these transfers, while possibly working in the underground economy.

4.4. Labor Market

The numerous regulations in the official labor market and the total wage costs are also driving forces for the shadow economy. Two main aspects the effects of the reduction in official working hours and the influence of the unemployment rate on the increase of the shadow economy are discussed quite often in this context:

- As in most OECD countries, unemployment is, to a large extent, caused by the fact that total labor costs are too high. This can be seen as a cause for an increase of the shadow economy.

- The reduction in working hours in the official economy was introduced by governments (e.g., France) and/or labor unions (e.g., Germany) in order to reduce the unemployment rate. The idea behind this is that there is only a limited quantity of work, and that this quantity has to be "redistributed." But this idea neglects a key factor that especially a forced reduction (but an increase in flexibility of working hours, too) increases the potential of hours that can be worked in the shadow economy.[19] Early retirements can also lead to more unofficial activities and part-time work offers great opportunities to the individual to adopt another job in the untaxed, unregulated economy, as argued by de Gijsel (1984) and Riebel (1983, 1984).[20]

4.5. Public Sector Services

An increase of the shadow economy leads to reduced state revenues, which in turn reduces the quality and quantity of publicly provided goods and services. Ultimately, this can lead to an increase in the tax rates for firms and individuals in the official sector, quite often combined with a deterioration in the quality of the public goods (such as the public infrastructure) and of the administration, with the consequence of even stronger incentives to participate in the shadow economy. Johnson et al. (1998b) present a simple model of this relationship. Their findings show that smaller shadow economies appear in countries with higher tax revenues, if achieved by lower tax rates, fewer laws and regulations, and less bribery facing enterprises. Countries with a better rule of the law, which is financed by tax revenues, also have smaller shadow economies. Transition countries have higher levels of regulation, leading to a significantly higher incidence of bribery, higher effective taxes on official activities, a large discretionary framework of regulations, and, consequently, to a higher shadow economy.

The overall conclusion is that "wealthier countries of the OECD, as well as some in Eastern Europe find themselves in the 'good equilibrium' of relatively low tax and regulatory burden, sizeable revenue mobilization, good rule of law and corruption control, and [relatively] small unofficial economy. By contrast, a number of countries in Latin American and the former Soviet Union exhibit characteristics consistent with a 'bad equilibrium': tax and regulatory discretion and burden on the firm is high, the rule of law is weak, and there is a high incidence of bribery and a relatively high share of activities in the unofficial economy." (Johnson et al., 1998a, p. I).

5. The Effects of the Shadow Economy on the Official Economy

In order to study the effects of the shadow economy on the official one, several studies integrate underground economies into macroeconomic models.[21] Houston (1987) develops a theoretical macro model of business cycle as well as tax and monetary policy linkages with the shadow economy. He concludes from his investigation of the growth of the shadow economy that, on the one side its effect should be taken into account in setting tax and regulatory policies, and, on the other side, the existence of a shadow economy could lead to an overstatement of the inflationary effects of fiscal or monetary stimulus. Adam and Ginsburgh (1985) focus on the implications of the shadow economy on "official" growth in their study concerning Belgium. They find a positive relationship between the growth of the shadow economy and the "official" one and, under certain assumptions (i.e., very low entry costs into the shadow economy due to a low probability of enforcement), they conclude that an expansionary fiscal policy has a positive stimulus for both the formal and informal economies. A study of the United States by Fichtenbaum (1989) argues that the United States productivity slowdown over the period 1970–89 was vastly overstated, as the underreporting of income due to the more rapid growth of the United States shadow economy during this period was *not* taken into account.[22]

Another hypothesis is that a substantial reduction of the shadow economy leads to a significant increase in tax revenues and therefore to a greater quantity and quality of public goods and services, which ultimately can stimulate economic growth. Some authors found evidence for this hypothesis. A recent study by Loayza (1996) presents a simple macroeconomic endogenous growth model whose production technology depends on congestable public services. The determinants and effects of the informal sector are studied, where excessive taxes and regulations are imposed by governments and where the capability to enforce compliance is low. The model concludes that in economies where (1) the statutory tax burden is larger than the optimal tax burden, and where (2) the enforcement of compliance is too weak, the increase of the relative size of the informal economy generates a reduction of economic growth. The reason for this correlation is the strongly negative correlation between the informal sector and public infrastructure indices, while public infrastructure is the key element for economic growth. For example, Loayza finds empirical evidence for Latin America countries that if the shadow economy increases by one percentage point of GDP ceteris paribus, the growth rate of official real GDP per capita decreases by 1.22 percentage points of GDP.

This negative impact of informal sector activities on economic growth is not broadly accepted.[23] For example, the key feature of the model has been criticized, because the model is based on the assumption that the production technology essentially depends on tax-financed public services, which are subject to congestion. In addition, the informal sector is not paying any taxes but must pay penalties which are not used to finance public services. Based on these assumptions the negative correlation between the size of the informal sector and economic growth is therefore not very surprising.

Depending on the prevailing view of the informal sector, one might also come to the opposite conclusion. In the neoclassical view, the underground economy is optimal in the sense that it responds to the economic environment's demand for urban services and small-scale manufacturing. From this point of view, the informal sector provides the economy with a dynamic and entrepreneurial spirit and can lead to more competition, higher efficiency and strong boundaries and limits for government activities. The informal sector may offer great contributions "to the creation of markets, increase financial resources, enhance entrepreneurship, and transform the legal, social, and economic institutions necessary for accumulation" (Asea, 1996, p. 166). The voluntary self-selection between the formal and informal sectors, as described above in microeconomic models, may provide a higher potential for economic growth and, hence, a positive correlation between an increase of the informal sector and economic growth. The effects of an increase of the shadow economy on economic growth therefore remain considerably ambiguous.

The empirical evidence of these hypotheses is also not clear. Since many Latin American countries had or still have a tradition of excessive regulations and weak government institutions, Loayza (1996) finds some evidence of the implications of his growth model in the early 1990s in these countries: the increase in the size of the shadow economy negatively affects growth (1) by reducing the availability of public services for everyone in the economy, and (2) by using the existing public services less efficiently, or not at all.

On the other side, the positive "side effects" of shadow economy activities must be considered. Empirical findings of Schneider (1998b) show clearly that over 66 percent of the earnings in the shadow economy are rather immediately spent in the official sector. The positive effects of this expenditure for economic growth and for the (indirect) tax revenues must be taken into account as well. Bhattacharyya (1993, 1999) found clear evidence for the United Kingdom (1960–84) that the hidden economy has a significant effect on consumer expenditures. He points out that the hidden economy has a positive effect on consumer expenditures of nondurable goods and services, but an even stronger positive effect on consumer expenditures of durable goods and services.[24]

6. Corruption and the Shadow Economy Substitutive or Complementary Effects?

Over the last 10 years, corruption has gained growing attention among scientists, politicians, and public officials regarding its origins, consequences, and ways to fight it.[25] Corruption has been defined in many different ways but "the most popular and simplest definition of corruption is that it is the abuse of public power for private benefit" (Tanzi, 1998, p. 8). From this definition the private sector seems to be excluded, which is, of course, not the case, a more general definition is "that corruption is the intentional non-compliance with arm's length relationship from this behavior for oneself or for related individuals" (Tanzi, 1998, p. 8). There are various kinds of corruption including cost reductions in response to bribes and cash payments, and there is an extensive literature about which factors stimulate corruption.[26] Activities in which corruption is sometimes involved include:

- regulations or licenses to engage in particular activities (e.g., opening a shop, a taxi license);
- land zoning and other similar official decisions;
- access to publicly provided goods and services;
- control over decision making regarding procurement of public investment contracts;
- control over the provision of tax incentives; and
- control over hiring and promotion within the public sector.

The effect of corruption on the official economy can be seen from different sides: Romer (1994) has suggested that corruption, as a tax on ex-post profits, may in general stimulate the entry of new goods or technologies, which require an initial fixed-cost investment. Mauro (1995) finds a significant negative correlation between the corruption index and the investment rate or rate of GDP growth. A one-standard-deviation improvement in the corruption index is estimated by Mauro to increase the investment rate by about 3 percent. Johnson et al. (1998b, p. 39) find a significant relationship between corruption and GDP growth (an increase in corruption on an indexed scale from 0 to 6 by only 1 point decreases GDP growth by 0.84 percentage points) but the relationship becomes insignificant if the shadow economy is entered as an independent variable. On the other side, Bardhan (1997, p. 1329) concludes that "it is probably correct to say that the process of economic growth ultimately generates enough forces to reduce corruption" a view supported by Rose-Ackermann (1997), who further argues that any reform that increases the competitiveness of the economy will help reduce incentives for corruption.

Thus, policies that liberalize foreign trade and remove entry barriers for industry promote competition and reduce corruption. Such reforms will also encourage firms to move from the shadow economy into the official economy, where they can obtain access to capital at market rates. Rose-Ackermann (1997, p. 21) concludes that "going underground is a *substitute* for bribery, although sometimes firms bribe officials in order to avoid the official states."

There are only a few studies which empirically investigate the relationship between the shadow economy and corruption, either in a country or over a sample of countries.[27] Johnson et al. (1998, p. 21) find, in their empirical investigation of 49 countries of Latin America, the OECD, and the post-communist countries of Eastern Europe and the former Soviet Union, a statistically highly significant relationship between the various measures of bribery or corruption and the shadow economy; a 1 point improvement (= less corruption) in the corruption index ICRG[28] leads to about an 8–11 percentage point decline in the shadow economy, ceteris paribus. Using another measure for corruption, the transparency International Corruption Index,[29] Johnson et al. found that a 1 point increase in this index (= less corruption) decreases the shadow economy by 5.1 percentage points, ceteris paribus. Friedman et al. (1999, p.27) conclude: "... In summary, the relationship between the share of the unofficial economy and rule of law (including corruption) is strong and consistent across eight measures provided by six distinct organizations. All eight of the indices suggest that countries with more corruption have a higher share of the unofficial economy." In their investigation, they show that a one point increase in the index of corruption increased the share of the unofficial economy by 7.6 percentage points in the year 1997.

To summarize, the relationship between the share (size) of the shadow economy and the amount of corruption is strong and consistent, as different measures show. Countries with more corruption and briberies have a higher share (size) of the shadow economy. Whereas Rose-Ackermann concludes from her work that going underground is a *substitute* for corruption (bribery), the empirical results of Johnson et al. point more to a complementary process: *countries with more corruption, ceteris paribus, have higher shares of the shadow economy.*

7. Summary and Conclusions

There are many obstacles to be overcome in measuring the size of the shadow economy and analyzing its consequences for the official economy. In this paper, it is shown that although it is difficult to estimate the size of the shadow economy, it is not impossible. I have demonstrated that with various methods (e.g., the currency demand, the physical input measure, and the model approach), some insights can be provided into the size and development of the shadow economy of developing, transition, and the OECD countries. The general impression from the results of these methods is that, for all countries investigated, the shadow economy has reached a remarkably large size. There is another common finding that the size of the shadow economy in most transition and all investigated OECD countries has been growing over the recent decade. Furthermore, the results in this essay show that an increasing burden of taxation and social security payments, combined with rising state regulatory activities, are the major driving forces behind the size and growth of the shadow economy. According to some studies, a growing shadow economy has a negative impact on official GDP growth and is linked to the amount of corruption.

To conclude: shadow economies are a complex phenomenon, present to an important extent even in the most industrialized and developed economies. People engage in shadow economic activity for a variety of reasons; among the most important, as far as I can tell, are government actions, most notably taxation and regulation. Along with these considerations goes a third, no less important one: a government aiming to reduce shadow economic activity has to first and foremost analyze the complex and frequently contradictory relationships that are among the consequences of its own policy decisions.

FRIEDRICH SCHNEIDER

NOTES

1. Compare with the feature "Controversy: on the hidden economy," in the Economic Journal, Vol. 109, No. 456, June 1999.
2. Compare the different opinions of Tanzi (1999), Thomas (1999), and Giles (1999a,b).
3. This figure has been derived from polls of the German and Austrian population about the (effects of) the shadow economy. For further information, see Schneider (1998a,b). These polls also show that two-thirds of the value added produced in the shadow economy would not be produced in the official economy if the shadow economy did not exist.
4. This definition is used, e.g., by Feige (1989, 1994), Frey and Pommerehne (1984), Schneider and Enste (2000), and Schneider (2001a,b,c).
5. For a detailed discussion, see Frey and Pommerehne (1984), Feige (1989), Thomas (1992), and Schneider (1986, 1994a,b, 1998a).
6. Compare also Feinstein (1999), who tries to close the gap between tax evasion and shadow economy research.
7. See Thomas (1992), Lippert and Walker (1997), Schneider (1994a,b, 1997, 1998a,b, 2001a,b,c), Schneider and Enste (2000), Johnson et al. (1998a,b), De Soto (1989); Zilberfarb

(1986); Tanzi (1999), and Giles (1999a), just to quote a few recent ones.
8. See Schneider (1994b, 1998b), for a similar result of the effects of a major tax reform in Austria on the shadow economy. Schneider shows that a major reduction in the direct tax burden did not lead to a major reduction in the shadow economy. Because legal tax avoidance was abolished and other factors, like regulations, were not changed; hence, for a considerable part of the taxpayers, the actual tax and regulation burden remained unchanged.
9. If leisure is assumed to be a normal good.
10. See Thomas (1992), p. 134B7.
11. For a broad survey, see Andreoni et al. (1998).
12. See Alm (1996), for an overview of tax compliance explanations in different studies. The theoretical literature on tax evasion is summarized in Cowell (1990); see also Allingham and Sandmo (1972), for their path-breaking study in this area.
13. The higher the top marginal tax rate, the lower the size of the shadow economy.
14. Friedman et al. (1999) found a similar result in a cross-country analysis that higher tax rates are associated with less official activity as percent of GDP. They argue entrepreneurs go underground not to avoid official taxes but they want to reduce the burden of bureaucracy and corruption. However, looking at their empirical (regression) results, the finding that higher tax rates are correlated with a lower share of the unofficial economy is not very robust and, in most cases, using different tax rates, they do not find a statistically significant result.
15. See Enste (1997), for further details on the (postponed) major German tax reform.
16. See, for a (social) psychological, theoretical foundation of this feature, Schmölders (1960, 1975), Brehm (1966, 1972); and for a (first) application to the shadow economy, see Pelzmann (1988).
17. See, e.g., Frey (1989), for a first application of the Public Choice Theory to the shadow economy.
18. See, e.g., Lemieux et al. (1994).
19. After Volkswagen in Germany reduced the working hours considerably, there is some evidence that in the area around the firm, much more reconstruction and renovation of houses took place compared to similar other regions.
20. See Becker (1965), Trockel (1987), and Werner (1990), for a more detailed analysis.
21. For Austria, this was done by Schneider et al. (1989), and Neck et al. (1989). For further discussion of this aspect, see Quirk (1996), and Giles (1999a).
22. Compare also the findings of Pommerehne and Schneider (1985), who come to similar conclusions.
23. See Asea (1996), for a more detailed criticism of the Loayza model.
24. A close interaction between official and unofficial economies is also emphasized in Giles (1999a), and in Tanzi (1999).
25. The literature is quite large and only some of it (mostly more recent) is given here: Rose-Ackermann (1978, 1997, 1999), Shleifer and Vishny (1993), Tanzi (1994, 1997, 1998), Johnson et al. (1998a,b), and Kaufmann and Sachs (1998). For the latest survey, see Bardhan (1997), Jain (1998), and Rose-Ackermann (1999).
26. See, e.g., Rose-Ackermann (1997, 1999), Jain (1998), Tanzi (1998), and Bardhan (1997).
27. See, e.g., Johnson et al. (1998a,b), Johnson et al. (1997), and Kaufmann and Sachs (1998).
28. This index ranks between 1 and 6 (best = no corruption), and was averaged by Johnson et al. (1998, p. 21) for the 1990s.
29. This index ranks between 0 and 10 (best = no corruption).

REFERENCES

Adam, Markus, C. and Victor Ginsburgh (1985). "The effects of irregular markets on macroeconomic policy: some estimates for Belgium." *European Economic Review*, 29(1): 15–33.

Allingham, Michael G. and Agnar Sandmo (1972). "Income tax evasion: a theoretical analysis." *Journal of Public Economics*, 1(3–4): 323–338.

Alm, James (1996). "Explaining tax compliance," in Pozo, Susan (eds.) *Exploring the Underground Economy*. Kalamazoo, Michigan, pp. 103–127.

Andreoni, James, Erard, Brian and Jonathan Feinstein (1998). "Tax compliance." *Journal of Economic Literature*, 36: 818–860.

Asea, Patrick K. (1996). "The informal sector: baby or bath water?" *Carnegie-Rochester Conference Series on Public Policy*, 45: 163–171.

Bardhan, Pranab (1997). "Corruption and development: a review of issues." *Journal of Economic Literature*, 35: 1320–1346.

Becker, Gary S. (1965), "A theory of the allocation of time." *The Economic Journal*, 75(299): 493–517.

Bhattacharyya, D.K. (1993). *How Does the "Hidden Economy" Affect Consumers Expenditure? An Econometric Study of the U.K. (1960–1984)*. Berlin: International Institute of Public Finance (IIPF).

Bhattacharyya, D.K. (1999). "On the economic rationale of estimating the hidden economy." *The Economic Journal*, 109(456): 348–359.

Brehm, J.W. (1966). *A Theory of Psychological Reactance*. New York: Academic Press.

Brehm, J.W. (1972). *Responses to Loss of Freedom. A Theory of Psychological Reactance*. Morristown: General Learning Press.

Cebula, Richard J. (1997). "An empirical analysis of the impact of government tax and auditing policies on the size of the underground economy: the case of the United States, 1993–94." *American Journal of Economics and Sociology*, 56(2): 173–185.

Cowell, Frank (1990). *Cheating the Government*. Cambridge, MA: MIT Press.

de Gijsel, Peter (1984). "Ökonomische Theorie des schwarzarbeitsangebots und der Mehrfachbeschäftigung," in Gretschmann, Klaus, Heinze, Rolf G., Mettelsiefen, Bernd (Hrsg.) *Schattenwirtschaft. Wirtschafts- und sozialwissenschaftliche Aspekte, internationale Erfahrungen*. Göttingen: Vandenhoeck und Rubrecht, pp. 76–96.

Enste, Dominik H. (1997). "Ökonomische Wirkungsanalyse der Einkommensteuerreform. Grundlegende Ziele, Wirkungen und Gegenfinanzierungsmöglichkeiten," in Institut für Wohnungsrecht und Wohnungswirtschaft an der Universität zu Köln (Hrsg.) *Ökonomische Wirkungsanalyse der Einkommensteuerreform*. Köln. INWO 14, pp. 9–25.

Feige, Edgar L. (ed.) (1989). *The Underground Economies. Tax Evasion and Information Distortion.* Cambridge, New York, Melbourne: Cambridge University Press.

Feige, Edgar L. (1994). "The underground economy and the currency enigma." *Supplement to Public Finance/ Finances Publiques,* 49: 119–136.

Feinstein, Jonathan S. (1999). "Approaches for estimating noncompliance: examples from federal taxation in the United States." *The Economic Journal,* 109(456): 360–369.

Fichtenbaum, Ronald (1989), "The productivity slowdown and the underground economy." *Quarterly Journal of Business and Economics,* 28(3): 78–90.

Frey, Bruno S. (1989). "How large (or small) should the underground economy be?" in Feige, Edgar (ed.) *The Underground Economies: Tax Evasion and Information Distortion.* New York: Cambridge University Press, pp. 133–149.

Frey, Bruno S. and Werner Pommerehne (1984). "The hidden economy: state and prospect for measurement." *Review of Income and Wealth,* 30(1): 1–23.

Friedman, E., Johnson, S., Kaufmann, D., and Zoido-Lobaton, P. (1999). "Dodging the grabbing hand: the determinants of unofficial activity in 69 countries." Discussion Paper, Washington, DC, World Bank.

Giles, David, E.A. (1999a). "Measuring the hidden economy: implications for econometric modeling." *The Economic Journal,* 109(456): 370–380.

Giles, David, E.A. (1999b). "Modeling the hidden economy in the tax-gap in New Zealand." Working Paper, Department of Economics, University of Victoria, Canada.

Hill, Roderick and Muhammed Kabir (1996). "Tax rates, the tax mix, and the growth of the underground economy in Canada: what can we infer?." *Canadian Tax Journal/ Revue Fiscale Canadienne,* 44(6): 1552–1583.

Houston, John F. (1987). "Estimating the size and implications of the underground economy." Working Paper 87–9, Federal Reserve Bank of Philadelphia, Philadelphia (N.J.).

Jain, Arvind, K. (ed.) (1998). *Economics of Corruption.* Boston: Kluwer Academic Publishers.

Johnson, Simon, Kaufmann, Daniel, and Andrei Shleifer (1997). "The unofficial economy in transition." Brookings Papers on Economic Activity, Fall, Washington D.C.

Johnson, Simon, Kaufmann, Daniel and Pablo Zoido-Lobatón (1998a). "Regulatory discretion and the unofficial economy." *The American Economic Review,* 88(2): 387–392.

Johnson, Simon, Kaufmann, Daniel and Pablo Zoido-Lobatón (1998b). *Corruption, Public Finances and the Unofficial Economy.* Discussion Paper, The World Bank, Washington, DC.

Kaufmann, Daniel and Jeffrey Sachs (1998). *"Determinants of Corruption."* Harvard University (Unpublished manuscript).

Kirchgaessner, Gebhard (1983). "Size and development of the West German shadow economy, 1955–1980." *Zeitschrift für die gesamte Staatswissenschaft,* 139(2): 197–214.

Kirchgaessner, Gebhard (1984). "Verfahren zur Erfassung des in der Schattenwirtschaft erarbeiteten Sozialprodukts." *Allgemeines Statistisches Archiv,* 68(4): 378–405.

Klovland, Jan (1984). "Tax evasion and the demand for currency in Norway and Sweden: is there a hidden relationship?" *Scandinavian Journal of Economics,* 86(4): 423–439.

Lemieux, Thomas, Fortin, Bernard and Pierre Fréchette (1994). "The effect of taxes on labor supply in the underground economy." *The American Economic Review,* 84(1): 231–254.

Lippert, Owen and Michael Walker (eds.) (1997). *The Underground Economy: Global Evidences of its Size and Impact.* Vancouver, B.C.: The Frazer Institute.

Loayza, Norman V. (1996). "The economics of the informal sector: a simple model and some empirical evidence from Latin America." *Carnegie-Rochester Conference Series on Public Policy,* 45: 129–162.

Mauro, Paolo (1995). "Corruption and growth." *Quarterly Journal of Economics,* 11093: 681–712.

Mogensen, Gunnar V., Kvist, Hans K., Körmendi, Eszter, and Soren Pedersen (1995). *The Shadow Economy in Denmark 1994: Measurement and Results.* Study No. 3, Copenhagen, The Rockwool Foundation Research Unit.

Neck, Reinhard, Hofreither, Markus and Friedrich Schneider (1989). "The consequences of progressive income taxation for the shadow economy: some theoretical considerations," in Boes, Dieter and Felderer, Bernhard (eds.) *The Political Economy of Progressive Taxation.* Heidelberg: Springer Publishing Company, pp. 149–176.

Pelzmann, Linde (1988). *Wirtschaftspsychologie.* Arbeitslosenforschung, Schattenwirtschaft, Steuerpsychologie. Wien, New York: Springer.

Pommerehne, Werner W. and Friedrich Schneider (1985). "The decline of productivity growth and the rise of the shadow economy in the U.S." Working Paper 85–9, University of Aarhus, Aarhus, Denmark.

Pommerehne, Werner, and Weck-Hannemann, Hannelore (1992). "Steuerhinterziehung: Einige romantische, realistische und nicht zuletzt empirische Befunde." *Zeitschrift für Wirtschafts- und Sozialwissenschaften,* 112(3): 433–466.

Quirk, Peter, J. (1996). "Macroeconomic implications of money laundering." IMF Working Paper 96/66, Washington, DC.

Riebel, Volker (1983). *Die Schwarzarbeit als Problem der Zeitallokation.* Frankfurt am Main, Bern, New York: Lang Publishing Company.

Riebel, Volker (1984). "Arbeitszeitverkürzung und Schwarzarbeit. Auswirkungen einer Verkürzung der Wochenarbeitszeit auf das individuelle Arbeitsangebot." *Zeitschrift für Wirtschafts- und Sozialwissenschaften,* 104(5): 515–538.

Romer, Paul (1994). "New goods, old theory, and the welfare costs of trade restrictions." *Journal of Development Economics,* 43(1): 5–38.

Rose-Ackermann, Susan (1978). *Corruption: A study in Political Economy.* New York: Academic Press.

Rose-Ackermann, Susan (1997). *Corruption and Development.* Annual Bank Conference on Development Economics. Washington DC. The World Bank.

Rose-Ackermann, Susan (1999). *Corruption and Government: Causes, Consequences and Reforms.* Cambridge, MA: Cambridge University Press.

Schmölders, Günter (1960). *Das Irrationale in der öffentlichen Finanzwirtschaft. Probleme der Finanzpsychologie.* Hamburg: Rowohlt-Publishing Company.

Schmölders, Günter (1975). *Einführung in die Geld- und Finanzpsychologie*. Darmstadt: Wissenschaftliche Buchgesellschaft.

Schneider, Friedrich (1986). "Estimating the size of the Danish shadow economy using the currency demand approach: an attempt." *The Scandinavian Journal of Economics*, 88(4): 643–668.

Schneider, Friedrich (1994a). "Measuring the size and development of the shadow economy. Can the causes be found and the obstacles be overcome?" in Brandstaetter, Hermann, and Güth, Werner (eds.) *Essays on Economic Psychology*. Berlin, Heidelberg: Springer Publishing Company, pp. 193–212.

Schneider, Friedrich (1994b). "Can the shadow economy be reduced through major tax reforms? An empirical investigation for Austria." *Supplement to Public Finance/ Finances Publiques*, 49: 137–152.

Schneider, Friedrich (1997). "The shadow economies of western Europe." *Journal of the Institute of Economic Affairs*, 17(3): 42–48.

Schneider, Friedrich (1998a). "Further empirical results of the size of the shadow economy of 17 OECD countries over time." Paper to be presented at the 54 Congress of the IIPF Cordowa, Argentina, and discussion paper, Department of Economics, University of Linz, Linz, Austria.

Schneider, Friedrich (1998b). Stellt das Anwachsen der Schwarzarbeit eine wirtschaftspolitische Herausforderung dar? Einige Gedanken aus volkswirtschaftlicher Sicht. Linz, *Mitteilungen des Instituts für angewandte Wirtschaftsforschung* (IAW), I/98, S. 4–13.

Schneider, Friedrich (2001a). "Die Schattenwirtschaft — Tatbestand, Ursachen, Auswirkungen," in Anton Rauscher (ed.) *Die Arbeitswelt im Wandel*. Mönchengladbacher Gespräche, Band 21, Köln, 2001.

Schneider, Friedrich (2001b). Arbeit im Schatten: Einige theoretische und empirische Überlegungen über die Schattenwirtschaft, *Perspektiven der Wirtschaftspolitik*, Blackwell Publishers, Band 2, Heft 4, 2001.

Schneider, Friedrich (2001c). "What do we know about the shadow economy?" Evidence from 21 OECD countries." *World Economics*, 2(4).

Schneider, Friedrich, and Dominik Enste (2000). "Shadow economies: size, causes, and consequences." *Journal of Economic Literature*, 38(1): 114–177.

Schneider, Friedrich, Markus F. Hofreither, and Reinhard Neck (1989). "The consequences of a changing shadow economy for the official economy: some empirical results for Austria," in Boes, Dieter and Bernhard Felderer (eds.) *The Political Economy of Progressive Taxation*. Heidelberg: Springer Publishing Company, pp. 181–211.

Shleifer, Andrei, and Robert W. Vishny (1993). "Corruption." *Quarterly Journal of Economics*, 108(4): 559–617.

Smith, Philip (1994). "Assessing the size of the underground economy: the Canadian statistical perspectives." *Canadian Economic Observer*, Catalogue No. 11–010, 3.16–33, at 3.18.

Spiro, Peter S. (1993). "Evidence of a post-GST increase in the underground economy." *Canadian Tax Journal/ Revue Fiscale Canadienne*, 41(2): 247–258.

Tanzi, Vito (1994). "Corruption, governmental activities, and markets." IMF Working Paper 99, pp. 1–20.

Tanzi, Vito (1998). "Corruption around the world: causes, consequences, scope, and cures." IMF Working Paper 63, pp. 1–39.

Tanzi, Vito (1999). "Uses and abuses of estimates of the underground economy." *The Economic Journal*, 109(456): 338–340.

Thomas, Jim J. (1992). "Informal economic activity." *LSE, Handbooks in Economics*. London: Harvester Wheatsheaf.

Thomas, Jim J. (1999). "Quantifying the Black economy: 'measurement without theory' yet again?" *The Economic Journal*, 109(456): 381–389.

Trockel, Jochen (1987). "Die Schattenwirtschaft in der Bundesrepublik Deutschland." *Eine ökonomische Analyze am Beispiel der Bauwirtschaft*. Bergisch-Gladbach, Köln, Eul.

Werner, Christian (1990). *Die Beschäftigungswirkungen der Schattenwirtschaft*. Pfaffenweiler, Centaurus.

Zilberfarb, Ben-Zion (1986). "Estimates of the underground economy in the United States, 1930–80." *Staff Papers* (International Monetary Fund), 33(4): 790–798.

SOCIAL CHOICE, CONTRACTS AND LOGROLLING

The problems connected with logrolling (Bernholz, 1974) and vote-trading (Kramer, 1973; McKelvey, 1976; Plott, 1967) are special cases of much wider phenomena (Bernholz, 1981; Schwartz, 1981, 1986). These phenomena are in fact the only reason for the inconsistencies of non-dictatorial societies described by Arrow's *General Impossibility Theorem* (Arrow, 1963/51; see Sen, 1987, for a review of Social Choice Theory) *if more than one issues are implied, if individuals have separable preference orderings and if such inconsistencies are not present concerning the alternatives of single issues*. Moreover, the respective "paradoxes" of voting and logrolling, usually distinguished in the literature, are identical (Bernholz, 2000). Also, the implied social inconsistencies can even occur if participating individuals have identical preferences but face different restrictions (Breyer, 1980). Finally, the problems put into the centre of attention by Arrow would not exist without the presence of negative externalities (in its broad sense, that is including also political externalities). But then, as suggested by the Coase Theorem, stable Pareto-optimal outcomes do result in the absence of transaction costs in spite of the validity of Arrow's Theorem, provided that binding contracts are possible. Consequently, the following statement by Sen (1987: 383) is only true if contracts are not binding: "...it would appear that there is no way of arriving at a social choice procedure specifying what is to be chosen..., satisfying the appropriately interpreted (i.e., in terms of choice) conditions specified by Arrow...."

1. Definitions and Assumptions

To consider the general nature of the phenomena, consider a decentralised society, in which $M = \{M_1, M_2, \ldots, M_n\}$ is the *set of issues* among whose *alternatives* humans can select. Each issue comprises at least two alternatives $a_{ik(i)}$, ($i = 1, 2, \ldots, n$; $k(i) = 1, 2, \ldots$). An *outcome* is defined as containing one alternative out of each issue: $a_s = (a_{1k(1)}, a_{2k(2)}, \ldots, a_{nk(n)})$. Consequently, $s = 1, 2, \ldots, q$, where $q = |M_1|*|M_2|*\ldots*|M_n|$. Further, let $V_i \subseteq V$ denote the n subsets of society to which the rights to decide the n issues M_i have been assigned. V is the set of all adult people in society. We assume, that these m individuals have weak, ordinal, complete and transitive preferences over all outcomes. In some cases we will assume that individual preference orderings are separable. This means that if an individual prefers alternatives of one or a number of issues to other alternatives of the same issue(s), where the alternatives of all other issues remain constant, then this is also true for different alternatives of the other issues held constant. Formally, consider four different vectors $a_f^h, a_f^{n-h} a_g^h, a_g^{n-h}$ such that $a_f \equiv (a_f^h, a_f^{n-h})$, $a_g \equiv (a_g^h, a_g^{n-h})$, $a_s \equiv (a_g^h, a_f^{n-h})$, $a_t \equiv (a_f^h, a_g^{n-h})$. The four vectors contain h and $n-h$ different alternatives, respectively, one out of each issue. Denote by R_j that individual j either prefers the first alternative to the second or is indifferent among them. Assume that $a_f R_j a_s$. Then individual preferences are separable if also $a_t R_j a_g$ holds. Or, similarly, if $a_s R_j a_g$, then $a_f R_j a_t$ is valid.

Return to the decision-making subsets of society. If $V_i > 1$ we call this an *organisation*. An organisation is supposed to have any consistent decision rule like simple majority voting, voting with the majority of stocks, or unanimous decision-making to decide among alternatives. Moreover, let $C_{i1}, C_{i2} \ldots \subseteq V_i$ be the "winning coalitions" of the organisation, that is the subset of people who, according to its decision rule, can take decisions for the organisation. Only one such coalition exists, namely $C_{i1} = V_i$, if unanimity is required. This is also the case, if V_i contains only one individual. Finally, dictatorship is excluded by assuming that there exists no individual $j \in V$ for which $\{j\} = C_{ij}$ for all i.

These definitions and notations comprise a very broad range of institutional settings. For instance, if $V_i = V$ for all i, and if simple majority voting is used throughout, we may speak of a *Total Direct Democracy*. For in this case all issues are collectively decided by all citizens by applying simple majority voting. On the other hand, if $m > n$ and if each individual j has assigned the right to decide at least one issue, one may call this *Pure Individualistic Liberalism*. Another form of *Pure Liberalism* would be present, if $V_i \subset V$, if $|V_i| \geq 1$ for all i, if $V_i \neq V_k$ ($i, k = 1, 2, \ldots, m$; $i \neq k$), and if each individual belonged to at least one V_i.

2. Logrolling and Cyclical Social Preferences

We prove first that a logrolling agreement beneficial to its participants implies always cyclical social preferences. It is assumed that individuals have complete, weak, transitive and separable individual preference orderings (the separability assumption makes the proof easier, but it can be removed, see below). A logrolling situation is given if all decisions are taken by majority (or qualified majority) voting of the members of a group; if two or more subsets of this group who prefer intensively certain alternatives of different issues to others would remain in a minority concerning their favoured issues, but could form a majority by agreeing to vote for each other's alternatives in an exchange of votes. This exchange of votes for the alternatives of different issues implies, however, that the decision in favour of the unwanted alternatives of other issues is not as important as that relating to the alternatives of the issues favoured by the members of the own subset of the group. This means that to assume separable individual preferences is adequate in such a situation. Subsequently only an agreement among two subsets of society will be analysed, but an extension to the case in which more than two subsets have to join to win a majority is straightforward.

Formally, assume that

$$(a_g^h, a_f^{n-h}) \equiv a_s R a_f \equiv (a_f^h, a_f^{n-h}), \qquad (2.1)$$

$$(a_f^h, a_g^{n-h}) \equiv a_t R a_f \equiv (a_f^h, a_f^{n-h}) \qquad (2.2)$$

where R means "the group prefers or is indifferent to". Note that "group indifference" can not only arise because all group members are indifferent among the respective outcomes, but also since no majority can be found for one of the two outcomes. This is especially possible if a qualified majority is required by the decision rule.

Now assume further that

$$(a_f^h, a_f^{n-h}) \equiv a_f P a_g \equiv (a_g^h, a_g^{n-h}). \qquad (2.3)$$

Then a logrolling situation allowing a successful agreement among a majority is present. For the last assumption means that a majority (or a qualified majority) of individuals in the group prefers a_f to a_g, $a_f P_m a_g$. But this implies together with the first two assumptions and the assumption of separable individual preferences that this majority is composed out of two subsets of the group who form each a minority and for whose members $a_f P_j a_s$, $a_f P_i a_t$ respectively.

The existence of cyclical social preferences can now be derived easily. For first, from (2.1) and (2.2) respectively, we get by using the assumption of separable individual preference orderings:

$$(a_g^h, a_g^{n-h}) \equiv a_g R a_t, \qquad (2.4)$$

$$(a_g^h, a_g^{n-h}) \equiv a_g R a_s \qquad (2.5)$$

And second, it follows from (2.3) together with (2.5) and (2.1), and with (2.4) and (2.2):

$$a_f P a_g R a_s R a_f, \qquad (2.6)$$

and

$$a_f P a_g R a_t R a_f. \qquad (2.7)$$

It is important to realise that the preferred, but dominated and consequently unstable outcome a_f can be reached in two different ways by the winning coalition composed out of the two subsets of society. First, with a_g being the status quo, the coalition can first vote on this outcome as compared to a_s or a_t in favour of one of the latter, and then in favour of a_f compared to these outcomes. This will be called *explicit logrolling* in contrast to *implicit logrolling*. Implicit logrolling takes place if the coalition votes directly in favour of a_f put against the status quo a_g. This presupposes that the changes in the alternatives of the issues at stake can be bundled together by the coalition into one bill. The different problems connected with implicit and explicit logrolling will be taken up in the next section.

3. Logrolling by Majorities and the Paradox of Voting

Let us turn next to prove the identity of logrolling and the paradox of voting, assuming that two or more issues are present. Consider the graphical representation in Figure 1. Two issues M_1 and M_2 with infinitely many alternatives are assumed. Society comprises only three members as voters. Also let $V_1 \equiv V_2 \equiv V \equiv \{1,2,3\}$, i.e., all members of society have the right to decide the two issues. As a decision rule simple majority rule is assumed for both issues. The most preferred outcomes for voters 1, 2 and 3 are x_1, x_2, x_3 respectively. The circles or ellipses around these points combine all outcomes for which the voter in question is indifferent. The further away such a curve from the most preferred outcome the less the outcomes on it are estimated by the voter.

This implies that all three voters have single-peaked preferences. But it is well-known that this is not a condition sufficient to secure a stable outcome if simple (and in this case even two-thirds) majority voting is used. True, if voting would take place independently on the two issues, $x_4 = \{M_1', M_2'\}$, which combines the two most preferred positions of the two different median voters, would be selected. But voters 2 and 3 prefer x_7 to this outcome, so

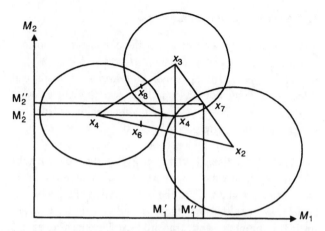

Figure 1: Logrolling and the paradox of voting.

that it will receive a majority if put to a vote against x_4. But the former is itself dominated by x_8, which is preferred by 1 and 3. Similarly, x_8 is dominated by x_6, itself dominated by x_4. Thus a cycle exists and no outcome is stable. It is easy to show that this is just one of infinitely many possible cycles, that the outcome may wander anywhere (McKelvey, 1976), and also, that the conditions for a stable outcome are very restrictive (Plott, 1967; Kramer, 1973).

Note next that by moving from one outcome to another, the respective majority is creating in each case a negative externality to the outvoted voter (minority). Thus, as will be proved in Section 4, negative externalities are here as always a precondition for a cycle. Moreover, the majorities in question have to follow an agreement as to their voting behaviour. This can be done in two ways: Either, an explicit logrolling contract is concluded for instance by 2 and 3 to bring about x_7 instead of x_4: Both agree to vote first for M_1'' of the first, and then for M_2'' of the second issue. In this case voting on the two issues takes place separately.

Or the two issues are bundled together (e.g., in one bill), so that only one vote takes place between x_4 and x_7, where $x_7 = \{M_1'', M_2''\}$. This is a contract which Gordon Tullock has named implicit logrolling. Explicit logrolling is problematic, since 2 would prefer not to keep his part of the bargain in the second vote and vote for M_2'. But even if x_7 is brought about (as is certainly the case if implicit logrolling is used), it is still unstable. For other contracts are better for different majorities, so that further logrolling agreements are favourable, which leads to cyclical social preferences. Thus logrolling contracts are a precondition for cyclical preferences. Moreover, it follows from the example, given the case of implicit logrolling, that the paradox of voting for two or more issues is identical to the fact that majority logrolling is possible.

With many voters present it will usually not be possible for them to conclude logrolling agreements. But in this case parties may exist which propose packages in their election platforms containing alternatives of several issues. If such a package is beneficial to a majority of voters, we have again a case of implicit logrolling, but with the contract now proposed by outsiders, the parties. As a consequence, cyclical social preferences are present again. And this means that any party program proposed by one party can be defeated by that of another party, as already recognised by Downs (1957: 55–60).

4. The General Relationship between Contracting and Cyclical Social Preferences

It has already been stated that logrolling is just a special case of a much more general phenomenon, which has now to be analysed. Assume that all individuals have separable individual preference orderings, and that no cyclical social preferences exist concerning single issues. That is, there is no collection of at least three different winning coalitions C_{ir} ($r = 1, 2, 3, \ldots$), such that for outcomes *different only in alternatives of issue i*:

$$a_{i1} R a_{i2} R \ldots R a_{ih} P a_{i,h+1} R a_{i,h+2} R \ldots R a_{i1}$$

is valid. Recall that P means "preferred by society", and R that "society" either "prefers" an outcome to the following one or is "indifferent" between them. Note again that the latter can also occur when no winning coalition exists for one of the two outcomes following each other in the sequence.

Given these assumptions, it follows that cyclical social preferences can only occur, if two or more winning coalitions exist, which may be called without loss of generality $C_{11}, C_{21}, C_{31}, \ldots$, who have the right by using their respective decision rules to decide *different* issues $M_1, M_2, M_3, \ldots$, and who agree to bring about an outcome preferred to the status quo by all of their members. This means that only by agreeing on such an outcome, that is by concluding a contract, cyclical social preferences arise.

This result holds for the following reasons. First, given separable individual preferences, it follows from the absence of cyclical social preferences in single issues, that such cycles can also not occur if only the alternatives of other issues are different. For since this does not influence the preferences of the members of the winning coalitions concerning their issues because of the assumption of separable individual preferences, this is also true for their decisions and consequently for the "preferences of society". Second, none of the winning coalitions can bring about the new desired outcome on its own, since it does not control the other issues, for which it is not a winning coalition. Otherwise the outcome would already have resulted

before. Consequently, if cyclical social preferences occur they can only result from contracts referring to more than one issues controlled by the winning coalitions to bring about preferred outcomes.

Let us illustrate this result with the help of an example. Assume three issues, each with two alternatives, and a society comprising three individuals, i.e., $V = \{1, 2, 3\}$. The number of outcomes is, therefore, eight. Moreover, we assume strong individual preference orderings (i.e., individuals are not indifferent among any pair of outcomes), and for individuals 1 and 3 *separable* individual preference orderings concerning issues M_1 and M_3, respectively, and for all individuals concerning issue M_2 (Table 1).

The right to decide issues one and three is assigned to individuals one and three, respectively. All members of society have the right to decide issue two by simple majority vote. Thus we assume $V_1 = \{1\}$, $V_3 = \{3\}$, $V_2 = V = \{1, 2, 3\}$. The resulting situation is sketched in Figure 2. Here the arrows point from the outcomes preferred by society to those dominated by them. For instance for individual 1, who has the right to decide the first issue, $a_7 P_1 a_5$, so that "society" also "selects" the former outcome. Concerning

Table 1: Preference orderings of the members of society

Individual	1	2	3
	a_3	a_2	a_8
Strong individual	a_1	a_1	a_6
Preference	a_4	a_6	a_2
Orderings over	a_7	a_4	a_4
Outcomes	a_5	a_5	a_5
	a_8	a_8	a_1
	a_6	a_7	a_7
	a_2	a_3	a_3

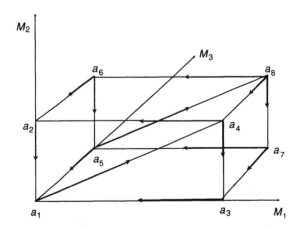

Figure 2: Contracting as causing cyclical social preferences.

the second issue, $a_2P_2a_3$, $a_2P_3a_3$ so that the former is chosen by majority voting. Note also, that all parallel arrows point into the same direction because of the separable preferences of individuals 1 and 3 concerning issues M_1 and M_2, and of all individuals concerning issue M_2, respectively.

Now without any contracts among different winning coalitions controlling different issues no cyclical social preferences are present and a_8 is the resulting stable outcome. But $a_5P_1a_8$, $a_5P_2a_8$. Note that 1 has the right to decide the first issue, and that 1 and 2 form a winning coalition for the second issue. As a consequence they can conclude an agreement to bring about a_5, which is, however, dominated by a_6, a_7, which are dominated by a_8. Thus cyclical social preferences are caused by the possibility to conclude a contract beneficial for its participants.

It remains to prove that cyclical social preferences will always result, whenever a contract between winning coalitions controlling different issues benefits all of their members. This is easy to prove. Without contracts and no cyclical social preferences among the alternatives of single issues there can also be no cyclical social preferences comprising alternatives of two or more issues. This follows from the separability of individual preferences, which implies that the decision by those controlling an issue will remain the same whatever decisions others take concerning the other issues they have the right to decide. This implies that in Figure 2 all parallel arrows point into the same direction. As a consequence a stable outcome results. But the conclusion of a contract changes this situation, since it leads to another outcome which is not stable relative to the decisions taken by the winning coalitions controlling individual issues. Otherwise it would have been selected before. Thus the decisions taken independently by these winning coalitions lead back to the originally stable outcome, which is itself dominated by that selected through the contract.

The situation is different and more complicated if non-separable individual preference orderings are present. This is the case for the preference orderings of individual 1 concerning issue M_3 in the above example (Table 1), for though $a_1P_1a_5$, $a_3P_1a_7$, $a_4P_1a_8$ we see that $a_6P_1a_2$. Similarly, inseparability of preference ordering concerning M_1 holds for individual 3. These inseparable preferences were unimportant for the relationships sketched in Figure 2 since 1 and 3 had only the right to decide M_1, M_3, respectively. But this is no longer the case if a different assignment of rights is considered. As an example, and to bring logrolling into the discussion, assume that $V_1 = V_2 = V_3 = V$ and that all issues are decided by majority voting. Then the situation of Figure 3 emerges for society.

As can be seen there exist now cyclical social preferences, namely $a_2Pa_4Pa_8Pa_6Pa_2$, without any contracts and this means, in this case, without a logrolling agreement

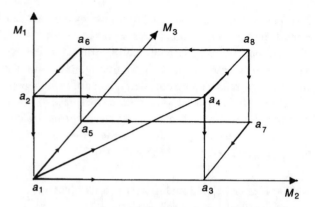

Figure 3: Non-separable individual preferences and cyclical social preferences.

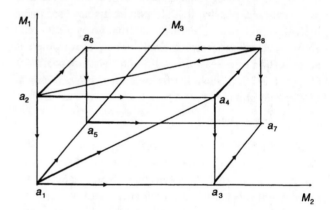

Figure 4: Non-separable individual preferences and cyclical social preferences: Case 2.

being concluded among different winning coalitions controlling different issues. This is a consequence of the fact that the non-separable preferences of individuals 1 and 3 are now decisive concerning M_1.

But note also that if a contract, in this case a logrolling agreement, is concluded between 1 and 2 to bring about a_1Pa_4, since they both have corresponding preferences and form together a majority, then an additional social preference cycle is created.

Consider next a third example, in which the preference ordering of individual 1 is changed concerning one pair of outcomes only, namely from $a_6P_1a_2$ to $a_2P_1a_6$. Moreover, whereas it is assumed as before that $V_1 = V_2 = V = \{1, 2, 3\}$, with majority voting as a decision rule, the right to decide M_3 is now assigned to individual 1, $V_3 = \{1\}$. Note that inseparable individual preference orderings are still present. In this example we get the situation of Figure 4.

It follows that no cyclical social preferences are present if no contracts are concluded and that a_2 is the only stable outcome. Now let us check whether contracting leads again to cyclical social preferences. This would be not the case, if 1 and 2 would conclude a contract implying a_1Pa_4, which they could do since they enjoy a majority for both issues M_1 and M_2. But such a contract would never be agreed on by 2, since the present stable outcome a_2 is preferred by it to a_1. This is different for a contract between 1 and 3 implying a_8Pa_2, since they both prefer the former outcome to the latter. Moreover, 1 has the right to decide M_3 and they both form a majority for a decision on M_1. And this contract leads again to cyclical social preferences. We conclude from this example that contracts bring only about cyclical social preferences if another outcome is "socially preferred" to an outcome which directly or indirectly dominates all other outcomes if no contracts are concluded. However, returning to the second example, this conclusion has to be changed somewhat. For in this example outcomes a_2, a_4, a_6, a_8 are members of a cycle, but dominate directly of indirectly all other outcomes if no contracts take place. And again, since a_1Pa_4, one of this set of dominant outcomes is dominated itself if a contract is concluded. And as a consequence a cyclical social preference cycle results.

The results derived with the help of the examples allow to formulate

Theorem 1. *Assume weak, ordinal, complete and transitive individual preferences and a society in which there exists a decentralised assignment of the rights to decide issues, together with appropriate decision rules for organisations. Then, if no cyclical social preferences are present without contracts being concluded on decision-making concerning different issues, then each conclusion of such contracts leads to cyclical social preferences. Moreover, if a subset of outcomes exists for which cyclical social preferences are present if no contracts are concluded, and which dominate directly and indirectly all other outcomes, then additional cycles result if contracts are concluded by which one of the latter outcomes dominates one of the former* (for general formal proofs see Bernholz, 1980; Schwartz, 1981, 1985).

Note that the special case of separable individual preferences is covered by Theorem 1. For in this case one stable dominating outcome exists without contracts, if no cyclical social preferences exist among outcomes different only in single issues. It then follows from the Theorem that the conclusion of contracts is the only reason for the emergence of cyclical social preferences.

5. Negative Externalities and Cyclical Social Preferences

In this Section we prove

Theorem 2. *Externalities are a necessary condition for the existence of cyclical social preferences.*

Define first negative externalities. Denote by C'_{ij} a winning coalition which can decide among outcomes a_i, a_j. Note that this can either be a coalition which has the right according to the assignment of rights and the prevailing decision rule to decide among alternatives of one issue, so that the two outcomes are only different in this issue. Or that the winning coalition could come about by a contract among such coalitions who agree on their preferences for the two outcomes which differ in more than one issue.

Definition of negative externalities: Assume that a C'_{ij} exists for all of whose members $a_iP_ha_j, (\forall h \in C'_{ij})$. In this case we get a_iPa_j. Thus this winning coalition can bring about the former outcome, whenever the latter is present. Then negative externalities exist for other members of society not belonging to the coalition if $a_jP_ha_i, (h \in V - C'_{ij})$.

This is a very broad definition. Negative externalities include not only the externalities usually considered in economics, but also the negative consequences for the individuals who have the right to participate in a decision, but who are "outvoted" according to the decision rules prevailing in the organisation(s). This latter phenomenon has been mentioned early by Buchanan (1962) and Buchanan and Tullock (1965) as stemming from the fact that collective decision-making not requiring unanimity may lead to negative externalities.

Let us prove now Theorem 2. We take into account that individuals may be indifferent between two outcomes, and denote by $a_iR_ha_j$ that individual h is either indifferent between these two outcomes or prefers the former to the latter outcome. Consider outcomes $a_0, a_1, \ldots, a_s$. Assume that cyclical social preferences exist:

$$a_sPa_{s-1}P\ldots Pa_1Pa_0Pa_s \quad \text{with } 3 \leq s \geq q. \tag{5.1}$$

Then there exist winning coalitions $C'_{s,s-1}, C'_{s-1,s-2}, \ldots, C'_{10}, C'_{0s}$ for whom

$$a_oP_ha_s, (\forall h \in C'_{0s}) \tag{5.2}$$

and

$$a_iP_ha_{i-1}, (h \in C'_{i,i-1}) \quad (i = 1, 2, \ldots, s) \tag{5.3}$$

is valid.

(5.1) implies, because of the transitivity of individual preferences:

$$(\overset{s}{\underset{i=1}{\text{I}}} C'_{i,i-1}) \cap C'_{0s} = \emptyset, \tag{5.4}$$

which implies the absence of dictatorship.

We assume now that no negative externalities exist for the members of society not belonging to the above winning coalitions, and show that this leads to a contradiction. It follows from the absence of negative externalities that

$$a_0R_ha_s, (\forall h \in V - C'_{0s}) \tag{5.5}$$

and

$$a_iR_ha_{i-1}, (\forall h \in V - C'_{i,i-1}) \quad (i = 1, 2, \ldots, s). \tag{5.6}$$

From (5.2) and (5.5) and from (5.3) and (5.6), respectively,

$$a_o R_h a_s, (\forall h \in V) \quad \text{and} \tag{5.7}$$

$$a_i R_h a_{j-1}, (\forall h \in V) \quad (i = 1, 2, \ldots, s). \tag{5.8}$$

Now consider any $C'_{i,i-1}$ ($i = 1, 2, \ldots, s$) or C'_{0s} for all of whose members (5.3) or (5.2) is valid. Since $C'_{0s}, C'_{i,i-1} \subset V$ (5.7) and (5.8) are true for all of their members. But then one can derive from (5.2) and (5.8) or from (5.3), (5.7) and (5.8), respectively:

$$a_s R_h a_{s-1} R_h \ldots R_h a_1 R_h a_0 P_h a_s, (\forall h \in C'_{0s}), \tag{5.9}$$

$$a_s R_h a_{s-1} R_h \ldots R_h a_i P_h a_{i-1} R_h \ldots R_h a_0 R_h a_s, (\forall h \in C'_{i,i-1}) \tag{5.10}$$
$(i = 1, 2, \ldots, s)$.

This result, however, contradicts the assumption of transitive individual preferences. Thus, cyclical social preferences can only exist if negative externalities are present.

Theorem 2 has far-reaching consequences. It suggests that the assignment of rights is of decisive importance for the occurrence of cyclical social preferences. Even more, according to the *Coase Theorem* the original assignment of rights is not important if no transaction costs for concluding contracts are present, since then all negative externalities can be removed by mutually beneficial agreements. Before returning to this problem in section 7, however, let us take up the influence of the kind of assignment of rights.

6. Cyclical Social Preferences and Assignment of Rights

Denote by a *profile of individual preference orderings* a m-tuple of individual preference orderings, one for each of the m members of society. Obviously there exists a huge number of such profiles, since people can have many different preference orderings. Subsequently we illustrate with the help of examples (for a general proof see Bernholz, 1986).

Theorem 3. *For each possible profile of individual preference orderings, there exists a non-oligarchic assignment of rights to decide among all pairs of outcomes, such that no intransitive social preferences exist, and that a stable Pareto optimal outcome results.*

Note that rights are referred to in the theorem as rights to decide among pairs of outcomes instead of among alternatives of issues. This is, however, not important. For if we add to the right to decide issues the right to conclude contracts, both rights together imply a right to decide among certain pairs of outcomes for the winning coalitions agreeing on the respective contract.

Consider first the examples of Table 1 and of Figures 2 and 3. In these cases the same individual preference

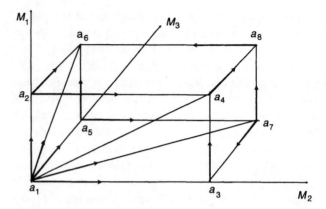

Figure 5: Reassignment of rights to decide issues prevents cyclical social preferences.

orderings lead through two different assignment of rights and the conclusion of contracts to cyclical social preferences. According to Theorem 3 there should, however, given the profile of individual preferences, exist an assignment of rights preventing cyclical social preferences. And this is indeed the case for the following assignment: $V_1 = \{3\}$, $V_2 = \{1\}$, $V_3 = \{2\}$. The resulting situation is presented in Figure 5 in which no cycles exist and in which a_1 is the stable, Pareto optimal outcome. The diagonal from a_1 to a_4 shows no arrow, since the preferences of the potential partners are opposed, so that no contract is concluded. For all other diagonals the same is true or the potential contracts do not imply cyclical social preferences. Moreover, they would not be concluded since they would not lead for the participants of such contracts to a better or another outcome than a_1.

Moreover, when analysing whether there exists an assignment of rights preventing cyclical social preferences in the example of Figure 4, we find that the assignment just given, and thus the situation depicted in Figure 5, is again a solution. This is not surprising, for the preferences of the three members of society are the same as in Table 1, except that for individual 1 $a_2 P_1 a_6$ instead of the opposite preference among these outcomes. But 1 has no right to participate in the decision concerning issue M_3, so that the situation of Figure 2 remains unchanged. It is important to point out, that within the framework of total direct democracy present in the logrolling case, no solution can be found for removing cyclical social preferences, except with unanimity as a voting rule, whereas an individualistic liberal reassignment of rights offers a solution. This is not the accidental result of our specific example, since it has been shown (Bernholz, 1986: 256f.) that:

Theorem 4. *For any possible profile of individual preferences there exists a purely liberal assignment of the rights* to decide among all pairs of outcomes, such that no intransitive or cyclical social preferences exist and that any outcome to which no other outcome is preferred is Pareto optimal. But the same result does not hold if we assign the rights to decide among all pairs of outcomes to all members of society (Total Direct Democracy), deciding with simple or qualified majorities.

Since the general approach presented here does include pure individualistic liberalism, it also covers Sen's (1970) well-known example concerning the conflict between mother and daughter whether they should read Lady Chatterley's Lover. Decision rights for the two issues are only assigned to individuals, namely mother and daughter. It will be shown that in this example, too, negative externalities are present, that the conclusion of a contract leads to cyclical group preferences, and that they can be removed by a different assignment of rights. Following Sen, let us assume $V_1 = \{1\}$ and $V_2 = \{2\}$, $V = \{1, 2\}$, where 1 denotes the mother and 2 the daughter. The two issues M_1 and M_2 refer to reading the book by mother and daughter, respectively. The two alternatives of each issue are "reading" and "not reading" by mother and daughter. Table 2 describes the strong preference orderings of mother and daughter over the four outcomes. As can be seen, the decisions by the mother lead to negative externalities for the daughter, and vice versa.

The resulting situation is sketched in Figure 6. The stable outcome without contract, a_3, is Pareto-inferior. This is Sen's celebrated theorem of the *Impossibility of a Paretian Liberal*. But if we allow a contract between mother and daughter, such an outcome will be agreed on, since both prefer a_2 to a_3. But the contract implies a social preference cycle, because the mother prefers a_1 (both do not read), and the daughter a_4 (both read the book) (Theorem 1). But a stable outcome is reached without a contract if the right to decide M_1 is assigned to the daughter and that to decide M_2 to the mother (Theorems 3 and 4).

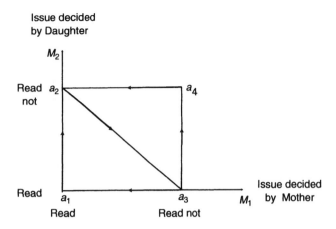

Figure 6: Reading Lady Chatterly's Lover.

It has been pointed out correctly that the results presented by Theorems 3 and 4 may be interesting logically, but that their relevance for reality is rather limited, since an assignment preventing cyclical social preferences would have to be based on a knowledge of all individual preference orderings in society. As a consequence, one has to ask whether the same or a similar result cannot be reached by individual decisions, given some original assignment of rights. This is, indeed, the case, as will be shown in the next section.

7. Cyclical Social Preferences, Negative Externalities and the Coase Theorem

Negative externalities are a precondition for the existence of cyclical social preferences. But then the possibility to conclude contracts should, according to the Coase Theorem (Coase, 1960), lead to stable Pareto optimal outcomes, whatever the original assignment of rights, provided that there are no transaction costs. And social choice theory as well as the theory of logrolling do not assume the presence of such costs. It seems to follow that the Coase Theorem contradicts Theorem 1, which asserts that contracts are a major reason of cyclical social preferences.

But this seeming contradiction can be removed, if *contracts are binding*, and if the Coase Theorem is generalised. Subsequently, a difference will be made between *internal* and *external contracts*. An external contract is a contract agreed on by organisations or individuals with other organisations or individuals. An internal contract, by contrast, is a contract concluded by the members of a winning coalition who have the right to decide an issue for an organisation according to its decision rule, to bring about a certain alternative. Note that this may but need not be done by agreeing to an external contract.

Table 2: Preferences for reading Lady Chatterly's Lover

	Members of society	
	Mother 1	Daughter 2
Strong	a_1	a_4
Separable	a_2	a_2
Individual	a_3	a_3
Preference Orderings	a_4	a_1

Let us now illustrate with several examples that the generalised Coase Theorem holds if internal as well external contracts are binding. Consider first the example of Table 2 and Figure 6. In this case only *external contracts* can be concluded, since no organisation is present. The contract to bring about a_2 is advantageous to both mother and daughter. If it is also binding, then this Pareto optimal outcome is also stable. For outcomes a_1, a_4 and thus cyclical social preferences could only come about, if mother or daughter, respectively could break the contract. This result demonstrates also that Sen's theorem of the *Impossibility of a Paretian Liberal*, though true, is based on a too narrow conception of liberalism. For if the possibility of binding contracts is included, the supposed paradox disappears.

Consider next the logrolling example of Table 1 and Figure 3. In this case only *internal contracts* can be agreed on by winning coalitions, since $V_1 = V_2 = V_3 = V$. 1 and 2, for whom $a_1 P_j a_4$, are minorities if issues M_1, M_2 are voted on separately. They thus have to conclude a contract to bring about a winning logrolling coalition for outcome a_1. But since 2 prefers a_2 it is motivated to b break this *internal* contract. This is, however, prevented if the contract is binding, and no cyclical social preferences result. Note also, that the resulting outcome is Pareto optimal. The same analysis is valid for the example of Figure 4.

Things are a little bit more complicated for the example of Table 1 and Figure 2. In this case only $V_2 = V$, whereas $V_1 = \{1\}$. As a consequence an external and an internal contract are involved in bringing about a_1 instead of a_4. An external contract concluded between V_1 and V_2; and an internal contract between 1 and 2 to vote for the respective alternative of M_2, though for 2 $a_2 P_2 a_1$. But a_1 is not stable, even if both contracts are binding. For 3 has the right to decide M_3 and prefers a_5. Obviously, Pareto optimal outcome a_4 is a candidate for an external contract by all V_i and an internal contract by 1, 2 and 3 to vote for the respective alternative of issue M_2. Note that in this case all participants to the contract have an incentive to break it. 3 prefers a_8 and has the right to bring it about. 1 and 2 would prefer to move to a_1 and could do it by the contract described above. This would imply that 1 would break the external contract for V_1, and that both would break the internal contract on how to vote on issue M_2, which would also violate the external contract concluded for V_2. But again, if both external and internal contracts are binding, stable Pareto optimal outcome a_4 comes about.

The results just discussed suggest (for a general proof see Bernholz, 1997, 1999).

Theorem 5. *Assume that weak, ordinal, complete and transitive individual preference orderings are present, that at least one finely divisible good exists, that any decentralised original assignment of rights to subsets of society is given to decide issues, and that no cyclical social preferences are present without contracts. Then if binding external and internal contracts can be concluded, a stable Pareto optimal outcome results from the decisions of the members of society.*

8. Conclusions

The conclusions drawn above underline first the importance of a clear and complete assignment of rights to decide issues, that is also of property rights. They show second the importance of the freedom to conclude binding contracts, and stress third the need for a legal system trying to prevent any violation of contracts by sufficiently strong sanctions. The results, therefore, cast doubt on the social opprobrium against concluding contracts concerning political decisions, and the absence of fines and penalties if such contracts are broken. Even the prohibition to exchange or sell votes seems to be problematic. The possibility to enforce "political" contracts under certain conditions within the framework of repeated games may not be sufficient to overcome the implied disadvantages in many empirical cases. Finally, the meta-rights of some organisations like parliament, government or bureaucracy to reassign decision rights more or less at their discretion, may have severe negative consequences for society. On the other hand, new issues and alternatives are coming up all the time, so that some organisation is needed to assign them. Connected to this may be a necessity to reassign some rights concerning the old issues. But much work remains to be done to clarify these problems.

Moreover, great caution is advisable concerning the interpretation of the conclusions. First, no strategically motivated decisions to bring about a preferred outcome were taken into account. Second, the absence of transaction costs has been assumed. This is a severe restriction, since binding contracts implying up to n issues may be needed to bring about the stable Pareto optimal outcomes. And transaction costs will generally increase with the number of issues and people involved. As a consequence, many binding contracts may not be concluded because of such costs. Note also that the presence of transaction costs may be a sufficient condition for the evolution of organisations in history. For we have shown that up to n-issue contracts may be necessary to get stable Pareto-optimal outcomes. But if transaction costs are no longer neglected, it is clear that they generally increase with the number of issues and of people involved. It follows that this is already a sufficient condition for the evolution of organisations in history, of organisations which control one or more issues, so that the number of people participating in negotiating contracts and thus contract costs are reduced. From this conclusion it follows that it is not possible to agree with Williamson's statement (1981: 1545): "that but for the *simultaneous existence of bounded rationality and opportunism*, all economic contracting problems are trivial and the study of economic institutions is unimportant. Thus, but for bounded rationality, all economic exchange could be effectively organized by contract."

PETER BERNHOLZ

REFERENCES

Arrow, K.J. (1963/51). *Social Choice and Individual Values*. New York: John Wiley & Sons.

Bernholz, P. (1974). "Logrolling, arrow-paradox and decision rules: a generalisation." *Kyklos* 27: 49–72.

Bernholz, P. (1981). A General Social Dilemma: Profitable Exchange and Intransitive Group Preferences. *Zeitschrift fuer Nationaloekonomie* 40: 1–23; reprinted in J.M. Buchanan and R.D. Tollison (eds.) (1984) *Public Choice II*, 361–381. Ann Arbor: University of Michigan Press.

Bernholz, P. (1982). "Externalities as a necessary condition for cyclical social preferences." *Quarterly Journal of Economics*, 47(4): 699–705.

Bernholz, P. (1986). "A general constitutional possibility theorem." *Public Choice*, 51: 249–265.

Bernholz, P. (1997). "Property rights, contracts, cyclical social preferences and the coase theorem: a synthesis." *European Journal of Political Economy*, 13(3): 419–464.

Bernholz, P. (1999). "The generalized coase theorem and separable individual preferences: a comment." *European Journal of Political Economy*, 15: 331–335.

Bernholz, P. (2000). "Instability of voting outcomes, logrolling, arrow, coase, and all that: a different interpretation," in P. Fishback et al. (eds.) *Public Choice Essays in Honour of a Maverick Scholar: Gordon Tullock*. Boston, Dordrecht, London: Kluwer Academic Publishers, pp. 83–97.

Breyer, F. (1980). "On the relevance of preference similarities for the paradox of voting—identical utility functions and cyclical majorities." *Kyklos*, 33: 523–530.

Buchanan, J.M. (1962). "Politics, policy and the pigovian margins." *Economica*, N.S. 29: 17–28.

Buchanan, J.M. and Tullock, G. (1962). *The Calculus of Consent*. Ann Arbor: University of Michigan Press.

Coase, R.H. (1960). "The problem of social cost." *Journal of Law and Economics*, 3: 1–44.

Downs, A. (1957). *An Economic Theory of Democracy*. New York: Harper and Row.

Kramer, G. (1973). "On a class of equilibrium conditions for majority rule." *Econometrica*, 41: 285–297.

McKelvey, R.D. (1976). "Intransitivities in multidimensional voting models and some implications for agenda control." *Journal of Economic Theory*, 12: 472–482.

Plott, C.R. (1967). "A notion of equilibrium and its possibility under majority rule." *American Economic Review*, 57: 787–806.

Schwartz, T. (1981). "The universal instability theorem." *Public Choice*, 37: 487–501.

Schwartz, T. (1986). *The Logic of Collective Choice*. New York: Columbia University Press.

Sen, A. (1970). "The impossibility of a paretian liberal." *Journal of Political Economy*, 78: 152–157.

Sen, A. (1987). "Social choice," in J. Eatwell, et al. (eds.) *The New Palgrave. A Dictionary of Economics*, Volume 4, pp. 382–393. London: Macmillan.

Williamson, O.E. (1981). "The modern corporation: origins, evolution, attributes." *Journal of Economic Literature*, 19: 1537–1568.

SPATIAL THEORY

Assume that every voter's preferences are single-peaked and slope downward monotonically on either side of the peak (unless his peak lies at one extreme of the scale)....The best way [for each party] to gain more support is to move toward the other extreme, so as to get more voters outside of it — i.e., to come between them and its opponent. As the two parties move closer together, they become more moderate and less extreme in policy in an effort to win the crucial middle-of-the-road voters, i.e., those whose views place them between the two parties. This center area becomes smaller and smaller as both parties strive to capture moderate votes; finally the two parties become nearly identical in platforms and actions. (Downs, 1957, pp. 116–117)

One of the fundamental building blocks in the analysis of political phenomena is the representation of preferences. Without some means of capturing the essence of goals and trade-offs for individual choices, the mechanics of the public choice method are stalled. While there are many ways of representing preferences, the single most commonly used approach is the "spatial" model. The idea of conceiving preference in a kind of "space" is actually quite ancient, as the quote from Aristotle's *Politics* below shows. Furthermore, there are hints of several topics of modern spatial theory, including the power of the "middle," and the problem of instability in political processes.

1. Origins of Spatial Political Competition

It is important to recognize that the spatial model is not just an "as-if" form of reasoning about political phenomena. One can quickly find myriad references to "left" and "right" in political discourse, both in the media and in elite accounts. Although "space" is a metaphor, it is one that is used so widely that it must connect quite closely with human cognition about political representation.

The origin of the "left" and "right" metaphors, as is well known, is a reference to the physical positions occupied by different factions in the French National Assembly after 1789. The Girondins on the "right" of the huge meeting hall held power, and ran the government. The more radical Jacobin allies of Robespierre sat in the "mountain" on benches rising up the wall on the far "left." The Jacobins on the left were constantly agitating for change, while the Girondins on the right defended stability and the status quo. With only a very little adjustment for time and circumstance, these meaning still attach to "left" and "right" in political discourse today.

An alternative meaning, mapping an ideological left and right onto positions with respect to ownership of capital (right) and defense of labor (left), was created by Karl Marx, and is used today in a wide variety of surveys. This meaning, however, is at best misleading and is often simply incorrect. The former Soviet Union, particularly Russia, had a clearly defined left and right at the end of the 20th century. But "left" was understood to mean liberal reformers who favored markets and democracy, whereas the "right" was composed of former communists who demanded a return to central planning and a secure and stable, if unelected, government.

2. The Problem of Representation

In economics, the problem of representation of preferences has been refined to the point that is simply a mathematical problem. Suppose that there are many alternatives, and that for each pair of alternatives, I prefer one, or like them equally. Then it is possible (assuming transitivity) to construct an aggregate weak ordering that allows the individual to "rank" alternatives from best to worst, with each alternative either uniquely or with a group of other alternatives associated with an ordinal level. If I like A better than B, we say, "A is preferred to B." If I like them equally well, then "I am indifferent between A and B."

"Representing" the preferences implied by this ranking requires the assignment of any mathematical function f that has the following properties: (1) If A is preferred to B, then $f(A) \geq f(B)$. (2) If A and B are equally preferred, then $f(A) = f(B)$. As should be obvious, if there exists at least one function that represents these preferences, there will be infinitely many (since, for example, f and $f' = (f/2) + 37$ both have the same ordering of the index numbers associated with alternatives). In other words, any order-preserving transformation of a function that represents the preferences is equally good.

The work on preferences in economics has shown that relatively few assumptions are required to ensure representability. One common, and plausible, type of preferences that is not representable by a mathematical function is "lexicographic" preferences, but most preferences that obey simply convergence criteria are representable. Economic preferences, however, generally assume either non-satiety or free disposal. Can something like the same approach be used to "represent" *political* preferences, which may very well require interior ideal points?

To understand the problem, consider the difference between preferences for apples and preferences for education. We generally model preference for apples as non-decreasing, so that more is preferred to less. What about education, or more accurately education budget? If asked, most citizens will not say that they think that the education budget should be infinite. Instead, they will select some finite number of dollars they think is the "best" budget, and will argue that either a larger or smaller budget is less preferred. This "interior" ideal point is illustrated in Figure 1. (The utility functions graphed in the figure are symmetric for the sake of simplicity, but there is nothing in spatial theory that requires symmetry.)

One important research question in public choice is the relation of political preferences to economic preferences. More specifically, can political preferences with interior ideal points be derived from economic preferences, with the connection being the opportunity cost of taxes used to finance public programs? Interestingly, though the initial findings were hopeful (see, e.g., Barr and Davis, 1966), the answer turns out to be "no" (see Denzau and Parks, 1977, 1979; Slutsky, 1977; for a review, see Hinich and Munger, 1994, chapter 2).

Consequently, the basis of political preferences in "representation" is more tenuous than for economic

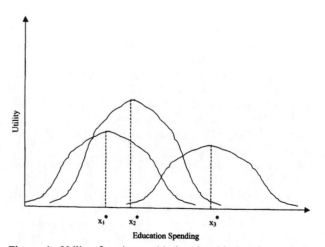

Figure 1: Utility functions with interior ideal points x_i^* for education, three citizens.

preferences: the only way to justify interior ideal points rigorously is to connect preferences for the good with the recognition that the financing scheme requires that citizens also pay for the good. This means that preferences are being defined simultaneously over the underlying good and the price of the good, rather than just preferences for the good alone.

On the other hand, the mathematical underpinnings for political preference representation in a "space" are well defined and consistent, requiring only minimal assumptions about the convexity of the sets of alternatives enclosed by indifference curves (Schofield, 1984). To the extent that government decisions on property rights, security, and a currency system are logically antecedent to the problem of representing economic preferences, the problem may go the other way. That is, there is a failure of duality in the representation problem: it is perfectly easy to take preferences in either the public or private sectors as primitive, and then use utility functions to represent them. As the literature cited in this section shows, once one starts with economic preferences, there is no consistent way to "induce" public sector preferences. However, it is equally true that if one takes political preferences as primitives, then it is the "induced" economic preferences that exhibit inconsistency. We will take spatial theory as a primitive, rather than induced or derived, means of representing public sector preferences.

3. The First Spatial Models

As Hinich and Munger (1994) point out, the first clear use of the spatial "model" appears in Aristotle's *Politics*, written down before 325 B.C.E., and perhaps amended and modified in several ways in the centuries that followed. Still, as the work comes down to us, it is clear that there is both a deep understanding of politics and stability, and a connection to the idea of a dimension, or simple space, that organizes political conflict.

> Now in all states there are three elements: one class is very rich, another very poor, and a third in a mean. It is admitted that moderation and the mean are best, and therefore it will clearly be best to possess the gifts of fortune in moderation; for in that condition of life men are most ready to follow rational principle...[T]hose states are likely to be well-administered, in which the middle class is large, and stronger if possible than both the other classes, or at any rate than either singly, for the addition of the middle class turns the scale, and prevents either of the extremes from being dominant...The legislator should always include the middle class in his government; if he makes his laws oligarchical, to the middle class let him look; if he makes them democratical, he should equally by his laws try to attach this class to the state. There only can the government ever be stable where the middle class exceeds one or both of the others, and in that case there will be no fear that the rich will unite with the poor against the rulers. (Aristotle, 1979, pp. 138–142)

As was discussed earlier, this understanding of politics seems to come naturally to human beings, with the clearest example deriving from the language used to describe the conflict in the French Assembly. But what of models? How are we to think of the idea of a "space," or dimension of conflict, in a way that gives us testable propositions about political behavior and institutions?

The early literature in economics on "spatial" competition addressed what seem like similar considerations. Hotelling (1929), Lerner and Singer (1937), and Smithies (1941) all addressed the problem of location, in the sense that a set of firms selling zero cost, undifferentiated products might compete by choosing the physical setting for the business. The classic metaphor is the choice of two hot dog stands on a street or beach, with potential patrons distributed along the linear dimension of competition. The key assumption is that, since the products are undifferentiated (all hot dogs are of the same make), patrons will choose solely based on location. The equilibrium set of locations, as was shown by various means in this literature, was achieved when (in the case of two firms), the businesses converged to a "central place." With more than three competitors, the results are ambiguous (there are many possible equilibria), and with arbitrarily many firms very little can be said.

The interesting thing about the early spatial models in economics was the fact that the authors worked to develop normative implications. An important controversy was Hotelling's rather strong claim that capitalism was "wasteful," at least compared to a planned economy. The prediction of convergence implied that both (or all) firms ended up as close together as they could manage, increasing the average distance traveled by consumers. Hotelling concluded: "Our cities become uneconomically large and the business districts within them are too concentrated. Methodist and Presbyterian churches are too much alike; cider is too homogeneous" (p. 57).

Lerner and Singer (1937) disputed this claim, pointing out that it rested on tenuous assumptions (particularly about transport charges and the extreme inelasticity of demand assumed by Hotelling). Smithies (1941) pursued the matter further, showing that under some plausible assumptions there exist nonconvergent equilibria.

Unfortunately, the problems of spatial location for firms and spatial preference representation in politics are not isomorphic. The analogies in results are not very useful, and can be misleading. The idea that voters might choose the candidate "closer" to their own ideal seems plausible enough, but it is by no means clear what "close" means once the idea of simple Euclidean distance is dispensed with. Euclidean distance makes good sense in the hot dog stand competition, since it takes just as long to walk one hundred yards north as it does to walk one hundred yards south. But it is by no means clear that we would want to build in this extreme kind of symmetry in representing political spatial preferences.

The problem is worse if there are multiple dimensions. Euclidean distance makes two assumptions about preferences:

(1) separability — My evaluation of issue i is not affected by the level of issue j I expect to result from the decision process.

(2) equal salience — Marginal changes in issue i have the same increment/decrement for my utility as marginal changes in issue j.

Neither of these is a problem for the spatial location problem, because my reaction to having to travel is based on distance, not whether the distance is in any one direction. But if we are to use a policy "space" to represent political preferences, the assumptions of separability and equal salience are both empirically unrealistic and theoretically limiting.

The extension of this kind of reasoning to political problems, particularly of party competition, was accomplished by Downs (1957). It is clear, however, that Downs' analysis is of a piece with the earlier work; consider Smithies' first paragraph:

> The very fact that Professor Harold Hotelling's pioneer article explained so successfully the close similarity of the Republican and Democratic platforms in 1928 indicates that something more was needed in 1936. It was probably true to say in 1928 that by moving to the center of electoral opinion neither party risked losing its peripheral support. The situation at the present time requires no elaboration; suffice it to say that neither party feels itself free to compete with the other for the undecided votes at the center, in full confidence that it will retain its support from the extremes of political opinion.

This is a very sophisticated statement, recognizing that equilibria, if they exist, will depend on the reliability of turnout and support from those at the extremes. If, to use the economic analogy for the last time, the "elasticity of demand" of citizens is high, moving toward the center may actually reduce one's vote share, as the ardent supporters out in the wings lose interest. To be fair, Downs concentrated on the problems of turnout, and information, but Downs has come to be associated with the result that candidates converge to the middle, or median, in two-party elections. It has since been shown (for a review, see Berger et al., 2000) that the convergence result is actually very fragile under the plausible set of "Downsian" assumption, and unlikely to be observed empirically.

4. A Rigorous Representation: Spatial Theory in the 1960s

The first rigorous statement of the spatial model as a representation of preferences, at a level of generality analogous to that of economics, was the result of the collaboration of Otto Davis and Melvin Hinich. In three papers (Davis and Hinich, 1966, 1967, 1968), they laid the groundwork for what is now thought of as spatial theory.

Using a generalized quadratic form for representing preferences, they were able to account for non-separability and differences in salience in an elegantly simple way. Further, in all three papers, but particularly in the 1968 piece, they addressed the normative problem of the "good" in the democratic choice problem: if we accept the idea of Aristotle's "mean" as the best choice for a democracy, there is a benchmark against which predicted outcomes in the spatial model can be compared. The most widely recognized paper in this collaboration, Davis et al. (1970) is a general exposition of all the results in the series of papers, with some extensions, and is the generic original reference in the spatial theory literature.

5. Social Choice Theory

Social choice theory and spatial theory are related subjects, but there are many important differences. Social choice theory tends to focus on the consequences of aggregation of individual "lists," using different aggregation ("voting") rules. Very little restriction is placed on the form that these lists can take, other than each weak order is transitive. Some of the most important work, such as Arrow (1963), actually assumes explicitly that preferences are characterized by "universal domain," so that any ordering over elements of the choice set is possible. There is no requirement, in social choice theory, that the preferences are "representable." Instead, social choice theorists work directly with preference orderings themselves.

Spatial theory, on the other hand, focuses on preferences that are single-peaked, and which are amenable to mathematical representation. The simplest kind of spatial preferences, Euclidean preferences, make a very restrictive set of assumptions about the kind of function that can represent the underlying ordering over alternatives. The simplest way to think of the difference, then, is that social choice theory takes preferences as primitive, and unknown, with any ordering equally likely. Spatial theory uses the notion that "closer" alternatives are more preferred, though spatial theory can account for weighted Euclidean distance, so that the function representing preferences exhibits nonseparability and different salience for different issues.

There are some important overlaps between spatial theory and social choice theory. An early work, in many ways ahead of its time, was Black and Newing (1951). This book introduced something very close to the analytical tool now called "win sets," but at the time too little was known about the problems of aggregation to give a coherent account. Black recognized the limitations in the earlier work, and published his seminal *Theory of Committees and Elections* in 1958, though this book took more of a social choice than a spatial perspective.

Probably the best known example of the intersection of spatial and social choice theory is Plott's (1967) then revolutionary exposition of the problem of the nonexistence of equilibrium under most arbitrarily chosen configurations of voter ideal points (for an extension, see Enelow and Hinich, 1983). This paper led to a new research agenda, trying to identify some subset of the policy space that is likely to contain outcomes, if not unique equilibria, of majority rule voting processes. For example, Schofield (1978, 1984) offered a mathematically more general treatment than that of Plott, but works mainly within the logic of the spatial representation of preferences. McKelvey (1976a,b, 1979, 1986) generalized the concept of spatial equilibrium, and distilled some important solution concepts, including covering and dominance. The notion of the "uncovered set" in a spatial context derives from Miller (1980); for a review and some extensions, see Cox (1987).

6. Extensions

The spatial model has been extended in a number of useful ways, a review of which would extend beyond the scope of this short essay. Useful, though very different, reviews of the literature can be found in Coughlin (1992), Enelow and Hinich (1984, 1990), Hinich and Munger (1997), and Ordeshook (1986, 1997). But a brief list of extensions is worthwhile.

- One of the earliest, and most interesting, is the extension of the spatial model to account for the turnout decision, allowing for rational abstention. Hinich et al. (1973) gather together many strands of literature, and raise some important questions about the notion of equilibrium in the spatial model.

- The idea of treating voter actions as outcomes of an idiosyncratic probability distribution function arises naturally from the Hinich, Ledyard, and Ordeshook work, and was taken up by Hinich (1977), and Enelow and Hinich (1989).

- The restriction of the "space" of conflict to only a few dimensions, based on the empirical phenomenon of clustering of issues, has resulted in two related, yet distinct, theoretical extensions of the spatial model. The idea that "ideologies" are important for explaining mass behavior was developed by Hinich and Pollard (1981), extended by Enelow and Hinich (1984), and given a firmer theoretical foundation by Hinich and Munger (1994). The claim that "ideology" is an important empirical predictor of both the vote of members in Congress and of the structure of the space of competition itself can be found in Poole and Rosenthal (1996), which reviews Poole and Rosenthal's many previous contributions to the development of this idea.

- The spatial model has an important policy implication for agenda control, because it allows analysis of the role of the "setter." There have been many contributions on this point, but the most important is Romer and Rosenthal (1978). A review of the larger literature, and its importance, can be found in Rosenthal (1990).

- Finally, the spatial model has given rise to a number of tests using experimental methods and human subjects. A review of this literature can be found in McKelvey and Ordeshook (1990). The important thing about experimental work in the spatial model is that it can suggest patterns of outcomes empirically, since many of the theoretical results are simply negative, because of the absence of equilibria.

7. Conclusion

Spatial theory is the single most important analytical construct for representing citizen preferences over policies, public goods, and government actions. Though the mathematical generality of spatial models falls short of the standards of preference representation in economics, it is important to recognize three things. First, the problem of representing political "preferences" is inherently more difficult than representing economic preferences. Thus, it is not clear whether our models are not very good, or the problem is just very hard. Second, spatial models perform very well in a wide variety of useful theoretical settings, and can be used to investigate the precise properties of different institutional arrangements, ranging from committee systems in legislatures to the assignments of ministry portfolios in parliamentary governments, and encompassing voting by the mass public on referenda or elections.

Finally, the spatial model is appealing because of its inherent verisimilitude. The notion of "left" and "right" as a description of the "location" of candidates or parties is nearly universal. The notion of "moving to the center" or "outflanking on the left/right" pervades media and elite discourse about politics. For all these reasons, knowledge of the basic results of spatial theory is one of the foundations of public choice theory.

MELVIN J. HINICH
MICHAEL C. MUNGER

REFERENCES

Aristotle ([c. 350 B.C.] 1979). *Politics and Poetics* (translated by Benjamin Jowett and S.H. Butcher, Norwalk, CT: Easton Press.

Arrow, Kenneth J. (1951, 1963). *Social Choice and Individual Values*. New Haven: Yale University Press.

Barr, James and Otto Davis (1966). "An elementary political and economic theory of the expenditures of local government." *Southern Economic Journal*, 33: 149–165.

Berger, Mark, Michael Munger, and Richard Potthoff. (2000). "The Downsian model predicts divergence." *Journal of Theoretical Politics*, 12: 78–90.

Black, Duncan ([1958], 1987). *The Theory of Committees and Elections*. Dordrecht: Kluwer Academic Publishers.

Black, Duncan and Newing, R.A. (1951). *Committee Decisions With Complementary Valuation*. London: Lowe and Brydon.

Coughlin, Peter (1992). *Probabilistic Voting Theory*. New York: Cambridge University Press.

Cox, Gary (1987). "The core and the uncovered set." *American Journal of Political Science* 31: 408–422.

Davis, Otto and Melvin Hinich (1966). "A mathematical model of policy formation in a democratic society," in J. Bernd (ed.) *Mathematical Applications in Political Science*, Volume II. Dallas: Southern Methodist University Press, pp. 175–208.

Davis, Otto and Melvin Hinich (1967). "Some results related to a mathematical model of policy formation in a democratic society," in J. Bernd (ed.) *Mathematical Applications in Political Science*, Volume III. Charlottesville: University of Virginia Press, pp. 14–38.

Davis, Otto A. and Hinich Melvin, J., (1968). "On the power and importance of the mean preference in a mathematical model of democratic choice." *Public Choice*, 5: 59–72.

Davis, Otto A., Hinich Melvin, J., and Ordeshook, Peter C. (1970). "An expository development of a mathematical model of the electoral process." *American Political Science Review*, 64: 426–448.

Denzau, Arthur and Robert Parks (1977). "A problem with public sector preferences." *Journal of Economic Theory*, 14: 454–457.

Denzau, Arthur and Robert Parks (1979). "Deriving public sector preferences." *Journal of Public Economics*, 11: 335–352.

Downs, Anthony (1957). *An Economic Theory of Democracy*. New York: Harper & Row.

Enelow, James M. and Hinich Melvin, J. (1983). "On plott's pairwise symmetry condition for majority rule equilibrium." *Public Choice*, 40(3): 317–321

Enelow, James and Melvin Hinich, J., (1984). *Spatial Theory of Voting: An Introduction*. New York: Cambridge University Press.

Enelow, James M. and Melvin Hinich, J. (1989). "A general probabilistic spatial theory of elections." *Public Choice*, 61: 101–113.

Enelow, James M. and Hinich, Melvin J. (eds.) (1990). *Advances in the Spatial Theory of Voting*. New York: Cambridge University Press, pp. 1–11.

Hinich, Melvin J. (1977). "Equilibrium in spatial voting: the median voting result is an artifact." *Journal of Economic Theory*, 16: 208–219.

Hinich, Melvin J., Ledyard, John O., and Ordeshook, Peter C. (1973). "A theory of electoral equilibrium: a spatial analysis based on the theory of games." *Journal of Politics*, 35: 154–193.

Hinich, Melvin and Michael Munger (1994). *Ideology and the Theory of Political Choice*. Ann Arbor, MI: University of Michigan Press.

Hinich, Melvin and Michael Munger (1997). *Analytical Politics*. New York: Cambridge University Press.

Hotelling, Harold (1929). "Stability in competition." *Economic Journal*, 39: 41–57.

Lerner, A.P. and Singer, H.W. (1937). "Some notes on duopoly and spatial competition." *The Journal of Political Economy*, 45: 145–186.

McKelvey, Richard (1976a). "General conditions for global intransitivities in formal voting models." *Econometrica*, 47: 1085–1111.

McKelvey, Richard (1976b), "Intransitivities in multidimensional voting bodies and some implications for agenda control." *Journal of Economic Theory*, 30: 283–314.

McKelvey, Richard (1979). "Covering, dominance, and institution-free properties of social choice." *American Journal of Political Science*, 30: 283–314.

McKelvey, Richard (1986). "General conditions for global intransitivities in formal voting models." *Econometrica*, 47: 1085–1111.

McKelvey, Richard and Peter Ordeshook (1990). "A decade of experimental results on spatial models of elections and committees," in Enelow and Hinich (eds.) *Advances in the Spatial Theory of Voting*. New York: Cambridge University Press, pp. 99–144.

Miller, Nicholas (1980). "A new solution set for tournament and majority voting." *American Journal of Political Science*, 24: 68–96.

Ordeshook, Peter C. (1986). *Game Theory and Political Theory*. New York: Cambridge University Press.

Ordeshook, Peter C. (1997). "The spatial analysis of elections and committees: four decades of research," in Dennis Mueller (ed.) *Perspectives on Public Choice: A Handbook*. Cambridge: Cambridge University Press, pp. 247–270.

Plott, C.R. (1967). "A nation of equilibrium and its possibility under majority rule." *American Economic Review*, 57: 787–806.

Poole, Keith and Howard Rosenthal (1996). *Congress: A Political-Economic History of Roll-Call Voting*. New York: Oxford University Press.

Riker, William (1980). "Implications from the disequilibrium of majority rule for the study of institutions." *American Political Science Review*, 74: 432–446.

Romer, Thomas and Howard Rosenthal (1978). "Political resource allocation, controlled agendas, and the status quo." *Public Choice*, 33: 27–43.

Rosenthal, Howard (1990). "The setter model," in Enelow and Hinich (eds.) *Advances in the Spatial Theory of Voting*. New York: Cambridge University Press, pp. 199–234.

Schofield, Norman (1978). "Instability of simple dynamic games," *Review of Economic Studies*, 45: 575–594.

Schofield, Norman (1984). "Social equilibrium and cycles on compact sets," *Journal of Economic Theory*, 33: 59–71.

Slutsky, Steven (1977). "A voting model for the allocation of public goods: existence of an equilibrium." *Journal of Economic Theory*, 14: 299–325.

Smithies, Arthur (1941). "Optimum location in spatial competition." *The Journal of Political Economy*, 49: 423–439.

T

TRADE LIBERALIZATION AND GLOBALIZATION

Trade liberalization is the reverse process of protectionism. After previous protectionist decisions, trade liberalization occurs when governments decide to move back toward free trade. Trade liberalization may take place unilaterally. Extensive trade liberalization that occurred among the richer countries in the second half of the 20th century was however reciprocal and multilateral. Countries' governments reciprocated each other's liberalization decisions, and the liberalization was non-discriminatory in applying to all liberalizing trading partners. The trade liberalization was accompanied by liberalization of international capital markets and by substantial international migration, both legal and illegal. International agreements and conventions also unified rules of conduct concerning protection of property rights, including intellectual property rights related to proprietary knowledge. The outcome of these liberalizing and integrating processes is known as globalization. The issues are why or how did globalization occur, and whether the outcome has been good for humanity.

1. Reciprocal Liberalization

A government can transfer income to an import-competing industry through unilateral protection. Incomes in export industries can be unilaterally increased through export subsidies. The articles of the pre-1995 General Agreement on Tariffs and Trade (GATT) and the rules of the successor World Trade Organization (WTO) do not view export subsidies favorably, and allow duties to be levied to counter export subsidies. If there has been past protection, income can instead be transferred to an export sector by unilateral liberalization, provided that exporters have access to foreign markets. Foreign protectionist barriers may limit access of exporters to foreign markets. When foreign import quotas limit exports, exporters need to be included in the quota to have market access and cannot sell more than the allowed quantities. Foreign tariffs impose additional costs of selling in the foreign markets. Exporters will regard the elimination or reduction of foreign import quotas and tariffs as providing them with market access, or market access under more favorable conditions.

Policy makers dealing with trade liberalization are in practice vitally concerned with such notions of market access. By exchanging market access for each other's exporters, governments hope to be seen as reciprocally providing benefits for each other's export sectors with an effectiveness or a visibility that may not be possible through unilateral liberalization. Each government benefits politically from the market access provided for its export industries by the other reciprocating government (Hillman et al., 1995; Hillman and Moser, 1996).

This practical concern with the exchange of market access reflects a mercantilist view of international trade by policy makers. The mercantilist view is that granting of access of foreign goods to the domestic market is not a socially beneficial policy for the liberalizing economy. Rather, allowing foreigners to sell in the home market under more favorable conditions of market access is a "concession" or "favor" that compromises the rights of domestic producers to their own market and requires a reciprocal favor of foreign market access in return.

How much protection each government retains after providing and receiving market access for exporters depends on the relative political influence, or political importance, of export and import-competing industries. Politically optimal exchange of market access need not therefore result in an agreement to eliminate all trade barriers to implement free trade. Reciprocal liberalization will in particular be gradual, if governments are constrained in the magnitude of the income losses that can be imposed at any point in time on the import-competing industries that lose from the reciprocal liberalization (Ethier, 2001, 2002).

Consider a country that is small relative to the world market. The world market consists of the combined national markets of all potential trading partners. With open access to the world market under conditions of free trade, exporters in such a small country have no problems of market access. They can sell all they wish at given world prices. If however the world market consists of segmented national markets with import quotas or tariffs, and if the small country is large in any of these markets, its exporters will benefit from improved conditions of foreign market access. This potentially provides governments of even small countries with incentives to participate in negotiations for reciprocal exchange of market access.

Any particular exporting firm in any country is likely to be grateful for perceived improvements in conditions of foreign market access, either through elimination or relaxation of quota restrictions or through reduced foreign tariffs. The firm may be able to receive a higher price for its exports, which from the country perspective is an improvement in the terms of trade. Improved foreign market access is beneficial for the firm even if new export sales take place without price increases. The benefit is evident if the firm is not capacity constrained. If the firm has no immediate excess capacity, new investment can increase capacity. With the firm's selling price providing a mark-up of costs, providing long-run average costs do not significantly increase when production capacity is expanded, profits increase through increased export sales. If the expansion of firms is at the expense of the import-competing sector, through diversion of investment and labor hired away from import-competing firms, incomes in the import-competing sector decline. A government that reciprocally liberalizes imposes losses on the domestic import-competing sector.

Since new markets that allow increased sales without increases in price are valuable to exporting firms, the exchange of market access that reciprocally benefits export firms in different countries does not require improvements in the terms of trade. Indeed, with only two countries, it is impossible for liberalization through reciprocal exchange of market access to improve the terms of trade of both countries. Each country benefits from more trade at unchanged terms of trade because protection causes each to value imports higher than what it must pay to buy them from its partner.

Unilateral liberalization would however deteriorate the terms of trade of the liberalizing country (if the country's population can collectively influence the terms of trade). Reciprocal liberalization through exchange of market access avoids significant terms of trade losses for any country. Reciprocal tariff liberalization could, for example, happen to leave the terms of trade unchanged. Export sectors in both countries will have however benefited from an increase in the relative domestic price of their products that is not neutralized even in part by a deterioration in the terms of trade.

Through reciprocal liberalization, two liberalizing governments forgo tax revenue to transfer income to their own exporters, while reciprocal liberalization prevents part of that revenue from being captured by foreign exporters. The reciprocal trade liberalization that occurs is also beneficial for society at large in each country, by moving countries closer to free trade. The social benefits of more liberal trade policies have come about, however, because of the political interest in opening foreign markets to export industries government (Hillman et al., 1995; Hillman and Moser, 1996).

2. Terms of Trade Changes

Trade liberalization as exchange of market access is consistent with the political-economy premises of a public choice view of policy determination, because of the focus on income distribution and political motives for policy decisions. An alternative view emphasizes the effects of terms of trade changes on social welfare. After governments have reciprocally imposed tariffs with the intent of improving the terms of trade, there are in general reciprocal incentives to liberalize trade. Countries can possibly be better off in the Nash equilibirum than in free trade (see *international trade policy: departure from free*), but losses incurred because of the tariffs through domestic inefficiencies and reduced volumes of trade more generally provide mutual gains from trade liberalization. Although mutual tariffs are the Nash equilibrium outcome in a single-move prisoners' dilemma game where governments impose tariffs with the intent of improving the terms of trade, applications of the theory of repeated games, and in particular the folk theorem of repeated games, show how mutually beneficial self-enforcing contracts to move toward free trade can be an equilibrium outcome. It is typically assumed that such contracts are supported by the threat that any deviation by a government would result in reversion to the static Nash equilibrium tariffs. However, in actual practice, deviations normally trigger negotiations (which in the WTO are governed by an elaborate dispute settlement procedure) to determine what retaliatory tariffs should be imposed. This raises the possibility that renegotiation could undermine the threats on which the contracts are based, and when tariff contracts are restricted to being "renegotiation proof", free trade cannot be achieved (Ludema, 2001).

When negotiations however take place to liberalize trade, the issues actually on the agenda involve willingness to reduce protectionist barriers in order to exchange market access, rather than how trade liberalization will affect the terms of trade. The contingent protection (see *international trade policy: departure from free trade*) that accompanies trade liberalization agreements confirms the political sensitivity to income distribution consequences of trade liberalization.

Still, if terms of trade changes are significant, governments would have incentives to take terms of trade changes into account when formulating policies to achieve domestic income distribution objectives (Bagwell and Staiger, 1999, 2001). Because of changes in the terms of trade, a government may not be prepared to liberalize unilaterally to assist export sectors. If the terms of trade are not determined in a broader world market, prices received by home exporters fall when the terms of trade decline because of unilateral liberalization. There are therefore two influences on prices of the export sector's output when trade liberalization is unilateral. The export sector benefits with unchanged terms of trade. If the terms of trade however deteriorate, the sensitive problem for a government may not be the social loss, but the compromise of the objective of liberalizing to benefit the export sector. Reciprocal liberalization avoids or moderates the deterioration in the terms of trade that would disadvantage exporters.

While terms of trade effects influence incentives to negotiate reciprocal liberalization when terms of trade effects are significant, the incentives for reciprocal trade liberalization are present without terms of trade changes, through the mutual political benefits from increasing exporters' incomes through reciprocal liberalization to exchange market access (Hillman et al., 1995; Hillman and Moser, 1996; Ethier, 2001, 2002).

3. Multilateral Liberalization

Trade liberalization has not been bilateral, but was negotiated in a sequence of multilateral agreements. The multilateral agreements were based on a most-favored nation clause (MFN), which required any market access for exporters from one country to be provided to exporters from all countries (Horn and Mavriodis, 2001). MFN is a means of confronting opportunism in the exchange of market access in a multi-country world (Ethier, 2001). Market access can be simultaneously exchanged with many countries, in principle at different terms. For example, two countries might negotiate trade liberalization and agree to levy tariffs of 20 percent on each other's trade, when trade with other countries is subject to higher tariffs. Afterwards, one of the two countries can proceed to negotiate further liberalization with a third country with (for example) reciprocal 10 percent import duties. The market access provided to the first trading partner is thereby devalued, since the first trading country still confronts the 20 percent tariff while the new trading partner is advantaged by the superior market access of a 10 percent tariff. The way to avoid such devaluation of benefit of negotiated market access is to insist that whatever "favors" are granted to one country are also granted to all other countries with whom trade agreements are in place. The outcome is multilateralism in trade liberalization.

Non-discrimination in trade liberalization through the MFN clause was therefore not due to principles of "fairness" and enlightenment in seeking equal treatment to establish a liberal international trading environment. The universal openness of multilateral liberalization was rather the equilibrium outcome of the non-sustainability of bilateralism in the face of potential opportunism in exchange of market access. Multilateralism protected the prior benefits of producers that had been negotiated by exchange of market access (Ethier, 2001, 2002).

4. Liberalization and Contingent Protection

Contingent protection (see *international trade policy: departure from free trade*) allows governments to protect selected industries even though prior commitments were made that trade was to be liberal. Contingent protection encourages ex-ante agreement on trade liberalization, since liberalization agreements do not have to be complete in covering all possible contingencies regarding future changes in international comparative advantage.

Contingent protection is therefore a form of political insurance when trade liberalization is negotiated. Future outcomes that are politically non-tenable can be addressed if the need arises through the provisions of contingent protection. Multilateralism adds a further dimension to the insurance role of contingent protection (Ethier, 2002). Countries negotiate trade liberalization realizing that, ex post, no sovereign government will do anything that is against its own interest. Negotiated liberalization therefore cannot exceed the liberalization preferred, ex post, by the country most reluctant to liberalize. When negotiations take place, it is not known how future changes in comparative advantage will affect different countries' exporters. Future outcomes can result in leaders (whose exporters are the most efficient), followers (whose exporters compete abroad with those of the leaders), and laggards (whose import-competing firms compete with exporters from both the leaders and the followers). The leaders will capture export markets from the laggards, and also from followers who export to the same markets. The followers, whose goods are less attractive to buyers for price or quality reasons, will then lose sales in export markets. Discriminatory protection by laggards against leaders through anti-dumping duties or voluntary export restraints protects the laggard's own home market and also protects followers from the advantages of the leaders. The form of protection however, provides the leaders with compensatory rent transfers. Adequate compensation provides leaders with incentives to accept the protection of the laggards without retaliation. Governments know at the stage of negotiation of liberalization agreements that, should their exporters in the future be followers rather than leaders, protection by the laggards will discriminate against the leaders. Under conditions of uncertainty about whose exporters will be leaders, followers, or laggards, contingent protection therefore makes liberalization more attractive than if the discriminatory contingent protection were not part of future policy possibilities. Thus, ex ante, more liberalization can be negotiated. In a multilateral context, the insurance against adverse comparative advantage outcomes provided through contingent protection is therefore also multilateral (Ethier, 2002).

5. Preferential Trading and Regionalism

Preferential trading arrangements (Pomfret, 1988) depart from MFN treatment in providing selective discriminatory exchange of market access to participating countries. While discriminatory preferences contradict MFN treatment, the arrangements are permissible in the GATT-WTO framework provided that participating countries substantially reduce internal trade barriers among themselves and that trade barriers against other countries not rise on average.

A preferential trading agreement can take the form of a customs union such as in the case of the European Union, or a free-trade area as in the case of NAFTA (North American Free Trade Agreement). The members of a customs union have a common foreign trade policy. A free-trade agreement permits each member country to maintain an independent trade policy with other non-member countries.

A free-trade agreement therefore requires internal border policing to certify the origin of goods, to prevent goods entering the free-trade area through the least protectionist country and then moving to more protectionist countries. Preferential trading arrangements are usually regional, and are part of a liberalizing process that has been called regionalism. A free-trade agreement avoids opportunist behavior in exchange of market access. By completely liberalizing all the way to free trade, the countries in the regional agreements are left with no scope for depreciating the value of the agreements by offering better terms of market access to others.

There is no assurance a customs union is on balance beneficial for a domestic population. A customs union provides benefits through liberal internal trade among member countries according to comparative advantage, and also provides benefits through a greater variety of products available to consumers in the expanded market (Levy, 1997). These gains are balanced against losses from trade diversion.

Trade diversion occurs when, because of the preference in market access to member countries, the customs union makes more expensive goods seem cheaper to a member country's consumers. For example, a good from the cheapest foreign source may cost $100, but the country is outside the customs union and an import duty of 50 percent is levied on the good. Consumers would therefore pay $150 if they purchased imports from the cheapest foreign source. Producers from a country within the customs union can supply the same good for $140, and there is no duty because of the free market access of the member country. Consumers therefore buy from the cheaper member country's producers. There is therefore a $40 loss on every unit of the good imported. If domestic consumers were to buy from the cheapest foreign source, the cost would be $100 paid to the foreign producer, and an import duty of $50 paid to the home government. A benevolent government would however return the $50 to consumers through public spending or reduced taxation, leaving a net cost to consumers of $100. In these circumstances, a country's consumers confront a multi-person prisoners' dilemma (Hillman, 1989). The country's consumers would all be better off if they collectively ignored the privately cheaper duty-free good, and bought the privately more expensive good that is less expensive at world prices.

Trade diversion can occur when a customs union complies with the GATT/WTO restriction that trade barriers against non-member countries do not increase. Under a first-best policy of non-discriminatory free trade, losses from trade diversion could not occur. A customs union is a case of the second-best, because free trade is not with everybody (Viner, 1950). Because of trade diversion, the question whether joining a customs union is beneficial for a country's population requires an empirical answer.

A free trade agreement allows each government to set import duties to avoid losses from trade diversion. If external duties in a customs union are low, prospects for trade diversion are also low: free trade within the European Union emerged in the latter parts of the 20th century in the aftermath of extensive multilateral trade liberalization that reduced the scope of anticipated losses from trade diversion. Changes in political will to protect after entry into a customs union can also diminish trade diversion (Richardson, 1993).

Although the formation of a customs union can result in net losses because of trade diversion, in principle every move towards world free trade through membership of countries in customs unions can be manipulated to be beneficial for members of the customs union without loss to other countries (Kemp and Wan, 1976). Whenever a group of countries forms a customs union, it is possible to find a common external tariff for the customs union and compensating lump-sum payments between members of the union that no person, whether in the customs union or not, is worse off than before the formation of the union. The lump-sum transfers are here among countries' governments in the first instance. Further lump-sum transfers would distribute the compensating payments to individuals. With the provision that lump-sum transfers among individuals are feasible, the path to world free trade through the formation of groups of countries into customs unions can be made Pareto-improving (that is, some people could always be made better off in each step without anyone being made worse off). A problem is that members of a customs union need have no particular incentive to constrain themselves o adopt a common external tariff that does not harm outsiders.

6. Non-economic Motives

The motives for preferential trading agreements are often non-economic. Regional governments do not usually commission measurement of gains from trade creation and losses from trade diversion. The motives for formation of the European Union were not principally economic. The intent of the founders was to end the European conflicts that had been due to past animosities among nation states, and to provide a counter to the United States. There was also a prescience that a united Germany would fit better within a united Europe.

7. Foreign Investment and Migration

Regional preferential trading arrangements are a means of poorer countries competing for foreign direct investment from richer countries (Ethier, 1998a,b). The attraction for foreign investment is that a free-trade agreement allows duty-free import of inputs and duty-free export of goods produced in poorer countries to markets of richer countries. For example, the exchange of market access through NAFTA was one sided, with low-income Mexico eliminating more protectionist barriers than the United States and Canada. In mercantilist terms, Mexico made more concessions or gave up more than it received, since it already had quite free access to the U.S. and Canadian markets. NAFTA however provided incentives for foreign investment to go into Mexico, rather than into other countries like Mexico, because of the marginal increase in market access to its northern neighbors that NAFTA gave to Mexico. From the vantage of the United States, foreign investment in Mexico, by increasing demand for local labor, could reduce incentives for illegal immigration.

8. Unilateral Trade Liberalization

Governments have sometimes liberalized trade policy unilaterally, without the strategic considerations of exchange of market access. By liberalizing unilaterally, a country's government places itself in a situation where there are no "concessions" left to exchange with foreign governments that have not likewise completely liberalized. Unilateral liberalization took place as a part of a process of development assistance to poorer countries, although evidence indicates that political influence affected the market-access concessions that were granted (Ray, 1987). Unilateral liberalization in poorer countries has also sometimes occurred as part of policy conditionality for World Bank assistance.

The most prominently researched case of unilateral trade liberalization is the repeal of the Corn Laws in 19th century England (Irwin, 1989; Schonhardt-Bailey, 1996, 1997). The Napoleonic Wars had provided natural protection for English agriculture. Afterwards, the natural protection was replaced by protection through government policy. One hypothesis is that repeal of the Corn Laws, as the protectionist polices were known, reflected enlightened liberal trade policy responding to the case for free trade that had been made by David Ricardo through his theory of comparative advantage. A political economy view looks in the direction of political popularity and private self-interest to explain the unilateral trade liberalization. England imported food, and the real wage was determined in terms of food. The agricultural interests who benefited from the protection provided by the Corn Laws had however successfully resisted trade liberalization for some decades. The trade liberalization took place when the previous stringent opposition of agricultural interests had subsided. An investigation of the asset composition in the estates left by landowners reveals diversification of asset ownership out of land and into transport and industry (Schonhardt-Bailey, 1991). No one in a country would have an interest in protectionist policies and there would be national consensus for free trade, if domestic asset markets permit the population of a country to perfectly diversify asset holdings to reflect the composition of national productive assets or resources. Free trade, which maximizes national income, would then also maximize each individual's personal income. It is *asymmetric* domestic asset ownership that defines special interests, and which underlies the political-economy relation between income distribution and endogenous protectionist policies. The asset diversification of prior landed interests is consistent with a change from previous support for protection to support for trade liberalization.

More generally, amenability to trade liberalization can be linked to development of domestic and global asset markets that have allowed diversification of personal income sources (Feeney and Hillman, 2001). The asset diversification moderates or eliminates the association between individuals' incomes and special-interest industry identities. Industry-specific factors of production continue to exist, but the income from the industry-specific factors is spread by opportunities for diversification in asset ownership. As asset markets became more developed in the second half of the 20th century, the asset diversification reduced industry-specific associations and changed personal interests to be more supportive of trade liberalization. When governments negotiated trade liberalization, asset markets moderated prior domestic opposition to liberal trade policy, and there were more beneficiaries of the expanded national income from exchange of market access.

Markets allowing people directly to diversify their human capital holdings do not exist, and there is a question whether opportunities for diversification of physical capital allow a fully diversified portfolio to be achieved by balancing non-diversifiable human capital against diversifiable physical capital. There will also be principal-agent problems when individuals are completely diversified. Risk-averse investors invest in mutual funds to diversify their asset portfolios, and if fully diversified have an interest in trade liberalization. At the same time, stock option schemes, which are intended to give managers an interest in the profitability of individual firms, also give managers an interest in lobbying for industry protection that increases the value of the stock options. Solving the shareholder-manager principal-agent problem through stock options therefore gives rise to another principal-agent problem where managers resist the liberal trade policies that benefit diversified shareholders (Cassing, 1996).

9. Globalization

Liberalization of international trade, and also of international capital transactions, resulted toward the end of the 20th century in a phenomenon known as globalization. The term globalization refers to the integration of national markets into global markets. Globalization occurred as multilateral trade liberalization and the regional agreements reduced trade barriers among the richer countries, and as restrictions on international capital market transactions were lifted. Globalization was also facilitated by new ease of international communications. Trade patterns changed that had previously been based on the richer countries trading among themselves and importing raw materials and low-valued goods from poorer countries. In the United States, the proportion of imports from the poorer countries to the richer countries increased from 14 percent in 1970 to 35 percent in 1990. In western Europe the increase was from 5 percent to 12 percent in the same period (inclusive of intra-European trade). The types of goods exported by the poorer countries also changed. By 1992, 58 percent of the exports from the developing countries to the developed world were light manufactured goods, compared with 5 percent in 1955 when many of the poorer countries were still colonies of European countries. The change in the volume and composition of the international trade of poorer countries was accompanied by increased international mobility of capital. Political risk was reduced in those poorer countries where the rule of law prevailed and private property rights were protected. Adherence to the rule of law provides assurance for foreign investors that their ownership rights were protected. At the same time, domestic changes in the poorer countries led to improvements in education and health of the local populations, which permitted domestic labor to be mobilized for organized market activity.

The changes affected domestic income distribution. Economic theory predicts that, without international investment and migration, free trade in goods in the long run equalizes real wages internationally or at least reduces wage differences. When liberalization of capital movements and foreign investment equalizes risk-adjusted returns to capital across countries, real wages tend to be equalized in the short run. As trade liberalization proceeds, domestic changes are in particular predicted to take place in income distribution to the detriment of the unskilled low-human capital workers in the richer human-capital abundant countries of the world. The equalizing tendencies in real wages become more pronounced when substantial migration from poorer to richer countries takes place, legally and illegally. When income distribution becomes globalized, personal incomes tend to depend more on individuals' personal capabilities and education rather than on where they live. Thus, in the latter part of the 20th century, real incomes of unskilled workers in richer countries declined absolutely, and also relative to skilled workers' incomes. For example, the U.S. male college-education high-school premium was 40 percent in 1979 and 74 percent in 1996. During the same period, the male college premium for completion of high school increased from 73 percent to 157 percent. For women, the college-high school graduation premium increased from 50 percent in 1979 to 72 percent in 1989, and then remained more or less constant throughout the remainder of the century. Inequality also increased in the relative incomes of younger and older workers: the mean annual income premium for male workers aged 45–54 relative to those aged 25–34 rose from a ratio of 1.15 in 1979 to 1.27 in 1989, and then to 1.35 by 1995 (source: Brauer, 1998). Such changes in income distribution in the United States have been described as an "economic disaster (that) has befallen low-skilled Americans, especially young men" (Freeman, 1995). In the "social markets" of Europe, the adverse effects for people with low skills were felt more in terms of unemployment levels than reduced market incomes.

Trade liberalization is not the sole reason for decline in incomes and employment of unskilled workers in the richer countries. Technological change also reduced demand for unskilled workers. The liberalization of international trade occurred simultaneously with a technological revolution in information technologies that required complementary skills and education (Krueger, 1993; Burtless, 1995). There were also new standards of employee responsibility, since capricious or inept employee behavior became extremely costly for employers. The changes in income distribution are a consequence of influences of both trade liberalization and technology. An approach to identifying the contribution of trade liberalization is to look for possible relative price changes that would have given rise to the income changes. Yet also reciprocal and multilateral liberalization through exchange of market access neutralizes or dampens any terms of trade changes that would be associated with unilateral liberalization.

Unskilled workers were disadvantaged by incentives for the introduction of the new technologies associated with trade liberalization (Wood, 1994). Through the new technologies, producers in high labor-cost countries sought ways to compete with low labor-cost foreign goods by substituting domestic unskilled labor with domestic skilled labor. Because domestic unskilled labor could not compete with the cheaper foreign unskilled labor used to produce lower-quality imports, a change to higher quality production also took place.

Demand for low-skill labor also declined in richer countries as producers responded to trade liberalization through outsourcing. Imports from foreign cheap-labor sources thereby replaced domestic production of intermediate goods that used low skilled labor, contracting employment opportunities and wages of local unskilled workers then declined. Evidence suggests that outsourcing explains some 20 percent of the substitution toward skilled nonproduction workers in the United States in the 1980s (Feenstra and Hansen, 1996). Outsourcing takes place when trade liberalization allows foreign intermediate goods to be used in place of domestic production without a penalty for use of foreign goods.

10. Opposition to Globalization

Low-skilled persons in richer countries have self-interested reasons to oppose globalization. Although low skilled, these people have had expectations of a standard of living that is due to them because they live in a country that is on aggregate wealthy. After globalization, the principal difference between being low skilled in rich and poor countries is in the role of the state in richer countries as a provider of last resort (Rodrik, 1998).

Trade liberalization and outsourcing increase incomes in the poorer countries of the world. Opponents of globalization have however pointed to adverse effects in the poorer countries through labor standards and the environment (Bhagwati and Hudec, 1996; Anderson, 1997). Where child labor is a social norm, trade liberalization increases the demand for child labor because of improved foreign market access for goods produced by children. The opposition to child labor as a matter of social conscience then becomes opposition to globalization (or trade liberalization).

Domestic industries in richer countries may confront competition from foreign goods produced by children or foreign investment may take place to take advantage of the low costs of using child labor. Higher labor standards in poor countries benefit domestic producers and workers in rich countries by increasing production costs in poor countries. Again economic and humanitarian objectives become intertwined (Hefeker and Wunner, 2002). Protectionist policies in richer countries would also protect producers and workers in richer countries and protect foreign workers from low foreign labor standards by denying market access for the foreign produced goods. If foreign labor standards cannot be changed, foreign labor standards become the basis for a case for protection to keep the foreign goods produced with the foreign labor standards out of the markets of richer countries (Agel and Lundborg, 1995). Coalitions composed of producers and groups seeking social policies can form to oppose globalization (Hillman and Ursprung, 1992). Producers and workers seeking protection from import competition can be bedfellows (wanted or unwanted) with groups seeking protection of the environment and seeking to improve working conditions and end child labor in poor countries. Opposition to globalization has been particularly fierce when multinational firms, whose owners are principally in richer countries, use child labor or employ foreign labor at prevailing market wages and conditions of the poorer countries.

Local employers in poorer countries have not been subject to the same scrutiny as multinational firms. Nor have local restrictions in poorer countries on the freedom and rights of women, nor practices such as genital mutilation of pubescent female children, been reasons for outrage of opponents of globalization. Opponents of globalization have not protested the corrupt behavior of rulers in poorer countries and the policies that keep the poor in poor countries in sustained poverty. Nor is the observation heralded that the highest inequality is in the poorer countries of the world where the political elites rule the poor. The opponents of globalization have an agenda that blames poverty in poor countries on open world markets, rather than calling for change in the behavior of political elites in poorer countries who sustain poverty by failing to use aid resources to improve living conditions of the general population (Rowley, 2000; Easterly, 1991; Hillman, 2002).

The environment is also an issue for opponents of globalization. Clearing of rain forests and destruction of animals and their habitats is linked to demand in international markets. The opponents of globalization blame open markets, rather than confronting the foreign political elites who sell rights to deforestation.

Preferences regarding labor standards, sending children to school, and for environmental quality can reflect income differences rather than cultural attributes. As incomes increase in poorer countries, preferences can consequently be expected to become more uniform over time. Globalization furthers this objective by increasing incomes in poorer countries through market integration with richer countries, and is therefore pro-environment (Grossman and Kreuger, 1993). Political rulers may however not be responsive to the preferences and wishes of their citizens who seek to end child labor and end clearing of rain forests and destruction of animal habitats. The source of the problems that concern social activists is then again not globalization, but governments in poor countries that do not provide adequate resources for schools and continue environmental degradation for personal profit. It is interesting that the opponents of globalization have preferred to blame markets rather than blaming governments and political elites in poorer countries for exploitative labor standards and damaging environmental policies.

ARYE L. HILLMAN

REFERENCES

Agel, J. and Lundborg, P. (1995). "Fair wages in an open economy." *Economica*, 62: 335–351.

Anderson, K. (1997). "Social policy dimensions of economic integration: environmental and labor standards," in I. Takatoshi and A.O. Krueger (eds.) *Regionalism versus Multilateral Trade Arrangements*. Chicago: The University of Chicago Press.

Bagwell, K. and Staiger R.W. (1999). "An economic theory of GATT." *American Economic Review*, 89: 215–248.

Bagwell K. and Staiger, R.W. (2001). "Reciprocity, non-discrimination and preferential agreements in the multilateral trading system." *European Journal of Political Economy*, 17: 281–325.

Bhagwati, J.N. and Hudec, R.E. (eds.) (1996). *Fair Trade and Harmonization: Prerequisites for Free Trade*. Cambridge, MA: MIT Press.

Brauer, D. (1998). "The changing US income distribution: facts, explanations, and unresolved issues." Working Paper No. 9811, Federal Reserve Bank of New York.

Burtless, G. (1995). "International trade and the rise in earnings inequality." *Journal of Economic Literature*, 33: 800–816.

Cassing, J.H. (1996). "Protectionist mutual funds." *European Journal of Political Economy*, 12: 1–18.

Easterly, W. (1991). *The Elusive Quest for Growth: Economists' Adventures and Misadventures in the Tropics*. Cambridge, MA: MIT Press.

Ethier, W.J. (1998a). "Regionalism in a multilateral world." *Journal of Political Economy*, 106: 1214–1245.

Ethier, W.J. (1998b). "The new regionalism." *Economic Journal*, 108: 1149–1161.

Ethier, W.J. (2001). "Theoretical problems in negotiating trade liberalization." *European Journal of Political Economy*, 17: 209–232.

Ethier, W.J. (2002). "Unilateralism in a multilateral world." *Economic Journal*, 112: 266–292.

Feeney, J. and Hillman, A.L. (2001). "Privatization and the political economy of strategic trade policy." *International Economic Review*, 42: 535–556.

Feenstra, R. and Hansen, G. (1996). "Globalization, outsourcing, and wage inequality." *American Economic Review, Papers and Proceedings*, 86: 240–245.

Freeman, R.B. (1995). "Are your wages being set in Beijing?" *Journal of Economic Perspectives*, 9: 15–32.

Grossman, G.M. and Krueger, A.B. (1993). "Environmental impacts of a North-American free trade agreement," in P. Garber (ed.) *The Mexican–U.S. Free Trade Agreement*. Cambridge, MA: MIT Press.

Hefeker, C. and Wunner, N. (2002). "The producer interest in foreign labor standards." *European Journal of Political Economy*, 18: 429–447.

Hillman, A.L. (1989). "Resolving the puzzle of welfare reducing trade diversion: a prisoners' dilemma interpretation." *Oxford Economic Papers*, 41: 452–455.

Hillman, A.L. (2002). "The World Bank and the persistence of poverty in poor countries." *European Journal of Political Economy*, 18.

Hillman, A.L., Long, N.V., and Moser, P. (1995). "Modeling reciprocal trade liberalization: the political-economy and national-welfare perspectives." *Swiss Journal of Economics and Statistics*, 131: 503–515.

Hillman, A.L. and Moser, P. (1996). "Trade liberalization as politically optimal exchange of market access," in M. Canzoneri, W.J. Ethier, and V. Grilli (eds.) *The New Transatlantic Economy*. New York: Cambridge University Press, pp. 295–312; reprinted in K. Anderson and B. Hoekman (eds.) *The Global Trading System*, Volume 2, *Core Rules and Procedures* I.B. Tauris and Co Ltd, London and New York, 2002.

Hillman, A.L. and Ursprung, H.W. (1992). "The influence of environmental concerns on the political determination of international trade policy," in R. Blackhurst and K. Anderson (eds.) *The Greening of World Trade Issues*. Brookfield. Wheatsheaf, pp. 195–220.

Horn, H. and Mavriodis, P. (2001). "Economic and legal aspects of the most-favored-nation clause." *European Journal of Political Economy*, 17: 233–279.

Irwin, D. (1989). "Political economy and Peel's repeal of the Corn laws." *Economics and Politics*, 1: 41–59.

Kemp, M.C. and Wan, H. (1976). "An elementary proposition concerning the formation of customs unions." *Journal of International Economics*, 6: 95–97; reprinted in M.C. Kemp (ed.) *The Gains From Trade and the Gains From Trade: Essays* in *International Trade Theory*. London: Routledge, 1995, pp. 37–40.

Krueger, A.B. (1993). "How computers have changed the wage structure: evidence from microdata 1984–1989." *Quarterly Journal of Economics*, 107: 33–60.

Levy, P.I. (1997). "The political economy of free-trade agreements." *American Economic Review*, 87: 506–519.

Ludema, R.D. (2001). "Optimal international trade agreements and dispute settlement procedures." *European Journal of Political Economy*, 17: 355–376.

Pomfret, R. (1988). *Unequal Trade: The Economics of Discriminatory Trade Agreements*. Oxford: Basil Blackwell.

Ray, E. (1987). "The impact of special interests on preferential trade concessions by the U.S." *Review of Economics and Statistics*, 69: 187–195.

Richardson, M. (1993). "Endogenous protection and trade diversion." *Journal of International Economics*, 34: 309–324.

Rodrik, D. (1998). "Why do more open economies have bigger governments?" *Journal of Political Economy*, 106: 997–1032.

Rowley, C. (2000). "Political culture and economic performance in sub-Saharan Africa." *European Journal of Political Economy*, 16: 133–158.

Schonhardt-Bailey, C. (1991). "Specific factors, capital markets, portfolio diversification, and free trade: domestic determinants of repeal of the Corn laws." *World Politics*, 43: 545–569.

Schonhardt-Bailey, C. (1996). *Free Trade: The Repeal of the Corn Laws*. Bristol: Thoemmes Press.

Schonhardt-Bailey, C. (1997). *The Rise of Free Trade*, Volumes 1–4. London: Routledge.

Tullock, G. (1991). "Accidental freedom," in A.L. Hillman (ed.) *Markets and Politicians: Politicized Economic Choice*. Boston and Dordrecht: Kluwer Academic Publishers, pp. 93–122.

Viner, J. (1950). *The Customs Union Issue*. New York: Carnegie Endowment for International Peace.

Wood, A. (1994). *North-South Trade, Employment, and Inequality: Changing Fortunes in a Skill-Driven World*. Oxford: Clarendon Press.

WILLIAM H. RIKER

William Harrison Riker, one of the founders of the Public Choice Society, arguably transformed the discipline of Political Science more than any single individual in the last half-century, creating the possibility of a genuine science of politics. It is difficult to measure the relative importance of his own scholarship, the vision of the scientific enterprise he imposed on the discipline, the training he gave a new generation of scholars, and the integration of this new understanding of political science into the social sciences. Each on their own was a legacy few achieve. Collectively, his contributions are, like the man himself, peerless.

Bill, as he was called, was born in Des Moines, Iowa, on September 22, 1920. He died June 26, 1993. His beloved wife, Mary Elizabeth (M.E.) whom he married in 1943, passed away on March 14, 2002. He had two daughters and two sons, one of whom died twenty years before Bill.

Bill graduated from DePauw University in 1942. He deferred an acceptance to attend the University of Chicago that was the leading graduate program in Political Science in the pre-War years so that he could work in support of the war effort at RCA. In 1944, he concluded that Harvard University had emerged as the leading program, and left RCA to enter Harvard's Ph.D. program. He received his degree from there in 1948. He took a position at Lawrence College (now Lawrence University) that year, rising to the rank of Professor before he left for the University of Rochester in 1962, his home for the rest of his life.

Bill's training at Harvard was conventional for its day, although one must credit his contact with Professor Pendleton Herring for association with a scholar who, while not "scientific" in the sense Riker came to believe in, nonetheless was systematic in his analyses (see Shepsle, 2002). It was therefore only later at Lawrence College, learning and working on his own, that he developed his views on the nature of political science and its place among the social sciences. In 1954, the leading journal of the discipline, the *American Political Science Review*, published "A Method for Evaluating the Distribution of Power in a Committee System," by L.S. Shapley and Martin Shubik. In it, they developed their "power index" and applied it to the bicameral U.S. Congress and to the U. N. Security Council. This Shapley-Shubik power index is a special case of the Shapley value, and the article provided citations to that original paper (1953), Von Neumann and Morganstern's *Theory of Games and Economic Behavior* (1944, 1947) and Arrow's *Social Choice and Individual Values* (1951). These works, Downs' *An Economic Theory of Democracy* (1957), Buchanan and Tullock's *The Calculus of Consent: Logical Foundations of Constitutional Democracy* (1962), Duncan Black's *The Theory of Committees and Elections* (1958) and Black and R.A. Newing's *Committee Decisions with Complementary Valuations* (1951) provided Bill the rational choice theory through which he would seek to achieve a scientific study of politics.

These studies had three major consequences for his work over the remainder of the 1950s. First, his studies led him to think deeply about the nature of science, resulting in two papers in the *Journal of Philosophy*, "Events and Situations" (1957) and "Causes of Events" (1958). Second, he began to consider the potential for rational choice theory, in general, and game theory in particular, to explain politics. He first did so by applying theories of others, beginning with "The Paradox of Voting and Congressional Rules for Voting on Amendments," published in the *American Political Science Review* (1958). Shortly thereafter, these considerations also led him to revise an introductory text on American government he had written earlier (originally published in 1953), transforming it into the first rational choice book aimed at undergraduate audiences in Political Science (1965). He would soon develop his own theory of political coalitions, based on game theory. But first came the third major consequence of his theoretical development, one that included recognition from the academy, via becoming a Fellow at the Center for Advanced Study in the Behavioral Sciences in 1960–61.

His thinking on how to study politics had now almost fully matured. In his application to the Center, he wrote (quoted in Bueno de Mesquita and Shepsle, 2001, p. 8):

> I describe the field in which I expect to work at the Center as 'formal, positive political theory.' By Formal, I mean the expression of the theory in algebraic rather than verbal symbols. By positive I means the expression of descriptive rather than normative propositions.... I visualize the growth in political science of a body of theory somewhat similar to...the neo-classical theory of value in economics. It seems to be that a number of propositions from the mathematical theory of games can be woven into a theory of politics. Hence, my main interest at present is attempting to use game theory for the construction of political theory.

His Fellowship year was devoted primarily to writing *The Theory of Political Coalitions* (1962) which served as the study that backed those hopes with results. This book marked a transition from applying the work of others to creation of his own theory. He recognized his account as taking off from ideas in *Theory of Games and Economic Behavior*, but unlike Von Neumann and Morgenstern, he developed the "size principle" for the case of n-person, zero-sum games. At this point he believed that politics was best understood as being a contest about winning and losing, and thus about zero-sum games, although later he would see that winning and losing did not necessarily lead to the zero-sum property. *The Theory of Political Coalitions* was more than the first fully developed rational choice theory by a political scientist. The book had a major impact on traditional political scientists and was widely used by the contemporary profession in guiding their empirical work, perhaps most heavily in the analysis of governing coalitions in multi-party parliaments. It thus was the first choice-theoretic (to say nothing of being the first game-theoretic) study to shape traditional scholarship in his discipline.

The 1960s were a time of even more dramatic changes in Bill's career. In 1962, not only was *The Theory of Political Coalitions* published, but he also accepted the position of chairman at the University of Rochester, beginning a 15-year tenure as department chair. His task was to create a new Ph.D. program in Political Science that reflected his understanding of what a science of politics could be. He took what was essentially a small-to-medium sized liberal arts college's department and expanded it considerably — all the way up to 13 members a decade later! He did so by adding young scholars such as Arthur Goldberg, Richard Niemi, and John Mueller, who were trained as close to the vision Riker held of the discipline as was then possible, to the more traditional scholars already on hand. Of these young scholars, Jerry Kramer most fully embodied this vision with serious mathematical capabilities, well beyond those of anyone else then in the discipline, tied to a deep interest in matters political.

Perhaps the most remarkable first achievement of his chairmanship was the ability to graft a new political science on to a standing department, and the greatest fruit of this tree was the long-running, intellectual and collegial departmental leadership coalition of Riker and Richard Fenno. This pairing created a remarkable training ground for new scholars almost immediately upon formation. The new program went from unranked to one ranked as number 14 in the nation by the end of the 1960s, that is, in under a decade of existence, and then to a "top ten" ranking the next time such comparisons were made a decade later. At the end of its first decade, Bill's program already had or was in the process of training scholars who would play a role in the Public Choice Society, would be elected to the American Academy of Arts and Sciences, and/or would join Riker and Fenno in the National Academy of Sciences. These included such as Peter Aranson, Morris Fiorina, Richard McKelvey, Peter Ordeshook, David Rohde, and Kenneth Shepsle (as well as this author).

The 1960s were, for Bill, fruitful not only in institutional creation, through the Ph.D. program he created and his role in forming the Public Choice Society, but also in terms of his own scholarship. In 1964, Little-Brown published his *Federalism: Origin, Operation, Maintenance* which some consider his greatest work. He, often with his graduate students, launched what are believed to be the first laboratory game experiments in political science (e.g., his "Bargaining in Three-Person Games," [1967] and with William James Zavoina, "Rational Behavior in Politics: Evidence from a Three-Person Game," [1970] both in the *American Political Science Review*). His 1968 article with then graduate student Ordeshook, "A Theory of the Calculus of Voting" (also in the *American Political Science Review*), remains controversial, heavily cited, and, it is fair to say, seminal over three decades later. In some ways, it could be said that this intellectual decade ended with the publication in 1973 of his and Ordeshook's *An Introduction to Positive Political Theory*. This last book has associated with the actual title on its dust jacket the informal subtitle, "A synthesis and exposition of current trends in descriptive political theory based on axiomatic and deductive reasoning." It stands as the first graduate-level text of the application of rational choice theory to political problems, reflecting how much work had been in the area Bill had launched in the discipline less than two decades earlier. To be sure, much of the original work considered had been done by social scientists in other disciplines (still mostly, but not exclusively, economics), but a substantial amount was done by political scientists. More to the point, the book covered a much wider variety of topics common to politics, especially democratic politics, than would have been possible a decade earlier. These included chapters on political participation, voting and elections, legislatures, and regulation and other aspects of bureaucracies.

While Bill had a truly far ranging intellect and therefore worked on a remarkable array of topics, he made unusual contributions to the study of three more questions that seem in retrospect to evolve naturally from what he had accomplished by 1973. Rational choice theory made its first and greatest impact (largely through Riker and the department he created) in the study of various aspects of the democratic process. In 1982, his *Liberalism Against Populism: A Confrontation Between the Theory of Democracy and the Theory of Social Choice* (W.H. Freeman) brought the increasingly wide ranging and deepening set of formal results to bear on the normative foundations of democracy. His basic claim was that the results from social choice theory essentially rendered democracy as a choice between or among competing platforms (or what he meant by "populism") meaningless. He found in the results, however, the basis for justification of Madisonian liberalism, by which he meant elections as a referendum on the incumbent office holders.

Liberalism Against Populism also included results about the second of the three topics, institutions. One of the things that made the formal study of government and politics different from the study of market economies, especially in this period of work under general equilibrium theory, was that institutions both structured political competition and were the result of that competition. In 1982, he began to develop the theoretical underpinnings of what he considered to be about as close to a law-like regularity in politics as could be found in his essay, "The Two-Party System and Duverger's Law: An Essay on the History of Political Science," (*American Political Science Review*). This, he suggested, was an institutional equilibrium resulting from the interactions of citizens and their political leaders taking place within a particular institutional context, in this case the context of plurality voting. While Duverger's Law was therefore an institutional equilibrium, it was not a general one, because it was quite possible to change the institutional context. Political leadership unhappy with the two-party system need only change its elections from plurality to proportional methods, as New Zealand did in the 1990s, for example. As the theory would predict, that system changed from an essentially exact two-party system, with one of the two winning majority control of their legislature, to one with two larger parties but sufficient smaller ones to deny either party majority control. This point about the "endogeneity" of institutions is general, he argued two years earlier. In 1980, he had made a devastating argument about the consequences of the general absence of voting (and other) equilibrium in politics (making politics, he claimed, the "truly dismal science"). In "Implications from the Disequilibrium of Majority Rule for the Study of Institutions" (*American Political Science Review*, 1980), he argued that the disequilibrium of voting was "inherited" by a sort of backwards induction onto the choices of rules. As a result, institutions were themselves as problematic as voting — the same problem that undermined "populism" in his thinking undermined institutions as well. He thus viewed institutions as little more than a temporary "congealing of tastes." They were no more a general equilibrium than was any other voting outcome, and they therefore carry no more moral weight.

Bill began his journey by seeking to establish a science of politics on the basis of game theory. That journey led him and his fellow scholars to discover that the science of politics was very different from the science of economics, from which his ideas originated. The political analogy to the market is the election, but the analogy does not lead to a general equilibrium outcome, but one in which disequilibrium (or, its essential equivalent in these terms, a seemingly infinite number of equilibria) are common place. In addition, the problem of government is that of power, and in particular that those who choose outcomes also choose large portions of the rules under which the government operates. The selection of these institutional features is just as fraught with instability (and lack ethical justification) as is the passage of ordinary legislation. Bill therefore turned to seek a new way to think about choice under disequilibrium (or a proliferation of equilibria). He turned to acts of political leadership, looking at what he called political "heresthetics." This term was his creation to cover instances of manipulation of the strategic context to turn uncertain outcomes in one's favor. He first made this sort of argument in his presidential address to the American Political Science Association, "The Heresthetics of Constitution Making: The Presidency in 1787, with Comments on Determinism and Rational Choice" (published in the *American Political Science Review* in 1984). It was itself a heresthetical act of Riker to put this art of strategy to the academy first in that most "sacred" of secular locations, the founding of this Republic. He then collected a series of case studies to illustrate and develop this account in his *The Art of Political Manipulation* (Yale, 1986). He continued the attempt to develop this part of the scientific explanation of politics to the end of his life, ending with a posthumously published account of the passage of the U.S. Constitution in the various states, *The Strategy of Rhetoric* (Yale, 1996).

While Bill succeeded in redefining the discipline of Political Science, his work began, as it ended, in the larger realm of social science more generally. He began by drawing from Economics and from game theory. In the middle, his and Ordeshook's *An Introduction to Positive Political Theory* (1973) was a rich application of the work of many social scientists, including those cited already and other prominent Public Choice scholars such as Mancur Olson. Indeed, it was often through the Society, its journal and its annual meetings that this work grew. Twenty years later, he and his students in political science were developing theories of social phenomena of sufficient originality and importance to return the favor to Public Choice scholars in other disciplines.

In the end, then, William H. Riker succeeded in placing political science within the set of scientifically-based social sciences. He was among the first social scientists to apply game theory systematically to any major set of problems in a sustained way. He extended this vision to the discipline through his own work and that of the students he directly trained at the University of Rochester and at the (increasing numbers of) graduate programs that have emulated his. He linked political science to the other scientific social sciences, once again through his own scholarship and through institution building, notably through the Public Choice Society. He then brought his considerable energies to bear on understanding the nature and ethical standing of democracy through implications of the scientific results of he and his students. He addressed the central problem of politics (who rules the rulers) by including the study of institutions and of leadership in that "formal, positive political theory" he had promised forty years earlier.

JOHN ALDRICH

REFERENCES

Arrow, Kenneth J. (1951). *Social Choice and Individual Values*. New York: John Wiley & Sons.

Black, Duncan (1958). *The Theory of Committees and Elections*. Cambridge, England: Cambridge University Press.

Black, Duncan and Newing, R.A. (1951). *Committee Decisions with Complementary Valuation*. London: William Hodge and Co.

Buchanan, James M. and Gordon Tullock (1962). *The Calculus of Consent*. Ann Arbor, MI. University of Michigan Press.

Bueno de Mesquita, Bruce and Kenneth Shepsle (2001). "William Harrison Riker: 1920–1993. *Biographical Memoirs*. National Academy of Sciences. 79: 3–22.

Downs, Anthony (1957). *An Economic Theory of Democracy*. New York: Harper and Row.

Riker, William H. (1962). *The Theory of Political Coalitions*. New Haven, CT: Yale University Press.

Riker, William H. (1957). "Event and situations." *Journal of Philosophy*, 54: 57–70.

Riker, William H. (1958). "Causes of events." *Journal of Philosophy*, 56: 281–292.

Riker, William H. (1958). "The paradox of voting and congressional rules for voting on amendments." *American Political Science Review*, 52: 349–366.

Riker, William H. (1953). *Democracy in the United States*. New York: MacMillan.

Riker, William H. (1964). *Federalism: Origin, Operation, Maintenance*. Boston: Little-Brown.

Riker, William H. (1965). *Democracy in the United States*, Second Edition. New York: MacMillan.

Riker, William H. (1967). "Bargaining in three-person games." *American Political Science Review*, 61: 342–356.

Riker, William H. (1980). "Implications from the disequilibrium of majority rule for the study of institutions." *American Political Science Review*, 74: 432–446.

Riker, William H. (1982). *Liberalism Against Populism: A Confrontation Between the Theory of Democracy and the Theory of Social Choice*. San Francisco, CA: W.H. Freeman.

Riker, William H. (1982). "The two-party system and duverger's law: an essay on the history of political science." *American Political Science Review*, 76: 753–766.

Riker, William H. (1984). "The heresthetics of constitution making: the presidency in 1787, with comments on determinism and rational choice." *American Political Science Review*, 78: 1–16.

Riker, William H. (1986). *The Art of Political Manipulation*. New Haven, CT: Yale University Press.

Riker, William H. (1996). *The Strategy of Rhetoric* (published posthumously with the assistance of R. Calvert, J. Mueller, and R. Wilson). New Haven, CT: Yale University Press.

Riker, William H. and Peter C. Ordeshook (1968). "A theory of the calculus of voting." *American Political Science Review*, 62: 25–42.

Riker, William H. and Peter C. Ordeshook (1973). *An Introduction to Positive Political Theory*. Englewood Cliffs, NJ: Prentice-Hall.

Riker, William H. and William James Zavoina (1970). "Rational behavior in politics." *American Political Science Review*, 64: 48–60.

Shapley, L.S. (1953). "A value for n-person games." *Annals of Mathematics Study*, 28: 307–317.

Shapley, L.S. and Martin Shubik (1954). "A method for evaluating the distribution of power in a committee system." *American Political Science Review*, 48: 787–792.

Shepsle, Kenneth A. (2002). "Political losers." Inaugural William H. Riker Lecture, Public Choice Society, San Diego, CA, March 23.

Von Neumann, John, and Oscar Morganstern (1944, 1947). *Theory of Games and Economic Behavior*. Princeton, NJ: Princeton University Press.

Biographies

ALDRICH, John Herbert

Born
September 24, 1947, Pittsburgh, Pennsylvania, USA

Current Position
Pfizer-Pratt University Professor of Political Science, Duke University, Durham, North Carolina, 1997–

Degrees
B.A., Allegheny College, 1969; M.A., Ph.D., University of Rochester, 1971, 1975.

Offices and Honors
Co-Editor, *American Journal of Political Science*, 1985–1988 (with John L. Sullivan).
President, Southern Political Science Association, 1988–1989.
Fellow, Center for Advanced Study in the Behavioral Sciences, 1989–1990.
Fellow, Bellagio Center, 2002.
Heinz Eulau Award (best article in the *American Political Science Review*), 1990 (with Eugene Borgida and John L. Sullivan).
Gladys Kammerer Award (best book on U.S. national policy, APSA), 1996.
CQ Press Award (Legislative Studies Section, APSA, best paper on legislative politics), 1996 (with David Rohde).
Pi Sigma Alpha Award (best paper, SPSA), 1997 (with David Rohde).
Fellow, American Academy of Arts and Sciences.

Principal Fields of Interest
American Politics; Democratic Theory; Political Economy; Methodology.

Selected Publications
Books
1. *Before the Convention: Strategies and Choices in Presidential Nomination Campaigns* (University of Chicago Press, 1980).
2. *Change and Continuity in the 1980 Elections* (CQ Press, 1982) (with Paul R. Abramson and David W. Rohde) (Revised edition, 1983).
3. *Analysis with a Limited Dependent Variable: Linear Probability, Logit, and Probit Models* (Sage Series on Quantitative Analysis, 1984) (with Forrest Nelson).
4. *Why Parties? The Origin and Transformation of Political Parties in America* (University of Chicago Press, 1995).
5. *Change and Continuity in the 2000 Elections* (CQ Press, 2002) (with Paul R. Abramson and David W. Rohde).

Articles
1. "A method of scaling with applications to the 1968 and 1972 U.S. presidential elections." *American Political Science Review*, 11(March):1977 (with Richard McKelvey).
2. "The dilemma of a paretian liberal: some consequences of Sen's theorem," and "Liberal games: further thoughts on social choice and game theory." *Public Choice*, 30(Summer):1977.
3. "Electoral choice in 1972: a test of some theorems of the spatial model of electoral competition." *Journal of Mathematical Sociology*, 5:1977.
4. "A dynamic model of presidential nomination campaigns." *American Political Science Review*, 14(September):1980.
5. "A spatial model with party activists: implications for electoral dynamics," and "rejoinder." *Public Choice*, 41:1983.
6. "A downsian spatial model with party activism." *American Political Science Review*, 17(December):1983.
7. "Southern parties in state and nation." *Journal of Politics*, August:2000.
8. "Challenges to the American two-party system: evidence from the 1968, 1980, 1992, and 1996 presidential elections." *Political Research Quarterly*, 53(3):2000 (with Paul R. Abramson, Phil Paolino, and David W. Rohde).
9. "Conditional party government in the States." *American Journal of Political Science*, 46(1):2002 (with James S. Coleman Battista).

Principal Contributions
John Aldrich has worked primarily on various aspects of democratic practices. These have included developing and applying theories of electoral politics in American and comparative elections and theories of individual political behavior. He then turned to institutional models. He developed a theory of political parties, particularly in the American setting, which led to a long series of collaborations with David Rohde, in which they have developed a theory of legislative politics in the presence of political parties. A final major project, in collaboration with a number of others, examines the impact of economic globalization (or other forms of uncertainty-inducing economic shocks) on the public's policy preferences and political demands. Aldrich has tried to combine methods and approaches from Economics, Psychology, and History, along with those from his own discipline, under the supposition that genuine progress in understanding human choices is most likely only through the most general application of the social and behavioral sciences.

ANDERSON, Lisa Reneé

Born
June 8, 1967, Petersburg, Virginia, USA

Current Position
Associate Professor of Economics, The College of William and Mary, 2002–.

Past Positions
Assistant Professor of Economics, The College of William and Mary, 1997–2002; Visiting Assistant Professor, American University, 1995–1997.

Degrees
B.S., M.A., Virginia Commonwealth University, 1988, 1989; M.A., Ph.D., University of Virginia, 1992, 1994.

Principal Fields of Interest
Experimental Economics; Economics of Information; Public Choice.

Selected Publications
Books
1. "Public choice as an experimental science," in Shughart and Razzolini (eds.) *The Elgar Companion to Public Choice* (Edward Elgar Publishing, 2001).
2. "Information cascades and rational conformity" forthcoming in McCabe (ed.) *The Encyclopedia of Cognitive Science* (Macmillan, 2003) (with C. Holt).
3. "Information cascade experiments" forthcoming in Plott and Smith (eds.) *The Handbook of Results in Experimental Economics* (North-Holland, 2003) (with C. Holt).

Articles
1. "Understanding Bayes' rule." *The Journal of Economic Perspectives*, 10(2):1996 (with C. Holt).
2. "Information cascades." *The Journal of Economic Perspectives*, 10(4):1996 (with C. Holt).
3. "Information cascades in the laboratory." *The American Economic Review*, 87(5):1997 (with C. Holt).
4. "Agendas and strategic voting." *The Southern Economic Journal*, 65(3):1999 (with C. Holt).
5. "Choosing winners and losers in a permit trading game." *The Southern Economic Journal*, 67(1):2000 (with S. Stafford).
6. "Cultural differences in attitudes towards bargaining." *Economics Letters*, 69(October):2000 (with Y. Rodgers and R. Rodriguez).
7. "Payoff effects in information cascade experiments." *Economic Inquiry*, 39(4):2001.
8. "An experimental analysis of rent seeking under varying competitive conditions" *Public Choice*, 115:2003 (with S. Stafford).

Principal Contributions
Lisa Anderson's thesis was an experimental investigation of how patterns of conformity might develop when people have private information and make public decisions in sequence. These patterns, known as information cascades, have been used to explain phenomena ranging from stock market bubbles to animal mating behavior. This work resulted in several publications and she continues to do research involving information processing. For example, she is currently using the cascade framework to compare majority rule and unanimity in a sequential voting framework. Also in the area of public choice, her research includes experimental studies of public goods provision and rent seeking. Finally, she is actively involved in promoting the pedagogical use of economics experiments. She has written six papers on this topic and has organized three national conferences on using experiments as a teaching tool.

BAUMOL, William J.

Born
February 26, 1922, New York, New York, USA

Current Positions
Professor of Economics, New York University, 1970–; Professor Emeritus and Senior Research Economist, Princeton University, 1992–.

Past Positions
Joseph Douglas Green Professor of Economics, Princeton University, 1949–1992; Assistant Lecturer, London School of Economics, 1947–1949; Junior Economist, U.S. Department of Agriculture, 1942, 1946.

Degrees
B.S.S, College of the City of New York, 1942; Ph.D., University of London, 1949.

Offices and Honors
Chairman, Committee on Economic Status of the Profession, 1962–1970.
Past Chairman and Member, Economic Policy Council, State of New Jersey, 1967–1975.
Past First Vice President, American Association of University Professors, 1968–1970.

Joseph Douglas Green 1895 Professorship of Economics, Princeton University, 1968.
Elected Member, American Academy of Arts and Sciences, 1971.
John R. Commons Award, Omicron Delta Epsilon, 1975.
Townsend Harris Medal, Alumni Assoc. of the City College of New York, 1975.
Eastern Economic Association, 1978–1979.
Association of Environmental and Resource Economists, 1979.
Past President, American Economic Association, 1981.
Atlantic Economic Society, 1985.
Winner, Assoc. of American Publishers Award for Best Book in Business, Management and Economics, *Superfairness: Applications and Theory*, 1986.
Recipient, Frank E. Seidman Distinguished Award in Political Economy, 1987.
Elected Member, National Academy of Sciences, 1987.
Winner, Assoc. of American Publishers Annual Awards for Excellence in Publishing, Honorable Mention in Social Sciences, *Productivity and American Leadership: The Long View*, 1989.
Recipient, First Senior Scholar in the Arts and Sciences Award, New York University, 1992.
Winner, Assoc. of Environmental and Resource Economists Award for Publication of Enduring Quality, *The Theory of Environmental Policy*, 1993.

Principal Fields of Interest
Innovation and Economic Growth; Theory of the Firm and Industrial Organization; Welfare Economics; Regulation and Antitrust, Economics; of the Arts; Environmental Economics.

Selected Publications
Books
1. *Economic Dynamics*, 1951, 1959, 1970 (with R. Turvey).
2. *Welfare Economics and the Theory of the State*, 1952, 1965.
3. *Business Behavior, Value and Growth*, 1959, 1966.
4. *Economic Theory and Operations Analysis*, 1961, 1965, 1972, 1976.
5. *Performing Arts: The Economic Dilemma*, 1966 (with W.G. Bowen).
6. *The Theory of Environmental Policy*, 1975, 1988 (with W.E. Oates).
7. *Contestable Markets and the Theory of Industry Structure*, 1982, 1988 (with R.D. Willig and J.C. Panzar).
8. *Superfairness: Applications and Theory*, 1986.
9. *Productivity and American Leadership: The Long View*, 1989, paperback, 1991 (with S.A. Batey Blackman and E.N. Wolff).
10. *Entrepreneurship, Management and the Structure of Payoffs*, 1993.
11. *Global Trade and Conflicting National Interests*, 2000 (with Ralph E. Gomory).

Principal Contributions
William Baumol's contributions include the sales maximization model which is used to demonstrate the possibility of formal analysis of the behavior of the firm with objectives other than profit maximization. His work with William Bowen on the economics of the arts led to formulation of the cost disease model that helps to explain the persistently rising real cost of services with handicraft components, including health care, education and live performing arts. Later work with other economists provided the Contestable Markets analysis that shows how under free entry and exit the market can determine industry structure, and how analysis can provide guidance to antitrust and regulation in industries with scale economies, in which large firms are unavoidable and can be desirable. Baumol's analysis of entrepreneurship as a critical input that can be allocated by payoff arrangements among productive, rent seeking and destructive (e.g., criminal) activities shows how policy can be used to stimulate productive entrepreneurship. His latest book studies the mechanism that enables the free market economy to achieve an unparalleled record of growth and innovation, and can help less affluent economies to begin to emulate that performance.

BAVETTA, Sebastiano

Born
March 27, 1964, Palermo, Sicilia, Italy

Current Positions
Associate Professor of Public Economics, University of Palermo, 2000–; Co-Director of the Research Program in Democracy, Business and Human Well-Being, London School of Economics, 2000–; Research Associate, London School of Economics, 2001–.

Past Positions
Professor of Microeconomics, Master in Economics and Institutions, Tor Vergata, University of Rome, 1999; Professor of Normative Assessments in Health Economics, Master in Health Economics, University of Messina, 1999; Visiting fellow at the Center for Public Choice, George Mason University, 1996; Visiting fellow at the THEMA, Universitè de Cergy-Pontoise, 1996.

Degrees
B.A., University of Palermo, 1987; M.Sc., University of Pennsylvania, 1990; Ph.D., London School of Economics, 1999.

Principal Fields of Interest
Normative Economics; Constitutional Political Economy, Institutional Economics; Philosophical Foundations of Freedom.

Selected Publications
Articles
1. "The measurement of specific freedom," *Notizie di Politeia*, 15:1999.
2. "Measuring autonomy freedom," with Vitorocco Peragine, Economic Series Working Paper n. 00/27, Universidad Carlos III de Madrid, May 2000.
3. "A model of the representation of interest in a compound democracy." *Constitutional Political Economy*, 11:2000 (with F. Padovano).
4. "Measuring autonomy freedom with globally relevant opportunities." London School of Economics, 2001 (with Vitorocco Peragine, mimeo).
5. "Autonomy freedom and deliberation." London School of Economics, 2001 (with Francesco Guala, mimeo).
6. "Constraints and the measurement of freedom of choice." *Theory and Decision*, 50:2001 (with M. Del Seta).

Principal Contributions
Sebastiano Bavetta has made several contributions on the analysis and measurement of freedom. His work has examined issues ranging from the axiomatic definition and measurement of individual freedom to the empirical measures of the degree of economic liberty. He is working on the impact of political institutions on international business and on the role played by special interest groups in determining policy outcomes.

BENNETT, James Thomas

Born
October 19, 1942, Memphis, Tennessee, USA

Current Positions
William P. Snavely Professor of Political Economy and Public Policy, George Mason University, 1984–; Director, John M. Olin Institute for Employment Practice and Policy, George Mason University, 1995–.

Past Positions
Professor of Economics, George Mason University, 1976–1983; Associate Professor of Economics, George Mason University, 1975–1976; Assistant Professor of Economics, George Washington University, 1970–1975.

Degrees
B.S., M.S., Ph.D., Case Institute of Technology, 1964, 1966, 1970.

Offices and Honors
1. Adjunct Scholar, The Heritage Foundation, 1979–.
2. Member, The Philadelphia Society, 1981.
3. Member, Mont Pelerin Society, 1982.

Editorial Duties
Editor and Founder, *Journal of Labor Research*, 1980–.

Principal Fields of Interest
Public Choice, Public Policy, Political Economy.

Selected Publications
Books
1. *Unhealthy Charities: Hazardous to Your Health and Wealth* (Basic Books, 1994; paperback, 1995) (with Thomas DiLorenzo).
2. *CancerScam: The Diversion of Federal Cancer Funds to Politics* (Transaction Publishers, 1998) (with Thomas DiLorenzo).
3. *The Food and Drink Police: America's Nannies, Busybodies and Petty Tyrants* (Transaction Publishers, 1999) (with Thomas DiLorenzo).
4. *From Pathology to Politics: Public Health in America* (Transaction Publishers, 2000) (with Thomas DiLorenzo).
5. *Public Health Profiteering* (Transaction Publishers, 2001) (with Thomas DiLorenzo).

BENSON, Bruce Lowell

Born
March 18, 1949, Havre, Montana, USA

Current Positions
DeVoe Moore Professor, 1997–; Distinguished Research Professor, 1993–; Department of Economics, Research Associate, 1994–; Oversight/Advisory Board Member, 2000–; DeVoe L. Moore Center, Florida State University; Senior Fellow, Independent Institute, Oakland, California, 1997–; Associate, Political Economy Research Center, Bozeman, Montana, 1982–.

Past Positions
Professor of Economics, 1987–1993; Associate Professor of Economics, 1985–1987; Faculty Associate, Policy Sciences Center, 1987–1993; Florida State University; Research Fellow, Independent Institute, Oakland,

California, 1991–1997; Associate Professor of Economics, Montana State University, 1982–1985; Visiting Assistant Professor of Economics, 1978–1979; Assistant Professor of Economics, 1979–1982; Associate Professor of Economics, 1982; Pennsylvania State University, College Park; Pacific Research Fellow, Pacific Research Institute for Public Policy in San Francisco, California, 1982–1990; Salvatori Fellow, Salvatori Center for Academic Leadership, Heritage Foundation in Washington, 1992–1994.

Degrees
B.A., M.A., University of Montana, 1973, 1975; Ph.D., Texas A&M University, 1978.

Offices and Honors
Georgescu-Roegen Prize for the best article in the *Southern Economic Journal*, 1989.
Honorable Mention Runner-up, H. L. Mencken National Book Award, 1991.
Ludwig von Mises Prize, 1992.
Board of Trustees of the Southern Economic Association, 1995–1997.
Professional Excellence Program Award, Florida State University, 1999.
The Journal of Private Enterprise Best Paper Award, 1999.
Executive Committee of the Association of Private Enterprise Education, 1999–2001.
Sir Antony Fisher International Memorial Award, 2000.
Association of Private Enterprise Education Distinguished Scholar Award, 2001.
Vice President, Association of Private Enterprise Education, 2001–2002 (President elect, 2002–2003).

Editorial Duties
Co-Editor, *Economic Journal Watch* (a refereed on-line journal), 2001–; Associate Editor, *Journal of Regional Science*, 1988–; Associate Editor, *The Journal of Drug Issues*, 1998–; Associate Editor, *Review of Austrian Economics*, 1998–; Contributing Editor, *The Independent Review: A Journal of Political Economy*, 1995–; Editorial Board Member, *Quarterly Journal of Austrian Economics*, 1997–; Editorial Board Member, *Quarterly Journal of Libertarian Studies*, 1999–; Member of the Comité Scientifique, *Journal des Economistes et des Etudes Humaines*, 2002–.

Principal Fields of Interest
Law and Economics; New Institutional Economics; Public Choice; Economics of Crime and Substance Abuse.

Selected Publications
Books
1. *American Antitrust Law in Theory and in Practice* (Avebury, 1989) (with M.L. Greenhut).
2. *The Enterprise of Law: Justice Without the State.* (Pacific Research Institute for Public Policy, 1990).
3. *The Economic Anatomy of a Drug War: Criminal Justice in the Commons* (Rowman and Littlefield, 1994) (with D.W. Rasmussen).
4. *To Serve and Protect: Privatization and Community in Criminal Justice* (New York University Press, 1998).

Articles
1. "Löschian competition under alternative demand conditions." *American Economic Review*, 70(December): 1980.
2. "Rent seeking from a property rights perspective." *Southern Economic Journal*, 51(October):1984.
3. "The political economy of government corruption: the logic of underground government." *Journal of Legal Studies*, 14(June):1985 (with J. Baden).
4. "The lagged impact of state and local taxes on economic activity and political behavior." *Economic Inquiry*, 24(July):1986 (with R. N. Johnson).
5. "The spontaneous evolution of commercial law." *Southern Economic Journal*, 55(January):1989.
6. "Integration of spatial markets." *American Journal of Agricultural Economics*, 70(February):1990 (with M.D. Faminow).
7. "On the basing point system." *American Economic Review*, 80(June):1990 (with M.L. Greenhut and G. Norman).
8. "Basing point pricing and production concentration." *Economic Journal*, 101(May):1991 (with M.L. Greenhut, G. Norman, and J.B. Soper).
9. "Are public goods really common pools: considerations of the evolution of policing and highways in England." *Economic Inquiry*, 32(April):1994.
10. "Emerging from the hobbesian jungle: might takes and makes rights." *Constitutional Political Economy* (Spring/Summer): 1994.
11. "Police bureaucrats, their incentives, and the war on drugs." *Public Choice*, 83(April):1995 (with D.W. Rasmussen and D.L. Sollars).
12. "An exploration of the impact of modern arbitration statutes on the development of arbitration in the United States." *Journal of Law, Economics, & Organization*, 11(October):1995.
13. "Deterrence and public policy: tradeoffs in the allocation of police resources." *International Review of Law*

and Economics, 18(March):1998 (with I. Kim and D.W. Rasmussen).
14. "To arbitrate or to litigate: that is the question." *European Journal of Law and Economics*, 8 (September):1999.
15. "Entrepreneurial police and drug enforcement policy." *Public Choice*, 104(September):2000 (with B.D. Mast and D.W. Rasmussen).
16. "Privately produced general deterrence." *Journal of Law and Economics*, 11 (October):2001 (with B.D. Mast).

Principal Contributions
M.L. Greenhut was Bruce Benson's graduate-school mentor, and as a consequence, much of his early work was on spatial price theory. He also studied with Randy Holcombe, Steve Pejovich, and Eirik Furubotn, however, so he developed an interest in public choice and neoinstitutional economics, and over time these interests expanded. When David Theroux asked him to contribute to a volume on gun control, Benson began documenting private responses to crime (initially to demonstrate that the dominant causal relationship ran from crime to guns for protection). As he explored this issue, he realized that the assumption dominating economics, that government provides and enforces the rules of the game, was not valid. This led to *The Enterprise of Law*, a number of articles on private policing, "the Law Merchant," arbitration, and customary law, and another book, *To Serve and Protect*. This research continues, with a major focus on the evolution of law, and another with Brent Mast on the relationships between private security regulation, security market performance, crime, and the demand for public policing. A new research focus also emerged in the late 1980s as Benson and David Rasmussen started exploring the economics and politics of illicit drug policy. This ongoing collaboration has generated a number of articles and a book. In the course of his career Benson has produced 4 books, over 110 academic journal articles, and more than 40 chapters for edited volumes, along with other publications (see http://garnet.acns.fsu.edu/~bbenson/).

BERNHOLZ, Peter

Born
February 18, 1929, Bad Salzuflen, Germany

Current Position
Professor Emeritus, Faculty of Economics, Center for Economics and Business (WWZ), Universitaet Basel, Switzerland, 1998.

Past Positions
Assistant at Universitaet Frankfurt and Universitaet Muenchen, 1956–1962; Dozent (Assistant Professor) at Universitaet Frankfurt, 1964–1966; Ordentlicher (Full) Professor, Technische Universitaet Berlin, 1966–1971; Ordentlicher Professor and Director, Institut fuer Sozialwissenschaften, Universitaet Basel, Switzerland, 1971–1988; Ordentlicher Professor and Director Institut fuer Volkswirtschaft, 1988–1997, Universitaet Basel, Switzerland.

Degrees
Diplomvolkswirt, (Master's Degree), Dr. rer. pol. Universitaet Marburg, 1953, 1955; Habilitation Universitaet Frankfurt, 1962.

Offices and Honors
Rockefeller Fellow at Harvard and Stanford Universities, 1963/64.
Guest professorships at Massachusetts Institute of Technology, 1969; Virginia Polytechnic Institute, 1974, 1978; Stanford University 1981; University of California, Los Angeles, 1986/87 and Irvine, 1998; Australian National University, Canberra, 1993.
President of *European Public Choice Society*, 1974–1980.
Member of *Wissenschaftlicher Beirat beim Bundesminister fuer Wirtschaft* (*Scientific Advisory Board of the German Minister of Economics*), 1974.
Member of *Macroeconomic Policy Group* of the European Community, 1988–1990.
Member of the Board of the *Mont Pelerin Society*, 1992–1998.
Research Fellow, Center for Study of Public Choice, George Mason University. Corresponding member of the Bavarian Academy of Sciences, 1994.
Dr. rer. pol. h.c. Universitaet Konstanz, 2000.
Fellow, Wissenschaftskolleg (Center for Advanced Studies) zu Berlin, 2000/2001.
Member of *Verein fuer Socialpolitik (German Economics Association)*.
Listed in *Who's Who in Economics: A Biographical Dictionary of Major Economists*. First edition, Second edition, Third edition.

Principal Fields of Interest
Public Choice; Social Choice; Austrian Capital Theory; Monetary History, Theory and Political Economy; International Relations; Totalitarianism.

Selected Publications
Books
1. *Aussenpolitik und internationale Wirtschaftsbeziehungen* (*Foreign Policy and International Economic Relations*).

Frankfurter wissenschaftliche Beitraege. (Klostermann, 1966).
2. *Waehrungskrisen und Waehrungsordnung* (*Currency Crises and International Monetary Regime*) (Hoffmann und Campe, 1974).
3. *Grundlagen der Politischen Oekonomie* (*Foundations of Political Economy*), two vol., Third, revised edition (with F. Breyer) (J.C.B. Mohr, 1993/94). Russian and Ukrainian Editions in two vols. (Kiel: Lybid, 1998 and 1997).
4. *Flexible Exchange Rates in Historical Perspectives*, Princeton Studies in International Finances No. 49, International Finance Section, Dept. of Economics (Princeton University, 1982).
5. *The International Game of Power* (Mouton Publishers, 1985).
6. *Economic Imperialism. The Economic Method Applied Outside the Field of Economics* (Paragon House, 1986) (edited, with G. Radnitzky).
7. *Political Competition, Innovation and Growth. A Historical Analysis.* (Springer, 1998) (edited, with M.E. Streit and R. Vaubel).

Articles
1. "Economic Policies in a Democracy." *Kyklos*, 19: 1966.
2. "Logrolling, arrow-paradox and decision rules. A generalization." *Kyklos*, 27(1):1974.
3. "A general two-period neo-Austrian model of capital." *Journal of Economic Theory*, 17:1978 (twith M. Faber and W. Reiss); reprinted in Malte Faber (ed.) *Studies in Austrian Capital Theory, Investment and Time* (Springer, 1986).
4. "A general social dilemma: profitable exchange and intransitive preferences." *Zeitschrift für Nationalökonomie*, 40:1980.
5. "Externalities as a necessary condition for cyclical social preferences." *Quarterly Journal of Economics*, 47(4):1982.
6. "A general constitutional possibility theorem." *Public Choice*, 51:1986; reprinted in G. Radnitzky and P. Bernholz (eds.) *Economic Imperialism* (Paragon House, 1986).
7. "Growth of government, economic growth and individual freedom." *Journal of Institutional and Theoretical Economics*, 142(4):1986.
8. "The implementation and maintenance of a monetary constitution." *The Cato Journal* 6(2): 1986, reprinted in James A. Dorn and Anna J. Schwartz (eds.) *The Search for Stable Money* (University of Chicago Press, 1987).
9. "The importance of reorganizing money, credit, and banking when decentralizing economic decision-making." *Economic Reform in China: Problems and Prospects* (edited by James A. Dorn and Wang XI) (University of Chicago Press, 1990).
10. "Currency competition, inflation, Gresham's Law and exchange rate." (edited by Pierre L. Siklos) *Great Inflations of the 20th Century. Theories, Policies and Evidence* (Edward Elgar publishing, 1995).
11. "The Bundesbank and the process of European monetary integration." *Fifty Years of the Deutsche Mark. Central Bank and the Currency in Germany since 1948* (edited by Deutsche Bundesbank) (Oxford University Press, 1999).
12. "The generalized Coase theorem and separable individual preferences: an extension." *European Journal of Political Economy*, 15:1999.
13. "Ideocracy and totalitarianism: a formal analysis incorporating ideology." *Public Choice*, 108: 2001.

Principal Contributions
Early interest in intertemporal problems encouraged work on Austrian capital and monetary theory. The former was reformulated and extended and shown that neo-classical capital theory is a special case covered by it. In public choice theory it was demonstrated that imperfect information of voters, economic growth, and interest groups bring about the support of stagnating industries. In social choice it was shown that logrolling benefiting majorities implies cyclical social preferences. A proof followed which generalized this result to all contracts on different issues agreed on by different subsets of decentralized society having the right to decide issues. Finally, it could be shown that the problems of the resulting cyclical social preferences can be solved by an adequate assignment of rights or by binding contracts if no transaction costs are present.

In monetary economics the reasons of the demand for paper money, the characteristics of inflations and the behavior of exchange rates (overshooting) was studied by using historical evidence. It was shown under which economic and political conditions stable monetary regimes can emerge and be maintained.

The study of the transition of political economic regimes to different regimes revealed the importance of military and political competition among states. Related to this was an effort to study the long-term political tendencies in democracies to intervene into the market economy, and studies of totalitarian regimes and of the workings of the international political system.

BESLEY, Timothy, John

Born
September 14, 1960, Kesteven, England

Current Positions
Professor of Economics, London School of Economics and Political Science, 1995–; Director, Suntory Toyota International Centres for Economics and Related Disciplines, 2001–; Research Fellow, Institute for Fiscal Studies, 1995–; Program Director in Public Policy, Centre for Economic Policy Research, 1998.

Past Positions
Fellow, All Souls College, Oxford, 1983–1991, 1995–2000; Visiting Assistant Professor of Public and International Affairs, Princeton University, 1988–1989; Assistant Professor of Economics and International affairs, Princeton University, 1989–1995; Lecturer in Economics, Keble College, Oxford, 1985–1987.

Degrees
B.A., M.Phil., D.Phil, Oxford University, 1983, 1985, 1987.

Offices and Honors
Fellow of the Econometric Society.
Fellow of the British Academy.
Elected Council Member, Royal Economic Society
Elected Council Member, European Economics Association.
Winner of Inaugural Richard Musgrave Prize (with Harvey Rosen) for paper "Sales Taxes and Prices: An Empirical Analysis" published in the *National Tax Journal*, 1999.

Editorial Duties
Co-Editor, *American Economic Review*, 1999–; Managing Editor, *Economic Journal*, 1996–1999; Editorial Boards of: *Oxford Economic Papers, Journal of Development Economics, Economics and Politics, Journal of Developing Areas, American Economic Review, International Tax and Public Finance, Review of Economic Studies, World Bank Economic Review, Review of Development Economics.*

Principal Fields of Interest
Development Economics; Political Economy; Public Economics.

Selected Publications
Articles
1. "Decentralizing public good supply." *Econometrica*, 59(6), November 1991 (with Ian Jewitt).
2. "Workfare versus welfare: incentive arguments for work requirements in poverty alleviation programs." *American Economic Review*, 82(1):1992 (with Stephen Coate).
3. "Taxes and bribery: the role of wage incentives." *Economic Journal* 103(1): 1993 (with John McLaren).
4. "The economics of rotating savings and credit associations." *American Economic Review*, 83(4):1993 (with Stephen Coate and Glen Loury).
5. "Incumbent behavior: vote seeking, tax setting and yardstick competition." *American Economic Review*, 85(1): 1995 (with Anne Case).
6. "The design of income maintenance programs." *Review of Economic Studies*, 62(2):1995 (with Stephen Coate).
7. "Does electoral accountability affect economic policy choices? Evidence from gubernatorial terms limits." *Quarterly Journal of Economics*, 110(3):1995 (with Anne Case).
8. "Property rights and investment incentives: theory and evidence from Ghana." *Journal of Political Economy*, 103(5): 1995.
9. "An economic model of representative democracy." *Quarterly Journal of Economics*, 112(1):1997 (with Stephen Coate).
10. "Sources of inefficiency in a representative democracy: a dynamic analysis." *American Economic Review*, 88(1):1998 (with Stephen Coate).
11. "Lobbying and welfare in a Representative democracy." *Review of Economic Studies*, 68(1):2001 (with Stephen Coate).
12. "Public versus private ownership of public goods." *Quarterly Journal of Economics*, 116(4):2001 (with Maitreesh Ghatak).

Principal Contributions
Timothy Besley's work in political economy has focused on developing models of the policy process that can ask welfare questions about the achievements of the political process in allocating resources. With Stephen Coate, he has developed an approach to the political process known as the "citizen-candidate" model. He has also worked on models that bring imperfect competition into the political process (political agency models). This lead to work on the using of yardstick political competition in federal systems (joint with Anne Case). This has also lead to an interest in the role of the press and independent agencies in information provision. Besley's work in development economics has focused on a range of issues including: property rights and investment incentives, indigenous savings institutions, technology adoption, and tax evasion. His work in public

economics has studied a range of issues including: income maintenance programs, tax competition, public provision of private goods, merit goods, and health insurance.

BESOCKE, Portia DiGiovanni

Born
July 7, 1965, Springfield, Massachusetts, USA

Current Positions
Doctoral Candidate in Economics, Claremont Graduate University.

Degrees
B.A., St. John's College, Annapolis, MD, 1986; M.A; Claremont Graduate University, 2001; Doctoral studies Claremont Graduate University, 2001–present.

Offices and Honors
Participant, Public Choice Outreach Conference, 2002.
Member, Student Executive Committee, School of Politics and Economics, Claremont Graduate University, 2001–2002.
Sustainable Communities Leadership Fellow, the Inland Empire Economic Partnership, 2000–2001.

Principal Fields of Interest
Public Choice; Public Finance; Regional Economics.

Principal Contributions
Portia Besocke has a B.A. in philosophy from St. John's College, the "great books" school, in Annapolis, MD. After working as an automotive mechanic, a visual effects camera-operator, and a production assistant at a National Public Radio affiliate, She obtained an M.A. in Politics, Economics and Business in the School of Politics and Economics at Claremont Graduate University in 2001. Courses taught by Virginia School scholars Thomas Borcherding, Arthur Denzau, and Thomas Willett linking politics and economics were so interesting that she stayed on as an Economics doctoral student. In her thesis, she will attempt to analyze the effects of changes in the federal vs. private funding formula and organizational structure on the behavior of public broadcasting using a public choice approach.

BOETTKE, Peter J.

Born
January 3, 1960, Rahway, New Jersey, USA

Current Positions
Deputy Director, James M. Buchanan Center for Political Economy, George Mason University, 1999–; Associate Professor of Economics, George Mason University, 1998–; Senior Research Fellow, Mercatus Center, George Mason University, 1999–.

Past Positions
Associate Professor of Economic and Finance, Manhattan College, 1997–1999; Senior Fellow, Austrian Economics Program, New York University, 1997–1998; Assistant Professor of Economics, New York University, 1990–1997; National Fellow, Hoover Institution on War, Revolution and Peace, Stanford University, 1992–1993; Assistant Professor of Economics, Oakland University, 1988–1990; Assistant Professor of Economics, George Mason University, 1987–1988.

Degrees
B.A., Grove City College, 1983; Ph.D., George Mason University, 1989.

Offices and Honors
Member, The Mont Pelerin Society, 1995.
President, Society for Development of Austrian Economics, 2000–2001.
1999 Smith Prize from the Society for the Development of Austrian Economics for "What Went Wrong with Economics?," *Critical Review* 11(1): 1997; 11–65.
1997 Otto Eckstein Prize (Honorable Mention) from the Eastern Economic Association for the paper "Hayek's *The Road to Serfdom* Revisited," *Eastern Economic Journal* (Winter 1995).
1995 Golden Dozen Teaching Award in recognition of excellence in undergraduate teaching, College of Arts and Science, New York University.
1994 F.A. Hayek Fellowship Award, The Mont Pelerin Society. First Place in international paper competition on the legacy of F. A. Hayek.
1989 William P. Snavely Award Winner — Outstanding Graduate Student in Economics, George Mason University.

Editorial Duties
Founding Editor, *Advances in Austrian Economics*, 1994–1998; Editor, *Review of Austrian Economics*, 1998–; Managing Editor, *Market Process*, 1984–1987.

Principal Fields of Interest
Comparative Political Economy; Market Process Theory; History of Economic Thought and Methodology.

Selected Publications
Books
1. *The Political Economy of Soviet Socialism: The Formative Years, 1918-1928* (Kluwer Academic Publishers, 1990).
2. *Why Perestroika Failed: The Politics and Economics of Socialist Transformation* (Routledge, 1993).
3. *The Elgar Companion to Austrian Economics* (ed.) (Edward Elgar Publishing, 1994).
4. *Market Process Theories*, 2 volumes (Edward Elgar Publishing, 1998) (Edited, with David L. Prychitko).
5. *The Legacy of F. A. Hayek: Politics, Philosophy and Economics*, 3 volumes (ed.) (Edward Elgar Publishing, 2000).
6. *Socialism and the Market: The Socialist Calculation Debate Revisited*, 9 volumes (ed.) (Routledge, 2000).
7. *Calculation & Coordination: Essays on Socialism and Transitional Political Economy* (Routledge, 2001).
8. *The Economic Way of Thinking*, 10th Edition (Prentice Hall, 2002) (with Paul Heyne and David Prychitko).

Articles
1. "Why are there no Austrian socialists? Ideology, science and the Austrian school." *Journal of the History of Economic Thought*, 17:1995.
2. "Where did economics go wrong: modern economics as a flight from reality." *Critical Review*, 11(1):1997.
3. "Promises made and promises broken in the Russian transition." *Constitutional Political Economy*, 9(2): 1998.
4. "Economic calculation: the Austrian contribution to political economy." *Advances in Austrian Economics*, 5: 1998.
5. "The Russian crisis: perils and prospects for Post-Soviet transition." *American Journal of Economics & Sociology*, 58(3):1999.
6. "Knight and the Austrians on capital and the problem of socialism." *History of Political Economy*, 34(1):2002 (with Karen Vaughn).
7. "Post classical political economy." *American Journal of Economics and Sociology*, 61(1):2002 (with Virgil Storr).
8. "From the philosophy of mind to the philosophy of the market." *Journal of Economic Methodology*, 9(1):2002 (with John Robert Subrick).
9. "Kirznerian Entrepreneurship and The Economics of Science." *Journal des Economistes et des Etudes Humaines*, 12(1):2002 (with William Butos).
10. "Entrepreneurship and development: cause or consequence?." *Advances in Austrian Economics*, 6:2002 (with Christopher Coyne).

Principal Contributions
Peter Boettke's work has focused on the origin, history, collapse and transition from socialism in Russia. The main thrust of his work in comparative political economy has been to bring the insights of Ludwig von Mises and F.A. Hayek to analyze the operation of the Soviet type economy. This work has highlighted the ideological aspirations of the Soviet experience, the inability of those aspirations to be realized in practice, the unintended consequences of the Soviet experience, the *de facto* operating principles in Soviet economic and political life, and the implications of transition policy of this *de facto* reality of black markets, vested interests and attenuated property rights.

In addition to this applied work in political economy, Boettke has maintained an active interest in history of economic thought and methodology. In particular, he has done several studies on the development of modern economics and the role of the Austrian economists in the debates that have shaped modern economics. In 1998, he took over the editorship of the *Review of Austrian Economics*.

BORCHERDING, Thomas Earl

Born
February 18, 1939, Cincinnati, Ohio, USA

Current Position
Professor, Economic and Politics, Claremont Graduate University, 1983–.

Past Positions
Associate Professor and Professor of Economics, Simon Fraser University, 1973–1983; Visiting Research Fellow, Hoover Institution, Stanford University, 1979–1980; Visiting Professor of Law and Economics, University of Toronto, 1968–1979; Post-doctoral Fellow, Hoover Institution, 1974–1975; Associate Professor of Economics, Virginia Polytechnic Institution, 1971–1973; Assistant Professor, University of Washington, 1966–1971; Post doctoral Fellow, Thomas Jefferson Center for Study of Political Economy, University of Virginia, 1965–1966.

Degrees
B.A., University of Cincinnati, 1961; Ph.D., Duke University, 1966

Offices and Honors
Phi Beta Kappa, 1961
Mont Pelerin Society, 1985
Listed in *Who's Who in Economics: A Biographical Dictionary of Major Economists* (1700–1998).
Listed in *Who's Who in America*.

Editorial Duties
Co-Editor, Managing Editor, and Senior Editor, *Economic Inquiry*, 1980–1997.

Principal Fields of Interest
Public Choice and Political Economy; Public Economics; Sociological Economics.

Selected Publications
Books
1. *Budgets and Bureaucrats: The Sources of Government Growth*, (ed.) (Duke University Press, 1977).
2. *The Egg Marketing Board: A Case Study of Monopoly and Its Social Costs* (The Fraser Institute, 1981).

Articles
1. "The demand for the services of non-federal governments." *American Economic Review*, 62 (December): 1972 (with R.T. Deacon).
2. "The economics of school integration: public choice with tie-ins." *Public Choice*, Fall(31):1977.
3. "Why do all the good apples go east? Alchian and Allen's substitution theorem revisited." *Journal of Political Economy*, February(76):1978 (with E. Silberberg).
4. "Expropriation of private property and the basis for compensation." *University of Toronto Law Journal*, Summer:1979 (with J. Knetsch).
5. "Comparing the efficiency of private and public production: a survey of the evidence from five federal states." *Zeitschrift fuer Nationaloekonomie/Journal of Economic Theory: Public Production* (edited by D. Boes et al.), Supplement: 1982 (with W. Pommerehne and F. Schneider).
6. "The causes of government expenditure growth: a survey of the U.S. evidence." *Journal of Public Economics*, December: 1985.
7. "Organizing government supply: the role of bureaucracy," in F. Thompson and M. Green (eds.) *Handbook of Public Finance* (Marcel Dekker, 1998) (with A. Khursheed).
8. "Market power and stable cartels: theory and empirical test." *Journal of Law and Economics*, 44 October: 2001 (with D. Filson, E. Fruits and E. Keen).
9. "Group consumption, free riding and informal reciprocity agreements." *The Journal of Economic Behavior and Organization*, Spring:2002 (with D. Filson).
10. "The growth of real government," in R. Wagner and J. Backhaus (eds.) *Handbook of Public Finance* (Edward Elgar Publishing, 2003) (with S. Ferris and A. Garzoni).

Principle Contributions
Thomas Borcherding's research has been concerned with the role of institutions in economic, political, and social choice. He considers himself a Virginia School economist, and uses middlebrow microeconomic theory to analyze a diversity of topics from the growth of government, the behavior of bureaucrats, the evolution of desegregation politics, the social costs of conscription, the operations of legal rent-seeking cartels, to his most recent work on group consumption without formal rules, and conflicts of interest in the Hollywood film industry. Borcherding's current work is concerned with the theory of investments in social capital, the political choice between regulation and fiscal instruments, and the effects that reduced deadweights of broad-based taxes have on the size of the public sector.

BRADBURY, John Charles

Born
September 28, 1973, Charlotte, North Carolina, USA

Current Positions
Visiting Assistant Professor of Economics, The University of the South, Sewanee, Tennessee, USA, 2001–.

Past Positions
Assistant Professor of Business Administration, North Georgia College & State University, 2000–2001; Research Associate, Mercatus Center, 1999–2000. Instructor of Economics, George Mason University, 1999–2000; Graduate Research Fellow, Political Economy Research Center (PERC), Bozeman, MT, 1998.

Degrees
B.A., Wofford College, 1996; M.A., Ph.D., George Mason University, 1998, 2000.

Principal Fields of Interest
Public Economics; Regulation.

Selected Publications
Articles
1. "ATM surcharges and the expansion of consumer choice." *Cato Briefing Paper*, March:1998.
2. "Legislative organization and government spending: cross-country evidence." *Journal of Public Economics*, 82(December):2001 (with W. M. Crain).
3. "Bicameralism and fiscal policy." *Southern Economic Journal*, 68(January):2002 (with W. M. Crain).
4. "Local government structure and public expenditures." *Public Choice*, in press. (with E.F. Stephenson).

Principal Contributions
John Bradbury's main area of research concentrates on the effects of legislative organization on fiscal policy. Principally, he has examined the importance of bicameralism and the median voter in representative democracy. Additionally, he worked on the Mercatus Center Regulatory Studies Program quantifying the costs of labor regulation. Bradbury also studied the prohibition ATM surcharges. His research in this area has been featured in the *Wall Street Journal, Journal of Commerce, Investors Business Daily*, and *USA Today*.

BRAMS, Steven J.

Born
November 28, 1940, Concord, New Hampshire, USA

Current Position
Professor of Politics, New York University, 1969–

Past Positions
Assistant Professor, Department of Political Science, Syracuse University, 1967–1969; Research Associate, Institute for Defense Analyses, 1965–1967.

Degrees
B.S., Massachusetts Institute of Technology, 1962; Ph.D., Northwestern University, 1966.

Offices and Honors
Social Science Research Council Research Training Fellowship, 1964–1965.
Guggenheim Fellowship, 1986–1987.
President, Peace Science Society (International), 1990–1991.
Fellow, American Association for the Advancement of Science, 1992.
Fellow, Public Choice Society, 1998.
Visiting Scholar, Russell Sage Foundation, 1998–1999.
Susan Strange Award, International Studies Association, 2002.

Principal Fields of Interest
Formal Modeling, principally in political science.

Selected Publications
Books
1. *Game Theory and Politics* (Free Press, 1975).
2. *Paradoxes in Politics: An Introduction to the Nonobvious in Political Science* (Free Press, 1976).
3. *The Presidential Election Game* (Yale University Press, 1978).
4. *Applied Game Theory: Proceedings of a Conference* (Physica-Verlag, 1979). (edited, with A. Schotter and G. Schwödiauer).
5. *Biblical Games: A Strategic Analysis of Stories in the Old Testament* (MIT Press, 1980) (Revised edition, 2002).
6. *Modules in Applied Mathematics: Political and Related Models*, vol. 2 (Springer-Verlag, 1983) (edited, with W.F. Lucas and P.D. Straffin, Jr.).
7. *Approval Voting* (Birkhäuser, 1983) (with P.C. Fishburn).
8. *Superior Beings: If They Exist, How Would We Know? Game-Theoretic Implications of Omniscience, Omnipotence, Immortality, and Incomprehensibility* (Springer-Verlag, 1983).
9. *Superpower Games: Applying Game Theory to Superpower Conflict* (Yale University Press, 1985).
10. *Rational Politics: Decisions, Games, and Strategy* (CQ Press, 1985) (Reprinted by Academic Press, 1989).
11. *Game Theory and National Security* (Basil Blackwell, 1988. Spanish translation, 1989) (with D.M. Kilgour).
12. *Negotiation Games: Applying Game Theory to Bargaining and Arbitration* (Routledge, 1990).
13. *Theory of Moves* (Cambridge University Press, 1994).
14. *Fair Division: From Cake-Cutting to Dispute Resolution* (Cambridge University Press, 1996) (with A.D. Taylor).

15. *The Win-Win Solution: Guaranteeing Fair Shares to Everybody* (W.W. Norton, 1999)

U.S. Patent
Computer-Based Method for the Fair Division of Ownership of Goods (with A.D. Taylor) #5983205, granted 11/9/99 and assigned to New York University.

Principal Contributions
Steven Brams has applied game theory and social choice theory to, among other fields, voting and elections, international relations, and the Bible and theology. He has written or edited 15 books and over 200 scholarly articles. He has also written a number of popular articles, most of which reflect his normative interests in voting and fair division. Specifically, he is an advocate of an election reform called approval voting, which has been adopted by several major professional societies with, collectively, over 600,000 members. Brams has also promoted a dispute-resolution procedure called adjusted winner, which is analyzed in his two books with Alan Taylor, *Fair Division* and *The Win-Win Solution*. The algorithm underlying this procedure has been patented by NYU and appears to be the only patent ever granted for a legal or dispute-resolution procedure.

BUCHANAN, James McGill

Born
October 3, 1919, Murfreesboro, Tennessee, USA

Current Positions
Advisory General Director, Center for Study of Public Choice, George Mason University, 1988–; Professor Emeritus of Economics, George Mason University, Virginia, 1999–; Professor Emeritus of Economics and Philosophy, Virginia Polytechnic and State University, 1999–.

Past Positions
Virginia Polytechnic Institute, 1969–1983; University of California, Los Angeles, 1968–1969; University of Virginia, 1956–1968.

Degrees
B.A., Middle Tennessee State College, 1940; M.S., University of Tennessee, 1941; Ph.D., University of Chicago, 1948.

Offices and Honors
Southern Economic Association, President, 1963.
Member, American Economic Association; Royal Economic Society; Southern Economic Association; Mt. Pelerin Society; Public Choice Society (cofounder), 1963.
Executive Committee (1966–1969); Vice President (1971), American Economic Association.
President, 1984–1986; Vice President, 1982–1984; Executive Committee, Member of the Board, 1976–1982 Mt. Pelerin Society.
Distinguished Fellow, American Economic Association, 1983.
President, 1983–1984; President-Elect, 1982–1983; Vice President, 1981–1982, Western Economic Association.
Frank Seidman Distinguished Award in Political Economy, 1984.
Alfred Nobel Memorial Prize in Economic Sciences, 1986.
Lord Foundation Award for Leadership in Wealth Creation, 1988.
Distinguished Senior Fellow, Cato Institute, 1987.
Legion de la Libertad, Instituto Cultural Ludwig von Mises, Mexico City, Mexico, 1992.
International Uberto Bonino Award for Science, Arts and Letters, Messina, Italy, 1993.
Honorary Professor, University of the Pacific, 1996.
Lifetime Achievement Award, Templeton Honor Rolls, 1997.
Distinguished Senior Fellow, Law and Economics Center, George Mason University, 1997.
Alumni Academic Hall of Fame, University of Tennessee, Knoxville, Tennessee, 1999.
Distinguished Professor Emeritus of Economics, George Mason University, Virginia, 1999.
University Distinguished Professor Emeritus of Economics and Philosophy, Virginia Polytechnic and State University, Virginia, 1999.

Principal Fields of Interest
Public Choice; Political Economy; Political Philosophy.

Selected Publications
Books
1. *Public Principles of Public Debt* (Richard D. Irwin, 1958).
2. *The Calculus of Consent* (University of Michigan Press, 1962) (with G. Tullock).
3. *Public Finance in Democratic Process* (University of North Carolina Press, 1967).
4. *Demand and Supply of Public Goods* (Rand McNally, 1968).
5. *Cost and Choice* (Markham Press, 1969).
6. *The Limits of Liberty* (University of Chicago Press, 1975).

7. *The Power to Tax* (Cambridge University Press, 1980) (with G. Brennan).
8. *The Reason of Rules* (Cambridge University Press, 1985) (with G. Brennan).
9. *Better than Plowing* (University of Chicago Press, 1992).
10. *Politics by Principle, Not Interest* (Cambridge University Press, 1998) (with R. Congleton).
11. *The Collected Works of James M. Buchanan* (Liberty Fund, 1999–2002).

Articles
All major papers have been republished in Volumes 1 and 12–19 of *The Collected Works of James M. Buchanan*. Liberty Fund, 1999–2001.

Principal Contributions
James Buchanan's concentration and early research was in public economics, which leads directly into inquiry as to how political decisions get made. His first paper called on economists to specify models of political structure before proferring advice on policy. This early work was followed by criticism of efforts to construct social welfare functions for a nonexistent collectivity. How do we derive a rational choice explanation for politics? The Buchanan–Tullock book *The Calculus of Consent*, 1962, addressed this question. This effort was followed, in 1975, by *The Limits of Liberty*, which examined the basic question concerned with the emergence of order from anarchy along with the control of political agents. Buchanan's emphasis has been on the importance of the set of constitutional rules under which ordinary politics is allowed to function. The follow-on research program in constitutional economics has occupied his attention in the 1980s, 1990s, and into the new century. (For additional information on Buchanan's personal and academic journies, see his series of autobiographical essays in *Better than Plowing: and Other Personal Essays* [University of Chicago Press, 1992].)

CAIN, Michael J.G.

Born
November 24, 1957 Philadelphia, Pennsylvania, USA

Current Positions
Associate Professor of Political Science, St. Mary's College of Maryland, 2001–; Woodrow Wilson Residential Fellow, Woodrow Wilson International Center for Scholars, 2002–.

Past Positions
Assistant Professor in Political Science, St. Mary's College of Maryland, 1999–2001; Assistant Professor in Political Science, University of Mississippi, 1993–1999; Visiting Professor in Public Policy, University of Warsaw, 1995–1996; Visiting Assistant Professor in Political Science, University of Mississippi, 1992–1993; Instructor in Government and Politics, University of Maryland, 1990–1992; Lecturer in Political Methodology, George Washington University, Spring 1989.

Degrees
B.A., Rutgers University, 1980; M.A., Ph.D., University of Maryland, 1990, 1993.

Offices and Honors
Excellence in Teaching Award, the College of Behavioral and Social Sciences, University of Maryland, May 1991.
Fellowship for Public Policy Development in Eastern Europe, the American Council of Learned Societies and the International Research and Exchange Board, August 1995.
Advisory Board Member, International Summer Program on the Holocaust, St. Mary's College of Maryland, 2001–.
Advisory Board Member, Center for the Study of Democracy, 2002–.

Principal Fields of Interest
Public Choice; Collective Action Theory; Political Economy of Transition; Post-Communist Social Policy.

Selected Publications
Articles
1. "Marginal cost sharing and the articles of confederation." *Public Choice*, 90(1–4):1997 (with Keith L. Dougherty). (Reprinted in *Constitutional Political Economy in a Public Choice Perspective* Kluwer Academic Publishing, 1997) (edited by Charles K. Rowley).
2. "An experimental investigation of motives and information in the prisoner's dilemma game." (JAI Press, 1998) *Advances in Group Processes*, Vol. 15 (edited by John Skvoretz and Jacek Szmatka).
3. "Suppressing Shays' Rebellion: collective action and constitutional design under the articles of confederation." *The Journal of Theoretical Politics*, 11(2):1999 (with Keith L. Dougherty).
4. "Transitional politics or public choice? an evaluation of stalled pension reforms in Poland." (edited by Linda J. Cook, Mitchell A. Orenstein, and Marilyn Rueschemeyer). *Left Parties and Social Policies in Post-Communist Societies*. (Westview Press, 1999). (with Aleksander Surdej).

5. "Globalizing tendencies in social policy." *Emergo: Journal of Transforming Economies and Societies*, 7(2): 2000.
6. "Social choice theory." (edited by William F. Shughart II and Laura Razzolini) *The Elgar Companion to Public Choice* (Edward Elgar Publishing, 2001).

Principal Contributions
Michael Cain's main theoretical contributions have focused on understanding collective action problems in various applied and experimental settings. After gaining experience in the political economy of transitions, his recent work has focus on applications of public choice theory to social policy in transitioning states. As a Resident Fellow at the Woodrow Wilson International Center for Scholars, he is currently working on a book manuscript entitled *Diffusing the Washington Consensus: Spreading Liberal Social Reforms in Post-Communist Societies*. This book explains why social welfare reforms spread so rapidly in East European states and investigates the mechanisms for these reforms using standard arguments from public choice theory.

CAPLAN, Bryan Douglas

Born
April 8, 1971, Los Angeles, California, USA

Current Position
Assistant Professor of Economics, George Mason University, 1997–.

Degrees
B.A., University of California at Berkeley, 1993; Ph.D., Princeton University, 1997.

Principal Fields of Interest
Public Economics; Public Choice; Public Opinion.

Selected Publications
Articles
1. "The Austrian search for realistic foundations." *Southern Economic Journal*, 65(4):1999.
2. "Rational irrationality: a framework for the neoclassical-behavioral debate." *Eastern Economic Journal*, 26(2): 2000.
3. "When is two better than one? how federalism amplifies and mitigates imperfect political competition." *Journal of Public Economics*, 80(1):2001.
4. "Rational ignorance versus rational irrationality." *Kyklos*, 54(1):2001.
5. "Has Leviathan been bound? a theory of imperfectly constrained government with evidence from the states." *Southern Economic Journal*, 67(4):2001.
6. "Rational irrationality and the microfoundations of political failure." *Public Choice*, 107(3/4):2001.
7. "What makes people think like economists? evidence from the survey of Americans and economists on the economy." *Journal of Law and Economics*, 44(2):2001.
8. "Systematically biased beliefs about economics: robust evidence of judgmental anomalies from the survey of Americans and economists on the economy." *Economic Journal*, 112:2002.
9. "Sociotropes, systematic bias, and political failure: reflections on the survey of Americans and economists on the economy." *Social Science Quarterly*, June:2002.
10. "The Logic of Collective Belief." *Rationality and Society*, forthcoming.

Principal Contributions
Much of Bryan Caplan's current work is positively inspired by Geoffrey Brennan and Loren Lomasky's *Democracy and Decision* and negatively inspired by Donald Wittman's *The Myth of Democratic Failure*. Brennan and Lomasky made Caplan realize that voters' low probability of decisiveness had wide-ranging and substantive implications. Analogizing voters and consumers, he came to see, is misleading at best. Wittman, on the other hand, convinced him of the weaknesses of a great deal of the earlier literature in public choice, but also led him to question the prevailing assumption of voter rationality. In terms of basic economic theory, we should actually *expect* agents to be less rational when they vote than when they participate in markets. Caplan explores this insight theoretically in a family of articles on "rational irrationality." In his more empirical work, he has demonstrated the existence of large and robust systematic belief differences between economists and the general public and investigated "what makes people think like economists." His long-run research goal is to reorient public choice to focus more on voter-driven political failure and less on the perverse influence of special interests. In the process, he hope to establish a tighter connection between economists who do public choice and political scientists who do empirical public opinion research.

CONGLETON, Roger Douglas

Born
November 13, 1951, Newton, New Jersey, USA

Current Positions
Professor of Economics, George Mason University; 1998; General Director, Center for Study of Public Choice, 2000–2002; Senior Research Associate, Center for Study of Public Choice; Senior Research Associate, SNS, Stockholm, Sweden.

Past Positions
Visiting Professor of Economics, Universitat Autonoma de Barcelona, Spain; Visiting Professor of Economics, Stockholm School of Economics, Stockholm, Sweden; Visiting Research Fellow, Research School for Social Science, Australian National University; Bradley Postdoctoral Fellow and Research Associate, Center for Study of Public Choice, George Mason University; Assistant Professor of Economics, Clarkson University; Post Doctoral Fellow and Adjunct Assistant Professor, New York University; Adjunct Assistant Professor of Economics, Albion College.

Degrees
B.A., M.A., Ph.D., Virginia Polytechnic Institute and State University, 1974, 1976, 1978.

Offices and Honors
Rensselaer Polytechnic Institute Medal for Mathematics and Science, 1970.
E B. Earhart Foundation Fellowship, Virginia Polytechnic Institute and State University, 1977–1978.
Post Doctoral Fellow in Austrian Economics, New York University, 1979–1980.
Bradley Post Doctoral Fellow, Center for Study of Public Choice, George Mason University, 1986–1987.
Director's Research Fellowship, Research School for Social Sciences, Australian National University, May–August 1993.

Principal Fields of Interest
Public Choice; Constitutional Economics; Environmental Economics; Public Finance; Social Evolution.

Selected Publications
Books
1. *The Economic Analysis of Rent Seeking* (Edgar Elgar Publishing, 1995) (edited, with R.D. Tollison).
2. *The Political Economy of Environmental Protection: Analysis and Evidence.* (ed.) (University of Michigan Press, 1996).
3. *Politics by Principle, Not Interest: Towards Nondiscriminatory Democracy*, (Cambridge University Press, 1998) (with James M. Buchanan).
4. *Att Förbättra Demokratin:* En Politisk-Economisk Analys av Sveriges Grundlag (Perfecting Parliament, A Political Economy Analysis of the Swedish Constitution). (SNS Förlag, 2002).
5. Improving Democracy through Constitutional Reform: Some Swedish Lessons (Kluwer, 2003).

Articles
1 "Economic conditions and national elections, post-sample forecasts of the kramer equations." *American Political Science Review*, 76:1982 (with H.S. Atesoglu).
2. "Committees and rent-seeking effort." *Journal of Public Economics*, 25:1984.
3. "An overview of the contractarian public finance of James Buchanan." *Public Finance Quarterly*, 16(April):1988.
4. "Efficient status seeking: externalities and the evolution of status games." *Journal of Economic Behavior and Organization*, 11:1989.
5. "The growth of social security expenditures, electoral push or political pull?" *Economic Inquiry*, 28(January):1990 (with W. Shughart).
6. "Information, special interests, and single-issue voting," *Public Choice*, 69(February):1991.
7. "Ideological conviction and persuasion in the rent-seeking society." *Journal of Public Economics*, 44(February):1991.
8. "The value of the veil, how much distributional information is enough?" *Public Choice*, 73(January): 1992 (with W. Sweetser).
9. "Rationality, morality, and exit." *American Political Science Review*, 86(June):1992 (with Viktor Vanberg).
10. "Political institutions and pollution control." *Review of Economics and Statistics*, 74(August):1992.
11. "Political efficiency and equal protection of the law." *Kyklos*, 50:1997.
12. "Voter discernment and candidate entry in pluralitarian elections." *Public Choice*, 95:1998 (with B. Steunenberg).
13. "Help, harm or avoid: on the personal advantage of dispositions to cooperate and punish in multilateral PD games with exit," *Journal of Economic Behavior and Organization*, 44:2001 (with V. Vanberg).
14. "Rational ignorance and rationally biased expectations: the discrete informational foundations of fiscal illusion," *Public Choice*, 107:2001.
15. "On the durability of King and Council: the continuum between dictatorship and democracy." *Constitutional Political Economy*, 12:2001.

Principal Contributions

Roger Congleton's main line of research has explored the interaction between various formal and informal institutions and the extent to which competition and conflict generate dead weight losses. That line of research has explored the role of institutions in democratic and non-democratic rent-seeking societies, rules for status seeking games, the role of formal and informal political constitutions in public policy formation, and the evolution of norms for participating in joint enterprises. A second line of research has explored the politics of national and international environmental policy formation. That research demonstrated that democratic politics clearly affects environmental policies. For example, democracies tend to have more rigorous environmental regulations and sign more environmental treaties than autocratic regimes. A third line of research uses history to determine the relationship between institutional structure and the emergence and failures of democratic regimes. Current research projects and a complete vita can be found on the web at rdc1.net.

COUGHLIN, Peter Joseph

Born
July 3, 1952; Hackensack, New Jersey, USA

Current Position
Associate Professor of Economics, University of Maryland at College Park, 1985–.

Past Positions
Assistant Professor of Economics, University of Maryland at College Park, 1982–1985; Postdoctoral Fellow at Harvard, Stanford, Oxford and Carnegie-Mellon Universities, 1978–1982; Assistant Professor of Economics, Middlebury College, 1976–1978.

Degrees
B.A., M.A., State University of New York at Albany, 1973, 1974; M.S., University of Vermont, 1978; Ph.D., State University of New York at Albany, 1976.

Offices and Honors
James L. Barr Award in Public Economics (from the Association for Public Policy Analysis and Management), 1984.
Fellow, Center for Advanced Study in the Behavioral Sciences at Stanford, 1987–1988.

Editorial Duties
Member, Editorial Board, *Economics Letters*, 1990–1992.

Principal Fields of Interest
Election Models; Social Choice; Voting Theory; Applied Game Theory.

Selected Publications
Book
1. *Probabilistic Voting Theory* (Cambridge University Press, 1992).

Articles
1. "Electoral outcomes with probabilistic voting and Nash social welfare maxima." *Journal of Public Economics*, 15:1981 (with S. Nitzan).
2. "Pareto optimality of policy proposals with probabilistic voting." *Public Choice*, 39:1982.
3. "Necessary and sufficient conditions for single-peakedness in public economic models." *Journal of Public Economics*, 25:1984 (with M. Hinich).
4. "Special majority rules and the existence of voting equilibria." *Social Choice and Welfare*, 3:1986.
5. "Rights and the private Pareto principle." *Economica*, 53:1986.
6. "Economic policy advice and political preferences." *Public Choice*, 61:1989.
7. "Candidate uncertainty and electoral equilibria." In *Advances in the Spatial Theory of Voting* (Cambridge University Press, 1990) (James Enelow and Melvin Hinich, eds).
8. "Electoral politics, interest groups and the size of government." *Economic Inquiry*, 28:1990 (with D. Mueller and P. Murrell).
9. "Pure strategy equilibria in a class of systems defense games." *International Journal of Game Theory*, 20:1992.
10. "Redistribution by a representative democracy and distributive justice under uncertainty." (ed.) *Markets, Information and Uncertainty* (Cambridge University Press, 1999) (edited by G. Chichilnisky).

Principal Contributions
Peter Coughlin's book and a number of his articles are about election models. In this area, he has been especially interested in probabilistic voting models. Among other things, his work on this topic has been concerned with conditions for electoral equilibria in probabilistic voting models, the locations of the equilibria, and welfare properties of the equilibria. He has also written articles on various aspects of majority voting. These articles address questions

about single-peakedness, voting equilibria and related topics. In addition, Coughlin has written about some other matters-including rights, systems defense games, and the relation between policy advice and political preferences.

COWEN, Tyler

Born
January 21, 1962, Kearny, New Jersey, USA

Current Positions
Holbert C. Harris Professor of Economics, George Mason University; General Director, Mercatus Center, James M. Buchanan Center for Political Economy.

Past Positions
Assistant and Associate Professor of Economics, University of California, Irvine, 1987–1990.

Degrees
B.S., George Mason University, 1983; Ph.D., Harvard University, 1987.

Principal Fields of Interest
Economics of the Arts; Public Choice; Economics and Philosophy; Applied Microeconomics.

Selected Publications
Books
1. *Explorations in the New Monetary Economics* (Basil Blackwell 1994) (with Randall Kroszner).
2. *Risk and Business Cycles: New and Old Austrian Perspectives* (Routledge, 1998).
3. *In Praise of Commercial Culture* (Harvard University Press, 1998).
4. *What Price Fame?* (Harvard University Press, 2002).
5. *Creative Destruction: How Globalization is Changing the World's Cultures* (Princeton University Press, 2002).

Articles
1. "Inconsistent equilibrium constructs: mises and rothbard on the evenly rotating economy." *American Economic Review*, 75 (September):1985 (with Richard Fink).
2. "The development of the new monetary economics." *Journal of Political Economy*, 95(June):1987 (with Randall Kroszner).
3. "Self-liberation versus self-constraint." *Ethics*, 10 (January): 1991.
4. "Law as a public good: the economics of anarchy." *Economics and Philosophy*, 8:1992.
5. "Against the social discount rate." In *Justice Across the Generations: Philosophy, Politics, and Society*, sixth series (Yale University Press, 1992) (Peter Laslett and James Fishkin, eds.) (with Derek Parfit).
6. "The scope and limits of preference sovereignty." *Economics and Philosophy*, 9: 1993.
7. "Rent-seeking promotes the provision of public goods," *Economics and Politics*, 6(2):1994 (with Amihai Glazer and Henry MacMillan).
8. "What do we learn from the repugnant conclusion?" *Ethics*, 106:1996.
9. "Why women succeed, and fail, in the arts." *Journal of Cultural Economics*, 20:1996.
10. "Discounting and restitution." *Philosophy and Public Affairs*, Spring:1997.
11. "Why do societies become more or less free?" (Mercatus Center publication) (George Mason University, 2000).
12. "An economic theory of avant-garde and popular art, or high and low culture." *Southern Economic Journal* 66:2000 (with Alex Tabarrok).

Principal Contributions
Tyler Cowen's current research interests concern the relations between commerce, creativity, capitalism, and freedom, as exemplified in his recent books on the economics of the arts. More generally, he is interested in the foundations of free societies and what makes them sustainable.

CRAIN, William Mark

Born
June 14, 1951, Port Arthur, Texas, USA

Current Positions
Professor of Economics, George Mason University, Virginia, USA, 1986–; Senior Research Associate, Center for Study of Public Choice, 1976–.

Past Positions
Associate Professor of Economics, George Mason University, 1982–1986; Special Assistant to the Director, US Office of Management and Budget, 1987–1988;

Associate Professor of Economics, Virginia Tech, 1979–1982; Visiting Assistant Professor of Economics, UCLA, 1978–1980.

Degrees
B.A., University of Houston, 1972; Ph.D., Texas A&M University, 1976.

Editorial Duties
Joint Editor, *Journal of Cultural Economics*, 1993–1998

Offices and Honors
Virginia Transportation Revenue Advisory Panel, 1990–98.
Virginia Retirement System Board of Trustees, 2001–.
Virginia Governor's Advisory Board of Economists, 1994–.

Principal Fields of Interest
Public Choice; Public Finance; Regulation.

Selected Publications

Books
1. *Vehicle Safety Inspection Systems: How Effective?* (American Enterprise Institute, 1980).
2. *Televised Legislatures: Political Information Technology and Public Choice* (Kluwer Academic Publishers, 1988) (with Brian L. Goff).
3. *Predicting Politics: Essays in Empirical Public Choice* (University of Michigan Press, 1990) (edited, with Robert D. Tollison).
4. *The Impact of Regulatory Costs on Small Firms*, (U.S. Small Business Administration, 2001) (with Thomas D. Hopkins).
5. *Volatile States: Institutions, Policy, and the Performance of American State Economies* (University of Michigan Press) in press.

Articles
1. "Campaign expenditures and political competition." *Journal of Law and Economics*, 19(April):1976 (with R.D. Tollison).
2. "On the structure of stability of political parkets." *Journal of Political Economy*, 85(4):1977.
3. "A test of the property rights theory of the firm: water utilities in the United States." *Journal of Law and Economics*, 21(2):1978 (with A. Zardkoohi).
4. "Constitutional change in the interest-group Theory of government." *Journal of Legal Studies*, 8(2):1979 (with R.D. Tollison).
5. "X-inefficiency and non-pecuniary rewards in a rent-seeking society: a neglected issue in the Property Rights Theory of the firm." *American Economic Review*, September: 1980 (with A. Zardkoohi).
6. "Final voting in legislatures." *American Economic Review*, 76(4):1986 (with D.R. Leavens and R.D. Tollison).
7. "Televising legislatures: an economic analysis," *Journal of Law and Economics*, 29(2):1986 (with B.L. Goff).
8. "Time inconsistency and fiscal policy: empirical analysis of US States, 1969–89." *Journal of Public Economics*, 51(2):1993 (with R.D. Tollison).
9. "Legislative committees as loyalty-generating institutions." *Public Choice*, 81(November):1994 (with D.C. Coker).
10. "The politics of infrastructure." *Journal of Law and Economics*, 38(1):1995 (with L.K. Oakley).
11. "Legislative organization of fiscal policy." *Journal of Law and Economics*, 38(2):1995 (with T.J. Muris).
12. "Fiscal consequences of budget baselines." *Journal of Public Economics*, 67(3):1998 (with Nicole V. Crain).
13. "Economic growth regressions for the American States: a sensitivity analysis," with K.J. Lee, *Economic Inquiry*, 37(2):1999.
14. "Districts, diversity and fiscal biases: evidence from the American States," *Journal of Law and Economics*, 23(2):1999.
15. "The constitutionality of race-conscious redistricting: an empirical analysis," *Journal of Legal Studies*, 30(1): 2001.

Principal Contributions
The common theme in Mark Crain's research is the empirical testing of economic and political hypotheses. This includes his early work on the property rights theory of the firm (public versus private utilities), regulation (vehicle safety inspections), his work on legislatures and legislative institutions (redistricting, final voting, television, and committees), and more recent work on budgetary and fiscal institutions (term limits, legislative organization and fiscal policy, taxation and economic growth, and budgetary processes). Crain's most recent book entitled *Volatile States* examines why American state economies grow at vastly different rates and manifest wide differences in living standards. The analysis elevates the role of economic and fiscal volatility, and identifies institutions and policies that are key determinants of economic success. The central contribution is the elevated role of volatility, which tracks the perspective in modern financial theory. Just as rates of return alone provide an incomplete basis for gauging portfolio performance, the level or growth in state economies

reveals an incomplete and perhaps distorted picture of performance. Taking the volatility of state economies explicitly into account refines the whole notion of "economic success." In addition to economic volatility, his research explores the importance of fiscal volatility: for example, the trade-off between the volatility of state budgets and the efficiency of public sector operations. Institutions such as balanced budget requirements, tax and expenditure limitations, biennial budgeting, and the item veto affect fiscal volatility and through this channel have indirect as well as direct effects on the size of government.

CREW, Michael Anthony

Born
May 28, 1942, Sedgley, Staffordshire, England

Current Positions
Professor II, Rutgers Business School, Newark and New Brunswick, Rutgers University, 1987–; Director of Center for Research in Regulated Industries, Graduate School of Management, Rutgers University, 1984–.

Past Positions
Visiting Professor of Economics, University of Texas at Arlington, 1984; Professor I (with tenure), Graduate School of Management, Rutgers University, 1987; Associate Professor of Business Administration (with tenure), Rutgers University, 1980; Visiting Professor of Economics, Wesleyan University, Spring 1976; Visiting Faculty Member in Economics, Harvard University, Summer 1975; Senior Lecturer in Economics, University of Strathclyde, 1974–1977; Associate Head, Department of Social Studies, Paisley College of Technology, 1972–1974; Lecturer in Economics, University of Southampton, 1971–1972; Lecturer in Economics, London Graduate School of Business Studies, 1970–1971; Lecturer in Economics, University of Kent at Canterbury, 1969–1970; Visiting Lecturer/Visiting Assistant Professor of Economics, Carnegie-Mellon University, 1968–1969; Assistant Lecturer/Lecturer in Management Studies, University of Bradford, 1965–1969; Assistant Lecturer in Business Economics, University of Strathclyde, 1964–1965.

Degrees
B.Com., University of Birmingham, 1963; Ph.D., University of Bradford, 1972.

Offices and Honors
Recipient with Paul Kleindorfer, on behalf of the Center for Research in Regulated Industries, of the Hermes Award, 1992. Distinguished Service Award 2002, Public Utility Research Center, University of Florida.

Editorial Duties
Editor and founder, *Journal of Regulatory Economics*, 1988–; Editor, Kluwer Series of books, *Topics in Regulatory Economics and Policy*, 1986–; Co-founder, *Applied Economics* and Executive Editor, Joint Editor and Editor 1968–1972.

Principal Fields of Interest
Regulatory Economics.

Selected Publications
Books
1. *Public Utility Economics* (Macmillan Press, St. Martin's Press, 1979) (with P.R. Kleindorfer).
2. *Problems in Public Utility Economics and Regulation* (ed.) (Lexington Books, 1979).
3. *Issues in Public Utility Pricing and Regulation* (ed.) (Lexington Books, 1980).
4. *The Economics of Public Utility Regulation* (Macmillan Press, M.I.T. Press, 1986) (with P.R. Kleindorfer).
5. *Regulating Utilities in an Era of Deregulation* (ed.) (Macmillan Press, 1987).
6. *The Economics of Postal Service*, (Kluwer Academic Publishers, 1992) (with P.R. Kleindorfer).
7. *Emerging Competition in the Postal and Delivery Sectors*, (ed.) (Kluwer Academic Publishers, 1999) (with P.R. Kleindorfer).
8. *Current Directions in Postal Reform* (ed.) (Kluwer Academic Publishers, 2000) (with P.R. Kleindorfer).
9. *Expanding Competition in Regulated Industries* (ed.) (Kluwer Academic Publishers, 2000).
10. *Future Directions in Postal Reform* (ed.) (Kluwer Academic Publishers, 2001) (with P.R. Kleindorfer).
11. *Postal and Delivery Services: Pricing, Productivity, Regulation and Strategy* (ed.) (Kluwer Academic Publishers, 2002) (with P.R. Kleindorfer).

Articles
1. "Pennine electricity board." (Nelson, 1966); reprinted in Ralph Turvey (ed.), *Public Enterprise* (Penguin, 1969).
2. "Marshall and Turvey on peak load or joint product pricing." *Journal of Political Economy*, November-December:1971 (with P.R. Kleindorfer).
3. "Peak load pricing with a diverse technology." *Bell Journal of Economics*, Spring:1976 (with P.R. Kleindorfer).
4. "Reliability and public utility pricing." *American Economic Review*, March:1978 (with P.R. Kleindorfer).

5. "Public utility regulation and managerial discretion." *Southern Economic Journal*, January:1979 (with P.R. Kleindorfer).
6. "Peak-load pricing in postal services." *Economic Journal*, September:1990 (with P.R. Kleindorfer and M.A. Smith).
7. "Economic depreciation and the regulated firm under competition and technological change." *Journal of Regulatory Economics*, March:1992 (with P.R. Kleindorfer).
8. "The theory of Peak-Load Pricing: a survey," *Journal of Regulatory Economics*, November:1995 (with C.S. Fernando and P.R. Kleindorfer).
9. "Incentive regulation in the United Kingdom and the United States: some lessons." *Journal of Regulatory Economics*, May:1996 (with P.R. Kleindorfer).
10. "Efficient entry, monopoly, and the Universal Service Obligation in postal service." *Journal of Regulatory Economics*, September:1998 (with P.R. Kleindorfer).

Principal Contributions
Michael Crew's early work was in the field of industrial organization and public policy, commencing with studies of the British electric utility industry. This provided the basis for his work on the theory and practice of peak load pricing with Paul Kleindorfer. Combining this with his interests in X-efficiency, institutional economics and government, Crew became increasingly interested in the role of regulation especially of natural monopoly. He has applied his work to all the network industries and more recently extensively to the postal sector with Paul Kleindorfer. As founder and Director of the Center for Research in Regulated Industries, Crew has aimed through conferences and studies to foster research and informed debate on regulation. He has written and edited over 25 books and published over 80 essays or articles. For details of his curriculum vitae and the work of the Center see http://crri.rutgers.edu

DA EMPOLI, Domenico

Born
September 24, 1941, Reggio Calabria, Italy

Current Positions
Chairman of the Scientific Committee of "Fondazione Luigi Einaudi per Studi di Politica ed Economia", 1985–; Professor of Public Finance, Università di Roma "La Sapienza", 1984–; Professor of Public Economics at Luiss Libera Università degli Studi Sociali — Roma, 1968–.

Past Positions
Assistant of Public Finance, Università di Roma "La Sapienza", 1967–1974; Professor of Public Finance, Univerità di Messina, 1975–1978; Professor of Public Finance, Università di Napoli, 1979–1983.

Degree
D.J., Università di Roma "La Sapienza", 1963.

Offices and Honors
Member, The Mont Pelerin Society, 1976.
Member, Board of SIEP (Public Economics Society), 1994–1999.
Vice-President SIEP (Public Economics Society), 1994–1999.
Vice-President (and then President) of the Economic Committee of CNR (National Research Council), 1994–1999.
Member, Finance Committee, International Seabed Authority (Kingston, Jamaica), 1995–.
Chairman, Finance Committee, International Seabed Authority (Kingston, Jamaica), 1998–.

Editorial Duties
Founding Editor, *Journal of Public Finance and Public Choice*, 1983–.

Principal Fields of Interest
Public Finance and Public Choice; History of Economic Thought.

Selected Publications
Books and Essays
1. *Analisi critica di alcuni effetti dell' imposta generale sulle vendite*, (Giuffrè, 1966.)
2. *Debito pubblico, imposte e tasso d'interesse*, (Giuffrè, 1974).
3. *Finanza pubblica e Contabilità nazionale su base trimestrale [1954–1975]* (ed.) (Cedam, 1979).
4. *Scelte Pubbliche* (Le Monnier, 1984). (edited with S. Carrubba).
5. *Il Bilancio dello Stato-La finanza pubblica tra Governo e Parlamento* (Sole-24 Ore, 1988, 3rd ed. 2000) (with P. De Ioanna and G. Vegas).

6. *Le Vie della Libertà-Il Liberalismo come teoria e come politica negli anni novanta* (ed.) (Fondazione Luigi Einaudi, 1993).
7. *Verso un nuovo Stato sociale-Tendenze e criteri*, (Angeli, 1997) (edited with G. Muraro).
8. *Concorrenza fiscale in un'economia internazionale integrata*, Angeli, 1999 (edited, with M. Bordignon).
9. *Politica fiscale, flessibilità dei mercati e crescita*, Angeli, 2001 (edited, with M. Bordignon).

Articles
1. "Note critiche sull'imposizione degli incrementi di valore patrimoniali." *Rivista di diritto finanziario e Scienza delle finanze*, 1964.
2. "Riforma tributaria e finanza locale." *Tributi*, 1971.
3. "Stato sociale e democrazia." *Rassegna economica del Banco di Napoli*, 1983.
4. "A science for liberty: public finance according to Luigi Einaudi's Thought." *Journal of Public Finance and Public Choice*, 1986.
5. "Beni pubblici e democrazia." *Teoria dei sistemi economici* (ed. B. Jossa), Utet, 1989.
6. "The Italian Law for the protection of competition and the market." *Journal of Public Finance and Public Choice*, 1990.
7. "Do ideas have consequences?." *Journal of Public Finance and Public Choice*, 2-3: 1992.
8. "Public choice in Italy." *Public Choice*, 77:1994.
9. "Federalismo fiscale e scelte pubbliche." *Attualità del federalismo fiscale*, Univ. of Cassino, 1996.
10. "Harmful tax competition." *International Tax Law Review*, 1999.
11. "Welfare state and income redistribution in democracy." *Review of Economic Conditions of Italy*, 2000.
12. "A public choice analysis of the international sea-bed authority." *Constitutional Economics*, 11:2000.
13. "The reduction of the Italian public debt: problems and opportunities." *Politica fiscale, flessibilità dei mercati e crescita* cit., 2001 (with C. De Nicola).

Principal Contributions
Domenico da Empoli's early work focused on traditional Public Finance subjects, such as sales taxation and public debt. Progressively, his interests in the economic study of institutions grew, under the influence of James M. Buchanan's and Gordon Tullock's teachings. Though he became acquainted with Public Choice in 1966 (his first year of study in American universities, mainly the University of Illinois and the University of Chicago, where he spent a second year), da Empoli waited some time before entering into this field of research, essentially because he thought that this approach might lower government's reputation and in this way it might weaken the foundations of the polity. He now thinks the opposite: Public choice helps in discovering the existing imperfections of the public system that can harm the use of national resources and sometimes also restrain individual liberties. Public choice provides the instruments to recognize the dangers of public policies and to prevent these dangers through appropriate constitutional reforms. His personal interests in this sector deal with the policy implications of public choice (in particular in the area of welfare), not only at national level, but also in international organizations. These views inspire his activity as editor of the *Journal of Public Finance and Public Choice* (see the web page: www.jpfpc.org).

DAVIS, Otto Anderson

Born
April 4, 1934, Florence, South Carolina, USA

Current Position
W.W. Cooper University Professor of Economics and Public Policy, Carnegie Mellon University, 1981–.

Past Positions
Dean and Professor of Political Economy, School of Urban and Public Affairs (now the Heinz School of Public Policy and Management), Carnegie Mellon University, 1975–1981; Associate Dean and Professor of Political Economy, School of Urban and Public Affairs, 1968–1975; Professor of Economics, Graduate School of Industrial Administration, Carnegie Mellon University, 1967–1968; Associate Professor of Economics, Graduate School of Industrial Administration, 1965–1967; Assistant Professor of Economics, Graduate School of Industrial Administration, 1960–1965.

Degrees
A.B., Wofford College, 1956; M.A., Ph.D., University of Virginia, 1957, 1960.

Offices and Honors
President, The Public Choice Society, 1970–1972.
Fellow of the Center for Advanced Study in the Behavioral Sciences, 1974–1975.
Fellow of the Econometric Society, elected 1978.
Research Director, Pennsylvania Tax Commission, 1979–81.
President, The Association of Public Policy Analysis and Management, 1983.

Listed in *Who's Who in Economics: A Biographical Dictionary of Major Economists 1700–1980.*

Principal Fields of Interest

Public Choice; Issues of Public Policy, including regulation, education, and urban problems; and a special interest in freedom, both economic and political, and its consequences for the organization of society.

Selected Publications

Articles

1. "The economics of urban renewal." *Law and Contemporary Problems*, 26(winter):1961 (with A. Whinston).
2. "Externalities, welfare and the theory of games." *Journal of Political Economy*, 70(June):1962 (with A. Whinston).
3. "Welfare economics and the theory of second best." *Review of Economic Studies*, 32(January):1965 (with A. Whinston).
4. "An elementary political and economic theory of the expenditures of local governments." *Southern Economic Journal*, 32(October):1966 (with J. Barr).
5. "On the process of budgeting: an empirical study of congressional appropriations." *Papers on Non-Market Decision Making*, 1:1966 (with M.A.H. Dempster and A. Wildavsky).
6. "A mathematical model of policy formation in a democratic society." In *Mathematical Applications in Political Science II* (Southern Methodist University Press, 1966) (J. Bernd, ed.) (with M.J. Hinich).
7. "A theory of the budgetary process." *American Political Science Review*, 60(September):1966 (with M.A.H. Dempster and A. Wildavsky).
8. "Urban property markets: some empirical results and their implications for municipal zoning." *Journal of Law and Economics*, 10(October):1967 (with J.P. Crecine and J.E. Jackson).
9. "Externalities, information and alternative collective action," (with M. Kamien), *The Analysis and Evaluation off Public Expenditures: the PPB System*, A compendium of papers submitted to the Subcommittee on Economy in Government of the Joint Economic Committee of the Congress of the U.S. (U.S. Government Printing Office, 1969.)
10. "An expository development of a mathematical model of the electoral process." *American Political Science Review*, 54(June):1970 (with M.J. Hinich and P.C. Ordeshook).
11. "Social preference orderings and majority rule." *Econometrica*, 40(January):1972 (with M.H. DeGroot and M.J. Hinich).
12. "The shrinkage in the stock of low quality housing in the central city: an empirical study of the U.S. experience over the last ten years." *Urban Studies*, 11(February):1974 (With C. Eastman and Chang-i Hua).
13. "Senate defeat of the family assistance plan." *Public Policy*, 3(summer):1974 (with J.E. Jackson).
14. "Towards a predictive theory of government expenditure: U.S. domestic appropriations." *British Journal of Politics*, 1975 (with M.A.H. Dempster and A. Wildavsky).
15. "Imperfect consumers and welfare comparisons of policies concerning information and regulation." *The Bell Journal of Economics*, 7(Autumn):1976 (with C.S. Colantoni and M. Swaminathan).
16. "A simultaneous equations model of the educational process." *Journal of Public Economics*, 1977 (with A.E. Boardman and P.R. Sanday).
17. "The jitneys: a study of grassroots capitalism." *Journal of Contemporary Studies*, 7(Winter):1984 (with N. Johnson).
18. "Private income security during a time of stress: a case study of U.S. Steel." *Labour and Society*, 15:1990 (with E. Montgomery).
19. "The two freedoms, economic growth and development: an empirical study." *Public Choice*, 100:1999 (with W. Wu).
20. "The two freedoms in a growth model." *The Journal of Private Enterprise*, XIV(Spring):1999 (with W. Wu).

Principal Contributions

Otto Davis's interest in the problems associated with public choice began in graduate school under the influence of James M. Buchanan, his advisor, and has been a constant theme in his intellectual life. Also, he has been consistently interested in public policy problems including the intellectual underpinnings, that make analysis of such problems possible. Otherwise, he refers to himself as an intellectual drifter, working on whatever strikes his fancy at one particular time. Recently, the quantification and measurement of the philosophy of classical liberalism, and democracy, have stimulated his latent interest in the study of these freedoms and he expects this interest to occupy much of his time in the future.

EKELUND, Robert Burton Jr.

Born

September 20, 1940, Galveston, Texas, USA

Current Positions

Edward K. and Catherine L. Lowder Eminent Scholar, Auburn University, 1988–; Vernon F. Taylor Distinguished Professor, Trinity University, 2003–.

Past Positions

Visiting Scholar, Hoover Institute, Stanford University, July 1992; Professor of Economics, Auburn University, January 1979–; Lowder Professor of Economics, Auburn University, 1977–1978; Liberty National Professor of Economics, 1987–1988; Visiting Professor of Economics, Auburn University, 1977–1978; From Assistant Professor (1967–1970) to Associate Professor (1970–1974) to Professor; (1974–1979) of Economics, Texas A&M University; Instructor of Economics, Louisiana State University; 1966–1967; Graduate Teaching Assistant, Louisiana State University, 1963–1966; Instructor of Economics, St. Mary's University, 1962–1963.

Degrees

B.B.A., St. Mary's University, 1962; M.A., St. Mary's University, 1963; Ph.D., Louisiana State University, 1967.

Offices and Honors

Member, Heritage Foundation, Cato Institute, Mises Institute.
Phi Kappa Phi, Elected 1974, Texas A&M University.
Executive Committee: Association for Social Economics (1977–1978).
Executive Committee: Southern Economic Association (1982–1983).
First Vice-President, Southern Economic Association, 1984.
1990 Sir Antony Fisher Memorial Award (Third Place).
Listed in *Who's Who in Economics: A Biographical Dictionary of Major Economists, 1700–1986*. second edition, third edition.
Advisory Board, Jule Collins Smith Museum of Art, Auburn University.

Editorial Duties

Permanent Associate Editor; *Review of Social Economy* (1977–1995); *History of Political Economy* (1983–1988); *Social Science Journal* (1984–present); *Review of Austrian Economics* (1985–1997); *Quarterly Journal of Austrian Economics* (1998–present).

Principal Fields of Interest

Political Economy of Regulation; Economic History and Public Choice; History of Economic Theory.

Selected Publications

Books

1. *The Evolution of Demand Theory: A Collection of Essays* (D.C. Heath and Co., 1972) (edited, with W.P. Gramm and Eirik Furubotn).
2. *A. History of Economic Theory and Method* (McGraw-Hill, Inc., 1975, 1983, 1990, 1997, with Spanish, Chinese, and Serbo-Croatian translations) (with R.F. Hebert).
3. *Mercantilism as a Rent-Seeking Society: Economic Regulation in Historical Perspective* (Texas A&M University Press, 1981) (with R.D. Tollison).
4. *Economics* (Little, Brown and Company, 1986, 1988, 1991, 1994, 1997, 2000) (with R.D. Tollison).
5. *Advertising and the Market Process: A Modern Economic View* (Pacific Institute, 1988, with French translation, 1992; Turkish translation, 1999) (with D.S. Saurman).
6. *Intermediate Microeconomics: Price Theory and Application* (D.C. Heath, Inc., 1995) (with R.W. Ault).
7. *Sacred Trust: The Medieval Church as an Economic Firm* (Oxford University Press, 1996) (with R.F. Hebert, R.D. Tollison, G. Anderson, and A. Davidson).
8. *Politicized Economies: Monarchs, Monopoly and Mercantilism* (Texas A&M University Press, 1997) (with R.D. Tollison).
9. *The Foundations of Regulatory Economics* 3 Volumes with introduction and readers guide (ed.) (Edward Elgar Publishing, 1998).
10. *Secret Origins of Modern Microeconomics: Dupuit and the Engineers* (University of Chicago Press, 1999) (with R.F. Hebert).

Articles

1. "Jules Dupuit and the early theory of marginal cost pricing." *Journal of Political Economy*, 76(May/June): 1968.
2. "Price discrimination and product differentiation in Economic Theory: an early analysis." *The Quarterly Journal of Economics*, 84(May):1970.
3. "Public economics at the *Ecole des Ponts et Chaussees*, 1830–50." *Journal of Public Economics*, 2(July):1973 (with R.F. Hebert).
4. "Joint Supply, the Taussig-Pigou controversy and the theory of public goods." *Journal of Law and Economics*, 16(October):1973 (with J.R. Hulett).
5. "Capital fixity, innovations, and long-term contracting: an intertemporal economic theory of Regulation." *American Economic Review*, March:1982 (with R.S. Higgins).

6. "Political choice and the child labor statute of 1938: public interest or interest group legislation?." *Public Choice*, 82:1995 (with A. Davidson and E. Davis).
7. "The *Economist* Dupuit on theory, institutions and policy: first of the moderns?." *History of Political Economy*, 32(Spring):2000.
8. "Market power in radio markets: an empirical analysis of local and national concentration." *Journal of Law and Economics*, 43(April):2000 (with G.S. Ford and T. Koutsky).
9. "The origins of neoclassical economics." *Journal of Economic Perspectives*, 16(May):2002 (with R.F. Hebert).
10. "An economic analysis of the protestant reformation." *Journal of Political Economy*, 110(June):2002 (with R.F. Hebert and R.D. Tollison).

Principal Contributions
Robert Ekelund's three overarching and interwoven interests in economics have remained the same from the beginning: in history of economic theory, in the political economy of regulation and in the economic history of institutions. With few exceptions, his entire career has been devoted to these three general areas. After a number of early contributions in the areas of history of theory, economic history and regulation he was confronted with two new approaches to these subjects: the seminal work of Stigler and Peltzman that generalized the supply and demand for regulation and the underlying principles of public choice, taught to him at Texas A&M by his friend Bob Tollison. These confrontations changed the directions and methods of his research. With Tollison (and others), large segments of the whole panoply of western economic history are being reexamined using refined tools of modern microeconomics, public choice, and property rights. New insights may be turned out utilizing these important tools that have implications for economic growth and development, a fundamental aim of the science. In a loose sense, Ekelund's entire output of some 200 papers and essays and 24 books is devoted to this quest.

FISCHEL, William A.

Born
April 10, 1945, Bethlehem, Pennsylvania, USA

Current Positions
Professor of Economics, Dartmouth College, Hanover, New Hampshire, 1973–; Faculty Associate, Lincoln Institute of Land Policy, Cambridge, MA, 1997–.

Past Positions
Visiting Professor, University of Washington (Seattle) Graduate School of Public Affairs, 1998–1999; Visiting Professor, University of California at Santa Barbara, 1985–1986; Visiting Associate Professor, University of California at Davis, 1980–1981; Adjunct Professor, Vermont Law School, 1984–1991; Olin Fellow in Law and Economics, School of Law (Boalt Hall), University of California, Berkeley, 1991–1992; Instructor, Economics Institute for Federal Judges and Law Professors, George Mason University School of Law, 1995–1998.

Degrees
B.A., Amherst College, 1967; Ph.D., Princeton University, 1973.

Offices and Honors
Phi Beta Kappa, 1967.
Honorable Mention [second prize], National Tax Association's Outstanding Doctoral Dissertation Competition, 1974.
Who's Who in America, 1988.

Editorial Duties
Editorial Boards: *Eastern Economic Journal*, 1992–; *Land Economics* 1985–; *Planning and Markets* (electronic journal) 1996– (charter board member); *Regulation* (Cato Institute) 1999–.

Principal Fields of Interest
Law and Economics of Local Government, including Land-Use Regulation, Property Taxation, and School Finance.

Selected Publications
Books
1. *The Economics of Zoning Laws: A Property Rights Approach to American Land Use Controls* (Johns Hopkins University Press, 1985).
2. *Regulatory Takings: Law, Economics, and Politics* (Harvard University Press, 1995).
3. *The Homevoter Hypothesis: How Home Values Influence Local Government Taxation, School Finance, and Land-Use Policies* (Harvard University Press, 2001).

Articles
1. "Takings, insurance, and Michelman: comments on economic interpretations of 'Just Compensation' Law." *Journal of Legal Studies*, 17:1988 (with Perry Shapiro).
2. "A Constitutional choice model of compensation for takings." *International Review of Law and Economics*, 9:1989 (with Perry Shapiro).

3. "Exploring the Kozinski paradox: why is more efficient regulation a taking of property?" *Chicago-Kent Law Review*, 67(3):1991.
4. "Property taxation and the Tiebout model: evidence for the benefit view from Zoning and voting." *Journal of Economic Literature*, 30:1992.
5. "The offer/ask disparity and just compensation for takings: a constitutional choice perspective." *International Review of Law and Economics*, 15:1995.
6. "How *Serrano* caused proposition 13." *Journal of Law and Politics*, 12:1996.
7. "The political economy of just compensation: lessons from the military draft for the takings issue." *Harvard Journal of Law and Public Policy*, 20:1996.
8. "Preferences for school finance systems: voters versus Judges." *National Tax Journal*, 49:1996 (with Colin Campbell).
9. "Why judicial reversal of apartheid made a difference." *Vanderbilt Law Review* (Colloquium Issue: Rethinking *Buchanan v. Warley*), 51:1998.
10. "Homevoters, municipal corporate governance, and the benefit view of the property tax." *National Tax Journal* 54:2001.

Principal Contributions
William Fischel has endeavored to understand the workings of local government through the lenses of neoclassical economics, law and economics, and public choice. Both the left and right sides of the political spectrum are skeptical about local government: liberals because it is local, conservatives because it is government. Both views undervalue the unique, hybrid nature of American municipalities. The smaller (less than 100,000 population) local governments in which most Americans live are best characterized as municipal corporations whose major stockholders are their resident homeowners. More than 25,000 local governments are scattered across in the United States, making it among the most competitive industries in the nation. Good and bad things local governments do raise and lower home values, but homeowners, unlike corporate stockholders, cannot diversify their holdings. This makes homebuyers attentive to the choice of municipality and school district, as suggested by Tiebout, and to the governance of the location they eventually choose. Homeowners use zoning laws to protect their investment, often at the expense of outsiders and owners of developable property. Fischel has shown how local governments use and abuse zoning in *The Economics of Zoning Laws* (1985), and has explained how courts have failed to police the legal boundaries between homeowners and owners of undeveloped land in *Regulatory Takings* (1995). Yet in *The Homevoter Hypothesis* (2001), he argues the local governments produce better schools and higher quality environments than the state or national government would, giving a guarded endorsement to what Tocqueville celebrated as the foundation of American democracy.

FROHLICH, Norman

Born
September 30, 1941, Winnipeg, Manitoba, Canada

Current Positions
Professor, I.H. Asper School of Business, University of Manitoba; Senior Researcher, Manitoba Centre for Health Policy, 1990–.

Past Positions
Professor, Department of Business Administration, University of Manitoba, 1990–; Professor, Department of Public Policy, University of Manitoba, 1981–1989; Head of Department 1982–1989; Associate Professor, Department of Public Policy, University of Manitoba, 1979–1981; Management Audit Officer, Department of Finance, Province of Manitoba, 1978–1979; Program Audit Officer, Management Committee of Cabinet Secretariat, Province of Manitoba, 1976–1978; Associate Professor, Department of Government, The University of Texas at Austin, 1974–1976; Assistant Professor, Department of Government, The University of Texas at Austin, 1970–1974.

Degrees
B.Sc., Mathematics, The University of Manitoba, 1963; M.S., Mathematics, Rutgers University, 1965; Ph.D., Politics, Princeton University, 1971.

Offices and Honors
Fellowship from the Japan Society for the Promotion of Science 1996.
Member of the Honorary Board of the Public Choice Society, Japan.
Duncan Black Prize for the best article of 1996 in *Public Choice*.

Editorial Duties
Charter member, Editorial Board, *Journal of Theoretical Politics*; Joint Book Review Editor (with Joe A. Oppenheimer and Oran Young), *Public Choice*, 1973–1975.

Principal Fields of Interest
Experimental Economics; Public Choice; Ethics; Distributive Justice; Collective Action/Social Dilemmas; Health Care Policy.

Selected Publications
Books
1. *Political Leadership and Collective Goods* (Princeton University Press, 1971) (with Joe A. Oppenheimer and Oran Young).
2. *Modern Political Economy*, in Robert A. Dahl (ed.) *The Foundation of Modern Political Science Series*, (Prentice-Hall Inc., 1978) (with Joe A. Oppenheimer).
3. *Economia Politica Moderna* (The University of Brasilia Press published a Portuguese translation of *Modern Political Economy* in its political thought series: Pensamento Politico, 1992); *Modern Political Economy*, 1991; a Japanese edition with updated suggested readings.
4. *Choosing Justice: an Experimental Approach to Ethical Theory* (University of California Press, 1992) (with Joe A. Oppenheimer).

Articles
1. "I get by with a little help from my friends." *World Politics*, 22(October): 1970 (with Joe A. Oppenheimer).
2. "Self-interest or altruism: what difference?" *Journal of Conflict Resolution*, 18(March):1974.
3. "The carrot and the stick: optimal program mixes for entrepreneurial political leaders." *Public Choice*, 19 (Fall):1974 (with Joe A. Oppenheimer).
4. "Individual contributions to collective goods: alternative models." *Journal of Conflict Resolution*, 19(March):1975 (with Thomas Hunt, Joe A. Oppenheimer, and R. Harrison Wagner).
5. "The instability of minimum winning coalitions." *American Political Science Review*, 69(September):1975.
6. "A test of downsian voter rationality: 1964 presidential voting." *American Political Science Review*, 72(March):1978 (with Joe A. Oppenheimer, Jeffrey Smith, and Oran R. Young).
7. "Beyond economic man: altruism, egalitarianism, and difference maximizing." *Journal of Conflict Resolution*, 28(1):1984 (with Joe A. Oppenheimer and with Pat Bond and Irvin Boschmann).
8. "Choices of principles of distributive justice in experimental groups." *American Journal of Political Science*, 31(3):1987 (with Joe A. Oppenheimer and Cheryl Eavey).
9. "Choosing justice in experimental democracies with production." *American Political Science Review*, 84(2):1990 (with Joe A. Oppenheimer).
10. "An impartial reasoning solution to the prisoner's dilemma." *Public Choice*, 74:1992.
11. "A regional comparison of socioeconomic and health indices in a Canadian Province." *Social Science and Medicine*, 42(9):1996 (with Cam Mustard).
12. "Experiencing impartiality to invoke fairness in the n-PD: some experimental results." *Public Choice*, 86: 1996 (with Joe Oppenheimer).
13. "Improving the effectiveness of gainsharing: the role of fairness and participation." *Administrative Studies Quarterly*, 37:1992 (with Christine Cooper and Bruno Dyck).
14. "A role for structured observation in ethical inquiry." *Social Justice Review*, 10(1):1997 (with Joe A. Oppenheimer).
15. "Some doubts about measuring self-interest using dictator experiments: the costs of anonymity." *Journal of Economic Behavior and Organization*, 46(3):2001 (with Joe Oppenheimer and J. Bernard Moore).

Principal Contributions
Norman Frohlich routinely collaborates with Joe Oppenheimer. Their initial interest in collective action led them to identify conditions under which rational self-interested individuals would contribute to public goods, to identify classes of public goods and (together with Oran Young) to define and develop the first formal characterization of the political entrepreneur. They also developed early experiments that demonstrated the existence of classes of other regarding behavior. They also utilized the tools of experimental economics to examine notions of distributive justice and show the potential of experimental methods for casting light on ethical problems. Frohlich and Oppenheimer's more recent work has focused on normative and cognitive aspects of decision making. They have been attempting to identify how generalized framing effects can impact individual and societal decisions, both from a normative and positive perspective.

GARRETT, Thomas A.

Born
January 18, 1971, Lancaster, Pennsylvania, USA

Current Position
Senior Economist, The Federal Reserve Bank of St. Louis.

Past Positions
Assistant Professor, Department of Agricultural Economics, Kansas State University, May 1999 to June

2002; Post-Doctoral Fellow, Department of Economics, West Virginia University, August 1998 to May 1999.

Degrees
B.S.B.A., Shippensburg University of Pennsylvania, May 1993; M.A., West Virginia University, May 1997; Ph.D., West Virginia University, August 1998.

Principal Fields of Interest
Public Choice, State and Local Public Finance, Economics of State Lotteries and Gambling.

Selected Publications
Articles
1. "Taxation and product quality: new evidence from generic cigarettes." *Journal of Political Economy*, 105(August):1997 (with R. Sobel).
2. "A test of shirking under legislative and citizen vote: the case of state lottery adoption." *Journal of Law and Economics*, 42(April):1999.
3. "Gamblers favor skewness, not risk: further evidence from United States' lottery Games." *Economics Letters*, 63(April):1999 (with R. Sobel).
4. "An introduction to state and local public finance," in Scott Loveridge (ed.) *The Web-Book of Regional Science* (Regional Research Institute, West Virginia University, 2000) (with J. Leatherman).
5. "An international comparison of lotteries and the distribution of lottery expenditures." *International Review of Applied Economics*, 15(April):2001.
6. "The leviathan lottery? testing the revenue maximization objective of state lotteries as evidence for leviathan." *Public Choice*, 109(October):2001.
7. "Economies of scale and inefficiencies in county extension councils: a case for consolidation?" *American Journal of Agricultural Economics*, 83(November): 2001.
8. "Earmarking lottery revenues for education: a new test of fungibility." *Journal of Education Finance*, 26(Winter):2001.
9. "On the measurement of rent seeking and its social opportunity cost." *Public Choice* 112:2002 (with R. Sobel).
10. "The revenue impacts of cross-border lottery shopping in the presence of spatial autocorrelation." forthcoming in *Regional Science and Urban Economics* (with T. Marsh). (2003)

Principal Contributions
Much of Thomas Garrett's research has focused on the economics of state lotteries from both a public finance and a public choice perspective. Given states' increasing reliance on non-traditional revenue sources such as lotteries, he has explored the impacts of cross-border lottery shopping and the effectiveness of earmarking lottery funds. This work has revealed there are significant lottery revenue gains and losses across state lines due to geographical convenience and differences in lottery jackpots, and that political incentives available to state politicians inhibit the proper earmarking of lottery revenues for education. Another piece provided evidence on the risk preferences of lottery players and how these preferences translate into the game design that maximizes lottery revenue. Garrett contributed to the literature on legislative shirking by exploring the political processes behind state lottery adoption. The empirical model and results are more robust than earlier works on legislative shirking since voting data is available for both the legislature and citizenry. He also developed a new empirical test for Leviathan, which is based on the construction of individual lottery games to maximize lottery revenues for the state. His recent research focus has been the inefficiency of public sector organizations such as public school districts and Land-Grant Extension services. Unique simulations are performed to measure the cost-savings to taxpayers from consolidating these public sector services.

GOFF, Brian L.

Born
March 26, 1961, San Diego, California, USA

Current Positions
Professor of Economics, Western Kentucky University, 1996–.

Past Positions
Associate Professor of Economics, Western Kentucky University, 1991–1996; Assistant Professor of Economics, 1986–1991.

Degrees
B.A., Western Kentucky University, 1983; M.A., George Mason University, 1985; Ph.D., George Mason University, 1986.

Offices and Honors
Research Award, Ford College of Business, Western Kentucky University, 1999.
Research Award, Ford College of Business, Western Kentucky University, 1992.

Vitale Award for Innovation and Creativity in MBA Curriculum, Ford College of Business, Western Kentucky University, 2001.

Principal Fields of Interest
Economics of Organizations; Macro Political Economy; Economics of Sports.

Selected Publications
Books
1. *Televised Legislatures: Political Information Technology and Public Choice* (Kluwer Academic Publishers, 1988) (with W.M. Crain).
2. *Sportometrics* (Texas A&M University Press, 1990) (edited, with R.D. Tollison).
3. *The National Collegiate Athletic Association: A Study in Cartel Behavior* (University of Chicago Press, 1992) (with A.A. Fleisher and R.D. Tollison).
4. *Regulation and Macroeconomic Performance* (Kluwer Academic Publishers, 1996).
5. *Spoiled Rotten: Affluence, Anxiety, and Social Decay in America* (Westview Press, 1999) (with A.A. Fleisher).

Articles
1. "Televising legislatures: an economic analysis." *Journal of Law and Economics*, 29(October):1986 (with W.M. Crain).
2. "Health and the economy: choice versus exogenous variables." *Kyklos*, 43(Fasc 3):1990.
3. "Federal deficit effects on short and long term rates." *Southern Economic Journal*, 57(July):1990.
4. "Optimal seigniorage, the gold standard, and central bank financing." *Journal of Money, Credit, and Banking*, 25(February):1993 (with M. Toma).
5. "On the (mis)measurement of legislator ideology and shirking." *Public Choice*, 76:1993 (with K.B. Grier).
6. "The political economy of prohibition in the United States, 1919–1933." *Social Science Quarterly*, 75(June):1994 (with G. Anderson).
7. "Batter-up: moral hazard and the effects of the dh rule on hit batsmen." *Economic Inquiry*, 33(July):1997 (with W.F. Shughart and R.D. Tollison).
8. "Persistence in government spending fluctuations: New Evidence on the Displacement Effect." *Public Choice*, 97(1–2):1998.
9. "Explaining U.S. federal deficits, 1889–1998." *Economic Inquiry*, forthcoming (with R.D. Tollison).
10. "Racial integration as an innovation: empirical evidence from sports leagues." *American Economic Review*, forthcoming (with R.E. McCormick and R.D. Tollison).

Principal Contributions
From the outset, much of Brian Goff's work has centered on the microeconomic structure and incentives of organizations. Through collaborations with others as well as on his own, the applications have covered a variety of policy and sports organizations including the U.S. Congress, bureaucratic agencies, the Supreme Court, the NCAA, Major League Baseball, and others. From 1990 onward, he also directed attention toward issues in macro political economy addressing basic measurement issues in regulation and government spending as well as the behavior of institutions such as the Federal Reserve. In several articles, Goff has dealt directly with either the effects of deficits or explanations for deficits. In recent years, he has also turned attention toward the measurement of basic standards of living and how growth in living standards have influenced socioeconomic outcomes such as family life, crime, and work.

GROFMAN, Bernard N.

Born
December 2, 1944, Houston, Texas, USA

Current Position
Professor of Political Science and Social Psychology, and Adjunct Professor of Economics, University of California at Irvine, 1980–.

Past Positions
Scholar-in-Residence, Department of Political Science, University of Bologna, (April-June, 2001); Scholar-in-Residence, Institute for Legal Studies, Kansai University, (June/July, 1990); Visiting Professor, Department of Political Science, University of Michigan (Fall, 1989); College Visiting Professor, Department of Political Science, University of Washington, (Spring, 1985); Guest Scholar, Governmental Studies Program, Brookings Institution (Winter, 1984); Visiting Lecturer (Gastdozent), Lehrstuhl für Politische Wissenschaft, University of Mannheim (Summer, 1973); Associate Professor of Political Science and Social Psychology, University of California at Irvine (1976–1980); Adjunct Assistant Professor, Applied Mathematics, SUNY at Stony Brook (Spring, 1975); Assistant Professor, Political Science, SUNY at Stony Brook (1971–1976); Instructor, Political Science, SUNY at Stony Brook (1970–1971).

Degrees
B.S., M.A., Ph.D., University of Chicago, 1966, 1968, 1972.

Offices and Honors

Member, American Academy of Arts and Science, 2001.
Chair, Section on Representation and Electoral Systems, American Political Science Association, 1991–1993.
Member, UCI Institute for Mathematical Behavioral Sciences, 1992–.
Founding Member, UCI Center for the Study of Democracy (1996).
Listed in *Who's Who in the World*.
Fellow, Institute for Advanced Study, University of Bologna, Spring, 2001.
President, Public Choice Society, 2001–2002.

Principal Fields of Interest

Individual/Group Decision Making Processes/Methods; Redistricting/Voting Rights; Models of Political Persuasion/Propaganda.

Selected Publications

Books

1. *Choosing an Electoral System* (Praeger, 1984) (edited, with Arend Lijphart).
2. *Electoral Laws and Their Political Consequences* (Agathon Press, 1986) (edited, with Arend Lijphart).
3. *The 'Federalist Papers' and the New Institutionalism* (Agathon Press, 1989) (edited, with Donald Wittman).
4. *Minority Representation and the Quest for Voting Equality* (Cambridge University Press, 1992) (with Lisa Handley and Richard Niemi).
5. *Quiet Revolution in the South: The Impact of the Voting Rights Act, 1965–1990* (Princeton University Press, 1994) (edited, with Chandler Davidson).
6. *Legislative Term Limits: Public Choice Perspectives* (Kluwer Academic Publishers, 1996).
7. *Elections in Japan, Korea and Taiwan under the Single Non-Transferable Vote: The Comparative Study of an Embedded Institution* (University of Michigan Press, 1999) (edited, with Sung-Chull Lee, Edwin Winckler, and Brian Woodall).
8. *A Unified Theory of Voting: Directional and Proximity Spatial Models* (Cambridge University Press, 1999) (with Samuel Merrill, III).
9. *Elections in Australia, Ireland and Malta under the Single Transferable Vote* (University of Michigan Press, 2000) (edited, with Shaun Bowler).
10. *Political Science as Puzzle Solving* (ed) (University of Michigan Press, 2001).

Articles

1. "On the possibility of faithfully representative committees." *American Political Science Review*, 80(3):1986 (with Scott L. Feld).
2. "Stability and centrality of legislative choice in the spatial context." *American Political Science Review*, 81(2): 1987 (with Guillermo Owen, Nicholas Noviello and Amihai Glazer).
3. "The core and the stability of group choice in spatial voting games." *American Political Science Review*, 82(1): 1988 (with Norman Schofield and Scott L. Feld).
4. "Rousseau's general will: A Condorcetian perspective." *American Political Science Review*, 82(2):1988 (with Scott L. Feld).
5. Ideological consistency as a collective phenomenon. *American Political Science Review*, 82(3):1988 (with Scott L. Feld).
6. "The committee assignment process and the conditional nature of committee bias." *American Political Science Review*, 84(4):1990 (with Richard L. Hall).
7. "Public choice, civic republicanism, and American politics: Perspectives of a 'reasonable choice' modeler." *Texas Law Review*, 71(7):1993 (with Bernard, Grofman).
8. "Modeling negative campaigning." *American Political Science Review*, 89(1):1995 (with Stergios Skaperdas).
9. "Modelling cabinet durability/cabinet termination: a synthetic literature review and critique." *British Journal of Political Science*, 27:1997 (with Peter van Roozendaal).
10. "Explaining Divided U.S. Senate Delegations, 1788–1994." *American Political Science Review* 92(2): 1998 (with Thomas Brunell).

Principal Contributions

Most of Bernard Grofman's work is co-authored, and his research has been very much influenced by long-term collaborations: with the sociologist, Scott Feld; the game theorist, Guillermo Owen; the economist, Amihi Glazer; the psychologist, Michel Regenwetter; the statistician, Samuel Merrill; and with two voting rights scholars, Lisa Handley and Chandler Davidson. Early work focused on aspects of individual and social choice, including theoretical work on the Condorcet jury theorem and empirical work on actual jury decision-making. Grofman shifted to the study of party competition and spatial models. About the same time, by happy accident, he also became involved in the study of redistricting and voting rights, which has now been a major aspect of his work for over two decades, and which has given me the opportunity to serve as an expert witness in a number of precedent-setting cases. Grofman's most recent work has dealt with empirical paradoxes in public choice theories, e.g., why we don't see cycles, why people vote.

HANSON, Robin Dale

Born
August 28, 1959, St. Charles, Illinois, USA

Current Positions
Assistant Professor of Economics, George Mason University, 1999–.

Past Positions
Robert Wood Johnson Foundation Scholar in Health Policy Research, University of California at Berkeley, 1997–1999; Research Scientist, NASA Ames Research Center, 1989–1993; Research Scientist, Lockheed Artificial Intelligence Center, 1984–1989.

Degrees
M.S., M.A., University of Chicago, 1984; B.S. University of California at Irvine, 1981; Ph.D., California Institute of Technology, 1997.

Offices and Honors
NASA Space Act Award, 1992.
Institute for Humane Studies Fellowship, 1993.
Prix Ars Electronica Golden Nica, WWW, 1995.
Alfred P. Sloan Dissertation Fellowship, 1996.

Principal Fields of Interest
Information Aggregation; Public Choice; Health Economics; Future Technology.

Selected Publications
Articles
1. "Can wiretaps remain cost-effective?" *Communications of the Association of Computing Machinery*, 37(12):1994.
2. "Buy health, not health care." *CATO Journal*, 14(1):1994.
3. "Could gambling save science? encouraging an honest consensus." with "Reply to Comments" and "comparing peer review to information prizes — a possible economics experiment." *Social Epistemology*, 9(1):1995.
4. 'Correction to McKelvey and Page, "Public and private information: an experimental study of information pooling." *Econometrica*, 64(5):1996.
5. "Consensus by identifying extremists." *Theory and Decision* 44(3):1998.
6. "Decision markets." *IEEE Intelligent Systems*, 14(3):1999.
7. "Why health is not special: errors in evolved bioethics intuitions." *Social Philosophy & Policy*, 19(2):2002.
8. "Warning Labels as Cheap Talk: Why Regulators Ban Drugs." *Journal of Public Economics*, 85(2):2002.
9. "Combinatorial Information Market Makers" *Information Systems Frontiers*, forthcoming, 2003.

Principal Contributions
Robin Hanson's main research has been in information aggregation. He has considered voter incentives to become informed, information transmission about product quality via warning labels, information pooling in experiments, and the common human neglect of information implicit in the fact that others disagree with them. He has designed information markets where speculators can aggregate information about the consequences of policies and has designed a form of government based on this concept. Hanson has also designed better incentives for health care providers and tried to make sense of puzzles in health economics by posting and evolved tendency to show that we care. He has explored the economic consequences of foreseeable future technologies, such as the web, uploads and space colonization.

HETTICH, Walter

Born
April 19, 1939, Zurich, Switzerland

Current Positions
Professor of Economics, California State University, Fullerton; Visiting Professor, Chuo University, Tokyo, 2003.

Past Positions
Research Fellow, University of Konstanz, June 1993; Professor of Economics, Carleton University, 1976–1985; Adjunct Professor, University of California at Santa Cruz, 1983; Visiting Professor, University of California at Berkeley, Fall 1982; Associate Professor, Carleton University, 1970–1976; Research Associate, Economic Council of Canada, Ottawa, 1969–1970; Research Associate, The Canada Council, Ottawa, 1968–1969; Visiting Fellow, International Institute of Education, UNESCO, Paris, Summer 1967; Assistant Professor of Economics, Queen's University, Kingston, Canada, 1966–1968.

Degrees
B.A., University of California, 1962; M.A., Ph.D., Yale University, 1963, 1967.

Offices and Honors
Earhart Foundation Fellowship in Economics, 1963–1964.
Dissertation Fellowship, Urban Economics, Resources for the Future, 1965–1966.
Outstanding Professor, School of Business and Economics, California State University, Fullerton, 1989–1990.
Outstanding Research and Creativity Award, Department of Economics, California State University, Fullerton, 2001.

Principal Fields of Interest
Economics of the Public Sector; Collective Choice; Applied Microeconomics.

Selected Publications
Books
1. *Expenditures, Output and Productivity in Canadian University Education* (Economic Council of Canada, Information Canada, 1971).
2. *Benefit-Cost Analysis for Air Transportation Projects: A Guide for the Canadian Air Transportation Administration.* (Transport Canada, Ottawa, 1983) (with Cary Swoveland).
3. *Democratic Choice and Taxation: A Theoretical and Empirical Analysis* (Cambridge University Press, 1999) (with Stanley L. Winer).

Articles
1. "Mixed public and private financing of education: comment." *American Economic Review*, 59(March):1969.
2. "Bureaucrats and public goods." *Public Choice*, 21(Spring):1975.
3. "Henry simons on taxation and the economic system." *National Tax Journal*, 32(March):1979.
4. "A theory of partial tax reform." *Canadian Journal of Economics*, 12(November):1979.
5. "A Positive model of tax structure." *Journal of Public Economics*, 24:1984 (with Stanley L. Winer).
6. "Economic and political foundations of tax structure." *American Economic Review*, 78(September):1988 (with Stanley L. Winer).
7. "Debt and tariffs: an empirical investigation of the evolution of revenue systems." *Journal of Public Economics*, 45:1991 (with Stanley L. Winer).
8. "The complexity of tax structure in competitive political systems." *International Tax and Public Finance*, 5:1998 (with George Warskett and Stanley L. Winer).
9. "What is missed if we leave out collective choice in the analysis of Taxation." *National Tax Journal*, 51:1998 (with Stanley L. Winer).
10. "Better than what? policy analysis, collective choice and the standard of reference," (edited with Stanley L. Winer and Hirofumi Shibata) *Political Economy and Public Finance* (Edward Elgar Publishing, 2002).

Principal Contributions
Walter Hettich began his career with research on the economics of education. This led to work on the theory and application of benefit-cost analysis and to the study of how such analysis is used in a bureaucratic setting. He also developed an interest in the writings of Henry Simons, particularly in his analysis of income taxation. After proposing a formal approach to the measurement of horizontal equity, Hettich began to combine tax analysis with collective choice. Together with Stanley Winer, he developed a systematic treatment of the major positive and normative aspects of taxation based on probabilistic voting, work that culminated in their book *Democratic Choice and Taxation*. Hettich remains interested in integrating the fields of public finance and collective choice and in studying a variety of public sector issues in a context where collective choice matters.

HINICH, Melvin J.

Born
April 29, 1939

Current Positions
Mike Hogg Professor of Government and Professor of Economics, University of Texas.

Past Positions
Professor of Government and Economics, University of Texas, 1982–; Professor of Economics, Virginia Polytechnic Institute and State University, 1974–1982; Expert Consultant, Naval Coastal Systems Center, Panama City, Fl., 1979; Sherman Fairchild Distinguished Scholar, California Institute of Technology, 1975–1976; Professor, Political Economy and Statistics, Carnegie Melon University School of Urban and Public Affairs and the Department of Statistics, 1970–1974; Assistant Professor, Associate Professor, Graduate School of Industrial Administration and the Department of Statistics, 1963–1968, 1968–1970; Analyst, strategic force deployments, Center for Naval Analysis, University of Rochester, Arlington, VA., Summer, 1969; Research in statistical signal processing, Columbia University-Hudson Laboratories, Dobbs Ferry, NY., 1965–67 (Consultant, 1965–1966,

1967–1968); Lecturer in Statistics, Business School MBA Program, Iona College, 1967; Signal Processing Research, Bell Telephone Laboratories, Whippany, NJ., Summer, 1974; Analysis of Jakowatz adaptive waveform recognition, General Electric Research Laboratories, Schenectady, NY., Summe, 1961; Linguistics Research, Bell Telephone Laboratories, Murry Hill, NY, 1960.

Degrees
B.S., M.S., Carnegie Institute of Technology, 1959, 1960; Ph.D., Stanford University, 1963.

Editorial Duties
Associate Editor, *Macroeconomic Dynamics*, 1997–present; Associate Editor, *Society of Nonlinear Dynamics and Economics*, 2001–present; Associate Editor, *Journal of the American Statistical Association*, 1984–1997; Associate Editor, *Journal of Mathematical Sociology*, 1970–1980; Special Issue Editor for Social Choice issue of JMS, July 1972.

Offices and Honors
Fellow of the Institute of Mathematical Statistics, December 1973.
Sherman Fairchild Distinguished Scholar at the California Institute of Technology, 1975–1976.
Listed in *Who's Who in America*, 1975–.
Listed in *Who's Who in the World*, 1995.
Fellow of the Public Choice Society, March 1988.
President of the Public Choice Society, 1992–1994.

Principal Fields of Interest
Time Series Analysis; Statistical Signal Processing; Econometrics; Statistics; Public Choice; Political Science.

Selected Publications
Books
1. *Consumer Protection Legislation and the U.S. Food Industry* (Pergamon Press, 1980) (with R. Staelin).
2. *The Spatial Theory of Voting: An Introduction* (Cambridge University Press, January, 1984) (with J. Enelow).
3. *Ideology and the Theory of Political Choice* (University of Michigan Press, 1994) (with M. C. Munger).
4. *Analytical Politics* (Cambridge University Press, 1997) (with M.C. Munger).
5. *Empirical Studies in Comparative Politics* (Kluwer Academic Publishers, 1999) (with M.C. Munger).

Articles
1. "A mathematical model of policy formation in a democratic society." *Mathematical Applications in Political Science II*, Monograph, J. Bernd (ed.), Arnold Foundation Monographs (Southern Methodist University Press, 1966) (with O. Davis).
2. "On the power and importance of the mean preference in a mathematical model of democratic choice." *Public Choice*, 5:1968 (with O. Davis).
3. "Abstentions and equilibrium in the electoral process." *Public Choice*, 7:1969 (with P.C. Ordershook).
4. "An expository development of a mathematical model of the electoral process." *American Political Science Review*, 64(2):1970 (with O. Davis and P.C. Ordeshook).
5. "Plurality maximization: a spatial analysis with variable participation." *American Political Science Review*, 64(3):1970 (with P.C. Ordeshook).
6. "Social preference orderings and majority rule." *Econometrica*, 40:1972 (with O. Davis and M. DeGroot).
7. "Equilibrium in spatial voting: the median voter result is an artifact." *Journal of Economic Theory*, 16(2): 1977.
8. "A new approach to the spatial theory of electoral competition." *American Journal of Political Science*, 25(2):1981 (with Walker Pollard).
9. "Necessary and sufficiently conditions for single-peakedness in public economics models." *Journal of Public Economics*, 25:1984 (with P. Coughlin).
10. "A spatial theory of ideology." *Journal of Theoretical Politics*, 4(1):1992 (with Michael Munger).

Principal Contributions
The Spatial Theory of Electoral Competition (with Otto Davis, Peter Ordeshook, James Enelow, Michael Munger); his solely authored papers; and the work of his doctoral students, Lawrence Cahoon, Walker Pollard, James Endersby, Jay Dow, and Hazem Ghobarah; Probabilistic Voting; and The Cahoon-Hinich Spatial Analysis Method MAP.

HOLCOMBE, Randall Gregory

Born
June 4, 1950, Bridgeport, Connecticut, USA

Current Position
DeVoe Moore Professor of Economics, Florida State University, Tallahassee, Florida, 1988–.

Past Positions
Assistant Professor, Associate Professor, Professor, and Lowder Professor of Economics, Auburn University, Auburn, Alabama, 1977–1988; Assistant Professor of Economics, Texas A&M University, 1975–1977.

Degrees
B.S., University of Florida, 1972; M.A., Ph.D., Virginia Polytechnic Institute and State University, 1974, 1976.

Offices and Honors
Member, Florida Governor's Council of Economic Advisors, 2000–.
Chairman of the Research Advisory Council, The James Madison Institute, 1991–; member of the Research Advisory Council, 1987–.
Adjunct Scholar, The Ludwig von Mises Institute, 1982–.
Listed in *Who's Who in America*.
Ludwig von Mises Prize for scholarship in Austrian Economics, 1992.
Georgescu-Roegen Prize in Economics for the best article in the *Southern Economic Journal*, 1992.
Best Article Award, *Atlantic Economic Journal*, 1996.

Editorial Duties
Editorial Board Member, *Public Finance Review*, 1995–; Editorial Board Member, *The Quarterly Journal of Austrian Economics*, 1998–; Editorial Board Member, *Public Choice and Constitutional Economics*, 2001–; Editorial Board Member, *The Review of Austrian Economics*, 1987–1997.

Principal Fields of Interest
Public Choice; Public Finance.

Selected Publications
Books
1. *Public Finance and the Political Process* (Southern Illinois University Press, 1983).
2. *An Economic Analysis of Democracy* (Southern Illinois University Press, 1985).
3. *Public Sector Economics* (Wadsworth, 1988).
4. *Economic Models and Methodology* (Greenwood Press, 1989).
5. *The Economic Foundations of Government* (New York University Press, 1994).
6. *Public Policy and the Quality of Life* (Greenwood Press, 1995).
7. *Public Finance: Government Revenues and Expenditures in the United States Economy* (West, 1996).
8. *Growth and Variability in State Revenue: An Anatomy of State Fiscal Crises* (Greenwood Press, 1997) (with Russell S. Sobel).
9. *Writing Off Ideas: Taxation, Foundations, and Philanthropy in America*. (Transaction Publishers, 2000).
10. *From Liberty to Democracy: The Transformation of American Government*. (University of Michigan Press, 2002).

Articles
1. "The Florida system: a Bowen equilibrium referendum process." *National Tax Journal*, 30(March):1977.
2. "An empirical test of the median voter model." *Economic Inquiry*, 18(April):1980.
3. "The median voter model in public choice theory." *Public Choice*, 61(May):1989.
4. "Measuring the growth and variability of tax bases over the business cycle." *National Tax Journal*, 49(December):1996 (with R.S. Sobel).
5. "The growth of the federal government in the 1920s." *Cato Journal*, 16(Fall):1996.
6. "Absence of envy does not imply fairness." *Southern Economic Journal*, 63(January):1997.
7. "Tax policy from a public choice perspective." *National Tax Journal*, 51(June):1998.
8. "Veterans interests and the transition to economic growth: 1870–1915." *Public Choice*, 99(June):1999.
9. "Economic freedom and the environment for economic growth." *Journal of Institutional and Theoretical Economics*, 155(December):1999 (with J. Gwartney and R. Lawson).
10. "The growth of local government in the United States from 1820 to 1870." *Journal of Economic History*, 61(March):2001 (with D.J. Lacombe).

Principal Contributions
Randall Holcombe's primary interest in economics has been the study of government allocation of resources, and much of his work has focused on how resources are allocated through democratic decision-making, and how constitutional rules for government decision-making are formulated. His earlier work dealt mainly with voting theory and constitutional theory, and more recently he has begun to look at American political history using the public choice framework. He has also applied public choice analysis to taxation issues. In addition to these theoretical interests, Holcombe

has worked on a number of more policy-oriented issues. In the 1970s he worked on energy policy, and in the 1990s he worked on growth management and land use planning. The examination of tax policy from a public choice perspective has been an interest of his throughout his career. He has also worked directly with policy-makers on taxation, expenditure, and land use planning issues, both in Florida and at the national level.

HOLLER, Manfred Joseph

Born
July 25, 1946, Munich, Germany

Current Position
Professor of Economics at the University of Hamburg, Germany, 1991–.

Past Positions
Dean of the School of Economics, University of Hamburg, Germany, 1997–1998 (Vice-dean, 1995–1997, 1998–1999); Associate Professor of Economics, University of Aarhus, Denmark, 1986–1991; Acting Professor of Economics, University of Munich, Germany, 1984–1985; Senior Researcher, University of Munich, 1983–1986; Senior Assistant, Department of Economics, University of Munich, 1975–1983.

Degrees
Diplom-Volkswirt, Doctorate (Dr. rer. pol.), Habilitation (Dr. rer. pol. habil), University of Munich, Germany, 1971, 1975, 1983.

Offices and Honors
Member, Board of Directors, *Munich Institute of Integrated Studies* (Gesellschaft für Integrierte Studien e.V., Munich), 1982–1994.
Director, Committee for Education, *International Academy of Science*, 1987–.
President, *European Academy for Standardization* (EURAS), 1994, Vice-President, 1994–1999, President, 1999–2001, Managing Director, 2001–.
Board Member, *European Public Choice Society*, 1996–1999.

Editorial Duties
Founding Editor, *Munich Social Science Review*, 1978–1979; Founding Editor, *Homo Oeconomicus*, 1983–; Founding Editor, *European Journal of Political Economy*, 1985–1993; Managing Editor, *EURAS Yearbook of Standardization*, 1998–; Editor, *Jahrbuch für Neu Politische Ökonomie*, 2000–; Assessing Editor, *Journal of Mind and Behavior*, 1980–; Assessing Editor, *Journal of Theoretical Politics*, 1989–; Member, Editorial Board, *Control and Cybernetics*, 1994–; Consultant Editor, *European Journal of Law and Economics*, 1989–; Associate Editor, *Central European Journal of Operations Research*, 1999–.

Principal Fields of Interest
Game Theory; Standardization and Network Economics; Law and Economics; Cultural Economics and the Economics of Art.

Selected Publications
Books
1. *Die Entscheidungen politischer Parteien. Modelle zur Bestimmung der Staatstätigkeit* (Dissertation 1975) (Verlag Ölschläger, 1979).
2. *Ökonomische Theorie der Politik. Eine Einführung*, (eds.) (Verlag Moderne Industrie, 1979) (with Claude Hillinger).
3. *Power, Voting, and Voting Power* (ed.) (Physica-Verlag, 1982).
4. *Coalitions and Collective Action* (ed.) (Physica-Verlag, 1984).
5. *The Logic of Multiparty Systems* (ed.) (Kluwer Academic Publishers, 1987).
6. *Arbeitsmarktmodelle* (Springer-Verlag, 1997) (with Laszlo Goerke).
7. (ed.), *Scandal and Its Theory* (Homo Oeconomicus 16) (Accedo-Verlag, 1999).
8. *Einführung in die Spieltheorie* (4th revised and extended edition) (Springer-Verlag, 2000) (with Gerhard Illing).
9. *Power Indices and Coalition Formation* (Kluwer Academic Publishers, 2001) (edited, with Guillermo Owen).
10. *Power and Fairness*, Jahrbuch für Neu Politische Ökonomie, 20, Mohr-Siebeck, forthcoming (edited, with H. Kliemt, D. Schmidtchen und M. Streit).

Articles
1. "Power in the European parliament: what will change?" *Quality and Quantity*, 11:1977 (with Johann Kellermann).
2. "Forming coalitions and measuring voting power." *Political Studies*, 30:1982.

3. "Power, Luck, and the Right Index." *Journal of Economics* (Zeitschrift für Nationalökonomie), 43: 1983 (with Edward W. Packel).
4. "The unprofitability of mixed-strategy equilibria in two-person games: a second folk-theorem." *Economics Letters*, 32:1990.
5. "Fighting pollution when decisions are strategic." *Public Choice*, 76:1993.
6. "Voting on standardisation," *Public Choice*, 83:1995 (with Laszlo Goerke).
7. "Two stories, one power index." *Journal of Theoretical Politics*, 10:1998.
8. "Tax Compliance Policy Reconsidered." *Homo Oeconomicus*, 15:1998 (with Bruno Frey).
9. "The value of coalition is power." *Homo Oeconomicus* 15:1999 (reprinted in Notizie di Politeia, 59: 2000) (with Mika Widgrén).
10. "Constrained monotonicity and the measurement of power." *Theory and Decision*, 50:2001 (with Rie Ono and Frank Steffen).

Principal Contributions
Manfred Holler's most prominent – although not always popular – contribution to public choice theory is the Public Good Index (also called the Holler-Packel index or Holler index). He introduced this measure of a prior voting power in an article in the *Munich Social Science Review* (1978). It has been reprinted in *Power, Voting and Voting Power* (1982, see above). In a contribution to *Politcal Studies* (1982), he added the public good interpretation to the measure. Holler and Packel (1983) contains an axiomatization of measure.

Holler's second contribution to public choice is the minimax interpretation of the inspection game. In 1990, when he published his first article on the unprofitability of mixed-strategy equilibria in two-person games, he thought this result an original contribution to game theory - which it was not. However, the analysis of the implications of this result and the minimax interpretation proved to be a powerful instrument for explaining "paradoxical" behavior. (See, e.g., Frey/Holler, 1998). More recent work focuses on voting and labor relations, and voting and standardization, and mediation. Contemporary work is in the economics of art.

HOLT, Charles A.

Born
October 2, 1948, Richmond, Virginia, USA

Current Positions
Merrill Bankard Professor of Economics, University of Virginia, 1996–; Honorary Professor, University of Amsterdam, 2003–; Director, Thomas Jefferson Center for Political Economy, 2001–.

Past Positions
Professor of Economics, University of Virginia, 1989–1996; Associate Professor of Economics, University of Virginia, 1983–1989; Associate Professor of Economics, University of Minnesota, 1982–1983; Assistant Professor of Economics, University of Minnesota, 1976–1982; Visiting Scholar, Georgia State University, Spring 2000; Federal Reserve Bank of Atlanta, Short Term Visitor, 2000–2001; Visiting Scholar, California Institute of Technology, Fall 1999; Visiting Scholar, University of Amsterdam, June 1996; Stanford University, Spring 1996; Universite Louis Pasteur, Strasbourg France, May 1995, 1996; Visiting Scholar, Economic Science Laboratory, University of Arizona, July 1989; Visiting Scholar, Autonomous University of Barcelona, CSIC, 1986–1987 and June 1988; Consultant, Federal Trade Commission, intermittent, 1983–1993.

Degrees
B.A., Washington and Lee University, 1970; M.S., Carnegie-Mellon University, 1974; Ph.D., Carnegie-Mellon University, 1977.

Offices and Honors
L.J. Savage Award (dissertation research in Bayesian analysis), 1977.
Alexander Henderson Award (Carnegie-Mellon), 1977.
President, Economic Science Foundation, 1991–1993.
Vice-President, Southern Economic Association, 1993–1994.
Charter Member, Game Theory Society, 1998.
American Economic Association, Committee on Economic Education, 1999–.
President, Southern Economic Association, 2001–2002.
Listed in *Who's Who in the United States*.
Listed in *Who's Who in Economics*.

Editorial Duties
Founding Co-Editor, *Experimental Economics*, 1997–; Board of Editors, *American Economic Review*, 1999–; Associate Editor, *International Journal of Game Theory*, 1995–2000; Associate Editor, *Economic Theory*, 1995–1998.

Selected Publications

Books

1. *Experimental Economics* (Princeton University Press, 1993).
2. "*Research in Experimental Economics, Emissions Permit Experiments*." Vol. 7 (JAI Press, 1999) (edited, with M. Isaac).
3. *Research in Experimental Economics, Emissions Permit Experiments*, Vol. 7 (JAI Press, 1999) (edited, with M. Isaac).

Articles

1. "Uncertainty and the bidding for incentive contracts." *American Economic Review*, 69(September):1979.
2. "An experimental test of the consistent-conjectures hypothesis." *American Economic Review*, 75(June): 1985.
3. "Preference reversals and the independence axiom." *American Economic Review*, 76(June):1986.
4. "Strategic voting in agenda-controlled committee experiments." *American Economic Review*, 79(September): 1989 (with C. Eckel).
5. "An experimental test of equilibrium dominance in signaling games." *American Economic Review*, 82 (December):1992 (with J. Brandts).
6. "The loser's curse." *American Economic Review*, 84: June, 1994 (with R. Sherman).
7. "Information cascades in the laboratory." *American Economic Review*, 87(December):1997 (with L. Anderson).
8. "Anomalous Behavior in a Traveler's Dilemma?" *American Economic Review*, 89 (June):1999 (with M. Capra, J. Goeree, and R. Gomez).
9. "Stochastic game theory: for playing games, not just for doing theory." *Proceedings of the National Academy of Sciences*, 96. (September):1999 (with J. Goeree).
10. "Ten little treasures of game theory and ten intuitive contradictions." *American Economic Review*, December:2001 (with Jacob Goeree).
11. "Risk aversion and incentive effects in lottery choices." *American Economic Review*, forthcoming 2003.

Principal Contributions

Charles Holt began working on models of auctions and the procurement process. In the process, he became interested in laboratory experiments. Anomalies in the data from these experiments led him to reject a number of theoretical refinements proposed by theorists and to develop and refine theories of behavior with elements of bounded rationality. This work on "stochastic game theory" (with coauthors Jacob Goeree and Tom Palfrey) consists of a set of related models of learning, introspection, and equilibrium.

KAEMPFER, William Hutchison

Born
March 4, 1951, West Chester, Pennsylvania, USA

Current Positions
Associate Vice Chancellor of Academic Affairs for Budget and Planning, University of Colorado, 1997–; Professor of Economics, University of Colorado, 1994–.

Past Positions
Associate Professor and Assistant Professor of Economics, University of Colorado, 1989–1994, 1981–1989; Associate Professor, The Economics Institute, Boulder, Colorado, 1991, 1992; Visiting Assistant Professor and Visiting Lecturer, Claremont Graduate School and Claremont McKenna College, 1985–1986, 1986–1988, 1991; Assistant Professor, University of Washington, 1979–1981; Visiting Assistant Professor, University of North Carolina at Greensboro, 1978–1979; Instructor, The College of Wooster, 1975–1976.

Degrees
B.A., The College of Wooster, 1973; M.A., Ph.D., Duke University, 1975, 1979.

Principal Fields of Interest
International Public Choice; International Trade Theory and Policy; Sports Economics.

Selected Publications

Books

1. *International Economic Sanctions: A Public Choice Perspective* (Westview Press, 1992) (with Anton D. Lowenberg).
2. *International Trade: Theory and Evidence* (McGraw-Hill, 1995) (with James R. Markusen, James R. Melvin, and Keith E. Maskus).
3. *The Origins and Demise of South African Apartheid: A Public Choice Analysis* (University of Michigan Press, 1998) (with Anton D. Lowenberg).

Articles

1. "The impact of monopoly pricing on the lerner symmetry theorem." *Quarterly Journal of Economics*,

XCVII(August):1983 (with Jonathan Eaton, Gene M. Grossman, and Edward Tower).
2. "The effect of unit fees on the consumption of quality." *Economic Inquiry*, XXIII(April):1985 (with Raymond T. Brastow).
3. "A model of the political economy of international investment sanctions: the case of South Africa." *Kyklos*, 39:1986 (with Anton D. Lowenberg).
4. "Divestment, investment sanctions and disinvestment: an evaluation of anti-apartheid policy instruments." *International Organization*, 41(Summer):1987 (with James A. Lehman and Anton D. Lowenberg).
5. "The theory of international economic sanctions: a public choice approach." *The American Economic Review*, 78(September):1988 (with Anton D. Lowenberg).
6. "Incremental protection and efficient political choice between tariffs and quotas." *Canadian Journal of Economics*, 22(May):1989 (with J. Harold McClure, Jr. and Thomas D. Willett).
7. "Sanctioning South Africa: the politics behind the policies." *The Cato Journal* 8(Winter):1989 (with Anton D. Lowenberg).
8. "A test of tariff endogeneity in the United States." *American Economic Review*, 81(September):1991 (with Alok Bohara).
9. "The welfare implications of exogenous policy constraints: a CGE analysis of tariffication." *Review of Development Economics*, 1(June):1997 (with Martin T. Ross and Thomas F. Rutherford).
10. "Income inequality and tax policy for south african race groups." Forthcoming in *Review of Economics and Statistics*, 2002 (with Gregory Berg).

Principal Contributions
A major focus of William Kaempfer's work has been to bring the principles of public choice analysis to international economics. International trade policy has long been a fertile field for applying public choice and his work has proceeded in this area with both theoretical and empirical contributions. For the past 15 years, more than 25 collaborations with Anton D. Lowenberg have introduced public choice analysis to the examination of international economic sanctions in particular. These contributions have not only helped to explain why sanctions are frequently such a futile instrument of international relations, but also have established why sanctions may have been successful where they seem to have worked.

KEIL, Manfred Werner

Born
1954

Current Position
Associate Professor of Economics, Claremont McKenna College.

Degrees
Zwischenprüfung, Johann Wolfgang Goethe Universität, 1975; M.A., University of Texas, 1977; Ph.D., London School of Economics, 1985.

Selected Publications
Articles
1. "Incomes policy in a political business cycle environment: a structural model for the U.K. economy 1961–1980," in Hughes-Hallet (ed.) *Applied Decision Analysis and Economic Behaviour: Advanced Studies in Theoretical and Applied Econometrics*, Vol. 3 (Dordrecht: Martinus Nijhoff Publishers) 1984 (with Meghnad Desai and Sushil Wadwhani).
2. "Is the political business cycle really dead?" *Southern Economic Journal*, July: 1988.
3. "An analysis of Canadian unemployment." *Canadian Public Policy*, March: 1990 (with James Symons).
4. "A comparison among partial adjustment, rational expectations and error correction estimates of the Canadian demand for money." *Journal of Applied Econometrics*, July:1990 (with William Richardson).
5. "A model of speculative efficiency with 'News' error components."*Applied Economics*, September:1993.
6. "Internal migration and unemployment in Germany: an Anglo-Irish perspective." *Weltwirtschaftliches Archiv*, September:1993 (with Andrew Newell).
7. "Variations in state unemployment rates: a comparative macroeconomic performance analysis." *Southern Business and Economic Journal*, January:1994 (with Louis Pantuosco).
8. "Lessons from the OECD experience of unemployment." *Labour Market Review*, Winter:1993/4 (with Andrew Newell).
9. "An aggregate model of the Canadian labor market." *Journal of Macroeconomics*, Fall:1994 (with James Symons).
10. "Canadian and U.S. unemployment rates: a comparison based on regional data." *Canadian Public Policy*, Supplement, 1998 (with Lou Pantuosco).
11. "An explanation of the recently experienced fall in the natural rate of unemployment." *Papers and Proceedings*, Western Decision Science Institute, Annual Meetings, 1999.

12. "Mean reversion recast as measurement error: lessons for finance from Galton's fallacy." *Papers and Proceedings*, Western Decision Science Institute, Annual Meetings, 2000.
13. "The sources of unemployment in Canada, 1967–1991: evidence from a panel of regions and demographic groups." *Oxford Economic Papers*, 53(1):2001 (with Pierre Fortin and James Symons).
14. "Capital mobility for developing countries may not be so high." *Journal of Development Economics*, 2002 (forthcoming) (with Y. Ahn and T. Willett).

Principal Contributions
Applications include papers on rent seeking, auctions, bargaining, public goods, signaling, and various coordination games. A typical example is the "traveler's dilemma" where the data for some treatments are quite close to the unique Nash prediction, whereas the data for other treatments are on the opposite side of the set of feasible decisions. The models (of stochastic potential and quantal response equilibrium) explain the convergence to Nash predictions in one case and the sharp divergence in another. Current work includes the programming of a series of Veconlab web-based interactive games and markets for teaching and research: http://veconlab.econ.virginia.edu/admin.htm

To date, he has written and edited several books and over a hundred articles on topics in experimental economics and related theory (see http://www.people.virginia.edu/~cah2k for details).

KENNY, Lawrence Wagner

Born
June 29, 1950, Baltimore, Maryland, USA

Current Positions
Professor of Economics, University of Florida, 1990–; Affiliate Professor of Political Science, University of Florida, 1996–.

Past Positions
Associate Professor of Economics, University of Florida, 1980–1990; Visiting Scholar, National Bureau of Economic Research, 1977–1978; Assistant Professor of Economics, University of Florida, 1975–1980.

Degrees
B.A., Wesleyan University, 1972; M.A., Ph.D., University of Chicago, 1975, 1977.

Offices and Honors
NIMH-USPHS Fellowships, 1972–1975.
Outstanding Teacher of the Year in Economics, 1989–1990. University of Florida.
TIP Award, for Outstanding Undergraduate Teaching 1990–1993. University of Florida.

Editorial Duties
Editorial Board, *Economic Inquiry*, 1997–2001.

Principal Fields of Interest
Public Choice; Economics of Education.

Selected Publications
Books
1. *Up the Political Ladder: Career Paths in U.S. Politics* (Sage Publications, 2000) (with W.L. Francis).

Articles
1. "Voter turnout and the benefits of voting." *Public Choice*, 35(5):1980 (with J.E. Filer).
2. "Voter reaction to city-county consolidation referenda." *Journal of Law and Economics*, 23(April):1980 (with J.E. Filer).
3. "Optimal tenure of elected public officials." *Journal of Law and Economics*, 29(October):1986 (with J.D. Adams).
4. "The retention of state governors." *Public Choice*, 62(July):1989 (with J.D. Adams).
5. "Redistribution, income, and voting." *American Journal of Political Science*, 37(February):1993 (with J.E. Filer and R.B. Morton).
6. "Retrospective voting and political mobility." *American Journal of Political Science*, 38(November):1994 (with W.L. Francis, R.B. Morton and A.B. Schmidt).
7. "Constituent errors in assessing their senators." *Public Choice*, 83(June):1995 (with T.A. Husted and R.B. Morton).
8. "Evidence on electoral accountability in the U.S. senate: are unfaithful agents really punished?," *Economic Inquiry*, 34(July):1996 (with A.B. Schmidt and R.B. Morton).
9. "The effect of the expansion of the voting franchise on the size of government." *Journal of Political Economy*, 105(February):1997 (with T.A. Husted).
10. "Did women's suffrage change the size and scope of government." *Journal of Political Economy*, 107(December):1999 (with J.R. Lott Jr.).

Principal Contributions

The success of a democracy hinges on well informed voters reelecting officials who have represented them well and tossing out officials who have been bad agents. Lawrence Kenny finds that senators who have been too liberal or too conservative and governors who have been unable to stimulate the state economy are less likely to be reelected. The punishment for poor representation is greater in states in which voters are better informed. In these states, the reelection mechanism works well, and term limits on governors are less common. Kenny's research also suggests that public schools are less efficient when states leave voters with less latitude in determining their schools' spending, causing voters to devote less effort to monitoring school districts. Using numerous measures of the benefits and costs from voting, in several papers Kenny finds strong support for the economic theory of voting and that it takes several decades for turnout to fully respond to new voting privileges.

Although the median voter model remains popular in economics, his research shows that it is dominated empirically by a model in which parties compete by selecting different platforms. Senators from a state often are chosen by different electoral constituencies, and legislators closer to the optimal state party platform are more likely to seek higher office and later to be reelected.

In other papers, Kenny has found that voters and legislators vote their self-interest and that government spending has risen as barriers to voting for the poor and for women, who tend to be poor, were lifted.

KLEINDORFER, Paul Robert

Born
May 12, 1940, Aurora, Illinois, USA

Current Positions
Universal Furniture Professor of Decision Sciences and Economics; Professor of Public Policy and Management; Co-Director of the Risk Management and Decision Processes Center; The Wharton School, University of Pennsylvania, 1977–.

Past Positions
Research Associate, Carnegie-Mellon University, (1968–1969); Assistant Professor, Sloan School of Management, MIT (1969–1972); Research Fellow, International Institute of Management (Berlin) (1972–1973); Associate Professor (1973–1977), Professor (1977–present), The Wharton School, University of Pennsylvania; Research Fellow, International Institute for Applied Systems Analysis (Vienna) (1984–1985); Johannes Herkules Haid Guest Professor, University of Ulm (Summer, 1986); Metzler Foundation Professor, University of Frankfurt, Germany (Summer, 1995); Visiting Scholar, INSEAD, Fontainebleau, France (1999–2000).

Degrees
B.S., U.S. Naval Academy; Ph.D., Carnegie-Mellon University.

Offices and Honors
Fulbright Fellowship for study in Mathematics, Karl-Eberhard Universität, Tübingen, Germany (1964–1965). Recipient with Michael Crew, on behalf of the Center for Research in Regulated Industries, of the Hermes Award (1992).

Editorial Duties
Associate Editor, *Journal of Regulatory Economics*, 1988–present; Associate Editor, *Review of Economic Design*, 1995–present.

Principal Fields of Interest
Regulatory Economics; Decision Sciences.

Selected Publications
Books
1. *Public Utility Economics* (Macmillan Press, St. Martin's Press, 1979) (with M.A. Crew).
2. *Applied Stochastic Control in Econometrics and Management Science* (North Holland, Amsterdam, 1980) (edited, with A. Bensoussan and C.S. Tapiero).
3. *The Economics of Public Utility Regulation* (Macmillan Press, M.I.T. Press, 1986) (with M.A. Crew).
4. *The Economics of Postal Service* (Kluwer Academic Publishers, 1992) (with M.A. Crew).
5. *Decision Sciences: An Integrative Perspective* (Cambridge University Press, 1993) (with H.C. Kunreuther and P.J. Schoemaker).
6. *Energy, Environment and The Economy: Asian Perspectives* (Edward Elgar Publishing, 1996) (edited, with H.C. Kunreuther and D.S. Hong).
7. *Emerging Competition in Postal and Delivery Services*, (Kluwer Academic Publishers, 1999) (edited, with M.A. Crew).

8. *Current Directions in Postal Reform*, (Kluwer Academic Publishers, 2000) (edited, with M.A. Crew).
9. *Future Directions in Postal Reform*, (Kluwer Academic Publishers, 2001) (edited, with M.A. Crew).
10. *Postal and Delivery Services: Pricing, Productivity, Regulation and Strategy*, (Kluwer Academic Publishers, 2002) (edited, with M.A. Crew).

Articles
1. "Marshall and Turvey on peak load or joint product pricing." *Journal of Political Economy*, November–December:1971 (with M.A. Crew).
2. "Peak load pricing with a diverse technology." *Bell Journal of Economics*, Spring:1976 (with M.A. Crew).
3. "Reliability and public utility pricing." *American Economic Review*, March:1978 (with M.A. Crew).
4. "Public utility regulation and managerial discretion." *Southern Economic Journal*, January:1979 (with M.A. Crew).
5. "Peak-load pricing in postal services." *Economic Journal*, September:1990 (with M.A. Crew and M.A. Smith).
6. "Economic depreciation and the regulated firm under competition and technological change." *Journal of Regulatory Economics*, March:1992 (with M.A. Crew).
7. "Auctioning the provision of an indivisible public good." *Journal of Economic Theory*, 1994 (with M.R. Sertel).
8. "Incentive regulation in the United Kingdom and the United States: some lessons." *Journal of Regulatory Economics*, May:1996 (with M.A. Crew).
9. "Efficient entry, monopoly, and the universal service obligation in postal service." *Journal of Regulatory Economics*, September:1998 (with M.A. Crew).
10. "The complementary roles of mitigation and insurance in managing catastrophic risks." *Risk Analysis*, 4:1999 (with H. Kunreuther).

Principal Contributions
Paul Kleindorfer's research has encompassed three broad areas: pricing and investment theory in regulated industries; methodological foundations of the decision sciences and related public choice problems; and public policy related to risk management, especially for catastrophe risks arising from natural hazards or major industrial accidents. He has written extensively on the first subject with M. A. Crew, with whom his collaboration over 30 years has led to many publications on the theory and practice of price and profit regulation in a variety of network industries, focused recently primarily on the electricity and the postal sectors. Kleindorfer co-directs the Wharton Risk and Decision Processes Center. For details of his curriculum vitae and the work of the Center see http://opim.wharton.upenn.edu/risk/

KURRILD-KLITGAARD, Peter

Born
October 11, 1966, Odense, Funen, Denmark

Current Positions
Associate Professor, Political Theory and Comparative Politics, Department of Political Science and Public Management, University of Southern Denmark, 2000–; Adjunct Associate Professor, Institute of Political Science, University of Copenhagen, 1997–.

Past Positions
Visiting Scholar, Institute for Social and Economic Research and Policy, Columbia University, and Department of Economics, New York University, 2001–2002; Assistant Professor, Department of Political Science, University of Aarhus, Denmark, 1998–2000; Research Assistant Professor, Institute of Political Science, University of Copenhagen, Denmark, 1996–1997; Research Fellow, Institute of Political Science, University of Copenhagen, Denmark, 1992–1996.

Degrees
B.A., M.Sc., University of Copenhagen, 1991, 1992; M.A., Columbia University, 1993; Ph.D., University of Copenhagen, 1997.

Offices and Honors
Member, Mont Pelerin Society, 1998.
Member, Philadelphia Society, 1999.
Member, Board, Danish Political Science Association, 2001–.
Member, Executive Board, European Public Choice Society, 2001–.

Editorial Duties
Associate Editor, *Advances in Austrian Economics*, 2001–; Member, Editorial Board, Journal of Libertarian Studies, 2000–; Editor, *Libertas*, 1986–1988, 1997–2001.

Principal Fields of Interest
Public Choice; Social Choice; Constitutional Economics.

Selected Publications
Books
1. *Etik, marked og stat: Liberalismen fra Locke til Nozick*. København: Handelshøjskolens Forlag, 1992 (with N.J. Foss).
2. *Rational choice, collective action and the paradox of rebellion*. (Institute of Political Science, University of Copenhagen & Copenhagen Political Studies Press, 1997).
3. *Valg, vælgere og velfærdsstat: Festskrift til Hans Jørgen Nielsen* (København: Politiske Studier, 2000) (with L. Bille and T. Bryder).

Articles
1. "Economic effects of political institutions, with special reference to constitutions." In *Why Constitutions Matter* (Stockholm: City University Press, 2000) (N. Karlson and J. Nergelius, eds.) (with N. Berggren).
2. "Self-ownership and consent: the contractarian liberalism of Richard Overton." *Journal of Libertarian Studies*, 15(1):2000.
3. "The constitutional economics of autocratic succession." *Public Choice*, 103(1–2):2000.
4. "An empirical example of the Condorcet paradox of voting in a large electorate." *Public Choice*, 107(1–2):2001.
5. "On rationality, ideal types and economics: Alfred Schütz and the Austrian School." *Review of Austrian Economics*, 14(2/3):2001.
6. "Velstandens grundlov: Magtdeling, rettigheder og gevinstsøgning." *Politica*, 33(1):2001.
7. "Opting-out: the constitutional economics of exit." *American Journal of Economics and Sociology* 61(1): 2002.

Principal Contributions
Peter Kurrild-Klitgaard's work on rebellion showed that while large-scale rebellious activities often may have the character of a collective action problem, this is not necessarily so. In particular, he demonstrated that even in an n-person Prisoners' Dilemma the presence of some cooperators may affect the behavior of other players, and that the solution to such problems in the real world often are produced by political entrepreneurs.

His current work deals primarily with two aspects of how institutions influences outcomes, specifically (a) how alternative voting systems tend to influence election outcomes, and (b) how alternative constitutional set-ups influence economic growth, public spending, taxation, regulation, etc.

LABAND, David Neil

Born
July 31, 1956, Newport News, Virginia, USA

Current Positions
Professor of Forest Economics, School of Forestry and Wildlife Sciences, Auburn University, 2000–; Research Associate, Forest Policy Center, Auburn University, 2000–.

Past Positions
Professor of Economics, Auburn University, 1994–2000 (Department Head, 1994–1999); Professor and Chair, Department of Economics and Finance, Salisbury State University, 1992–1994; Associate Professor of Economics, Clemson University, 1986–1992; Assistant Professor of Economics, University of Maryland Baltimore County, 1982–1986; Visiting Assistant Professor, Virginia Polytechnic Institute and State University, 1981–1982.

Degrees
B.A., M.A., Ph.D., Virginia Polytechnic Institute and State University, 1978, 1980, 1981.

Offices and Honors
Phi Beta Kappa, 1978.
President, Gamma Chapter of Alabama, 2001–2002.

Principal Fields of Interest
Public Choice; Law and Economics; Labor Economics; Economics of Science.

Selected Publications
Books
1. *Foreign Ownership of U.S. Farmland: An Economic Perspective of Regulation* (Lexington Books, 1984).
2. *The Roots of Success: Why Children Follow in Their Parents' Career Footsteps*, (Praeger, 1985) (with B.F. Lentz).
3. *Blue Laws: The History, Economics, and Politics of Sunday Closing Laws* (Lexington Books, 1987) (with D.H. Heinbuch).
4. *Patterns of Corporate Philanthropy* (Capital Research Center, 1988) (with R. Meiners).
5. *Sex Discrimination in the Legal Profession* (Quorum Books, 1995) (with B.F. Lentz).

6. *Transfer Activity in the United States* (The Cato Institute, 2001) (with G.C. McClintock).

Articles
1. "Like father, like son: toward an economic theory of occupational following." *Southern Economic Journal*, 50(October):1983 (with B.F. Lentz).
2. "Favorite sons: intergenerational wealth transfers among politicians." *Economic Inquiry*, 23:1985 (with B.F. Lentz).
3. "Why so many children of doctors become doctors: nepotism versus human capital transfers." *Journal of Human Resources*, 24(3):1989 (with B.F. Lentz).
4. "Is there value-added from the review process in economics?: preliminary evidence from authors." *Quarterly Journal of Economics*, 105(2):1990.
5. "Self-recruitment in the legal profession." *Journal of Labor Economics*, 10(2):1992 (with B.F. Lentz).
6. "An estimate of resource expenditures on transfer activity in the United States." *Quarterly Journal of Economics*, 107(3):1992 (with J.P. Sophocleus).
7. "Favoritism versus search for good papers: empirical evidence on the behavior of journal editors." *Journal of Political Economy*, 102(1):1994 (with M.J. Piette).
8. "Are economists more selfish than other 'Social' scientists?" *Public Choice*, 100(1–2):1999 (with R.O. Beil).
9. "Intellectual collaboration." *Journal of Political Economy*, 108(3):2000 (with R.D. Tollison).
10. "The impact of unfunded environmental mandates when environmental quality and timber are produced jointly." *European Journal of Law and Economics*, 10(3):2000.

Principal Contributions
David Laband has had a career-long interest in the economics of science, which has culminated in a substantial number of papers with numerous colleagues, especially Bob Tollison. In addition, he has longstanding interests in the area of public choice, most notably in the areas of rent seeking and transfer activity. In recent years Laband has developed an interest in expressive behavior, in regards to voting. He has had a long and fruitful collaboration with Barney Lentz. In their early years, they contributed extensively to development and application of an economic theory of occupational following. This was followed by development of an economic theory of the mentor/protege relationship and analyses of discrimination on intangible margins.

LANGBEIN, Laura

Born
March 1, 1943, Washington, DC, USA

Current Positions
Professor, School of Public Affairs, American University, 1973–present; Director, School of Public Affairs Ph.D. Program, 1990–present; Private Consultant on Statistics, Research Design, Survey Research and Program Evaluation, 1972–.

Past Positions
Associate Professor, School of Government and Public Administration, American University, 1978–1983; Assistant Professor, School of Government and Public Administration, American University, 1973–1978; Assistant Professor, Maxwell School, Syracuse University, 1970–1973.

Degrees
B.A., Oberlin College, 1965; Ph.D., University of North Carolina, 1972.

Offices and Honors
Hooker Fellow, McMaster University, January, 2002.
Performing member (clarinet), Friday Morning Music Club.

Editorial Duties
Editorial Board, *Policy Studies Review; Journal of Public Administration Theory and Research*.

Principal Fields of Interest
Public Choice; Quantitative Methods and Research Design; Policy Analysis.

Selected Publications
Books
1. *Ecological Inference* (Sage University Paper Series on Quantitative Applications in the Social Sciences, Sage Publications, Inc., 1977) (with A. Lichtman).
2. *Discovering Whether Programs Work: A Statistical Guide to Program Evaluation* (Goodyear, 1980).

Articles
1. "Across the great divide: inferring individual level behavior from aggregate data." *Political Methodology*, 3(4):1976 (with A. Lichtman).
2. "The section 8–existing housing program's administrative fee structure: a formal model of bureau behavior with empirical evidence." *Public Choice* 39:(1983).

3. "Negotiation, compliance and environmental regulation." *Journal of Politics*, August:1985 (with C. Kerwin).
4. "Money and access: some empirical evidence." *Journal of Politics*, November:1986.
5. "Wage differentials among regulated, private, and government sectors: a case study." *Eastern Economic Journal* 15(3):July–September 1989 (with I. Broder).
6. "The political efficacy of lobbying and money: gun control in the house, 1986." *Legislative Studies Quarterly*, 15(3):1990 (with M. Lotwis).
7. "PAC's, lobbies, and political conflict: the case of gun control." *Public Choice*, 77(3):1993.
8. "Grounded beefs: monopoly prices, minority business, and the Price of Hamburgers at U.S. Airports" *Public Administration Review*, 54(3):1994 (with L. Wilson).
9. "Estimating the impact of regulatory enforcement: practical implications of positive political theory." *Evaluation Review*, 18(5):1994.
10. "Shirking and ideology: defense in the Senate." *Congress and The Presidency* 22(1):1995.
11. "Rethinking ward and at-large elections: total spending, the number of locations of selected city services, and policy types." *Public Choice* 88:1996 (with P. Crewson and C.N. Brasher).
12. "Pay, productivity and public sector: the case of electrical engineers." *Journal of Public Administration Research and Theory*, 8(3):1998 (with G. Lewis).
13. "Politics, rules, and death row: why states eschew or execute executions." *Social Science Quarterly*, 80(4): 1999 (lead article).
14. "Regulatory negotiation versus conventional rulemaking: claims and counter-claims." *Journal of Public Administration Research and Theory*, 10(3):2000 (with Cornelius Kerwin).
15. "Ownership, empowerment and productivity: some empirical evidence on the causes and consequences of employee discretion." *Journal of Policy Analysis and Management*, 19(3):2000.
16. "Responsive bureaus, equity and regulatory negotiation: an empirical view." *Journal of Policy Analysis and Management*, forthcoming, 2002.
17. "Sports in school: source of amity or antipathy?" *Social Science Quarterly*, forthcoming, 2002 (with R. Bess).
18. "Why do white Americans support the death penalty?" *Journal of Politics*, forthcoming, 2003 (with Joe Soss and Alan Metelko).

Principal Contributions
Laura Langbein's early research centered on problems of aggregation bias in applied policy research. Her current research centers on using quantitative methods to test individual choice models of policy formation and implementation. She also has published articles on the validity of student evaluations of teaching. Her current work includes a paper that examines public school music education as a quasi-private good.

LEE, Dong Won

Born
February 26, 1972, Seoul, S. Korea

Current Positions
Doctoral Candidate in Economics, Claremont Graduate University.

Past Positions
Mentor, 1998 and Assistant Program Coordinator, 1998–1999, Peter F. Drucker Graduate School of Management.

Degrees
B.S., California State Polytechnic University-Pomona, 1997; M.B.A., Claremont Graduate University, 1999; Doctoral studies Claremont Graduate University 1999–.

Offices and Honors
First Place, Wall Street Journal Achievement Award, 1997.
Member, Drucker Student Advisory Council, 1998–1999.
President, Korean Student Association of Claremont Colleges, 2000–2001.

Principal Fields of Interest
Public Choice; Public Finance; Empirical Finance.

Principal Contributions
Dong Won Lee's dissertation research concerns the relationship of tax choices and efficiency to the size and growth of government, and the effects of regulation as an alternative policy instrument to public spending on budgets and their growth.

LEE, Dwight R.

Born
May 12, 1941, Fayetteville, North Carolina, USA

Current Position
Bernard Ramsey Professor of Free Enterprise and Economics, Terry College of Business, University of Georgia, 1985–.

Past Positions
Visiting Scholar, Liberty Fund, Inc., Jan-July 1999; John M. Olin Visiting Scholar, Center for Study of American Business, Washington University, 1988–1989; Associate Professor & Research Fellow, Center for Study of Public Choice, George Mason University, 1983–1985; Associate Professor, Research Fellow, and Executive Director; Center for Study of Public Choice, Virginia Polytechnic Institute & State University, 1981–1983; Associate Professor, Department of Economics, Virginia Polytechnic Institute & State University, 1978–1980; Assistant and Associate Professor, Department of Economics, University of Colorado, 1972–1978.

Degrees
B.A., San Diego State University, 1964; Ph.D., University of California at San Diego, 1972.

Offices and Honors
Second prize, N. Goto Essay Contest, Mont Pelerin Meeting, West Berlin, September 5–10, 1982.
Member, The Mont Pelerin Society, 1984.
Adjunct Research Associate, Center for Study of Public Choice, 1985–.
Winner, North American Region of N. Goto Essay Contest, Mont Pelerin Meeting, Saint Vincent, Italy, August 31–September 6, 1986.
Member, Executive Board, Southern Economic Association, 1987–1989.
First Vice President, Southern Economic Association, 1991–1992.
Winner, Distinguished Scholar Award, Association of Private Enterprise Education, 1992.
Vice President, Association of Private Enterprise Education, 1993–1994.
President, Association of Private Enterprise Education, 1994–1995.
Winner, National Federation of Independent Businesses Essay Contest on Entrepreneurship and Public Policy, April 1, 1996 (with Candace Allen).
President Elect, Southern Economic Association 1996–1997.
President, Southern Economic Association 1997–1998.
Kent-Aronoff Award, Outstanding Service to Association of Private Enterprise Education, 1997.
Named to the Templeton Honor Roll for Education in a Free Society, 1997–1998.
Winner, Association of Private Enterprise Education Essay contest on Private Enterprise, Entrepreneurship, and Society, April 7, 1998 (with Candace Allen).

Principle Fields of Interest
Economics of the Environment and Natural Resources; Economics of Political Decision Making; Public Finance; Law and Economics; Labor Economics.

Selected Publications
Books
1. *Taxation and the Deficit Economy: Fiscal Policy and Capital Formation in the United States* (Pacific Research Institute for Public Policy, 1986) (contributing editor).
2. *Regulating Government: A Preface to Constitutional Economics* (Lexington Books, D.C. Heath and Company, 1987) (with Richard B. McKenzie).
3. *The Market Economy: A Reader* (Roxbury Publishing Company, 1991) (edited, with James Doti). Named to the Templeton Honor Roll, 1997–1998.
4. *Quicksilver Capital: How the Rapid Movement of Wealth has Changed the World* (Free Press, 1991) (with Richard McKenzie).
5. *Failure and Progress: The Bright Side of the Dismal Science* (Cato Institute, 1993) (with Richard McKenzie).
6. *Managing Through Incentives: How to Develop a More Collaborative, Productive, and Profitable Organization* (Oxford University Press, 1998) (with Richard McKenzie).
7. *Getting Rich in America: 8 Simple Rules for Building a Fortune and a Satisfying Life* (Harper Business, 1999) (with Richard McKenzie).

Articles
1. "Discrimination and efficiency in the pricing of public goods." *Journal of Law and Economics*, 29(2): 1977.
2. "Price controls, binding constraints and intertemporal decision making." *Journal of Political Economy*, 86(2): 1978.
3. "Politics, time and the Laffer curve." *Journal of Political Economy*, 90:1982 (with James Buchanan).
4. "Politics, ideology, and the power of public choice." *Virginia Law Review*, 74(2):1988.
5. "Free riding and paid riding in the fight against terrorism." *The American Economic Review: Papers and Proceeding*, 78(2):1988.

6. "Status versus Enforcement: the case of the optimal speed limit." *American Economic Review*, 79(4):1989 (with Phil Graves and Robert Sexton).
7. "Private interest support for efficiency enhancing antitrust policies." *Economic Inquiry*, 30:1992 (with James M. Buchanan).
8. "How the client effect moderates price competition." *Southern Economic Journal*, 64(3):1998 (with Richard B. McKenzie).
9. "Free cash flow and public governance: the case of Alaska." *Journal of Applied Corporate Finance*, 14(3): 2000 (with Jim Verbrugge).
10. "How digital economics revises antitrust thinking." *The Antitrust Bulletin*, Summer:2001 (with Richard McKenzie).

Principle Contributions
Dwight Lee's early work began with dynamic models of firm behavior, which quickly evolved into work on the optimal use of natural resources, both renewable and non-renewable, and on environmental problems and policy. From his work on these issues it was natural to start thinking about public goods and public choice issues. Public choice has made up the greatest part of his body of research. In addition to his professional writing, Lee has devoted a significant amount of his effort to communicating to nonacademic audiences basic economic concepts and an understanding of how markets work.

LOHMANN, Susanne

Born
September 24, 1961, Bremen, Germany

Current Positions
Professor of Political Science, University of California, Los Angeles, 1998–; Director, Center for Governance, University of California, Los Angeles, 2000–.

Past Positions
Professor of Policy Studies, School of Public Policy and Social Research, University of California, Los Angeles, 1998–2001; Director, Center for Comparative Political Economy, University of California, Los Angeles, 1998–2000; Visiting Professor, Anderson School of Business, University of California, Los Angeles, Spring Quarter 2000; Visiting Professor, Department of Economics, University of California, Los Angeles, Winter Quarter 2000; Visiting Associate Professor of Political Science, California Institute of Technology, Fall Semester 1996; Visiting Associate Professor of Law, University of Southern California, Spring Semester 1996; Associate Professor of Political Science, University of California, Los Angeles, 1995–1998; Assistant Professor of Political Science, University of California, Los Angeles, 1993–1995; Assistant Professor of Political Science (courtesy), Stanford University, 1992/93; Assistant Professor of Political Economy and Business, Graduate School of Business, Stanford University, 1990–1993.

Degrees
Diplom Volkswirtschaftslehre (M.S.), University of Bonn, 1986; M.S., Ph.D., Carnegie Mellon University, 1988, 1991.

Offices and Honors
John M. Olin Doctoral Fellowship, Carnegie Mellon University, 1986–1989.
Best Ph.D. Student Teacher Award, Carnegie Mellon University, 1989.
Alfred P. Sloan Doctoral Dissertation Fellowship, 1989/90.
James and Doris McNamara Faculty Fellowship, Stanford University, 1991/92.
Faculty Career Development Award, University of California, Los Angeles, 1994/95.
Olin Fellowship, University of Southern California, 1996.
Deutscher Akademischer Austausch Dienst Prize for Distinguished Scholarship in German Studies, 1998.
Fellowship, Center for Advanced Study in the Behavioral Sciences, 1998/99.
Fellowship, John Simon Guggenheim Memorial Foundation, 2000/01.

Principal Fields of Interest
Collective Action; Central Banking; Ethics and Governance; Higher Education.

Selected Publications
Articles
1. "Optimal commitment in monetary policy: credibility versus flexibility." *American Economic Review*, 82: 1992.
2. "A signaling model of informative and manipulative political action." *American Political Science Review*, 88:1993.
3. "Electoral cycles and international policy cooperation." *European Economic Review*, 37:1993.

4. "Information aggregation through costly political action." *American Economic Review*, 84:1994.
5. "Dynamics of informational cascades: the monday demonstrations in Leipzig, East Germany, 1989–1991." *World Politics*, 47:1994.
6. "Divided government and U.S. trade policy." *International Organization*, 49:1994 (with Sharyn O'Halloran).
7. "A signaling model of competitive political pressures." *Economics and Politics*, 5:1995.
8. "Information, access and contributions: a signaling model of lobbying." *Public Choice*, 85:1995.
9. "Fire-alarm signals and the political control of regulatory agencies." *Journal of Law, Economics, and Organization*, 12:1996 (with Hugo Hopenhayn).
10. "Linkage politics." *Journal of Conflict Resolution*, 41:1997.
11. "Partisan control of the money supply and decentralized appointment powers." *European Journal of Political Economy*, 13:1997.
12. "Federalism and central bank independence: the politics of German monetary policy, 1957–1992." *World Politics*, 50:1998.
13. "Rationalizing the political business cycle: a workhorse model." *Economics and Politics*, 10:1998.
14. "Delegation and the regulation of risk." *Games and Economic Behavior*, 23:1998 (with Hugo Hopenhayn).
15. "Institutional checks and balances and the political control of the money supply." *Oxford Economic Papers*, 50:1998.
16. "An information rationale for the power of special interests." *American Political Science Review*, 92:1998.
17. "What price accountability? the Lucas Island model and the politics of monetary policy." *American Journal of Political Science*, 43(2):1999.
18. "Setting the agenda: electoral competition, commitment of policy, and issue salience." *Public Choice*, 99:1999 (with Amihai Glazer).
19. "Collective action cascades: an informational rationale for the power in numbers." *Journal of Economics Surveys*, 14:2000.
20. "Sollbruchstelle: deep uncertainty and the design of monetary institutions." *International Finance*, 3:2000.

Principal Contributions
In the first decade of her career, Susanne Lohmann developed a signaling theory of collective action, which found its empirical expression in an article on the Leipzig Monday demonstrations. In parallel, she worked on issues of monetary policy and central bank banking, with an empirical application to the Deutsche Bundesbank. She is currently interested in exploring issues of ethics and governance, with special emphasis on higher education. She is writing a book titled *How Universities Think*.

LÓPEZ, Edward John

Born
November 28, 1969, San Antonio, Texas, USA

Current Position
Assistant Professor, Department of Economics, University of North Texas.

Past Positions
Visiting Scholar, Center for Study of Public Choice, James Buchanan Center for Political Economy, George Mason University, Summer 2001; Earhart Post Doctoral Fellow, Department of Economics, George Mason University, 1997–98; Instructor, Department of Economics, George Mason University, 1995–1998; Manager, Public Policy Programs, Center for Market Processes, George Mason University, 1994–1996; Professional Staff Member, Joint Economic Committee, United States Congress, 1993–1994.

Degrees
B.S., Texas A&M University, 1992; M.A., George Mason University, 1995; Ph.D., George Mason University, 1997.

Offices and Honors
Recipient, three fellowships from Earhart Foundation (dissertation fellowship 1996–1997; post-doctoral fellowship 1997–1998; fellowship research grant 2001–2002).
Salvatori Fellow, *Foundations of American Liberty*, Salvatori Center for Appreciation of the Founding Fathers, The Heritage Foundation, June 1999.
Faculty Coordinator, American Institute for Foreign Study, Prague, Czech Republic, Summer 2000.

Editorial Duties
Guest Co-Editor, *Review of Austrian Economics* 15(2–3), 2002. Special Issue on Austrian Economics and Public Choice; Reviewer, *Educational Evaluation and Policy Analysis, Electoral Studies, Journal of Theoretical Politics,*

Political Research Quarterly, Public Choice, Review of Austrian Economics.

Principal Fields of Interest
Public Choice; Industrial Organization.

Selected Publications
Journals
Guest editor with introduction, *Review of Austrian Economics* 15, Summer 2002 (Special Issue on Austrian and Public Choice Economics).

Articles
1. "New anti-merger theories: a critique." *Cato Journal*, 20(3): 2001.
2. "Committee assignments and the cost of party loyalty." *Political Research Quarterly*, 55. (March):2002 (with Wayne A. Leighton).
3. "The Legislator as Political Entrepreneur: Investment in Political Capital." *Review of Austrian Economics* 15(2–3): 2002.
4. "Congressional voting on term limits." forthcoming in *Public Choice*.
5. "Term limits: causes and consequences." forthcoming in *Public Choice*.

Principal Contributions
Edward López's research may be characterized as using standard economic tools to investigate the role of institutions in political and social change. In his research he has emphasized congressional voting, legislative organization, the role of ideology, and specific institutions such as term limits and campaign finance. He also does research in industrial organization, with an emphasis on price discrimination and recent developments in antitrust regulation. The majority of his research has involved empirical studies of congressional voting, ideology, and legislative organization. He has begun to work more on theoretically modeling the effects of political institutions on the lobbying/rent-seeking efforts of firms and individuals. Lopez has served as the guest co-editor (with Peter J. Boettke) of a symposium on Austrian and public choice economics that recently appeared as a special issue of the *Review of Austrian Economics*. He is interested in developing his research such that it has a positive impact on the way societies shape their institutions. While he was in graduate school, for example, he served on the staff of the Joint Economic Committee of the U.S. Senate, where his work was instrumental in the debate over President Clinton's proposed health care plan.

MATSUSAKA, John G.

Born
July 5, 1964.

Current Positions
Professor of Finance and Business Economics, Marshall School of Business, University of Southern California, 1990; Senior Research Fellow and member of Board of Directors, Initiative and Referendum Institute, Washington, D.C.

Past Positions
John M. Olin Visiting Professor of Economics, George J. Stigler Center for the Study of the Economy and the State, University of Chicago, 2001; Visiting Associate, California Institute of Technology, 2000; Visiting Scholar, Anderson School of Management, UCLA, 1996; National Fellow, Hoover Institution, Stanford University, 1994–1995; Lecturer, Department of Economics, University of Chicago, 1987–1989.

Degrees
B.A., University of Washington, Seattle, Washington, 1985; M.A., Ph.D., University of Illinois, 1991.

Selected Publications
Articles
1. "Economics of Direct Legislation." *Quarterly Journal of Economics*, 107(May):1992.
2. "Fiscal effects of the voter initiative: evidence from the last 30 years." *Journal of Political Economy*, 103(June):1995.
3. "Systematic deviations from constituent interests: the role of legislative structure and political parties in the states." *Economic Inquiry*, 84(July):1995 (with T.W. Gilligan).
4. "Demand for environmental goods: evidence from voting patterns on California Initiatives." *Journal of Law and Economics*, 40(April):1997 (with M.E. Kahn).
5. "Voter turnout: how much can we explain?." *Public Choice*, 98(March):1999 (with F. Palda).
6. "Fiscal effects of the voter initiative in the first half of the twentieth century." *Journal of Law and Economics*, 43(October):2000.
7. "Fiscal policy, legislature size, and political parties: evidence from the first half of the twentieth century." *National Tax Journal*, 54(March):2001 (with T.W. Gilligan).
8. "Political resource allocation: benefits and costs of voter initiatives." *Journal of Law, Economics, and Organization*, 17(October):2001 (with N.M. McCarty).

9. "Problems with a methodology used to test the responsiveness of policy to opinion in initiative states." *Journal of Politics*, 58(November):2001.
10. *For the many or the few: how the initiative process changes American Government*. Book manuscript in progress.

McCHESNEY, Fred Sanderson

Born
November 19, 1948, Washington, DC, USA

Current Positions
Northwestern University, 1999–; Class of 1967 / James B. Haddad Professor of Law; Professor, Department of Management & Strategy, Kellogg School of Management.

Past Positions
Professor of Law, Cornell University, 1997–1999; Robert T. Thompson Professor of Law and Business, Emory University, 1987–1997 (Assistant Professor, 1983–1985; Associate Professor 1985–1987); Professor of Economics, Emory University, 1987–1997.

Degrees
B.A., Holy Cross College, 1970; J.D., University of Miami, 1978; Ph.D., University of Virginia, 1982.

Offices and Honors
Consumer Advisory Council, Federal Reserve Board, 1984–1987.
General Counsel, Southern Economic Association, 1984–.
Member, American Law Institute, 1988–.
Executive Committee, Section on Antitrust, Association of American Law Schools, 1996–1997.
Affiliate, Center for Study of Industrial Organization, Northwestern University, 2000–.

Editorial Duties
Editorial Board: *Public Choice, Managerial and Decision Economics, Journal des Economistes et des Etudes Humaines*.

Principal Fields of Interest
Virginia Political Economy; Property Rights; Law and Economics; Industrial Organization; Corporate Law and Finance; Empirical Methods.

Selected Publications
Books
1. *Causes and Consequences of Antitrust: The Public Choice Perspective* (University of Chicago Press, 1995) (edited with W. Shughart).
2. *Money for Nothing: Politicians, Rent Extraction and Political Extortion* (Harvard University Press, 1997).
3. *Economic Inputs, Legal Outputs: The Role of Economists in Modern Antitrust* (edited) (John Wiley & Sons, 1998).
4. *Antitrust Law: Interpretation and Implementation* (Michie/Lexis, 1st ed. 1998, 2nd ed. 2002) (with C. Goetz).
5. *Property Rights: Cooperation, Conflict and Law* (Princeton University Press, 2002) (edited with T. Anderson).

Articles
1. "Prohibitions on volunteer fire-fighting in nineteenth century America: a property rights perspective." 15 *Journal of Legal Studies*, 69:1986.
2. "Rent extraction and rent creation in the economic theory of regulation." *Journal of Legal Studies*, 101: 1987.
3. "Sensationalism, newspaper profits, and the marginal value of Watergate." *Economic Inquiry*, 135:1987.
4. "Government as definer of property rights: Indian land ownership, ethnic externalities, and bureaucratic budgets." *Journal of Legal Studies*, 297:1990.
5. "Bureaucracy and politics in FTC merger challenges." *Journal of Law and Economics*, 463:1990 (with M. Coate and R. Higgins).
6. "Bargaining costs, bargaining benefits and compulsory non-bargaining rules." *Journal of Law, Economics, and Organization*, 334:1991 (with D. Haddock).
7. "Rent extraction and interest-group organization in a Coasean Model of regulation." *Journal of Legal Studies*, 73:1991.
8. "Raid or trade? an economic model of Indian-White relations." *Journal of Law and Economics*, 39: 1994 (with T. Anderson).
9. "Why do firms contrive shortages?: the economics of intentional underpricing." *Economic Inquiry*, 39: 1994 (with D. Haddock).
10. "Government as definer of Property Rights: tragedy exiting the commons?" in *Property Rights: Cooperation, Conflict and Law* (T. Anderson & F. McChesney, eds., forthcoming).

MUDAMBI, Ram

Born
October 18, 1954, Maharashtra, India

Current Position
Associate Professor of Strategic Management, Temple University, USA, 2000–; Reader in International Business, University of Reading, UK, 1997–.

Past Positions
Associate Professor of Economics, Case Western Reserve University, 1998–2000; Senior Lecturer in Strategy, University of Buckingham, 1992–1997; Assistant Professor of Economics, Lehigh University, 1985–1991; Visiting Assistant Professor of Economics, University of North Carolina, 1988–1989.

Degrees
B.A., Elphinstone College, University of Bombay, 1974; M.S., London School of Economics and Political Science, 1977; Ph.D., Cornell University, 1986.

Principal Fields of Interest
Public Choice; Politics of International Business; Strategies of Multinational Firms.

Selected Publications
Books
1. The Organisation of the Firm: International Business Perspectives (Routledge, 1998) (edited, with M. Ricketts).
2. *Party Strategies and Voting Behaviour: The Political Economy of Italian Electoral Reform* (Edward Elgar Publishing, 2001), (edited, with P. Navarra and G. Sobbrio).
3. *Rules and Reason: Perspectives in Constitutional Political Economy* (Cambridge University Press, 2001), (edited, with P. Navarra and G. Sobbrio).

Articles
1. "Plurality versus proportional representation: an analysis of Sicilian elections." *Public Choice*, 86:1996 (with P. Navarra and C. Nicosia).
2. "A complete information index for measuring the proportionality of electoral systems." *Applied Economics Letters*, 4:1997.
3. "Voter information and power dilution: evidence from Sicilian provincial elections." *Public Choice*, 92:1997 (with P. Navarra and G. Sobbrio).
4. "Changing the rules. Political competition under proportionality and plurality". *European Journal of Political Economy*, 15(3):1999 (with P. Navarra and G. Sobbrio).
5. "Political culture and foreign direct investments: the case of Italy." *Economic of Governance*, 2003 forthcoming (with P. Navarra).
6. "Institutions and market reform in emerging economies: a rent-seeking perspective." *Public Choice*, 2003 (with P. Navarra and C. Paul).

Principal Contributions
Ram Mudambi has made several contributions on the impact of electoral systems on party strategies and voting behavior. His work has examined issues involved in electoral system change, from the normative perspective (constitutional political economy) as well as the positive perspective (public choice). In particular, he has studied the electoral system changes in Italy during the 1990s in great detail. Currently he is working on the impact of political institutions on international business.

MUNGER, Michael Curtis

Born
September 23, 1958, Orlando, Florida, USA

Current Positions
Professor and Chair, Department of Political Science, Duke University, 1997–; Director, MicroIncentives Research Center, Duke University; joint appointments in: Department of Economics, and Sanford Institute in Public Policy, Duke University; and Curriculum in Public Policy Analysis, University of North Carolina.

Past Positions
Associate Professor of Political Science and Director of Master of Public Administration Program, University of North Carolina, 1990–1997; Assistant Professor, University of Texas, 1986–1990; Visiting Assistant Professor, Dartmouth College, 1985–1986; Staff Economist, U.S. Federal Trade Commission, 1984–1985; Research Associate, Center for Study of American Business, Washington University, 1982–1983.

Degrees
B.A., Economics, Davidson College, 1980; M.A., Ph.D., Washington University, 1982, 1984.

Offices and Honors
National Merit Scholar, Davidson College (1976).
Political Economy Fellow, Washington University (1984).
Co-winner, Duncan Black Prize (best paper in *Public Choice*, 1995: "Win, Lose, or Withdraw,": (with D. Coates).
President, Public Choice Society, 1996–1998.

Principal Fields of Interest
Public Choice; American Politics and Institutions; Political Economy; Policy Analysis.

Selected Publications
Books
1. *Ideology and the Theory of Political Choice* (University of Michigan Press, 1994) (with Melvin J. Hinich). (paperback edition published September 1996).
2. *Analytical Politics* (Cambridge University Press, April 1997) (with Melvin J. Hinich). (Reprinted in Japanese and Spanish).
3. *Empirical Studies in Comparative Public Choice*, (Kluwer Academic Press, 1998) (edited, with Melvin J. Hinich).
4. *Analyzing Policy: Choices, Conflicts, and Practices.* (W.W. Norton, 2000).

Articles
1. "Legislators and interest groups: how unorganized interests get represented." *American Political Science Review*, 80(March):1986 (with Arthur T. Denzau).
2. "Allocation of desirable committee assignments: extended queues vs. committee expansion." *American Journal of Political Science* 32(2):1988.
3. "The rationality of ideology." *Journal of Law and Economics*, 32(April):1989 (with William R. Dougan).
4. "Contributions, expenditure, turnout: the 1982 U.S. House Elections." *American Political Science Review*, 83:1989 (with Gary Cox).
5. "Committee assignments, constituent preferences, and campaign contributions to House incumbents." *Economic Inquiry* 29:1991 (with Kevin Grier).
6. "Economic models of interest groups: an introductory survey." *American Journal of Political Science* 35: 1991 (with William Mitchell).
7. "The determinants of industry political activity, 1978–1986." *American Political Science Review*, 88: 1994 (with Kevin Grier and Brian Roberts).
8. "The prohibition and repeal amendments: a natural experiment in interest group influence." *Public Choice*, 90:1997 (with Thomas Schaller).
9. "The Downsian model predicts divergence." *Journal of Theoretical Politics*, 12:2000 (with Mark Berger and Richard Potthoff).
10. "Investigating the incidence of killer amendments in Congress." *Journal of Politics*, 2002 (with Jeff Jenkins).

Principal Contributions
Michael Munger's primary interests are in the functioning and stability of political institutions, including ideologies, and the way that they connect with market processes. In several published pieces, he has argued that the main focus in the social sciences should be on one large question: The fundamental is the construction, or maintenance, of institutions that make self-interested individual action not inconsistent with the welfare of the society. There are two ways to approach this problem: take perceptions of self-interest as given, and allow (as Madison suggested) ambition to counteract ambition. The alternative (as Rousseau suggested) is to try to mold people's perceptions of their self-interest, so that they value community and cooperation. Ideologies exist because they serve this second function, but they also constrain the development of societies. Munger was heavily influenced by three very different, scholars: Melvin Hinich, Douglass North and Barry Weingast.

NAVARRA, Pietro

Born
August 30, 1968, Messina, Sicilia, Italia

Current Positions
Research Associate, Center for Philosophy of Natural and Social Sciences, London School of Economics, UK, 2001–; Associate Professor of Public Economics, University of Messina, Italia, 2000–; Co-Director of the Research Program in 'Democracy, Business and Human Well-Being, London School of Economics, UK, 2000.

Past Positions
Visiting Fellow, Wisenschaftkollege, Institute for Advanced Studies, Berlin (Germany); Jan 2002; Visiting Scholar, Department of General and Strategic Management, Temple University, Spring 2001; Fulbright Research Fellow, Carnegie Mellon University Fall 2000; Visiting Scholar, Department of Economics, Case Western Reserve University, Fall 1999; Visiting Scholar, ISMA Centre, University of Reading, Fall 1997, Spring 1999; Visiting Scholar, School of Social Sciences, University of California at Irvine, Fall 1998; Visiting Scholar, Department of Economics, George Mason University, Spring 1995.

Degrees
B.A., University of Messina, 1990; M.S., Ph.D., University of Buckingham, 1994, 1997; M.S., by Research, University of York, 2000.

Principal Fields of Interest
Public Choice; Constitutional Political Economy; Institutional Economics; Health Economics.

Selected Publications
Books
1. "*Rules and Reason: Perspectives in Constitutional Political Economy.*" (Cambridge University Press; 2001). (edited, with R. Mudambi and G. Sobbrio).
2. *Party Strategies and Voting Behaviour: The Political Economy of Italian Electoral Reform* (Edward Elgar Publishing, 2001) (edited, with R. Mudambi and G. Sobbrio).

Articles
1. "Plurality versus proportional representation: an analysis of Sicilian elections." *Public Choice*, 86:1996 (with R. Mudambi and C. Nicosia).
2. "Voter information and power dilution: evidence from Sicilian provincial elections." *Public Choice*, 92:1997 (with R. Mudambi and G. Sobbrio).
3. "The strategic behaviour of the Italian left in a risk-sharing framework." *Public Choice*, 93:1997 (with D. Lignana).
4. "Changing the rules. Political competition under proportionality and plurality." *European Journal of Political Economy*, 15(3):1999 (with R. Mudambi and G. Sobbrio).
5. "Local pork-barrel politics in national pre-election dates: the case of Italy." *Public Choice*, 106:2001 (with M. Limosani).
6. "Election re-running and the nature of constitutional choices: The case of Italian Electoral Reform." *Constitutional Political Economy*, 12(1):2001 (with G. Sobbrio).
7. "Institutions and Market Reform in Emerging Economies: A Rent-Seeking Perspective." *Public Choice*, forthcoming 2003 (with R. Mudambi and C. Paul).
8. "Political culture and foreign direct investments: the case of Italy." *Economic of Governance*, forthcoming (with R. Mudambi).

Principal Contributions
Pietro Navarra has made several contributions on the impact of electoral systems on party strategies and voting behavior. His work has examined issues involved in electoral system change, from the normative perspective (constitutional political economy) as well as the positive perspective (public choice). In particular, he has studied the electoral system changes in Italy during the 1990s in great detail. Currently he is working on the impact of political institutions on international business.

OPPENHEIMER, Joe

Born
June 20, 1941, New Rochelle, New York, USA.

Current Positions
Professor, Department of Government and Politics, University of Maryland, and Director of the University's Collective Choice Center.

Past Positions
Faculty member, Department of Government and Politics, University of Maryland, 1976–present; Associate Professor, Department of Government, The University of Texas, 1974–1976; Assistant Professor, Department of Government, The University of Texas, 1970–1974.

Degrees
B.A., Cornell University, 1962; M.A., University of Michigan, 1964; Ph.D., Princeton University, 1971.

Offices and Honors
Member, Honorary Board, Public Choice Society, Japan. Duncan Black Prize for best article of 1996 in the journal *Public Choice* for "Experiencing Impartiality to Invoke Fairness in the n-PD: Some Experimental Results" (with Norman Frohlich).
Prize winner for experimental authoring software (C&C, VOTE).

Editorial Duties
Charter Member, Editorial Board, *Journal of Theoretical Politics*; Book Review Editor, *Public Choice*, 1975–1977; Joint Book Review Editor (with Norman Frohlich and Oran Young), *Public Choice*, 1973–1975.

Principal Fields of Interest
Experimental Economics; Public Choice; Ethics; Distributive Justice; Collective Action/Social Dilemmas; Social Welfare Policy.

Selected Publications
Books
1. *Political Leadership and Collective Goods* (Princeton University Press, 1971) (with Norman Frohlich and Oran Young).
2. *Modern Political Economy* (Prentice-Hall Inc. 1978) in the *Foundation of Modern Political Science Series*, Robert A. Dahl (ed.), (with Norman Frohlich).

Economia Politica Moderna, 1982; The University of Brasilia Press published a Portuguese translation of *Modern Political Economy* in its political thought series: Pensamento Politico. *Modern Political Economy*, 1991; a Japanese edition with updated suggested readings.
3. *Choosing Justice: an Experimental Approach to Ethical Theory*, (University of California Press, 1992) (with Norman Frohlich).
4. *Transboundary Freshwater Dispute Resolution: Theory, Practice and Annotated References.* (Tokyo: United Nations University Press, 2000) (with Heather Beach, Jesse Hamner, J. Joey Hewitt, Edy Kaufman, Anja Kurki, and Aaron Wolfe).

Articles
1. "I get by with a little help from my friends." *World Politics*, 22(October): 1970 (with Norman Frohlich).
2. "The carrot and the stick: optimal program mixes for entrepreneurial political leaders." *Public Choice*, 19(Fall):1974 (with Norman Frohlich).
3. "Individual contributions to collective goods: alternative models." *Journal of Conflict Resolution*, 19(March):1975 (with Thomas Hunt, Norman Frohlich, and R. Harrison Wagner).
4. "A test of Downsian voter rationality: 1964 Presidential Voting." *American Political Science Review*, 72(March):1978 (with Norman Frohlich, Jeffrey Smith, and Oran R. Young).
5. "Universalism and majority rule committees." *American Political Science Review*, 76(3):1982 (with Gary Miller).
6. "Liberating the industrious tailor: ideology and Science in the Social Sciences." *Political Methodology*, 8(1): 1982 (with R. Able).
7. "Beyond economic man: altruism, egalitarianism, and difference maximizing." *Journal of Conflict Resolution*, 28(1): 1984 (with Norman Frohlich and with Pat Bond and Irvin Boschmann).
8. "Choices of principles of distributive justice in experimental groups." *American Journal of Political Science*, 31(3):1987 (with Norman Frohlich and Cheryl Eavey).
9. "Choosing justice in experimental democracies with production." *American Political Science Review*, 84(2):1990 (with Norman Frohlich).
10. "Experiencing impartiality to invoke fairness in the n-PD: Some Experimental Results." *Public Choice*, 86:1996 (with Norman Frohlich).
11. "A role for structured observation in ethical inquiry." *Social Justice Review* 10(1):1997 (with Norman Frohlich).
12. "Using bargaining theory and economic analysis as an aid to trans-boundary water cooperation," in R.E. Just and S. Netanyahu (eds.) *Conflict and Cooperation on Trans-Boundary Water Resources* (Kluwer Academic Publishers, 1998) (Co-authored with Richard E. Just, George Frisvold, Verna Harrison, William Matuszeski, and David Zilberman) Reprinted in *The Management of Water Resources*. Charles W. Howe, series editor. (Edward Elgar Publishing, 2001).
13. "Some doubts about measuring self-interest using dictator experiments: the costs of anonymity." *Journal of Economic Behavior and Organization*, 46(3):2001 (with Norman Frohlich and J. Bernard Moore).

Principal Contributions
The vast majority of Joe Oppenheimer's contributions have been made in full collaboration with Norman Frohlich. Their initial interest in collective action led them to identify conditions under which rational self-interested individuals would contribute to public goods, to identify classes of public goods and (together with Oran Young) to define and develop the first formal characterization of the political entrepreneur. They also developed early experiments that demonstrated the existence of classes of other regarding behavior. They also utilized the tools of experimental economics to examine notions of distributive justice and show the potential of experimental methods for casting light on ethical problems. Substantively, they along with various replicators of their experiments, were able to demonstrate broad, cross-national rejection of the Rawlsian maximin criterion in deference to a principle that balances support for a guaranteed minimum for the needy while taking into account just desserts and the principal of social efficiency. Their more recent work has focused on normative and cognitive aspects of decision making. They have been attempting to identify how generalized framing effects can impact individual and societal decisions, both from a normative and positive perspective. Opppenheimer also co-authored a software suite which lets the professor or researcher author and run experiments on networked PCs.

PADOVANO, Fabio

Born
September 23, 1966, Florence, Italy

Current Position
Adjunct Professor of Public Finance, Facoltà di Giurisprudenza, Università di Lecce, 2002–; Associate

Professor of Public Finance, Facoltà di Scienze Politiche, Università Roma Tre, Roma, Italy, 2001–.

Past Positions
Assistant professor of Economics, Università Roma Tre, 1997–2001; Adjunct Professor of Public Finance, Università de L'Aquila, 1998–1999; Lecturer in Macroeconomics and Economic Growth, Graduate School of the Università di Roma La Sapienza, 1996 onwards; Lecturer in Mathematics for Economics, Università Roma Tre 1995–1997.

Research: Visiting Professor, Center for Study of Public Choice, George Mason University, 2001; Academic Visitor, London School of Economics and Political Science, 1997; Founder, Center for Economics of Institutions, Università Roma Tre, 1997; Graduate Research Assistant, Center for Study of Public Choice, George Mason University, 1992–1994.

Degrees
B.S., 1989, LUISS Guido Carli, Roma, Italy; M.A., Ph.D., George Mason University, 1993, 1995; Ph.D., University of Rome La Sapienza, Italy, 1995.

Offices and Honors
Member, The Mont Pelerin Society, 2002.
William T. Snavely Award, Outstanding Graduate Student in Economics, George Mason University, 1995.
Member, Public Choice Society, European Public Choice Society, American Economic Association, Società Italiana di Economia Pubblica, Società Italiana degli Economisti.

Principal Fields of Interest
Public Choice; Public Finance; Economic Growth.

Selected Publications
Books
1. "Deregulation, welfare state and competition in the goods and labor markets," in *Equity, Efficiency and Growth: the Future of the Welfare State* (Macmillan, 1996) (M. Baldassarri, L. Paganetto, and E.S. Phelps, eds.) (with Francesco Forte).
2. "Budget rules and fiscal performance in the European Union: a non-metric principal component analysis," in *Istituzioni Politiche e Finanza Pubblica* (Franco Angeli, 2000) (V. Dardanoni, G. Sobbrio, eds.) (with Francesco Lagona).

Articles
1. "Corporatist vs. decentralized Governance and economic growth." *Journal for Institutional Innovation, Development and Transition*, 3: 1999 (with Emma Galli).
2. "A model of the representation of interests in a compound democracy." *Constitutional Political Economy*, 11(1):2000 (with Sebastiano Bavetta).
3. "Wars of attrition in government coalitions and fiscal performance: a test on italian 1948–1994 data." *Public Choice* 109(1):2001 (with Larissa Venturi).
4. "Tax rates and economic growth in the OECD (Countries): 1951–1990." *Economic Inquiry*, 39(1): 2001 (with Emma Galli).
5. "Comparing the growth effects of marginal and average tax pressure and of tax progressivity." *European Journal of Political Economy*, 2002 (with Emma Galli).
6. "A comparative test of alternative theories of the determinants of public deficits." *Public Choice*, 113:2002 (with E. Galli).

Principal Contributions
Fabio Padovano's early research agenda aimed to use positive public choice models to explain structural problems of the Italian economy, especially in the field of public finance, economic growth and policy decision-making. He concentrated on empirical research because until the early 1990s in Italy public choice was mainly known and appreciated as a theory, but found difficulties to penetrate the Italian scientific culture, since very little work had been done to show how these theories could explain Italian phenomena. In order to overcome this problem, Padovano has provided public choice analyses of public debt and deficits, of the financial effects of alternative budget approbation procedures, and of the impact on output growth alternative systems of governance of the labor market. To the same end, he has founded the Center for Economics of Institutions with his colleagues of the Università Roma Tre, to promote the growth of young scholars interested in public choice related research.

An obstacle to perform empirical research in public choice in Italy has always been the availability of political and institutional data. Padovano has thus started to assemble a databank on the legislative production of the Italian Republic, in order to study the existence of a political legislation cycle; he is also assembling a databank on local tax rates and electoral outcomes, to monitor the effects of the progressive shift of Italy from a centralized to a more decentralized, almost federalist organization of the tax system.

In the field of public finance Padovano has devised a new approach to test the effects of marginal tax rates on economic growth.

His theoretical work has concentrated on the internal composition of government. The aim is to understand when the various government bodies compete with each other to enhance electoral accountability, and what conditions lead the government bodies to collude, doing away with the constitutional principles of the separation of powers and of checks and balances.

PALDA, Filip

Born
May 12, 1962, Montreal, Quebec, Canada

Current Positions
Visiting Professor, Center for Economic Research and Graduate Education of the Charles University, Prague, 2002–; Associate Professor, École nationale d'administration publique, Montreal, Canada, 1994–; Senior Fellow, The Fraser Institute, Vancouver 1994–.

Past Positions
Senior Economist, The Fraser Institute, Vancouver, 1991–1994; Assistant Professor, Department of Economics, University of Ottawa, 1989–1991.

Degrees
B.A., M.A., Queen's University at Kingston 1983, 1984; Ph.D., University of Chicago, 1989.

Editorial Duties
Contributing Editor, *The Next City Magazine*, 1997–2000; Founding Editor, *Journal for Institutional Innovation and Development*, 1997–2001.

Principal Fields of Interest
Public Choice; Public Finance.

Selected Publications
Books
1. *Election Finance Regulation in Canada: A Critical Review* (The Fraser Institute, 1991).
2. *Provincial Trade Wars: Why the Blockade Must End* (The Fraser Institute, 1994) (ed).
3. *The New Federalist.* Gordon Tullock (ed.) (The Fraser Institute, 1994). (Adapted for Canadian readers by Filip Palda).
4. *How Much is Your Vote Worth? The Unfairness of Campaign Spending Limits* (Institute for Contemporary Studies, 1994).
5. *It's No Gamble: The Social Benefits of the Stock Market* (The Fraser Institute, 1995) (ed).
6. *Essays in Canadian Surface Transportation* (Vancouver: The Fraser Institute, 1995) (ed.)
7. *Tax Facts Ten* (The Fraser Institute, 1997) (with I. Horry, J. Emes, and M. Walker).
8. *Here the People Rule: A Toolbook for Reforming Democracy* (Paragon House Publishers, 1997).
9. *Home on the Urban Range: An Idea Map for Reforming the City* (The Fraser Institute, 1998).
10. *Tax Evasion and Firm Survival in Competitive Markets* (Edward Elgar Publishing, 2001).

Articles
1. "Campaign spending and the government jackpot." *Economic Inquiry*, October:1992.
2. "The Downsian voter meets the ecological fallacy." *Public Choice*, 77:1993 (with J. Matsusaka).
3. "Can repressive regimes be moderated through foreign aid?" *Public Choice*, 77:1993.
4. "Fiscal churning and political efficiency." *Kyklos*, 50: 1997.
5. "Evasive ability and the efficiency costs of the underground economy." *Canadian Journal of Economics*, 31:1999.
6. "Voter turnout: how much can we explain?." *Public Choice*, 98:1999 (with J.G. Matsusaka).
7. "Property Rights vs. Income Redistribution: which path to national wealth?" *Public Choice*, 101:1999.
8. "Improper selection of high-cost producers in the rent-seeking Contest." *Public Choice*, 105.
9. "Some deadweight losses from the minimum wage: the cases of full and partial compliance." *Labour Economics*, 7:2000.
10. "Are campaign contributions a form of speech? the case of recent house elections." In press, *Public Choice*, 2002 (with Dhammika Dharmapala).

Principal Contributions
Filip Palda's principal contribution is to have discovered and elaborated the notion of displacement deadweight loss. An inefficient producer with a good ability to evade the tax may displace from the market the efficient producer who is an inept evader. The difference in costs between the two is the displacement deadweight loss from the tax. This concept has possibilities in public choice. Palda showed how it gives rise to a new form of rent-seeking cost, namely the cost of having a good lobbyist snatch a government contract or regulatory ruling from an inept lobbyist who would be the most efficient choice for the job. In the field of campaign finances his original contribution has been to point out that voters punish candidates who rely on a concentrated source of funds. He has also done extensive work on the political economy of campaign spending laws to show that these laws may serve the interests of the legislators who write them

more than they serve the public interest. Finally, Palda has brought attention to the phenomenon of "fiscal churning", which occurs when government simultaneously transfers money to a person and taxes that money back. He has pointed out that this is a major activity of government that has received almost no theoretical treatment.

PARISI, Francesco

Born
May 31, 1962, Rome, Italy

Current Positions
Distinguished Professor of Law and Economics, University of Milan (Italy), 2002–; Professor of Law, George Mason University, Virginia, USA, 1998–.

Past Positions
Associate Professor of Law, George Mason University, 1993–1998; Assistant Professor of Law, Louisiana State University, 1991–1993; Lecturer in Law, University of California Berkeley, School of Law (Boalt Hall), 1990–1991.

Degrees
D. Jur., University of Rome, 1985; LL.M., J.S.D., M.A., University of California, Berkeley; 1988, 1990, 1995, Ph.D., George Mason University, 1998.

Offices and Honors
Honorary Member, Bulgarian Hayek Society, 2002–.
Vice-President, Henry Capitant Association, 1993–.
Member, Board of Directors, American Society of Comparative Law, 1993–.
Member, Board of Academic Advisors, University of Milan (Bocconi), 1999–.
Member, Board of Advisors, University of Virginia, Law and Economic Development Center, 1999–.

Editorial Duties
Editor, *International Legal Theory*, 1994–2000; Member, Board of Editors, *American Journal of Comparative Law*, 1994–; Member, Board of Advisors, *Journal of International Legal Studies*, 1995–2000; Member, Board of Editors, *International Review of Law and Economics*, 1997–; Editor, *Comparative Law Abstracts (Social Sciences Research Network)*, 2001–; Editor, *Supreme Court Economic Review*, 2002–.

Principal Fields of Interest
Law and Economics; Public Choice and Constitutional Political Economy; Comparative Legal Theory.

Selected Publications
Books
1. *Il Contratto Concluso Mediante Computer* ("The Formation of Contracts Via Computer"), (CEDAM, 1987).
2. *Liability for Negligence and Judicial Discretion*, 1st edn., (California, 1990); 2nd edition, (California, 1992).
3. *Law and Economics*. Volumes I-III (Edward Elgar Publishing, 1997) (edited, with R.A. Posner).
4. *The Economic Structure of the Law* (The Collected Papers of Richard A. Posner: Volume I), (ELGAR, 2000).
5. *The Economics of Private Law* (The Collected Papers of Richard A. Posner: Volume II), (ELGAR, 2001).
6. *The Economics of Public Law* (The Collected Papers of Richard A. Posner: Volume III), (ELGAR, 2001).
7. *The Economic Foundations of Private Law* (Edward Elgar Publishing, 2002) (edited, with R.A. Posner).
8. *The Law and Economics of the European Union* (Lexis Publishing, 2002) (with P. Stephan and B. Depoorter).
9. *Law and Economics: Essays By the Founding Fathers* (Edward Elgar Publishing, forthcoming) (co-edited with C.K. Rowley).

Articles
1. "Alterum non Laedere: an intellectual history of civil liability." *American Journal of Jurisprudence*, 39: 1994.
2. "Toward a theory of spontaneous law." *Constitutional Political Economy*, 6:1995.
3. "Choice of Law." *The New Palgrave Dictionary of Economics and the Law* (Macmillan, 1998) (with Larry Ribstein).
4. "The cost of the game: a taxonomy of social interaction." *European Journal of Law and Economics*, 9:2000.
5. "The genesis of liability in Ancient law." *American Law and Economics Review*, 3:2001.
6. "Entropy in property." *American Journal of Comparative Law*, 2002.
7. "Freedom of contract and the Laws of entropy." *Supreme Court Economic Review*, 9:2002.
8. "Rent-seeking through litigation: adversarial and inquisitorial systems compared." *International Review of Law and Economics*, 2002.
9. "Reciprocity-induced cooperation." *Journal of Institutional and Theoretical Economics*, 159:2003 (with Vincy Fon).

10. "The political coase theorem." *Public Choice* (forthcoming).

Principal Contributions

Francesco Parisi's early work was in the field of comparative law and economics, commencing with a study on the emergence and evolution of liability rules, started while he was at the University of California at Berkeley. In 1993, he joined the law faculty at George Mason University. This offered him an opportunity to work at the interface of law and economics and public choice theory. Since then, his academic research has applied these methodologies to a broad range of legal and institutional issues. During the late 1990s his research explored the relationship between different sources of law, with special emphasis on customary law and choice of law. In recent years, the focus has shifted towards the formulation of economic models of legal evolution and the institutional design of lawmaking. Parisi has written and edited some 10 books and authored over 100 scholarly papers in support of this research agenda.

PEACOCK, Alan Turner

Born
June 26, 1922, Newcastle, England

Current Positions
Honorary Research Professor in Public Finance, Edinburgh Business School, Heriot Watt University, 1987–; Professor Emeritus in Economics, University of Buckingham; Honorary Professor of Economics, University of York, 1978–; Economic Consultant, The David Hume Institute, Edinburgh, 1992–.

Past Positions
Joint Founder and Executive Director, The David Hume Institute, 1985–1991; Principal and Professor of Economics, University of Buckingham 1979–1984; Foundation Professor of Economics (Deputy Vice Chancellor 1963–1969) University of York, 1962–1978 — on secondment as Chief Economic Adviser, Department of Trade and Industry, UK Government, 1973–1976; Professor of Economic Science and Head of Department of Political Economy, University of Edinburgh, 1956–1962; Reader in Public Finance, 1951–1956 and Lecturer in Economics, 1948–1951, London School of Economics and Political Science, Lecturer in Economics, University of St. Andrews, 1947–1948.

Degrees
M.A., University of St. Andrews, 1947.

Offices and Honours
President, International Institute of Public Finance, 1966–1969 (Hon. President, 1975–).
Member of Royal Commission on the Constitution, 1971–1973.
Social Science Research Council 1971–1973.
Honorary Doctorates: Universities of Stirling (1974), Zurich (1984), Buckingham (1986), Brunel (1987), Edinburgh (1990), St. Andrews (1990), Dundee (1990), Catania (1991), York (1997), Lisbon (2000) and Turin (2001).
Institute of Economic Affairs: Academic Advisory Committee (1962–1988), Trustee (1988–1993), Honorary Fellow (1993–).
Hon.Pres. Atlantic Economic Society, 1981–1982.
Chairman, Home Office Committee on Financing of the BBC, 1985–1986.
Chairman, Scottish Arts Council and Member Arts Council of Great Britain, 1986–1992.
Chairman, UN Advisory Mission on Social Protection in the Transition to a Market Economy, Moscow, 1992.
Elected: Fellow of the British Academy, 1979 (Keynes Lecturer 1994).
Honorary Fellow, London School of Economics, 1980.
Fellow of the Royal Society of Edinburgh, 1989.
Foreign Member of the Italian Academy (Academia Nazionale dei Lincei), 1996.
Official Honours: Distinguished Service Cross (Royal Navy), 1945.
Knighthood for Public Service, 1987.

Editorial Duties
Assistant Editor, *Economica*, 1950–1956; Joint Editor, *Scottish Journal of Political Economy*, 1960–1962; Joint Editor, *International Economic Papers*, 1951–1967; Joint Editor, York University Series on Economics, 1964–1977; Editor, The David Hume Institute, Occasional Papers Series, 1985–1991.

Principal Fields of Interest
Economics of Public Finance; Public Choice; Economic Thought and Policy; Cultural Economics.

Selected Publications
Books
1. *The Economics of National Insurance* (Wm. Hodge, 1952).
2. *Classics in The Theory of Public Finance* (Macmillan, 1958) (edited, with Richard Musgrave).

3. *The Growth of Public Expenditure in the United Kingdom* (National Bureau of Economic Research inc., 1961: Revised Edition, George Allen and Unwin, 1967) (with Jack Wiseman).
4. *The Economic Theory of Fiscal Policy* (George Allen and Unwin, 1971: Second Edition, 1976) (with G.K. Shaw).
5. *Welfare Economics: A Liberal Restatement* (Martin Robertson, 1975) (with Charles Rowley).
6. *The Composer in the Market Place* (Faber Music, 1975) (with Ronald Weir).
7. *The Economic Analysis of Government* (Martin Robertson, 1979).
8. *Public Choice Analysis in Historical Perspective* (Mattioli Lectures) (Cambridge University Press, 1992).
9. *Paying the Piper: Culture, Music and Money* (Edinburgh University Press, 1993).
10. *The Political Economy of Economic Freedom* (Edward Elgar, 1997).

Articles
1. "The national insurance funds." *Economica*, New Series, August: 1949.
2. "The economics of dependence." *Economica*, New Series, November:1954 (with F.W. Paish).
3. "A note on the balanced budget multiplier." *Economic Journal*, June:1956.
4. "Economics of a net wealth tax for Britain." *British Tax Review*, (November-December):1963.
5. "Consumption taxes and compensatory finance." *Economic Journal*, March:1967 (with John Williamson).
6. "Welfare Economics and Public Subsidies to the Arts." *Manchester School*, December:1969.
7. "Approaches to the analysis of public expenditure growth." *Public Finance Quarterly*, January:1979 (with Jack Wiseman).
8. "Bargaining and the regulatory system." *International Review of Law and Economics*, June:1986 (with Martin Ricketts).
9. "Wicksell and Public Choice." *The New Palgrave Dictionary of Economics and The Law*, 3:1998.
10. "The communitarian attack on economics." *Kyklos*, 52:1999.

Principal Contributions
Nurtured in the Scots tradition in political economy, Alan Peacock has had an abiding interest in the formulation of liberalist ideas on the good society and their translation into determining the limits of government intervention. His contributions lie in three areas: (i) improving understanding of the forces underlying the growth of the public sector, together with my colleague Jack Wiseman; (ii) clarifying the meaning of a liberal approach to defining the role of the public sector and distinguishing it from standard welfare economics, in partnership with Charles Rowley; (iii) trying to translate the goals of a liberal approach into practical action in a number of fields. This included serving as the first Vice Chancellor (i.e. President) of the only independent university in the United Kingdom, helping to liberalise parts of the welfare state (e.g. pensions), and attempting to introduce greater freedom of choice in the arts and broadcasting.

PECORINO, Paul

Born
June 14, 1964, Manhasset, New York, USA

Current Positions
Professor of Economics, University of Alabama, Tuscaloosa, Alabama, USA, 2001–; J. Reese Phifer Faculty Fellow, University of Alabama, 2000–.

Past Positions
Associate Professor of Economics, University of Alabama, 1998–2001; Assistant Professor of Economics, University of Alabama, 1994–1998; Assistant Professor of Economics, University of Mississippi, 1991–1994; Student Intern, Board of Governors of the Federal Reserve System, 1990.

Degrees
B.A., State University of New York at Stony Brook, 1986; Ph.D., Duke University, 1990.

Principle Fields of Interest
Law and Economics; Public Choice; International Economics.

Selected Publications
1. "Tax structure and growth in a model with human capital." *Journal of Public Economics*, 52(September): 1993.
2. "Tax rates and tax revenues in a model of growth through human capital accumulation." *Journal of Monetary Economics*, 36(December):1995.
3. "Bargaining with informative offers: an analysis of final offer arbitration." *Journal of Legal Studies* 27(June):1998 (with Amy Farmer).

4. "Is there a free-rider problem in lobbying? Endogenous tariffs, trigger strategies, and the number of firms." *American Economic Review*, 88(June):1998.
5. "The effect of group size on public good provision in a repeated game setting." *Journal of Public Economics*, 72(April):1999.
6. "Legal expenditure as a rent-seeking game." *Public Choice*, 100(September):1999 (with Amy Farmer).
7. "Market structure, tariff lobbying and the free-rider problem." *Public Choice*, 106(March):2001.
8. "Bargaining and information: an empirical analysis of a multistage arbitration game." *Journal of Labor Economics*, 19(October):2001 (with Mark Van Boening).
9. "Can by-product lobbying firms compete?" *Journal of Public Economics*, 82(December):2001.
10. "Should the U.S. permit reimport of prescription drugs from Canada?" *Journal of Health Economics*, forthcoming.

Principle Contributions
One area of Paul Pecorino's research has focused on questions raised by Mancur Olson's *The Logic of Collective Action*. One such question concerns of the relationship between group size and the free-rider problem. In the context of infinitely repeated games, Pecorino has found that there is no presumption that cooperation becomes more difficult as group size increases. It is quite possible that there are factors not captured in these simple repeated games, such as asymmetric information, which do cause the free-rider problem to become worse as group size increases. What his work shows, however, is that there is nothing systematic in evolution of payoffs under cooperation, defection and punishment, which dictates that cooperation must break down in large groups or that cooperation will become more difficult, as group size increases. One mechanism, discussed by Olson, that can be used to overcome the free-rider problem is by-product lobbying. Under by-product lobbying, an industry association sells private goods and uses the resulting profits to finance industry lobbying. It has been argued that competition will prevent the survival of by-product firms. However, for monopolistically competitive markets Pecorino has shown that by-product firms can compete with for-profit firms and still retain profits to be used for lobbying purposes.

RATHBONE, Anne Elissa

Born
February 23, 1973, Alexandria, Virginia, USA

Current Positions
Ph.D., Graduate Student of Economics, George Mason University, 2000–; Research Assistant for Dr. Charles K. Rowley, George Mason University, 2000–; Research Assistant for Dr. Peter Boettke, George Mason University, St. Charles University, Prague, 2000–2001.

Degrees
B.S., James Madison University, 1995.

Principal Fields of Interest
Austrian Economics; Public Choice; Constitutional/Institutional Economics; Comparative Political Economy; Law and Economics.

Selected Publications
1. "Terrorism." *Public Choice*, 111(1–2):2002 (with Charles K. Rowley).
2. "al-Quaeda". (with Charles K. Rowley). *The Encyclopedia of Public Choice*. (Edited by Charles K. Rowley and Friedrich Schneider) (Kluwer Academic Publishers, September, 2003).

REKSULAK, Michael

Born
March 18, 1972, Erfurt, Thüringen, Germany

Current Positions
Doctoral Candidate, Department of Economics, University of Mississippi.

Past Positions
Research Fellow, Max-Planck-Institute for Research into Economic Systems, Jena, Germany, 1998–1999.

Degrees
Diploma in European Management Science, University of Kent at Canterbury, England, 1996; B.A. (equivalent), Friedrich-Schiller-Universität Jena, Germany, 1997; M.A., University of Mississippi, 1998.

Offices and Honors
Fellow of the Konrad-Adenauer-Foundation, Germany, 1994–1998; Honors Fellow of the Graduate School, University of Mississippi, 1999–2002.

Principal Fields of Interest
Public Choice; Public Economics; Managerial Economics; Experimental Economics.

Publications

"The Political Economy of the IRS." *Economics and Politics*, 13(July):2001 (with M. Young and W.F. Shughart II).

ROMER, Thomas

Current Positions
Director, Research Program in Political Economy, Princeton University, 2001–; Professor of Politics and Public Affairs, Princeton University, 1991–.

Past Positions
Visitor, Institute for Advanced Study, 2001–2002; Chairman, Department of Politics, Princeton University, 1993–1997; Visiting Scholar, Hoover Institution, Stanford University, 1998; Fellow, Center for Advanced Study in the Behavioral Sciences, 1994–1995; Professor of Economics and Political Economy, Carnegie Mellon University, 1983–1991; Visiting Scholar, Hoover Institution, Stanford University, 1988–1989; Associate Professor of Economics and Political Economy, Carnegie-Mellon University, 1979–1983; Associate Head, Department of Economics, Carnegie-Mellon University, 1980–1982; Visiting Economist, Federal Trade Commission, Washington, 1979–1980; Assistant Professor of Economics, Carnegie-Mellon University, 1975–1979; Assistant Professor of Economics, University of Western Ontario, 1974–1975.

Degrees
B.S., Massachusetts Institute of Technology, 1968; M.Phil., Yale University, 1971; Ph.D., Yale University, 1974.

Offices and Honors
Joint Council on Economic Education Award, 1975.
Duncan Black Award (Public Choice Society), 1980.
Member, National Science Foundation Economics Advisory Panel, 1985–87.
Listed in *Who's Who In Economics: A Biographical Dictionary of Major Economists 1700–1986* (Second Edition).
Listed in *Who's Who In Economics*, (Third Edition).

Editorial Duties
Co-Editor, *Carnegie Papers on Political Economy*, 1981–1987; Member, Board of Editors, *American Economic Review*, 1990–1993; Member, Editorial Board, *Public Choice*, 1991–.

Principal Fields of Interest
Political Economy; Public Economics; Intergovernmental Relations.

Selected Publications
Articles

1. "Individual welfare, majority voting, and the properties of a linear income tax." *Journal of Public Economics*, 4(May):1975.
2. "Political resource allocation, controlled agendas, and the status quo." *Public Choice*, 33, (Winter):1978 (with H. Rosenthal). Reprinted in J.M. Buchanan and R.D. Tollison (eds.), *The Theory of Public Choice-II* (University of Michigan Press, 1984. Also reprinted in C.K. Rowley (ed.), *Public Choice Theory*, vol. I. Edward Elgar Publishing Co., 1994).
3. "The elusive median voter." *Journal of Public Economics*, 12(October):1979 (with H. Rosenthal). (Reprinted in C.K. Rowley (ed.), *Public Choice Theory*, I. Edward Elgar Publishing Co., 1994.)
4. "Bureaucrats vs. voters: on the political economy of resource allocation by direct democracy." *Quarterly Journal of Economics*, 93(November):1979 (with H. Rosenthal).
5. "Asymmetric information and agenda control: the bases of monopoly power in Public Spending." *Journal of Public Economics*, 17(February):1982 (with R. Filimon and H. Rosenthal).
6. "A constitution for solving asymmetric externality games." *American Journal of Political Science*, 27 (February):1983 (with H. Rosenthal).
7. "Warranties, performance, and the resolution of buyer-seller disputes." *Bell Journal of Economics*, 14(Spring):1983 (with T. Palfrey).
8. "Equilibrium among local jurisdictions: toward an integrated treatment of voting and residential choice." *Journal of Public Economics*, 24(August):1984 (with D. Epple and R. Filimon).
9. "Patterns of political action committee contributions to the 1980 Campaigns for the U.S. House of Representatives." *Public Choice*, 47:1985 (with K.T. Poole).
10. "Political foundations of the thrift debacle," in A. Alesina and G. Carliner (eds.) *Politics and Economics in the Eighties* (University of Chicago Press, 1991) (with Barry R. Weingast). (Reprinted in J. Barth and D. Brumbaugh (eds.), *The Reform of Deposit Insurance*, Harper/Collins, 1992.)
11. "Mobility and Redistribution." *Journal of Political Economy*, 99(August):1991. (with D. Epple) (Reprinted in T. Persson and G. Tabellini (eds.) *Monetary and Fiscal Policy*, Volume 2: *Politics*, MIT Press, 1994.)

12. "Economic incentives and political institutions: spending and voting in school budget referenda." *Journal of Public Economics*, 49(October):1992 (with H. Rosenthal and V. Munley).
13. "Polarization, incumbency, and the personal vote." In *Political Economy: Institutions, Competition, and Representation* (Cambridge University Press, 1993) (W. Barnett, M. Hinich, and N. Schofield, eds.) (with J. Londregan).
14. "An empirical investigation of the dynamics of PAC contributions." *American Journal of Political Science*, 38(August):1994 (with James Snyder).
15. "Interjurisdictional sorting and majority rule: an empirical investigation." *Econometrica*, 69(November):2001 (with Dennis Epple and Holger Sieg).

Principal Contributions
The focus of Thomas Romer's research has been the interaction of market and nonmarket forces in resource allocation, particularly in the political economy of the public sector. This has involved both theoretical and empirical investigation. Early work dealt with determinants of income tax rates, using a highly streamlined representation of the political process. The structure of political decision-making is modelled in greater detail in his work on local public spending (in collaboration with H. Rosenthal), where considerations of agenda control and asymmetric information play important roles. With D. Epple, Romer has studied the political economy of systems of multiple jurisdictions among which households can move, focusing especially on questions of land use control, taxation, and redistributive policies in such settings. In another line of research, he has investigated the connections of between political campaign finance and political/economic outcomes.

ROWLEY, Charles Kershaw

Born
June 21, 1939, Southampton, Hampshire, England

Current Positions
Duncan Black Professor of Economics, George Mason University 2000–; General Director, The Locke Institute, Fairfax, Virginia, 1990–; Senior Research Associate, James M. Buchanan Institute, 1999–.

Past Positions
Professor of Economics, George Mason University, 1984–1999; Senior Research Associate, Center for Study of Public Choice, 1984–1994; Dean of the Graduate School, George Mason University, 1986–1988; David Dale Professor of Economics, University of Newcastle upon Tyne, England, 1972–1983; Dean of the Faculty of Social Sciences, University of Newcastle upon Tyne, 1978–1981 and 1983; Senior Lecturer and Reader, in Economic and Social Statistics, University of York, England, 1970–1971 and 1971–1972; Lecturer and Senior Lecturer in Economics, University of Kent at Canterbury, England, 1965–1969 and 1969–1970; Lecturer in Industrial Economics, University of Nottingham, England, 1962–1965.

Degrees
B.A., Ph.D., University of Nottingham, 1960, 1964.

Offices and Honors
Member, The Mont Pelerin Society, 1971.
President, European Public Choice Society, 1980–1982.
First Place, Sir Antony Fisher International Memorial Awards, 1994, 1996.
Member, Board of Trustees of the Virginia Outdoors Foundation, 1996–2004.
Listed in *Who's Who in Economics: A Biographical Dictionary of Major Economists 1700*–1986 (Second Edition).
Listed in *Who's Who In Economics*. (Third Edition).

Editorial Duties
Founding Editor Publishing, *International Review of Law and Economics*, 1980–1986; Joint Editor, *Public Choice*, 1990–.

Principal Fields of Interest
Public Choice; Law and Economics; Classical Liberal Political Economy.

Selected Publications
Books
1. *The British Monopolies Commission* (G. Allen and Unwin, 1966).
2. *Welfare Economics: A Liberal Restatement* (Martin Robertson, 1975) (with A.T. Peacock).
3. *Deficits* (Basil Blackwell, 1987) (edited, with J.M. Buchanan and R.D. Tollison).
4. *Democracy and Public Choice* (ed.) (Basil Blackwell, 1987).
5. *The Political Economy of Rent Seeking* (Kluwer Academic Publishers, 1988) (edited, with R.D. Tollison and G. Tullock).

6. *The Right to Justice* (Edward Elgar Publishing, 1992).
7. *Property Rights and the Limits of Democracy* (ed.) (Edward Elgar Publishing, 1993).
8. *Public Choice Theory* Volumes I–III (ed.) (Edward Elgar Publishing, 1993).
9. *Trade Protection in the United States* (Edward Elgar Publishing, 1995) (with W. Thorbecke and R.E. Wagner).
10. *Classical Liberalism and Civil Society* (ed.) (Edward Elgar Publishing, 1998).

Articles
1. "Mergers and public policy." *Journal of Law and Economics*, 11(April) 1968.
2. "The monopolies commission and rate of return on capital." *Economic Journal*, 79(March): 1969.
3. "On allocative efficiency, x-efficiency and the measurement of welfare loss." *Economica* NS 38(May): 1971 (with M.A. Crew).
4. "Pareto optimality and the political economy of liberalism." *Journal of Political Economy*, 80(May–June): 1972 (with A.T. Peacock).
5. "Welfare economics and the public regulation of natural monopoly." *Journal of Public Economics*, 1(June): 1972 (with A.T. Peacock).
6. "The economics of human exchange." *Journal of Legal Studies*, 17(January): 1988 (with G. Anderson and R.D. Tollison).
7. "Toward a public choice theory of monopoly regulation." *Public Choice*, 57(January): 1988 (with M.A. Crew).
8. "Law and economics from the perspective of economics." *The New Palgrave Dictionary of Economics and the Law* (Macmillan, 1998) (edited by P. Newman).
9. "Political culture and economic performance in sub-Saharan Africa." *European Journal of Political Economy*, 16(March):2000.
10. "Terrorism." *Public Choice*, 111(April):2002 (with Anne Rathbone).

Principal Contributions
Charles Rowley's early work was in the field of industrial organization and public policy, commencing with studies of the British Monopolies Commission. An interest in the concept of x-inefficiency shifted his attention to welfare economics where his collaboration with Alan Peacock led to a range of contributions in classical liberal political economy. His attention then shifted to public choice and law and economics where he has made many contributions. Rowley is especially interested in exploring, through a systematic application of rational choice theory, why political markets typically fail to provide either economic efficiency or individual freedom. Since 1990, through The Locke Institute, Rowley has launched a series of studies into various aspects of classical liberalism, focusing on the intellectual framework provided in the late seventeenth century by John Locke. At a time when the large majority of the economics profession is focused narrowly on technical issues raised by neoclassical economics, Rowley believes it is important to ensure that the still small candle of liberty is not extinguished in a lemming-like pursuit of wealth. He has so far written and edited some 30 books and some 160 scholarly essays in support of this research agenda (see *www.thelockeinstitute.org* for further details).

RUBIN, Paul Harold

Born
August 9, 1942, Boston, Massachusetts, USA

Current Position
Professor of Economics and Law, Emory University.

Past Positions
Emory University: Professor of Economics, 1991–1999; Acting Chair, Economics, 1993–1994; Adjunct Professor: VPI, 1984; Adjunct Professor George Washington University Law Center, 1985–1989; Professor Baruch College and the Graduate Center, City University of New York, 1982–1983; Assistant to Professor of Economics, University of Georgia, 1968–1982; Glassman-Oliver Economic Consultants: Vice President, 1987–1991; U.S. Consumer Product Safety Commission: Chief Economist, 1985–1987 (Senior Executive Service); Federal Trade Commission: Director of Advertising Economics, 1983–1985; President Reagan's Council of Economic Advisers: Senior Staff Economist, 1981–1982.

Degrees
B.A., University of Cincinnati, 1963; Ph.D., Purdue University, 1970.

Offices and Honors
Fellow, Public Choice Society.
Adjunct Scholar: American Enterprise Institute, 1992.
Adjunct Scholar, Georgia Public Policy Foundation, 1993.
Adjunct Scholar, Cato Institute, 1992–1998;
Senior Fellow, Progress and Freedom Foundation, 2000.

Listed in *Who's Who in Economics: A Biographical Dictionary of Major Economists 1700–1986* (Second Edition) (Second Edition, Third Edition).
First Vice-President, Southern Economics Association, 1994–1996.
Vice-President, Georgia Chapter, National Association of Scholars, 1994–2002.
Chairman's Award, Consumer Product Safety Commission, 1987.

Editorial Duties
Editor In Chief, *Managerial and Decision Economics*, 1994; Editorial Boards: *Public Choice; Regulation; Journal of Bioeconomics; Journal of Research in Pharmaceutical Economics; Journal of Real Estate Finance and Economics.*

Principal Fields of Interest
Public Choice; Law and Economics; Human Evolution and Economic and Political Behavior.

Selected Publications
Books
1. *Congressmen, Constituents, and Contributors* (Nijhoff, 1982) (with James B. Kau).
2. *Evolutionary Models in Economics and Law* (Edited, Central paper by Jack Hirshleifer), Vol. 4 of *Research in Law and Economics*, 1982).
3. *Business Firms and the Common Law* (Praeger, 1983).
4. *Managing Business Transactions: Controlling the Costs of Coordinating, Communicating, and Decision Making* (Free Press, 1990; paperback, 1993).
5. *Tort Reform by Contract* (American Enterprise Institute, 1993).
6. *Promises, Promises: Contracts in Russia and Other Post-Communist Economies*, Shaftesbury Papers (No. 11), (Edward Elgar Publishing and the Locke Institute, 1998, expanded version of "Growing a Legal System in the Post-Communist Economies." *Cornell International Law Journal*, Winter: 1994).
7. *Deregulating Telecommunications: The Baby Bells Case for Competition* (Wiley, 1995) (edited, with Richard Higgins).
8. *Privacy and the Commercial Use of Personal Information* (Kluwer Academic Publishers and Progress and Freedom Foundation, foreword by Senator Orrin Hatch, 2001) (with Thomas Lenard).
9. *Darwinian Politics: The Evolutionary Origins of Freedom*. Rutgers Series in Human Evolution, (Rutgers University Press, 2002).

Articles
1. "The expansion of firms." *Journal of Political Economy*, July:1973.
2. "Why is the common law efficient?" *Journal of Legal Studies*, January:1977.
3. "The theory of the firm and the structure of the franchise contract." *Journal of Law and Economics*, April:1978.
4. "Self interest, ideology and logrolling in congressional voting." *Journal of Law and Economics*, November:1979 (with James B. Kau).
5. "A general equilibrium model of congressional voting." *Quarterly Journal of Economics*, May:1982. (with James B. Kau and Donald Keenan).
6. "Matching prescription drugs and consumers: the benefits of direct advertising." *New England Journal of Medicine*, 22(August):1985 (with Alison Masson).
7. "Some implications of damage payments for nonpecuniary losses." *Journal of Legal Studies*, June:1992 (with John Calfee).
8. "The role of lawyers in changing the law." *Journal of Legal Studies*, June:1994 (with Martin Bailey).
9. "Litigation versus lobbying: forum shopping by rent-Seekers." *Public Choice*, 107(3–4):2001 (with Christopher Curran and John Curran).
10. "Effects of criminal procedure on crime rates: mapping out the consequences of the exclusionary rule." *Journal of Law and Economics*, forthcoming 2003, (with Raymond A. Atkins).

Principal Contributions
Paul Rubin's initial work was in the theory of the firm, industrial organization, and regulation. Studying regulation led to an interest in the source of the observed inefficiencies, and thus to research in public choice. His major contributions there, mainly with James Kau, were on the importance of ideology and the growth of government. Upon reading Richard Posner's *Economics Analysis of Law*, he began to do research in law and economics, where his major contribution was the evolutionary theory of legal change. He has examined several substantive areas of law, including franchising (the most cited paper on this topic), covenants not to compete, (the first application of human capital theory to this issue), advertising, privacy, and crime. Rubin spent time in government, and while at the FTC he wrote with Alison Masson the first paper explaining the benefits of direct to consumer advertising of pharmaceuticals. The FDA ultimately adopted the positions they advocated, and this may be his most important contribution to public policy. With John Calfee, he wrote on the inefficiency of tort law. This led to several papers (with his late colleague Martin Bailey and with Chris and John

Curran) on the interrelationship between rent seeking and the common law, building on my earlier work on the evolution of law. Rubin has also pursued a long standing interest in the relation between human evolution and economic behavior, and recently completed a book on this topic, which he hopes will influence public choice in the future.

SASS, Tim Roger

Born
December 28, 1956, Oakland, California, USA

Current Position
Professor of Economics, Florida State University, Florida, USA, 2000–.

Past Positions
Associate Professor of Economics, Florida State University, 1993–2000; Assistant Professor of Economics, Florida State University, 1990–1993; Visiting Assistant Professor of Economics, San Jose State University, 1987–1990; Assistant Professor of Economics, University of New Mexico, 1984–1987; Instructor, University of Washington, 1980–1984.

Degrees
B.A., University of California at Davis, 1979; M.A., University of Washington, 1981; Ph.D., University of Washington, 1984.

Principal Fields of Interest
Applied Microeconomics; Industrial Organization; Public Choice.

Selected Publications
Articles
1. "A note on optimal price cutting behavior under demand uncertainty." *Review of Economics and Statistics*, 70(May): 1988.
2. "Agency cost, firm size, and exclusive dealing." *Journal of Law and Economics*, 32(October): 1989 (with Micha Gisser).
3. "The allocation of resources by voting." *Quarterly Journal of Economics* 105(August): 1990 (with Yoram Barzel).
4. "The market for safety regulation and the effect of regulation on fatalities: the case of motorcycle helmet laws." *Review of Economics and Statistics*, 73(February): 1991 (with J. Paul Leigh).
5. "The choice of municipal government structure and public expenditures." *Public Choice*, 71(August): 1991.
6. "Constitutional choice in representative democracies." *Public Choice*, 74(December): 1992.
7. "Mandated exclusive territories and economic efficiency: an empirical analysis of the malt beverage industry." *Journal of Law and Economics*, 36(April): 1993 (with David S. Saurman).
8. "Advertising restrictions and concentration: the case of malt beverages." *Review of Economics and Statistics*, 77(February): 1995 (with David S. Saurman).
9. "The voting rights act, district elections, and the success of black candidates in municipal elections." *Journal of Law and Economics*, 38(October): 1995 (with Stephen L. Mehay).
10. "The changing impact of electoral structure on black representation in the south, 1970–1996." *Public Choice*, 104(September): 2000 (with Bobby J. Pittman, Jr.).

Principal Contributions
The focus of Tim Sass' research is the nexus of political choice and laws affecting economic behavior, particularly antitrust and regulation. In recent years his research has been concentrated in three specific areas: vertical contractual relationships, voting systems and voting rights law, and economic regulation. His research interest in vertical contractual relationships began with a study of exclusive dealing arrangements in the insurance industry in 1989. This led to an exploration of other vertical restrictions, particularly exclusive territories in the beer industry and quasi-vertical contractual relationships in health care.

Sass' research on voting rights and voting systems began early in his career, with a study of the voting rules used in condominium owner associations. More recently he has become interested in the issue of minority voting rights and the effects of the Voting Rights Act. He has written three papers that look at the effect of district elections on the electoral success of minorities in municipal elections and how the impact of different election schemes has changed over time.

The third specific area of research, economic regulation, is where sass' dual interests in economic behavior and collective decision-making overlap. His work on regulation encompasses both the direct impact of laws affecting economic behavior and the political decisions that determine which laws are adopted. Articles in this line of research cover a variety of regulations, including motorcycle helmet laws, zoning regulation, advertising restrictions, and professional licensure statutes.

SCHMID-LUEBBERT, Stefanie

Born
July 19, 1971

Current Position
Ph.D. Program ("Graduiertenkolleg") Law and Economics, Institute for Law and Economics, University of Hamburg, Germany, 2002–.

Past Positions
Research Associate, Institute for Law and Economics, University of Hamburg, Germany, 1998–2002; Visiting Scholar, School of Law, University of California at Berkeley, 1999–2000; Student Research Assistant, Institute for World Economics, Kiel, Germany, 1995–1997.

Degrees
Diplom-Volkswirtin, University of Kiel, 1998.

Principal Fields of Interest
Law and Economics of the European Union; Public Law and Economics; Environmental Economics.

Selected Publications
Books
1. *Umweltpolitik und internationale Wettbewerbsfähigkeit* (National environmental policy and the international competitiveness of industries), (Öko-Institut Verlag, Freiburg 1998).
2. *Beiträge zur Ökonomischen Analyse im Öffentlichen Recht* (Economic Analysis of Public Law) (edited with A. van Aaken), Wiesbaden, forthcoming.

Articles
"Constitutional economics and the federal constitution of the European union," in A. van Aaken and S. Schmid-Lübbert (eds.) *Beiträge zur Ökonomischen Analyse im Öffentlichen Recht*, Wiesbaden, forthcoming.

SCHNEIDER, Friedrich Georg

Born
February 16, 1949, Konstanz, Germany

Current Positions
Professor of Economics, Department of Economics, Institute of Economic Policy, Johannes Kepler University of Linz.

Degrees
Bachelor of Economics, Bachelor of Political Science, University of Konstanz, 1972; Diplom-Volkswirt, Master of Economics, University of Konstanz, 1973; Dr.rer.soc. (Ph.D.), University of Konstanz, 1976; Habilitation (Promotion of being able to compete for a full professor ("Chair" in Europe), University of Zürich, 1983.

Offices and Honors
President, Austrian Economic Association, 1997–1999; Vice-President for Foreign Affairs, Johannes-Kepler-University of Linz, Austria, 1996–; European Editor, *Public Choice*, 1990–.

Principal Fields of Interest
General Economic Policy; Taxation; Shadow Economy; Environmental Economics; Privatization and Deregulation Policies.

Selected Publications
Books
1. *Current Issues in Public Choice* (Edward Elgar Publishing, 1996) (with José Casas Pardo).
2. *The Shadow Economy: Theoretical Approaches, Empirical Studies, and Political Implications* (zusammen mit Dominik H. Enste) (Cambridge University Press, 2002).

Articles
1. "Free riding and collective action: a laboratory experiment in public microeconomics." *The Quarterly Journal of Economics*, 95(4): 1981 (with Werner W. Pommerehne).
2. "Economic theory of choice and the preference reversal phenomenon: a reexamination." *American Economic Review*, 72(3): 1982 (with Werner W. Pommerehne and Peter Zweifel).
3. "The development of the shadow economy under changing tax systems and structures: Some Theoretical and Empirical Results for Austria." *Finanzarchiv*, 50(3): 1993 (with Reinhard Neck).
4. "Deficits, Bailout and Free Riders: Fiscal Elements of a European Constitution." Special Issue *Kyklos*, Heft 3: 1994.
5. "Tragic choices and collective decision-making: an empirical study of voter preferences for alternative collective decision-making mechanisms." *The Economic Journal*, 1997 (with Werner W. Pommerehne and Albert Hart).
6. "The shadow economies of Western Europe." *Economic Affairs*, 17(3): 1997.

7. Zunehmende Schwarzarbeit — Eine wirtschafts- und staatspolitische Herausforderung? *Volkswirtschaftliche Korrespondenz der Adolf Weber Stiftung* 5/99, München, 1999.
8. "No chance for incentive-oriented environmental policies in representative democracies?" *Ecological Economics*, 1999.
9. "Shadow economies: sizes, causes, and Consequences." *Journal of Economic Literature* 38(1): 2000 (with Dominik Enste).
10. "The Bundesbank's reaction to policy conflicts." In *50 Years of Bundesbank: Lessons for the ECB* (London: Routledge, 2000) (Jakob de Haan, ed.) (with Helge Berger).
11. "Informal and underground economy. In *International Encyclopedia of Social and Behavioral Science*, Bd. 12 Economics (Elsevier Science Publishing Company, 2001) (Orley Ashenfelter, ed.) (with Bruno S. Frey).
12. "State and local taxation." In *International Encyclopedia of Social and Behavioral Science*, Bd. 12 Economics (Elsevier Science Publishing Company, 2001) (Orley Ashenfelter, ed.) (with Lars P. Feld).
13. "The role of a new international monetary institution after the EMU and after the Asian Crises: some preliminary ideas using constitutional economics." In *Method and Morals in Constitutional Economics: Essays in Honor of James M. Buchanan* (Springer, 2002) (Geoffrey Brennan, Hartmut Kliemt und Robert D. Tollison (Hrsg.) eds.).

SCHOFIELD, Norman James

Born
January 30, 1944, Rothesay, Bute, Scotland

Current Positions
Fulbright Distinguished Chair in American Studies, Humboldt University, Berlin, Germany, 2002–2003; Dr. William Taussig Professor of Political Economy, Professor of Economics and of Political Science, Director of the Center in Political Economy, Washington University 1991–.

Past Positions
Fellow, Center for Advanced Study in the Behavioral Sciences, Stanford, 1988–1989; Sherman Fairchild Distinguished Scholar, California Insitute of Technology, 1983–1984, and Visiting Professor, California Insitute of Technology, 1984–1986; Reader in Economics, Essex University, 1979–1986; Visiting Lecturer and Associate Professor, Political Science, University of Texas 1976–1979; Visiting Lecturer, Political Science, Yale University, 1972; Fellow and Lecturer, Government, Essex University, 1969–1976.

Degrees
B.S., Liverpool University, 1966; Ph.D., Essex University, 1976; Ph.D., Essex University, 1985; Litt. D., Liverpool University, 1986; D.Sc., Universite de Caen, France, 1991.

Offices and Honors
Recipient of the Riker Prize for contributions to political theory, Rochester University, 2002.
Listed in *Who's Who in Economics*, Second Edition, Third Edition.

Editorial Duties
Editorial Board, *Social Choice and Welfare: Politics, Philosophy and Economics*.

Principle Fields of Interest
Social Choice Theory; Political Economy.

Selected Publications
Books
1. *Mathematical Methods in Economics* (New York University Press, 1984).
2. *Social Choice Theory and Democracy* (Springer, 1985).
3. *Statistical Methods in the Social Sciences* (Holt, Rinehart, Winston, 1986) (with P. Whitely, S. Satchell, and M. Chatterji).
4. *Multiparty Governments* (Oxford University Press, 1990) (reprinted Michigan University Press, 1998) (with M. Laver).
5. *Political Economy: Institutions, Competition and Representation* (Cambridge University Press, 1993) (edited, with W. Barnett and M. Hinich).
6. *Social Choice, Welfare and Ethics* (Cambridge University Press, 1995) (edited, with W. Barnett, H. Moulin, and M. Salles).
7. *Collective Decision-Making* (ed.) (Kluwer, 1996).

Articles
1. "Ethical decision rules for uncertain voters." *British Journal of Political Science*, 2(October): 1972.

2. "Generalized bargaining sets for cooperative games." *International Journal of Game Theory*, 7(October): 1978.
3. "Instability of simple dynamic games." *Review of Economic Studies*, 45(October): 1978.
4. "Social equilibrium and cycles on compact sets." *Journal of Economic Theory*, 33(June): 1984.
5. "Existence of equilibrium on a manifold." *Mathematics of Operations Research*, 9(November): 1984.
6. "Anarchy, altruism, and cooperation." *Social Choice and Welfare*, 2(November): 1985.
7. "Structural instability of the core." *Journal of Mathematical Economics*, 15(December): 1987 (with R.D. McKelvey).
8. "Generalized symmetry conditions at a core point." *Econometrica*, 55(July): 1987 (with R.D. McKelvey).
9. "Political competition and multiparty coalition governments." *European Journal of Political Research*, 23(January): 1993.
10. "Evolution of the constitution. *British Journal of Political Science*, 32(January): 2002.

Research Interests
Norman Schofield's early work was in formal social choice theory, and with Richard McKelvey (both independently and in collaboration), he proved certain "chaos" theorems applicable to voting. At the same time, he worked with Michael Laver on theory and empirical studies on coalition formation in European multiparty systems. Since 1993, in collaboration with a number of colleagues of Washington University, he has focused on estimating voter choice under various electoral laws. From 1997 or so, Schofield became more interested in the significance of the notion of chaos for democratic political processes. Increasingly, he has worked on combining the insights of Douglass North and William Riker in an attempt to understand historical developments in Britain and the U.S. in the early modern period. He is currently working on a book of essays, provisionally titled, *Beliefs, Constitutions and Democracy*.

SCULLY, Gerald William

Born
June 13, 1941, New York, New York, USA

Current Position
Professor of Economics, University of Texas at Dallas, 1985–2002; Emeritus Professor, 2002–.

Past Positions
Distinguished Visiting Professor, Inland Revenue, Wellington, New Zealand, 1996; Distinguished Visiting Scholar, International Center for Economic Research, Turin, Italy, 1995; Bradley Foundation Distinguished Resident Scholar, Heritage Foundation, 1990–1991; Professor of Economics, Southern Methodist University, 1972–1985; Harvard Institute for International Development, 1975–1976; Associate Professor of Economics, Southern Illinois University, 1969–1972; Assistant Professor of Economics, Ohio University, 1966–1969; Lecturer, Modern European History, Fairleigh Dickinson University, 1962–1963.

Degrees
B.A., Fairleigh Dickinson University, 1962; M.A., The New School for Social Research, 1965; Ph.D., Rutgers University, 1968.

Offices and Honors
Senior Fellow, National Center for Policy Analysis, 1975
Member, The Mont Pelerin Society, 1986.
Listed in *Who's Who in Economics: A Biographical Dictionary of Major Economists 1700–1995*. Third Edition.

Editorial Duties
Member, Editorial Board *Public Choice, Pacific Economic Review, Managerial and Decision Economics, Journal of Sports Economics*.

Principal Fields of Interest
Public Choice; Economics of Institutions; Economic Growth; Sports Economics.

Selected Publications
Books
1. *The Business of Major League Baseball* (University of Chicago Press, 1989).
2. *Measuring the Quality of Life Across Countries: A Multi-dimensional Analysis* (Westview Press, 1991) (with D. Slottje).
3. *Constitutional Environments and Economic Growth* (Princeton University Press, 1992).
4. *Advances in the Economics of Sport* (ed.) (JAI Press, 1992).
5. *The Market Structure of Sports* (University of Chicago Press, 1995).

6. *Taxation and the Limits of Government* (Kluwer Academic Publishers, 2000) (senior editor, with P. Caragata).

Articles
1. "Interstate wage differentials: A cross section analysis." *American Economic Review*, 59(5): 1969.
2. "Pay and performance in major league baseball." *American Economic Review*, 64(5): 1974.
3. "Static vs. dynamic Phillips curves." *Review of Economics and Statistics*, 56(3): 1974.
4. "Mullahs, muslims, and marital sorting." *Journal of Political Economy*, 87(5): 1979.
5. "The institutional framework and economic development." *Journal of Political Economy*, 96(3): 1988.
6. "The size of the state, economic growth, and the efficient utilization of national resources." *Public Choice*, 63(2): 1989.
7. "Rights, equity, and economic efficiency." *Public Choice*, 68(1–3): 1991.
8. "The growth tax in the United States." *Public Choice*, 85: 1995.
9. "Government expenditure and quality of life." *Public Choice*, 108(1–2): 2001.
10. "Economic freedom, government policy and the trade-off between equity and economic growth." *Public Choice*: 113, 2002.

Principal Contributions
Gerald Scully's earliest work was on inter-regional wage differentials, which showed the effect of physical and human capital, discrimination, and unionization on income convergence. This work led into international trade theory, with contributions on immiserizing growth, technical change, and the theory of optimal intervention. In the early 1970s, he wrote several papers, that formed the foundation of the economics of sport, now a sub-field in economics. These papers measured the extent of salary discrimination in sport, the marginal revenue productivity of players and their rate of monopsonistic exploitation under player reservation, and the technical efficiency of managers and coaches. A recent contribution is on the effect of rule changes on the distribution of player earnings using a rank-order tournament model.

In the last ten years Scully's focus has been on measuring inefficiency, examining the roles of institutional technology and policy on growth and equity, and other issues in public choice and constitutional political economy. The work on inefficiency mainly is related to the effects of different property rights regimes and issues of vertical integration and multi-nationality. He has shown that the extent of economic freedom and the rule of law are preconditions for a high rate of economic progress in the Third World.

In public choice and constitutional political economy, Scully's main contributions have been on the theory of rent-seeking, the political market for income redistribution, measuring the equality-efficiency tradeoff, estimating the effect of the distribution of rights on economic efficiency and equity, further work on the theory of the rule space and economic growth, and estimating the growth-maximizing tax rate for the advanced industrial countries.

SENED, Itai

Born
May 4, 1955, Israel

Current Position
Associate Professor of Political Science, Washington University; Director, Center for New Institutional Social Sciences, Washington University.

Past Positions
Senior Lecturer with Tenure, Tel Aviv University, 1996–1999; Visiting Associate Professor, Washington University, 1994–1999; Visiting Lecturer, Haifa University, 1993–1996; Lecturer, Tel Aviv University 1991–1996; Post-Doctoral Fellow, Washington University, 1990–1991.

Degrees
B.A., Philosophy and Political Science, Tel Aviv University, 1986; M.A., Ph.D., Political Science, University of Rochester: 1998, 1990.

Offices and Honors
Fulbright Award, U.S. – Israel Educational Foundation, 1986; Post Doctoral Fellowship, Center in Political Economy, Washington University, 1990–1991; Allon Grant, Most Promising Young Faculty in Israel, 1991–1994; Phi Sigma Alpha award, Best Paper in the Midwest Political Science Association meetings, 1995.

Selected Publications
Books
1. *Explaining Social Institutions* (The University of Michigan Press, 1995) (edited, with Jack Knight).
2. *The Journal of Theoretical Politics*, 7(3): 1995 (Special Issue on "Coalitions and Political Bargaining") (edited, with Gideon Doron).
3. *The Political Institution of Private Property* (Cambridge University Press, 1997).

4. *Political Bargaining: Theory Practice and Process* (Sage Publications, 2001) (with Gideon Doron).

Articles
1. "Rational voting and candidate entry under plurality rule." *American Journal of Political Science*, 34(4): 1990 (with T.J. Feddersen and Stephen G. Wright).
2. "A political theory of the origin of property rights." *American Journal of Political Science*, 35(4): 1991 (with W.H. Riker).
3. "Contemporary theory of institutions in perspective." *The Journal of Theoretical Politics*, 3(4): 1991.
4. "The role of lobbyists: entrepreneurs with two audiences." *American Journal of Political Science*, 37(3): 1993 (with S.H. Ainsworth).
5. "A model of coalition formation: theory and evidence." *The Journal of Politics*, 58(2): 1996.
6. "Common property and private property: the case of air slots." *The Journal of Theoretical Politics*, 8(4): 1996 (with William H. Riker).
7. "Nash equilibria in multiparty competition with 'Stochastic' voters." *Annals of Operations Research*, 84: 1998 (with N. Schofield and D. Nixon).
8. "Ingegneria istituzionale" ("Institutional engeneering") *Politeia* Anno, XV(53): 1999 (in Italian).

Principal Contributions
Itai Sened was until recently a senior lecturer of political science at Tel Aviv University and a regular visiting scholar at Washington University in St. Louis. Since 1997 he has moved permanently to St. Louis and is currently an associate professor of political science and the Director of the Center for New Institutional Social Sciences (CNISS) at Washington University. His main interests are theory of institutions, game theory and applied mathematical modeling.

SHUGHART, William Franklin II

Born
December 3, 1947, Harrisburg, Pennsylvania, USA

Current Positions
Frederick A.P. Barnard Distinguished Professor of Economics, University of Mississippi, 1998–.

Past Positions
Professor of Economics and P.M.B. Self, William King Self and Henry C. Self Free Enterprise Chair, University of Mississippi, 1988–1998; Associate Professor of Economics and Research Associate, Center for Study of Public Choice, George Mason University, 1985–1988; Assistant Professor and Associate Professor of Economics, Clemson University, 1983–1984 and 1984–1985; Economist and Special Assistant to the Director, Bureau of Economics, Federal Trade Commission, 1979–1982 and 1982–1983; Visiting Lecturer in Economics, University of Arizona, 1978–1979.

Degrees
B.A., M.S., Ph.D., Texas A&M University, 1969, 1970, 1978.

Offices and Honors
Elected to Phi Kappa Phi, 1991.
Member, Governor-Elect's Education Task Force and co-chair, Subcommittee on Institutions of Higher Learning, 1991.
Gubernatorial appointee, Mississippi State Job Training Coordinating Council, 1992–1994.
Member, Mississippi State Auditor's Task Force on Privatization and chair, Subcommittee on Privatization Criteria, 1992.
Research Fellow and member, Board of Advisors, The Independent Institute, 1995– and 1998–.
Member, Board of Trustees of the Southern Economic Association, 1996–1998.
"Honorable Mention", Sir Anthony Fisher International Memorial Award, 1998.
Frederick A.P. Barnard Distinguished Professor, The University of Mississippi, 1998–.
Recipient, Business Week Award, Economic Faculty Association of Rotterdam, Erasmus University, 1999.
Policy Advisor, The Heartland Institute's Center on the Digital Economy, 1999–.

Editorial Duties
Book Review Editor, *Public Choice*, 1991–2003; Book Review Editor, *Managerial and Decision Economics*, 1994–; Associate Editor, *Southern Economic Journal*, 1996–2001; Editor, *Public Choice*, 2004–.

Principal Fields of Interest
Public Choice; Public Finance; Industrial Organization.

Selected Publications
Books
1. *The Organization of Industry* 1990) (with Richard D. Irwin).
2. *Antitrust Policy and Interest-Group Politics* (Quorum Books, 1990).
3. *Modern Managerial Economics: Economic Theory for Business Decisions* (South-Western Publishing Co., 1994) (with W.F. Chappell and R.L. Cottle).
4. *The Causes and Consequences of Antitrust: The Public-Choice Perspective* (University of Chicago Press, 1995) (edited, with F.S. McChesney).

5. *The Organization of Industry*, 2nd ed (Dame Publications, Inc., 1997).
6. *Taxing Choice: The Predatory Politics of Fiscal Discrimination* (ed) (Transaction Publishers, 1997).
7. *The Political Economy of the New Deal* (Edward Elgar Publishing, 1998) (with J.F. Couch).
8. *The Elgar Companion to Public Choice* (Edward Elgar Publishing, 2001) (edited, with L. Razzolini).
9. *The Economics of Budget Deficits* Volumes I–II (Edward Elgar Publishing, 2002) (edited, with C.K. Rowley and R.D. Tollison).

Articles
1. "Preliminary evidence on the use of inputs by the Federal Reserve System." *American Economic Review*, 73(June): 1983 (with R.D. Tollison).
2. "The disinterest in deregulation." *American Economic Review*, 74(December): 1984 (with R.E. McCormick and R.D. Tollison).
3. "Adam Smith in the customhouse." *Journal of Political Economy*, 93(August): 1985 (with G.M. Anderson and R.D. Tollison).
4. "Free entry and efficient rent seeking." *Public Choice*, 46: 1985 (with R.S. Higgins and R.D. Tollison).
5. "On the incentives of judges to enforce legislative wealth transfers." *Journal of Law and Economics*, 32(April): 1989 (with G.M. Anderson and R.D. Tollison).
6. "Going for the gold: Property rights and athletic effort in transitional economies." *Kyklos*, 46: 1993 (with R.D. Tollison).
7. "The reformer's dilemma." *Public Finance Review*, 27(September): 1999.
8. "Reversal of fortune: the politics and economics of the superconducting supercollider." *Public Choice*, 100(September): 1999 (with P. Pecorino and A. Basuchoudhary).
9. "The political economy of the IRS." *Economics and Politics*, 13(July): 2001 (with M. Young and M. Reksulak).
10. "September 11, 2001." *Public Choice*, 111(April): 2002.

Principal Contributions
William Shughart's lifelong interest in bringing public choice principles to bear in analyzing antitrust and regulatory policies commenced during his time at the Federal Trade Commission, where he began a fruitful collaboration with Robert Tollison. A subsequent three-year appointment at the Center for Study of Public Choice, where he was associated with a group of scholars that included James Buchanan, Gordon Tullock, Charles Rowley, and Mark Crain, as well as a highly talented collection of graduate students and distinguished visitors, deepened Shughart's interest in helping extend the public choice model to a wider set of problems. It was there that he first studied positive explanations underlying the propensities of democratic governments to run chronic budget deficits, explored the interest-group politics that shape excise tax policy choices, and participated in elaborating the theory and applications of the Tullockian rent-seeking insight. However, the bulk of his attention remains devoted to showing that, conventional wisdom and Chicago-school thinking notwithstanding, enforcement of the antitrust laws does not systematically promote economic efficiency. To the contrary, placing public policies toward 'monopoly' in public-choice perspective suggests that, like regulation in general, the antitrust laws afford opportunities for protection *from* competitive market forces to firms able to exploit the logic of collective action, demands to which rationally self-interested politicians and policymakers predictably respond. Shughart has written some 150 scholarly articles and is working on his tenth book (see *http://faculty.bus.olemiss.edu/wshughart*).

SMITH, Vernon L.

Born
January 1, 1927, Wichita, Kansas, USA

Current Positions
Professor of Economics and Law, George Mason University, 2001–.

Past Positions
Instructor of Economics, University of Kansas, 1951–1952; Economist, Harvard Economics Research Project, 1954–1955; Assistant Professor, Purdue University, 1955–1958; Associate Professor, Purdue University, 1958–1961; Visiting Professor, Stanford University, 1961–1962; Professor, Purdue University, 1961–1967, Professor (Krannert Outstanding Professorship), Purdue University, 1964–1967; Professor, Brown University, 1967–1968; Professor, University of Massachusetts, 1968–1975; Visiting Professor, USC and Cal Tech, 1974–1975; Professor, University of Arizona, 1975–2001; Regent's Professor of Economics, University of Arizona, 1988–2001; McClelland Professor of Economics, University of Arizona, 1998–2001.

Degrees
B.S.E.E., California Institute of Technology, 1949; M.A., University of Kansas, 1952; Ph.D., Harvard University, 1955.

Offices and Honors
Best Economic Inquiry Article, Western Economic Association, 1980–1982.
Vice President, Southern Economic Association, 1985–1986.
Founding President, Economic Science Association, 1986–1987.
Research Director, Economic Science Laboratory, 1986–2001.
Vice President, Economic Science Association, 1987–1989.
President, Public Choice Society, 1988–1990.
Fellow, Econometric Society, 1988–.
Vice President, Western Economic Association, 1988–1989.
President Elect, Western Economic Association, 1989–1990.
Honorary Doctor of Management, Purdue University, 1989.
President, Western Economic Association, 1990–1991
Fellow, American Association for the Advancement of Science, 1990.
Fellow, American Academy of Arts and Sciences, 1991.
Distinguished Fellow, American Economic Association, 1992.
Adam Smith Award, Association of Private Enterprise Education, 1995.
Elected Member, National Academy of Science, April 15, 1995.
President, Association for Private Enterprise Education, 1997.
President, International Foundation for Research in Experimental Economics, 1997–.
Templeton Honors Rolls for Education in a Free Society, Intercollegiate Studies Institute, May 1997.
Nobel Symposium, Behavioral and Experimental Economics, Speaker, December 4–6, 2001.
Alfred Nobel Memorial Prize in Economic Sciences, 2002.

Editorial Duties
Contributing Editor, *Business Scope*, 1957–1962; Board of Editors, *American Economic Review*, 1969–1972; Editorial Board, *The Cato Journal*, 1983; Associate Editor, *Journal of Economic Behavior and Organization*, 1985–; Board of Reviewing Editors, *Science*, 1988–1991; Editorial Board, *Economic Theory*, 1992–; Editorial Board, *Economic Design*, 1994–; Editorial Board, *Journal of Economic Methodology*, 1995–2000; Advisory Editor, *Journal of Experimental Economics*, 1998–.

Principal Fields of Interest
Experimental Economics; Property Rights; Industrial Organization.

Selected Publications
Books
1. *Economics: An Analytical Approach*, 1st ed. (Richard D. Irwin, 1958), (with K. Davidson and J. Wiley).
2. *Investment and Production* (Harvard University Press, 1961).
3. *Research in Experimental Economics*, Vol. 1 (ed.), (JAI Press, 1979).
4. *Research in Experimental Economics*, Vol. 1 (JAI Press 1980) (supplement, by J. Friedman and A. Hoggatt).
5. *Research in Experimental Economics*, Vol. 2 (ed.) (JAI Press, 1982).
6. *Research in Experimental Economics*, Vol. 3, (ed.) (JAI Press, 1985).
7. *Schools of Economic Thought: Experimental Economics*, editor (Edward Elgar Publishing, 1990).
8. *Papers in Experimental Economics* (Collected works) (Cambridge University Press, 1991).
9. *Experiments in Decision, Organization and Exchange*, (Elsevier Science Publishers, 1993), (edited, with R. Day).
10. *Bargaining and Market Behavior*, Essays in Experimental Economics (Collected works) (Cambridge University Press, 2000).

Articles
1. "The Theory of Investment and Production." *Quarterly Journal of Economics*, February: 1959.
2. "An experimental study of competitive market behavior." *Journal of Political Economy*, April: 1962.
3. "Effect of market organization on competitive equilibrium." *Quarterly Journal of Economics*, May: 1964.
4. "Experimental auction markets and the Walrasian hypothesis." *Journal of Political Economy*, August: 1965.
5. "Experimental studies of discrimination versus competition in sealed bid auction markets." *Journal of Business*, January: 1967.
6. "Economics of the primitive hunter culture with applications to pleistocene extinction and the rise of agriculture." *Journal of Political Economy*, July/August: 1975.
7. "Experimental economics: Induced Value Theory." *American Economic Review*, May: 1976.
8. "Microeconomic systems as an experimental science." *American Economic Review*, December: 1982.
9. "Theory and individual behavior in first price auctions." *Journal of Risk and Uncertainty*, 1(April): 1988 (with J. Cox and J. Walker).
10. "Bubbles, crashes and endogenous expectations in experimental spot asset markets." *Econometrica*, September: 1988 (with G. Suchanek and A. Williams).

11. "Auction institution design: theory and behavior of simultaneous multiple unit generalizations of the dutch and english auctions." *American Economic Review*, December: 1990 (with Kevin A. McCabe and Stephen J. Rassenti).
12. "Designing call auction institutions: is double dutch the best?" *Economic Journal*, 202(January): 1992 (with Kevin A. McCabe and Stephen J. Rassenti).

Principal Contributions
Production and Investment Theory
Experimental Economics
Natural Resource Economics
Financial Market Theory and Behavior; the M-M non theorem
Auction Theory and Behavior
Deregulation of Network Industries: pipelines, electricity, water
Trust, Reciprocity and Exchange
Brain Function and Behavior

SOBBRIO, Giuseppe

Born
July 26, 1942, Gualtieri Sicaminò, Sicilia, Italia

Current Position
Professor of Public Economics, University of Messina, Italia; President of the Scientific Committee "MSc in Health Economics," University of Messina, Italia; Vice-President Italian Society of Public Economics.

Past Positions
Director of the Istituto of Economics and Finance, University of Messina 1981–1999; President Sientific Committee "MSc in Evironmental Economics" University of Messina 1997–1999; Professor of Public Economics, Scuola Superiore della Pubblica Amministrazione, Presidenza del Consiglio, Roma 1997–1998; Professor of Public Finance University of Messina 1980–1996; Professor of Economics University of Messina 1978–1988, 1991–1997; Advisor of the Ministry of European Affairs, 1983; Advisor of Provincia di Messina, 1994–1997; Advisor of Provincia di Reggio Calabria, 1997–2001.

Degrees
B.A., University of Messina

Principal Fields of Interest
Public Choice; Constitutional Political Economy; Institutional Economics; Health Economics.

Selected Publications
Books
1. *La Riqualificazione dell'Intervento Pubblico nell'Europa del 1992* (Cacucci, 1991) (edited by G. Palmerio and G. Sobbrio).
2. *Public Policy After 1992* (CMS Publishing, 1991) (edited by G. Palmerio and G. Sobbrio).
3. *Modelli Organizzativi e Intervento Pubblico* (Giuffrè, 1994) (edited by G. Sobbrio).
4. *La Finanza delle Regioni e degli Eenti Locali* (Cacucci, 1997) (edited by G. Sobbrio).
5. *Federalismo Fiscale e Bilancio per Obbiettivi* (Giuffrè, 1998) (edited by G. Sobbrio).
6. *Economia del Settore Pubblico* (Giuffrè 1999) (edited by G. Sobbrio).
7. *Efficienza ed Efficacia nell'Offerta di Servizi Sanita* (Franco Angeli, 2000) (edited by G. Sobbrio).
8. *Istituzioni Politiche e Finanza Pubblica* (Franco Angeli, 2000) (edited by V. Dardanoni and G. Sobbrio).
9. *Rules and Reason: Perspectives in Constitutional Political Economy* (Cambridge University Press, 2001) (edited by R. Mudambi, P. Navarra, and G. Sobbrio).
10. *Rules, Choice and Strategy: The Political Economy of Italian Electoral Reform*, R. Mudambi, P. Navarra and (Edward Elgar Publishing, 2001) (edited by G. Sobbrio).

Articles
1. "Voter Information and Power Dilution: Evidence from Sicilian Provincial Elections." *Public Choice*, 92: 1997 (with R. Mudambi and P. Navarra).
2. "The Italian electoral reform from the perspective of constitutional political economy," *Notizie di Politeia*, 55: 1999 (with R. Mudambi and P. Navarra).
3. "The nature of organizations and the economics of constitutional rules." *Rivista di Scienza delle Finanze*, 1: 1999.
4. "Changing the rules: political party competition under plurality ad proportionality." *European Journal of Political Economy*, 15: 1999.
5. "The impact of legislative and electoral institutions on economic policy change: theory and evidence from emerging market countries," *Istituzioni Politiche e Finanza Pubblica* (Milano, Franco Angeli, 2000) (V. Dardanoni and G. Sobbrio, eds.) (with R. Mudambi and P. Navarra).
6. "Election re-running and the nature of constitutional choices: the case of Italian electoral reform," *Constitutional Political Economy*, 12: 2001; 1–24 (with P. Navarra).
7. "The role of the European Central Bank: Independence, Control Regulations and European Institutions." *Rivista di Scienza delle Finanze*, 3: 2001.

8. "The electoral cost imposed on political coalitions by constituent parties: the case of Italian national elections," *Rules and Reason: Perspectives on Constitutional Political Economy* (Cambridge, University Press, 2001) (R. Mudambi, P. Navarra, and G. Sobbrio, eds.) (with R. Mudambi and P. Navarra).

Principal Contributions

Giuseppe Sobbrio's research explores several areas of public economics focusing especially on public choice and local public finance. He has examined issues dealing with fiscal federalism, optimal allocation of local public goods and income distribution. His most recent work concerns positive and normative political economy. He has published several papers and a book on the effects produced by the change of the Italian electoral rules on both the voting behavior and electoral competition. Currently he is investigating the effects of political instability on policy decision at the local level.

SOBEL, Russell Steven

Born
June 19, 1968, Des Moines, Iowa, USA

Current Position
Associate Professor of Economics, West Virginia University, USA, 2000–.

Past Positions
Assistant Professor of Economics, West Virginia University, 1994–2000.

Degrees
B.B.A., Francis Marion College, 1990; M.S., Florida State University, 1993; Ph.D., Florida State University, 1994.

Offices and Honors
Atlantic Economic Journal Best Article of the Year Award, 1995.
The West Virginia University Golden Apple Award for Outstanding Teaching, 1996, 2001.
The West Virginia University Foundation Award for Outstanding Teaching, 1997.
Mont Pelerin Society Earhart Fellow, 1998.
WVU College of Business and Economics Outstanding Researcher Award, 1998.
The June Harless Teaching Award for Exceptional Teaching, 1999, 2001.

Principal Fields of Interest
Public Choice; Constitutional Economics; State and Local Public Finance.

Selected Publications
Books
1. *Growth and Variability in State Tax Revenue: An Anatomy of State Fiscal Crises* (Greenwood Press, 1997) (with R.G. Holcombe).
2. *Economics: Private and Public Choice* (Dryden Press, 2000) (with J.D. Gwartney and R.L. Stroup).

Articles
1. "Political incentives and legislative voting." *Journal of Public Finance and Public Choice*, 10(December): 1992.
2. "The League of Nations Covenant and the United Nations Charter: an analysis of two international constitutions." *Constitutional Political Economy*, 5(Spring/Summer): 1994.
3. "Measuring the growth and variability of tax bases over the business cycle." *National Tax Journal* 49(December): 1996 (with R.G. Holcombe).
4. "Taxation and product quality: new evidence from generic cigarettes." *Journal of Political Economy* 105(August): 1997 (with T.A. Garrett).
5. "Optimal taxation in a federal system of governments." *Southern Economic Journal*, 64(October): 1997.
6. "Exchange rate evidence on the effectiveness of U.N. policy." *Public Choice*, 95(April): 1998.
7. "The political costs of tax increases and expenditure reductions: evidence from state legislative turnover." *Public Choice*, 96(July): 1998.
8. "In defense of the articles of confederation and the contribution mechanism as a means of government finance: a general comment on the literature." *Public Choice*, 99(June): 1999.
9. "Theory and evidence on the political economy of the minimum wage." *Journal of Political Economy*, 107(August): 1999.
10. "The unanimous voting rule is not the political equivalent to market exchange." *Public Choice*, 106(March): 2001 (with R.G. Holcombe).

Principal Contributions

Russell Sobel's early work focused on applying public choice models to international organizations, particularly the United Nations. He defended the U.N. system in terms of how it relies on contributions, rather than taxation, to finance its activities, and on the ease of member nations to opt out of the organization and its specific programs individually. His next major research area (with Randy Holcombe) focused on the growth and variability of state tax revenue and on the role of state rainy day funds. Since that time he has taken a particular interest in applying public choice theory to models of taxation in a federal system of governments. Sobel has been a staunch defender of alternative forms of government financing like were present under the Articles of Confederation. More recently, he has worked on applying public choice models to state lotteries (with Tom Garrett) and to state rainy day funds (with Gary Wagner). He has also published a series of papers (with Randy Holcombe) exploring the impact of pecuniary externalities on the efficiency of market (and public sector) action. His recent empirical work has focused on showing how seemingly public-minded policies such as the minimum wage and FEMA disaster expenditures are better explained by public choice models than by altruistic models of the public sector. Sobel also lectures on the merits of free-markets and authors principles of economics textbook with Jim Gwartney and Rick Stroup.

STEPYKINA, Ekaterina

Born
April 6, 1976, Leningrad, USSR

Current Positions
Ph.D. graduate student of Economics, George Mason University.

Past Positions
Research Assistant for Dr. Peter Boettke 2000–; Assistant archivist, Ludwig von Mises papers, Hillsdale College, Michigan; Assistant editor, *1995 Annual Report*, Parallel Computer Technologies Centre, St. Petersburg, Russia.

Degrees
B.A., Hillsdale College, 2000.

Principal Fields of Interest
Institutional Economics; Comparative Political Economy; Austrian Economics

Selected Publications
"Is Russia a market economy?" *The Encyclopedia of Public Choice*. (Edited by Charles K. Rowley and Friedrich Schneider.) (Kluwer Academic Publishers, September 2003.)

STRATMANN, Thomas

Born
February 22, 1959, Muenster, Germany

Current Positions
Professor of Economics, George Mason University, Virginia, USA, 1999–; Senior Research Associate, James M. Buchanan Center, 1999–; CESifo Research Fellow 2002–.

Past Positions
Assistant and Associate Professor of Economics, Montana State University, 1990–1999; Visiting Professor, University of Munich, Center for Economic Studies, December 2001–January 2002; Visiting Professor, University of Vienna, Austria 1998–99; Visiting Professor, University of Konstanz, Germany, May-July 1996; John M. Olin Visiting Assistant Professor, Center for the Study of the Economy 1993–94.

Degrees
B.A., Free University of Berlin, 1985; M.A., Ph.D., University of Maryland, 1988, 1990.

Editorial Duties
Co- Editor, *Southern Economic Journal*; Associate Editor, *European Journal of Economics*

Principal Fields of Interest
Public Choice; Public Economics; Health Economics

Selected Publications
Articles
1. "The economic effects of democratic participation." *Journal of Public Economics* (forthcoming 2003) with Dennis C. Mueller).
2. "Can special interests buy congressional votes?: evidence from financial services legislation." *Journal of Law and Economics*, October:2002.
3. "Plurality rule, proportional representation, and the german bundestag: how incentives to Pork-barrel differ across Electoral Systems." *American Journal of Political Science*, July:2002 (with Martin Baur).
4. "Congressional voting over legislative careers: shifting positions and changing constraints." *American Political Science Review*, September:2000.
5. "Competition among political pressure groups and the organization of congress: theory and evidence from financial service political action committees." *American Economic Review*, December: 1998 (with Randall S. Kroszner).
6. "The market for congressional votes: is timing of contributions everything?" *Journal of Law and Economics*, April: 1998.

7. "How reelection constituencies matter: evidence from Political Action Committees' contributions and congressional voting." *Journal of Law and Economics*, October: 1996.
8. "Instability in collective decisions? a test for cyclical majorities." *Public Choice*, July: 1996.
9. "Campaign contributions and congressional voting: does the timing of contributions matter?" *The Review of Economics and Statistics*, January: 1995.
10. "Informative and persuasive campaigning." *Public Choice*, October: 1994 (with Dennis C. Mueller)
11. "The effects of logrolling on congressional voting." *American Economic Review*, December: 1992.
12. "Are contributors rational: untangling strategies of Political Action Committees." *Journal of Political Economy*, June: 1992.

THOMPSON, Earl

Born
1938

Current Position
Professor of Economics, University of California, Los Angeles, 1965–.

Degrees
Ph.D., Harvard University, 1961.

Selected Publications
Books
1. *Ideology and the Evolution of Vital Institutions: Guilds, The Gold Standard, and Modern International Cooperation* (Kluwer Academic Publishers, 2001) (with Charles Hickson).

Articles
1. "A pareto optimal group decision process." *Papers on Non-Market Decision Making*, Vol. 1 (Later Named *Public Choice*): 1966 (edited with G. Tullock).
2. "Debt instruments in both macroeconomic theory and capital theory." *American Economic Review*, 57(December): 1967.
3. "The perfectly competitive production of collective goods." *Review of Economics and Statistics*, XLX (February):1968.
4. "Taxation and national defense." *Journal of Political Economy*, July/August:1974.
5. "On taxation and the control of externalities." *American Economic Review*, June: 1974 (with Ron Batchelder).
6. "An economic basis for the 'National Defense Argument's for protecting certain industries." *Journal of Political Economy*, February:1979.
7. "Social interaction under truly perfect information." *Journal of Mathematical Sociology*, November: 1980 (with Roger Faith).
8. "Divisionalization and entry deterrence." *Quarterly Journal of Economics*, May: 1986 (with M. Schwartz).
9. "A New Theory of Guilds and European Economic Development." *Exploration in Economic History*, 28: 1991 (with C.R. Hickson).

Principal Contributions
During the first 20 years of his career, Earl Thmpson published articles on pure and applied economic theory in all major U.S. economic journals. Increasingly, his models resulted in the conclusion that contemporary U.S. economic institutions — rather than being the inefficient result of an inefficient social process that almost all economists interpreted them to be — were largely the efficient result of an efficient social process. Then, in the early 1980s, his work turned toward the study of history. Although this redirection initially was simply used to test new theories of guilds, economic underdevelopment, and social organization, it eventually became apparent that the various histories were realizations of an underlying evolutionary process. A marriage of this process to the burgeoning field of evolutionary game theory generated his recent book, written with Charles Hickson.

THORNTON, Mark

Born
June 7, 1960, Geneva, New York, USA

Current Positions
Associate Professor of Economics, Abbott Turner College of Business, Columbus State University, 1999–; Senior Faculty, Ludwig von Mises Institute, Auburn, Alabama, 1999–.

Past Positions
Assistant Superintendent of Banking, State Banking Department of Alabama, 1997–1999; Adjunct Professor of Economics, Auburn University at Montgomery, 1997–1999; O.P. Alford Chair of Economics, Ludwig von Mises Institute, 1993–1997; Assistant Professor of

Economics, Auburn University, 1990–1993; Instructor of Economics, Auburn University, 1988–1990.

Degrees
B.S., St. Bonaventure University, 1982; Ph.D., Auburn University, 1989.

Offices and Honors
Abbott Turner College of Business, Columbus State University, Research Award, 2001.
Columbus State University Research and Scholarship Award, 2002.
Tenure at Columbus State University, 2002.

Editorial Duties
Editor, *Austrian Economics Newsletter*, 1983–1982; Book Review Editor, *Quarterly Journal of Austrian Economics*, 1999–.

Principal Fields of Interest
Austrian Economics; Political Economy; History.

Selected Publications
Books
1. *The Economics of Prohibition* (University of Utah Press, 1991).
2. *Alcohol Prohibition was a Failure* (Cato Institute, 1991).
3. "Prohibition," *The Handbook of Austrian Economics* (Edward Elgar Publishing, 1994) (edited by P.J. Boettke).
4. "The Repeal of Prohibitionism," *Liberty for the Twenty-First Century: Contemporary Libertarian Thought* (Rowman & Littlefield, 1995) (edited by T.R. Machan and D.B. Rasmussen).
5. "Prohibition: The Ultimate Sin Tax," *Taxing Choice: The Predatory Politics of Fiscal Discrimination* (Transaction Publishers, 1997) (edited by W.F. Shughart).
6. "Perfect Drug Legalization," *How to Legalize Drugs: Public Health, Social Science, and Civil Liberties Perspectives* (Jason Aronson, Inc. Publishers, 1998) (edited by J. Fish).

Articles
1. "Economists on illegal drugs." *Atlantic Economic Journal*, 19(June): 1991.
2. "The Pope and the price of leather." *Journal of Institutional and Theoretical Economics*, 148(September): 1992.
3. "The Union blockade versus demoralization of the South: relative prices in the Confederacy." *Social Science Quarterly*, 73(December): 1992 (with R.B. Ekelund, Jr.) .
4. "The fall and rise of Puritanical policy in America." *Journal of Libertarian Studies*, 12(Spring): 1996.
5. "The economics of prohibition-related crime: contests with externalities." *Advances in Applied Microeconomics*, 7: 1998 (with R.O. Beil).
6. "Constituency size and government spending." *Public Finance Quarterly*, 27(November): 1999 (with M. Ulrich).
7. "The 'Confederate' blockade of the South." *Quarterly Journal of Austrian Economics*, 4(Spring): 2001 (with R.B. Ekelund, Jr).
8. "The Great Depression tax revolts revisited." *Journal of Libertarian Studies*, 15(Summer):2001 (with C.D. Weise).
9. "A new perspective on antebellum slavery: public policy and slave prices." *Atlantic Economic Journal*, 29 (September):2001 (with M.A. Yanochik and B.T. Ewing).

Principal Contributions
Mark Thornton began his career with the topic of prohibition and continues to write on that subject. Using price theory, he has shown that prohibition makes products such as alcohol and drugs more dangerous, is counterproductive to the public interest and, in a real economic sense, is impossible. Applying the concept of relative prices to the Union blockade he and Robert Ekelund explained why luxury items tended to dominate in blockade running and dubbed this the "Rhett Butler Effect." They have subsequently examined other economic and public choice issues of the American Civil War. His third major ongoing research interest is examining the impact of public policy on slavery where, in contrast to Fogel and Engerman, et al., we have been able to show that public policy was largely responsible for the "profitability" of antebellum slavery. Finally, Thornton has an ongoing interest in the lost contributions of innovators in economic science such as Richard Cantillon, Frederick Bastiat, Jules Dupuit, William Thornton, Benjamin Anderson, and Ludwig von Mises.

TIDEMAN, Thorwald Nicolaus

Born
August 11, 1943, Chicago, Illinois, USA

Current Position
Professor of Economics, Virginia Polytechnic Institute and State University, 1985–.

Past Positions
Associate Professor of Economics, Virginia Polytechnic Institute and State University, 1975–1985; Post-Doctoral Fellow, Center for Study of Public Choice, 1973–1975; Senior Staff Economist, President's Council of Economic Advisors, 1970–1971; Assistant Professor of Economics, Harvard University, 1969–1973.

Degrees
B.A., Reed College, 1965; Ph.D., University of Chicago, 1969.

Offices and Honors
Member, Board of Directors, Robert Schalkenbach Foundation, 1989–; President, 1996–2001; Vice President, 2001–.
Listed in *Who's Who In Economics: A Biographical Dictionary of Major Economists*.
Listed in *Who's Who In Economics*.

Principal Fields of Interest
Economic Justice; Public Choice; Public Finance.

Selected Publications
Books
1. *Land and Taxation* (Shepheard-Walwyn, 1994).
2. *Constitution for a Future Country* (Palgrave, 2001) (edited, with Martin Bailey).

Articles
1. "A new and superior process for making social choices." *Journal of Political Economy*, 84(December):1976 (with G. Tullock).
2. "A tax on land value *is* neutral." *National Tax Journal*, 35(March):1982.
3. "Independence of clones as a criterion for voting rules." *Social Choice and Welfare*, 4:1987.
4. "Takings, moral evolution and justice." *Columbia Law Review*, 88(December):1988.
5. "Commons and commonwealths: a new framework for the justification of territorial claims." *Commons Without Tragedy*, (Barnes and Noble, 1991) (edited by R. Andelson).
6. "The economics of efficient taxes on land" *Land and Taxation* (Shepheard-Walwyn, (1994) (edited, with N. Tideman).
7. "Taxing land is better than neutral: land taxes, land speculation and the timing of development," in *Land-Value Taxation: The Equitable and Efficient Source of Public Finance* (M.E. Sharpe, 1999) (edited, wth K. Wenzer).
8. "Better voting methods through technology: the refinement-manageability trade-off in the single transferable vote" *Public Choice*, 103(April):2000 (with D. Richardson).
9. "Global economic justice," *Geophilos* 00 (Autumn): 2000.
10. "The avoidable excess burden of broad-based U.S. taxes" *Public Finance Review*, September: 2002 (with A. Johns, E. Akobundu, and P. Wutthicharoen).

Principal Contributions
The theme that unifies most of Thorwald Tideman's work is identifying appropriate collective action. His doctoral dissertation dealt with ways of achieving efficient land use despite interdependency in the most efficient uses of neighboring parcels of land. One chapter dealt with the efficient size and spacing of a local public good. Another developed the properties of a self-assessed property tax. Much of his work has explored novel voting rules, such as the demand-revealing process (which motivates people to report truthfully the intensities of their preferences) and the single transferable vote (which is useful for electing multiple persons from a single constituency). Other work has explored the best ways of cutting through majority-rule cycles. More recently, Tideman has concentrated on issues of social justice, and in particular on issues emerging from the framework, developed most notably by Henry George, that begins with the axioms that people have rights to themselves and that all people have equal rights to natural opportunities. Thus he has written about the neutrality of taxes on land, about measures of the excess burden of taxes on labor and capital, and about the implications of Georgist theory for a just world order.

TOLLISON, Robert Dewitt

Born
November 27, 1942, Spartanburg, South Carolina, USA

Current Positions
Adjunct Research Associate, James M. Buchanan Center, 2000–; Professor of Economics and BB & T Senior Fellow, Clemson University.

Past Positions
Robert M. Hearin Professor of Economics, University of Mississippi, USA, 1998–; Duncan Black Professor of

Economics, George Mason University, 1984–1998; Director, Center for Study of Public Choice, 1984–1998; Abney Professor of Economics, Clemson University, 1981–1983; Director, Bureau of Economics, Federal Trade Commission, 1981–1983; Professor of Economics, Virginia Tech, 1976–1981; Executive Director, Center for Study of Public Choice, 1976–1981; Visiting Professor of Law and Economics, University of Miami Law School, 1975–1976; Associate Professor and Professor of Economics, Texas A&M University, 1972–1976; Department Head, Texas A&M University, 1974–1976; Senior Staff Economist, President's Council of Economic Advisers, 1971–1972; Assistant Professor, Business School, Cornell University, 1969–1972.

Degrees
B.A., Wofford College, 1964; M.A., University of Alabama, 1965; Ph.D., University of Virginia, 1969.

Offices and Honors
President, Southern Economic Association, 1985.
President, Public Choice Society, 1994–1996.

Editorial Duties
Joint Editor, *Public Choice*, 1990–; Board of Editors, *Constitutional Political Economy*, 1988–; Board of Editors, *Journal of Sports Economics*, 1999–.

Principal Fields of Interest
Public Choice; Industrial Organization; Political Economy.

Selected Publications
Books
1. *Politicians, Legislation, and the Economy: An Inquiry into the Interest-Group Theory of Government.* (Martinus Nijhoff, 1981) (with R. McCormick).
2. *Mercantilism as a Rent-Seeking Society* (Texas A&M University Press, 1982) (with R. Ekelund).
3. *The National Collegiate Athletic Association: A Study in Cartel Behavior* (University of Chicago Press, 1992) (with A. Fleisher and B. Goff).
4. *Sacred Trust: The Medieval Church as an Economic Firm* (Oxford University Press, 1996) (with R. Ekelund, R. Hebert, G. Anderson, and A. Davis).
5. *Politized Economies: Monarchy, Monopolies, and Mercantilism* (Texas A&M Press, 1997) (with R. Ekelund).
6. *The Economic Approach to Public Policy: Selected Readings* (Cornell University Press, 1976) (edited with R. Amacher and T. Willett).
7. *Towards a Theory of the Rent-Seeking Society* (Texas A&M University Press, 1980) (edited, with James M. Buchanan and Gordon Tullock).
8. *Predicting Politics: Essays in Empirical Public Choice* (University of Michigan Press, 1990) (edited, with M. Crain).
9. *Sportometrics*. (Texas A&M University Press, 1990) (edited, with B. Goff).
10. *The Collected Works of James M. Buchanan*. (Liberty Fund, 1999–2002) (edited, with G. Brennan and H. Kliemt).

Articles
1. "Legislatures as Unions." *Journal of Political Economy*, 86(February):1978 (with Robert McCormick).
2. "An Economic Theory of Issue Linkages in International Negotiations." *International Organization*, 33(Autumn):1979 (with T. Willett).
3. "A Theory of Legislative Organization: making the most of your majority." *Quarterly Journal of Economics* 94(March):1980 (with Arleen Leibowitz).
4. "The homogenization of heterogeneous inputs." *American Economic Review*, 71(March):1981 (with J.M. Buchanan).
5. "Preliminary evidence on the use of inputs by the federal reserve system." *American Economic Review* 73(June):1983 (with W. Shughart).
6. "Crime on the Court." *Journal of Political Economy*, 92(April):1984 (with R. McCormick).
7. "Final voting in legislatures." *American Economic Review*, 76(September):1986 (with M. Crain and D. Leavens).
8. "Intellectual collaboration." *Journal of Political Economy*, 108(June):2000 (with D. Laband).
9. "Racial integration as an innovation: empirical evidence from sports leagues." *American Economic Review*, 92:2002 (with B. Goff and R. McCormick).
10. "An economic analysis of the protestant reformation." *Journal of Political Economy*, 2002 (with R. Ekelund and R. Hebert).

Principal Contributions
Early on, Robert Tollison turned his attention to empirical work in public choice and other areas. His primary research agenda has been to show how economics can be used to explain behavior in unlikely settings. These settings or actors to date have included religion, the medieval church, politics, legislatures, popes, coaches, sports, war, coauthorship, polygamy, music, language, mercantilism, judges, executives, bureaucrats, and athletes. He has written or edited numerous books and articles on these as well as other subjects.

TOWER, Edward

Born
January 16, 1943, Fitchburg, Massachusetts, USA

Current Position
Professor of Economics, Duke University, North Carolina, USA, 1977–.

Past Positions
Associate Professor, Duke University, 1974–1977; Visiting Professor, Nanjing University 1991–1992; Visiting Professor, Helsinki School of Business and Economics, 1993; Visiting Professor, Economics Institute, Boulder, Colorado, 1989; Assistant Professor, Associate Professor, and Visiting Professor, Simon Fraser University 1972–1974 and various summers thereafter; Visiting Lecturer, Visiting Senior Lecturer, and Visiting Professor, University of Auckland 1971–1972, and various northern summers thereafter; Assistant Professor, Fletcher School of Law and Diplomacy at Tufts University, 1970–1971, Visiting Assistant Professor, New Mexico State University, 1966; Teaching Fellow and Resident Tutor in Economics, Lowell House, Harvard University, 1966–1970.

Degrees
B.A., M.A., Ph.D., Harvard University, 1964, 1967, 1971.

Offices and Honors
Consultant to U.S. Treasury, 1972–1977.
Treasurer, Carolina Friends School, 1976–1979.
Member and Chair for one year: Advisory Screening Committee for Fulbright Fellowships in Economics for the Council for International Exchange of Scholars, 1979–1982.
Vice President, Southern Economic Association, 1982–1983.
President, Eno River Press, 1980–present.
Consultant, World Bank, March 1982–1997.
Research Associate, Claremont Center for Economic Policy Studies, January 1983–present.
Consultant to Governor of the Bank of Sudan under the Auspices of the U.S. Agency for International Development, 1983–1985.
Consultant to the Harvard Institute for International Development in Indonesia, 1984–1985.
Visiting Fellow, Department of Economics, Research School of Pacific Studies, Australian National University, June–August 1986.
Consultant to USAID Malawi and the Government of Malawi, April – May 1987.
Member of Advisory Board, Centre for International Economics,1986–present.
Consultant to USAID Nairobi, March 1989.
Visiting Fellow, Research School of Social Sciences. Australian National University January–August 1992.
Vice President, International Economics and Finance Society, 1995.

Editorial Duties
Southern Economic Journal, 1980–1982; *Eastern Africa Economic Review*, 1986–1995; *Economic Inquiry*, 1987–1996; *Contemporary Policy Issues*, 1988–1996; *North American Review of Economics and Finance*, 1989–1999; Westview Press, Political Economy of Global Independence Series, 1989–1999; *Journal of Economic Integration*, 1991–1999; *Review of International Economics*, 1992–; *Journal of Economic Development*, 1997–; *Journal of Policy Reform*, 2001–; *Rivista Internazionale di Scienze Economiche e Commerciali*, 2002–.

Principal Fields of Interest
Politics of Protection; Development Economics; Equity Valuation.

Selected Publications
Books
1. *The Theory of Optimum Currency Areas and Exchange-Rate Flexibility*, Special Paper in International Economics, Vol. 11 (Princeton University, May 1976) (with T.D. Willett).
2. *Effective Protection, Domestic Resource Cost and Shadow Prices: A General Equilibrium Perspective*, World Bank Staff Working Paper No. 664, September, 1984.
3. *On Shadow Pricing*, World Bank Staff Working Paper No. 792, January 1986 (with G. Pursell).
4. *Judging Economic Policy: Selected Writings of Gottfried Haberler* (Westview Press, 1997) (with Richard J. Sweeney and Thomas D. Willett).

Articles
1. "The economic impact - industrial and regional — of an arms cut." *Review of Economics and Statistics*, August 1965. (with W.W. Leontief, A. Morgan, K. Polenske and D. Simpson).
2. "Commercial policy under fixed and flexible exchange rates." *Quarterly Journal of Economics*, August: 1973.
3. "The optimum quota and retaliation." *Review of Economic Studies*, October:1975.
4. "Dynamic stability and the choice between fixed and flexible exchange rates." *Economic Journal*, March:1977.

5. "Trade policy and the American income distribution." *Review of Economics and Statistics*, May:1982 (with J.C. Hartigan).
6. "The Textile Bill of 1985: determinants of congressional voting patterns." *Public Choice*, May:1987 (with S.C. Toscini).
7. "On shadow pricing foreign exchange, non-traded goods and labor in a simple general equilibrium model." *Oxford Economic Papers*, June:1987 (with G.G. Pursell).
8. "Does trade liberalization benefit young and old alike?" *Review of International Economics*, February:1998 (with Omer Gokcekus).
9. "A golden jubilee note on Graaff's optimum tariff structures," *History of Political Economy*, Fall:2000. (with John Gilbert).
10. "Protectionism, labor mobility, and immiserizing growth in developing countries," *Economics Letters*, March:2002 (with John Gilbert).

Principal Contributions
Edward Tower's research topics have included the choice between fixed and flexible exchange rates; commercial policy in macro models; tariff and quota warfare; tariffs and quotas and imperfect competition, and political economy of protection. His current research is on valuing US and foreign equity markets.

TULLOCK, Gordon

Born
February 13, 1922, Rockford, Illinois, USA

Current Positions
Professor of Law & Economics, George Mason University, Fall 1999–.

Past Positions
1947–1956 Various far eastern positions in the US Foreign Service; 1956–1958 Research and Writing Various Places; 1958–1959 Post Doctoral Fellow, University of Virginia; 1959–1962 Asst. & Assoc. Professor, University of South Carolina; 1962–1967 Associate Professor, University of Virginia; 1967–1968 Professor of Economics and Political Science, Rice University; 1968–1972 Professor of Economics and Public Choice VPI & State University; 1972–1983 University Distinguished Professor VPI & State University; 1983–1987 Holbert R. Harris University Professor George Mason University; Spring 1987 Philip Morris Visiting Distinguished Scholar Baruch University; 1987–1999 Karl Eller Professor of Economics and Political Science, University of Arizona.

Degrees
J.D., University of Chicago Law School, 1947.

Offices and Honors
President, Public Choice Society.
President, Southern Economic Association.
President, Western Economic Association.
Secretary, Public Choice Society.
Member, Board of American Political Science Association.
Academic Advisor Hong Kong Center for Economic Research.
President of Atlantic Economic Society.
President of Association for Free Enterprise Economics.
President of International Bio Economics Society.
First recipient of the Leslie T. Wilkins Award, presented for "The Outstanding Book in the Field of Criminology and Criminal Justice," for 1982, by the Criminal Justice Research Center, Albany, New York.
Honorary Doctor Laws, University of Chicago, 1992.
Was presented the 1993 Adam Smith Award, in Washington, DC, April, 1993, and at the Western Economic Association conference held in Lake Tahoe, June, 1993, an award dinner held in honor "Re: Works of Gordon Tullock".
Honorary Doctor of Philosophy, Basle, 1995.
Member of the American Political Science Review Hall of Fame, March 1996. *PS: Political Science & Politics*.
Award for Outstanding contributions in law and economics by George Mason University Law School, 1996.
Distinguished Fellow, January 1998 — American Economics Association.

Editorial Duties
Founding editor, *Public Choice*, Active Editor 1962–1990, Contributing Editor 1990–present; Publisher, *Public Choice* Monograph Series of 1965–1980; Editor, *Frontiers of Economics*.

Principal Fields of Interest
Public Choice; Law and Economics; Classical Liberal Political Economy; Bio Economics.

Selected Publications
Books
1. *The Calculus of Consent: Logical Foundations of Constitutional Democracy* (University of Michigan Press, 1962) (with J.M. Buchanan).
2. *The Politics of Bureaucracy* (Public Affairs Press, 1965).

3. *The Organization of Inquiry* (Duke University Press, 1966; University Press of America, 1987).
4. *The Logic of the Law* (Basic Books Inc., 1971; University Press of America, 1988).
5. *The Social Dilemma: The Economics of War and Revolution* (Center for Study of Public Choice, 1974).
6. *Toward a Theory of the Rent-Seeking Society* (Texas A&M University Press, Series 4, 1980) (with James Buchanan and Robert D. Tollison)
7. *Economics of Income Redistribution* (Kluwer-Nijhoff Publishing, 1983).
8. *Autocracy* (Martinus Nijhoff, 1987).
9. *The Economics of Non-Human Societies* (Pallas Press, 1994).
10. *The New Federalist.* (Fraser Institute, 1994).

Articles
1. "Paper money: a cycle in Cathay." *Economic History Review*, 9(June):1956.
2. "Problems of majority voting." *Journal of Political Economy*, 67(December):1959.
3. "Information without profit." *Papers on Non-Market Decision Making*, 1:1966.
4. "The general irrelevance of the general impossibility theorem." *Quarterly Journal of Economics*, 81(May): 1967.
5. "The welfare costs of tariffs, monopolies and theft." *Western Economic Journal*, 5(June):1967.
6. "The Cost of Transfers." *Kyklos*, 24(Fasc. 4):1971.
7. "Competing for aid." *Public Choice*, 21(Spring):1975.
8. "A new and superior process for making social choices." *Journal of Political Economy*, 84(6):1976 (with T. Nicolaus Tideman).
9. "The rhetoric and reality of redistribution." *Southern Economic Journal*, 47(4):April 1981.
10. "The initial emergence of states." *Values and the Social Order*, Volume 3: Voluntary versus coercive orders. (Avebury, 1997) (Gerard Radnitzky, ed.).

Principal Contributions
Gordon Tullock has wandered in many fields. When he left the diplomatic service, he began work on how bureaucracies work, which led to his first independent publication. The actual functioning of democracies (and autocracies) has probably been his major preoccupation. In addition to many books and articles, he was the founding editor of *Public Choice*, a journal he edited for 28 years. He has also written in international affairs, with particular reference to wars and revolutions. As a law graduate, he has maintained a keen interest in law and economics, publishing three books and numerous articles in that field. Most recently, he has become interested in bio-economics and has written one book and several articles in that field. Tullock also written on the political economy of income redistribution with special reference to the pension system. As a final example of the diverse nature of his career, for many years he has been an active member of the board of directors of a small company in Iowa.

TWIGHT, Charlotte Augusta Lewis

Current Positions
Adjunct Scholar, Cato Institute, Washington, D.C., 2002–; Professor of Economics, Boise State University, Boise, Idaho, USA, 1991–.

Past Positions
Chairman, Department of Economics, Boise State University, 1994–1996; Associate Professor, Department of Economics, Boise State University, 1988–1991; Assistant Professor, Department of Economics, Boise State University, 1986–1988; Lecturer/Visiting Assistant Professor of Business Economics, Department of Finance and Business Economics, University of Washington, Seattle, Washington, 1983–1986; Predoctoral Teaching Associate, Department of Economics, University of Washington, 1981–1983; Consultant to Professor Steven N.S. Cheung, Department of Economics, University of Washington, 1978–1981; Lecturer (Law), Department of Business, Government, and Society, University of Washington, 1975–1978; Computer Programmer/Analyst, GS-11, Naval Command Systems Support Activity, Washington, D.C., 1966–1970; Teaching Assistant, Department of English, University of Washington, 1965–1966.

Degrees
B.A., California State University at Fresno; J.D., M.A., Ph.D., University of Washington, 1973, 1980, 1983.

Offices and Honors
Executive Editor, *Washington Law Review*, University of Washington School of Law, 1972–1973.
Member, Washington State Bar Association, 1973–.
Listed in *Who's Who in American Law*, First Edition, 1977.
Professor of the Year, awarded by Alpha Kappa Psi, University of Washington Chapter, 1986.
Professor of the Year, awarded by Alpha Kappa Psi, Boise State University Chapter, 1992.
Lecturer, Foundation for Teaching Economics, 1996–1997.
Member, Advisory Council, *Econ Journal Watch*.

Member, Academic Advisory Board, Institute for Health Freedom.
Member, Humane Studies Fellowship Academic Review Committee, Institute for Humane Studies.

Editorial Duties
Contributing Editor, *The Independent Review: A Journal of Political Economy*.

Principal Fields of Interest
Public Choice; Political Economy; Law and Economics; Growth of Government.

Selected Publications
Books
1. *America's Emerging Fascist Economy* (Arlington House, 1975).
2. *Dependent on D.C.: The Rise of Federal Control Over the Lives of Ordinary Americans*. (Palgrave/St. Martin's Press, 2002).

Articles
1. "Government manipulation of constitutional-level transaction costs: a general theory of transaction-cost augmentation and the growth of government." *Public Choice*, 56:1988.
2. "On the efficiency of law: a public choice perspective." *Public Choice*, 66:1990 (with M.A. Crew).
3. "Constitutional renegotiation: impediments to consensual revision." *Constitutional Political Economy*, 3:1992.
4. "Channeling ideological change: the political economy of dependence on government." *Kyklos*, 46:1993.
5. "Political transaction-cost manipulation: an integrating theory." *Journal of Theoretical Politics*, 6:1994.
6. "Evolution of federal income tax withholding: the machinery of institutional change." *Cato Journal*, 14(Winter):1995.
7. "Federal control over education: crisis, deception, and institutional change." *Journal of Economic Behavior and Organization*, 31(December):1996.
8. "Medicare's origin: the economics and politics of dependency." *Cato Journal*, 16(Winter):1997.
9. "Watching you: systematic federal surveillance of ordinary americans." *The Independent Review*, 4(Fall):1999.
10. "Health and human services 'Privacy' standards: the coming destruction of American Medical Privacy." *The Independent Review*, 6(Spring):2002.

Principal Contributions
For decades, Charlotte Twight's overriding interest has been the growth of government power and its liberty-eroding consequences for private individuals. Her first book examined the transformation of America's political economy that was already evident in 1975, examining historical counterparts of the prevalent U.S. system of nominal deference to private markets coupled with almost unlimited federal power to intervene in those markets. In her Ph.D. dissertation, she developed a theory of government manipulation of constitutional-level transaction costs as an explanation of the growth of government, examining the theory's applicability to the federal government's off-budget expenditure through the Federal Financing Bank. Subsequently, she has had the opportunity to study that theory's relevance to many different U.S. policy areas, including the creation and implementation of Social Security, income tax withholding, federal education laws, Medicare and other federal health care legislation, and statutory laws establishing federal databases and other forms of surveillance of law-abiding Americans. This theory, which Twight now calls political transaction-cost manipulation, helps to explain why rational choices in political contexts erode both liberty and economic efficiency. The book *Dependent on D.C.* summarizes her principal contributions in this area.

URKEN, Arnold Bernard

Born
November 26, 1941, Trenton, New Jersey, USA

Current Positions
Professor of Political Science, Stevens Institute of Technology, Hoboken, New Jersey; Researcher, Cyber-Security Laboratory, Stevens Institute of Technology, 2001–; Founder and President, Choice Logic Corporation, 1996–.

Past Positions
Associate Dean for Academic Affairs, Stevens Institute of Technology, 1999–2000, Director, Stevens Engineering Assessment Center, Charles V. Schaefer School of Engineering, 1997–1999, Research Professor, Advanced Telecommunications Institute, Stevens Institute of Technology, 1992–1993, Fellow in Computer Policy, State of New Jersey, 1979–1980, Associate Professor of Political Science, Stevens Institute of Technology, 1979–1983, Assistant Professor of Political Science, 1973–1979, Research Fellow, Philosophy and Social Science, London School of Economics, 1965–1966.

Degrees
A.B., Oberlin College, 1963; M.A., Rutgers University, 1964; Ph.D., New York University, 1973

Principal Fields of Interest
Voting Theory; History of Social Choice Theory; Computers and Decision Theory.

Selected Publications
Books
1. *Classics of Social Choice*, (University of Michigan Press, 1995) (edited, translated, and introduced with Iain Mclean).

Articles
1. "Optimal jury design." *Jurimetrics*, 1984 (with Steven Traflet).
2. "Social Choice Theory and distributed decision making." *Proceedings of the International Conference on Office Information Systems* (IEEE/ACM, 1988) (edited by R. Allen).
3. "Condorcet-Jefferson: un chaînon manquant dans la théorie du choix social?" *Condorcet: Mathématicien, Économiste, Philosophe, Homme Politique* (Paris: Minerve, 1989) (edited by Pierre Crépel and C. Gilain).
4. "Condorcet's 1785 Essai and the origins of social Choice Theory." *Proceedings of the Annual Meeting of the Public Choice Society* (Tuscon, AZ, 1989).
5. "Coordinating agent action via voting." *Proceedings of the International Conference on Office Information Systems* (Cambridge: IEEE/ACM, 1990).
6. "The Condorcet-Jefferson connection and the origins of Social Choice Theory," *Public Choice*, 1991.
7. "The impact of computer-mediated voting." *National Conference on the Social and Ethical Aspects of Computing* (Southern Connecticut University: The Research Center on Computing and Society, 1992).
8. "Did Jefferson or Madison Understand Condorcet's Social Choice Theory?" *Public Choice*, 1992 (with Iain McLean).
9. "Voting methods in context: the development of a science of voting in French Scientific Institutions, 1699–1803." (Rochester: International Conference on Social Choice and Welfare, 1994).
10. "Polls, surveys, and choice processor technology." *World Wide Web Journal*, (Cambridge, 1996).
11. "La réception des oeuvres de Condorcet sur le choix social 1794–1803: Lhuilier, Morales, et Daunou," *Nouvelles Recherches sur Condorcet* (Paris: Minverve, 1996).
12. "The Stevens Assessment Center: Web-based Educational Assessment." *The Future of Voting on the World Wide Web* (Vienna: Austrian Academy of Sciences, 1998) (edited by Peter Paul Sint).

Principal Contributions
Arnold Urken's interest in models of collective choice began with the application of game theoretic, coalition formation ideas to explain the Chinese Civil War. He began using Monte Carlo computer simulation models to study the properties of voting processes. While studying approval voting, he discovered that classical works in social choice seemed to be widely cited, but rarely read. A project on Condorcet's 1785 Essai with colleagues in 18th century French science and probability theory expanded his awareness of the scope and implications of Condorcet's work, the social context of French scientific and political institutions, and intellectual connections to Jefferson, L'Huillier, and others. Archival work in the French Academy of Sciences and Institute of France uncovered many discoveries, including a previously unknown analysis of voting rules in the Institute of France by Pierre Claude Daunou. Urken's collaboration with Iain McLean made these works accessible to English readers and produced clarifications of underlying developments in social choice theory. This work overlapped with Urken's interest in the normative and analytical aspects of computer-mediated voting by revealing how organizations choose and change voting systems. His investigations of voting rules in computer-mediated environments analyzed the implications of using social choice principles to solve problems of collective decision making. His work developed a social choice approach to managing tasks in which the decision makers could be humans, machines, or programs. His work on computing environments led him to collaborate on a laboratory for certifying election systems (which they closed because the standards for testing software were too lax) and problems of conducting Web-based assessment of educational outcomes for engineering to meet accreditation. His book on the evolution of computers and voting began before the breakdowns of the 2000 US presidential election and before the flurry of interest in Internet voting in government and industry. A unifying thread in all of Urken's work is that there is no generally optimal voting method.

VACHRIS, Michelle Albert

Born
June 1, 1962, Norfolk, Virginia, USA

Current Position
Associate Professor of Economics, Christopher Newport University, 2000–.

Past Positions
Director of International Business, Christopher Newport University, 1998–2001; Assistant Professor of Economics, Christopher Newport University, 1994–1999; Consultant, International Monetary Fund, 1995; Adjunct Assistant Professor of Economics, Loyola College of Maryland, 1993; Economist, U.S. Bureau of Labor Statistics, 1984–1994; Consultant, Organization for Economic Cooperation and Development, 1986.

Degrees
B.A., College of William and Mary, 1984; M.A., Ph.D., George Mason University, 1988, 1992.

Offices and Honors
George Mason University Outstanding Graduate Student in Economics, 1992.
Christopher Newport University Brout Professor, 1996.
John S. McClure Continuing Education Scholarship Foundation Directorial Board, 1996–
Virginia Association of Economists Board Member 1998–; President-elect 2002–.
Christopher Newport University nominee for State Council for Higher Education in Virginia Outstanding Faculty Award, 2000, 2001.
Virginia Beach Libertarian Party, Chair 2002; Vice-Chair, 2001.
Virginia Institute for Public Policy, Academic Advisory Board, 2002–.

Principal Fields of Interest
Public Choice Economics; Industrial Organization; International Economics; Teaching of Economics.

Selected Publications
Articles
1. "New international price series by nation and region." *Monthly Labor Review*, June: 1992.
2. "Snake oil economics versus public choice." *Public Choice Theory, III*: 1993 (Edward Elgar Publishing). (with C.K. Rowley).
3. "Why democracy in the United States does not necessarily produce efficient results." *Journal of Public Finance and Public Choice*, December:1995 (with C.K. Rowley).
4. "The Virginia school of political economy." *Beyond Neoclassical Economics: Heterodox Approaches to Economic Theory*, (Edward Elgar Publishing, 1996) (Fred Foldvary, ed.) (with C.K. Rowley).
5. "Federal antitrust enforcement: a principal-agent perspective." *Public Choice*, September:1996.
6. "Teaching economics in a virtual classroom." *Virginia Economic Journal*, September:1997.
7. "Teaching economics without 'chalk and talk': the experience of CNU online." *Journal of Economic Education*, 30(3):1999.
8. "International comparisons of incomes and prices: 1996 results." *Monthly Labor Review*, October:1999 (with J. Thomas).
9. "More evidence that university administrators are utility maximizing bureaucrats." *Economics of Governance*, forthcoming (with D. Coates and B.R. Humphries).

Principal Contributions
Michelle Vachris' research interests involve the three varied fields of public choice economics, international economics, and teaching pedagogy. Her work in public choice stems from her dissertation, "The political economy of antitrust," in which she uses theory of the firm to analyze political markets. In collaboration with Charles K. Rowley, she broadened this work to explore inefficiencies inherent in democratic political markets, and she has recently applied theory of the firm to governance problems in academia. As an international economics consultant, Vachris worked with the International Monetary Fund (IMF) to assist the Russian Federation with the development and implementation of import and export price indexes during the first years of their transition to a market economy. She is currently the Academic Advisor to the U.S. Bureau of Labor Statistics (BLS) for Purchasing Power Parities. In this capacity, she performs research concerning the international comparison of incomes and prices published by the Organization for Economic Cooperation and Development (OECD). The third area of research in which she is engaged is distance learning, where she develops online courses and assesses student outcomes.

VANBERG, Viktor J.

Born
August 12, 1943, Aachen, Germany

Current Positions
Director, Walter Eucken Institut, Freiburg i.Br., Germany, 2001–; Professor of Economics, University of Freiburg i.Br., Germany, 1995–.

Past Positions
Professor of Economics, George Mason University, and Editorial Director, Center for Study of Public Choice, 1988–1995; Associate Professor of Economics, George Mason University, and Research Associate, Center for Study of Public Choice, 1985–1988; Visiting Professor, Department of Economics, George Mason University, 1984–1985; Visiting Research Associate, Center for Study of Public Choice, 1983–1985; Visiting Professor, Sociology, University of Mannheim, Germany, 1981–1982; Visiting Professor, Sociology, University of Hamburg, Germany, 1976–1977; Research Associate/Academic Assistant, Department of Economics, University of Muenster, Germany, 1974–1983; Academic Assistant, University of Berlin (TU), 1968–1974.

Degrees
Dipl.Soz., University of Muenster, Germany, 1968; Dr.Phil., University of Berlin (TU), Germany, 1974; Dr.Phil.Habil., University of Mannheim, Germany, 1981.

Editorial Duties
Joint Editor, *Constitutional Political Economy*, 1990–2001.

Principal Fields of Interest
Constitutional Political Economy; Evolutionary Economics.

Selected Publications
Books
1. *Die zwei Soziologien — Individualismus und Kollektivismus in der Sozialtheorie* [The Two Sociologies — Individualism and Collectivism in Social Theory] (J.C.B. Mohr (Paul Siebeck) 1975).
2. *Markt und Organisation — Individualistische Sozialtheorie und das Problem Korporativen Handelns* [Market and Organization — Individualist Social Theory and the Problem of Corporate Action] (J.B.C. Mohr (Paul Siebeck) 1982).
3. *Rules and Choice in Economics* (Routledge, 1994).
4. *The Constitution of Markets — Essays in Political Economy* (Routledge, 2001).

Articles
1. "Organization Theory and Fiscal Economics: Society, State, and Public Debt." *Journal of Law, Economics, and Organization*, 2: 1986 (with J.M. Buchanan).
2. "Interests and Theories in Constitutional Choice." *Journal of Theoretical Politics*, 1: 1989 (with J.M. Buchanan).
3. "Rationality, morality and exit." *American Poltical Science Review*, 86 (June):1992 (with Roger D. Congleton).
4. "Rational choice, rule-following and institutions: an evolutionary perspective." *Rationality, Institutions and Economic Methodology*, (Routledge 1993) (edited by B. Gustafson, C. Knudsen, U. Mäki).
5. "Cultural evolution, collective learning and constitutional design," *Economic Thought and Political Theory* (Kluwer Academic Publishers, 1994) (edited by D. Reisman).
6. "Globalization, democracy and citizens' sovereignty: can competition among governments enhance democracy?" *Constitutional Political Economy*, 11:2000.
7. "Freiburg School of Law and Economics." *The New Palgrave Dictionary of Economics and the Law*, Vol. 2 (Macmillan, 1998) (edited by P. Newman).
8. "Functional Federalism: Communal or Individual Rights?" *Kyklos*, 53:2000.
9. "Markets and the Law." *International Encyclopedia of the Social and Behavioral Sciences* Vol. 14, (Elsevier, 2001) (edited by N.J. Smelser and P.B. Baltes).
10. "Rational choice vs. program-based behavior: alternative theoretical approaches and their relevance for the study of institutions." *Rationality and Society*, 14: 2002.

Principal Contributions
Starting his academic career as a sociologist, Viktor Vanberg's interest in the role of rules and institutions on the one side and his dissatisfaction with what went under the name of "sociological theory" on the other made him look for ways to combine the sociologists' focus on the institutional dimension with the methodological individualism of theoretical economics. Vanberg's early work is concerned with the history and the explanatory potential of an individualistic approach to social phenomena in general and to social norms and institutions in particular, drawing extensively on literature in the economic tradition of social theory (notably the work of F.A. Hayek) and seeking to extend the individualistic perspective from the study of market-like spontaneous interaction to the study of organisations and corporate action. As the emergence of a new institutionalism in economics (including, in particular, public choice theory and other, related, approaches) provided a more hospitable environment for his ambitions than sociology, Vanberg very much welcomed the opportunity, offered to him by J.M. Buchanan in 1983, to join the Center for Study of Public Choice and to pursue research interests, henceforth, as an economist by academic affiliation. Vanberg's main work since has been within the paradigm of constitutional political economy, initiated by Buchanan, seeking to clarify issues at the foundation of a constitutional

economics approach — including its adequate behavioural foundation — and to explore its implications for economic policy. The focus of his ongoing research is on issues of constitutional choice and competition among constitutions on the national and international level, on the relation between the constitutional economics perspective and ethics, and on the paradigm of rule- or program-based behaviour as an alternative to the rational choice paradigm.

VAUBEL, Roland

Born
January 5, 1948, Obernburg/Main, FR Germany

Current Position
Professor of Economics, University of Mannheim, Germany, 1984–.

Past Positions
Visiting Professor, Graduate School of Business, University of Chicago, 1981; Associate Professor and Professor, Erasmus University Rotterdam, 1979–1980; Researcher, Institute of World Economics, Kiel, FR Germany 1973–1979, 81–84.

Degrees
B.A., M.A., University of Oxford, 1970; Columbia University, New York, 1972; Dr., Dr. habil., University of Kiel, FR Germany, 1977, 1980.

Offices and Honors
Member and Rapporteur, Study Group "European Monetary Unity," Commission of the European Communities, Brussels, 1974–1976.
Board of Directors, Mont Pelerin Society, 1980–1986, 1994–2000.
Cato Institute, Adjunct Scholar, 1980–1990.
Member of Advisory Council, Institute of Economic Affairs, London, 1980–.
Member, Academic Advisory Council, Federal Ministry of Economics, 1993–.
Chairman, Research Group "Institutionalization of International Negotiation Systems," German Science Foundation, 2001–.

Editorial Duties
Panel Member, *Economic Policy*, 1986–1987; Editorial Board, *Constitutional Political Economy*, 1989–; Editorial Board, *European Journal of Political Economy*, 1995–.

Principal Fields of Interest
Public Choice, Constitutional Economics, International Organizations, European Integration, International Finance, Monetary Policy, Social Policy.

Selected Publications
Books
1. *Strategies for Currency Unification. The Economics of Currency Competition and the Case for a European Parallel Currency* (Siebeck, 1978).
2. *Choice in Monetary Union*, Ninth Wincott Lecture (Institute of Economic Affairs, London, Occasional Papers, 55, 1979).
3. *The Political Economy of International Organisations in International Money and Finance*, Tenth Henry Thornton Lecture (City University, London, 1988).
4. *The Political Economy of International Organizations. A Public Choice Approach* (Westview Press, 1991) (edited, with T.D. Willett).
5. *The Centralisation of Western Europe* (Institute of Economic Affairs, London, Hobart Papers, 1995).
6. *Political Competition, Innovation and Growth: A Historical Analysis* (Springer, 1998) (edited, with P. Bernholz and M.E. Streit).

Articles
1. "Real exchange-rate changes in the European Community: A new approach to the determination of optimum currency areas." *Journal of International Economics*, 8(May):1978.
2. "The return to the New European Monetary System." *Monetary Institutions and the Policy Process* (Carnegie-Rochester Series on Public Policy, 13, North Holland, 1980) (edited by K. Brunner, A.H. Meltzer).
3. "Coordination or competition among national macroeconomic policies?" *Reflections on a Troubled World Economy* (Macmillan, 1983) (edited by F. Machlup, G. Fels, H. Müller-Groeling).
4. "Competing currencies: the case for free entry." *The Search for Stable Money* (University of Chicago Press, 1987) (edited by J.A. Dorn, A. Schwartz).
5. "A public-choice approach to international organization." *Public Choice*, 51:1986.
6. "Currency competition and European monetary integration." *Economic Journal*, 100(September): 1990 (reprinted in P. de Grauwe (ed.) *The Political Economy of Monetary Union*, The International

Library of Critical Writings in Economics, 134, Edward Elgar Publishing, 2001).
7. "The political economy of the International Monetary Fund: A public choice analysis," *The Political Economy of International Organizations*, (Westview Press, 1991) (edited by R. Vaubel, T.D. Willett).
8. "The political economy of centralization and the European Community." *Public Choice*, 81:1994.
9. "Constitutional safeguards against centralization in federal states: an international cross-section analysis." *Constitutional Political Economy*, 7:1996.
10. "The bureaucratic and partisan behavior of independent central banks." *European Journal of Political Economy*, 13:1997.

Principal Contributions
The main theme of Roland Vaubel's research has been interjurisdictional competition among policy makers and its opposite, the coordination and centralisation of economic policies through international organizations and political integration. Inspired by F.A. Hayek, Vaubel's initial focus was on the efficiency of competition in the field of monetary policy. Later on, he turned to public-choice explanations of political centralization and international organization. The last few years have been devoted to the comparative analysis of constitutional provisions to preserve interjurisdictional competition in federal states and in the European Union. (For a complete list of his publications and further details see www.vwl.uni-mannheim.de/vaubel).

WAGNER, Richard E.

Born
28 April 1941, Jamestown, North Dakota, USA

Current Positions
Senior Fellow and Chairman of Academic Advisory Board, Public Interest Institute, 1995–; Holbert L. Harris Professor of Economics, George Mason University, 1988–.

Past Positions
Professor of Economics, Florida State University, 1981–1988; Professor of Economics, Auburn University, 1979–1981; Professor of Economics, Virginia Polytechnic Institute and State University, 1975–1979; Associate Professor of Economics, Virginia Polytechnic Institute and State University, 1973–1975; Senior Research Associate, The Urban Institute, 1972–1973; Associate Professor of Economics, Tulane University, 1968–1972; Assistant Professor of Economics, University of California, Irvine, 1966–1968.

Degrees
B.S., University of Southern California, 1963; Ph.D., University of Virginia, 1966.

Offices and Honors
Listed in *The Templeton Honor Roll for Education in a Free Society.*
Listed in *Who's Who in America.*

Editorial Duties
Book Review Editor, *Public Choice, 1974–1978;* Editor, *Constitutional Political Economy*, 1989–1997.

Principal Fields of Interest
Catallactical Public Finance; Institutional Political Economy; Spontaneous Order Macroeconomics.

Selected Publications
Books
1. *The Public Economy* (Chicago: Markham, 1973).
2. *Democracy in Deficit: The Political Legacy of Lord Keynes* (Academic Press, 1977) (with James M. Buchanan).
3. *Inheritance and the State: Tax Principles for a Free and Prosperous Commonwealth* (American Enterprise Institute, 1977).
4. *Public Finance: Revenues and Expenditures in a Democratic Society* (Little, Brown, 1983).
5. *Public Choice and Constitutional Economics* (JAI press, 1988) (edited, with James D. Gwartney).
6. *To Promote The General Welfare: Market Processes vs. Political Transfers* (Pacific Research Institute, 1989).
7. *The Economics of Smoking* (Kluwer Nijhoff, 1991) (with Robert D. Tollison).
8. *Charging for Government: User Charges and Earmarked Taxes in Principle and Practice* (Routledge, 1991).
9. *Trade Protection in the United States* (Edward Elgar Publishing, 1995) (with Charles K. Rowley and Willem Thorbecke).
10. *Federalist Government in Principle and Practice* (Kluwer Academic Publishers, 2001) (edited, with Donald P. Racheter).

Articles
1. "Revenue structure, fiscal illusion, and budgetary choice." *Public Choice*, 25 (Spring):1976.

2. "Wagner's Law, fiscal institutions, and the growth of government." *National Tax Journal* 30(March):1977 (with Warren E. Weber).
3. "Economic manipulation for political profit: macroeconomic consequences and constitutional implications." *Kyklos*, 30 (3):1977.
4. "The cameralists: a public choice perspective." *Public Choice*, 53 (1):1987 (with Jürgen Backhaus).
5. "*The calculus of consent*: a Wicksellian retrospective." *Public Choice*, 56(February):1988.
6. "Romance, realism, and economic reform" *Kyklos*, 44 (1):1991 (with Robert D. Tollison).
7. "Grazing the budgetary commons: the rational politics of budgetary irresponsibility." *Journal of Law and Politics*, 9 (Fall):1992.
8. "Crafting social rules: Common Law vs. Statute Law, once again." *Constitutional Political Economy* 3(Fall):1992.
9. "Austrian cycle theory: saving the wheat while discarding the chaff." *Review of Austrian Economics*, 12(1):1999.
10. "Complexity, governance, and constitutional craftsmanship." *American Journal of Economics and Sociology* 61(January):2002.

Principal Contributions
While Richard Wagner's work has treated a large number of particular topics, most of it has pursued the vision that economic phenomena within a society are emergent and not choice-theoretic phenomena, which in turn generates both spontaneous order and unintended consequences. This overall theme has been pursued mainly with respect to three topic areas: public finance, political economy, and macroeconomics. His work in public finance has pursued the argument that fiscal phenomena in democratic polities do not reflect some ruler's maximizing or minimizing choices, but rather reflect some combination of exchange and domination, with the mixture between the two being governed by the framework of fiscal and political institutions in place. His work in political economy has been animated by the classical recognition that morality is habit that is formed through practice, whether for good or for bad. Public policy is thus a constitutive enterprise because of the learning through institutionalized practice that takes place. His work on macroeconomics similarly treats macro phenomena as emerging through complex interaction among market participants. Where a Robinson Crusoe will face numerous exogenous shocks, the aggregation of Crusoes that we call a society will face almost none. Rather, societies face a continual clashing among intentions and plans. On occasion, Wagner has referred to this vision as systemic or emergent macroeconomics. (For further elaboration, see my home page at *www.mason.gmu.edu/~rwagner*.)

WECK-HANNEMANN, Hannelore

Born
August 2, 1954, Ravensburg, Germany

Current Positions
Professor of Political Economy, University of Innsbruck, Austria, 1994–; Lecturer at the University of Zurich, Switzerland, 1990–.

Past Positions
Professor of Economics/Public Finance, Humboldt-University of Berlin, 1994; Associate Professor, Swiss Federal Institute of Technology (ETH) in Zürich, 1992–1994; Assistant Professor, Research Program of the Deutsche Forschungsgemeinschaft (DFG), University of Constance, 1987–1992; Fellow at the Wissenschaftskolleg of Berlin, 1984–1985; Assistant Professor of the Swiss National Foundation at the University of Zurich, 1982–1984 and 1985–1987; Research Assistant, University of Zurich, 1978–1982; Research Assistant at the Wissenschaftszentrum Berlin (WZB), 1977–1978.

Degrees
Master of Economics (lic.rer.soc.), University of Constance (Germany), 1977; Ph.D. (Dr.oec.publ.), University of Zurich (Switzerland), 1982; Dr.habil. University of Zurich (Switzerland), 1990.

Offices and Honors
Member, Research Council, European University Institute, Florence/Italy, 1994–2000.
Member, Board, Austrian Economic Association, 1995–.
Member, Board, European Public Choice Society, 1997–2000.
Member, Board (Kuratorium/Rat), Austrian College/European Forum Alpbach, 1998–
Member, Austrian Accreditation Council, 2000–2007.
Vicepresident, Austrian Accreditation Council, 2002–.

Editorial Duties
Member of the Editorial Board, *Public Choice*, 1992–; Member of the Editorial Board, *Perspektiven der*

Wirtschaftspolitik, 1998–; Member of the Editorial Board, *Public Finance and Management* (electronic journal), 1998–.

Principal Fields of Interest
Public Choice; Public Finance; Environmental Economics; Experimental Economics.

Selected Publications
Books
1. *Schattenwirtschaft: Eine Möglichkeit zur Einschränkung der öffentlichen Verwaltung? Eine ökonomische Analyse.* (Peter Lang, 1983).
2. *Schattenwirtschaft* (Franz Vahlen, 1984) (with W.W. Pommerehne and B.S. Frey).
3. *Die heimliche Wirtschaft. Struktur und Entwicklung der Schattenwirtschaft in der Schweiz.* (Paul Haupt, 1986) (with W.W. Pommerehne and B.S. Frey).
4. *Politische Ökonomie des Protektionismus. Eine institutionelle und empirische Analyse.* (Campus, Frankfurt/New York, 1992).
5. *Global Environmental Change in Alpine Regions. Recognition, Impact, Adaptation and Mitigation.* (Edward Elgar Publishing, 2002) (edited, with K. Steininger).

Articles
1. "What produces a hidden economy? an international cross section analysis," *Southern Economic Journal*, 118(3): 1982 (with B.S. Frey).
2. "A statistical study of the effect of the great depression on elections: the Weimar Republic, 1930–1933," *Political Behavior*, 5(4): 1983 (with B.S. Frey).
3. "The hidden economy as an "Unobserved" Variable," *European Economic Review*, 26: 1984 (with B.S. Frey).
4. "Protectionism in direct democracy," *Journal of Institutional and Theoretical Economics*, 146(3): 1990.
5. "Determinants of foreign aid under alternative institutional arrangements," (with F. Schneider) R. Vaubel and T.D. Willett *The Political Economy of International Organizations* (Westview Press, 1991).
6. "The Contribution of Public Choice Theory to International Political Economy," (with B.S. Frey) in C. Polychroniou (ed.) *Perspectives and Issues in International Political Economy* (Praeger 1992).
7. "Are incentive instruments as good as economists believe? some new considerations," (with B.S. Frey) in L. Bovenberg and S. Cnossen (eds.) *Public Economics and the Environment in an Imperfect World* (Kluwer Academic Publishers, 1995).
8. "Tax rates, tax administration and income tax evasion in Switzerland." *Public Choice*, 88(1–2): 1996 (with W.W. Pommerehne).
9. "Do people care about democracy? an experiment exploring the value of voting rights." *Public Choice*, 91(1): 1997 (with W. Güth).
10. "Globalization as a challenge for Public Choice Theory." *Public Choice*, 106(1–2): 2001.
11. "Pricing road use: politico-economic and fairness considerations." *Transportation Research D: Transport and Environment*, forthcoming, 2002 (with F. Oberholzer-Gee).

Principal Contributions
The cooperation with Bruno S. Frey and his co-workers at the University of Constance and Zurich was decisive for Hannelore Weck-Hannemann's interest in public choice and the economic analysis of human behavior at the borders of economics from the beginning of her studies and her academic career. Main topics she has focused on are politico-economic modeling, explaining tax evasion and the shadow economy, the political economics of protectionism and environmental policy. Her interest in ongoing work concentrates on the analysis of non-market decision-making in politics and in the family, as well as in empirical and experimental economics. A major concern these days is also individual and collective decision-making under risk and the focus on new instruments in natural hazard management and the chances for implementation.

WILLETT, Thomas Dunaway

Born
November 15, 1942, Staunton, Virginia, USA

Current Positions
Director, The Claremont Institute for Economic Policy Studies, Claremont Colleges, Claremont, CA, January 1983–; Horton Professor of Economics, Claremont Graduate University and Claremont McKenna College, September 1977–.

Past Positions
Director of Research and Senior Advisor for International Economic Affairs; Director of International Monetary Research, U.S. Treasury, July 1975–August 1977; Deputy Assistant Secretary of the Treasury for International Affairs — Research, December 1972–July 1975; Professor, Associate Professor of Economics and Public Affairs, Graduate School of Business and Public Administration, Cornell University, 1970–1972; Senior Staff Economist, Council of Economic Advisors, 1969–1970, on leave from

Harvard University; Assistant Professor of Economics, Harvard University, 1967–1970.

Degrees
B.A., College of William and Mary, 1964; Ph.D., University of Virginia, 1967.

Editorial Duties
Economics Editor, *Public Policy*, 1969–1972; Co-Editor, *Economic Inquiry*, 1989–1996; Series Editor, *The Political Economy of Global Interdependence*, Westview Press. 1991–2001.

Principal Fields of Interest
Comparative and International Political Economy; International Money and Finance; Public Choice.

Selected Publications
Books
1. *U.S. Balance-of-Payments Policies and International Monetary Reform* (American Enterprise Institute for Public Policy Research, 1968) (with Gottfried Haberler).
2. *The Theory of Optimum Currency Areas and Exchange Rate Flexibility*, Princeton Special Papers in International Finance, 11 (May):1976 (with Edward Tower).
3. *The Economic Approach to Public Policy* (Cornell University Press, 1976) (edited, with Ryan C. Amacher and Robert Tollison).
4. *Floating Exchange Rates and International Monetary Reform* (American Enterprise Institute for Public Policy Research, 1977).
5. *International Liquidity Issues* (American Enterprise Institute for Public Policy Research, 1980) (sponsored by American Enterprise Institute and Joint Economic Committee Special Study on Economic Change).
6. *Political Business Cycles: The Political Economy of Money, Inflation, and Unemployment* (ed.) (Duke University Press for the Pacific Research Institute, 1988).
7. *International Trade Policies: The Gains from Exchange Between Economics and Political Science* (Proceedings of the Ford Foundation-funded, Claremont-U.S.C. conference on international political economy held in March 1987), (University of Michigan Press, 1990) (edited, with John Odell).
8. *The Political Economy of International Organizations: A Public Choice Perspective* (Westview Press, 1991) (edited, with Roland Vaubel).
9. *Establishing Monetary Stability in Emerging Market Economies* (Westview Press, 1995) (edited, with Richard Burdekin, Richard Sweeney, and Clas Wihlborg).
10. *Exchange Rate Policies for Emerging Market Economies* (Westview Press, 1999) (edited, with Richard Sweeney and Clas Wihlborg).

Articles
1. "International specie flows and American monetary stability: 1834–1960." *Journal of Economic History*, March:1968.
2. "Interest-rate policy and external balance." *Quarterly Journal of Economics*, May:1969 (with Francesco Forte).
3. "A note on the relation between the rate and predictability of inflation." *Economica*, May:1976 (with Dennis Logue).
4. "An economic Theory of Mutually Advantageous Issue Linkages in International Negotiations." *International Organization*, Autumn:1979 (with Robert Tollison).
5. "Presidential politics, budget deficits, and monetary policy in the United States:1960–1976." *Public Choice*, 40(1):1983 (with Leroy O. Laney).
6. "Incremental protection and efficient political choice between tariffs and quotas." *Canadian Journal of Economics*, May:1989 (with William H. Kaempfer and J. Harold McClure, Jr.).
7. "Inflation uncertainty and the optimal inflation tax." *Kredit und Kapital*, 1994, Heftl; (with King Banaian and J. Harold McClure, Jr.).
8. "International financial markets as sources of crisis or discipline: the too much, too late hypothesis." *Princeton Essays in International Finance*, (May: 2000).
9. "Upping the ante for political economy analysis of international financial institutions." *The World Economy*, March:2001.
10. "Truth in advertising and the great dollarization scam." *Journal of Policy Modeling* 23 (April):2001.

Principal Contributions
Thomas Willett's early work covered a wide range of areas in applied microeconomics, public choice, international economies, and the analysis of micro and macroeconomic policy issues. Starting in the 1980s, much of his work turned to public choice analyses of monetary and international economic policies and the integration of this with the work of political scientists on comparative and international political economy. His recent research has focused

on two interested areas. One is a range of international monetary and financial issues including the behavior of international capital flows, currency crises, optimum currency area theory and the analysis of alternative exchange rate regimes and reform of the international financial system. A major focus of a good bit of this research is the need to take political economy considerations into account. The second area is explicit public choice or political economy analysis of different possible methods of fostering monetary discipline such as central bank independence, fixed exchange rates, financial integration, and the policy conditionality program of the International Monetary Fund.

WILLIAMS, Walter E.

Born
March 31, 1936, Philadelphia, Pennsylvania, USA

Current Position
John M. Olin Distinguished Professor of Economics, George Mason University.

Past Positions
Professor of Economics, George Mason University, 1980–present, Economics Department Chairman 1995–2001, Associate Professor of Economics, Temple University 1973–1980, Senior Research, Urban Institute, 1971–1973, Assistant Professor of Economics, California State University, Los Angeles, 1967–1971, Instructor, Los Angeles City College, Los Angeles, 1967–1969, Group Supervisor, Los Angeles County Probation Department, 1963–1967.

Degrees
B.A., California State University, Los Angeles, 1965; M.A., Ph.D., University of California Los Angeles, 1967, 1972.

Offices and Honors
Member, Mont Pelerin Society.
National Service Award 1980 (Institute for Socioeconomic Studies).
George Washington Medal of Honor 1983 (Freedoms Foundation).
Doctor of Humane Letters, Virginia Union University, 1984.
Faculty Member of the Year (1984–1985).
California State University 1987 Distinguished Alumnus Award.
Los Angeles City Commendation Award 1987.
Adam Smith Award, Association of Private Enterprise Education (1989).
Doctor of Humane Letters, *Honoris Causa*, Grove City College.
Veterans of Foreign Wars of the U.S. News Media Award (1993).
Doctor of Laws, *Honoris Causa*, Washington & Jefferson College.

Principle Field of Interest
Labor Economics, Regulation and Law and Economics.

Selected Publications
Books
1. *The State Against Blacks* (McGraw-Hill, 1982).
2. *South Africa's War Against Capitalism* (Praeger, 1989).

Articles
1. "Political decentralization." *American Economic Review*, May: 1971.
2. "Why the poor pay more: an alternative explanation." *Social Science Quarterly*, September: 1973.
3. "Some hard questions on minority businesses." *Negro Educational Review*, April/July: 1974.
4. "Racial price discrimination: a note." *Economic Inquiry*, January: 1977.
5. "Racial price discrimination: a further note." *Economic Inquiry*, July: 1978.
6. "Legal restriction on black progress." *Howard University Law Journal* January: 1978.
7. "Male-female earnings differentials: a critical reappraisal." (with Walter Block) *The Journal of Labor Research*, II(2): 1981.
8. "Good intentions-bad results: the economy pastoral—and America's disadvantaged." *Notre Dame Journal of Law, Ethics & Public Policy*, II (1): 1985.
9. "Why urban problems persist." *Southern California Law Review*, 66 (4): 1993.
10. "The economics of the colour bar." *Journal of Labor Research*, Spring: 1997.

Principle Contributions
Walter Williams has made economic principles accessible and understandable to literally millions upon millions of Americans through his 20-plus years syndicated column and his syndicated radio appearances to a worldwide audience of over 20 million listeners, and as economic commentator on numerous television programs.

WINER, Stanley Lewis

Born
November 29, 1947, Toronto, Canada

Current Positions
Canada Research Chair Professor in Public Policy, School of Public Policy and Administration and Department of Economics, Carleton University, Ottawa, Canada, 2001–.

Past Positions
Lecturer in Political Economy, Policy Studies Program, Department of Political Science, Hebrew University of Jerusalem, April–May 2002; Cross Appointment, Professor, Department of Economics and School of Public Policy and Administration, Carleton University, 1999 — Visiting Research Fellow, Statistics Canada, Ottawa, 1997–2000; Lecturer in Taxation, Ministry of Finance, Hanoi, August 1999, November 1999, May 2000, July 2000, May 2001; Visiting Professor, Départements de sciences économiques and Centre de recherche et developpement en economique, University of Montreal, Fall 1996; Visiting Fellow, Director's Section, Research School of the Social Sciences, Australian National University, May — August 1996; Lecturer in Microeconomics, Local Government Program, Department of Political Science, University of Western Ontario, Fall 1990; Lecturer in Microeconomics and cost-benefit Analysis, Institute of Public Administration, Renmin University, Beijing, Summer 1990; Professor, School of Public Administration, Carleton University, 1988–2001; Visiting Associate Professor, Graduate School of Industrial Administration, Carnegie-Mellon University, 1982–1983; Associate Professor, School of Public Administration, 1981–1988; Assistant Professor, Department of Economics, Carleton University, 1976–1978; Research Economist, Economic Council of Canada, 1975–1976.

Degrees
B.A., Carleton University 1971; M.A., Ph.D., Johns Hopkins University, 1973, 1975.

Offices and Honors
Carleton University Stitt and Linch Scholarships 1967 and 1969.
Canada Council Doctoral Fellowship, 1972–1975.
Merit Award, Carleton University, 1981.
Social Sciences and Humanities Research Council (of Canada) Leave Fellowship,1982–1983.
Scholarly Achievement Award, Carleton University, 1985.
Scholarly Achievement Award, Carleton University, 1986.
Supervisor, Doctoral Program in Public Policy, School of Public Administration, 1991–1996.
Research Achievement Award, Carleton University, 1998–1999.
Canada Research Chair, Tier I, July 2001.
Member, Canada Research Chairs College of Reviewers, 2001–.
Elected Executive Vice-President, International Institute of Public Finance, 2002–2005.

Editorial Duties
Editorial Board, *Carleton Library Series* (McGill-Queens University Press), 2000–2003; Guest Editor, *International Tax and Public Finance* volume 9(4), August 2002; Chair of scientific committee, 57th Congress of the International Institute of Public Finance, Linz, Austria, August 27–30, 2001.

Principal Fields of Interest
Public Economics, Collective Choice; Applied Microeconomics; Applied Econometrics.

Selected Publications
Books
1. *Internal Migration and Fiscal Structure: An Econometric Study of the Determinants of Inter-Provincial Migration in Canada* (Ottawa: Economic Council of Canada, 1982) (with Denis Gauthier).
2. *Knocking on the Back Door: Canadian Perspectives on the Political Economy of Freer Trade with the United States.* (Institute for Research on Public Policy, 1987) (edited, with Allan Maslove).
3. *Democratic Choice and Taxation: A Theoretical and Empirical Analysis* (Cambridge University Press, 1999) (with Walter Hettich).
4. *Political Economy in Federal States: Selected Essays of Stanley L. Winer* (Edward Elgar Publishing, 2002).
5. *Political Economy and Public Finance: The Role of Political Economy in the Theory and Practice of Public Economics* (Edward Elgar Publishing, 2002) (edited, with Hirofumi Shibata).

Articles
1. "Optimal fiscal illusion and the size of government." *Public Choice*, 35:1980 (with E.G. West).
2. "Some evidence on the effect of the separation of spending and taxing decisions." *Journal of Political Economy*, 9 (February):1983.

3. "A positive model of tax structure." *Journal of Public Economics*, 24:1984 (with Walter Hettich).
4. "Money and politics in a small open economy." *Public Choice*, 51:1986.
5. "The role of exchange rate flexibility in the international transmission of inflation in long and shorter runs: Canada 1953 to 1981." *Canadian Journal of Economics*, 19:1986.
6. "Economic and political foundations of tax structure." *American Economic Review*, 78 (September):1988 (with Walter Hettich).
7. "Debt and tariffs: an empirical investigation of the evolution of revenue systems." *Journal of Public Economics*, 45:1991 (with Walter Hettich).
8. "The complexity of tax structure in competitive political systems." *International Tax and Public Finance*, 5: 1998 (with George Warskett and Walter Hettich).
9. "Political influence, economic interests and endogenous tax structure in a computable equilibrium framework: with application to the united states, 1973 and 1983." *Public Choice* 109(1):2001 (with Louis Hotte).
10. "Tinpots, totalitarians (and democrats): an empirical investigation of the effects of economic growth on civil liberties and political rights." *Public Choice*, forthcoming 2003 (with Muhammed Islam).

Principal Contributions
Stanley Winer's early work is on the econometrics of macroeconomic policy in small, open federal economies under alternative exchange regimes. This led to research on the role of the exchange rate in the transmission of inflation from the United States to Canada, and on the role of the exchange regime in determining the link between monetary growth and politics in Canada. In other work, a long-standing interest in the political economy of federalism led him to study policy-induced internal migration, and the effects of intergovernmental grants. The latter research involved one of the first empirical applications of the median voter model in Canada. During the early 1980's, Winer began to work with Walter Hettich developing models of fiscal systems as a whole. Irwin Gillespie was also working on related matters at Carleton. They began to move away from the median voter model in order to deal with the complexity of actual fiscal structures. A longstanding and still ongoing collaboration with Hettich lead to a systematic treatment of the major positive and normative aspects of tax systems based on probabilistic voting, work that culminated in their 1999 book *Democratic Choice and Taxation*. This included computable general equilibrium applications developed with Thomas Rutherford. Most recently, *Democratic Choice and Taxation* has provided the basis for joint work with Stephen Ferris on time series models of the evolution of permanent and transitory components of fiscal systems, and for research with Lawrence Kenny on the pattern of tax systems in the world as a whole.

WITTMAN, Donald Alan

Born
April 11, 1942

Current Position
Professor of Economics, University of California, Santa Cruz, 1980–.

Past Positions
Associate Professor of Economics, University of California, Santa Cruz, 1976–1980; Assistant Professor of Political Science, University of Chicago, 1974–1976; Assistant Professor of Economics, University of California, Santa Cruz, 1969–1974.

Degrees
B.A., University of Michigan, 1964; M.A., Ph.D., University of California at Berkeley, 1966, 1970.

Editorial Duties
Economics of Governance, 1997–.

Principal Fields of Interest
Politics, Law, Microeconomic Theory.

Selected Publications
Books
1. *The Federalist Papers: The New Institutionalism and the Old*, (Agathon Press, 1989) (edited, with B. Grofman).
2. *The Myth of Democratic Failure: Why Political Institutions are Efficient* (University of Chicago Press, 1995). "American Political Science Association: Best Book or Article in Political Economy–1994, 1995 or 1996." Translated into Portuguese by Alvaro de Sa and Renata Eugenia Alves de Lima *O Mito do Fracasso da Democracia* (Bertrand Brasil, 1999) (Japanese version (Forthcoming).
3. *Economic Analysis of Law: Selected Readings* (ed.) (Blackwell Publishers, Forthcoming).

Articles
1. "Candidates with policy preferences: a dynamic model." *Journal of Economic Theory*, 1977.

2. "How a war ends." *Journal of Conflict Resolution*, 1979.
3. "Efficient rules of thumb in highway safety and sporting activity." *American Economic Review*, 1982.
4. "Candidate motivation: a synthesis." *American Political Science Review*, 1983.
5. "Multicandidate equilibria." *Public Choice*, 1985.
6. "Arms control and other games involving imperfect detection." *American Political Science Review*, 1989.
7. "Pressure group size and the politics of income redistribution." *Social Choice and Welfare*, 1989.
8. "Why democracies are efficient." *Journal of Political Economy*, 1989 (reprinted in C. Rowley (ed.) *Public Choice Theory*, Edward Elgar Publishers, 1993).
9. "Why voters vote for incumbents but against incumbency: a rational choice explanation." *Journal of Public Economics*, 1995 (with D. Friedman).
10. "The size and wealth of nations." *Journal of Conflict Resolution*, 2000.

WU, Wenbo

Born
August 23, 1968, Lishui, Zhejiang Province, P.R. China

Current Position
Assistant Professor of Public Policy, National University of Singapore, Republic of Singapore, 1999–.

Degrees
B.S., Peking University, 1990; M.S., Peking University, 1993; Ph.D., Carnegie Mellon University, 1999.

Principal Fields of Interest
Public Choice; Economics and Public Policy.

Selected Publications
1. "Policies for green design." *Journal of Environmental Economics and Management*, 36:1998 (with Don Fullerton).
2. "The two freedoms, economic growth and development: an empirical study." *Public Choice*, 100(1/2):1999 (with Otto Davis).
3. "The two freedoms in a growth model." *Journal of Private Enterprise*, XIV(2):1999 (with Otto Davis).

Principal Contributions
Wenbo Wu's academic interests are inspired by dramatic transformations occurring in China. He regards the transition fundamentally as changes in degrees of freedom. Through his empirical analyses on the simultaneous relationships among economic freedom, political freedom, and economic development, he is able to demonstrate that economic freedom is important in promoting economic growth and that political freedom is related to economic development.

INDEX

Note: Page numbers in **bold** type indicate individual articles and biographies

abrogative custom 226
absolutism 80, 88
abstention 238
    rational 110, 207, 231–2
academia 105
accountability 71, 73–5, 216
Adam, M. C. 291
adaptation 114
adaptive expectations 152, 153, 155
    inflation 160
adverse selection 253
advertising 12
affective bonds 124
agency problems 10, 217
    and political dilemma 220
    common 100
    minimization of 214
agenda-setting 218
agent-principal problem 199
aggregation preference 39
agriculture 132, 136
aid to dictators 85–6
airlines 274–5
Albert, Hans 235, 246, 249
Alchian, A. 62, 106
Aldrich, J. H. 6, **327**
Alesina, A. 160
alignment theorem 227
alliances 124, 140
allocation of resources 36, 63, 222, 252
    improving 185
    optimal 183
    scarce 61, 265
all-pay auctions 100, 120
Althusius, J. 64
altruism 119, 192
ambition 112
amenities 257
American Association of Retired Persons 212
American Economic Association 149, 155
American Medical Association 148
American Political Science Association 323
American Sociological Association 247
amoral behavior 112
anarchy 82, 142
Anderson, G. M. 143, 196, 197, 274
Anderson, L. R. **328**
Andreoni, J. 286
Andvig, J. C. 67
anticorruption 70, 72, 74
anti-dumping duties 133, 134
anti-Semitism 148
antitrust, regulation and **263–83**
"any leader" rule 25
apples 265
Aranson, P. H. 6, 7, 322
arbitrariness 72
Arendt, Hannah 235

Argentina 70
Aristotle 305, 307, 308
Armentano, D. T. 278
Arrow, Kenneth J. 3. 4, 5, 9, 24, 34, 35, 37, 140, 146, 158, 203, 204, 205, 217, 296, 308
    insight 204
Arrow paradox 36
articulation 230
Asea, P. K. 292
Ashworth, J. 181
asset diversification 132, 316
auctions 16, 132
    all-pay 100, 120
    menu 121
Aumann, R. 119
Austen-Smith, D. 6, 122, 123, 124
Australia 181
Austria 141, 148, 289
autocracy 80, 81, 84, 115, 207
    corrupt 69
    overthrown 82
autonomous individuals 64, 65

bads 10, 14, 61, 65
Baker, P. J. 181
balance of payments 52, 54
Ball, L. 168
bankers or peasants controversy 53
banking system deregulation 155
bankruptcies 275
Banks, J. S. 123
Bardhan, Pranab 67, 292
bargaining 21, 111, 174, 215, 217, 290
    Coasian 218, 220, 223
    failures, free riding and 219–20
    framework for 217
    legislative 121
    power 68, 71, 198
    strategic 209
Barr, J. 306
barriers to entry 94, 272, 274, 293
Barro, R. 81, 83, 85, 88, 160, 161, 166
Barry, N. 237
Baumol, W. J. 91, 268, 276, **328–9**
Bavetta, S. **329–30**
Becker, G. S. 7, 8, 14, 83, 106, 120, 121
bedrock theory 49
bees 25, 265
beggar-thy-neighbor policy 130
behavioral analysis 205
Belgium 287, 291
benefits 130, 205
    defense 25
    dispersed 5
    expected 112, 207
    hydrodynamic 25
    marginal 55, 92, 112
    political 134

benefits *contd.*
  scarce 68
  selective 212
  social 134
  trade-off 92
Bennedsen, M. 123
Bennett, J. T. **330**
Benson, B. L. 228, **330–2**
Bentham, Jeremy 64, 113, 204
Bergemann, D. 121
Berl, J. 101
Berlin, Sir Isaiah 157
Bernheim, B. D. 121
Bernholz, Peter 79–80, 142, 217, 301, 302, **332–3**
Bernstein, L. 230
Besley, T. J. 124, **334–5**
Besocke, P. D. **335**
Bhansali, R. J. 50
bias 64
  ideological 20
  inflation 160, 162, 163, 164, 166
  stabilization 161–4
bicameralism 13, 211
bidders 195
  disappointed 72
  highest 68
bifurcation 83
Bill of Rights 13, 73
binding contracts 303, 304
bio-economics 25, 106, 114
Black, Duncan 3, 4, 9, 12, 14, 34, 43, 105, 110, 177, 201–2, 203–4, 204–5, 309
  insights 203–4
black box theory 11, 120, 121, 198
blacks 82
Blacksburg 110, 141–3
Bloom, H. S. 56
"blue" dividend 94
Boadway, R. 173
Board of Trade (UK) 277
Boettke, P. J. 335–6
Bolivia 49
booms 153
Borcherding, T. E. 141, 336–7
Borda, Jean-Charles de 32, 34, 202–3
Borda-count rule 34
border officials 136
Bornstein, G. 99
Borooah, V. 119
Bosman, R. 101
Bottomore, T. B. 118
Boudon, R. 247
bounded rationality 10, 101, 265
Bovenberg, A. L. 94
Bowen, H. R. 34
Bradbury, J. C. **337–8**
Brams, S. J. **338–9**
Breit, W. 156
Brennan, H. G. 24, 141, 142, 143, 239
Breton, A. 39
bribery 67, 71–2, 73, 74, 75, 218, 291, 293
  impeachment for 222
  incentives and consequences of 68–70
Britain see United Kingdom

brokerage fees 16, 17, 20
  and wealth transfers 17
brokerage function 115
Brown, Pam 143
Brzezinski, Z. 77
Buchanan, James M. 4, 5, 6, 9, 23, 24, 25, 34, 35, 91, 106, 115, **139–45**, 149, 153, 173, 185, 211, 212, 221, 230, 236, 238, 240, 244, 246, 275, 284, 301, **339–40**
  insight 207–11
budget constraint 93
budget deficits 52, 54, 153, 259
  perennial 142
budget restraint 182, 183
budgets
  artificially fixed 78
  dictator's 87
  maximization 21
Bueno de Mesquita, B. 321
Bundesbank 167
"bundled" choice 140
bureaucracy 20–3, 93, 112–13, 198–9
  biased 124
  demand-revealing 115
  economic analysis of 112
  legislative control of 123
Burgess, Jo Ann 143
Burns, Arthur F. 147, 148, 150, 153
Bush, G. W. 197
Bush, Winston 141, 142
business cycles 153, 154, 156
  political 39–40, 52, 91, 160–1
Butler, E. 156

Cain, M J. G. **340–1**
Cairns, R. 120
Caldwell, M. 198
California Institute of Technology 101
Calvo, G. 165
Cambodia 82
campaign contributions 17, 123, 124, 132, 273
  common agency models of 121–2
  manipulating voters' preferences 213
  support models of 120
campaign expenditures 12
Canada 42, 181, 182, 316
  indirect taxes 289
capacity utilization 268, 275
capital 266, 293
  accumulation 83
  ownership of 306
  social 55
  stock 83
capital gains 175, 179, 257
capital-intensive firms 274
capital markets 132
capitalism 83, 148
  bleak future for 146
Caplan, B. D. **341**
cartels 134, 135–6
cash-flow tax 258–9
Cason, T. 99
Castro, Fidel 77, 87

Celler-Kefauver Act (US 1950) 277
censorship 84
Central America 136
Central and Eastern Europe 69–70, 72, 291, 293
central banks 156
 monetary policy and **159–72**
central planning 306
central rationality precept 65
certainty 236
Chamberlin, Edward 150
chaos 70, 207
charity 110
Charlottesville 140–1
Charney, J. I. 226–7
Chernick, H. 181
Chicago School 7–9, 10, 14, 15, 16, 93, 113, 147–8, 149, 150, 151, 153–4, 155, 285
child labor 318, 319
Chile 81, 83
China 15, 86, 87, 105, 110
 waste and corruption 70
civil law 221
civil service pay 72–3
Clarida, R. 166
Clark, John Maurice 148
Clarke, E. H. 38
Clayton Act (US 1914) 277, 278
Clinton, Bill 219
coalitions 17, 40
 formal, instability of 111
 inconsistent 56
 logrolling 211
 majority 217, 218
 minority 56, 206
 supportive 124
 unstable 41
 see also winning coalitions
Coase, Ronald H. 9, 91, 106, 113, 149, 222, 246, 249
Coase theorem 41, 218, 219, 265, 296, 303–4
Coate, S. 93, 124
coercion 185
 limiting 174
 made possible by majority rule 177
 state 64
 structural 123
 under majority rule 184
 ways to reduce 174
Coggins, J. 120
cognitive psychology 250
cointegration 52
Coleman, J. S. 247, 249, 250
collective action 65, 109, 112, 132, 213
 expected costs of most efficient form of 208
 logic of 35, 212, 285
 making decisions through 108
 potential 209–10
 problems in customary legal regimes 232
 rational choice approach to analysis of 213
 rational individual will not endorse 209
collective choice 61, 62, 108, 183–4
 entrustment of decision-making to 210–11
 normative analysis and **173–91**
collective decision-making 62, 174, 211, 220, 253
 arbitrary or dictatorial 37

 cost minimization of 214
 individual preferences captured by 215
 indivisibility of 24
 justification for making with simple majority rule 32
 rules of 23, 63, 208, 210
collective outcomes 216
Collier, K. 101
collusion 72
Columbia University 148, 149
Colwell, Ernest 149
command and control measures 93
commitment power 238
committees 17–18
 oversight 198, 199
common agency models 121–2, 124
common law 197, 215, 276
 adversarial procedures 113
 and economics of judicial lawmaking 221–5
 rules 214
communism 77, 306
communitarianism 64, 65
comparative advantage 131, 214, 222, 274, 315
 informational 215
 international 314
 lost 133, 134
compensation 134, 256–7
competition 268, 275
 electoral 121, 178
 foreign 133, 135, 318
 freedom from 267
 groups 5, 120
 imperfect 131
 import 133, 195
 lessening of 277
 lobbyists 100
 pairwise 204
 perfect 151, 265, 266
 spatial 307
 tax 182
 two-party 38–9
 unfair 133, 135, 277
 see also political competition
competitive markets 70, 175, 246, 268
compliance 229, 232, 285
 tax 286, 289, 291
 voluntary 136
compromise 81, 118–19
computable equilibrium modeling 182–3
Comte, Auguste 245
Condorcet, Nicolas Caritat, Marquis de 32, 34
Condorcet jury theorem 32, 33
Condorcet paradox of cyclical majorities 203, 204
Condorcet winners 32, 101, 177, 204, 216, 220
conflict 227, 229
 class 63, 212
 losses from 80
 trade 136
conflicts of interests 33, 122
Congleton, Roger 80, 142, 143, 185, **341–3**
congressional dominance theory 22
consensus 23
consistency 227
constant-cost conditions 266
constitutional choice 210

constitutional democracy   107, 210, 211
    and public choice   238–41
constitutional political economy   3–31, **60–7**, 109, 238
consuetudo secundum legem   226
consumer groups   84
consumption   78, 79, 224, 254, 257
    decisions are repetitive   192
    function Keynesian   152
    permanent   152
    "princely"   82
    ratio of   152
    regimes whose rulers are uninterested in   85
    world   130
contingent protection   133–4, 314
contracts   20, 265
    legislative   194–5, 196
    performance   162
    social choice, logrolling and   **296–305**
converts   80
cooperation   62, 114, 227
    economics and   63
    evolutionary theories of   225
    gains from   99
    no efficiency gain to be made from   98
    voluntary   210
Cooter, R. D.   216, 218, 219, 220–1, 223, 225, 227
Corn Laws, Repeal of (England 19th c.)
corruption   **67–76**, 285
    and shadow economy   290, 292–3
    gains from   136
    judges   194
Cosa Nostra, La   16
cost-benefit analysis   224
cost curves   266, 268
cost minimization   224
costs
    administrative   179
    agency   225
    avoidance   94
    deadweight   174
    decision-making   4, 23, 25, 108, 211
    direct   215
    efficiency   134, 120, 184
    environmental   131
    information   25, 55, 182, 215, 239
    labor   318
    legislation   220–1
    lobbying   122
    opportunity   109, 224
    political   179
    production   318
    reputational   228
    rulemaking   214–15
    subjective   141
    trade-off   92
    voting   207
    welfare   266–7
    see also external costs; marginal costs; transaction costs
Coughlin, P.   38, 182, 309, **343–44**
counterfactuals   182, 183, 184
Cournot duopoly model   131
Cournot equilibrium output   131
courts   195, 196, 221, 225, 230, 278
    informational advantages   215

Cowen, Tyler   143, **344**
Cox, G.   309
CPI (consumer price index)   271
Crain, W. M.   19, 141, 196, **344–6**
creativity   141
credibility   19, 80, 168
Crew, M. A.   **346–7**
crime   81, 286
Cuba   86, 87
Cukierman, A.   166
customary law   214, 215, 216
    and economics of decentralized lawmaking   225–32
customs union   315
cutbacks   70
cycles   17, 33
    economic   119
    election   52, 57
    interrelationships between   203
    macro-economic, election-related   160
    monetary   105
    normative and positive implications of existence of   32
    partisan   52
    political   18
    voting   37
    see also business cycles
cyclical social preferences
    and assignment of rights   302–3
    contracting and   299–301
    logrolling and   297–8
    negative externalities and   301–2, 303–4
cycling   32, 34, 35, 37, 39, 178
    endless   177
    potential for   204
Czechoslovakia (former)   287

Da Empoli, D.   **347–8**
D'Amato, A.   230
Darwinian selection   114, 231
Davis, D. D.   97, 98, 100
Davis, O. A.   306, 308, **348–9**
Davis, Toby   141
"deadweight triangle"   36
de Alessi, L.   276
debt   156, 179, 259
    crises   49
decision-making   297
    constitutional   24
    delegating   196
    government, logic of   205
    non-market   97
    opportunity cost of   224
    political   92, 95, 120, 217
    topdown   112
    see also collective decision-making
decision rules   155, 209, 210, 297, 303
declining industries   134
defection strategies   228, 229
defense   136
    anti-predator   25
deference   18, 224
    enhanced   20
deficit-finance   153, 154, 259–60
de Haan, J.   181

della Porta, D. 68
demand 191, 268, 270
  child labor 318
  currency 289
  derived 194
  elasticity of 268, 270
  excess 92
  money 155
  public goods 140
  reduced domestic 130
  "revelation" processes 38
  transfer 198
demand constraint 21
demand curves 265
  all-or-none 198
  downward-sloping 266
democracy
  arises out of dictatorship 82
  basic difference between dictatorship and 84
  economic theory of 205
  falsifiable theory of 4
  inefficient because dominated by interest groups 83
  justification for 33
  populist 37
  see also constitutional democracy; representative democracy
democratic inaction 81
demonstrations 84
DeMooij, R. A. 94
Demsetz, H. 245, 265
Deng Xiaoping 86
Denmark 54, 289
Denzau, A. 141, 306
depoliticization 63
deregulation 71, 274–6, 269, 272, 274–6
  banking system 155
desuteudo 226
deterrence strategy 72
developing countries 72–3
De Vroey, M. 155
Dharmapala, D. 124
dictators 36, 82
  behavior of 77–80
  benevolent 52
  fear on the part of 77
  time horizons 82
  utility maximizing 79
Dictator's Dilemma 77–9, 84, 85, 88
dictatorship **77–90**, 136, 209
Director, Rose 148, 149
  see also Friedman, R. D.
discount rate 52
discretion 68, 71, 199
  agency 23
  judicial 196
  monetary 162
discretionary power 21, 22, 92, 93, 156, 224
discrimination 136, 314, 315
  price 266, 270, 277
dishonesty 72
disloyalty 84
dispute resolution 224
distortions 94, 131
di Tella, Rafael 70

Dittmer, R. 165
diversification 132, 316, 317
dividends 257, 258
division of labor 240, 245, 249
  within legislature 17
Dixit, A. 121
Dodgson, Charles L. (Lewis Carroll) 34, 203
dogma 149
Dorussen, H. 51
Douglas, Paul 147
Down, W. 84
Downs, Anthony 3, 4, 9, 12, 35, 38, 39, 40, 99, 105, 110, 211, 284, 299, 305, 308
  insight 204–7
Drazen, A. 118
Drissen, E. 119
dumping 133
duopoly 132
Durkheim, Emile 245, 246, 250
duty 239
Duvalier, Papa Doc 81, 83, 84

East Asia 83
Easterbrook, F. H. 218
Eastern Europe see Central and Eastern Europe
Eavey, C. 101
econometrics 96
economic efficiency 62, 79, 267, 268
  under dictatorship 80–5
economic growth 78, 197, 291, 292
  enormous 86
  marginal interventions on 79
  producers benefit from 85
  spectacular 87
  under dictatorship 81
economic imperialism 244, 248–9
economic man 49, 52, 53
  see also homo oeconomicus
economics
  behavioral foundations, as a social science 249–50
  constitutional 23, 60–3
  experimental 41–2, 97–8
  institutional 18
  nonconstitutional 60–2
  positive 150–1
  public choice from the perspective of **191–201**
  sociology and 244–7, 248–9
  theodicy problem of 49
  welfare 9, 15, 23–4, 144, 252
Economic Science Association 97
economic theory 317
economic theory of regulation 272–4
  agency problem impact on 19
economies of scale 215, 268
  potential importance of 131
economies of scope 215
Edgeworth, F. Y. 174
education 317, 318
efficiency 223, 224, 254
  allocative 265, 266, 268, 270
  enhancing 255
  evolution toward 231
  free trade 130

efficiency *contd.*
  political market 211
  productive 265, 266, 270
  public sector 185
  taxation 174, 175
  see also economic efficiency
effort 134
egotropic question 53
Ehrlich, I. 224
Eisenhower, Dwight D. 24
Ekelund, R. B. **349–51**
Ekins, P. 94
Electoral College 18, 197
elementary social behavior 247
Elhauge, E. R. 219
endangered species 269
endorsements 123, 124
endowment 98
Enelow, J. M. 6, 12, 309
enemies 80
enforcement 228, 232
  compliance, weak 291
  credible 72
  legal or political 74
England 80, 316
  legal system 113
  separation of powers 196
Enlightenment 211
Enron 110
entitlements 223, 275
entrenchment 84
entrepreneurs 69, 267
  discouraged 69
entry barriers 71
environmental damage/degradation 131, 319
environmental politics **91–6**, 121
equality 254
equilibria 49, 192
  "bad" 291
  general 119, 180, 182, 184, 323
  inefficient 231
  labor market 155
  legislative 17
  long-run, zero-profit 266
  mixed 238
  multiple 69
  partial 175, 226
  political 5, 12, 19, 92–3, 111, 115, 175, 176–80, 184, 185
  political market 8, 10
  problem of establishing 178
  rational-expectations 160
  sequential 122
  simultaneous, money and power 79
  structure-induced 111
  unique 3, 309
  zero-inflation 163
  see also Nash equilibrium
Erikson, Robert S. 53
essences 144
estate tax 259
estimation problems 52
ethnic groups 77, 79, 81
EU (European Union) 54, 136, 182, 277, 316

Euclidean distance 308, 309
Europe 17, 258, 317
  natural monopolies 269
European Public Choice Society 43, 97
evolution 231
exchange rate 158
executive branch 10, 20, 194, 197–8
exile 80
exit 73, 74
expectations 22, 164, 318
  adaptive 152, 153, 155, 160
  naïve 153
  static 52–3
  stationary 56
  see also rational expectations
experimental public choice **96–104**
experts 64
exploitation of minorities 111
exports 312, 313
  restraints/restrictions on 133, 134, 135, 136
external costs 25, 91
  expected 4, 108, 208, 209, 210, 211
  lawmaking 215–16
  tradeoff between direct and 215
externalities 10, 253, 265
  beneficial 130–1, 132
  environmental 131
  free markets plagued by problems of 24
  negative 92, 301–2, 303–4
  Pareto-relevant 208, 225
  uncompensated private learning 130
extortion 72, 73, 74

factors of production 134–5
Fairfax 141, 142, 143–4
fairness 42, 254, 255, 257, 314
Faith, Roger 141
farmers 193, 195
  poor 9
fascists 157
favoritism 72
Federal Communications Commission 271
Federal Reserve System 147, 154, 156, 167
federalism 69
Fehr, E. 98
Feldmann, S. E. 123
Ferejohn, J. A. 6
Ferguson, Adam 244
Fichtenbaum, R. 291
filibusters 195
"financial paradises" 74
Findlay, R. 120
Fiorina, M. 6, 7, 101, 322
first-order conditions 168, 183
First Theorem of Welfare Economics 175
fiscal federalism 119, 121, 140, 260–1
fiscal policy 123, 155, 175
  overrated 151–3
  Friedman's plans for coordinating monetary and 156
Fischel, W. A. **351–2**
fish 25
Fisher, Irving 152
Fitts, M. A. 178
folk theorem 237, 313

Forman, Frank   143
France   226, 287, 290, 306, 307
fraud   67, 68, 74
freedom
   economic, Friedman's defense of   158
   individual   146, 147, 158
   political   81, 158
free lunch fallacy   152
free markets   146
   attack on   23–4
   Friedman's success in promoting   155
   predictable tension between democracy and   158
   presumption against   15
free riding   37, 42, 174, 212, 213, 229, 236, 284, 285
   and bargaining failures   219–20
   costly punishment of   98
   diffuse groups and   14
   interest-groups   93
   negative   120
   selfish individually rational prediction of   99
free trade
   departure from   **129–38**
   trade policy might compromise efficiency of   130
   see also NAFTA
French revolution   80
"fresh-water economics"   7
Frey, B. S.   39, 50, 92, 246, 250
Friedman, David   110
Friedman, E.   290
Friedman, Milton   7, 8, 10, 24, 107, **146–59**
   Friedman rule   167
Friedman, R. D.   157
Friedrich, K.   77
Frisch, Ragnar   204
Frohlich, N.   41, **352–3**
FTC (Federal Trade Commission)   198, 199, 277, 278
full employment   156
Fuller, L. L.   228
full integration problem   258

Gächter, S.   98
gains
   aggregated   63
   cooperation   99
   efficiency   131, 267
   foreign government can neutralize   131
   social   278
   transitional   275
   see also capital gains
gains-from-trade   18
   positive   24
Galbraith, John Kenneth   146, 158, 212
game theory   40, 225, 322, 323, 324
games
   bargaining   290
   Battle of the Sexes   229
   conflict   227
   cooperative   118–19
   non-cooperative   119
   participation   99–100
   persuasion   122, 123
   redistributive voting   177
   repeated   121, 122, 313
   sender-receiver   122
   signaling   123, 124
   zero-sum   63, 322
   see also prisoner's dilemma Gans, J. S.   177
Garber, P. M.   276
Gardner, R.   119
Garrett, T. A.   **353–4**
Gastil data   83
"gate keeping"   18
GATT (General Agreement on Tariffs and Trade)   133, 312, 315
Gauthier, D.   230
Gavin, W. T.   165
GDP (gross domestic product)   49, 52, 55, 286, 289–92 passim
   nominal   167, 168
generality   204, 227
genocide   79
Germany   226, 287, 289, 290, 316
   Nazi   78, 81, 82
Ghiselin, Michael   114
Gibbard, A.   37
Giddens, A.   245
Ginsburgh, V.   291
Girondins   306
globalization   137
   trade liberalization and   **312–20**
Glorious Revolution (England 1688)   80
GNP (gross national product)   85, 286, 287, 288
Goeree, J.   100
Goetz, Charles J.   106, 141
Goff, B. L.   143, **354–5**
Goldberg, Arthur   322
Goodhart, C. A. E.   50
goodness   61
goods and services   61, 252, 286, 292
Gordon, D.   160, 161, 166
Gore, A.   197
Gould, A. C.   181
Goulder, L. H.   94
government   3
   failure   10
   good   33
   views of   136–7
   vote-maximizing   205
   votes to rule   56
   wasteful spending   130
government intervention   132, 157, 268, 285
   exotic methods of   10
grandfathering   94, 95
Great Depression (1930s)   146, 147, 148, 154
Great Society programs (1960's)   158
Greece   287
greed   236
"green" dividend   94
Grier, K. B.   197
grievance asymmetry   57
Grofman, B. N.   203, **355–6**
Großer, J.   100
Grossman, G. M.   118, 121, 122
groups see interest-groups
Groves, Harold   148
Groves, T.   38, 41

habits   250
Habyarimana regime   79

Hagen, J. von 182
Hahn, Robert 91
Haig-Simons criterion 257
Haiti 81, 84
Hanson, R. D. **357**
Harberger fallacy 109
harm 133
Harsanyi, J. C. 124, 230
Harsanyi-Shapley-Nash value 118
Hart, H. L. A. 226
Hart-Scott-Rodino Antitrust Improvement Act (US 1976) 277
Hayek, F. A. von 245
Hay, D. A. 277
health/health care 254, 317
Hechter, M. 247
Heckathorn, D. D. 247
Heiner, Ron 143
Helpman, E. 118, 121, 122
Henderson, D. R. 273
Henderson, D. W. 167
hereditary monarchy 83
heresthetics 323
Herman, V. M. 41
Hettich, W. 173, 181, 182, **357-8**
Heyndels, B. 181
Hibbs, D. A. 39, 50, 52, 160
Hicks, J. R. 113
Hill, R. 289
Hinich, M. J. 6, 12, 141, 306, 307, 308, 309, **358-9**
Hirsch, A. 150
Hirshleifer, J. 114, 119
historicism 245
history of thought **201-14**
Hitler, Adolf 77, 82, 85, 88, 157, 235
Hobbes, Thomas 24, 64, 107, 109, 115, 195
Hobbesian problem of social order 236-8
Hoffman, E. 41, 101
Hojnacki, M. 124
Holcombe, R. G. 142, **359-61**
hold-out strategies 229
Holler, M. J. **361-2**
Holt, C. A. 97, 98, 100, **362-3**
Holtz-Eakin, D. 182
Homans, G. C. 246-7, 248, 249
homo oeconomicus 7, 24, 55, 65, 107, 108, 109, 114, 208, 246
honesty 72
horizontal equity 257
Hotelling, Harold 4, 148, 149, 205, 206, 207, 307, 308
"hot lines" 73-4
Hotte, L. 182
Houston, J. F. 291
Hoyt, W. H. 124
human capital 259, 289
  diversification of 317
  under-investment in 69
human rights 83, 84, 87
  economic justification of 85
Hume, David 107, 235, 237, 238, 244
Hylland, A. 38
hyperinflation 105
hyperinflationary 154

ICC (Interstate Commerce Commission) 269, 273, 274, 275
idealism 62

ideals 274
ideology 21
  credibility of 80
  political parties 206
ignorance *see* rational ignorance; veil of ignorance
illegal activities 73
  deals 69
  gambling 74
  mergers 278
Illinois 269
"immiserization" 84
imperialistic aims 80
implicit agreements 195
imports
  competition from 133
  from poorer countries 317
  relative price of 130
  restrictions on 136
  taxes on 132
impossibility theorem 37, 204
incentive alignment
  perfect 217
  reciprocity and 227-8
incentive effect 95
incentives 223, 228, 271, 285
  corruption 71, 72, 75
  economic 92, 94
  ex ante 22
  financial 67
  free-riding 99
  judicial 224
  participants react to a change of 100
  payoff 71-2
  political 153
  redistribution 174
  selective 93, 212
income
  capital 259
  future 163
  labor 259
  marginal utility of 161, 164
  median 181
  national 316
  permanent 152, 154
  potential 166, 167
  rational-expectations solutions for 161
  real, cyclical movements in 156
  redistribution 119
  rise in 86
  skewness of 177, 178
  utility 205
  variance of 177
income distribution 119, 135, 136, 267
  domestic 33, 317
  fair 254, 255
  how taxes affect 255
income persistence 163-4, 165
income redistribution 254-5, 266
  trade policy and 135-6
income tax 289
  corporation 257-8
  negative 157
inconvertibles 80
independence-of-irrelevant-alternatives axiom 37

individual behavior   191
individual choice   140, 144
    primacy of   211
individual preferences   34, 97, 297, 299, 302
    aggregating   38
    captured by collective decision-making   215
    more fully satisfied   63
    strategic concealment of   37
individual rights   24, 210, 240, 241
    guaranteeing   216
    protection of   238
inefficiency   84, 100, 136
    allocative   267, 270
    domestic   130, 131, 135
    organizational   112
    second-best corrections for   132
    tax instruments   174
inequality   317
infant industries   130–1, 132
inflation   39, 51–2, 53, 54, 154, 160
    economy-wide rate of   271
    expected rate of   166
    future, preemptive strikes against   167
    rational-expectations solutions for   161
    unemployment and   155
    variance of   162
inflation targets   162–5
influence functions   12
information
    asymmetric   5, 133, 134, 265
    costly to acquire   265
    deficiencies, free markets plagued by problems of   24
    imperfect   91, 232
    marginal benefits of   54–5
    specialized   270
    strategic misrepresentation of   270
    untruthful   100
information transmission models   122–3
informed choice   33
injury   133
in-kind services   254, 257
Inman, R. P.   178
insects   114
insiders   25
instability   18, 179
    formal coalitions   111
    majority rule   204
institutional choices   144
institutions
    building blocks of   250
    democratic   86
    economic   69
    knave-proof   235–6
    market   43
    monetary   159
    political   43, 69, 78, 208
    role of   181–2
    socialist   114
    stylized facts about the role of   181
instrument rules   166, 167, 168
insurance   134, 212, 213, 253–4
interactions
    market   106
    political   62

interest function approach   118
interest-groups   10, 12, 196, 198, 274, 284
    behavior and influence   **118–29**
    competition among   5, 84
    democracy inefficient because dominated by   83
    free-rider problem associated with   93
    group votes   217
    opportunities for   200
    political   194
    pressures   14
    private business   94–5
    rational choice approach to analysis of   212
    redistributory demands of   81
    Virginia School theory   6
    willing to pay for wealth transfers   195
    see also special interests
interest rates   156
intermediate goods   318
international law   226
international relations   229
international trade
    liberalization of   317–18
    negotiations   123
international trade policy   121
    departure from free trade   **129–38**
investment
    discouraged   69
    foreign   316
    return on   271
invisible hand theorem   38, 81, 175
Iraq   87
Ireland   287
irrationality   56
IRS (Internal Revenue Service)   289
Isaac, R. M.   98
Islam, M.   79
IS-LM curves   153
issue bundling   219
Italy   56, 72, 287
    tradition in public finance   140

Jacobins   306
Japan   56, 287
Japanese Public Choice Society   43
Jews   82
Johnson, L. B.   24, 284
Johnson, P. E.   124
Johnson, Simon   70, 289, 290, 291, 292, 293
joint ventures   74
Jones, Homer   147
Jordahl, H.   54
journals   98, 106, 114, 115, 140, 148
judges   114, 221
    appointed through political process   19
    corrupt   72
    economic self-interest of   194
    function of   20
    salaries of   196
judicial independence   194, 196
judicial review   222
judiciary   10, 19–20, 194–7, 215
jurors   114
justice   42, 224

Kabir, M. 289
Kaempfer, W. H. 84, 87, **363-4**
Kagel, J. H. 98
Kahneman, D. 56, 236
Kaldor, Nicholas 113
Kaldor-Hicks efficient 222
Kaldor-Hicks-Scitovsky potential compensation test 146
Kaysen, C. 278
Keefer, P. 82
Keen, M. 173
Keil, M. W. **364-5**
Kennedy, J. F. 24
Kennedy (Justice) 20
Kenny, L. W. 173, 181, **365-6**
Keynes, John Maynard 146, 152
Keynesian economics/Keynesians 9, 140, 142, 146, 149, 153, 155, 156, 158
  Friedman's critique 151-2
Kiewiet, D. R. 51, 53-4
Kimball, D. C. 124
Kimenyi, M. S. 94
Kinder, D. R. 51, 53-4
Kirchgässner, G. 91, 94, 95, 181, 289
Kirchsteiger, G. 100
Klein, B. 223
Kleindorfer, P. R. **366-7**
Kliemt, H. 238
Klitgaard, Robert 67-8
Klovland, J. 289
Knight, Frank 7, 139, 140, 147, 148, 150, 153
Kramer, G. H. 39, 50, 52, 54, 56, 322
Krueger, Anne 15, 36, 109
Kuhn, T. 114
Kurrild-Klitgaard, P. **367-8**
Kuznets, Simon 148, 150, 152
Kydland, F. E. 160, 161, 166
Kyoto protocol 91

Laband, D. N. 16, 142, **368-9**
labor
  child 318, 319
  cost of 131, 288
  defense of 306
  foreign 318
  intensity of 274
  unskilled 318
labor market 94, 193, 290-1
  equilibrium 155
  imperfections in 161
  monopoly power 194
  policies 121
  temptation to inflate anticipated by 163-4
labor unions 85, 193, 194, 199, 290
  closed shop and picket lines 213
Laffer curve 289
Lakatos, I. 64
Lambsdorff, Johann Graf 69
Landa, Janet 25, 114, 142
Landes, William 7, 8-9, 194, 195, 196, 221, 222
Langbein, L. **369-70**
Latin America 291, 292, 293
  see also Argentina; Bolivia; Chile; Mexico
law enforcement 72, 276
  fixed supply of personnel 69

lawmaking
  and political representation 216-17
  decentralized, economics of 225-32
  institutional design of 214-16
  judicial 221-5
law(s) 20, 113-14
  anticorruption 72
  anti-dumping 133, 135
  contingent-protection 133
  durability of 17
  predatory-pricing 133
  public choice from the perspective of **214-35**
lawyers 193
  self-seeking 114
leaders and laggards 314
Leavens, Don 143
Ledyard, J. O. 38, 41, 98, 99, 309
Lee, Dong Won **370**
Lee, Dwight 141, 143, **370-2**
Lee Kwan Yew 81
left-right issue space 206, 207
legal rules 224-5, 226
  common law 214
  customary law 216, 226, 230
  default 215, 227
  inefficient 223
legislatures 10, 16-18, 192-4, 199
  assign property rights in wealth transfers 195
  bicameral 23, 107, 211
  infested with parasites 13
  negotiating budgets with 21
  political instability in 178
  taking advantage of rational ignorance 213
  unicameral 211
  wealth-maximizing 195
legitimacy 37, 68, 239-40
  corrupt governments lack 69
Leibenstein, H. 228, 267
leisure-seeking 224
Lemieux, T. 289
Lerner, A. P. 307
Letwin, W. 276
Leviathan 142
Levy, David 143
Lewis, D. 228
Lewis-Beck, M. S. 51, 53
Li, Wei 70
liability 222, 223
liberalism
  classical 148, 149, 154, 157, 158
  Madisonian 323
  pure individualistic 297, 303
liberalization 133, 137, **312-20**
liberty 64, 108, 115
  demand for 86
  economic 146
  Friedman on 156-8
  individual 149
Liberty Fund 139
licenses 71
lies/lying 112, 123
  paid 114
Lindahl, E. 173, 174
Lindenberg, S. 244, 247

Lindsay, Matt 141
litigation 222, 224
  as a rule selection mechanism 223
"load shedding" 70
Loayza, N. V. 291, 292
lobbying 94, 212, 272–3, 285
  agenda stage 124
  basic signaling model of 122
  costs and benefits of 198
  emergence of lobbyists 123
  interest group abstains from 122–3
  models of 123
Locke, John 64, 107, 108, 115
logrolling 216, 217, 218
  and cyclical social preferences 297–8
  by majorities and paradox of voting 298–9
  committees substitute for 17
  institutional opportunities for 211
  relevance of 111
  social choice, contracts and **296–305**
Lohmann, S. **372–3**
Lomasky, L. E. 238, 239
Londregan, J. 86
López, E. J. **373–4**
loss aversion 56
losses
  aggregated 63
  deadweight 15, 109, 110, 266, 267
  domestic efficiency 134
  economic 84
  from conflict 80
  trade-related income 134
  utility 63
  welfare 124, 174, 179, 183, 266, 267
loyalty 77, 79, 87
  absolute 85
  high/low 78
  short-run fall in 86

Machiavelli, N. 112
Machlup, F. 148
Mackay, Bob 141
MacRae, C. D. 39, 160
macroaggregation 61
macroeconomic policies 39, 40, 152–3
macroeconomics 61
  income persistence and 163–4
  Keynesian 9
Madison, James 13, 19, 107, 323
Mafia 81
majority rule 80, 111, 140
  coercion under 177, 184
  instability of 204
  limiting 185
  normative advantages 4
malfeasance 72, 73, 74
Manhattan 49
Marchi, N. de 150
Marcos, Ferdinand 85
marginal costs 54, 79, 183, 232, 270
  expected 109
  price equals 265, 266
  price exceeds 266
market capitalization 110

market economies 14, 267, 323
market efficiency theory 54
market failure 5, 183, 265, 277
  near-universal 10
  policy responses to 264–7
market forces 267, 272
  decentralized 175
market power 265, 266, 267
  abuses of 277
markets 70, 175, 246, 306
  corrupt 68
  efficient 196
  highly stylized 249
  imperfect 130, 131
  insurance, incomplete 134
  international 131
  intervention-free determination of 136
  non-competitive 131, 132
  social function of 35
  under-provision of 212
  world/global 130, 312–13, 317
markups 275, 313
Markus, G. B. 54
Marshall, A. 109, 110, 155
Marvel, H. P. 194, 274
Marx, Karl 118, 285
Marxian theory 63, 212
Maryland school 285
Matsusaka, J. G. **374–5**
Mauro, P. 292
Mazza, I. 119, 124
McCallum, B. T. 167
McChesney, F. S. 375
McClintock, G. C. 16
McGarrity, J. 143
McGraw, T. K. 275, 276
McKelvey, R. 6, 37, 100, 101, 142, 177, 309, 322
McKibbin, W. J. 167
media
  censoring 84
  independent 73
median gap model 56
median voter 14, 21, 184, 298
  and extensions 176–8
  experiments 101
  identified 181
  model 180, 185
  policy preferences 11
median voter theorem 11, 34, 182, 203, 204, 205
Medicare/Medicaid 254
Mehta, Nimai 143
Meltzer, A. H. 177, 180
Menger, C. 248
mercantilism 63, 312
mergers 277, 278
merit 112, 134
methodological individualism 24, 65, 244–5, 247, 249
Mexico 316
MFN (most-favored nation) treatment 314, 315
microeconomics 175, 191
migration 316
Milesi-Ferretti, G. M. 181
Mill, John Stuart 34, 107, 157
Miller, G. 101

Miller, N. R. 217
Miller, William 70
Millis, Harry A. 147
Millner, E. L. 100
Milosevic, Slobodan 87
Minnesota, University of 149
minorities
  coalition of 56, 206
  exploitation of 111
  long-term 108
Mints, Lloyd 147, 148, 153
Mirrlees, J. 174
Mises, Ludwig von 112, 158
mistrust 86
Mitchell, Wesley C. 148
MMC (UK Monopolies and Mergers Commission) 277, 278
Mobutu, S. 83
Moe, T. M. 118, 124, 198
Mogensen, G. K. 286
monarchies 82, 83
monetary policy 153, 154
  and central bank behavior **159–72**
  as fundamental basis for individual freedom 146
  Friedman's views on 156
money 153–5
  demand for 155
  opportunity to make more 85
  quantity theory of 153, 154, 156
money supply 156, 167
money-to-power relation 78
monitoring 73, 216
monopoly 10, 15, 21, 130, 252, 276
  abuses of 272
  attacks on 109
  creation of 277, 278
  dead hand of 275
  deadweight losses due to 267
  free markets plagued by problems of 24
  incentive to create 110
  social costs of 36
  trumped-up claims of 268
  welfare costs of 266–7
  see also natural monopolies
monopoly power 71, 73
  in labor market 194
monopsony power 130, 132, 136
Moomau, P. H. 181
Moore, M. O. 124
moral goals 112
moral hazard 5, 131, 133, 141
moral suasion 75
morality 227, 230, 250
moral philosophy 244, 245, 285
Moran, M. J. 113, 198
Morris, Dick 220
Morris, D. J. 277
Morris, S. 93
Morton, R. 101, 181
Moselle, B. 82
most-preferred points 38–9
motivations 97, 238
Mudambi, R. **375–6**
Mueller, D. C. 38, 142, 249–50
Mueller, J. E. 50, 55, 56, 322

Mui, V. 99
multidimensional policies 122
multilateral liberalization 314, 318
multinational firms 318
multiparty systems 40, 41
multiple means 123–4
Munger, M. C. 6, 306, 307, 309, **376–7**
Musgrave, R. 9, 173
Myerson, R. B. 235
myopia 52, 113, 158

NAFTA (North American Free Trade Agreement) 315, 316
Nannestad, P. 53, 54, 56
Napoleon Bonaparte 113
Nash Bargaining Solution 119
Nash equilibrium 99, 100, 183, 230, 313
  truthful 121
National Health Service (UK) 254
national security 136
natural monopolies 268, 269, 270, 271, 272
  regulation will target 273
naturalistic fallacy 66
Navarra, P. **377–8**
NBER (National Bureau of Economic Research) 148, 150, 153
Nechyba, T. J. 182
Nef, John 147
negative campaigning 112
Nelson, R. R. 250
neoclassical economics 9, 14, 107, 151, 166, 289
  "model-Platonism" of 249
  price theory 148
  welfare 183
nervous system 114
Netherlands 56, 276, 287
Neustadt, R. E. 197
New Classical or Lucas aggregate supply 167
New Deal 148
new entrants 110, 194
Newing, R. A. 204, 309
New Jersey 182
New Keynesian aggregate supply curve 164, 165–6
New Political Macroeconomics 160
New York 148, 149, 269
New Zealand 323
Niemi, Richard 322
Nietzsche, F. 66
nirvana fallacy 265, 266
Niskanen, William 22, 36–7, 101, 112, 113, 198
Nitzan, S. 38, 120, 182
Nixon, R. 24
Nobel prizes 39, 143, 149, 150, 204
non-cooperative (Cournot-Nash) behavior 120
non-discretionary rule 155
non-opportunistic behavior 237–8, 241
nonprofit organizations 73, 114, 224
Nordhaus, W. D. 39, 52, 159, 160, 161
normative analysis 183–5
norm-compliant behavior 237
norms 228, 230, 231–2, 250
  behavior 177
  cooperative 225, 231
  internalized 237, 238
  optimal 230
  overarching 65

protection and 132–3
rent-seeking 109–10
taxation **173–91**
political markets 8, 10–12, 175, 219
   advocacy a highly predictable activity in 112
   atomistic demand in 118
   effects of uncertainty on behavior of 206
   efficiency 211
   failures 175, 184
   indivisibilities in 5
   inherently stable 4
   inherently unstable 3
   officials have a considerable influence in 93
   riddled by weaknesses 24
   transaction costs of contracting in 17
political parties
   central 40
   competition between 92, 205
   forced to compete for votes 178
   group behavior 208
   ideology 206
   left-of-center/right-of-center 39
   opposition 84, 87, 179, 181, 206
political philosophy 62, 63
political power 108, 158
   development and distribution of 83
   rational abstentions and 207
political pressure 212
political science 208
"political support function" 183
politics
   conflictual 63
   congressional 19
   constitutional 62–3
   environmental **91–6**
   interest-group theory of 20
   presidential 19
"politics-as-it-is" 18
politics-like-markets analogues 219
pollution 71, 253
Pommerehne, W. W. 181
Poole, K. T. 86, 309
Popper, Karl 150, 151
popularity 92
   dictators 77, 78
   see also VP-function
pork barrel projects 67, 77, 278
Portugal 287
Posner, Richard 7, 8–9, 36, 113, 194, 195, 196, 221, 222, 224, 268, 271, 272, 273, 278
possibility theorem 217
Poterba, J. M. 181
Potters, J. 100, 120, 122, 123–4
poverty 157, 318
power
   contest for 83–5
   costs of accumulating 78
   regime, frustrated by loss of 79
   secular 80
   struggle for 35, 178
   see also political power
power to tax model 118
PR (proportional representation) 99, 181
   closed-list 69

Prat, A. 100, 121, 124
Pratt, M. D. 100
praxeology 158
predators/predatory behaviour 25, 81–3, 109, 133
predictions 150, 198, 224
preference aggregation procedure 37
preference functions 61
preferences 192, 266, 319
   aggregating 34
   central bank 163
   collective 217
   dictator's 78, 79, 82
   forcing lobbies to reveal 122
   intransitive 218
   litigants' 215
   meddlesome 61
   party constituencies 160
   personal, judges indulge their own 195, 196
   presidential 198
   representation of 306–7, 308, 309
   revelation of 37–8, 174, 225
   unique majority 221
   well-behaved 177
   see also cyclical social preferences; individual preferences; single-peaked preferences; voter preferences
preferential trading 315–16
preferredness 65
Prescott, E. J. 160, 161, 166
Presidency (US) 18–19, 197–8
presidentialism 69
pressure groups 15
Price, H. D. 56
Price, S. 54
price-cap regulation 271
price-fixing agreements 276, 277
prices 155, 256, 265, 266, 270
   artificially high 275
   efficient 225
   raised above competitive levels 273
   Ramsey-optimal 268
   sticky 165
   world 135, 315
Priest, G. L. 223
principal-agent relationship 93, 317
prison 68
prisoner's dilemma 228, 229, 236, 315
private goods 120, 177
private markets 8, 10, 70, 174, 175, 183
   contract-enforcing mechanisms in 195
private sector 36, 73, 175, 269
privatization 67, 70, 71, 253, 254, 269
privileges
   monopoly 77
   regulatory 275
   special 110
prizes 100
probability 32, 33, 111, 112, 120, 122, 238
   exogenous 124
   fixed 165
   miscalculation of 12
   zero 100
procurements 70, 71, 73
product differentiation 266

production 271
  expanded capacity 313
  labor-intensive 274
productivity 94, 154, 156, 291
  marginal 224
profitability 317
profits 132, 271
profits
  above-normal 266, 267, 270, 272
  below-normal 266
  competitive struggle for 35
  eroded 275
  excess 275
  foreign producer 134
  maximizing 68
  shadow economy 288–9
promises 238
property rights 62, 82, 83, 85, 175, 210, 312, 317
  clearly defined 22
  committee structure of Congress grounded in 17–18
  imprescriptible 108
protectionism see trade protection
Przeworski, A. 81, 85, 119
psychology 249, 250
pubic goods 82
public administration 112
public choice 3–48
  experimental **96–104**
  from the perspective of economics **191–201**
  from the perspective of history of thought **201–14**
  from the perspective of law **214–35**
  from the perspective of philosophy **235–44**
  from the perspective of sociology **244–51**
  public finance and 261
Public Choice Society 97, 141, 247, 249, 322, 324
public debt theory 140
public expenditure 180, 181, 252–5
public finance **252–62**
  Italian tradition in 140
  Musgravian 9
public goods 5, 10, 14, 97, 121, 174, 252–3, 265
  "demand" for 140
  experiments 98–9
  free markets plagued by problems of 24
  group-specific 120
  inducing people to reveal preferences for 38
  optimal supply of 214
  Pareto optimal allocation of 37
  provision of 78, 179
public interest 8, 15, 191, 224, 227, 273
  government should act in 137
  private property affected with 269
public opinion 92, 206
public sector 10, 119, 269
  comparatively low 287
  efficiency 185
  services 291
  those who want to get wealthy choose 69
public services 67, 292
public utilities 270, 271, 272
punishment 70, 123, 238
purposive actor model 247
puzzle-solving 114

quantity theory of money 153, 154, 156
quasi-dictatorships 136
quotas
  adherence to limit on 133
  domestic market 134
  export 135
  import 132, 135, 312

Ramsey, F. P. 174
Ransom, R. L. 156
rates of return 271
  fair 275
Rathbone, A. **385–6**
rational actor models 43
rational choice 3–7 passim, 11, 21, 24, 64, 65, 66, 106, 107, 110, 114, 239, 248, 249, 250, 322
  collective action analysis 213
  forward-looking 241
  interest group analysis 212
  positive 112
rational expectations 10, 153
  discretionary 160
  full information 52
  inflation 160
  one way to define 54
  solutions for inflation and income 161
rational ignorance 10, 12, 92, 111, 112, 136, 200
  legislatures taking advantage of 213
rational voter model 35, 206
rationality 51, 55, 65, 123, 60, 238
  see also bounded rationality
Raub, W. 247
Rawls, John 9, 24, 41–2, 108, 142, 230
Reagan, Ronald 19
reality 151, 245
  no natural way of observing 66
receivers 122
recession 152
reciprocal liberalization 312–13, 314, 318
reciprocity 98, 227–9, 237
"red tape" 69
redistribution 121, 267, 285
  coercive 177, 180, 181, 185
  incentives for 174
  tax 239
  see also income redistribution; wealth redistribution
redistributory pressures 81
re-election constraint 92, 94
referenda 193, 323
reforms 70–5, 87, 293
  constitutional 10
  economic 15
  factionalist 275
  institutional 10
  legal 113
  tax 94, 149, 180
regionalism 315–16
regulation
  agency problem impact on economic theory of 199
  and antitrust **263–83**
  dictator's power may be used through 78

inefficient 15–16
labor market 290
Reilly, R. J. 100
Reinikka, Ritva 70
religion 158
Renaud, P. 119
rent-extraction 14–16
rents 14
  intramarginal 274
  legislative 222
  monopoly 36, 70, 109, 110, 113
  sanctions 84, 87
rent-seeking 14–16, 20, 81, 120, 134–5, 218
  and lobbying 100–1
  flat taxes reduce 143
  minimization of 214
  political economy of 109–10
  social costs of 36
  special interests targeting 19
repetition 100
representation 124, 306–7, 308
representation theorem 182–3, 184
representative democracy 92, 95, 205, 206
  citizen-candidate model of 124
repression 78, 77, 79, 80, 85, 86, 87
reputation 121, 122, 147, 149–50, 196, 224, 228, 238
  honest 72
  lobbying used to maintain 123
  pressure typically exerted to build up 123
reputational forces 160
Reschovsky, A. 181
resource misallocation 16, 272
  see also allocation of resources
responsibility hypothesis model 50, 52
retaliation 131
retirement 212, 254
  early 291
revenue motives 132
revenue raising instruments 257–60
"revolving doors" 124
rewards 18, 50, 72, 131, 238, 257
Ricardo, D. 63, 245, 316
Richard, S. F. 177, 180
rights
  assignment of 302–3
  constitutional 115
  contract 82
  grazing 71
  pollution 71
  quota 135
  scarce 68
  see also human rights; individual rights; property rights
"rights revolution" 84
Riker, William H. 6, 7, 36, 37, 39, 40, 191, **321–4**
risk aversion 56, 110
Ritzer, G. 248
rivals 265, 266
  intent of eliminating 133
Robbins, Lionel 113, 150
Roberts, J. M. 165
Roberts, K. W. S. 177
Robertson, D. H. 235

Robinson, James 83
Robinson, Joan 146, 158
Robinson-Patman Act (US 1936) 277, 278
Rochester school 6–7, 321
Roe, M. 231
Rogoff, K. 161
role reversibility 227, 228, 229
Roman Corpus Juris 216
Romer, P. 292
Romer, T. 6, 177, 309, **386–7**
Root, H. 80
Rose-Ackerman, S. 67, 69, 72, 292, 293
Rosenthal, H. 99, 238, 309
Roth, A. E. 98
Rothenberg, L. S. 124
"roving bandits" 82, 284
Rowley, Charles K. 7, 142, 143, 154, 196, 198, 244, **387–8**
Rubin, P. H. 222–3, 278, **388–90**
Rubinfield, D. C. 223
rule-following 250
rule of law 238, 317
  compensatory function of 226
  democracy does not necessarily promote 81
  weak 2961
rules
  choices over 5
  constitutional 9, 63, 108, 112, 194
  instrument 166, 167, 168
  legislative 177, 181
  monetary policy 166–7
  power conferring 241
  public choice 240–1
  reason of 156
  redistribution 41–2
  supra-majority 108
  targeting 166, 167–8
  transparent 71
  see also legal rules; voting rules
Rustichini, A. 121
Rutgers University 147
Rutherford, T. 182
Rwanda 79
Ryle, Gilbert 240

Saddam Hussein 77, 84, 87
Sadiraj, 123
"salt-water economics" 8
Samaritan's Dilemma 142
Samuelson, Paul 5, 23–4, 37–8, 61, 146, 150, 151, 158, 285
sanctions 84, 85, 87
Sanders, D. 54, 56
Sargent, T. J. 156
Satterthwaite, M. A. 37
savings 152, 219, 257
  cost 271
Scandinavian countries see Denmark; Norway; Sweden
scarcity 61, 70, 71
  artificial creation of 60
Schagrodsky, Ernesto 70
Scherer, F. M. 268
Schmid-Luebbert, S. **391–2**
Schmoller, G. 248

Schneider, F. 39, 50, 91, 95, 142, 181, 289, 292
Schofield, N. J. 6, 37, 177, 309, **392–3**
Schotter, A. 228
Schram, A. 97, 98, 99
Schultz, Henry 147, 148
Schumpeter, J. A. 34, 35, 38, 105
Schwartz, Anna 153, 154
Schwartz, T. 217, 301
Scottish Moralists 245
Scully, G. W. **393–4**
SEC (Securities and Exchange Commission) 199, 271
second-best case 130, 132, 133, 134, 161, 163
secret funds 73
seignorage 179
self-dealing 67, 70
self-enforcing mechanisms 195
self-interest 64, 92, 107, 108, 191, 199, 223, 238, 316
   ambitious 112
   breadth of 82
   individual 211
   judges, economic 194
   rational 225
selfishness 99, 235, 236, 238
self-selection mechanism 69
Sen, Amartya 61, 36, 81, 85, 113, 230, 296, 303
Sened, I. **394–5**
separation of powers 17, 18, 107, 196, 214, 221–2
Serbia 87
shadow economy **286–96**
Shapley-Shubik power index 321
Shapley value 119
Shepsle, K. A. 6, 7, 17, 197, 321, 322
Sherman Antitrust Act (US 1890) 276–7, 278
Shleifer, A. 67
shocks 181
   exogenous 175, 231
   external 50
   fiscal policy 153
   inflation 163
   supply 159, 161, 166
Shoup, Carl 149
Shubik, M. 217
   see also Shapley-Shubik
Shughart, W. F. 143, 269, **395–6**
side payments 217, 218, 221
SIE (structurally-induced-equilibrium) models 197
signal extraction problem 152
Simons, Henry 7, 105, 113, 147, 153, 156, 185
simple majority rule 23, 32, 34
Singapore 81
Singer, H. W. 307
single-peaked preferences 3, 204, 207, 298, 308
Sloof, R. 118, 122, 123, 124
Slutsky, S. 306
Smart, M. 177
Smith, Adam 63–4, 58, 244, 245
Smith, Philip 286
Smith, Vernon L. 41, 97, **396–9**
Smithies, Arthur 206, 307
smuggling 136
Sobel, R. S. **399–400**
social choice 61, 204, 308–9
   Arrovian 9

contracts, logrolling and **296–305**
social costs
   monopoly 36, 110
   rent-seeking 36
   severe 68
social exchange theory 247
social interaction 66, 229
"social market" revolution 86
social norms
   adjudicating 225
   stochastic origin of 227
social order 236–8
social philosophy 63
social security 119, 288–90
social welfare 131, 265, 278, 290
   Arrow's famous work on 140
   deadweight losses 267
   failure of free markets to maximize 146
   government maximizing 134
   maximize 133
   political decision makers can maximize 131
   tax systems that maximize 174
social welfare function 38, 52
socialism 269
   democratic 158
   dogma 149
socialist countries (former) 69
sociology **244–51**
sociotropic/egotropic controversy 53–4
Socratic technique 114
Solow, Robert 146, 158
Sonnemans, J. 99
Souter (Justice) 20
South Africa 82
   Apartheid 81
   sanctions against 87
Southern Economic Association 141
Soviet Union (former) 72, 82, 291
   breakdown/collapse of 24, 110, 269
Spagat, M. 79, 83
Spain 287
spatial theory **305–11**
spatial voting models/experiments 6, 239, 101
special interests 13–14, 19, 316
   legislation 67
   per capita stakes of 132
   unconstrained by free-rider considerations 21–2
specificity 224, 225
Speck, S. 94
spillovers 92, 95
Spinoza, B. de 64, 237
Spiro, P. S. 289
Spitzer, M. L. 41
Staaf, R. J. 276
Staayer, J. A. 192
stability 20, 111, 177, 218, 306
   collective outcomes 216
   logrolling as an instrument of 216
   political 3, 285
   price 154, 156, 160, 161–2, 167
stabilization 153, 161–4
   of contracts 20
   policy 150
   shock 166

stagflation 154
Stalin, Josef 82, 85, 88, 157, 235, 285
Standard Oil 277
Stanford University 149
stare decisis 224, 226
"stationary bandits" 81, 82, 88, 284, 285
statistical research 180–2
Stearns, M. L. 216, 228
Steinmo, S. 182
Stepykina, E. **400–1**
Stigler, George J. 5, 8, 52, 83, 107, 119, 148, 149, 194, 199–200, 267–8, 273, 274, 275
Stiglitz, Joseph E. 110
stigma moral 69
strategic behavior 122
strategic trade policy 131–2
structure-induced paradigm 111
Stubblebine, Craig 141
stylized facts 125, 181
sub-Saharan Africa 69
subsidies 85, 131, 195, 312
   agricultural 132, 136
   competition among groups for 84
   groups can more readily obtain 120
   import duties that neutralize 133
substitution 318
suffrage 108
super-majorities 18, 196
supply 21, 140, 198, 268
   foreknowledge of 134
   labor 177, 289
   money 154, 156
Supreme Court (US) 13, 19, 109
   Mogul Steamship (1815) 269
   Munn (1934) 269
   West Coast (1937) 109
Suranovic, S. M. 124
surplus 218, 266
   budget 21
   consumers' 109
   future 156
"survival of the fittest" 231
sustainability 270
Svendsen, G. T. 94–5
Svensson, Jakob 70
Svensson, Leo 164, 165, 168
Swedberg, R. 244, 246, 247
Sweden 54, 56, 289
   tax structures 182
Switzerland 135, 287, 288

Tabellini, G. 118, 160, 181
Tanzi, V. 292
targets 164–5
   inflation 162–3, 167–8
tariff and non-tariff barriers 195
tariffs 85, 109, 179, 314
   optimum 130, 131, 132, 135
   retaliatory 130, 313
   transfer of income 136
   see also GATT
taxation
   consumption 258–9
   corporation 257–8
   corruption in collection of 71
   dictator's power may be used through 78
   dispersed 5
   ecological/environmental 93, 94
   export 136
   flat 143, 179
   incentive effects of 119
   international trade 132
   optimal 185, 256–7
   political economy of **173–91**
   unconstitutional 196
   wealth 259
   see also income tax
tax burdens 178, 184, 257
   excess 255–6
   increase of 288–90
tax evasion 74, 143, 286
tax redistribution 239
Taylor, M. J. 41, 51
Taylor rule (J. B. Taylor) 167, 168
teams 99
terms of trade 130, 135, 312
   changes 313–14
   domestic political objectives and 134
terror 80
theft reduces wealth 81–2
Theil, H. 160, 169
theodicy problem of economics 49
theory of second best 131
third markets 131
Thomas (Justice) 20
Thompson, E. **401**
Thornton, M. **401–2**
threat 95, 238
   enforcement of 123
   exit 73
   from foreign aggressors 136
TI (Transparency International) 68
Tideman, T. N. 141, **402–3**
Tillman, Betty 141, 143
timocrats 78, 79
Tinbergen, J. 160, 169
tinpots 78, 85, 86
Tirole, J. 268
tit-for-tat strategy 229
Tobin, James 146, 158
"tokens" 98
Tollison, R. D. 19, 120, 196, 197, 274, **403–4**
Toma, Genia 142
Toma, Mark 142, 181
tort law 8–9
torture 84
totalitarian regimes 78, 85, 86–7, 157
   evolution of 79–80
Tower, E. **405–6**
tradable permits 93, 94
trade 86–7
   restraint of 276
   unfair 133
trade diversion 315, 316
trade liberalization and globalization **312–20**
trade-offs 219
   among desired goods 191
   choice of targets and effect on 164–5

trade-offs contd.
  direct and external costs 215
  electoral 199
  inflation bias and stabilization bias 162
  macroeconomic variables 168
  political 199
  price inflation and unemployment 155
  tariffs and other sources of revenue 179
trade protection 130–1, 132, 136, 179, 313, 318
  contingent 133–4, 314
Train, K. E. 271
transaction costs 182, 215, 225
  contracting in political markets 17
  minimized 223
  positive 208, 219
  vote-trading 220
  zero 266
transfers 92, 290
  converting rent-seeking costs into 110
  cost of 93
  demand for 198
  hidden income 136
  in-kind 254
  lump-sum 14, 94, 315
  social 290
  surreptitious or hidden income 135
  welfare neutral 15
  see also wealth transfers
transition countries 72
transivity 37, 216
transparency 71, 75
Treaty of Rome (1957) 277
trend factor 205
triangulation 219–20
trust 55, 236
truth 61
Tullock, Gordon 3, 4, 5, 6, 9, 15, 23, 24, 25, 35, 36, 76, 91, 93, 105–17, 140, 141, 142, 143, 149, 212, 221, 236, 238, 301, 406–7
  insight 207–11
Turner, D. F. 278
Tutsis 79
Tversky, A. 236
Twight, C. A. L. **407–8**
tying 219
tyrannies 78, 79, 85, 87, 157
tyranny of the majority 211

Uganda 70
Ullmann-Margalit, E. 230
unanimity 23, 25, 108, 113, 215, 297, 301
  qualified 174
unanimity rule 34, 41, 140, 208, 209, 210
uncertainty 24, 57, 178, 210
  augmented 115
  effects on behavior of political markets 206
  extraneous 132
  future comparative advantage 133
  generalized 9, 23
  group size 100
  receiver 122
  veil of 108, 230
underground economy see shadow economy
unemployment 51–2, 53, 160, 290, 317

  and inflation 155
  strategy of reducing when going into election 39
unfair practices 133
unicameralism 211
unilateral liberalization 312, 313, 316–17
United Kingdom 54
  antitrust legislation 277
  Factory Acts (1830s) 274
  health services 254
  privatization 269
  regulation 271
  tax structures 182
  underground economy 287, 292
United States 4, 42, 87, 95
  Act to Regulate Commerce (1887) 269
  annual cost of rent-seeking and rent protection 16
  estimates of saving 152
  farm associations 212–13
  federal farm program 9
  freedom of information acts 73
  government growth 149
  illegal gambling 74
  imports from poorer countries 317
  income distribution 33, 317
  judiciary 19–20, 221
  legislature 17
  presidency 197–8
  separation of powers 196
  state legislator pay 194
  sulfur emissions 253
  taxation 181, 182, 256
  underground economy 287, 288, 291
  see also US Congress; US Constitution; also under names of individual states
universality 226–7
"universal service" requirements 272
unskilled workers 318
Urken, A. B. **408–9**
US Civil Aeronautics 274, 275
US Congress 195, 219, 221, 278
  budgets appropriated by 22
  bureaucracy monitored and controlled by 199
  committee assignments 17
  interest group constituencies 19
  regulatory powers delegated to President 18
  stability to protect itself 111
US Constitution 13, 17, 323
  Buchanan's support for balanced budget amendment 142
  collapse (1860) 108
  President's veto power 18
utilitarianism 64, 204, 245
utility
  expected 8, 108
  future 152
  interpersonal comparability and aggregate measurability of 64
  limitations posed by the ordinal nature of 113
  marginal 162, 164
  median voter's 182
  problem of measuring across individuals 211
  short-term loss of 113
utility functions 161, 166
  central bank 164, 165, 167, 168
  derived 162, 163, 224

procedural 195
shared 66
spontaneous 226, 227, 229
supraindividualistic 64
see also social norms
Norpoth, Helmut 53
North, D. 80
Norway 289
NRC (National Resources Committee) 148, 150
Nutter, Warren 9

Oates, W. E. 91
Oberholzer-Gee, F. 92
observed behavior 65
OECD countries 181, 290, 291, 293
Office of Fair Trading (UK) 277
Olson, Mancur 5, 13, 14, 35, 42, 81–2, 83, 88, 98, 101, 220, 239, 323
 insights 212–13
 scholarly legacy **284–6**
Ombudsmen 74
one man, one vote 217–18
OPEC embargos 136
"openness" 86
opinio iuris 227, 230
opinion polls 239
Opp, K.-D. 247
Oppenheimer, J. **378–9**
opportunism 228, 238
opportunities
 corrupt 68, 70, 73
 employment 318
 for interest groups 200
 job 291
optimality 175
optimization 182, 183
 global 219
Ordeshook, P. C. 6, 13, 101, 309, 322, 323
Ordover, J. A. 276
Ortega y Gasset, J. 66
Osborne, M. J. 119
output 21, 131, 266
outsiders 73
overdissipation 100
oversight 20, 22, 23, 271
 committee 198, 199
 relaxed 21

Padovano, F. **379–81**
Palda, F. **381–2**
Paldam, M. 51, 53, 54, 56
Palfrey, T. R. 99, 100, 238
paradox of voting 55, 110, 200, 296
 logrolling by majorities and 298–9
parasites 13
Pareto, V. 18
Pareto improvement 85, 184, 315
Pareto optimality/efficiency 37, 41, 175, 111, 184, 222, 252, 303, 304
Pareto principle 146
 modified 113, 115
 weak 204
Parisi, F. 216, 217, 218, 219, 229, **382–3**
Parkinson's Law 112
Parks, R. 306

Parsons, Talcott 236, 245
"partisan effects" 40
partisan theory 160
part-time work 291
path dependence 231
patronage 21, 213
Pauly, Mark 141
payoffs 73, 97, 98, 99, 101, 111, 228, 229
 day-to-day interactions riddled with 69
 monetary 194
 projects designed to make them easy to hide 68
 reducing incentives for 71–2
Peacock, Sir A. T. **383–4**
peak-load pricing 270
Peck, R. 119
Pecorino, P. **384–5**
peer pressure 225
Peltzman, S. 7, 12, 83, 119, 273, 274, 275
penalties 68, 72, 73
perceptions 66
perfect knowledge 266
performance 206
 future, competing parties 205
 judiciary, Latin America 70
 long-term political stability hurts 285
Persson, T. 118, 160, 181
persuasion 111, 112, 206
Peterman, J. A. 278
Philippines 85
Phillips curve 52, 160, 165–6
 fallacy of 155
philosophy 208
 public choice from the perspective of **235–44**
 see also moral philosophy; political philosophy; social philosophy
Pigou, A. C. 9, 91, 174
Pinochet, Augusto 81
Plato 61, 108
pleasure and pain 64
Plott, C. 41, 98, 101, 141, 309
plurality 178, 202
Polak, B. 82
Poland 42
police 72
 honest 74
 political 77
policy
 anticorruption 70
 competition 277, 278
 environmental 121
 stabilization 166, 167
 tax 177, 179
 trade 86, 315, 317
 see also fiscal policy; international trade policy; monetary policy
political bargains 218–19
political campaigning 123
political choice 61
political competition 92, 184, 217, 323
 political parties 92, 205
 politicians 16
 spatial 305–6
political economy 245
 constitutional 3–31, **60–7**, 109, 238
 legislation 216–21

political economy *contd.*
  employed piecewise 166
  single-peaked 203
utility-maximizing 9, 106, 111, 175, 192, 199, 223, 249
  self-seeking 21

Vachris, M. A. **409–10**
validity 151, 227, 231
  external 98
Välimäki, J. 121
value judgements 158
values 224
  core 220
  internalization of 238
  shared 65, 66
  supreme 79–80
Vanberg, V. J. 143, 244, 245, 247, 248, **410–12**
van der Ploeg, F. 119
van Dijk, F. 124
Vannucci, A. 68
van Roozendaal, P. 40–1
van Velthoven, B. 119
van Winden, F. 101, 119, 120, 122, 123, 124
VAT (value-added tax) 258, 289
Vaubel, R. **412–13**
veil of ignorance 24, 230
veil of insignificance 238
veil of tears 37
velocity 154
Verwimp, Philip 79
veto power 215
Vickrey, William 38
Vienna Convention (1969) 229
Viner, Jacob 7, 147, 149, 153
Virginia School 6, 9–11, 14, 15, 193, 244, 285
Vishny, R. 67
Volcker, P. A. 167
Volkerink, B. 181
voluntary contributions 98–9
voluntary export restraint 132
Voss, T. 247
vote functions 120–1
vote motive 11–13, 110–12
voter participation 238–40
voter preferences 3, 4, 211, 217
  campaign contributions utilized to manipulate 21
  capacity for democratic procedures to aggregate information on 37
  distributions 205, 206
  median 92, 111
voters 199–200
  backward-looking 160
  disorganized 133
  grievance asymmetry 55–6
  middle-of-the-road 40
  minority 218
  myopic 52
  retrospective 52–3
  rich 18
  short-sighted 39
  sociotropic 53–4
  swing 52
  uninformed 54–5
  unpredictable 199
  well-informed 33

voter turnout 99–100, 199
votes
  group 217
  market for 217–18
  money buys 121
  trading 111, 218, 220, 296
vote-seeking behavior 112
voting 135
  benefits of 199
  costs of 199, 207
  deterministic 38, 178
  expressive 112, 239
  majority 202
  paradox of 55, 110, 200, 296, 298–9
  probabilistic 38, 176, 178–80, 183, 184, 185
  rational 111, 205
  rationality of 55
  simple majority 211
  sociotropic 57
voting behavior 239
  campaign contributions offered to affect 124
  plausible approach to 200
voting rules 37–8, 97–8, 308
  Pareto-optimal 25
VP- (vote and popularity) function **49–59**, 91

wages 155, 257
  legislative 193–4
  minimum 131
  monopoly 194
  public sector 72–3
  real 317
  relative 193
Wagner, R. E. 24, 141, 142, 143, 153, **413–14**
Wald, Abraham 149
Wallerstein, M. 119
Wallis, Allen 148, 149
Walras, L. 245–6
Walters, A. 150, 154
"warm glow" 239
Washington 148
Watergate crisis (1974) 24, 109
wealth 8
  accumulation 192
  expected 21
  inherited, Buchanan's antipathy towards 139
  interest group with an interest in 119
  loss of 110
  of the nation 63
  theft reduces 81–2
wealth maximization 7, 192, 195, 196, 228, 273
wealth redistribution 7, 18
  political 15
wealth taxes 259
wealth transfers 199, 275
  coercive 196
  durability of 194
  interest groups willing to pay for 195
Weaver, Carolyn 142
Weber, Max 112, 245, 248
websites 68
Weck-Hanneman, H. 194, **414–15**
Weingast, B. R. 6, 7, 80, 113, 197, 198

Welch, W. 120
welfare 218, 253, 254, 255, 289
  aggregate 184
  changes in 92, 175
  expected 230
  group 98
  joint 121
  loss in 256
  maximized 52, 225, 230
  voter 185
  see also social welfare
welfare function
  exogenously given 174
  political 118, 121
well-being 80, 112
Wellington, Arthur Wellesley, 1st Duke of 113
Wellisz, S. 120
Wells, A. 248
West, Eddie 142
Westminster 17
Wheeler-Lea Act (US 1938) 277
Whinston, M. D. 121
whistleblower protection 74
Wicksell, Knut 34, 107, 139, 140, 173, 174, 185
Willett, T. D. **415–17**

Williams, W. E. **417**
willingness-to-pay 68
"will of the people" 217
Wilson, Edward O. 114
Wilson, Woodrow 112
Winer, S. L. 79, 173, 181, **418–19**
winners and losers 131, 132
winner-takes-all election 99
winning coalitions 301, 304
  minimum 40, 191
Wintrobe, R. 79, 83, 87, 88, 173, 198, 199
Wittman, D. 14, 39, **419–20**
Wolfowitz, Jacob 149
working hours 290–1
World Bank 69, 70, 316
World War I 86
Wright, G. 197
WTO (World Trade Organization) 133, 312, 313, 315

xenophobia 25
X-inefficiency 267

Zambia 49
Zavoina, W. J. 322
Zeckhauser, R. 38